KU-662-143

DICTIONARY OF BANKING AND FINANCE

DICTIONARY OF BANKING AND FINANCE

A Commentary on Banking,
Financial Services and Corporate and Personal Finance

Derrick G. Hanson, LL.M.
of Lincoln's Inn, Barrister;
Fellow of the Institute of Bankers

PITMAN

PITMAN PUBLISHING LTD
128 Long Acre, London WC2E 9AN

PITMAN PUBLISHING INC
1020 Plain Street, Marshfield, Massachusetts 02050

Associated Companies
Pitman Publishing Pty Ltd, Melbourne
Pitman Publishing New Zealand Ltd, Wellington
Copp Clark Pitman, Toronto

First published in Great Britain 1985

Library of Congress Cataloging in Publication Data

Hanson, D. G. (Derrick G.)
Dictionary of Banking and Finance.
1. Finance—Dictionaries. 2. Banks and Banking—Dictionaries. I. Title.
HG151.H37 1985 332'.03'21 85–12299

ISBN 0–273–01859–0

British Library Cataloguing in Publication Data

Hanson, D. G.
Dictionary of banking and finance: a commentary on banking, financial services and corporate and personal finance.
1. Finance—Dictionaries
I. Title
332'.03'21 HG151

ISBN 0–273–01859—0

Printed at The Bath Press, Avon

CONTENTS

AUTHOR'S NOTE

In the world of finance nothing stands still. Even as this work was being printed, the new consolidating Companies Act (747 Sections, 25 Schedules and 630 pages) arrived on the Statute Book. Wherever practicable the Dictionary has been updated to include the Section references and quotations from the new Act. In similar vein, the Finance Bill, the Insolvency Bill, the Social Security Bill and the Trustee Savings Banks Bill are making their way through Parliament and references have been made in the Dictionary to what is thought to be the Legislature's intention.

To add to the changing scene, the main provisions of the Consumer Credit Act came into force last month and the Data Protection Act begins to come into effect in a few months' time.

Lastly, we have had the massive Green Paper on Social Security, the Government's announcements on building societies' enhanced powers, the continuing discussion and anticipated legislation on investor protection and the 'Big Bang' on the Stock Exchange.

In the light of these and other changes, I have included a short Supplement which follows the main text and which, as far as practicable, updates the Dictionary to June 1985.

DGH
June 1985

INTRODUCTION

The older generation of bankers grew up with *Thomson's Dictionary of Banking*. They did not necessarily refer to it very often (having passed their examinations at an early age), but it was a comfort to know that it was there on the bookshelf. At first, therefore, it seemed surprising to discover, with a little market research, that a generation of bankers had emerged who relied not at all on Thomson and indeed, in some cases, confessed not to have heard of his famous dictionary, notwithstanding that the twelfth and last edition was published in 1974 and the most recent reprint was in 1978. Thus, there was a danger that Thomson would become a museum piece. Older bankers would mourn its passing: younger ones might not notice its absence. Yet, Thomson still stands as the only commentary of its kind on the language and practices of British banking in its traditional forms over the 70 years or so since the first edition was published. What then has changed?

The biggest change of all is in the scope of the business of banking. If some bankers today, as we have said, plead ignorance of Thomson, how much more would Thomson himself have failed to recognize the 'universal' banks of our time. Banking in its traditional form is concerned with the taking of deposits, the lending of money and the transmission of payments. Those are still the primary functions of banking, albeit on a much larger map, on a much larger scale and in a much more technologically advanced way than could have been contemplated years ago. More than that, however, bankers have ventured into activities which have taken them into the far corners of the whole world of finance. So far as the British banks are concerned, it is difficult to think of any legitimate financial service which banking does not now encompass. Thus, the banker of today needs at least a working acquaintance with trusts, insurance, merchant banking, unit trusts, computer services, credit cards, leasing, factoring, hire purchase and the whole world of international trade. After many generations, indeed a few centuries, of comparatively orthodox and stereotyped banking the newer, universal image of the banks has appeared in the last 20 years or so. Thus, the biggest change in the British banking scene is the increased catholicity of bank services.

The second major change is that brought about by automation. Not only is a high proportion of routine banking work now done by electronic means, but this in turn has led to the employment of a higher proportion of non-career staff. Not all that long ago a bank cashier would not only be able to recite, for example, Section 82 of the Bills of Exchange Act by heart, but would be conscious of its relevance in his day's work as he 'collected' cheques for the credit of a customer's account. Not all bank cashiers of today will necessarily have heard of the Bills of Exchange Act nor, in all fairness, does it matter. Yet those who have a senior responsibility for protecting the bank's legal position in relations with its customers still need to know the rules. Furthermore, although vast numbers of cheques are 'paid' daily by mechanical or electronic means, the use of trade bills of exchange has increased considerably and the banker ignores the Act at his peril.

There is a third area of change which extends far beyond the borders of banking. In former days, there were clearer demarcations between differing skills. Nowadays, it seems to be a feature of the financial world that the participants 'trespass' quite readily on each other's preserves and there seems to be a cheerful acceptance of the fact that there are few, if any, boundaries between complementary skills. So it was that until the passing of the Banking Act 1979 almost anyone could establish a bank and did! Even today there is no great difficulty, within the Bank of England guidelines, in becoming a deposit-taking institution. Banks themselves have, as we have said, spread their net widely into related and sometimes unrelated fields. Banks have become insurers: some insurance companies own banks. Banks, insurance companies and stockbrokers all manage unit trusts. Banks, solicitors and accountants give taxation advice. At least one bank has entered the estate agency field and estate 'agents' have become 'principals' in property development. Insurance brokers have moved into the wider field of advisory services, whilst banks and finance houses have moved into insurance broking. Some building societies offer cheque book and money transmission services and the Trustee Savings Banks found themselves, at least for a while, owning a commodity exchange. Accountants, stockbrokers and merchant banks give corporate financial advice. Banks, stockbrokers and accountants provide computer services. There are times when it seems to have become a jolly free-for-all.

INTRODUCTION

Whatever boundaries may have been crossed, the real truth of the matter, however, is that finance is not compartmentalized nor can it be. Almost any person or institution offering any financial service, however single-mindedly, must today have an awareness of a wide range of related financial matters.

Even as this book is being completed the City is taking on a new look and has indeed already moved into a new dimension. Banks have taken significant stakes in firms of jobbers and stockbrokers and new alliances have been forged among merchant banks, stockbrokers, investment trusts, money brokers and discount houses. At least one insurance company has established a link with a major US securities firm and, on the domestic front, building societies are seeking enhanced powers to enable them to move into new fields. Both the Government and the Bank of England have welcomed and indeed encouraged these newer groupings and thus a new Leviathan is emerging—the financial conglomerate.

This work is, therefore, concerned with finance rather than banking alone. Finance, we are told by the *Oxford English Dictionary*, means the money resources of state, company or person. It therefore encompasses the entire business world, whether institutional or personal and whether seen from the angle of the participant or the professional advisor. The aim here, therefore, is to provide a commentary on financial terms and usages, for the guidance of all concerned with money in their own right or on behalf of customer or client.

Lastly, the word 'dictionary' may be a misnomer. The present work is designed to be not merely a glossary of financial terms, but an exposition, albeit condensed, of each financial subject. To that extent it is more in the nature of a modest encyclopaedia. Indeed, Thomson's work had attained encyclopaedic proportions over the years. I am indebted to Thomson and his distinguished editors and I have incorporated many entries from the last edition of that work.

In a work of this nature there were inevitable difficulties in setting the parameters for the subject matter. How much history should be included? How long should each entry be? To whom is the work directed? As I have said above, we are dealing here with subjects rather than words and I have therefore included historical references wherever they have added genuine interest to and made for a better understanding of a particular subject. It was more difficult, however, to determine the length and content of each entry and I have worked on the assumption that anyone turning to these pages in a spirit of inquiry will hope to find a reasonably comprehensive answer—at least enough for his or her purpose—and will not wish necessarily to be referred to a number of other works. On the other hand, some of the subjects are so vast, e.g. taxation, company law, that it is impossible to treat each of them comprehensively in the space available. I have therefore sought to provide adequate if not always exhaustive, treatment for the benefit of the typical inquirer and I judge that person to be for the most part, a professional man or woman who seeks information on a financial subject outside his or her own immediate expertise. Thus, the chartered accountant is unlikely to turn to these pages for an exposition of the Companies Act 1985 nor will the solicitor look here for guidance on the wills aspect of the Administration of Justice Act 1982, but I hope that others will find such entries helpful and interesting. I have therefore tried to make the book useful to anyone and everyone whose work or studies take them across the thresholds of finance in the hope that, more often than not, they may find the answer they are seeking.

With the generous consent of the respective publishers, I have drawn freely on my own contemporary works: *Service Banking: The Arrival of the All-Purpose Bank*, published by the Institute of Bankers, 10 Lombard Street, London (second edition 1982) and *Moneyguide: The Handbook of Personal Finance*, a loose-leaf publication with an updating service from Kluwer Publishing Limited, 1 Harlequin Avenue, Great West Road, Brentford, Middlesex.

I am very grateful for the help I have received from a number of sources in the preparation of this work. In particular I am indebted to Mr Eynon Smart, LL.B., Hon. FIB, who so meticulously read the entire typescript of this work and made numerous suggestions which, almost without exception, I have incorporated. As always, I am indebted to my secretaries, Jennifer Ray and Shelagh Page, for their immaculate typing, to my daughter and her husband, Rosemary and Paul Baines, for reading the proofs and making numerous helpful suggestions, and to my daughter, Heather Witherington, for checking the amendments.

Lastly, I shall always be in the debt of those good friends in almost every financial sphere who, in the years in which I have been less of a participant and more of an observer of and commentator on the financial scene, have opened their doors to me as readily as they have shared their vast experience. They are too numerous to list but they are not forgotten.

D.G.H.
June 1985

ABATEMENT Where the estate of a deceased person is insufficient to pay all the legacies in full, the legacies must normally be reduced, or abated, in equal proportions according to the amount available. If, for example, an estate is sufficient only to pay one-half of the legacies bequeathed by the testator, all the legacies will be abated by 50 per cent. A testator may indicate that a particular legacy is to be paid in priority to other legacies, but such an indication must be clear and unequivocal. An indication that a particular legacy is to be paid at an earlier date than the others does not of itself give any priority in the event of abatement.

If an annuity is given by will and it is necessary for the legacies to abate, the value of the annuity will be abated proportionately with the general legacies. Thus, it will be necessary for the annuity to be valued and the capital sum reduced pro rata. The annuitant will then be entitled to receive the capital sum so reduced.

Specific legacies (SEE *Legacy*) do not abate with general (i.e. pecuniary) legacies unless the estate is insolvent, i.e. insufficient to pay the debts and expenses, in which case the specific legacies will abate *inter se*.

A demonstrative legacy (q.v.) does not abate with the general legacies. Abatement may be necessary, however, if the particular fund out of which the demonstrative legacy is payable is not sufficient for the purpose.

ABSCONDING DEBTOR SEE *Act of Bankruptcy*

ABSOLUTE TITLE Land may be registered under the Land Registration Act 1925, with an Absolute Title. A grant of an Absolute Title gives the proprietor a state-guaranteed title against all the world. The Land Certificate thereafter is the sole document of title and the previous title deeds are obsolete. To evidence this fact it is impressed with the Land Registry stamp. Absolute Title is granted for the most part in respect of freehold land, but in certain circumstances may be granted in respect of a leasehold estate. A possessory title may be converted into an absolute freehold title after 15 years or, if leasehold, to a good leasehold title after ten years. SEE *Land Registration*

ABSORPTION COSTING A system of costing sometimes used by companies with a wide product range. The products may arise from the common manufacturing facilities of the group or company, but in unequal and perhaps erratic proportions depending on the nature of the products and the fluctuation in demand. It becomes necessary to 'absorb' the overhead expenses in the cost of the products made or partly made in each centre. This may be an arbitrary judgment depending on the nature of each business. It is quite usual to arrive at a common unit of production expressed in labour hours, which takes into account all the production, marketing and overhead costs of the operation.

ABSTRACT OF TITLE A document prepared by the vendor's solicitor and delivered to the purchaser's solicitor on the transfer of land. It is an epitome of the vendor's deeds and subsidiary documents, but is not part of the title. The abstract should commence with the deed—the root of title—stipulated in the contract of sale for commencement of title. If there is no such stipulation, the abstract should ordinarily cover a minimum period of 15 years (Law of Property Act 1969, Section 23). Previously the period was 30 years. An abstract of title will disclose, in addition to the deeds in the vendor's possession, documents not usually handed over to a purchaser, but necessary to show an unbroken chain of title, such as probates, marriage and death certificates, settlements, etc. An acknowledgment of the right to production of any missing deeds or documents mentioned in the abstract of title should be obtained.

ACCEPTANCE This word is commonly used as meaning a bill of exchange, that is, the actual bill itself; but an acceptance is really the writing across the face of a bill by which the drawee agrees to the order of the drawer. The drawee is the person to whom a bill is addressed by the drawer, and who is required to pay on demand, or at a fixed or determinable future time, a sum certain in money to or to the order of a specified person, or to bearer. If the drawee agrees to the drawer's order he signifies his assent by accepting the bill. When the drawee has accepted a bill he is called the acceptor.

An acceptance is defined by Section 17 of the Bills of Exchange Act 1882 as follows:

> (1) The acceptance of a bill is the signification by the drawee of his assent to the order of the drawer.
> (2) An acceptance is invalid unless it complies with the following conditions, namely:
> (*a*) It must be written on the bill and be signed by the drawee. The mere signature of the drawee without additional words is sufficient.
> (*b*) It must not express that the drawee will perform his promise by any other means than the payment of money.

As a rule a drawee accepts a bill after it has been fully completed and signed by the drawer; but by Section 18,

> A bill may be accepted—
> (1) Before it has been signed by the drawer, or while otherwise incomplete:
> (2) When it is overdue, or after it has been dishonoured by a previous refusal to accept, or by non-payment:
> (3) When a bill payable after sight is dishonoured by non-acceptance and the drawee subsequently accepts it, the holder, in the absence of any different agreement, is entitled to have the bill accepted as of the date of first presentment to the drawee for acceptance.

There are two kinds of acceptances:
1 General acceptance SEE *Acceptance, General.*
2 Qualified acceptance SEE *Acceptance, Qualified.*

> A general acceptance assents without qualification to the order of the drawer. A qualified acceptance in express terms varies the effect of the bill as drawn. [Section 19(2)]

An acceptance is usually upon the face of the bill, but the drawee's signature placed upon the back of it is regarded as sufficient. In such a case it is usual to make a reference on the front of the bill to the fact that acceptance is on the back. A drawee may accept a bill by merely writing his name across it, without any further words, but it is customary for the word 'accepted' to be used. When the bill is domiciled, the name of the bank where it is payable follows the word 'accepted' and then the acceptor signs his name. The commonest form of acceptance (a general acceptance) is 'Accepted, payable at the X & Y Banking Co. Ltd, London, John Brown'.

If the bill is payable at so many days after sight, the drawee must add the date of sighting to his acceptance. SEE *Sighting a Bill*

If there are several drawees named on a bill, each one of them must sign the acceptance; but an order addressed to two drawees in the alternative, or to two or more drawees in succession, is not a bill of exchange. SEE *Drawee*

Section 17 states that the acceptance must be signed by the drawee, but anyone who holds a proper authority from the drawee to accept bills may accept on his behalf. A bill cannot be drawn on one person and accepted by another.

Where the drawee is a firm, the partner who accepts must do so in the name of the firm. Where the drawee is a limited company, the acceptance should contain the name of the company as well as the signatures of the authorized officials. If officials in signing do not show that they sign for and on behalf of the company they may render themselves personally liable.

The rules as to presentment of a bill for acceptance, are dealt with under *Presentment for Acceptance.*

When a bill is duly presented for acceptance and is not accepted within the customary time (that is by the close of business on the day following presentation for acceptance), the person presenting it must treat it as dishonoured by non-acceptance. SEE *Dishonour of Bill of Exchange*

Until a drawee has accepted the bill he is not liable thereon; but in Scotland where the drawee has funds available for its payment, the bill operates as an assignment of the amount of the bill in favour of the holder from the time when the bill is presented to the drawee (Section 53).

An acceptor is at liberty to cancel his acceptance provided that the bill is still in his own hands, and that he has not led anyone to believe that he would accept it.

The liability of an acceptor is defined by Section 54:

> The acceptor of a bill, by accepting it—
> (1) Engages that he will pay it according to the tenor of his acceptance:
> (2) Is precluded from denying to a holder in due course: [q.v.]
> (*a*) The existence of the drawer, the genuineness of his signature and his capacity and authority to draw the bill:
> (*b*) In the case of a bill payable to drawer's order, the then capacity of the drawer to indorse, but not the genuineness or validity of his indorsement;
> (*c*) In the case of a bill payable to the order of a third person, the existence of the payee and his then capacity to indorse, but not the genuineness or validity of his indorsement.

As an acceptor is responsible for the genuineness of the drawer's signature, a drawee consequently incurs an unnecessary liability if he accepts a bill before it has been signed by the drawer. If the bill is drawn 'per pro' or on behalf of the drawer, the drawee ought to satisfy himself before accepting the bill, that the drawer has authorized the bill to be drawn in that way. He is not liable for signatures, such as the payee's or an indorser's, which do not, in the ordinary course of things, appear upon a bill until after it has been accepted.

No person is liable as acceptor of a bill who has not signed it as such: provided that (1) where a person signs a bill in a trade or assumed name, he is liable thereon as if he had signed it in his own name; (2) the signature of the name of a firm is equivalent to the signature by the person so signing of the names of all persons liable as partners in that firm (Section 23). In the case of a non-trading partnership, an acceptance by a partner binds himself alone and not the firm.

If there are several acceptors on a bill they are jointly liable, not jointly and severally.

Where a bill is accepted payable at the acceptor's bankers, that is a sufficient authority for the banker to debit it to his customer's account; but in practice, country bankers often require particulars of acceptances falling due to be given, and a written order from the customer to pay them. Such an order does not require to be stamped. London bankers pay inland bills without advice, but foreign bills domiciled in London require advice.

Notice of the death, bankruptcy or mental incapacity of an acceptor revokes a banker's authority to pay an acceptance.

If the banker is a holder for value (q.v.), he may debit an acceptance to the acceptor's account, even if the acceptor has sent instructions not to pay the bill.

Where a bill is accepted, say, by John Brown payable at the British Bank, Leeds, although no drawee's name is mentioned in the bill, it may be debited to his account. A bill may also be charged to the acceptor's account which is accepted simply 'John Brown,' if there is an indication elsewhere on the bill that it is payable at the British Bank, Leeds.

A banker is not obliged to pay a bill accepted payable with him or to retire an acceptance payable in London, except by instructions or by custom. In *Bank of England* v *Vagliano Brothers* [1891] AC 107, it was held that 'if a banker undertakes the duty of paying his customer's acceptances, the arrangement is the result of some special agreement, expressed or implied.'

An order signed by a customer to retire an acceptance (whether his own or another person's) does not require a stamp to be affixed.

A drawer often indicates in the body of the bill, or below the drawee's name, where it shall be payable, e.g. 'payable in London,' but if there is no such indication, the drawee accepts it payable in the place where he lives, unless he follows the recognized custom and makes it payable in London.

If a bill is accepted payable at, say, the British Bank Plc, and no town is mentioned, it should be presented at the British Bank in the town where the drawee is described as living.

As to the practice of banks accepting bills on behalf of customers, SEE *Confirmed Credit, Documentary Bill.*

In Scotland, acceptors sign their names under the drawer's signature, but when they accept the bill payable at their bankers, the acceptance is generally across the bill. SEE *Bill of Exchange*

ACCEPTANCE, GENERAL When a drawee writes his name across a bill agreeing to the order of the drawer, it is called an acceptance of the bill. The Bills of Exchange Act 1882, Section 19, defines two kinds of acceptance:

> (1) An acceptance is either (*a*) general or (*b*) qualified. [SEE *Acceptance, Qualified*]
>
> (2) A general acceptance assents without qualification to the order of the drawer.
>
> (*c*) ... An acceptance to pay at a particular place is a general acceptance, unless it expressly states that the bill is to be paid there only and not elsewhere.

The following are specimens of general acceptances:

John Brown
Accepted, John Brown
Accepted John Brown, 2 King Street, Leeds
Accepted, payable at X & Y Bank Plc, Leeds, John Brown
Sighted, 16 June, John Brown, Leeds
Accepted, payable at A & B Bank Plc, London per pro John Brown, W. Robinson

A holder of a general acceptance may present it to the acceptor himself, but, if there is a place of payment mentioned on the bill, unless it is presented at that place he will lose his recourse against all the other parties to the bill. SEE *Acceptance; Acceptance, Qualified; Bill of Exchange*

ACCEPTANCE, QUALIFIED An acceptance is either general (SEE *Acceptance, General*) or qualified. Section 19 of the Bills of Exchange Act 1882, defines a qualified acceptance as follows:

> (2) ... A qualified acceptance in express terms varies the effect of the bill as drawn.

In particular an acceptance is qualified which is—

(*a*) conditional, that is to say, which makes payment by the acceptor dependent on the fulfilment of a condition therein stated:

(*b*) partial, that is to say, an acceptance to pay part only of the amount for which the bill is drawn:

(*c*) local, that is to say, an acceptance to pay only at a particular specified place:

An acceptance to pay at a particular place is a general acceptance, unless it expressly states that the bill is to be paid there only and not elsewhere:

(*d*) Qualified as to time:

(*e*) The acceptance of some one or more of the drawees, but not of all.

The following are specimens of qualified acceptances:

Conditional: 'Accepted, payable on delivery of bills of lading. J. Brown'

Partial—bill drawn for £100: 'Accepted for £50 only. J. Brown'

Local: 'Accepted, payable at the X & Y Bank Plc, Leeds, and there only. J. Brown'. In order to charge the acceptor and other parties, the bill must be presented for payment at the place named.

As to time—bill drawn at three months' date. 'Accepted, payable at X & Y Bank Plc, W. Brown.'

Not accepted by all the drawees—bill drawn on W. Brown, J. Jones, and W. Robinson: Accepted, payable at X & Y Bank Plc, W. Robinson'. In this case W. Robinson is liable to pay the bill.

The duties of the holder, the drawer, or the indorser of a qualified acceptance are set forth in Section 44 as follows:

(1) The holder of a bill may refuse to take a qualified acceptance, and if he does not obtain an unqualified acceptance may treat the bill as dishonoured by non-acceptance.

(2) Where a qualified acceptance is taken, and the drawer or an indorser has not expressly or impliedly authorised the holder to take a qualified acceptance, or does not subsequently assent thereto, such drawer or indorser is discharged from his liability on the bill.

The provisions of this sub-section do not apply to a partial acceptance, whereof due notice has been given. Where a foreign bill has been accepted as to part, it must be protested as to the balance.

(3) When the drawer or indorser of a bill receives notice of a qualified acceptance, and does not within a reasonable time express his dissent to the holder he shall be deemed to have assented thereto.

Where by the terms of a qualified acceptance, presentment for payment is required, the acceptor, in the absence of an express stipulation to that effect, is not discharged by the omission to present the bill for payment on the day that it matures (Section 52(2).) If a bill be accepted with a qualified acceptance as to place, the holder cannot sue the acceptor before he has presented the bill for payment.

ACCEPTANCE CREDIT A credit whose terms involve the drawing of time bills needing acceptance either by the bank issuing the credit or by the customer. SEE *Documentary Credit*

ACCEPTANCE FOR HONOUR The drawer of a bill and any indorser may insert in the bill the name of a person to whom a holder may resort in case of need that is in case the bill is dishonoured by non-acceptance or non-payment. Such a person is called the referee in case of need. (See Bills of Exchange Act 1882, Section 15.) If the bill is not accepted by the drawee the holder may, after the bill is protested for non-acceptance, present it to the referee in case of need. When the referee accepts it, he becomes an acceptor for honour.

After protest for non-acceptance (q.v.) any person may, with the consent of the holder, accept a bill 'supra protest' for the honour of any party thereon. Section 65 of the Bills of Exchange Act 1882 provides as follows:

(1) Where a bill of exchange has been protested for dishonour by non-acceptance, or protested for better security, and is not overdue, any person, not being a party already liable thereon, may, with the consent of the holder, intervene and accept the bill supra protest, for the honour of any party liable thereon, or for the honour of the person for whose account the bill is drawn.

(2) A bill may be accepted for honour for part only of the sum for which it is drawn.

(3) An acceptance for honour supra protest in order to be valid must—

(*a*) be written on the bill, and indicate that it is an acceptance for honour:

(*b*) be signed by the acceptor for honour.

(4) Where an acceptance for honour does not expressly state for whose honour it is made, it is deemed to be an acceptance for the honour of the drawer.

(5) Where a bill payable after sight is accepted for honour, its maturity is calculated from the date of the noting for non-acceptance, and not from the date of the acceptance for honour.

An acceptance for honour is written across the bill as, 'Accepted for the honour of John Brown, Thomas Jones', or 'Accepted supra protest, Thomas Jones', or 'Accepted for the honour of John Brown with £ for notarial charges, Thomas Jones', or, 'Accepted S.P. [i.e. supra protest], Thomas Jones'.

The liability of an acceptor for honour is dealt with in Section 66 as follows:

(1) The acceptor for honour of a bill by accepting it engages that he will, on due presentment, pay the bill according to the tenor of his acceptance, if it is not paid by the drawee, provided it has been duly presented for payment, and protested for non-payment, and that he receives notice of these facts.

(2) The acceptor for honour is liable to the holder and to all parties to the bill subsequent to the party for whose honour he has accepted.

As to presentment for payment to an acceptor for honour, see Section 67 under *Presentment for Payment*. SEE *Acceptance; Bill of Exchange*

ACCEPTING HOUSES These are financial institutions which specialize in accepting bills drawn on them under credits established in favour of approved customers. They are a major part of the merchant banking scene in the UK, although not all merchant banks are accepting houses. The term had its origin in the merchanting activities of the late eighteenth and early nineteenth centuries when trade between countries would be financed by bills of exchange drawn on the principal merchanting houses. At that point the merchants were merely financing their own trading activities. As international trade developed and other lesser known names wished to import goods from abroad, the established merchants lent their names to the newcomers by agreeing to accept bills of exchange on their behalf. The accepting house would charge a commission for this service and thus there grew up the business of accepting bills to finance the trade not merely of themselves but of others. Acceptance business thus became, and to a degree always has been, the hallmark of the true merchant bank. The acceptance 'credit' was primarily a means of financing international trade until the 1930s, but the use of acceptance credits for domestic business was given an impetus by the MacMillan Report in 1931. The MacMillan Committee recommended that commercial bills be used more widely as a means of financing domestic trade and, either for this reason or because of the falling off in foreign trade and the difficulties of a number of countries, bills of exchange became more widely used as a means of financing domestic trade. Today, the accepting houses are a major and indeed essential part of the London money market. Sixteen of the leading merchant banks constitute the Accepting Houses Committee, which acts as the regulatory and disciplinary body for its members. The principal qualifications for membership of the Committee are that a substantial part of the business of each house shall consist of accepting bills to finance the trade of others, that the bills when accepted can command the finest rates on the discount market and that the acceptances are freely taken by the Bank of England.

ACCEPTOR When the drawee of a bill (that is the person to whom the bill is addressed) agrees to the order of the drawer, he shows his assent by signing his name across the bill. That is, he accepts it, and when that is done he is called the acceptor. The acceptor is the person who is expected to pay the bill at maturity.

In applying the provisions of Part IV of the Bills of Exchange Act 1882, dealing with promissory notes (q.v.), the maker of a note is to be deemed to correspond with the acceptor of a bill. If there are several acceptors of a bill they can only be liable jointly, but in the case of a promissory note the makers may be liable jointly, or jointly and severally, according to the wording of the note.

An acceptor is not discharged through any failure of a holder to present the bill to him at maturity for payment. He is liable thereon for six years from its maturity. If an acceptor becomes bankrupt, his acceptances should be withdrawn by any customer for whom they have been discounted, though legally the withdrawal cannot be enforced before the bills mature. SEE *Acceptance; Bill of Exchange*

A cheque, albeit a bill of exchange, does not require acceptance and thus a banker does not become the acceptor of his customer's cheque. This is because the relationship of banker and customer is that of debtor and creditor and a customer with funds in his current account is entitled to draw on those funds on demand. SEE *Banker and Customer*

ACCESS This is the name of the credit card scheme introduced by a number of leading banks in October 1972. The original sponsors were National Westminster Bank, Midland Bank and Lloyds Bank. Together these three banks promoted the Joint Credit Card Company, in which they share the equity. Before the launch of Access, Williams & Glyn's Bank, Clydesdale Bank, Northern Bank, Ulster Bank and Royal Bank of Scotland joined in the scheme. The scheme is run as a joint venture by the participating banks, who are responsible for the recruitment and control of their own cardholder files. The Joint Credit Card Company is responsible for dealing with the merchants who accept Access cards and for the computer operations.

At the end of 1983, there were approximately 6.5 million Access cardholders in the UK.

In March 1975, Access became a member of the Inter-Bank Card Association with, then, 32 million cardholders around the world. This group, now operating under the name Mastercard, is one of the two large credit card groupings in the world, the other being Visa (q.v.) SEE *Credit Card*. SEE ALSO Supplement

ACCIDENT INSURANCE This is a loosely used term to include personal accident insurance (q.v.) or other forms of insurance in which accident may be a factor, e.g. accidents at sea (SEE *Marine Insurance*), accidents on the highway (SEE *Motor Vehicle Insurance*) and accidents involving buildings (SEE *Household Insurance*).

In general, the term accident for insurance purposes is meant to exclude the operation of natural causes such as old age or physical or mental disease. It has been suggested that the term covers any unlooked for mishap or an untoward event which is not expected or designed (Lord MacNaghten in *Fenton* v *Thorley & Co Ltd* [1903] AC 443 HL at p. 448). On the other hand, an accident may arise from an 'act of God', e.g. death from lightning or earthquake. It may also arise from a deliberate act—as in the case of a murder, which may be 'accidental' so far as the victim is concerned. The term is discussed fully under *Personal Accident Insurance*.

ACCOMMODATION BILL A bill to which a person, called an accommodation party, puts his name to oblige or accommodate another person without receiving any consideration for so doing. The position of such a party is, in fact, that of a surety or guarantor. Bills of this type used to be called 'kites,' or 'windmills,' or 'windbills'. A may accept a bill for the accommodation of B the drawer, who is in need of money. A receives no consideration and does not expect to be called upon to pay the bill when due. B raises the necessary funds by discounting the bill, expecting that, at maturity, he will be in a position to meet the bill himself. If, however, he fails to do so, a holder for value (q.v.), even though he knew it was an accommodation bill when he took it, can sue the acceptor and prior indorsers. But until value has been given no one is liable on such a bill. When a banker discounts an accommodation bill he becomes a holder for value.

The Bills of Exchange Act 1882, Section 28, defines an accommodation bill and the liability of an accommodation party as follows:

(1) An accommodation party to a bill is a person who has signed a bill as drawer, acceptor, or indorser, without receiving value therefor, and for the purpose of lending his name to some other person.

(2) An accommodation party is liable on the bill to a holder for value; and it is immaterial whether, when such holder took the bill, he knew such party to be an accommodation party or not.

By Section 46(2), presentment for payment is dispensed with

(c) As regards the drawer, where the drawee or acceptor is not bound, as between himself and the drawer, to accept or pay the bill, and the drawer has no reason to believe that the bill would be paid if presented.

(d) As regards an indorser, where the bill was accepted or made for the accommodation of that indorser and he has no reason to expect that the bill would be paid if presented.

Notice of dishonour is dispensed with, by Section 50(2),

(c) (4) Where the drawee or acceptor is as between himself and the drawer under no obligation to accept or pay the bill;

(d) As regards the indorser,

(3) Where the bill was accepted or made for his accommodation.

But to preserve the holder's rights against any prior parties the bill should be presented for payment at maturity.

By Section 59(3): 'Where an accommodation bill is paid in due course by the party accommodated, the bill is discharged.'

ACCOMMODATION PARTY The person who signs the bill as drawer, acceptor, or indorser, without receiving any value therefor, for the purpose of accommodating some other person. An accommodation party is liable to a holder for value. SEE *Accommodation Bill*

ACCORD AND SATISFACTION The substitution of one agreement for another, one party to a contract being willing to waive his claim under the contract for something different.

There cannot be a good accord and satisfaction of the whole of a debt by payment of part unless there be valuable consideration for giving up the remainder. The delivery and acceptance in satisfaction of a negotiable instrument for a less sum than the total sum due is good accord and satisfaction—the consideration being the getting of something different from legal tender in the shape of a negotiable instrument.

ACCOUNT In financial terms the word account is used in four senses: (1) entries in a ledger, e.g. capital account, drawings account, motor vehicles account or, indeed, cash account, which was historically part of the ledger; (2) a statement or bill requiring payment for goods or services, e.g. the butcher or the builder may 'render his account'; (3) a statement of stewardship such as an executor's account or a liquidator's account and, in the plural, the financial accounts of public companies to their shareholders are in this category; (4) the reckoning and recording of a debtor–creditor relationship. This last is the basis of modern banking. It is the existence of the account which establishes the banker–customer relationship. For a person to be a customer of a bank within the meaning of Section 4 of the Cheques Act 1957, there must be either a deposit or a current account or some similar relationship (*Great Western Railway* v *London & County Banking Company* [1901] AC 414). SEE *Current Account; Customer; Deposit Account*

ACCOUNT, STOCK EXCHANGE For the purpose of settling Stock Exchange bargains in company securities (as distinct from government stocks, local authority issues, etc.), the year is divided into 24 accounts consisting in most cases of a fortnight with the occasional three-week account. All transactions taking place within an account are due for settlement on the Settlement Day or Account Day, which is 10 days after the last Friday of the account, and thus falls on the second Monday after the last day of dealings. It is a day when securities should be delivered and payment made.

No stamp duty is payable on shares which are bought and sold within an account and normally only one commission charge is made by the stockbroker. On the last day of an account the client may deal for the next account, thereby extending the settlement period. SEE *Settlement, Stock Exchange*

ACCOUNT DAY SEE *Account, Stock Exchange*

ACCOUNT PAYEE These words, or their equivalent, such as a 'a/c AB,' are frequently added to the crossing of a cheque with the idea of safeguarding it in transmission. The phrase has no mention in the Bills of Exchange Act 1882, and does not render a cheque not transferable (*National Bank* v *Silke* [1891] 1 QB 435). Furthermore, the words have no effect on the negotiable quality of a cheque (*A. L. Underwood Ltd* v *The Bank of Liverpool & Martins Ltd* (1924) 40 TLR 302).

The efficacy of the phrase lies in its warning effect on a collecting banker, for the collection of a cheque bearing an 'a/c payee' crossing for anyone but the payee will enable the latter to claim damages for conversion if the cheque has been used in fraud of him. It has been held that the collection of a cheque so crossed for someone other than the payee is negligence disentitling the banker to the protection of Section 2, Bills of Exchange Act 1882 [now replaced by Section 4, Cheques Act 1957]. (*Bevan* v *National Bank Ltd* (1907) 23 TLR 65; *House Property Co. of London, Ltd and Others* v *London County & Westminster Bank Ltd* (1915) 31 TLR 479.) But where an English bank collected a cheque crossed 'a/c payee' for a foreign banking correspondent who remitted it for credit in its account in London and the cheque had been paid into the foreign bank by one of its customers in fraud of the payee, it was held that the English bank had not acted negligently (*Importers Co. Ltd* v *Westminster Bank Ltd* (1927) 43 TLR 325). It is not clear beyond all doubt whether sufficient enquiry can eliminate the risk for the collecting banker, despite this so-called crossing. However, at least the duty of enquiry is much heavier than it would otherwise have been.

The fact that a cheque is payable to a specified person or to bearer and crossed 'a/c payee' does not minimize the significance of the words.

The paying banker is not concerned with the special features of an 'a/c payee' crossing, and evidence in the shape of further indorsements that the cheque has not gone to the payee's account does not put him on enquiry.

An uncrossed cheque marked 'a/c payee' and presented across the counter for payment should not be paid.

The Committee of London Clearing Bankers agreed in 1958 that the drawing of non-transferable cheques would create serious practical difficulties for the banks and might expose them to unacceptable risks. For example, a paying banker would have no statutory protection in respect of non-transferable cheques cashed at the counter and would in each case be obliged positively to identify the payee; while the collecting banker could not become the holder for value of a non-transferable cheque and would not be able to enforce payment in his own name. For these and other reasons, therefore, it recommended that in appropriate cases customers should be approached with a request that the practice should be discontinued.

ACCOUNT STATED This term has two meanings. It may mean the simple acknowledgment of a debt, which acknowledgment is considered merely prima facie evidence of the existence of the debt and rebuttable by further evidence. In its second sense it means that parties who have had a series of mutual transactions have agreed expressly or implicitly to a set-off (q.v.) of the items against each other and to be answerable only for the balance.

In this latter sense the courts have consistently refused to hold that the pass book was evidence of an account stated. It is even less likely that the present-day loose-leaf statement, which is not returned by the customer to his banker, would be so considered.

ACCOUNTANT According to the *Oxford English Dictionary*, an accountant is a professional keeper and inspector of accounts. Thus, the term has no very precise meaning and is used loosely throughout the financial world to indicate any person who has a responsibility for recording or supervising financial matters. The principal accounting bodies in the UK are the Institute of Chartered Accountants in England and Wales, the Institute of Chartered Accountants in Scotland and the Association of Certified Accountants. These three bodies are participants in the Joint Disciplinary Scheme which was established in 1981, the objectives of which are

> to promote the highest possible standards of professional and business conduct, efficiency and competence (a) by members in the performance of their professional or business activities (including duties as a servant or employee of any organisation), and (b) by member firms in the provision of the services which they offer to the public, by providing a system for the investigation and regulation of the activities of members and member firms so as to secure their adherence to all professional criteria, including but not limited to, all relevant recommendations and standards promulgated from time to time by or with the approval of the councils of the participants.

In the early 1970s, the accountancy institutes set up the Accounting Standards Committee charged with the task of improving the technical quality of financial reporting, and up to the present time, the Committee has issued 20 *Statements of Standard Accounting Practice* (SSAPs). Whilst the Accounting Standards Committee has no power to enforce conformity with the SSAPs, it does have a considerable persuasive influence and, in general, it is a requirement of the Stock Exchange that quoted companies will comply with the standards under the terms of their listing agreements. SEE ALSO *Current Cost Accounting; Inflation Accounting*

ACCRUED INCOME The cumulative running of interest, usually on a day-to-day basis, on a capital asset. Thus, for example, on the death of a shareholder, it may be necessary to apportion dividends received after the death over the period to which the dividends relate, if the income and the capital of the estate pass to different people. SEE UNDER *Apportionment*

ACCRUED INTEREST Interest may accrue on a day-to-day basis on a capital asset or liability. On a bank overdraft or on a bank deposit account, the interest, although calculated, say, quarterly, is deemed to accrue from day to day.

In the case of Government stocks and most other fixed interest securities, the accrued interest is reflected in the quoted price. This is not so, however, in the case of 'short' Government securities, i.e. those with a life up to five years to maturity. These are quoted 'clean'. This means that the gross amount of accrued interest since the last interest date must be added or subtracted (depending on whether the price is ex dividend or cum dividend) in order to arrive at the total consideration.

ACCUMULATION UNITS Units in a unit trust (q.v.) where net income, instead of being distributed to the unit-holders, is automatically reflected in the increased value of the units. This can be done only if the trust deed makes provision for accumulation units as such. This has the advantage that income may be re-invested without the incurring of an initial charge on each occasion. In other cases, unit-holders may if they wish arrange for income distributions to be invested in further units, but these are not accumulation units as such and on each occasion an initial charge will be incurred, as with any new purchase of units.

ACT OF BANKRUPTCY An act of bankruptcy is one of the many steps defined by statute which, if taken by a debtor, may lead to a bankruptcy petition and subsequent bankruptcy proceedings. When a debtor commits an act of bankruptcy, the court may, on a bankruptcy petition being presented either by a creditor or by the debtor, make a receiving order for the protection of the estate. The act must have been committed within three months before the presentation of the petition.

Eight various acts of bankruptcy are detailed in Section 1 of the Bankruptcy Act 1914:

> (1) A debtor commits an act of bankruptcy in each of the following cases—
>
> (*a*) If in England or elsewhere he makes a conveyance or assignment of his property to a trustee or trustees for the benefit of his creditors generally:
>
> (*b*) If in England or elsewhere he makes a fraudulent conveyance, gift, delivery, or transfer of his property, or of any part thereof:
>
> (*c*) If in England or elsewhere he makes any conveyance or transfer of his property or any part thereof, or creates any charge thereon, which would under this or any other Act be void as a fraudulent preference if he were adjudged bankrupt:
>
> (*d*) If with intent to defeat or delay his creditors he does any of the following things, namely, departs out of England, or being out of England remains out of England, or departs from his dwelling-house, or otherwise absents himself, or begins to keep house:

(*e*) If execution against him has been levied by seizure of his goods under process in an action in any Court, or in any civil proceeding in the High Court, and the goods have been either sold or held by the sheriff for twenty-one days:

Provided that, where an interpleader summons has been taken out in regard to the goods seized, the time elapsing between the date at which such summons is taken out and the date at which the proceedings on such summons are finally disposed of, settled, or abandoned, shall not be taken into account in calculating such period of twenty-one days:

(*f*) If he files in the Court a declaration of his inability to pay his debts or presents a bankruptcy petition against himself:

(*g*) If a creditor has obtained a final judgment or final order against him for any amount, and, execution thereon not having been stayed, has served on him in England, or, by leave of the Court, elsewhere, a bankruptcy notice under this Act, and he does not, within seven days after service of the notice, in case the service is effected in England, and in case the service is effected elsewhere, then within the time limited in that behalf by the order giving leave to effect the service, either comply with the requirements of the notice, or satisfy the Court that he has a counter-claim set-off or cross demand, which equals or exceeds the amount of the judgment debt or sum ordered to be paid, and which he could not set up in the action in which the judgment was obtained, or the proceedings in which the order was obtained:

For the purposes of this paragraph and of Section 2 of this Act, any person who is, for the time being, entitled to enforce a final judgment or final order, shall be deemed a creditor who has obtained a final judgment or final order.

(*h*) If the debtor gives notice to any of his creditors that he has suspended, or that he is about to suspend, payment of his debts.

The phrase 'begins to keep house' in subsection (*d*) means to shut himself up in the house, or to refuse to see his creditors with the intention of delaying them.

There are three further acts of bankruptcy:

(*i*) The County Courts Act 1959 allowed an application to be made for an Administration Order (q.v.) over assets of the debtor. The Administration of Justice Act 1965 provided that the making of such an application was to be treated as an act of bankruptcy.

(*j*) When a County Court is hearing an application for an Attachment of Earnings Order and considers that an Administration Order may be appropriate, the Court may order the debtor to submit a list of all his debts. By the Administration of Justice Act 1970, such an action is deemed to be an act of bankruptcy.

(*k*) The Criminal Justice Act 1972, Sections 7 to 9, and the first schedule of the Act, provides that a person against whom a criminal bankruptcy order is made is to be treated as a debtor who has committed an act of bankruptcy on the date on which the order is made. Criminal bankruptcy occurs where a person is convicted of an offence before the Crown Court and it appears to the Court that, as a result of the offence(s), loss or damage other than personal injury has been suffered by one or more persons, whose identity is known to the Court, and the amount or aggregate amount of the loss or damage exceeds £15,000. The petition is presented in the High Court but the proceedings may be transferred

An available act of bankruptcy means any act of bankruptcy available for a bankruptcy petition at the date of the presentation of the petition on which the receiving order is made (Section 167).

It is often difficult to decide whether a certain state of things does or does not constitute an act of bankruptcy. A mere statement by a debtor that, in certain events, he will be obliged to suspend payment is not of itself, an act of bankruptcy. Where a doctor, through his solicitor, sent a circular letter calling together a meeting of his creditors it was held that the position of a non-trader, such as a doctor, differed greatly from that of a trader, and that in the case of a non-trader a declaration of inability to pay his debts was not necessarily a notice to his creditors of an intention to suspend payment. (*Re a Debtor; ex parte the Petitioning Creditors* (1912) 106 LT 812).

In *Anglo-South American Bank Ltd* v *Urban District Council of Withernsea* (1924) KB, a debtor had admitted at a creditors' meeting that he was insolvent and asked his creditors to accept a composition. He refused to file his petition and indicated that his intention was to carry on as long as he could and not to suspend payment of his debts generally unless he was forced into bankruptcy by his creditors. After the meeting he obtained money from the plaintiffs by means of the defendant's cheque. It was held that there was no act of bankruptcy, and that the plaintiffs were bona fide holders for value without notice of any defect in the title of the debtor. Greer, J, in the course of his judgment, referring to paragraph (*h*) in Section 1, said

It seems reasonably clear

(1) That the bankrupt's statement must be something more than a mere casual remark. It must be a statement that by its form appears to be an intentional statement by the bankrupt of something that he has already done or something he intends to do. This, at least, is involved in the use of the word 'notice'.

(2) That a statement by or on behalf of the debtor that he is insolvent, whether the deficiency be great or small,

is not of itself an act of bankruptcy, unless it amounts to a statement of inability to pay each and every one of his creditors.

(3) That a statement of insolvency may be made on such an occasion and with such surrounding circumstances that a reasonably minded creditor would understand it as an intimation that the debtor had suspended, or was about to suspend, payment of his debts generally, and if it be so made it is an act of bankruptcy.

By an act of bankruptcy a bill which has been given in payment of a debt becomes immediately payable, and where any person liable upon a bill commits an act of bankruptcy a holder can present a petition upon his debt (*Ex parte Raatz* [1897] 2 QB 80).

In a bankruptcy, the whole of the bankrupt's property devolves on the trustee and the trustee's title to that property relates back to the act of bankruptcy on which the receiving order is made, or if there are more acts of bankruptcy than one, to the time of the first of the acts of bankruptcy committed within three months next preceding the date of the presentation of the bankruptcy petition; but no bankruptcy petition, receiving order or adjudication shall be rendered invalid by reason of any act of bankruptcy anterior to the debt of the petitioning creditor. SEE SECTION 37 UNDER *Adjudication in Bankruptcy*.

A payment by a bankrupt to any of his creditors or a payment to a bankrupt is not invalidated by bankruptcy provided that the payment takes place before the date of the receiving order, and provided that the person (other than the debtor) to, by, or with whom the payment was made has not, at the time of the payment, notice of an available act of bankruptcy committed by the bankrupt before that time. (SEE SECTION 45 UNDER *Bankruptcy*.)

By Section 46

Validity of certain payments to bankrupt and assignee

A payment of money, or delivery of property, to a person subsequently adjudged bankrupt, or to a person claiming by assignment from him, shall, notwithstanding anything in this Act, be a good discharge to the person paying the money or delivering the property, if the payment or delivery is made before the actual date on which the receiving order is made and without notice of the presentation of a bankruptcy petition, and is either pursuant to the ordinary course of business or otherwise bona fide.

By this Section a payment of money to a person subsequently adjudged bankrupt, or to a person claiming by assignment from him, is protected if the payment is made before the date of the receiving order and without notice of the presentation of a bankruptcy petition. It is to be noted, however, that the payment must, apparently, be made to the person himself or to a person claiming by assignment from him. Payment of a cheque, drawn by a person who is subsequently adjudged bankrupt, in favour of a third party does not come within the words of this Section. The payee of a bankrupt's cheque is not a person claiming by assignment from the bankrupt. A banker is protected by this Section in paying over any balance on a customer's account to the trustee under a deed of assignment.

There is some doubt as to whether a banker paying cheques to third parties is protected by Section 46. (See *Paget: Law of Banking*, 9th Edition, p. 94 for discussion of the point and the view that he is not protected.

In *Re Dalton (a Bankrupt)* [1962] 3 WLR 140, an insolvent debtor had goods seized and held by the sheriff for 21 days. This was an act of bankruptcy. His business was sold, the proceeds going to his solicitor, who had notice of the act of bankruptcy. The solicitor paid certain creditors out of the proceeds, in the belief that these were all the creditors there were. It subsequently transpired that there were further debts totalling £4,000. Finally, the debtor was adjudicated bankrupt on his own petition. The trustee in bankruptcy applied for an order for an account of the moneys passing through the hands of the solicitor. A Divisional Court held that the solicitor was protected by Sections 45 and 46. In dealing with the latter section, Russell, J, said

The payment by one who holds funds for A to B on the request or order or direction of A, seems to us to be out of the ordinary and natural scope of the phrase 'payment to A.' If it be considered a mischief that a banker be not able to meet demands from the customer for cash, it is surely no less a mischief that the banker be not able to honour cheques drawn by the customer in favour of other persons, always remembering the safeguard that for the section to operate it must be shown that the payment is made pursuant to the ordinary course of business or otherwise bona fide. (We observe that, of course, the payee of the cheque would not be a person claiming by assignment.) It would, in our judgment, be very strange if Parliament had enacted that a banker (with the relevant notice) must say to his customer: 'I cannot honour your cheques to tradesmen totalling £50, but here is £50 in cash for you to post or send or take to them'.

As a result of these dicta, if not of the decision itself, the distinction between Section 45 and Section 46 has become very blurred, and the position must await further clarification.

In *Re Wigzell, ex parte the Trustee* (1921) 37 TLR 373, a debtor, against whom a receiving order was made, obtained an order staying the advertisement pending an appeal, which was subsequently dismissed. The debtor was afterwards adjudicated bankrupt. After the receiving order, payments into his banking account were made by the debtor, and payments out were also made, the bankers not knowing of the receiving order. Held that the effect of Sections 18, 37 (SEE UNDER *Adjudication in Bankruptcy*) and 38 was to make the money paid into the account the property of the trustee, and that these transactions were not protected by Sections 45 or 46 (see above). The bankers were not entitled to credit themselves with anything paid out to the bankrupt during the same period. This decision was affirmed by the Court of Appeal (1921, 37 TLR 526). Younger, LJ, in his judgment said that the affirmation does not preclude the bank from claiming the right, by a proper application, to trace into the pockets of persons, who, but for the payment to them, would have been creditors in the bankruptcy, the sums so paid to them, to the intent that the bank may stand in the shoes of those persons so paid and receive from the trustee in bankruptcy the dividend to which but for the payment they would have been entitled.

Section 4 of the Bankruptcy (Amendment) Act 1926, partially remedies this harshness; its effect is that where money has been paid to a third party in ignorance of a receiving order and before its advertisement, the trustee must, where reasonably practicable, recover such money from such third party.

By the Deeds of Arrangement Act 1914

> Section 24(1). If the trustee under a deed of arrangement, which either is expressed to be or is in fact for the benefit of the debtor's creditors generally, serves in the prescribed manner on any creditor of the debtor notice in writing of the execution of the deed and of the filing of the statutory declaration certifying the creditors' assents, with an intimation that the creditor will not, after the expiration of one month from the service of the notice, be entitled to present a bankruptcy petition against the debtor founded on the execution of the deed, or on any other act committed by him in the course or for the purpose of the proceedings preliminary to the execution of the deed, as an act of bankruptcy, that creditor shall not, after the expiration of that period, unless the deed becomes void, be entitled to present a bankruptcy petition against the debtor founded on the execution of the deed, or any act so committed by him as an act of bankruptcy. [SEE *Deed of Arrangement*]

SEE *Assignment for Benefit of Creditors, Bankruptcy, Fraudulent Conveyance, Fraudulent Preference, Receiving Order*

ACTIVE CIRCULATION The notes which are in circulation, that is, notes which have been issued from a bank of issue and are in the hands of the public, as distinguished, for example, from those held by the Banking Department of the Bank of England as part of the reserve.

ACTIVE SERVICE, DEATH ON The estate of a deceased person is exempt from capital transfer tax if the deceased

1) was at some time a member of the armed forces of the Crown or of certain ancillary organizations or was subject to the law governing the armed forces, and

2) died at any time as a result of a wound inflicted, an accident occurring or a disease contracted when on active service or on other service of a warlike nature, or

3) whose death was caused by or hastened by the activation on active service, etc. of a disease contracted at some earlier date.

In order to claim relief, the personal representatives of the deceased must obtain from the Ministry of Defence a certificate stating that the requisite conditions have been satisfied.

ACTUARY An actuary is defined in the *Oxford English Dictionary* as an expert in statistics, especially one who calculates insurance risks and premiums. From the mid-eighteenth century onwards, the role of the actuary was concerned almost exclusively with the calculation of mortality risks for the purpose of life assurance. It seems that one James Dodson played a leading part in the development of mortality tables in the mid-eighteenth century by the simple expedient of taking sample dates from gravestones. In modern times, the major part of actuarial activity is still concerned with life assurance but actuaries have extended their statistical methods significantly into areas of general insurances, such as fire, accident and marine. Actuaries have also played a major role in the development of pension schemes and now have a statutory obligation in relation to occupational pension schemes.

In general, actuaries in Britain are either Fellows of the Institute of Actuaries in England, or Fellows of the Faculty of Actuaries in Scotland. Their principal field of activity is still in insurance companies but in recent years an increasing number have become consulting actuaries or pension consultants or have taken up employment in the public sector, industry or the financial sector.

A number of statutory duties have been imposed on actuaries by various acts of Parliament, of which the following are some of the principal examples.

By Section 19, Insurance Companies Act 1982, every company which undertakes long-term business (principally life and annuity business, linked long-term business, permanent health insurance and pension fund management) is required to appoint an actuary as actuary to the company and to notify the Secretary of State within 14 days whenever such an appointment is made or terminated. In respect of every accounting year commencing on or after 1st January, 1981, the appointed actuary must sign a certificate, annexed to the balance sheet of the company, stating that adequate records have been kept for the purpose of valuing the long-term business liabilities and that the liabilities in respect of long-term business do not exceed the long-term business assets (Regulation 18(b) of Statutory Instrument 1980, No. 6).

For accounting years ending after 14th March, 1984, the certificate is to state, if such be the case, that adequate records have been kept for the purpose of valuing the long-term business liabilities, that the mathematical reserves, together with any amount specified (being part of the excess of the admissible assets representing the long-term business funds over the amount shown in the relevant form) constitute proper provision for the liabilities, including liabilities arising from any distribution of surplus, that the liabilities have been assessed in the context of the assets valued in accordance with the appropriate regulations and the certificate should also state the required solvency margin.

Under Section 18 of the Act, every company transacting long-term business must once in every 12 month period, cause an investigation to be made into its financial condition by the appointed actuary and an abstract of the actuary's report must be set out in the form prescribed in Regulation 17(a) of Statutory Instrument 1980, No.6.

Section 18 of the Act also requires the company at least once every five years to prepare in the prescribed form the statement of its long-term business at the date to which the accounts were made up for the actuarial investigation.

Under Section 49 of the Act, it is provided that the court shall not entertain an application for the transfer of the whole or part of the long-term business of one insurance company to another unless the petition is accompanied by a report on the scheme by an independent actuary.

Section 90 of the Act provides for regulations to be made regarding the determination of the value of the assets and the amount of the liabilities in any case in which the value or amount is required by any provision of the Act to be determined in accordance with valuation regulations.

Under the Superannuation and Other Trust Funds (Validation) Act 1927, it is provided (Section 5) that the financial condition of every fund registered under the Act must be investigated and reported on at least once every five years by an actuary. A similar provision is contained in the Local Government Superannuation Regulations 1974.

Under the Friendly Societies Act 1974, all registered societies are required to have a valuation undertaken by an actuary at least every five years, or if required by the Chief Registrar of Friendly Societies, at least once every three years. SEE *Expectation of Life; Friendly Societies; Life Assurance*

ADDITIONAL VOLUNTARY CONTRIBUTION (AVC) A contribution made by an employee to an occupational pension scheme over and above the general level of employees' contributions to the scheme. If the rules of the scheme permit (and in many instances they may be amended for this purpose), an employee may make additional contributions in order to increase his pension benefits provided the employee's total contributions do not exceed 15 per cent of his total remuneration (including all taxable benefits such as motor cars and private health insurance contributions). There are a number of ways in which an employee may benefit by making AVCs. For example, an employee who does not have a sufficient number of years' service to qualify for a full pension under the scheme may augment his pension up to the permitted maximum by making additional contributions. Similarly, by making AVCs, an employee may facilitate early retirement and also secure future increases in pension as at least a partial hedge against inflation. It may also be possible to secure greater benefits for widows and children than would otherwise be available under the main scheme. SEE *Pensions*

ADEMPTION The gift by will of a specific legacy is 'adeemed' and can therefore no longer take effect if the item in question no longer exists in the testator's ownership at the date of the death. A gift by will may also be adeemed where, after making his will, a testator makes a disposition of the item in question to the legatee during the testator's lifetime. Also, because of the principle of equity that a testator does not wish to benefit his children unequally (in the absence of evidence to the contrary), a gift to a child by will may be adeemed by a gift, albeit of other property, to a child during the testator's life.

The normal case of ademption, however, arises where a particular asset given to a particular legatee or devisee no longer exists or is otherwise no longer in the testator's ownership at the date of death. It has been held that a gift of 'my piano' refers to the piano owned by the testator at the date of the will and thus the gift was adeemed when the testator sold the piano and purchased another one (*Re Sikes, Moxon* v *Crossley* [1927] 1 Ch 364). A gift of a Government security which changes its character because, for example, of its conversion into another form of security will be adeemed unless the authorizing statute provides that ademption shall not take place (*Re Jenkins, Jenkins* v *Daves* [1931] Ch 218). A gift of shares will be adeemed if they become the subject of a capital reorganization or takeover, etc. of a kind which completely destroys the identity of the original shareholding (*Kuypers, Kuypers* v *Kuypers* [1925] Ch 244). On the other hand, the conversion or subdivision of shares within a company will not normally result in the ademption of a gift of those shares by will.

Ademption can only apply to specific gifts by will and not to general or demonstrative legacies (q.v.).

ADJUDICATION IN BANKRUPTCY Where a receiving order has been made against a debtor (SEE *Receiving Order*), though he is not at that date adjudged bankrupt, it means that, unless a composition or scheme of arrangement is accepted by the creditors, the court will, shortly, make an order adjudicating the debtor bankrupt.

Section 18 of the Bankruptcy Act 1914 enacts

(1) Where a receiving order is made against a debtor, then, if the creditors at the first meeting or any adjournment thereof by ordinary resolution resolve that the debtor be adjudged bankrupt, or pass no resolution, or if the creditors do not meet, or if a composition or scheme is not approved in pursuance of this Act within fourteen days after the conclusion of the examination of the debtor or such further time as the Court may allow, the Court shall adjudge the debtor bankrupt; and thereupon the property of the bankrupt shall become divisible among his creditors and shall vest in a trustee.

(2) Notice of every order adjudging a debtor bankrupt, stating the name, address, and description of the bankrupt, the date of the adjudication, and the Court by which the adjudication is made, shall be gazetted and advertised in a local paper in the prescribed manner, and the date of the order shall, for the purposes of this Act, be the date of the adjudication.

The court has power in certain cases to annul an adjudication. Section 29 provides

(1) Where in the opinion of the Court a debtor ought not to have been adjudged bankrupt, or where it is proved to the satisfaction of the Court that the debts of the bankrupt are paid in full, the Court may, on the application of any person interested by order annul the adjudication.

(3) Notice of the order annulling an adjudication shall be forthwith gazetted and published in a local paper.

The creditors may, if they think fit, at any time, after a debtor is adjudicated a bankrupt, entertain a proposal for a composition in satisfaction of the debts due to them or for a scheme of arrangement of the bankrupt's affairs (Section 21(1)).

Section 37(1) relates to the date when a bankruptcy is deemed to commence. Thus

The bankruptcy of a debtor, whether it takes place on the debtor's own petition or upon that of a creditor or creditors, shall be deemed to have relation back to, and to commence at, the time of the act of bankruptcy being committed on which a receiving order is made against him, or, if the bankrupt is proved to have committed more acts of bankruptcy than one, to have relation back to, and to commence at, the time of the first of the acts of bankruptcy proved to have been committed by the bankrupt within three months next preceding the date of the presentation of the bankruptcy petition; but no bankruptcy petition, receiving order, or adjudication shall be rendered invalid by reason of any act of bankruptcy anterior to the debt of the petitioning creditor.

See Section 46, Bankruptcy Act 1914, under *Act of Bankruptcy* as to validity of certain payments to the bankrupt or his assignee. See also Section 45 under *Bankruptcy*.

ADJUDICATION STAMPS Where a doubt exists as to the stamp duty with which any instrument is chargeable, the opinion of the Board of Inland Revenue may be obtained as to the proper stamp. The instrument itself, and also a sufficient abstract thereof, must be lodged with the Controller of Stamps, and a separate abstract must be lodged with each deed. No document can be received for adjudication until it has been executed by all necessary parties.

ADMINISTRATION OF ESTATES (SMALL PAYMENTS) ACT 1965 The chief purpose of this Act was to raise to a more realistic figure the limit below which, in the case of small estates, sums could be paid out without production of a grant of representation. Prior to the passing of the Act, such powers were contained in a number of statutes dealing with assets such as money with building societies, friendly societies, industrial and provident societies, National Savings Certificates, Premium Savings Bonds, Post Office Savings Bank Accounts (now National Savings Bank accounts) and funds in court. The limits imposed by the former statutes were £100 or £200.

The 1965 Act raised these limits to £500 in relation to deaths on and after 5th September, 1965, and the same figure applied also to certain powers of nomination exercised after that date. The Treasury was given power to raise the limit above £500 by order and also to raise to a similar figure a limit imposed by any statute not specifically referred to in the new Act. By the Administration of Estates (Small Payments) (Increase of Limit) Order 1975, the limit was increased to £1,500 in respect of deaths on or after 9th August, 1975 and by the Administration of Estates (Small Payments) (Increase of Limit) Order 1984, the limit was increased to £5,000 with effect from 11 May 1984. SEE *Excepted Estates*

ADMINISTRATION ORDER Where a debtor is unable to pay the amount of a county court judgment forthwith and claims that his total indebtedness does not exceed £2,000 (inclusive of the debt for which the judgment was obtained), the court may make an order providing for the administration of his estate. The order is granted under Section 148 of the County Courts Act 1959, and under Section 21 of the Administration of Justice Act 1965, an application for such an Administration Order is the equivalent of an act of bankruptcy (q.v.). Such an Administration Order should be distinguished from an order made under Section 130 of the Bankruptcy Act 1914, for the administration in bankruptcy of a deceased's estate.

The application by a debtor is made in the form of an affidavit setting out a list of all his creditors and the amount of their debts, his income, outgoings and personal circumstances and his proposals for payment of the whole or part of the debts by instalments. Unless the court otherwise directs, the debtor must attend a hearing and he must answer all questions put to him or permitted by the court. If an Administration Order is made, no creditor thereafter has any remedy against the debtor in respect of any debt which has been notified in the proceedings, except with the leave of the court. An Administration Order is designed for the benefit of a debtor who has several creditors and it may be set aside if he fails to fulfil his part of the Order. He then ceases to be protected by the Order and is exposed to the risk of proceedings by his creditors.

Under Section 4 of the Attachment of Earnings Act 1971, where, on an application for an Attachment of Earnings Order to secure payment of a judgment debt, it appears that the debtor has other debts, the court is required to consider whether the case may be one for the making of an Administration Order.

ADMINISTRATOR The court will appoint an administrator to wind up the estate of a deceased person in cases where (1) the deceased has died intestate or (2) the deceased left a will, but (a) did not name an executor or (b) the executor died before the testator or (c) the executor is unwilling or unable to act. Thus, an administrator either acts (1) on intestacy or (2) 'with the will annexed' (*cum testamento annexo*). An administrator appointed on intestacy is responsible for administering the estate in accordance with the rules of intestacy (q.v.). An administrator 'with the will annexed' will administer an estate in accordance with the terms of the will.

An executor's authority stems from the will itself (although it has to be confirmed in the grant of probate when the will is 'proved') and he may act in the affairs of the estate immediately the death occurs whereas an administrator has strictly speaking, no authority until appointed by the court, although he will have to undertake *de facto* a number of duties on behalf of the estate, e.g. valuing the assets, in order to apply for the grant of letters of administration (q.v.).

A banker has no authority to allow any dealings on the account of a customer who died intestate, nor to deal with any securities held on behalf of the deceased's estate until the administrator has obtained a grant of letters of administration.

Upon the death of the sole or last surviving administrator his executors, if any, do not undertake his duties. A new grant of letters of administration may be necessary. SEE *Administrator De Bonis Non; Executor; Letters of Administration; Personal Representatives*

ADMINISTRATOR AD LITEM An administrator of a deceased person's estate appointed for the purpose of litigation only.

ADMINISTRATOR CUM TESTAMENTO ANNEXO An administrator with the will annexed. SEE *Administrator*

ADMINISTRATOR DE BONIS NON A contraction of administrator *de bonis non administratis*, which means administrator of effects not administered. Where an administrator dies, or an executor dies without appointing an executor, and the duties connected with the administration have not been completed, the court will appoint another person, called an administrator *de bonis non*, to complete the winding up of the estate.

ADMINISTRATOR DURANTE ABSENTIA An administrator appointed to act during the absence abroad of an administrator.

ADMINISTRATOR DURANTE MINORE AETATE An administrator appointed to act during the minority of the executor or of the person legally entitled to a grant of letters of administration.

ADMINISTRATOR PENDENTE LITE An administrator appointed to administer an estate pending any suit respecting the validity of a will or any other matter in dispute.

ADOPTION The regulations regarding the adoption of children in England and Wales are consolidated in the Adoption Act 1976. From the financial point of view, the principal consideration is the devolution of property on death or *inter vivos*. In general, once an adoption order has been made, the adopted child is to be considered, for the purposes of the devolution of property, as if he or she were, in all respects, the child of the adopter, born in lawful wedlock. Under the Act, an adopted child is to be treated as the child of no person other than the adopter but this does not affect any vested interest which the child might have before the date of adoption. In those cases where a disposition depends on the date of birth of a child or children of an adoptive parent, it takes effect as if the adopted child had been born on the day of the adoption (but this does not affect any reference to the child's age).

Under the Adoption Act, there are provisions for the protection of a trustee or personal representative who distributes property in ignorance of the fact that an adoption order has been made, provided he has not received notice of the circumstances before the distribution.

AD VALOREM Latin for 'according to value'. An *ad valorem* stamp duty is a duty calculated by reference to a certain scale according to the value of the subject-matter to which the document relates. All cheques, bills of exchange, and promissory notes were charged with a fixed duty of 2d until 1st February, 1971, after which date this duty ceased to be payable, but duty is *ad valorem* upon many other documents: assignments of leases, conveyance, transfers of stocks and shares, etc.

By the Stamp Act 1891, Section 6

(1) Where an instrument is chargeable with *ad valorem* duty in respect of—

- (*a*) any money in any foreign or colonial currency, or
- (*b*) any stock or marketable security, the duty shall be calculated on the value, on the day of the date of the instrument, of the money in British currency according to the current rate of exchange, or of the stock or security according to the average price thereof.

(2) Where an instrument contains a statement of current rate of exchange, or average price, as the case may require, and is stamped in accordance with that statement, it is, so far as regards the subject-matter of the statement, to be deemed duly stamped, unless or until it is shown that the statement is untrue, and that the instrument is in fact insufficiently stamped.

By the Finance Act 1899, Section 12

(1) Where an instrument is charged with an *ad valorem* duty in respect of any money in any foreign or colonial currency, a rate of exchange for which is specified in the schedule to this Act, the stamp duty on that instrument shall, instead of being calculated as provided by Section 6 of the Stamp Act, 1891, be calculated according to the rate of exchange so specified.

(2) The Commissioners may substitute, as respects any foreign or colonial currency mentioned in the Schedule to this Act, any rate of exchange, for that specified in the Schedule, and may add to the Schedule a rate of exchange for any foreign or colonial currency not mentioned therein, and this Act shall be construed as if any rate of exchange for the time being substituted or added were contained in the said Schedule, and in the case of the substitution of a rate of exchange as if the rate for which the new rate is substituted were omitted from that Schedule.

(3) Any substitution or addition so made by the Commissioners shall not take effect until it has been advertised in the *London Gazette* for two successive weeks. SEE *Adjudication Stamps; Stamp Duty*

ADVANCE CORPORATION TAX (ACT) This was introduced by the Finance Act 1973 and applied to all companies resident in the UK with effect from 5th April, 1973. It is the corporation tax which a company must pay to the Inland Revenue when it makes a dividend payment or other 'qualifying' distribution to its shareholders. It is known as *advance* corporation tax because it is paid in advance of, and ultimately deducted from, the company's total corporation tax liability for the year in question. With effect from accounting periods ending on or after 1st April, 1984, if a company does not have sufficient taxable profits to cover the ACT, the excess may be carried back over the six preceding accounting periods of the company. Prior to 1st April, 1984, the excess could be carried back over only the two preceding accounting periods, Any excess may be carried forward indefinitely. This situation may arise, for example, where a company has not been trading profitably, but has paid a dividend out of distributable reserves, or where it has 'sheltered' its profits with capital allowances or stock relief.

The rate of ACT depends on the basic rate for the time being of income tax. It is calculated by grossing back the amount of the distribution to the shareholder by the basic rate of tax then in force. Thus, if the basic rate of tax is 30 per cent the ACT will be 30 per cent of the grossed-up dividend, i.e. $3/7$ of the net dividend. At the time of the distribution the shareholders receive a tax credit for the amount of ACT so paid. Depending on the tax liability of the shareholder, this tax may be recoverable wholly or in part.

ADVANCEMENT A payment made by a trustee out of the capital of trust funds to a beneficiary for the purpose of establishing him in life. Thus the payment must be for some reason which will assist the recipient in his career or assist him in building up his capital assets. Suitable opportunities for an advancement would be the purchase of equipment for a new business, or the purchase of a share in a partnership, or the provision of funds for a settlement on the marriage of the beneficiary. There must be some element of permanent or long-term provision for the beneficiary.

The instrument setting up the trust may provide for advancement or the trustee may act under the powers conferred by Section 32 of the Trustee Act 1925, subsection (1) of which is as follows.

> Trustees may at any time or times pay or apply any capital money subject to a trust, for the advancement or benefit in such manner as they may in their absolute discretion think fit of any person entitled to the capital of the trust property or of any share thereof, whether absolutely or contingently on his attaining any specified age or on the occurrence of any other event, or subject to a gift over on his death under any specified age or on the occurrence of any other event, and whether in possession or in remainder or reversion, and such payment or application may be made notwithstanding that the interest of such person is liable to be defeated by the exercise of a power of appointment or revocation, or to be diminished by the increase of the class to which he belongs:
>
> Provided that—
>
> (*a*) the money so paid or applied for the advancement or benefit of any person shall not exceed altogether in amount one-half of the presumptive or vested share or interest of that person in the trust property; and
>
> (*b*) if that person is or becomes absolutely and indefeasibly entitled to a share in the trust property the money so paid or applied shall be brought into account as part of such share; and
>
> (*c*) no such payment or application shall be made so as to prejudice any person entitled to any prior life or other interest, whether vested or contingent, in the money paid or applied, unless such person is in existence and of full age and consents in writing to such payment or application.

The Section does not apply to capital money arising under the Settled Land Act 1925, or to trusts created or constituted before 1st January, 1926. The powers which it confers are in addition to the powers (if any) conferred on the trustees by the instrument creating the trust, but apply if and so far only as a contrary intention is not expressed in that instrument and have effect subject to the terms thereof.

It will be observed that the wording of Section 32 refers to 'advancement or benefit'. Benefit is a much wider term and covers on the face of it almost any kind of payment. Where the advance is for the benefit of an infant, however, trustees should not advance capital for an object for which the parents of the infant can themselves pay, such as school fees, for the result would be for the benefit, not of the infant, but of his parents. Nor should trustees fetter the possible exercise of their discretion in the future. Where the advance is for the benefit of a beneficiary of full age and *sui juris*, it appears that the trustees may hand over the capital provided that they are satisfied as to the use which the beneficiary is going to make of it, or at any rate consider the beneficiary to be the sort of person who would not make an imprudent use of the money.

It was decided in *Re Ropner's Settlement Trusts* [1956] 3 All ER 332, that the application of capital for a contingent beneficiary by paying it to trustees of a settlement in favour of that beneficiary with the object of lightening the burden of estate duty was a 'benefit'.

Consequently the practice has grown of transferring money to other settlements by exercise of a power of advancement for the primary purpose of saving capital transfer tax (supported by the House of Lords decision in *Re Pilkington's Will Trusts*, [1962] 3 All E.R. 622.

ADVANCEMENT, PRESUMPTION OF The term advancement is also used in a sense different from the previous entry. It refers to the rule of equity that where there is a transfer of an asset by a person to or into the name of his wife or child or adopted child, there is a presumption that a gift is intended. This is contrary to the general rule in all other cases that where a person transfers an asset into the name of another person, there is prima facie no gift and there is a resulting trust in favour of the donor. Thus, in this context the term advancement merely means that the transfer is by way of gift. There is no presumption of advancement in the case of a transfer by a wife to her husband, nor by a mother to her child, although it seems that it may be so in the case of a widowed mother. In all cases, the presumption of advancement may be rebutted if it can be shown that there is no intention to benefit the donee at the time the transfer was made.

ADVANCES A general term embracing various categories of lending by the banks in the UK. SEE *Lending by Banks*

ADVICE When a banker issues a draft, he sends an advice, called a letter of advice, to the banker upon whom the draft has been drawn, giving him particulars of the amount, number, date and payee, so that, when the instrument is presented for payment, the drawee banker may be able to satisfy himself that the draft is in order. In the absence of an advice, a banker would hesitate to pay a draft: at least, this would be so when the practice has been followed previously.

The word 'advice' applies also to many other forms of intimation which a banker in the course of his business has to make to customers, other banks, and his own head office or London agents, such as advices of credits received, payments to be made, bills to be paid, etc.

ADVICE, FINANCIAL Financial advice in one form or another is given by virtually all persons and institutions engaged in business of a financial nature. Thus, banks, accountants, stockbrokers, insurance brokers, and investment counsellors advise their customers or clients on matters relevant to their immediate business. Similarly, those not immediately engaged in financial activity, e.g. solicitors and estate agents, may also have occasion to advise their clients on the financial aspects of the business on hand. There is no one profession dedicated to the giving of financial advice per se but professional accountants come nearest to that role. Traditionally, banks have been hesitant over the giving of advice, particularly on investment matters, but in the case of *Woods v Martins Bank Ltd and Another* [1958] 3 All ER, Mr Justice Salmon said, 'I have found that it is part of the defendant's business to advise customers and potential customers on financial matters of all kinds'. Whilst that was a conclusion drawn from the particular facts of that case, there has been a notable movement in modern times towards the giving of financial advice 'of all kinds' by banks although more usually by specialist departments or companies or subsidiary companies, rather than by individual bank managers. Thus, nowadays, banks provide extensive advisory services, covering Stock Exchange investment, insurance, business management, taxation, pensions and personal financial planning. SEE *Estate Planning; Investment Management Services; Merchant Banking*

ADVISE FATE Where early notice is required as to the payment, or non-payment, of a cheque, the cheque is sent direct to the banker on whom it is drawn with a request to 'advise fate'. A banker is not under any obligation to advise the fate of a cheque, but it is done as a matter of courtesy between bankers.

Alternatively, the enquiring banker may telephone the banker on whom the cheque is drawn to ascertain its fate.

When an enquiry is received asking if a certain cheque will be paid when presented, a banker should be careful to qualify an affirmative reply, otherwise he may find that, by the time the cheque is actually presented, the customer's account has altered so as not to admit of its payment, or that payment of the cheque has been stopped by the drawer, or that the balance of the account has been attached by a legal order, and yet he will, if he gave an unqualified reply, be liable to pay it. The Council of the Institute of Bankers recommend some such reply being made as: 'Would pay if in our hands and in order.'

A banker must not set aside or 'earmark' a sum out of the customer's balance to meet a cheque about which another banker has enquired. The cheque cannot be dealt with till it arrives. SEE *Appropriation of Payments*

AFFREIGHTMENT A contract of affreightment is the agreement made by a shipowner to carry goods in consideration of a certain payment called the freight. When the contract relates to the use of the whole ship for the cargo, the terms are embodied in the charter party (q.v.), but if the contract is merely to convey certain goods, as part of the ship's cargo, the agreement is contained in the bill of lading (q.v.).

À FORFAIT This a form of export finance which has traditionally been more common among banks in continental Europe but which some British and US banks have actively developed in recent years. The term (meaning literally to relinquish, e.g. a right, to something) applies to a type of export facility where a bank on behalf of an exporter, agrees to buy the debt due from the foreign customer. Generally, à forfait finance, or forfaiting is appropriate to fixed-price contracts for, say, two to five years, e.g. for manufactured goods. It is also used, however, for shorter-term commodity finance. It is not appropriate to contracts under which payment depends upon performance clauses. The advantage to the exporter is that he receives payment more or less immediately and he is no longer concerned with obtaining payment under the contract. The return to the forfaiting bank lies in the discount at which the trade debt is purchased. To that extent there is a similarity to factoring (q.v.)

Over the years there was comparatively little interest in forfaiting in Britain because of the overall coverage for exports provided by the Export Credits Guarantee Department (q.v.) but the practice has developed in more recent times with the active encouragement of a number of leading banks.

AFTER ACQUIRED PROPERTY SEE *Bankrupt Person*

AGE ADDITION A term applicable to certain state benefits under the Social Security regulations. Persons who have reached the age of 80 and are in receipt of any one of the following social security benefits receive automatically an additional payment (currently 25p per week): retirement pension; industrial disablement (or widow's) pension; war disablement (or widow's) pension; non-contributory invalidity pension; invalid care allowance; supplementary pension.

The age addition is allowed only in relation to any one of these benefits and would normally be attached to the retirement pension. Age addition is subject to income tax (ICTA 1970, Section 219). (SEE Appendix 2).

AGE ADMITTED SEE *Life Assurance*

AGE ALLOWANCE An allowance for income tax purposes (in lieu of the personal allowance) applicable to persons aged 64 or over at the commencement of an income tax year on 6th April (SEE Appendix 1)

The full age allowance is paid only to those person whose total income for tax purposes does not exceed a stipulated sum (SEE Appendix 1). If the income exceeds that amount, the age allowance is reduced by two-thirds of the excess over that figure until the age allowance is completely eliminated. The allowance is then reduced to the single personal allowance level or married personal allowance level, as the case may be.

AGENT An agent is a person who acts under authority from his principal, and the extent of his powers to bind his principal is limited to the terms of that authority. It is therefore necessary in dealing with an agent, in matters of any importance, to ascertain exactly what are his powers. If an agent is authorized to enter into a contract under seal, he must be appointed by deed. He may have authority to act only in some particular or special duty, as in the case of an agent empowered to purchase a house; or the authority may be of a much wider nature and constitute a person a general agent.

When a banker employs a correspondent or agent in carrying out a transaction for a customer, the banker is responsible to his customer for any loss arising from the conduct of the agent (*Mackersy* v *Ramsays* [1843] 9 Cl and Fin 818.) This is probably not the case when the customer has nominated the sub-agent; of course, the banker may cover the eventuality by specific stipulation. The banker, however, will have a right of recourse against his correspondent, by whose default the banker has incurred the loss.

Where a person's authority is unlimited, he is called a universal agent, and the principal is bound by whatever his agent does, so long as it is in accordance with the law of the land.

An agent has no power to delegate his authority to another person, although this power may occasionally be implied.

Where an agent, in exercise of his authority, affixes his name to a bill of exchange, as drawer, acceptor, or indorser, he must be careful to sign in such a manner that no personal liability will attach to him. The addition of such words as 'manager', 'agent', 'secretary' would not be sufficient to clear him from personal liability.

In *Leadbitter* v *Farrow* (1816) 5 M & S, at p. 349 Lord Ellenborough said

> Is it not a universal rule that a man who puts his name to a bill of exchange thereby makes himself personally liable, unless he states upon the face of the bill that he subscribes it for another, or by procuration of another, which are the words of exclusion? Unless he says plainly, 'I am the mere scribe,' he is liable.

The Bills of Exchange Act 1882, Section 26, provides as follows:

> (1) Where a person signs a bill as drawer, indorser, or acceptor, and adds words to his signature, indicating that he signs for or on behalf of a principal, or in a representative character, he is not personally liable thereon; but the mere addition to his signature of words describing him as an agent, or as filling a representative character, does not exempt him from personal liability.
>
> (2) In determining whether a signature on a bill is that of the principal or that of the agent by whose hand it is written, the construction most favourable to the validity of the instrument shall be adopted.

In signing for a company it is much better if an agent states definitely the capacity in which he signs, and prefixes the words 'per pro' or 'For and on behalf of', for example:

per pro T. Brown & Sons Ltd,
R. Jones, Secretary

per pro British Banking Co. Plc,
T. Smith Manager

For and on behalf of the
.... Co. Ltd
R. Brown, Director
R. Jones, Secretary

But the form of signature, 'T. Brown & Sons Ltd, R. Jones, Secretary', without a prefix is very common.

With regard to a procuration signature, Section 25 enacts

A signature by procuration operates as notice that the agent has but a limited authority to sign, and the principal is only bound by such signature if the agent in so signing was acting within the actual limits of his authority.

In *A. Stewart & Son of Dundee Ltd* v *Westminster Bank* [1926] *Weekly Notes*, p. 126, Rowlatt, J, said, in the course of his judgment, with reference to Section 25 (see above), that he was of opinion that the expression 'by procuration' must be understood as limited to agency on behalf of a natural person and not as extending to a signature on behalf of a company which cannot sign by itself. In the Court of Appeal (*Weekly Notes*, p. 271) the Court did not express any opinion whether the provisions of Section 25 were limited to the case of agency on behalf of a natural person. In this case the bank collected cheques payable to the limited company (the cheques being indorsed 'For and on behalf of' the limited company by Sir John S, the managing director, who held the whole of the ordinary capital of the company), and credited the proceeds to an account in the name of the old private firm, A. S. & Son, the business of which had been taken over by the limited company. On the death of Sir John it was found that he had used the proceeds of the cheques for his own purposes in fraud of the limited company. It was held that the bank had no defence to an action by the company for the recovery of the amount of such cheques. There was no authority for Sir John to indorse the cheques and pay them into the old firm's account (of which firm he was formerly sole partner). His actual authority could only be to indorse cheques for the benefit of the company, and at the time that he indorsed them he intended to steal the proceeds. By Section 24 the signature was wholly inoperative and the defendants acquired no rights under that signature unless it could be shown that Sir John had ostensible authority to indorse the cheques. But there was no ostensible authority. The appeal was allowed and judgment entered for the plaintiffs.

Where a signature is placed on a bill without the authority of the person whose signature it purports to be, the unauthorized signature is wholly inoperative. The supposed principal is not bound because it is not his signature; and the supposed agent is not bound on the bill because the signature pretends to be that of a principal. Apart from the bill, a person so signing would be liable for false representation of authority.

No person is liable as drawer, indorser, or acceptor of a bill who has not signed it as such, except where a person signs in a trade or assumed name, or in the name of a firm.

An agent may have authority, instead of signing per pro, to sign the actual name of his principal, or to impress the signature with a rubber stamp. Section 91 enacts

(1) Where, by this Act, any instrument or writing is required to be signed by any person, it is not necessary that he should sign it with his own hand, but it is sufficient if his signature is written thereon by some other person by or under his authority.

(2) In the case of a corporation, where, by this Act, any instrument or writing is required to be signed, it is sufficient if the instrument or writing be sealed with the corporate seal.

But nothing in this Section shall be construed as requiring the bill or note of a corporation to be under seal.

An infant may act as an agent. An undischarged bankrupt may also act as agent.

In *Bradford* v *Price* (1923) 39 TLR 272, the following extract from *Leake on Contracts* was quoted with approval by McCardie, J., in the course of his judgment:

An agent is not justified in accepting a cheque on behalf of his principal in lieu of a payment in cash unless he has authority to do so; but if an agent authorised to receive payment in cash accepts a cheque which is met upon presentation, and before his authority to receive cash is revoked, the debtor is discharged.

An agent should not place to the credit of his own private account cheques payable to his principal. Where the business requires this to be done, there should be a written authority from the principal. When cheques are drawn, under authority, by an agent and he pays them into his own private account, the banker is put on enquiry.

Where cheques are to be signed by an agent, an authority or mandate should be given by the principal requesting the banker to honour such cheques, and if the agent is to have power to sign when the account is overdrawn the authority should include that power (SEE *Mandate*). In the case of a limited company, a resolution should be passed by the directors as to the method in which cheques are to be signed, and a copy of the resolution, signed by the chairman, should be furnished to the banker along with specimens of the authorised signatures. SEE *Company*

In entering into a contract with anyone purporting to act on behalf of a limited liability company it is essential to ascertain that the official has the requisite authority. In *Kreditbank Kassel GmbH* v *Schenkers Ltd*, where bills were drawn by an official of the defendants without authority, it was held that, in the absence of evidence that he had ostensible authority to draw bills on behalf of the company, the plaintiffs (who had discounted the bills) were not entitled to assume that he had such authority. (See the case under *Company*.)

On the death of the principal, any authority given to an agent to sign cheques is cancelled. The death of an agent does not prevent a banker paying a cheque signed by the agent on the account of his principal, and presented for payment after the agent's death. The authority is also determined by the bankruptcy or insanity of the principal.

The board of directors, council, or other governing body of a corporation aggregate may by resolution appoint an agent, either generally or in any particular case, to execute on behalf of the corporation any agreement or other instrument not under seal in relation to any matter within the powers of the corporation (Law of Property Act 1925, Section 74(2)).

The following cases show how necessary it is that an agent should, in order to avoid all risk, sign in such a manner that there may be no question that he does so merely as an agent.

In *Chapman* v *Smethurst* [1909] 1 KB 73, an action was brought on a promissory note: 'Six months after demand I promise to pay to Mrs N. Chapman the sum of £300 for value received, together with six per cent interest per annum. J. H. Smethurst's Laundry and Dye Works (Limited), J. H. Smethurst, Managing Director.' The words 'J. H. Smethurst's Laundry and Dye Works (Limited)' and 'Managing Director' were placed on the note by means of a rubber stamp. Mr Justice Channell held that the defendant was personally liable on the promissory note, because he had not added any words to show that he signed merely as the agent of the company. On appeal, however, it was held that the company could be sued on the note.

In *Landes* v *Marcus & Davids* (1909) 25 TLR 478, a cheque was signed by the defendants (directors of Marcus & Co.), in favour of the plaintiff, in the following way: 'B. Marcus, Director.' 'S. H. Davids, Director,' The space for the secretary's signature was left blank. The name of the company was printed only at the top of the cheque. Although the directors added words to show their representative capacity, it was held that, in signing the cheques, they did not indicate that they did so on behalf of the company, and that they were personally liable on the cheque. (See the case of *Elliot* v *Bax-Ironside* under *Indorsement*.)

An agent cannot borrow money on behalf of his principal unless authorized to do so; and if a banker, with knowledge of the extent to which an agent may borrow permits him to exceed his authority, the principal will not be liable. (See further under *Negotiable Instruments*.)

In *Lloyd* v *Grace, Smith & Co.* (1912) 107 LT 531, where a fraud was committed by an agent for his own benefit, the House of Lords held that the principal is liable for the fraud of his agent acting within the scope of his authority. Lord Macnaghten, in the course of his judgment, said:

> The only difference, in my opinion, between the case where the principal receives the benefit of the fraud, and the case where he does not, is that in the latter case the principal is liable for the wrong done to the person defrauded by his agent acting within the scope of his agency; in the former case he is liable on that ground and also on the ground that by taking the benefit he has adopted the act of his agent. [SEE *Per Pro*]

In *Freeman and Lockyer* v *Buckhurst Park Properties Ltd* [1964] 2 QB 480. Diplock, LJ, said that in the absence of actual authority of an agent acting on behalf of a company, it had to be established

> (1) That a representation that the agent had authority to enter on behalf of a company into a contract of the kind sought to be enforced was made to the contractor.
>
> (2) That such representation was made by a person or persons who had actual authority to manage the business of the company either generally or in respect of those matters to which the contract relates.
>
> (3) That he (the contractor) was induced by such representation to enter into the contract, that is, that he in fact relied upon it.
>
> (4) That under its memorandum or articles of association the company was not deprived of the capacity either to enter into a contract of the kind sought to be enforced or to delegate authority to enter into a contract of that kind to the agent.

As to the banker acting in the capacity of an agent, see *Banker as Agent*.

AGRICULTURAL BUILDINGS ALLOWANCE An allowance for income tax purposes under Section 68 and 69, Capital Allowances Act 1968 as amended by Section 39, Finance Act 1978 in respect of capital expenditure on farm buildings. The allowance applies to farm houses, cottages, fences, etc. on agricultural land, smallholdings and forestry holdings. From April 1978, an initial allowance of 20 per cent of the capital expenditure could be claimed for the purpose of tax relief and therafter an annual writing down allowance of 10 per cent of the expenditure cost could be claimed each year. From 1st April 1986, however, the initial allowance is abolished and the writing down allowance reduced to 4 per cent per annum.

AGRICULTURAL CREDIT CORPORATION LIMITED The corporation was formed in 1959 to assist farmers by providing guarantees to the farmers' banks. In March 1965, the activities under the original scheme were transferred to a new company, Farming Loans Guarantees Limited. The ACC is now Government-sponsored and initially assisted only horticultural businesses However, in October 1965, the corporation agreed to provide further support to the agricultural industry. The guarantees entered into relate either to loans made by the clearing banks to approved applicants for specific capital expenditure or alternatively for general working capital.

AGRICULTURAL HOLDING The aggregate of agricultural land comprised in a contract of tenancy, not being a contract under which the land is let to the tenant during his continuance in any office, appointment or employment held under the landlord. Agricultural land is land used for agriculture in the course of a trade or business and any other land which is so designated by the Minister of Agriculture. By statutes, termination of such tenancies, as well as compensation and other matters associated with a change in tenants, are subject to special provisions. Unpaid compensation due to a tenant can form a charge taking priority over a mortgage (Agricultural Holdings Act 1948, Section 72). The Agricultural Holdings Act 1984 amended in a number of respects the law relating to agricultural holdings. In particular, the 1984 Act abolished the statutory succession to agricultural holdings under the Agriculture (Miscellaneous Provisions) Act 1976, as regards new tenancies, and amended the law relating to existing agricultural tenancies.

AGRICULTURAL LAND, INVESTMENT IN Over the years, agricultural land values in the UK have, by and large, kept pace with inflation. From an investor's point of view there is of course a scarcity value in land and, particularly in proximity to urban areas, there is a 'hope' value. Farming methods have improved considerably in the UK over the years with the result that agriculture in the UK is now among the most efficient in the world and farm businesses are able to sustain more economic rents than was the case years ago.

There are, however, some disadvantages in investment in agricultural land, notably that there are limited opportunities for smaller investors as a degree of supervision of the investment is necessary, which may not always be convenient. Yields tend to be lower than in other forms of property investment and farm tenants enjoy statutory protection which can be a problem if the land is not farmed efficiently.

In 1982 sales of land with vacant possession, as reported for stamp duty purposes, averaged £1,330 per acre. This figure, however, would reflect a wide disparity between a few hundred pounds per acre for hill farms, up to over £3,000 per acre for good arable land.

In general, the values of tenanted land have been a little more than one-half of vacant possession prices, but this is far from being an accepted rule and the difference varies widely from time to time and from one part of the country to another.

There is a degree of relief for capital transfer tax purposes in cases where the transferor was the occupier of the agricultural land or where it was owned by him and let as agricultural property during the seven years preceding the date of the transfer. SEE *Capital Transfer Tax*

AGRICULTURAL MORTGAGE CORPORATION PLC This came into being in 1928 under the provisions of the Agricultural Credits Act of that year. Under that Act and the Act of 1932, the corporation is empowered to make loans on the security of first mortgage of agricultural or forestry properties in England and Wales. The loans may not exceed two-thirds of the certified value of the mortgaged property at the time of the advance. Loans are available up to periods of 40 years in the case of farms, and 60 years for forestry purposes. Typical agricultural purposes for which loans may be made are: the purchase of farm property, the repayment of other borrowing, capital improvements, the provision of working capital and the provision of capital for forestry purposes. Loans may be at a fixed or variable rate of interest and, in general, variable rate loans may be converted to fixed rate at any time at the option of the borrowers.

The Corporation is also empowered to make improvement loans under the Improvement of Land Act 1864 and 1899. These loans are secured by rent charges on the land improved, created in each case with the approval of the Minister of Agriculture, Fisheries and Food. In 1982 the Corporation also introduced a new facility under which it cooperates with tenants' consortia and, in appropriate cases, bids for estates with the objectives of providing the majority of tenants with loan capital to acquire their individual farms.

The share capital of the Corporations is held by the Bank of England and the five major clearing banks. The Corporation's resources are augmented by loans from the Ministry of Agriculture, Fisheries and Food (approximately £14½ million in 1983) and issues of debenture stocks and loans (of which approximately £389 million was outstanding in 1983).

AIR FINANCE LIMITED A private company established in 1953 by three merchant banks and the Finance Corporation for Industry Limited, to assist manufacturers of aircraft and aero engines to develop exports by enabling them to offer extended credit terms to suitable overseas customers.

AIRLEASE INTERNATIONAL A consortium of banks formed for the purpose of the equipping of the world's airlines and shipping lines by leasing finance. SEE *Leasing*

ALIMONY A payment made by one party to a marriage for the maintenance, benefit, etc. of the other party to the marriage on the break-up of the marriage by divorce or separation. SEE *Maintenance Payments*

ALL MONEYS DEBENTURE SEE *Debenture*

ALL–RISKS INSURANCE This may take the form of a separate policy of insurance or it may be part of the insurance policy covering the contents of a house. In either case, it covers loss or in some case damage to personal belongings in circumstances where cover would not normally be available under a household contents policy. An all-risks policy would, for example, cover the loss of personal possessions in the home in circumstances other than the normal perils of theft or fire covered by the contents policy. It would also cover personal possessions being carried or worn on the person. The cover might be on a limited geographical basis, e.g. UK only, or on a worldwide basis. Typical examples of articles for which all-risks insurance would be appropriate are jewellery, furs, watches, cameras, binoculars and other intrinsically valuable articles of personal use or ornament.

All-risks cover is now generally available on a 'new-for-old' basis and may be inflation-linked. Premiums vary considerably depending on the nature of the articles to be insured and the geographical location.

ALL SHARE INDEX SEE *Financial Times Actuaries All-share Index*

ALLOTMENT An applicant for shares which are being issued by a company generally fills up a printed form of application supplied by the company, in which he requests that the shares he requires be allotted to him. At the same time, he either sends a cheque to the company for the amount payable on application, or pays in the amount to the company's bankers. If his application is successful, he will, in due course receive a letter of allotment stating the number of shares which have been allotted to him, and requesting payment of the amount due per share upon allotment. SEE *Application for Shares*

The Companies Act 1985, Section 83, provides:

(1) No allotment shall be made of any share capital of a company offered to the public for subscription unless:

(a) there has been subscribed the amount stated in the prospectus as the minimum amount which, in the opinion of the directors, must be raised by the issue of share capital in order to provide for the matters specified in paragraph 2 of Schedule 3 (preliminary expenses, purchase of property, working capital, etc.); and

(b) the sum payable on application for the amount so stated has been paid to and received by the company.

(2) For the purposes of subsection (1)(b), a sum is deemed paid to the company, and received by it, if a cheque for that sum has been received in good faith by the company and the directors have no reason for suspecting that the cheque will not be paid.

(3) The amount so stated in the prospectus is to be reckoned exclusively of any amount payable otherwise than in cash and is known as 'the minimum subscription'.

(4) If the above conditions have not been complied with on the expiration of 40 days after the first issue of the prospectus, all money received from applicants for shares shall be forthwith repaid to them without interest.

(5) If any of the money is not repaid within 48 days after the issue of the prospectus, the directors of the company are jointly and severally liable to repay it with interest at the rate of 5 per cent per annum from the expiration of the 48th day; except that a director is not so liable if he proves that the default in the repayment of the money was not due to any misconduct or negligence on his part.

(6) Any condition requiring or binding an applicant for shares to waive compliance with any requirement of this section is void.

(7) This section does not apply to an allotment of shares subsequent to the first allotment of shares offered to the public for subscription.

When a company limited by shares, or a company limited by guarantee and having a share capital, makes any allotment, the company must, within one month thereafter, file with the Registrar of Companies a return of the allotment in accordance with Section 88 of the Act. SEE *Companies, Letter of Allotment; Prospectus*

ALLOTMENT LETTER SEE *Letter of Allotment*

ALLOTTEE The person to whom shares in a company are allotted in response to an application for shares.

ALTERATIONS TO BILLS OF EXCHANGE All material alterations in a bill must be initialed or signed by all the parties liable on the bill, and all alterations in a cheque must be confirmed by the drawer. It is not sufficient, in the case of a limited company's cheque, if a material alteration is initialed only by the secretary, unless, of course, the banker has authority to accept the signature of the secretary alone.

Section 64, Bills of Exchange Act 1882, enacts

(1) Where a bill or acceptance is materially altered without the assent of all parties liable on the bill, the bill is avoided except as against a party who has himself made, authorised, or assented to the alteration, and subsequent indorsers:
Provided that,

Where a bill has been materially altered, but the alteration is not apparent, and the bill is in the hands of a holder in due course, such holder may avail himself of the bill as if it had not been altered, and may enforce payment of it according to its original tenor.

(2) In particular the following alterations are material, namely, any alteration of the date, the sum payable, the time of payment, the place of payment, and, where a bill has been accepted generally, the addition of a place of payment without the acceptor's assent.

By Section 78

A crossing authorised by this Act is a material part of the cheque; it shall not be lawful for any person to obliterate or, except as authorised by this Act, to add to or alter the crossing.

The alterations authorized by the Bills of Exchange Act 1882 are

1 Any holder may convert a blank indorsement into a special indorsement (Section 34(4)).
2 Where a cheque is uncrossed, the holder may cross it generally or specially (Section 77).
3 Where crossed generally, the holder may cross it specially (Section 77).
4 Where crossed generally or specially, the holder may add the words 'not negotiable' (Section 77).
5 Where crossed specially, a banker to whom it is crossed may cross it specially to another banker for collection (Section 77).
6 Where an uncrossed cheque, or a cheque crossed generally, is sent to a banker for collection, he may cross it specially to himself (Section 77).
7 Where a bill payable at a fixed period after date is issued undated, or an acceptance of a bill payable at a fixed period after sight is undated, any holder may insert the true date (Section12).
8 A cheque which is payable to 'bearer' may be altered by the payee to 'order', but an alteration of a cheque from 'order' to 'bearer' must be initialed by all the drawers, and of a bill by all parties liable thereon. In *Aldous* v *Cornwell* [1868] LR 3 WB 573, where no time of payment was stated on a bill, it was held that the words 'on demand' could be inserted. (Subsequently covered by the Bills of Exchange Act 1882, Section 10(1)(*b*).)

As to cancellation of a crossing, see *Opening a Crossing*.

Various protections have been devised in order to prevent, or to make difficult, the fraudulent alteration of a cheque. Words such as 'under one hundred pounds' or 'not exceeding one hundred pounds' are often written across, or stamped upon, a cheque; or the cheque may be perforated with those words.

The body of a cheque may also be tinted, or printed over with words or a design to show more readily if an erasure takes place, and the paper may be made with a 'fugitive' surface, that is, a paper which loses its surface if any attempt is made to rub out what is written thereon. Cheque paper is also specially prepared to prevent chemicals being used to effect an alteration.

As to the various points to be observed when drawing a cheque, see *Drawing a Cheque*.

The following case illustrates the importance of seeing that any material alteration in a cheque is initialed by all the persons by whom the cheque is drawn.

In the *Kepitigalla Rubber Estates Ltd* v *The National Bank of India Ltd* [1909] 2 KB 1010, the plaintiffs had given the defendants a written authority to honour cheques drawn by two directors and the secretary. A cheque for £150 was altered from 'order' to 'bearer' and initialed by the secretary, and the initials of one of the directors were forged by means of a rubber stamp. The other director signed the cheque, but did not initial the alteration. Mr Justice Bray said

With regard to the payment of the cheque for £150, where Mr Lauder had not initialled the alteration from 'order' to 'bearer,' the accountants stated that it was usual for bankers to pay if two out of the three initialled the alteration. It seemed to me, however, that they would do this at their own risk; if Mr Lauder never initialled or authorized the alteration the payment of the cheque by the bank would not be authorized.

In *Souchette Ltd* v *London County Westminster & Parr's Bank Ltd* (1920) 36 TLR 195, a cheque 'Pay self or order' was signed for the Souchette Company by two directors, Frank Matthews and another. The cheque went through Mr Matthews's account and was forwarded by the defendant bank for collection. The cheque was returned and sent back to Mr Matthews to be put in order. When it came back for collection it was altered to read 'Pay self, F. Matthews, or order'. The addition of the words 'F. Matthews' was in that person's writing and was not authenticated by the initials of the other signing director. Mr Justice Greer in his judgment said that when the cheque came to the defendant bank if they thought about it at all they would have seen that it was an alteration of a cheque which was payable only to the order of the company itself, into a cheque payable to the order of F. Matthews, one of the directors who had signed it, without apparently the concurrence of the other director. The defendant bank were negligent in cashing that cheque without making any enquiries to see whether or not the other bank or company were willing that the cheque should be placed to the credit of Mr Matthews's account. (Other points in this case are referred to under *Collecting Banker, Conversion.*)

In *Young* v *Grote* (1827) 4 Bing 253, the amount of a cheque drawn by the plaintiff had been fraudulently increased after the cheque had been signed. An arbitrator found that the plaintiff had been negligent in causing his cheque to be handed to his clerk in such a state that he could, by the mere insertion of words, make it appear to be a cheque for the larger sum. It was held by the Court of Common Pleas that the defendants, the plaintiff's bankers, were not liable for the loss sustained by the plaintiff.

In *London Joint Stock Bank Ltd* v *Macmillan and Arthur* [1918] AC 777, the respondents had a confidential clerk to whom was entrusted the duty of filling in cheques for signature. The clerk presented to Mr Arthur for signature a bearer cheque for petty cash. There were no words at all in the space left for words, and in the space for figures there appeared the figures 2–0–0. The clerk having obtained Mr Arthur's signature to the cheque in this condition, added the words 'One hundred and twenty pounds' in the space left for words and the figures 1 and 0 on either side of the figure 2. (This was an appeal by the bank to the House of Lords from an order of the Court of Appeal [1917] 2 KB 439, which affirmed a judgment of Sankey, J, [1917] 1 KB 363, who decided that Macmillan and Arthur were not guilty of any negligence which misled the bank.)

The Lord Chancellor, in the course of his judgment, said

> The relation between banker and customer is that of debtor and creditor, with a superadded obligation on the part of the banker to honour the customer's cheques if the account is in credit. A cheque drawn by a customer is in point of law a mandate to the banker to pay the amount according to the tenor of the cheque. It is beyond dispute that the customer is bound to exercise reasonable care in drawing the cheque to prevent the banker being misled. If he draws the cheque in a manner which facilitates fraud, he is guilty of a breach of duty as between himself and the banker and, and he will be responsible to the banker for any loss sustained by the banker as a natural and direct consequence of this breach of duty. ... The question whether there was negligence as between banker and customer is a question of fact in each particular case, and can be decided only on a view of the cheque as issued by the drawer, with the help of any evidence available as to the course of dealings between the parties or otherwise. ... If *Young* v *Grote* is right, the judgment now appealed from is wrong. In my opinion, the decision in *Young* v *Grote* is sound in principle and supported by a great preponderance of authority, and must be treated as good law. ... In the present case, the customer neglected all precautions. He signed the cheque, leaving blank the space where the amount should have been stated in words, and, where it should have been stated in figures, there was only the figure '2' with blank spaces on either side of it. In my judgment, there was a clear breach of the duty which the customer owed to the banker. ... No one can be certain of preventing forgery, but it is a very simple thing in drawing a cheque to take reasonable and ordinary precautions against forgery. If, owing to the neglect of such precautions, it is put into the power of any dishonest person to increase the amount by forgery, the customer must bear the loss as between himself and the banker. But, further, it is well settled law that if a customer signs a cheque in blank and leaves it to a clerk or other person to fill it up, he is bound by the instrument as filled up by the agent. ... For all practical purposes, the cheque was in blank, as the figure '2' in its isolated position afforded no security whatever against a fraudulent increase. ... For these reasons I think that judgement should be entered for the bank.

Viscount Haldane, in the course of his judgment, said

> The obligation of the customer to avoid negligence was, I think, well expressed by Kennedy, J, in *Lewes Sanitary Steam Laundry Co.* v *Barclay* (1906) 95 LT 444, when that very accomplished judge defined it as including 'a duty to be careful not to facilitate any fraud, which, when it has been perpetrated, is seen to have in fact flowed in natural and uninterrupted sequence from the negligent act'.

Viscount Haldane held that it was immediately due to the action of the respondents, and not to any other cause, that the clerk was able to make additions to the cheque; and

> I am of the opinion that in putting as much as they did within his power, the took the risk of failure in the discharge of their duty to the bank of which they were customers. It follows that they cannot now recover the amount of a loss which was due to their own negligence.

In *Adelphi Bank* v *Edwards* (1882) 26 Sol J 360, where the amount of a bill had been fraudulently altered by a holder, spaces having been left in drawing the bill, which enabled this to be done, Lord Justice Baggallay said

It seems to me impossible to say that there was any duty on the part of the acceptor of the bill towards the party who might subsequently become the holder of the bill so to criticise, and so to examine the bill before he signed, as to put it out of the possibility of any additional words being afterwards inserted in it.

The case was cited with approval in the case of *Schofield* v *Earl of Londesborough* (1896) 75 LT 254; [1896] AC 514, where it was held that the acceptor of a bill of exchange is not under a duty to take precautions against fraudulent alterations in the bill after acceptance. In referring to this case (in *London Joint Stock Bank Ltd* v *Macmillan and Arthur*), the Lord Chancellor said

The decision of the House of Lords in the Schofield case proceeded on the ground that the duty which *Young* v *Grote* affirmed to exist as between banker and customer had no relation to any supposed duty on the part of the acceptor of a bill of exchange to those into whose possession the bill might pass. The decision of the House of Lords does not infringe upon the authority of *Young* v *Grote*. On the contrary, I think it recognises it.

If a customer has not been negligent in drawing a cheque and the amount has been fraudulently increased, the loss will fall upon the banker who has paid the cheque.

Where a solicitor prepared a cheque for the signatures of trustees, making it payable to 'John Prust & Co.,' and after receiving the cheque duly signed, added to the payee's name 'per Cumberbirch & Potts,' it was held that this unauthorized addition was a material alteration voiding the cheque. The signing of the cheque by the trustees with a space after the payee's name was not negligence and the drawee bank was liable (*Slingsby and Others* v *District Bank Ltd* [1932] 1 KB 544).

ALTERNATE DIRECTORS If the articles of association of a company permit, a director can nominate an alternate or substitute director, who can act when his principal is absent, and his acts done within the scope of his authority are binding on the company. The appointment of an alternate director should be in writing and notice given. Unless provided by the articles, an alternate director cannot look to the company for his fees, which are the responsibility of his principal. Particulars of alternate directors must be included in the annual return to Companies House.

ALTERNATIVE DRAWEE An order addressed to two drawees in the alternative, or to two or more drawees in succession, is not a bill of exchange. SEE *Drawee*

ALTERNATIVE INVESTMENT An expression coined in the 1970s to denote some of the less traditional forms of investment. The term has no precise definition, but would normally be used in relation to non-financial assets. Thus, as an alternative to investment in stocks and shares, building societies, life policies and national savings, one might 'invest' in stamps, antique silver, claret, firearms, Chinese ceramics and works of art. In recent times, almost anything which is collectable has come to be regarded as an avenue for investment. This includes not only the more traditional collectors' items such as glass, books, maps, prints and old furniture, but also such modern artefacts as toy soldiers, children's comics, old share certificates and art nouveau.

The surge of interest in these more tangible forms of investment had its impetus in the hyperinflation of the early 1970s. That, together with the stock market's slump of 1973–74, brought about a general disillusionment with financial assets and the desire to invest in 'things'. Since then there have been some equally dramatic swings in the values of some of the more tangible investments, e.g. stamps, silver, gold coins and in a wide range of 'collectables' sold in the auction rooms, but the search for alternative investments continues. Perhaps the main reason is the continuing failure of the stock market to perform in line with inflation. This in itself reflects a lack of growth in the UK economy and the absence of any significant improvement in productivity and profitability of British industry. That aside, many forms of alternative investment have the attraction that they can be used and enjoyed because of their intrinsic qualities. For the most part, they do not have the advantage of yielding any income, but they enjoy reasonable exemption from capital gains tax (q.v.). They are reasonably portable and transferable and can be passed on to future generations. SEE ALSO *Coins, Investment in; Gold; Silver; Stamps*

ALTERNATIVE PAYEE A bill of exchange may be made payable in the alternative to one of two, or one or some of several payees. SEE *Payee*

AMERICAN EXPRESS CARD This is a payments card issued by the American Express Company. It is one of the travel and entertainment (T & E) category of cards (q.v.) and is in fact in wider use than any other card of its class. It is not a credit card as such, but a method of payment, i.e. there is no provision for extended credit as there is with credit cards.

American Express opened offices in the UK in 1963 and shortly afterwards entered into an arrangement for the promotion of its cards through Lloyds Bank and Martins Bank. This move was overtaken, however, by the subsequent mergers of the major banks in the UK and the issue by the banks of their own credit cards.

At the present time, American Express cards are accepted by over 700,000 merchants in 165 countries.

In 1982, American Express introduced its Gold Card in the UK. This provides the holder with standby overdraft facilities at Lloyds Bank, together with substantial travel accident insurance and cheque encashment facilities around the world. Since then, American Express has introduced similar arrangements with Royal Bank of Scotland Group, Bank of Ireland and Grindlays Bank.

AMERICAN SHARE CERTIFICATES One type of these certificates has the nature of a registered holding and also of a bearer security. On the face is given the name of the registered holder of the shares and on the back is supplied a blank form of transfer, which, when signed by the registered holder, makes the certificate transferable by delivery like a bearer bond. The registered holder, however, is the person to whom the company sends the dividends, and the owner of the certificate (unless he gets registered himself) must apply to him for the dividend, producing the certificate to show that he is entitled to it. It is usual for the shares to be registered in the name of a London institution in order to facilitate handling. In those cases, a commission is charged by the registered holder for receiving and paying over the dividend to the owner of the certificate. SEE *Marking Names*

These certificates differ from a bearer bond, in that a bearer bond is a 'negotiable instrument', which a certificate of this description is not, and therefore they do not give to the owner any better title than the previous owner had. In practice, however, they pass from one person to another by mere delivery, and may perhaps now be accepted by courts as bearer instruments by usage if the indorsements are genuine, although it was held otherwise in *London and County Banking Company Ltd* v *London and River Plate Bank Ltd* (1887) 20 QBD 232. Such certificates deposited with a bank appear to be good security unless the banker has been placed on enquiry (*Fuller* v *Glyn* [1914] 2 KB 168).

AMORTIZATION, AMORTIZEMENT The redemption of loans or bonds by annual payments from a sinking fund. The sinking fund is built up for the purpose of redeeming annually such an amount of bonds as are due to be paid off, along with the interest on outstanding bonds. An amortization table is printed on certain bonds which are repayable in this manner, showing the amount redeemable each year.

ANNUAL GENERAL MEETING A general meeting of every company shall be held once at the least in every calendar year, and not more than 15 months after the last preceding general meeting. SEE *Meetings, Companies—annual general meetings*

The usual business at the annual meeting of shareholders is: reading the notice convening the meeting, reading the auditor's report, adopting the directors' report and balance sheet, sanctioning a dividend, electing directors in place of those retiring by rotation, and appointing the auditors.

ANNUAL RETURN Under ss 363 and 365 of the Companies Act 1985 every company having a share capital shall once at least in every year send to the registrar of companies a return (called the Annual Return) of all persons, who, on the fourteenth day after the annual general meeting for the year, are members of the company, and of all persons who have ceased to be members since the date of the last return. The return must state the names and addresses of all the past and present members therein mentioned, and the number of shares held by each of the existing members at the date of the return, specifying shares transferred since the date of the last return and the dates of registration of the transfers, and must contain a summary specifying various particulars regarding the shares.

The return must be completed with 14 days after the fourteenth day, above mentioned, and forwarded forthwith to the Registrar of Companies.

ANNUITANT A person who is in the receipt of an annuity.

ANNUITY Literally, a sum of money payable yearly, but it may in fact be payable half-yearly, quarterly or monthly. An annuity may be payable in perpetuity, in which case it would normally have to be of a charitable nature, e.g. for the upkeep of graves. More usually, an annuity is payable during and for the duration of a person's life. The sale of annuities constitutes an important part of the business of life assurance companies. An annuity purchased from a life office is, in essence, the reverse of a life policy. Whereas under a life policy the insurance company agrees to pay a capital sum in return for premiums paid over a number of years, under an annuity contract the annuitant pays a capital sum to the life office as consideration for annual payments to be made by the life office over subsequent years. To some extent, annuities and life policies are complementary in the books of life offices. For example, an unfavourable mortality experience in relation to life policies may be off-set by a favourable experience on the annuity side. The cost of an annuity contract decreases with the age of the annuitant whereas, in the ordinary way, the cost of life assurance becomes greater with age.

Evidence of health also acts in a contrary fashion—ill health will normally give rise to a loading of life assurance premiums, whereas ill health in a prospective annuitant may permit more advantageous rates to be granted.

A guaranteed annuity may be one which is stated to take effect for a guaranteed minimum number of years, e.g. an annuity for life payable for a minimum period of five years (the payments being made to the annuitant's estate in the event of death in that period). The term is also applied to annuities which guarantee the return of the original purchase money over a period of years, or to the annuitant's estate in the event of death in that time.

The principal advantages of annuities are that they secure an annual return normally much higher than would otherwise be obtained on other forms of capital investment. Also, the fact that the annuity payments include in each case a return of capital minimizes the tax liability on the annual or other periodic payments.

The principal disadvantage of an annuity purchase is that it is irrevocable and neither the annuitant nor his family can recover the purchase price except to the extent that there is a guaranteed return of capital (see above).

A *variable annuity* is one which contains provision for annual increases (or other variation) in the annuity payments. This is useful in times of inflation, but the degree of increase can only be limited, usually up to, say, five per cent per annum of the annual sum.

A *deferred annuity* is one which is to take effect at some future date. In the case of an annuity purchased commercially, payment may commence at some future date in return for consideration paid now or over the intervening years. Such deferred annuities are the basis of private pension plans. SEE *Pensions, Pension Schemes — personal pension schemes*

A *reversionary annuity* is one which commences on the death of one person and is payable during the lifetime of another person, e.g. an annuity to be paid to a wife on the death of her husband.

Joint annuities may be taken out on the lives of two or more persons, usually husband and wife, to be payable during their joint lives and the life of the survivor.

It was possible until 31st August, 1962 to purchase annuities from the government and some such government annuities are still in course of payment to the annuitants concerned.

Annuities may also be created by will or by lifetime gift. Annuities bequeathed by will are for the most part regarded as general legacies and abate equally with other general legacies if the estate is insufficient. SEE *Abatement; Home Loan Plans*

ANTE-DATED Ante-dating is the placing of a date on a document prior to that on which it is actually signed. A bill of exchange is not invalid by reason only that it is ante-dated (Section 13(2), Bills of Exchange Act 1882). SEE *Date*

APPEALS (AGAINST TAXATION ASSESSMENTS) A taxpayer who does not agree with the amount of an income tax assessment may appeal against the assessment within 30 days of the date of the Notice of Assessment. An extension of this period will usually be allowed for good reasons, such as absence from home. The appeal must be in writing and should indicated in brief terms the grounds of the appeal.

Even if an appeal is made, the amount of tax which has been assessed is still payable, although the taxpayer may apply for postponement of payment of some or all of the tax on the grounds that the assessment is excessive.

If it should still prove impossible to reach agreement between the taxpayer and the Inland Revenue, the appeal will normally go the General Commissioners of Inland Revenue, but the taxpayer may apply for the appeal to be heard by the Special Commissioners of Inland Revenue provided he gives notice of such a request within 30 days from the Notice of Assessment.

As a general rule, the more straightforward and factual types of appeal will be heard by the General Commissioners, who are local lay people. More difficult cases and particularly those involving points of law will normally be heard by the Special Commissioners.

There is no appeal from the Commissioners of Inland Revenue on questions of fact, but on questions of law the taxpayer or the Commissioners may appeal to the High Court and from there to the Court of Appeal and the House of Lords.

APPLICATION FOR SHARES A form of application for shares usually accompanies a prospectus offering to the public for subscription or purchase shares in a company.

When the form is filled up by an applicant, it is

dispatched, along with the sum payable on application to the company or the company's bankers. If the application is successful, a letter of allotment (q.v.) is sent to the applicant in due course.

APPORTIONMENT The word is used in a number of contexts to indicate the division of financial benefit or responsibility. Thus, there may be an apportionment of general rates and water rate on the completion of the sale of a property, there may be an apportionment of damages as a result of a legal claim and the apportionment of a chief rent or ground rent where part of a leasehold passes into separate ownership.

Two particular categories of apportionment may arise on the adminstration of an estate or trust. The first is *statutory apportionment* under the Apportionment Act 1870. This relates to the time apportionment of interest and dividend payments where ownership of an asset has changed hands, e.g. on a death. The most typical instance is the apportioning of dividend payments received after the death of a shareholder, but relating to an accounting period in which the death occurred. The proportion of the dividend to the date of death is strictly part of the capital of the estate and not income of the estate itself.

The second category, that of *equitable apportionment*, arises from a number of rules of equity formulated by the courts over the years to maintain a proper balance between the rights of life tenants (q.v.) and remaindermen on the administration of an estate or trust. Examples of such cases are *Howe* v *Dartmouth* (1802) 7 Ves 137, dealing with property of a wasting or hazardous nature in a trust; *Re Earl of Chesterfield's Trusts* (1883) 24 ChD 643, dealing with property of a reversionary nature in a trust, *Allhusen* v *Whittell* (1867) LR 4 Eq 295, dealing with the apportionment of debts, legacies and expenses between the capital and income of a trust; *Re Perkins* (1907) 2 Ch 596, dealing with the apportionment of an annuity between life tenants and remaindermen; and *Re Atkinson* (1904) 2 Ch 160, dealing with the apportionment of the proceeds of mortgaged property between life tenant and remaindermen where the proceeds are insufficient to repay both capital and interest in full.

In the interests of simplicity, it is quite common nowadays for statutory apportionment and all forms of equitable apportionment to be specifically excluded under the terms of a will or trust instrument.

APPROPRIATION OF PAYMENTS Certain rules have evolved over the years regarding the appropriation or allocation of payments made by a debtor to a creditor. The basic rule is that if A owes B two or more debts, then in making a payment to B, A may choose the debt to which he wishes the payment to be applied. If, for example, a customer pays in funds to his banker to meet a specified cheque or bill, the funds must be used for that purpose, irrespective of the overall state of the customer's account and of any views which the banker may himself have on the subject.

The second rule which evolved in the case of *Simson* v *Ingham* (1823) is that if the debtor does not make any specific appropriation at the time of payment, the creditor may allocate the payment as he pleases even in the satisfaction of a debt which is statute-barred.

The third rule is that if a customer has mixed up his own funds and trust moneys in a bank account, any cheques which he draws on the account for his own use are deemed to have been drawn first on the customer's own funds rather than the trust's moneys.

Of particular importance to bankers is the appropriation of payments in a running or current account. In such an account, if neither the debtor nor the creditor has made an appropriation (as mentioned above), the rule is that payments into and out of the account are set off against each other in the order in which they occur, e.g. the first item on the debit side of the account is discharged, wholly or in part, by the first item on the credit side. This is known as the Rule in Clayton's Case (q.v.).

ARBITRAGE The purchase of foreign exchange bullion or securities in one centre for sale forthwith in another centre where higher prices are ruling. Thus, it is the taking advantage of the difference in prices between two markets. The term is often used in a wider sense to include stocks and shares or, indeed, any goods or commodities where there is the opportunity of taking advantage of different prices between markets. SEE ALSO *Arbitration of Exchange*

ARBITRATION This is defined in Halsbury as

> the reference of a dispute or difference between not less than two parties for determination, after hearing both sides in a judicial manner, by a person or persons other than a court of competent jurisdiction.

Persons to whom such reference is made are called arbitrators. Where there is provision for reference to yet another person in the event of disagreement among the arbitrators, that other person is usually referred to as an umpire.

Provision for arbitration may rise by statute or under some formal institutional umbrella or, in some cases, by *ad hoc* agreement among the parties. Arbitration is possible only in relation to issues which would otherwise be triable under the civil law. It is not possible to have arbitration in relation to criminal acts or other offences of a public nature.

In general, arbitration proceedings are now governed by the Arbitration Act 1979.

Most arbitrations are conducted under the auspices and supervision of a formal institution. These include, for example,

1. The London Court of International Arbitration, which is managed by the Chartered Institute of Arbitrators. The Chartered Institute is the main arbitration institute in Britain and has about 5,000 members drawn from all relevant professions and vocations, including a number of experienced international arbitrators.
2. The London Maritime Arbitrators Association, located at the Baltic Exchange in London. This Association does not administer arbitration but it provides a panel of experienced members covering maritime arbitrations.
3. The Institution of Civil Engineers, the Royal Institute of British Architects and the Royal Institution of Chartered Surveyors all provide arbritation arrangements and standard forms of contract incorporating arbitration clauses within their own spheres of activity.
4. The International Federation of Consulting Engineers provide model forms of contract incorporating arbitration clauses for work which is tendered for internationally.
5. The commodities markets also provide arbitration facilities for their members.

Because of its pre-eminence in international commerce, London has a highly developed system of arbitration. This is partly because of the high level of commercial expertise centred in London and partly because of the highly developed system of mercantile law in Britain. Arbitration in London has a reputation for flexibility, expedition and relatively low cost. Approximately 50,000 arbitrators are appointed each year in this country and about 10,000 arbitration awards made annually in London, covering a wide field of international commercial activity and involving disputes which may not necessarily have any connection with London or Britain.

In 1981 The London International Arbitration Trust Limited was set up to encourage and promote the use of arbitration facilities in London. The Trust will advise on suitable arbitration clauses, the choice of arbitrators, and the general conduct and adminstration of arbitration in London.

ARBITRATION OF EXCHANGE (Frequently called arbitrage.) The operation by which a merchant pays a debt in one country by means of a bill payable in another. The price of bills payable in different centres is taken into account, and if it is found that it is cheaper to settle a debt in, say, Paris, by means of a bill upon, say, Amsterdam or Berlin, than by a bill upon Paris, the merchant takes advantage of that fact and makes payment accordingly.

Simple arbitration is where only one intermediate place is included in the transaction; where there are several places it is called compound arbitration.

Similar operations are conducted by bankers in order to make exchange profits.

ARIEL (AUTOMATED REAL-TIME INVESTMENTS EXCHANGE) This was a system introduced by the Accepting Houses Committee in 1974 for the purpose of matching buying and selling orders in stocks and shares. The system was designed for dealings of £5,000 and above and was intended to facilitate the matching of bargains between institutions with some savings in costs, particularly for larger deals. ARIEL does not have, however, the number of subscribers originally hoped for and the level of institutional investment turnover passing through ARIEL is believed to be less than ½ per cent.

ARRANGEMENT WITH CREDITORS (MEMBERS) Where a person is unable to pay his debts he may (apart altogether from the Bankruptcy Act) endeavour to make an arrangement with his creditors with respect to the money he owes to them. A debtor usually offers

1. To pay the creditors so much in the pound in full satisfaction of his debts to them (SEE *Composition with Creditors*); or
2. To transfer his property to a trustee to be realized and the proceeds divided amongst the creditors. SEE *Assignment for Benefit of Creditors*

If such an arrangement is made by deed or agreement, the deed of arrangement must be registered within seven days at the Department of Trade and Industry. SEE *Deed of Arrangement*

In the case of a proposed arrangement between a company and its creditors, or between the company and its members, the Companies Act 1985, Section 425, enacts.

(1) Where a compromise or arrangement is proposed between a company and its creditors or any class of them, or between the company and its members or any class of them, the Court may, on the application in a summary way of the company or of any creditor or member of the company or, in the case of a company being wound up, of the liquidator, order a meeting of the creditors or class of creditors, or of the members of

the company or class of members, as the case may be, to be summoned in such manner as the Court directs.

(2) If a majority in number representing three-fourths in value of the creditors or class of creditors, or members or class of members, as the case may be, present and voting either in person or by proxy at the meeting, agree to any compromise or arrangement, the compromise or arrangement is, if sanctioned by the court, binding on all the creditors or the class of creditors, or on the members or class of members, as the case may be, and also on the company, or, in the case of a company in the course of being wound up, on the liquidator and contributories of the company.

The expression 'company' means any company liable to be wound up under this Act and the expression 'arrangement' includes a reorganization of the share capital by consolidation of shares of different classes or by the divison of shares into shares of different classes or by both those methods (subsection (6)). An order under subsection (2) shall have no effect until an office copy of the order has been delivered to the Registrar of Companies, and a copy of every such order shall be annexed to every copy of the memorandum of the company issued after the order has been made (subsection (3)).

The Companies Act 1985, makes provisions for facilitating reconstruction and amalgamation of companies. Where application is made to the court for sanction of a compromise or arrangement under Section 425 and the court is satisfied that the scheme is for reconstruction or amalgamation, the court may, either by an order sanctioning the compromise or arrangement, or by any subsequent order, make provision, amongst other things, for the transfer of the property and liabilities from the one company to the other company, the allotment and appropriation of shares and other interests, and the dissolution, without winding up, of the transferor company (Section 427). Any conveyance or assignment by a company of all its property to trustees for the benefit of all its creditors shall be void to all intents (Companies Act 1985, Section 615(2). SEE *Winding Up*

ARTICLES OF ASSOCIATION The articles of association are the regulations or by-laws of a company by which its affairs are governed.

The memorandum forms the boundary to the company's powers, but within that boundary the company can, subject to the provisions of the Companies Acts, make its own rules and regulations, and these are contained in the articles of association. The articles

accept the memorandum of association as the charter of incorporation of the company, and so accepting it the articles proceed to define the duties, the rights, and the powers of the governing body as between themselves and the company at large, and the mode and form in which the business of the company is to be carried on, and the mode and form in which changes in the internal regulations of the company may from time to time be made. [*Ashbury Railway Carriage Co.* v *Riche* [1875] LR 7 HL 653]

Every person dealing with a company is deemed to have notice of the contents of the memorandum and articles.

The following sections of the Companies Act 1985 apply to the Articles of Association of a company:

7. (1) There may in the case of a company limited by shares and there shall in the case of a company limited by guarantee or unlimited, be registered with the memorandum articles of association signed by the subscribers to the memorandum and prescribing regulations for the company.

(2) In the case of an unlimited company having a share capital the articles must state the amount of share capital with which the company proposed to be registered.

(3) Articles must:

(*a*) be printed,

(*b*) be divided into paragraphs numbered consecutively, and

(*c*) be signed by each subscriber of the memorandum in the presence of at least one witness who must attest the signature (which attestation is sufficient in Scotland as well as in England and Wales).

8. (1) Table A is as prescribed by regulations made by the Secretary of State; and a company may for its articles adopt the whole or any part of that Table.

(2) In the case of a company limited by shares, if articles are not registered or, if articles are registered, in so far as they do not exclude or modify Table A, that Table (so far as applicable, and in force at the date of the company's registration) constitutes the company's articles, in the same manner and to the same extent as if articles in the form of that Table had been duly registered.

(3) If in consequence of regulations under this section Table A is altered, the alteration does not affect a company registered before the alteration takes effect, or repeal as respects that company any portion of the Table.

(4) The form of the articles of association of:

(*a*) a company limited by guarantee and not having a share capital,

(*b*) a company limited by guarantee and having a share capital, and

(*c*) an unlimited company having a share capital, shall be respectively in accordance with Table C, D or E prescribed by regulations and made by the Secrtary of State, or as near to that form as circumstances admit.

9. (1) Subject to the provisions of this Act and to the conditions contained in its memorandum, a company may by special resolution alter its articles.

(2) Alterations so made in the articles are (subject to this Act) as valid as if originally contained in them, and are subject in like manner to alteration by special resolution.

Table A, which is contained in the Companies Act 1985 and referred to in the above sections, contains regulations which may be adopted for a company's articles of association, but in many companies special articles are prepared. Articles of association deal with the following matters: share capital, lien on shares, calls on shares, transfer and transmission of shares, forfeiture of shares, conversion of shares into stock, alteration of capital, general meetings, proceedings at general meeting, votes of members, directors powers and duties of directors, the seal, disqualifications of directors, rotation of directors, proceedings of directors, dividends and reserve, accounts, audit, notices.

A company's Articles of Association, along with the Memorandum of Association (q.v.), must be registered with the registrar of companies for England and Wales. The following are the major provisions in the 1985 Act regarding registration and its effect:

10. (1) The company's memorandum and articles (if any) shall be delivered:

(a) to the registrar of companies for England and Wales, if the memorandum states that the registered office of the company is to be situated in England and Wales, or that it is to be situated in Wales; and

(b) to the registrar of companies for Scotland, if the memorandum states that the registered office of the company is to be situated in Scotland.

(2) With the memorandum there shall be delivered a statement in the prescribed form containing the names and requisite particulars of:

(a) the person who is, or the persons who are, to be the first director or directors of the company; and

(b) the person who is, or the persons who are, to be the first secretary or joint secretaries of the company;

and the requisite particulars in each case are those set out in Schedule 1.

(3) The statement shall be signed by or on behalf of the subscribers of the memorandum and shall contain a consent signed by each of the persons named in it as a director, as secretary or as one of joint secretaries, to act in the relevant capacity.

(4) Where a memorandum is delivered by a person as agent for the subscribers, the statement shall specify that fact and the person's name and address.

(5) An appointment by any articles delivered with the memorandum of a person as director or secretary of the company is void unless he is named as a director or secretary in the statement.

(6) There shall in the statement be specified the intended situation of the company's registered office on incorporation.

12.—(1) The registrar of companies shall not register a company's memorandum delivered under section 10 unless he is satisfied that all the requirements of this Act in respect of registration and of matters precedent and incidental to it have been complied with.

(2) Subject to this, the registrar shall retain and register the memorandum and articles (if any) delivered to him under that section.

(3) A statutory declaration in the prescribed form by—

(a) a solicitor engaged in the formation of a company, or

(b) a person named as a director or secretary of the company in the statement delivered under section 10(2),

that those requirements have been complied with shall be delivered to the registrar of companies, and the registrar may accept such a declaration as sufficient evidence of compliance.

13.—(1) On the registration of a company's memorandum, the registrar of companies shall give a certificate that the company is incorporated and, in the case of a limited company, that it is limited.

(2) The certificate may be signed by the registrar, or authenticated by his official seal.

(3) From the date of incorporation mentioned in the certificate, the subscribers of the memorandum, together with such other persons as may from time to time become members of the company, shall be a body corporate by the name contained in the memorandum.

(4) That body corporate is then capable forthwith of exercising all the functions of an incorporated company, but with such liability on the part of its members to contribute to its assets in the event of its being wound up as is provided by this Act.

This is subject, in the case of a public company, to section 117 (additional certificate as to amount of allotted share capital).

(5) The persons named in the statement under section 10 as directors, secretary or joint secretaries are, on the company's incorporation, deemed to have been respectively appointed as its first directors, secretary or joint secretaries.

(6) Where the registrar registers an association's memorandum which states that the association is to be a public company, the certificate of incorporation shall contain a statement that the company is a public company.

(7) A certificate of incorporation given in respect of an association is conclusive evidence—

(a) that the requirements of this Act in respect of registration and of matters precedent and incidental to it have been complied with, and that the association is a company authorised to be registered, and is duly registered, under this Act, and

(b) if the certificate contains a statement that the

company is a public company, that the company is such a company.

14.—(1) Subject to the provisions of this Act, the memorandum and articles, when registered, bind the company and its members to the same extent as if they respectively had been signed and sealed by each member, and contained covenants on the part of each member to observe all the provisions of the memorandum and of the articles.

(2) Money payable by a member of the company under the memorandum or articles is a debt due from him to the company, and in England and Wales is of the nature of a specialty debt.

SEE *Resolutions;* SEE ALSO *Companies; Memorandum of Association; Table A*

ASIAN DOLLARS The term applies to United States dollars dealt in, whether by deposit or loans, in Asian countries, notably Japan, Hongkong and the Pacific Basin. SEE *Eurocurrency*

ASSENT SEE *Personal Representatives*

ASSENTED A term used to describe stocks and shares and, in some cases, bonds where the investor has agreed to an offer or proposal changing the nature of the investment, e.g. a merger or capital reconstruction or, particularly in the case of foreign government bonds, an agreement to accept some modified terms, perhaps as to interest or capital repayment, hence assented bonds.

ASSESSMENT OF INCOME TAX The determination by an Inspector of Taxes of the amount of a taxpayer's income tax liability. Assessments made under Schedule E of the Income Tax Acts relate to income from an office or employment and income tax is normally deducted in such cases under the PAYE system (q.v.). In all other cases, the Inspector of Taxes will normally issue a Notice of Assessment indicating the tax liability in that year of assessment.

The normal date for payment of income tax other than under Schedule E is 1st January in the year of assessment. In the case of Schedule D assessments on business profits, income tax is normally payable in two instalments, namely, on 1st January and 1st July in the year of assessment.

Higher-rate income tax on any income not taxed at source is payable on 1st January in the year of assessment. Higher-rate income tax on income which has suffered the basic rate of income tax at source is normally payable on 1st December in the year following the year of assessment. SEE ALSO *Income Tax*

ASSET STRIPPING A situation which arises where a company rich in assets is taken over and the assets are sold off at a profit. If the company making the bid has a high share price, it is usually possible to acquire the asset-rich company at a modest price and then realize substantial gains on the sales of the assets. Such acquisitions are usually made as a financial operation and not for any industrial logic as such. Asset stripping was common in the 1970s, but understandably came to be a matter of some opprobrium.

ASSET VALUE The value of a company calculated by reference to the current value of the underlying assets, from which is then deducted the amount of the company's liabilities. The asset value per share is the amount of the net assets so calculated divided by the number of ordinary shares in issue.

The asset value of a company will usually be of some relevance in arriving at the share value, but the current quoted price of the shares, if listed on a stock exchange, may differ widely from the asset value, depending on the company's profit record, dividend policy, trading prospects and all other relevant factors.

The asset value of a company's shares has a particular significance for capital transfer tax purposes where a controlling shareholder makes a disposition of his shares, whether by lifetime gift or on death. SEE *Capital Transfer Tax*

ASSETS The goods, property and resources of all kinds of a company, a partnership or an individual which are available for the payment of debts and liabilities. For accounting purposes in balance sheets these are usually categorized as fixed assets (e.g. freehold and leasehold property, plant and machinery) and current assets (e.g. stock, work in progress, debtors and bank balances). The assets of a company or an individual may be those which are in some obvious and tangible form, or those which are intangible such as goodwill or intellectual property (patents, copyrights, etc.). SEE *Balance Sheets; Balance Sheets of the Personal Sector*

ASSIGNMENT To assign a right or property is to transfer it, or make it over, to another person. An assignment may be absolute or by way of charge.

As to the difference between 'assignability', and 'negotiability' see *Negotiable Instruments.* As to the assignment of a life policy, see *Life Policy.* SEE *Debts, Assignment of; Equitable Assignment.*

ASSIGNMENT FOR BENEFIT OF CREDITORS A person who is unable to pay his debts may legally call his creditors together and offer to transfer his assets to a trustee, in order that they may be realized and the proceeds apportioned amongst the creditors, according to the amount of their claims, in full discharge of the amount owing.

The deed assigning the property to the trustee must be registered at the Department of Trade and Industry within seven days, otherwise it is void. SEE *Deed of Arrangement*

Where the assignment is of company property, the position is governed by Section 615 of the Companies Act 1985. SEE UNDER *Arrangement with Creditors*.

An assignment of the debtor's property for the benefit of his creditors is an arrangement quite apart from proceedings under the Bankruptcy Acts.

Where a debtor assigns his property to a trustee for the benefit of creditors generally, it is an act of bankruptcy (SEE *Act of Bankruptcy*), and a debtor may be adjudged a bankrupt upon a bankruptcy petition presented within three months from the date of an act of bankruptcy (SEE *Receiving Order*). When such a petition is presented and the debtor is made bankrupt, the deed of assignment becomes void. SEE *Bankruptcy; Composition with creditors*

ASSIGNMENT OF DEBTS SEE *Debts, Assignment of*

ASSIGNMENT OF LIFE POLICY SEE *Life Policy*

ASSOCIATED BANKS OF EUROPE CORPORATION (ABECOR) An association of European Banks, sometimes referred to as a banking 'club'. ABECOR consists of Barclays Bank, Banque Nationale de Paris, Banque Bruxelles Lambert, Algemene Bank Nederland, Dresdner Bank, Bayerische Hypotheken- und Wechsel-Bank and Banca Nationale del Lavoro. The purpose of this and similiar associations is to facilitate the services which the individual banks offer to their customers and this is achieved by consortium lending and reciprocity of other lending arrangements.

ASSOCIATED COMPANY This is a term without any precise legal definition, but in general means a company in which another company has from 20 per cent to 50 per cent of the share capital. If, for example, the investment exceeded 50 per cent, the 'associated company' would rank as a subsidiary company for accounting purposes. If the investment was less than 20 per cent, it would normally be regarded as no more than a trade or portfolio investment.

ASSOCIATION OF BRITISH CHAMBERS OF COMMERCE This association was formed in 1860 as a focal point for the chambers of commerce which had evolved in Britain from the end of the eighteenth century onwards. Today there are 87 chambers of commerce affiliated to the Association, representing over 57,000 manufacturing, merchanting and service and professional businesses.

In Britain the chambers of commerce are not, as in continental Europe established as part of the administrative law of the state. The UK chambers are voluntary organizations financed by members' subscriptions. Their objects are the promotion and protection of trade, commerce and industry in the area represented, the representation of the interests of those engaged in trade, commerce and industry, and the provision of services or facilities for members. Every member company or firm is represented (1) locally through the local chamber, (2) regionally through the regional chamber, and (3) nationally and internationally through the Association.

Chambers of commerce provide their members with a wide range of information on both local and national business matters, including economic forecasts and details of changes in the law affecting business activities. Most chambers issue newsletters or bulletins and arrange seminars and conferences for their members. In particular, they organize trade promotion events in cooperation with the Department of Trade and Industry and other public bodies. They provide an important link with other chambers and similar organizations in other countries.

A particular role of the chambers of commerce is the administration of the export documentation system in the UK. They are the only body who are authorized by the Department of Trade and Industry to issue certificates of origin (q.v.) for goods which are exported. (SEE ALSO *Uniform Customs and Practice for Documented Credits*) The Association is a member of the Permanent Conference of Chambers of Commerce of the European Economic Community and of the International Chamber of Commerce which was founded in 1919.

The Association plays a major role in the provision of information for members, the training of younger members, the development of commerce generally and the representation of members' interests to the Government and other public bodies.

ASSOCIATION OF BRITISH FACTORS LIMITED The business of factoring is described under the entry *Factoring*. In 1977, the Association of British Factors Ltd was formed to bring together the leading organizations engaged in factoring and invoice discounting. The principal objectives of the Association are

1. to establish and maintain the highest level of professional standards for the factoring industry;

2. to deal with legal, regulatory and other matters of common interest in the development of factoring services;
3. to assist members of the factoring industry in their contacts with other professional bodies, the Government and other interested parties;
4. to seek to improve efficiency further within the factoring industry through formalized staff training procedures.

At the time of writing, the Association is made up of the eight leading factoring houses in the UK.

ASSUMED NAME The Bills of Exchange Act 1882 permits a bill to be signed in an assumed name. By Section 23

(1) Where a person signs a bill in a trade or assumed name, he is liable thereon as if he had signed it in his own name.

A purchaser of a business often assumes, for a time at any rate, the name of the person who built up the connection. Where a person trades in an assumed name, and signs cheques and bills in that name, it is customary for a banker to receive a written authority from him to honour cheques or bills when signed in the trade name. The authority is signed by the person in his real name and a specimen signature of the assumed name is given. SEE *Registration of Business Names*

ASSURANCE SEE *Life Assurance*

ATTACHMENT Where a person has obtained a judgment for the recovery of money, he may, by application to the court, obtain a garnishee order, which, when served upon a banker, will attach any money in the banker's hands belonging to the person against whom judgment was given. SEE *Garnishee Order*

The expression is also used in a wider connotation relating to other assets attached in satisfaction of a judgment.

ATTACHMENT OF EARNINGS ACT 1971 Under this Act the High Court may make an Attachment of Earnings Order to secure payments under a High Court Maintenance Order. In addition, a County Court may make an Attachment of Earnings Order to secure

1. payments under a High Court or a County Court Maintenance Order;
2. payment of a judgment debt of £5 or more;
3. payments under a County Court Administration Order.

A Magistrates' Court may make an Attachment of Earnings Order to secure

1. payments under a Magistrates' Court Maintenance Order;
2. payment of a sum to be paid under a conviction, such as a fine;
3. payment of a sum under a Legal Aid Contribution Order.

The term 'judgment debt' means a sum payable under

1. a judgment or order enforceable by a court in England and Wales (not being a Magistrates' Court);
2. an order of a Magistrates' Court for payment of money recoverable summarily as a civil debt;
3. an order of any court which is enforceable as if it were for the payment of money so recoverable.

The court determines the protected earnings rate, i.e. the minimum rate below which the earnings actually paid should not be reduced and also the normal deduction rate.

In practice it is found that the debtor can delay or defeat the object of the Act by constantly changing his employment. SEE *Act of Bankruptcy*

ATTENDANCE ALLOWANCE Attendance allowance is designed for persons who are seriously disabled, whether through physical or mental illness, and who need a lot of attention. The allowance may be payable to any person above the age of two, provided the various requirements are satisfied. This type of benefit is not contributory, it is not means-tested and is not subject to tax (SEE Appendix 2).

In order to qualify for attendance allowance the disabled person must require attention (1) during the day, or (2) during the night, or (3) both during the day and night. The allowance will be paid only if the following conditions are met:

Attention by day This is interpreted as frequent attention throughout the day in connection with the disabled person's bodily functions, e.g. eating and drinking, walking, keeping clean and keeping warm, or continual supervision throughout the day in order to avoid substantial danger to the disabled person or others. In a Court of Appeal judgment, it has been held that the performance of domestic duties such as cooking or shopping does not constitute attention in connection with bodily functions (*Times*, 14th April, 1981).

Attention by night This is interpreted as prolonged or repeated attention during the night in connection with the disabled person's bodily functions or continual supervision throughout the night to avoid substantial danger to the disabled person or others.

Attention by day and night A higher rate of attendance allowance is paid in cases where attention is required by day and night (SEE Appendix 2).

A disabled person cannot qualify for allowance

until the attendance rules have been satisfied for six months, although a claim may be made after a period of four months in order that, if the allowance is granted, it may be paid immediately at the end of the six-month period.

There is also a residence requirement in that the disabled person (1) must normally live in the UK, the Isle of Man or the Channel Islands, (2) must be living there when the claim is made, and (3) must have lived there for six months out of the last 12 months.

Special residence rules apply to members of HM Forces and their families accompanying them abroad, people going abroad for medical treatment, people moving to the UK from another EEC country, and nationals of countries which have reciprocal agreements with the UK on attendance allowance.

Attendance allowance is not payable to disabled persons who are in hospitals run by the National Health Service, homes run by a local authority or other forms of accommodation financed from public funds. It is payable, however, to private patients in hospital.

ATTESTATION A formal witnessing of a signature. In the case of a will, the testator's signature must be made, or acknowledged, by the testator in the presence of two or more witnesses each of whom must attest or witness the will. There is no special form of attestation necessary, but the following is a common attestation clause:

Signed by the said , the testator, in the presence of us, both present at the same time, who in his presence and at his request and in the presence of each other have hereunto submitted our names as witnesses.
A.B.
C.D.

(BUT SEE Administration of Justice Act 1982 under *Will*.)

The witnesses give their names, addresses, and descriptions. A legacy to a witness or to the spouse of a witness is void.

Where a signature is witnessed, as in the case of a transfer of shares, the form is usually

Signed, sealed and delivered by the above named in the presence of

Signature
Address
Occupation

When a document is executed by a person acting under a power of attorney, the form is

Signed, sealed, and delivered by the above-named John Brown by his attorney John Jones in the presence of, etc.

A transferee should not witness a transferor's signature. A minor is not a suitable witness. There is no legal objection to a wife witnessing her husband's signature, or a husband witnessing that of his wife, but there are many companies that will not accept such witnesses.

Where any material alterations or interlineations have been made in a deed, they should be referred to in the attestation clause as having been made before execution of the document.

In a document under hand, a witness often signs simply as: 'Witness, John Brown', and gives his address and description.

When a signature by 'mark' is witnessed, the form is

His
John × Brown
mark

Witness
John Jones
Warwick Road
Carlisle, Builder

In the case of a deed which is executed by a 'mark', the words used are to the following effect:

Signed, sealed, and delivered by the above-named John Brown, he having signed by a mark in consequence of being unable to sign his name, in the presence of us, the deed having first been read over and explained to him when he appeared perfectly to understand the same.

Several signatures on a document may be witnessed by the same person.

ATTORNEY, LETTER AND POWER OF
SEE *Power of Attorney*

ATTORNMENT An attornment clause in a mortgage deed is one in which the mortgagor attorns tenant, i.e. acknowledges himself to be the tenant of the mortgaged property, normally at a rent equal to the periodic instalments under the mortgage. The original idea was to confer on the mortgagee the right of distrain for rent in the event of non-payment of the mortgage instalments. This is no longer possible and attornment clauses have largely fallen into disuse among banks and building societies. One of the few remaining benefits of an attornment clause is that the mortgagee may bring an action for possession under the Small Tenements Recovery Act 1838. If an attornment clause is included, it should provide for a peppercorn rent, otherwise the mortgagee may run into problems of Rent Acts protection.

AUCTION, BUYING AT The three largest auction houses in the UK are

Sotheby, Parke, Bernet Group Limited (Sotheby's)
Christie's International Limited (Christie's)
Phillips Son & Neale (Phillips)

There are, of course, many other auction houses operating throughout the British Isles.

London is the acknowledged centre of the international art market and has been since the 1950s. The other principal centres are Paris and New York, but a number of factors have contributed to the dominance of London. This was partly the movement of French treasures to London during the French Revolution, partly in later years the effect of the US slump on the auction market in New York, partly the disposal of collections by aristocratic families in this country, and partly the convenience of London as a centre of communications. In more recent years, the favourable level of commissions in London has no doubt been a major factor in the increasing dominance of the London auction rooms.

Auctioneers' commissions in the UK have traditionally been lower than in other countries and continue to be so. Until 1975, the seller of goods in this country would pay a commission of 12½ per cent–15 per cent and no commission would be charged to the buyer. In more recent years, it has been the practice to charge a buyer's premium at the rate of 10 per cent and the vendor's commission is usually charged at 12½ per cent on proceeds up to £500 and 10 per cent above that figure. On special lots, the vendor's commission will usually be negotiable. In most cases, there is no buyer's premium on coins and medals, wines, motor vehicles and certain other special items.

For all practical purposes, therefore, the average cost of buying an article at auction is 10 per cent plus VAT and, if the article is subsequently resold at auction, a vendor's premium of 10 per cent plus VAT will be payable. Thus, from an investor's point of view, anything bought at auction will normally have had to increase by 20 per cent in value before the cost price is recovered. Depending on the nature of the article, this could, however, be very much less than the mark-up if it had been bought and sold through a dealer.

The levels of commissions in London continue to be lower than the rest of the world. In West Germany, the combined vendor's and buyer's commissions total 30 per cent and they can be approximately that high in Switzerland and the USA. In France, the combined commissions rise to approximately 23 per cent.

The buyer at auction will normally be required to make payment immediately for his purchase and, if he does not remove his goods within a stipulated period, typically five days, he may become liable for storage and insurance costs.

AUDIT The examination, usually yearly or half-yearly, of books of account, by a person specially appointed the auditor for the purpose of ascertaining the correctness of the books. SEE *Auditors*

AUDITORS The auditors of a company are appointed by the shareholders and their function is to make an independent investigation of the company's affairs and to report to the shareholders.

The appointment, powers and duties of auditors are contained in Sections 159 to 163 of the Companies Act 1948, as amended by the Companies Acts of 1957, 1976 and, to a minor degree, 1981.

Appointment of Auditors

Under Section 384, Companies Act 1985:

(1) Every company shall, at each general meeting of the company at which accounts are laid in accordance with section 241, appoint an auditor or auditors to hold office from the conclusion of that meeting until the conclusion of the next general meeting at which the requirements of section 241 are complied with.

This is subject to section 252 (exemption for dormant companies).

(2) The first auditors of a company may be appointed by the directors at any time before the first general meeting of the company at which accounts are laid; and auditors so appointed shall hold office until the conclusion of that meeting.

(3) If the directors fail to exercise their powers under subsection (2), those powers may be exercised by the company in general meeting.

(4) The directors, or the company in general meeting, may fill any casual vacancy in the office of auditor; but while any such vacancy continues, the surviving or continuing auditor or auditors (if any) may act.

(5) If at any general meeting of a company at which accounts are laid as required by section 241 no auditors are appointed or reappointed, the Secretary of State may appoint a person to fill the vacancy; and the company shall, within one week of that power of the Secretary of State becoming exercisable, give to him notice of that fact.

If a company fails to give the notice required by this subsection, the company and every officer of it who is in default is guilty of an offence and liable to a fine and, for continued contravention, to a daily default fine.

Removal of Auditors

Auditors may be removed from office by an ordinary resolution of a company, of which 28 days' notice must be given. An auditor who wishes to make representations relating to his removal from office may do so in writing and request the company to send copies of his representations to the members. If for any reason this is not done, the auditor can require that his representations be read out at the general meeting of the company.

Resignation of Auditors
The resignation of an auditor is governed by Section 390, Companies Act 1985, which provides that an auditor may resign from office but in doing so he must provide a statement of any circumstances which he considers should be brought to the notice of the members or provide a statement to the effect that there are no such circumstances. If he does not do this, his resignation is not valid.

Remuneration of Auditors
Where, as is usual, the first auditor of a company is appointed by the directors, they will also fix his remuneration. Thereafter, the auditors' remuneration is fixed by the company in general meeting or in such a manner as the company in general meeting may determine. It is usual for a general meeting to authorize the directors to fix the auditors' remuneration.

Duties of Auditors
The duties of an auditor are onerous. He must report on the statutory accounts laid by the directors before the members and state whether, in his opinion, the balance sheet and profit and loss accounts and group accounts, where appropriate, have been properly prepared in accordance with the Companies Act and give 'a true and fair view' of the company's state of affairs for the financial year.

Under Section 237, Companies Act 1985, The auditor of a company is required to carry out such investigations which will enable him to form an opinion on whether proper accounting records have been kept and whether the company's accounts are in accord with the accounting records and returns. In reporting on the accounts of a company, the auditor will have regard to the various requirements of the Companies Acts and the standards laid down by the accounting bodies. He must report on the consistency of the directors' report with the accounts and he must make a statement on any non-compliance with the requirement of that Act regarding disclosure of directors' dealings.

Lord Justice Lindley in (*Re London & General Bank Ltd* (No. 2) [1895] 2 Ch 673) said

> It is no part of an auditor's duty to give advice, either to directors or shareholders as to what they ought to do. His business is to ascertain and state the true financial position of the company at the time of the audit ... an auditor, however, is not bound to do more than exercise reasonable care and skill in making enquiries and investigations.

There is little doubt that auditing standards have risen over the years, particularly since the secondary bank crisis of the early 1970s. Much more is expected of an auditor than used to be the case, partly because of the statutory obligations imposed by successive Companies Acts and partly because of the standards imposed by the professional bodies. The liability of an auditor is considerable. He may be liable for breach of contract or for the tort of negligence to the members of the company and may conceivably incur responsibility to third parties who rely on the auditor's report. He is also guilty of a statutory offence if he fails to comply with the Companies Act in relation to the duties of auditors.

Qualifications of Auditors
Under the Companies Act, an auditor must be a member of one of those bodies of accountants recognized for auditor purposes by the Department of Trade and Industry. At the present time, this embraces members of the Institute of Chartered Accountants of England and Wales, the Institute of Chartered Accountants of Scotland, the Association of Certified Accountants and the Institute of Chartered Accountants in Ireland.

AUDITOR'S REPORT SEE *Auditors*

AUTHORIZED BANK Any office in the UK or the Channel Islands of a banker who was for the time being authorized by an Order of HM Treasury to act for all purposes of the Exchange Control Act 1947 (q.v.) as an authorized dealer in relation to gold and foreign currencies and to whom various general permissions were given to implement certain types of Exchange Control transactions. They included most of the commercial banks in the UK (both British and foreign) but not offices abroad of such banks. The term should not be confused with that of 'recognized bank' under the Banking Act 1979 (q.v.).

AUTHORIZED CAPITAL The capital of a company as authorized by its memorandum of association. It is called also the 'nominal' and 'registered' capital. SEE *Capital*

AUTHORIZED DEALERS IN GOLD Any office in the UK or the Channel Islands of a banker or firm who was for the time being authorized by an Order of HM Treasury to act for all purposes of the Exchange Control Act 1947 (q.v.) as an authorized dealer in relation to gold, i.e. they were permitted to hold, and deal in, gold bullion. They included all the authorized banks (q.v.) and two firms of bullion brokers.

AUTHORIZED DEPOSITARY The exchange Control Act 1947 provided that bearer securities should be deposited with an authorized depositary. This is no longer necessary consequent upon the suspension of the Exchange Control Regulations in 1979. The Regulations may, however, be reintroduced at some future date and the relevant Sections (15 and 42) of the Act are, therefore, quoted as follows:

> 15.—(2). It shall be the duty of every person by whom or to whose order ... a certificate of title is held in the United Kingdom, and of every person resident in the United Kingdom by whom or to whose order ... a certificate of title is held outside the United Kingdom, to cause the certificate of title to be kept at all times ... in the custody of an authorised depositary.
>
> (3) An authorised depositary shall not part with any certificate of title or coupon required under this Section to be in the custody of an authorised depositary. Provided that this subsection shall not prohibit an authorised depositary—
>
> (*a*) from parting with a certificate or title or coupon to or to the order of another authorised depositary, where the person from whom the other authorised depositary is to receive instructions in relation thereto is to be the same as the person from whom he receives instructions;
>
> (*b*) from parting with a certificate of title, for the purpose of obtaining payment of capital moneys payable on the security to the person entrusted with payment thereof;
>
> (*c*) from parting with a coupon in the ordinary course for collection.
>
> (4) No capital moneys, interest or dividends shall be paid in the UK on any security except to the order of an authorised depositary having the custody of the certificate of title to that security, so, however, that this subsection shall not be taken as restricting the manner in which any sum lawfully paid on account of the capital moneys, interest or dividends may be dealt with by the person receiving them.
>
> (5). An authorised depositary shall not do any act whereby he recognises or gives effect to the substitution of one person for another as the person from whom he receives instructions in relation to a certificate of title or coupon, unless there is produced to him the prescribed evidence that he is not by so doing giving effect to any transaction which is prohibited by this Act.
>
> 42. 'Authorised Depositary' means a person for the time being authorised by an order of the Treasury to act as an authorised depositary for the purposes of Part III of this Act. [SEE *Exchange Control Act 1947*]

Besides banks, this category includes members of the London and Associated Stock Exchanges, certain specialist financial institutions, and solicitors practising in the UK.

AUTHORIZED UNIT TRUST A unit trust authorized by the Department of Trade and Industry under the Prevention of Fraud (Investments) Act 1958 (q.v.). SEE *Unit Trusts*

AUTOMATED TELLER MACHINE (ATM) This is a robot which dispenses cash and, in some cases, deals with certain other basic banking transactions of a kind which traditionally would have been handled by a cashier or teller over a bank counter. The first ATMs to be introduced anywhere in the world were installed in the UK in 1967. These early dispensers were designed to receive vouchers of £10 each, obtained by a customer from his bank and used in the dispensers when the need arose. Since then, far more sophisticated types of machine have been introduced.

Perhaps the main distinction between modern ATMs and the early cash dispensers is that the newer machines are on line to the computer centres of the banks or their credit card companies. By inserting a plastic card and keying in a personal identification number, the customer is able to draw cash, usually up to £50 or £100, provided the computer accepts the debit. Some of the machines will also accept cheques and other vouchers paid in for the credit of an account and some of them will provide the customer with details of his or her bank balance.

Some ATMs are 'through the wall', i.e. they are installed in the wall of a banking branch; others are located at various points of sale such as stores, filling stations and airports.

By the end of 1982 there were approximately 3,500 ATMs in Britain, out of an approximate total of 11,000 throughout Europe. By that time, in the USA, there were nearly 30,000 machines in use and approximately 27,000 in Japan.

It has been a feature of the development of ATMs in the UK that the individual banks developed their own ATMs and did not share each other's machines as was done in the United States. In September 1982, however, Midland Bank and National Westminster Bank announced the reciprocal use of their ATMs and in March 1983 a similar announcement was made by the Bank of Scotland, Barclays Bank, Lloyds Bank and the Royal Bank of Scotland Group.

A number of building societies have also introduced ATMs and at the time of writing, there are indications of a wider use throughout the building society movement.

AVERAGE (IN SHIPPING) The amount payable by the owner of a ship and by the owners of the cargo, in proportion to their individual interests, to make good any loss caused by throwing part of the cargo overboard or cutting away the masts or such like things, in order to prevent the loss of the ship and the rest of the cargo. SEE *General Average*

AVERAGE ADJUSTER A person who settles or adjusts the amount to be paid by the owner of the ship and the owners of the cargo, in connection with any intentional losses which have been made for the safety of the ship or the cargo. SEE *General Average*

AVERAGE CLAUSE The clause in a marine insurance policy which may provide that certain articles are free from average, unless general, or the ship be stranded, and that other articles are free from average under, say, three per cent, unless general, or the ship be stranded, sunk, burnt, or on fire.

Under an average clause in a fire policy, in the event of a fire, the amount payable by the insurance company will be, if the property is only partially destroyed, and has not been insured up to the full value of the property, a proportioned amount of the damage, based upon the proportion which the amount insured bears to the full value of the property. Where a property, value £30,000, is insured for £15,000, and damage by fire occurs to the extent of £9,000, the amount which the company will pay will be £4,500 — that is, half the loss, because the property was insured for only half its value.

AVERAGING (STOCK EXCHANGE) A 'bull' speculator on the Stock Exchange buys more of a certain stock he holds, when the price has fallen, so as to make the average price of the whole purchase less than the price paid for the original purchase; and a 'bear' speculator, when the price rises against him, sells more of the stock so as to average the price.

AVIATION INSURANCE A category of insurance covering, as the name implies, risks arising from aviation. An operator of aircraft may insure against loss of, or damage to, the aircraft, but most forms of aviation insurance have grown out of public liability insurance. The insurable risks of an aircraft (or airline) operator stem from the various categories of liability which the operator may incur. In some cases, these are absolute liabilities, i.e. not depending on proof of negligence or other legal responsibility, and in some cases that liability is limited as to amount. The main categories of public liability attaching to the operating of aircraft or an airline are

1. liability to persons on land or water who have sustained personal injury or damage to their property,
2. liability to passengers being carried on international or internal flights,
3. liability to passengers through wilful misconduct,
4. liability in respect of registered luggage or goods carried, and
5. liability for negligence to other aircraft or its passengers.

Certain categories of aviation insurance are obligatory, very much in the same way as third-party motor insurance.

B

BACK-TO-BACK LOAN A term applied to any loan which is supported by an equivalent deposit. More usually, however, it refers to a loan in one currency backed by a deposit in another currency, possibly in a different country. When the Exchange Control Regulations were in force in the UK, overseas investments were sometimes purchased by means of back-to-back loans as an alternative to the purchase of premium currency. The overseas securities would be purchased with currency borrowed for the purpose and an equivalent sum in sterling deposited with a bank in the UK. The Bank of England required such foreign loans to be covered by foreign securities to the extent of 115 per cent, the margin of 15 per cent having to be topped up as necessary from time to time by the purchase of foreign securities through the premium currency pool. SEE *Premium Currency; Premium Dollar*

BACKING A BILL The indorsement of a bill or cheque by a party who is not the payee or indorsee, for the purpose of acting as surety for the drawer, payee or other party to the instrument. Such a 'stiffening' indorsement will make the person so signing liable on the bill although his indorsement was not necessary for its negotiation.

If the bank is the holder of a bill or note payable to its own order, and requires the indorsement of an additional party to the bill for better security, such third party is not liable as indorser to the bank.

If the bank has indorsed the bill or note as payee before getting the 'stiffening' indorsement, the bank is a *prior* indorser to the third party, and the latter is only bound to reimburse *subsequent* indorsers (Bills of Exchange Act 1882, Section 55(2)(*a*)). If, however, the bank gets the surety's indorsement before indorsing the bill or note itself, it cannot claim to be a holder in due course, because it does not take the bill from the surety 'complete and regular on the face of it', in that its own indorsement as payee is lacking.

Hence, when a party becomes surety to the drawer of a bill payable to the latter's own order or to the payee of a bill, it is necessary to have evidence additional to the surety's indorsement, showing explicitly if such indorsement was made to secure the drawer or payee, or was merely for the benefit of subsequent holders. Such evidence should take the form of a separate letter acknowledging liability or a note written on the bill by the surety. An oral understanding is insufficient, for, being a contract of suretyship, such an engagement must, by the Statute of Frauds 1677, be in writing. SEE ALSO *Law Reform (Enforcement of Contracts) Act*

In the case of *Lombard Banking Ltd* v *Central Garage & Engineering Ltd & Others* [1962] 3 WLR 1199, it was held that it was open to the court to receive evidence as to the order in which indorsements were made, where this was different from the order appearing on the bill.

BACKWARDATION The charge made to a 'bear' on the Stock Exchange (i.e. a person who sells shares which he may not possess in anticipation of being able to purchase them at a lower price) for the loan of stock to enable him to carry over a transaction from one Stock Exchange Account to the next. SEE ALSO *Contango*

BAIL BOND A bond given by a banker on behalf of his customer in order to secure the release of the latter's ship after it has been arrested as a consequence of a collision.

BAILEE The person to whom goods are entrusted for a specific purpose by another person called the bailor. SEE *Bailment*

BAILMENT The delivery of goods or chattels to another person for a particular purpose other than on a sale. The law of bailment is derived almost entirely from the Roman law on the subject, but it touches and concerns a great many aspects of business life. For example, auctioneers, innkeepers, common carriers, pawnbrokers, drycleaners and bankers are all involved in contacts of bailment. In the financial world, the principal examples of bailment are safe custody (q.v.) and hire purchase (q.v.).

BAILOR The person who entrusts goods or chattels to another (the bailee) for a specific purpose. SEE *Bailment*

BALANCE CERTIFICATE The certificate received by a shareholder for the remainder of his holding when he has sold part of his holding.

BALANCE OF PAYMENTS In its simplest terms, the balance of payments represents the difference in the values of a country's imports and exports. The UK balance of payments, therefore, reflects all transactions between the UK and the rest of the world. Such transactions are made up of (1) current account (trade in goods and services), (2) capital account (direct and portfolio investment overseas) and (3) official financing (movements in the official reserves and other public sector transactions).

The balance of *trade* in goods and services normally reflects, in the case of the UK, a very high level of invisible earnings such as shipping, banking, insurance, tourism, air transport and dividends from overseas investments.

BALANCE SHEET A balance sheet shows the assets and liabilities *at a point in time* of a company or other incorporated body or of a private person. It is usually a picture of a trading enterprise, but may just as well be a statement drawn up by a charity, a club, a partnership or a private individual. It is essentially a 'still' photograph at a particular date and should not be confused (although it quite often is in common parlance) with a profit and loss account or trading account, which are, to use the same analogy, a moving film of the enterprise throughout the accounting period.

A balance sheet must be so drawn up as to exhibit a truthful statement of the position. The position should not be represented as being better than it actually is, but the position may be better than is disclosed in the statement. Lord Justice Buckley said, 'The purpose of the balance sheet is primarily to show that the financial position of the company is at least as good as there stated, not to show that it is not and may not be better.'

The balance sheet of a company must be signed on behalf of the board by two directors, or, if there is only one, by that director, and the auditors' report must be attached to the balance sheet, and must be read before the company in general meeting and shall be open to inspection by any shareholder (Sections 238 and 241 of the Companies Act 1985).

Under the Companies Act 1985 the directors of every company shall once at least in every year lay before the company in general meeting a profit and loss account, also a balance sheet as at the date to which the profit and loss account is made up. There shall be attached to every such balance sheet a report by the directors with respect to the company's affairs, the amount which they recommend should be paid by way of dividend and the amount, if any, which they propose to carry to a reserve fund.

Schedule 8 to the Companies Act 1948, as amended, contained the basic principles which for many years governed the content and format of company balance sheets in the United Kingdom. The general rules regarding the form and content of company accounts are now set out in Schedule 4 of the Companies Act 1985.

In general, every balance sheet of a company must now show the items listed in one of the two formats set out in the Schedule (see over). Where a balance sheet has been prepared by reference to one of those formats, it is required that the directors of the company adopt the same format in preparing the accounts for subsequent financial years unless, in their opinion, there are special reasons for a change, in which case the reasons for the change must be explained in a note to the accounts in which the new format is first adopted. A balance sheet may include items not listed in the statutory format but certain items, viz. preliminary expenses, expenses of and commission on any issues of shares or debentures, and costs of research, may not be included as assets in any company's balance sheet.

It is also required that a company shows in its balance sheet the corresponding amounts for the financial year immediately preceding that to which the balance sheet relates.

By Schedule 5 of the Companies Act 1985, there must be included or annexed particulars of the identity, place of incorporation and of shareholding of subsidiaries, unless exemption in respect of a foreign subsidiary is granted by the Department of Trade and Industry. By Schedule 5 of the Act similar particulars have to be provided of companies in which one-tenth or more of the nominal shareholding is held and provides for a statement to be provided of the identity of a subsidiary company's ultimate holding company. Sections 235 and 261 call for additional information regarding the year's activities, whilst Schedule 10 of the 1985 Act requires information regarding employees and political or charitable payments.

Every member and every debenture holder of a company, public or private, must be sent a copy of the company's balance sheet, profit and loss account and auditor's report not less than 21 days before the general meeting at which the accounts are to be laid.

See other sections under *Directors*.

The Companies Act 1981, which was designed to give effect to the Fourth Directive of the EEC, introduced far-reaching changes in the content and format of company accounts. Many of the new provisions were contained in Schedule 1 to the 1981 Act which replaced Schedule 8 of the 1948 Act. As mentioned above, the 1985 Act provides for companies to adopt one of two formats for the presentation of their balance sheets. The content of the more usual vertical style is shown below. The alternative permitted by the Act includes the same headings in horizontal layout.

A *Called up share capital not paid*

B *Fixed assets*
- I Intangible assets
  - 1 Development costs
  - 2 Concessions, patents, licences, trade marks and similar rights and assets
  - 3 Goodwill
  - 4 Payments on account
- II Tangible assets
  - 1 Land and buildings
  - 2 Plant and machinery
  - 3 Fixtures, fittings, tools and equipment
  - 4 Payments on account and assets in course of construction
- III Investments
  - 1 Shares in group companies
  - 2 Loans to group companies
  - 3 Shares in related companies
  - 4 Loans to related companies
  - 5 Other investments other than loans
  - 6 Other loans
  - 7 Own shares

C *Current assets*
- I Stocks
  - 1 Raw materials and consumables
  - 2 Work in progress
  - 3 Finished goods and goods for resale
  - 4 Payments on account
- II Debtors
  - 1 Trade debtors
  - 2 Amounts owed by group companies
  - 3 Amounts owed by related companies
  - 4 Other debtors
  - 5 Called-up share capital not paid
  - 6 Prepayments and accrued income
- III Investments
  - 1 Shares in group companies
  - 2 Own shares
  - 3 Other investments
- IV Cash at bank and in hand

D *Prepayments and accrued income*

E *Creditors: amounts falling due within one year*
- 1 Debenture loans
- 2 Bank loans and overdrafts
- 3 Payments received on account
- 4 Trade creditors
- 5 Bills of Exchange payable
- 6 Amounts owed to group companies
- 7 Amounts owed to related companies
- 8 Other creditors including taxation and social security
- 9 Accruals and deferred income

F *Net current assets (liabilities)*

G *Total assets less current liabilities*

H *Creditors: amounts falling due after more than one year*
- 1 Debenture loans
- 2 Bank loans and overdrafts
- 3 Payments received on account
- 4 Trade creditors
- 5 Bills of exchange payable
- 6 Amounts owed to group companies
- 7 Amounts owed to related companies
- 8 Other creditors including taxation and social security
- 9 Accruals and deferred income

I *Provisions for liabilities and charges*
- 1 Pensions and similar obligations
- 2 Taxation, including deferred taxation
- 3 Other provisions

J *Accruals and deferred income*

K *Capital and reserves*
- I Called-up share capital
- II Share premium account
- III Revaluation reserve
- IV Other reserves
  - 1 Capital redemption reserve
  - 2 Reserve for own shares
  - 3 Reserves provided for by the articles of association
  - 4 Other reserves
- V Profit and Loss account

The 1985 Act also incorporates a number of recommendations contained in the Statements of Standard Accounting Practice (SSAP) issued by the accounting bodies and these are dealt with under their respective headings throughout this work.

BALANCE SHEETS OF THE PERSONAL SECTOR Until comparatively recent times little information was available regarding the value and nature of assets owned by private individuals in the UK. A considerable amount of work was done on this subject by the Royal Commission on the Distribution of Income and Wealth (Chairman: Lord Diamond, HMSO, Cmnd 6171, 1975) using sample surveys and information available to the Inland Revenue. The Diamond Report stressed that the methods used were 'subject to a number of deficiencies and weaknesses'. Nevertheless, it provided a platform for further refinement of the figures by the Central Statistical Office so that the values and composition of personal wealth are now published on a regular basis.

The principal categories of assets in private hands at the end of 1983 are given in the table below.

	£ million
National Savings	26,431
Bank current accounts	20,030
Bank deposit accounts	31,655
Building society shares and deposits	66,993
British government securities	17,857
UK ordinary shares	45,035
Unit trusts	4,570
Private equity in life assurance and pension funds	138,000
Houses (estimated)	345,900

Source: Financial Statistics.

BALANCE TICKET Where a certain number of shares has been sold and the certificate, which is sent by the seller's broker to the company's office for certification, is for a larger number than has been sold, a balance ticket is given to the broker for the remaining shares. When the new certificate for the unsold shares is ready, it can be obtained on delivery of the balance ticket. SEE *Certified Transfer*

BALANCING CHARGE A term usually used in relation to income tax where, for example, taxation relief on a particular asset is recoverable because the asset has been sold for more than the written-down value. If, for example, in relation to a motor car writing-down allowances (q.v.) have been allowed for tax purposes and the proceeds of sale exceed the residual, i.e. written-down value, there will be a balancing charge for tax in respect of that excess.

BALTIC EXCHANGE The full name is the Baltic Mercantile and Shipping Exchange. The mercantile aspect is accounted for by dealings in commodities, principally grain, oil, fats and oil seeds. The shipping side of the house is a market for vessel chartering and cargo space and a market in secondhand ships. Since 1949, the Baltic has also operated a market for air chartering.

BANK The word 'bank' is said to be derived from the Italian word *banco*, a bench. The early bankers, the Jews in Lombardy, transacted their business at benches in the market-place. When a banker failed, his *banco* was broken up by the people whence our word 'bankrupt'.

One of the earliest Italian banks, the Bank of Venice, was originated for the management of a public loan, or *monte*, as it was called. Macleod, in his *Elements of Banking*, says

> At that period the Germans were masters of a great part of Italy; and the German word *banck* came to be used as its Italian equivalent *monte*, and was Italianised into *banco*, and the loans were called indifferently *monti* or *banchi*.

There is no adequate statutory definition of a bank in this country. The Bills of Exchange Act 1882, the Bankers' Books Evidence Act 1879 and the Companies Act 1948 all describe a banker as a person or institution 'carrying on the business of banking'. There are similar definitions in the Bank Charter Act 1844, the Stamp Act 1891 and the Agricultural Credits Act 1928. It is not surprising, therefore, that in the case of *United Dominions Trust* v. *Kirkwood* [1966] 1 All ER, Lord Denning, MR, said, 'A banker is easier to recognise than to define.' In that case, the time-honoured view of Sir John Paget, KC was confirmed, namely, that the four tests of banking business are (1) the taking of deposits, (2) the taking of current accounts, (3) the payment of cheques, and (4) the collection of cheques.

However, the overriding consideration which emerged in that particular case was that of 'reputation'. Denning, MR, said

> In such a matter as this, when Parliament has given no guidance, we cannot do better than look at the reputation of the concern amongst intelligent men of commerce. . . . UDT has only succeeded in this case because of their reputation and standing in the City of London as bankers.

The problem of recognition, if not of definition, has been resolved by the Banking Act 1979 (q.v.). Subject to certain exceptions, no person carrying on a business of any description in the UK may describe himself as a bank or banker, or indicate that he is carrying on a banking business unless the business is recognized as a bank by the Bank of England under the Banking Act (Section 36).

We may say, therefore, that a bank is a business recognized as a bank by the Bank of England under the Banking Act 1979. SEE ALSO *Banker and Customer*

BANK ACCEPTANCE A bill accepted by a bank. A merchant in this country, purchasing goods overseas, may arrange for his bankers to accept a bill drawn on them by the shippers, the various shipping documents being attached to the bill. The shipper may then sell the bill and thus receive immediate payment for the goods (SEE *Documentary Credit*). Banks show the total of these acceptances in their balance sheet as a liability with a contra entry on the asset side of the customers' liability to the bank.

BANK BILL A bill which is drawn or accepted by a bank.

BANK CHARGES The term is used loosely to describe interest charges on bank loans and overdrafts (SEE *Bank Interest*), but more correctly refers to the fees and commissions charged by banks for services to their customers. It is the latter meaning which is dealt with here. For many years, bank charges were applied on a not very scientific and indeed rather a subjective basis. A typical basis of charging for the conduct of a business bank account would be, and still is, calculated as a percentage, e.g. $\frac{1}{8}$ per cent of the turnover on the account. In other cases, particularly for personal accounts, the charge would be on the basis of so much per item on the ledger sheet. In all cases, charges would reflect to some extent the general conduct of the account, the standing of the customer and the balances held with the bank.

Nowadays, the banks all publish their respective scale of tariffs for personal accounts. Certain of the banks make no charges for personal accounts which are maintained in credit. Some of the banks, however, require a minimum balance to be maintained, e.g. £100 before allowing 'free banking'. It is in any case usual for *credits* to a bank account to be free of charges, but charges are made for withdrawals and electronic payments. The charges per item vary from bank to bank, but are in the range of 12p to 35p. Where a charge is made because the minimum credit balance has not been maintained, there is usually provision for the charge to be reduced by a notional interest allowance for the average cleared balance on the account during the period in question. Bank charges are usually applied on a quarterly basis, but some banks apply them half-yearly.

In their evidence to the Wilson Committee (q.v.) the banks estimated that only 20 per cent of the total costs of money transmission was recouped in the form of bank charges (*Committee of London Clearing Bankers: The London Clearing Banks—Evidence to the [Wilson] Committee to Review the Functioning of Financial Institutions*, Longman, 1978). In 1978, the Price Commission enquired into the subject of bank charges for money transmission and recommended that the charges should more closely relate to the cost of the service provided and that fuller credit should be given to the customer for the benefits accruing to the bank from investment of the credit balances. In more recent times, the banks have sought to bring their charges more in line with the true costs of the service and it is estimated that bank charges now account for approximately 30 per cent of the total costs of the banking service.

BANK CHARTER ACT 1844 An Act to regulate the issue of bank notes and for giving to the Governor and Company of the Bank of England certain privileges for a limited period. The Act was passed on 19th July, 1844. By the Currency and Bank Notes Act 1928, various Sections of the Bank Charter Act were repealed (SEE *Bank of England; Currency and Bank Notes Act 1928*). The main provisions of the Bank Charter Act, before these repeals, were: the Bank of England was to be divided into two departments, the issue department and the banking department. The directors were to transfer to the issue department securities to the extent of £14,000,000, of which the debt due by the public was to be a part, and also so much of the gold coin, gold and silver bullion as should not be required for the banking department, in exchange for bank notes.

The Act gave the Bank of England a monopoly of note issue within a radius of three miles from the City of London.

After the passing of the Act there were to be no new banks of issue in any part of the UK, and, if a banker ceased to issue his own notes, the Bank of England was empowered to increase its note issue against public securities by two-thirds of the amount of such issue withdrawn from circulation. A bank issuing notes on 6th May, 1844, was allowed to continue to issue to an average amount as ascertained by the average amount of the bank's notes in circulation for 12 weeks preceding 27th April. Issuing banks were to render accounts to the Commissioners of Inland Revenue.

By Section 11, 'it shall not be lawful for any banker to draw, accept, make, or issue, in England or Wales, any bill of exchange or promissory note or engagement for the payment of money payable to bearer on demand,' except in the case of those banks which were issuing their own notes in 1844. (The exception was repealed by the Currency and Bank Notes Act 1928.)

Previous to the passing of this Act bankers issued notes without restrictions, and it was anticipated that the restrictions imposed by the Act would have a beneficial effect in preventing the evils from which the country had suffered through an unrestricted issue. The working of the Act was soon tested. In 1847 a severe crisis occurred, but the Act did not fulfil its expectations and in order to save the situation the Government had to intervene and authorize the Bank to issue notes in excess of the amount fixed by the Act. This is called the 'Suspension of the Bank

Act', and it was successful in restoring confidence. In November 1857, another crisis occurred, and again the Government gave permission to the Bank to exceed its authorized issue, with the same result as on the previous occasion. In May 1866, the Act was suspended for the third time, and, as before, the trouble soon passed away.

On the outbreak of war with Germany in August, 1914, the Government issued an emergency paper currency of £1 and 10s notes (SEE *Moratorium*). On 1st August, 1914, the Prime Minister and the Chancellor of the Exchequer sent a letter to the Bank of England authorizing the suspension of the Bank Act. In answer to a question in the House of Commons (9th November, 1915) as to whether the Bank Act was, in fact, suspended in August, 1914, the Prime Minister said

The authority of 1st August was never acted upon, and was succeeded by Section 3 of the Currency and Bank Notes Act, 1914, which received the Royal Assent on 6th August. On 7th and 8th August, as adequate supplies of currency notes were not for the moment available, certain notes of the Bank of England were used, at the request of the Treasury, for the purpose of advances to bankers under the Currency and Bank Notes Act, the maximum excess involved being £3,043,000. By 10th August the position as regards the bank notes had become normal in all respects.

Section 3 provided that

the Governor and Company of the Bank of England and any persons concerned in the management of any Scottish or Irish bank of issue may, so far as temporarily authorised by the Treasury and subject to any conditions attached to that authority, issue notes in excess of any limit fixed by law; and those persons are hereby indemnified, freed, and discharged from any liability, penal or civil, in respect of any issue of notes beyond the amount fixed by law which has been made by them since 1st August, 1914, in pursuance of any authority of the Treasury, or of any letter from the Chancellor of the Exchequer, and any proceedings taken to enforce any such liability shall be void.

In 1928 the currency note issue of the Treasury was transferred to the Bank of England. SEE *Currency and Bank Notes Act 1928*

The Act regulating the issue of notes in Northern Ireland is 8 & 9 Vict c 37, and the corresponding Act for Scotland is 8 & 9 Vict c 38. SEE *Bank Notes; Bank of England; Bank of Issue*

BANK OF ENGLAND In 1691, William Paterson, a native of Dumfriesshire, submitted to the Government a plan for the establishment of a national bank, and in 1694 the Bank of England was incorporated by Act 5 & 6 William & Mary. The Act is entitled 'An Act for granting to their Majesties several duties upon tonnage of ships and vessels, and upon beer, ale, and other liquors, for securing certain recompenses and advantages in the Act mentioned, to such persons as shall voluntarily advance the sum of fifteen hundred thousand pounds towards carrying on the war with France'. The Act authorized the raising of £1,200,000 by voluntary subscription, the subscribers to be incorporated under the style of The Governor and Company of the Bank of England. The sum of £300,000 was also authorized to be raised by subscription and annuities granted to the subscribers. All the money was quickly subscribed, and a charter was granted on 27th July, 1694, for 11 years, and it has since then been renewed from time to time.

In 1708, when the Bank Charter was renewed, a clause was inserted constituting the Bank of England the only joint stock bank in England. In 1718 subscriptions for Government loans were for the first time received at the Bank, and the Bank has been employed by the Government in similar transactions ever since such time.

In 1720 the Bank found itself in danger of being involved in the South Sea Company's ruin. In 1734 its business was transferred from the Grocers' Hall to a newly erected building in Threadneedle Street. The Bank commenced to issue Bank Post Bills in 1738. The Bank began to issue notes for £10 and £15 in 1759; previous to that year it would appear that the lowest amount of note issued was £20. In 1780 the Gordon Riots occurred, and for protection a company of Foot Guards did duty in the Bank, and until quite recent years a picket of Grenadier or Coldstream Guards mounted guard at the Bank each night. In 1793, practically one hundred years after the Bank was founded, notes for £5 were first issued. The capital of the Bank had by that time increased to £11,642,400. In 1797, owing to the effects of the unusual demand for specie, an Order in Council was issued 'that it is indispensably necessary for the public service, that the Directors of the Bank of England should forbear issuing any cash in payment, until the sense of Parliament can be taken on the subject'.

Notes for £1 and £2 appeared for the first time in 1797. In the same year Peel's Restriction Act was passed. It is entitled 'An Act for continuing for a limited time the restriction contained in the minute of Council of the 26th of February, 1797, of payment of cash by the Bank'.

In 1810, the Bullion Committee reported to the House of Commons upon the high price of bullion and the state of the circulating medium. In 1816, the Bank was authorized to increase its capital to £14,553,000, at which amount it stood until public ownership in 1946. In 1819 the Bank Restriction Act was further continued till 1820. On 1st May, 1821, the Bank began to pay its notes in gold. In December, 1825, the Bank passed through a very severe time, and it appears that the credit of the Bank was saved by the finding of a box containing a quantity of one-pound notes. In 1825 at a time of general financial crisis, the Bank of England was authorized to open branches in the larger provincial towns and to issue notes therefrom. Accordingly, branches were opened at Gloucester, Manchester, and Swansea. At the present time, branches are established at Birmingham, Bristol, Law Courts (London), Leeds, Liverpool, Manchester, Newcastle upon Tyne, and Southampton. In 1826 notes under £5 were abolished; and the monopoly which the Bank had hitherto enjoyed was done away with except in London and within a radius of 65 miles thereof. In 1844, the Bank Charter Act was passed. It separated the Bank into two departments, the Issue Department and the Banking Department. The Bank's note issue was limited to £14,000,000 against securities, part of which was the debt due from the public; for any notes issued in excess of that amount gold coins, or gold or silver bullion must be deposited in the issue department. The net profit on any issue of notes against securities exceeding £14,000,000 was paid to the State. The Bank Act has been suspended on three occasions—in 1847, 1857, and 1866. On the outbreak of war with Germany in 1914, the Bank was authorized to suspend the Bank Act, but the authority was not acted upon. SEE *Bank Charter Act 1844*

The Bank of England's advertised rate of discount, known as 'bank rate', was the rate on which all money rates hinged. SEE *Bank Rate*

For many years prior to public ownership, the Bank of England had assumed the functions of a Central Bank (q.v.), and in pursuance of this policy had gradually shed its private and commercial business, selling its Western Branch in Burlington Gardens, London, to the Royal Bank of Scotland.

The Bank kept the national reserve of bullion, and as all other banks throughout the country keep an account with the Bank of England, either directly or indirectly (by keeping an account with a London agent, which agent keeps an account there), the Bank of England occupied the unique position of being the holder of the ultimate banking reserve. In a time of panic all banks fell back upon the Bank of England for supplies of gold.

On 14th February, 1946, the Bank of England Act 1946 was passed which brought the capital stock of the Bank into public ownership, subjected the Bank to public control, and made provision with respect to the relations between the Treasury, the Bank of England, and other banks.

BANK OF ENGLAND MINIMUM LENDING RATE SEE *Minimum Lending Rate*

BANK OF ENGLAND NOTES The Bank of England is a bank of issue, and may issue notes in England and Wales. The Bank is separated into two departments, the Issue Department and the Banking Department. By the Currency and Bank Notes Act 1928, the currency note issue of the Treasury was transferred to the Bank of England, the Bank was empowered to issue bank notes for £1 and for 10s, such notes to be legal tender in Scotland and Northern Ireland as in England, and the Bank's note issue against securities (the 'fiduciary note issue') was fixed at £260,000,000. SEE *Currency and Bank Notes Act 1928; Fiduciary Issue*

By the Gold Standard Act 1925, until otherwise provided by Proclamation, the Bank of England shall not be bound to pay any note of the Bank in coin. SEE *Gold Standard Act 1925*

Bank of England notes may be signed by machinery instead of being written (16 & 17 Vict c 2, Section 1).

Notes of the Bank of England are not subject to any stamp duty. They are issued for £1, £5, £10, £20 and £50. Until 30th April, 1945, notes for £100, £200, £500 and £1,000 were also in circulation, but on that date they were withdrawn in connection with the Government's policy to stamp out black market operations and to check income tax evasion. These high value notes are now no longer legal tender, but are still repayable at the Bank of England. Owing to the prevalence of forged £5 notes in Europe, at the close of the Second World War, a new type of note of better protective character was issued in October 1945.

As from 1st March, 1946, the old type of £5 note was called in and from that date was no longer legal tender, although encashable at the Bank of England.

Where notes of the Bank of England issued more than 40 years ago (or in the case of notes for £1 or 10s, 20 years, see the 1928 Act) have not been presented for payment, the Bank of England is empowered by the Bank Act 1892, Section 6, to write off the amount, or any proportion of it, of such notes from the total amount issued by the issue department, and the Bank Charter Act 1844, is to apply as if the amount so written off had not been issued, provided that

(a) A return of the amount of notes so written off shall be forthwith sent to the Treasury and laid by them before Parliament; and
(b) This Section shall not affect the liability of the Bank to pay any note included in the amount so written off, and if it is presented for payment the amount shall either be paid out of the bank notes, gold coin, or bullion in the banking department; or, if it is exchanged for gold coin or bullion in the issue department, or for a note issued from the issue department, a corresponding amount of gold coin or bullion shall be transferred from the banking department and appropriated to the issue department.

Lord Mansfield, in *Miller* v *Race* (1758) 1 Burr 452, said

> Bank notes are not goods, nor securities, nor documents for debts, nor are they so esteemed, but are treated as money, as cash, in the ordinary course and transaction of business by the general consent of mankind.

A material part of a Bank of England note, and of all bank notes, is the number. If a note is lost or stolen, the number often enables the loser who has kept a record of it to trace the note.

In *Suffell* v *Bank of England* (1882) 9 QBD 555, the numbers upon certain notes had been fraudulently altered before they had been bona fide purchased by the plaintiff for value. It was held that, although the alteration did not vary the contract, it was material in the sense of altering the notes in an essential part, and that therefore the notes were vitiated so that the plaintiff could not recover.

In *Hongkong and Shanghai Banking Corporation* v *Lo Lee Shi* (1928) 44 TLR 233, one of its notes had been accidentally mutilated and the number was missing. The Judicial Committee of the Privy Council held that there was nothing to destroy the liability of the bank upon a document which was admitted to be one of its notes. They added

> It is not possible in this case to lay down any general principles of law; they desire their judgment to be limited to this point, that in the special circumstances of this case it is possible, by means of the fragments of the document, assisted by oral evidence, to establish a claim against the bank for the $500 due upon the note.

In this case the number had been accidentally defaced, and it was pointed out that the case of *Suffell* v *Bank of England* was different, as in that case the notes had been intentionally and fraudulently altered.

Mutilated bank notes are referred to under *Mutilated Notes.*

BANK OF ENGLAND RETURN By the Bank Charter Act 1844 (q.v.), Section 6, it is provided that the Bank of England issue a weekly return as to its financial position

> An account of the amount of Bank of England notes issued by the Issue Department of the Bank of England and of gold coin and of gold and silver bullion respectively, and of securities in the said Issue Department, and also an account of the capital stock, and the deposits, and of the money and securities belonging to the said Governor and Company in the Banking Department of the Bank of England, on some day in every week to be fixed by the Commissioners of Stamps and Taxes, shall be transmitted by the said Governor and Company weekly to the said Commissioners in the form prescribed in the schedule hereto annexed marked (A) and shall be published by the said Commissioners in the next succeeding *London Gazette* in which the same may be conveniently inserted.

By the Currency and Bank Notes Act 1928, the form prescribed under the above section may be modified to such an extent as the Treasury, with the concurrence of the Bank, consider necessary, having regard to the provisions of this Act (Section 10). The Weekly Return is still published in the *Gazette*, and is also issued to the Press and public. It is published on Thursdays and is made up to the close of business on the previous day.

BANK AS EXECUTOR AND TRUSTEE The British banks entered the field of executorship and trustee business in the years from 1908 to 1912. This followed the passing of the Public Trustee Act of 1906 which created the office of the Public Trustee with power to charge for his services, as well as empowering other trust corporations (q.v.) to act as custodian trustees with power to charge for their services. Although little advantage was taken in later years of the custodian trustee provisions, the Act introduced the concept of the trading trustee. There was apparently some fear that the Public Trustee would be in a monopoly position and that very substantial bank balances would pass from the private sector to the Bank of England. In the following years, therefore, a number of banks and insurance companies set up trustee departments to provide executor and trustee services for their own shareholders and customers.

Nowadays, the business embraces the administration of estates and the trusteeship of private and corporate trusts. The latter category includes the trusteeship of unit trusts, pension funds, debenture trusts and trusteeships for insurance companies under the Insurance Companies Act 1974 (Section 32).

At the end of 1981, the clearing banks in England and Scotland were responsible for the administration of approximately 80,000 trusts of all kinds with a total value of approximately £15,000 million. The number of outstanding appointments under the wills of living customers was approximately 965,000.

Out of the traditional trust business of the clearing banks emerged a very substantial investment management business, which in turn was a factor in the entry of the banks into the management of unit trusts. SEE *Investment Management Services; Unit Trusts*

BANK FOR INTERNATIONAL SETTLEMENTS The BIS was created in May, 1930, chiefly for the purpose of facilitating the transfer and mobilization of German reparation payments arising out of the First World War. In addition, it was formed in order to study the problems arising out of international indebtedness and to devise methods of securing exchange stability. Its office is at Basle and it has no branches. The share capital (Swiss gold francs authorized 1,500,000,000, of which 280,203,125 is paid up) was subscribed by the Central Banks (q.v.) of the nations chiefly interested in the reparations, and nominees of those nations constitute the board of directors. A year after its foundation it was faced by the European banking crisis of 1931. In an effort to avert the crisis, the BIS granted substantial credits to the Central Banks of Germany, Austria, Hungary, and Yugoslavia, but it had not the resources to allow it to intervene on a large enough scale, and its ability to grant further help ceased when its Central Bank depositors proceeded to withdraw their deposits.

In 1932 reparations were cancelled, leaving the BIS wih its function of trustee-administrator of various funds and its agency business on behalf of certain international organizations. Its international banking business continued on a limited scale and its services proved useful as a clearing institution for transfers of gold. The Bank also provided frequent opportunities for meetings of the heads of the various central banks. But difficulties in the field of international payments in the years preceding the Second World War dashed any hopes that may have been held at the time of its foundation that the BIS might come to occupy a key position in international finance.

The position of the Bank was greatly complicated by the Second World War. Its official attitude was one of strict neutrality, but not unnaturally its neutrality was suspect when Switzerland was completely surrounded by nations under German domination or influence. It was thought that in any case its position was anomalous and that it should be liquidated. That process, however, presented difficulties once the war had begun, and the Bank continued in being though no British representative took any part in its management. British participation was not completely withdrawn, as it was not desired that control should pass into enemy hands.

As the war neared its conclusion and proposals were put forward for the future conduct of international finance, the question once more arose of what useful purpose the BIS could serve, particularly when the International Bank of Reconstruction and Development (q.v.) came into being. It was argued, however, that the BIS could carry through certain classes of transactions which were not within the legal powers of its new rival. It might usefully grant small credits to central banks, in certain circumstances, to the extent of its limited resources. The Bank, therefore, continues in business.

The statistical work of the BIS has always been of a high quality, and its Annual Report is a very full and informative document on many aspects of international finance.

In particular, the figures published by the BIS for international settlements provide a measure for the extent of the eurocurrency market. The figures show the foreign currency liabilities to foreign residents of commercial banks in each of the principal countries where eurocurrency business is conducted. SEE *Eurocurrency*

BANK GIRO The increase in the volume of standing orders and traders' credits led in 1960 to the establishment by the banks of a credit clearing which enabled them to handle a far greater number of transfers and to extend their facilities to a wider public. In 1967, the name of the credit transfer system was changed to Bank Giro, which included the newly introduced direct debiting system (q.v.), in order to anticipate the expected competition from the National Giro (q.v.) which became operative in 1968.

Credit transfers fall under three headings in practice:

1. Those comprising cash and/or cheques, etc., paid in at one branch by a customer, or his agent, for the credit of his account at another branch of the same bank or of another bank in the UK.
2. Those comprising cash paid in by non-customers, or a cheque drawn by a customer on the branch where the credit is being paid in, for the credit of another customer's account at another branch of the same bank or of another bank in the UK.
3. Those made periodically, perhaps by standing

order when made manually, or comprising salaries and payments to suppliers, to other customers' accounts at other branches of the same bank or of other banks in the UK.

SEE ALSO *Bankers' Automated Clearing Services Limited; Credit Clearing*

BANK HOLIDAYS The Banking and Financial Dealings Act 1971 replaced the Bank Holiday Act 1871 and conferred power

to suspend financial and other dealings on bank holidays or other days, and to amend the law relating to bills of exchange and promissory notes with reference to the maturity of bills and notes and other matters affected by the closing of banks on Saturdays, and for purposes connected therewith.

The days which were appointed under the Act to be bank holidays are

In England and Wales

Easter Monday
The last Monday in May
The last Monday in August
26th December if it is not a Sunday
27th December in a year in which 25th or 26th December is a Sunday

In Scotland

New Year's Day if it is not a Sunday, or if it is a Sunday, 3rd January
2nd January, if it is not a Sunday, or if it is a Sunday, 3rd January
Good Friday
The first Monday in May
The first Monday in August
Christmas Day if it is not a Sunday, or if it is a Sunday, 26th December

In Northern Ireland

17th March, if it is not a Sunday or, if it is a Sunday, 18th March
Easter Monday
The last Monday in May
The last Monday in August
26th December, if it is not a Sunday
27th December in a year in which 25th or 26th December is a Sunday

The Act also provides for other days to be declared bank holidays by Royal Proclamation from time to time (e.g. the first Monday in May).

One of the provisions in the Act is to introduce Saturday as a non-business day as well as Sunday for the purpose of the Bills of Exchange Act.

The Act also gives the Treasury wide powers by statutory instrument to prohibit on specified days any banking transactions, dealings in foreign currency, gold, silver bullion or commodities, or dealings on the Stock Exchange.

BANK HOURS Since July 1969 the normal hours of business of the banks in this country have been from 9.30 a.m. until 3.30 p.m. from Monday to Friday inclusive, excluding bank holidays (q.v.). Additionally, in certain areas banks are open for one evening per week, usually from 4.30 p.m. until 6.00 p.m. In some local areas, there is evening opening by prior arrangement and in market towns it is quite usual to open for an additional period on market days. In very small towns or villages, the hours may be shorter and are regulated according to local needs. Sub-branches are in some cases open for only two or three hours once a week.

Although in general banks have not been open for business on Saturday mornings since 1969, there have been some instances of Saturday opening, particularly in the London area for bureaux de change purposes and at airports. As from August 1982, Barclays Bank decided to open a number of branches on Saturday mornings throughout the country and since then all the major clearing banks have resumed a degree of Saturday opening.

A transaction which occurs after the bank doors have been closed for business is deemed to have taken place 'after hours'. Although in some cases this may be harmless, e.g. the cashing of a customer's own cheque, a banker will normally exercise considerable discretion in accepting transactions 'after hours'. In particular, a drawer of a cheque has a right to stop payment of the cheque and to give notice during business hours and if such a cheque is cashed 'after hours', the bank will be liable in the event of a notice to stop payment being received the following morning. Also, the banker would lose the protection of Section 60, Bills of Exchange Act 1882 and Section 1, The Cheques Act 1957 (SEE *Payment of Bill* as the cheque would not have been paid 'in the ordinary course of business'.

BANK INTEREST This falls into two categories: credit interest and debit interest. Two of the main ingredients of banking are the taking of deposits and the lending of money. The profit to the banker lies in the interest differential between these two activities less the costs of running the business. Interest is the cost of money. Bank interest is either the cost to the banker of borrowing money from his customer, or the cost to the customer of borrowing money from the bank.

Credit Interest

It has been the custom in the UK to pay interest on deposit accounts, typically those held by the bank on seven days' notice, and on various forms of savings accounts, but not on current accounts. The current account in Britain has been linked with the unique and highly developed cheque clearing system, which has grown in this country on a national basis for over 200 years and, on a local basis, for much longer than that. It was the widespread acceptance of cheques and the efficiency of the clearing system which gave the special characteristics to current accounts. In a current account money is put to work, it circulates freely and for all practical purposes it is as good as cash. Traditionally, money was not put into a current account to earn interest—it was there to pay bills. The banker had the use of the money and in return provided the facilities for payment by cheque.

Seldom, if ever, would a London banker allow interest on a current account as such, but it was not unknown in country districts for interest to be paid on current account balances, depending on the amount of the balance and the level of activity on the account. Since December 1945, however, it has not been the practice to allow interest on current accounts conducted with the major clearing banks. The high interest rates of the 1970s and early 1980s led to a demand for interest on current accounts, but the inflation of those years also led to a considerable increase in the cost of current account operation (SEE *Bank Charges*). The cost to a bank of operating current accounts is of the order of 9 per cent of the total current account balances. This obviously leaves little scope for the payment of interest: indeed, it would be possible to pay interest on a current account only if a realistic charge were made for the operations on the account.

Banks have, however, traditionally paid interest on deposit accounts, i.e. moneys placed with them on seven days' notice or longer. But the balances are not normally available for money transfer purposes.

In recent times, most of the banks have introduced 'money' accounts under a variety of names. These accounts normally offer a rate of interest at or near money market rates but have a fairly high minimum balance, e.g. £1,000. Some of these accounts offer limited withdrawal and money transfer facilities. They were introduced by the banks in response to competition from building societies and the Department of National Savings.

Prior to the introduction of Competition and Credit Control in 1971, the rate of interest on seven-day deposit accounts (the London Bankers' Deposit Rate) was agreed among the London clearing banks and was traditionally 2 per cent below the level of bank rate. Since 1971, banks have been free to fix their own interest rates, but the degree of competition in a highly developed market prohibits any wide divergence on rates from one bank to another.

The main factor in determining the level of interest rates on bank deposits is the ability of the banks to deploy the funds profitably. Thus, there has always been a relationship between deposit rates of interest and the rates obtainable by the banks on advances. The differential between deposit rate and base lending rate has been as low as 1½ per cent but has varied over the years between that figure and 4½ per cent with a tendency for the margin to widen in recent times. An increasingly important factor is the level of interest rates in the wholesale money market.

Debit Interest

Throughout the Middle Ages in England, the lending of money at interest was considered to be unchristian and was forbidden to Englishmen. The taking of interest was stigmatized with the name of usury and appears to have been based on a rather strict interpretation of the Mosaic Law. However, successive monarchs in this country were glad of the services first of the Jews and then of the Lombards and were among their principal borrowing customers. The usury laws were partly abolished by Henry VIII in 1545 and the taking of interest on loans was made legal. The rate was fixed at 10 per cent per annum. It was reduced to 8 per cent in 1624, to 6 per cent in 1651, and to 5 per cent in 1714. It was not until 1900, in the Moneylenders Act, that legislation was again introduced to regulate the lending of money and the charging of interest. By that time however, bankers were excluded from the definition of 'moneylenders'.

In more recent times, it was the practice of banks to quote their lending rates by reference to the old Bank Rate (q.v.) but with the introduction of Competition and Credit Control in 1971, this practice was abandoned and the banks now determine independently their own base lending rates. These will reflect the general level of interest rates in the economy, but each bank will have regard to both the average cost and the marginal cost of the funds it borrows. It is primarily the rate at which the banks can obtain deposits which determines the general level of bank interest rates, both debit and credit.

In most cases, the interest on advances will be quoted by reference to the bank's own base rate and may vary from, say, 1 per cent over base rate to 5 per cent over base rate. The rate will normally reflect the financial standing of the customer, the nature of the loan and the priority which the bank gives to a particular category of business.

Personal loans and other formalized categories of lending, usually for a fixed term of, say, two to five years with monthly repayments, are subject to a fixed rate of interest on the original amount of the loan and the rate is determined at the time the loan is taken. Because the loan is reducing, the true rate of interest is appreciably more than the rate quoted at the outset. The true rate is approximately twice the quoted rate so that, for example, a loan granted at 10 per cent on the amount borrowed repayable over two years by monthly reductions would incur a true rate of interest of 18.7 per cent.

Interest on credit card loans is calculated on a similar basis.

Under the Consumer Credit Act 1974 (q.v.), banks and other institutions making loans to the public must state the true rate of interest to the borrower in relation to all loans up to £15,000.

The rate of interest on larger loans to the corporate sector tend nowadays to be quoted by reference to London Inter-Bank Offered Rate (LIBOR), especially in relation to term loans which reflect the general level of interest rates in the money market. SEE *Banking Supervision*

BANK NOTES Bank notes are promissory notes issued by a bank and payable to bearer on demand, but unlike promissory notes they may be re-issued after payment.

The definition of a bank note by 17 & 18 Vict. c. 83, Section 11, is: 'All bills, drafts, or notes other than notes of the Bank of England which shall be issued by any banker, or the agent of any banker for the payment of money to the bearer on demand; and all bills, drafts, or notes so issued which shall entitle or be intended to entitle the bearer or holder thereof, without indorsement, or without any further or other indorsement that may be thereon at the time of the issuing thereof, to the payment of any sum of money on demand, whether the same shall be so expressed or not, in whatever form and by whomsoever such bills, drafts or notes shall be drawn or made, shall be deemed to be bank notes of the banker by whom or by whose agent the same shall be issued within the meaning of the 7 & 8 Vict. c. 32, and 8 & 9 Vict. cc. 37 & 38.'

The Chinese are said to have been the inventors of bank notes about the year 119 B.C.

The origin of bank notes in England is to be found in the receipts which goldsmiths gave for money left with them for safe keeping. At first they were special promises with regard to some particular money in their possession, but afterwards they became general promises to deliver a sum of money on demand.

Notes for less than £5 were prohibited in England by an Act of 1826 (7 Geo. IV, c. 6, Section 3). By the Currency and Bank Notes Act 1928, the Bank of England was empowered to issue bank notes for £1 and for 10s. (Section 1(1).)

The note issue of England and Wales is now in the sole hands of the Bank of England as a result of the provisions of the Bank Charter Act 1844 (the last note-issuing bank (Fox Fowler & Co.) being absorbed by Lloyds Bank in 1921), and of the Currency and Bank Notes Act 1928, which transferred the issue of £1 and 10s. notes from the Treasury to the Bank of England. In 1844, when the Bank Charter Act was passed there were 279 banks issuing notes in England. That same year there were 19 banks issuing notes in Scotland, but now only three Scottish banks, Clydesdale, the Bank of Scotland and the Royal Bank of Scotland, issue notes.

The currency note issue of the Treasury was transferred to the Bank of England in 1928. SEE *Currency and Bank Notes Act 1928*. SEE ALSO *Bank Charter Act; Bank of Issue; Forgery; Indorsement of Bank Note; Legal Tender; Stolen Bank Notes; Currency and Bank Notes Act 1928*

BANK OF ISSUE A bank which issues its own notes payable to bearer on demand. Principally through amalgamations, the banks of issue in England have disappeared, leaving only the Bank of England.

The issue of bank notes in Ireland was regulated by the Act of 1845 (8 & 9 Vict c 37). A banker in Ireland was prohibited from issuing notes in excess of the amount certified by the Commissioners of Stamps and Taxes (that is, the average amount of notes in circulation for one year prior to 1st May, 1845) except against the monthly average amount of gold and silver held by such banker at the head office and four principal places of issue.

The issue of bank notes in Scotland is regulated by the Act of 1845 (8 & 9 Vict c 38). Bankers issuing notes on 6th May, 1844, were empowered to continue to issue them to the extent of the amount certified by the Commissioners (that is, the average amount of notes in circulation for one year prior to the passing of the Act) and the monthly average of gold and silver coin held by such banker at the head office or principal place of issue.

In each of those Acts of 1845 it is provided that the silver against which notes may be issued must not exceed one-fourth part of the gold coin; that notes for one pound and upwards may be issued; and that Bank of England notes, though they may circulate in Ireland and Scotland, are not a legal tender in those countries.

By the Currency and Bank Notes Act 1928, for the purpose of any enactment which, in the case of a bank in Scotland or Northern Ireland, limits by reference to the amount of gold and silver coin held by any such bank the amount of notes which that bank may have in circulation, Bank of England notes held by that bank, or by the Bank of England on account of that bank, shall be treated as being gold coin held by that bank (Section 9(1)).

A bank in Scotland or Northern Ireland may hold the coin and Bank of England notes, by reference to which the amount of notes which it is entitled to have in circulation is limited, at such of its offices in Scotland or Northern Ireland respectively, not exceeding two, as may from time to time be approved by the Treasury (Section 9(2)).

By Section 1 of the same Act, Bank of England notes for £1 may be put into circulation in Scotland and Northern Ireland, and shall be current and legal tender there as in England.

BANK RATE The Bank Rate was the advertised minimum rate at which the Bank of England would discount approved bills of exchange (of not more than three months' currency), but the rate which was actually charged to customers who kept their accounts with the Bank was the current market rate, which was, as a rule, lower than the Bank Rate. The Bank Rate was fixed by the directors at their weekly meeting each Thursday, though alterations were sometimes made, when necessary, upon other days. The Rate was regulated according to the supply of money, on the one hand, and the demand for it, on the other. When the Bank reserve got too low, the directors raised the Rate, but when the directors found that they were in a position to increase their loans or discounts, the Rate was lowered. The reserve in the banking department was the most important cause of the rise or fall of the Bank Rate. A small reserve indicated a high Rate, and a large reserve a low Rate. When gold standards were in operation, a rise in the Bank Rate tended to attract gold to the UK; a fall in the Rate encouraged gold to go abroad. The Bank Rate was, therefore, of the utmost importance in protecting the national reserve of gold. The rates, whether for loans, discounts, or deposits, of all the other banks in the country were regulated more or less, according to the Bank Rate.

The Bank Rate was, in more recent times, used as a weapon in the hands of the Government to check inflation and stimulate demand as and when necessary.

On 9th October, 1972, the Chancellor of the Exchequer abolished Bank Rate with effect from 16th October, 1972. It had been largely inoperative since greater competition between banks was introduced in the autumn of 1971. At that time each bank introduced its own Base Rate (q.v.) to which it linked its lending instead of, as previously, linking its lending rates to Bank Rate. The remaining function of Bank Rate, that of 'last resort' cost of lending to discount market, had ceased to be related to reality because as a national 'penalty' rate it was latterly lower than the average market rate. SEE *Minimum Lending Rate*

BANK STATEMENT The description applied to the periodical, mechanized statement sheet supplied by the banks to their customers. This has almost wholly supplanted the former hand-written pass book.

BANKER AS AGENT The relationship of the banker *vis-à-vis* his customer is primarily that of debtor and creditor, with a superadded obligation to repay his customer when called upon to do so. However, there will be many occasions in the contractual relationship when the banker is acting as the agent of his customer. In general, this will be so when a third party enters into the transaction. Thus, the banker is an agent when he collects for his customer cheques paid in for the credit of his customer's account.

Again, the relationship of agency arises when the banker pays on his customer's instructions money of his customer to a third person. Under this head come the payment of third-party cheques, the remitting of money abroad by means of drafts or mail or cable transfers, the purchase of stock exchange securities, or payments under standing orders. In such cases, the banker will normally be able to point to a specific instruction from his customer to make the payment in question, but where he cannot do this equity may come to his assistance if it can be shown that the payment had to be made by his customer in any case.

In *B. Liggett (Liverpool) Ltd* v *Barclays Bank* (1928) 137 LT 443, the company instructed the bank to honour cheques signed by any two directors. This instruction was later varied by M, one of the directors to the effect that his signature was to appear on all cheques paid. Nevertheless, the bank later honoured a number of cheques signed in some cases by one director only and in others by two directors, neither of whom was M. The plaintiff company subsequently claimed these amounts from the bank as money paid without authority. The bank relied on the equitable doctrine under which a person who has in fact paid the debts of another without authority is allowed to take advantage of his payment.

Wright, J, held that this doctrine was applicable to the extent to which the payments made were in respect of goods supplied to the company and in the ordinary course of business. 'The customer in such a case is really no worse off, because the legal liability which has to be discharged is discharged, though it is discharged under circumstances which at common law would not entitle the bank to debit the customer.'

The bank may also act as agent for another bank, as where it receives bills for presentation to its customer, or where, owing to the absence of a suitable branch of that other bank, it is asked to witness a signature to another bank's form of guarantee or to make payments under a credit established by that other bank. In such a case, the agent bank is responsible only to the bank acting as principal and sustains no direct responsibility to the customer, who has no direct contractual link with the agent bank.

A Clearing House bank may act as agent for a bank not represented in the clearing house, so that the latter's cheques may be duly cleared.

A bank also acts as agent for a customer when it engages in insurance broking on the customer's behalf, or where it acts for the customer in the management of investments, making travel arrangements or submitting income tax returns to the Inland Revenue on behalf of a customer. A bank is not an agent for its customer, however, where it acts as executor or trustee, nor when it acts as an insurer under a life policy, nor when it pays a cheque or leases plant and equipment.

In recent times, there has been a significant move by banks into an agency field with the acquisition by some banks of a number of estate agency businesses.

BANKER AND CUSTOMER The ordinary relationship between a banker and a customer is that of debtor and creditor. When a customer pays in money to the credit of his account, the banker becomes the debtor and the customer the creditor, but when the banker makes a loan to a customer the position is reversed, as the customer is then the debtor and the banker the creditor. The money which a banker receives from a customer is at the free disposal of the banker. He may preserve it in his till, invest it in some security, or lend it out to another customer; but the customer retains the right to demand back a similar amount or to draw cheques upon the banker up to that sum, the cheques being payable either to the customer himself or to some other person. The obligation of a banker to pay his customer's cheques is in addition to the relationship of debtor and creditor. The right to overdraw an account, however, only arises from a special agreement. The customer may also accept bills and arrange with the banker that they be charged to his account at maturity, or he may, in certain cases, make arrangements for the banker to accept bills on his behalf. In order to constitute a person a customer, Lord Davy said, in *Great Western Railway* v *London and County Banking Co.* [1901] AC 414, 'I think there must be some sort of account, either a deposit or a current account or some similar relation'. See other cases under *Customer*. SEE ALSO *Bank*

In *Swiss Bank Corporation* v *Joachimson* (1921) 37 TLR 534, the Court of Appeal held that express demand by a customer for repayment of a current account is a condition precedent to the right to sue the banker for the amount. A banker may, therefore, have to face legal claims for balances which have remained dormant for more than six years. This decision will not have much practical effect, as a banker never takes advantage of the Limitation Act 1939. Atkin, LJ, in his judgment, summarized the relations between a banker and his customer as follows:

> The bank undertakes to receive money and to collect bills for its customer's account. The proceeds so received are not to be held in trust for the customer, but the bank borrows the proceeds and undertakes to repay them. The promise to repay is to repay at the branch of the bank where the account is kept and during banking hours. It includes a promise to repay any part of the amount due, against the written order of the customer addressed to the bank at the branch, and, as such written orders may be outstanding in the ordinary course of business for two or three days, it is a term of the contract that the bank will not cease to do business with the customer except upon reasonable notice. The customer, on his part, undertakes to exercise reasonable care in executing his written orders so as not to mislead the bank or to facilitate forgery. I think it is necessarily a term of such contract that the bank is not liable to pay the customer the full amount of his balance until he demands payment from the bank at the branch at which the current account is kept. [SEE *Limitation Act 1939; Unclaimed Balances*]

This summary by Atkin, LJ, of the implied terms of the banking contract is a most important statement for the banking world. Additions to the terms have been made by later cases. The duty of the banker to keep his customers' affairs secret is discussed in *Tournier* v *National Provincial and Union Bank of England Ltd* (1924). (See below.)

In *Greenwood* v *Martin's Bank* (1932) 48 TLR 601, the plaintiff discovered that his wife had withdrawn the whole of his bank balance by means of forged cheques. She said she had taken it to lend to her sister, who was involved in litigation. She appealed to her husband not to reveal the forgeries to the bank and said he would get his money back when her sister had won her case. Greenwood therefore did not inform the bank of the forgeries, and there were no more forgeries after that date. Some months later the wife asked her husband for more money and when he refused and said he was going to the bank, she committed suicide. Greenwood then went to the bank and told the manager about the forged cheques. When the manager asked why he had not been told about them before, Greenwood said he did not want to give his wife away. He subsequently brought an action against the bank to recover the amount of the forged cheques. It was held by the House of Lords that there was a duty on the part of the customers to inform the bank of the forgeries as soon as he knew of them.

> There is a continuing duty on either side to act with reasonable care to ensure the proper working of the account. The banker, if a cheque were presented to him which he rejected as forged, would be under a duty to report that to the customer to enable him to inquire into and protect himself against the circumstances of the forgery. That would involve a corresponding duty on the customer, if he became aware that forged cheques were being presented to his banker, to inform the banker in order that the banker might avoid loss in the future.

There could be no question of ratification by the customer, and there was no consideration for the adoption of the transactions. The bank were therefore entitled to set up an estoppel (q.v.). Owing to the wife's suicide they had lost their right of recourse to her which they should rightly have if they were obliged to make good the plaintiff's losses. The plaintiff's silence was a direct cause of this, and therefore he could not succeed.

In some states in Canada and USA there is, either by law or by stipulation of the banker at the time the account is opened, an obligation to draw attention to forgeries when paid cheques are received—otherwise the banker is not responsible for subsequent forgeries perpetrated by the same hand.

In *Woods* v *Martins Bank* [1958] 3 All ER 166, the plaintiff brought a successful action against the bank on the grounds that financial advice had been negligently given him by the manager. The plaintiff was a man of little business experience who looked to his manager for advice and relied upon him. He was advised to invest money in a company which was also in account at the same branch, but which was not doing well and in respect of whose overdraft the manager was under pressure from his head office to show a reduction. These facts were not disclosed to the plaintiff by the manager: on the contrary, he was advised that the company was financially sound and that the investment would be a wise one.

The bank in defence claimed that it was no part of the bank's duty to give advice on investments, and, therefore, however careless or incompetent the advice which their manager gave the plaintiff, they were not responsible for any loss which might have been caused by that advice.

Salmon, J, in considering what was and what was not within the scope of the bank's business, quoted from the bank's advertising booklet various passages which suggested that good financial advice from the best available source was to be had from any manager of the bank. As a result of his perusal, the judge held that it was part of the defendant's business to advise customers and potential customers on financial matters of all kinds.

> No doubt the manager could have refused to advise the plaintiff, but as he chose to advise him, the law in these circumstances imposes an obligation on him to advise with reasonable care and skill.

This case imposes on bankers no general duty to advise on financial matters or investments, but does establish that when a bank advertises that it will give financial advice to customers, it is a term of the banking contract that such advice should be given honestly and without negligence.

If a customer leaves with his banker a parcel of securities for safe custody, the banker's position is that of a bailee, and his liability depends, to a certain extent, upon whether he undertakes the duty gratuitously or for reward. The difference between a banker as a debtor to his customer and as a bailee may be illustrated as follows. If John Brown pays in £20 to the credit of his account, the banker becomes Brown's debtor and is liable to repay to Brown £20 on demand, but until the demand is made the banker can do what he likes with the money, and the £20 which is ultimately repaid to Brown does not, of course, consist of the same notes as were originally handed by Brown to the banker. But if Brown gives to the banker a sealed bag containing, say, notes to the value of £20 and leaves it for custody, the banker becomes a bailee and must take care of the bag as entrusted to him, and return it, with the contents untouched, to the customer when required (SEE *Safe Custody*). Bankers are probably adding to their established obligations by advertisement as to what they will undertake. In *Conway Corporation* v *Midland Bank Ltd* [1965] 2 All ER 972, it was held that the banker borrowed money received for the credit of an account. He did not hold it as his customer's agent and therefore could not be sued (as could an estate agent receiving the rent) for failing to carry out sanitary repairs where the rent was paid into the landlord's banking account by the tenant.

A banker and his staff are bound to secrecy regarding the business and accounts of the customers, but a banker may, in certain cases, be compelled to give evidence in a court of law, and he may also be required to give a copy of entries in the books of the bank. SEE *Bankers' Books (Evidence) Act 1879*

In *Tournier* v *National Provincial and Union Bank of England Ltd* (1924) 40 TLR 214, Bankes, LJ, said in the course of his judgment, with regard to the claim for damages for breach of the confidence existing between banker and customer, that the duty of a banker towards his customer not to disclose his affairs is a legal one arising out of contract and that the duty is not absolute, but qualified. The qualifications of the contractual duty of secrecy implied in the relation of banker and customer can be classified under four headings:

1. Where disclosure is under compulsion of law (e.g., where a bank is required under Section 29, Income Tax Act 1952, to disclose to the tax authorities amounts of deposit interest exceeding £15 paid or credited without deduction of income tax.
2. Where there is a duty to the public to disclose (e.g., where danger to the State or public duty may supersede the duty of the agent to his principal).
3. Where the interests of the bank require disclosure (e.g., where a bank issues a writ claiming payment of an overdraft, stating on the face of the writ the amount of the overdraft).
4. Where the disclosure is made by the express or implied consent of the customer (e.g., where the customer authorizes a reference to his banker).

The duty does not cease the moment a customer closes his account. Information gained during the currency of the account remains confidential, unless released in circumstances bringing the case within one of the above four classes of qualification. Again, the confidence is not confined to the actual state of the customer's account. It extends to information derived from the account itself.

> A more doubtful question is whether the confidence extends to information in reference to the customer and his affairs derived not from the customer's account, but from other sources, as, for instance, from the account of another customer of the customer's bank. . . . I cannot think that the duty of non-disclosure is confined to information derived from the customer himself or from his account.

In the case of *Bankers Trust Company* v *Shapira and Others* [1980] 1 WLR 1274, the Bankers Trust of New York sought to obtain discovery of all documents in the hands of Discount Bank (Overseas), Hatton Garden, in connection with a transfer of $700,000 to Discount Bank by Bankers Trust on the strength of forged cheques paid in to Bankers Trust.

In the Court of Appeal, Lord Denning said, 'Though banks have a confidential relationship with their customers, it does not apply to conceal the fraud and iniquity of wrongdoers', and quoted Lord Reid's remarks of 1942:

> If through no fault of his own a person gets mixed up in the tortious acts of others, he may incur no personal liability but he comes under a duty to assist the person who has been wronged by giving him full information and disclosing the identity of the wrongdoers.

In the present case, therefore, Discount Bank owed such a duty to Bankers Trust.

As to a banker's position when he is requested by another banker to supply an opinion as to the status or sufficiency of a customer, see *Banker's Opinions*.

There is, of course, no presumption in the banker and customer relationship that the bank will allow the customer to borrow. It would seem, however, that there is a risk of liability to a bank if, however inadvertently, it gives a customer the impression that a loan has been agreed when in fact that is not the case. In *Box* v *Midland Bank Ltd* [1979] 2 Lloyds Rep 391, the plaintiff claimed that the bank manager had given him to understand that a loan would be granted but, in the result, the loan was refused. The plaintiff had altered his position in that he had entered into a contract relying on the availability of the loan and when it was not forthcoming he became bankrupt. The manager had, in fact, agreed to make the loan subject to production of an ECGD policy but had not made it clear that he was referring to an ECGD bankers' guarantee which, in the result, was not available. The judge agreed that the bank manager could have disclaimed liability for his statement but he did not do so and he should have known that his prediction regarding the loan would be relied on. In the result, the damages which accrued directly from the representation were minor but the basic point was accepted, i.e. that the bank was liable for its misrepresentation, however innocent.

It is not unusual for the banker–customer relationship to be described as 'special'. It is characterized by such words as 'trust' and 'confidence' and although the banker–customer relationship is not one of those in which undue influence may be presumed (e.g. solicitor and client, trustee and beneficiary, doctor and patient) there is at least a suggestion of a fiduciary relationship. This view was given expression in *Lloyds Bank Ltd* v *Bundy* [1975] QB 36, a case in which a father had given a guarantee and a charge over his farm to a bank (which was also his own bank) to secure the account of his son. When a receiving order was made against the son, the bank sought to recover against the father by the sale of the farm property. The Court of Appeal, reversing the judgment of the Country Court, held that the bank was in breach of the fiduciary duty of care arising from the special relationship between themselves and their customer, the father. Sir Eric Sache said

> It not infrequently occurs in provincial and country branches of great banks that a relationship is built up over the years and, in due course, the senior officials may become trusted counsellors of customers, of whose affairs they have an intimate knowledge. Confidential trust is placed in them because of a combination of status, goodwill and knowledge. ... The situation was thus one which, to any reasonable person ... cried aloud the defendant's need for careful independent advice.

In the Court of Appeal, Cairns, LJ, questioned the existence of a fiduciary relationship but supported Sir Eric Sache in the unusual circumstances of the case. Lord Denning based his view primarily on the 'inequality of bargaining power' but thought that, in any case, a presumption of undue influence arose in the special circumstances of the case. All the members of the Court of Appeal based their judgments on the very unusual circumstances of the case but had no difficulty in reaching the view that the relationship of banker and customer is, or can be, a very special one.

Another interesting aspect of the banker–customer relationship arose as a result of the decision in *British Bank of the Middle East* v *Sun Life Assurance of Canada (UK) Ltd* [1983].

In that case, the manager of a life assurance company had purported to confirm the authority of an under-manager to lend £150,000 to the plaintiff bank. Neither the manager nor the under-manager had the authority to sanction such a loan. The plaintiff bank appealed against the decision of the Court of Appeal, which had upheld the decision in the High Court, that the bank was unable to recover payment of the sum in question from the life assurance company. The House of Lords dismissed the Appeal on the grounds that neither the manager nor the under-manager had either the authority or the ostensible authority, to sanction such a loan. This decision was followed almost immediately by a statement on behalf of the London clearing banks to the effect that the banks will honour, in all but the most extraordinary circumstances, a written commitment by the manager of a banking branch, even if the branch manager had exceeded his loan sanctioning limit. This aspect of the banker–customer relationship was summed-up by the spokesman of the Banking Information Service, who said 'since the traditional banking relationship in the UK is between the customer and his bank manager, then by talking to the bank manager you are talking to your bank'.

Further information respecting the various matters and positions by which a banker is brought into more or less direct contact with his customers will be found under the respective headings, in particular the following: *Account; Advances; Bank; Bankrupt Person; Collecting Banker; Companies; Death of Bank Customer; Deposit Receipt; Partnerships; Paying Banker; Promissory Note; Security*

BANKERS' AUTOMATED CLEARING SERVICE LIMITED (BACS) In April, 1968, the clearing banks set up the Inter-Bank Computer Bureau, later to become a separate company, Bankers' Automated Clearing Services Limited (BACS), to handle payments between banks on an electronic basis. This has become the largest automated clearing house in the world. It deals with those transfers between banks which are entirely automated to the extent that they are on magnetic tape rather than vouchers. With the computerization of current accounts throughout the banks, it became possible for inter-bank and inter-branch transfers to be effected by the exchange of magnetic tapes. Nearly all standing order payments are now processed in this way, as are a large volume of direct debits and an increasing volume of individual automated credit transfers. Within each bank, magnetic tapes are prepared daily in respect of transfers to be made between banks, or between branches of the bank. In the case of inter-bank transfers, the tapes are sent to BACS where they are integrated and a tape produced for each bank for credits to be made to its own customers.

BACS is, however, much more than a process of settlement and distribution of credit payments between banks. It provides a similar service to other financial institutions and to the customers of the banks. Thus, a company which has a large volume of credit transfer payments to be made regularly may deliver an electronic tape direct to

BACS. From the banks' point of view, there are considerable savings in the use of BACS instead of the older methods of transfer. It has been estimated that the cost of processing a paper voucher such as a cheque is three times that of making the payment through BACS. SEE *Banker's Order; Direct Debiting*

BANKERS' BOOKS (EVIDENCE) ACT 1879 This Act was passed on 23rd May, 1879.

In *Rex* v *Bono & Another* (1913) 29 TLR 635, it was held that this Act was for the benefit of bankers, and its object was to relieve them of the necessity of actually attending in court with their books; it was not passed to increase facilities for discovery. It was clearly a matter of judicial discretion as to which were proper cases in which to afford such facilities; certainly the case of a defendant seeking to justify a libel was not such a case. The main provisions of the Act are

1. A copy of any entry in a banker's book shall in all legal proceedings be received as prima facie evidence of such entry, and of the matters, transactions, and accounts therein recorded.
2. A copy of an entry in a banker's book shall not be received in evidence unless it be first proved that the book was at the time of the making of the entry one of the ordinary books of the bank, and that the entry was made in the usual and ordinary course of business, and that the book is in the custody or control of the bank.

Such proof may be given by a partner or officer of the bank, and may be given orally or by an affidavit sworn before any commissioner or person authorized to take affidavits.

3. A copy of an entry in a banker's books shall not be received in evidence unless it be further proved that the copy has been examined with the original entry and is correct.

Such proof shall be given by some person who has examined the copy with the original entry, and may be given either orally or by an affidavit sworn before any commissioner or person authorized to take affidavits.

4. A banker or officer of a bank shall not in any legal proceedings to which the bank is not a party, be compellable to produce any banker's books, the contents of which can be proved under the Act, or to appear as a witness to prove the matters, transactions, and accounts therein recorded, unless by order of a judge made for special cause.
5. On the application of any party to a legal proceeding, a court or judge may order that such party be at liberty to inspect and take copies of any entries in a banker's book for any of the purposes of such proceedings. Such an order may be made either with or without summoning the bank or any other party, and shall be served on the bank three clear days before the same is to be obeyed, unless the court or judge otherwise directs.
6. The expressions 'bank' and 'banker' mean any person, persons, partnerships, or company carrying on the business of bankers and also any savings bank certified under the Acts relating to savings banks, and also any Post Office Savings Bank (now the National Savings Bank). Expressions relating to 'bankers' books' include ledgers, day books, cash books, account books, and all other books used in the bank's ordinary business.

In *Waterhouse* v *Barker* (1924) 40 TLR 805, the plaintiff applied under Section 7 of the above Act for liberty to inspect and take copies of certain entries in the female defendant's bankers' books. The defendant objected to producing those entries, swearing that they might tend to incriminate her and subject her to a criminal prosecution. It was held that a litigant who swears that an inspection might tend to incriminate him (or her) is privileged from inspection, and, therefore, as the defendant had sworn that the entries in question might tend to incriminate her, no order for inspection could be made before the trial of the action.

This Act does not apply to the Bank of England, which is not a company carrying on the business of bankers within the meaning of the Act.

Under the Banking Act 1979, Schedule 6, paragraph 1, it is provided that for the purpose of the 1879 Act, bankers' books include records used in the ordinary business of the bank, whether written or 'micro-film, magnetic tape or any other form of mechanical or electronic data retrieval mechanism'.

In *Williams and Others* v *Summerfield* [1972] 2 QB 513, the first case in which the application of the Act in criminal proceedings was tested, Lord Widgery said that in civil cases 'the courts have set their face against Section 7 being used as a kind of searching enquiry or fishing expedition beyond the ordinary rules of discovery', and he made it clear that in criminal cases also, orders should be made only 'after the most careful thought and on the clearest ground'. The order sought was allowed in that case, but his cautionary words were repeated and amplified in *R* v *Marlborough Stipendiary Magistrate* (1980) 70 Cr App R 291, where the Divisional Court quashed 26 orders obtained by the police under the Act. SEE Supplement

BANKER'S CARD SEE *Cheque Card*

BANKERS' CLEARING HOUSE SEE *Clearing House*

BANKER'S DRAFT A person who wishes to remit money to someone in another place may, if he does not send his own cheque, obtain from his banker a draft on demand payable to the person who is to be paid the money. It may be drawn upon the banker's London office or London agents, or upon one of the banker's own branches, or upon some other bank where an arrangement exists for drafts to be drawn. Whenever a draft is drawn, an advice is dispatched the same day, advising the London agents, bank or branch, as the case may be, of the particulars of the draft, so that the banker on whom it is drawn may recognize the draft when it is presented.

A draft on demand drawn by one branch upon another branch or upon the head office is not a cheque within the meaning of the Bills of Exchange Act 1882, as it is not addressed by one person to another, which is part of the definition of a cheque.

By the Cheques Act 1957, Section 5, it is provided that the crossed-cheque sections of the Bills of Exchange Act 1882 (Sections 76–81) shall apply to the 'instruments' mentioned in Section 4 of the Cheques Act in the same way as they apply to cheques, as far as is applicable. The instruments there listed include (in subsection (2)(*d*)) a banker's draft, which is defined as 'any draft payable on demand drawn by a banker upon himself, whether payable at the head office or some other office of the banks'. Bankers' drafts may therefore be effectively crossed in any of the ways mentioned in Section 76, Bills of Exchange Act.

A banker paying a crossed banker's draft is protected against a forged indorsement by Section 80 of the Bills of Exchange Act (as extended by Section 5, Cheques Act). In paying an uncrossed draft, he is not protected by Section 60, inasmuch as the Cheques Act only extends Sections 76 to 81 to bankers' drafts, and reliance must still be placed on Section 19 of the Stamp Act 1853, in respect of protection against forged indorsements and this is as follows:

> Provided always, that any draft or order drawn upon a banker for a sum of money payable to order on demand which shall, when presented for payment, purport to be indorsed by the person to whom the same shall be drawn payable, shall be a sufficient authority to such banker to pay the amount of such draft or order to the bearer thereof; and it shall not be incumbent on such banker to prove that such indorsement, or any subsequent indorsement, was made by or under the direction or authority of the person to whom the said draft or order was or is made payable, either by the drawer or any indorser thereof.

It is considered by some authorities that this section protects a banker in paying not only drafts drawn by one branch on another or on the head office, but also drafts drawn abroad on the head office in England.

A banker paying in good faith and in the ordinary course of business such a draft which is not indorsed or is irregularly indorsed, does not in doing so incur any liability by reason only of the absence of, or irregularity in, indorsement (Cheques Act 1957, Section 1).

It may be that protection is given by this Section in the case of payment of crossed or uncrossed bankers' drafts having a forged indorsement. This depends on whether the phrase 'absence of, or irregularity in, indorsement' is construed to include forged indorsements.

Where a banker's draft has been lost, a new one will be issued only on a satisfactory indemnity being provided. Countermand of payment will not be accepted by a bank of its own draft, but if lost before indorsement, advice of its loss would virtually make it impossible for the draft to be cashed at the drawee's office. If, however, it was negotiated abroad, this would not necessarily follow, as a title can be made through a forgery in some foreign countries.

Where a customer applies for a banker's draft, an authority to debit his account should accompany the application, unless a cheque accompanies it.

The mere production of a cheque by the customer's agent without other authority is not sufficient. In *Dominion & Gresham Guarantee Co* v *Bank of Montreal*, a Privy Council case (see *Financial News*, 18th July, 1930), an official of a company procured the proper complement of signatures to a cheque payable to the company's bankers and obtained, in exchange for the cheque and an application form signed by himself, a bank draft on New York in fraud of his company. It was held that the bank was liable for issuing drafts without the company's authority.

In the case of *Commercial Banking Company of Sydney Ltd* v *Mann* [1961] AC 1, a partner, in excess of his authority and in fraud of his copartner, drew cheques on the partnership account in payment for bankers' drafts which he then passed to a third party, who cashed them with the appellant bank. This bank was sued by the injured partner for conversion. On appeal, the Privy Council decision turned on the question whether the fraudulent partner was authorized to obtain the drafts; only if this question could be answered in the affirmative did the drafts become the property of the plaintiff. It was held that there was no authority, and thus the property did not pass, and accordingly the plaintiffs could not sue in conversion.

BANKER'S OPINIONS One of the cases where a banker is absolved from the duty of secrecy regarding his customer's affairs, given in *Tournier* v *National Provincial & Union Bank of England Ltd* (SEE UNDER *Banker and Customer*) is where the disclosure is made by the express or implied consent of the customer. Frequently customers give their banker's name as a reference—this is express consent—but a large number of enquiries are made which are not at the instance of the customer. Some authorities consider that the consent of the customer is implied in such cases, inasmuch as by opening an account he impliedly agrees to the established usages of bankers obtaining as regards his account. In the above case, Atkin, LJ, said, 'It appears to me that if it (i.e. the practice of bankers to give information about their customers to other bankers) is justified it must be upon the basis of an implied consent of the customer'. In *Parsons* v *Barclay & Co. and Another* (1910) 26 TLR 628, Baron Bramwell's opinion in *Swift* v *Jewsbury* LR 9 QB 301, was quoted with approval, to the effect that the giving of opinions by one banker to another was a well-established custom among bankers.

Replies to inquiries should be carefully worded so as to avoid any possibility of an action for libel by the customer. Legal proceedings have more usually arisen, however, at the instance of the party at whose request the enquiry was made.

Actions may be for fraudulent misrepresentation or for innocent misrepresentation. The first term connotes something wider than criminal fraud—there can be a legal fraud, and in this sense, fraudulent misrepresentation is one made 'knowing it not to be true or without belief that it is true or . . . recklessly or carelessly as to whether it was true or false' (Ridley, J, in *Parsons* v *Barclay & Co. and Another*). But by Lord Tenterden's Act 1828,

> no action shall be brought whereby to charge any person upon or by reason of any representation or assurance made or given concerning or relating to the character, credit, ability, trade or dealings of any other person to the intent or purpose that such other person may obtain credit, money or goods upon it, unless such representation or assurance be made in writing, signed by the party to be charged therewith.

Hence a bank cannot be charged with fraudulent misrepresentation unless the opinion bears its signature. If the opinion is signed by the manager, he will be liable if his answer can be construed as fraudulent misrepresentation. If, as is sometimes done, the opinion is unsigned, neither bank or manager will be liable.

The more usual risk comes from innocent misrepresentation. This, in itself, is not a cause of action unless it can be shown that the answer was given negligently. This means that it must be shown that the banker is under a duty to take care, and the duty is to answer honestly from the facts immediately before the banker; it does not extend to seeking out information from sources beyond the banker's immediate province. In *Parsons* v *Barclay & Co. and Another* (above) the Appeal Court held that no further duty was required of a banker than that of answering honestly and to the best of his ability and judgment from the facts immediately before him.

In *Batts Combe Quarry Co.* v *Barclays Bank Ltd* (1913) 48 TLR 4, the plaintiffs alleged that the bank was negligent and guilty of a breach of duty in answering an enquiry made on their behalf by another bank. The jury found, on the direction of the judge, for the defendants, on the ground that there was no evidence that the defendants owed a duty to the plaintiffs and that there was in fact no evidence of negligence.

In a number of cases where banks had given negligent or at least imprudent answers to enquiries, it was consistently held that in the absence of some contractual, special or fiduciary relationship between the enquirer and the responding bank there was no duty of care and therefore any negligence was immaterial. This principle was maintained in the lower court and also in the Court of Appeal in the case of *Hedley, Byrne & Company Ltd* v *Heller & Partners Ltd* [1964] AC 465, but the House of Lords decided differently [1964] AC 465. The appellants, who were advertising agents, enquired through their bankers of the respondents, who were the bankers of Easipower Ltd, as to the financial stability of Easipower Ltd, and received satisfactory references from the respondents, which were not justified, as a result of which the appellants undertook very substantial orders for Easipower Ltd, for which that company could not pay. In August 1958, when the first of two references was given, Easipower Ltd had a substantial overdraft with the respondents and the company was in serious difficulties with its trade creditors. A satisfactory reply to an enquiry in these circumstances amounted to negligence. The appellants submitted that when references were given by one bank to another for the benefit of a customer of the enquiring bank, there was a sufficient proximity between the answering bank and the customer to impose a duty of care.

This argument was rejected. The facts in this case did not give rise to a special relationship. The authorities showed that the special relationship must be one between the enquirer and the referee, and the fact that there was some relationship between the referee and the subject of the reference did not create a duty of care.

In the House of Lords, Lord Reith said that both the references given were given in confidence and without responsibility. In general, an innocent but negligent representation gave no cause of action. There had to be something more than mere mis-statement to establish liability. There had to be expressly, or by implication from the circumstances, an assumption by the speaker or writer of some responsibility for the words in question. Where, however, it was plain that the party seeking information or advice trusted the party supplying it to exercise such a degree of care as the circumstances required, and it was reasonable so to trust the person supplying the information, and the latter knew or ought to have known that the enquirer was relying on him, the law imposed a duty of care on the party making the statement or giving the advice.

A reasonable man, who knew that his skill and judgment were being relied upon, could decline to give the information or advice sought, or he could give it with the clear qualification that he accepted no responsibility for it, or he could answer without qualification. If he chose the last course, he accepted a relationship with the enquirer which required him to take such care as the circumstances demanded, but in this test the plaintiffs could not succeed. There had been an express disclaimer of responsibility by the defendants when the references were given.

Lords Morris, Hodson, Devlin and Pearce concurred.

> If a professional man such as a banker voluntarily undertakes a service by giving deliberate advice he is under a duty to exercise reasonable care. It matters not that there is no contract or fiduciary relationship between them. It must now be taken as settled that if someone possessed of a special skill undertakes, quite irrespective of contract, to apply that skill for the assistance of another who relies upon such skill, a duty of care will arise. [Lord Morris]

> A modern example of the principle would be the giving of negligent advice by a bank on investments when advising on investments was part of its business. The fact that the advice was given to someone not a customer or in any fiduciary relationship with the banker would not matter. But in this case the language of the disclaimer of responsibility prevents the plaintiffs from recovering. [Lord Hodson]

The House of Lords was unanimous in its decision and, if banks are, as it seems, liable for honest negligence, they can rely now with confidence only upon the express disclaimer printed upon the reply form. Oral replies given over the telephone may carry a dangerous implication unless written confirmations are scrupulously sent subsequently, although bankers may possibly be able to establish from a course of dealing that the reservation is to apply. Moreover, the principle so clearly stated obviously has wider applications than to the answering of status enquiries. Any stranger who seeks the advice of any bank on any matter, with which the bank may be assumed, by virtue of its position in the community, its experience and knowledge, to have a special aptitude for dealing, may be able to claim a duty of care on the bank's part, to rebut which will require proof of communication of an express disclaimer of responsibility. The banker's liability will also be affected by his advertisements. SEE *Banker and Customer*

Suitable records are kept by banks of answers given to enquiries and of answers received to enquiries. A note should be made of any reports given orally and not in writing. Answers are usually given only to bankers whose names appear in the *Bankers' Almanac* and to certain recognized trade protection societies. Any enquiries received from other sources are returned with a request for them to be put through a banker.

Enquiries are sometimes received direct from an inquirer with a request that the reply should be sent to his or their bankers, the intention being to save a day on the receipt of the reply. The practice of banks on this point differs. Legally it is considered that the bankers are protected when the application is made by one bank to another, and the reply is honestly and carefully made by the receiving bank to the enquiring bank. An express disclaimer of responsibility should, of course, be included in the reply.

The police have no more right than other persons to information unless they produce a Court Order, except perhaps where a public duty to disclose can be established. The Department of Trade and Industry and the Director of Public Prosecutions have certain rights to information concerning a company whose affairs are the subject of an inspection or which is in liquidation, by Sections 164–71 and 334 of the Companies Act 1948. SEE ALSO *Banker and Customer; Secrecy*

BANKER'S ORDER A banker's order, sometimes known as a standing order, is a written request from a customer to the bank to make a series of payments, usually monthly or annually, either for a limited period or 'until further notice'. The banker is under no obligation to make a payment unless the account is in credit or operating within an agreed overdraft facility. Standing order payments are now dealt with through Bankers' Automated Clearing Services (q.v.). All payments are processed electronically, each bank preparing each day a magnetic tape for payments to be made to other banks.

BANKING ACT 1979 This Act established the criteria by which the Bank of England may recognize an institution as a bank and brought the supervision of banks and deposit-taking institutions into line with the requirements of the EEC.

The principal critera for the recognition of a deposit-taking institution as a bank are

1. that the institution enjoys, and has for a reasonable period of time enjoyed, a high reputation and standing in the financial community; and
2. that the institution provides in the UK a wide range of banking services, or a 'highly specialized banking service';
3. that at least two individuals effectively direct the business of the institution;
4. that the institution has net assets of £5 million if providing a wide range of banking services and £250,000 if providing a highly specialized banking service.

An institution is not to be regarded as providing a wide range of banking services within the meaning of the Act unless it provides all of the following:

(a) current or deposit account facilities, or the acceptance of funds in the wholesale money markets;
(b) finance in the form of overdraft or loan facilities, or the lending of funds in the wholesale money markets;
(c) foreign exchange services;
(d) finance through the medium of bills of exchange and promissory notes, together with finance for foreign trade; and
(e) financial advice or investment management services and facilities for arranging the purchase and sale of securities.

For the purpose of determining whether an institution is providing 'a wide range of banking services' or a 'highly specialized banking service', the Bank of England may disregard the fact that the institution does not provide one or two of the services listed above.

An institution seeking to carry on a deposit-taking business which does not qualify for recognition as a bank may nevertheless be licensed by the Bank of England as a deposit-taking institution. Thus, the Act envisages two categories of deposit-taking business: a recognized bank as outlined above, or a licensed deposit-taking institution. The Bank will not grant a full licence unless the requirements of the Act in relation to licensed institutions are satisfied, namely:

1. Every person who is a director, controller or manager of the business must be a fit and proper person to hold that position.
2. Two individuals must effectively direct the business of the institution.
3. The institution must have net assets of at least £250,000 (unless it was carrying on a deposit-taking business prior to 9th November, 1978).
4. The institution conducts, or will conduct, its business in a prudent manner and, in particular, maintains net assets and other financial resources as are considered appropriate by the Bank and maintains adequate liquidity and makes adequate provision for bad and doubtful debts.

The relevant sections of the Banking Act 1979 came into effect on 1st October, 1979.

At the time of writing, there are approximately 280 institutions recognized as banks and approximately 295 institutions licensed to carry on a deposit-taking business.

Under Section 34 of the Act, the Treasury after consultation with the Bank may make regulations by statutory instrument regarding the issue, form and content of advertisements inviting the making of deposits. In this context, 'advertisement' means every form of advertising

> whether in a publication, by the display of notices, signs, labels, showcards or goods, by distribution of samples, by means of circulars, catalogues, price lists or other documents, by an exhibition of photographic or cinematographic films, or of pictures or models, by way of sounding broadcasting or television, or any other manner.

At the present time, no such statutory instrument has been issued. Under Section 35, however, if the Bank considers that an advertisement for deposits, whether issued or proposed to be issued, is misleading, it may give the institution directions on the subject of including the prohibition of a particular advertisement.

No person carrying on a business of any kind in the UK may use any name or in any other way so describe himself as to indicate, or reasonably be understood to indicate, that he is a bank or banker or is carrying on a banking business unless the business is that of a recognized bank, or certain other statutory exceptions, e.g. the National Savings Bank. A licensed deposit-taker may not, therefore, be described as a bank, but there are limited circumstances in which it might indicate that it provides banking services (Section 36, Banking Act 1979).

The Bank of England has indicated that a licensed institution may insert in its published literature and on its notepaper the expressions 'licensed deposit-taking institution' or 'licensed under the Banking Act 1979 to take deposits'.

The Banking Act 1979 also contained provisions for the setting-up of the Deposit Protection Scheme for the protection of persons making deposits with recognized banks and licensed institutions. Under the scheme, which came into effect in February 1982, the amount of contribution payable by each bank or institution will be at an overall percentage rate fixed by the Deposit Protection Board in relation to the deposit base of the bank or licensed deposit-taker. There is provision for minimum and maximum contributions of £2,500 and £300,000 respectively and for the fund to be maintained at a minimum of £5 million and maximum of £6 million. In the event of a bank or licensed deposit-taking institution becoming insolvent, the fund guarantees up to 75 per cent of the first £10,000 of a depositor's sterling deposits with the institution concerned.

BANKING INFORMATION SERVICE This is a unit set up under the auspices of the Committee of London Clearing Bankers for the purpose of disseminating to the press and public information of general interest on banking as a whole and particularly in relation to the activities of the member banks of the Committee of London Clearing Bankers.

BANKING SUPERVISION Prior to the passing of the Banking Act 1979 (q.v.), there was little formalized control of banking institutions in the UK. The Bank of England's supervisory role was exercised in a very informal way and, under the Bank's general guidance, the commercial banks were expected to maintain high standards of self-regulated prudential controls. There were, however, a large number of deposit-taking institutions which were not within the Bank of England's advisory and supervisory arrangements. Matters came to a head with the secondary banking crisis of 1973–74. This had two significant effects. One was the presentation to Parliament in August 1976 of a White Paper on *The Licensing and Supervision of Deposit-Taking Institutions*, which led to the passing of the Banking Act in 1979. The crisis also led to discussions between the clearing banks and the Bank of England in 1975, culminating in a general agreement on such matters as the adequacy of capital and liquidity. A flexible approach is still maintained by the Bank of England in these matters in relation to the major banks and is based on a continuing process of bank-by-bank assessment.

The whole system of bank recognition and the licensing of deposit-taking institutions is now firmly within the Bank of England's statutory powers, as described under the entry *Banking Act 1979*. The Deposit Protection Scheme introduced under that Act for the protection of bank depositors is also described under that heading.

On the wider international scene there is, in Basle, a Supervisors' Committee under the auspices of the Bank of International Settlements. This Committee seeks to secure international agreement on the harmonization of standards on such subjects as capital ratios and levels of gearing. At the time of writing, there is no general agreement as to what is an adequate level of capital for a bank. A bank's capital may, in any case, be in two categories, viz. its primary capital consisting of equity and reserves and a secondary level of capital consisting of subordinated debt. There are also problems in modern times with banks entering into commitments which are not always reflected in their balance sheet, e.g. the underwriting of note issues, and the fact that many banks, at home and abroad enter into a wide range of financial activities, which take them into areas of risk beyond those which are traditionally associated with banking.

BANKRUPT PERSON A person who has been adjudicated a bankrupt by the Court of Bankruptcy. In the early days of banking, when a banker failed, his bench, or banco, at which he did business, was broken by the people, whence the word 'bankrupt' (Italian *banco*, a bench; Latin *ruptus*, broken).

As to the validity of certain payments to a person subsequently adjudged bankrupt, or to his assignee, see under *Act of Bankruptcy*.

As soon as a person is adjudicated a bankrupt, he is an undischarged bankrupt until he receives his discharge.

The main aspects of bankruptcy law are enshrined in the Bankruptcy Act 1914, which includes the following provisions:

Obtaining Credit by Undischarged Bankrupt

Under Section 155 of the Act, an undischarged bankrupt commits a misdemeanour if he

1. either alone or jointly with any other person obtains credit to the extent of £50 or upwards from any person without informing that person that he is an undischarged bankrupt; or
2. engages in any trade or business under a name other than that under which he was adjudicated bankrupt without disclosing to all persons with whom he enters into any business transaction the name under which he was adjudicated bankrupt.

Dealings with an Undischarged Bankrupt
All transactions by a bankrupt with any person dealing with him bona fide and for value, in respect of property, whether real or personal, acquired by the bankrupt after the adjudication, shall, if completed before any intervention by the trustee in bankruptcy, be valid against the trustee.

Where a banker has ascertained that a person having an account with him is an undischarged bankrupt then, unless the banker is satisfied that the account is on behalf of some other person, it shall be his duty forthwith to inform the trustee in the bankruptcy or the Department of Trade and Industry of the existence of the account and thereafter he shall not make any payments out of the account except under an order of the court or in accordance with instructions from the trustee in bankruptcy, unless by the expiration of one month from the date of giving the information no instructions have been received from the trustee.

Disqualification of a Bankrupt
An undischarged bankrupt may not sit in the House of Lords or be elected to, or sit in, the House of Commons or be appointed a Justice of the Peace or hold the office of mayor, alderman or councillor.

Under the Companies Act 1948 (Section 187(1)), it is a criminal offence for an undischarged bankrupt to act as a director or to take any direct or indirect part in the management of a company without the leave of the court by which he was adjudicated bankrupt.

A minor can be made a bankrupt only in respect of debts legally binding on him. If there is no debt legally enforceable against him, he cannot be made a bankrupt even on his own petition. A minor is not liable to bankruptcy proceedings in respect of a debt contracted by a firm of which he is a partner.

Both married and single women are subject to the same bankruptcy laws as a man, regardless of whether or not they are carrying on a business.

A partnership is dissolved in the event of the bankruptcy of one of the partners. In the event of a bankruptcy of a firm, the individual partners are bankrupts and no further operations may be conducted by the partnership.

The bankruptcy of an executor or trustee does not affect his ability to deal with the estate or trust under his control.

An undischarged bankrupt may apply to the court at any time for his discharge and the court may grant it or refuse it at its discretion. Under Section 26, Bankruptcy Act 1914, if the bankruptcy was occasioned by misfortune without any misconduct on the part of the bankrupt, he may be granted a 'certificate of misfortune'. Under the Insolvency Act 1976, Section 7, the court may make an order providing for the automatic discharge of a bankrupt after a five year period.

In *R* v *Miller* [1977] 1 WLR 1129, it was held that an undischarged bankrupt who entered into a hire purchase agreement without disclosing that he was an undischarged bankrupt was not guilty of an offence under Section 155, Bankruptcy Act 1914 (see above) because obtaining goods under a hire purchase agreement was not obtaining them 'on credit'. The theory is that, under hire purchase agreement, each instalment falls due for payment on the due date and no credit as such is given. Indeed, as the court said, if there had been default in paying an instalment, the finance company would have an immediate cause of action for the overdue amount which was the antithesis of giving credit.

BANKRUPTCY When a person is unable to pay his debts, his property is, in certain circumstances, taken possession of by the official receiver or trustee in bankruptcy, who realizes it and distributes the proceeds amongst the creditors.

The law of bankruptcy in England is contained in the Bankruptcy Act 1914, an Act to consolidate the law relating to bankruptcy, and in several unrepealed Sections in previous Acts.

By the 1914 Act, Section 1(2) provides

> In this Act, the expression 'a debtor,' unless the context otherwise implies, includes any person, whether a British subject or not, who at the time when any act of bankruptcy was done or suffered by him—
> (*a*) was personally present in England; or
> (*b*) ordinarily resided or had a place of residence in England; or
> (*c*) was carrying on business in England, personally, or by means of an agent or manager; or
> (*d*) was a member of a firm or partnership which carried on business in England.

Where a debtor has committed an act of bankruptcy (q.v.) a creditor, or creditors, whose debt or debts amount to not less than £750, may petition the court which has bankruptcy jurisdiction over the debtor, to make a receiving order (q.v.) with the object of having the debtor's estate administered under the bankruptcy law for the benefit of the creditors. A bankruptcy petition may also be presented by the debtor himself. A debtor is not adjudged a bankrupt immediately upon the making of a receiving order, but a general meeting of creditors (q.v.) is held shortly after the order is made, to consider whether a composition or scheme of arrangement shall be entertained or whether he shall be adjudged bankrupt.

After a receiving order is made, the debtor must make out and submit to the official receiver (that is, the official of the court who takes control of the debtor's estate) a statement of his affairs. (SEE Section 14, under *Receiving Order*. SEE ALSO *Official Receiver*)

As soon as convenient after the expiration of the time for the submission of a debtor's statement of affairs, the court shall hold a public sitting for the examination of the debtor, but the court shall not declare that his examination is concluded until after the day appointed for the first meeting of creditors. SEE *Public Examination of Debtor*.

If a debtor intends to make a proposal to his creditors for a composition in satisfaction of his debts, or a proposal for a scheme of arrangement of his affairs, he must, within four days of submitting his statement of affairs, or within such time as the official receiver may fix, lodge his proposal with the official receiver, embodying the terms of the composition or scheme and setting out particulars of any sureties or securities proposed. SEE *Compositions* (Bankruptcy Act)

If the debtor's proposal is accepted by the creditors, the receiving order is discharged. If a trustee is not appointed, the official receiver acts as trustee for the purpose of receiving and distributing the composition, or for the purpose of carrying out the terms of the scheme. A creditor under a composition or scheme must lodge his proof of debt with the trustee.

If the composition or scheme is not accepted within 14 days after the conclusion of the debtor's examination, or such time as is allowed by the court, or if the creditors resolve that the debtor be adjudged bankrupt, or if they do not pass any resolution, the court shall adjudge the debtor bankrupt (SEE *Adjudication in Bankruptcy*), and thereupon his property shall vest in a trustee (see *Trustee in Bankruptcy*), and be divisible amongst his creditors. As to any money or securities in a banker's hands at the time of adjudication, or ceived afterwards, see under *Bankrupt Person*.

The bankruptcy of a debtor, whether it takes place on his own petition or that of a creditor, dates back to the time of the act of bankruptcy being committed on which the receiving order was made against him (Section 37 of the Bankruptcy Act 1914, see under *Adjudication in Bankruptcy*).

The creditors may appoint a committee of inspection to superintend the administration of the bankrupt's property by the trustee. SEE *Committee of Inspection*

A trustee may be authorised by the Board of Trade to open a local banking account (SEE Section 89 of the 1914 Act, see under *Trustee in Bankruptcy*).

Where the committee of inspection approve, the trustee of a bankrupt's estate may pledge any deeds belonging to the estate, if the money is required for the payment of the bankrupt's debts.

A creditor's claim against a bankrupt's estate must be made on oath and upon the prescribed form called the proof of debt (q.v.).

A bankrupt may, at any time after being adjudged bankrupt, apply to the court for an order of discharge, and the court shall appoint a day for hearing the application. SEE *Discharge of Bankrupt*

If a debtor gives a creditor a preference over other creditors, and he is adjudged a bankrupt on a petition presented within six months thereafter, the preference shall be deemed fraudulent and void as against the trustee. SEE *Fraudulent Preference*

Any settlement of property shall, if the settlor becomes bankrupt within two years after the date of the settlement, be void against the trustee, or if he becomes bankrupt at any time within ten years after that date, be also void against the trustee, unless it is proved that the settlor was able to pay all his debts at the time he made the settlement, without the aid of the property comprised therein. SEE *Settlements—(Settlor Bankrupt)*

Section 45 of the Bankruptcy Act 1914, with respect to bona fide transactions without notice, provides as follows:

> Subject to the foregoing provisions of this Act with respect to the effect of bankruptcy on an execution or attachment, and with respect to the avoidance of certain settlements, assignments, and preferences, nothing in this Act shall invalidate, in the case of a bankruptcy—
>
> (*a*) Any payment by the bankrupt to any of his creditors;
> (*b*) Any payment or delivery to the bankrupt;
> (*c*) Any conveyance or assignment by the bankrupt for valuable consideration;
> (*d*) Any contract, dealing, or transaction by or with the bankrupt for valuable consideration:
>
> Provided that both the following conditions are complied with, namely—
>
> (1) that the payment, delivery, conveyance, assignment, contract, dealing, or transaction, as the case may be, takes place before the date of the receiving order; and
>
> (2) that the person (other than the debtor) to, by, or with whom the payment, delivery, conveyance, assignment, contract, dealing, or transaction was made, executed, or entered into, has not at the time of payment, delivery, conveyance, assignment, contract, dealing, or transaction, notice of any available act of bankruptcy committed by the bankrupt before that time.

But see Section 46, Bankruptcy Act 1914, as to the validity of certain payments to a bankrupt or his assignee, under *Act of Bankruptcy*.

It is the duty of the trustee to declare and distribute dividends amongst the creditors who have proved their debts. SEE *Dividends in Bankruptcy*

A debtor who is unable to pay his creditors is not always dealt with under the Bankruptcy Acts. He may call his creditors together and offer a composition, that is, to pay each creditor only so much in the pound (SEE *Composition with Creditors*), or he may offer to assign his property to a trustee, in order that it may be realized and the proceeds divided amongst the creditors (SEE *Assignment for Benefit of Creditors*). When an arrangement is made in either of those ways and is embodied in a deed or agreement, the deed of arrangement (q.v.) or agreement must be registered within seven days.

As to dealings with an undischarged bankrupt, see *Bankrupt*; and as to the avoidance of general assignments of book debts unless registered, see *Debts, Assignment of*.

An advertisement in the *London Gazette* of a receiving order or an adjudication order is conclusive evidence of the order having been made. SEE *Gazetted*

In the case of *Re Turner, a Bankrupt, ex parte The Trustee of the Property of the Bankrupt* v *Turner* [1974] 1 WLR 1556, a husband and wife had purchased a house jointly and it was acknowledge that the wife was entitled to one half of the beneficial interest. The husband was adjudicated bankrupt and it was held that the trustee in bankruptcy was entitled to vacant possession of the property in order that it may be sold with vacant possession. The matter, said Goff, J, was entirely within the discretion of the court. A similar decision was arrived at in *Re McCarthy, a Bankrupt* [1975] 1 WLR 807.

SEE *Acts of Bankruptcy; Adjudication in Bankruptcy; Administration Order; Assignment for Benefit of Creditors; Bankrupt Person; Committee of Inspection; Composition with Creditors; Compositions (Bankruptcy Act); Cork Committee; Death of Insolvent Person; Debts, Assignment of; Deed of Arrangement; Discharge of Bankrupt, Dividends in Bankruptcy; Fraudulent Preference; Insolvency; Interest; Married Woman; Meeting of Creditors; Official Receiver; Preferential Payments; Proof of Debts; Public Examination of Debtor; Receiving Order; Settlements (Settlor Bankrupt); Trustee in Bankruptcy; Undischarged Bankrupt.*

BANKRUPTCY NOTICE Where a creditor has obtained a final judgment or final order against a debtor and execution has not been stayed, he may serve on the latter a bankruptcy notice. If this is not complied with within seven days of its service or a counterclaim entered for an equal or greater amount of the judgment debt, the debtor has committed an act of bankruptcy. Under the Bankruptcy Act 1914, a bankruptcy notice has to be in a prescribed form and this is now contained in the Bankruptcy Rules 1952. Use of the statutory form is mandatory. SEE ALSO *Act of Bankruptcy*

BANKRUPTCY PETITION SEE *Receiving Order*

BAR GOLD A bar of gold is 400 oz fine. Smaller 'bars', usually 200 oz fine, are known as 'tablets'. Central bank reserves and international exchange settlements employ bar gold in large proportion, and it is measured at so much fine gold per unit of the currency of the country quoting. Bar gold is practically fine gold and is rejected if it contains too much alloy. Certain signatures of recognized assayers are well known and are passed in the market, but where there is any doubt as to the bar gold's origin it is assayed afresh. In the UK, before the Gold Standard Act of 1925, bar gold of not less than £20,000 in value could be sold to the Mint at £3 17s 10½d per oz of standard gold and minted free, but it was often more convenient to sell it to the Bank of England at £3 17s 9d, which was its statutory buying price. The difference of 1½d was to cover the loss of interest during the time the bullion was being minted. Between 1925 and 1931 the Bank of England ceased to convert its notes into coin, but would sell or exchange bars containing 400 oz of fine gold at £3 17s 10½d per oz of standard gold, which means in minimum amounts of nearly £1,700. The Gold Standard (Amendment) Act of 1931 released the Bank from any obligation to sell gold. London quotations were changed in September 1919 from the standard to the fine ounce basis. SEE ALSO *Bank of England; Central Bank; Gold; Gold Standard*

BARCLAYCARD This is the credit card introduced by Barclays Bank in 1966. It was the first bank credit card to be issued in Great Britain. Barclaycard was launched by Barclays in cooperation with Bank Americard ,and Barclaycard is now part of the worldwide Visa Group.

Barclaycards also serve as cheque cards (q.v.) guaranteeing cash withdrawals up to £100 from Barclays Group branches and the purchase of goods and services up to £50 per transaction.

At the present time, there are approximately 6.5 million Barclaycard holders in the UK including those who use Barclaycard only as a cheque card.

SEE ALSO *Access; Cheque Cards; Credit Cards; Supplement*

BARE TRUSTEE A person who holds an asset on behalf of another person in circumstances where that other person is absolutely entitled to the beneficial ownership of the asset. If, for example, A holds property for B and B is entitled to call for it any time or to instruct A in the way he must deal with the property, A is a bare trustee for B. A nominee such as a bank's nominee company is in the position of a bare trustee for the customer whose stocks and shares they may hold.

BARGAIN A transaction carried out on a stock exchange between a stockbroker and a jobber. Bargains in individual shares are reported in *The Stock Exchange Official List* and, to some extent, in the public press. The activity of a stock exchange on a particular day is measured in terms of the number of bargains transacted. The number of bargains in a day can vary from 5,000 to 30,000 and in the course of the year the total of The number of bargains on The London Stock Exchange now exceeds 6 million.

BARRATRY The word, as used in a bill of lading (q.v.) or a charter party (q.v.), means any wilful wrongdoing by the master or crew of a ship by which the interests of the shipowner are injured.

BASE COINS A banker is justified in breaking or destroying any base coins which came into his hands. Section 26 of 24 & 25 Vict c 99 enacts:

Where any coin shall be tendered as the Queen's current gold or silver coin to any person who shall suspect the same to be diminished otherwise than by reasonable wearing, or to be counterfeit, it shall be lawful for such person to cut, break, bend, or deface such coin, and if any coin so cut, broken, bent or defaced shall appear to be diminished otherwise than by reasonable wearing, or to be counterfeit, the person tendering the same shall bear the loss thereof, but if the same shall be of due weight, and shall appear to be lawful coin, the person cutting, breaking, bending, or defacing the same is hereby required to receive the same at the rate it was coined for; and if any dispute shall arise whether the coin so cut, broken, bent, or defaced be diminished in manner aforesaid, or counterfeit it shall be heard and finally determined in a summary manner by any Justice of the Peace, who is hereby empowered to examine upon oath as well the parties as any other person, in order to the decision of such dispute; and the Tellers at the Receipt of Her Majesty's Exchequer, and their deputies and clerks, and the Receivers-General of every branch of Her Majesty's Revenue, are hereby required to cut, break, or deface or cause to be cut, broken, or defaced every piece of counterfeit or unlawfully diminished gold or silver coin which shall be tendered to them in payment of any part of Her Majesty's Revenue.

Counterfeit coins are rarely encountered nowadays as their value is hardly sufficient to repay the counterfeiter for the trouble of making and uttering them. A suspected counterfeit coin may, however, be tested by trying to bend it, or by scraping the milled edge with a genuine coin, or by throwing it down on the counter. A counterfeit coin will bend easily. The soft metal will mark and 'give' when scraped. The sound of such a coin will not ring true when thrown down, but will appear dull or dead. SEE *Coinage, Coins; Coinage Offences*

BASE RATE Following the issue of the Bank of England paper, *Competition and Credit Control* in May 1971, the London and Scottish clearing banks agreed to abandon their collective agreements on interest rates with effect from 16th September, 1971. Individual banks were enabled to quote their own deposit rates for seven-day money and to quote for term deposits. They also became free to quote lending rates linked to their own Base Rates instead of to Bank Rate (q.v.) and this has become the normal pattern. SEE *Bank Interest*

BASIS PRICE This is the 'striking' price in an option, particularly in commodity dealing. Where, for example, A has the right to buy or sell to B an agreed amount of a particular commodity at any time within an agreed period, the price agreed at the time of the contract is the 'basis' or 'striking' price. The buyer of the option will pay a premium over and above the basis price in return for receiving the option and this is the amount of his risk. SEE *Options*

BEAR A speculator on the Stock Exchange. The name applies to someone who anticipates a fall in a certain security and who, therefore, sells stocks which he does not possess in the hope of buying them back at a lower price and thereby making a profit. One may of course have a 'bearish' view of the whole market and not merely of particular securities. A bear market is a falling market or one which is thought likely to fall. SEE *Bull*

BEARER (CHEQUE OR BILL) Bearer, in the Bills of Exchange Act 1882, means the person in possession of a bill or note which is payable to bearer (Section 2).

A bill is payable to bearer which is expressed to be so payable, or on which the only or last indorsement is an indorsement in blank. [Section 8(3)]

Where the payee is a fictitious or non-existing person the bill may be treated as payable to bearer. [Section 7(3)]

A bill in these sections includes a cheque.

Where the holder of a bill payable to bearer negotiates it

by delivery without indorsing it, he is called a transferor by delivery. [Section 58(1)]

A bill (or cheque) payable to bearer does not require to be indorsed. A person, other than the drawer, cannot be sued upon a cheque, so long as it is not indorsed by him. If, however, he indorses it, he may be sued thereon by any subsequent holder. Although a transferor by delivery is not liable on the instrument in the event of its dishonour, he would be liable if there was a forged signature at the time of the transfer, because by Section 58(3), a transferor by delivery warrants to his immediate transferee being a holder for value that the bill is what it purports to be, that he has a right to transfer it, and that at the time of transfer he is not aware of any fact that renders it valueless.

If a cheque drawn payable to bearer is indorsed 'Pay J. Brown or order', it does not require John Brown's signature or any indorsement, as it is on the face of it a bearer cheque.

In practice, a bearer cheque may be altered by the payee from bearer to order, by simply striking out the printed word 'bearer', or by striking it out and writing the word 'order'. Such an alteration does not require to be initialed.

An order cheque, however, can be altered on the face into a bearer cheque only by the drawer, who must sign the alteration; if there are more drawers than one, each must sign.

When an order cheque is indorsed in blank, that is, not made payable to anyone else by the payee or indorser, it becomes a cheque payable to bearer. Any holder may convert the blank indorsement into a special indorsement, and the cheque (or bill) would again become payable to order.

A cheque or bill payable to a fictitious or non-existing person is payable to bearer. In the case of *Bank of England* v *Vagliano Brothers* [1891] AC 107, it was held that a fictitious or non-existing person included a real person who never had nor was intended to have any right to the bills. Lord Herschell said

> I have arrived at the conclusion that whenever the name inserted as that of the payee is so inserted by way of pretence merely, without any intention that payment shall only be made in conformity therewith, the payee is a fictitious person within the meaning of the statute, whether the name be that of an existing person or of one who has no existence.

A banker incurs no liability in paying, to the person presenting, an uncrossed cheque made payable to bearer by the drawer, even if the person who presents such cheque has stolen it. In *Charles* v *Blackwell* (1877) 2 CPD 151, it was held that where the banker paid the bearer of a lost or stolen cheque, he obeyed the mandate of his customer, the drawer, and could charge him accordingly; while on the other hand, the customer was protected, and this even though the bearer so paid had no property in the cheque, but was himself a thief who had stolen it. The drawer was entitled to say to the payee, 'I gave you an instrument which you were willing to take in satisfaction of your debt if the drawee paid the amount to the bearer and this the drawee has done'. (SEE *Agent*) But in an exceptional case, such as where a cheque is payable to the 'British Bank Ltd or bearer', a banker would require to be exceedingly careful in making enquiries before paying such a cheque to a stranger, for although it is payable to the bearer the banker knows that it is not the custom for a bank to send a cheque by a stranger to be cashed. SEE *Crossed Cheque*

Where a person takes a cheque payable to bearer, it is advisable for him to get the transferor to indorse it and so make him a party to the cheque, as without the indorsement the transferor could not be sued upon the cheque in the event of its dishonour.

A cheque payable to 'Wages or order', 'Cash or order', 'House or order', etc., is in some quarters mistakenly considered to be payable to bearer under Section 6(3) of the Bills of Exchange Act 1882, which states that bills payable to fictitious or non-existing persons are payable to bearer. Such designations, however, are not fictitious payees, but impersonal payees, and in some cases the drawer's indorsement is desirable. Instruments so drawn, however, are not cheques, for they are not payable to the order of a specified person (*North and South Insurance Corporation Ltd* v *National Provincial Bank Ltd, Times*, 9th November, 1935). SEE *Impersonal Payees*

A cheque payable to 'Bearer or order', the word 'bearer' being written in the space for a payee's name, is payable to the bearer. *Orbit Mining & Trading Co. Ltd* v *Westminster Bank Ltd* [1962] 3 All ER 565.

In Scotland, it is customary to request the person receiving cash for a bearer cheque to indorse it. SEE *Bills of Exchange; Cheque*

BEARER BONDS A bearer bond, that is a bond which is payable to the bearer, in contradistinction to a bond which is registered in the name of the holder, passes by mere delivery the full benefits conferred by the bond, so long as the transferee takes it in good faith and for value and without notice of any defect in the transferor's title. If it should ultimately appear that the transferor had stolen the bond, or had otherwise a defective title, the transferee's right to retain the bond would not be affected. A bearer bond belongs to the class of documents called negotiable instruments (q.v.). Formerly, only bearer bonds which were issued in foreign countries and treated in the UK by merchants as negotiable were regarded by the courts as negotiable instruments, but in modern times, debentures to bearer of an English company have been recognized by the courts as negotiable instruments.

In *Edelstein* v *Schuler* [1903] 2 KB 144, Bigham, J, said, 'In my opinion the time has passed when the negotiability of bearer bonds, whether Government bonds or trading bonds, foreign or English, can be called in question in our courts'.

Attached to the bond, or in a separate sheet, is a series of coupons, each one being dated, if the interest is payable half-yearly, for a different half-year, and forming the warrant, upon the production of which the holder will be paid the interest represented by that coupon. When the coupons are exhausted a fresh supply may be obtained in exchange for the 'talon' which is usually attached to the bond. Some coupons are not dated, being payable according to advertisement. A coupon sheet should not be detached from the bond. Securities to bearer, without the current coupon, are not a good delivery on the Stock Exchange. The possessor of bearer bonds should never write his name upon them, as it might cause them to form a bad delivery.

Certain bonds are drawn as being payable to the bearer, or 'when registered, to the registered holder'. In such cases, the name of the registered holder is entered in a place provided on the back of the bond.

Where bearer bonds are given as security, a banker usually takes a memorandum or agreement showing the purpose for which they are lodged. No deed of transfer is necessary, as they pass to the holder by simple delivery, and even if the bonds form part of a trust and the banker had no notice of the trust when he took them as security, his title will not be affected. An advance should not, of course, be made against coupons without the bond.

When bonds are left for safe custody in joint names, particularly when the parties are trustees, the banker should be most careful not to part with the bonds unless upon the signature of all the parties. It has been held that trustees may give authority to one of their number to cut off coupons from bonds deposited for safe custody as they fall due. In such a case, it is the banker's duty to see that nothing more is removed than the coupons which are falling due. SEE *Safe Custody*

The Exchange Control Act 1947 (q.v.) provided that bearer securities had to be lodged with or to the order of an approved bank chosen by the owner of the security. This new control was imposed to prevent the transfer of British-owned securities to foreign ownership except for value received. The ownership of such bearer securities was not affected by this regulation, but the depositee bank was under a duty to ensure that no illegal transfer of such items took place. This requirement no longer applies during the suspension of the Exchange Control Regulations.

BEARER SCRIP This is a document issued by a government or a company, upon a new issue of capital, until such time as all instalments have been paid and the definitive bond is ready. The bearer scrip, like the bearer bond which is eventually received, is treated as a negotiable instrument: that is, a holder for value, without notice of any defect in the transferor's title, obtains a good title thereto. In some cases, however, bearer scrip is exchanged for registered bonds or certificates. SEE *Bearer Bonds; Script Certificate*

BED AND BREAKFASTING The selling of a security one day and the repurchase of it almost immediately in order to establish either a gain or loss for capital gains tax purposes, or for some accounting purpose. For tax purposes, the asset is deemed to be disposed of (provided the sale is at arm's length) and the repurchase constitutes a new base price for the asset. Under the Finance Act 1982, indexation of a capital gain will commence to run afresh if an investment is sold and repurchased. SEE *Capital Gains Tax*; Supplement

BENEFICIAL OWNER In a conveyance for valuable consideration, other than a mortgage, where the vendor conveys as 'beneficial owner', these words have the meaning (Schedule 2, Law of Property Act 1925) that he impliedly covenants that he has full power to convey the property expressed to be conveyed, that the property shall be quitely entered upon and enjoyed by the person to whom the conveyance is made, that the property is freed and discharged from all incumbrances and claims other than those subject to which the conveyance is expressly made, and that he will execute any further deeds for further or more perfectly assuring the property to the person to whom the conveyance is made.

If the property is leasehold the 'beneficial owner' also impliedly covenants that it is a good, valid and effectual lease, and that all rents and covenants have been paid and observed.

In the case of a conveyance of freehold property by way of mortgage, the 'beneficial owner' impliedly covenants that he has power to convey, that, if default was made in payment of the money intended to be secured, it should be lawful for the mortgagee to enter into and hold the property, that the property was freed from all incumbrances other than those to which the mortgage was expressly made subject, and that he would execute any further necessary deed.

In a mortgage of leasehold property, he impliedly covenants that he will pay all rents and observe all covenants, so long as any money remained unpaid.

More generally a beneficial owner is a person entitled to the substance of any real or personal property, where the formal or legal title is vested in a third person who is a trustee or nominee, the 'beneficial owner' being entitled *absolutely* to the substance of the property.

BENEFICIARY A person who benefits under a will is called a beneficiary. He may receive either 'real' property (SEE *Realty*), in which case he is a devisee, or he may receive 'personal' property (SEE *Personal Estate; Personalty*), when he is named a legatee. The term is also used in relation to a person who benefits under a trust.

BENEFITS IN KIND The term is usually used in relation to those emoluments of an office or employment which are paid other than in money. Thus, benefits in kind might include a motor car, petrol for private motoring, private living accommodation, interest-free or low-interest loans, medical insurance, free suits of clothes and other so-called 'perquisites' of a particular employment. In some cases, the benefits attach to particular types of employment, e.g. free coal enjoyed by miners and free travel enjoyed by British Rail employees. Under the law as it stands at present, benefits in kind paid to company directors and higher-paid employees are taxable almost without exception. At the present time, a 'higher-paid employee' is a person in receipt of earnings of more than £8,500. For lower-paid employees, not being directors, a wide range of benefits in kind, e.g. motor cars, medical insurance, are not taxable. SEE *Income Tax*

BEQUEST A gift or legacy of personal property by a will.

BEST TERMS Under Rule 212(2) of Appendix 41 of the Rules and Regulations of the Stock Exchange, the commissions earned by stockbrokers may be shared with banks and other approved agents through whom business is introduced. In general, a higher rate of commission applies in such cases, particularly for the larger transactions. For a transaction to be on 'best terms' from the client's standpoint, it is better that commissions should not be shared and that the lower rates of commissions under Appendix 39 of the Rules be applied. Above a certain level, therefore, currently £7,000 in the case of ordinary share transactions, it is more economical for the investor to deal direct with the broker or to ask his agent to deal through the broker on 'best terms', i.e. on a non-divisible basis.

BID AND OFFER BASES A method of calculation of unit trust prices. SEE *Unit Trusts*

BID PRICE The price at which stocks and shares, commodities and indeed any item of property may be sold, i.e. it is the price 'bid' by the prospective buyer. In the case of quoted securities, it would be the jobber who made the bid price. The difference between the bid and offer prices (SEE *Offer Price*) is the 'jobber's turn' in the case of transactions on the Stock Exchange. This is not necessarily the measure of his profit, however, because for example on a falling market he may have to sell shares at a lower price in order to balance his book. The skill of the jobber lies to a considerable extent in anticipating the balance in the market of buyers and sellers.

BILL BROKER Bill brokers are merchants whose traditional business is the buying and selling of bills. They are more usually referred to nowadays as discount houses. The London discount market comprises the ten houses of the London Discount Market Association (q.v.). They make the market in treasury bills, trade bills and bills of local authorities, public sector institutions and banks. They act as principals, buying and selling for their own account and stand between the Bank of England and the money markets.

The discount houses maintain contact with the banks and other institutions in the money markets and provide them with funds as necessary against their own bills and the discount houses themselves sell short-term bills to the Bank of England for cash.

The discount houses have a special role in relation to the issue, each Thursday, of Treasury Bills by the Bank of England. By agreement, the members of the Discount Houses Association underwrite the entire weekly issue, which nowadays is of the order of £500 million. This aspect of the discount houses' role has diminished now that the bills of the banks themselves have become more important as an instrument in monetary policy.

In addition to making the market in public sector and trade bills, the discount houses enjoy a special relationship with the Bank of England. The regular meetings between the Governor of the Bank and the Chairman of the London Discount Market Association provide a forum for the discussion of interest rates and a channel of communication between the authorities on the one hand and the City institutions on the other.

Bill brokers deal in short-dated Government bonds and these are now accepted by the banks as cover for short-term loans. The brokers also participate in market dealings in London dollar certificates of deposit (q.v.) and sterling certificates of deposit (q.v.). The brokers require substantial funds with which to trade, this being provided by their own capital, loans from bankers repayable at call or short notice and, in many cases, deposits from the public.

Under the present arrangements, the Bank of England requires all eligible banks (SEE *Eligible Bills*) to keep at least 4 per cent of their eligible liabilities in the form of secured deposits (called club money) with members of the London Discount Market Association, thus ensuring a source of funds for the discount houses.

BILL OF EXCHANGE A bill of exchange is defined by the Bills of Exchange Act 1882, Section 3, as follows:

(1) A bill of exchange is an unconditional order in writing, addressed by one person to another, signed by the person giving it, requiring the person to whom it is addressed to pay on demand or at a fixed or determinable future time a sum certain in money to or to the order of a specified person, or to bearer.

(2) An instrument which does not comply with these conditions, or which orders any act to be done in addition to the payment of money, is not a bill of exchange.

(3) An order to pay out of a particular fund is not unconditional within the meaning of this Section; but an unqualified order to pay, coupled with (*a*) an indication of a particular fund out of which the drawee is to reimburse himself or a particular account to be debited with the amount, or (*b*) a statement of the transaction which gives rise to the bill, is unconditional.

(4) A bill is not invalid by reason–

(*a*) That it is not dated;
(*b*) That it does not specify the value given, or that any value has been given therefor;
(*c*) That it does not specify the place where it is drawn or the place where it is payable.

Section 9 provides that

(1) The sum payable by a bill is a sum certain within the meaning of this Act, although it is required to be paid—

(*a*) With interest.
(*b*) By stated instalments.
(*c*) By stated instalments, with a provision that upon default in payment of any instalment the whole shall become due.
(*d*) According to an indicated rate of exchange or according to a rate of exchange to be ascertained as directed by the bill.

(2) Where the sum payable is expressed in words and also in figures, and there is a discrepancy between the two, the sum denoted by the words is the amount payable.

In *Cohn* v *Boulken* (1920) 36 TLR 767, where a cheque had been drawn for '7680 francs (Paris)', it was held to be a bill of exchange, being for a sum of money certain or which can be made certain within Section 9(1)(*d*) of the Act. 'The rate of exchange was sufficiently indicated on the face of the cheque. In any event the rate of exchange was sufficiently indicated by the practice of banking which had been proved.' It was stated that the settled practice of bankers with cheques drawn in England on an English bank for an amount in French currency was to debit the drawer in sterling at the rate of exchange ruling on the day and at the hour of presentation, and to give the payee the equivalent in sterling. It was also held that the drawer cannot as between himself and an indorsee of the cheque set up an oral agreement between himself and the original payee that the rate of exchange should be that ruling at the date of the cheque (q.v.). Where a bill is drawn payable in the UK in a foreign currency without stipulation as to the rate of exchange, a tender in payment of notes and coin in the currency of the bill is not a legal tender.

A bill may be written, printed, or typewritten.

There is no particular form prescribed by the Act, but bills are nearly always drawn in the same way. The following are specimens of the ordinary forms of bills of exchange:

Leeds, 10 June 19 . .
£100
Three months after date pay
to { me or to my order / John Brown or order / bearer } the
sum of one hundred pounds for value received.
John Jones

To Mr Thomas Smith
24 River Street, London

Leeds, 10 June 19 . .
£100
On demand pay to John Brown or order the sum of one hundred pounds for value received.
John Jones

To Mr W Robinson
London

The first record of the use of bills of exchange in England is stated to be in a statute of 3 Rich. II, c. 3, in 1379. The original use of bills in the UK appears to have been for the settlement of debts between merchants in England and those in another country. For example, where Brown in England owed money to Dumont in, say, France, he would draw a bill upon Hugo in that country, who happened to owe him money, requesting Hugo to pay the money to Dumont. In this way Brown paid his debt to Dumont without the necessity of sending gold from England to France.

It is said that bills were in common use in Venice as early as the thirteenth century, and that they were first used by the Florentines in the twelfth century. Inland bills were made legal in England in 1697.

The persons whose names appear upon a bill of exchange are the drawer, the drawee (who by accepting the bill becomes the acceptor), the payee (who may also be the drawer), and the indorser. These persons are called the parties to the bill. In addition there may also be the name of the banker at whose office the acceptor makes the bill payable, but he is not one of 'the parties' to the bill.

The parties who are closely related, as the drawer and the acceptor, an indorser and the indorser immediately preceding him, are the 'immediate parties'. The parties who are not closely related, as the drawer and an indorsee, are the 'remote parties'.

A bill may be an inland bill (that is, one both drawn and payable within the British Islands, excluding Eire, or drawn within the British Islands upon some person resident therein), or a foreign bill (that is, one drawn otherwise than as an inland bill).

The holder of a bill of exchange may hold it till it is due and present it for payment himself; or he may negotiate the bill, that is, transfer it to another person; or he may leave it with his banker with a request that the bill be collected at maturity and the proceeds credited to his account; or he may take it to his banker, or to a bill broker, and after indorsing it have it discounted. By discounting a bill he receives at once the amount of the bill (which may not be payable by the acceptor for some months to come), less the amount charged for discounting it.

A bill drawn payable on a contingency, such as at a certain period after the arrival of a ship is not valid.

SEE *Bills of Exchange Act 1882* [where a reference is given to the articles which include the various sections of the Act]; *Acceptance; Acceptance, General; Acceptance, Qualified; Acceptance for Honour; Acceptor; Accommodation Bill; Agent; Alterations to Bill of Exchange; Antedated, Bearer; Bills for Collection; Bill in a Set; Cancellation of Bill of Exchange; Cheque; Consideration for Bill of Exchange; Date; Days of Grace; Delivery of Bill; Dishonour of Bill of Exchange; Documentary Bill; Draft; Drawee; Drawer; Foreign Bill; Forgery; Holder for Value; Holder in Due Course; Holder of Bill of Exchange; Inchoate Instrument; Indorsement; Indorser; Inland Bill; Lost Bill of Exchange; Negotiation of Bill of Exchange; Noting; Order (Cheque or Bill of Exchange); Overdue Bill; Part Payment; Parties to Bill of Exchange; Payee; Paying Banker; Payment for Honour; Payment of Bill; Presentment for Acceptance; Presentment for Payment; Promissory Note; Protest; Referee in Case of Need; Retiring a Bill; Supra Protest; Time of Payment of Bill; Transferor by Delivery*

BILL OF LADING A receipt for goods, upon shipment, signed by some person authorized to sign the same on behalf of the shipowner. The document states that the goods have been shipped in good order, and quotes the rate at which the freight is to be paid by the consignees. A note is usually made upon a bill of lading that the weight, quantity and quality of the cargo is unknown. The shipowner undertakes to deliver the goods at their destination in the same condition as they were when he received them.

Bills of lading are usually drawn in sets of three and, in addition, there are two 'copies'. Of these copies, one is given to the master and the other is retained by the loading brokers. The copies are of no value. Copy bills of lading are sometimes marked 'Copy—not negotiable' to ensure that no confusion shall arise between the unsigned copies and the valid parts. One of the three bills of lading is sent by the shipper to the consignee by one mail, and another is sent to him by another route, if possible, or by the following mail, and the third is retained by the shipper as evidence in support of a claim for insurance, in the event of the ship being lost, that the goods were in that ship. On the arrival of the ship at its destination, the consignee may, by handing the bill of lading to the master of the ship and paying all claims for freight and other charges, obtain possession of the goods. If the consignee wishes to transfer the goods to some other person, he can, by simply indorsing the bill of lading and delivering it to that person, constitute him the absolute owner of the goods. If such a transfer is made by the consignee in good faith and for value, the consignor's right to stop the goods in transit is cancelled. As a bill of lading is not a negotiable instrument, it follows that if the person who transfers it has no title or a defective title to the goods, the person to whom it is transferred obtains no better title than the transferor had.

As to a vendor's right of stoppage *in transitu*,

see under *Factors Act; Sale of Goods Act.* Those Acts include a bill of lading under the expression 'document of title'.

In the USA, the Bills of Lading Act 1916, makes all bills of lading, issued by any common carrier for the transportation of goods in the USA to a place in a foreign country, if to order, fully negotiable instruments.

During the time a cargo is at sea, the bill of lading is the symbol of the cargo, and 'the indorsement and delivery of the bill of lading operate as a symbolical delivery of the cargo'.

A pledgee can also defeat the claim of a third party who has seized the goods after landing if he or his agent still retains the bill (*Barclays Banks* v *Commissioners of Inland Revenue* [1963] Lloyd's List Rep 81).

If the consignee's name is not inserted in the bill of lading, the ownership of the goods remains in the consignor. If a bill of lading is not drawn to 'order to assigns' it is not assignable.

When the goods received on board are in good order and no adverse remarks, such as 'boxes broken', etc., are made upon the bill of lading, it is called a clean bill of lading.

In *Evans* v *J. Webster and Bros Ltd* (1928) 45 TLR 136, the plaintiff, a shipowner, shipped timber for which he issued a clean bill of lading held by defendants as indorsees. The timber was delivered short and damaged. The defendants submitted that the statement in the bill of lading that the proper quantity of timber had been shipped in good order was conclusive evidence against the shipowner. The plaintiff replied that the clean bills of lading had been issued in reliance on a fraudulent statement by the shipper to the master that, unless he signed bills of lading in that form he would not get clearance, and that therefore the statements in the bill of lading were not binding on the shipowner. It was held that the plaintiff was estopped from disputing the statement in the bill of lading. Wright, J, said

> A shipowner should not be allowed to say that a bill of lading holder could not rely on the statement in the bill of lading unless the information in the possession of the bill of lading holder contradicting the statement was of at least as much weight as the statement itself. There might possibly be cases where the holder knew from independent knowledge that the bill of lading was inaccurate, but such cases must be rare.

In *Brown, Jenkinson and Co Ltd* v *Percy Dalton (London) Ltd* [1957] 2 All ER 844, the plaintiffs as agents for the shipowners agreed with the defendants for the shipment of 100 barrels of orange juice f.o.b. London to Hamburg, freight to be paid by the defendants. The defendants stipulated that they should have clean on-board bills of lading. The barrels were in fact old and leaking, as the defendants knew and as the plaintiffs learned when the barrels were brought to the dock. At the request of the defendants the plaintiffs agreed to issue and did issue bills of lading describing the goods as 'in apparent good order and condition', the defendants agreeing to indemnify the shipowners against all losses or damage arising from the issue of clean bills of lading. Owing to the condition of the barrels a considerable quantity of the orange juice leaked away before they were delivered to the ultimate purchasers. The shipowners having paid the amount of the loss so arising assigned to the plaintiffs their rights under the agreement of indemnity. The plaintiffs, when they issued clean bills of lading, knew that bankers would not ordinarily advance money against bills of lading unless the bills were clean bills of lading, but the plaintiffs had not contemplated that anyone should be defrauded by the issue of these bills of lading and did not know what was intended to be done with the bills of lading by any purchasers of the goods from the defendants.

It was held that the court would not enforce the defendants' promise to indemnify the shipowners, since the promise arose out of a transaction which contained all the elements of the tort of deceit and was thus given for an unlawful consideration, namely, the plaintiffs' making at the request of the defendants a false representation, which they both knew to be false but on which they intended that others should act; and the fact that the plaintiffs did not contemplate that anyone would be defrauded did not render the agreement enforceable by them.

Morris, LJ, in his judgment said

> the practice of giving indemnities on the issuing of clean bills of lading is not uncommon . . . there may perhaps be some circumstances in which indemnities can properly be given. Thus, if a shipowner thinks that he has detected some faulty condition in regard to goods to be taken on board, he may be assured by the shipper that he is entirely mistaken; if he is so persuaded by the shipper, it may be that he could honestly issue a clean bill of lading while taking an indemnity in case it was later shown that there had, in fact, been some faulty condition. Each case must depend on its circumstances.

The strict legal meaning of 'clean' in relation to a bill of lading was emphasized in *M. Golodetz & Co Inc* v *Czarnikow Rionda Co Inc* [1980] 1 WLR 495, where in the Court of Appeal it was held that a clean bill of lading 'is one in which there is nothing to qualify the admission that the goods were in apparent good order and condition at the time of shipment'. In that case, a fire on the ship had damaged 200 tonnes of sugar after part-loading had taken place. In the result, two bills of lading were presented, one for 200 tonnes acknowledging shipment in good order, but carrying a note that the cargo had been discharged because of damage. Both the banks and the buyers had rejected the bill as not being 'clean' but the Court held that the bill was clean within the strict legal meaning. The Court rejected the argument of the defendants that 'clean' meant 'marketable'. When the dispute went to arbitration it had been open to the arbitrators to find against its marketability but they had merely found that the bill was not 'clean', a view which the Court of Appeal could not uphold. It appears that this was the first case where the courts had had to consider a bill of lading, the fate of which had been recorded in this particular way and it seems to run contra to the dictum of Lord Sumner in 1922:

These documents have to be handled by banks, they have to be taken up or rejected promptly and without any opportunity for prolonged enquiry, they have to be such as can be retendered to sub-purchasers, and it is essential that they should so conform to the accustomed shipping documents and to be reasonably and readily fit to pass current in commerce.

The issue of clean bills of lading where 'claused' bills of lading should rightfully be issued is clearly wrong where the damage to the goods is serious, and if an indemnity is given in these circumstances and clean bills of lading are issued, there is a risk that innocent third parties will act in reliance on the clean bills of lading to their detriment.

It is the general policy of the clearing banks not to give an indemnity of the character indicated above. It is to be noted that by tendering a bill of exchange with accompanying documents the banker does not warrant that such documents (e.g. a bill of lading) arc genuine (*Guaranty Trust Company* v *Hannay* [1918] 2 KB 623).

As already stated, the master of the ship delivers the goods to the person who presents the bill of lading, but if it should happen that two different purchasers have each received one of the bills of lading, the master is not liable if he delivers the goods to the purchaser who comes first with a bill of lading, provided, of course, he acts in good faith and has no notice of the conflicting claims. From an examination of the bill of lading it will be noticed that the master or purser affirms to two (or three, as the case may be) bills of lading, 'one of which bills being accomplished, the others to stand void'. It is therefore necessary, in order to have a complete security, that all the bills of lading should be held.

In addition to holding all the bills of lading, a 'stop-order' upon the goods may be lodged by the person about to make an advance upon them.

As to the three parts of a bill of lading Earl Cairns said in *Glyn, Mills, Currie & Co* v *East and West India Dock Co* (1882) 7 App Cas 591,

All that any person who advances money upon a bill of lading will have to do, if he sees, as he will see on the face of the bill of lading, that it has been signed in more parts than one, will be to require that all the parts are brought in—that is to say, that all the title deeds are brought in. I know that that is the practice with regard to other title deeds, and it strikes me with some surprise that any one would advance money upon a bill of lading without taking that course of requiring the delivery up of all the parts. If the person advancing the money does not choose to do that, another course which he may take is to be vigilant and on the alert, and to take care that he is on the spot at the first arrival of the ship in the dock. If those who advance money on bills of lading do not adopt one or other of those courses, it appears to me that if they suffer, they suffer in consequence of their own act.

A banker who advances against wool (for example) which has been imported from abroad, may adopt the following course. He may take up the bills of lading and instruct the shippers to send the wool by rail to his order. He may then direct the railway board to deliver it to the combers, on his behalf, who will ascertain and advise the banker as to the various qualities and quantities 'tops', 'middles', 'bottoms', etc., so that he may see what it will realize at present quotations. When the customer sells the wool, the banker then orders it to be delivered in accordance with the customer's instructions against payment of the purchase price.

By Section 19(3), Sale of Goods Act 1979.

Where the seller of goods draws on the buyer for the price, and transmits the bill of exchange and the bill of lading to the buyer together to secure acceptance or payment of the bill of exchange, the buyer is bound to return the bill of lading if he does not honour the bill of exchange, and, if he wrongfully retains the bill of lading, the property in the goods does not pass to him.

Instead of sending bills of lading direct to the consignee, the consignor may draw a bill of exchange upon the consignee for the value of the goods dispatched and attach the bills of lading to the bill. Those documents may then be sent by the consignor's bankers to their correspondents in the town where the consignee lives, with a request to present the bill to the consignee for acceptance; and instructions are often given that the bills of lading may be handed to the consignee upon his accepting the bill. The consignee can then obtain the goods, sell them and be in a position to meet his acceptance at maturity.

Frequently the consignor draws a bill upon the consignee and discounts it at his bankers, pledging the indorsed bills of lading as security, and the banker has to send forward the bill to his correspondents to obtain the drawee's acceptance (SEE *Documentary Bill*); or the consignor may, under instructions, draw upon the consignee's banker, the bills of lading being attached to the bill of exchange.

When bills of lading are given as security, a memorandum of deposit, or letter of lien is taken, which provides that, in default of payment, the banker may sell the goods represented by the bills. In some cases, where an advance has been made upon bills of lading, the bills are handed to the borrower upon his signing a trust receipt. SEE *Trust Letter or Receipt*

Where a bill of lading is taken as security containing such a clause as 'all conditions of every character as per charter party' (see below), the lender should ascertain what are the conditions in the charter party, as that document may reserve to the owners of the vessel the right of lien upon the cargo for payment of freight, demurrage and other charges.

A bill of lading pledged as security should be indorsed either in blank or to the banker, and be deposited, as stated above, under a letter of lien or hypothecation (q.v.). To avoid any liabilities that may attach to an indorser of the bill with respect to the goods, it is preferable for the banker to take it indorsed in blank. It has, however, been held by the House of Lords that, where a bill of lading is indorsed and pledged by way of security, a banker indorsee is not subject to the same liabilities in respect of the goods as a person to whom a bill of lading is indorsed upon a sale of the goods (*Sewell* v *Burdick* [1884] 10 App Cas 74). But if the banker claims the goods in order to realize his security, he is then liable for the freight, warehouse charges, and all charges payable in accordance with the terms of the bill of lading. When the banker indorses and delivers the bill to a holder for value the banker's liability under the bill then ceases.

When a banker has claimed and received delivery of the goods, the addition of the words 'without recourse' to his indorsement does not relieve him from liability under the bill of lading.

Where a transfer of a bill of lading takes place, upon a sale of the goods, Section 1 of the Bills of Lading Act 1855 enacts

> Every consignee of goods named in a bill of lading, and every indorsee of a bill of lading to whom the property in the goods therein mentioned shall pass, upon or by reason of such consignment or indorsement, shall have transferred to and vested in him all rights of suit, and be subject to the same liabilities in respect of such goods as if the contract contained in the bill of lading had been made with himself.

Where a banker, by instructions of a customer, accepts a bill drawn by a client of that customer against bills of lading, the banker will not be liable if the bills of lading should afterwards prove to be forgeries.

Along with the bill of lading there should be the insurance policy (SEE *Marine Insurance*), and the detailed description of the goods in the policy should agree with that in the bill of lading.

A 'port bill of lading' is one which is signed by an authorized person after the goods have been received by that person at the port of shipment.

A 'through bill of lading' is one which provides (or ought to provide) for the continuous responsibility of several railway and shipping undertakings from one place to another. There should be attached to every through bill of lading a certificate by the railway authority stating that the authority's agent who has signed the bill of lading is authorized to sign and verifying his signature.

A 'berth bill of lading' is the term used to distinguish a bill of lading issued by a liner, or by a vessel trading under liner conditions, from a bill of lading issued by a vessel carrying cargo under a charter party.

At the International Conference on Maritime Law, held in Brussels in October 1922, recommendations were made for the unification of certain Rules relating to bills of lading. At another meeting, in 1923, the Rules were amended. The Rules as so amended are set out, with modifications, in the Schedule to the Carriage of Goods by Sea Act 1924, and by that Act given the force of law with a view to establishing the liabilities, rights, and immunities attaching to carriers under bills of lading.

The Act applies to carriage of goods by sea from any port in Great Britain or Northern Ireland to any other port, whether in or outside Great Britain or Northern Ireland. By Section 3

> Every bill of lading or similar document of title, issued in Great Britain or Northern Ireland, which contains or is evidence of any contract to which the Rules apply shall contain an express statement that it is to have effect subject to the provisions of the said Rules as applied by this Act.

The Rules provide, among other things, that after receiving the goods into his charge the carrier, or the master or agent of the carrier shall, on demand of the shipper, issue to the shipper a bill of lading showing

1. the lading marks necessary for identification of the goods;
2. either the number of packages or pieces, or the

quantity, or weight, as the case may be, as furnished in writing by the shipper;
3. the apparent order and condition of the goods.

Such a bill of lading shall be prima facie evidence of the receipt by the carrier of the goods.

After the goods are loaded, the bill of lading to be issued by the carrier shall, if the shipper so demands, be a 'shipped' bill of lading, provided that if the shipper shall have previously taken up any document of title to such goods, he shall surrender the same as against the issue of the 'shipped' bill of lading, but at the option of the carrier such document of title may be noted at the port of shipment by the carrier with the name of the ship and the date of shipment, and when so noted it shall be deemed to constitute a 'shipped' bill of lading.

The provisions of the Rules shall not be applicable to charter parties, but if bills of lading are issued in the case of a ship under a charter party they shall comply with the terms of the Rules. Nothing in the Rules shall be held to prevent the insertion in a bill of lading of any lawful provision regarding general average.

Any agreement in a contract of carriage relieving the carrier from liability under the Rules shall be null and void; but where goods are to be carried from a port in Great Britain or Northern Ireland to any other port in Great Britain or Northern Ireland or to a port in the Irish Free State a special agreement may be entered into as to the liability and rights of the carrier, provided that no bill of lading is issued and that the terms agreed are embodied in a non-negotiable receipt (Section 4 of the Act and Article VI of the Schedule).

A carrier shall be liable for any loss exceeding £100 per package or unit, unless the nature and value of such goods have been declared by the shipper and inserted in the bill of lading.

The Caspiana Clause was inserted in bills of lading to cover shipowners from Mr Justice McNair's decision in *G. H. Renton & Co Ltd* v *Palmyra Trading Corporation of Panama* [1955] 3 WLR 535, where owing to strikes in the ports of London and Hull, cargoes destined according to the bill of lading for these ports were taken on to Hamburg and unloaded there, the shipowners leaving it to the cargo-owners to bring the goods from Hamburg to the UK at their own expense. The bill of lading provided for discharge at other ports in the events of the contract ports being closed by strike, but the strike clause was held inconsistent with, and repugnant to, the main purpose of the contract. The decision was reversed in the Court of Appeal, the reversal being confirmed in the House of Lords.

Stamp duty on bills of lading was abolished by the Finance Act 1949.

SEE *Charter Party; Mate's Receipt*

BILL OF SALE An assignment of personal chattels as security for a debt. Personal chattels include goods, furniture, and other articles capable of complete transfer by delivery. Trade machinery is deemed to be personal chattels. (See definition, as given in Bills of Sale Act 1878, of 'personal chattels' under *Chattels*.) Bills of sale are very rarely taken by bankers as security. A bill of sale may be absolute, or conditional by way of mortgage, the former evidencing an out and out transfer. The registration of a bill of sale by a debtor should act as a danger signal to a banker.

Section 4 of the Bills of Sale Act 1878 interprets the meaning of bill of sale as follows:

> The expression 'bill of sale' shall include bills of sale, assignments, transfers, declarations of trust without transfer, inventories of goods with receipt thereto attached, or receipts for purchase moneys of goods, and other assurances of personal chattels, and also powers of attorney, authorities, or licences to take possession of personal chattels as security for any debt, and also any agreement, whether intended or not to be followed by the execution of any other instrument, by which a right in equity to any personal chattels, or to any charge or security thereon, shall be conferred, but shall not include the following documents; that is to say, assignments for the benefit of the creditors of the person making or giving the same, marriage settlements, transfers, or assignments of any ship or vessel, or any share thereof, transfers of goods in the ordinary course of business of any trade or calling, bills of sale of goods in foreign parts or at sea, bills of lading, India warrants, warehouse-keepers' certificates, warrants or orders for the delivery of goods, or any other documents used in the ordinary course of business as proof of the possession or control of goods, or authorising or purporting to authorise, either by indorsement or by delivery, the possessor of such document to transfer or receive goods thereby represented.

The Bills of Sale Act does not apply to any debentures issued by any mortgage, loan or other incorporated company, and secured upon the capital stock or goods, chattels, and effects of such company (Section 17 of Bills of Sale Act (1878) Amendment Act 1882). By the Companies Act 1985, Section 396, a mortgage or charge, by a company, created or evidenced by an instrument which, if executed by an individual would require registration as a bill of sale, must be registered with the registrar of companies. (SEE *Registration of Charges*) A society incorporated under the Industrial and Provident Societies Act 1893 is not an incorporated company within the exceptions in Section 17 of the Bills of Sale Act 1882. (See the case under *Industrial and Provident Societies*.)

As to the avoidance of a general assignment of book debts unless registered as if it were a bill of sale, see Section 43, Bankruptcy Act 1914, under *Debts, Assignment of*.

A bill of sale given by way of security for the payment of money by the grantor must be in accordance with the form given in the Schedule to the Bills of Sale Act (1878) Amendment Act 1882.

It has been held, in the case of a bill of sale void because it was not drawn in accordance with the legal form, that the covenant in the bill to pay principal and interest was also void.

A bill of sale given in consideration of any sum under £30 shall be void (Section 12 of the Act).

A bill of sale must be registered at the Central Office of the Supreme Court within seven clear days after its execution; and requires reregistration once at least every five years. An assignment of a registered bill of sale does not require registration. Any person is entitled to search the register on payment of a fee of five pence.

Documents void as unregistered *conditional* bills of sale, that is bills of sale given as security and not out and out assignments, usually are also not in the required form. An example would be a simple document purporting to create a mortgage of goods. This would be void for two reasons: it is not in the required form; it is not registered. Only bills in the stipulated form may be registered. Certain specific documents have been held to be outside the scope of the Act (e.g. *North Western Bank* v *Poynter* [1895] AC 56).

The grantee of a bill of sale may seize the chattels thereby assigned if the grantor makes default in payment of the sums secured by the instrument, or becomes bankrupt, or suffers any of the goods to be distrained for rent, rates, or taxes, or fraudulently removes any of the goods, or fails, without reasonable execuse, to produce to the grantee his last receipts for rent, rates and taxes, or if execution has been levied against the grantor's goods under any judgment at law (Section 7, Bills of Sale Act (1878), Amendment Act 1882).

If two bills of sale are given upon the same property, priority is decided according to the order of the date of their registration.

A bill of sale by way of gift is void if the grantor becomes bankrupt within two years after the date, or at any time within ten years unless the claimants can prove that the grantor was solvent at the time he made the settlement. SEE *Settlements—(Settlor Bankrupt)*

BILL OF SALE, SHIP A registered ship, or a share therein, is transferred to a purchaser by a bill of sale in the prescribed form as required by the Merchant Shipping Act 1894. SEE *Ship*

BILL AS SECURITY Where a bill of exchange has been deposited or pledged as security for an advance, the holder of the bill is 'deemed to be a holder for value to the extent of the sum for which he has a lien' (Section 27(3), Bills of Exchange Act 1882). Where the holder, e.g. a banker, sues upon the bill at maturity and recovers the amount of it, if the sum recovered is greater than the debt owing by the person who deposited the bill, he must pay over the difference to that person. If the depositor's title to the bill was in order, the banker can recover the whole amount of the bill, but if the depositor's title was defective the banker can recover the amount of the bill to the extent of his lien, provided he had no notice of the depositor's defective title when he took the bill.

When a bill is lodged as security, it should be indorsed by the person depositing it, and a memorandum of deposit should be signed by the depositor to make it clear that the bill is pledged as security. When a banker holds a bill as security, he must present it for payment at maturity, and if it is dishonoured, he must give due notice of the dishonour.

A banker may, if necessary, sue for repayment of an overdraft at any time before the maturity of the bill which he holds as security (*Peacock* v *Pursell* (1863) 32 LJ CD 266).

BILL IN A SET Foreign bills are usually drawn in several parts, and, for safety, the parts may be transmitted by separate mails. Where a bill is drawn in that way it is said to be drawn in a set, and the various parts constitute one bill.

The rules regarding a bill drawn in a set are dealt with in Section 71 of the Bills of Exchange Act 1882, which is as follows:

> (1) Where a bill is drawn in a set, each part of the set being numbered, and containing a reference to the other parts, the whole of the parts constitute one bill.
>
> (2) Where the holder of a set indorses two or more parts to different persons, he is liable on every such part, and every indorser subsequent to him is liable on the part he has himself indorsed as if the said parts were separate bills.
>
> (3) Where two or more parts of a set are negotiated to different holders in due course, the holder whose title first accrues is as between such holders deemed the true owner of the bill; but nothing in this subsection shall affect the rights of a person who in due course accepts or pays the part first presented to him.
>
> (4) The acceptance may be written on any part, and it must be written on one part only. If the drawee accepts more than one part, and such accepted parts get into the hands of different holders in due course, he is liable on every such part as if it were a separate bill.

(5) When the acceptor of a bill drawn in a set pays it without requiring the part bearing his acceptance to be delivered up to him, and that part at maturity is outstanding in the hands of a holder in due course, he is liable to the holder thereof.

(6) Subject to the preceding rules, where any one part of a bill drawn in a set is discharged by payment or otherwise, the whole bill is discharged.

Where a bill is drawn in two parts, to save time one may be sent at once to the drawee for acceptance. The other part may be negotiated and contain a reference that the accepted part is in the possession of a certain firm as 'First and in need with Messrs Blank & Co, London'. If the bill is dishonoured, the agents named in the reference will, after it has been protested for non-payment, pay the bill for the honour of their principal.

A bill of lading is usually issued in a set, and each one is signed by some person authorized to sign the same on behalf of the shipowner, but he is liable only for one of them. As soon as one has been presented and the goods delivered, the others are void. But if the drawee of a bill of exchange accepts more parts than one, he is not discharged by paying one of them, but is liable on every such part. SEE *Bill of Lading*

BILLS FOR COLLECTION Bills left for collection (or 'short bills', as they are sometimes called—a term which originated in the custom of entering the bills in the cusomer's account in a column 'short' of the cash column) are bills which a customer leaves with his banker to be collected at maturity and of which the proceeds are to be credited to his account. Such bills may be entered to the credit of an account for bills received for collection and to the debit of a contra account, so that a proper record may be preserved. Bills for collection are also received from other bankers, frequently a day or two before maturity.

Where bills are paid to the credit of an account and are neither discounted nor drawn against, the bills remain the property of the customer. If the account becomes overdrawn, the banker has a lien upon them to that extent. If the bills are discounted, they become the absolute property of the banker.

Bills left for collection, even if indorsed to the bank, do not form part of the bank's assets, and if the bank should fail the owner may, subject to any lien of the bank, recover the bills.

When bills sent by correspondents for collection are accompanied by instructions, such as 'Deliver documents against payment', 'Incur no expense', 'If unpaid do not protest', the instructions must be carefully attended to.

When a bill is sent out for collection, many bankers place the word 'received' upon the back of the bill as a safeguard against the loss of the bill. A banker collecting a bill of exchange other than a cheque has no statutory protection against conversion. SEE *Bill of Exchange*

BILLS OF EXCHANGE ACT 1882 45 & 46 Vict c 61 An act 'to codify the law relating to bills of exchange, cheques and promissory notes' which received the Royal Assent on 18th August, 1882. It has been described as the 'perfect' Act of Parliament because of its masterly drafting and the fact that over 100 years it has required very little amendment and presented comparatively few problems of interpretation. SEE *Cheques Act 1957*

In view of the continuing importance of the Act to the financial and business community, all the Sections of the Act are listed below with a note of the relevant entries in this work.

Preliminary

1. This Act may be cited as the Bills of Exchange Act 1882.

2. In this Act, unless the context otherwise requires

'Acceptance' means an acceptance completed by delivery or notification.

'Action' includes counterclaim and set-off.

'Banker' includes a body of persons whether incorporated or not who carry on the business of banking.

'Bankrupt' includes any person whose estate is vested in a trustee or assignee under the law for the time being in force relating to bankruptcy.

'Bearer' means the person in possession of a bill or note which is payable to bearer.

'Bill' means bill of exchange, and 'note' means promissory note.

'Delivery' means transfer of possession, actual or constructive, from one person to another.

'Holder' means the payee or indorsee of a bill or note who is in possession of it, or the bearer thereof.

'Indorsement' means an indorsement completed by delivery.

'Issue' means the first delivery of a bill or note, complete in form to a person who takes it as a holder.

'Person' includes a body or persons whether incorporated or not.

'Value' means valuable consideration.

'Written' includes printed, and 'writing' includes print.

BILLS OF EXCHANGE ACT 1882

Section of Act		Entry to consult
PART I		
Preliminary		
1 Short title		See above
2 Interpretation of terms		See above
PART II		
Bills of Exchange		
Form and interpretation		
3 Bill of exchange defined		Bill of Exchange
4 Inland and foreign bills		Inland Bill, Foreign Bill
5 Effect where different parties to the bill are the same person		Drawer Drawee
6 Address to drawee		Drawee
7 Certainty required as to payee		Payee
8 What bills are negotiable	s.s. (1), (2)	Negotiation of Bill of Exchange
	s.s. (3)	Bearer
	s.s. (4), (5)	Order
9 Sum payable	s.s. (1), (2)	Bill of Exchange
	s.s. (3)	Interest on Bill
10 Bill payable on demand		Time of Payment of Bill
11 Bill payable at a future time		Time of Payment of Bill
12 Omission of date in bill payable after date		Date
13 Ante-dating and post-dating		Date
14 Computation of time of payment		Time of Payment of Bill
15 Case of need		Referee in Case of Need
16 Optional stipulations by drawer or indorser		Drawer
17 Definition and requisites of acceptance		Acceptance
18 Time for acceptance		Acceptance
19 General and qualified acceptances		Acceptance, General Acceptance, Qualified
20 Inchoate instruments		Inchoate Instrument
21 Delivery		Delivery of Bill
Capacity and authority of parties		
22 Capacity of parties		Parties to Bill of Exchange
23 Signature essential to liability		Parties to Bill of Exchange
24 Forged or unauthorised signature		Forgery
25 Procuration signatures		Agent
26 Person signing as agent or in representative capacity		Agent
The consideration for a bill		
27 Value and holder for value	s.s. (1)	Consideration for Bill of Exchange
	s.s. (2), (3)	Holder for Value
28 Accommodation bill or party		Accommodation Bill
29 Holder in due course		Holder in Due Course
30 Presumption of value and good faith		Holder in Due Course
Negotiation of bills		
31 Negotiation of bill		Negotiation of Bill of Exchange
32 Requisites of a valid indorsement		Indorsement
33 Conditional indorsement		Indorsement
34 Indorsement in blank and special indorsement		Indorsement
35 Restrictive indorsement		Indorsement
36 Negotiation of overdue or dishonoured bill		Negotiation of Bill of Exchange
37 Negotiation of bill to party already liable thereon		Negotiation of Bill of Exchange
38 Rights of the holder		Holder in Due Course
General duties of the holder		
39 When presentment for acceptance is necessary		Presentment for Acceptance
40 Time for presenting bill payable after sight		Presentment for Acceptance
41 Rules as to presentment for acceptance and excuses for non-presentment		Presentment for Acceptance
42 Non-acceptance		Dishonour of Bill of Exchange

Section of Act	Entry to consult
43 Dishonour by non-acceptance and its consequences	Dishonour of Bill of Exchange
44 Duties as to qualified acceptances	Acceptance, Qualified
45 Rules as to presentment for payment	Presentment for Payment
46 Excuses for delay or non-presentment for payment	Presentment for Payment
47 Dishonour by non-payment	Dishonour of Bill of Exchange
48 Notice of dishonour and effect of non-notice	Dishonour of Bill of Exchange
49 Rules as to notice of dishonour	Dishonour of Bill of Exchange
50 Excuses for non-notice and delay	Dishonour of Bill of Exchange
51 Noting or protest of bill	Protest
52 Duties of holder as regards drawee or acceptor	Presentment for Payment
Liabilities of parties	
53 Funds in hands of drawee	Drawee
54 Liability of acceptor	Acceptance
55 Liability of drawer or indorser s.s. (1)	Drawer
s.s. (2)	Indorser
56 Stranger signing bill liable as indorser	Indorser
57 Measure of damages against parties to dishonoured bill	Dishonour of Bill of Exchange
58 Transferor by delivery and transferee	Transferor by Delivery
Discharge of bill	
59 Payment in due course	Payment of Bill
60 Banker paying demand draft whereon indorsement is forged	Payment of Bill
61 Acceptor, the holder at maturity	Payment of Bill
62 Express waiver or renunciation	Payment of Bill
63 Cancellation	Cancellation of Bills of Exchange
64 Alteration of bill	Alterations to Bills of Exchange
Acceptance and payment for honour	
65 Acceptance for honour supra protest	Acceptance for Honour
66 Liability of acceptor for honour	Acceptance for Honour
67 Presentment to acceptor for honour	Presentment for Payment
68 Payment for honour supra protest	Payment for Honour
Lost instruments	
69 Holder's right to duplicate of lost bill	Lost Bill of Exchange
70 Action on lost bill	Lost Bill of Exchange
Bill in a set	
71 Rules as to sets	Bill in a Set
Conflict of laws	
72 Rules where laws conflict	Foreign Bill
PART III	
Cheques on a banker	
73 Cheque defined	Cheque
74 Presentment of cheque for payment	Presentment for Payment
75 Revocation of banker's authority	Payment of Cheque
Crossed cheques	
76 General and special crossings defined	Crossed Cheque
77 Crossing by drawer or after issue	Crossed Cheque
78 Crossing a material part of cheque	Crossed Cheque
79 Duties of banker as to crossed cheques	Crossed Cheque
80 Protection to bankers and drawer where cheque is crossed	Crossed Cheque
81 Effect of 'not negotiable' crossing on holder	Crossed Cheque
82 Repealed	Cheques Act, 1957 (Section 4)
PART IV	
Promissory Notes	
83 Promissory note defined	Promissory Note
84 Delivery necessary	Promissory Note
85 Joint and several notes	Promissory Note
86 Note payable on demand	Presentment for Payment
87 Presentment of note for payment	Presentment for Payment
88 Liability of maker	Promissory Note
89 Application of Part II to notes	Promissory Note

BILLS OF EXCHANGE (TIME OF NOTING) ACT 1917

Section of Act		Entry to consult
PART V		
Supplementary		
90	Good faith	Good Faith
91	Signature by agent	Agent
92	Computation of time	Time of Payment of Bill
93	When noting equivalent to protests	Protest
94	Protest when notary not accessible	Protest
95	Dividend warrants may be crossed	Crossed Cheque
96	(Repealed by Statute Law Revision Act, 1898, 61 & 62 Vict. c. 22.)	
97	Savings in relation to certain other Acts	
98	Savings of summary diligence in Scotland	
99	Construction with other Acts, etc.	
100	Parol evidence allowed in certain judicial proceedings in Scotland	
	Schedule 1. Form of protest	Protest

BILLS OF EXCHANGE (TIME OF NOTING) ACT 1917 This Act repealed Section 51(4), Bills of Exchange Act 1882, which required a dishonoured bill to be noted on the day of its dishonour and provided instead that a bill of exchange 'may be noted on the day of its dishonour and must be noted not later than the next succeeding business day'.

BIMETALLISM A double standard, of gold and silver, circulates gold and silver coins containing the full weight of metal represented by their face value. The fluctuating value of silver in relation to gold makes this a difficult system to control, and it was abandoned in England in 1816 after nearly a century of experiment, during which time chipped and debased coins drove out of circulation the full-weight coins. Gold in particular was always worth melting down for sale as metal. This is unlike 'symmetalism' which is an amalgamated standard, combining units of gold and silver as the basis of the currency with no coins related only to one metal.

BLANK CHEQUE A cheque which is signed by the drawer without any amount being filled in. When such a cheque is issued, it is usually with the intention that the payee or some other authorized person should fill in an amount as sanctioned by the drawer. A blank cheque is an unsatisfactory document to give to anyone, as it might easily fall into the hands of some person who would make a wrong use of it. See the case of *London Joint Stock Bank Ltd* v *Macmillan and Arthur* under *Alterations to Bills of Exchange*. See also the provisions of Section 20 of the Bills of Exchange Act 1882 under *Inchoate instrument*.

BLANK INDORSEMENT Where an indorsement on a bill of exchange specifies no indorsee, it is an indorsement in blank. A bill so indorsed becomes payable to bearer. The same term applies to the indorsement of cheques. Any holder may convert a blank indorsement into a special indorsement by writing above the indorser's signature a direction to pay the bill or cheque to, or to the order of, himself or some other person. SEE *Indorsement*

BLANK TRANSFER A blank transfer of stock or shares is a transfer on which a material particular is lacking: the date is not, in this sense, a material particular. It is sometimes used when shares are given as security for a debt, the intention being that if default is made in payment the lender may fill in his own name, as transferee, or insert the date, and send the instrument forward for registration. If a blank transfer is to be held unstamped, it should not be dated, otherwise it cannot after 30 days from execution, be stamped except under a penalty.

A blank transfer, however, in those companies where the transfer must be under seal, is not a satisfactory security. In the case of *Powell* v *London and Provincial Bank* [1893] 2 Ch 555, a stock certificate and a blank transfer were given to the bank as security. The bank subsequently inserted its own name in the transfer and executed it, and was duly registered by the company. Lord Justice Lindley said

> in order to acquire the legal title to stock or shares in companies governed by the Companies Clauses Consolidation Act 1845, you must have a deed executed by the transferor, and you must have that transfer registered. Until you have got *both* you have not got the legal title in the transferee. Now what took place here was this: Mr Edwards gave to the bank a transfer sealed by him, and, so far as form goes, probably delivered by him to the bank, but with blanks. It was not in a complete form. It was never in that form in which such an instrument, however much wax there might be at the bottom, could amount to a deed by the transferor. We all know that both at common law and under these statutes if you execute a transfer in blank, that instrument with the blanks is not a deed. Then what happened is this. That document so executed by Edwards in blank was

filled up afterwards by the bank, probably as was intended, and the bank itself was put in as the transferee and the bank got itself registered. ... What was the effect of what had been done? It was not that the bank got a good title. The registration of the stock in the bank, unless preceded by a valid deed transferring the stock from the owner of it, does not give the transferee a good title at all. We have not to consider the effect of documents executed in blank as agreements enforceable in equity. We have nothing to do with that, but we are considering the legal title of the bank. The bank had no legal title at all.

In that case the stock certificate proved to be part of a trust estate, and the bank, although it had no notice of the trust, had its title postponed to the prior equitable title of the persons interested under the trust.

In *France* v *Clark* (1884) 50 LT 1, 26 Ch Div 256, the Court of Appeal held that a person who without enquiry takes from another an instrument signed in blank by a third party, and fills up the blank, cannot, even in the case of a negotiable instrument, claim the benefit of being a purchaser for value without notice, so as to acquire a greater right than the person from whom he himself received the instrument. In *Fry & Mason* v *Smellie & Taylor* (1912) 106 LT 405, where a principal handed to his agent the documents of title to shares together with a transfer signed in blank, and gave the agent authority (though limited) to borrow thereon, and the agent borrowed in excess of his authority, the lender being ignorant of any limitation of the authority, it was held by the Court of Appeal that the principal could not take advantage of any limitation in point of amount which he placed upon the authority to raise money as against the lender who had no notice of it. Kennedy, LJ, said

One of two innocent persons had to suffer by the misconduct of the agent; and the burden of loss ought in equity to fall upon him who intended his agent to obtain money from the other party, and clothed his agent with an apparently unqualified authority to obtain the documents for that purpose.

In the case of those companies where debentures and shares are transferable by an instrument under hand (a deed under seal not being required), a blank transfer does form a satisfactory security, and the transferee's name can subsequently be filled in. In the event of the transferor's death, however, before the blanks are filled up, the banker's authority to do so is cancelled.

The reason why a blank transfer under seal cannot legally have any blanks subsequently filled in by a banker is that a document under seal is a deed and takes effect from its delivery. To enable a blank transfer under seal to be effectually completed, the blanks should be filled in the presence of the transferor, or by his authority under seal, or the deed should be redelivered by him.

In *Coleman* v *London County and Westminster Bank* [1916] 2 Ch 353, the bank suffered where trustees charged with blank transfers shares belonging to the Trust for a private liability of the settlor. It was held that the prior equitable title of the beneficiaries prevailed. The transfer into the name of a bank or its nominee company will usually avoid this risk in the absence of contrary notice at the time the charge is taken. That is to say the bank becomes the legal mortgagee. SEE *Certificate; Transfer of Shares*

BLIND PERSONS There are two categories of financial assistance for blind persons: blind person's relief for income tax purposes and a 'blindness addition' under the supplementary benefits scheme.

Blind person's relief for income tax purposes may be claimed by any person who is registered as a blind person with the local authority during all or part of a particular tax year. If both husband and wife are blind, they may both claim. A married man living with his wife who is blind may claim relief unless the wife's income is separately taxed. Total blindness is not necessary: it is sufficient that the eyesight is so poor that it is impossible to perform any work for which eyesight is normally used.

'Blindness addition' under the supplementary benefits scheme will be payable to any blind person who qualifies in other respects for supplementary benefit as a person of limited means.

A blind person may also be entitled to disablement benefit (q.v.).

BLOCKED CURRENCY A currency of a country is said to be blocked when the government of that country creates categories of its currency that can be used only for purchases within the country. A further extension is seen when the government decrees that some of the blocked currency arising from particular transactions can be utilized only for certain specific purposes. This type of regulation was carried furthest in Germany during the Hitler regime, where there were numerous categories of 'internal' marks, such as the Travelmark, which could only be used by visitors to Germany, and the Askimark, which was used to pay for imports from certain South American states, such states having to spend such marks in the purchase of German manufactures.

The price of blocked currencies such as these is quoted at so much discount in the 'free' currency, which itself tends in course of time to become little more than a bookkeeping unit. SEE *Exchange Restrictions Control Act 1947*

BLOOD STOCK, INSURANCE OF A number of insurance companies will provide cover for death or injury to animals which are valuable for racing or breeding.

BLUE CHIPS Literally, the higher value blue chips used in poker, but applied loosely to ordinary shares in first-class industrial companies.

BOLTON COMMITTEE The Committee of Inquiry on Small Firms (Chairman: J. E. Bolton) appointed in July 1969 with the following terms of reference:

1. To consider the role of small firms in the national economy, the facilities available to them and the problems confronting them; and to make recommendations. For the purpose of the study, a small firm might be defined broadly as one with not more than 200 employees, but this should not be regarded as a rigid definition.
2. In the course of the study, it will be necessary to examine in particular the profitability of small firms and the availability of finance. Regard should also be paid to the special functions of small firms, for example as innovators and specialist suppliers.

The Committee issued its report in September 1971. The Committee considered such matters as the characteristics and performance of small firms, their place in the economy, small firms in other countries, their particular problems, sources of finance and the impact of taxation, industrial training, monopolies and restrictive practices legislation and the impact of Government and local authority requirements in matters of form-filling and planning applications, etc. The Committee's Research Unit published the results of 16 separate surveys covering the activities of small firms in particular industries and the financial facilities available for small firms. The Committee arrived at a number of major conclusions, including the following:

> The small firm sector remains one of substantial importance in the UK economy: its output is equivalent to about one-fifth of the GNP and it employs more people than the entire public sector.
> The contribution of small businessmen to the vitality of society is inestimable. The qualities of vigour, enterprise and ambition which characterise so many of them have made them natural community leaders and they have been benefactors to their localities, to the arts and in many other ways which help to make life meaningful and pleasant. Above all, their spirit of independence is a strength to the nation . . .
> The small firm is in many ways a highly efficient organism, better adapted to the exploitation of certain kinds of economic opportunity than larger units and having some special advantages which derive from the intense commitment of the owner-manager.

The Committee made a number of wide-ranging recommendations on such subjects as taxation, company law, industrial development and planning controls and recommended that a Small Firms Advisory Bureau should be established. Many of the recommendations were subsequently adopted as Government policy and a Small Firms Advisory Bureau was in fact set up to assist smaller companies with advice on technical, financial and management problems.

The Bolton Committee and its Research Unit came to the conclusion that there was no 'institutional deficiency' in the provision of finance for small companies (SEE *Wilson Committee*). It was of the opinion, however, that: 'Small businessmen, and to some extent their professional advisers, have a lamentable ignorance of the sources available to meet specific financial needs! The Report did suggest that the clearing banks might improve their services to the small businessmen in two particular respects:

1. To impose as a normal condition for the grant of an overdraft to a firm the production of regular cashflow statements, or the employment of adequate estimating and budgetary systems.
2. 'The bank manager should be ideally placed to advise such small businessmen on the availability, the cost and the advantages of different forms of finance in cases where an overdraft facility is not the appropriate kind of finance for the purpose in mind.'

It was these recommendations in particular that prompted the leading banks to introduce business advisory services, particularly for the smaller customers.

BONA FIDE Latin for 'in good faith'. The opposite of bona fide is *mala fide*, in bad faith. The Bills of Exchange Act 1882 (q.v.) states that a thing is deemed to be done in good faith, within the meaning of the Act, where it is in fact done honestly, whether it is done negligently or not.

BOND(S) The correct and traditional use of the word means a binding engagement (*Oxford English Dictionary*). Hence, the Stock Exchange motto 'My word is my bond'. In its more tangible, i.e. written, form a bond is a deed by which one person binds himself to another, either to pay a certain sum of money or to fulfil a certain contract. Hence, Shylock, in the Merchant of Venice, 'let him look to his bond'. Bonds may also be issued in respect of obligations entered into by institutions and governments (SEE *Bearer Bonds; Busted Bonds*). The shorter-dated securities of the British Government, i.e. those with maturity dates of five years hence or less, are usually referred to as bonds, as are the fixed interest securities issued by corporations and governments throughout the world. SEE *Eurobonds*

A less obvious but now widely accepted use of the term is in relation to single-premium life policies. These are in the form of linked life assurance (q.v.) for lump sum investment purposes and may take the form of gilt bonds, money bonds, etc. SEE *Managed Bond; Property Bond*

The term nowadays is used in wide variety of situations, usually indicating a certificate or other document evidencing a money obligation, e.g. granny bonds (index-linked savings certificates (q.v.)). SEE ALSO *Performance Bond*

BOND-WASHING The practice of bond-washing is thought to have begun on any scale in the early 1930s. The transaction took place in the period during which it was possible to deal in, mainly, gilt-edged stocks both cum-dividend and ex-dividend. The bond-washer purchased stock cum-dividend and sold it immediately afterwards ex-dividend, thus taking the benefit of the taxed dividend. If he were a dealer in securities, he could take the benefit of the 'loss' between the buying and selling prices of the stock, which would enable him to reclaim the tax deducted from the dividend. The purchase of a dividend for the difference between the two prices was beneficial to those not liable to income tax, including non-residents and charities.

A further stage entailed the artificial creation of dividends by jobbing firms who had an arrangement with the Inland Revenue whereby the complications which arose through jobbers having a balance of dividends either due to them or from them through buying more stock cum-dividend than they had sold, or vice versa, were ironed out. This arrangement incidentally enabled jobbers to collect net dividends through the market, purporting to be taxed at source, which had never existed. This tax had never been paid to the Inland Revenue but was nevertheless reclaimable from them. The second artificial dividend arose where the seller of ex-dividend stock and the buyer of cum-dividend stock were both entitled to a dividend.

The practice was stopped by the Finance Acts of 1959 and 1960. SEE Supplement

BONUS CERTIFICATE On a division of profits by an insurance company, a policy holder, who partakes in the profits, receives a bonus certificate from the company certifying that the sum of £. . . has been added to and will be payable with the sum assured under the policy. A policy holder may, instead of having the bonus added to the policy, elect to have the bonus paid in cash or used to reduce the annual premium. SEE *Life Assurance*

BONUS SHARES (BONUS ISSUE) This is the capitalization by a company of reserves or undistributed profits and the issue of new additional shares to the members. The term 'bonus' is not appropriate because there is no element of bounty in such a distribution—a better term is 'capitalization issue'.

A company may capitalize its reserves in this way provided there is a power to do so in the articles of association. Since 1948, Table A (as now amended by the 1980 Companies Act) has contained such power.

An issue of bonus shares is not a 'distribution' within the meaning of the 1980 Act and is, therefore, not governed by the special rules contained in that Act. SEE *Distribution*

The main purpose of a bonus issue is to bring the capital of a company more closely in line with the level of the company's assets. In general, a simple bonus issue is regarded as 'capital' for tax purposes in the UK (*Commissioners of the Inland Revenue* v *Blott* (1920) 36 TLR 575). There are circumstances, however, in which such a capitalization issue may be subject to income tax and reference should be made to Sections 234 and 235, Income and Corporation Taxes Act 1970.

BOOK DEBTS The item 'book debts', which appears in the balance sheet of a trade or a trading concern, represents the amount owing for goods sold, etc., as shown by the books.

The definition of a book debt is not, however, entirely free from doubt. Buckley, J, in *Independent Automatic Sales Ltd* v. *Knowles & Foster* [1962] 3 WLR 974, expressed the view that it was a debt that now or in the future *could* be entered in the books of the company or trader to whom it was due, which is a very wide definition. SEE *Debts, Assignment of*

This principle, however, was varied by the decision in *Paul and Frank Ltd and Another* v *Discount Bank (Overseas) Ltd* [1966] 2 All ER 922, where it was held that a charge on money due under an Export Credit Guarantee Department policy was not registrable as a charge on a book debt.

BORROWING POWERS (COMPANIES) The component aspects of a company's borrowing powers are (1) the power as such to borrow, (2) the nature of the permitted borrowing and (3) the extent of the borrowing. The power to borrow is usually expressly given in the objects clause of the memorandum of association. Trading companies have implied power to borrow, but nevertheless borrowing powers are invariably included in the objects clause of such companies.

The power to borrow extends only to the furtherance of those objects set out in the company's memorandum of association. This was well illustrated in the case of *Introductions Ltd* v *National Provincial Bank Ltd* [1970] Ch 199. This concerned a company which was originally set up to assist visitors to the Festival of Britain in 1951 but subsequently went into the business of pig farming. The company failed in 1965, with liabilities of £2 million, including an overdraft at the bank for which debentures had been given as security. The liquidator of the company claimed that the security was invalid because the business conducted by the company was *ultra vires* and thus the borrowing must also be *ultra vires*. In upholding the High Court judgment against the bank, Harman, LJ, in the Court of Appeal said 'borrowing is not an end in itself and must be for some purpose of the company; . . . you cannot convert a power into an object merely by saying so'. SEE *Ultra Vires*

As regards the method of borrowing, the articles of association generally put the exercise of the company's borrowing powers in the directors' hands either by a clause authorizing them to exercise all such powers of the company as are not required by the articles or the 1948 Companies Act to be exercised by the general meeting (see Article 79 of Table A), or by a separate clause authorizing them to borrow. Infrequently, however, it is provided that borrowing powers must be exercised by the company in general meeting.

If, as rarely happens, there is in the memorandum of association a limitation on a company's borrowing powers and a company exceeds such limit, the result may be serious for the lender, as such borrowing will be *ultra vires* the company and incapable of ratification. Occasionally, if there is a stipulation in a loan stock agreement or a preference share issue as to a company's borrowing, it is reflected in the memorandum of association, although more frequently it is recapitulated in the articles of association which set out the directors' borrowing powers.

In most cases, however, limitation is found in the articles; this will be a limitation to the extent to which the directors may exercise the company's borrowing powers. If the articles are silent upon this point, the position is governed by Table A (q.v.), which in the 1948 Companies Act provided that the directors may exercise all the borrowing powers of the company up to the amount of the company's issued capital. The article further provides that in computing such borrowing, temporary loans obtained from a company's bankers in the ordinary course of business are excluded. A lender is not concerned to see or enquire if the limit is observed. If the powers prescribed in the articles are exceeded, the company in general meeting may ratify such excess.

In reckoning the extent to which a company has availed itself of its borrowing powers, discounted bills and trade debts are excluded. Public companies may not exercise borrowing powers until they have received their certificate of authority to commence business. The receipt of application moneys for debentures is not a borrowing in this connection.

Where a corporation has been created by an individual statute, the borrowing powers are to be found in that statute. In the case of the nationalized industries, for example, the borrowing powers of the Transport Commission are to be found in the Transport Act 1962; of the Gas Council, in the Gas Act 1948; of the Electricity Council, in the Electricity Act 1957; and of the Coal Board, in the Coal Industry Nationalisation Act 1946.

As to the borrowing powers of administrators and executors, infants, liquidators, trustees and undischarged bankrupts, see under those entries.

BOTTOMRY BOND The word 'bottomry' means a system of lending money to a shipowner for the purposes of a voyage on the security of the ship, the lender losing his money if the ship is lost (*Oxford English Dictionary*). A bottomry bond is a document by which the master or captain of a ship charges or hypothecates (q.v.) the ship as security for the repayment of a loan. The circumstances under which such an instrument could be created are where the ship is in a foreign port and certain repairs are absolutely necessary in order to enable the ship to continue its voyage, and the captain has no other means of raising the money required to effect the repairs, and is unable to communicate with the owners. The money borrowed upon a bottomry bond is repayable only in the event of the ship reaching its destination. A lender must exercise the greatest care, as a captain has no authority to bind the shipowner, except in case of necessity.

BOURSE The name of the principal place in each country (or large town doing an active foreign trade) where the balance of trade between that country and others is settled by the mutual interchange of bills, and where merchants resort to buy and sell merchandise. They are international clearing houses.

At a bourse, an exporter of goods to another country sells his draft, so getting payment for the goods exported; and it is there also that an importer goes to buy a draft (the same that the above exporter sells) which he remits to the foreign seller, so making payment for the goods imported.

In Britain, foreign bill business was, prior to 1921, done as the Royal Exchange, London, but is now conducted through the individual houses in the City. In Continental Europe, stock exchange business is also conducted at the bourses and, in common parlance, the Paris Stock Exchange is usually referred to as the Bourse.

BRANCHES OF BANKS For some purposes the branches of a bank are treated as though they were separate banks, e.g. one branch is not obliged to pay a cheque drawn upon another branch, and one branch, may, in giving notice of dishonour, treat the other branch, in the matter of time, as a separate institution. On the other hand, branches are regarded as parts of one body in certain cases, e.g. a credit balance at one branch may be used to reduce an overdrawn account of the same customer at another branch (SEE *Set Off*); and where a customer has two accounts, one in credit at one branch and one overdrawn at another branch, and he presents a cheque at the branch with the credit balance, the banker is entitled, in considering whether he should pay the cheque, to regard the two accounts as one account, but if there has been an agreement, or the practice in the past has been to treat the two accounts as quite distinct, the banker could not, without due notice, suddenly change his method of dealing. A customer, however, has no right to demand that any accounts he may have at different branches be treated as one account with respect to cheques drawn. His cheque is (in the absence of express agreement) payable only at the branch on which drawn, and that branch may, if necessary, dishonour the cheque, even though the customer has adequate funds at another branch.

It has been held that notice of the stopping of a cheque at one branch of a bank is not notice to the other branches. SEE *Payment Stopped*

For most purposes the head offices and branches are regarded as one body. It has been held that notice to the head office of an act of bankruptcy is equivalent to notice to the branches, allowing for reasonable time to communicate the notice to the branches. SEE *Acts of Bankruptcy*

Service of a Garnishee Order *nisi* on the head office is service on the bank, but reasonable time to communicate with the branches must be allowed. SEE *Garnishee Order*

Where a crossed cheque drawn on one branch is paid to credit of a customer's account at another branch of the same bank, the branches in such a case may be regarded either as one bank (in which case protection against a forged indorsement is obtained by Section 60 of the Bills of Exchange Act) or as practically two different banks, payment being made by one to the other (in which case the payment fulfils the requirements of Section 80).

A customer may pay in at any branch to his credit at the branch where he keeps his account, but the amount is not available to meet cheques until advice of the credit has been received. A bank may incur liability if a cheque is dishonoured at one branch consequent upon the neglect of another branch in dispatching promptly an advice of such credit.

A customer may also, as a rule, arrange to have his cheques cashed at other branches. In such a case the branch where his account is kept advises the branch where they are to be cashed to pay them up to a certain limited amount in any one day, or as may be desired, and furnishes at the same time a specimen of the drawer's signature. When a cheque drawn on one branch is paid, under advice, by another branch, it is considered that the bank obtains the protection (*inter alia*) of Section 60 of the Bills of Exchange Act (SEE UNDER *Payment of Cheque*). But if a branch cashes a cheque on another branch, without an advice to do so, the former branch does not act in the matter of cashing it as the bank of the drawer and can rely only upon the credit of the person who presented it. SEE *Open Credits*

BREACH OF TRUST A breach of trust may arise from some act or default of a trustee in carrying out the terms of his trust, e.g. by his neglecting, contravening or exceeding his duties. A trustee commits a breach of trust if he acts contrary to the conditions laid down in the deed or will under which the trust is created, or if he invests trust funds in securities other than those authorized either by law or the trust deed. It is the duty of a trustee to acquaint himself with the affairs of the trust and the nature of the trust property, to satisfy himself that the trust fund is properly invested and that his predecessors have not committed breaches of trust. If, through his omission to enquire into these matters, the trust suffers a loss, a trustee may be liable although he was not a party to the breach as such. It is the duty of a trustee to obtain control of, and preserve, the trust's property for the benefit of the beneficiaries. He must not, therefore, leave any part of the trust assets in the names of unauthorized persons.

A breach of trust by one trustee does not of itself render a co-trustee liable for that breach. In all cases of breach of trust, the trustee committing the breach is personally liable for the loss or damage to the trust fund.

By the Trustee Act 1925, if it appears to the court that a trustee is personally liable for any breach of trust, but has acted honestly and reasonably, and ought fairly to be excused for the breach, the court may relieve him either wholly or partly from personal liability (Section 61).

The court may authorize dealings with trust property which cannot be effected by trustees by reason of the absence of any power for that purpose in the trust instrument (Section 57). SEE *Trustee; Trustee Investments*

BRETTON WOODS The name given to a conference of the United Nations held in 1944 at Bretton Woods, USA, for the formulation of a post-war international financial policy. The two main problems it considered were the provision of international machinery to ensure economic equilibrium and the creation of stable currency and exchange conditions.

Its deliberations resulted in the establishment of an International Monetary Fund (q.v.) for establishing stable relations between currencies, and of an International Bank for Reconstruction and Development (q.v.) to enable former occupied countries to get finance for productive enterprises.

BRIDGING LOAN A short-term advance to a customer pending the receipt by him of funds from another source. The most common example is the loan of the whole or part of the purchase money for a house pending the receipt of the proceeds of a house which is being sold.

Early in 1973, with the agreement of the Law Society, a new form (Form 4) of solicitors' undertaking for use in connection with bridging finance was introduced, embodying an irrevocable authority from the customer to the solicitor for him to pay to the bank the net proceeds of sale after all disbursements have been made. It is thought that such authority acts as an equitable assignment of the proceeds of sale, valid against a trustee in bankruptcy (q.v.).

BRITISH BANKERS' ASSOCIATION (BBA) This is the representative trade association for recognized banks operating in the UK. The association was formed in 1920 by a reorganization of the Central Association of Bankers into which was merged the Association of English Country Bankers. However, it was not until 1972, when membership was extended to cover the UK banking industry as a whole and when Britain's entry into the EEC was negotiated, that its present functions developed.

Membership is divided into two categories. Full members, of whom in 1983 there were 64, consist of recognized banks established under British law with their head offices in the UK and which are British controlled. Branches or subsidiaries in the UK of banks with head offices in other member states of the EEC may also apply for full membership. Other banks operating in the UK are associate members, of which there are currently 221.

The affairs of the BBA are managed by a General Council, chaired by the President, and by an Executive Committee appointed by the General Council. The Association represents the views of its members to the Bank of England, to Government departments and to other bodies where it is appropriate for a common banking industry approach to be made.

In Europe, the principal functions of the Association are to participate in the work of the Banking Federation of the Community and to represent the views of the UK banking industry to the institutions of the Community.

A wide range of subjects is dealt with by the BBA, including banking law, banking supervision, company law, consumer protection, capital markets and fiscal matters.

BRITISH INSURANCE ASSOCIATION (BIA) The Association was founded in 1917 and now has approximately 330 members. It is the central association of insurance companies authorized to transact any class or classes of insurance or reinsurance business in the UK. The constitution of the BIA defines its objects as 'the protection, promotion and advancement of the common interests of all classes of insurance business'. When the BIA was founded, the essential object was to create an organization which would handle problems of wide common interest without encroaching on the rights of individual member companies or of the other market bodies. The Association's prime purpose, therefore, is to deal with those matters which are beyond the scope of, or uneconomic for, any one company or any other insurance body to handle alone, and in this way to further the interests of member companies.

The BIA sets out to achieve this by

1. acting as a single authoritative voice for members and as a channel of communication between them and the Government, financial and other bodies which seek to consult the insurance market;
2. conducting a public relations programme de-

signed to improve public appreciation and understanding of insurance;
3. studying a wide variety of technical subjects on behalf of members;
4. operating a system whereby complaints against member companies can be investigated at senior level within the company concerned.

There are some matters which are outside the scope of the BIA, for example, the fixing of premium rates, underwriting, and staff matters.

Much of the work of the BIA is conducted through a system of specialized committees, panels and units comprising executives or technicians from insurance companies serving in a voluntary capacity and contributing their particular knowledge and experience for the benefit of the whole company market.

The worldwide premium income of BIA members in 1982–83 was approximately £11,000 million.

In 1969, jointly with Lloyd's, the Association set up the Motor Insurance Repair Research Centre at Thatcham in Berkshire. The Centre deals with repairs to damaged vehicles and issues recommendations on repair times and methods. These recommendations are made available to insurers, the repair trade and motor manufacturers.

In 1967, the BIA established, near Oxford, its first Motor Engineers Unit, employing staff engineers to inspect damaged vehicles on behalf of BIA member companies transacting motor business. Since then, 10 more units have been established to cover a wide band of the country stretching from Cornwall to the Wash. A unit based on Chester serves the whole of North Wales, another at Lancaster covers North Western England as far north as Carlisle, and there is now a unit covering Newcastle upon Tyne.

The units between them employ 50 motor engineers, inspecting damaged vehicles at the rate of around 60,000 a year. The main function of the staff motor engineer is to inspect damaged vehicles to ensure that the extent of the damage and the estimated cost of repair have been correctly calculated and to negotiate accordingly on behalf of the insurance company concerned.

BRITISH INSURANCE BROKERS' ASSOCIATION (BIBA) This is the professional trade body for insurance brokers. Its membership consists of firms and companies registered under the Insurance Brokers (Registration) Act 1977 (q.v.).

The BIBA was formed in 1977 by amalgamation of the former organizations for insurance brokers, the Corporation, Association and Federation respectively of Insurance Brokers and the Lloyd's Insurance Brokers Association.

The objects of the BIBA are to provide a central organization for insurance brokers and

> generally to do all such things as from time to time may be calculated to safeguard the interests of the community and promise the efficiency and proper professional conduct of insurance brokers, with a view to ensuring for the community the existence of a class of insurance intermediary, known as insurance brokers, who can be relied upon as being trustworthy and duly qualified to perform the duties of their profession.

SEE *Insurance Broking*

BRITISH OVERSEAS AND COMMONWEALTH BANKS' ASSOCIATION (BOCBA) The Association was founded in 1917 as the British Overseas Banks' Association, and the name was changed in 1964 in recognition of the fact that a number of its members, as the Commonwealth developed, had moved their place of incorporation from London to their countries of main activity. All British banks with a substantial proportion of their business conducted through their own offices overseas and all Commonwealth banks with offices in London are eligible for membership.

The Association serves as a forum for the exchange of ideas on subjects which particularly concern its membership. It is affiliated to the British Bankers' Association (q.v.) and nominates representatives to serve on most of that association's committees. It liaises direct in its members' interests with the Bank of England and Government ministries.

BRITISH SAVINGS BONDS These were a British Government security issued by the Department for National Savings and were on sale from 1st April, 1968 to 31st December, 1979. The last issue of the bonds was 9½ per cent British Savings Bonds (2nd Issue) repayable five years after purchase with a premium of £4 for every £100 invested. The maximum holding was £10,000.

BRITISH TECHNOLOGY GROUP SEE *National Enterprise Board*

BROKEN ACCOUNT An account is said to be 'broken' when operations upon it are stopped, and all subsequent transactions are passed through a new account. This takes place, for example, upon the death of a guarantor, when a banker wishes to preserve his recourse against the estate of the deceased. Unless the debtor's account is broken, all payments to credit go to release the guarantor, and all debits form a fresh unsecured advance. A banker cannot break an account arbitrarily; the necessary circumstances must first have arisen. Whenever possible the written consent of the customer should be obtained to the opening of the new account. An account should also be broken on the bankruptcy or insanity of a guarantor. SEE *Clayton's Case; Collateral Security; Notice of Second Mortgage; Partnerships; Winding up*

Care should be exercised where there is a current account in credit, a wages account, and a 'stopped' account also in debit. SEE *Wages Cheques of a Company*

In the case of *Re E. J. Morel (1934) Ltd* [1962] 1 Ch 21, a stopped account was treated like a loan account and the bank was not allowed to combine accounts to its best advantage. SEE *Set Off*

BROKERAGE The charge of so much per cent or per share made by a broker for carrying out the instructions of a client to buy or sell stocks or shares. SEE *Stockbroker*

BROKERS Persons who buy and sell goods, bills, stocks and shares, etc. on behalf of other person. SEE *Bill Broker; Stockbroker*

BRONZE COINS Bronze coins were issued by the Mint for a penny, a halfpenny and a farthing. Copper coins (which were first issued in 1672) were replaced by bronze in 1860, but the latter continued commonly to be called copper coins. The farthing ceased to be legal tender from 31st December, 1960 and the halfpenny from 1st August, 1969. The 'old' penny continued in circulation after decimalization on 15th February, 1971, although no more were issued by the Mint after that date. It continued for a time to be legal tender only to the extent of twelve coins valued formerly at one shilling, now five new pence. Old pennies (and old threepenny pieces) ceased to be legal tender from 1st September, 1971.

The new bronze coins, which have circulated since 15th February, 1971, comprise three denominations, twopence, penny and halfpenny (now withdrawn), weighing respectively 7.128 grams, 3.564 grams and 1.782 grams. The coins are thus weight-related with one twopence piece weighing the same as two pennies or four halfpennies. The coins are legal tender to the extent of 20 pence.

The composition of the bronze is 95 parts of copper, 4 parts of tin, and 1 part of zinc. SEE *Coinage*

BUCKET SHOP A pejorative term used to describe share dealers who are not members of the Stock Exchange and it belongs really to the days when 'share pushing' was not so severely proscribed and regulated. It is thought the term may have had its origin in the bucket shops of America in the days of prohibition when customers collected their alcohol in their own buckets. The term nowadays has a wider application than share dealing and is used, for example, to refer to travel agents who are not members of the International Air Transport Association. SEE *Share Pushing; Prevention of Fraud (Investments) Act 1958*

BUDGET The name given to the annual statement of the Chancellor of the Exchequer in which he estimates the revenue to be received during the year from existing taxes to meet the estimated expenditure. He may propose increased taxation if additional revenue is required, or if the estimated revenue is more than the estimated expenditure, he may propose reduced taxation or indicate new schemes of the Government to utilize the excess revenue.

According to the *Oxford English Dictionary*, the word 'budget' is derived from 'budge', an anglicized form of the French 'bouge', an obsolete word meaning a small bag. In a pamphlet issued in 1733, Sir Robert Walpole, the Prime Minister and Chancellor, is satirically pictured opening a bag filled with medicines and charms.

The Budget is presented by the Chancellor to Parliament around the beginning of the financial year and used to be presented to the House sitting as the Committee of Ways and Means. The authority of the Committee of Ways and Means to continue existing taxation was challenged in 1913 and the problem was resolved by the Provisional Collection of Taxes Act 1913, which enabled the introduction of new taxes or the renewal of existing taxes to come into effect on the day they are proposed by the Chancellor, provided:

1. the resolutions are agreed to by the House within 10 sitting days;
2. the Bill is read a second time within 20 sitting days after it has been agreed to by the House;
3. the Bill receives the Royal Assent within four months after the resolution has been voted; and
4. the resolution does not impose a new tax.

Since 1967, the Budget has been delivered in the House as such, rather than in Committee and the Provisional Collection of Taxes Act amended accordingly. That Act still remains in force, however, and without it it would not be possible to put into effect any changes in taxation, nor to continue with the tax structure from the previous year.

BUDGET ACCOUNTS Budget accounts were introduced by some banks in the late 1960s mainly to assist monthly-paid customers to make provision for regular bills received at longer intervals. For example, a customer might list on a schedule the estimated cost of electricity, gas, water, rates, clothing, holidays and insurance, together with his vehicle excise licence and season ticket—where it is cheaper to pay for an annual rather than a lesser period, for the ensuing twelve months. These items are then totalled and a percentage service charge is added. The total is divided by 12 and the resulting amount is transferred monthly from the ordinary current account to the budget account for the next 12 months. After the first transfer, the service charge is taken from the budget account and from then on any bills received which appear on the schedule may be paid from the budget account. Whether or not the budget account becomes overdrawn during the year, no other charge for interest or commission is made. At the end of the 12 month period any remaining credit balance or overdraft is adjusted by transfer to or from the ordinary current account.

A number of stores also operate budget accounts for their customers as a form of revolving credit.

BUILDING SOCIETIES Building societies were first developed in the late eighteenth century after what has often been referred to as the spirit of self-help. The first society was established in Birmingham in 1775.

The early societies were 'terminating' societies in that they were designed to terminate at a fixed date or when some objective specified in the rules had been attained. With one or two exceptions, all modern building societies are 'permanent'.

In the early societies, which were small and local, the members would subscribe funds which would be used first to buy some land and then to build a house. Further money would be used to buy further land and build further houses. The houses would be allocated by ballot among the members, or in some cases the 'right' to a house would be sold by auction among the members.

In time, money was subscribed by other people who had money to invest but did not necessarily wish to buy a house through the society. Thus, the members of a building society became its investors and its borrowers, and this is still the situation today.

By 1900 there were 2,286 building societies in existence, but with the termination and merger of societies over the years the number had reduced to 190 by the end of 1984. The following table shows the growth in the number of share accounts and the number of borrowers over the years.

Year	Number of societies	Number of share accounts 000s	Number of borrowers 000s
1900	2,286	585	
1910	1,723	626	
1920	1,271	748	
1930	1,026	1,449	720
1940	952	2,088	1,503
1950	819	2,256	1,508
1960	726	3,910	2,349
1970	481	10,265	3,655
1971	467	11,568	3,896
1972	456	12,874	4,126
1973	447	14,385	4,204
1974	416	15,856	4,250
1975	382	17,916	4,397
1976	364	19,991	4,609
1977	339	22,536	4,836
1978	316	24,999	5,108
1979	287	27,878	5,251
1980	273	30,640	5,383
1981	251	33,371	5,484
1982	227	36,609	5,634
1983	206	37,713	5,928

Source: Building Societies Association.

Building societies have become the major channel of personal, short-term savings in the UK. The following table shows how the building societies' share of personal savings rose from 9 per cent in 1950 to 46.4 per cent in 1983.

At the end of 1982, investment in building societies accounted for 18 per cent of all personal financial assets, second only to the combined

Institution	1950 Amount £m	1950 Share per cent	1960 Amount £m	1960 Share per cent	1970 Amount £m	1970 Share per cent	1983 Amount £m	1983 Share per cent
National Savings Banks and	6,131	46	6,965	42	8,362	30	24,606	15
Savings Banks	6,060 (1951)	45	6,884	41	10,062	35	64,887	39
Building Societies	1,160	9	2,793	17	10,059	35	77,482	46
Total:	13,351	100	16,642	100	28,483	100	166,975	100

Source: Financial Statistics. See Supplement.

figure for life assurance and pension funds (33 per cent). The total assets of building societies increased from £370m in 1930 to over £97,000m in 1984. The 20 largest societies account for over 80 per cent of the total assets of the movement.

At the end of 1983 there were 6,644 building society branches in the UK.

In recent times, the question of building society powers has been very much the subject of discussion. Under Section 1(1) of the Building Societies Act 1962, the only purpose for which a building society may be established is for

> Raising, by the subscriptions of the members, a stock or fund for making advances to members out of the funds of the society upon security by way of mortgage of freehold or leasehold estate.

Thus, as the law stands at present, building societies may not lend money other than on mortgage, and thus may not allow an investor's account to become overdrawn. For the same reason, it may not issue a cheque guarantee card because this obliges the society to pay a cheque which may have the effect of overdrawing an account and thus, the society would be acting *ultra vires*. Similarly, a society may not enter into any business activity of a kind which is not clearly incidental to or consequential upon the statutory purposes for which the society has been formed. It may not therefore, conduct insurance business on behalf of an insurance company, except to the extent that it does so to provide life cover or, e.g. house insurance related to the mortgage loans to its members. Again, a society may own property for its own occupation and lease out surplus capacity, but may not otherwise enter into property owning or property development schemes.

In July 1984 the Government published a Green Paper, *Building Societies: A New Framework*. This discussion document was issued to fulfil the Government's promise in its election manifesto to consider how building societies could play a fuller part in providing people with new housing and how the law in relation to building societies might be brought up to date. The Green Paper took into account proposals made by the Building Societies Association (q.v.) in earlier discussion documents issued in January 1983 and February 1984.

In summary, the Green Paper contemplated the following changes in the legal and functional structure of building societies:

1. Up to 10 per cent of a society's 'commercial assets' could be lent on second mortgages or other security and up to five per cent could be lent on unsecured loans, but 90 per cent of the society's assets would continue to be lent only on first mortgage, as is required at present for all building society loans.
2. Up to one-fifth of a society's funds could come from the money markets.
3. Societies could own land and develop properties for renting.
4. Societies would be able to invest in subsidiaries provided there were no potentially heavy contingent liabilities as, for example, in the case of underwriting.
5. Societies would be able to offer fuller money transmission and banking services, including the provision of a cheque books, cheque guarantee cards and cash dispensers.
6. Discussion would be invited on the possibility of undertaking integrated house-buying services, e.g. conveyancing, surveying, estate-agency work, insurance broking and other agency services.
7. The present interest rate 'cartel' (SEE *Building Societies Association*) would end.
8. Societies would have the right to become limited companies if the members so wished, in which case they would require a deposit taking licence from the Bank of England and would come within the supervision of the Bank.
9. There would be a statutory investment protection scheme as exists in the case of banks (SEE *Deposit Protection Scheme*).

It is contemplated that a new legal framework will be introduced within the life of the current Parliament. In the meantime, the discussion continues.

BUILDING SOCIETIES, INVESTMENT IN

As mentioned above, building societies have become the major repository of short-term, personal savings in the UK. The principal method of investment in a building society is by the acquisition of shares. Over 80 per cent of investment in the larger societies is by this method. Most societies issue term shares (under various names) to permit fixed investment for periods up to five years. The rate of interest on the ordinary shares of building societies normally follows the 'recommended rate' of the Building Societies Association, other categories of shares usually carrying a differential rate of interest, depending on the term of the investment or the period of notice for withdrawal. Ordinary shares are repayable on demand. Most building societies offer savings schemes of one kind or another.

Until April 1985, the maximum investment permitted in a single building society by one person was £30,000 (£60,000 for an investment in joint names). An investor may now invest up to the maximum sum permitted by individual societies.

It is a feature of building societies in the UK that the societies pay to the Inland Revenue income tax at what is known as the 'composite rate' on the interest which they allow to their investors. The rate is calculated each year according to a number of factors, including the basic rate of tax currently in force, the reliefs available and the typical income levels of a cross-section of building society investors. This arrangement is not intended to give building society investors any special relief from tax, but rather to calculate in a composite way the level of taxation which would be payable if interest were paid gross to individual investors.

Thus, income tax is paid by the building societies and no further income tax at the basic rate is paid by the investor on the interest received. Investors who are liable for higher rates of income tax will, however, have to pay higher-rate tax and, where appropriate, investment income surcharge on their building society interest. With effect from the fiscal year 1985/86, a similar composite rate scheme was introduced in relation to interest paid by banks on personal accounts. The scheme operates in very much the same way as has applied to building societies for many years, and at the same level of composite rate.

BUILDING SOCIETIES ACT 1962 Virtually all the law relating to building societies is now codified in this Act. The Act imposes conditions affecting the functions, operation and dissolution of societies, provides for audit and the publication of detailed yearly accounts, restricts borrowing and lending powers, and confers certain privileges such as the limitation of liability of members and exemption from certain stamp duties. The Act is administered by the Registrar of Friendly Societies. The Chief Registrar of Friendly Societies (q.v.) is ex officio Registrar of Building Societies, and has powers to undertake investigations into the affairs of societies in the interests of depositors or investors and if he thinks fit, to prohibit particular societies from advertising for additional funds. He controls the formation of new societies and advertising for funds. The Act limits the advances which may be made on non-domestic property and to companies, and ensures that the investment of surplus funds is regulated.

BUILDING SOCIETIES ASSOCIATION This was constituted in its present form in 1936. Membership is open to building societies which conform to certain minimum financial criteria, approximately the same criteria as those which qualify any society for trustee status but without the same minimum requirement as to size. The Association is in effect the trade association for building societies of Britain. It is a forum for discussion on building society matters and disseminates a wide range of building society statistics to its members and to the public. The Association acts as a channel of communication between the building society movement and the Government. The Association represents approximately 70 per cent in number but 99 per cent in asset value of the societies in Britain.

The Association acts through a council which is elected in a way which reflects the varying size of societies as well as the regional representation. Until 1983, the Council of the Building Societies Association operated a system of 'recommended' rates of interest, which the major societies agreed to follow and which, for the most part, other societies followed with slight variations. This arrangement, often referred to as the 'building society cartel', was discontinued in 1983 and a system of 'advised' rates substituted. In practice, the pattern has continued of following the advised rates in very much the same way as societies previously followed the recommended rates.

The Association does not, in general, exercise a supervisory role in relation to the conduct of building societies, this being a matter for the Chief Registrar of Friendly Societies (q.v.). The Council has however acted to co-ordinate rescue arrangements on those rare occasions when a building society has fallen into financial difficulty. Also, in 1982, the Association introduced the Building Societies Investors' Protection Scheme.

BUILDING SOCIETY LINKED POLICY SEE *Life Assurance—conventional and linked life assurance*

BUILDING SOCIETY MORTGAGE LOANS The primary purpose of building societies is to lend money on mortgage to their members for the purpose of house purchase. This was from the beginning, and still is, the raison d'être of building societies. In earlier days, groups of people would come together to form a society and pool their savings for the purpose of buying plots of land and building houses for their members. SEE *Building Societies*

When enough had been saved to house all the members, the society would be brought to an end. Hence, the term 'building societies' and the term 'terminating societies' as distinct from those of the present day which are 'permanent'.

BUILDING SOCIETY MORTGAGE LOANS

Building societies are governed in the conduct of their business and the nature of their lending by the Building Societies Act 1962 (q.v.) and subsequent amendments.

The principal or primary security for an advance by a building society must be freehold or leasehold property, but societies are empowered to take into account additional security of the kind specified in Schedule 3 to the Building Societies Act 1962, e.g. a charge on a life assurance policy or certain categories of guarantees. A building society may not lend money on second mortgage unless the first mortgage is in favour of the same society.

Most building societies are prepared to lend on the security of most types of residential property, whether freehold or leasehold, whether old or new and whether in one part of the country or another. Naturally, however, a society is concerned with the quality of its security and thus will expect its mortgage properties to have (or to be brought up to forthwith) certain basic standards, such as indoor sanitation. A society will be reluctant to lend in an area where the deterioration in property values will affect the safety of the loan.

In general, societies will not consider lending on the security of properties which have prospective lives of less than 30 years and, in the case of leasehold property, the lease should have a reasonable time to run, e.g. 20–30 years beyond the term of the mortgage.

Most societies will lend on purpose-built flats as readily as on houses. They will not always be willing, however, to lend on the security of converted flats. In recent times, some building societies have entered into schemes with local authorities in order to finance the purchase of domestic dwellings in some of the run-down areas of the inner cities.

Rates of interest charged by building societies to their borrowers tend to follow the 'advised' rate agreed by the Council of the Building Societies Association from time to time. This is the rate which the largest societies adopt by common consent and which most societies follow as a close guideline. All societies are free, however, to fix whatever rate they please and a number of societies charge marginally more than the recommended rate. Some societies also charge differential rates of interest in relation to particular levels of borrowing, e.g. the larger the loan the larger the rate of interest, but this practice has become less common in recent years.

On a new mortgage, the rate of interest will be that which is in force for loans with that particular building society at that date. It is a feature of building society loans in the UK, however, that the rate of interest varies from time to time depending on the level of interest which societies have to pay on their shares and deposits in order to attract money, and that rate will, in turn, reflect the general level of interest rates in the economy. Thus, at the time of purchase, a house buyer will not know how much interest will be payable in future years. It is a reasonable assumption, however, that building society rates will continue to go up or down according to the general level of interest rates in the market, so that the house owner will find his interest charges increased only at times when the cost of money in general increases. Rates will not go up and down at the mere caprice of the building society.

When interest rates increase, many societies will allow their borrowers, if they so wish, to continue their monthly payments at the existing level, notwithstanding that this will lengthen the mortgage repayment term. This, of course, cannot apply on every occasion, nor for an indefinite period, but it is helpful at a time when interest rates are high and expected to return to a lower level before long.

Building society loans may be taken out over very long periods, quite often for the remainder of the working life of the borrower. Thus, the term of the loan may be for 25 or 30 years, but seldom beyond 35 years. In fact, with annuity loans (see below) there is very little saving in terms of the monthly repayments by extending a loan beyond the 25-year period, depending of course on the rate of interest payable.

In practice, the life of a building society loan is often comparatively short, partly because of the increased mobility of people perhaps in the course of their employment and partly because of the natural desire to change houses with changing needs. In the course of a lifetime, a person may own a succession of houses. When a house is sold, the mortgage is repaid and the new purchase will be the subject of an entirely new mortgage arrangement, either with the same building society or a different one.

The average building society mortgage term is, therefore, to some extent a reflection of the turnover of houses. For many years the average period was around seven to eight years, but a recent survey has suggested that this figure is as low as five and a half to six.

Building society loans are repaid in one of two ways: the annuity method or the endowment method.

Annuity method This is the more common method of repayment. Over the life of the mortgage, the borrower makes monthly payments which are made up partly of interest and partly of capital repayments.

The amount of the monthly payments will of course vary according to the period of the mortgage and the rate of interest. The table below shows the monthly mortgage payments for a £10,000 loan at varying rates of interest and over varying periods.

Interest rate per cent	20-year term £	25-year term £	30-year term £
10.00	97.90	91.90	88.40
10.25	99.60	93.60	90.30
10.50	101.30	95.40	92.20
10.75	103.00	97.20	94.00
11.00	104.70	99.00	95.90
11.25	106.40	100.80	97.80
11.50	108.10	102.60	99.70
11.75	109.90	104.50	101.60
12.00	111.60	106.30	103.50
12.25	113.40	108.10	105.40
12.50	115.10	110.00	107.40
12.75	116.90	111.90	109.30
13.00	118.70	113.70	111.20
13.25	120.50	115.60	113.20
13.50	122.30	117.50	115.10
13.75	124.10	119.40	117.10
14.00	125.90	121.30	119.10
14.25	127.70	123.20	121.00
14.50	129.50	125.10	123.00
14.75	131.30	127.00	125.00
15.00	133.20	129.00	127.00

Source: Building Societies Association.

Endowment method Under the endowment method of repayment, the amount of the mortgage loan remains fixed for the term of the mortgage and is repaid at the end of that time from the proceeds of an endowment assurance policy. There are three categories of endowment mortgages:

1. Without-profits endowment mortgage. The sum assured will be the amount required to repay the loan at maturity.
2. With-profits endowment mortgage. In this case also, the sum assured will be the amount required to repay the loan at maturity, but at the end of the term the borrower will receive the bonuses declared on the policy and thus will enjoy the benefits of this additional means of saving.
3. Low-cost endowment mortgage. A with-profits endowment scheme under (2) can be very attractive because it gives the borrower a cash sum in addition to taking care of the mortgage loan. On the other hand, because the benefits are more than are strictly necessary for the purpose of paying off the loan, it can be an expensive way of buying a house. Recognizing this, most assurance companies have introduced the so-called low-cost endowment policies under which the sum assured is less than the amount of the loan, but some allowance is made for a modest level of bonuses in order to bring the policy proceeds up to the amount of the loan at maturity. As the sum assured is less than the mortgage debt, the position would be uncovered in the event of the death of the borrower. The assurance company, therefore, combines in the package sufficient term assurance to make up the necessary cover.

Until recent years, approximately 95 per cent of all house purchase loans outstanding in this country were arranged through building societies. In more recent years, the proportion of building society lending fell to approximately 80 per cent as other lending institutions, particularly the banks, entered this field.

BULL A person who takes an optimistic view of the stock market or of commodity markets and who, therefore, buys stock (or commodities) in anticipation of a rise in price, probably hoping to sell out at a profit before having to pay for his purchase. A bull market is one which appears to be on a rising trend. SEE ALSO *Bear; Backwardation; Contango; Stock Exchange*

BULLDOG BONDS A colloquialism applied to domestic bonds issued by overseas countries but raised in London and denominated in sterling.

BULLION Gold and silver in bars or in the mass. The word is also used when speaking of large quantities of gold, silver and copper coins, especially when regarded by weight. Bullion is said to have been originally the name of the office or mint where the metal was stamped into coins.

By the Bank Charter Act 1844, Section 4, all persons were entitled to demand from the Issue Department of the Bank of England notes in exchange for gold bullion, at the rate of £3 17s 9d per ounce of standard gold:

> Provided always that the said Governor and Company shall in all cases be entitled to require such gold bullion to be melted and assayed by persons approved by the said Governor and Company at the expense of the parties tendering such gold bullion.

Under the Coinage Act of 1870, anyone had the right to take bar gold, if of sufficient fineness, to the Mint and have it coined, free of expense, at the rate of £3 17s 10½d per ounce of standard gold, provided that the value was not less than £20,000, but the owner of the gold bullion had to wait for payment until it was coined. Anyone requiring coins for gold bullion would take it to the Bank of

England, where, as stated above, notes at the rate of £3 17s 9d per ounce were given at once.

By the Gold Standard Act 1925, the Section of the Coinage Act 1870, which enabled any person bringing gold bullion to the Mint to have it assayed and coined, ceased to have effect. The right to tender bullion to be coined is thus confined by law, as it has long been confined in practice, to the Bank of England. The same Act put the Bank of England under the obligation to sell gold bullion, in amount not less than 400 fine ounces, in exchange for legal tender at the fixed price of £3 17s 10½d per standard ounce. Section 1(2) of the Gold Standard Act 1925 was suspended on 21st September, 1931, relieving the Bank of England from the obligation to sell gold bullion.

After many years of restriction, residents of the UK and of the USA may invest freely in gold, including gold bullion. SEE *Bar Gold; Gold, Investment in*

BULLION COINS Gold coins, such as sovereigns, Krugerrands and ductas, which are made from bullion gold with a high degree of fineness. SEE *Gold, Investment in*

BUREAU DE CHANGE This is a shop or sometimes merely a counter where one type of currency may be exchanged for another. It is primarily a service for tourists. With the growth of tourism in London in recent years, coupled perhaps with the closing of the banks on Saturday mornings, there has been an increase in the number of independent bureaux de change opened in London and, to a lesser degree, in the provinces. It is thought that in 1980 there were approximately 200 shops, stores and hotels offering bureau de change facilities in London and other centres in the UK. The banks have in some cases extended their hours of business to provide bureau de change facilities in the evenings and at weekends. Barclays Bank, for instance, opened its first bureau de change in Oxford Street, London, in September 1977 to provide a six-day service from 8 am until 10 pm. Lloyds Bank introduced bureau de change facilities through their Lewis' Bank subsidiary in Lewis' Group stores and Midland Bank offer separate bureau de change facilities through their subsidiary, Thomas Cook.

BUSINESS ADVISORY SERVICES This is a term widely used to apply to the advisory services provided by the banks in the UK for, in particular, smaller businesses. The provision of such services had its origin in the Bolton Committee on Small Firms (q.v.) and now most of the clearing banks, in varying degrees, provide advisory help to small and medium-sized concerns. In their evidence to the Wilson Committee (q.v.), the clearing banks said:

> The clearing banks are the main, and in many cases the only, point of contact with the financial system for the 1¼ million businesses in the country believed to meet the Bolton Committee's definition of a small firm. . . . One of the most important features of the development of the clearing banks over the past twenty years has been the increasing range of facilities available through their branch outlets to meet the needs of smaller businesses at each successive stage of their development.

The advisory services of the banks include such subjects as business objectives, budgeting, costing, pricing policy, credit control, cashflow, stock control, management control, use of resources and provision of finance.

Although these services are often referred to in the context of the clearing banks, they do not by any means have a monopoly of business advisory work. Many firms of accountants provide comparable services, either direct or through associated consultancy firms. Also, the provision of advice to larger companies has for long enough been a province of the merchant banks.

BUSINESS EXPANSION SCHEME This was introduced by the Chancellor of the Exchequer in his Budget Speech on 10th March, 1981, under the title Business Start-Up Scheme and subsequently enacted in the Finance Act of the year. In the Budget and subsequent Finance Act of 1983, the scope of the Scheme was broadened and the title changed to Business Expansion Scheme. It is designed to encourage the investment of risk capital in unquoted trading enterprises.

The main aspect of the Scheme is that a private investor may obtain tax relief in respect of investments up to £40,000 per annum in companies which qualify under the Scheme. The amount of the investment is treated as a deduction from the investor's income in the year in which the investment is made. Thus tax relief applies at the investors' marginal rate. The original Scheme was designed to continue until April, 1984 but it was subsequently extended to April, 1987.

The following are some of its principal characteristics.

1. The Scheme applies only to companies carrying on certain qualifying trades. Broadly, these exclude leasing and financial operations, dealing in commodities or land or futures farming, and businesses conducted on a non-profit basis.
2. The investor must not be an employee or a paid director of the company, nor must he or his associates own more than 30 per cent of the

company's capital. An associate in this context includes husband or wife, parents, grandparents, children or grandchildren. It does not include brothers, sisters, uncles and aunts or their children. A business partner is deemed to be an associate.

3. More than one shareholder may claim relief in respect of investments in the same company.

4. The company must be resident in the UK and must be carrying on a qualifying trade 'wholly or mainly in the United Kingdom'. In general, this means that the major part, i.e. over one-half of the company's total activities must take place within the UK.

5. The Scheme does not apply to companies whose shares are listed on an authorized Stock Exchange or which are dealt in on the Unlisted Securities Market.

6. Relief is given to the taxpayer for the year in which the shares are issued, provided in the case of a new company, that it has been trading for four months. There is a time limit of two years in which the claim must be made.

7. During the first five years, relief may be lost if any value is withdrawn from the company by the shareholder other than proper expenses, reasonable interest on loans and normal dividends, etc.

8. If, within the five year period, there is a withdrawal of value from the company, whether by the shareholder or any third party, such as the repayment of redemption of share capital or loans (except loans made after the subscription date of the qualifying shares) the relief is correspondingly reduced. The winding-up of the company in the five year period will have a similar effect.

9. If the shareholder sells the shares at an arm's length price within five years of issue, the relief is withdrawn proportionately to the amount which is received for the sale. On the disposal of the shares, other than at arm's length, the whole of the relief is withdrawn. The death of the shareholder does not constitute a disposal.

10. All the issued shares must be fully paid and, in the period from two years before the issue of the qualifying shares until three years after the issue, the company may have only ordinary share capital and fixed interest preference shares.

11. The minimum qualifying subscription is £500. Where the subscription is made by husband and wife, the minimum and maximum investment is available to them jointly. If the wife has applied for a separate assessment or elected for separate taxation of her earnings, relief on a qualifying investment is given to the wife separately, but only within the overall maximum of £40,000 for husband and wife together.

12. Relief under this Scheme is available only for bona fide commercial investments and not for tax avoidance reasons.

BUSINESS EXPENSES The term may relate to those expenses incurred by (1) a company in the course of its business activities, (2) a partnership or self-employed person in the course of their business activities, or (3) expenses incurred by an employed person in connection with their employer's business activities. The main point for consideration in relation to business expenses is whether or not they are allowable for tax purposes. A company or a self-employed person engaged in a trade, business or profession may deduct for tax purposes those expenses which are 'wholly and exclusively' related to the business. An employed person, however, may only deduct for tax purposes those expenses which are 'wholly, exclusively and *necessarily*' incurred in connection with his employment. SEE ALSO *Income Tax*

BUSINESS NAMES SEE *Registration of Business Names*

BUSINESS PROPERTY A term used in relation to those business assets which, in certain circumstances, enjoy relief from capital gains tax (q.v.) and capital transfer tax (q.v.).

BUSINESS RETIREMENT RELIEF If the proprietor of a family business disposes of the business on his retirement, whether by gift or sale, there is no capital gain tax on the disposal value provided (1) the proprietor is over 65 years of age, and (2) he has owned the business for the past ten years. The exemption applies to the first £100,000 of the disposal value. The relief applies only to 'chargeable business assets', i.e. those used in the business as distinct from investments made by the business.

If the proprietor is between 60 and 65 years of age, the relief is reduced by £20,000 for each year between his current age and age 65 with a corresponding adjustment for odd months.

If the business has not been owned for ten years, there is a graduated form of relief, i.e 10 per cent exemption for one year's ownership rising to 100 per cent for ten years' ownership.

This form of retirement relief also applies to a director of a family company, i.e. one in which he has 25 per cent of the voting rights or in which he has at least five per cent of the vótes out of a total of at least 51 per cent held by his family. SEE ALSO *Capital Gains Tax; Capital Transfer Tax; Business Property;* Supplement

BUSTED BONDS The bonds (q.v.) issued by foreign governments who have failed to meet their obligations under the bonds, or issued by companies and other incorporated bodies who have gone into liquidation or otherwise ceased to exist. Sometimes, such bonds are held in hope of some future return, but more often nowadays are collectors' items, the actual bond certificate having acquired an intrinsic value in itself.

BUYING IN A Stock Exchange term. Where securities have not been delivered by a seller to a purchaser at the appointed time, they may be 'bought in' by an official of the Stock Exchange. In the case of registered securities, if not delivered within ten days, they may be bought in against the seller on the eleventh day after the Ticket-day, or on any subsequent day, and the loss occasioned by such buying in must be borne by the seller. SEE *Selling out; Stock Exchange*

C

CABLE TRANSFER SEE *Telegraphic Transfer*

CALL A Stock Exchange term meaning the right to buy a specified security at a certain price within an arranged period (SEE *Option; Stock Exchange*). Also, the amount payable on a share originally issued as nil paid or partly paid. Calls made on partly paid government stocks would be made in accordance with the terms of the issue. In the case of a partly paid share of a company, calls must be made in accordance with the company's articles of association. A limited company may, by special resolution, declare that any portion of its uncalled capital shall not be called up except in the event of the company being wound up. SEE *Reserve Liability*

Even after a shareholder has sold his partly paid up shares he continues to be liable in some circumstances in the event of the company being wound up within one year after the shares have been transferred. SEE *Contributories*

CALL MONEY SEE *Money at Call and Short Notice*

CALL OPTION Such an option gives the purchaser a right to buy the shares or commodities over which the option has been given at an agreed price. A call option is purchased, therefore, in the expectation of a future rise in price. The opposite is a 'put' option, which is the right to sell in the future at a price agreed at the time of the option. SEE *Option*

CANCELLATION OF BILL OF EXCHANGE A bill of exchange is discharged when it is intentionally cancelled. The Bills of Exchange Act 1882, Section 63, provides

(1) Where a bill is intentionally cancelled by the holder or his agent, and the cancellation is apparent thereon, the bill is discharged.

(2) In like manner any party liable on a bill may be discharged by the intentional cancellation of his signature by the holder or his agent. In such case any indorser who would have had a right of recourse against the party whose signature is cancelled, is also discharged.

(3) A cancellation made unintentionally, or under a mistake, or without the authority of the holder, is inoperative; but where a bill or any signature thereon appears to have been cancelled the burden of proof lies on the party who alleges that the cancellation was made unintentionally, or under a mistake, or without authority.

Where a bill, or cheque, has been accidentally cancelled by a banker, a note should be made near to the cancellation that it has been 'cancelled in error', and the words should be initialed, or signed, by the banker who has made such cancellation.

Where a cheque is torn in two, a banker treats it as cancelled and will not pay it unless the mutilation is confirmed by a banker as accidental. SEE *Mutilated Cheque or Bill*

By Section 3, Cheques Act 1957, 'an unindorsed cheque which appears to have been paid by the banker on whom it is drawn is evidence of the receipt by the payee of the sum payable by the cheque.'

When a bill is paid, the acceptor's signature is cancelled.

The cancellation of a signature should be decisive, but should not make the signature illegible. SEE *Cancelled Cheques and Bills*

CANCELLED CHEQUES AND BILLS When a cheque is paid, it becomes the property of the drawer, but the banker is entitled to keep it as a voucher till the account is settled, or the customer agrees that the entries in the statement are correct. A paid cheque is useful evidence for the drawer of the payment of the money. (See Section 3, Cheques Act 1957 (q.v.) It is also evidence for the banker that he has repaid money belonging to the drawer, to the amount of the cheque.

The cancellation is usually effected by the drawer's signature on a cheque and the acceptor's signature on a bill being marked through with ink, often with the initials of the officer responsible, and an impression is made on each document of the paid date stamp, the date being that of the day of payment. The signatures should not be obliterated, and the date stamp should be distinct.

If the cancelled cheque is required as evidence in a court of law, the drawer, as being the owner of the paid cheque, if it is in the custody of the banker, must take steps to obtain it from the banker. This, in practice, would never be refused, if a receipt is given to protect the banker.

It is increasingly the practice of banks not to return paid cheques to the customer unless they are specifically requested to do so, in view of the improved narratives on computerized statements. SEE *Cancellation of Bill of Exchange*

CAPITAL In the early stages of civilization, sheep and cattle acted as a currency. Being counted *by the head*, the livestock was called *capitale*, whence the economic term *capital*, the law term *chattel*, and our common name *cattle*.

In business situations, the term capital is usually used to represent the total resources employed in the business; thus 'shareholders' capital', 'proprietors' capital', 'partners' capital'. In more general terms, however, it is the net worth of a person or institution, i.e. the total value of the assets less the amount of liabilities. The word is often used in contradistinction to 'income'. In that sense, capital is the amount of an asset, e.g. land, property, a shareholding or a bank balance; income is the current accrual of value obtained by putting the capital to work, i.e. the rent or dividend or interest, or indeed the fruits of an asset such as the yield from arable farming. Generally, income takes on the colour of capital when it is itself put to work to produce a return. However, such a distinction is rather arbitrary, particularly in relation to 'stock-in-trade', growing crops and the goods to which value is in course of being added. Their value at any one point of time is 'capital'—on sale, the proceeds less costs are income.

In a company, the capital is the sum subscribed by the members of the company—that is, the shareholders—for the purposes of the business. The amount which is authorized by the memorandum of association is the 'authorized', 'nominal', or 'registered' capital. Of the nominal capital there is often only a part of it issued, called the 'issued' capital, the remainder being referred to as 'unissued'. Further portions may be issued from time to time, until the full nominal capital has been issued. Of the capital which has been 'issued' (called also the 'subscribed' capital), only that part of it is paid up, or subscribed by the shareholders, which the directors have 'called up'. The part which has been called up and paid is called the 'paid up' capital, the remaining part being termed the 'uncalled' capital; and it remains unpaid until a 'call' is made for it by the directors. If the whole has been called up, the shares are said to be 'fully paid'. A company may mortgage its uncalled capital. Of the uncalled capital, a certain portion may, if the company has so resolved, form a reserve liability, which is not called up except in the event of the company being wound up. This reserve capital cannot be mortgaged (Section 120, Companies Act 1985).

A shareholder's liability in the company is limited to the nominal value of the shares held by him, and if the shares are fully paid his loss, in the event of the failure of the company, will not exceed the amount he has invested in the company (but SEE *Contributories*). In the case of a private trader, however, he stands to lose not only the money he has put into the business, but also his private means so far as they may be required to meet the demands of the creditors. A trader's capital is usually treated as being the difference between the assets and the actual liabilities.

CAPITAL ALLOWANCES The amount allowed for taxation purposes on the cost of capital assets. Until 1971, the taxation allowances on expenditure on capital assets were roughly in line with the standard methods of annual depreciation. Under the 1971 Finance Act, however, 60 per cent of the cost of acquisition of a business asset was treated as a first year allowance, deductible for tax purposes in the year of acquisition or carried forward at the discretion of the taxpayer in whole or in part against future profits. In July 1971, the allowable deduction was increased to 80 per cent and in March 1972, the relief was extended to 100 per cent of the acquisition costs. The Finance Act 1984 introduced a number of changes in the rates of capital allowances including:

1 First year allowances for plant and machinery, commercial vehicles and other equipment are reduced

(a) to 75 per cent in respect of expenditure incurred on or after 14th March, 1984,

(b) to 50 per cent in respect of expenditure incurred on or after 1st April, 1985, and

(c) to nil in respect of expenditure incurred on or after 1st April, 1986.

2 Writing-down allowances on industrial buildings are reduced

(a) to 50 per cent in respect of expenditure incurred on or after 14th March, 1984,

(b) to 25 per cent in respect of expenditure incurred on or after 1st April, 1985, and

(c) to nil in respect of expenditure incurred on or after 1st April, 1986

3 Residual expenditure not qualifying for first year allowances continue to be eligible for writing down allowances (q.v.) at the rate of 25 per cent per annum of the reducing balance.

4 Expenditure incurred before 1st April, 1987, under a binding contract entered into on or before 13th March, 1984 qualifies for 100 per cent first year allowance.

The Chancellor also announced that legislation would be introduced, to take effect from 1st April, 1985, to enable writing down allowances to be claimed from the time when the capital expenditure is incurred, whether or not the assets have yet been brought into use in the business. Subsequently in a Written Answer, the Financial Secretary to the Treasury indicated that official practice is to treat the date that the expenditure has been incurred as the earlier of

(i) the date of payment made after issue of the invoice, and
(ii) the date on which the vendor becomes entitled to take legal action to enforce payment by the purchaser.

Thus, if payment is not made in a particular accounting period and the legal obligation to pay has not arisen because, for example, of an agreed period of credit, or other usage of the trade extending into the next accounting period, the capital expenditure will be deemed to have been incurred in that later period.

Different rules apply to motor cars. SEE *Writing Down Allowances*

SEE *Agricultural Buildings Allowance; Industrial Allowance and Supplement*

CAPITAL/DEPOSIT RATIO Among the clearing banks in the UK, the ratio of capital to bank deposits has been traditionally of the order of six to eight per cent. One of the problems of recent years has been that of maintaining an adequate capital base in relation to the level of deposits and, in particular, it has been difficult to maintain an adequate level of free capital, i.e. shareholders' capital less those assets such as premises which are locked up in the infra-structure of a bank. In their evidence to the Wilson Committee (q.v.), the banks maintained that bank profits had not been running at a sufficient level to maintain an adequate free capital base allowing for increased costs of preserving the asset infrastructure, notwithstanding that dividends had been paid at no more than a fair level. SEE ALSO *Banking Supervision*

CAPITAL DISTRIBUTION This may refer to the distribution to shareholders of capital profits, i.e. profits made on the sale of capital assets as distinct from trading profits, or it may refer to a distribution to shareholders of the nominal capital of a company. SEE *Company Purchase of Own Shares; Reduction of Share Capital*

CAPITAL GAINS TAX This was introduced in the UK in the Finance Act 1965 and the relevant legislation was subsequently consolidated in the Capital Gains Tax Act of 1979. There is now only one category of capital gains tax; the former tax on so-called short-term capital gains no longer exists. (Tax on short-term capital gains had in fact been introduced in April 1962, i.e. prior to the main capital gains tax legislation of the Finance Act 1965, but the short-term gains tax legislation was repealed in the Finance Act of 1971.)

Subject to the statutory exemptions and reliefs, there is a prima facie charge to capital gains tax on any gain resulting from the disposal of an asset by a resident of the UK. The charge to tax arises if the taxpayer is either resident in the UK or ordinarily resident in the UK for any part of the year of assessment. Capital gains tax is paid by all taxpayers whether companies, other corporate bodies, unincorporated associations, partnerships, trusts or private individuals. The increase in the value of an asset which is retained in the same ownership does not *per se* give rise to any charge to tax. It is the *disposal* of an asset at a value in excess of its acquisition price (or basic value) which gives rise to a chargeable gain.

The Nature of a Disposal

A disposal for capital gains tax purposes may be wholly or in part. The following are examples of disposals on which there would be a prima facie charge for tax on any gain:

Sale of an asset.
Part-exchange of an asset.
Gift of an asset.
Loss or destruction of an asset, e.g. by fire.
Sale or leasing of some interest in an asset.
Sale or surrender of some right in an asset.
Death of the owner of an asset.

Exemptions

While all the above constitute disposals, there are certain statutory exemptions for capital gains tax purposes, principally the following:

1. Transfers between husband and wife. Whether this is by sale, gift or exchange, the transfer of assets between husband and wife does not constitute a disposal for capital gains tax purposes. There is deemed to be a continuing ownership so that if the husband or wife to whom the asset has been transferred subsequently disposes of it any charge for tax is calculated in relation to the value of the asset when the spouse who made the transfer to his or her husband or wife first acquired it.
2. Gifts of assets to charities are exempt from capital gains tax in all circumstances.
3. The transfer of an asset to a nominee for the benefit of the transferor does not constitute a

disposal because there is no change in the beneficial ownership.
4. The transfer of an asset as security for a debt, e.g. the mortgage of a house, does not constitute a disposal for tax purposes.
5. While the death of the owner of an asset constitutes a disposal, there is in fact now no capital gains tax on death. Because there is technically a disposal, any beneficiary who acquires the assets on death is deemed to have done so at their value at the date of death.

The following assets are exempt from capital gains tax, subject to the qualifications shown in each case:

The taxpayer's own principal residence (but see below).
Any other home or homes of the taxpayer lived in rent-free by a dependent relative.
Private motor cars, motor cycles and other private vehicles.
National Savings Certificates, Save-As-You-Earn Certificates and certain other National Savings.
Gambling gains.
Damages or compensation awarded for injury to a person or reputation.
British Government securities held for a year or more or acquired on death.
Bonds, debentures or loan stock issued by a listed company after 13th March, 1984 and held for 12 months before disposal. This applies only to bonds etc., issued as a 'debt on security' as, for example, a debenture. It does not apply to convertible stocks and the bond etc., must be capable of being marketed and not merely an issue between two companies in the same group.
Policies of life assurance or deferred annuity policies, provided these are not purchased from another owner.
Personal chattels (i.e. furniture, jewellery, works of art and other movable property) provided the value of each object at the time of disposal does not exceed £3,000. For example, a set of chairs would constitute an individual item, but not if sold separately to different persons.
Other movable assets with a wasting life (typically with a probable life of 50 years or less) such as horses, boats.
Foreign currency acquired for expenditure abroad.
British money, including for example sovereigns dated post 1836.
Unsecured debts, provided the transferor is the original creditor.
Gifts to the nation of assets considered to be of national, scientific or historic interest.
Gifts of historic houses and other similar property for access by the public.
Gifts of shares in a close company or gifts by the company of its assets for the benefit of the employees of the company. (Broadly speaking, 'close' companies are those which are under the control of five or fewer persons and their 'associates', i.e. close family such as husband, wife, children, parents, brother, sister.)
Any individual gifts, of any asset, to one person of not more than £100 in value during the tax year.

Disposals of Private Residences

As mentioned above, the disposal of the taxpayer's principal private residence does not give rise to a chargeable gain for capital gains tax purposes.

In the ordinary way, for a house to be so exempted it must have been the main or only residence of the taxpayer throughout the period of his ownership since 6th April, 1965. This exemption will not be lost, however, as a result of the following absences:

The last 24 months of ownership, provided the owner has intended to sell the house during this period, e.g. consequent upon a move to another property.
Time spent in employment abroad.
Time spent away from the property by reason of employment elsewhere.
Time spent living in property related to a particular employment (with effect from 31st July, 1978).
Periods of absence for any reason up to a total of three years (in addition to the other exempt periods mentioned above).

The exemption from capital gains tax for a principal residence will normally apply not only to the property itself but to an appropriate amount of garden or grounds. In general, an area up to one acre would qualify for exemption, but beyond that it would be necessary to show that the area is appropriate to a particular property and enjoyed with it as a domestic residence.

A principal residence that has been wholly or partly let during the period of ownership would normally have suffered a proportionate reduction in the capital gains tax exemption on the sale of the property. With the passing of the Finance Act 1980, however, any chargeable gain which arises because of the letting of the property will be reduced by either £20,000 or the amount of the gain which qualifies for the 'main residence' exemption, whichever is the less. The Inland Revenue have let it be known, however, that relief does not extend to property which, although it may be part of the same building, forms a dwelling house separate from that which is, or has been, the owner's dwelling house, e.g. a self-contained flat with separate access from the road.

If the owner of the house, being his or her principal residence, acquires a second property, he may regard the second residence as his principal home provided he gives written notice to the Inland Revenue within two years of acquiring the second property. In the absence of any such election by the taxpayer, the Inland Revenue will decide on the disposal of a property whether or not it has been the principal residence of the taxpayer in the light of all the surrounding circumstances. If part of a principal residence is used for business purposes there will be a proportionate reduction in the capital gains tax relief on the sale of the property. This will not normally apply, however, if no part of the house has been used exclusively for business.

If a taxpayer has been absent from his home for lengthy periods, he must normally return to his home at the end of such absences in order to qualify for the exemptions set out above. This does not apply, however, to the last two years of ownership in which, as indicated above, relief will be granted even though the house has not necessarily been occupied. If an owner has been living in job-related accommodation and bought a house with a view to ultimate retirement, the capital gains tax relief will be allowed, notwithstanding that the house may be sold before the owner actually lives in it.

In a case before the Court of Appeal in 1982, it was confirmed that a residence may comprise several dwellings which are not physically joined together. In that case, a separate chalet bungalow had been used for the occupation of a caretaker and housekeeper while the owner was absent from the main residence. On the sale of the bungalow, exemption from capital gains tax applied because it was deemed to be part of the main residence.

Relief for Small Gains (Personal Taxpayers Only)

For personal taxpayers there is relief for small capital gains. The amount of this relief is normally increased each year by the amount of any percentage increase in the general index of retail prices for the 12 months to the previous December. The level of small gains relief is shown in Appendix 1. This applies to private individuals and trusts for the mentally disabled or for a person in receipt of attendance allowance. The small gains exemption for other trusts is shown in Appendix 1.

Apart from these exemptions, the rate of capital gains tax is 30 per cent and this is applied to the taxpayer's total capital gain in the fiscal year after deducting the small gains allowance.

The small gains exemption (at the personal taxpayer's rate) also applies to personal representatives in respect of gains accruing to them in the year of death and in the two following years of assessment.

For the purpose of computing the liability for capital gains tax, it is necessary to arrive at the value of the asset at the date of disposal (see valuation of assets, below). In the case of an arm's-length sale of an asset, the value will normally be the sale proceeds. In the case of a disposal of an asset other than by sale, e.g. gift, the value of the disposal will be the open market value of the asset at the date of disposal.

From the value of the asset at the date of disposal it is then necessary to deduct the value at the date of acquisition. This may have been the purchase price, or in the event of acquisition by gift or other means it will be the open market value of the asset at that date. In simplest terms, the charge to capital gains tax arises on the difference between the disposal value and the acquisition value. In addition there may be deducted

1. any costs incidental to the acquisition or disposal of the asset, e.g. solicitor's charges, stamp duty, surveyor's costs, etc., and
2. any expenditure incurred in the enhancement of the property during the time of ownership. This does not, however, extend to normal repairs and maintenance or other expenditure of a revenue nature nor, in view of a High Court decision in 1980, does it extend to the value of the owner's time in improving the asset.

Deductible Losses

Any losses incurred by an individual on the disposal of assets or incurred by his wife on the disposal of her assets, may be set off against any gains made by him or his wife on the disposal of assets in the same tax year. If the losses in any year are not relieved by chargeable gains, they may be carried forward against future capital gains of either husband or wife.

Valuation of Assets

For capital gains tax purposes, the acquisition or disposal value of any asset is deemed to be the open market valuation on the day in question.

In the case of Stock Exchange securities, the 'quarter-up' basis is normally used, as with probate valuations. This means that the value of a particular share is the bid price, i.e. the lower price, quoted in the Stock Exchange Official List for that day plus a quarter of the differences between the bid price and the offer price. Where, however, the half-way price between the highest and lowest prices at which bargains were done in those shares on that day is lower than the 'quarter-up' basis, this lower price is taken.

In the case of unquoted securities and other assets for which there is no public market, the valuation must be agreed with the Capital Taxes Office of the Inland Revenue and will normally be on the basis of the price which an arm's-length purchaser would pay in possession of all the relevant facts.

Unit Trusts and Investment Trusts

With effect from 1st April, 1980, authorized unit trusts, approved investment trusts and court investment funds are exempt from capital gains tax on disposals within such trusts or funds.

An investor in unit trusts or investment trusts is now accountable for capital gains tax in the ordinary way on the disposal of his or her units or shares, subject to the exemptions which apply to all disposals.

Prior to 1st April, 1980, authorized unit trusts and investment trusts paid capital gains tax at 10 per cent on investment gains within their funds and investors in such trusts were given a deduction of 10 per cent from the rate of tax payable on the disposal of their units or shares. If, for example, the taxpayer were liable for capital gains tax at 15 per cent, the rate of tax which he would pay on unit trust or investment trust gains would have been five per cent.

Unit trusts which have not been authorized by the Department of Trade and Industry and investment trusts which have not been approved by the Inland Revenue do not enjoy the current exemption from capital gains tax and thus pay tax on capital gains at the appropriate corporation tax rate.

Business Assets

Special rules apply to family companies. A family company is one in which the proprietor has at least 25 per cent of the voting rights, or his or her immediate family have at least 51 per cent of the voting rights including five per cent held by the proprietor. In such a family company, four major aspects of capital gains tax relief apply:

Roll-over relief Where business assets are sold there is a prima facie charge to capital gains tax on any resulting profit. If, however, the proceeds of the business assets are re-invested in the replacement of those assets within one year before the sale or within three years afterwards, any capital gains tax liability is 'rolled-over' to the extent that any gain on the disposal is deducted from the cost of the new assets. (This form of relief is available to all trading companies and not merely family businesses.)

Where a trader ceases carrying on a trade and commences carrying on another trade, the Inland Revenue are prepared to regard the trades as being carried on successively, provided that the interval between ceasing the one trade and commencing the other does not exceed three years.

Business Expansion Scheme Under the Business Expansion Scheme (q.v.) introduced in the Finance Act 1981, special rules apply to the sale of a qualifying shareholding. Under the 1981 Act, if the shareholding was disposed of after the five year qualifying period and the proceeds exceeded the allowable costs, the cost was reduced for capital gains tax purposes by one-half of the amount of the income tax relief. Under the 1982 Finance Act, however, this provision has been withdrawn and the whole of the original cost will now rank as allowable for capital gains tax purposes, in those cases where the shares are sold at cost or at a profit after the five year period.

Gifts of family businesses If shares in a family company, or the assets of that company, are given to near relatives, no capital gains tax is payable on the disposal. The liability is 'rolled-over' with the result that the recipient of the shares or assets takes them virtually at the original acquisition cost of the transferor. This is achieved by deducting the notional gain on the disposal from the value of the shares or assets for the purpose of determining the recipient's acquisition value.

Business retirement relief If the proprietor of a family business disposes of the business on his retirement, whether by gift or sale, there is no capital gains tax on the disposal value provided (1) the proprietor is over 65 years of age, and (2) he has owned the business for the past ten years.

The exemption applies to the first £100,000 of the disposal value. The relief applies only to 'chargeable business assets', i.e. those used in the business as distinct from investments made by the business.

If the proprietor is between 60 and 65 years of age, the relief is reduced by £10,000 for each year between his current age and age 65 with a corresponding adjustment for odd months.

If the business has not been owned for 10 years, there is a graduated form of relief, i.e. 10 per cent exemption for one year's ownership rising to 100 per cent for 10 years' ownership.

This form of retirement relief also applies to a director of a family company, i.e. one in which he has 25 per cent of the voting rights or in which he has at least 5 per cent of the votes out of a total of at least 51 per cent held by his family. SEE Supplement

Gifts Between Individuals

The Finance Act 1980 extended the roll-over relief on gifts of business assets to include all gifts (or sales which are not at arm's-length) between individuals. The effect of this relief is that if the transferor and transferee so elect, the chargeable gain on the disposal may be held over. The acquisition value in the hands of the donee will then be reduced by the amount of the held-over gain for the purpose of calculating capital gains tax on a future disposal of the assets. If a gain qualifies for business retirement relief (see above), the amount of the held-over gain cannot exceed the chargeable gain after allowing for retirement relief.

Gifts to a Trust

With effect from 6th April, 1981, a gift made by an individual to a trust is eligible for roll-over relief similar to that which applies to gifts between individuals. Under the 1982 Finance Act, roll-over relief is made available in relation to property coming out of a settlement if the relief is claimed by both the transferor and the transferee. The Act also removes the charge to capital gains tax on the termination of a life interest where the underlying assets remain settled.

Piecemeal Gifts

Section 151, Capital Gains Tax Act 1979, contains certain provisions relating to the transfer of assets in a piecemeal or fragmented way, from one person to a 'connected' person (which broadly means husband or wife, close family or trusts and companies controlled by such people). The effect of the Section is that capital gains tax is computed by reference to the market value of all the assets transferred, i.e. taken collectively, if that value is greater than the sum of the individual market values of each transfer. Thus a person may transfer over a period individual parcels of shares in a company, which taken together, represent a controlling interest and would have in most cases a higher value than the sum of the individual transfers. The Financial Secretary to the Treasury confirmed on 20th December, 1984, that Section 151 applied only to transactions which occurred within a two year period, i.e. for the purpose of piecemeal or fragmented gifts, the capital gains tax liability on earlier transactions will not be affected if those transactions are more than two years before the current transaction.

Acquisitions of Quoted Securities Prior to 6th April, 1982

Prior to this date, if purchases of quoted securities were made in the same stock but at different times and at different prices, the acquisitions were 'pooled' for the purpose of calculating the acquisition value. On the sale of part of the combined holding, there was no assumption of a 'first-in-first-out' basis. The acquisition price is deemed to be the average price of the pooled shares.

In the case of shares purchased before 7th April, 1965, different rules apply in that shares held before that date are deemed to be sold on a 'first-in-first-out' basis. The taxpayer may, however, elect to have all the shares treated for capital gains tax purposes as if they were acquired on 6th April, 1965 (the year in which capital gains tax was introduced), in which case the quoted valuation of the individual shares on that day will apply.

In the case of acquisitions on or after 6th April, 1982, the rules regarding the pooling of assets do not apply. Share pools existing on that day are treated as single assets and are subject to special rules under the indexation provisions (see below and Supplement).

Joint Interests in Land

Where two or more persons share the beneficial ownership of land, there is a prima facie charge to capital gains tax if the joint owners enter into an exchange of their interests, e.g. if they each become entitled to separate parts of the land. To alleviate this situation, the Chancellor of the Exchequer, on 19th December, 1984, announced an extra-statutory concession to enable any capital gains tax in such circumstances to be deferred. Thus, by concession, an owner of land may claim rollover relief (similar to that provided for in Sections III(A) and III(B), Capital Gains Tax Act 1979), where

(i) a holding of land is held jointly and as a result of an exchange, each joint owner becomes sole owner of part of the land, formerly owned jointly, or
(ii) a number of separate holdings of land are held jointly and as a result of the exchange, each joint owner becomes sole owner of one or more holdings.

The relief does not apply if the interest acquired is or becomes a dwellinghouse or part of a dwellinghouse. Where, however, individuals are joint beneficial owners of dwellinghouses which are their respective residences, and they enter into an exchange of interests in consequence of which they become the sole owners of those houses, concessionary relief may be claimed in certain circumstances (notably if Sections 101 and 102, Capital Gains Tax Act 1979, apply).

In order to obtain this extra-statutory concession, each owner must undertake to accept for capital gains tax purposes, that he is deemed to have acquired the other's interest in the dwelling-house at the original base cost, and the original date on which that joint interest was acquired.

Indexation of Capital Gains

In his Budget Speech in March 1982, the Chancellor of the Exchequer introduced a new element in the calculation of capital gains for tax purposes. In order to take account of inflation, the expenditure allowable in calculating the gain on the disposal of an asset will be adjusted to take into account any percentage increase in the general index of retail prices in the period since March 1982.

Relief is not given, however, in respect of the first year of ownership, e.g. if an asset is held for three years subsequent to March 1982, only the increase in the retail prices index in the last two years is relevant. In the case of an asset held for more than 12 months prior to March 1982, the allowable expenditure is increased by reference to any increase in the RPI between March 1982 and the date of disposal. SEE Supplement

Indexation does not apply to losses, nor can it be applied in such a way as to create or increase losses. SEE Supplement

The following particular points should be noted:

1. Indexation applies only to disposals on or after 6th April, 1982 in the case of individuals (1st April, 1982 in the case of companies).
2. In the case of transfers between husband and wife, it is not necessary for a transferee to hold the shares for an additional 12 months' qualifying period.
3. The indexation allowance is applied not only to the base cost of an asset, but also in relation to any allowable expenses in connection with the ownership of that asset. All such items are separately indexed from the date the expenditure is incurred (e.g. improvement to a property) up to the date of disposal.
4. In the case of roll-over relief (see above), on gifts between individuals and on replacement of business assets, the amount to be 'rolled-over' will take account of any relief available to the transferor under the indexation rules, but the donee will have to hold the asset for a further qualifying period of 12 months before further relief accrues.
5. In the case of shares acquired before 6th April, 1965 in respect of which no pooling election has been made (see above), the securities are dealt with for indexation purposes on a 'last-in-first out' basis.
6. In the case of securities acquired after 5th April, 1982, the following provisions apply:

(a) Each acquisition is considered separately and the pooling provisions no longer apply (see above).

(b) Transactions in quoted securities within the same stock exchange account are matched against each other.

(c) Under the indexation rules, disposals are considered in chronological order. If shares have been acquired in the previous 12 months, the disposals are dealt with on a 'first-in-first-out' basis. If shares have been held for more than 12 months, they are dealt with on a 'last-in-first-out' basis.

CAPITAL ISSUES COMMITTEE Since 1932, there has been control, to a greater or less degree, over capital issues in the UK. The 1932 controls, and such modifications as were made up to 1939, were without a statutory basis, but resulted from public requests by the Chancellor, which the various markets observed. At the outbreak of war in 1939, the Foreign Transactions (Advisory) Committee, which had been set up in 1936 to advise the Treasury on issues involving remittances to countries outside the Commonwealth, was renamed the Capital Issues Committee and was given the wider task of advising the Treasury on the administration of the statutory control of capital issues (and analogous transactions), for which provision was made in Regulation 6 of the Defence (Finance) Regulations 1939.

The end of the war in 1945 saw the retention of the Capital Issues Committee with its primary function unchanged; permanent provision for capital issues control was made the following year with the passing of the Borrowing (Control and Guarantees) Act 1946.

The exemption limit below which application to the Committee was not required was initially for issues of £10,000 in any period of 12 months. This was raised by regulation to £50,000, at which level it remained until March 1956, when it was reduced to £10,000. In July 1958, the limit reverted to £50,000. On 4th August, 1961, the Treasury under its statutory powers gave a general consent whereby it became no longer necessary for any person or company resident in the UK to apply individually for Treasury consent before borrowing money in Great Britain or before issuing shares or other securities (other than redeemable shares issued by way of capitalization of profits and reserves). The Capital Issues Committee was dissolved in November 1967, when it was decided that its continued retention was no longer justified in view of the number of cases for consideration.

Under the present procedure, applications for consent should be addressed in the first instance to the Bank of England, who will consult the Treasury from whom the applicants will receive a letter giving either consent or refusal.

The control currently exercised by the Treasury over borrowing in Great Britain is based on the Control of Borrowing Order 1958 (Statutory Instrument No. 1208 of 1958) as amended by the Control of Borrowing (Amendment) Order 1967 (SI No. 69 of 1967) and the Control of Borrowing (Amendment) Order 1970 (SI No. 708 of 1970). These Orders specify the few types of transaction which remain subject to control.

A General Consent which came into operation on 1st February, 1968, gave an exemption for certain transactions effected by local authorities.

CAPITAL TRANSFER TAX This was introduced in the UK by the Finance Act 1975. It replaced the former estate duty legislation, which was repealed by the 1975 Act, but capital transfer tax goes further than estate duty in that, subject to the statutory exemptions, it applied to all transfers of capital whether during life or on death.

Capital transfer tax owes much to the former estate duty law and many of the complexities of estate duty still apply. An entry of this nature can, therefore, contain no more than an outline of the principal aspects of the tax.

The old estate duty provisions ceased to apply with effect from 12th March, 1975. In that case of death after that date, the capital transfer tax regulations apply. In the case of deaths on or before 12th March, 1975 but subsequent to 12th November, 1974, estate duty would be payable (subject to the statutory exemptions and reliefs), but it would be payable at the capital transfer tax rates. In the case of deaths on or before 12th November, 1974, the old estate duty regulations applied in full.

Transitional provisions were also introduced in relation to gifts, the operative date being 27th March, 1974. Gifts made before that date, but within seven years of the death of the donor, would be chargeable to capital transfer tax as would have been the case under the old estate duty rules. But a degree of relief was introduced so that

1. the gift was reduced by 15 per cent if death occurs over four years later,
2. the gift was reduced by 30 per cent if death is over five years later, and
3. the gift is reduced by 60 per cent if death occurred more than six years later.

Subject to the transitional provisions and subject to the statutory reliefs and exemptions, capital transfer tax is payable on all transfers of value on deaths occurring after 12th March, 1975 and on lifetime gifts made after 26th March, 1974.

If the transferor is domiciled in the UK, the capital transfer tax rules will apply to transfers of property wheresoever situated in the world. If the transferor is not domiciled in the UK, the tax will apply only in relation to the transfer of assets situated in the UK. Special rules apply in relation to domicile (q.v.) The general concept is that capital transfer tax is payable on the amount by which the transfer reduces the transferor's personal estate. In the case of a lifetime transfer, this will usually be the amount of the gift. In the case of a transfer on death, the transfer of value will be the total amount of the deceased's estate.

The amount of tax payable will depend on the cumulative total of gifts made by a transferor in his lifetime and the value of his estate passing on death, subject in each case to the statutory exemptions and reliefs. With effect from 6th April, 1981 (under the provisions of the Finance Act of that year), the period within which cumulative transfers are taken into account for the purpose of determining the rate of tax is limited to ten years.

Lifetime Transfers

Capital transfer tax is prima facie payable on transfers of value by an individual in his or her lifetime to the extent that this results in a reduction in the transferor's personal estate. This applies to outright gifts and to transfers to settlements or other trusts.

The tax does not apply in the case of sales of assets for full consideration, but there may be a charge to tax in all cases where there is an intended gratuitous bounty in favour of the transferee, including for example

1. sales of assets for less than the full consideration (but not if it is merely accidental that the value turns out to be more than the sale price),
2. the release of a debt,
3. transactions which, although not transfers of value in themselves, are so linked to 'associated operations' that a benefit is conferred on another person,
4. the failure to exercise a right, e.g. an option, as a result of which failure some benefit accrues to another person.

As mentioned above, the amount of the transfer is deemed to be the loss to the transferor. The amount of any tax payable on a lifetime gift may be paid by the donor or the donee. If, however, the donor pays the tax, the loss to the donor's estate is deemed to be the net amount of the gift grossed up at the rate of tax payable. If the transferee bears the tax on a particular gift, the loss to the transferor's estate is the actual amount of the gift not the grossed-up sum.

The donor and donee are free to decide who shall pay the capital transfer tax, if any, but the Inland Revenue may claim from either if the need arises.

Although the amount of the gift for tax purposes is deemed to be the total loss to the donor, in calculating that loss no account is taken of the costs of making the gift, e.g. legal expenses or stamp duty, nor of any other taxes which the donor may be called upon to pay, such as capital gains tax or development land tax.

The tax, if any, payable on the occasion of a particular transfer is determined by the cumulative level of transfers to that date. The rates of tax on lifetime gifts are shown in Appendix 1. With effect from 13th March, 1984, no capital transfer tax was payable on the first £64,000 of cumulative, chargeable transfers and this threshold is subject to annual indexation (See Appendix 1). Credit will not be given, however, for tax paid prior to that date under the earlier scales of capital transfer tax (but see below in relation to transfers on death).

The exemptions and reliefs applicable to lifetime gifts are shown in Appendix 1.

Transfers on Death

Capital transfer tax is prima facie payable on the net value of an estate on death. The net value is ascertained by valuing the assets of the estate at their open market value and deducting the liabilities of the deceased at the date of death. The rate of capital transfer tax is then applied after allowing for the appropriate reliefs and exemptions.

Transfers made by a deceased within three years before death are chargeable to tax at the rate applicable to transfers on death. In some cases, therefore, the death of the transferor within three years of the gift will give rise to an additional charge to tax. This tax is payable by the recipient of the gift, but relief is available where the object of the gift has fallen in value in the intervening period.

As with lifetime gifts, the rate of duty appropriate to transfers on death will depend on the cumulative total of lifetime and death transfers, i.e. the net value of the estate at the date of death plus transfers made during the deceased's lifetime or, in the case of deaths on or after 10th March, 1981, transfers made during the previous ten years. If, for example, the deceased had made transfers of £40,000 within ten years of death (no capital transfer tax payable) and died leaving a net estate of, say, £30,000, tax would be payable by reference to the combined total of £70,000.

If in the case of a person dying after 25th March, 1980, an additional charge for tax arises as a result of gifts having been made within three years of death, credit will be given for tax already paid on those gifts at the rate of tax in force at the time of transfer.

Where tax has been paid on chargeable transfers during the deceased's lifetime, it would clearly be unfair to charge his estate with tax on death on the full amount of the cumulative value. Equally, it would be unfair to give his estate credit only for that tax paid during life, bearing in mind the difference in rates of duty between lifetime and death transfers. Accordingly, credit is given for duty on the lifetime gifts at the 'transfer on death' rate of duty.

Exemptions and Reliefs

The following transfers are exempt from capital transfer tax whether they are made by the transferor during life or on death.

Transfers between husband and wife The general rule is that transfers between husband and wife are absolutely exempt from capital transfer tax.

There is a qualification to this rule where the husband or wife making the transfer is domiciled in the UK and the spouse receiving the gift is domiciled abroad. In that event tax is payable on transfers above the cumulative exemption figure, currently £55,000.

There is another limitation in the case of gifts between husband and wife subject to a condition which is not satisfied within a 12 month period. In such cases the exemption is lost, but this does not apply to gifts between husband and wife under a will where the surviving spouse is only to benefit in the event of his or her surviving for a stated period.

The exemption in favour of transfers between husband and wife also applies to settled property, i.e. where there is a provision for one to benefit from funds provided by the other.

Gifts and bequests to charities Gifts to charities, on death or in life, are wholly exempt from capital transfer tax. Prior to 15th March, 1983, gifts to charities, on death, or in the year prior to death were exempt from tax up to a total of £250,000 if made subsequent to 9th March, 1982. The exemption limit prior to that date was £200,000.

Gifts to political parties The rules for charities apply also to gifts or bequests to political parties provided that at the last general election before the gift takes effect at least two members of the political party were elected to the House of Commons, or at least one member elected and at least 150,000 votes cast for the party's candidates.

Gifts and bequests to certain national bodies Gifts and bequests are free of capital transfer tax if made to national museums, the National Trust, the National Gallery, any university, any government department or any local authority, and a number of other national institutions as listed in Schedule VI to the Finance Act 1975.

Gifts and bequests of 'National Heritage property' to a non-profit making body approved by the Treasury Such gifts must relate to property of outstanding scenic, historic, scientific or artistic interest, including land, buildings, antiques, works of art and the like.

The following exemptions apply only to lifetime gifts:

Small gifts With effect from 6th April, 1980, gifts up to a total value of £250 per person in any one tax year are exempt from capital transfer tax (prior to April 1980 the limit was £100). In the case of larger gifts, the first £250 per person per tax year was also exempt prior to the year 1981–82 (see below).

Annual exemption With effect from the fiscal year 1981–82, gifts amounting in aggregate to £3,000 per donor became exempt from tax. (Prior to that year the exemption was £2,000 per annum and prior to the fiscal year 1976–77, the exemption was £1,000 per annum.) With effect from the fiscal year 1981–82, the small gifts exemption (see above) is not available to form part of an exempt slice of a larger gift (See Appendix 1).

If any part of the annual exemption is not used in a particular year it may be carried forward to the following year. Thus, in that second year a donor may make aggregate transfers equal to twice the annual exemption. The exemption can be carried forward for one year only and each year the exemption for that year is deemed to be used up in priority to any part of the previous year's exemption which has been carried forward.

Normal expenditure out of income In keeping with the old estate duty rules, a transfer is not taxable as a gift if it is clearly made out of income. It must be possible to show that

1. Taking one year with another, the transfer was made from income and not from capital.
2. The transferor was left with sufficient income out of which to maintain his normal standard of living.
3. The gift was part of his normal expenditure, which in this context means that the gift was typical or habitual.

A life assurance premium is a good example of 'normal expenditure out of income' because of its recurring nature. A person may now, however, apply capital in the purchase of an annuity and use the annual payments to pay life assurance premiums unless it can be shown that the transactions were completely independent.

Similarly, if a person buys an annuity and makes payments by way of gift out of the annual annuity payments, the 'normal expenditure' exemption will apply only to the extent that the transfers are made out of the income content of the annuity payments.

The word 'income' is construed as meaning net income after income tax.

Gifts of assets other than cash do not normally come within this exemption unless a particular asset has been purchased for the purpose of the gift out of available income.

Gifts in consideration of marriage Gifts made in consideration of marriage are exempt from capital transfer tax to the extent shown below.

The gift must be made to, or for the benefit of, either or both parties to the marriage and must be a gift which takes effect only on the marriage. The limits on this exemption are

1. £5,000 if the donor is a parent of either party to the marriage,
2. £2,500 if the donor is a grandparent or remoter ancestor of one of the parties to the marriage,
3. £1,000 in any other circumstances.

Gifts by way of marriage settlement may also qualify for this exemption provided the persons who may benefit under the settlement are the parties to the marriage, their issue and the wife or husband of any issue, or certain other persons as defined in Paragraph 6 of Schedule 6 of the Finance Act 1975.

Gifts for the maintenance of the family As a general rule, the following lifetime gifts are exempt from tax:

1. Gifts for the maintenance of a spouse or former spouse.
2. Gifts for the maintenance of children up to the age of 18 or until the completion of full-time education. (This exemption applies to legitimate, illegitimate, adopted children or stepchildren, whether or not in the legal care of the parent donor.)
3. Gifts for the maintenance of dependent relatives. In this context, the definition of dependent relative is the same as for the income tax laws, but without the same restriction as to the relative's

financial circumstances. The maintenance payments must, however, be reasonable in relation to the relative's circumstances.

Valuations
The rules for valuing assets for capital transfer tax purposes follow broadly those that applied to estate duty. Section 38 of the Finance Act 1975 provides that subject to the provisions of the Act 'the value at any time of any property shall, for the purposes of capital transfer tax, be the price which the property might reasonably be expected to fetch if sold in the open market at that time'. Schedule 10 of the Act contains detailed provisions regarding the valuation of assets for the purpose of the tax.

Section 38 of the Act provides that the value of any property shall be the price which it might reasonably be expected to fetch if sold in the open market at the time of the transfer, but that the price shall not be assumed to be reduced on the ground that the whole property is to be placed on the market at one and the same time.

Quoted investments Stocks and shares quoted on a stock exchange are valued on the 'quarter-up' basis, i.e. at the lower quoted price plus one-quarter of the difference between the lower and higher quoted prices or, if lower, the half-way price between the highest and lowest recorded bargains for the day.

Unit trusts are valued at the managers' bid price on the day of valuation.

Unquoted securities The normal open market rule of valuation applies and the price is deemed to be that which a normal prudent buyer in possession of all the relevant facts would pay on an arm's-length basis.

Cash assets Balances at banks, the Post Office, building societies, etc. are taken at their face value. Debts due to the transferor, whether transferred by him in life or on death, are taken at their full value unless it can be shown that recovery of all or some part of the debt is not reasonably practicable, provided that the difficulty has not arisen through some action of the transferor.

Life assurance policies If the policy is on the life of the transferor, the value on death is the sum payable under the terms of the policy. In the case of a lifetime gift of the life policy, the value is that which it would fetch in the open market.

If the transferor has taken out a life policy on his own life in trust for named beneficiaries, the proceeds will not be part of his estate and the liability for capital transfer tax, if any, will attach to the amounts of the individual premiums. If these were within the 'normal expenditure' or 'annual exemption' rules, no liability would arise.

Personal chattels The normal open market valuation rule applies.

Freehold and leasehold properties The normal open market valuation will apply, taking into account any special restrictions affecting the property, e.g. a service tenancy.

Liabilities of the transferor Any liabilities of the transferor in relation to the property transferred will be taken into account in valuing the transfer. For example, if a freehold property is subject to a mortgage, the amount of the mortgage debt is deductible from the open market valuation of the property for the purpose of arriving at the value of the asset transferred.

In the case of a transfer on death, the whole of the transferor's liabilities are taken into account because they are a diminution in the total value of the assets. Also, on death a reasonable sum is allowed for funeral expenses as a deduction from the value of the estate.

The expenses of transfer Any expenses of transferring an asset, e.g. legal charges, stamp duty, etc., are ignored in arriving at the value of the transfer for capital transfer tax purposes if the expenses are borne by the transferor. If, however, they are borne by the transferee, they are allowed as a deduction from the value of the transfer.

Related property In arriving at the value of the transfer of property, whether during life or on death, regard is had to any other related property which, if sold together with the transferred property, would enhance the value of the transfer. This extends not only to property actually owned by the transferor, but also property which (1) is owned by his or her wife or husband, (2) has been subject of an exempt transfer to a charity or national institution since 15th April, 1976 by the transferor or his or her wife or husband.

The effect of this rule is that unquoted shares may, for example, have a limited value to the extent of the transferor's own shareholding, but the value of the combined shareholdings, taking into account those held by his or her spouse or in trust, etc., may be very considerable. Tax is payable only on the property transferred, but the value as a proportion of the total related property may be much higher than the value of the transferred property standing alone.

Example A might have, say, 10,000 shares valued at £20,000 and gives these to a third party. A's wife, however, might also have 10,000 of the shares and a settlement set up by the transferor or his wife may hold another 50,000 shares. Together the shareholdings might well confer a controlling interest in the company and be far more valuable than the minority holdings. If, for example, the total of 70,000 shares was worth £245,000, the value of A's shares for capital transfer tax purposes would be one-seventh of that figure, i.e. £35,000 instead of the figure of £20,000 which would otherwise have been the value of his minority holding.

A similar situation might arise with assets other than shares. A husband and wife might own adjoining properties, or a house with an adjoining field, each in their respective names, where the combined value of the two assets is greater than the sum of the individual parts. On a transfer by either of them to a third party, the value for capital transfer tax purposes is not the value of the transferred asset standing alone, but is the proportionate value of the total when held with the related property.

The principle throughout is that the measure of value is the diminution which the transfer occasions in the transferor's estate and this is not necessarily the same as the value of the transferred asset in the hands of the transferor.

There is a departure from this general principle in the case of certain assets passing on death. In some instances, a greater value may attach to the transfer on death than was enjoyed by the deceased immediately before his death. A typical case would be that of a life assurance policy where the proceeds on death might far exceed the surrender value immediately before death. Similarly, in the case of damages payable to the personal representatives of a deceased under the Law Reform (Miscellaneous Provisions) Act 1934 in respect of the deceased's loss of expectation of life through injury, the value of the assets transferred on death would thus be enhanced, notwithstanding that the assets passing are greater than those owned by the deceased in his lifetime.

Settled Property

The rules relating to settled property for the purpose of capital transfer tax are set out in Schedule 5 of the Finance Act 1975.

A settlement is a disposition of property

1. to be held in trust for persons in succession or for any person subject to a contingency, or
2. held by trustees on trust to accumulate the whole or any part of the income of the property or to make payments out of that income at the discretion of themselves or any other person, or property burdened with an annuity or other periodical payment for a person's life or other terminable period (other than transactions for full consideration).

The transfer of assets to a trust will in itself give rise to a charge for capital transfer tax, subject to the usual reliefs and exemptions. The situation is the same as any other chargeable transfer. No tax liability would arise, however, if the property were to be held in trust for the transferor's own absolute benefit because in that case there would be no transfer of the beneficial interest.

The rules governing capital transfer tax on settlements vary according to whether or not there is, at the time in being, an interest in possession. This expression is not defined in the Act but is a concept well known to the old estate duty law. In view of the doubts that arose as to the scope of the expression in relation to capital transfer tax, the Board of Inland Revenue issued an explanatory press notice on the subject on 12th February, 1976.

In general terms, a person has no interest in possession in settled property if he or she has the immediate entitlement to any income produced by that property as it arises. Thus, the most usual form of an interest in possession in settled property is a life interest, but the interest may be for someone else's life or for any fixed or terminable period.

If there is no interest in possession, either because the income is to be applied at the discretion of the trustees or because there is a direction to accumulate the income, different rules apply for capital transfer tax purposes. These types of settlement are normally known as discretionary or accumulation trusts.

Settlements where there is an interest in possession

The general rule is that capital transfer tax is payable on the value of the settled property whenever an interest in possession comes to an end or is disposed of. This may be because of the death of the person owning the interest in possession, e.g. the death of a life tenant, or the termination of that interest in possession on some other event in accordance with the terms of the settlement. The gift, sale, surrender or other disposal of an interest in possession by the person so entitled would all be chargeable events for capital transfer tax.

If the chargeable event is the death of the person owning the interest in possession, the value of the settled property in which he or she had that interest is aggregated with his or her estate for capital transfer tax purposes. As a general rule, however, the settled property will bear its own proportion of the total tax payable. The rate of tax payable will be that appropriate to transfers on death. The calculation is the same as if the settled property had formed part of the beneficiary's own estate. The cumulative chargeable transfers made in his lifetime will, therefore, be taken into account in arriving at the rate of tax.

The statutory exemptions for transfers between husband and wife and for transfers to charities and national institutions, etc. apply to settled property when an interest in possession comes to an end, whether the chargeable event is the death of the beneficiary or some event in his lifetime.

The exemptions applicable to transfers for the maintenance of children, the transferor's spouse or dependent relatives are also available if the interest in possession is disposed of by the beneficiary but not where it comes to an end on the happening of some other event.

With effect from the fiscal year 1981–82, the annual exemption applicable to lifetime gifts and the exemption relating to gifts in consideration of marriage are extended to settled property to the extent that an interest in possession is terminated.

If a person has a beneficial interest in part only of settled property, e.g. if he is entitled to, say, one-third of the income of a trust fund, it is that proportion of the fund which is deemed to be transferred on the happening of the chargeable event.

A more difficult situation may arise where the beneficiary is entitled to a fixed interest in possession, e.g. a fixed annuity, and other beneficiaries are entitled to the remaining income of the settled fund. In accordance with the Schedule 5 to the 1975 Finance Act, the interest of the annuitant will be deemed to be that proportion of the settled property as his or her part of the income bears to the whole income. Thus, the value of the annuitant's interest in possession (or that of the other beneficiaries) could be varied almost capriciously depending on the manner of investment of the settled property. There is, however, provision for the regulation by statutory instrument of the limits of income to be taken into account for this purpose. Under the regulations in force at present, if the tax is chargeable by reference to the value of the annuity, it must be treated as yielding not less than the gross dividend yield of the Financial Times Actuaries All-Share Index (q.v.) on the date of the chargeable event. For the purpose of calculating any tax on the remainder of the settled property, it shall be deemed to be yielding not more than the yield on 2½ per cent Consols.

If a beneficiary entitled to an interest in possession sells that interest, tax will be payable on the value of the property in which the interest subsisted, but the amount of the consideration will be allowed as a deduction.

Discretionary Settlements

Special rules apply to this category of settlements and these were revised extensively under the Finance Act 1982. The detailed provisions are outside the scope of this work, but the rules are broadly as follow.

1. When property 'enters' a discretionary trust, there is a charge to capital transfer tax at the lifetime rate of tax as in the case of other lifetime transfers.
2. On each tenth anniversary occurring after 31st March, 1983, a charge will be levied on the settled property at 30 per cent of the effective lifetime rate.
3. The exit of property from a discretionary trust will not of itself give rise to a charge to tax, but a proportion of the ten-year periodic charge will usually be payable.

Calculation of the periodic charge For the purpose of the periodic charge, the amount of the value assumed to be transferred is the total of the following:

1. the value of the funds in the discretionary trust,
2. the value at the time the trust was set up of any property in the trust which has remained outside the discretionary part of the trust, and
3. the value of property in any other trusts set up by the settlor on the same day (excluding charitable and exempted trusts).

The charge to tax will relate only to the discretionary trust property during the period in which it was within the discretionary trust. For this purpose, the ten-year period is divided into 40 three-monthly periods. If, for example, the relevant property has been outside the terms of the discretionary trust for three out of 10 years, the charge to tax will be reduced by twelve-fortieths. In the case of settlements made between 26th March, 1974 (when the Capital Transfer Tax provisions relating to gifts came into effect) and 9th March, 1982 (from which date the provisions set out above came into effect) for the purpose of calculating the first periodic charge, any distributions of capital made from the trust in the preceding 10 years are taken into account in the calculation.

Exemptions from Capital Transfer Tax

Approved superannuation schemes Under Section 89, Finance Act 1976, contributions made by an employer to an approved superannuation scheme for the purpose of providing retirement benefits for his employees are not subject to capital transfer tax.

Even if retirement benefits are made for an employee or employees other than under an approved scheme, relief from capital transfer tax will apply to the extent that the benefits received by the recipient do not exceed those which could have been provided under an approved scheme. This latter relief applies, however, only where the employer and employee are not 'connected' persons. In general, for this purpose a person is connected with another person if he or she is the person's wife or husband, or a relative, or a husband or wife of a relative. The term 'connected with' is a wide one and extends to a trustee of the trust fund, members of the same partnership and their relatives, companies under the same ultimate control, and a company controlled by a person either alone or with other connected persons.

The foregoing applies to the provision of sums for retirement benefits. Approved pension schemes are themselves exempt, however, notwithstanding that they may be settled property under the trust deed. There may, however, be a charge for tax in cases where

1. a member of the scheme gives up part of his pension to provide for a dependant other than his or her spouse.
2. a member of the scheme has a discretionary power to say who shall receive benefit on his death.
3. a benefit under the scheme becomes payable to the personal representatives of the member's estate.
4. a sum payable under a scheme is resettled.

Employee trusts As with superannuation funds, there is a considerable degree of exemption from capital transfer tax not only in relation to the transfer of funds for the provision of employees of a company but also to dispositions thereafter from such funds.

Under Section 90, Finance Act 1976, a disposition by a close company to trustees for the benefit of the company's employees will be exempt from capital transfer tax provided

1. the persons entitled to benefit from the trust are all or most of the persons employed by or holding office with the company or its subsidiaries;
2. the terms of the trust exclude from benefit any participator in the company, or anyone who has been a participator at any time after, or during, the 10 years before, the transfer or anyone who is a connected person.

A 'participator' for this purpose has the same meaning as in Section 39, Finance Act 1975, which in turn adopts the definition in Chapter 3 of Part XI of the Income and Corporation Taxes Act 1970. In general terms, a participator in a company is any person having a share or interest in the capital or income of the company, including shareholders, loan creditors or any persons who possess or acquire a right to participate in a company's distributions. For the purpose of employee trusts, loan creditors are excluded by the 1975 Act and under the 1976 Act, Section 90, the definition excludes any participator who, on a winding-up of the company, would not be entitled to five per cent or more of its assets.

Under Section 90(2) of the 1976 Act, no capital transfer tax will be payable on a disposition to trustees by a person beneficially entitled to shares in a company whereby the shares are to be held on trust for the benefit of the employees. For the exemption to apply

1. the transfer must relate to all the shares or other securities of the company to which the transferor is beneficially entitled,
2. immediately after the transfer there must be no shares or securities of the company to which the transferor or his or her spouse are beneficially entitled,
3. as a result of the transfer, the trustees must hold all or substantially all the ordinary shares of the company and have the exercise of the majority of the voting power

As with transfers by a close company, the persons for whose benefit the trusts are declared must include all or most of the employees of the company.

In the case of such a transfer by a private individual, the exemption will only apply if the same considerations are observed in relation to participators and connected persons as described above.

Exemption from capital transfer tax will apply to any distributions by an employee trust during any period within which the settled property can be applied only for the benefit of (1) employees, (2) the relatives or dependants of employees, or (3) charities.

The exemption is wider than that available in the case of transfers *to* employee trusts in that a trust itself enjoys exemption from tax if the beneficiaries are defined by reference to employment in a particular trade, profession or undertaking, or by reference to employment by or office with a body carrying on a trade, profession or undertaking. In this latter category, however, the class must comprise all or most of the persons employed by or holding office with that body.

Protective trusts Protective trusts may arise under Section 33 of the Trustee Act 1925 or under some more specific provision in the trust instrument. Under a protective trust, the beneficiary has an interest in possession in the income of the settled fund during his life, subject to the proviso that if he becomes bankrupt or charges his interest, or in the event of a number of other similar circumstances, his right to the income ceases and certain discretionary trusts come into operation.

If such an interest comes to an end in this way, there is no charge for capital transfer tax, nor does a charge for tax arise if the trustees exercise their discretion in favour of the original beneficiary and continue to distribute the income to him or her. During the continuance of the discretionary trusts so created, there is no periodic charge for tax. Under the provision of the 1975 Finance Act, the periodic charge is deferred until such time as there is a capital distribution or a chargeable event.

Trusts for the mentally disabled No capital transfer tax is payable if a property has been transferred to a trust during the lifetime of a mentally disabled person, and at least one-half of the settled property is secured for the benefit of the disabled person during his or her life.

A discretionary trust satisfying these requirements is exempt from the periodic charge. With effect from 10th March, 1981, a disabled person under such a trust will be deemed to have an interest in possession in the settled property, thus enabling an appointment of the settled funds to be made to the disabled person without incurring a tax charge.

Not only is any distribution from the trust in such circumstances free of tax, but the transfer of funds to the settlement will also be exempt if the disabled person is the settlor. He or she will be deemed to be the settlor if the court has made the settlement on his or her behalf. Under Section 51, Finance Act 1977, these provisions will apply if a trust has been set up for the benefit of a person who is in receipt of an attendance allowance.

Business property There is a degree of relief available for the transfer of business property whether it is a lifetime transfer or a transfer on death, and whether or not the business property is settled property.

The relief was introduced by Section 73 in Schedule 10 of the Finance Act 1976. It applies to what is defined as 'relevant business property', that is

1. property consisting of a business or interest in a business,
2. shares in or securities of a company, which by themselves or with other holdings gave the transferor control of the company immediately before the transfer, and
3. any land or building, machinery or plant which immediately before the transfer was used wholly or mainly for the purpose of a business carried on by a company of which the transferor then had control, or by a partnership of which he then was a partner.

The relief does not extend to businesses engaged wholly or mainly in dealing in securities or in land or buildings unless the business is (1) that of a jobber or discount house in the UK or (2) that of a holding company and the group as a whole is not wholly or mainly engaged in investment or property dealing.

The original provisions gave relief of 30 per cent in the value of relevant business property for capital transfer tax purposes, but with effect from 26th October, 1977 new rates of relief apply.

On the transfer of the whole or part of a business, e.g. that of a sole proprietor or partner, the relief is 50 per cent. On the transfer of a controlling interest of shares in an unquoted company, the relief is 50 per cent. Land, buildings, plant and machinery and other property used in a business or in a company controlled by the transferor or in a partnership in which the transferor is a partner qualify for relief at 30 per cent. Minority shareholdings in unquoted companies qualify for relief at 20 per cent. Securities dealt in on the Unlisted Securities Market are deemed to be 'unquoted' shares.

The appropriate rate of relief takes the form of a reduction in the value of the relevant business property before deducting the amount of the annual exemption or any other relevant reliefs.

Relief is available only if the transferor owned the business or the business property for two years or more immediately before the transfer, or the property transferred replaced other relevant business property and that either one property or the other had been held for at least two years in the five years prior to the transfer.

For the purpose of relief on business property, the business assets are valued on the normal basis for the purpose of capital transfer tax, i.e. at open market value less liabilities. If any of the business assets have not been used wholly or mainly in the business in the last two years or are not required at the time of the transfer for the future use of the business, they are excluded from the relief. The same applies to assets used wholly or mainly for the personal benefit of the transferor or persons connected with him.

With effect from 10th March, 1981, relief on business property at the rate of 30 per cent is available on land, buildings, plant, etc. used for business purposes by a transferor, but comprised in a settlement in which he was beneficially entitled to an interest in possession, e.g. where the transferor is the tenant for life of business property.

Agricultural property In the tradition of the old estate duty laws, a degree of relief is available on transfers of agricultural property for the purpose of capital transfer tax. With effect from 6th April, 1976 the relief for tax purposes is 50 per cent of the agricultural value of the land.

For the purpose of the relief, agricultural property means agricultural land or pasture in the UK (including in this instance the Channel Islands and the Isle of Man) and any farmhouses, farm cottages or other buildings appropriate to the business of agriculture. Thus, a farmhouse appropriate to the overall size of the farm will qualify. On the other hand, former farm cottages let for holiday purposes will not. Woodlands are eligible for relief if they are connected with the agricultural business. For the purpose of the relief, market gardening is treated as farming.

The relief applies to lifetime gifts as well as transfers on death. It applies also to agricultural property held in settlements, provided that there is an interest in possession, but not if it is a discretionary trust.

The rules governing agricultural relief were amended in the Finance Act 1981 and the relief will apply if either of the following two primary conditions are satisfied:

1. The transferor occupies the property. Under this heading, the transferor, or a company controlled by the transferor, must have occupied the agricultural property for agricultural purposes for at least two years prior to the transfer. If he acquired the property by inheritance, the time is deemed to run from the date of death. If the transferor had moved from one agricultural property to another, it is sufficient that for at least two years out of the previous five he had occupied one or other of the agricultural properties. If a farmer ceases to occupy agricultural property, e.g. through retirement or illness, but continues to own it, he may still obtain the agricultural relief on the transfer of the property provided
(a) relief would have been available if he had transferred the property at the time he vacated it,
(b) the transfer is to a member of his family (which in this context is construed widely, including nephews and nieces of the farmer or his wife and adopted and illegitimate children).
2. The property was owned by the transferor for the seven years ending at the date of transfer and occupied as agricultural property during that period. Thus, the transferor need not himself be engaged in agriculture. Under the 1981 Act, it is sufficient that the property be let and occupied as agricultural property during the qualifying period. If the seven year qualifying period is not satisfied, it is sufficient that the property was occupied for agricultural purposes for seven out of the ten years immediately prior to the transfer.

The relief applies only to the agricultural value of the property. If, for example, part of the property has a development or 'hope' value, this factor will be excluded from the relief. The essence of the relief is that the property will be used for agricultural purposes in perpetuity.

Prior to 10th March, 1981, agricultural relief was limited to a total agricultural value of £250,000 or 1,000 acres, whichever gave the greater relief. Rough grazing land, however, counted as one-sixth of its actual area for the purpose of calculating the 1,000 acres. A hill-farmer might, therefore, be able to claim relief on a 6,000 acre farm. The limit has been removed under the Finance Act 1981 but there are transitional provisions where a transferor became entitled to agricultural property on the death of a spouse after 10th March, 1981. In general, the 50 per cent relief will apply where the transferor occupies the property for agricultural purposes and can offer vacant possession at the time of the transfer, or within 12 months. In other cases, which will normally mean agricultural land that is let, the relief is restricted to 20 per cent.

Agricultural relief may also be obtained in relation to shares or debentures in a company engaged in agriculture provided the company was controlled by the transferor and the general requirements of farming are met, as described in relation to an individual farmer.

Agricultural relief must be claimed within two years of the transfer by such person as may be liable for payment of all or part of the tax.

On the transfer of assets forming part of an agricultural business, it will usually be possible to claim either business relief or agricultural relief, or in some cases both. It will not be possible, however, to claim business relief on assets for which agricultural relief is claimed. The following points should be borne in mind:

1. Any business conducted on the agricultural estate, but not qualifying for agricultural relief, may qualify for business relief.
2. Business relief may in certain circumstances be more favourable than agricultural relief. (This is primarily because business relief is applied to the value of the business asset before deduction of available exemption. Agricultural relief, however, is applied to that part of the chargeable transfer which relates to the agricultural property.)

Where a farm is transferred subject to a mortgage, the relief applies to the net value. If part of the mortgage property is not agricultural, the relief is calculated proportionately.

Woodlands Certain relief from capital transfer tax applies to the transfer of woodlands on death.

Where death gives rise to a transfer of woodlands, the executors (or other persons liable for payment of the capital transfer tax) may elect to have the value of the timber (not the underlying land) excluded from the estate for tax purposes. This will apply only if

1. the election is made within two years of the death, and
2. the deceased owned the woodlands beneficially for at least five years before his death, or acquired it other than by purchase, e.g. by gift or inheritance.

The effect of the relief is that no capital transfer tax is paid on the value of the growing timber until it is sold or otherwise disposed of, or until it is transferred again on another death.

If the timber is disposed of, tax is charged on the market value at a rate of tax calculated by adding the value of the disposed timber to the value of the transferor's estate.

Where the owner of the timber makes a gift of part of it, there will be a charge to tax partly by reference to the value of the estate out of which the timber came and partly by reference to his own previous chargeable transfers.

Woodlands may qualify for business relief whether on a lifetime transfer or a transfer on death. Business relief may not be obtained in addition to woodlands relief on the growing timber, but may be claimed in lieu of it or may be claimed on the other assets, including the land itself, employed in the business.

Falls in value after death Where capital transfer tax is payable on the estate of a deceased person and the executors, or other persons, sell, within 12 months of the death, quoted investments held by the deceased at the time of death, the executor or other person may claim that the sale prices of the investments may be substituted for the valuation at the date of death. This relief does not apply, however, only to those investments which have been sold and fallen in value. If such a claim is made all the quoted securities in the estate which have been sold within the 12 month period must be revalued and tax paid according to the new gross figure.

Example If a person's investments at the date of death were valued for probate purposes at, say, £20,000 but sold within 12 months for £15,000, the overall loss of £5,000 is allowed as a reduction in the value of the estate for capital transfer tax purposes.

If, however, within two months of the sale of quoted securities the executors purchase other quoted securities, the loss on sale is reduced by the proportion which the amount of the re-investment bears to the amount of the proceeds. If, therefore, in the example above further investments had been purchased within two months at a cost of, say, £3,000, the relief would be reduced by £3,000/£15,000, i.e. from £5,000 to £4,000. Tax would be paid on £16,000.

Where land or buildings in a deceased's estate are sold within three years after the death, the sale price may be substituted for the probate value.

Where, because of the death of a transferor within three years of the transfer of property, additional tax becomes payable, because of the higher appropriate rate, a reduction is made in the amount of the additional tax if the value of the property has fallen between the date of the transfer and the date of death or, if the property has been sold before death, the date of sale.

The relief is limited to the difference between the tax already paid on the lifetime scale and the additional tax payable on the death scale calculated according to the lower value of the property. The relief does not apply to wasting assets such as motor cars and certain household goods.

As indicated above, the value of property passing on a death may be enhanced because of taking into account 'related property' or other property of the same kind passing on the death, e.g. unquoted shares held in a trust. If, in those circumstances, part of that particular property held in the estate is sold within three years of the date of death, the estate property may be revalued without regard to the other related property or other property passing. The sale must, however, be at arm's-length and the executors of the estate and the trustees of any settlement must not be the same persons.

Quick succession relief In accordance with the relief granted under the former estate duty rules, a degree of relief was granted from capital transfer tax on the death of someone who, within the previous four years, had received property which was the subject of a chargeable transfer. Under the Finance Act 1981, the period of relief was extended from four to five years with effect from 10th March 1981 and the same rules apply whether the assets in question are in direct ownership or settled property. The effect of the relief is that, where there are two or more chargeable events affecting the same property in a short period, the tax on the second event will be reduced by a percentage of the tax paid on that property on the previous chargeable event. If the successive events arise within one year, the relief is 100 per cent. The relief is reduced to 80 per cent, 60 per cent, 40 per cent and 20 per cent respectively depending on whether the event occurs in the second, third, fourth or fifth years.

In the case of settled property, the relief is obtainable whether or not the charge arises on death or on the termination of an interest in possession. The transferor must, however, have had an interest in possession in the settled property and the first charge to tax must not have arisen prior to the making of the settlement.

Gratuitous disclaimers If, within two years of the date of a person's death, any beneficiary under the estate disclaims gratuitously the amount of his or her interest, the disclaimer does not amount to a chargeable transfer.

A disclaimer by a beneficiary of an interest in settled property is similarly regarded. It is not a chargeable transfer and the person concerned is treated as not having been entitled to the interest. In the case of settled property, there is no statutory period within which the disclaimer, to be effective for tax purposes, must be made. The passing of time may, however, make it increasingly difficult for the beneficiary to establish that the disclaimer is genuine.

Deeds of family arrangement Where the beneficiaries under a will or intestacy come to an arrangement among themselves to rearrange the beneficial interests, that arrangement does not constitute a chargeable transfer by the beneficiaries themselves, but takes effect for capital transfer tax purposes as if the terms of the arrangements had been incorporated into the terms of the will or intestacy (Section 47, Finance Act 1975 (as amended)).

It is not essential that such an arrangement should be by deed provided it is properly evidenced by some instrument or a formal exchange of correspondence. Nor is it necessary that the beneficiaries be in all cases members of the deceased's family in the narrow sense. It is a practice of the Inland Revenue to interpret the section widely and it would extend to any member of the deceased's family and to any beneficiary under the will or intestacy, but the section would not apply where, under the arrangement, some new beneficiary had been introduced who was not a member of the deceased's family.

For the section to apply, the deed of family arrangement must have been executed within two years of the death.

This relief will not be available where a beneficiary has already had some advantage from that part of the estate which is the subject of the arrangement, i.e. a beneficiary cannot take a gift and then redirect it to someone else.

The same section of the Act extends similar treatment to certain other situations:

1. A person may disclaim an interest in settled property, in which case the capital transfer tax rules will apply as if he had not been entitled to such interest.
2. An election by a surviving spouse under the Administration of Estates Act 1925, i.e. the redemption of a life interest in the residuary estate in return for a capital sum, is not a transfer for value and takes effect under this Section as if the capital sum had been payable on intestacy.
3. Where a beneficiary has taken property under a will and passed it to another person in accordance with some non-binding bequest by the testator, this is not a chargeable transfer and the gift takes effect as if it had not been incorporated in the terms of the will.

Death on active service The estate of a deceased person is exempt from capital transfer tax if the deceased

1. was at some time a member of the armed forces of the Crown or of certain ancillary organizations or was subject to the law governing the armed forces, and
2. died at any time as a result of a wound inflicted, an accident occurring or a disease contracted when on active service or on other service of a warlike nature, or
3. his death was caused by or hastened by the recurrence on active service, etc. of a disease contracted at some earlier date.

In order to claim relief, the personal representatives of the deceased must obtain from the Ministry of Defence a certificate stating that the requisite conditions have been satisfied.

Capital taxes on works of art Reference has already been made to circumstances in which gifts of works of art may enjoy freedom from capital transfer tax. Freedom from both capital gains tax and capital transfer tax can be obtained in relation to property held for the National Heritage and in recent times, the rules on this subject have been relaxed and more widely publicized.

Exemption from capital taxes may be granted for 'any pictures, prints, books, manuscripts, works of art, scientific collections or other things not yielding income which appear to the Treasury to be of national, scientific, historic or artistic interest'. Whether or not particular objects meet this standard depends on the advice which the

Capital Taxes Office takes from expert advisers in national museums and galleries.

In general, a person who *acquires* a work of art may obtain a conditional exemption from tax provided he or she undertakes

1. to keep the object permanently in the UK apart from temporary exhibitions abroad with the approval of the Treasury;
2. to take reasonable steps to preserve the object; and
3. to take reasonable steps to secure public access to the object.

A person who wishes to apply for such conditional exemption should do so immediately on receiving the object in question, whether by gift or inheritance. If exemption is allowed, it will apply to any taxes which might otherwise have been payable on the gift or transfer. The exemptions may be renewed on subsequent transfers provided that the three basic undertakings are observed.

'Reasonable public access' may be provided by

1. opening a house or a room to the public for a reasonable number of days each year for the purpose of viewing the object; or
2. arranging for the object to be lent to a public collection for display on a reasonably long-term basis; or
3. arranging for the details of the object to be entered in a list of conditionally exempt items maintained at the Victoria & Albert Museum with an undertaking that the object will be made available on request to interested persons and on loan to a public collection for not more than one special exhibition of up to six months' duration every two years.

A person wishing to *dispose* of a work of art may do so in the ordinary way, in which case capital gains tax and capital transfer tax may be payable. If the object in question is subject to a conditional exemption granted after 1st September, 1982 and the owner wishes to sell it on the open market, he or she must give public collections three months' notice of the intention by writing to the Museums and Galleries Commission. If this is not done, an export licence for the article may be withheld indefinitely.

On the disposal of a work of art, etc. exemption from capital taxes may be obtained

1. if the object is given or bequeathed to someone who renews the conditional exemption undertaking; or
2. if it is given or bequeathed to a public collection such as a national or local museum (as set out in Paragraph 12 of Schedule 6, Finance Act 1975); or
3. if it is sold by private treaty to one of such public bodies; or
4. if the object is acceptable to the Government in lieu of capital taxes on other property.

Sale by private treaty If the article is sold by private treaty to one of the public bodies listed in the 1975 Act, the proceeds will not attract capital taxes. The public body concerned will not normally pay as high a price as might be obtained on the open market because of the freedom from tax which the vendor will enjoy. The government have advised museums and galleries that they should in general offer the seller an amount equal to 25 per cent of the tax exemption over and above the net amount which the vendor would have received had the full tax been payable. In each case, however, the price will be the subject of negotiation.

Acceptance in lieu of tax If capital transfer tax is payable on other assets, the Treasury may accept a work of art in satisfaction of the tax liability. This again will depend on the advice of the expert advisers, but the standard will be much higher than that which applies to conditional exemption, mentioned above. In general, the advisers will have regard to the following guidelines:

1. Does the object have an especially close association with our history and national life?
2. Is the object of especial artistic or art-historical interest?
3. Is the object of especial importance for the study of some particular form of art, learning or history?
4. Does the object have any especially close association with a particular historic setting?

Indexation of Capital Transfer Tax Thresholds
From December 1982 onwards, if the general index of retail prices for the month of December exceeds that for the previous December, the bands of tax in Appendix 1 are increased by the percentage increase in the retail prices index. New tables are published by the Treasury before 6th April each year and the adjusted rates apply to chargeable transfers made on or after 6th April in that year.

CAPITALIZATION ISSUE An issue of shares consequent upon a reorganization of, but not an increase in, a company's capital. It normally takes the form of an issue of shares to existing shareholders in proportion to their existing shareholdings, the shares being created by a capitalization of existing reserves. SEE *Bonus Shares (Bonus Issue)*

CAPTIVE INSURANCE COMPANY This is usually a subsidiary company of a larger group and is set up for the purpose of handling the group's insurance risks. In this way, the group or parent company undertakes its own insurance, thereby retaining the profit element of the insurance contracts. It is thus a form of self-insurance, but the larger risks are usually laid off in the re-insurance market. In recent years, it has become the practice to establish captive insurance companies in those financial centres of the world where there is little or no tax liability. Bermuda and Guernsey in particular developed an expertise in this field of operation and, in more recent times, both the Isle of Man and Jersey have introduced legislation to permit insurance companies to operate with freedom from local tax. The main purpose of such off-shore captive insurance companies is that profits can be built up free from the tax structure and other constraints which may apply in the country where the parent company is registered.

CARAT A measure by which goldsmiths and assayers denote the fineness of gold. Any portion of gold is supposed to be divided into 24 parts, each part being called a carat, and if it is all pure gold it is said to be '24 carats' fine. English gold coins contain 11 parts pure gold and one part of copper; that is, standard gold is eleven-twelfths fine, and eleven-twelfths of 24 carats equal 22 carats fine.

The word is believed to have its origin in the name 'carob', the black bean pod of the locust tree, the beans being used historically as a measure of weight. So far as gold is concerned, a carat does not now represent any particular weight, but merely states the proportion of gold there is in any given weight. The carat used for weighing diamonds, however, has a fixed weight equal to 3.17 grains Troy.

The word also applies to the internationally accepted measurement of diamonds. In this case, it is the measurement of weight and a carat is equivalent to 0.2 gram. SEE *Diamonds, Investment in Gold*

CARRIAGE OF GOODS BY SEA ACT 1924 SEE *Bill of Lading*

CARRY OVER, CARRYING OVER On the Stock Exchange, to 'carry over' means to continue a bargain until next account, instead of paying for stock bought, or delivering stock which has been sold, as the case may be. In the former case the client may be required to pay contango (q.v.) and in the latter, backwardation (q.v.)

CARTE BLANCHE A payment card used for travel and entertainment and similar purposes, now owned by Citicorp. SEE *Credit Card*

CARTEL An agreement between manufacturing or trading organizations to control output, or to combine marketing operations, or to control prices, or to take other steps to dominate a market and restrict competition. Examples are the Krupps steel cartel in pre-war Germany and the manufacture of cement in pre-war Britain, the Central Selling Organisation controlled by the de Beers Group, which seeks to match the supply and demand for diamonds, and such international bodies as the Organisation of Petroleum Exporting Countries (OPEC) and International Air Transport Association (IATA). Such organizations are not necessarily antisocial or unlawful. Their position depends on the legislators' view in the country in which they operate and, to some extent, upon the circumstances of each individual case. Such agreements would normally be registrable in the UK under the Restrictive Trade Practices Act (q.v.) and might be referred to the Monopolies Commission by the Office of Fair Trading.

In the USA, cartels are referred to as 'trusts' and are governed by the anti-trust legislation of that country.

CASH A word believed to have its origin in an old French word *casse* meaning box, or the Italian *cassa* meaning case (*Oxford English Dictionary*). In everyday use, the term may refer now either to (1) ready money being bank notes or coins or (2) the payment aspect of a transaction which may be cash in the ready money sense, or payment by cheque (or other bill of exchange), or even by credit card. Hence, cash book and cash account.

We will limit our comment here to cash as ready money. As such, it is a measure of value and a token of exchange. All that is necessary for a commodity to be used as money is that it should be accepted as such by a community. Money becomes necessary in a primitive society when there are surpluses of goods of one kind or another or, in one area or another, beyond a level where exchange can be by barter. In the transition from barter to coinage, the artefacts of particular societies may be used as a medium of exchange as metallic tools were used by the early Chinese. In other societies, cattle, shells, cigarettes, postage stamps and a variety of other goods or tokens have been used as money. SEE *Coins*

Metallic coins were not supplemented by the use of bank notes to any significant degree until the twentieth century. SEE *Currency and Bank Notes Act 1928*

A bank note is a promissory note made by a banker payable to bearer and payable on demand. SEE *Bank of England Notes*

Of the 50,000 million or so payments made in the British Isles each year, some 95 per cent are made in coin or notes. All such cash is collected from the Bank of England by the clearing banks and distributed throughout the country. The banks are responsible for the entire cash distribution, i.e. not only for their own customers, but for other financial institutions including the building societies and the Post Office.

It is estimated that in the USA 87 per cent of all payments are still made in cash, amounting to approximately 200,000 million payments per annum. Nevertheless, this very considerable volume of payments constitutes only three per cent or so of the total value.

The first automatic dispensers of cash to be used anywhere in the world were introduced into the UK in 1967. SEE *Automated Teller Machines*

CASH DISPENSERS SEE *Automated Teller Machines*

CASH MANAGEMENT This is the management of the liquid resources of a business in order to maximize the return on those resources. In a simple case, it may be no more than the consolidation of a number of bank balances in order to minimize the net borrowing or to maximize the cash position for short-term investment. In the case of an international or multinational company, there may be many balances held in differing currencies around the world and the management of those cash resources can be a major operation. It entails the netting of balances among companies in the group, whether in one currency or a number of currencies. This in itself normally involves a computerized operation in one central place with telegraphic transmission for the recording of day-to-day balances. A number of banks offer computerized facilities to their customers for the day-to-day management of multicurrency balances. In some cases, this can be done in a 'neutral' tax area, thus enabling net balances to be accumulated with a degree of tax freedom.

CASH RATIO A bank maintains a cash reserve consisting of bank notes, coin and balances, available on demand with the Bank of England, in order to meet the demands of its customers for ready cash. The ratio between the total of such reserves and the bank's liabilities to the public on current, deposit, and other accounts is known as the cash ratio. It shows, therefore, the percentage of the total amount of money lodged with the bank by its customers that is held in the form of cash in the till or as balances at the Bank of England, convertible at will into cash.

Since cash so held is a non-earning asset, banks endeavour to keep its amount to a minimum. This, however, is determined by the banks' experience of their daily cash requirements in the ordinary course of business. A cash ratio of approximately 10 per cent was traditionally regarded as desirable, though such a percentage was purely conventional. However, in December 1946, the London Clearing Banks announced that as from 1st January, 1947

> Taking into account the general disposition of bank assets now ruling, it has been agreed in consultation with the Bank of England that the *daily* ratio of cash balances to deposit liabilities will be maintained on the basis of 8 per cent.

SEE *Competition and Credit Control*

CASH SETTLEMENT A Stock Exchange term applied to those cases where payment is required for securities on the business day following the day of the transaction. This applies to British Government securities and local Government stocks, but also to certain other cases, e.g. new issues in allotment letter form.

CASHFLOW The term is used loosely to indicate the transfer of cash over a period into or out of a person's hands, but in business terms it is usually the net accrual to the resources of a business in the course of a trading period. It is thus the net profit of the enterprise plus such provisions which may have been allowed in arriving at the net profit, but which do not in themselves represent an outflow of funds. The most typical item in this category is depreciation, but there may also be provision for deferred taxation. In most businesses, net cashflow means the net profit after tax plus depreciation added back.

In recent times, the term is used increasingly to refer to the literal cashflow of a business, i.e. the difference between the money coming in and the money going out. Usually a developing business would have a small or even negative cashflow as profits are ploughed back in the purchase of further assets. SEE ALSO *Discounted Cashflow*

CASHLESS SOCIETY For many years, people have spoken of the coming of a 'cashless society', meaning a society in which payment for goods and services would be made by one of the modern methods of settlement (e.g. cheques, standing orders, direct debits, electronic funds transfer) with a reduction in the number of payments made in cash. Indeed, in 1871 J. W. Gilbart in *The History and Principles of Banking* prophesied that 'Were every man to keep a deposit account at a bank and make all his payments by cheques, money might be superseded and cheques become the sole circulating medium'. In fact, that has not happened and at the present day 95 per cent of all payments in the UK are made in coin or notes. In the USA, 87 per cent of all payments are made in cash, i.e. over 200,000 million payments per annum. SEE *Cash*

Whilst there has been no significant decrease in the *number* of payments made in cash, the actual *value* of cash payments is small. In the USA, for example, only three per cent by value of payments are made in cash.

Although there is no foreseeable prospect of a cashless society, there has been increasing encouragement in recent years for the payment of wages by cheque (q.v.). This is partly because of the natural wish of the banks to encourage the banking habit, but it is also seen as a more efficient means of paying wages and a means of reducing the security risk.

CAUTION A method of protecting certain interests in registered land by lodging a notice at the Land Registry. Thus a party to a pending action affecting registered land may lodge a caution at the Land Registry against dealings in the land at issue. SEE ALSO *Mortgage Caution*

CAVEAT From the Latin, let him beware. A notice of warning given usually to some official authority indicating the interest in a particular matter of the person issuing the caveat. The term was used, for example, in relation to the Yorkshire Registry of Deeds (q.v.). The principal use of the term nowadays is in relation to applications for grants of probate and/or letters of administration. A person may give notice to the Principal Probate Registry or to any of the district registries to ensure that no grant of probate or letters of administration in a particular estate is sealed without notice being given to the caveator. The caveat must contain the name and last address of the deceased, the date and place of death, the name of the caveator and an address for service of the notice. An index of caveats is maintained at the Principal Probate Registry, including all caveats entered in district registries.

If a caveat has been entered, the person applying for a grant of probate or letters of administration must apply for the issue of a warning to the caveator. Indeed, any person interested in the proposed issue of a grant may also apply. A warning is then sent to the caveator requiring him to enter an appearance, indicating his interest in the matter. A caveator may withdraw his caveat at any time before entering an appearance, but if a warning has been issued the caveator must give notice of withdrawal to the person issuing the warning. If the time for entering an appearance has expired and the caveator has not entered an appearance, the person issuing the warning may file an affidavit showing that the warning was duly served and that he has not received a summons for directions. The caveat then ceases to have effect.

It is normal for a caveat to remain in force for a period of six months from the date on which it is entered. At one time it was not possible to renew or extend a caveat but under the Non-Contentious Probate (Amendment) Rules 1976, a person who has entered a caveat may apply for an extension of the existing caveat, provided he does so in the registry in which the caveat was originally entered. He must do so within the last month before the existing caveat is due to expire. The extension will be for a further period of six months from the original caveat's expiry date. A caveat may be extended more than once.

CENTRAL BANK The name given to a bank which (1) holds its government's liquid funds and the reserves of the commercial banks, (2) has a monopoly (or virtual monopoly) of the note issue and the custody and control of the gold reserve of the country, and (3) controls and regulates the supply of credit. In some countries, the central bank is a privately owned joint stock company, which issues its own notes, subject to certain legal restrictions. In other countries, it is owned by the state. In either case, its function is to control the volume of credit by raising or lowering its rate of discount and by buying or selling securities on the market. Latterly, central banks in certain countries have been charged by their governments with the management of large funds set aside for use in safeguarding the currency against undue short-term fluctuations. SEE *Exchange Equalization Account*

Central banks also undertake the negotiation of international monetary agreements. The understanding reached between England, France and the USA in September 1936, regarding exchange stabilization was a good example of this type of co-operation.

The last 50 years have seen a great increase in the number of central banks, principally because of the emergence of new self-governing nations. The USA in 1913 set up a reserve banking system, rather than a central bank proper, for by the Federal Reserve Act a series of government banks was established and membership of the Reserve System was optional. Members were under an obligation to keep certain specified reserves with their local reserve bank, and submit to inspection, receiving certain privileges (such as status) in return. Membership of national banks is now compulsory and the activities of the various reserve banks are coordinated and very largely controlled by the Federal Reserve Board, which, though part of the original plan has in recent years acquired greater powers and has also become less of an organ of the banking profession and much more a department of government.

CERTIFICATE The document which is issued by a company, to a member of the company, specifying the shares or stock held by him. It is usually signed by two directors, countersigned by the secretary, and impressed with the company's seal. Under the Stock Exchange (Completion of Bargains) Act 1976, companies are authorized to use a separate seal for the purpose of sealing certificates. This is a facsimile of the common seal with the addition of the word 'securities'.

Certificates are of many different sizes, and usually papers of different colours are used for the various classes or issues of shares and stocks.

A certificate under the common seal of the company, specifying any shares held by any member, shall be prima facie evidence of the title of the member to the shares (Section 184 of the Companies Act 1985). SEE *Share Capital*

Before an official quotation for stocks and shares can be obtained, the Committee of the Stock Exchange require that the certificates must conform to certain conditions SEE *Quotation on London Stock Exchange*

Section 185 of the Companies Act 1985, provides that:

> ... every company shall—
> (a) within 2 months after the allotment of any of its shares, debentures or debenture stock, and
> (b) within 2 months after the date on which the transfer of any such shares, debentures or debenture stock is lodged with the company
>
> complete and have ready for delivery the certificates of all shares, the debentures and the certificates of all debenture stock allotted or transferred (unless the conditions of issue of the shares, debentures or debenture stock otherwise provide).

The Section contains certain exemptions in relation to transfers under the Stock Transfer Act 1982 and allotments or transfers to Stock Exchange nominees.

Under Section 183(5), if a company refuses to register a transfer of any shares or debentures, the company shall, within two months after the date on which the transfer was lodged with the company, send to the transferee notice of the refusal.

Where certificates are lodged as security, a blank transfer (q.v.) and qualifying agreement or letter of deposit, are taken by some banks, but the most satisfactory way is to take a completed transfer and letter of deposit and have the shares registered in the names of the nominees of the bank or in the name of a nominee company. If, however, a banker does not wish to register at once, he often takes a fully completed transfer with a letter of deposit and gives notice of his charge to the company. When this is done and he retains possession of the certificate, he has, as a rule, a good security. (See however, the remarks under *Transfer of Shares* with reference to the giving of notice to the company.) A simple deposit of certificates as security even without a memorandum of deposit, constitutes an equitable mortgage, and the banker can, when necessary, apply to the court for power to sell. In nearly all cases, the certificates must be surrendered before a transfer of the shares can be effected.

A deposit of a certificate with or without blank transfers will be defeated if it transpires that the depositor holds as a trustee.

At the time of writing, a proposal is before the Stock Exchange for the voluntary elimination of share certificates. The suggestion is that a Central Stock Office of the Stock Exchange will record all dealings on behalf of the scheme's members who will be stockbrokers, banks and large institutions. The system will be entirely computerized and designed to eliminate the paper work at present involved in share dealings. A private investor would join the scheme only through an agent who would be a member of the Central Stock Office and who would act as the investor's nominee.

CERTIFICATE TO COMMENCE BUSINESS When a public company is entitled to commence business, the Registrar of Companies issues a certificate that the company is entitled to commence business, and that certificate is conclusive evidence thereof. Any advance made by a banker to a company before the date of that certificate cannot be recovered from the company. A private company, however, is entitled to commence business immediately after incorporation and the above certificate is not required. The regulations regarding the commencement of business and the exercise of any borrowing powers are contained in Section 109 of the Companies Act 1948, now re-enacted in Section 117 Companies Act 1985.

A company limited by guarantee and not having a share capital does not require to obtain a certificate before commencing business or exercising its borrowing powers.

CERTIFICATE OF DEDUCTION OF INCOME TAX SEE *Income Tax*

CERTIFICATE OF DEPOSIT A Certificate of Deposit was defined in the Finance Act 1968 as

> a document relating to money, in any currency, which has been deposited with the issuer or some other

person, being a document which recognises an obligation to pay a stated amount to bearer or to order, with or without interest, and being a document by the delivery of which, with or without indorsement the right to receive that stated amount, with or without interest, is transferable.

SEE *London Dollar Certificates of Deposit; Sterling Certificates of Deposit*

CERTIFICATE OF EXISTENCE A company paying an annuity to a person will often require, before making the payments, a certificate that such person was alive on a certain day. Such a certificate will quite often be given by a bank on behalf of a customer and the bank will of course satisfy themselves that their customer is alive. (This is sometimes known as a life certificate.)

CERTIFICATE OF INCORPORATION On the registration of the memorandum of a company, the registrar of companies shall certify under his hand that the company is incorporated, and in the case of a limited company that the company is limited. From the date of incorporation, mentioned in the certificate of incorporation, the subscribers to the memorandum, and others who may become members, shall be a body corporate, capable of exercising all the functions of an incorporated company, and having perpetual succession and a common seal, with power to hold land, but with such liability on the part of the members to contribute to the assets of the company, in the event of its being wound up, as is provided for in the Companies Act.

Such a certificate is conclusive evidence that all the requirements of the Act, in respect of registration and of matters precedent and incidental thereto, have been complied with, and that the association is a company authorized to be registered and is duly registered under the Act. (See Section13, Companies Act 1985, and also under *Articles of Association and Memorandum of Association.*)

CERTIFICATE OF INSCRIPTION (OR STOCK RECEIPT) A certificate of inscribed stock. It is of value as a memorandum only, the stockholder's title being the entry in the books of the registrar.

CERTIFICATE OF INSURANCE SEE *Insurance Certificate*

CERTIFICATE OF MORTGAGE OF SHIP A registered owner, if desirous of disposing by way of mortgage or sale of the ship or share in respect of which he is registered, at any place out of the country in which the port of registry of the ship is situate, may apply to the registrar, and the registrar shall thereupon enable him to do so by granting a certificate of mortgage or a certificate of sale (Section 36, Merchant Shipping Act 1894). The instrument gives particulars of the ship and an account of mortgages or certificates of mortgages granted in respect of the ship.

A person who advances money under a certificate of mortgage, when there is a previous mortgage or certificate of mortgage indorsed on the said certificate, does so at his own risk. His title is liable to be defeated by the person claiming under the incumbrance so indorsed. SEE *Ship*

CERTIFICATE OF ORIGIN OR MANUFACTURE A document issued at a custom house or by a chamber of commerce (q.v.). The object of the certificate is to satisfy an importer in certain foreign countries that the goods he is to receive are of British origin or manufacture. When sending goods to certain countries, exporters must include among the documents a certificate of origin bearing the visa of the consul of the consignee's country.

CERTIFICATE OF REGISTRATION A certificate given by the Registrar of Companies of any mortgage or charge registered in pursuance of Section 401 of the Companies Act 1985 (SEE *Registration of Charges*), and stating the amount thereby secured. The certificate is conclusive evidence that the requirements of the Act as to registration have been complied with. A copy of every certificate of registration is to be indorsed by the company on every debenture or certificate of debenture stock which is issued by the company, and the payment of which is secured by the mortgage or charge so registered. In the case of *Re C. L. Nye Ltd* [1970] 3 WLR 158, a certificate was held to be good despite the charge not having been delivered within 21 days of its execution and the date of the charge wrongly stated. There was, however, no suggestion of fraud in the case.

CERTIFICATE OF SEARCH A certificate issued by the Registrar of a Deeds or Charges or Land Register in response to an application for an official search in respect of certain properties or names. Certificates of search are also issued by local authorities in respect of local land charges. SEE ALSO *Land Charges*

CERTIFICATED BANKRUPT A bankrupt who holds a release from the Court of Bankruptcy. SEE *Bankruptcy*

CERTIFICATION OF CHEQUES In the USA cheques are freely 'certified' by bankers, the certification being equal to an acceptance by the banker. When a US banker accepts or certifies a cheque, he charges the amount at once to the drawer's account and holds it in a special account against his liability upon the cheque. By the law of that country 'where the holder of a cheque procures it to be accepted or certified, the drawer and all indorsers are discharged from liability thereon'.

In the UK, cheques were sometimes for the convenience of bankers in connection with the local clearing of cheques, 'marked' as good. Instead of 'marking' a cheque some bankers paid it, if in order, and gave in exchange a clearing voucher to be passed through the next local clearing.

Marking has been treated in the UK as not being the equivalent of acceptance, and does not render the banker liable to the holder. (See *Bank of Baroda Ltd* v *Punjab National Bank Ltd* [1944] AC 176, which, although a Privy Council case relating to India and hence not binding, did not differentiate from English law.) SEE *Marked Cheque*

CERTIFICATION OF TRANSFERS SEE *Certified Transfer*

CERTIFIED CHEQUE A cheque which is marked or certified by a banker that it is good for the amount for which it is drawn. The 'marking' of a cheque for the drawer or a holder is not a desirable practice. It is better to debit the cheque to the drawer's account and issue a banker's draft. SEE *Certification of Cheques, Marked Cheque*

CERTIFIED TRANSFER Transfers are often certified upon the margin by the secretary or registrar of a company, that the certificates for the shares dealt with in the transfer are in the company's office. The words generally used are

Certificate for ... shares, ... paid, has been lodged at the company's office. Date.
The ... Company Limited
..., Secretary

Or sometimes the words are 'Coupon for £ ... received at the company's office by '.

The custom of certifying transfers grew out of the exigencies of Stock Exchange practice when, for example, part only of a holding of shares is sold and the certificate has to be split. The relative transfer is certified by the company that the relative certificate has been lodged with it, thus providing assurance to the buyer that the seller is, in fact, able to deliver the shares in question. Alternatively, the Secretary of the Share and Loan Department of the Stock Exchange will by means of a facsimile signature certify that a specified certificate has been forwarded to the company's office. Many transfer forms have this form of certificate printed on them.

The method of certification varies, and sometimes the secretary or registrar signs or initials the transfer; more often a subordinate official or a clerk signs or initials it. A rubber stamp is used, often with a facsimile signature, which is sometimes initialled.

Cases have arisen where a duly authorized agent has certified transfers in fraud of the company, the relative certificates not having been lodged.

In *Bishop* v *Balkis Consolidated Co* [1890] 25 QBD 512, Lindley, LJ, said

In my opinion, it is proved that to give 'certifications' is incidental to the transaction, in the ordinary business way, of part of the legitimate business of all companies having capital divided into shares which are transferable by deed or other instrument.

Such a certification, however, does not appear to put much responsibility upon the company. In *Peat* v *Clayton* [1906] 1 Ch 659, Joyce, J, said

It only amounts to a representation that a document has been lodged with the company, apparently in order, and showing, prima facie, that the transferor is entitled to the shares, but it is no warranty of the transferor's title to the shares, or as to the validity of any of the documents, or that the company has received no notice in lieu of distringas, or any other notice affecting the matter.

In *George Whitechurch Ltd* v *Cavanagh* [1902] AC 117, Lord MacNaghten said

There is no obligation on a company to certify transfers at all. The certification is not passed by the directors or brought before the board. A certification, in fact, is only required for a temporary purpose, to meet the exigencies of business on the Stock Exchange, which has stated days and fixed periods for the different stages of a business transaction intended to be carried out under its rules.

In this case, it was held that the authority given by a company to certify transfers only extends to cases where certificates are actually lodged and the company is not bound by any fraudulent act of its secretary in connection with such transfers. Hence certified transfers are not usually acceptable as banking security and if taken should be sent to the registrar without delay.

Section 184 of the Company Act 1985 provides that the certification by a company of any transfer will be a representation by the company that there have been produced to the company such documents as show a prima facie title to the shares or debentures, but not that the transferor has any title thereto. The Section goes on to provide that a transfer will be certificated if it bears the words 'certificate lodged' or like words and is signed or initialled by an authorized person. Such signature need not be handwritten.

By the rules of the Stock Exchange, the buyer of securities may refuse to pay for a transfer deed unaccompanied by the certificate, unless it be officially certified that the certificate is at the office of the company. SEE *Balance Ticket; Transfer of Shares*

CESTUI QUE TRUST A person in whose favour a trust operates, that is, who is beneficially interested in the estate. If A holds land in trust for B, A is the trustee and B is the *cestui que trust*. Plural, *cestuis que trustent*.

CHAPS SEE *Clearing House Automated Payments System*

CHARGE CERTIFICATE The certificate issued under seal by the Land Registry when a charge on registered land is registered. It contains the original charge and is the equivalent of a legal mortgage of un-registered land. SEE *Land Registration*

CHARGE BY WAY OF LEGAL MORTGAGE A method of effecting a mortgage of freeholds or leaseholds. If the mortgage recites that 'A as beneficial owner hereby charges by way of legal mortgage all and singular the property mentioned in the schedule, etc.', the mortgagee will be in the same position as if a mortgage had been effected by a demise of freeholds or a subdemise of leaseholds. See Schedule 5 to Law of Property Act 1925. SEE ALSO *Legal Mortgage, Mortgage*

CHARGES SEE *Bank Charges*

CHARGING ORDER Where a creditor has obtained judgment against a debtor for the payment of a debt, he may obtain from the court an order charging, with the payment of the judgment debt, any shares or stock standing in the name of the debtor, or in the name of any person in trust for him. The effect of the order is to prevent a company from registering any transfer, or paying any dividend to the shareholder, in respect of the shares or stock so charged. A lender against the shares concerned, if served with notice of the Charging Order, must not lend further sums against the security. At the expiration of six calendar months from the date of the order *nisi*, the judgment creditor may proceed to take the benefit of the charge after obtaining from the court an order for sale.

This way of seeking satisfaction of a judgment debt has been available in relation to land since the Administration of Justice Act 1956, which abolished the old form of 'Writ of Elegit'. In order to obtain the benefit in the event of insolvency or as against a third party, it is necessary to appoint a receiver of the land (*Re Overseas Aviation Engineering Ltd* [1963] Ch 24).

CHARITABLE COMPANIES Under Section 19, Companies Act 1948, companies formed for the purpose of promoting art, science, religion, charity or any other like object could be licensed by the Board of Trade (now the Department of Trade and Industry) to be registered as a company with limited liability without the addition of 'limited' to its name.

Section 19 was repealed by the Companies Act 1981 and a company is entitled to the exemption from the use of 'limited' only if

1. its objects are the promotion of commerce, art, science, education, religion, charity or any profession and anything incidental or conducive to any of those objects, *and*
2. its memorandum or articles of association
(a) require its profits or other income to be applied in promoting its objects,
(b) prohibit the payment of dividends to its members, *and*
(c) require all the assets which would otherwise be available to its members generally to be transferred on winding up, either to another body with objects similar to its own or to another body whose objects are the promotion of charity and anything incidental or conducive thereto (Section 25, Companies Act 1981, re-enacted in Section 30 of the Companies Act 1985).

In order to secure this exemption, a statutory declaration should be delivered to the Registrar of Companies (by a director or secretary of the company or a solicitor acting for the company) when application is made to register the company. A company to which this exemption applies will also be exempt under Section 108 of the 1948 Act, from publishing the company's name and places of business on business documents and from sending lists of members to the Registrar.

CHARITABLE TRUST A trust for the relief of poverty, the advancement of education or religion, or for the benefit of the community in some other way (Lord MacNaghten's definition in *Re Pemsel*, [1891] AC 531). Such a trust, as opposed to a private trust, is not subject to the rule against perpetuity, i.e. it can continue indefinitely. With changing social conditions, it has in many cases become difficult for the trustees of old charities to apply their funds in pursuance of the original intention of the settlor, and much case law has resulted from such trustees seeking power to vary the conditions of their trusts and from personal representatives or beneficiaries under a will wishing to establish whether a trust is, in fact, charitable or not.

Thus, in *Re Cole: Westminster Bank* v *Moore* [1958] 3 All ER 102, Lord Evershed, MR, said

Notwithstanding the passage of three centuries during which the Courts have been able to attach the charitable label to large numbers and varieties of dispositions and reject the claim to qualify in no less a number of cases, the underlying idea seems to remain as elusive as ever. The truth may be that the possible variations of expressed intention by testators and settlors are as the sands of the sea and that no catalogue of illustrations, however long, can exhaust or confine charity's scope.

In the same case, Romer, LJ, restated the settled legal principle in his judgment. 'It is clear beyond controversy that if trust property is vested in trustees to apply income for purposes, some of which are charitable and some are not and the trust involves a perpetuity, then the whole gift fails.'

Thus, in *Re Diplock* [1941] Ch 253, large sums of money had been distributed to charities by trustees directed to benefit 'charitable or benevolent objects'. The gift failed because benevolent objects are not necessarily charitable, and the trustees incurred heavy liability.

In more recent times, the Charity Commissioners (Annual Report 1983) have considered whether trusts and other organizations set up for the benefit of the unemployed were entitled to charitable status. Whilst it was clear that the relief of poverty among the unemployed is a charitable purpose, the Commissioners came to the conclusion that organizations providing long-term work (even organizations of a kind which are non-political and non-profit making) are not regarded as charitable.

The Charities Act 1960 enlarges the powers of the Charity Commissioners and makes them responsible to Parliament, to whom they must make an annual report. A Register of Charities is established on which every charity not exempted by the Act must be registered, and such registration is conclusive proof of charitable status. (This status carries with it certain exemptions from tax, distribution of income for charitable purposes being tax-free.) The obligation to register is placed on the charity trustees, who, under the Act, are defined as the persons having the general control and management of the administration of the charity. A custodian trustee is, therefore, not under any duty to register the charity.

Section 22 of the Act authorizes the establishment of common investment funds for charities. By virtue of this power, a common fund is already in existence for certain almshouses, and the Charities Official Investment Fund has been set up for the benefit of charities generally. Large charities may well prefer to continue to manage their own investments, but the common fund is of considerable attraction to trustees of smaller funds.

Under Section 23, where it appears to the Commissioners that any action proposed or contemplated in the administration of a charity is expedient in the interests of that charity, they may by an order sanction that action. Such an order may give directions as to the manner in which any expenditure is to be borne. Banks asked to lend against the security of a mortgage of land held under a charitable trust should, therefore, either see a clear power to mortgage in the instrument, whether deed or will, setting up the trust, or make certain that the consent of the Commissioners to the proposed mortgage has been given.

Under Section 24, the Commissioners may give an opinion or advice to a charity trustee on matters affecting the performance of his duties. A trustee acting on such advice shall be deemed to have acted in accordance with his trust unless he knows, or should suspect, that the opinion or advice was given in ignorance of material facts; or the decision of the court has been obtained in the matter, or proceedings are on foot to obtain one.

The Trustee Investment Act 1961 gives authority to trustees to invest up to one-half of a trust fund in a wide range of investments, including certain equities. This proportion of the fund may be increased to a maximum of three-quarters if the Treasury should by an order so direct. This Act applies to all trusts, including charitable trusts, with a few exceptions. SEE *Trustee Investments*

Where bankers or others lend to a charity and anticipate recovering from the assets of the charity, if need be, the consent of the Charity Commissioners will be necessary in relation to any charge on land. Also, it is thought, if the assets are endowed, the trustees being restricted to the use of the *income*, the consent may be necessary whether these endowed assets are mortgaged or not. SEE ALSO *Official Custodian for Charities*

CHARTS, CHARTISTS This refers to the practice of forecasting share price movements by interpreting charts or graphs of the historical share price. The theory of chartism is that share performances tend to follow recurring patterns, although in each case the particular pattern may not always be easily discernible. The practice was introduced by Charles H. Dow, founder of the Dow Jones Index, towards the end of the last century. The theory is that at any one time there is a main or primary trend in the market, i.e. a bull market or a bear market (q.v.) which may last over a period of a few years. Within that general trend there are secondary movements lasting perhaps for a few months and within that secondary pattern there are the day-to-day fluctuations.

Charts take various forms, but there are three main categories: *line* charts which are merely straight graphs of price movements over a period of time, usually plotted against some other relevant data, e.g. the market level generally, for purposes of comparison; *bar* charts made up of vertical lines showing the highest and lowest prices over, say, a particular week; and *point-and-figure* charts on which no time scale is shown, but on which movements in a share price up and down are recorded as they happen.

The usefulness of charts depends on the individual interpretation by chartists. Generally, however, they will look for a trend line to indicate a continuing bull or bear market. A chart may show that a particular share registers a 'resistance level' at a particular peak and that a share may show a particular 'support level', at which point buyers seem consistently to be forthcoming.

The chartist pays no direct regard to economic trends, the fiscal or legislative environment, social attitudes, changes of management, or any of the other factors to which an investment analyst would have regard. Chartists are criticized, therefore, for being 'unscientific' and for paying too little regard to the performance of individual companies. On the other hand, there is little doubt that a share price may go up or down depending on overall sentiment regardless of short-term company performance. It is thought to be the mass behaviour of investors which for the chartist produces cyclical patterns.

CHARTER PARTY An agreement by which the owners of a ship, or their agents, agree to place the vessel at the disposal of a merchant, the charterer, for the conveyance of a full cargo of goods. A charter party may be for one or more voyages or for a definite period of time, or it may effect a demise of the ship for any length of time that may be agreed upon.

The term 'charter party' is said to be derived from the Latin *charta partita* (divided parchment). In former times, the document was cut into two parts, one part being kept by the owner of the ship and the other part by the charterer.

The wording of the agreement varies somewhat according to the trade in connection with which it is used.

CHATTELS Chattel is a modern form of the word cattle. In primitive communities, cattle sometimes performed the function of money.

The Bills of Sale Act 1878, Section 4, defines personal chattels as follows:

> The expression 'personal chattels' shall mean goods, furniture, and other articles capable of complete transfer by delivery, and (when separately assigned or charged) pictures and growing crops, but shall not include chattel interests in real estate nor fixtures (except trade machinery as hereinafter defined), when assigned together with a freehold or leasehold interest in any land or building to which they are affixed, nor growing crops when assigned together with any interest in the land on which they grow, nor shares or interests in the stock, funds, or securities of any government, or in the capital or property or incorporated or joint stock companies, nor choses in action, nor any stock or produce upon any farm or lands which by virtue of any covenant or agreement or of the custom of the country ought not to be removed from any farm where the same are at the time of making or giving of such bill of sale.

By Section 5

> Trade machinery shall, for the purposes of this Act, be deemed to be personal chattels, and any mode of disposition of trade machinery by the owner thereof which should be a bill of sale as to any other personal chattels shall be deemed to be a bill of sale within the meaning of this Act.

Under the Administration of Estates Act 1925 'personal chattels' mean carriages, horses, motor cars (not used for business purposes), china, books, furniture, jewellery, wines, etc., but do not include any chattels used at the death of the intestate for business purposes nor money or securities for money (Section 55(1)(x)).

In the case of *Re Crispin's Will Trusts, Arkwright* v *Thurley* [1974] 3 WLR 657, the Court of Appeal, reversing the decision of the Palatine Court, held that a collection of clocks fell within the definition of 'personal chattels' under the Administration of Estates Act, notwithstanding that, in this instance, the clocks were worth about £51,000, out of a total estate of £83,000.

CHECK TRADING A system of instalment credit which had its origin in the North of England. Under a check trading scheme, customers are issued with vouchers which they use at shops on an approved list, payment for the vouchers being made on a regular instalment basis to a representative of the check trading company who will call at the customer's home. Check trading was first introduced into the UK by the Provident Clothing Company, now the Provident Financial Group. Check trading is regarded as the forerunner of credit cards (q.v.), partly in that payment was made by a voucher and secondly that the customer enjoys the benefit of revolving credit.

CHEQUE The cheque first came into use about 1780. It was then written 'check'. According to J. W. Gilbart

The word is derived from the French *echecs*, chess. The chequers placed at the doors of public-houses were intended to represent chessboards, and originally denoted that the game of chess was played in those houses. Similar tables were employed in reckoning money, and hence came the expression 'to check an account'; and the government office where the public accounts were kept was called the exchequer.

Another explanation is that the word 'check' arose from the consecutive numbers which were placed upon the forms to act as a check or means of verification. In the USA the word 'check' is used at the present day.

Section 73 of the Bills of Exchange Act 1882 defines a cheque as 'a bill of exchange drawn on a banker, payable on demand'. Section 3 contains a definition of a bill of exchange (q.v.). Thus, taking the two Sections together, a cheque is an unconditional order in writing, drawn on a banker, signed by the drawer, requiring the banker to pay on demand 'a sum certain in money' to or to the order of a specified person or to bearer.

A cheque differs from a bill in several points: it does not require acceptance; it is drawn upon a banker; the banker may be protected if he pays it bearing a forged indorsement; the drawer is the person liable to pay it, and the drawer, as a rule, is not discharged by delay in presenting it for payment. The intention of a cheque is that it be paid at an early date. The drawee's authority to pay is determined by notice of the drawer's death, and the drawer may stop payment of the cheque.

There is no legal requirement as to the material on which a cheque is written. It does not strictly have to be on the standardized cheque form and a cheque written out on a piece of paper is sufficient provided it is correctly worded. In practice, however, it is unlikely to be accepted by a bank in these days of automated clearing systems. Even less likely to be accepted are those cheques which have been drawn over the years on eggs, slabs of stone, the side of a cow and ladies' underwear.

The members of the British Bankers' Association (q.v.) agreed in June 1946 to standardize cheque forms. As regards size, they were not to exceed 8 inches by 4 inches or be less than 6 inches by 3 inches.

Prior to this time, the amount was usually inserted in figures on the left-hand side; as from June 1946, the space for the amount in figures has been shown on the right-hand side, immediately above the signature of the drawer.

The customary form of cheque should be adhered to as much as possible, though legally any form which fulfils the requirements of the Bills of Exchange Act would be sufficient as, for example, where the drawer instead of signing his name at the bottom signs it at the top, 'I, John Brown, direct you to pay to John Jones the sum', etc.

Some cheques have a notice upon them that they are payable only if presented within a certain period. Such a condition may possibly exclude the document from being considered a cheque under the Bills of Exchange Act. In *Thairlwall* v *Great Northern Railway Company* [1910] 2 KB 509, where a dividend warrant had a condition at the bottom of it that 'it will not be honoured after three months from date of issue unless specially indorsed for payment by the secretary', it was argued that the document was not a cheque because of this condition. Mr Justice Bray said

I have felt a great deal of doubt on this point because of this statement. But, on the whole, I am inclined to think that this document is a cheque, and is within the meaning of Sections 73 and 3 of the Bills of Exchange Act 1882, a cheque and an unconditional order in writing .... And I think it is none the less a cheque because of that statement at the bottom of the document. I do not consider that statement makes the order conditional.

There are also forms of cheques, or rather documents, which make the payment dependent upon a certain receipt being signed. Conditional documents of this kind are not cheques as defined by the Bills of Exchange Act. They may, however, be crossed like a cheque. SEE *Receipt on Cheque*

Since the passing of the Cheques Act 1957 (q.v.), indorsement is necessary for various reasons only in the following cases:

1. where cheques are cashed or exchanged across counter;
2. where cheques have been negotiated;
3. where cheques payable to joint payees are tendered for the credit of an account to which all are not parties;
4. where a cheque acts as a combined cheque and receipt form;
5. in the case of bills of exchange other than cheques, and promissory notes.

Some of the categories stem from the London Clearing Bankers' circular rather than from the Act and it is not certain that in all cases the courts would insist on indorsement. See, for example, *Westminster Bank Ltd* v *Zang* [1966] 1 All ER 114.

With regard to alterations in cheques and fraudulent alterations, see *Alterations to Bills of Exchange*.

If there is a difference between the amount in writing and the figures on a cheque, the cheque may be paid according to the amount in writing, but it is the usual custom to return the cheque unpaid marked 'amounts differ'. If the figures have been omitted and the amount only appears in writing, a banker is justified in paying the cheque according to the words, though if the words have been omitted and the amount is given only in figures, the cheque should not be paid.

If the payee himself presents a cheque for payment and declines to indorse it, he has probably a legal right to do so, and the banker paying the cheque will be protected under Section 1(1), Cheques Act 1957, if the cheque is otherwise in order. However, the circular dated 23rd September, 1957 of the Committee of London Clearing Bankers included the following:

> Indorsement will continue to be necessary in the following cases:
> (a) Cheques cashed or exchanged across the counter. It is considered that the public interest will best be served by continuing existing practice in regard to cheques cashed or exchanged. The Mocatta Committee set up by the Government to examine the whole question of indorsement attached importance to indorsement of such cheques as possibly affording some evidence of identity of the recipient and some measure of protection for the public.

If the balance of a customer's account will not allow of the full payment of a cheque which is presented, the cheque may be dishonoured. A cheque cannot be paid in part. In England, if such a cheque is dishonoured and another cheque is presented subsequently for a smaller amount, which the account will stand, it may be paid. In Scotland, however, when a cheque is presented for payment and there is not a sufficient balance to meet it, the cheque attaches such funds as there may be in the banker's hands belonging to the drawer, and subsequent cheques, though for a less amount than the balance of the account, will be returned unpaid. The amount attached is transferred by the banker to a separate account.

A cheque which has been cut, or torn, into two or more portions, or torn sufficiently to suggest cancellation, is not, as a rule, paid by a banker. But if a mutilated cheque bears a note upon it signed by a collecting banker, such as 'accidentally torn', it is customary to pay it.

A person is liable to be charged under the Theft Act 1968 if he gives a cheque in payment of a purchase when he has no account with the banker on whom the cheque is drawn.

As to an overdue cheque, see Section 36, Bills of Exchange Act (under *Negotiation of Bill of Exchange*), and Sections 45 and 74 (under *Presentment for Payment*).

A cheque is not invalid solely by reason that it is post-dated or ante-dated.

When the London clearing banks introduced electronic sorting and posting, they agreed that a code line should be printed in magnetic ink across the foot of the cheque. The code line contains symbols and numbers which, reading from left to right, will give the serial number of the cheque, the bank and branch sorting code number, the customer's account number, a transaction code number and the amount of the cheque.

Approaching 3,000 million cheques and other vouchers are handled by the British banks each year and the number continues to grow. Where a cheque is paid into a customer's account at a particular branch, that bank is said to 'collect' the cheque for the customer, which means that it is sent off through the clearing system to the branch of the bank on which it is drawn, i.e. the 'paying' bank. If for any reason the paying bank is not prepared to pay the cheque, either because there are no funds to meet it or the signature is irregular or there is some other defect, payment will be refused and the cheque will be returned to the collecting bank who will debit the customer's account. If the cheque is in order, it will be paid the day it is received at the paying bank and the payee's account will be credited. Nowadays, however, many cheques are supported by a cheque card and thus cannot be returned by the paying banker. Also, it is increasingly difficult to check signatures because cheques are sorted by mechanical means and by automated means and accounts debited according to the account number.

Whether the bank has a duty to scrutinize automated cheques which may have been altered manually, as in *Burnett v Westminster Bank Ltd* [1966] 1 QB 742, is not clear. In Burnett's case, the bank had printed warnings in their cheque books that the automated cheques would be debited to the accounts so designated, but Mocatta, J, held that the warning on the cheque book cover as to what was then a novel procedure could not be regarded as sufficient. The procedure is now well established and specific warnings are not given; but as there is clearly a duty to examine signatures to cheques it might be held that a bank must take notice of a clear alteration to the code line, coupled with the printed name of the account.

SEE *Alterations to Bills of Exchange; Antedated; Bearer; Bill of Exchange; Bills of Exchange Act 1882; Cancellation of Bill of Exchange; Cancelled Cheques and Bills; Cheques Act 1957;*

Clearing House; Collecting Banker; Consideration for Bill of Exchange; Countermand of Payment; Crossed Cheque; Date on Bill of Exchange; Delivery of Bill; Dishonour of Bill of Exchange; Drawee; Drawer; Foreign Bill; Forgery; Holder for Value; Holder in Due Course; Holder of Bill of Exchange; Inchoate Instrument; Indorsement; Indorser; Inland Bill; Lost Bill of Exchange; Marked Cheque; Negotiation of Bill of Exchange; Not Negotiable Crossing; Order (Cheque or Bill of Exchange); Overdue Bill; Part Payment; Parties to Bill of Exchange; Payee; Paying Banker; Payment of Bill; Payment of Cheque; Post-dated; Presentment for Payment; Receipt on Cheque, Returned Cheque or Bill; Stale Cheque; Time of Payment of Bill, Transferor by Delivery, Travellers' Cheques.

CHEQUE CARD The purpose of a bank cheque card is, in effect, to guarantee payment of a cheque within prescribed limits, whether presented for cash at a branch of the paying bank or to a trader for goods or services. The first cheque card was introduced by National Provincial Bank in October 1965, guaranteeing payment of cheques up to £30. In March the following year Midland Bank introduced their cheque card, and in the following month Lloyds Bank, Martins Bank, Williams Deacon's Bank, National Bank, Yorkshire Bank, Glyn Mills & Co., Lewis's Bank, Bank of Scotland, Royal Bank of Scotland, National Commercial Bank of Scotland, Bank of Ireland and Hibernian Bank, representing in all 4,600 branches, issued their joint Bankers' Card, similarly guaranteeing payment of cheques up to £30. In 1969, it was estimated that one million cheque cards were in use in Great Britain. With the merger of Barclays Bank and Martins Bank that year, the Bankers' Card was withdrawn from the former Martins Bank customers (Barclays Bank having already issued their Barclaycard, although at that stage this was not a cheque card).

An inevitable corollary of the cheque card's arrival was the reluctance of traders to accept cheques without a supporting card. It was suggested in *The Banker* that

> The decline in the cheque's acceptability is in part connected with the growing number of people with bank accounts. Until fairly recently, banks served a rather privileged section of the community—the same section as, rightly or wrongly, shopkeepers deferentially expected to be honest. The extension of the market has been accompanied by an increase of dud cheques and a greater degree of suspicion on the part of shopkeepers.

For a few years after the re-alignment of the banks in the postmerger period, only Barclays Bank operated without a cheque card as such. This led to the strange but perhaps predictable result that some traders refused to accept Barclays Bank cheques. As a result, Barclays Bank arranged for Barclaycards to serve the dual role of credit card and cheque card, and thus nowadays cheque cards are available in support of cheques issued by all the British clearing banks. The limit of the 'guarantee' is normally £50 for the purchase of goods and services and for cash withdrawals at other banks. Some banks offer a higher limit of £100 for cash withdrawals from their own branches.

For the 'guarantee' to apply, the conditions printed on the reverse of the cheque card must be satisfied:

1. The cheque must be signed in the presence of the payee.
2. The signature on the cheque must correspond with the specimen signature on the card.
3. The cheque must be drawn on a bank cheque form bearing the code number shown on the card.
4. The cheque must be drawn before the expiry date of the card.
5. The card number must be written on the reverse of the cheque.

Of great concern is the fraudulent use of cheque books and cheque cards. At the end of 1981, there were approximately 16 million cheque cards in issue in the UK. It is believed that in that year the loss to the British clearing banks through the fraudulent use of cheque cards was of the order of £12 million. A high proportion of fraud arises from the use of cheque cards outside the UK and it came as no great surprise when in April 1982 the clearing banks announced that the use of cheque guarantee cards would be restricted to the British Isles from May 1983. Even though the cheque card limit has been retained at £50 for purchases over the counter, a stolen book of 30 cheques is worth potentially £1,500 to a thief with the aid of a stolen or faked cheque card. Approximately 70 per cent of all card frauds take place over retail counters, not in the banks themselves. SEE *Credit Cards* and Supplement

CHEQUES ACT 1957 After many years of public discussion of the time spent in the indorsement of cheques that were paid in by the payee to his own account, the Mocatta Committee was appointed in 1955 to examine the possibility of change. The Committee rejected the suggestion, which had been widely canvassed, for a new non-transferable instrument, preferring to retain the negotiability of the cheque. The Committee's recommendations were the basis of the Cheques Act, the main effect of which was that cheques paid in to the credit of the payee's account no longer required indorsement and an unindorsed cheque paid by the banker on whom it was drawn became evidence of the receipt by the payee of the amount in question. The legislature took the opportunity of tidying up one or two other points in relation to cheques.

Sections 1, 2 and 3 of the Act provide as follows.

1.—(1) Where a banker in good faith and in the ordinary course of business pays a cheque drawn on him which is not indorsed or is irregularly indorsed, he does not, in doing so, incur any liability by reason only of the absence of, or irregularity in, indorsement, and he is deemed to have paid it in due course.

(2) Where a banker in good faith and in the ordinary course of business pays any such instrument as the following, namely—

(*a*) a document issued by a customer of his which, though not a bill of exchange, is intended to enable a person to obtain payment from him of the sum mentioned in the document;

(*b*) a draft payable on demand drawn by him upon himself, whether payable at the head office or some other office of his bank;

he does not, in doing so, incur any liability by reason only of the absence of or irregularity in, indorsement, and the payment discharges the instrument.

2. A banker who gives value for, or has a lien on, a cheque payable to order which the holder delivers to him for collection without indorsing it, has such (if any) rights as he would have had if, upon delivery, the holder had indorsed it in blank.

3. An unindorsed cheque which appears to have been paid by the banker on whom it is drawn is evidence of the receipt by the payee of the sum payable by the cheque.

Section 4 of the Act extends the crossed cheques provision of Section 82 of the Bills of Exchange Act 1882 to cover uncrossed cheques and certain other instruments such as Inland Revenue warrants, whether they are unindorsed or irregularly indorsed.

CHIEF REGISTRAR OF FRIENDLY SOCIETIES This official function had its origin in the Friendly Societies Act 1896. The Chief Registrar, together with the assistant registrars, constitute the Central Office of the Registry of Friendly Societies (SEE *Friendly Society*). The office of the Chief Registrar deals with applications by friendly societies for registration and receives the annual returns and valuations in the form which the Chief Registrar prescribes. The Chief Registrar appoints inspectors to investigate the affairs of societies as may be necessary and generally exercises an oversight of the friendly society movement in the UK.

Under the Building Societies Act 1962, the Chief Registrar of Friendly Societies is given a special responsibility and considerable powers in relation to building societies. It is perhaps the growth of the building society movement in the UK which has given special emphasis to the role of the Chief Registrar and the Central Office.

Under the Building Societies Act, the Chief Registrar has *inter alia* the power to

1. approve statements made by building societies under Section 20(1) of the Act in connection with the merging of building societies or the transfer of engagements between societies;
2. increase the limits for special advances (q.v.) with the consent of the Treasury;
3. extend the types of security which may be taken by building societies for advances, again with the consent of the Treasury;
4. approve arrangements for guarantee funds to protect investors from loss (SEE *Investors' Protection Scheme*);
5. authorize, with Treasury consent, a building society to lend money to another society in financial difficulty;
6. prohibit a society from accepting further funds;
7. control advertising by building societies;
8. demand production of books and other records from societies.

SEE *Building Societies*

CHIEF RENT Freehold land in Lancashire and around Bristol is sometimes subject to a perpetual rent charge called a 'chief rent'. The payment of the rent is secured to the owner of the rent charge by a right of re-entry. A chief rent must not be confused with a ground rent, where the freehold rests in the party receiving the rent, the party paying it having merely a leasehold interest. With a chief rent the party paying it is the owner of the freehold but is under a liability to pay an annual charge thereon.

CHILD ALLOWANCE This was a form of income tax allowance available to parents of children under the age of 18 or undergoing full-time education. The allowance was gradually phased out over a number of years and terminated completely after the fiscal year 1981–82.

CHILD BENEFIT This was introduced with effect from 5th April, 1977 and replaced the earlier system of family allowances. It is payable to persons who have the responsibility of bringing up a child or children. There is no means test and the benefit is free of income tax.

In the case of a married couple, it is the wife who should make the claim, but if the husband wishes to do so he should provide a signed statement from his wife that she does not wish to make the claim herself. If the parents of the child are unmarried, the mother should make the claim. If the child lives with one parent, that parent should make the claim and if the child lives with a couple who are not its parents, they may decide between themselves who should make the claim.

The child benefit is payable in respect of all children: under the age of 16 years, or aged 16–18 years if pursuing a full-time course of study at school or college up to A-Level or Ordinary National Diploma standard, but not if the child is studying at a higher level. Generally, child benefit will not be payable if

1. the child is in the care of the local authority, or
2. a child has been boarded out by the local authority with foster parents, or
3. the parents were exempt from UK income tax in the previous tax year, e.g. by virtue of employment for a foreign government, or
4. the parents or the child have not lived in the UK for more than 26 weeks in the past year.

With effect from 6th August, 1984, a child is deemed to be receiving full-time education if he or she is attending a course of education at a recognized educational establishment and in the pursuit of that course, the time spent receiving instruction or tuition, undertaking supervised study, examination or practical work or taking part in any exercise, experiment or project for which provision is made in the curriculum, exceeds 12 hours per week, excluding meal breaks and periods of unsupervised study.
The benefit is non-contributory. (See Appendix 2)

CHILD'S SPECIAL ALLOWANCE This is a weekly payment payable to a woman on the death of her former husband if

1. the marriage was dissolved or annulled, and
2. at the time of his death the woman had a child towards whose support the former husband was contributing or was liable to contribute.

The mother will be entitled to this special allowance if

1. she has not been married since the divorce or annulment, and
2. she is entitled to child benefit for the child, and
3. she or her former husband were entitled to child benefit when he was alive, and
4. her former husband was contributing at least 25p a week towards the child's support, or was obliged to do so under a Court Order or other agreement.

Child's special allowance is subject to a qualifying contribution record on the part of the former husband. (See Appendix 2)

CHOSE IN ACTION Property which a person has not got in his actual possession, but which he has a right to demand by an action at law. Money due upon a bill of exchange, book debts, insurance policies, legacies, and stocks and shares in a company are examples of a chose in action, sometimes referred to unnecessarily and uglifyingly as a *thing* in action. Where the money or goods are in actual possession, they are called choses in possession. SEE *Debts, Assignment of*

CHOSE IN POSSESSION SEE *Chose in Action*

CIRCULAR LETTER OF CREDIT At one time these were issued quite widely for the use of persons travelling abroad. A circular letter of credit is one which is addressed to all the correspondents of the issuing bank, whereas a direct letter of credit is addressed to a particular correspondent bank. It is an authority to the correspondent bank to provide the bearer of the letter of credit with facilities within the terms of the letter. Once the amount of the letter has been exhausted, the letter of credit is cancelled. With the increased use of travellers' cheques and credit cards, there is little need nowadays for letters of credit.

CITY CODE ON TAKE-OVERS AND MERGERS SEE *Take-overs and Mergers*

CLASSIFICATION OF BANK ADVANCES SEE *Lending by Banks*

CLAWBACK The withdrawal of income tax relief in certain circumstances where life assurance policies cease to be 'qualifying life policies' (q.v.). It has been the practice for very many years in the UK for life assurance premiums to qualify for a degree of income tax relief. With effect from 6th April, 1979, the tax relief (currently 15 per cent up to the permitted maximum—see below) is automatically deducted from all qualifying life assurance premiums. The maximum relief available to each taxpayer is £1,500 per annum or one-sixth of his or her total taxable income, whichever is the larger.

If a qualifying life policy on which the relief has been granted is surrendered or converted to a paid-up policy during the first four years of the policy's life, the Inland Revenue will 'clawback' some or all of the tax relief already allowed. In the event of surrender in the first two years, the clawback will be the full 15 per cent of the premiums paid; in the event of surrender in the third year, the clawback will be two-thirds of that 15 per cent, i.e. 10 per cent and in the event of surrender in the fourth year, the clawback will be one-third of 15 per cent, i.e. five per cent of the premiums paid. The insurance company will be required to deduct the amount of the clawback from the policy surrender proceeds. Similar rules apply to the converting of a life policy to a paid-up policy, or to the surrender of a bonus on a life policy.

Premiums on policies taken out after 13th March, 1984 do not qualify for tax relief (SEE *Income Tax*): thus clawback applies only to policies taken out on or before that date.

CLAYTON'S CASE This case, decided in 1816, and reported in 1 Mer 529 *et seq.* (sometimes quoted as *Devaynes* v *Noble*), is the leading authority on the subject of the appropriation of payments (q.v.). If a debtor owes more than one debt to his creditor, and pays him a sum of money insufficient to liquidate the whole of the debts, it is sometimes a matter of importance, e.g. in relation to the Limitation Act 1939, to know to which debts the payment is to be appropriated. From Clayton's Case, the following rules are derived, mainly taken from the Roman Law: (1) A debtor making a payment has a right to appropriate it to the discharge of any debt due to the creditor; (2) if at the time of payment there is no express or implied appropriation thereof by the debtor, then the creditor has a right to make the appropriation; (3) in the absence of any appropriation by either debtor or creditor, an appropriation is made by presumption of law, according to the items of account, the first item on the debit side being the item discharged or reduced by the first item on the credit side. The principle of the case was thus explained (see p. 608 of the report):

> This is the case of a banking account, where all the sums paid in form one blended fund, the parts of which have no longer any distinct existence. Neither banker nor customer ever thinks of saying, 'This draft is to be placed to the account of the £500 paid in on Monday, and this other to the account of the £500 paid in on Tuesday.' There is a fund of £1,800 to draw upon, and that is enough. In such a case, there is no room for any other appropriation than that which arises from the order in which the receipts and payments take place, and are carried into the account. Presumably, it is the sum first paid in that is first drawn out. It is the first item on the debit side of the account that is discharged, or reduced, by the first item on the credit side. The appropriation is made by the very act of setting the two items against each other. Upon that principle all accounts current are settled, and particularly cash accounts. When there has been a continuation of dealings, in what way can it be ascertained whether the specific balance due on a given day has, or has not, been discharged, but by examining whether payments to the amount of that balance appear by the account to have been made? You are not to take the account backwards, and strike the balance at the head, instead of the foot, of it. A man's banker breaks, owing him, on the whole account, a balance of £1,000. It would surprise one to hear the customer say, 'I have been fortunate enough to draw out all that I paid in during the last four years; but there is £1,000 which I paid in five years ago that I hold myself never to have drawn out; and, therefore, if I can find anybody who was answerable for the debts of the banking house, such as they stood five years ago, I have a right to say that it is that specific sum which is still due to me, and not the £1,000 that I paid in last week.'

The Earl of Selborne, LC, in *In re Sherry, London and County Banking Company* v *Terry* (1884) 25 ChD 692, said

> The principle of Clayton's Case, and of the other cases which deal with the same subject, is this, that where a creditor having a right to appropriate moneys paid to him generally, and not specifically appropriated by the person paying them, carries them into a particular account kept in his books, he prima facie appropriates them to that account, and the effect of that is, that the payments are *de facto* appropriated according to the priority in order of the entries on the one side and on the other of that account. It is, of course, absolutely necessary for the application of those authorities that there should be one unbroken account, and entries made in that account by the person having a right to appropriate the payment to that account; and the way to avoid the application of Clayton's Case, where there is no other principle in question, is to break the account and open a new and distinct account. When that is done, and the payment is entered to that new and distinct account, whatever other rule may govern the case, it certainly is not the rule of Clayton's Case.

SEE *Broken Account*

In *Deeley* v *Lloyds Bank Ltd* (1912) 107 LT 465, Lord Shaw quoted (in connection with the above rule) the following with approval:

> According to the law of England the person paying the money has the primary right to say to what account it shall be appropriated; the creditor, if the debtor makes no appropriation, has the right to appropriate, and if neither of them exercises the right, then one can look on the matter as a matter of account and see how the creditor has dealt with the payment, in order to ascertain how he did in fact appropriate it; and if there is nothing more than this, that there is a current account kept by the creditor, or a particular account, kept by the creditor, and he carries the money to that particular account, then the Court concludes that the appropriation has been made, and having been made, it is made once for all, and it does not lie in the mouth of the creditor afterwards to seek to vary that appropriation.

SEE *Notice of Second Mortgage*

In *Bradford Old Bank* v *Sutcliffe* (1918) 34 TLR 299, where there were two accounts, a loan account and a current account, it was held that the two accounts could not be considered as one, and that 'payments to the credit of the current account are appropriated to that account and cannot be taken in reduction of the loan account'. SEE *Broken Account*

The principle of Clayton's Case does not apply where a person has mixed trust moneys with his own moneys in his account. The money which he first withdraws from the account is taken to be his own money, leaving the trust funds intact (*In re Hallet's Estate* (1879) 13 ChD 696). But if the trust moneys of several persons have been paid into a customer's account the position is different. Where a solicitor had paid into his account moneys belonging to various clients, it was held that the rule in Clayton's Case applied as between the claimants to the trust moneys; that is, that the first trust money paid in is the first money drawn out (*In re Stenning, Wood* v *Stenning* [1895] 2 Ch 433.) The rule in Clayton's Case is a rule of evidence and not of law, and if it can be shown that the intention of the parties was to avoid appropriation under the rule, it will have no application. Some banks include in their forms of charge or guarantee a clause designed to avoid the operation of the rule; such a clause proved efficacious in *Westminster Bank* v *Cond* (1940) 46 Com Cas 60. SEE *Appropriation of Payments, Partnerships*

Indirectly, the principle sometimes operates for the benefit of bankers: in relation to floating charges for which money has to be advanced subsequently to the charge, if there is an insolvency within 12 months, the turnover on a current account will be sufficient although there is no increase in the debit balance (*Re Yeovil Glove Co. Ltd* [1965] Ch 148).

CLEAN ACCEPTANCE A general acceptance. SEE *Acceptance, General*

CLEAN BILL A bill of exchange which is unsupported by shipping documents or other security. SEE *Documentary Bill*

CLEAN BILL OF LADING SEE *Bill of Lading*

CLEAN CREDIT A credit opened by a banker under which persons abroad may draw bills upon the banker, the banker undertaking to accept the bills if drawn in accordance with the conditions in the credit. It is called 'clean' because the bills have no documents attached. Such a credit is granted only to firms of the highest standing, or against securities.

CLEAR DAYS Section 141(2) of the Companies Act 1948 provided, *inter alia*, that a resolution shall be a special resolution when it has been passed by such a majority as is required for the passing of an extraordinary resolution and at a general meeting of which *'not less than twenty-one days' notice'*, specifying the intention to propose the resolution as a special resolution, has been duly given. In *Re Hector Whaling Ltd* (*Times*, 3rd December, 1935), Bennett, J. held that the italicized words mean 21 clear days, exclusive of the day of service and exclusive of the day on which the meeting is held. It is usual in the articles of association of a company to provide that a notice of a meeting may be served by the company either personally or by sending it through the post, and that if a notice is served by post, it shall be deemed to have been served at the latest within 24 hours after the time of posting. In such cases, therefore, 'clear days' will exclude the day of posting and the following day and the day of the meeting itself. SEE Supplement

CLEARING BANKS The London clearing banks are those banks which have a seat in the Bankers' Clearing House. They are

Bank of England
Barclays Bank plc
Co-operative Bank plc
Coutts & Co. Ltd
Lloyds Bank plc
Midland Bank plc
National Girobank
National Westminster Bank plc
Central Trustee Savings Bank
Williams & Glyn's Bank Ltd

The criteria established by the clearing banks for membership of the Clearing House (q.v.) are (1) the existence of a branch network, (2) a sufficient volume of items passing through the clearing system (this proportion was fixed in 1974 at one per cent of the total volume), (3) an ability to accept and conform to the functional requirements and timetable of the clearing system, including the setting-up of a town clearing branch and a clearing department within a reasonable distance of the Clearing House and (4) an acceptance of the costs of participation.

The Scottish 'clearing' banks and the Yorkshire Bank are not members of the Clearing House.

Membership of the Clearing House is not synonymous with membership of the Committee of London Clearing Bankers (q.v.).

In 1984, a committee set up under the auspices of the Committee of London Clearing Bankers, published its report which proposed that a new bank clearing system be set up which would permit institutions, in addition to the 10 banks listed above, to become members, subject to certain criteria, the main one being that the institution concerned was dealing with $\frac{1}{2}$ per cent by volume of total clearings passing through the new company. Such institutions would have full membership of the new umbrella body, alongside the existing members. Additionally, it was proposed that other institutions accounting for a smaller amount of total clearings be enabled to join with other institutions in applying for associate membership of the new body.

CLEARING HOUSE The first Clearing House was built in 1833 on part of the site occupied by the present building at 10 Lombard Street. The system of clearing cheques on a national basis originated in or about 1770 and the clerks from the private banks met daily at a central point in the City to exchange drafts drawn on each other's houses. The net balances were settled in cash and this method continued until the present system of settlement through the Bank of England was introduced in 1854.

The correct title of the institution, as distinct from the building, is Bankers' Clearing House. This is a limited company owned by the banks which constitute the Committee of London Clearing Bankers (q.v.).

The term 'clearing bank' had its origin in the system of 'clearing' cheques and settling the balances, as described above. Until 1969, there was a system of local clearings in the principal cities, in addition to the Town Clearing and General Clearing. Today, there are two clearing systems: Town Clearing which deals with cheques for £10,000 or more drawn on a 100 or so branches in the City of London, and the General Clearing which deals with the rest of the country. The purpose of the Town Clearing is to enable major transfers of funds to be dealt with in London on the same day. Although the number of items is small in relation to the whole country, the value of cleared items on the Town Clearing is very considerable and represents approximately 90 per cent of the total value of cleared cheques in the country. The clearing system throughout the country is now automated to the extent that cheques are automatically sorted and listed on computers. SEE *Bankers' Automated Clearing Services Limited; Credit Clearing*

The number and value of paper items passing through the Bankers' Clearing House in 1984 were as shown below.

	Value £ million	Number thousands
Credit clearing	362, 735	419,993
Debit clearing	8,977,693	2,332,358

Source: CLCB.

CLEARING HOUSE AUTOMATED PAYMENTS SYSTEM (CHAPS) In 1977, the clearing banks took the decision to proceed with the development of an electronic system for the Town Clearing (SEE *Clearing House*) and this came into full operation in February 1984. Under this system, known as Clearing House Automated Payments System (CHAPS), banks using the Town Clearing are able to initiate payments by electronic means, thus dispensing with paper vouchers and achieving almost instant money transfers. CHAPS is owned and operated by the London clearing banks and the Bank of England, and at the time of writing a number of other banks have joined the scheme as participants. Each member bank may make immediate payments to other member banks and the daily differences between banks are adjusted in the books of the Bank of England at the close of business. A non-member bank, e.g. an overseas bank, may make arrangements with a member bank for a transfer of funds to another member bank for the credit, e.g. of a non-member bank's account. Each member bank is free to make its own arrangements with its own customers on a commercial basis for the instantaneous transfer of funds through CHAPS. Thus, any payment of £10,000 or more may be made in this way, e.g. for the settlement of security transactions, and the system is useful in many cases where a banker's draft would otherwise be necessary, e.g. on the settlement of a property purchase.

CLIENTS' ACCOUNT This is a bank account in which moneys belonging to clients of a professional firm are held as, for example, in the case of solicitors and accountants. The balances of such accounts are in the nature of trust moneys, i.e. they belong to the clients concerned, they do not belong to the professional firm in whose name the balances may be held and they are not available for set-off against any liability of that firm to the bank. The Solicitors' Acts 1974, the Employment Agencies Act 1973, the Insurance Brokers' (Registration) Act 1977, the Estate Agencies Act 1979 and the Rules of the National Association of Share Dealers and Investment Managers (NASDIM) all require clients' moneys to be held in separate bank accounts. SEE ALSO *Solicitor's Accounts*

CLOSE COMPANY This is defined in Section 282 of the Income and Corporation Taxes Act 1970 as amended by the Finance Act 1972. The Section provides that a close company is one 'which is under the control of five or fewer participators, or of participators who are directors'. There is a number of exceptions to the definition, principally the exclusion of companies not resident in the UK.

Also under Section 283 of the Act, a company is a close company if, on the assumption that it is a close company, 'more than half of any amount falling to be apportioned under Schedule 16 to the Finance Act 1972 ... could be apportioned among five or fewer participators or among participators who are directors'.

A company is not to be treated as a close company if it is controlled by a company which is not a close company, or by two or more companies none of which is a close company *and* it could not be treated as a close company except by taking as one of the five or fewer participators requisite for its being so treated, a company which is not a close company.

Under Section 283, a company is not to be treated as a close company if

(*a*) shares in the company carrying not less than 35 per cent of the voting power in the company (not being shares entitled to a fixed rate of dividend, whether with or without a further right to participate in profits) have been allotted unconditionally to, or acquired unconditionally by, and are at that time beneficially held by, the public.

(*b*) any such shares have within the preceding twelve months been the subject of dealings on a recognised stock exchange, and the shares have within those twelve months been quoted in the official list of a recognised stock exchange.

This does not apply, however, to a company at any time when the total percentage of the voting power in the company possessed by all of the company's 'principal members' exceeds 85 per cent. A person is a principal member of a company if he possesses more than five per cent of the voting power and, where there are more than five such persons, if he is one of the five persons who possesses the greatest percentages or if, because two or more persons possess equal percentages of the voting power of the company, there are no such five persons, he is one of the six or more persons (so as to include those two or more who possess equal percentages) who possess the greater percentages.

Whether or not a company is a close company is relevant for taxation purposes in relation to a number of matters, including *inter alia*,

1. distributions to participators in a close company and associates (Section 284, ICTA);
2. interest paid to directors and their associates (Section 285);
3. loans to participators or their associates (Section 286);
4. shortfall in distributions (Section 289 *et seq.*);
5. transfers by close companies (Section 39, Finance Act 1975, as amended).

CLOSING PRICES The prices for stocks and shares which are quoted on a Stock Exchange at the close of business.

CODICIL A supplement to a will, by which a testator is able to add to what is contained in the will or to make any alteration which he may desire. A codicil must be dated and signed by the testator and attested by two witnesses in the same manner as a will. SEE *Will*

The general rule is that the execution of a codicil brings the effective date of the will down to the date of the codicil. This may be particularly relevant in relation to the gift of a specific legacy, e.g. 'my piano'. SEE *Ademption*

COINAGE, COINS The first issue of coins in the western world is believed to have been in the reign of King Ardys of Lydia in Asia Minor in the seventh century BC. Systems of coinage were also developed in the same century in China and India, although there is some suggestion, as yet unsubstantiated, that metallic coins were in use in China at a much earlier date. It was in the reign of Croesus, last King of Lydia, in the sixth century BC, that a bimetallic system of coinage was first introduced, i.e. gold and silver, and this led in time to a system of exchange throughout the Persian Empire and later the Greek world.

All that is necessary for a commodity to be used as money is that it should be accepted as such by a community. Money becomes necessary in a primitive society when there are surpluses of goods of one kind or another, or in one area or another, beyond the level where exchange can be by barter. In the transition from barter to coinage, the artefacts of a particular society may be used as a medium of exchange, e.g. the metallic tools used by the Chinese. In many societies, cattle have been a standard medium of exchange, as have shells and, in more recent times, cigarettes. The use of metallic tokens or coins as a means of exchange has the advantage of durability, portability, homogeneity and the ability for the supply to be controlled.

The history of coinage embraces the coins engraved by Sicilian artists in the fourth and fifth centuries BC (still rated as perhaps the most beautiful coins ever struck) through the introduction of a uniform coinage by Alexander the Great, the silver denarius of the Roman Empire and the bronze bars bearing cattle symbols which gave us the word *pecunia* from the *pecus* of cattle, the Dark Ages with some rather ugly, almost primitive coins, the Gothic Art of the Middle Ages, the advent of American gold and silver in great quantities in the sixteenth century, the milling processes introduced in France and then in England to prevent counterfeiting, the enormous demands for coins arising from the Industrial Revolution through to the issue of non-circulating commemorative coins issued by a number of countries in recent times.

The token coinage (q.v.) of Great Britain was silver and bronze, but by the Coinage Act 1946, cupro-nickel coins were substituted for the silver coinage, consisting of three-quarters copper and one-quarter nickel. The silver coinage originally consisted of 37/40 silver and 3/40 alloy. After the First World War the high price of silver resulted in the silver content being reduced to one-half. After 1945, however, the world shortage of silver and its high price, coupled with the liability to repay the USA 88,000,000 oz borrowed during the Second World War on lease-lend, forced the Government to withdraw the silver coinage and substitute cupro-nickel coins.

Following the decision to introduce decimal coinage the half-crown (q.v.) ceased to be legal tender on 1st January, 1970. The 50p entered circulation on 14th October, 1970 subsequently the 20p piece and the £1 coin were introduced by Royal Proclamation of 10th February, 1982. The old halfpenny had been withdrawn from circulation in August 1969.

Below is Schedule 1 of the Decimal Currency Act 1967. It gives the denominations, weight, diameter and composition of new coins.

The Currency Act 1982, amending the 1967 Act, provided that the term 'the penny' may now be substituted for 'new penny'. SEE *Decimal Coinage; Legal Tender*

COINAGE OFFENCES Offences relating to the UK's coinage are now governed by the Forgery and Counterfeiting Act 1981, which repealed earlier legislation on the subject, principally, the Coinage Offences Act 1936.

Under the Act, it is an offence for a person to make a counterfeit of a currency note or of a protected coin, intending that he or another shall pass or tender it as genuine. For the purposes of the Act, a currency note means, in general terms, the bank notes lawfully issued in England and Wales, Scotland, Northern Ireland, the Channel Islands, the Isle of Man or the Republic of Ireland. A protected coin means any coin which is customarily used as money in any country or is specified by the Treasury for such purpose but by statutory instrument.

Under the Act, it is also an offence for a person to pass or tender as genuine anything which is, and which he knows or believes to be, a counterfeit of a currency note or protected coin or to deliver to another anything which is, and which he knows or believes to be, such a counterfeit, intending that the person to whom it is delivered or another shall pass or tender it as genuine.

It is also an offence under the Act for a person to have in his custody or under his control, anything which is, and he knows or believes to be, a counterfeit of a currency note or of a protected coin, intending either to pass or tender it as genuine or to deliver it to another with the intention that he or another shall pass it or tender it as genuine.

Further, it is an offence for a person to make, or to have in his custody or under his control, any thing which he intends to use, or to permit any other person to use, for the purpose of making a counterfeit of a currency note or of a protected coin with the intention that it be passed or tendered as genuine.

The Act also makes it an offence for any person to reproduce on any substance whatsoever, whether or not on the correct scale, any British currency note or any part of one unless the 'relevant authority', i.e. the lawful issuing author-

1 Metal and denominations	2 Standard weight grams	3 Standard diameter cm	4 Standard composition	5 Weight variation grams
Cupro-nickel			Three-quarters copper one-quarter nickel	
Ten new pence	11.31036	2.8500		0.0646
Five new pence	5.65518	2.3595		0.0375
Bronze			Mixed metal: copper, tin and zinc	
Two new pence	7.12800	2.5910		0.1500
New penny	3.56400	2.0320		0.0750
New halfpenny	1.78200	1.7145		0.0375

ity for that particular note, has previously consented in writing. Similarly, it is an offence for a person to make an imitation British coin or to sell or distribute imitation British coins or to have them in his custody or under his control unless the Treasury have previously consented in writing.

For the purpose of the Act, a British coin is any coin which is legal tender in any part of the UK and 'imitation British coin' means anything which resembles a British coin in shape, size and the substance of which it is made.

COINS, INVESTMENT IN The extensive purchase of coins for investment purposes is a comparatively recent feature going back only to the 1960s. The presence of investors and the need for dealers to cater for investors' requirements has led to wide swings in coin prices, which are not always welcomed by the genuine collector. The modern tendency to invest in things rather than paper securities has given a boost to coin collecting, as to much other fine art investing and perhaps the greatest upsurge in prices of coins was that which coincided with the slump in the stock market in 1973–74.

The advantages of investing in coins are

1. They are easily portable and transferable.
2. They have an international market.
3. Collectable coins are well documented and catalogued.
4. Many have aesthetic appeal.
5. To some people they have historical appeal, e.g. the tribute penny of the Bible, the Queen Anne farthing and the Spanish 'pieces of eight'.
6. There is a uniform style of grading.
7. They are easily marketable.

Some disadvantages are

1. The very real risk of forgery.
2. The value of a coin may be upset by the discovery of a new 'hoard'.
3. Good collections become a security risk.
4. Insurance costs tend to be high.
5. Dealing costs tend to be high compared with more traditional investments.

The factors which affect the value of a coin are rarity, its substance, e.g. gold, silver, the craftmanship or art work, historical or other associations, and condition.

Coins are graded depending on their condition, in accordance with the following scale which is accepted more or less internationally:

FDC (Fleur de Coin)	absolutely perfect condition as it left the mint
UNC (Uncirculated)	new from the mint but with perhaps small imperfections
EF (Extremely fine)	design and inscription sharp and clear, but faint traces of wear
VF (Very fine)	design and inscription clear, but with some minor damage or rubbing
F (Fine)	signs of wear apparent to the naked eye or badly centred or with minor damage such as scratches through harsh cleaning, but inscription and date easily distinguishable
Fair	design, inscription and date still distinguishable, but coin seriously worn or damaged or faultily struck
Poor	so worn or damaged or badly struck that little detail can be made out

Coins have always been the subject of forgery, originally for their use as money but now more usually to deceive collectors. Older forgeries can often be detected under a microscope because of minute air bubbles in the metal, but later forgeries done in pressure casts are more difficult to detect. The forgery of coins is very wide-spread and only the experts can detect a skilled forgery. Nowadays, reports of counterfeit coins are circulated by the International Bureau for the Suppression of Counterfeit Coins. The International Association of Professional Numismatists conducts a very sophisticated forgery detection service and, for a modest fee, will give a signed opinion on any coin submitted to it.

COLLATERAL SECURITY This term is used in three senses: in the Stamp Act 1891, it means additional as opposed to primary security SEE *Collateral Stamping*; occasionally it is used colloquially to signify impersonal security (such as stocks and shares) as opposed to personal security (such as a guarantee); more usually it is used to describe security lodged by a third party. Collateral security, in this last sense, has the advantage over security lodged by the borrower, that in the case of the latter's failure its value does not have to be deducted for the purpose of proving in the bankruptcy, but a claim can be made against the debtors' estate for the whole sum due and recourse made on the collateral security for the deficiency.

COLLATERAL STAMPING This method particularly applied to instruments expressly drawn to cover all sums due or to become due. The word 'collateral' is loosely used in relation to securities, but it had the specific meaning of 'secondary' (as opposed to primary), 'auxiliary' or 'additional' in relation to stamping.

Ad valorem stamping of mortgages was abolished by the Finance Act 1971, Section 64. Prior to the passing of that Act, where two or more mortgages were taken as security at the same time, one of them, or where a further mortgage was taken in addition to one already held, the earliest dated document was treated as the primary security and stamped *ad valorem* to cover the highest amount of the total advance. The remaining or subsequent mortgages were treated as collateral securities and stamped at a lower rate with 50p maximum. Both the stamps mentioned so far were red impressed stamps showing the amount of stamp duty paid. On the collateral documents, blue stamps were impressed denoting the value of the primary (red) stamps impressed on the primary document.

When the primary security was withdrawn, the first collateral security became the primary security.

COLLECTING BANKER When a cheque is paid into a customer's account at a particular branch of a bank, that bank is said to 'collect' the cheque for the customer which means that it is sent off through the clearing system to the branch of the bank on which it is drawn, i.e. the 'paying' bank.

A banker must act with due care and diligence in presenting for payment cheques paid in for collection, and neglect to use the customary and recognized channels may involve him in loss. Where a cheque payable alternatively in London or Norwich was passed through the Country Clearing, and the customer's cheque drawn in reliance on its clearance in London, was dishonoured, evidence was called showing that it was banking custom to pass cheques so marked through the Town Clearing and damages were awarded to the customer accordingly (*Forman* v *Bank of England* (1902) 18 TLR 339).

The collecting banker must give his customer due notice of any cheques paid in for collection returned unpaid and cannot debit his customer with such cheques if notice is not duly given. Notice of dishonour should be given notwithstanding that the banker confirms any irregularity and re-presents the cheque without returning it to the customer.

A banker collecting a cheque drawn on another bank or branch may be a holder for value (q.v.) or an agent for collection depending on whether he is collecting the cheque for himself or for his customer. He is a holder for value where he exchanges or cashes the cheque forthwith for his customer, where he is the indorsee or the payee other than as agent for collection, where he collects expressly or implicitly in reduction of a customer's overdrawn account, where he has a lien over the cheque, and where he expressly or impliedly allows his customer to draw against the cheque before clearance.

In *Barclays Bank Ltd* v *Harding* (*Journal of the Institute of Bankers*, April, 1962) a Mr Walker, who at all material times concealed the fact that he was an undischarged bankrupt, persuaded the defendant to draw a cheque for £4,500 payable to Geoffrey Roberts. A company called Waytrade Ltd was trading under that name and paid the cheque, together with another for £4,000, into its account with Barclays Bank. Against these two cheques the bank paid a total of £8,926 in cheques drawn by the company, whose account at the end of these transactions was overdrawn £320. The cheque for £4,000 was paid, but that for £4,500 was stopped by order of the defendant, who had discovered that he had been deceived. The bank, who had given value for the two cheques, claimed to be holders for value and holders in due course. The cheque on which the defendant was sued had not been indorsed, but by virtue of Section 2 of the Cheques Act 1957, the bank was held to have the same rights in relation to the cheque as it would have had if the cheque had been duly indorsed, and judgment was given in its favour. (SEE ALSO *Midland Bank Ltd* v *Charles Simpson Motors Ltd*, under LIEN)

In *A. L. Underwood Ltd* v *Barclays Bank Ltd* [1924] KB 775, Scrutton, LJ, in the course of his judgment said

> The cases where an agent for collection becomes a holder for value must turn on an express or implied agreement between bank and customer that the latter may draw against the cheques before they are cleared. Though the cheques were in fact credited to the customer's account before they were cleared, the customer was not informed of this, and I can see nothing to prevent the bank from declining to honour the cheque if the payment in, against which it was drawn, had not been cleared.

Atkin, LJ, said

> The mere fact that the bank in their books enter the value of the cheques on the credit side of the account on the day on which they receive the cheques for collection does not, without more, constitute the bank a holder for value. To constitute value, there must be, in such a case, a contract between banker and customer, express or

implied, that the bank will, before receipt of the proceeds, honour cheques of the customer drawn against the cheques.

On the other hand, the placing of a cheque to the credit of a customer's account before clearance does not deprive a banker of his protection as collecting agent, by virtue of the Cheques Act 1957, Section 4(1)(*b*).

The above-mentioned Section, which has since 1957 taken the place of the repealed Section 82 of the Bills of Exchange Act 1882, places the collecting banker in a more advantageous position than was the case prior to the passing of the Cheques Act 1957 (q.v.). Not only is the collecting banker now protected in the case of both crossed and open drafts, but the Section has been widened to include those instruments analogous to cheques which for one reason or another cannot satisfy the definition of a bill of exchange.

A banker should not collect a cheque for a stranger, as he will be liable to the true owner if the stranger had no title to the cheque. In collecting a cheque, to gain the protection of Section 4 of the Cheques Act 1957, the banker must act in good faith and without negligence, and must collect for a customer. He will then be protected against any action by a true owner. As to what constitutes a person a customer, SEE *Customer*.

In *Lloyds Bank Ltd* v *Savory & Co.*, the House of Lords by a majority of 3 to 2, affirmed the decision of the Court of Appeal (reversing the decision of the Lower Court) that it is negligence not to enquire as to the nature of a customer's employment and the name of his employer, if any. Likewise, the same enquiries are necessary where the account of a wife of an employee is involved.

The particular facts concerned two clerks employed by a firm of stockbrokers who stole the firm's cheques payable to third parties or bearer. In the one case, the cheques were paid into the clerk's own account; in the other case, they were paid into his wife's account. In the first case, the bank knew that its customer was a stockbroker's clerk but did not know who were his employers, relying on the introduction of another clerk, well known locally. In the second case, the wife of the clerk was introduced by her landlady. The case was complicated by the use of the branch credit system, the bulk of the cheques having been paid in at City Offices for the credit of the respective accounts at country branches.

In the House of Lords the case was dealt with on the lines that the cheques were paid in at the branches where the accounts were conducted, on the grounds that the branch credit system was of the bank's own devising, and that if adequate safeguards were not taken to prevent this system being used in fraud of the true owners of cheques, banks must suffer any loss arising.

As a result of this decision, it became the practice of banks to make enquiries as to a new customer's employer, if any, and in the case of women customers, as to their husband's employment and employer, if any.

In a judgment of the Privy Council in *Commissioners of Taxation* v *English Scottish and Australian Bank Ltd* (1920) 36 TLR 305, Lord Dunedin said

> The test of negligence is whether the transaction of paying in any given cheque, coupled with the circumstances antecedent and present, was so out of the ordinary course that it ought to have aroused doubts in the bankers' minds and caused them to make inquiry.

See further remarks in this case under *Customer*

A banker should not collect for the credit of an agent's private account cheques payable to his principal, unless authorized in writing by the principal.

Where a cheque is payable to 'A B per X', 'X is not authorized to receive the money as his own, or to deal with it except for his principals'. (See the case *Slingsby and Others* v *The District Bank Ltd*, under *Indorsement*.)

It has been held to be negligence to take a cheque payable to a partnership for the credit of the private account of one of the partners without enquiring from the other partners whether he is entitled to deal with it as owner (*Bevan* v *National Bank* (1906) 23 TLR 65).

In *Souchette Ltd* v *London County Westminster & Parr's Bank Ltd* (1920) 36 TLR 195, where cheques payable to a third party 'or bearer' were credited to the account of T. Matthews, one of the directors who had drawn the cheques on behalf of the company, it was held that the collecting banker was not negligent in collecting those cheques as the banker was entitled to suppose that the directors who drew these cheques drew them to 'bearer' for convenience in order that they might be dealt with by the bearer for the benefit of the company. But where the cheques were payable to a third party 'or order', and they were credited to the account of T. Matthews, who had forged the indorsements, it was held that the bank was negligent. (Other points in this case are referred to under *Alterations to Bills of Exchange*; *Conversion*.)

(See the case of *A. Stewart & Son of Dundee Ltd* v *Westminster Bank*, under *Agent*.)

It is contrary to ordinary business procedure for a limited company to pay a debt due to an official by means of a cheque payable to itself. In *Hannan's Lake View Central Ltd* v *Armstrong & Co.*

(1900) 16 TLR 236, the secretary of the plaintiff company indorsed a crossed cheque, payable to the company, and paid it into his private account. It was held that the bank had not acted 'without negligence', seeing that they knew the company had an account at another bank and that it was apparent that the secretary was using for himself a valuable document which was, upon its face, the property of his employers.

In *A. L. Underwood Ltd* v *Bank of Liverpool and Martins* (1924) 40 TLR 302, the sole director and practically the sole shareholder of the company indorsed for the company cheques payable to the company and paid them into his private account. In the action brought by the company against the bank for conversion of the cheques, the bank claimed the protection of Section 82 of the Bills of Exchange Act on the ground that they collected the cheques in good faith and without negligence, and they relied on the ostensible authority of the sole director to deal with the cheques in that way. Bankes, LJ, in the course of his judgment said that the cheques were plainly on the face of them the property of the company. Held that there was not only negligence on the part of the bank, but such an absence of ordinary enquiry as to disentitle the bank from relying on a defence founded on the ostensible authority of the director.

> I feel satisfied that the obvious enquiry whether the company had not got its own banking account would have put a stop to the fraudulent system adopted by the director, and I do not think that it lies in the mouth of the bank to say that an inquiry would have been useless.
>
> If banks for fear of offending their customers will not make inquiries into unusual circumstances, they must take, with the benefit of not annoying their customer, the risk of liability because they do not inquire.

(On 'Inquiry', see also the case of *Baker* v *Barclays Bank Ltd* [1955] 2 All ER 571, under *Negligence*.)

A banker may be liable if an account is not conducted in consonance with the description which the customer gave of himself at the time the account was opened. (SEE *Nu-Stilo Footwear Ltd* v *Lloyds Bank Ltd* [*Journal of the Institute of Bankers*, 1956, p. 239] under *Negligence*.)

In *Orbit Mining Company Ltd* v *Westminster Bank Ltd* [1962] 3 WLR 1256 (which see also under *Negligence*) Harman, LJ, quoting with approval an earlier decision speaking of the standard of care to be shown, said, 'If a standard is sought, it must be the standard to be derived from the ordinary practice of bankers.'

Where a cheque is paid into an account at the same branch on which the cheque is drawn, the protection of Section 60, Bills of Exchange Act 1882, is not available to the banker to the exclusion of Section 4, Cheques Act 1957. The bank cannot be treated merely as a paying bank. It is also a collecting bank protected or not by Section 4, Cheques Act, according to whether the statutory conditions for protection can be satisfied, or not. SEE *Worshipful Company of Carpenters of the City of London* v *British Mutual Banking Co. Ltd* [1937] 3 All ER 811, where an employee in fraud of the company paid into his account cheques drawn by the company on the same office payable to third parties. On appeal it was held that the bank in collecting the cheques was liable for conversion, being without the protection of Section 82, Bills of Exchange Act 1882, on the ground of negligence.

To escape liability for conversion, the bank must show that it is within the protection of both Section 60 (or 80) of the Bills of Exchange Act 1882, and 4 of the Cheques Act 1957.

Where there has been a series of fraudulent dealings with cheques, undetected by the true owner, it is no defence to say that the bank was 'lulled to sleep'. 'Neglect of duty does not cease by repetition to be neglect of duty.' (*Bank of Montreal* v *Dominion Gresham Guarantee & Casualty Co.* [1930] AC 659.)

An interesting claim against a collecting banker occurred in the case of *Universal Guarantee Company* v *National Bank of Australasia* [1965] All ER 98. The collecting banker was there sued for negligence. This was an action that had no connection with his statutory protection; it was a common law action for the tort of negligence. A fraudulent clerk forged the indorsement of cheques drawn by his employers in favour of third parties, to whom payment was due. These cheques he then paid into his employers' *own* account, adjusting the internal office accounts to his own advantage. In an action against the bank, in which it was suggested that it was negligent to take such drafts, the decision went in favour of the bank. Similarly, quite irrespective of the statutory protection, in the case of the *Australia and New Zealand Bank* v *Ateliers etc.* [1966] 2 WLR 1216 PC, there was a successful defence to an action for conversion on the grounds that the alleged conversion was by the indirect authority of the party who had lost by the conversion. The case of *Marfani* v *Midland Bank Ltd*, [1967] 3 All ER, was however a decision on Section 4 of the Cheques Act; in particular it was as to whether the bank had been negligent by not following up references. There had been one reference that was not followed up, but the other referee had called and the evidence of his conversation with the manager was regarded as sufficient to allay the need for further investigation. This was on its particular facts and it does not, therefore, follow beyond doubt that an answer from one referee is sufficient; nevertheless, many banks, feasibly with justification, do regard the one reference in practice as being sufficient so long as its authenticity is confirmed. In the case of *Lumsden & Co.* v *London Trustee Savings Bank* [1971] Lloyd's Law Reports 114, a new avenue of defence, and incidentally a new basis for negotiation of dispute in such cases, emerged for a collecting banker. Although where stockbrokers had been somewhat negligent in drawing cheques the collecting banker himself could not dispute his own negligence, and thus lost his statutory protection, he was afforded a measure of relief. The Contributory Negligence Act 1945, was pleaded as applying to any tort, including conversion. Because the measure of respective responsibility was regarded by the judge as being ninety per cent on the part of the stockbrokers and ten per cent on the part of the bankers, the latter were obliged to pay only ten per cent of the loss despite not being able to put any reliance on Section 4 of the Cheques Act. The Banking Act 1979, Section 47, now provides that in any circumstances in which proof of absence of negligence on the part of a banker would be a defence in proceedings by reason of Section 4 of the Cheques Act 1957, a defence of contributory negligence shall also be available to the banker.

Cheques are often crossed 'account payee' or 'account John Jones'. Such words are not provided for in the Bills of Exchange Act 1882, but a collecting banker has been held to be negligent for placing a cheque so crossed to an account other than that indicated in the crossing. SEE *Account Payee*

In the case of a cheque payable on condition of a receipt being signed, it should be collected only for the payee, as the document is not considered to be transferable. SEE *Receipt on Cheque*

See the case of *Morison* v *London County & Westminster Bank* under *Per Pro*. SEE *Holder for Value*

SEE Supplement

COMBINING ACCOUNTS SEE *Set-Off*

COMEX The commodity exchanges in New York. In practice, the term is used more particularly in relation to the copper price on the New York Exchange.

COMMERCIAL PROPERTY A term usually applied to shops and offices as distinct from factories, warehouses and other forms of industrial property. SEE *Property, Investment in*

COMMISSION ON CURRENT ACCOUNTS
SEE *Bank Charges*

COMMISSIONERS OF INLAND REVENUE
This title embraces the General Commissioners of Inland Revenue and the Special Commissioners of Inland Revenue. The General Commissioners are lay people who deal with taxation appeals on the more routine matters and straightforward matters of fact. The Special Commissioners are full-time Civil Servants with taxation experience who, as a general rule, will deal with the more complicated appeals, particularly if a legal point is involved. The taxpayer has a degree of choice whether he appeals to the General Commissioners or the Special Commissioners but the more technical cases will normally go automatically to the Special Commissioners. There is no appeal from the Commissioners on questions of fact but on questions of law; either the taxpayer or the Commissioners may appeal to the High Court and from there to the Court of Appeal and the House of Lords.

COMMITTEE OF INSPECTION The persons appointed by the creditors to superintend the administration of a bankrupt's property by the trustee. SEE *Trustee in Bankruptcy*

Section 20 Bankruptcy Act 1914 provides *inter alia*:

(1) The creditors qualified to vote may, at their first or any subsequent meeting, by resolution appoint a committee of inspection for the purpose of superintending the administration of the bankrupt's property by the trustee.

(2) The committee of inspection shall consist of not more than five nor less than three persons. Such a person may be a creditor or the holder of a general proxy or general power of attorney from a creditor, but he cannot act until the creditor has proved his debt and the proof has been admitted; or he may be a person to whom a creditor intends to give a general proxy or general power of attorney, but he cannot act until he holds such proxy or power, and until the creditor has proved his debt and the proof has been admitted.

(3) The committee of inspection shall meet at such times as they shall from time to time appoint, and, failing such appointment, at least once a month; and the trustee or any member of the committee may also call a meeting of the committee as and when he thinks necessary.

(4) The committee may act by a majority of their members present at a meeting, but shall not act unless a majority of the committee are present at the meeting.

(5) If there be no committee of inspection, any act or thing or any direction or permission by this Act authorized or required to be done or given by the committee may be done or given by the Board of Trade on the application of the trustee.

The Department of Trade and Industry may, on

application by the committee of inspection, authorize the trustee to have an account with a local bank. SEE UNDER *Trustee in Bankruptcy*

In connection with the winding up of a company, a committee may be appointed to supervise the liquidation. It shall consist of creditors and contributories of the company in such proportions as may be agreed on by the meetings of creditors and contributories, or as, in case of difference, may be determined by the court (Section 253(1) of the Companies Act 1948, re-enacted in Section 547 of the Companies Act 1985.

COMMITTEE OF LONDON CLEARING BANKERS (CLCB) The Committee consists of the chairmen of the six London clearing banks—Barclays, Coutts, Lloyds, Midland, National Westminster and Williams & Glyn's. The other members of the Clearing House (q.v.) are not members of the CLCB. The Bankers' Clearing House is a limited company which is jointly owned by the member banks of the CLCB.

Prior to the introduction of Competition and Credit Control (q.v.) in May 1971, there were a number of collective agreements in force among the clearing banks, principally in relation to interest rates and the CLCB was very much concerned with the management of these agreements. At their weekly meeting on Thursdays, they would fix the London Bankers' Deposit Rate. Until 1971, there was a considerable number of inter-bank agreements in force, but many of these were abolished with the introduction of Competition and Credit Control. Although this removed part of the *raison d'être* of the CLCB, the Committee continues as a 'trade association' for the banking industry as well as retaining the very considerable responsibility for the Clearing House.

In particular, the CLCB is the official link between the banks, the Bank of England and the Treasury. It is the principal forum for consultation and avenue of communication between the authorities and the banking industry. It operates through a number of committees, the principal one below chairman level being the Chief Executive Officers Committee.

COMMITTEE TO REVIEW NATIONAL SAVINGS (PAGE COMMITTEE) This Committee was appointed in June 1971 under the Chairmanship of Sir Harry Page and it reported in June 1973. Its terms of reference were

1. To consider the future role and development of the National Savings movement, the Department for National Savings and the Trustee Savings Banks in their provision to the public of savings, money transmission and other financial services.
2. To consider the suitability of the broad structure and organization of the institutions for carrying out their functions; including their relationships with each other, with the Government and Government agencies, and with other financial organizations, and taking into account the demand on national resources involved in their operations.

The Committee's report was wide-ranging, covering the entire savings field in the UK at the time.

The main recommendations of the Committee were

1. that there should be a major restructuring of the Trustee Savings Banks, in the course of which 'they would cut loose from Government and become a "third force" in banking, standing mid-way between the National Savings Bank and the clearing banks',
2. the National Savings Bank should remain under Government control, channelling all its funds into public sector securities and without any material change in its services,
3. that a new form of National Savings security should be introduced combining most of the features of the existing National Savings certificates but incorporating some elements of the British Savings Bonds (a recommendation not, in fact, adopted),
4. that the National Savings voluntary movement should be wound up, and
5. that the Government should experiment with the issuing of index-linked bonds for the small saver 'on the grounds that he is least able to protect his capital against inflation'.

These recommendations led, in particular, to the reform and development of the Trustee Savings Banks (q.v.) and the introduction by the Government of index-linked securities (q.v.). (SEE *Report of the Committee to Review National Savings*, Cmnd 5273, HMSO 1973)

COMMODITIES A commodity is usually a basic substance such as cotton, wool, rubber, cocoa, sugar or some form of mineral. It does not have to be so basic. A commodity market can exist in virtually any substance or product which is produced in quantity somewhere in the world and for which there is a demand, probably in some other part of the world. It must, however, be an homogeneous substance of consistent quality throughout so that it may be sold by sample. A wide range of commodities are traded in the USA, including such unlikely items as plywood and frozen pork bellies. In London, the principal markets are in silver, tin, lead, copper, zinc, nickel and aluminium, and the soft commodities (i.e. non-metallic) of coffee, cocoa and sugar. Other active markets are wool, rubber, soya beans and grain.

There are three categories of operators in the commodity markets. They are

1. the producers of commodities who seek to sell them,
2. the users of commodities in their various businesses, and
3. the investors or traders who operate in the market between the producer and the user, and who indeed help to make the worldwide market.

The investors do not expect to take delivery of the commodity which they have bought. They buy only in anticipation of being able to sell at a higher price.

The principal aspects of the commodity market are spot trading, forward contracts, futures, options.

Spot Trading

The spot price for a commodity is the current cash price. If the commodity markets consisted only of spot trading, there would be very little interest for investors and speculators. When a commodity has been purchased for cash, the ownership passes to the buyer together with the holding costs until such time as the commodity is sold at the then spot price. This limited type of activity would not support much interest in the market and it is the forward contracts and dealings in futures which give commodity markets their appeal.

Forward Contracts

This is a contract between the supplier and the user of a particular commodity for the supply of the commodity at some future date, e.g. in six month's time, at a price now agreed between the parties. At the time of the contract, the commodity may not have been produced, but the supplier will have the benefit of knowing that he will receive an agreed price in six months' time. The user will have the advantage of being able to budget for the known cost of the commodity in his own manufacturing business.

If the parties contemplate that the price of that particular commodity will rise, they will fix the forward contract price above the current spot price. This is known as a 'contango' (q.v.) situation. If they expect prices to fall, they fix a price lower than the current spot price. This is known as 'backwardation' (q.v.).

A forward contract is a fixed arrangement between the parties concerned. The supplier and the buyer have to be in the market at the same time with matching situations and there is little scope for variation, or the interposing of third parties. Out of the concept of the forward contract emerged the futures market.

Futures

Present day commodity trading is based very largely on the concept of futures. A futures contract arises when an investor agrees on, say, 1st January to buy cocoa for delivery nine months hence on 30th September at a predetermined price, believing that the spot price of cocoa on 30th September will be greater than the agreed price. On the terminal date of the contract, he will take delivery and sell the cocoa immediately at the spot price. If prices have moved against him, he will make a loss. If he was right in his judgment, he will make a profit. In fact, he will not necessarily wait for the terminal date. If before 30th September he sees an opportunity for selling the cocoa 'future' at a profit, he may do so. A converse situation may arise in that an investor expecting a fall in commodity prices may agree to sell cocoa, or whatever, in nine months' time at an agreed price. Before the terminal date, he will hope to buy the commodity at a lower price for delivery on the same terminal date. He thus matches his book or is said to 'cancel' his contract. It is understood that about 90 per cent of all futures contracts are matched in this way, i.e. do not run through to the settlement date.

Trading in futures enables a large number of people to invest or speculate in commodity markets, without being involved as suppliers or users of the commodities. This helps to maintain an active and continuous market, so that prices for most commodities are always available. The clearing house for all trading in soft commodities on the London exchanges is the International Commodities Clearing House Limited (q.v.). In the case of metals, there is no clearing house as such. The members of the London Metal Exchange deal as principals, albeit on behalf of other individual clients.

Options

In broad terms, trading in commodity options is the same as trading in options on the Stock Exchange. A 'call' option gives the investor the right to buy at the agreed price at any time between the date of the option and its expiry date.

A 'put' option gives the investor the right to sell at the agreed price between the date of the option and the expiry date. On the whole, commodity options run for longer periods than share options, e.g. three years in the case of certain commodities, and the cost of commodity options is proportionately lower than share options.

Options are a means of limiting the investor's risk to a fixed sum, while securing the possibility of substantial profits. Commodity options are not, however, a large proportion of the total commodity trading on the London exchanges.

Some advantages of commodity trading are

1. The principles of commodity investment are more easily followed and the investment more easily managed than with many other forms of investment, including the Stock Exchange.
2. Most commodity trading is on 'margins' or 'deposits'. Usually the investor will be required to pay 10 per cent of the amount of the contract. This in itself does not limit his risk—he is still liable for the full amount of the contract, but in terms of cashflow only 10 per cent of the total position taken is committed at any one time.
3. An investor may always liquidate his contract and either take his profits, or cut his losses.
4. Commodity prices tend to follow trends, although they may fluctuate considerably on a day-to-day basis.
5. The profit in percentage terms in the course of a year can be very considerable.
6. The 'stop–loss' system is a protection to the investor. It is possible for the investor to limit contingent losses to predetermined levels. The investor's instruction to his broker comes into effect when the market reaches a particular level (or as near to that level as an order can reasonably be given).

On the other hand, there are some disadvantages of commodity trading. They are

1. Many potential investors have little knowledge of commodities and the commodity markets.
2. Investors may be tempted to 'trade up' and take a very exposed position.
3. Commodity investment is speculative—the risks are very real.

COMMON AGRICULTURAL POLICY (CAP) The Treaty of Rome, on which the European Economic Community is founded, lays down five basic objectives for the development of agriculture in the Community. This is known as the Common Agricultural Policy and the aims are

1. to increase agricultural productivity by technical progress and by improving the structure of agricultural businesses to allow the best use to be made of resources;
2. to ensure a fair standard of living for the agricultural community;
3. to stabilize agricultural markets;
4. to ensure the availability of supplies; and
5. to ensure the consumer pays a fair price.

The EEC seeks to achieve these objectives partly by a tariff wall to restrict imports and partly by maintaining prices of agricultural products at a level which is determined annually. The prices are underpinned by the European Agricultural Guidance and Guarantee Fund which provides price support for about 90 per cent of the total agricultural output of the EEC

In 1969, when the devaluation of the French franc and the revaluation of the German mark would have had a major impact on agricultural prices in the two countries, it was decided to express the support prices for agricultural products at the old rates of exchange. This led to the introduction of two sets of exchange rates, the one being the normal market rate between countries and the other being the agricultural or 'green' rate, which came to be expressed in terms of the European Currency Unit (Ecu). The 'green' rate applicable to sterling is the 'green pound'. The effect of this is that the support or intervention prices for agricultural products in the UK is converted at the green pound rate which, from time to time, may be above or below the market exchange rate. The differences between the green rate and the market rate would in the ordinary way lead to the movement of products within the Community in order to take advantage of the anomaly. To correct this, there is a system of border taxes or refunds, known as 'monetary compensatory amounts' (MCAs).

COMMON MARKET SEE *European Economic Community*

COMMORIENTES Where two or more persons die more or less simultaneously and it is uncertain which was the last to die, there is a presumption in law that the deaths occurred in order of seniority (see Law of Property Act 1925, Section 184). The application of this rule occasionally resulted in a double claim for estate duty. The Intestates' Estates Act 1952 provided in Section 1(4) that where husband and wife die in such circumstances intestate, the presumption does not apply and the estate of each passes direct to the next of kin. This enactment offered some relief, but did nothing to alleviate the cases in which one of the spouses survived for a definite period of time and then died, or the cases in which a will had been made. In *Re Beare* (*Times*, 4th October, 1957), a husband and wife both died as a result of a motor accident, and the court was unable to hold that the husband survived the wife. Consequently, the husband, being the elder, was presumed to have died first. The wife, therefore, inherited under his will the whole of his estate, and the combined property then passed under the wife's intestacy to the children. Estate duty was payable on the husband's property which, as it passed to the wife, was again liable to duty by reason of her death.

The Finance Act of 1958 accordingly provided (in Section 29) that in all cases after 15th April 1958 where two or more persons die in circumstances rendering it uncertain which of them survived the other or others, the property chargeable with estate duty in respect of each death shall be ascertained as if they had died at the same instant and all relevant property had devolved accordingly. It is also provided that for deaths after 15th April, 1958, where Section 33 of the Wills Act 1837 operates to prevent the lapse of a bequest, a claim for duty shall not arise in respect of the property posthumously acquired by reason of that Act.

COMMUTATION The word 'commute' means to interchange two things (*Oxford English Dictionary*) such as commuting one form of punishment for another one of less severity. In finance, the word indicates the changing of one method of payment for another, e.g. the commuting of an annual income payment to a capital sum. It is used principally in relation to the commuting of part of a pension under an occupational pension scheme in return for a lump sum payment on retirement. Under the Inland Revenue Code, with which all occupational schemes have had to comply since 1980, the maximum lump sum benefit which may be taken under a pension scheme is one and a half times final salary. SEE *Pensions*

COMPANIES ACT 1947 This Act was the result of the report of the Cohen Committee of 1943. It amended and amplified the Act of 1929, and was itself repealed by the 1948 Act (see below) save for those Sections dealing with matters not relating to companies, e.g. bankruptcy and registration of business names.

COMPANIES ACT 1948 This Act came into operation on 1st July, 1948, and repealed the whole of the Companies Act 1929, and the major part of the Companies Act 1947.

COMPANIES ACT 1967 To a limited extent this statute implemented recommendations of the Jenkins Committee (q.v.). Its main effects were

1. the provision of stricter rules for the control of insurance companies;
2. the abolition of the exempt private company, with its exception for borrowing by directors against security provided by their companies (incidentally, all accounts had to be publicly available);
3. the controversy regarding publication of bank accounts was left to the Board of Trade (now Department of Trade and Industry);
4. the limitation on the number of partners in firms of stockbrokers, accountants and solicitors was removed;
5. a certificate from the Board of Trade (Department of Trade and Industry) that a person or company was a banker was to be conclusive for the purpose of exemption alone from the Moneylenders Acts, although such a certificate was not necessary to establish that a person or company was a banker (but see *Banking Act 1979*).

COMPANIES ACT 1976 This Act dealt in particular with a number of accounting and procedural matters, of which the following are the most important.

Section 1 imposes an obligation on the directors of a company to prepare accounts in respect of each period exceeding six months and not exceeding 18 months since the company's last accounting reference date and the accounts must be laid before the company in general meeting within ten months of the end of the accounting reference period in the case of a private company and within seven months in the case of a public company. Provision is made for each director to be fined up to £400 in the event of default in laying the company's accounts before the general meeting and delivering them to the Registrar of Companies and £40 for each day during which the default continues. (Sections 1–6)

Section 13(1) lists the recognized bodies of accountants for the purposes of company audits. (Section 14 requires every company to appoint auditors at each general meeting, at which the company's accounts are laid before the meeting. The auditors hold office until the end of the next such meeting and the automatic re-appointment of auditors ceased.)

Section 16 requires an auditor who resigns to state in writing if there are any circumstances connected with his resignation which should be brought to the notice of shareholders, or the new auditors.

Section 17 empowers a resigning auditor to requisition a meeting of the company to consider the circumstances of his resignation.

Section 19 makes it a criminal offence for an officer of a company deliberately to make false or misleading statements to an auditor.

Section 24 reduces from 14 days to five days the period in which a director is required under the 1967 Act to notify the company of his acquisition of shares in the company.

Section 27 introduced to quoted companies the right to require registered shareholders to disclose whether or not they are the beneficial owners of the shares and, if not, who else is interested in them. SEE *Disclosure of Interests in Shares*

COMPANIES ACT 1980 This was an important Act in that it contained the first major impact of EEC law on English company law. The Act is concerned principally with (1) matters concerning share capital (q.v.), (2) certain matters concerning duties of directors (q.v.) and (3) rules governing 'insider dealing' (q.v.). The Act also contained a number of provisions relating to the registration and re-registration of companies.

COMPANIES ACT 1981 This Act introduced the most far-reaching changes in company law since the reforms of 1947. In particular, it gave effect to the EEC Fourth Directive on the form and content of company accounts.

The main subjects covered by the Act are

1. Company accounting and disclosure requirements.
2. Company and business names. SEE *Registration of Business Names*
3. Regulations regarding share capital. SEE *Account Company Purchase of Own Shares; Share Premium*
4. Regulations regarding the disclosure of interest in shares. SEE *Disclosure of Interest in Shares*

COMPANIES ACT 1985. SEE Supplement

COMPANY (COMPANIES) The words 'company' and 'companies' have little, if any, legal significance. The words suggest an association of two or more people in some common enterprise, but even that cannot be assumed. The firm of Smith & Company, being a partnership is not a company under the Companies Acts. In fact, Smith & Company may be a sole proprietorship so that it is not even an association of two or more people.

In business parlance, however, 'company' normally denotes an incorporated body registered under the Companies Acts. Thus, there are companies limited by shares (q.v.) and companies limited by guarantee (q.v.). Lastly, there are unlimited companies (q.v.), incorporated under the Companies Acts, but not enjoying limited liability.

It is well established that incorporated companies are separate legal persons distinct from the individual members. This well established principle was enunciated in *Salomon* v *Salomon & Co* [1897] AC 22 HL and in numerous other cases over the years. However, an association of persons can acquire separate legal status only in so far as the legislature permits, and thus there have been (and still are) only three fundamental methods of incorporation in the UK: by Royal Charter, by special Act of Parliament or by incorporation under the Companies Clauses Acts of 1845–1889 or, in more recent years, the Companies Acts.

For all practical purposes, we are concerned here with companies regulated by the Companies Acts, although there are still a number of trading corporations which owe their corporate status either to a Royal Charter or to a special Act of Parliament.

A company is governed in its dealings with the outside world by the terms of its memorandum of association. This must state the name of the company, the location of its registered office and the company's objects. If the company is to have a share capital, the memorandum must include the names of the original subscribers and the number of shares (at least one per subscriber) which each is to hold. If the company has a share capital, the proposed amount thereof must be stated, together with the number of shares into which the capital is to be divided. If the company is limited by shares or by guarantee, the memorandum must state that the liability of the members is limited. The objects clause in the memorandum sets out the objects which the company is to pursue and thereafter governs the company's legal position. Any acts performed outside those powers is not binding upon the company (SEE *Ultra Vires*). In *Mahony* v *East Holyford Mining Co Ltd* [1875] LR 7 HL 869, Lord Hatherley said that those who deal with joint stock companies must be affected with notice of all that is contained in the memorandum and articles of association.

In the case of *In re Jon Beauforte (London) Ltd* [1953] 1 All ER 634, a liquidator was held able to refute liability for debts incurred in activities outside the ambit of the memorandum of association, although they were commercial debts for transactions entered into in complete good faith.

The *ultra vires* doctrine was modified by the provisions of Section 9 of the European Communities Act 1972.

The conduct of a company's internal affairs are governed by the articles of association (q.v.). If a company does not register its own articles of association, the terms of Table A of the Companies Act 1948 are deemed to be adopted. If the company does register its own articles, Table A still applies to the extent that it is not excluded or modified by those articles. SEE *Articles of Association*; Supplement

There is a distinction in law between a private company and a public company. Under the 1948 Companies Act (and previous Companies Acts), there was no definition of a public company, but by implication it was a company which was not a private company. A private company, within the meaning of the 1948 Act, was a company which by its articles restricted the right to transfer its shares, limited the number of its members to 50 (not including employees and former employees) and prohibited any invitation to the public to subscribe for any shares or debentures in the company. Any two or more persons could form a private company (which is still the case), whereas the minimum number of members for a public company was seven, but two is now sufficient.

Under the Companies Act 1980, the definitions of public and private companies were changed to bring the law into line with the requirements of the Second EEC Directive in company law. Under the 1980 Companies Act, companies are henceforth to be classified as (1) public or (2) private, whether or not they are companies limited by shares or by guarantee.

Under the 1985 Act, a definition of a public company is one which is limited by shares or limited by guarantee and has a share capital, being a company

1. the memorandum of which states that the company is to be a public company, and
2. in relation to which the provisions of the Companies Acts as to the registration or re-registration of a public company have been complied with, (Section 1(3))
3. the nominal value of the allotted share capital of which is not less than an authorized minimum (currently £50,000) (sections 117 & 118)

A private company now means a company that is not a public company, but is generally precluded from offering its shares or debentures to the public.

Under Section 1(2) of the 1980 Act, no new companies limited by guarantee are permitted to have a share capital. SEE *Companies Limited by Guarantee*

Under Section 25 of the 1985 Act, all public companies are required to include at the end of their name the words 'public limited company' (or the Welsh equivalent) or the abbreviation 'plc'.

A private company is required to include the word 'limited' (or the abbreviation 'Ltd') at the end of its name.

The number of companies registered in the UK has risen almost continually over this century and at the end of 1981 there were 788,846 companies registered, of which 8,018 were public companies. It is not known how many companies are dormant but the Inland Revenue's estimate of active companies is in the region of 600,000.

COMPANY CARS A term loosely applied to motor cars provided for employees by their employers, whether companies or not. It has become the practice to provide employees with cars in certain types of employment as it has been, and still is, more tax effective to the employee than an equivalent payment in cash.

If a car is made available by an employer for the exclusive use of an employee, no tax will be payable by the employee on either the value of the car as a benefit in kind or the amount of any running costs paid by the employer unless the employee is a director or higher-paid employee. (At the present time, this means an employee in receipt of £8,500 or more per annum.)

In the case of directors or such employees, tax is payable according to a scale of benefits depending on the value of the car when new and its cubic capacity. (See Appendix 1)

This scale of benefits is designed to cover the capital cost of the car and all running costs (other than petrol or other fuel).

1. Where the employee's use of a company car for business purposes is regarded as insubstantial—business mileage in year does not exceed 2,500 miles (prior to 6th April, 1982 10 per cent or less of the car's total use)—the employee will be assessed on one and a half times the scale of benefits in the table (previously the benefit was calculated by reference to the cost and age of the car).
2. If the employee uses a car for business purposes for 18,000 miles (prior to April 1981 25,000 miles) or more in the course of a year, the scale of benefits shown in Appendix 1 is reduced by half.
3. Where an employee or members of his family or household have the use of additional car(s), then the scale of benefits will be increased to one and a half times for each car, other than the car most used for business purposes, even though the business mileage of each car exceeds 2,500 miles.
4. If the car is part of a company car pool there is no assessment on the employee, but in order to satisfy this requirement, the car must be available to and used by more than one employee, it must

be used only for business and not normally kept at the employee's home address.

If the employer provides free petrol or other fuel for the employee, an additional tax charge is made in accordance with the current scale. (See Appendix 1)

If an employee is required to reimburse for the full cost of all company fuel used for private purposes, the scale will be cancelled. The scale charge will apply wherever free petrol for private motoring is provided by the employer regardless of how much or how little petrol is so supplied. If the employee uses his car for more than 18,000 miles a year and qualifies for the one-half reduction in the car scale charge (see above), he will also be entitled to the one-half reduction in the car *fuel* scale charge.

COMPANY HOUSES The general rule is that an employee is taxed (whether a director or higher-paid employee, or not) on the value of any living accommodation made available by the employer, and that the employee pays tax on the gross annual value (the figure from which the rateable value is derived) plus any expenses, e.g. heating and cleaning, paid by the employer. The employee will be exempt from tax on this presumed benefit, however, if

1. he has to live in the accommodation in order to carry out his duties properly, e.g. the caretaker of a property, or
2. it is customary in that class of employment to have accommodation provided and it helps the employee to do his job better, e.g. a resident nurse at an old people's home, or
3. the employment involves a security risk and the accommodation is provided for the employee's safety.

In the case of a director or higher-paid employee, only this last category will entitle him to exemption from tax. Additionally, a director or higher-paid employee will be assessed for tax on any expenses paid by the employer in connection with the accommodation (up to 10 per cent of the employee's net emoluments from that company excluding the expenditure in question).

COMPANY LIMITED BY GUARANTEE WITH OR WITHOUT A SHARE CAPITAL A company where the liability of its members is limited, by the memorandum of association, to such amount as the members may respectively thereby undertake to contribute to the assets of the company, in the event of its being wound up. Such companies are now only registered where they exist otherwise than for profit. They are usually formed for the purpose of clubs and societies which are not intended to make a profit.

The word 'limited' must generally be the last word in the name of the company. But see *Charitable Companies*.

Section 15 of the Companies Act 1985 provides:

(1) In the case of a company limited by guarantee and not having a share capital, every provision in the memorandum or articles, or in any resolution of the company purporting to give any person a right to participate in the divisible profits of the company otherwise than as a member, is void.

(2) For purposes of provisions of this Act relating to the memorandum of a company limited by guarantee, and for those of Section 1(4) and this section, every provision in the memorandum or articles, or in any resolution, of a company so limited purporting to divide the company's undertaking into shares or interests is to be treated as a provision for a share capital, notwithstanding that the nominal amount or number of the shares of interests is not specified by provision.

Section 1(4) referred to above (re-enacting Section 1(2) of the Companies Act 1980), provides that with effect from 22nd December 1980, a company cannot be formed as, or become, a company limited by guarantee with a share capital.

By Section 7 of the 1985 Act in the case of a company limited by guarantee, articles of association must be registered with the memorandum.

Under the Companies Act 1985, a company limited by guarantee may be a public company if (1) it has a share capital, (2) in its memorandum it states that the company is to be a public company and (3) the registration details appropriate to a public company have been completed. As mentioned above, however, no new companies limited by guarantee will be permitted to have a share capital. This follows the recommendation of the Jenkins Committee (q.v.) which considered it inappropriate for a company formed with the intention of making distributions of profits to its members to register as a company limited by guarantee. SEE *Articles of Association; Memorandum of Association; Names of Companies*

COMPANY LIMITED BY SHARES A company where the liability of its members is limited by the memorandum of association to the amount, if any, unpaid on the shares respectively held by them.

Under the Companies Act 1985, each public company is required to include as the last part of its name the words 'public limited company' or the abbreviation 'plc' (or the Welsh equivalent). Each private limited company must include as the last part of its name the word 'limited' or the abbreviation 'ltd'.

A private limited company formed for promoting commerce, art, science, religion, charity or other useful object, where any profits or income are to be used in promoting its objects, may be licensed by the Department of Trade and Industry (formerly the Board of Trade) as a company with limited liability, without the addition of the word 'limited' to its name. SEE *Charitable Companies*

Under the Companies Act, a private company limited by guarantee does not need to include the word 'limited' in its title, nor do certain charitable companies (q.v.). SEE *Articles of Association; Memorandum of Association; Names of Companies; Share Capital*

COMPANY PURCHASE OF OWN SHARES Under Section 54, Companies Act 1948, it was unlawful

> for a company to give, whether directly or indirectly, and whether by means of a loan, guarantee, the provision of security or otherwise, any financial assistance for the purpose of, or in connection with, a purchase or subscription made, or to be made, by any person of or for any shares in the company or, where the company is a subsidiary company, in its holding company.

There were certain exceptions to this prohibition, principally where the lending of money was part of the ordinary business of a company and also where a company was lending the money for employees other than directors to buy shares in the company.

Section 54 was strictly interpreted in the courts with the result that the Section came to have a very restrictive effect on what might otherwise have been desirable and certainly bona fide transactions.

The Section is repealed by the Companies Act 1981, although the principle remains that a company may not give financial assistance for the purchase of its own shares.

Under Section 152 of the Companies Act 1985, financial assistance means

1. financial assistance given by way of gift,
2. financial assistance given by way of guarantee, security or indemnity, other than an indemnity in respect of the indemnifier's own neglect or default, or by way of release or waiver,
3. financial assistance given by way of a loan or any agreement under which any of the obligations of the person giving the assistance are to be fulfilled at a time when, in accordance with the agreement, any obligation of any other party to the agreement remains unfulfilled or by way of the novation of, or the assignment of, any rights arising under any such loan or agreement, or
4. any other financial assistance by a company whose net assets are as a result reduced to a material extent or which has no net assets.

The general prohibition does not prevent

1. a company from giving financial assistance if
   (a) the company's principal purpose is not to give financial assistance for the acquisition of its shares or shares of its holding company or the financial assistance is just an incidental part of some larger purpose of the company; and
   (b) the financial assistance is given in good faith in the interests of the company;
2. where the lending of money is part of the ordinary business of the company, the lending of money by it in the ordinary course of business;
3. the provision by a company of money for the acquisition of fully paid shares in the company under an employee's shares scheme;
4. the making by a company of loans to persons, other than directors, employed in good faith by the company so that those persons may acquire for beneficial ownership fully paid shares in the company or its holding company; and
5. the payment of dividends, the making of distributions in a winding up, the allotment of bonus shares, the acceptance of shares by the liquidator, any reduction of capital approved by the court, and compromise under Section 137 of the 1985 Act with creditors and any redemption or purchase of own shares.

In the case of a public company, the exceptions in (2), (3) and (4) above only apply if the company has net assets which are not reduced or, to the extent that they are reduced, the financial assistance must be provided out of distributable profit.

Subject to certain conditions (see below), a *private company* may give financial assistance for the acquisition of its shares or shares of its holding company in any circumstances where the company has net assets and, to the extent that those assets are reduced, the financial assistance is provided out of distributable profits. Such financial assistance may only be given to a holding company if that holding company and any intermediate holding company are also private companies.

Conditions of Exceptions

The conditions referred to above are

1. Except where the company is a wholly-owned subsidiary, a special resolution is required. Similarly, except if those companies are wholly-owned subsidiaries, special resolutions are also required by the holding company and all intermediate holding companies where financial assistance is given for the acquisition of shares in a holding company.
2. The directors of the company and, where appropriate, the holding company and intermediate holding companies must make a statutory declaration in the prescribed form:

(a) containing particulars of the assistance proposed to be given and identifying the person to whom it is given as well as giving particulars of the business of the company; and
(b) stating that the directors have formed the opinion that, immediately after the financial assistance is given the company will be able to pay its debts and, during 12 months following the giving of the financial assistance, that it will continue to be able to pay its debts as they fall due (or, if it is intended to commence winding up within 12 months, that it will be able to pay its debts in full within 12 months of the commencement of winding up).

3. A report by the auditors addressed to the directors should be attached to the declaration stating that they have enquired into the state of affairs of the company and are not aware of anything to indicate that the opinion expressed by the directors (see 2(b)) is unreasonable in all the circumstances.
4. The financial assistance must not be given earlier than four weeks after the resolution is passed (or the latest resolution is passed, if there are two or more resolutions) unless all voting members voted in favour of the resolution (or resolutions).
5. The financial assistance must not be given more than eight weeks after the statutory declaration (or the earliest statutory declaration, if there are two or more declarations) is made. Each special resolution must be passed on the date of, or within the week immediately following, the related statutory declaration.
6. In the case of each resolution, the statutory declaration and auditors' report must be available for inspection by members at the meeting where the resolution is passed.
7. The statutory declaration and auditors' report must be delivered to the registrar (with the resolution, if one is required).

Where a special resolution is passed in accordance with the above conditions, an application for its cancellation may be made to the court within 28 days by the holders of not less than 10 per cent of the nominal value of any class of the company's issued share capital. An application may not be made by anyone who consented to or voted in favour of the resolution.

On hearing such an application, the court may make such order as it thinks fit. Notice of the application and a copy of the order must be delivered by the company to the registrar.

Section 54 of the old Act and Sections 151 and 152 of the 1985 Act are concerned with the provision of *financial assistance* for the purchase of companies' shares. The direct purchase by a company of its own shares prior to the Companies Act 1981 was prohibited in the UK without the sanction of the court because this would amount to a reduction of capital. Under Section 58 of the 1948 Act, it was possible to issue redeemable preference shares which could in fact have been ordinary shares with a degree of preference in respect of capital repayment or dividends. Section 159, Companies Act 1985 empowers companies to issue redeemable equity shares. SEE *Redeemable Preference Shares*

Of particular importance is the power granted in the Act to enable companies to purchase their own shares. Public and private companies may, in certain circumstances, purchase their own fully paid shares for cancellation, whether out of distributable profits or out of the proceeds of the issue of further shares. Private companies may also purchase their own shares out of capital, subject to the requirements listed below.

The following are the principal conditions to be satisfied for a company to purchase its own shares:

1. The company must be authorized to do so by its articles.
2. If it is an off-market purchase (i.e. not through a recognized stock exchange), the purchase must be authorized by a special resolution of the members.
3. Such a special resolution for an off-market purchase will not be effective if it would not have been passed but for the votes of members holding shares to which the resolution relates (unless those votes were cast on a poll relating to other shares).
4. A record of the contracts for the off-market purchase must be available at the registered office of the company for members to inspect for at least 15 days before the meeting at which it is proposed that a special resolution shall be passed.
5. In the case of a *market* purchase by a company of its own shares, an ordinary resolution of members is sufficient authority.
6. A copy of the resolution conferring, varying, revoking or renewing any authority for a market purchase must be delivered to the Registrar of Companies within 15 days of being passed.
7. When shares are purchased by a company out of profits, the transfer must be made to 'capital redemption reserve' equal to the nominal value of the shares so purchased less the proceeds of any new issue.

A *private* company may, if authorized to do so by its articles, make a payment out of capital for the redemption or purchase of its own shares, but distributable profits must be exhausted first before resorting to capital.

A company may not purchase any of its own shares if, as a result of that purchase, there would no longer be any member of the company holding shares other than redeemable shares.

In all cases where shares are being purchased out of capital, the directors must make a statutory declaration specifying the amount of the capital payments so applied and stating that

having made full enquiries into the affairs and prospects of the company, they are of the opinion that:
(i) there will be no grounds on which the company could be found unable to pay its debts immediately after the payment is due; and
(ii) the company will be able to continue its business as a going concern throughout the year immediately following the payment and will thus be able to pay its debts as they fall due.

The statutory declaration must be accompanied by a report from the auditors of the company to the directors, stating that

1. they have enquired into the company's state of affairs;
2. the permissible capital payment, as specified in a declaration, has in their view been properly determined in accordance with Sections 171 and 172 of the Companies Act 1985; and
3. they are not aware of anything to indicate that the opinion expressed by the directors in the declaration is unreasonable.

In all cases of the purchase of shares out of capital, a notice in the form prescribed in the Act must be published in the *Gazette* and in a national newspaper, although the latter publication may be dispensed with if notice is given to each of the company's creditors.

But for the saving provision of the Finance Act 1982, the purchase of a company's shares would amount to a distribution under the Corporation Tax Acts and would thus attract advance corporation tax. Section 53 of the Finance Act 1982, however, exempts such payments if

1. the company is an unquoted company and either a trading company or the holding company of a trading group; and
2. the redemption or repayment or purchase is made wholly or mainly for the purpose of benefiting a trade carried on by the company or by any of its 75 per cent owned subsidiaries and does not form part of the scheme or arrangement for the purpose of
(a) enabling the owner of the shares to participate in the profits of the company without receiving a dividend; or
(b) the avoidance of tax;
3. the conditions of Paragraphs 1–9 of Schedule 9 to the Finance Act 1982 have been complied with: principally, this relates to the obtaining of approval from the Board of Inland Revenue to the proposed transaction.

Purchase by companies of their own shares has been a significant feature of United States companies for some years, and has now become an increasingly popular move in the UK. At the time of writing, over 1,000 companies have taken advantage of the provisions in the 1981 Act to repurchase some of their own shares. On the whole, this is a tax-efficient way of passing funds to shareholders, because the proceeds are taxed as capital gains, rather than income in the hands of the shareholder. A return of capital to shareholders in this way can also have beneficial effects on the company's figures, e.g. earnings per share and assets per share are effectively increased by the re-purchase of some of a company's shares.

COMPANY, UNLIMITED A company not having any limit to the liability of its members for the debts of the company. Very few companies are now registered with unlimited liability. Many banking and other companies which were originally unlimited have been re-registered as limited companies.

In the event of an unlimited company being wound up, though the liability of the members is unlimited, the members are, as between themselves, only liable to contribute in proportion to their holdings. A past member is under no liability at all if he had ceased to be a member for a year before the winding-up. SEE *Contributories*

Section 51 of the Companies Act 1985 provides:

51.—(1) Subject as follows, a company which is registered as unlimited may be re-registered as limited if a special resolution that it should be so re-registered is passed, and the requirements of this section are complied with in respect of the resolution and otherwise.

(2) A company cannot under this section be re-registered as a public company; and a company is excluded from re-registering under it if it is unlimited by virtue of re-registration under section 43 of the Companies Act 1967 or section 49 of this Act.

(3) The special resolution must state whether the company is to be limited by shares or by guarantee and—
(a) if it is to be limited by shares, must state what the share capital is to be and provide for the making of such alterations in the memorandum as are necessary to bring it (in substance and in form) into conformity with the requirements of this Act with respect to the memorandum of a company so limited, and such alterations in the articles as are requisite in the circumstances;
(b) if it is to be limited by guarantee, must provide for the making of such alterations in its memorandum and articles as are necessary to bring

them (in substance and in form) into conformity with the requirements of this Act with respect to the memorandum and articles of a company so limited.

COMPENSATION FOR LOSS OF OFFICE OR EMPLOYMENT The payment made for loss of an office or employment is prima facie an emolument of that office or employment.

With effect from 6th April, 1981, the first £25,000 of a loss of office payment will normally be free of income tax. (Prior to that date, the exemption limit was £10,000 and prior to April 1978, £5,000.) In certain circumstances, however, the *full amount* of the payment will be taxed including, in particular, the following instances:

1. payments made before employment actually ceases,
2. payments expressed to be for past services,
3. payments in return for restrictive covenants,
4. payments which take the form of waiver of loans,
5. compensation payments which are precisely stated in a contract of service.

In most other cases, however, the £25,000 exemption will apply and the method of taxation of any balance above that figure will follow the rules introduced in the Finance Act 1981 with effect from 6th April, 1981 as amended by Finance Act 1982. Prior to April 1981, a distinction was drawn between compensation payments and *ex gratia* payments, but this no longer applies. Also prior to that date, the tax on the excess payment was calculated according to a 'top-slicing' formula, but this too no longer applies.

The balance above £25,000 is added to the employee's other taxable income for the tax year in which it is received and the tax charge on the lump sum is then half the difference between (1) the amount of tax payable before bringing the lump sum into account and (2) the amount of tax which would be payable if the whole of the taxable part of the lump sum were treated as additional income for that year. Thus, if the tax payable by A regardless of any lump sum is, say, £6,000 and if, bringing into account the non-exempt part of a lump sum, his tax liability would be £8,000, the additional tax payable by virtue of the termination payment will be one-half of the difference between the two figures, i.e. £1,000.

With effect from 6th April, 1982, the 50 per cent reduction in tax applies to any excess over the initial £25,000 exemption up to a figure of £50,000. Between £50,001 and £75,000 the exemption is reduced to one-quarter. Any excess over £75,000 is fully taxable with no relief.

COMPETITION AND CREDIT CONTROL A new system of credit control for the financial system was introduced on 16th September, 1971. This entry sets out the old and new forms of control with comparisons and presents some of the implications for the clearing banks.

Prior to September 1971, control of credit operated through official controls on the liquidity of the banks and a series of quantitative and qualitative restraints on the lending activities of the banks and finance houses. In particular:

1. The banks maintained a ratio of eight per cent between cash held in tills and at the Bank of England and their gross deposits.
2. The total of cash and other liquid assets, including money at call and short notice, Treasury Bills, other commercial bills and refinanceable credits, was maintained at a minimum level of 28 per cent of each bank's gross deposits.
3. To reduce bank liquidity, independently of open market operations, the Bank of England had power to call for Special Deposits from the London Clearing and Scottish banks. In August 1971, the London Clearing Banks had $3\frac{1}{2}$ per cent of gross deposits lodged as Special Deposits on which they received interest at the going Treasury bill rate.
4. The level of clearing bank advances was subject to various official ceilings apart from some exempt categories such as loans to nationalized industries and fixed rate finance for exports and shipbuilding.

Changes in the system of control were considered desirable for a number of reasons. The development of the banking system and the growth of financial institutions outside the scope of official credit controls had led to a relative decline in the importance of the clearing banks. The application of controls had become only partially effective, and a uniform and more equitable system was called for. The authorities also recognized that continued restrictions on clearing bank lending inhibited competition and produced economic inefficiency in the use of resources. They were therefore prepared to consider other methods of controlling the economy paying more attention to money supply and the allocation of credit through the price mechanism.

The Changes

The changes in the methods of credit control were outlined in the Bank of England papers *Competition and Credit Control* (May 1971) and *Reserve Ratios and Special Deposit* (September 1971). They apply to all banks operating in the UK.

Interest Rates
The London and Scottish Clearing Banks abandoned their collective agreements on interest rates. Individual banks were enabled to quote their own deposit rates for seven day money and quote for term deposits. They were also free to quote lending rates linked to their own Base Rates.

Credit Controls
All existing lending restrictions and liquidity constraints were abandoned. Existing Special Deposits were repaid and much of the excess liquidity mopped up by clearing bank subscription to £750 million short dated government securities. A new concept of total eligible liabilities was evolved to replace gross deposits as a basis for control.

Eligible liabilities consist of sterling deposits, other than those with an original maturity of over two years, and the net of interbank transactions and sterling certificates of deposit of whatever maturity. Sterling resources obtained by switching foreign currencies into sterling are included. There is also an adjustment for items in transit.

In place of the former liquidity ratio the banks were required to observe a reserve asset ratio which was fixed at a minimum of 12½ per cent of total eligible liabilities. Reserve assets comprise

Balances at the Bank of England.
British Government and Northern Ireland Treasury Bills.
Money at call with the London Discount Market.
British Government stocks and nationalized industries' stocks guaranteed by HM Government with 1 year or less to maturity.
Local authority bills eligible for rediscount at the Bank of England.
Commercial bills eligible for rediscount at the Bank of England—up to a maximum of 2 per cent of eligible liabilities.

In more recent times, the system of reserve asset ratios has been abandoned and following discussions between the Bank of England and the major banks, a system of prudential controls has taken its place based on continuing dialogues with each bank and a degree of supervision appropriate to each individual case.

Competition and credit control was in a number of respects a major turning point in British banking. One early effect was the upsurge in the level of the money supply in 1972 and 1973 consequent upon the considerable expansion in bank lending. The increase in lending, which the authorities encouraged, was arguably a factor in the build-up to the secondary bank crisis of 1974–75. More particularly, however, the new system introduced a degree of competitiveness which had not hitherto been seen in modern banking and which, for the most part, was widely welcomed. The banks were now free to bid for deposits and to some extent, therefore, the *raison d'être* of their bidding subsidiaries disappeared. New and profitable outlets for bank finance were sought and new skills developed, banks became more aggressive and moved increasingly towards the concept of the all-purpose bank.

COMPOSITION WITH CREDITORS
Where a debtor is unable to pay his creditors he may, legally, call his creditors together and make an arrangement with them, by which he may obtain relief from his debts, and one of the usual methods by which this is done is to offer to pay a composition, that is, to pay so much in the pound in full discharge of the debts due to the creditors. The composition is usually payable in a number of instalments, upon specified dates, and is guaranteed by sureties. In some cases promissory notes are given for the various instalments, and are made payable at the various dates on which the instalments are due.

If the arrangement is agreed to by the creditors in a deed or instrument, called a deed of arrangement, it must be registered within seven days, otherwise it is void. SEE *Deed of Arrangement*

An arrangement of this kind between a debtor and his creditors is quite independent of proceedings under the Bankruptcy Acts, but, if he fails to pay the agreed instalments, the arrangement does not prevent proceedings in bankruptcy being subsequently taken. SEE *Act of Bankruptcy; Assignment for Benefit of Creditors; Bankruptcy*

As regards compositions made by companies, the position is governed by Section 425, Companies Act 1985:

(1) Where a compromise or arrangement is proposed between a company and its creditors or any class of them or between the company and its members or any class of them, the Court may, on the application of the company or any creditor or member of it or, in the case of a company being wound up of the liquidator, order a meeting of the creditors or class of creditors, or of the members of the company or class of members, as the case may be, to be summoned in such manner as the Court directs.

(2) If a majority in number representing three-fourths in value of the creditors or class of creditors or members or class of members, as the case may be, present and voting either in person or by proxy at the meeting, agree to any compromise or arrangement, the compromise or arrangement, if sanctioned by the Court is binding on all the creditors or the class of creditors, or on the members or class of members, as the case may be, and also on the company or, in the case of a company in the

course of being wound up, on the liquidator and contributories of the company.

(3) The court's order under sub-section (2) has no effect until an office copy of it has been delivered to the Registrar of Companies for registration, and a copy of every such order shall be annexed to every copy of the Company's memorandum issued after the order has been made, or, in the case of a company not having a memorandum, of every copy so issued of the instrument constituting the company or defining its constitution.

(4) If a company makes default in complying with subsection (3), the company and every officer of it who is in default is liable to a fine.

Power to effect a compromise with the creditors of a company in course of winding up by the court is given to a liquidator by Section 539, Companies Act 1985, in the following terms:

(1) The liquidator in a winding up by the court shall have power, with the sanction either of the court or of the committee of inspection—

(*e*) to make any compromise or arrangement with creditors or persons claiming to be creditors, or having or alleging themselves to have any claim, (present or future, certain or contingent, ascertained or sounding only in damages) against the company, or whereby the company may be rendered liable;

(*f*) to compromise all calls and liabilities to calls, debts and liabilities capable of resulting in debts, and all claims, present or future, certain or contingent, ascertained or sounding only in damages, subsisting or supposed to subsist between the company and a contributory or alleged contributory or other debtor or person apprehending liability to the company, and all questions in any way relating to or affecting the assets or the winding up of the company, on such terms as may be agreed, and take any security for the discharge of any such call, debt, liability or claim and give a complete discharge in respect of it.

COMPOSITIONS (BANKRUPTCY ACT) When a receiving order has been made against a debtor, he must, within a certain time, submit a statement of his affairs to the official receiver. (SEE *Receiving Order*) If the debtor wishes to submit to his creditors a proposal for a composition—that is, a payment of so much in the pound—or for a scheme of arrangement, the Bankruptcy Act 1914 provides as follows:

16.—(1) Where a debtor intends to make a proposal for a composition in satisfaction of his debts, or a proposal for a scheme of arrangement of his affairs, he shall, within four days of submitting his statement of affairs, or within such time thereafter as the official receiver may fix, lodge with the official receiver a proposal in writing, signed by him, embodying the terms of the composition or scheme which he is desirous of submitting for the consideration of his creditors, and setting out particulars of any sureties or securities proposed.

(2) In such case the official receiver shall hold a meeting of creditors, before the public examination of the debtor is concluded, and send to each creditor, before the meeting, a copy of the debtor's proposal with a report thereon; and if at that meeting a majority in number and three-fourths in value of all the creditors who have proved resolve to accept the proposal, it shall be deemed to be duly accepted by the creditors, and when approved by the court shall be binding on all the creditors.

The court has power to approve or to refuse to approve the proposal (subsection (11)).

If the debtor's proposal is accepted by the creditors, the receiving order is discharged by the court. If a trustee is appointed to carry out the scheme, the official receiver hands the debtor's property to him, but if no trustee is appointed the official receiver acts as trustee.

If the proposal is not accepted within fourteen days after the conclusion of the debtor's examination, the Court shall adjudge the debtor bankrupt. SEE *Adjudication in Bankruptcy*

A composition or scheme of arrangement may be accepted by the creditors, if they think fit, at any time after the debtor is adjudicated bankrupt, and the court may annul the bankruptcy (Section 21(1) and (2)).

If default is made in payment of an instalment, under the composition or scheme the court may adjudge the debtor bankrupt, and annul the composition or scheme, but without prejudice to the validity of any sale, disposition, or payment duly made in pursuance of the composition or scheme (Section 16(16)).

Debts are proved in the same way as in the case of bankruptcy. SEE *Bankruptcy; Proof of Debts; Scheme of Arrangement*

COMPOUNDING WITH CREDITORS SEE *Composition with Creditors*

COMPULSORY LIQUIDATION SEE *Winding Up*

CONDITIONAL ACCEPTANCE SEE *Acceptance, Qualified*

CONDITIONAL INDORSEMENT Where a condition is attached to an indorser's signature on a bill of exchange, the condition may be disregarded by the paying banker, and payment to the indorsee is valid whether the condition has been fulfilled or not. As between the indorser and indorsee, however, the condition is thought to be operative; and if the indorsee receives payment without the condition being fulfilled, he holds the money in trust for the indorser. An indorsement 'Pay John Brown or order, on the arrival of the ship Swallow at Calcutta' would be conditional. SEE *Indorsement*

CONDITIONAL ORDERS A bill of exchange is an unconditional order. An order upon a banker to pay a certain sum, provided that a form of receipt is signed, is not unconditional, and therefore does not comply with the definition of a cheque in the Bills of Exchange Act 1882. See Section 3 under *Bill of Exchange* and Section 73 under *Cheque*.

Such documents are not protected by Section 60 of the Bills of Exchange Act 1882, although they come within the ambit of Section 80 of that Act by virtue of the extension (by Section 5 of the Cheques Act 1957) of the provisions of the crossed cheque sections of the Bills of Exchange Act 1882 to (*inter alia*) documents issued by a customer of a banker which are intended to enable a person to obtain payment from the banker of the sum mentioned in the document.

There is, probably, no protection for the banker who pays an uncrossed conditional order having a forged indorsement (unless some can be construed from Section 1 of the Cheques Act), and consequently it is usual for a banker to require an indemnity from a customer who wishes to issue such documents. Under Section 1 of the Cheques Act 1957, a banker paying a conditional order drawn on him which is not indorsed or is irregularly indorsed, does not, in doing so, incur any liability by reason only of the absence of, or irregularity in, indorsement.

A conditional order is probably an equitable assignment. It is possible, therefore, that as between banker and customer its presentation operates as notice of an assignment of funds and, as with a cheque in Scotland, results in the earmarking of the balance for the person entitled to the cheque if the balance is insufficient (Cf. Section 53, Bills of Exchange Act 1882). The point however has not been before the courts.

An unqualified order to pay, coupled with an indication of a particular account to be debited, is unconditional (Section 3(3)).

(SEE *Receipt on Cheque* for further information regarding conditions on cheques.)

CONFIRMED CREDIT The nature of a confirmed credit can best be illustrated by example. A Norwegian importer may arrange to buy goods from West Africa and undertakes to make payment by opening a sterling credit in London in favour of the exporter. The Norwegian will request his own banker to arrange with a London banker to establish the credit on the terms, say, of payment against delivery of documents by the African exporter. The latter may desire to be assured that payment will be made with absolute certainty, in which case the importer by paying a small extra commission can arrange for the London banker to give his confirmation to the exporter that payment will be forthcoming.

This will be a confirmed credit. A confirmed credit is not necessarily the same as an irrevocable credit, since it is possible for the latter to be unconfirmed, as when a banker in country A instructs another banker in country B to open a credit in favour of a merchant C, the credit to be irrevocable as regards the first banker but not confirmed by the second; but the phraseology is now reconciled by the Uniform Customs (q.v.). SEE *Documentary Credit*

CONGLOMERATE A company engaged in a variety of business activities, sometimes seemingly unrelated to each other. Conglomerates have been more common in the USA than in the UK and on the whole have not been particularly successful. On the other hand, some Japanese conglomerates have succeeded very well.

CONSIDERATION Valuable consideration has been defined as 'some right, interest, profit, or benefit, accruing to one party, or some forbearance, detriment, loss or responsibility given, suffered, or undertaken by the other'.

A simple contract, that is a contract not under seal, in order to be enforceable at law, must be supported by a valuable consideration. In a contract under seal, a valuable consideration is not essential. 'Natural love and affection' is called good consideration, but it is not sufficient to support a simple contract. A contract based upon an illegal consideration, that is one which is contrary to the law or is against public policy or morality, cannot be enforced. SEE *Contract*

Upon a sale of property, the purchase price is the consideration, and that amount is inserted in the deed of conveyance and the stamp duty, *ad valorem*, calculated thereon.

In a deed of gift, as, for example, where a property is the subject of a gift from, say, a father to his son, the consideration may be 'natural love and affection'. The Finance (1909–10) Act, Section 74, enacts that any conveyance operating as a voluntary disposition *inter vivos* shall be chargeable with the same duty as if it were a conveyance on a sale, with the substitution of the value of the property conveyed for the amount of the consideration.

Where shares are specifically left in a Will, the consideration in a transfer from the executors to the legatee will be a nominal one; but where a legatee agrees to accept a transfer of certain shares, instead of receiving the cash to which he is entitled the consideration must be the price agreed upon between the legatee and executors, and the stamp duty will be *ad valorem*.

Consideration need not be stated in writing in the case of a guarantee (Mercantile Law Amendment Act 1856, Section 3).

CONSIDERATION FOR BILL OF EXCHANGE There must be a valuable consideration for a contract not under seal, though it is not necessary in a bill of exchange that the consideration be stated in writing.

The Bills of Exchange Act 1882, Section 3(4), enacts that a bill is not invalid by reason 'that it does not specify the value given, or that any value has been given therefor'.

The word 'sterling' was at one time usually written after the amount, but it is now very rarely met with on inland bills.

By Section 27

(1) Valuable consideration for a bill may be constituted by:

- (a) Any consideration sufficient to support a simple contract;
- (b) An antecedent debt or liability. Such a debt or liability is deemed valuable consideration whether the bill is payable on demand or at a future time.

In the case of *Re Keever* [1967] Ch 182, the bank was held to be a holder in due course (q.v.) because of the antecedent debt; the case was followed on this point in *Barclays Bank* v *Astley* [1970] *Sol J*, 6th February.

Where a person signs a bill as drawer, acceptor or indorser, without receiving value therefor, he is an accommodation party. SEE *Accommodation Bill*

A total failure of consideration is a defence between 'immediate parties', but it is not a defence between remote parties, when the holder is a holder in due course.

Where a cheque is given as a gift, the receiver cannot sue the giver thereon, because of the absence of consideration.

The title of a person who negotiates a bill is defective if he obtained the bill for an illegal consideration (Section 29(2)).

Where a consideration is affected with fraud or illegality, that would form a good defence against an immediate party, but not against a remote party who is a holder in due course, that is, one who took the bill for value, in good faith and without knowledge of any defect in the title. SEE *Holder in Due Course*

A bill, or cheque, given for a wagering or gaming debt cannot be sued upon by a holder who took it with knowledge of the illegal consideration, but a holder, in due course, who took it without such knowledge, can sue upon it. In the case of *Ladup Ltd* v *Shaikh (Nadeem) and Another* [1982] 3 WLR 172, the plaintiffs, who operated a casino, cashed a cheque for £45,000 for the first defendant, the cheque having been drawn by the second defendant and crossed 'not negotiable'. The second defendant stopped payment of the cheque because certain bank drafts which had been given to them by the first defendant were not met. McCowan, J, held that when the plaintiffs cashed the cheque they knew it had been given originally for an illegal consideration, i.e. for gaming purposes and they could therefore have no better title to the non-negotiable cheque than had the first defendant himself.

It was decided in *Moulis* v *Owen* [1907] 1 KB 746, that even when a cheque is drawn in a foreign country on a banker in the UK, for a consideration which is legal in the country where it is drawn, but illegal in the UK, the action on the cheque fails. SEE *Bill of Exchange*

CONSOLIDATED FUND The Consolidated Fund of the United Kingdom is the fund into which is paid the whole of the revenue, and out of which payments are made, as provided by Parliament. The account at the Bank of England is called the Exchequer Account. At one time, all monies borrowed by the Government or lent by the Government were respectively paid into and out of the Consolidated Fund but since 1968 a separate account had been conducted at the Bank of England under the title National Loans Fund, which deals with all borrowing and domestic lending by the central Government.

CONSOLIDATED FUND ACT An Act passed annually by Parliament to enable the Treasury to apply out of the Consolidated Fund a sum for the supply services of the ensuing financial year. This Act does not appropriate the sum to any particular services, but the Appropriation Act passed at the end of the session shows how all the grants made during the session are appropriated.

CONSOLS A contraction of 'consolidated funds' and 'consolidated annuities'. The Government borrowed money at different times and set aside a portion of the revenue to pay the interest or annuity upon each separate loan. The various loans were, in 1751, made uniform and consolidated into one fund, called the Three Per Cent Consolidated Annuities or Three Per Cent Consols. In 1888 the rate became $2\frac{3}{4}$ per cent, and in 1903 $2\frac{1}{2}$ per cent. Consols became redeemable at par in, or after, 1923 at the option of the Government.

The interest is due on 5th January, 5th April, 5th July, 5th October. Consols are marked ex dividend about four weeks before the interest is due. The Bank does not deduct income tax from interest on Consols when the interest does not exceed £5 per annum.

Consols were originally in inscribed form, but some 50 years ago were permitted to be held in bearer form. By the Finance Act 1911 they could be registered as transferable by deed. During 1940, holders of bearer Consols were encouraged to convert them into registered or inscribed stock for safety purposes. As from 1st January, 1943 inscribed stock for British Government securities, including Consols, was abolished. The term 'Consols' is also applied to the British Government 4 per cent Consolidated Stock redeemable 1957 or after, the interest on which is due on 1st February and 1st August.

The price of 2½ per cent Consols has been used traditionally as a barometer of Government stock price movements in relation to changing levels of interest rates. Being an undated stock, it is a 'pure' income investment having no redemption yield (q.v.) as such. The difference between the yield on Consols and the yield on equities is the reverse yield gap (q.v.).

CONSORTIUM BANKS These are banks set up in London and in other parts of the world, usually with a few main shareholders who are themselves banks or major financial institutions. A number of consortium banks were set up in London in the 1960s and early 1970s to give their shareholder banks the opportunity of doing business in London. They also provided the English bank shareholders with the opportunity of doing banking business outside the then interest rate cartel. They are essentially wholesale banks with virtually no retail operations. They raise their money either from their shareholders or in the money market and specialize in medium-term loans, project finance, leasing and other wholesale money operations. According to *The Banker*, in November 1982 there were 30 consortium or joint venture banks operating in London, owned in part by 70 overseas banks who had no other direct presence in the UK. In recent years, a number of consortia have been discontinued, usually by the outright purchase by one of the major shareholders.

CONSTANT ATTENDANCE ALLOWANCE This is a form of social security disablement benefit payable where the disablement is 100 per cent and the person concerned requires constant care and attention. SEE *Disablement Benefit*

CONSUMER CREDIT Although 'consumer credit' does not have any precise meaning, the terms of reference to the Crowther Committee (Report of the Committee on Consumer Credit. Chairman: Lord Crowther, Cmnd 4596 HMSO 1971) identifies consumer credit as the 'provision of credit to individuals for financing purchases of goods and services for personal consumption'. Thus, the term embraces hire purchase (q.v.), credit sales, personal loans, check trading (q.v.), credit cards (q.v.) and a very considerable proportion of bank lending to the personal sector (SEE *Lending by Banks*). On the other hand, it excludes loans for house purchase because that is not 'personal consumption' as such and it excludes many bank loans in the personal and professional sector, which are used for business purposes.

It can no longer be assumed that hire purchase is entirely consumer credit. Indeed, approximately 60 per cent of the business of the finance houses is in the industrial hire purchase field.

The total amount of consumer credit outstanding at the end of each year for the five years to 1984 are

Year	£ million
1979	£9,869
1980	£11,444
1981	£13,935
1982	£15,791
1983	£19,251
1984	£21,479 (est.)

Source: Financial Statistics (Central Statistical Office).

SEE ALSO *Crowther Committee on Consumer Credit; Finance Houses Association*

CONSUMER CREDIT ACT 1974 This was passed to give effect, at least in part, to recommendations of the Crowther Committee (q.v.). In the preamble to the Act, it is described as

> An Act to establish for the protection of consumers a new system, administered by the Director-General of Fair Trading, of licensing and other control of traders concerned with the provision of credit, or the supply of goods on hire or hire-purchase, and their transactions, in place of the present enactments regulating moneylenders, pawnbrokers and hire purchase traders and their transactions; and for related matters.

Part I of the Act (Sections 1–7) provides for the appointment of a Director-General of Fair Trading and sets out the powers and duties of the Director.

Part II (Sections 8–20) deal with credit agreements, hire agreements and linked transactions. In particular, Section 8 defines the Consumer Credit Agreement as an agreement whereby an individual is provided with credit not exceeding

£5,000 (now £15,000) and states that such an agreement is a regulated agreement within the Act unless it is an exempt agreement by virtue of Section 16 (below).

Sections 9, 10 and 11 define credit, running account credit and fixed sum credit and restricted-use and unrestricted-use credit agreements.

Sections 12 and 13 define debtor–credit supplier and debtor–creditor agreements in relation to the purpose for which the credit is to be used.

Section 14 defines a credit-token as

a card, check, voucher, coupon, stamp, form, booklet or other document or thing given to an individual by a person carrying on a consumer credit business who undertakes:

(a) that on the production of it (whether or not some other action is also required) he will supply cash, goods and services (or any of them) on credit, or

(b) that where, on the production of it to a third party (whether or not any other action is also required) the third party supplies cash, goods and services (or any of them) he will pay the third party for them (whether or not deducting any discount or commission) in return for payment to him by the individual.

Section 15 defines consumer hire agreement as

an agreement which

(a) is not a hire purchase agreement, and

(b) is capable of subsisting for more than three months, and

(c) does not require the hirer to make payments exceeding £5,000 (now £15,000).

The Section states that consumer hire agreements are regulated agreements under the Act.

Section 16 provides that the Act does not regulate a consumer credit agreement where the creditor is a local authority or building society or other body being an insurance company, friendly society, charity etc., as specified by the Secretary of State, provided the agreement is secured by a land mortgage.

Section 17 deals with small agreements and contains provisions to prevent the use of several small agreements where it appears probable that the parties would have made a single agreement but for the desire to avoid the operation of provisions of the Act. A small agreement is

1. a regulated consumer credit agreement for credit not exceeding £30 (now £50), other than a hire purchase or conditional sale agreement; or
2. a regulated consumer hire agreement which does not require the hirer to make payments exceeding £30 (now £50).

Sections 18 and 19 define multiple agreements and linked transactions.

Section 20 contains power for the Secretary of State to make regulations for the determination of the 'total charge for credit', including sums payable in respect of a linked transaction.

Part III, Sections 21–42, relates to the licensing of credit and hire business.

Section 21 provides

1. a licence is required to carry on a consumer credit business or consumer hire business;
2. a local authority does not need a licence to carry on a business; and
3. a corporate body empowered by a public general Act naming it to carry on a business does not need a licence to do so.

The remaining Sections in this part contain detailed provisions as to the content of the licence, the persons entitled to hold a licence, determination of applications, renewal, variation, suspension and revocation of licences, maintenance of a register by the Director of Fair Trading and the effect of carrying on a business when unlicensed.

Part IV, Sections 43–54, deals with the power of the Secretary of State to make regulations as to the form and content of advertisements for consumer credit or consumer hire purchase. These sections define canvassing and make the canvassing of debtor–creditor agreements an offence in certain circumstances, make it an offence to circulate to a minor documents relating to credit with a view to financial gain, prohibit the sending of unsolicited credit tokens and provide for other regulations relating to the display of information and conduct of business etc.

Part V, Sections 55–74, governs entry into agreement or hire agreement. In particular, Sections 62 and 63 provide that, in cerain circumstances, the debtor or hirer must be presented with copies of the unexecuted and the executed agreements.

Sections 67 to 69 enable a debtor or hirer to serve a notice of cancellation within a specified 'cooling-off' period to bring an end to the agreement and any linked transactions, provided that some conditions are satisfied.

Part VI, Sections 75–86, relates to matters arising during the currency of credit or hire agreements and deals, in particular, with the giving of information to the debtor or hirer, the appropriation of payments and restricts the actions that may be taken under the agreement on the death of the debtor or hirer.

Part VII, Sections 87–104, deals with default and termination. In particular, Section 90 provides that when one-third of the total price has been paid in respect of goods held under a regulated hire purchase or conditional sale agreement, the goods become protected and the creditor can only recover possession by an order of the court.

Section 92 prohibits the entry into any premises to take possession of goods or to recover possession of land without an order of the court.

Section 99 gives the debtor under a regulated hire purchase or conditional sale agreement, the right to terminate the agreement any time before the final payment falls due.

Part VIII, Sections 105–126, deals with security. These sections deal with the form and content of any security provided in relation to a regulated agreement.

Section 123 provides that a creditor or owner shall not take a negotiable instrument other than a banknote or cheque in discharge of any sum payable

1. by the debtor or hirer under a regulated agreement; or
2. by any person as surety in relation to the agreement (this Section does not apply where the regulated agreement is a non-commercial agreement, i.e. one not made by the creditor or owner in the course of a business carried on by him).

Part IX, Sections 127–144 deals with judicial control, Part X, Sections 145–160, deals with ancillary credit bill business, which is defined in Section 145 as 'any business so far as it comprises or relates to credit brokerage, debt-adjusting, debt-counselling, debt-collecting, or the operation of a credit reference agency'.

Under the same section, credit brokerage is the effecting of introductions

1. of individuals desiring to obtain credit
   (a) to persons carrying on businesses to which the Act applies, or
   (b) in the case of an individual desiring to obtain credit to finance the acquisition or provision of a dwelling occupied, or to be occupied, by himself or his relative, to any person carrying on a business, in the course of which he provides credit secured on land, or
2. of individuals desiring to obtain goods on hire to persons carrying on businesses to which the Act applies, or
3. of individuals desiring to obtain credit or to obtain goods on hire to other credit brokers.

Part XI, Sections 161–173, deals with enforcement of the Act and Part XII, Sections 174–193, deals with various supplementary provisions.

This far-reaching Act came into effect on 31st July, 1974, apart from certain provisions which came into effect on appointed days between 1974 and 1977.

The system of licensing under the Act commenced on 3rd August, 1976, and licences were issued for three-year periods. With effect from 1st August, 1979, however, the Government decided to extend the validity of licences from three years to ten years.

The licensing arrangements do not apply to credit business done with limited companies, e.g. lending money to limited companies or giving advice on sources of credit, etc; nor is a licence required where a trader merely commits a customer to take normal trade credit, e.g. to pay bills monthly or quarterly. In general, however, anyone engaged in a credit business under any of the following headings must be licensed under the Act:

Consumer credit business That is, the lending of money or the allowing of credit, in all cases where the amount of the credit does not exceed £15,000. This category covers hire purchase, credit sales, overdrafts, budget accounts, credit cards, check trading, etc.

Consumer hire business In cases where the total amount of the payments does not exceed £15,000.

Credit brokerage That is, the arranging of credit for other persons, e.g. where an estate agent arranges a mortgage through a building society. Again the £15,000 limit applies.

Debt adjusting and debt counselling In cases where the amounts involved are within the £15,000 limit.

Debt collecting That is, taking steps to procure the payment of debts under a consumer credit or hire agreement.

Credit reference business That is, the supplying of information regarding the financial standing of individuals (not companies) but this does not apply to the giving of information about the customers gained in the normal course of business, such as the giving of a trade reference.

Anyone engaged in credit business under two or more of these headings will require separate licences for each category.

SEE Supplement

CONTANGO The charge made by a stockbroker for carrying over or continuing a bargain from one Stock Exchange settlement until another. The charge was based on money market rates, and was fixed on 'contango day'—the first of the Stock Exchange settling days—also known as 'carry over day', 'making up day', or 'continuation day'.

The contango system was abolished on the

outbreak of war in 1939 and was not restored when the Council of the Stock Exchange re-instituted the system of fortnightly settlements on 10th January, 1947.

The word is used in a rather different sense in the commodity markets when it is expected that the price of a particular commodity will rise. In such a case, the forward contract price will be fixed above the current spot price, the differential being the contango. SEE ALSO *Backwardation*

CONTENTS INSURANCE SEE *Household Insurance*

CONTINGENT LIABILITY A liability which is uncertain, usually one which may crystallize on the happening of a particular event. Perhaps the most typical example of a contingent liability is that of a guarantee (q.v.). The liability under the guarantee crystallizes and ceases to be a *contingent* liability only when the principal debtor fails to meet his liability and the bank 'calls up' the guarantee. SEE ALSO *Discounting a Bill* in relation to the contingent liability which may arise in that connection.

In matters of company accounting, it is a requirement of Schedule 9 to the Companies Act 1985 that the amount, or estimated amount, of any contingent liability, its legal nature and whether or not security has been provided, be shown in the company's accounts. Under Schedule 4 to the Companies Act 1985, all material contingencies, whether potential gains or not, should be disclosed with, if possible, an estimate of the financial effect on the company.

CONTINGENT REMAINDER SEE *Remainder*

CONTINUATION DAY The first of the five days of a Stock Exchange settlement. Also called contango day (q.v.). SEE *Stock Exchange*

CONTRACT A contract is an agreement between two parties with the intention that it shall be legally binding. According to the learned editors of Halsbury, whilst it is probably impossible to give one absolute and universally correct definition of a contract, the most commonly accepted definition is 'a promise or set of promises which the law will enforce'.

There must be at least two parties to a contract. There cannot, for example, be a contract between two departments of the same company because no person may make a contract with himself. The persons entering into the contract must have the legal capacity to do so. There are, for example, limitations on the capacity of infants, bankrupts, drunken persons and persons of unsound mind to enter into binding contracts. Legally binding contracts are entered into every day in the financial world and it would be impossible in a work of this nature to cover all aspects of the subject.

A contract may be made in a document under seal, as in a conveyance of property or transfer of shares; or it may be a simple contract made either by word of mouth or by a writing not under seal, as in a bill of exchange. In a contract under seal, there is no necessity to prove consideration. In a simple contract, there must be a consideration of value. A valuable consideration has been defined as 'some right, interest, profit, or benefit accruing to one party, or some forbearance, detriment, loss, or responsibility given, suffered, or undertaken by the other' (*Currie v Misa* [1875] LR10 Exch. 153). A past benefit is not a consideration sufficient to support a simple contract. When a guarantee is taken by a banker to secure an existing overdraft, the consideration is usually expressed as the banker's forbearance not to press for repayment of the money or as the granting of further time to the debtor, or as opening or continuing an account with the principal debtor.

By the Bills of Exchange Act 1882, a bill of exchange (q.v.), a cheque (q.v.), and a promissory note (q.v.), must be in writing. By the Statute of Frauds, a guarantee (q.v.) must be in writing, if it is to be enforceable at law. There are also other contracts which must be in writing.

In the case of a bill of exchange, it is not necessary to specify in writing the value given or that any value has been given. There must, however, be a valuable consideration, which may be any consideration sufficient to support a simple contract. An antecedent debt or liability is deemed a valuable consideration in a bill of exchange, whether the bill is payable on demand or at a future date. SEE *Consideration for Bill of Exchange*

Certain contracts are void because they are illegal, e.g. a contract to commit fraud or entered into for an immoral purpose. Other contracts are void because, for example, they are contrary to a particular Act of Parliament, e.g. contracts of gaming or wagering. The distinction between contracts which are illegal and those which are merely void may be of importance in relation to collateral agreements and the position of third parties. For example, security given for payment of a debt which arises from an illegal contract is tainted with illegality of the main transaction. On the other hand, security given for an obligation which is unenforceable in itself under a void contract, may nevertheless be enforceable provided there is separate consideration or the agreement is under seal.

A contract under seal is a specialty contract, and an action must be brought within 12 years from the date when the cause of action first arose. In a simple contract, the action must be brought within six years, except in relation to land, when the period is 12 years. SEE *Limitation Act 1939*

Section 36 of the Companies Act 1985 enacts that

(1) Contracts on behalf of a company may be made as follows:

(*a*) A contract which if made between private persons would be by law required to be in writing, and if made according to English law to be under seal, may be made on behalf of the company in writing under the common seal of the company:

(*b*) A contract which if made between private persons would be by law required to be in writing, signed by the parties to be charged therewith, may be made on behalf of the company in writing signed by any person acting under its authority, express or implied:

(*c*) A contract which if made between private persons would by law be valid although made by parol only, and not reduced into writing, may be made by parol on behalf of the company by any person acting under its authority, express or implied.

(2) A contract made according to this section:

(*a*) is effectual in law, and binds the company and its successors and all other parties to it;

(*b*) may be varied or discharged in the same manner in which it is authorised by this section to be made.

(3) A deed to which a company is a party is held to be validly executed according to the law of Scotland on behalf of the company if it is executed in accordance with this Act or is sealed with the company's common seal and subscribed on behalf of the company by two of the directors, or by a director and the secretary; and such subscription on behalf of the company is binding whether attested by witnesses or not.

(4) Where a contract purports to be made by a company, or by a person as agent for a company, at a time when the company has not been formed, then subject to any agreement to the contrary the contract has effect as one entered into by the person purporting to act for the company or as agent for it, and he is personally liable on the contract accordingly.

CONTRACT NOTE (STOCKBROKER'S) The note or memorandum which is given by a broker to the person for whom an order to buy or sell certain stocks or shares has been carried out, and which gives particulars of the transaction. SEE *Stockbroker*

CONTRACTING OUT Although the term may no doubt be used in a variety of situations, 'contracting out' normally refers nowadays to the facility under the Social Security Pensions Act 1975 for employers to contract out of, i.e. not to enter, the then new state pension scheme. There are in effect two state schemes: provision for the basic pension and the additional or earnings-related pension calculated according to the employee's level of earnings. It is not possible for an employer to contract out of those contributions which go towards the basic state pension, but under the Act employers were given the opportunity of contracting out of the earnings-related state scheme. In order to do so, the employer must provide pensions under an occupational scheme, which must be approved by the Occupational Pensions Board and, to be approved, the occupational scheme must provide benefits at least equivalent to the minimum benefits under the state scheme. SEE *Pensions*

It has been estimated that as many as 11 million employees were contracted out of the state scheme, i.e. approximately one-half of the total pensionable workforce.

CONTRIBUTORIES In the event of a company being wound up, the persons who are liable to contribute to the liabilities are called the contributories. Sections 502–504 of the Companies Act 1985 deals with the liability of present and past members as follows.

502.—(1) When a company is wound up, every present and past member is liable to contribute to its assets to any amount sufficient for payment of its debts and liabilities, and the costs, charges and expenses of the winding up, and for the adjustment of the rights of the contributories among themselves.

(2) This is subject as follows—

(*a*) a past member is not liable to contribute if he has ceased to be a member for one year or more before the commencement of the winding up;

(*b*) a past member is not liable to contribute in respect of any debt or liability of the company contracted after he ceased to be a member;

(*c*) a past member is not liable to contribute unless it appears to the court that the existing members are unable to satisfy the contributions required to be made by them in pursuance of this Act;

(*d*) in the case of a company limited by shares, no contribution is required from any member exceeding the amount (if any) unpaid on the shares in respect of which he is liable as a present or past member;

(*e*) nothing in this Act invalidates any provision contained in a policy of insurance or other contract whereby the liability of individual members on the policy or contract is restricted, or whereby the funds of the company are alone made liable in respect of the policy or contract;

(*f*) a sum due to any member of the company (in his character of a member) by way of dividends, profits or otherwise is not deemed to be a debt of the company, payable to that member in a case of competition between himself and any other creditor not a member of the company, but any such sum may be taken into account for the purpose of the final adjustment of the rights of the contributories among themselves.

(3) In the case of a company limited by guarantee, no contribution is required from any member exceeding the amount undertaken to be contributed by him to the company's assets in the event of its being wound up; but if it is a company with a share capital, every member of it is liable (in addition to the amount so undertaken to be contributed to the assets), to contribute to the extent of any sums unpaid on shares held by him.

503.—(1) In the winding up of a limited company, any director or manager (whether past or present) whose liability is under this Act unlimited is liable, in addition to his liability (if any) to contribute as an ordinary member, to make a further contribution as if he were at the commencement of the winding up a member of an unlimited company.

(2) However—

(*a*) a past director or manager is not liable to make such further contribution if he has ceased to hold office for a year or more before the commencement of the winding up;

(*b*) a past director or manager is not liable to make such further contribution in respect of any debt or liability of the company contracted after he ceased to hold office;

(*c*) subject to the company's articles, a director or manager is not liable to make such further contribution unless the court deems it necessary to require that contribution in order to satisfy the company's debts and liabilities and the costs, charges and expenses of the winding up.

504.—(1) This section applies where a company is being wound up and—

(*a*) it has under Chapter VII of Part V made a payment out of capital in respect of the redemption or purchase of any of its own shares (the payment being referred to below as 'the relevant payment'), and

(*b*) the aggregate amount of the company's assets and the amounts paid by way of contribution to its assets (apart from this section) is not sufficient for payment of its debts and liabilities and the costs, charges and expenses of the winding up.

(2) If the winding up commenced within one year of the date on which the relevant payment was made, then—

(*a*) the person from whom the shares were redeemed or purchased, and

(*b*) the directors who signed the statutory declaration made in accordance with section 173(3) for purposes of the redemption or purchase (except a director who shows that he had reasonable grounds for forming the opinion set out in the declaration),

are, so as to enable that insufficiency to be met, liable to contribute to the following extent to the company's assets.

(3) A person from whom any of the shares were redeemed or purchased is liable to contribute an amount not exceeding so much of the relevant payment as was made by the company in respect of his shares; and the directors are jointly and severally liable with that person to contribute that amount.

(4) A person who has contributed any amount to the assets in pursuance of this section may apply to the court for an order directing any other person jointly and severally liable in respect of that amount to pay him such amount as the court thinks just and equitable.

CONTROLLED FOREIGN COUNTRIES

The Finance Act 1984, Sections 82–91, introduced a charge to corporation tax in the United Kingdom on the profits of foreign companies controlled by companies in the United Kingdom. For the purpose of the Act, a controlled foreign company is one which (a) is resident outside the United Kingdom (b) is controlled by a UK resident company, and (c) is subject to a lower level of taxation in the country of residence than would apply in the United Kingdom. This last requirement means that the local tax paid in the country of residence is less than one half of the tax which would have been payable if the controlled company had been resident in the United Kingdom.

For the purpose of the Act 'control' is widely defined and includes a range of instances where a company in the UK, either alone or jointly with associates, either now or in the future, is able to control the affairs of the foreign company or in certain cases, has the right to the distributed income of that company or certain rights on the company's winding up.

There is no presumption that a charge to tax will arise in all cases where an overseas company is controlled from the United Kingdom. A charge to tax arises only if the Board of the Inland Revenue directs. In general, the tax will be charged on the profits of the controlled foreign company, as if it were a UK company. No charge will arise where the foreign company's profits for a twelve-month accounting period do not exceed £20,000.

The provisions of the Act do not apply to controlled foreign companies whose shares are publicly quoted on a recognized stock exchange in the controlled company's country of residence, provided the shares were public quoted within the twelve months preceding the end of the accounting period and provided that throughout the accounting period, at least 35% of the voting ordinary shares have been beneficially held by the public.

A direction for payment of corporation tax may be made on a UK company only if, together with connected or associated persons, it has at least a 10% interest in the controlled foreign company. For this purpose, those connected or associated persons are widely defined to include anyone with voting rights, the right to the income of the controlled company, a person who has control of the foreign company and, in certain cases, a loan creditor of that company.

No charge to corporation tax will arise on the controlled foreign company if one of the following tests is satisfied:

1. *The acceptable distribution test*: The controlled company remits 90% of its profits to the UK company, or 50% in the case of a trading controlled company, including companies trading in shares, land, commodities, etc.
2. *The exempt activities test*: The controlled company is regarded as being engaged in exempt activities. The rules under this heading are complex but are designed to cover those companies which have permanent premises in an overseas country and effectively manage their business in that country, with an adequate number of employees to deal with the company's business.

   If the controlled company satisfies those tests it will be exempt from UK tax if, either (a) it is a holding company which derives at least 90% of its total income from its controlled subsidiaries resident in the same country and which satisfy the exempt activities test, or in certain circumstances, are subsidiaries wherever resident which, not being holding companies themselves, satisfy the exempt activities test or are local holding companies, or (b) the main business consists neither of investment business nor dealing in goods for delivery either to or from the United Kingdom. Also, to satisfy this latter test, if the controlled company is engaged in wholesale, distributive or financial business, less than 50% of its gross trading receipts must be derived from connected or associated persons.
3. *The motive test*: No tax charge will arise if the company satisfies the motive test, i.e. that it appears to the Board of Inland Revenue that the transactions in question have resulted in only a minimal reduction in United Kingdom tax or that it was not one of the main purposes of the transactions to secure a reduction in UK tax. Similarly, the motive test will be satisfied if it was not one of the main reasons for the company's existence to achieve a reduction in United Kingdom tax by a diversion of profits away from the United Kingdom.

The Inland Revenue have published a list of 76 countries in which a controlled company will be deemed automatically to satisfy the motive test. If a company is resident in one of these countries and carries on business there, it will be regarded as meeting the conditions necessary for exclusion from the charge to corporation tax. The list of excluded countries is in two parts. Part I includes countries to which automatic exclusion from the charge to corporation tax will arise, provided the foreign company is resident and carrying on business in one of those countries. Part II is a list of countries to which the exclusion will apply provided the foreign company is not entitled to any of the specified taxation reliefs applicable to certain of those countries.

The list of countries and regulations applying to them may be amended from time to time.

CONVERSION Conversion is a legal term signifying wrongful interference with another person's property, inconsistent with the owner's right of possession. It has been defined as follows:

> Any person who, however innocently, obtains possession of goods the property of another who has been fraudulently deprived of the possession of them and disposes of them whether for his own benefit or that of another person, is guilty of a conversion.

A banker will be liable for conversion if he delivers to an unauthorized person articles left with him by a customer for safe custody. When he collects a cheque for a party who has no title or a defective title to it, he is guilty of conversion; whether he incurs liability to the true owner for such conversion depends on whether he is entitled to the protection of Section 4 of the Cheques Act 1957.

The damages for conversion of a negotiable instrument are its face value, but in *Souchette Ltd* v *London County Westminster & Parr's Bank Ltd* (1920) 36 TLR 195, an action by the plaintiff company to recover damages for the conversion of certain cheques or alternatively for 'money had and received' against the defendant bank, Mr Justice Greer said 'it has been frequently laid down as a general rule that the measure of damages is the value of the thing converted at the time of its conversion'.

In this case, a director of the plaintiff company paid into his own account cheques drawn by the company in favour of a certain payee, whose signature he forged. That director then paid a smaller amount by his own cheque to the payee. The bank was allowed the benefit of these sums which the payee had received, and the damages for the conversion of the cheques referred to was held to be the ultimate loss which the plaintiffs suffered. (See this case also under *Alterations to Bills of Exchange; Collecting Banker*.)

In *A. L. Underwood Ltd* v *Barclays Bank Ltd* [1924] 1 KB 775, the bank was held to have been negligent and to be liable for conversion, in receiving for collection on behalf of the sole director of the company, for his own personal account, cheques payable to the company, without making any enquiry. A paying banker may also be sued for conversion by a third party whose cheque has been stolen, but in practice this seldom happens because the banker is so well protected statutorily. SEE UNDER *Collecting Banker*

See also the case of *A. Stewart & Son of Dundee Ltd* v *Westminster Bank*, under *Agent*

CONVERTIBILITY The word was formerly used in relation to the ability to exchange paper money for gold on demand at the Bank of England. Any paper currency in any country which was convertible into gold on demand was known as a convertible paper currency.

The term is used more widely nowadays in relation to the ability to convert the currency of one country into that of another. Freedom of convertibility was adopted in principle by the main trading nations in 1958, but this was always subject to the Exchange Control Regulations of individual countries and such devices as investment premium for overseas portfolio investment and separate currencies for tourists.

The date on which the major world currencies became freely convertible was 27th December, 1958. In the post-war years until then there had been steady progress towards freedom of movement of currencies and freedom of world trade. The dollar had always been freely convertible and the world role of the dollar was not disputed. From 1958 onwards, however, there was a shift in emphasis from the USA to Europe and money began to move around the world in very large quantities. The formation of the European Economic Community (q.v.) gave a new stimulus to the economies of the major continental countries and this led to a major transfer of funds to Europe and a reduction in the gold reserves of the USA. Matters came to a head with the devaluation of sterling in 1967 followed six months later by the gold crisis of spring 1968. There was a run on gold and even the physical movement of gold between countries. The US was forced to introduce the two-tier price structure for gold—for currency purposes the price was maintained at $35 per ounce, but the market price of gold as a commodity was allowed to move freely.

CONVERTIBLE SECURITIES The term is usually applied nowadays to convertible loan stocks, i.e. fixed interest securities which carry the right to convert into the ordinary shares of the company concerned at some future date, or possibly over a given period of years, usually in accordance with a predetermined price formula. Such securities offer the attraction of a reasonably high yield with the opportunity to secure a capital gain by exercising the conversion rights. If, however, the company does not prosper so that the conversion rights become unattractive, the holder retains a reasonably high yielding loan stock.

CONVERTIBLE TERM ASSURANCE This is a term assurance contract (SEE *Life Assurance*) with the option to convert to an endowment policy or whole life policy during the term of the assurance without further medical examination.

COOLING OFF PERIOD This is the time in which a person who has taken out a life assurance policy may change his mind and cancel the contract. Under the Insurance Companies Regulations issued under the Insurance Companies Acts of 1974 and 1981, an insurer of a person's life must issue to the proposer a statutory notice in a prescribed form at or before the time the contract is entered into and the proposer may serve a notice of cancellation on the insurer within ten days of receiving the statutory notice, or on the earliest day that he knows that the contract has been entered into or the first or only premium paid. This period of ten days is the so-called cooling off period. SEE ALSO *Consumer Credit Act 1974*

COPPER COINS Real copper coins were first issued in 1672, and were replaced by bronze in 1860, though bronze coins are still commonly spoken of as 'coppers'. They are made of an alloy of 95 parts copper, four parts tin and one part zinc. The new decimal bronze coins are legal tender only to the amount of 20p. The figure of Britannia upon the old coins is said to have been originally modelled from the beautiful Frances Stuart, afterwards Duchess of Richmond. SEE *Coinage*

COPYHOLD In copyhold tenure, the freehold interest in land belonged to the lord of the manor, the copyhold tenant having practically an estate in fee simple subject, however, to certain customary rights and services due to the lord of the manor, such as 'fines' on admittance of a new tenant, quit rents payable annually, and the right of 'heriot', i.e. the right of the lord of the manor to take the best beast or chattel on the death of the copyholder.

By the Law of Property Act 1922, all copyholds were converted into freeholds on 1st January, 1926 and all manorial incidents, services, and rights were abolished subject to compensation payable to the lord and steward of the manor.

The right of the lord to manorial incidents was kept alive until the end of 1936, unless compensation had been agreed upon voluntarily meanwhile, after which time they were no longer payable. But the right to compensation persisted until 1st January, 1941. Until that time, either the lord or the tenant could apply to the Ministry of Agriculture to determine the amount of compensation, which was determined in accordance with the Copyhold Act 1894, as modified by the Law of Property Act 1922. If no application was made by 1st January, 1941, no compensation was payable for extinguished manorial incidents.

CORK COMMITTEE The Cork Committee was appointed on 27th January, 1977 and its report was presented to Parliament in June 1982. The Committee's terms of reference were

1. to review the law and practice relating to insolvency, bankruptcy, liquidation and receiverships in England and Wales and to consider what reforms are necessary or desirable;
2. to examine the possibility of formulating a comprehensive insolvency system and the extent to which existing procedures might, with advantage, be harmonized and integrated;
3. to suggest possible less formal procedures as alternatives to bankruptcy and company winding-up proceedings in appropriate circumstances; and
4. to make recommendations.

The Committee reviewed the entire field of insolvency law and the attendant procedures, both in relation to company liquidations and bankruptcy of individuals. The far-reaching report contains approximately 100 recommendations for changes in insolvency law and practice but at the present time no major legislation incorporating these recommendations has been introduced. In broad terms, the Committee recommended a simplification of the existing insolvency law and procedures, based as they are for the most part on a system introduced over 100 years ago. It recommended that there should be greater differentiation between insolvency which arises through misconduct and that which arises from incompetence or misfortune. The report recommended the creation of a new insolvency court and the introduction of minimum qualifications for insolvency practitioners. It also suggested that a greater emphasis should be placed on the preserving of an insolvent's business (and therefore of employment) by the appointment of 'administrators' (rather like receivers (q.v.)) with power to continue the business. The Committee also recommended a reduction in the number of preferential creditors in bankruptcy and liquidation proceedings and that some proportion, e.g. 10 per cent, of the net assets held under a floating charge be made available to unsecured creditors. Other recommendations were (1) a widening of the definition of 'family home', (2) the abolition of the concept of the 'act of bankruptcy' (q.v.), (3) changes in the 'after acquired property' rule, (4) changes in the law relating to fraudulent conveyances and fraudulent preferences and voluntary dispositions, (5) changes in the rules relating to interest on judgment debts, and (6) more stringent rules relating to delinquent directors.

All in all, the Cork Committee's report is a masterly review of insolvency law and practice and it will be interesting to see the extent to which the recommendations pass into law.

In February 1984, the Government published a White Paper entitled *A Revised Framework for Insolvency Law* (Cmnd 9175, HMSO). This proposed a number of legislative changes incorporating some but not by any means all of the Cork Report recommendations. SEE *Insolvency*

CORPORATION TAX Corporation tax is payable on profits made by corporate bodies such as companies registered under the Companies Acts, chartered companies and building societies and unincorporated associations such as clubs and private societies. The tax is not payable, however, by private individuals, nor by partnerships.

Corporation tax was introduced by the Finance Act 1965 to replace income tax and profits tax previously paid by companies resident in the UK. In general, a company or other corporation is charged to corporation tax on all its profits wherever arising, although the tax charge on capital gains is effectively at a lower rate than on income because, under Section 55 of the Finance Act 1965, chargeable gains are computed for corporation tax purposes in accordance with the principles applying to capital gains tax.

In April 1973, an imputation system of corporation tax was introduced, the effect of which is that (1) companies pay a single rate of tax on their profits whether distributed or retained, (2) when a company pays a dividend, it must make an advance payment of corporation tax (ACT) to the Inland Revenue, (3) the ACT is set off against the company's overall liability for corporation tax for that accounting period, and (4) the UK shareholders who have received the dividend are entitled to a tax credit for the amount of the ACT. SEE *Advance Corporation Tax*

For corporation tax purposes, the financial year of companies runs from 1st April to 31st March in the following year (regardless of the dates of the company's accounting year). If a company's accounting year does not coincide with the financial year and there is a change in the rate of corporation tax, the profits for the year will have to be apportioned and the two separate rates of tax applied. Corporation tax is payable on 1st January in the financial year beginning after the end of the company's accounting year for which the tax has been assessed. Thus, a company whose accounting year ends on, say, 30th April, 1984 will not pay corporation tax on the profits of that year until 1st January, 1985.

UK resident companies are subject to corporation tax on their total profits wheresoever earned. Under the various double taxation agreements, however, between the UK and the major trading countries overseas, a UK resident company with overseas earnings will receive a credit against their UK corporation tax for the amount of any foreign tax which may have been paid. In general, a company is regarded as resident in the UK if it is managed and control in that country. A non-resident company will be liable to corporation tax on its trading income arising through a branch or an agency in the UK.

The rates of corporation tax for the financial years 1983–86 are given in the table below.

	Rate %			
Financial year	1983	1984	1985	1986
Corporation tax rate	50	45	40	35
Small companies rate	30	30	30	30

A company may claim the benefit of the small companies rate if its profits do not exceed £100,000. If the profits exceed that figure but are less than £500,000, the tax is reduced by a fraction of the difference between £500,000 and the actual amount of the profits. The fractions for the years 1983–86 are given in the table below.

Financial year	1983	1984	1985	1986
Small companies relief fraction	$\frac{1}{20}$	$\frac{3}{80}$	$\frac{1}{40}$	$\frac{1}{80}$

In the years prior to 1986, insurance companies carrying on life business paid corporation tax at the rate of 37½ per cent on that part of their investment income allocated to or reserved for policy holders. This special rate ceases to apply, however, with effect from 1986, when the rate of corporation tax for all companies (other than smaller companies) is reduced to 35 per cent. SEE ALSO *Advance Corporation Tax, Capital Allowances, Depreciation, Stock Relief*

CORRESPONDENT BANKS The international banking system has been built up in former years on a network of correspondent banks, i.e. banks which have an agency relationship with each other and act for each other in their respective parts of the world. A large part of this correspondent banking relationship is based on London and the overseas banks acting for the London clearing banks in various parts of the world carry substantial balances with the London banks. A considerable amount of world trade was and still is financed by payments made through the correspondent banking network throughout the world.

On the whole, the international business of the London banks has been built up through their correspondent bank connections. For the most part, international banking from London meant servicing the correspondent bank relationships. With, however, the very considerable increase in world trade and greater capital transfers between countries, it became increasingly difficult to provide customers of, say, the UK banks with substantial finance overseas, by means of the correspondent bank connections. In order to provide on-the-spot services in other countries, the banks have therefore established branches, or at least representative offices, in overseas countries wherever this seemed to be justified. In other cases, the banks have set up subsidiaries or joint operations or consortium operations with correspondent banking friends in those other countries. Nevertheless, the vast international network of correspondent banks remains the main avenue of international payments in support of worldwide trading activities.

CORSET The correct name is 'the supplementary special deposit scheme'. This was first introduced by the Bank of England in November 1973 in order to slow down the growth in the money supply by curtailing the growth in bank lending. Each bank was required to lodge non-interest-earning special deposits with the Bank of England if its interest-bearing eligible liabilities (IBELS) exceeded a ceiling prescribed by the Bank. IBELS are essentially those bank deposits on which the banks pay interest and by inhibiting the banks from increasing these deposits, the Bank of England was able to restrict the capacity of the banks to lend. The fact that excess IBELS (i.e. beyond the permitted target growth which by definition cost the banks interest) could end up as non-interest-bearing special deposits for the Bank of England, was a powerful constraint. The scheme was not popular with the London banks, especially as it was introduced so soon after Competition and Credit Control (q.v.), which in 1971 gave the banks greater freedom of competition. The 'corset' was also unpopular because it was not related to the banking system as a whole, but to individual banks. In 1975, the 'corset' was suspended only to be re-introduced again in 1976 and then suspended again the following year.

COST OF LIVING 'The cost of living', as it is colloquially known, is measured on a monthly basis by the Retail Prices Index or, to give its full title, the General Index of Retail Prices. The Index is published by the Department of Employment and reflects the monthly price changes in those items which make up the Index. The Index is itself based on the pattern of household expenditure throughout the country, as revealed in the latest Family Expenditure Survey. Varying weightings are used for different categories of household expenditure in the composition of the Index. The individual weightings have varied quite considerably over the years. For example, food is shown as representing 20.6 per cent of the Index in 1982; in 1950, food accounted for nearly 35 per cent of the Index. Housing costs now account for 14.4 per cent of the Index, compared with only 10.8 per cent in 1975. Transport costs are now 15.4 per cent, compared with less than seven per cent in 1960.

At intervals over the years, a new base of 100 has been established for the Index. The Index of 100 established in January 1962 had risen to 191.8 by January 1974. The current Index was established with a base of 100 on 15th January, 1974. Since then, the movements in the Index have been as set out below:

January 1974	100.0
January 1975	119.9
January 1976	147.9
January 1977	172.4
January 1978	189.5
January 1979	207.2
January 1980	245.3
January 1981	277.3
January 1982	310.6
January 1983	325.9
January 1984	342.6
January 1985	359.80

COUNCIL FOR THE SECURITIES INDUSTRY (CSI) The Council for the Securities Industry is a self-regulatory body set up in 1978 with the support of the Bank of England and the major City institutions. It has the stated objectives of 'supervising, maintaining ethical standards, resolving differences between, and initiating new codes of conduct in relation to, the various parts of the securities industry; considering and examining proposals for new legislation; and ensuring liaison with the European Commission'. The setting up of the Council was to some extent a response to the Green Paper *The Community and the Company* issued in 1974 by the Labour Party, advocating the setting up of a commission in the UK on the lines of the Securities and Exchange Commission in the USA. The latter is a very large statutory body with considerable powers.

The setting up of the CSI reflects the British preference for self-regulatory rather than statutory control of the commercial life of the country.

The Chairman and Deputy Chairman of the CSI are appointed by the Governor of the Bank of England and it has a small secretariat seconded by the Bank. The Council embraces the Takeover Panel and the Markets Committee. It sets up other investigative panels as necessary, and works closely with the Quotations Committee of the Stock Exchange and the other Stock Exchange Committees. SEE *Gower Report; Take Overs and Mergers*

COUNTERFEIT COINS SEE *Base Coins*

COUNTERMAND OF PAYMENT A banker is obliged to honour the cheque of his customer, if there is a sufficient balance in the account to meet it, and the cheque is in order. The drawer may, however, instruct the banker to stop payment of a cheque, and the banker will be liable if he neglects to attend to the instructions.

In the Bills of Exchange Act 1882, Section 75 states that the duty and authority of a banker to pay a cheque drawn on him by his customer are determined by countermand of payment.

A countermand of payment can be given only by the drawer, but notice from a holder that a cheque has been lost by him would put a banker on his guard, pending instructions from the drawer.

Any cheque drawn upon a joint account may be stopped by any one of the joint parties, and one trustee or executor may stop payment of a cheque drawn by all the trustees or executors.

An order to stop payment of a cheque should be in writing and be signed by the customer, and if the order is subsequently cancelled, the fresh instructions should also be in writing. The drawer cannot stop payment of a cheque which a banker has, at the drawer's request, already certified, or marked, for payment.

As to countermand of payment by wire, etc SEE *Payment Stopped*. SEE *Bill of Exchange; Lost Bill of Exchange; Payment of Bill*

COUNTERPART A duplicate of an instrument. The word is used chiefly in connection with leases, e.g. where a house is leased for a period of years, the lessee receives the lease signed by the lessor and the lessor receives a counterpart or copy of it signed by the lessee.

COUNTERSIGN A frequent arrangement made by a company with its bankers is that all cheques shall be signed by two directors and countersigned by the secretary. The countersignature is as necessary as the other signatures before payment of a cheque. Where the secretary is also a director, the company's resolution as to the signing of cheques should state whether or not the secretary may sign in both capacities. In cases where cheques are to be signed by, say, one director and countersigned by the secretary, it is usually the intention of the company that two persons are to sign and not one person in two capacities. SEE UNDER *Company*

COUNTRY CLEARING The section of the Clearing House (q.v.) which, until September 1939, dealt with the clearance of all cheques drawn on banking offices outside the London postal area, i.e. outside the Town and Metropolitan Clearing areas.

Immediately before the outbreak of war in September 1939, the Clearing House was evacuated to Stoke-on-Trent and the Country Clearing merged into one general clearing that was set up as an emergency measure.

On the return of the Clearing House at the end of World War 2, the Country Clearing was not restored, country cheques being merged into the General Clearing.

COUPON From French *couper*, to cut. Literally a piece cut off. A coupon is a warrant for the payment of interest. It is usually attached to a bond or debenture, and requires to be cut off when the time has arrived for its presentment for payment. Where the interest on debentures and bonds is paid by means of coupons, a sheet of coupons is supplied. The sheet contains a series of coupons, there being a coupon with a different date for each payment of interest, quarterly or half-yearly, as the case may be, for several, and, in cases of large coupon sheets, for many years to come. Where no date of payment appears upon the coupons, they are payable on advertised dates. If the date of payment falls upon a Sunday or a bank holiday, they are payable on the succeeding business day.

Some coupons are payable either in the UK or abroad, as, for example, in London in sterling, or in New York (or other places) at the current rate of exchange in London.

There are also coupons payable at a fixed exchange, for example, in London in sterling, or 'in New York at the fixed exchange of $x per one pound sterling'. A holder of such coupons may present them for payment in London or, if there is an advantage to be secured from the exchange, he may instruct his bankers to collect them in New York and have the proceeds remitted to the UK, or if the holder looks for a fall in the sterling value of the dollar he may secure the exchange profit at once by having the coupons sold in the UK. A banker should take his customer's instructions when such coupons are handed in for collection.

When the last coupon has been detached, the part of the sheet which remains is called the 'talon', and it is forwarded to the address given thereon to be exchanged for a fresh sheet of coupons. A 'talon' is not, however, attached in all cases, and the bond must then be sent to obtain the new coupons.

In the event of any coupons being lost, notice should be given to the bank where they are payable. The banker will no doubt exercise care before paying them, but he cannot really refuse to pay them, unless an order to do so is received from the customer who gave the instructions for the bank to pay the coupons. As a matter of routine the banker will normally take an indemnity before making such payment.

In addition to being attached to bearer bonds, coupons are attached to Registered Coupon-Bonds.

A coupon is exempt from stamp duty. The exemption is contained in Section 40, Finance Act 1894:

> A coupon for interest on a marketable security as defined by the Stamp Act, 1891, being one of a set of coupons, whether issued with the security or subsequently issued in a sheet shall not be chargeable with any stamp duty.

A coupon attached to a scrip certificate is not exempt. In *U.G.S. Finance* v *National Mortgage Bank of Greece* (December 1963) the view was expressed by the Court that in London sterling coupons were not bearer documents. SEE *Bearer Bonds; Drawn Bonds*

The word 'coupon' is used nowadays in a loose sense to denote the amount of interest payable on a fixed interest stock or bond. For example, it might be said that a particular loan stock has been issued with a nine per cent coupon. This is merely a modern derivation from the original meaning of coupon described above.

COVENANT This is, strictly speaking, an agreement under seal or a clause in such an agreement. There are cases, however, where covenants may be implied from the construction of the document or the surrounding circumstances, or where they are implied by statute.

COVER SEE *Cover Note; Dividend Cover*

COVER NOTE This is the usual form in which interim insurance is granted, pending completion of a detailed proposal for insurance or, in some cases, pending consideration of a proposal which has been submitted to an insurer. If a cover note has been issued, there is a contract of insurance in existence, and both proposer and insurer are bound by the terms of the cover note. The cover note might, for example, refer to some standard form of policy, even though a policy as such has not been issued. A cover note continues in force for the period stated in the note, even if a full policy is not issued at the end of that time.

COVERED BEAR A person who sells shares in anticipation of a fall in price (SEE *Bear*), but who actually owns the shares he is selling so that he is not at risk if the fall does not happen.

CRAWLING PEG The gradual movement of exchange rates within predetermined margins or 'pegs'. This was in a sense a compromise arrangement in order to get away from the rigid system of fixed international currency parities under the Bretton Woods Agreement (q.v.). The idea was that instead of fixed exchange rates throughout the world, the rates would be allowed to move very slowly, perhaps one per cent or two per cent per annum. However, once the principle of moving exchange rates was accepted, it was natural to move towards floating exchange rates, leaving the rates to find their own level.

CREDIT BANKS, CREDIT SOCIETIES Credit banks or agricultural cooperative credit societies, as they are often called, have proved unsuccessful in Britain, but in continental Europe and in many other parts of the world much of the financing of agriculture is carried out by these societies.

They are especially well-developed in Germany, where the system began with the formation of a semi-philanthropic organization by F. W. Raiffeisen in 1849. The first efforts were slow in making progress, but by 1865 a number of similar societies had been formed. The main principles of these early societies were: (1) none but persons of the highest character might become members, (2) each society might operate only in a small area where the members would be mutually well-known, (3) money to be raised from amongst the members themselves, (4) unlimited liability, (5) no paid officials, (6) all profits to go to reserve.

Societies based upon similar principles now occupy an important place in German rural economy and the Raiffeisen-type of organization has spread to every part of the world. An adaptation of the system did particularly good work in India in helping to free the peasants from usurers.

Shortly after the first experiments of Raiffeisen in the Rhineland, F. H. Schulze of Delitzsch in Saxony began a more strictly commercial system of cooperative credit. These banks lent to both urban and rural borrowers and obtained part of their capital by the issue of shares.

A third foundation organization dating back to 1866 was that of Luzzatti in Italy. This has some of the characteristics of both the Raiffeisen and the Schulze–Delitzsch systems.

Upon these early cooperative efforts there was based in almost every Continental country a network of agricultural credit banks which did very useful work among the poorer populations. They also formed the inspiration for rural credit systems in the USA, India, Japan and the Dominions.

Yet in Britain the movement is practically dead. Owing largely to the strenuous personal pioneering efforts of the late Sir Horace Plunkett there was established a good number of such societies in Ireland, but the movement was never so strong in the rest of the British Isles. From the end of the nineteenth century, enthusiastic efforts were made by a small group of pioneers to introduce some system of agricultural credit cooperation in England. In 1893 the Agricultural Banks Association was formed and this combined early in the present century with the Agricultural Organisation Society (founded 1900) which was interested in agricultural cooperation generally. In 1908 a Central Cooperative Bank was established and by 1911 the movement had achieved a measure of success in that about 45 small cooperative credit societies were in operation, but the total amount of their loans was under £1,500.

Very little progress was made after that time in spite of the fact that the Government began to take an interest in the work. In 1913 the Board of Agriculture and Fisheries commenced an annual grant to the Agricultural Organisation Society. In the same year it was announced in the House of Commons that this Board had been in communication with the leading joint-stock banks which had branches in the rural districts, with regard to the assistance which the banks could offer, in accordance with ordinary banking principles, to registered Cooperative Credit Societies, consisting mainly of small-holders and allotment holders.

It was stated that most of the banks were willing to assist in the formation of a society and to give advice on matters of bookkeeping. They would also favourably consider the acceptance by managers of the post of unpaid treasurer, provided that it did not involve membership of the society.

These banks were prepared to allow as good rates as possible on balances in their hands. They would also be prepared to give favourable consideration to applications for advances from such societies, subject to the usual conditions as to repayment and to their being satisfied that the liability of the members of the society formed a good security. Interest charged on such advances would be at a favourable fixed rate subject to a year's notice of alteration.

Very few, if any, advances were ever made on these lines for the reason that the movement made very little progress subsequently.

In 1923 the Government subsidy to the Agricultural Organisation Society ceased and by 1925 the Society had to cease functioning as its income from voluntary contributions was insufficient to keep it going. Yet in the same year that this subsidy ceased the Committee on Agricultural Credit reported (Cmnd 1810) and recommended that an endeavour to meet the short term credit requirements of agriculture should be made by means of local Credit Societies to be subsidized by the Ministry of Agriculture to the extent of £1 for each £1 share, 5s paid.

These recommendations were made law by the Agricultural Credits Act 1923, but this failed to achieve any success. A mere three or four small societies were formed and by 1927 it was officially admitted that the Act had been a failure (*Report on Agricultural Credit*, by R. R. Enfield.) The Agricultural Credits Act 1928 has superseded these schemes by establishing the Agricultural Mortgage Corporation (q.v.) and by making statutory provision for the giving of fixed or floating agricultural charges on farming stock. SEE ALSO *Credit Unions*

CREDIT BROKERAGE Under Section 145 of the Consumer Credit Act 1974 (q.v.), credit brokerage is defined as

> the effecting of introductions—
> (*a*) of individuals desiring to obtain credit—
> (i) to persons carrying on businesses to which this sub-paragraph applies, or
> (ii) in the case of an individual desiring to obtain credit to finance the acquisition or provision of a dwelling occupied or to be occupied by himself or his relative, to any person carrying on a business in the course of which he provides credit secured on land, or
> (*b*) of individuals desiring to obtain goods on hire to persons carrying on businesses to which this paragraph applies, or
> (*c*) of individuals desiring to obtain credit, or to obtain goods on hire, to other credit-brokers.

Subsection (a)(i) above applies to

> (*a*) a consumer credit business;
> (*b*) a business which comprises or relates to consumer credit agreements being, otherwise than by virtue of Section 16(5)(a), exempt agreements;
> (*c*) a business which comprises or relates to unregulated agreements where—
> (i) the proper law of the agreement is the law of a country outside the United Kingdom, and
> (ii) if the proper law of the agreement were the law of a part of the United Kingdom it would be a regulated consumer credit agreement.

Under the Act 'a credit broker', means a person carrying on a business of credit brokerage. Persons carrying on such a business require to be licensed under the Consumer Credit Act 1974 (q.v.).

CREDIT CARD A credit card is a credit-token within the meaning of Section 14(1), Consumer Credit Act 1974, which defines a credit-token as a

> card, check, voucher, coupon, stamp, form, booklet or other document or thing given to an individual by a person carrying on a consumer credit business, who undertakes—
> (*a*) that on the production of it (whether or not some other action is also required) he will supply, cash, goods and services (or any of them) on credit, or
> (*b*) that where, on the production of it to a third party (whether or not any other action is also required), the third party supplies cash, goods and services (or any of them), he will pay the third party for them (whether or not deducting any discount or commission), in return for payment to him by the individual.

It is believed that the first credit card of a kind was introduced by the Provident Clothing Company (now the Provident Financial Group) in England in the 1880s. It was the earliest check trading scheme (q.v.)—customers were issued with vouchers which they could use at shops on the approved list and payment for the vouchers was made on a weekly instalment basis to the Provident Clothing representative who called at the customer's home. It was the forerunner of credit cards in two respects, in that payment was made by a voucher and the customer enjoyed the benefit of revolving credit.

It was in the USA, however, that the credit card as we know it today was developed. In the early 1900s, some of the US department stores issued credit coins or tokens which enabled customers to pay for goods, and the oil companies introduced 'courtesy cards' to be honoured at their petrol stations. To this day, the largest issuers of credit cards are the retail stores in North America. In recent years, it was estimated that out of 600 million credit cards in use in the USA, 85 per cent were issued by non-banking groups. Their cards differ from the bank cards in that their use is limited to purchases from the store issuing the card and associated stores. John Biggins of the Flatbush National Bank, New York, is credited with introducing the bank credit card. Under his 'Charge-It' plan, the credit for retail purchases was provided by the bank. That was in 1946 and in the next few years cards were introduced by Diner's Club, American Express and Carte Blanche. These were primarily for travel and entertainment purposes and became known as 'T and E' cards. They were a method of payment rather than a source of credit and did not provide a credit limit as such.

The first bank credit card as we know it today was issued by Franklin National Bank in 1952 and numerous bank cards were issued in the following years. The Bank of America issued Bank Americard in 1958 and eight years later, in 1966, the banks comprising the Western States Bankcard Association issued the Mastercharge Card. Bank Americard and Mastercharge became the focal points for the eventual groupings of all bank cards throughout the world.

In the UK, there are three categories of cards associated with the clearing banks. These are (1) travel and entertainment cards, (2) cheque cards and (3) credit cards. (Cash dispenser cards are in a different category, being *debit* cards rather than credit cards. There is an increasing tendency for one card to serve as a cheque guarantee card and a cash dispenser card.) Cheque cards are also in a different category from credit cards, their purpose being to guarantee payment of a cheque. SEE *Cheque Card*

Travel and Entertainment Cards

In the first category, as already mentioned, the Diner's Club card was the first to appear in the USA and was introduced to Great Britain in 1951, a year after its launch. In 1965, the then Westminster Bank took a minority shareholding in the Diner's Club in the UK, increasing this holding to 47.8 per cent of the equity in the following year. Thus, Westminster Bank, now National Westminster Bank, became the only British bank with a significant interest in a travel and entertainment card as such. Ultimately, it held 49.7 per cent of the UK-based operations of the Diner's Club. In 1981, Citicorp entered into an agreement to buy the Diner's Club, which had approaching 3.3 million members. Citicorp already owned Carte Blanche with about 1 million card holders.

American Express opened offices in England in 1963 and a few years later entered into an agreement for the promotion of its cards through Lloyds Bank and Martins Bank, but this move was overtaken and overshadowed by the subsequent development of card business among the clearing banks. Some ten years later, American Express had 4.8 million cardholders around the world generating over $4,000 million of business per annum. The number of cardholders was doubling every two years or so, but nevertheless the 'T and E' cards were not destined to grow at the rate of bank credit cars as such in the UK, and at the time of writing the Diner's Club has approximately 200,000 UK cardholders and American Express had approximately 600,000. A charge is normally made for travel and entertainment cards.

Bank Credit Cards

The first bank credit card issued in Great Britain was Barclaycard, launched in 1966 in co-operation with Bank Americard. By 1972, Barclaycard had over 1.7 million cardholders and 52,000 merchant outlets. At the present time, there are believed to be approximately 7.5 million Barclaycard holders in the UK and 220,000 merchants who accept the card. Barclaycard is now part of the world-wide Visa group, which is represented in 141 countries and is understood to have 120 million cardholders and over 4 million merchant outlets. In 1972, the other leading UK banks announced the introduction of the Access card. The original sponsors were National Westminster Bank, Midland Bank and Lloyds Bank. Together the three banks promoted the Joint Credit Card Company, in which they share the equity. Before the launch, Williams and Glyn's Bank, Clydesdale Bank, Northern Bank, Ulster Bank and Royal Bank of Scotland joined in the scheme. Within the first year, Access had 3.3 million cardholders and 65,000 merchant outlets. The following year, 1973, the group negotiated an agreement with Eurocard (a travel and entertainment card) which gave a link with a further 60,000 shops, hotels and restaurants throughout Europe. The truly international nature of the card was established with effect from March 1975 when Access became a member of the Interbank Card Association with, then, 32 million cardholders around the world. The Interbank Group, now known as Mastercharge, is believed to have over 100 million cardholders. The card is accepted in 160 countries by over 4 million merchants.

There are three quite distinct parties to a credit card operation: the cardholder, the merchant and the bank or other card-issuing organization.

Credit cardholders Any credit-worthy adult may be a credit cardholder. When a person applies for a credit card, he will be asked to supply details of his financial circumstances and, subject to satisfactory references, he will be given a card with an appropriate credit limit. Some limits, for example, in the case of student cardholders, are very small, but very substantial limits may be allowed for cardholders of considerable personal means. Many cardholders will have applied for a card not in order to obtain credit as such, as a means of postponing payment for goods, but in order to have the convenience of a card as a method of payment as an alternative to cash or cheques. In the early days of credit cards in the UK one of our major banks reported that the majority of cardholders 'continue to settle their accounts monthly' and were not availing themselves of continuing credit. In more recent times, however, another major group has estimated that about 70 per cent of its cardholders use their cards as a means of obtaining instalment credit.

There is, in any case, an element of free credit granted to cardholders because (1) accounts are sent out monthly covering purchases of goods or services since the last monthly statement and (2) the cardholders are allowed 25 days from the date of their monthly statement in which to settle the outstanding amount. It follows that if a cardholder's statement is normally sent out on, say, the 15th of the month, any purchases he makes on the 16th of the month could carry the benefit of 55 days' free credit.

The following are some of the advantages to a cardholder under the credit card system:

1. A card is a convenient method of payment as an alternative to cash or cheques. It is simple to operate, convenient to carry and reasonably immune to financial loss compared with losing cash or a cheque book.
2. It is a convenient source of credit if desired, involving no formalities and no interview with the bank manager. Owing to the revolving nature of the credit, the customer can take advantage of it as and when he pleases within, of course, the overall limit.
3. Because all monthly purchases are covered by one payment, the activity on the customer's banking account is considerably reduced with possible savings in commission charges.
4. It is an aid to budgeting because the cardholder can pay a fixed amount each month according to his circumstances, and plan accordingly.
5. The monthly statements in narrative form are a great help to domestic and even business bookkeeping.
6. The acceptability of the leading cards in so many countries of the world is an aid to business and holiday travel.
7. Under the Consumer Credit Act 1974, Section 75, the credit card companies may be held jointly and severally liable with the supplier in respect of defects in goods purchased on credit cards where the purchase price exceeds £50 and is not more than £15,000. This added protection became available to those who became cardholders after the relevant section of the Act came into force on 1st July, 1977.

It is no doubt inevitable that a large number of cards get lost and some stolen. If the finder or thief uses the card fraudulently, the cardholder may be held responsible for the first £25 of loss up to the time that he reports the circumstances to the card company. SEE Supplement

The merchants The second 'party' to the credit card transaction is the merchant. There are approximately 300,000 merchant outlets in the UK who accept credit cards in payment for the goods or services. From the merchants' point of view, there is a number of advantages in operating a credit card system:

1. By accepting a credit card, the merchant has a guarantee of payment and his account is immediately credited with the cleared funds on payment of the vouchers into his bank.
2. He can use the card system as an alternative to other means of allowing credit and thus avoid bad debts.
3. The acceptance of a card in lieu of cash reduces the security risk.
4. A merchant who accepts credit cards may expect to increase his turnover, as more and more people accept the practical advantages of credit cards and turn to those traders who will accept cards in settlement.
5. A credit card system permits the merchant to offer his customers the facility of taking credit without involving himself in the expense, administration or risk of setting up his own credit arrangements.
6. The merchant is able to expand his business to include overseas visitors.
7. He will also have the support of the credit card company in advertising campaigns and other promotional activities.
8. The credit card record of purchases is convenient for book-keeping.

Each retailer will be given by the card company an agreed 'floor limit' up to which he may accept customers' cards at his own discretion. Beyond that, he must telephone one of the principal card centres where a 24 hour service is operated, to confirm whether or not a card may be accepted for a particular purchase.

Early in 1984, the principal card companies introduced a joint company for authorizing credit card purchases by telephone. This is known as Cardlink. Under this scheme, retailers contribute to the installation of a telephone link to the joint company, On Line Card Services Limited (OLCS), so that card transactions for the principal groups may be dealt with in a uniform way. The card is passed through a magnetic strip reader on the telephone and the amount of the transaction is relayed via Cardlink to the appropriate card company. The card company then flashes a response on the display panel on the user terminal. This eliminates the need for the merchant to dial an authorization centre quoting the merchant number and the card number, etc. Also, there is no need for the merchant to refer to warning notices regarding lost and stolen cards because the transaction is automatically checked by the card-issuing company.

The cardholder does not pay a fee for his card, but the merchant will pay a service charge of up to 5 per cent on his credit card turnover. The average charge is about 2½ per cent.

The level of charge will vary according to the nature of the business. In general, goods sold on a small margin with a rapid turnover will suffer a lower service charge than, say, luxury items with a wider margin of profit.

The card companies The two principal credit cards in operation in the UK are Barclaycard and Access. At the time of writing, there are approximately 7.4 million Barclaycard holders (including those who use Barclaycard as a cheque card) and 7.6 million Access cardholders.

The service charge paid by merchants provides some income towards meeting the costs of running a credit card scheme, but the real source of profit to a card company lies in the interest charge made to customers who use their cards to take extended credit. If all cardholders paid their monthly accounts within the stipulated period, there would be little profit to the companies and indeed they would probably operate at a loss. It is estimated that the average period of credit taken by cardholders is between four and six months, and it is in the interests of the card companies to encourage cardholders not only to make more use of their cards but to avail themselves of the revolving credit facility.

In-house Cards

There is yet another main growth area which, at this point in time, has achieved only modest proportions. It is the development of credit card-schemes among retailers, i.e. the introduction of in-house cards. The largest issuer of cards in America are the department stores, whereas in the UK it has been a predominantly bank-dominated industry. Debenhams was one of the first stores to introduce a credit card, followed in 1978 by Marks & Spencer who introduced a credit card scheme financed by Citibank. The first national supermarket to adopt their own credit card was International Stores, whose scheme was administered by Barclays. On the whole, such schemes have been administered and financed by the clearing bank groups, e.g. Marley by Lloyds Bank, Associated Dairies and Boots by National Westminster Bank, Tesco by Midland and Burtons by Lloyds & Scottish.

British Airways have introduced their own card as part of Visa and Yorkshire Bank are also involved in the development of in-house schemes through their 60 per cent interest in North British Finance Group.

Some Legal Aspects

It is a term of the contract between a credit card company and a merchant that a credit card customer will be charged the same price for goods or services as a cash customer. In other words, a merchant may not add a surcharge to a credit card sale. In 1977, a number of garages complained to the Office of Fair Trading that this constituted an unfair practice on the part of the leading credit card companies. The matter was referred to the Monopolies and Mergers Commission, which reported in September 1980. The Commission concluded

> that it is against the public interest for a credit card company to exclude or restrict a trader's freedom to charge for goods and services, on presentation of a credit card, prices different from those charged in the case of other means of payment. This practice has the effect of preventing a trader from competing with other traders by offering different prices to credit card users and other customers, so depriving the customer of an important choice in purchasing goods or services, and in some cases possibly leading to increased prices generally to all a trader's customers, whether or not they are cardholders.

The Commission went on to recommend that any exclusion or restriction on the ability of a trader to charge different prices should be unenforceable and that it should be illegal to include such terms in any new contracts.

The Commission also criticized Barclaycard and the Joint Credit Card Company (Access) for exchanging information on charges made to particular traders and rates of interest to be paid by cardholders. The Commission considered

> that such discussion about policy, or arrangements with particular traders or groups of traders, are intended to

maintain or exploit the monopoly situation in favour of Barclaycard and the Joint Credit Card Company by restricting such competition as exists between them.

The leading credit card companies had in fact undertaken to the Commission that it was not now their policy to discuss with their rivals matters affecting competition and that dealings between the leading companies would in future be limited to procedural methods, such as technological developments and the training of the staff of traders.

So it was that the policy of 'dual pricing', i.e. the surcharging of credit card customers appeared to have official blessing and it became the practice among garages and, to a degree, among other retailers to add a surcharge, usually up to 25p per transaction, to credit card sales, in breach of their 'no-discrimination' clause with the credit card companies.

Over a year later, in December 1981, the Minister for Consumer Affairs announced that the Government was not going to act on the Monopolies and Mergers Commission's recommendation because 'the absence of surcharges makes for general convenience'.

After a period of some confusion, the credit card companies made it clear that traders were expected to observe the terms of their contracts if they wished to retain their credit card franchises and the system of dual charging has now disappeared.

The principal statute affecting the issue and use of credit cards is the Consumer Credit Act 1974 (q.v.). In particular, mention has been made above of the liability of credit card companies where defective goods are purchased by cardholders. Comparatively few cases on the subject of credit cards have so far come before the courts.

There was, however, one particular case which came before the House of Lords in June 1981 and it concerned the dishonest use of a credit card (*R* v *Lambie* [1981] 3 WLR 88). The case involved the purchase of goods by a young woman with a credit card when her credit limit was £200 and she was already overdrawn with the credit card company in excess of £800. The prosecution had been brought under Section 16 of the Theft Act 1968, on the grounds that the accused had obtained a pecuniary advantage by deception. The House of Lords, allowing the Appeal from the Court of Appeal, had no difficulty in concluding that the presentation of the credit card was a representation of authority to make a contract on the bank's behalf that the bank would honour the voucher. The only remaining question was whether the shop was induced by the representation to complete the transaction. Would the shop have allowed the transaction to go through if it had been known that the accused was acting dishonestly. It was held that the jury had been perfectly entitled to conclude that the answer was 'No'. In the Court of Appeal, the case had been distinguished from that of *R* v *Charles* [1977] AC 177, which concerned the dishonest use of a *cheque* card. That, too, was a House of Lords' case, in which their Lordships concluded that the manager of a gaming club, in accepting cheques backed by a cheque card, believed that the accused was entitled to use the card but, in the result, the amounts of the cheques greatly exceeded the accused's overdraft facility at his bank. In the Lambie case, the main question before the House of Lords was whether or not there was any essential difference between a cheque card transaction (as in *R* v *Charles*) and a credit card transaction. It is no doubt a comfort to the credit card companies and, indeed, to the public that the House of Lords took the same view of both cases, but it must be very doubtful whether cheque cards and credit cards are accepted in an essential belief that the customer has sufficient funds at the bank. The cheque and/or card is no doubt accepted because the shopkeeper knows that it will be paid by the bank or card company (assuming the customer is not on the 'stop' list).

CREDIT CLEARING The traditional banks' clearing system in the UK (SEE *Clearing House*) was a *debit* clearing, i.e. it is a *debiting* process because a cheque ends up as a debit to an account, even though in the mind of the drawer of the cheque it is issued with the intention of crediting the payee. There was thus no system other than the issuing of a number of cheques for a person to initiate credit transfers to other people. In the 1930s, however, the banks developed, somewhat tentatively, a system of 'traders' credit', a means by which a business customer could instruct his bank to make a number of payments, in accordance with a list supplied by the customer, to the banking accounts of the creditors concerned. Out of this grew the 'credit transfer' system, which in time enabled the customer of any branch of any bank in the country to pay in money for the account of a third party at any branch of any other bank. Each 'credit' was sent to the branch concerned accompanied by a branch payment voucher, i.e. a *debit* voucher for the amount involved which was then passed through the clearing system. The facility for making payments to branches of other banks in this way led to a very considerable increase in the number of standing orders (SEE *Banker's Order*) and other recurring items such as monthly salary payments. The volume of these transactions led to the formation in 1960 of the credit clearing. This operates in the same way as the debit clearing system, the only difference being that the net balances which the banks settle among themselves in the course of the clearing process represent the difference in the value of credit vouchers instead of debit vouchers.

The name of the credit clearing was changed in 1967 to Bank Giro in anticipation of the foreseen competition from the National Giro introduced the following year. The Bank Giro embraced the newly devised system of direct debiting. This enabled business customers, e.g. insurance companies, to initiate regular monthly payments which hitherto had been initiated by the customer as part of the standing-order system. SEE *Direct Debits*

The credit clearing or Bank Giro thus became the normal means of making credit transfers over bank counters for customers of other banks and other branches (as was the origin of the credit transfer system) both for (1) the immense volume of standing-order payments and direct debits used for all regular periodic payments in both the private and public sector, and (2) the vast majority of all regular payments initiated in the business sector for salaries, pensions, trade debts and the like. The credit clearing now handles well in excess of one million items each day. SEE *Bankers' Automated Clearing Services Limited; Bank Giro; Clearing House*

CREDIT CONTROLS SEE *Monetary Policy*

CREDIT INSURANCE A method of insuring the payment of commercial debts. By taking out a policy, a seller of goods may be relieved of the whole, or part, of any loss he may sustain should the buyer become insolvent and thereby be unable to pay the seller the full amount of the debt. Policies are granted to cover bills of exchange drawn in respect of goods sold and delivered. All duly accepted bills must be declared to the insurance company. In the event of dishonour of any duly accepted bill, the agreed proportion of such bill as is covered by the policy is paid to the assured on satisfactory proof of such dishonour and assignment of the debt to the company. Any amount collected by the company from the estate of the defaulter in excess of the amount paid by the company (plus interest and charges) is returned to the assured.

The Crowther Committee on Consumer Credit (q.v.) commented 'that there are no statistics available of the insurance of individual credit transactions—neither the number of policies issued nor the total of premiums charged. Nor are there any figures on the proportion of credit transactions in short'. Mortgage protection policies (q.v.) are a reasonably well-known form of credit insurance. SEE ALSO *Export Credits Guarantee Department; Factoring*

CREDIT SALE AGREEMENT This is defined under Section 189(1), Consumer Credit Act 1974 as 'an agreement for the sale of goods, under which the purchase price or part of it is payable by instalments, but which is not a conditional sale agreement'.

On a credit sale, the title in the goods sold normally passes to the buyer immediately, the price being paid by instalments over a period. Thus, it differs from hire purchase in that, under a contract of hire purchase, the goods are hired to the hirer over a period and the title passes to the hirer at the end of the hire period. For most practical and legal purposes, this distinction is no longer very significant. Both credit sale agreements and hire purchase agreements are within the scope of the Hire Purchase Act 1965 provided the purchase price does not exceed £15,000. Similarly, both types of arrangement and conditional sales are brought within the Consumer Credit Act 1974.

CREDIT SCORING This is a statistical method of appraising the credit-worthiness of an applicant for credit. To some extent credit scoring has replaced the traditional interview between bank manager and customer for the more straightforward type of personal (and in some cases business) borrowing. In the case of personal lending, whether by banks or finance houses, a system may be followed of allocating points for various aspects of the applicant's lifestyle, e.g. age, nature of property occupied, occupation, how long with the present employer and how long at the present address. The previous credit experience of the applicant will also be taken into account. The system of measurement is based on the statistical probability that the credit will be repaid. Most systems of credit scoring are now operated by computer and to some extent the more traditional subjective aspects of lending have been reduced to a fairly basic statistical approach.

CREDIT TRANSACTION In common parlance, this is any business transaction where payment of the money consideration is deferred over a period. There is a specific definition. however, in Section 65, Companies Act 1980, in relation to the prohibition of loans to directors.

Under Section 49 of that Act (Section 330, 1985 Act), a public company or its subsidiaries are prohibited from making loans to their directors, or entering into a 'credit transaction' as creditor for such a director or a person connected with a director. SEE *Loans to Directors*

Under Section 331 of the Act, 'a credit transaction' is a transaction under which one party ('the creditor')

(a) supplies any goods or sells any land under hire purchase agreement or conditional sale agreement;
(b) leases or hires any land or goods in return for periodical payments;
(c) otherwise disposes of land or supplies goods or services on the understanding that payment (whether in a lump sum or instalments or by way of periodical payments or otherwise) is to be deferred.

CREDIT TRANSFER This method of payment grew out of traders credits. Customers and the public generally are able to pay in money at any clearing bank for the account of a third party having an account at any other branch of any bank within the group. The intention was that the credit should be of cash, although in practice this is not always observed with the possibility of legal complication if the cheque received is dishonoured. There are a number of legal complexities that could be envisaged and that occasionally arise, although the system works very satisfactorily generally. The possible difficulties, such as countermand of instruction, conversion on collection of a cheque for a non-customer, and dishonour of a cheque received, are all dependent on the question as to whose agent the banker may be. In the absence of specific agreement between the ultimate recipient and the payer, in which case the banker will be the agent of the party, perhaps a local authority, due to receive the money, it is probable that the banker is the agent of the person from whom he receives the payment. So far there has been no litigation on this subject. SEE *Bank Giro; Bankers' Automated Clearing Services Limited; Credit Clearing*

CREDIT UNIONS These have been referred to as do-it-yourself banks. In broad terms, a credit union is a financial cooperative which accumulates members' savings and provides the members with low-cost credit. Credit unions are now governed by the Credit Unions Act of 1979. Prior to that, they were not the subject of any special legislation, but operated within the Industrial and Provident Societies Acts. The following are the essential features of credit unions in the UK, as now regulated by the 1979 Act:

1. They come within the overall supervision of the Chief Registrar of Friendly Societies.
2. The members of each union must be united by some common bond, e.g. members of the same trade union or club or residents in the same area or employees of the same firm.
3. There must be at least 21 members in each union, but no more than 5,000.
4. The maximum permitted savings per member is £3,000.
5. The maximum permitted loan to a member is the amount of his personal investment plus £2,000.
6. The rate of interest is limited to 1 per cent per month on the outstanding balance of the loan, i.e. a little over 12 per cent per annum.
7. Income earned by the union may be accumulated or paid out to members. Interest is free of tax for the first six years and then taxed in the ordinary way at the basic rate.
8. The unions must be non-profit-making in the sense that they are mutual societies for the purpose of providing a service to their members.

Like building societies, credit unions grew out of a spirit of self-help and their aim is to lend money to members for provident and productive purposes. Traditionally, they have sought to meet a social need, not only in the provision of loans but in an educational and advisory way on matters of finance.

There are believed to be approximately 70 credit unions in Britain but the movement was given an impetus by the 1979 Act. The Crowther Committee on Consumer Credit (q.v.) said

> We think there is a case for encouraging the credit union movement and for taking steps to make its existence, its aims and its methods widely known in the hope it may take root here and more credit unions be formed in Britain.

In the USA there are believed to be over 40 million members of credit unions, with total savings of over £23,000 million. In Canada also the movement has been widespread and approximately one-third of the population are members of credit unions.

CROSS-FIRING Cross-firing is where one person draws a bill or cheque upon another, and the latter, at the same time, draws a bill or cheque upon the former. If the banker allows drawings against uncleared effects, this device can continue unchecked. When a banker detects signs of such a practice, it will act as a danger signal and put him at once on his guard.

In the case of *Arora* v *Barclays Bank Ltd* in 1978 (an unreported case), Judge Leonard, in the

Mayor's and City of London Court, said

Cross-firing has been described as the drawing of corresponding cheques by two persons on different branches of the same bank—or on different banks—unsupported by any consideration other than the mutual giving and receiving of cheques. This practice, due to the normal delay in clearing the cheques—if they are honoured—results in the temporary augmentation of the credit in each account. The practice is not illegal in itself provided that it is not used for fraud or some illegal purpose. But it obviously can be used for some such purpose, and the defendants (i.e. the bank) want to discourage it so far as they can.

CROSSED CHEQUE A crossed cheque is defined by the Bills of Exchange Act 1882, Section 76, as follows.

(1) Where a cheque bears across its face an addition of—

(*a*) The words 'and company' or any abbreviation thereof between two parallel transverse lines, either with or without the words 'not negotiable'; or

(*b*) Two parallel transverse lines simply, either with or without the words 'not negotiable'; that addition constitutes a crossing and the cheque is crossed generally.

(2) Where a cheque bears across its face an addition of the name of a banker, either with or without the words 'not negotiable,' that addition constitutes a crossing, and the cheque is crossed specially and to that banker.

By Section 77

(1) A cheque may be crossed generally or specially by the drawer.

(2) Where a cheque is uncrossed, the holder may cross it generally or specially.

(3) Where a cheque is crossed generally, the holder may cross it specially.

(4) Where a cheque is crossed generally or specially, the holder may add the words 'not negotiable.'

(5) Where a cheque is crossed specially, the banker to whom it is crossed may again cross it specially to another banker for collection.

(6) Where an uncrossed cheque, or a cheque crossed generally, is sent to a banker for collection, he may cross it specially to himself.

By Section 78

A crossing authorised by this Act is a material part of the cheque; it shall not be lawful for any person to obliterate or, except as authorised by this Act, to add to or alter the crossing.

The duties of a banker with regard to crossed cheques are set forth in Section 79:

(1) Where a cheque is crossed specially to more than one banker except when crossed to an agent for collection being a banker, the banker on whom it is drawn shall refuse payment thereof.

(2) Where the banker on whom a cheque is drawn which is so crossed nevertheless pays the same, or pays a cheque crossed generally otherwise than to a banker, or if crossed specially otherwise than to the banker to whom it is crossed, or his agent for collection being a banker, he is liable to the true owner of the cheque for any loss he may sustain owing to the cheque having been so paid.

Provided that where a cheque is presented for payment which does not at the time of presentment appear to be crossed, or to have had a crossing which has been obliterated, or to have been added to or altered otherwise than as authorised by this Act, the banker paying the cheque in good faith and without negligence shall not be responsible or incur any liability, nor shall the payment be questioned by reason of the cheque having been crossed, or of the crossing having been obliterated or having been added to or altered otherwise than as authorised by this Act, and of payment having been made otherwise than to a banker or to the banker to whom the cheque is or was crossed, or to his agent for collection being a banker, as the case may be.

A banker paying a crossed cheque is afforded protection by Section 80:

Where the banker, on whom a crossed cheque is drawn, in good faith and without negligence pays it, if crossed generally, to a banker, or if crossed specially, to the banker to whom it is crossed, or his agent for collection being a banker, the banker paying the cheque, and, if the cheque has come into the hands of the payee, the drawer shall respectively be entitled to the same rights and be placed in the same position as if payment of the cheque had been made to the true owner thereof.

As to the effect of crossing upon the holder, Section 81 provides

Where a person takes a crossed cheque which bears on it the words 'not negotiable,' he shall not have and shall not be capable of giving a better title to the cheque than that which the person from whom he took it had.

A collecting banker is afforded protection by Section 4 of the Cheques Act 1957. (SEE UNDER *Cheques Act 1957. See also cases under Collecting Banker.*)

The word 'customer' in Section 4 includes another bank. (See the case of *Importers Company Ltd* v *Westminster Bank Ltd*, under *Account Payee.*)

The words 'without negligence' in Section 4 'cannot mean without breach of duty on the part of the banker towards himself or towards the person who is his customer. They must mean without taking due care to protect the person whose name appears in the cheque as being the payee'. (Bailhache, J, in *Ladbroke & Co.* v *Todd* (1914) 19 Com Cas 256)

However, it was indicated in the case of *Orbit Mining Company Ltd* v *Westminster Bank Ltd* [1962] 3 WLR 1256, that the duty of care depends on 'the ordinary practice of bankers'.

It has been held that to make a person a customer of a banker there must be some sort of account, either a deposit or a current account or some similar relation. (See cases under *Customer.*)

A dividend warrant may be crossed. Section 95 says 'The provisions of this Act as to crossed cheques shall apply to a warrant for payment of dividend.' The provisions do not apply to bills, which cannot, therefore, be crossed like cheques. If a bill should be crossed, the crossing is of no effect. Money orders and postal orders may be crossed.

The provisions of the Bills of Exchange Act 1882, relating to crossed cheques shall, so far as is applicable, have effect in relation to instruments (other than cheques) to which the last foregoing section applies as they have effect in relation to cheques (Section 5, Cheques Act 1957).

These instruments are: (1) cheques; (2) any document issued by a customer of a banker which, though not a bill of exchange, is intended to enable a person to obtain payment from that banker of the sum mentioned in the document; (3) any document issued by a public officer which is intended to enable a person to obtain payment from the Paymaster-General or the Queen's and Lord Treasurer's Remembrancer of the sum mentioned in the document, but is not a bill of exchange; (4) any draft payable on demand drawn by a banker upon himself, whether payable at the head office or some other office of his bank.

Below are specimens of crossings which come under the definition of a general crossing. But any of these, or similiar, words across a cheque, without the transverse lines or with only one transverse line, do not constitute a crossing.

It is to be noted that where such words as 'Under fifty pounds' are written across a cheque, if a line is drawn above and below those words the lines constitute a general crossing, although it may not have been the intention to cross it.

Below are specimens of crossings which are included in the definition of a special crossing.

There are many varieties of general and special crossings. As a rule, the transverse lines go right across the cheque, but frequently they are drawn only a half or a third way across, and in extreme cases the lines are so short as to be easily overlooked. The position of the lines is usually about the middle of a cheque, but they are sometimes drawn across a corner of it.

The place of any words added to the transverse

General crossings

and Company

& Co.

not negotiable

not negotiable | *& Co.*

under Fifty Pounds

For the credit of John Brown's account

not negotiable | *under Twenty Pounds*

Payee's account only

not negotiable | *& Co.*

Special crossings

The British Banking Co. plc

Payee's account at the X & Y Bank plc

not negotiable. X & Y Bank plc

X & Y Bank plc and Co.

The British Banking Co. plc not negotiable

& Co. X & Y Bank plc

X & Y Bank plc under Twenty Pounds

Remitted by the X & Y Bk. plc, to the British Banking Co. plc for collection lines is usually between or immediately above or immediately below the lines, but in some cases they are found at a considerable distance from the crossing, and occasionally are found written even below the amount. It is questionable, however, whether words which are not written between or near to the transverse lines could be held to be a part of the crossing.

Crossings may be written, stamped, printed, or perforated. Many mistakes as to the amount would be prevented if customers avoided drawing the crossing lines through the figures of a cheque.

By the above sections it is seen that a crossed cheque can be paid by the banker on whom it is drawn, if crossed generally, only to another banker—if crossed specially, only to the banker whose name appears in the crossing. If the holder of a crossed cheque is a customer of the banker on whom it is drawn, the banker may place such cheque, if it is so desired, to the credit of that customer's account, though he should not pay cash for it. The customer, however, may forthwith draw a cheque upon his account for the cash required.

Where a cheque crossed generally and drawn upon one branch is presented for payment at another branch of the same bank, the two branches are, for this purpose, considered to be two banks, and the banker paying such a cheque fulfils the requirements of the Act to pay it only to another banker. In *Gordon* v *London City and Midland Bank* [1902] 1 KB 242, the Master of the Rolls, referring to cheques of that description, said

> The defendants, whose branch bank receives payment from another branch, are certainly a bank. It may be that the payment is to themselves; still, it is a payment made to a bank, and the payment is also made by a bank.

Where a cheque is crossed, and a payee wishes to obtain cash for it from the banker on whom it is drawn, it is customary for the drawer to cancel the crossing and to write 'pay cash' upon the cheque. The alteration, called 'opening the crossing', should be signed by the drawer. A banker, however, should be on his guard when requested to cash a cheque where the crossing has been cancelled, lest by doing so he renders himself liable to a true owner who took the cheque in a crossed condition. SEE *Opening a Crossing*

The words 'not negotiable', added to a general or a special crossing, do not operate as a restriction upon the transfer of a cheque, but merely give notice to anyone taking the cheque that he cannot obtain a better title than the person had from whom he received it. The words 'not negotiable' do not by themselves constitute a crossing. SEE *Not Negotiable Crossing*

Many cheques have such words as 'place to credit of John Brown's account', 'account of payee', 'account John Jones' added to the crossing. The Bills of Exchange Act does not make any particular reference to an addition of that nature, though it does say at Section 78 that it shall not be lawful for any person to obliterate or, except as authorized by the Act, to add to or alter the crossing. If the paying banker carries out his duty, as prescribed by the Act, and pays a cheque crossed generally to a banker, and a cheque crossed specially to the banker named, he is not concerned at all as to whether, or not, the collecting banker carried out the instructions to place the proceeds to any account indicated. If a cheque drawn on the British Banking Co. and crossed 'X & Y Bank, for the account of John Brown', is paid in to the X & Y Bank, by Tom Jones to his own credit, it is difficult to believe that the X & Y Bank would be exonerated from blame if they ignored the clear indication upon the cheque and passed it to the credit of Jones. Accordingly, in practice, a banker who receives such a cheque for collection, requires that it be placed to the credit of the account as named in the crossing. In *National Bank* v *Silke* [1891] 1 QB 435, where a cheque was crossed 'account of Moriarty, National Bank', Lord Justice Lindley said, with reference to those words,

> It cannot be contended that they prohibit transfer, and I do not think that they indicate an intention that the cheque should not be transferable. They amount to nothing more than a direction to the plaintiffs to carry the amount of the cheque to Moriarty's account when they have received it.

In *Akrokerri (Atlantic) Mines Ltd* v *The Economic Bank* [1904] 2 KB 465, where certain cheques were crossed 'account Economic Bank', Mr Justice Bigham said

> In my opinion these words are not in any sense an addition to the crossing. A crossing is a direction to the paying bank to pay the money generally to a bank, or to a particular bank, as the case may be, and when this has been done the whole purpose of the crossing has been served. The paying bank has nothing to do with the application of the money after it has once been paid to the proper receiving banker. The words 'account A B' are a mere direction to the receiving bank as to how the money is to be dealt with after receipt.

With reference to the words 'how the money is to be dealt with after receipt', as a collecting banker may now pass crossed cheques at once to the credit of his customer, it would appear to follow that the words 'Account A B' are a direction to the receiving banker as to how he must deal with the cheques when he receives them. SEE *Account Payee*

The object of crossing cheques is to insure the safe transmission of the money from the sender to the receiver. A general crossing would prevent a thief from obtaining value from a banker for a cheque, unless he had a banking account. The usual special crossing would prevent him from obtaining value unless he had an account with the banker to whom the cheque was crossed. Thus the thief's chance of profiting by his plunder becomes still further remote. In the case of *Ringham* v *Hackett and Another* (*Times*, 9th February, 1980), it was emphasized that the crossing on a cheque was for the protection of the bank and its customer and did not necessarily affect the respective rights of the drawer and the payee. In that case, when the payee took a crossed cheque to the drawee bank, rather than presenting it for collection through his own bank, it was held that this was a valid presentation of the cheque under Section 45, Bills of Exchange Act, although the bank could not pay on such presentation, and that it was a misconception that presentation should be made 'through a bank'.

If a collecting banker gives cash over the counter for a crossed cheque on another banker, he does so at his own risk, because if an indorsement is forged he is liable to the true owner. SEE *Cheque; Collecting Banker* (and cases cited therein)

CROSSED TO TWO BANKERS An answer which is sometimes marked upon a cheque by the drawee banker, who is returning it unpaid for this reason. Where a cheque is crossed to two bankers, except when crossed to an agent for collection being a banker, the banker on whom it is drawn shall refuse payment thereof (Section 79, Bills of Exchange Act 1882). But a cheque crossed 'X & Y Bank, Leeds', and also stamped 'X & Y Bank, York', is not crossed to two bankers, as Leeds and York are branches of the same banker.

CROWN A crown is of the value of 25p and its standard weight is 436.36363 grains troy. Its standard fineness is thirty-seven-fortieths fine silver, three-fortieths alloy; altered by the Coinage Act 1920, to one-half fine silver, one-half alloy. No crowns were struck between 1902 and 1928. Silver crowns were first coined in 1551. SEE *Coinage*

CROWTHER COMMITTEE ON CONSUMER CREDIT REPORT After over two years' work the Crowther Committee's report on consumer credit was published on 24th March, 1971. The terms of reference of the Committee, announced in July 1968, were

1. to enquire into the present law and practice governing the provision of credit to individuals for financing purchases of goods and services for personal consumption;
2. to consider the advantages and disadvantages of existing and possible alternative arrangements for providing such credit, having regard to the interests of consumers, traders and suppliers of credit, including depositors;
3. to consider in particular whether any amendment of the Moneylenders Act is desirable; and
4. to make recommendations.

The Report was a prelude to the passing in due course of the Consumer Credit Act 1974 (q.v.). This entry therefore, is included as a matter of historical interest in relation to the social and legal aspects of consumer credit in the UK.

Economic and Social Aspects of Consumer Credit

The Committee found no reason to view with concern the growth of consumer credit. Moreover, the evidence examined showed that the proportion of borrowers who get into difficulty with their payments was very small and did not provide grounds for restrictive measures. The Committee considered that the correct line for economic policy should be to allow consumer credit the maximum freedom to develop under competitive conditions induced by increasing the amount of information available to the consumer, especially by mandatory disclosure of the effective rate of annual interest (including all charges), and by stimulating the education of consumers in the use of credit.

From the social aspect, users of consumer credit should be treated as adults capable of managing their own financial affairs. There should be no restriction on the freedom of access to credit but measures should be taken to prevent debtors from falling into default and to assist those who do.

Credit Law

The Committee found the existing law relating to credit transactions deficient in several ways and, in general, failing to provide just solutions to common problems. A great need was found for rationalization.

A new legal framework was therefore proposed which rests on two fundamental points:

1. Recognition that the extension of credit in a sale or hire-purchase transaction is in reality a loan and that the reservation of title under a

hire-purchase or conditional sale agreement or finance lease is in reality a chattel mortgage securing a loan.

2. Replacement of what are at present distinct sets of rules for different security devices by a legal structure applicable uniformly to all forms of security interest. Standard forms of instrument are not proposed but all forms of agreement serving a similar purpose should be regulated alike.

Two new statutes were therefore proposed. A Lending and Security Act and a Consumer Sale and Loan Act. Together these two Acts would involve the outright repeal of several existing Acts—notably the Hire Purchase Acts, the Moneylenders Acts, the Pawnbrokers Acts and the Bills of Sale Acts—and the amendment of many others.

Lending and Security Act

The proposed Lending and Security Act would contain provisions applicable to credit transactions generally and cover the loan aspect of all credit transactions (other than loans on the security of land). This would include unsecured loans; instalment sales; revolving credits; check trading and credit cards; hire-purchase and conditional sale agreements; finance leases; mortgages and charges of goods, documents and intangibles; and pledges of goods and documents. It was intended that the formal requirement for a valid security agreement should be only (1) that it is evidenced by a memorandum in writing or (2) that the secured party has taken possession of the security. In general, the secured party should be free to take a security interest, not only in the debtor's existing property, but in his after-acquired property but not where consumer goods are concerned. The relationship between the parties should be essentially that of mortgagee and mortgagor.

The Committee recommended that there should be a simple and flexible filing system of security interests in personal property. This would be administered by a Credit Commissioner and would be designed both to give notice to third parties of the existence of such interest and to protect the secured party. Consumer goods (other than motor vehicles) should be excluded from the system which should only be for sums secured of over £300.

Consumer Sale and Loan Act

The Consumer Sale and Loan Act would contain special provisions considered necessary for the protection of the consumer.

The definition of a consumer loan is necessarily complicated but roughly the Committee recommended that the Act should apply to credit transactions where

1. the borrower (buyer or hirer) is not a body corporate, and
2. the whole or part of the price of the goods or services purchased is advanced by the seller or a connected lender (a connected lender would be defined as one who, pursuant to a regular business relationship with one or more sellers, makes a loan which is used to buy goods or services from one such seller. It would embrace *inter alia* check traders and issuers of three-party credit cards) and
3. the sum advanced does not exceed £2,000, and
4. repayment is to be made by three or more instalments.

Such transactions, irrespective of the rate of interest, would fall within the scope of the Act as 'financed consumer sales'. Additionally, any loan to an individual of less than £2,000 and not made in connection with a financed consumer sale would come within the definition of a consumer loan if the (true) rate of interest (including charges) was more than $2\frac{1}{2}$ per cent above Bank rate. A loan by an independent lender at a rate not exceeding $2\frac{1}{2}$ per cent above Bank rate would, however, be outside the Act even if the loan was specifically advanced for the purchase of particular goods and even if its application to that purpose were to be controlled by the lender.

One important suggestion was that where the price payable under a consumer sale agreement is advanced wholly or in part by a connected lender, he should be liable for misrepresentations relating to the goods made by the seller, and for defects in title, but he should have a right of indemnity from the supplier.

In the matter of repossession and realization, the new Act should broadly follow the principles of the present Hire Purchase Act of which the most important is that, where the borrower has repaid one-third or more of the total debt, repossession can only be enforced with a Court Order.

Administrative and Fiscal Measures

The Committee recommended that all the functions of the Government in respect of consumer credit should come under the auspices of a Consumer Credit Commissioner appointed by the Secretary of State for Trade and Industry. This Commissioner would deal with the administration of the licensing system under which anyone carrying on the business of granting consumer credit, as principal, broker or agent, or counsellor would require a licence from the Commissioner, who would have the power to refuse renewal of or to revoke or suspend a licence.

The Committee felt it would be helpful if they included in their Report some observations on what they felt the impact of the Consumer Sale and Loan Act might be on the activities of different financing institutions. Those sections dealing with Banks, Finance Houses, Building Societies and Credit Card Issuers are quoted below.

Banks

Consumer loans by banks as independent lenders would be unaffected by the Act if the interest or charge did not exceed 2½ per cent over Bank rate in force at the date of the loan agreement. On this basis bank loans by way of overdraft or ordinary loan account with a clearing bank would at present rates of charge be outside the Act, whereas advances made under one of the special personal loans schemes would be within the statutory provisions, as would almost all advances by Section 123 banks on second mortgage.

Loans by a bank as a connected lender—including credit extended by means of credit cards—would be governed by the Consumer Sale and Loan Act if made in connection with a financed consumer sale. In such cases the bank would be liable for defects in the goods supplied and for misrepresentations by the seller relating to the goods but would have a right of indemnity against the seller. Loans by a bank made otherwise than in connection with a financed consumer sale—e.g. for house purchase or by way of an advance repayable by fewer than four instalments—would not be controlled, even if made by the bank as a connected lender, if interest was limited to 2½ per cent above Bank rate.

A bank would not have to be licensed unless it carried on the business of making loans within the Consumer Sale and Loan Act—which, in practice, can be taken to mean unless it operated a personal loans scheme or a credit card scheme providing for the repayment of debt by instalments. If it did carry on that business, its banking status would not exempt it from licensing requirements.

It would be illegal for a bank to canvass applications for non-purchase-money consumer loans on the door-step, whether directly or through brokers or other agents, except in response to a written request from the prospective borrower. This would be unlikely to affect the clearing banks but might affect certain Section 123 banks. A bank wishing to canvass personally unsolicited applications for purchase-money loans would require to hold a separate licence for that purpose. No such licence would, however, be necessary for postal canvassing, e.g. the unsolicited mailing of credit cards to account holders.

Finance Houses

The term 'finance house' is here used to denote a company of the kind now engaging in consumer hire-purchase or credit sale transactions. Such transactions, at the consumer level, would almost always fall within the Consumer Sale and Loan Act, both in relation to the lending aspect of the transaction and in relation to the sale aspect. The finance house would thus have to be licensed. It would also, as at present, be liable for defects in the goods and for misrepresentations by the dealer relating to the goods and it is proposed that this liability should be extended to services, though in a modified form. If the finance house, instead of entering into a hire-purchase or credit sale agreement with the consumer, were to advance the price by way of loan, thus enabling the consumer to pay the supplier in cash, the finance house would be responsible for defects and misrepresentations, if it was a connected lender and the sale was a financed consumer sale. The finance house would have a right of indemnity against the supplier. If the finance house were completely independent of the supplier, then whilst the loan of the price would attract the provisions of the Consumer Sale and Loan Act relating to loans, the finance house would not be responsible for any breaches of contract or misrepresentations by the supplier. Finance houses carrying on purely commercial transactions and not engaging in the business of making consumer loans or consumer sales would not be affected by the Consumer Sale and Loan Act at all.

Building Societies

So long as consumer loans by a building society were limited to advances for the purchase of real property or were made by the society as an independent lender, and the rate of interest charged did not exceed 2½ per cent above Bank rate, such loans would be outside the Consumer Sale and Loan Act and the building society would not require to be licensed. If, however, a building society were to lend money for the purchase of goods or services under a financed consumer sale, the Act would apply, and the society would require to be licensed, even if interest never exceeded 2½ per cent above Bank rate. A sale would not, of course, be a financed consumer sale if the society was not a connected lender but a lender wholly independent of the seller. Loans in excess of £2,000 would be outside the Act regardless of the rate of interest and whether or not such loans were made by the society as a connected lender.

Credit Card Issuers
Issuers of cards which offered only a monthly account facility would not be within the Consumer Sale and Loan Act at all but issuers of cards where the card-holder was given a credit ceiling and the option to repay by instalments would require to be licensed.

The Future
As for the future, the Committee foresaw a growth in competition among the different forms of granting credit. They expected a continuing shift away from forms of lending involving taking security on goods in a borrower's possession, and towards unsecured lending based on the general credit-worthiness of the borrower. This they felt would put a premium on a settled relationship between the consumer and one or two financial institutions.

To improve the credit market the Committee saw the main prescription as the fostering of competition among credit-grantors and in this respect they anticipated an important role for the banks. As the Report said,

> The commercial banks, with their traditional emphasis on knowledge of their customers and experience in making loans on the basis of personal assessment of the borrower rather than the security offered, would be ideally equipped for greater direct participation in the field of consumer credit.

The recommendation of the Crowther Committee for two new statutes to consolidate and amend the law relating to these various matters (see above) was not accepted in its entirety, but many of the recommendations were embodied in the Consumer Credit Act 1974 (q.v.).

CUM DIV Short for cum dividend, with dividend. It means that the purchaser of shares bought on this understanding is entitled to the dividend due to be paid, and if the dividend warrant is sent by the company to the seller, the latter must hand over the amount to the purchaser. Most stocks are cum div until the pay day following the declaration of dividend. SEE *Pay Day*

CUM DRAWING With any benefit there may be from a drawing of bonds for payment which is due to be made.

CUM RIGHTS A purchaser of shares 'cum rights' acquires any rights attaching to the shares, e.g. to take up further issues, etc.

CUMULATIVE DIVIDEND Preference shares have a preferential right to dividend before ordinary shares, and if the profits of the company in one year are not sufficient to pay the full dividend, the profits of succeeding years are used for that purpose, and, until the preference shares receive a full dividend for each year, the ordinary shares receive nothing. The dividend in such cases is said to be cumulative.

If, however, the preferential right as to dividend is confined merely to the profits of each year, the dividend is non-cumulative.

CUMULATIVE PARTICIPATING PREFERENCE SHARES SEE *Preference Stock or Shares*

CUPRO-NICKEL COIN By the Coinage Act 1946, cupro-nickel coins were substituted for silver coins, which were gradually withdrawn from circulation. Cupro-nickel coins are composed of three-quarters copper and one-quarter nickel. The change was made on account of the high price of silver after the Second World War and the necessity for paying back silver loaned from the USA under the lease-lend arrangement.

CURRENCY The word was originally applied to the currency, or passing from hand to hand, of money, but it has now come to be applied to the money itself, gold, silver and copper etc. Bills of exchange, bank notes, cheques and any other documents which act as a substitute for coins are also included under that term.

The term is also used to distinguish payments in foreign money from payments in sterling. Thus, a currency bill is one expressed other than in sterling.

A distinction is sometimes drawn between 'hard' and 'soft' currencies. A 'hard' currency is one which is strong in the sense that it commands confidence and is widely accepted as a means of settlement of international payments. A 'soft' currency is one which is not so universally accepted, usually because of some underlying weakness or immaturity in the economic system of the country concerned.

The currency, or circulating medium, by which sales and purchases were effected in former times, was represented in different countries by articles such as sugar, furs, fish, cloth, etc. and even at the present day in certain underdeveloped countries, cowries, salt and blocks of tea may be found in use.

The currency of a bill of exchange is a period for which it still has to run before maturity. The currency of a bill payable after sight begins when the bill is accepted. SEE *Coinage; Money*

CURRENCY AND BANK NOTES ACT 1928 The principal purpose of this Act was to transfer the currency note issue of the Treasury to the Bank of England, and this was effected on 22nd November, 1928.

CURRENCY AND BANK NOTES ACT 1939 The principal purposes of this Act, operative on 1st March, 1939, were to amend the law governing the amount of the fiduciary note issue and to provide for the weekly valuation of the assets of the Issue Department of the Bank of England.

CURRENCY AND BANK NOTES ACT 1954 This Act was brought into operation on 22nd February, 1954. It raised the statutory fiduciary note issue of the Bank of England to £1,575 million, subject to variations by the Treasury, though an upward change lasting for over two years has to be confirmed by Parliament. On the same day, the Defence Finance Regulations, which had hitherto governed the note issue, were revoked. The Financial Secretary to the Treasury commented during the passage of the new legislation through Committee that the 'promise to pay the bearer' made by the Bank of England on bank notes was of practical importance when notes of a particular series were demonetized or called in and ceased to be legal tender. If such notes were subsequently presented at the Bank of England, they would be paid.

The Fiduciary Note Issue (Extension of Period) Order 1968 made provision for the extension of the note issue level for successive two year periods, which has been continued by subsequent Orders through to the present day. SEE *Bank of England Return; Fiduciary Issue*

CURRENCY BILLS Bills which are drawn in foreign currency.

CURRENCY BONDS Bonds which are repayable in the currency of the country where they are issued.

CURRENT ACCOUNT A current or running account at a bank is an active account on which cheques are drawn and to which credits are paid, as opposed to a deposit account on which normally cheques are not drawn.

In the ordinary way, interest is not paid on current accounts with the clearing banks, although some banks have introduced special categories of accounts on which interest is paid and on which limited drawings are permitted.

The current account is perhaps the dominant feature of the British banking system. The money transfer system, built up by the joint stock banks over the years, is central to the financial system in the UK and one effect of this is that current account balances are so readily available for the payment of debts that they are almost as good as cash. In fact, current account balances are included in the narrowest definition of the money supply, M1 (q.v.) along with notes and coin in circulation. Approximately one-half of the retail deposits of the London clearing banks tend to be on current account. The balances are withdrawable on demand and may be used to meet cheques, standing orders, direct debits and similar money transfers through the banking system. A current account may be in credit or in debit, the term 'overdraft' being normally used to denote an overdrawn current account.

Most banks in the UK will normally require at least one reference from a reliable source before opening a banking account for a new customer. In the ordinary way, a cheque book will not be issued to a customer until the references have been obtained. This is to guard against the possibility of the proposed customer paying in cheques to which he may have no right or title, in which case the bank would be held to have been negligent in not obtaining a proper introduction or reference and thus lose the protection of Section 4 of the Cheques Act 1957.

Private persons opening banking accounts in joint names will be required to furnish the bank with an authority as to whether or not cheques are to be signed by either or both parties. When accounts are opened on behalf of companies or institutions and unincorporated associations, an appropriate mandate will be required by the bank governing the signing arrangements. SEE *Advances; Agent; Appropriation of Payments; Bankrupt Person; Clayton's Case; Company; Customer; Death of Bank Customer; Executor; Garnishee Order; Infants; Joint Account; Partnerships; Signature; Solicitors' Accounts; Trustee*

CURRENT ASSETS These are the assets used in the day-to-day running of a business and which, by their nature, move or circulate with the business activity. They include, for example, stocks, debtors, bank balances and cash. Current assets may be contrasted with fixed assets (q.v.) which, by their nature, tend to remain static, e.g. freehold and leasehold buildings, plant and machinery. Under Paragraph 75 of Schedule 1 to the Companies Act 1981, any assets not intended for use on a continuing basis in a company's activities are deemed to be current assets. Under the company accounting regulations brought in under that Act, current assets must be valued in the balance sheet at the lower of purchase price or production cost and net realizable value. Distribution costs may not be included in the production cost of current assets (Paragraphs 26(4) of Schedule 1). (Re-enacted in Schedule 4 of the Companies Act 1985.)

CURRENT COST ACCOUNTING The essence of current cost accounting (CCA) is the portrayal in the balance sheet of a company of the replacement costs of assets rather than the historic cost. The proposals for CCA arose out of the discussions in the 1970s on inflation accounting (q.v.). One school of thought was that company balance sheets should be adjusted for annual changes in the purchasing power of the pound. The effect of inflation was such that (1) most balance sheet figures no longer reflected the true value of a company's fixed assets, (2) operating profits were inflated by the rise in value of stocks and (3) company results did not necessarily reflect the true cost of replacing stocks.

The form of inflation accounting eventually adopted was that proposed by the Institute of Chartered Accountants in their *Statement of Standard Accounting Practice 16* (SSAP 16), based primarily on valuing assets for balance sheet purposes at replacement cost. SSAP 16 has been adopted as standard accounting practice for all major companies, including all companies listed on the Stock Exchange, and came into effect in respect of accounting periods beginning on 1st January, 1980 or later.

The Companies Act 1981 implementing the EEC Fourth Directive on company accounts does not impose current cost accounting, but provides alternative accounting rules for valuation purposes. The position at the moment, therefore, is that listed and other public companies may present their accounts on an historic basis showing adjustments for current cost accounting in accordance with SSAP 16 (in which case the accounting standards under the Companies Act 1981 must be applied to the historic accounts) or they may present their accounts entirely on a CCA basis, in which case SSAP 16 will apply.

On the whole, SSAP 16 met with widespread opposition and was the subject of considerable discussion and debate in the accountancy profession. In June 1984, the Accounting Standards Committee released an exposure draft for a proposed new current cost accounting standard to replace SSAP 16. It was intended that the new standard would take effect in relation to company accounting periods beginning on or after 1st January, 1985. It applies to all public companies, other than those which are 'value-based', such as life offices and investment trusts. The new Exposure Draft (ED 35) is based on the original concept of SSAP 16, i.e. that the profit of a company is the surplus after sufficient funds have been set aside to maintain the operating capability of the business. ED 35 has four main requirements:

1. depreciation adjustments to reflect the current cost of consuming fixed assets;
2. cost of sales adjustments to reflect the current cost of replacing stocks;
3. adjustments to reflect the increased monetary working capital required when a company's input prices are rising; and
4. a gearing adjustment to take into account the effect of debt capital.

ED 35 does not require companies to provide full current-cost balance sheets. The required information is to be provided in notes to the main historical cost accounts. The cumulative effect of the current cost accounting adjustments should be stated but it is not necessary to calculate the actual current cost accounting profit.

The proposed standard does not apply to private companies.

At the time of writing ED 35 has encountered a fair amount of opposition from professional bodies and a view has been advanced that inflation-adjusted figures are not essential to a 'true and fair view' in company accounts. The whole subject therefore, is back in the melting pot.

CURRENT LIABILITIES These are the obligations of a company which arise from its normal trading activities and which fluctuate in the course of those activities, as distinct from longer term obligations such as fixed loans, preference shares, etc. SEE *Current Assets*

CUSTODIAN TRUSTEE By the Public Trustee Act 1906, which came into operation on 1st January, 1908, the office of Public Trustee was established.

The Public Trustee may, amongst other duties, if he thinks fit, act as custodian trustee, if appointed by order of the court, or by the testator, settlor or other creator of a trust, or by the person having power to appoint new trustees.

Section 4 of the Public Trustee Act is as follows.

(1) Subject to rules under this Act the Public Trustee may, if he consents to act as such, and whether or not the number of trustees has been reduced below the original number, be appointed to be custodian trustee of any trust—

(*a*) by order of the Court made on the application of any person on whose application the Court may order the appointment of a new trustee; or

(b) by the testator, settlor, or other creator of any trust; or

(c) by the person having power to appoint new trustees.

(2) Where the Public Trustee is appointed to be custodian trustee of any trust—

(a) The trust property shall be transferred to the custodian trustee as if he were sole trustee, and for that purpose vesting orders may, where necessary, be made under the Trustee Act, 1893:

(b) The management of the trust property and the exercise of any power of discretion exercisable by the trustees under the trust shall remain vested in the trustees other than the custodian trustee (which trustees are hereinafter referred to as the managing trustees):

(c) As between the custodian trustee and the managing trustees, and subject and without prejudice to the rights of any other persons, the custodian trustee shall have the custody of all securities and documents of title relating to the trust property, but the managing trustees shall have free access thereto and be entitled to take copies thereof or extracts therefrom:

(d) The custodian trustee shall concur in and perform all acts necessary to enable the managing trustees to exercise their powers of management or any other power or discretion vested in them (including the power to pay money or securities into Court), unless the matter in which he is requested to concur is a breach of trust, or involves a personal liability upon him in respect of calls or otherwise, but, unless he so concurs, the custodian trustee shall not be liable for any act or default on the part of the managing trustees or any of them:

(e) All sums payable to or out of the income or capital of the trust property shall be paid to or by the custodian trustee: Provided that the custodian trustee may allow the dividends and other income derived from the trust property to be paid to the managing trustees or to such person as they direct, or into such bank to the credit of such person as they may direct, and in such case shall be exonerated from seeing to the application thereof and shall not be answerable for any loss or misapplication thereof:

(f) The power of appointing new trustees, when exercisable by the trustees, shall be exercisable by the managing trustees alone, but the custodian trustee shall have the same power of applying to the Court for the appointment of a new trustee as any other trustee:

(g) In determining the number of trustees for the purposes of the Trustee Act, 1893, the custodian trustee shall not be reckoned as a trustee:

(h) The custodian trustee, if he acts in good faith, shall not be liable for accepting as correct and acting upon the faith of any written statement by the managing trustees as to any birth, death, marriage, or other matter of pedigree or relationship, or other matter of fact, upon which the title to the trust property or any part thereof may depend, nor for acting upon any legal advice obtained by the managing trustees independently of the custodian trustee:

(i) The Court may, on the application of either the custodian trustee, or any of the managing trustees, or of any beneficiary, and on proof to their satisfaction that it is the general wish of the beneficiaries, or that on other grounds it is expedient, to terminate the custodian trusteeship, make an order for that purpose, and the Court may thereupon make such vesting orders and give such directions as under the circumstances may seem to the Court to be necessary or expedient.

(3) The provisions of this Section shall apply in like manner as to the Public Trustee to any banking or insurance company or other body corporate entitled by rules made under this Act to act as custodian trustee, with power for such company or body corporate to charge and retain or pay out of the trust property fees not exceeding the fees chargeable by the Public Trustee as custodian trustee.

With regard to corporate bodies acting as custodian trustees, Rule 30 of the Public Trustee Rules, as amended in 1926, is

(1) Any corporation constituted under the law of the United Kingdom or any part thereof and having a place of business there and empowered by its constitution to undertake trust business, and being either,

(a) a company incorporated by special Act or Royal Charter,

(b) a company registered (whether with or without limited liability) under the Companies Act, 1929, having a capital (in stock or shares) for the time being issued of not less than £250,000, of which not less than £100,000 shall have been paid in cash, or

(c) a company registered without limited liability under the Companies Act, 1929, whereof one of the members is a company within any of the classes hereinbefore defined.

shall be entitled to act as a custodian trustee.

A trust corporation can act as custodian trustee and managing trustee without requiring another party to be associated with it in the capacity of managing trustee (*Forster and Another* v *Williams Deacon's Bank Ltd*, 1934).

Although Section 4(3) quoted above empowered corporate bodies, such as banking and insurance companies, to act as custodian trustees, little use of this provision has been made by corporate trustees because of the burdensome and restrictive nature of the statutory provisions. Generally, they have preferred to accept custodian trusteeships under express powers in the trust deed and thus, in this way, they act for companies and other corporations and unincorporated groups of people such as clubs and local societies.

Perhaps the most important aspect of these statutory provisions is that they were the first instance in which an institution was authorized by statute to charge for acting as a trustee and thus, the concept of the 'trading' trustee was introduced into the UK. SEE *Banks as Executor and Trustee; Public Trustee; Trustee*

CUSTODY BILL OF LADING SEE *Bill of Lading*

CUSTOMARY FREEHOLDS These were converted into absolute freeholds as from 1st January, 1926, on the same principle as the enfranchisement of copyholds. Customary freeholds were akin to copyholds (q.v.), subject to the exception that the tenant's disposition of the land was not subject to the will of the lord of the manor.

CUSTOMER There is no statutory definition of a customer from a banking point of view. It has been held that in order to make a person a customer of a bank, within the meaning of Section 4 of the Cheques Act 1957 (which has replaced Section 82 of the Bills of Exchange Act 1882), there must be either a deposit or a current account or some similar relation. (*Great Western Railway* v *London and County Banking Co.*, [1901] AC 414.)

In the case of *Hampstead Guardians* v *Barclays Bank Ltd* (SEE *Current Account*), it was held that the fact that there was a flaw in the chain of identification of the customer ought to have put the bank on inquiry and that the bank was not protected by Section 82, Bills of Exchange Act 1882.

In *Ladbroke & Co.* v *Todd* (1914) 111 LT 43, Bailhache, J, said that he was of opinion that the relation of banker and customer begins as soon as a cheque or money is paid in, and the bank accepts it and is prepared to open an account.

In the case of *Commissioners of Taxation* v *English, Scottish, and Australian Bank Ltd* (1920) 36 TLR 305, which came before the Judicial Committee of the Privy Council, T opened an account with the bank, paying in cash £20; next day he paid in a crossed cheque payable to 053 or bearer (the cheque was subsequently discovered to have been stolen by someone from a letter box) and the following day cheques withdrawing the money were paid. The point was raised as to whether T was a customer within the meaning of the Section. It was held that

> the word 'customer' signifies a relationship in which duration is not of the essence. A person whose money has been accepted by the bank on the footing that they undertake to honour cheques up to the amount standing to his credit is a customer of the bank in the sense of the statute, irrespective of whether his connection is of short or long duration. T was therefore a customer, though one of short standing.

It was further held that the bank had acted without negligence in collecting the cheque. (See remarks on this point under *Collecting Banker*.)

The question of a reference must be remembered when considering whether a person is a customer or not. Until the bank has received a suitable reference, the banking contract may not be complete, or perhaps it would be more correct to say that the banking contract is made subject to an implied condition subsequent, that the reference given proves satisfactory to the banker. If the reference is satisfactory, then the person is a customer and probably always has been, and the protective Section will apply to the very first cheque he paid in. On the other hand, if no satisfactory reference can be obtained, the banker will be taking a risk if he keeps the account, and usually he will close it. In this case, the person is not a customer and probably never was one. Any cheques collected in this interim period are probably handled at the banker's risk. To meet this contingency some bankers refuse to collect a cheque paid in at the first interview, holding it on a suspense account until the reference is shown to be satisfactory.

Money paid in by a customer to his account is really lent to the banker, the banker becoming, not the trustee for that money, but the debtor of the customer. In the event of the banker's failure, the customer claims upon the estate as an ordinary creditor. The Lord Chancellor said, in *London Joint Stock Bank Ltd* v *Macmillan and Arthur* [1918] AC 777,

> The relation between banker and customer is that of debtor and creditor, with a superadded obligation on the part of the banker to honour the customer's cheques if the account is in credit. SEE *Current Account*

It is to be noted that it is possible for there to be a contractual relationship between banker and customer without the person being a customer for the purpose of Section 4 of the Cheques Act 1957. For example, the banker may have agreed specifically that the potential customer may have the right to operate the account and pay in cheques as soon as the enquiries on references have resulted in satisfactory answers. (Cf. *Stony Stanton Supplies (Coventry) Ltd* v *Midland Bank Ltd* [1966] 2 Lloyd's Rep 373.) SEE *Current Account*

CY PRÈS As nearly as possible. When the terms of a trust are incapable of being carried out absolutely, the courts have power to order that they be carried out *cy près*, as nearly as possible.

In fact, in modern times the *cy près* doctrine applies only to charitable gifts. If, for some reason, it is impossible to carry out the terms of a charitable gift and it can be shown that the donor had a general charitable intention, the court in exercise of its jurisdiction will carry out the charitable intention as nearly as possible to the apparent intentions of the donor. The doctrine will not be applied where a gift is not charitable in law, nor where some contrary intention has been displayed by the donor, e.g. an indication by a testator that if a charitable gift fails, the amount thereof shall fall into the residuary estate.

The Charities Act 1960 provided in Sections 13–31 for the widening of the application of property *cy près* where the original charitable purpose for which a charity was established has failed and also made provision for the assistance and supervision of charities by the court and central authorities.

D

DATA PROTECTION ACT 1984 SEE Supplement

DATE ON BILL OF EXCHANGE The Bills of Exchange Act 1882 provides that a bill is not invalid by reason that it is not dated (section 3)

Section 2 provides 'where a bill expressed to be payable at a fixed period after date is issued undated, or where the acceptance of a bill payable at a fixed period after sight is undated, any holder may insert therein the true date of issue or acceptance, and the bill shall be payable accordingly.'

'Provided that (1) where the holder in good faith and by mistake inserts a wrong date, and (2) in every case where a wrong date is inserted, if the bill subsequently comes into the hands of a holder in due course the bill shall not be avoided thereby, but shall operate and be payable as if the date so inserted had been the true date.'

The section applies only to time bills, but in the case of cheques on which the date has been omitted, it is generally considered that a holder may insert what he takes to be the true date. (See Section 20 under *Inchoate Instrument*.)

13.—(1) Where a bill or an acceptance or any indorsement on a bill is dated, the date shall, unless the contrary be proved, be deemed to be the true date of the drawing, acceptance, or indorsement, as the case may be.

(2) A bill is not invalid by reason only that it is ante-dated or post-dated or that it bears date on a Sunday.

Ante-dating is placing a date prior to the true date; post-dating, placing a date subsequent to the true date. A cheque with a Sunday date should not be paid until after the Sunday.

The difference between the insertion of an omitted date and the alteration of a date should be noted. The above Section permits any holder to insert a date, but Section 64 (SEE UNDER *Alterations to Bills of Exchange*) requires all parties to agree to an alteration.

The date is a material part of a bill and any alteration in a date, unless with the assent of all the parties liable on the bill, voids the bill except as against the party who had made or assented to the alteration, and subsequent indorsers; but where a date has been altered and the alteration is not apparent, a holder in due course may avail himself of the bill as if it had not been altered.

A cheque dated, say, 31st June, may be paid on or after 30th June.

Where a post-dated bill is discounted, and the acceptor dies or becomes bankrupt before the arrival of the date of the bill, the bill is not invalid by reason only that it is post-dated.

It is not permissible to give a bill or promissory note, undated, for say three months, and after payment of the bill or note, still undated, to issue it again for another three months, and so on. The only date which can be inserted in an undated bill is the true date of issue. A fresh debt requires a new bill or note.

The dates on bills of exchange and cheques are usually in figures, but they would be quite valid if written in words. SEE *Ante-Dated; Bill of Exchange*

A bill of exchange is incomplete and revocable until delivery of the instrument in order to give effect thereto. SEE *Delivery of Bill*

In *Williams* v *Rider* [1962] 3 WLR 119, it was held that a promise to pay made payable 'on or before December 31st, 1956', was not a promissory note because the date was not fixed or determinable.

In *Griffiths* v *Dalton* [1940] 2 KB 264, it was decided that a banker is not bound to pay a cheque that is undated and that the right of the holder to fill in the date lasts only for a reasonable time.

DATE OF DEED A deed takes effect from the date of its delivery and not necessarily from the date on which it is stated to have been executed. It is open to a party to a deed to show that it was delivered at some time other than the date of execution shown in the deed. In fact, an undated deed which has been executed and delivered is perfectly complete without the need to insert a date (per Sargant J, in *Esberger & Son Ltd* v *Capital & Counties Bank Ltd* [1913] 109 LT 140).

On the other hand, if the date of a lease is altered after the lease was executed, the lessor cannot deny that the date inserted by himself in the lease is the correct one if this would prejudice anyone claiming under the lease (*Rudd* v *Bowles* [1912] 2 Ch 60).

DATE OF WILL It would appear that there is no strict need in law for a will to be dated, although clearly as a matter of prudence and good order a date should be inserted. The omission to insert a date or the insertion of a wrong date will not invalidate a will, but in any instance where the date of a will is uncertain, the Registrar of the Probate Court will require evidence to be produced to establish the date.

A codicil to a will has the effect of republishing the will provided the codicil makes reference to the will. Thus, in such cases, the will takes effect as if it were made at the same date as the codicil. (SEE *Specific Legacy*) All wills and codicils 'speak from the date of death' and thus become operative only at that time regardless of the date of execution. SEE *Attestation; Codicil; Will*

DAYS OF GRACE Before the Banking and Financial Dealings Act 1971 came into operation, where a bill of exchange was not payable on demand, three days, called 'days of grace', were allowed. Partly to bring the UK in line with the rest of the Continent, and in order to rectify the anomalous position arising when bills of exchange become payable on a Saturday, the abovementioned Act was passed. Section 3 enacts as follows.

(1) Section 92 of the Bills of Exchange Act, 1882 (which, in a case in which the time limited by that Act for doing any act or thing is less than three days, excludes non-business days from the reckoning of that time, and defines such days for the purposes of the Act) shall have effect as if, in paragraph (a) of the definition of non-business days, 'Saturday' were inserted immediately before 'Sunday'.

This subsection shall not operate to extend any period expiring at or before the time it comes into force.

(2) For Section 14(1) of the Bills of Exchange Act, 1882 (under or by virtue of which the date of maturity of a bill or promissory note that does not say otherwise is arrived at by adding three days of grace to the time of payment as fixed by the bill or note, but is advanced or postponed if the last day of grace is a non-business day) there shall be substituted, except in its application to bills drawn and notes made before this subsection comes into force, the following paragraph—

(1) The bill is due and payable in all cases on the last day of the time of payment as fixed by the bill or, if that is a non-business day, on the succeeding business day.

(3) This Section shall come into force at the expiration of one month beginning with the date on which this Act is passed.

Insurance companies allow a number of days of grace within which premiums due upon policies may be paid, usually 15 days for fire insurance, and 30 days for life assurance. The due date of a premium is the date specified in the body of the policy, and not the last day of grace.

DEALER IN SECURITIES SEE *Licensed Dealer*

DEATH SEE *Administrator; Capital Transfer Tax; Executor; Death Grant*

DEATH GRANT Subject to the contribution conditions being satisfied (see below), death grant (currently £30) is payable on the death of any man born on or after 5th July, 1883 (i.e. who was 65 or under on 5th July, 1948 when the National Insurance Act came into force) and any woman born on or after 5th July, 1888 (i.e. who was 60 or under on 5th July, 1948). Death grant is payable at half the normal rate on the death of a man born between 5th July, 1883 and 4th July, 1893, or on the death of a woman born between 5th July, 1888 and 4th July, 1898. Death grant is not payable only on the death of a contributor. It may be payable

1. on the death of a male contributor, his wife, his child or his widow,
2. on the death of a female contributor, her husband, her child or her widower,
3. on the death of a handicapped person who has never been able to work (in which case the grant will be paid on the contribution record of any near relative with whom the deceased was living or would have been living but for his or her admission to a handicapped person's home).

In the case of the death of a child, the grant is normally payable on the contributions of the father or mother, but may be payable on some other person's contributions if that person was entitled to child benefit for the child at the time of the death.

The person on whose contribution record the death grant is claimed must have

1. paid, or been credited with, at least 25 contributions of any Class at any time between 5th July, 1948 (or the date of entry into insurance, if later) and 5th April, 1975 (or the date on which he or she reached normal retirement age or died, whichever is the earlier date), or
2. paid since 6th April, 1975 contributions in any one tax year (before the end of the claim) on earnings of at least 25 times the lower earnings limit.

In the case of the death of a person between 16 and 20 who does not satisfy either of the contribution conditions, death grant may be payable if at any time during the tax year in which he or she died, or during the previous tax year, he or she was under 19 and still at school or other full-time education (or would have been but for illness), or under 19 and unable to work because of illness or disability.

The purpose of death grant is primarily to cover the cost of funeral expenses and thus the grant will normally be paid to the person who has paid or who is responsible for those expenses. Thus, the grant is normally payable

1. to the executor or administrator who takes out a Grant of Representation, or
2. to the person who has paid the funeral expenses if there is no executor or administrator, or
3. if the funeral expenses have not been paid, to any person or institution who accepts the responsibility for the funeral expenses, or
4. to the next of kin if, for any reason, there is no funeral or if the funeral costs have been met by a burial society or for example the armed services.

In the case of death abroad, the grant will normally be payable if

1. the death occurred in another EEC country, or
2. the death occurred in Austria, Cyprus, Jamaica, Jersey or Guernsey, Norway, Portugal, Spain, Turkey or Yugoslavia, or
3. the death occurred in any other country and the deceased was receiving a national insurance benefit from the UK at the time of his death, or was ordinarily resident in Great Britain and died within 13 weeks of going abroad.

Death grant is not subject to income tax or capital transfer tax.

DEATH OF ACCEPTOR Where an acceptor is dead and no place of payment is specified, presentment (of a bill) must be made to a personal representative, if such there be, and if with the exercise of reasonable diligence he can be found. If he cannot be found, it should be presented at the house of the deceased.

The death of the acceptor cancels a banker's authority to pay a bill accepted by him, and any bill falling due after his death must be returned with answer 'acceptor deceased'.

A banker's authority to pay acceptances is revoked by his customer's death, but if, without notice of such death, he pays an acceptance, he can claim against the customer's estate for the amount, or, it would seem, reimburse himself out of the funds of the customer in his hands. [*Rogerson* v *Ladbrooke* [1822] 1 Bing 93]

DEATH OF ADMINISTRATOR On the death of an administrator the surviving administrator, if any, acts, but, on the death of the only or last one, fresh letters of administration require to be taken out, and a new bank account should be opened by the new administrator. SEE *Administrator De Bonis Non*

DEATH OF AGENT An agency contract is terminated by the death of the agent. Where, however, a cheque is signed by an agent or a person in an official capacity, payment should not be refused merely because the agent or official has died since the cheque was issued. For example, if Jones has authority to draw cheques upon Brown's account, a cheque so drawn should be paid, although Jones may have died before its presentation. Cheques signed by a secretary, treasurer, director, manager or other person signing in an official capacity must also be paid, irrespective of the death of the official before presentation.

DEATH OF BANK CUSTOMER A banker may receive formal notice of a customer's death, but it is sufficient notice of the death if he sees an announcement in the papers or hears of it from a reliable source. A mere rumour that his customer John Brown is supposed to be dead is not sufficient to warrant a banker returning a bill or cheque unpaid, though a banker in that case would usually take steps to confirm or disprove the rumour.

After notice of death, no further debits should be passed to the account, except where a banker has, prior to the death, made himself responsible, e.g. by marking a cheque for payment at the request of the drawer, or another bank, or by making a purchase of stock or shares according to the customer's order.

If the deceased customer leaves a will appointing executors, the executors can, after probate has been obtained and exhibited to the banker, deal with the account and securities of the deceased, subject to any claims by the banker.

Where there is no executor by reason of intestacy or otherwise, letters of administration must be obtained, and, after exhibition thereof to the banker, the administrators can act in the same way as executors. If the estate is a very small one, bankers sometimes pay the small balance in their hands, without letters of administration, on receiving a satisfactory indemnity. SEE ALSO *Death of Drawer*

DEATH OF DRAWEE Where the drawee of a bill is dead, presentment may be made to his personal representative, although presentment is excused and the bill may be treated as dishonoured by non-acceptance (Bills of Exchange Act 1882, Section 41(1)(*c*) and (2)(*a*)).

DEATH OF DRAWER The authority of a banker to pay a cheque drawn on him by his customer is determined by notice of the customer's death (Section 75, Bills of Exchange Act 1882). All cheques received after notice of his death must be returned with answer 'drawer deceased', except in the case of a cheque which has been 'marked' for payment by a banker at the request of the drawer. Such a cheque may be paid when presented, even though the drawer has died since the cheque was marked, as the 'marking' was, to all intents and purposes, a payment of the cheque (SEE *Marked Cheque*). Where a customer dies before settlement of a purchase of stock or shares effected by the banker on the customer's instructions, the account may be debited with the cost.

The notice of death does not affect any cheques which may have been debited to the deceased's account after his death, but prior to the time when the banker first heard of it. If a cheque is received in the morning's clearing and, before it is actually debited to the drawer's account, notice of his death is received, the cheque should be returned.

Before any transfer of the credit balance of the deceased's account can take place, probate or letters of administration must be exhibited. SEE *Death of Bank Customer*

Any cheques signed by the deceased in an official capacity, as treasurer, secretary, agent, director, etc., are not affected by his death.

If he has signed a cheque along with others on a joint credit account, the cheque would be paid, but if he signed alone upon the joint account it should not be paid. If the joint account is overdrawn, or the payment of the cheque would overdraw it, the banker should not pay it (if signed by the deceased with another of the joint holders), unless arrangements were made with the other drawer. On a joint account, only the survivors are responsible at common law for any overdraft. Joint and several liability is invariably imposed, however, by the terms of the mandate signed when the account is opened. SEE *Death of Joint Bank Customer*

Where the drawer of a bill is dead, and a party requiring to give notice of dishonour knows of it, the notice must be given to a personal representative if such there be, and with the exercise of reasonable diligence he can be found.

The death of AB, who has given CD a mandate to sign on his account, cancels the mandate, and the banker will, after receipt of notice of AB's death, return all cheques signed by CD under the mandate, with answer 'AB deceased' or 'customer deceased'.

DEATH OF EXECUTOR Upon the death of one executor the surviving executor, if there is one, continues to act. If the last executor is dead, his duties are undertaken by *his* executors, unless there is some special provision in the Will. In the event of the last executor dying intestate, letters of administration for the estate for which the deceased was executor must be taken out. SEE *Administrator De Bonis Non*

If, when probate was granted, power was reserved to another person to prove, the executors of the last surviving acting executor should not act unless the person to whom power was reserved is dead or has renounced probate.

When a cheque is signed by two, or more, executors, the death of one of them does not affect the payment of the cheque when presented, unless the account is overdrawn and the executors are personally liable.

By the Administration of Estates Act 1925, an executor of a sole or last surviving executor of a testator is the executor of that testator. So long as the chain of such representation is unbroken, the last executor in the chain is the executor of every preceding testator. The chain is broken by an intestacy, or failure of a testator to appoint an executor, or failure to obtain probate of a will.

DEATH OF GUARANTOR On receipt of notice of the death of a guarantor (whether sole guarantor or one of several) the banker will, if he is relying upon that surety (unless the guarantee provides that it shall not be determined by death), at once stop the account and open a fresh one for all further transactions. If the guarantee was to secure the customer's general indebtedness, all the customer's accounts, if he has more than one account, should be broken, credit as well as debit. (See the case of *Bradford Old Bank* v *Sutcliffe* under *Clayton's Case*.) This prevents the payments to credit from extinguishing the guarantor's liability. If the account is not stopped, all fresh debits will be unsecured. The personal representatives of the deceased guarantor should be advised of the position and of the terms under which the guarantee can be determined, if notice is required. SEE *Guarantee*

DEATH OF HOLDER Upon the death of the holder of a bill or cheque, all his rights are transmitted to his executor or administrator, and the executor or administrator, can sue upon the bill, or cheque, and negotiate it in the same way that the holder himself could have done. When an executor, or an administrator, indorses a bill or cheque, he should state the capacity in which he signs, otherwise he may render himself personally liable.

An indorsement by an executor or administrator should be confirmed by his banker.

If a cheque is payable to two persons and one of them dies, the cheque is payable to the surviving holder, after satisfactory evidence has been produced of the death of the other.

DEATH OF INDORSER Where an indorser is dead and the party requiring to give notice of dishonour knows of it, the notice must be given to a person representative, if he can be found.

DEATH OF INFANT SEE *Death of Minor*

DEATH OF INSOLVENT PERSON By the Administration of Estates Act 1925, where the estate of a deceased person is insolvent, his real and personal estate shall be administered in accordance with the following rules as to payment of debts (Section 34(1), and Rules in Part 1 of Schedule 1)

(1) The funeral, testamentary, and administration expenses have priority.

(2) Subject as aforesaid, the same rules shall prevail and be observed as to the respective rights of secured and unsecured creditors and as to debts and liabilities provable, and as to the valuation of annuities and future and contingent liabilities respectively, and as to the priorities of debts and liabilities as may be in force for the time being under the law of bankruptcy with respect to the assets of persons adjudged bankrupt.

DEATH OF JOINT BANK CUSTOMER Where an account is opened in the names of John Brown and John Jones, and Brown dies, Jones may withdraw the balance, but the banker would require proof of Brown's death, e.g. the death certificate.

This procedure is justified by the law relating to joint debts, which enables the survivor of two joint creditors to give a discharge for any balance due. It is customary in a mandate for a joint account to find a clause that the account is 'with benefit to survivor'. This is not so much an agreement between the parties as an admission that this is the law on the subject. There is an exception to this general rule, however, in the case of husband and wife.

Where an account is in the joint names of a husband and wife, when the wife dies the balance may be withdrawn by the husband if the account had been fed by him. If the husband dies first, the wife has power to draw a cheque for the balance, if it was the husband's intention that the money should be hers at his death. But if that was not the husband's intention, there appears to be some doubt as to whether the wife may draw the balance. In a case (*Marshal* v *Crutwell* [1875] LR 20 Eq 328) where the husband transferred his account into the names of himself and wife, with authority for either to sign cheques thereon, Sir George Jessel said

I think, the circumstances show that this was a mere arrangement for convenience, and that it was not intended to be a provision for the wife in the event which might happen, that at the husband's death there might be a fund standing to the credit of the banking account .... I come to the conclusion that it was not intended to be a provision for the wife, but simply a mode of conveniently managing the testator's affairs, and that it leaves the money, therefore, still his property

To prevent any question arising at the death of the husband, a banker should always have a clear arrangement made with the customers when such accounts are opened, as to whether or not the balance is to belong to the survivor. There seems little doubt that a bank is safe in paying over the balance of a joint account to the survivor if the mandate is in the normal form and has been observed and if the bank is without notice that the balance does not belong to the survivor.

If the personal representatives of a deceased joint account holder make claim to the balance, they will usually be informed that their remedy against the banker paying away the balance to the survivor(s) is by way of injunction. If an action were threatened, the banker would interplead.

Where both, or all, the joint holders are dead, the balance is repayable to the legal representatives of the one who died last. A cheque on a joint account drawn by one of the parties, under authority, prior to his death, should not be paid, if notice of death has been received. But if a cheque is signed by all the joint parties, and one has died, the cheque may be paid, as the money belongs to the survivors.

A mandate is terminated by the death of the person, or one of the persons, who gave it and cheques drawn thereunder and presented after notice of the death should not be paid.

In the case of a joint account which is overdrawn, the estate of the deceased is not, in the ordinary way, legally liable for the debt. It has been held that, where a cheque was signed by the three parties to a joint account and one of them died, the survivors only were liable and not the estate of the deceased. The usual form of mandate taken on the opening of a joint account provides for joint and several liability, and provided a debit account is broken the estate of the deceased joint account-holder will be liable.

In the case of articles which are left for safe custody in joint names, upon the death of one of the depositors, the articles should not be given up except on the signatures of the survivor and of the executor, or administrator of the deceased unless otherwise provided for in the form of mandate. SEE *Joint Account: Set-Off*

DEATH OF JOINT DEPOSITOR SEE *Death of Joint Bank Customer*

DEATH OF JOINT SHAREHOLDER Upon the death of one, the survivor becomes sole owner. Proof of death is required.

DEATH OF JOINT TENANT The interest of a deceased person under a joint tenancy where another tenant survives the deceased is an interest ceasing on his death (Administration of Estates Act 1925, Section 3(4)). The effect of this is that the legal title passes to the survivor or survivors, but the estate of the deceased joint tenant may be entitled to a beneficial interest in the property, depending on the terms of the joint tenancy. If the joint tenants held the property for themselves as beneficial tenants in common, the beneficial interest of the deceased joint tenant will pass to his or her estate. SEE *Joint Tenants*

DEATH OF MINOR A person under the age of 18 cannot make a valid will (except in the case of a soldier, sailor or airman on active service), so that on the death of a person under that age leaving personal estate, it is necessary for a grant of letters of administration to be taken out.

DEATH OF PARTNER Subject to any agreement between the partners, every partnership is dissolved as regards all the partners by the death of any partner. (See Section 33, Partnership Act 1890, under *Partnerships.*) The death of a limited partner does not dissolve the partnership.

The estate of a partner who dies is not liable for partnership debts contracted after the date of the death (Section 36), but may be indirectly affected by a valid pledge of the assets by the surviving partner(s) for the purpose of continuing the business before winding up the old partnership.

If the firm's account is overdrawn and the banker desires to retain his claim against the estate of the deceased partner, or if securities belonging to the deceased partner are held for the firm's account, the account should be stopped and a new one opened for future transactions, otherwise, according to the rule in Clayton's Case (q.v.), all sums paid to credit will release the deceased's estate to the amount of such credits, and all debits will form a fresh debt against the new partnership. This rule commences to apply from the actual date of death, even though the banker is quite unaware that the death has taken place. In such a case, the banker should, as soon as he knows of the death, alter the account as from the date of death so as to avoid the operation of the rule unless the statement has already been written up and delivered to the customers. Where the deceased partner is not relied upon, the account may be continued unbroken. If it is apparent that the survivors are continuing the business, i.e. that a new firm is created, enquiries should in due course be made as to the proposals for discharging the claims of the dead partner's estate. By Section 43 of the Partnership Act, the amount due from surviving or continuing partners to the representatives of a deceased partner in respect of the deceased partner's share is a debt accruing at the date of the death. It is not uncommon to find provision in the Articles of Partnership for the deceased partner's interest to remain as a loan in the firm.

On the death of a partner, the account should also be broken where a guarantee is held from a third party, until fresh arrangements are made with the firm and with the guarantor, unless the guarantee specially provides that it shall not be affected by any change in the partnership. (See Section 18, Partnership Act 1890, under *Partnerships.*)

If the firm's account is in credit, the banker need not break the account, though the surviving partners may, for their own convenience, desire to open a new account. When that is done and the balance has to be transferred, it should be drawn by cheque. Usually, however, the old account is simply continued with the name of the deceased partner dropped out of the account heading. The surviving partners have power to deal with any balance on the partnership account.

Cheques signed by a partner on the firm's account, and not presented for payment till after his death, should be paid, unless the account is overdrawn and his estate is to be held liable, in which case the cheques should be returned 'partner deceased'. The continuing partners may, however, give the banker written authority to charge any outstanding cheques to their new account. SEE *Partnerships*

DEATH OF PAYEE SEE *Death of Holder*

DEATH OF PRINCIPAL The death of a principal under a contract of agency automatically terminates the agency. Bankers and others dealing with agents can no longer act on the agent's authority, therefore, when they receive notice of the principal's death. SEE ALSO *Power of Attorney*

DEATH OF SHAREHOLDER On the death of a shareholder, the shares become part of the deceased's estate and may be dealt with by the executor or the administrator. An executor is entitled to receive the dividends without the shares being transferred into his name. Many companies require administrators or executors to transfer the shares of the deceased shareholder into their own names, unless they intend to sell the shares at an early date.

By Section 183(3), Companies Act 1985

A transfer of the share or other interest of a deceased member of a company made by his personal representative, although the personal representative is not himself a member of the company, is as valid as if he had been such a member at the time of the execution of the instrument of transfer.

Upon production of probate or letters of administration to a company, the certificate is indorsed with the names of the personal representatives. When personal representatives are registered as members, a new certificate is issued.

In the case of shares carrying an uncalled liability, the executor is not personally liable upon the shares of the deceased merely because he receives the dividends thereon, or is noted in the register as the executor of the deceased. If, however, the shares are transferred into the executor's name, he is liable for any calls there may be, though if he has become registered on behalf of the deceased's estate he may look to the estate to refund any payment. SEE *Death of Joint Shareholder; Transmission of Shares*

DEATH OF SURETY Where title deeds, or certificates, or other securities, are deposited with a banker by one person to secure an overdraft to another person, upon the death of the party giving the security, the account of the debtor should be stopped and arrangements made for a new account to be opened for future transactions. If this is not done, all credits to the account will release the security to the extent of the amounts paid in, and all fresh debits will be unsecured. The new account should be kept in credit till a fresh arrangement is made. If shares have been transferred to the banker and registered in his name, the same rules apply, because the transfer was given merely as a security.

Most bankers' forms of guarantee provide for three months' notice from the personal representative, which probably protects the banker who carries on the account after he has received notice of the death of the surety. However, the practice of stopping the account is preferable and is the usual policy. SEE ALSO *Death of Guarantor*

DEATH OF A TRUSTEE Section 18 of the Trustee Act 1925 provides

(1) Where a power or trust is given to or imposed on two or more trustees jointly, the same may be exercised or performed by the survivor or survivors of them for the time being.

(2) Until the appointment of new trustees, the personal representatives or representative for the time being of a sole trustee, or, where there were two or more trustees, of the last surviving or continuing trustee, shall be capable of exercising or performing any power or trust which was given to, or capable of being exercised by, the sole or last surviving or continuing trustee, or other the trustees or trustee for the time being of the trust.

(3) This Section takes effect subject to the restrictions imposed in regard to receipts by a sole trustee, not being a trust corporation. [SEE UNDER *Trustee*]

The above powers apply if and so far only as a contrary intention is not expressed in the instrument, if any, creating the trust (Section 29(2)).

DEBENTURE Derived from the Latin *debeo*, I ower. A debenture is an acknowledgment of indebtedness. It is usually given by an incorporated company, but may be given by anyone. It is usually given under seal, but can be given under hand. There is no statutory definition of a debenture in the Companies Act or anywhere else. A debenture is usually accompanied by a charge on the assets of the borrower (a mortgage debenture), but it may be a simple acknowledgment of a debt, in which case it is called a 'naked' debenture—rarely, if ever, met with in practice.

Debentures usually bear a specified rate of interest which is payable whether the company makes profits or not; sometimes income debentures are issued which stipulate that interest is only payable out of profits. Sometimes guaranteed debentures are issued wherein the payment of interest is guaranteed by another company.

Debentures are usually expressed to be transferable free from equities, that is, the company cannot as against a holder set off any debt due to it by the transferor; unless transfer free from equities is acknowledged in the instrument, the debenture is subject to equities, i.e. subject to any claim that the company may have against the transferor.

Debentures may be payable to bearer or may be in registered form and then the mode of transfer is specified in the instrument. Bearer debentures are recognized by the courts as being negotiable instruments transferable by delivery (*Bechuanaland Exploration Co.* v *London Trading Bank* [1898] 2 QB 658: *Edelstein* v *Schuler & Co.* [1902] 2 KB 145).

Debentures may be issued at a discount or at a premium or at par. This, together with the rate of interest offered, is an index of the company's credit. Sometimes, where a fixed charge is given on the company's assets, a trust deed is executed by the company whereby such specific assets are held by designated trustees in trust for the debenture holders. SEE *Debenture Trusts*

Debentures may be issued for one lump sum or in a series of, say, £100 each, in which each one of the series is expressed to rank *pari passu* with the others.

Debenture stock differs from debentures in that it is transferable in odd amounts and not in round sums. Usually the assets hypothecated to the service of debenture stock are the subject of a trust deed in favour of the stockholders.

Debentures may be redeemable at a stipulated time or after a certain period of notice, and it should be noted whether the company is under an obligation to redeem at the appointed time or whether it has merely the option to redeem.

Debentures may be perpetual or irredeemable, that is to say there is no date at which they are repayable, and unless the company defaults, the holder has no rights as regards principal against the company.

Debentures containing a charge on the company's assets require to be delivered for registration with the Registrar of Companies at Companies House within 21 days of their creation. Where a series of debentures containing or giving by reference to any other instrument any charge to the benefit of the debenture holders is created by a company, the required particulars must be delivered to the Registrar within 21 days after the execution of the deed containing the charge, together with the deed, or if there is no such deed, one of the debentures. The Registrar shall give a certificate of the registration of any such charge and the Company must indorse a copy thereof on every debenture or certificate of debenture stock (Companies Act 1985, Sections 401 and 402). In addition, a company must enter a debenture containing a charge on its own register of charges (Section 406).

A debenture issued by an industrial and provident society giving a charge on chattels, etc., requires registration as a bill of sale (*In re North Wales Produce & Supply Society Ltd* [1922] 2 Ch 340).

By Section 191 the company's own register of holders of debentures shall be open to the inspection of any debenture holder or shareholders of the company without fee and such holder may require a copy, or part of a copy, of the register on payment of a fee.

Where a debenture gives a fixed charge, the company, like any other mortgagor, cannot deal with the assets so charged and subsequent lenders cannot jeopardize the debenture holders' security. But where a floating charge is given, the company is at liberty to deal with the assets so covered as it pleases; indeed this is one of the advantages attaching to an incorporated company that it can charge its chattels and book debts without the necessity of a bill of sale or assignment. Likewise the company can create fixed charges subsequently, to take priority over the floating charge.

But usually a debenture giving a floating charge contains a proviso such as this:

> The debentures of the said series are all to rank *pari passu* as a first charge on the property hereby charged without any preference or priority over one another and such charge is to be a floating security, but so that the company is not to be at liberty to create any mortgage or charge on its undertaking *pari passu* with or in priority to the said debentures.

If a lender subsequently obtains a charge on a specific asset and has notice of such a condition his charge will be postponed to the floating charge, but without notice he will get priority. To ensure that such a floating charge will not be jeopardized in such a manner, it is desirable to include in the particulars of the floating charge registered at Companies House the clause above referred to; it is thought that this registration will then be notice to all the world.

As to the invalidity of a floating charge given within 12 months of a company's liquidation see *Floating Charge*.

By Section 194 of the Companies Act 1985, a company may re-issue redeemed debentures unless any provision to the contrary is contained in the Articles or other contract or unless the company has, by passing a resolution to that effect or by some other act, manifested its intention that the debentures shall be cancelled. On such a re-issue the holder will get the priorities that originally attached to the debentures. Particulars of debentures capable of such reissue must be given in a company's balance sheet. A lender should insist on such debentures being cancelled.

Debentures given to secure advances from time to time on current account or otherwise are not redeemed merely because the account goes into credit.

Default in payment of interest and/or principal will give the debenture holder the right

1. to sue the company for the amount due;
2. to apply to the Court for an order for foreclosure or for sale;
3. to appoint a receiver.

If there is a trust deed, the trustee may take possession of the assets charged and sell them for the benefit of the debenture holders. SEE ALSO UNDER *Receiver for Debenture Holders*

DEBENTURE (BANK) These are of two main types—fixed sum debentures and 'all moneys' debentures. A fixed sum debenture will either be a single instrument or a series of debentures making up the total sum lent. The advantage of this type over an 'all moneys' debenture is that where there is to be a transfer of the debenture rather than the sale of assets charged it can be effected for a fixed sum without stopping the running account.

It is considered that a fixed sum debenture might be looked upon as an investment by the bank, thus limiting the bank's right to that of an ordinary debenture holder. This might mean that the bank would be unable to sue on the banking account as opposed to the debenture. Hence it is customary to have the debenture accompanied by a form of agreement linking it up with the banking account and making it available for a fluctuating advance by way of loan or overdraft. The agreement provides that the debenture shall be held as a continuing security for all moneys owing now or in the future; it provides for interest at the banker's usual fluctuating rate, as opposed to the fixed rate that may be containing in the debenture; it gives the bank an express power of sale over the debenture.

An 'all moneys' debenture probably appeals more to a company than a fixed debenture plus a memorandum agreement, because it is more flexible if facilities are to be increased. The registration of a fixed sum debenture means publishing a figure which may never be reached, with detrimental effect on the company's creditors. An 'all moneys' debenture will suffice if increased advances are required, whereas with a fixed sum debenture increases over the amount inserted means a further debenture and agreement.

Practice differs among banks as to the type of debenture used; some banks have a standard printed form whilst others have a debenture drafted to meet the particular circumstances. In any case the main contents are as follows: reference will be made to the resolution of the company or directors authorizing the debenture; it will be drawn in favour of the bank or its nominee company or sometimes it is drawn in blank; it will be expressed to be payable on demand and interest will be stipulated for at a fixed rate or a fluctuating rate with quarterly or half-yearly rests. Then the company charges as security all its undertaking and property present and future, including its uncalled capital. This is followed by the conditions of issue, namely that the debentures shall be a first charge on the undertaking and property of the company and shall constitute a fixed charge on specific property listed in a schedule and also on any fixed machinery and plant, goodwill and uncalled capital. Such a charge, though specific, is equitable only and the bank gets none of the remedies of a legal mortgagee other than the power to appoint a receiver. Hence it is becoming customary to take a legal mortgage over the company's land and buildings by using the statutory formula of 'a charge by way of legal mortgage'. The company should in any case covenant to deposit the relative title deeds with the bank. Then will follow a floating charge on all the other assets, with a covenant not to create any further mortgages or charges to rank side by side with or in front of the bank's debenture. By including this covenant in the details registered at Companies House or by insisting on the debenture being authorized by special resolution (which requires registration), subsequent proposed lenders are warned. Finally, the conditions under which the moneys secured shall become payable are enumerated. They include written demand by the bank, default of the company with interest for, say, two months, the commencement of voluntary or compulsory winding up, cessation of business by the company, appointment of a receiver, and the alteration or attempted alteration of the company's memorandum and articles of association in a manner prejudicial to the bank. A right to inspect the company's books is desirable where a floating charge is given. Powers to appoint a receiver are taken and he is expressed to be the agent of the company and not of the bank so as to make the company responsible for his acts, default, and remuneration.

Where a banker takes a debenture from a newly incorporated company formed to acquire the assets of a sole trader or firm, he should ascertain that all the creditors of the old concern have been satisfied or have consented to the transfer of the assets to the newly incorporated company. Otherwise such transference may be used by an unsatisfied creditor as an act of bankruptcy in the shape of a fraudulent conveyance. If such creditor presents a petition within three months founded on this act of bankruptcy and a receiving order results, the trustee's title will relate back to the date of the transfer of the assets to the company and thus the debenture will be void. 'A transfer by a debtor of substantially the whole of his property, whether by way of charge or by way of sale, will be an act of bankruptcy if the necessary consequences of the transfer will be to defeat or delay his creditors.' (*In re Sims* [1930] 2 Ch 22.)

See under *Directors* the case of *Victors Ltd* v *Lingard*, with reference to the giving of a debenture by a company where a joint and several guarantee of the directors was already held SEE ALSO *Floating Charge; Receiver*

DEBENTURE HOLDER The person who holds a debenture or debenture stock. He may be either a registered holder, or a holder of a debenture payable to bearer. In the former case, a document of transfer is necessary to pass the ownership to another person, but in the latter case the debenture is transferable by simple delivery.

A debenture holder is a creditor of the company, as the debenture represents a loan to the company, and the interest thereon must be paid before any dividend is received by the shareholders. SEE *Debenture*

DEBENTURE STOCK Debenture stock is essentially the same as debentures, and both are usually secured by a charge or mortgage. Debentures, however, are for definite round sums, as separate debts, whereas certificates of debenture stock are for different amounts, as parts of one large debt.

When a certificate of debenture stock is given as security, a transfer from the registered holder to the bank's nominees, accompanied by a qualifying agreement, should be taken, and to make the security fully satisfactory, the transfer should be registered. SEE *Blank Transfer; Debenture; Share Capital; Transfer of Shares*

DEBENTURE TRUST When a company seeks to issue debenture or debenture stock, or even unsecured loan stock, it is customary to appoint a trustee to protect the interests of the debenture holders or stock-holders. The issue is normally constituted under a trust deed entered into between the company and the trustee. The powers and duties of the trustee will be set out in the deed. In general, it is the concern of the trustee to see that the obligations of the company are duly performed. The debentures or stock may carry a fixed charge over certain fixed assets, or a floating charge over the undertaking generally, or both. The trustee would normally hold the documents of title to any specifically charged assets and in some cases may be required to ensure that the floating assets of the undertaking are maintained at a stipulated level. If there is a sinking fund for the redemption of the debentures or stock, the trustee will be responsible for seeing that the fund is operated in accordance with the deed. The trustee may have a particularly active role where there are a number of dealings in the charged assets by way of sales, purchases, leases, etc. The security property can be released only with the consent of the trustee and such consent would also be necessary where, for any reason, it is proposed to reduce the value of the security property by the withdrawal of assets from behind the debentures or stock without replacement. The trustee will also be responsible for seeing that freehold and leasehold properties are properly insured and that all outgoings are duly met.

The trustee's role will be comparatively passive unless and until the security becomes enforceable, when some action will be necessary by the trustee, usually the appointment of a receiver, to protect the security property for the benefit of the debenture holders or stockholders. The trust deed will specify the circumstances in which the security shall become enforceable and these will normally include default in payment of principal or interest on the debentures or stock, the winding up of the company, the cessation of business or breaches of covenant by the company.

Debenture trusts are usually of long duration and call for trustees of standing and business experience. It is, therefore, more or less universal practice to appoint a trust corporation such as a bank or insurance company. The Public Trustee (q.v.) cannot act in this role.

It was not uncommon for a bank to accept debenture trusts in the prewar and immediate post-war years, but it became a matter for comment in the report of the Cohen Committee on company law amendment in 1945, which suggested that a conflict of interest might arise in cases where a bank was both the creditor of a company and trustee for the debenture holders. Following the Report, the Rules of the Stock Exchange were amended to provide that the trustee for the debenture holders of a listed company must not have an interest in relation to the company which might conflict with the trustee's role as such.

In more recent times, however, the Stock Exchange rule has been relaxed.

DEBTS, ASSIGNMENT OF A customer may assign to a banker any money which is due, or will be due, to him. This may be effected by an irrevocable letter signed by the customer, addressed to the person who owes him money, requesting that the debt be paid to the banker. The letter will be retained by the banker, who should give written notice at once to the debtor of the assignment, and ascertain from him if the debt is as stated, and if it is free from any prior charge. It is desirable to obtain an acknowledgment from the debtor. The banker should be able to prove that he sent the notice in case the debtor does not acknowledge it. In an equitable assignment of a debt 'all that is necessary is that the debtor should be given to understand that the debt has been made over by the creditor to some third person. If the debtor ignores such a notice he does so at his peril.' (*William Brandt's Sons & Co.* v *Dunlop Rubber Co.* [1905] AC 454.)

Although an assignment of a debt may take the form of an irrevocable order or a letter, the more satisfactory method is to have executed a mortgage assigning the debt absolutely, subject to the right of redemption, and notice should be given at once to the party owing the money. Until notice is given, the debtor may pay the debt direct to the assignor. A legal assignment must be absolute (not by way of charge only), must be in writing, and signed by the assignor. In order that the banker, as assignee, may not be held liable to the assignor for any loss which might arise from the banker's failure to enforce the necessary remedies for payment of the debt, there should be a clause in the deed to the effect that it shall not be incumbent on the banker to sue for the debt.

It was held that an assignment by way of mortgage made in the form of an absolute conveyance with a provision for redemption is an 'absolute assignment' (*Durham Bros.* v *Robertson* [1898] 1 QB 765), but it would now be considered a charge.

In the Court of Appeal (*Hughes* v *Pump House Hotel Co. Ltd* [1902] 2 KB 190] Mathew, L J said

> If, on consideration of the whole instrument, it is clear that the intention was to give a charge only, then the action must be in the name of the assignor; while, on the other hand, if it is clear from the instrument as a whole that the intention was to pass all the rights of the assignor in the debt or *chose in action* to the assignee, then the case will come within Section 136 [see below] and the action must be brought in the name of the assignee.

In this case an assignment of debts was given 'by way of continuing security'. It was held that the assignment was absolute and not by way of charge only.

The banker's right to the debt dates from the date of the notice (see Section 136 below), and until the notice has been given a subsequent assignee might, by giving notice, obtain priority to the banker; but an assignee cannot, by giving notice, obtain priority over a previous assignment if he knew of the former charge at the time when he obtained his own assignment. When notice has been given, it will, in the event of the bankruptcy of the assignor, prevent the debt passing to the Trustee in Bankruptcy under Section 38, Bankruptcy Act 1914. SEE *Reputed Owner*

By Section 136(1) of the Law of Property Act 1925 it is enacted as follows.

> Any absolute assignment, by writing under the hand of the assignor (not purporting to be by way of charge only), of any debt or other legal thing in action, of which express notice in writing has been given to the debtor, trustee, or other person from whom the assignor, would have been entitled to claim such debt or thing in action, is effectual in law (subject to equities having priority over the right of the assignee) to pass and transfer from the date of such notice, the legal right to such debt or thing in action, all legal and other remedies for the same, and the power to give a good discharge for the same, without the concurrence of the assignor: Provided that, if the debtor, trustee, or other person liable in respect of such debt or thing in action has notice that the assignment is disputed by the assignor or any person claiming under him, or of any other opposing or conflicting claims to such debt or thing in action, he may if he think fit, either call upon the persons making claim thereto to interplead concerning the same, or pay the debt or other thing in action into court under the provisions of the Trustee Act, 1925.

The notice required by the above subsection must be in writing. A verbal notice of the assignment is not sufficient (*Hockley and Papworth* v *Goldstein* (1921) 124 LT 277).

If the debtor at the time of the assignment has a counter claim against the assignor, the assignee will be entitled only to the balance of the debt after allowing for the counter claim. The banker should, therefore, before taking an assignment, ask the debtor if he has a counter claim and also, as mentioned above, ask what is the actual amount of the debt and whether there is any prior charge.

A cheque is not an assignment of money in favour of the payee, as the banker is liable only to the drawer; but if a customer formally assigns his balance to a third party and the banker receives notice thereof, his liability is then to the assignee. In Scotland, the presentment of a cheque attaches any balance there may be in the drawer's account to the extent of the cheque. SEE UNDER *Drawee*

A document which purports to transfer the property in goods as well as to assign the proceeds of their sale, constitutes a bill of sale and must be registered as such (*National Provincial and Union Bank of England* v *Lindsell* (1921) 66 Sol J 48). An assignment merely of the proceeds of a sale of goods does not require registration as a bill of sale (*Walker* v *Capital and Counties Bank and Others* (1910) *Times*, 16th December, 1910).

In *Bank of Liverpool & Martins Ltd* v *Holland* (1926) 43 TLR 29, the defendant owed £285 to W, who owed money to the plaintiff bank. W assigned to the bank the debt due to him by the defendant. Due notice of the assignment was given to the defendant. The assignment declared, 'that the amount recoverable under these presents shall not at any time exceed the sum of £150'. Wright, J, in his judgment, said that even if it was an assignment of only part of the debt it would still be a good equitable assignment, but in his view it was not an assignment of part of the debt but was an absolute assignment to the bank of the whole debt with a proviso that if the bank should recover more than £150 from the debtor, they must hold the balance in excess of £150 as trustees for the assignor. The assignment was held to be a good legal assignment and judgment was given for the bank.

When a company assigns to a bank as security a

book debt due to the company, the assignment must be registered under Section 395 of the Companies Act 1985. SEE *Registration of Charges*

An irrevocable authority is an equitable assignment (See *re Kent and Sussex Sawmills Ltd* [1947] Ch 177).

As to a general assignment of book debts, Section 43, Bankruptcy Act 1914, provides

(1) Where a person engaged in any trade or business makes an assignment to any other person of his existing or future book debts or any class thereof, and is subsequently adjudicated bankrupt, the assignment shall be void against the trustee as regards any book debts which have not been paid at the commencement of the bankruptcy, unless the assignment has been registered as if the assignment were a bill of sale given otherwise than by way of security for the payment of a sum of money, and the provisions of the Bills of Sale Act, 1878, with respect to the registration of bills of sale shall apply accordingly, subject to such necessary modifications as may be made by rules under that Act;

Provided that nothing in this Section shall have effect so as to render void any assignment of books debts due at the date of the assignment from specified debtors, or of debts growing due under specified contracts, or any assignment of book debts included in a transfer of a business made bona fide and for value, or in any assignment of assets for the benefit of creditors generally.

(2) For the purposes of this Section, 'assignment' includes assignment by way of security and other charges on book debts.

Under Section 136 of the Law of Property Act, a customer may assign to a third party any balance on his current account or deposit account, or the amount of a deposit receipt. On receipt of notice of the assignment the account should be 'stopped'. See further as to an assignment of a debt to a banker under *Transfer of Mortgage*. An assignment is subject to *ad valorem* conveyance duty if on sale or in consideration *pro tanto* of any debt under Section 57 of the Stamp Act 1891 (Alpe's *Law of Stamp Duties*). SEE *Registration of Charges*

DECIMAL COINAGE The change to a decimal currency had been advocated in various quarters for many years. The first practical step was the introduction of the florin—one-tenth of a pound. Many years later a special meeting of the Council of the Institute of Bankers, held on 2nd May, 1917, adopted the report of a committee appointed to enquire into the adoption of decimal coinage, and the metric system of weights and measures. The following is from the report:

Your Committee are of opinion that the existing system of weights and measures in this country is an obstacle in the way of the extension of our foreign trade, and more especially of our export trade.

Your Committee are convinced that no decimal system of coinage which is not based on the pound sterling can possibly be accepted by the bankers of this country .... The pound sterling is universally recognised in the settlement of international transactions throughout the world, and any abandonment, even in name only, of its use as our standard unit, could be fraught with risks which your Committee consider it would be unwise to incur.

The decimal system then recommended was based on the gold sovereign. For the next 40 years the question was kept under discussion, but it was undoubtedly the decision to apply for membership of the Common Market which finally impelled the Government to commit themselves to a policy of change. On 19th December, 1961, the Chancellor of the Exchequer announced in Parliament that the Government had accepted in principle the introduction of a decimal currency.

Discussion on the value of the major unit was then rekindled. Australia, New Zealand and South Africa had all decided to adopt a major unit to the value of the old ten shillings. The units were renamed dollars, dollars and rands respectively. When divided into one hundred parts the smallest coin became worth 1.2d. However in the UK, as the result of the report of a special committee in 1963 the decision was taken to retain the pound as the major unit, subdivided into 100 minor units—'new pence', as they were later named—with three new coins being introduced, 2p, 1p and ½p, the corresponding values being 4.8d, 2.4d and 1.2d. The reintroduction of a half-penny was the main criticism against this system. The old halfpenny was withdrawn from circulation in August 1969. It was considered that to have had the smallest coin, 1p, of the equivalent of 2.4d, would have proved inflationary. The banks decided to work, as they had done previously, for bookkeeping purposes, in whole pence.

Following the Decimal Currency Act 1967, the Mint began to issue 10p pieces and 5p pieces of the same size and weight as the old cupro-nickel two shillings and one shilling pieces respectively. The obverse was similar to the old coins with a new, slightly larger portrait of the Queen and smaller lettering. The reverse was redesigned and included the inscription 10 new pence and 5 new pence. The token values remained the same.

The half-crown, which would have been an awkward 12½p, was demonetized from 1st January, 1970. A new coin, the 50 pence piece, of radical design—an equilateral, curved heptagon in cupro-nickel without milled edges—entered general circulation 14th October, 1970. It replaced the ten shilling note, and has an expected life of 50 years as against the note's five to six months.

Detailed provisions for the change-over were set out in the Decimal Currency Act 1969. The appointed day was 15th February, 1971.

The banks arranged for all their branches to have a sufficient supply of the three new bronze coins for issuing for circulation for the first time on 15th February, 1971. They closed their doors at 3.30 p.m. on 10th February, and did not open again until 9.30 a.m. on 15th February, 1971. This gave sufficient time to clear all the cheques drawn in £ s d, to convert all accounting machines and to convert all balances to decimal mode.

Shopkeepers and others needing the three new bronze coins for change had been permitted to draw sufficient from the banks before 15th February, 1971, for their use. A majority of shops commenced trading that Monday morning in the new style and had converted their prices to decimal mode. They accepted the old pennies and threepenny pieces but gave change in the new coinage. These two old coins were paid into the banks in large quantities during the remainder of February and, three months later they had virtually ceased to circulate.

The immense amount of planning, preparation and publicity that took place before Decimal Day enabled the change-over to be made smoothly.

Since decimal currency was introduced, only two new denominations of coins have been introduced, namely, the 20 pence coin and the one pound coin.

The extract below is from Schedule 1 of the Decimal Currency Act 1967, covering the denominations, weight, diameter and composition of the new coins.

1 Metal and denomination	2 Standard weight grams	3 Standard diameter cm	4 Standard composition	5 Weight variation grams
Cupro-nickel				
Ten new pence	11.31036	2.8500	Three-quarters copper, one-quarter nickel	0.0646
Five new pence	5.65518	2.3595		0.0375
Bronze				
Two new pence	7.12800	2.5910	Mixed metal copper, tin and zinc	0.1500
New penny	3.56400	2.0320		0.0750
New halfpenny	1.78200	1.7145		0.0375

It will be noticed that the new bronze coins are weight and value related, i.e. one two pence piece weighs the same as two pennies and four halfpennies.

The Decimal Currency Act 1969, enacted, *inter alia*

1.—(1) Coins made by the Mint in accordance with Section 2 of the Decimal Currency Act, 1967, or in accordance with the Coinage Acts, 1870 to 1946, and not called in by proclamation under paragraph (5) of Section 11 of the Coinage Act, 1870, shall be legal tender as follows, that is to say—

(*a*) coins of cupro-nickel or silver of denominations of more than ten new pence or two shillings, for payment of any amount not exceeding ten pounds;

(*b*) coins of cupro-nickel or silver of denominations of not more than ten new pence or two shillings, for payment of any amount not exceeding five pounds;

(*c*) coins of bronze, for payment of any amount not exceeding twenty new pence or four shillings.

(2) In the foregoing subsection 'coins of bronze' includes threepences of mixed metal.

(3) Subject to subsection (6) of this Section and to any direction given by virtue of Section 15(5) of this Act, coins of the old currency other than gold coins shall not be legal tender after the end of the transitional period.

(4) For the purpose of being used for any payment in accordance with the foregoing provisions of this section a coin of either the old or the new currency may be treated as being a current coin of the other currency of equal value.

(5) The powers exercisable by proclamation by virtue of Section 11 of the Coinage Act, 1870, shall include power to direct that any coins of the new currency made by the Mint in accordance with Section 2 of the Decimal Currency Act, 1967, other than coins of cupro-nickel, silver or bronze shall be current and be legal tender for payment of any amount not exceeding such amount (not greater than ten pounds) as may be specified in the proclamation.

(6) For the purposes of this section silver coins of the Queen's Maundy money made in accordance with Section 3 of the Coinage Act, 1870, shall be treated as made in accordance with Section 2 of the Decimal Currency Act, 1967, and, if issued before the appointed day, shall be treated as denominated in the same number of new pence as the number of pence in which they were denominated.

2.—(1) A bill of exchange or promissory note drawn or made on or after the appointed day shall be invalid if the sum payable is an amount of money wholly or partly in shillings or pence.

(2) A bill of exchange or promissory note for an amount wholly or partly in shillings or pence dated 15th February, 1971, or later shall be deemed to have been drawn or made before 15th February, 1971, if it bears a certificate in writing by a banker that it was so drawn or made.

3.—(1) On and after the appointed day any reference to an amount of money in the old currency contained in an instrument to which this section applies shall, in so far as it refers to an amount in shillings or pence, be read as referring to the corresponding amount in the new currency calculated in accordance with the provisions of Schedule 1 to this Act.

(2) If a reference to an amount of money in the old currency contained in an instrument to which this section applies is altered so as to make it read as it would otherwise fall to be read in accordance with subsection (1) of this Section, the alteration shall not affect the validity of the instrument and, in the case of a bill of exchange or promissory note, shall not be treated as a material alteration for the purposes of Section 64 of the Bills of Exchange Act, 1882.

SEE *Coins, Coinage*

DECREASING TERM ASSURANCE A type of term assurance (SEE *Life Assurance*) under which the sum assured decreases over the period of the assurance, usually to coincide with some diminishing obligation of the life assured. SEE ALSO *Mortgage Protection Policy*

DEED A deed is a document in writing, or printing, on paper or parchment, which is signed, sealed and delivered by the parties thereto. The fact of a document being under seal does not necessarily constitute it a deed, e.g. a will under seal and a certificate of shares under the seal of a company are not deeds. An instrument is a deed when it is sealed and delivered as a deed.

Deeds are now signed and sealed, though at one time it was sufficient if they were merely sealed and delivered. When illiteracy was more common, the sealing of a document with a private seal would be of the first importance, but now that nearly all persons can write, the signature to a deed is the principal matter, the seal being merely a formality. The deed must be sealed, but it is no longer necessary that it should be the seal of the person who is sealing. It may be the seal of anyone, or a drop of wax, or simply a red wafer. The seals may be put on a deed before the parties sign, and touching a seal with the finger at the time of signing has the effect of sealing. There must be a separate seal for each person.

It is usual nowadays for blank deeds to bear a printed circle in which is printed the letters *l.s.* (*locus sigillii*). In the case of *First National Securities Ltd* v *Jones* [1978] 2 WLR 475, a mortgagor had signed his name across such a printed circle and the document was inscribed 'signed, sealed and delivered by the above-named mortgagor in the presence of ...'. The document was attested by a witness but bore no seal, wafer or other impression. It was held by the Court of Appeal that the printed circle and the letters *l.s.*, the signature across the circle and the wording of the attestation clause amounted to sufficient evidence that the document was a deed.

If a deed is read over to a person who cannot read, the attestation clause should be 'signed, sealed and delivered by the said John Brown, the document having first been read over to him when he appeared fully to understand the same'.

In addition to being signed and sealed, a deed must be delivered, and this is usually accomplished by the party placing a finger on the seal and saying, 'I deliver this as my act and deed'. A deed takes effect from the date of delivery. It is not necessarily an essential part of a deed that there should be a date upon it. The date of execution can be proved. SEE *Date of Deed*

A special note in the attestation clause of any material alteration or erasure in the deed should be made at the time the deed is signed and witnessed.

It is customary for a deed to be witnessed, but the absence of the attestation by a witness does not invalidate it.

There are two kinds of deeds, an indenture (q.v.), which is made between two or more parties, and a deed poll (q.v.), which is made by only one person, or by more than one if their interests are the same.

Blackstone says it is called a deed

> 'because it is the most solemn and authentic act that a man can possibly perform with relation to the disposal of his property; and therefore a man shall always be estopped by his own deed, or not permitted to aver or prove anything in contradiction to what he has once so solemnly and deliberately avowed.'

By the Law of Property Act 1925, any deed, whether or not being an indenture, may be described as a deed simply, or as a conveyance, mortgage, transfer of mortgage, lease or otherwise according to the nature of the transaction (Section 57). Thus, instead of starting with the words 'This Indenture', a deed may start 'This Conveyance', 'This Legal Charge', 'This Deed'.

Where a person executes a deed, he shall either sign or place his mark upon it; sealing alone shall not be deemed sufficient (Section 73).

Any alteration or erasure which appears on the face of a deed is presumed, in the absence of contrary evidence, to have been made before the deed was executed. If, after execution, a deed is altered in any material way without the consent of all parties, the deed becomes void from that point on. If a deed is altered after execution by consent of all parties, it does not become void, but if in consequence of the alteration, it has become virtually a new document, it must be resubmitted for stamping. (The stamp duties on various deeds are given under *Stamp Duty*.) SEE *Escrow*

DEED OF ARRANGEMENT A deed of arrangement whether under seal or not, made by a debtor for the benefit of his creditors, otherwise than under the Bankruptcy Acts, includes (1) an assignment of his property to a trustee, in order that it may be realized and the proceeds divided amongst the creditors (SEE *Assignment for Benefit of Creditors*); and (2) a deed or agreement under which the creditors agree to accept a composition—that is, a payment of so much in the pound in full discharge of the debts due by the debtor to them (SEE *Composition with Creditors*); and, in cases where creditors of a debtor obtain any control over his property or business, it also includes a deed of inspectorship entered into for the purpose of carrying on or winding up the business; and a letter of licence authorizing the debtor or any other person to manage, carry on, realize, or dispose of a business, with a view to the payment of debts; and any agreement or instrument authorizing the debtor or any other person to manage, carry on, realize, or dipose of the debtor's business, with a view of the payment of his debts (Section 1 to the Deeds of Arrangement Act 1914).

A deed of arrangement is void unless registered at the Department of Trade and Industry within seven clear days after the first execution thereof by the debtor or any creditor (Section 2 of the above Act).

By the Deeds of Arrangement Act 1914, Section 3, a deed of arrangement shall be void unless, before or within 21 days after the registration thereof, or within such extended time as the High Court or the court having jurisdiction in bankruptcy in the district in which the debtor resided or carried on business at the date of the execution of the deed may allow, it has received the assent of a majority in number and value of the creditors of the debtor (subsection (1)).

The assent of a creditor shall be established by his executing the deed of arrangement or sending to the trustee his assent in writing attested by a witness (subsection (3)).

The trustee shall file with the Department of Trade and Industry when the deed is registered, or in the case of a deed assented to after registration, within 28 days after registration or such extended time as the court may allow, a statutory declaration by the trustee that the requisite majority of the creditors have assented to the deed (subsection (4)).

In calculating a majority of creditors for the purposes of this Section a creditor holding security upon the property of the debtor shall be reckoned as a creditor only in respect of the balance due to him after deducting the value of such security, and creditors whose debts amount to sums not exceeding ten pounds shall be reckoned in the majority in value but not in the majority in numbers (subsection (5)).

By Section 11(1), it is enacted that the trustee under a deed of arrangement shall give security to the registrar of the bankruptcy court, in a sum equal to the estimated assets available for distribution among the unsecured creditors, to administer the deed properly, unless a majority in number and value of the creditors dispense with his giving such security.

'All moneys received by a trustee under a deed of arrangement shall be banked by him to an account to be opened in the name of the debtor's estate.' (Section 11(4))

The deed, if an assignment, is an available act of bankruptcy; and if any dissentient creditor petitions within three months, or within one-month under Section 24 (SEE *Act of Bankruptcy*) and bankruptcy follows, the trustee in bankruptcy can claim all moneys paid into the account referred to in Section 11(4). During that period, therefore, cheques should not be drawn upon the account. As the section indicates, the account should be opened 'in the name of the debtor's estate'.

The trustee shall at the expiration of every six months send to each creditor who assented to the deed of arrangement, a statement of the trustee's accounts and of the proceedings under the deed (Section 14).

As to the validity of certain payments to a person, who has committed an act of bankruptcy, or to his assignee, see Section 46, Bankruptcy Act 1914, under *Act of Bankruptcy*.

The register may be searched on payment of a fee. The registrar transmits a copy of each deed to the registrar of the County Court in the district of which the place of business or residence of the debtor is situate, and any person may search such registered copy on payment of a similar fee. SEE *Bankruptcy*

A deed of arrangement affecting land should be registered under the Land Charges Act 1925. SEE *Land Charges*.

If AB (who has executed a deed of arrangement and whose creditors have agreed that he may carry on the business) wishes to continue his banking account, the bank should consult the trustee as to the exact position. If all the creditors of AB have agreed to the arrangement, the bank would be safe in continuing the account, but there is always the possibility that, unknown to the assenting creditors, there may be a creditor who has not agreed to the arrangement, and this creditor may, if his debt amounts to £15 or over, take advantage of the act of bankruptcy during the available period to throw the estate into bankruptcy. In such an event, the title of the trustee in bankruptcy would relate back to the time of the first act of bankruptcy committed within three months preceding the date of the presentation of the bankruptcy petition. SEE UNDER *Adjudication in Bankruptcy*

DEED OF ASSIGNMENT SEE *Assignment for Benefit of Creditors*

DEED OF COVENANT A covenant is a document setting forth the terms of a contract or agreement between two or more persons. One of the categories of covenant referred to in the Stamp Act 1891 is 'in relation to any annuity or to other periodical payments'. And it is this type of deed of covenant which is normally encountered nowadays. Its principal use is the transfer of income from one person to another in a tax-effective way. Thus, A may covenant to pay B a sum of money for a period of years with the result that A's income is reduced and B's increased. If B pays income tax at a lower rate than A or perhaps pays no tax at all (as in the case of a charity), there is an overall saving of tax.

For a deed of covenant to be effective in this way, it must be capable of continuing for more than six years (three years in the case of charities), hence the practice of executing seven-year covenants. The recipient will receive from the covenantor an income tax certificate Form R.185 AP) showing the gross amount of the payment and the tax deducted at basic rate. If the recipient is not liable to income tax at the basic rate, he will be able to recover all or part of the tax deducted from the covenant payment. This does not apply, however, in the case of a covenant by a parent in favour of his or her own children under the age of 18 because the income of the child in that situation will still be deemed to be that of the parent.

In the case of charitable gifts, a deed of covenant may be even more effective. Under the Finance Act 1980, it is sufficient that a charitable deed of covenant can exceed three years, thus the effective period for a deed of covenant in favour of a charity is now a minimum of four years. In the case of such a charitable covenant, the basic rate of tax will be recoverable by the charity, as outlined above, and the amount of the gift will also be a valid deduction against the donor's liability for higher rate tax.

DEED OF FAMILY ARRANGEMENT A family arrangement is an agreement between members of the same family intended to be generally and reasonably for the benefit of the family (Halsbury). Such an arrangement may be implied from a long course of dealing, but in most cases a family arrangement is by deed. A typical example of a deed of family arrangement would be an agreement between members of a family to divide equally (or in some other way) property to which they are entitled under a will or intestacy. However, there are many other examples and, on the whole, the courts look favourably on such deeds. However, they may be set aside if there has been any undue influence, particularly by a parent over a child, or if some material fact has not been disclosed.

A deed of family arrangement may have particular relevance to capital transfer tax liability. Where the beneficiaries under a will or intestacy come to an agreement among themselves to rearrange the beneficial interests, that arrangement does not constitute a chargeable transfer by the beneficiaries themselves, but takes effect for capital transfer tax purposes as if the terms of the arrangements had been incorporated into the terms of the will or intestacy (Section 47, Finance Act 1975 (as amended)).

It is not essential that such an arrangement should be by deed provided it is properly evidenced by some instrument or a formal exchange of correspondence. Nor is it necessary that the beneficiaries be in all cases members of the deceased's family in the narrow sense. It is the practice of the Inland Revenue to interpret the Section widely and it would extend to any member of the deceased's family and to any beneficiary under the will or intestacy, but the Section would not apply where, under the arrangement, some new beneficiary had been introduced who was not a member of the deceased's family.

For the Section to apply, the deed of family arrangement must have been executed within two years of the death.

This relief will not be available where a beneficiary has already had some advantage from that part of the estate which is the subject of the arrangement, i.e. a beneficiary cannot take a gift and then re-direct it to someone else.

The same Section of the Act extends similar treatment to certain other situations:

1. A person may disclaim an interest in settled property, in which case the capital transfer tax rules will apply as if he had not been entitled to such interest.
2. An election by a surviving spouse under the Administration of Estates Act 1925, i.e. the redemption of a life interest in the residuary estate in return for a capital sum, is not a transfer for value and takes effect under this Section as if the capital sum had been payable on intestacy.
3. Where a beneficiary has taken property under a will and passed it to another person in accordance with some non-binding bequest by the testator, this is not a chargeable transfer and the gift takes effect as if it had not been incorporated in the terms of the will.

DEED OF GIFT The conveyance of a property as a gift. In the case of a voluntary deed of gift, the deed is void against the Trustee in Bankruptcy if the settlor becomes bankrupt within two years from the date thereof, and if he becomes bankrupt within ten years, it is void, unless it can be proved that he was, at the time of making the gift, able to pay all his debts without the property comprised in the deed of gift. (But see under *Settlements—Settlor Bankrupt*, as to taking such property as security.)

Where shares are transferred as a gift, the consideration is expressed as a nominal one, say, £1. The stamp duty on gifts *inter vivos* is the same as on a conveyance or transfer on sale, with the substitution in each case of the value of the property conveyed or transferred for the amount or value of the consideration. SEE *Capital Transfer Tax; Gifts* Inter Vivos

DEED POLL A deed to which there is only one party or one set of parties. A deed poll was cut or 'polled' straight at the edge. A deed poll usually commences 'Know all men by these presents', etc., and the date appears at the end. In an indenture the date is at the beginning. For the most part, it is used as evidencing a change in surname. Anyone can decide to change his surname with or without executing a deed poll, but the latter is better evidence and usually accepted without the enquiries which would be raised in its absence. SEE *Indenture*

DEEP DISCOUNT SECURITY This is defined in the Finance Act 1984, as any redeemable security that a company issues at a discount of either more than 15 per cent of its redemption value or more than ½ per cent a year over the term of the security. Thus, if a company issues at say 80, a bond redeemable in, say, 20 years at par (100) this would be deemed to be a deep discount bond for the purpose of the Act. Under the Act, a bond holder is taxed on the income of the bond in the ordinary way, but taxed on the amount of the discount only when he either redeems or disposes of the security. He is then taxed as though he had received investment income equal to the accrued discount spread over the period of ownership. The normal capital gains tax rules will apply in determining whether or not there has been a disposal, subject to the exception that in the case of the death of the owner of a deep discount bond he will be deemed to have disposed of it immediately prior to death (contrary to the general rule that capital gains tax is not payable on death).

In general, a company issuing a deep discount bond will be entitled to tax relief in each accounting period for the amount of the discount accrued over that period, but this is subject to a number of provisions in the 1984 Act, notably that the bond has been issued for the trading purposes of a company, or that the company is an investment company.

Special rules also apply under the Act, where deep discount securities are issued to replace existing securities.

DEFACED COINS Gold, silver, or copper coin which is defaced by being stamped with any name or words thereon, whether such coin is or is not thereby diminished in weight, is not a legal tender (24 & 25 Vict c 99, Section 7). (SEE *Legal Tender*) It was an offence (punishable by imprisonment for life or any shorter period) for any person to

1. gild or silver or wash or case over or colour any coin resembling any current gold or silver coin or any current copper coin with intent to make it resemble or pass for any current gold or silver coin;
2. gild or wash, case over or colour any current silver coin with intent to make it resemble or pass for any current gold coin; or
3. file or in any manner alter any current silver coin with intent to make it resemble or pass for any current gold coin or file or alter any current copper coin with intent to make it resemble or pass for any current gold or silver coin.

(Coinage Offences Act 1936, as amended by the Criminal Justice Act 1948 and the Criminal Law Act 1967. Now repealed by Forgery and Counterfeiting Act 1981.) SEE *Coinage, Coins*

DEFERRED ANNUITY SEE *Annuity; Pensions*

DEFERRED PENSION A pension payable at some future date, usually under an occupational pension scheme, but in the meantime 'frozen' because of the happening of some event, e.g. the resignation of the employee. The amount of the pension will be determined by the years of service, actual or credited, of the employee up to the date of leaving. In some pension schemes, there is a degree of escalation in relation to inflation in respect of the years before the pension actually becomes payable.

As an alternative to receiving a deferred pension, an employee may take the actuarial value of the deferred pension and invest it in an approved pension plan elsewhere and, in some cases, he may be able to transfer that value to the pension scheme of his new employer. SEE *Pensions*

DEFERRED SHARES, DEFERRED STOCK Shares or stock which do not receive a dividend until the shares or stock which rank in front have been satisfied. The capital of a company may be divided into preference, ordinary, and deferred shares or stock, or the ordinary stock may be split up (by, for example, statutory companies which have special powers to do so) into preferred and deferred ordinary.

DEFERRED TAXATION The term is normally used only in relation to corporation tax payable by a company and relates, as the name implies, to the postponed payment of corporation tax owing to some relief or allowance introduced by the Government. The earliest instance of deferred taxation arose under the 1973 Finance Act, which gave relief to companies and unincorporated traders in respect of tax on the inflationary appreciation of stock values (SEE *Stock Relief*). As the payment of such tax could be 'deferred' it became the practice to include 'deferred tax' in the assets of the balance sheet. Under the 1978 Finance Act, where stock relief had been given between the years 1973 and 1975, the deferred tax was allowed to be retained in the business forever and thereafter, each year's deferred tax ceased to be payable at all after a six-year period.

The treatment of deferred tax in the accounts of companies is governed by SSAP 15 issued by the Accounting Standards Committee (q.v.). In April 1984 the Committee issued a further draft Standard concerning the treatment of deferred tax consequent upon the reduction in capital allowances in the 1984 Finance Bill. The statement indicated that where changes in taxation result in significant adjustments to the deferred tax account of a company, the adjustment should be treated as an extraordinary item in the profit and loss account. The statement also says that companies should assess the dates of deferred tax liability by reference to their own circumstances. In some cases, a three-year period would be sufficient but where it is known that tax rates and the effect of tax reliefs will change in future years, companies should look further ahead and 'consider the timing of events'.

DEFUNCT COMPANY When the Registrar of Companies ascertains that a company has ceased to carry on business, or if he fails to receive any reply to his letters of inquiry addressed to the company, he may publish in the *Gazette* a notice that, at the expiration of three months from the date of the notice, the company's name will, unless cause is shown to the contrary, be struck off the register, and the company will be dissolved (Section 652, Companies Act 1985). By virtue of Section 651 of the Companies Act 1985, it is possible to restore a struck-off company by application to court within two years of the dissolution whereupon the court may declare the dissolution to have been void. SEE *Company*

DEL CREDERE A *del credere* commission is an extra commission paid by a principal to an agent when the agent guarantees the solvency of a customer to whom he has sold goods on credit. SEE ALSO *Factoring*

DELIVERY OF BILL 'Delivery' means transfer of possession, actual or constructive, from one person to another (Section 2, Bills of Exchange Act 1882).

Section 21 of the same Act provides

(1) Every contract on a bill, whether it be the drawer's, the acceptor's, or an indorser's, is incomplete and revocable, until delivery of the instrument in order to give effect thereto.

Provided that where an acceptance is written on a bill, and the drawee gives notice to or according to the directions of the person entitled to the bill that he has accepted it, the acceptance then becomes complete and irrevocable.

(2) As between immediate parties, and as regards a remote party other than a holder in due course, the delivery—

(*a*) in order to be effectual must be made either by or under the authority of the party drawing, accepting, or indorsing, as the case may be:

(*b*) may be shown to have been conditional or for a special purpose only, and not for the purpose of transferring the property in the bill.

But if the bill be in the hands of a holder in due course a valid delivery of the bill by all parties prior to him so as to make them liable to him is conclusively presumed.

(3) Where a bill is no longer in the possession of a party who has signed it as drawer, acceptor, or indorser, a valid and unconditional delivery by him is presumed until the contrary is proved.

Just as a deed is of no legal effect until it has been delivered, so, it is seen from this section, that a bill of exchange is incomplete and revocable until delivery of the instrument. Where a cheque is stolen from, or lost by, the drawer before he has issued it, the thief or finder of the cheque has no claim against the drawer.

In *Baxendale* v *Bennett* (1878) 3 QBD 525, where an acceptance in blank by the defendant had been stolen and a drawer's name was filled in, an action was brought on it by the plaintiff as indorsee for value. It was held that the defendant was not liable on the bill, as he had not authorized anyone to fill in a drawer's name and had not issued the acceptance. SEE *Bill of Exchange; Issue of Bill; Stolen Bill; Stolen Cheque; Transferor by Delivery*

DELIVERY OF CHEQUE SEE *Delivery of Bill*

DELIVERY OF DEED SEE *Deed*

DEMAND DRAFT SEE *Banker's Draft*

DEMONETIZE When a coin is officially withdrawn from circulation it is said to be demonetized. Pre-Victorian gold coins were demonetized when they were withdrawn from circulation under the Coinage Act of 1889, and the Royal Proclamation of 1890. Such a demonetized coin is no longer legal tender.

Recent examples include farthings which were demonetized from 1st January, 1961, old halfpennies from 1st August, 1969, half-crowns from 1st January, 1970, and the new halfpenny from 1st October, 1984.

DEMONSTRATIVE LEGACY A gift of money under a will, in which the testator indicates a particular fund or asset out of which the legacy is to be paid, e.g. £1,000 'out of my holding of ICI Stock'. On the other hand, a legacy of '£1,000 of my ICI Stock' would be a specific legacy. The distinction is important because a demonstrative legacy will not be adeemed if the fund out of which it is payable does not exist at the date of death (SEE *Ademption*). It is also relevant in relation to abatement (q.v.). If the fund out of which the legacy is payable still exists at the date of death, the legacy is payable in full even though the estate may be insufficient to pay the general legacies in full. If, on the other hand, the fund does not exist at the date of death, the legacy is treated as a general legacy and abates pro rata with the general legacies. SEE *Legacy*

DEPENDENT RELATIVE ALLOWANCE This is a category of income tax relief under the Income and Corporation Taxes Act 1970.

A person who looks after, at his or her own expense, a dependent relative may claim the dependent relative allowance. For this to apply, a relative must be

1. A relative (of the husband or wife) who is incapacitated by old age, i.e. who is at least 64 years of age at the beginning of the tax year, or
2. such a relative who is incapacitated by infirmity, or
3. the widowed, divorced or separated mother of either the husband or wife (regardless of age or infirmity).

Provided the husband or wife supports the relative financially, it is not necessary for him or her to live with the husband or wife. An additional allowance is made for each dependent relative so supported.

If the husband and wife are taxed on their separate earnings, the relief is obtainable by each of them for their own relatives.

The amount of the allowance is £100 per annum, but if the income of the dependent relative exceeds the amount of the basic retirement pension the allowance is reduced by £1 for every £1 in excess of the basic retirement pension.

If the claimant is a single woman or a woman whose earnings are taxed separately, the amount of the allowance is £145, reduced as above in respect of any excess in the dependent relative's income above the basic retirement pension.

DEPOSIT ACCOUNTS These are accounts opened for the purpose of earning interest as opposed to current or drawing accounts opened for the purpose of making payments by cheque, standing order, etc. Deposit accounts were known historically as deposit receipts (q.v.), whereas current accounts were known as drawing accounts. By far the most important category of deposit account in the UK banks is the seven-day deposit, e.g. they are subject to withdrawal at seven day's notice, although it has long been the practice to waive notice on request on payment of an interest penalty. Until the late 1960s, nearly all clearing bank deposits in the UK were on either current account or deposit account. This was partly because of the interest rate cartel which had operated over the years, and partly because of the difficulty of employing more costly deposits, e.g. higher rates for a longer term, on a profitable basis when the banks were required to maintain a 28 per cent liquidity ratio.

However, since the introduction of Competition and Credit Control (q.v.) in 1971, the banks have competed for deposits in the money markets and have obtained large 'wholesale' deposits.

Deposit accounts are among the most liquid forms of savings and are comparable to (and in competition with) some building society accounts and savings bank accounts.

Over the years, deposit accounts have accounted for approximately one-half of the total sterling deposits of the London clearing banks, although the proportion has varied slightly over the years usually depending on the level of interest rates. The following table shows the level of current and deposit accounts in relation to total sterling deposits over recent years.

£ millions

	1976	1977	1978	1979	1980	1981	1982	1983
Sterling deposits								
Sight principally current a/cs	11,491 (37.6)	13,919 (40.7)	16,240 (42.0)	19,409 (41.5)	18,565 (35.2)	21,323 (34.6)	25,084 (31.9)	28,944 (33.7)
Less than 8 days	10,937 (35.8)	11,095 (32.4)	12,332 (31.9)	15,739 (33.7)	19,863 (37.6)	22,075 (35.8)	24,965 (31.8)	25,287 (29.5)
8 days up to 1 month	2,712 (8.9)	2,589 (7.6)	3,360 (8.7)	3,874 (8.3)	5,537 (10.5)	6,259 (10.1)	10,727 (13.6)	10,981 (12.8)
1 month up to 3 months	2,721 (8.9)	2,607 (7.6)	3,342 (8.6)	3,960 (8.5)	4,214 (8.0)	6,106 (9.9)	8,244 (10.5)	9,800 (11.4)
3 months up to 6 months	1,318 (4.3)	1,693 (5.0)	1,777 (4.6)	1,733 (3.7)	2,164 (4.1)	2,669 (4.3)	4,042 (5.1)	4,189 (4.9)
6 months up to 1 year	966 (3.2)	1,534 (4.5)	993 (2.6)	1,109 (2.4)	1,543 (2.9)	1,396 (2.3)	2,851 (3.6)	3,384 (3.9)
1 year and over	420 (1.4)	753 (2.2)	643 (1.7)	924 (2.0)	899 (1.7)	1,897 (3.1)	2,714 (3.5)	3,226 (3.8)
Total sterling deposits	30,565	34,191	38,687	46,749	52,785	61,735	78,627	85,811

Source: CLCB Statistical Unit.

Until 1971, the rate of interest on deposit accounts was agreed among the clearing banks and it was known as the London Bankers' Deposit Rate. It was traditionally 2 per cent below Bank Rate. Since 1981, the banks have been free to fix their own interest rates, but the degree of competition in a highly developed market prohibits any wide divergence on rates from one bank to another. SEE Supplement

DEPOSIT PROTECTION BOARD The authority which administers the Deposit Protection Scheme (q.v.).

DEPOSIT PROTECTION FUND The fund set up under the Banking Act 1979 in connection with the Deposit Protection Scheme (q.v.).

DEPOSIT PROTECTION SCHEME The scheme was set up under the Banking Act 1979 and came into effect in February 1982. Under the scheme, all recognized banks and licensed deposit-taking institutions are required to contribute to the Deposit Protection Fund at an overall percentage rate fixed by the Deposit Protection Board. There is provision for minimum and maximum contributions of £2,500 and £300,000 respectively and for the Fund to be maintained at a minimum of £5 million and a maximum of £6 million. In the event of a bank or licensed deposit-taking institution becoming insolvent, the Fund guarantees up to 75 per cent of the first £10,000 of a depositor's sterling deposits with the bank or institution concerned.

DEPOSIT RATE A rather loose term to indicate the rate of interest paid by the clearing banks on deposit accounts (q.v.).

DEPOSIT RECEIPT This was the forerunner of the modern deposit account, but the term is still used in relation to a receipt given by a bank for a fixed deposit to be repaid at an agreed date. Interest at current rates will be paid on the deposit, either at agreed intervals or at expiry of the deposit. The 'rolling up' of interest on such an account may be useful to a customer for tax planning purposes, or for income equalization.

Deposit receipts are not transferable or negotiable (but see *Certificate of Deposit*). It is thought that the debt represented by the deposit receipt is capable of assignment and that a banker would have to pay the assignee on being given notice of assignment.

DEPOSIT-TAKING INSTITUTION SEE *Banking Act 1979*

DEPRECIATION The word is sometimes used in its literal sense to mean the diminution in value of an asset, usually from a combination of age and 'wear and tear'. In an accountancy sense, however, the word means the financial provision for that diminution in value out of the profits of the enterprise.

Accountancy practice has varied over the years in the treatment of depreciation, but on the whole an asset should be depreciated as a matter of business prudence. An asset with a short life should be written off over a short period; an asset with a long life may be written off over a longer period, either by an annual percentage of the residual cost or by the so-called 'straight line' method.

The depreciation of fixed assets is now governed by Schedule 4, Companies Act 1985 and Statement of Standard Accounting Practice 12 (SSAP 12). Paragraph 18 of Schedule 4 requires that the depreciable amount of a depreciating asset should be allocated on a systematic basis to each accounting period during the useful life of the asset. It is not necessary, however, to depreciate freehold land unless its residual value is expected to be less than book value. On the revaluation of an asset, the revalued amount, less any residual value, should be depreciated over the remaining useful life.

Under SSAP 12, a statement of accounting policies, including the treatment of depreciation, is to be included in a note to the company's accounts and this is now a statutory requirement under the 1981 Act. SEE ALSO *Capital Allowances*

DESTROYED BANK NOTE Where notes have been partly or wholly destroyed, their value can be recovered from the bank which issued them, provided that full particulars, including the numbers, are supplied, and that the bank is otherwise satisfied. The bank will require a sufficient indemnity to be given before paying notes which are stated to have been destroyed. See the law cases under *Bank of England Notes*. SEE *Mutilated Notes*

DEVALUATION This is the deliberate reduction in the value of a nation's currency in relation to the currencies of other countries. In the days of fixed exchange rates, members of the International Monetary Fund (q.v.) could devalue only after 'consultation' with the Fund. The par values of currencies were expressed in terms of weight in gold and on 18th September, 1949 the pound sterling was devalued, the par value being reduced from 3.58134 grams of fine gold (403 US cents) to 2.48828 grams of fine gold (280 US cents). On 18th November, 1967, sterling was again devalued, the par value being further reduced to 2.13281 grams of fine gold (240 US cents). In January 1972, the dollar was devalued so that the pound was revalued at US $2.6057, although the par value remained unchanged in terms of gold.

Under the present system of floating exchange rates, currencies, at least in theory, are free to fluctuate so that devaluation would arise from gradual depreciation of a currency. The value of a currency is now usually expressed in terms of some other major currency, e.g. the pound in relation to the dollar, or against a 'basket' of currencies weighted according to their trade significance to the UK.

Devaluation is usually sparked off by a serious widening of a country's trade gap, possibly because of rising costs making the country's exports uncompetitive. This, in turn, may be accompanied by an overall lack of confidence in the home currency and the movement of funds to other countries (when legally possible) which, in turn, exacerbates the payments deficit. Devaluation provides a country with the opportunity to offer its goods to other countries at a cheaper rate in terms of its own currency. It also means that the cost of importing foreign goods, in terms of the importing country's currency, increases. Thus, the boost to exports and the constraint on imports tends to rectify the balance of payments deficit. Nevertheless, devaluation is merely a palliative and does not remove whatever may be the basic cause of the imbalance, e.g. rising costs, heavy Government expenditure overseas, flight of funds or general lack of confidence in the currency. SEE *Floating Currency*

DEVELOPMENT LAND TAX This was introduced in the Development Land Tax Act 1976, and came into force from 1st August that year. There have been modifications in subsequent Finance Acts.

In essence, the tax is payable where a person who has an interest in land realizes the development value of the land. In very broad terms, development value is the difference between the disposal proceeds and the current use value. More precisely, it is the disposal proceeds (net after relevant expenses) and the *highest* of the following base values:

Base A The cost of acquiring the interest in the land, together with any increase in its *current* use value over the period of ownership, plus any expenditure on relevant improvements.
Base B 115 per cent of the *current* use value of the interest in the land at the date of the disposal, plus any expenditure on relevant improvements.
Base C 115 per cent of the cost of requisition plus expenditure on improvements.

Development land tax becomes payable

1. on the occasion of a disposal or part disposal of an interest in land, or
2. on the commencement of what is known as a 'project of material development'. This means any developments except those which are specifically exempted, e.g. the enlargement of the cubic content of a building by no more than one-third, the rebuilding of an existing building with an increase in the cubic content of no more than one-tenth, the use of buildings or land for forestry or agriculture and the use of land for car parking for a period of up to six years.

In other words, development land tax becomes prima facie payable when development value is realized on a sale or a development project is commenced.

No tax is payable on the disposal of land by charities, nor on the development of land for agricultural purposes.

The first £75,000 of development value realized in any financial year ending 31st March, is exempt from tax and this exemption is available annually. The exemption does not apply, however, to each disposal or development but up to the total development value realized by an owner in the year.

No development land tax is payable on the realization by a person of all or part of his principal or only private residence, together with gardens or grounds up to 1 acre or such larger area as may be appropriate for the reasonable enjoyment of the residence (effectively the same rule as for capital gains tax disposals). The normal rule is that the house must have been the principal or only residence of the individual concerned for at least 12 of the 24 months preceding the disposal (or one-half of the total period of ownership if less than 24 months, with a minimum of six months).

There is no liability for development land tax on an owner's death, nor on the gift of an interest in land.

Development land tax is normally payable three months after the event which gives rise to the charge, i.e. a disposal or the commencement of a project of material development (see above). In certain circumstances, e.g. where the consideration for sale is a rent spread over a number of years or where a development is to take a number of years, the tax may be paid over ten equal annual instalments. Interest is payable on the unpaid instalments, i.e. from the date the instalments fall due. Development land tax is currently chargeable at 60 per cent. SEE Supplement

DEVISE The gift by will of freehold property SEE *Devisee*

DEVISEE The person to whom 'real' property is left, or devised, in a will, is called the devisee. The person who takes all the real property remaining after the devisees have received their shares is called the residuary devisee.

The general rule with specific devises and bequests of property is that the beneficiary takes the gift in the condition in which it is found at the date of death and subject to all liabilities. So, with a specific devise of a house, the devisee—unless he is prepared to disclaim any benefit—must take the property in its then state of repair and subject to any covenants and other liabilities attaching to it. It is a principle of long standing, however, that if the testator has entered into a contract for work to be carried out to the property before his death, but dies before the work is completed, a specific devisee of the property by his will is entitled to have the work carried out at the expense of the estate (*Holt* v *Holt* [1694]). The deceased must, however, have actually entered into a contract if the devisee is to benefit (*re Day's Will Trusts, Lloyds Bank Ltd* v *Shape & Others* [1962] 3 All ER 699). SEE *Legatee; Personal Estate*

DIAMONDS, INVESTMENT IN Diamonds were first discovered somewhere around 1,000 BC in India and were used both for decorative purposes and for hardening the tips of tools for cutting. India remained the only source of diamonds throughout the world until they were discovered in Brazil early in the eighteenth century. For the next 150 years or so, Brazil was the main supplier of diamonds to be overtaken eventually by South Africa following the discovery of diamonds there in the 1860s. The first major discovery of diamonds in the USSR was in 1954 and about one-quarter of the world's output now comes from that country.

Some Characteristics of Diamonds

Diamond is one of the crystalline forms taken by carbon. Its geological origin is not known for certain, but it is believed to have been formed at extremely high temperatures and pressures below the crust of the earth and eventually forced upwards to its present deposits. Diamond is the hardest substance known and indeed to polish a diamond, a diamond's own dust is used.

Diamonds have been used for various purposes over the years, sometimes for personal adornment, sometimes to keep evil spirits at bay, sometimes to work magic and sometimes taken, in powdered form, for medicinal purposes. In addition to their ornamental and mystical value, diamonds are used widely for industrial purposes, such as cutting and polishing, bearings and styluses.

The four principal characteristics of a diamond are

Weight Diamonds are measured in carats (based historically on the weight of the black bean pod of the locust tree). The carat is now standardized internationally at 0.2 grams. The largest diamond ever found was the Cullinan Diamond from South West Africa in 1905, weighing 3,106 carats. This was cut into 105 stones, the two largest being part of the Crown Jewels.

Cut Diamonds may be cut or uncut. There are various ways in which diamonds are cut, the intention being to achieve a degree of symmetry and to maximize the return of light which reflects from the facets of the diamond. The traditional cut originating in the seventeenth century was the Brilliant Cut, which gave a diamond 58 facets. Other types of cut are the Point Cut, the Table Cut (in which one of the main points is flattened) and the Lozenge Cut. Not only is the reflectivity of a diamond high when properly cut, but the light falling on to the facets is dispersed into the colours of the spectrum, giving the diamond its 'fire'.

Clarity Anything which diminishes the light in a diamond is regarded as a flaw and no diamond is flawless (although there is a 'flawless' grading). There is a number of international scales in force for expressing the grades of diamonds, but only in the lower grade diamonds can the flaws be seen with the naked eye.

Colour Any impurities in a diamond absorb some of the natural (white) light falling on it and give the diamond a yellowish tinge. As with the scales of 'clarity', there are scales for determining the shades of colour of diamonds from pure white to light yellow.

Advantages and Disadvantages of Diamonds

Some advantages are

1. There is a degree of rarity, albeit artificially controlled (see below).
2. They last for ever.
3. They have romantic and emotional associations.
4. They are exceedingly compact (almost certainly the smallest unit of wealth in terms of value per cubic capacity).
5. They are universally acceptable.
6. They have increased in value steadily over the years.

Some disadvantages are

1. Only the expert can judge the quality of a diamond.
2. The mark-up is considerable in the retail price of mounted diamonds.
3. Mountings can become unfashionable.
4. Imitations are difficult for the layman to detect.
5. Prices fall during economic recession, both for gem diamonds and industrial ones.
6. The supply, and therefore the price, of diamonds is artificially controlled.
7. The world's stock of diamonds is growing.

It is now possible to produce diamonds by synthetic means, both for jewellery and industrial purposes. They are not fakes: they are diamonds in all respects, but they are man-made (principally in the USA) rather than being dug out of the earth. At present, they are no cheaper to produce than natural diamonds, but when they are it will be a point for the investor to watch.

Simulated diamonds made from paste, rock-crystal and the like are easily detected by the expert, but no doubt have found their way into much personal jewellery.

The Price of Diamonds

All the main producers of diamonds throughout the world are members of the Central Selling Organisation, which is controlled by the de Beers Group. The Organisation accounts for approximately 80 per cent of all uncut diamonds, sold throughout the world. They nearly all come to the diamond trade in London where they are sold to 300 or so dealers at ten sales or 'sights' a year. Through the Central Selling Organisation, the producers are able to match supply to demand and thus ensure a degree of stability in prices. This has certainly been to the advantage of the producers, the traders and retailers over the years and it may be argued that it is to the advantage of the investor. On the other hand, the degree of control is itself an artificially imposed one and the stability of diamond prices depends on its continued existence. The price list of the Central Selling Organisation covers over 2,500 grades of diamonds and the prices are not negotiable. So long as the present system continues, the prices of diamonds will almost certainly increase because the Central Selling Organisation is able to relate the supply to the demand.

Rough diamonds purchased by the main dealers in London will, in some cases, be sold to other dealers and they may go through many hands before being cut and polished. The mark-up may be quite considerable before the diamonds are mounted. There will then be the cost of mounting and the sale to the retailer, with the result that the final sale price may be 1,000 per cent up on the original price of the rough diamond at the London 'sight'. It follows that the investor should deal as closely as possible with the main dealers in London and indeed, they will accept commissions to buy on behalf of investors. The investor should buy only through dealers of the highest standing, he should buy only the top quality stones and he should obtain, in each case, a certificate from one of the recognized laboratories, e.g. the Gemological Institute of America or HRD (Hoge Raad voor Diamant).

DINER'S CLUB This is the name of the first of the US 'travel and entertainment' credit cards. It was introduced in 1950 and came to the UK in 1951. In 1965, the then Westminster Bank took a minority shareholding in the Diner's Club in the UK and increased its holding to 47.8 per cent of the equity in the following year. Subsequently, National Westminster Bank held 49.7 per cent of the UK-based operations of the Diner's Club. In 1981, Citicorp entered into an agreement to buy Diner's Club, which then had about 3¼ million members. SEE *Credit Card*

DIRECT DEBITING The direct debiting scheme is designed for the benefit of a company or other organization which receives large numbers of regular payments of fixed amounts by standing orders from its debtors, and which would prefer itself to originate debits on the accounts of its debtors with the banks concerned. Additionally, if the debtors agree, an organization which receives large numbers of payments not by standing order but by cheque because the amounts are variable may also avail itself of the scheme.

Bank customers wishing to use the scheme apply to their main bankers and, if permission is granted, they sign an indemnity addressed to all the clearing banks and the Scottish banks by name, and, if they wish to debit non-clearing banks, another indemnity addressed to them by name. In the indemnities the organizations concerned confirm that they will keep each of the banks concerned indemnified upon their respective first demands against all actions, claims, damages, costs and expenses arising directly or indirectly from such direct debiting and without their requiring proof of their agreement to the validity of such demand and that they will forthwith pay the amount thereof. The banks are also authorized to admit, compromise or reject any claims made upon them without reference to the customer. The banks are absolved from the necessity of verifying or checking that instructions given by bank customers have been given and remain in force in respect of any debits made at the request of the initiating organization. If the indemnities are given by limited companies the usual resolutions of the boards are necessary.

The banks need their customers' authorities before placing direct debits to their accounts. If there is a standing order already in existence a new authority is not required, so long, of course, as the indemnity is completed by the recipient. The initiating organization advises the branch banks concerned of their intention to change to direct debiting on a form agreed by the banks, in duplicate. One half is retained at the branch and the other half is completed by the bank and returned to the initiating organization giving the branch title, sorting code number and customer's account number in the lower half of the form. The top half contains details of the standing order which is compared with the original authority. The date on which the first direct debit is to be initiated is given, preferably at least six weeks in advance, to enable the bank to cancel the standing order and to avoid duplication of payment.

Where there is no standing order in existence individual customers complete an authority giving details of the payments and incorporating permissions to accept direct debits. The lower half of the form is dealt with as outlined in the previous paragraph.

The authorities of individual customers can also be taken in similar form to those described above to accept direct debits of variable amounts.

Lodgement of direct debits is normally made through the clearing departments of the banks. The creditor organization can either provide vouchers made out in the correct form, or, by arrangement, may pass computer-prepared magnetic tape.

Direct debits may be returned unpaid in the same way as cheques to the branch bank mentioned for that purpose on the voucher. If the voucher cannot be paid because of lack of funds, the answer written thereon will be 'unpaid'. In all other cases the same answers as those placed on cheques will be used, e.g. 'orders not to pay', 'account holder deceased', 'account transferred to Y Bank, branch', etc.

SEE *Bankers' Automated Clearing Service Limited.*

DIRECTORS Members of a joint stock company appointed to conduct its affairs. They may be appointed in the first instance by name in the articles, or more usually by the signatories to the memorandum in accordance with express power given therein. Subsequently they are usually appointed by the shareholders in general meeting.

Section 282 of the Companies Act 1985 provides:

(1) Every company registered on or after 1st November 1929 (other than a private company) shall have at least two directors.

(2) Every company registered before that date (other than a private company) shall have at least one director.

(3) Every private company shall have at least one director.

Section 228(2) provides:

(2) The company shall, within the period of 14 days from the occurrence of:

(*a*) any change among its directors or in its secretary, or

(*b*) any change in the particulars contained in the register,

send to the registrar of companies a notification in the prescribed form of the change and of the date on which it occurred; and a notification of a person having become a director or secretary, or one of joint secretaries, of the company shall contain a consent, signed by that person, to act in the relevant capacity.

The powers of directors are limited to the provisions of the memorandum and articles of association of the company.

Directors have been called trustees for the company, but in *Smith* v *Anderson* (1880) 15 Ch D 247, Lord Justice James said

A trustee is a man who is the owner of the property, and deals with it as a principal, as owner, and as master, subject only to an equitable obligation to account to some persons to whom he stands in the relation of trustee, and who are his *cestuis que trustent*. The same individual may fill the office of director and also be a trustee having property, but that is a rare, exceptional, and casual circumstance. The office of director is that of a paid servant of the company. A director never enters into a contract for himself, but he enters into contracts for his principal, that is, for the company of whom he is a director, and for whom he is acting. He cannot sue on such contracts, nor be sued on them, unless he exceeds his authority.

Jessel, MR said (in *In re Forest of Dean Coal Company* (1879) 10 Ch D 450)

Directors have sometimes been called trustees or commercial trustees, and sometimes they have been called managing partners; it does not matter much what you call them, so long as you understand what their true position is, which is that they are really commercial men managing a trading concern for the benefit of themselves and of all the other shareholders in it. They are bound, no doubt, to use reasonable diligence having regard to their position, though probably an ordinary director, who only attends at the board occasionally, cannot be expected to devote as much time and attention to the business as the sole managing partner of an ordinary partnership, but they are bound to use fair and reasonable diligence in the management of their company's affairs, and to act honestly. But where without fraud and without dishonesty they have omitted to get in a debt to the company by not suing within time, or because the man was solvent at one moment and became insolvent at another, I am of opinion that it by no means follows as a matter of course, as it might in the case of ordinary trustees of trust funds or of a trust debt, that they are to be made liable.

In *Re Brazilian Rubber Plantations Co. Ltd* (1910) 103 LT 697, it was held that

A director's duty requires him to act with such care as is reasonably to be expected from him, having regard to his knowledge and experience. He is not bound to bring any special qualification to his office, but if he is acquainted with the particular business carried on by the company, he must give the company the advantage of his knowledge when transacting the company's business. He is not bound to take any definite part in the conduct of the company's business, but so far as he does undertake it he must use reasonable care in its dispatch. Such reasonable care must be measured by the care an ordinary man might be expected to take in the same circumstances on his own behalf. He is not responsible for errors of judgment.

It appears to be no answer to the suggestion that a director has failed in his duty, for him to establish that he acted upon the directions of the majority of shareholders (*Selangor United Rubber Estates Ltd* v *Cradock (No. 3)* [1968] 1 WLR 1555).

See also the case of *Dey* v *Pullinger Engineering Co. Ltd* under *Company*.

The number of shares which a director must hold in the company to qualify him for the post of director, depends upon the terms of the articles of association. The Companies Act does not provide for any special qualification.

Table A, Article 77, provides that in default of a qualification being fixed by the company in general meeting, none shall be required.

It shall be the duty of every director who is by the regulations of the company required to hold a specified share qualification, and who is not already qualified, to obtain his qualification within two months after his appointment or such shorter time as may be fixed by the regulations of the company. The office of director shall be vacated if he does not obtain his qualification within that time, or if after the expiration of such period he ceases at any time to hold his qualification (Section 182).

Every company must keep a register of the names, any former Christian name or surname, nationality, addresses, and occupations of its directors and secretaries, and furnish a copy thereof to the registrar of companies and notify any changes (Section 200).

In a limited company the liability of the directors may, if so provided by the memorandum, be unlimited (Section 202).

A limited company, if so authorized by its articles, may, by special resolution, alter its memorandum so as to render unlimited the liability of its directors or managers (Section 203).

The balance sheet of a company must be signed by two directors, or if there is only one director, by that director (Section 155). In the case of a banking company registered after 15th August, 1879, the balance sheet must be signed by at least three directors (Section 155).

The following are some of the rules where Table A of the 1948 Act is adopted.

The directors may appoint one of their number to be managing director at such remuneration as they think fit and he shall not, while holding that office, be subject to retirement by rotation (Article 107).

The amount borrowed by the directors for the purposes of the company (otherwise than by the issue of share capital) shall not at any time exceed the issued share capital without the sanction of the company in general meeting, apart from temporary loans obtained from the company's bankers. No lender or other person dealing with the company shall be concerned to see or inquire whether this limit is observed (Article 79).

Every director present at a meeting or committee of directors shall sign his name in a book kept for that purpose (Article 86).

Every year at the annual general meeting one-third of the directors for the time being, or if their number is not three or a multiple of three, then the number nearest to one-third, shall retire from office. The directors to retire shall be those who have been longest in office since their last election. A retiring director shall be eligible for re-election. (Articles 89, 90, 91)

A minute book of all proceedings of directors must be kept.

Any casual vacancy may be filled up by the directors. SEE *Company*

The annual returns of a company must include the name, address, nationality, occupation, age, and particulars of other directorships of each director. (See Sixth Schedule, Part II, Companies Act 1948. See also Companies Act 1981 below.)

Every company registered on or after 1st November, 1929 (other than a private company) shall have at least two directors, and every company registered before that date (other than a private company) and every private company shall have a director (Section 176).

Every company shall have a secretary and a sole director shall not also be secretary (Section 177).

The acts of a director or manager shall be valid notwithstanding any defect that may afterwards be discovered in his appointment or qualifications (Section 180). This was held in *Morris* v *Kanssen* [1946] AC 459, not to cover a case where there has been a total absence of appointment or a fraudulent usurpation of authority.

In *Freeman & Lockyer* v *Buckhurst Park Properties (Mangol) Ltd* [1964] WLR 618, a case concerning the ostensible authority of directors, Diplock LJ stated, that for a party to enforce a contract against a company entered into on its behalf by an agent having no actual authority, it must be established

1. that a representation that the agent had authority to enter on behalf of the company into a contract of the kind sought to be enforced was made to the contractor;
2. that such representation was made by a person or persons who had 'actual' authority to manage the business of the company either generally or in respect of those matters to which the contract relates;
3. that he (the contractor) was induced by such representation to enter into the contract, that is, that he in fact relied upon it;
4. that under its memorandum or articles of association the company was not deprived of the capacity either to enter into a contract of the kind sought to be enforced or to delegate authority to enter into a contract of that kind to the agent.

If a director enters into a transaction which is within the company's powers, but outside the director's own authorization, and if the other contracting party knows of that lack of authority, the company is not bound by the contract, notwithstanding that it was within the powers of the company. (*Rolled Steel Products (Holdings) Limited* v *British Steel Corporation* [1984], *Financial Times, 15th June.*)

Section 190 prohibited the making of loans by a company to a director or to a director of its holding company. Likewise, the giving of a guarantee or of security by a company to secure advances by other people to such parties was prohibited (see also Companies Acts 1980 and 1981 below.)

By section 185 of the Companies Act 1948, now Section 293 of the 1985 Act, no person can be appointed a director of a public company if he has attained the age of 70. A director automatically relinquishes his office at the conclusion of the annual general meeting next after he attains the age of 70. These prohibitions do not apply to directors appointed or approved by the company in general meeting and are, moreover, subject to what the company's articles prescribe. The Section also does not apply to a private company.

By Section 184, a director may be removed from office by ordinary resolution of the company before the expiration of his period of office and notwithstanding anything in its articles or any service agreement. (See now sections 303 and 304 Companies Act 1985.)

A director who is, in any way, whether directly or indirectly, interested in a contract with the company shall declare the nature of his interest at a meeting of the directors. Nothing shall be taken to prejudice the operation of any rule of law restricting directors of a company from having any interest in contracts with the company. (See Section 317 of the 1985 Act.)

Some articles provide that no director shall vote on any contract in which he is interested. Hence where a guarantee of directors is held for a company's bank account, care must be exercised if any of the company's assets are subsequently charged, for such additional security lessens the director's guarantee liability, and to this extent they are personally interested in the charging of the assets. Hence unless the company's articles provide that the directors may vote on contracts in which they are personally interested, there is a danger that the charge will be held to be invalid (*Victors Ltd (in liquidation)* v *Lingard* [1927] 1 Ch 323).

An undischarged bankrupt must not act as director, or take any part in the management of any company except with the leave of the Court by which he was adjudged bankrupt (Section 187).

The Companies Act 1980 introduced a number of major provisions in relation to company directors, partly to implement the Second Directive in Company Law of the EEC and partly to give effect to some of the recommendations of the Government white paper *The Conduct of Company Directors* (Cmnd 7037, HMSO). They include the following:

1. In relation to Part IV of the Act (which is concerned with transactions between a company and its directors), a person may be treated as a director if the directors are accustomed to act on his directions or instructions. Such a person is sometimes described as a 'shadow director'. A person is not within this category, however, if a company merely acts on his professional advice.
2. No company, public or private, may enter into any contract of employment with a director for a period of more than five years if during that period his employment cannot be terminated by the company by the giving of notice, or his employment can only be so terminated in specified circumstances. The rule does not apply where the term of the contract has first been approved by the company in general meeting. The rule applies equally for contracts *for* services between a director and a company, e.g. a consultancy arrangement. (It may be noted that the provisions of the Act go further than those of the Stock Exchange Listing Agreement, which prohibits service contracts with a director of a company for a period of 10 years or longer without the prior approval of the company in general meeting.)
3. Section 48 of the Act prohibits any arrangement whereby a director of a company or of its holding company (but not of any subsidiary company) or any person connected with a director is to acquire any non-cash assets from the company, or any arrangement whereby a company acquires any non-cash assets from such a director or connected person. The prohibition does not apply if the value of the non-cash asset at the time of the arrangement is less than £1,000, or, if greater, is less than the lower of £50,000 and 10 per cent of the company's net assets. Again, the prohibition does not apply if the arrangement is first approved by a resolution of the company in general meeting. (See Sections 320–322, 1985 Act.)

Where the Section is contravened, the director and any connected person is liable to account to the company for any gain he has made as a result of the arrangement and to indemnify the company for any loss or damage resulting from the arrangement. The liability extends to any director who authorized the arrangement.

A connected person for this purpose is any spouse, child or stepchild under the age of 18, of the director, or any body corporate with which the director is associated. It also includes any person who is acting in his capacity as a trustee of any trust that includes the director or any connected person among the beneficiaries, or that confers a power on the trustees that may be exercised for the benefit of the director or any connected person. A person who is acting as a partner of a director or of any other person connected with him is also a connected person for this purpose.
4. The Act revises the rules relating to the provision of loans and other forms of credit by companies to their directors. SEE *Loans to Directors*
5. Section 60 of the Act (Section 317, 1985 Act) widens the provisions of Section 199, Companies Act 1948 regarding the disclosure to the board of a company by any director of his interest in contracts to which the company is a party. This is now extended to cover any transaction or arrangement of a loan or credit nature as defined in Section 330, 1985 Act.
6. Part V contains provisions *inter alia* relating to 'insider dealing' by a director of a company. SEE *Insider Dealing*
7. Section 46 (Section 309, 1985 Act) of the Act imposes a duty on directors to have regard to the interest of the company's employees. This is an addition to the directors' obligation to take account of the interests of the shareholders. Under the Act, the obligation to have regard to the interests of the employees is an *obligation* to the company and thus, is enforceable only at the suit of a shareholder—something which a minority shareholder cannot normally do under the rule in *Foss v Harbottle* [1843] 2 HARE 461.

The Companies Act 1981 implementing *inter alia* the Fourth Directive of the EEC in Company Law contains the following provisions relating to directors:

1. The register of directors must contain details of other directorships held by directors in the past five years other than directorships of dormant companies (Section 95—Sections 288–290 1985 Act).
2. The Department of Trade and Industry inspectors may require a director or past director of a company under investigation to produce documents under his control relating to bank accounts

through which cash derived from transactions between the director and the company is thought to have passed.
3. Section 111 made certain amendments to the law relating to loans to directors.

Section 9 of the Insolvency Act 1976, provides that the court may make an Order that a person shall not be a director of a company without the leave of the court for a maximum of five years from the date of the Order. The power exists where a person

1. is or has been a director of a company which has gone into liquidation at a time when it was insolvent; and
2. is or has been a director of another company which has similarly gone into liquidation within five years of the date on which the first company went into liquidation; and
3. the court is satisfied that his conduct as director of any of the companies makes him unfit to be concerned in the management of a company.

DIRECTORS' PENSIONS Prior to 1973 it was not possible for a director who held more than 5 per cent of the voting power of a company that was director-controlled, i.e. where the directors held more than 50 per cent of the voting rights, to be a member of the company's pension scheme. Nor was it possible for the company to take out a separate scheme on such a director's behalf. With the passing of the Finance Act 1973, however, this rule was changed and it is possible now for a controlling director to join the company's scheme or to benefit from a separate, individual pension arrangement.

In the case of such controlling director schemes, substantial sums may be built up outside the company with complete freedom from capital transfer tax. Such schemes are very flexible and the company may make larger transfers in the more profitable years, thereby reducing corporation tax liability. Indeed, the funds built up under such a scheme need not be separately invested; they may be used in the company's business provided they are under the control of acceptable trustees and up to one-half of the contributions may be put out on loan to the company. The Inland Revenue will require an undertaking from the trustees that they will not agree to the winding-up of the pension scheme other than in accordance with the terms of the trust deed. As an added safeguard to ensure that the trustees (who will in some cases be the directors of the company) do not wind up the fund and distribute the assets among themselves or their families, the Superannuation Funds Office requires that one of the trustees be what is now known as a 'pensioneer trustee'. This is a person or institution with professional experience of pension trusts who must be approved by the Superannuation Funds Office as a suitable trustee. This rule applies to all smaller pension schemes, which are defined as those with fewer than 12 members.

There is no fundamental difference between the two categories of individual pension schemes, i.e. the voluntary topping-up scheme for a company executive and the scheme devised for controlling directors. The original difference in treatment arose from the former rule that controlling directors could not be members of their main company scheme. There are, however, differing needs and attitudes between the executives of a large company on the one hand and the controlling directors of a family business on the other. SEE *Pensions*

DISABLEMENT BENEFIT Disablement benefit takes the form of a weekly pension or lump sum payment, depending on the degree of disablement. It is designed to cover industrial injuries and diseases where the disablement extends beyond the period of Statutory Sick Pay and sickness benefit. Where appropriate, it comes into operation at the point that injury benefit ceases.

Disablement benefit is payable for loss of physical or mental faculty as a result of an industrial accident or disease. This means, in general, the impairment of the power to enjoy life compared with the condition of a normal healthy person of the same age and sex. It is not related to the nature of the employment nor the loss of the injured person's earning power. It may be payable whether or not the injured person has returned to work.

The degree of disablement is assessed in percentage terms and no disablement benefit is payable where the loss of a particular faculty is assessed at less than 1 per cent. In general, in the case of disablement assessed at 20 per cent or more, a weekly pension will be payable. In the case of a lesser degree of disablement, a lump sum will be payable.

Once disablement benefit has been paid, no further claims can be considered for injury benefit. It is not necessary, however, for injury benefit to precede disablement benefit and it is not necessary that the claimant should have been off work, in which case he would not have received injury benefit or sickness benefit.

There is a scale laid down for certain clearly defined injuries. For example, the loss of sight or both hands ranks as a 100 per cent disablement.

The loss of one hand is normally 60 per cent and of an index finger 14 per cent.

The degree and duration of a disablement will be assessed by an independent medical board. If the claimant is not satisfied with the board's decision, there is a right of appeal to a medical appeal tribunal. If, however, the medical board has made a provisional assessment there is no right of appeal until two years have passed since the case first went to the medical board.

If disablement benefit is awarded, the recipient may also be entitled to one or more of the following additional allowances:

Special hardship allowance This is payable if, because of the injury or disease, the disabled person cannot return to his original job or one of a similar standard.

Constant attendance allowance This is payable if the disablement is 100 per cent and the disabled person requires constant care and attention.

Exceptionally severe disablement allowance This is an extra allowance for the severely disabled who are already receiving constant attendance allowance at a rate above the normal maximum and where the need for attendance is likely to be permanent.

Hospital treatment allowance If the disabled person is receiving disablement benefit at less than the full 100 per cent rate and is also a hospital in-patient for the purpose of receiving treatment for the injury or disease, there is a hospital treatment allowance which has the effect of raising the disablement benefit to 100 per cent during the period of the treatment.

Unemployability supplement This is payable if the disabled person is likely to be permanently unable to work because of the industrial injury or disease.

Unemployability supplement and special hardship allowance cannot both be paid in respect of the same period.

Basic disablement benefit is payable in addition to other National Insurance benefits such as sickness benefit (q.v.), invalidity benefit (q.v.) or retirement pension (q.v.), but none of these can be paid in addition to unemployability supplement.

During the period that unemployability supplement is paid, the claimant is entitled to have contributions credited and a self-employed person is also exempted from liability to pay contributions.

DISCHARGE OF BANKRUPT The regulations regarding the discharge of a bankrupt are contained in Section 26 of the Bankruptcy Act 1914 (as amended by the Bankruptcy (Amendment) Act 1926):

(1) A bankrupt may, at any time after being adjudged bankrupt, apply to the Court for an order of discharge, and the Court shall appoint a day for hearing the application, but the application shall not be heard until the public examination of the bankrupt is concluded. The application shall, except when the Court in accordance with rules under this Act otherwise directs, be heard in open Court.

(2) On the hearing of the application the Court shall take into consideration a report of the official receiver as to the bankrupt's conduct and affairs (including a report as to the bankrupt's conduct during the proceedings under his bankruptcy), and may either grant or refuse an absolute order of discharge, or suspend the operation of the order for a specified time, or grant an order of discharge subject to any conditions with respect to any earnings or income which may afterwards become due to the bankrupt, or with respect to his after-acquired property: Provided that where the bankrupt has committed any misdemeanour under this Act or any enactment repealed by this Act, or any other misdemeanour connected with his bankruptcy, or any felony connected with his bankruptcy, or where in any case any of the facts hereinafter mentioned are proved, the Court shall either—

(i) refuse the discharge; or
(ii) suspend the discharge for such period as the Court thinks proper; or
(iii) suspend the discharge until a dividend of not less than fifty pence in the pound has been paid to the creditors; or
(iv) require the bankrupt as a condition of his discharge to consent to judgment being entered against him by the official receiver or trustee for any balance or part of any balance of the debts provable under the bankruptcy which is not satisfied at the date of the discharge, such balance or part of any balance of the debts to be paid out of the future earnings or after acquired property of the bankrupt in such manner and subject to such conditions as the Court may direct, but execution shall not be issued on the judgment without leave of the Court, which leave may be given on proof that the bankrupt has since his discharge acquired property or income available towards payment of his debts:

Provided that, if at any time after the expiration of two years from the date of an order made under this Section the bankrupt satisfies the Court that there is no reasonable probability of his being in a position to comply with the terms of such order, the Court may modify the terms of the order, or of any substituted order, in such manner and upon such conditions as it may think fit.

(3) The facts hereinbefore referred to are—

(*a*) That the bankrupt's assets are not of a value equal to fifty pence in the pound on the amount of his unsecured liabilities, unless he satisfies the Court that the fact that the assets are not of a value equal to fifty pence in the pound on the amount of his unsecured liabilities has arisen from circumstances for which he cannot justly be held responsible:

(*b*) That the bankrupt has omitted to keep such

books of account as are usual and proper in the business carried on by him and as sufficiently disclose his business transactions and financial position within the three years immediately preceding his bankruptcy:

(c) That the bankrupt has continued to trade after knowing himself to be insolvent:

(d) That the bankrupt has contracted any debt provable in the bankruptcy without having at the time of contracting it any reasonable or probable ground of expectation (proof whereof shall lie on him) of being able to pay it:

(e) That the bankrupt has failed to account satisfactorily for any loss of assets or for any deficiency of assets to meet his liabilities:

(f) That the bankrupt has brought on, or contributed to, his bankruptcy by rash and hazardous speculations, or by unjustifiable extravagance in living, or by gambling, or by culpable neglect of his business affairs:

(g) That the bankrupt has put any of his creditors to unnecessary expense by a frivolous or vexatious defence to any action properly brought against him:

(h) That the bankrupt has brought on or contributed to his bankruptcy by incurring unjustifiable expense in bringing any frivolous or vexatious action:

(i) That the bankrupt has, within three months preceding the date of the receiving order, when unable to pay his debts as they become due given an undue preference to any of his creditors:

(j) That the bankrupt has within three months preceding the date of the receiving order, incurred liabilities with a view of making his assets equal to fifty pence in the pound on the amount of his unsecured liabilities:

(k) That the bankrupt has, on any previous occasion, been adjudged bankrupt, or made a composition or arrangement with his creditors:

(l) That the bankrupt has been guilty of any fraud or fraudulent breach of trust.

(5) For the purposes of this Section a bankrupt's assets shall be deemed of a value equal to fifty pence in the pound on the amount of his unsecured liabilities when the Court is satisfied that the property of the bankrupt has realised, or is likely to realise, or with due care in realisation might have realised, an amount equal to fifty pence in the pound on his unsecured liabilities, and a report by the official receiver or the trustee shall be prima facie evidence of the amount of such liabilities.

A discharged bankrupt shall, notwithstanding his discharge, give such assistance as the trustee may require in the realization of such of his property as is vested in the trustee, and if he fails to do so the court may, if it thinks fit, revoke discharge (Subsection (9)).

By Section 7 of the Insolvency Act 1976, the court is enabled to make an order providing for the automatic discharge of a bankrupt five years after his adjudication, and Section 8 of that Act imposes a duty on the Official Receiver to apply to the court for a hearing of discharge within one year after the fifth anniversary of the adjudication unless, within the five year period, the bankrupt has applied for an order of discharge under Section 26, Bankruptcy Act 1914 (see above) or an order has been made under Section 7 of the Insolvency Act.

In *Re Reed (a Debtor)* [1979] 2 All ER 22, it was held that an order under Section 7 of the Insolvency Act 1976, was not a mere formality. If the court was in doubt whether it was proper to dispense with the ordinary machinery of discharge, it would be right not to grant automatic discharge. It was intended that the court should adopt a broad approach, look at the matter as a whole, and adopt and apply its own judicial concept of fair application of the bankruptcy law. SEE *Bankrupt Person; Bankruptcy*

DISCHARGED BILL A bill of exchange is discharged when payment is made in due course by or on behalf of the drawee or acceptor (Bills of Exchange Act 1882, Section 59(1)). Where the acceptor of a bill is or becomes the holder of it at or after its maturity, it is discharged (Section 61). Where the holder of a bill at or after its maturity absolutely and unconditionally renounces his rights against the acceptor, the bill is discharged (Section 62).

Where a bill is intentionally cancelled by the holder or his agent, the bill is discharged. (See Section 63, Bills of Exchange Act 1882, under *Cancellation of Bill of Exchange*. See other Sections under *Payment of Bill*.)

When a banker has paid his customer's acceptance, he cancels the acceptor's signature in the same way as he would cancel the drawer's signature on a cheque. SEE *Payment of Bill*

DISCLAIMER A renunciation. An example of a disclaimer is found in connection with bankruptcy proceedings. By Section 54 of the Bankruptcy Act 1914, a trustee may disclaim any portion of the bankrupt's land of any tenure which is burdened with onerous covenants, or any shares or stock in companies, or unprofitable contracts, etc.

The term may be applied to other matters where a renunciation or repudiation is desired. For example, a person may disclaim an interest in settled property, in which case the capital transfer tax rules will apply as if he had not been entitled to that interest. SEE ALSO *Deed of Family Arrangement*

DISCLOSURE OF BANK PROFITS In September 1969, the clearing and Scottish banks announced that 'after a careful re-examination of the problems involved, and after discussions with the authorities', they had decided that 'their future annual accounts will be prepared in accordance with the provisions of the Companies Acts applicable to the generality of companies', and that they would 'cease to take any advantage of the exemptions hitherto available to them under Part III of the Eighth Schedule to the Companies Act, 1948'.

Profit figures on the new basis were announced on 20th February, 1970 by the London clearing banks, the Scottish banks and the banks with head offices in Northern Ireland. Broadly, the main changes in practice were that profits were shown without transfers to or from undisclosed contingency accounts, and the accumulated totals of such inner reserves were shown. Uniform accounting treatment had been achieved by prior agreement and this was seen in the creation of provisions for bad debts on the average experience of the latest five years, and the spreading of gains and losses on investments realized, also over five years, beginning with the year of realization.

The results of individual banks led to some adjustments of the prices of their shares on the Stock Exchange.

DISCLOSURE OF INTERESTS IN SHARES The Companies Act 1981, amending the relevant provisions of the 1967 and 1976 Companies Acts, requires the disclosure of a shareholder's interests in shares in a public company where the aggregate nominal value of the shares, in which the shareholder is interested, is equal to or more than five per cent of the total of the share capital, or any class thereof. (See Sections 198—210, 1985 Act.)

A person is deemed to be interested in shares where

1. his or her spouse, or child, or stepchild under the age of 18 is interested in the shares; or
2. a corporate body is interested in the shares and either that body or its directors are accustomed to act in accordance with the interested shareholder's directions, or he or she is entitled to exercise or control the exercise of one-third or more of the voting power at any general meeting of that body corporate; or
3. the interested shareholder is acting together with another person who is interested in the shares; or
4. he or she is a beneficiary of a trust which holds an interest in the shares; or
5. he or she enters into a contract to buy the shares; or
6. not being the registered holder, he or she is entitled to exercise or control the exercise of any right conferred by the holding of those shares; or
7. otherwise than by virtue of having an interest under a trust
(a) he has a right to call for delivery of the shares, or
(b) he has a right to acquire or is under an obligation to take the interest in them.

Persons are deemed to be acting together for the purpose of the Act if there is an agreement between them for the acquisition by any one or more of them for interests in shares in a public company and the agreement imposes any obligations or restrictions on one of the parties concerning the disposal or otherwise of the shares and any interest in that company's shares is in fact acquired by any of those persons in pursuance of the agreement.

Not only must a notifiable interest be disclosed when the shares are acquired, but the company must be informed when that interest has ceased, or when there is a change of more than one per cent in the aggregate nominal value.

Notification must be made in writing to the company, giving all the relevant details required by the Act, and this is to be done within five working days from the date the obligation to notify arises.

Every public company must keep a register of the information notified under the Act and the notifications of interests must be recorded in chronological order under the interested shareholder's name.

If a public company knows, or has reasonable cause to believe, that a person has, or had during the past three years, a notifiable interest in the company's share capital, it may make a written request to that person to indicate whether he or she holds, or has held, a notifiable interest. If a person fails to comply with a notice to disclose a notifiable interest, the company may apply to the court for an order imposing restrictions on the shares. The restrictions would be

1. Any transfer of the shares would be void.
2. No voting rights would be exercisable in respect of the shares.
3. No further shares may be issued to the holder.
4. Except in a liquidation, no payment may be made in respect of sums due from the company on those shares.

Failure to report a notifiable interest in response to a notice from the company may also lead to an unlimited fine or a maximum prison sentence of two years.

DISCOUNT SEE *Discounting a Bill*

DISCOUNT HOUSES SEE *Bill Broker*

DISCOUNTING A BILL When a banker discounts a bill, he buys it outright for a sum less than its face value, the difference comprising discount based on the unexpired term of the bill. Sometimes the face value of the bill is credited to the customer's account and a debit charged to the account by way of discount; in other cases the net amount of the bill is credited to the account. The transaction is in effect an advance on the security of the bill, the discount being, in effect, the interest charged for the loan until the maturity of the bill.

When trade bills are brought to a banker to be discounted, there are many points which require to be carefully observed in order that a banker may avoid taking bills which are unmarketable, or which may eventually cause problems.

If a bill drawn by Jones on Brown is brought to be discounted, a banker will consider the position of the acceptor Brown. If Brown's account is at another bank, what sort of a banker's opinion is held regarding him, is the opinion a recent one, and how many other bills accepted by Brown are in the bill case? Have any of Brown's acceptances ever been dishonoured? If Jones is the person who wants the bill discounted, the banker will note the total amount of bills already discounted for him and the quality of them. A certain number of the bills may be dishonoured at maturity, and the question arises, will Jones's account admit of the bills on which there is a risk, being debited to it, if they are returned unpaid?

If the parties to the bill are quite satisfactory, other points will arise in the banker's mind. Is the bill a genuine trade bill, that is, a bill accepted by Brown because he has received value for it from Jones, or has Brown accepted it merely for the accommodation of Jones, on the understanding that Jones himself must meet it at maturity? The banker may be informed that it is an accommodation bill when it is offered to him, or he may be left to find out that fact for himself. A scrutiny of Jones's account may show, perhaps, that a bill for practically the same amount appears regularly every three or six months, suggesting that it is the same bill which is being renewed time after time. Is there any cross drawing between Brown and Jones, that is does Brown accept bills for Jones and Jones accept them for Brown? Is the business between the two parties such as would justify Jones drawing on Brown? If Jones is an iron merchant, for example, and Brown a grocer, it is not very likely that the bill would arise out of the ordinary course of business between an iron merchant and a grocer, and the banker is put on inquiry.

In the words of George Rae, in his *Country Banker*:

> It is not the province of banking to discount bills, the proceeds of which are to provide the acceptors with fixed capital. A man may properly be drawn upon against goods, produce, or commodities which he is turning over in his business from day to day; but not against his buildings or machinery. These are not floating capital.

Again:

> A shipowner, or ship's husband, may properly be drawn upon for sails, or cordage, or stores supplied to ships, because there is a tangible fund in his incoming freights to meet this class of marine paper; but when he accepts against the hull of a ship, he passes the recognised limits of negotiable value, and his paper becomes discredited in the estimation of the bill market.

A bill which is payable to John Brown *only* should not be discounted, as the bill is not a negotiable instrument, and the banker could not, if necessary, sue upon it.

A banker who discounts a bill is a 'holder for value' (q.v.) and at maturity he obtains the full proceeds. The banker has no lien on the customer's credit balance for the contingent liability on any maturing bills except by agreement. (SEE *Lien*) But where a customer is bankrupt, the banker may set-off a credit balance against the contingent liability, by virtue of Section 31, Bankruptcy Act 1914. (See that Section under *Set-off*). This right of set-off against the contingent liability applies in the winding up of a company, but not in the case of the appointment of a receiver. SEE *Receiver, Winding Up*

The person for whom a bill is discounted must indorse it, as by indorsement he becomes one of the parties to the bill and liable thereon if the acceptor fails to pay it. If not indorsed or drawn by him, he is not liable on the bill, unless the bill proves to be a forgery, though he may become liable to the banker by custom or special agreement. SEE *Dishonour of Bill of Exchange; Transferor by Delivery*

When an advance is made upon the deposit of a bill as security, the banker is a 'holder for value' only to the extent of the sum he has lent upon it.

The discounter of a bill may, if he wishes, re-discount it. Bill brokers frequently re-discount bills with bankers, and instead of indorsing each bill they usually give a guarantee to cover all the bills re-discounted, for example, 'In consideration of your discounting for us any bills you may approve and think fit from time to time, we hereby guarantee the due payment of them as they respectively fall due.' An agreement in this form was held (*in ex parte Bishop* (1880) 15 Ch D 400) to be equal to an indorsement of each bill by the brokers.

In the money market, Treasury Bills (q.v.) and bills or drafts which bear the names of houses of the highest standing, are classed as first-class bills, or first-class paper. Where the names are not so well known, or financially strong, the bills are called second or third class paper, as the case may be.

If a banker discounts a bill of exchange, the discount is the amount of the deduction made by the banker for the present use of money which would not otherwise be received until the bill matured. It is thus in the nature of an interest charge, but unlike interest on a loan which is normally payable quarterly or half-yearly in arrear, the discount on a bill is received when the bill is discounted.

The following table shows the difference in profit per cent per annum between lending money by way of interest and by way of discount.

Interest %	Discount %
1	1.010101
2	2.040816
3	3.092783
4	4.166666
5	5.263157
6	6.382968
7	7.526881
8	8.695652
9	9.890109
10	11.111111
20	25.000000
30	42.857142
40	66.666666
50	100.000000

From this table it is seen that if a sum of £100 is lent at 20 per cent the lender would receive £100 at the end of a year plus £20 for interest, that is a profit of 20 per cent; but if he discounted a bill for £100 at the rate of 20 per cent he would advance only £80 and at the year end he would receive payment of £100, that is he would receive £20 for a loan of £80, or a profit of 25 per cent.

The rate at which a bill is discounted is partly dependent upon rates in the market, the length of time which will elapse before the bill matures, and the quality of the bill. If there is any doubt as to payment of the bill at maturity, the risk is taken into account by charging a higher rate than in the case of a bill which may be regarded as practically certain to be paid when due.

DISCOUNTED CASH FLOW In its simplest terms, this is the value today of money receivable in the future. Thus, the present value of £1,000 to be received in a year's time will depend on ruling interest rates and possible inflation. Disregarding inflation, the present value of funds to be received in the future depends only on the time factor and the rate of interest chosen. The discounted figure may be the present value of a single fixed sum receivable at a future date discounted at a given rate of interest over the intervening years. More usually in commercial situations, it is the present value of a series of variable cash sums receivable over a number of years. It is a useful calculation, therefore, when comparing the present value of a number of alternative industrial investment possibilities. Investment A may yield a given cash flow over a particular period of years and investment B yield a different cash flow over a different period of years. Applying a chosen discount rate to each of the two projects allows them to be evaluated on a comparable basis, not only in relation to each other but also in relation to other possible uses of the money. SEE *Cash Flow; Cash Management; Cash Ratio*

DISCRETIONARY ACCOUNT A term frequently applied to the account of an investment client held by a stockbroker or investment manager who is empowered to act at his own discretion in the management of the client's portfolio. Over the years there has been an increasing tendency for professional investment managers to act in this discretionary way, partly because investment clients do not always wish to be troubled with the investment decisions but also because reference to the client can cause delay and uncertainty. Discretionary accounts are also conducted by commodity brokers for their clients.

DISCRETIONARY TRUST A discretionary trust exists when a trustee has power to appropriate either the income or the capital, or both, of a trust fund to or for the benefit of any one or more of a class of beneficiaries, entirely at the trustee's own discretion. The discretionary power may apply to the whole trust fund or to some part of it. It may apply throughout the whole life of the trust or may arise at some particular point of time, e.g. on the death of a life tenant. A discretionary trust normally arises under the terms of the will or settlement deed but may arise in one statutory instance if property is left on 'protective trusts' (q.v.) under Section 33, Trustee Act 1925.

It is of the essence of a discretionary trust that no beneficiary has an 'interest in possession' for the time being in the trust fund, i.e. no person is entitled to either the income or the capital at the present time as of right.

A trustee of a discretionary trust has a considerable responsibility and should therefore be a person or institution of integrity and good sense. Two particular advantages of discretionary trusts are that they are flexible, enabling the trustee to exercise discretion according to changing circumstances over the years, and secondly, the settlor may have at least a moral influence on the destination of the funds. If he has made an irrevocable settlement, he has surrendered all right to fetter the trustee's discretion but the trustee is entitled to have regard to the settlor's wishes so far as these are known, always bearing in mind that the trustee must act in the best interests, not of the settlor, but of the beneficiaries.

Years ago, discretionary trusts had a certain appeal because of their tax-saving advantages but these were eaten into by successive legislation to the point where such trusts became positively disadvantageous. The capital transfer tax aspects were revised however in the Finance Act 1982 (SEE *Capital Transfer Tax*) and discretionary trusts are no longer at a disadvantage in relation to other forms of settlement. Indeed, they still have an important place in the total tax planning concept but their principal virtue must always be that of flexibility.

DISENTAIL To disentail was to bar or bring to an end an entail. Land was entailed when it was granted to a person and the heirs of his body. The deed barring an entail was called a disentailing deed, and the land thereafter might be dealt with at the will of the owner.

On 1st January, 1926, any legal estate tail then existing was, by the Law of Property Act 1925, converted into an equitable estate. SEE *Estate Tail*

DISHONOUR OF BILL OF EXCHANGE A bill is dishonoured either by non-acceptance or by non-payment, that is, where the person on whom a bill is drawn (the drawee) refuses to accept it, or where the person who, by accepting the bill (the acceptor) agreed to pay it, fails to do so on the day on which it is due, the bill is said to be dishonoured.

As to dishonour by non-acceptance, the Bills of Exchange Act 1882 provides as follows:

42. When a bill is duly presented for acceptance and is not accepted within the customary time, the person presenting it must treat it as dishonoured by non-acceptance. If he do not, the holder shall lose his right of recourse against the drawer and indorsers.

A drawee is by that Section entitled to the 'customary time', that is, until the close of business on the day following presentation for acceptance, within which to accept the bill or to refuse acceptance.

43. A bill is dishonoured by non-acceptance—
(*a*) When it is duly presented for acceptance, and such an acceptance as is prescribed by this Act is refused or cannot be obtained: or
(*b*) When presentment for acceptance is excused and the bill is not accepted.

(2) Subject to the provisions of this Act, when a bill is dishonoured by non-acceptance, an immediate right of recourse against the drawer and indorsers accrues to the holder, and no presentment for payment is necessary.

By Section 18, a bill may be accepted

(2) When it is overdue, or after it has been dishonoured by a previous refusal to accept, or by non-payment:

(3) When a bill payable after sight is dishonoured by non-acceptance, and the drawee subsequently accepts it, the holder, in the absence of any different agreement, is entitled to have the bill accepted as of the date of first presentment to the drawee for acceptance.

By Section 44

The holder of a bill may refuse to take a qualified acceptance, and if he does not obtain an unqualified acceptance may treat the bill as dishonoured by non-acceptance.

As to dishonour by non-payment, Section 47 provides

(1) A bill is dishonoured by non-payment (*a*) when it is duly presented for payment and payment is refused or cannot be obtained, or (*b*) when presentment is excused and the bill is overdue and unpaid.

(2) Subject to the provisions of this Act, when a bill is dishonoured by non-payment, an immediate right of recourse against the drawer and indorsers accrues to the holder.

Notice of dishonour must be given. Section 48 provides as follows:

Subject to the provisions of this Act, when a bill has been dishonoured by non-acceptance or by non-payment, notice of dishonour must be given to the drawer and each indorser, and any drawer or indorser to whom such notice is not given is discharged; Provided that—

(1) Where a bill is dishonoured by non-acceptance, and notice of dishonour is not given, the rights of a holder in due course subsequent to the omission, shall not be prejudiced by the omission.

(2) Where a bill is dishonoured by non-acceptance and due notice of dishonour is given, it shall not be necessary to give notice of a subsequent dishonour by

non-payment unless the bill shall in the meantime have been accepted.

Notice to the various parties of the dishonour of a bill must be given in strict conformity with the regulations set forth in Section 49, otherwise the drawer and indorsers may be discharged. The Section is as follows:

Notice of dishonour in order to be valid and effectual must be given in accordance with the following rules—

(1) The notice must be given by or on behalf of the holder, or by or on behalf of an indorser who, at the time of giving it, is himself liable on the bill.

(2) Notice of dishonour may be given by an agent either in his own name, or in the name of any party entitled to give notice whether that party be his principal or not.

(3) Where the notice is given by or on behalf of the holder, it enures for the benefit of all subsequent holders and all prior indorsers who have a right of recourse against the party to whom it is given.

(4) Where notice is given by or on behalf of an indorser entitled to give notice as hereinbefore provided, it enures for the benefit of the holder and all indorsers subsequent to the party to whom notice is given.

(5) The notice may be given in writing or by personal communication, and may be given in any terms which sufficiently identify the bill, and intimate that the bill has been dishonoured by non-acceptance or non-payment.

(6) The return of a dishonoured bill to the drawer or an indorser is, in point of form, deemed a sufficient notice of dishonour.

(7) A written notice need not be signed, and an insufficient written notice may be supplemented and validated by verbal communication. A misdescription of the bill shall not vitiate the notice unless the party to whom the notice is given is in fact misled thereby.

(8) Where notice of dishonour is required to be given to any person, it may be given either to the party himself, or to his agent in that behalf.

(9) Where the drawer or indorser is dead, and the party giving notice knows it, the notice must be given to a personal representative if such there be, and with the exercise of reasonable diligence he can be found.

(10) Where the drawer or indorser is bankrupt, notice may be given either to the party himself or to the trustee.

(11) Where there are two or more drawers or indorsers who are not partners, notice must be given to each of them, unless one of them has authority to receive such notice for the others.

(12) The notice may be given as soon as the bill is dishonoured and must be given within a reasonable time thereafter.

In the absence of special circumstances notice is not deemed to have been given within a reasonable time unless—

(*a*) where the person giving and the person to receive notice reside in the same place, the notice is given or sent off in time to reach the latter on the day after the dishonour of the bill;

(*b*) where the person giving and the person to receive notice reside in different places, the notice is sent off on the day after the dishonour of the bill, if there be a post at a convenient hour on that day, and if there be no such post on that day then by the next post thereafter.

(13) Where a bill when dishonoured is in the hands of an agent, he may either himself give notice to the parties liable on the bill, or he may give notice to his principal. If he gives notice to his principal, he must do so within the same time as if he were the holder, and the principal upon receipt of such notice has himself the same time for giving notice as if the agent had been an independent holder.

(14) Where a party to a bill receives due notice of dishonour, he has after the receipt of such notice the same period of time for giving notice to antecedent parties that the holder has after the dishonour.

(15) Where a notice of dishonour is duly addressed and posted, the sender is deemed to have given due notice of dishonour, notwithstanding any miscarriage by the post office.

The case of *Hamilton Finance Co. Ltd* v *Coverley Westray Walbaum and Tosetti Ltd and Portland Finance Co. Ltd* [1969] 1 Lloyd's Rep. 53, gives some assistance in the interpretation of the Section.

The question arose as to whether Upper Brook Street, W1, where Hamilton's offices were situated and Seething Lane, EC3, where Coverley's offices were situated, were to be regarded as 'in the same place' for the purpose of Section 49(12) of the Bills of Exchange Act dealing with notice of dishonour. It was held that they were, although had one of the offices been in the suburbs there was the possible suggestion that the decision would have been different.

With regard to another bill, Hamiltons had been informed by their bank on Tuesday, 15th February of the dishonour. They had written a letter the same day to be sent by Registered Post. They were unable to prove, however, from their post book that the letter had been despatched before 5pm and, therefore, they could not rely upon the notice.

In the case of a third bill notice of dishonour had been sent by letter on 4th February and received at noon on Monday, 7th February, it was accepted on the particular facts that the delay was occasioned by the Post Office.

In the unusual circumstances of *Eaglehill Ltd* v *Needham Builders Ltd* [1973] AC 992, it was held by the House of Lords that notice of dishonour is not vitiated by the fact that it was posted before the due date of the bill. It is good notice unless it is received before the bill is dishonoured. It was further held that notice is given at the time when the drawer receives it, which is when it is opened in the ordinary course of business.

In order to render the acceptor of a bill liable it is not necessary that notice of dishonour should be given to him. (Section 52(3), SEE UNDER *Presentment for Payment.*)

Under certain circumstances the Act excuses non-notice of dishonour, or delay in giving notice. Section 50 provides

(1) Delay in giving notice of dishonour is excused where the delay is caused by circumstances beyond the control of the party giving notice, and not imputable to his default, misconduct, or negligence. When the cause of delay ceases to operate the notice must be given with reasonable diligence.

(2) Notice of dishonour is dispensed with—

(*a*) When, after the exercise of reasonable diligence, notice as required by this Act cannot be given to or does not reach the drawer or indorser sought to be charged:

(*b*) By waiver express or implied. Notice of dishonour may be waived before the time of giving notice has arrived, or after the omission to give due notice:

(*c*) As regards the drawer in the following cases, namely, (1) where drawer and drawee are the same person, (2) where the drawee is a fictitious person or a person not having capacity to contract, (3) where the drawer is the person to whom the bill is presented for payment, (4) where the drawee or acceptor is as between himself and the drawer under no obligation to accept or pay the bill, (5) where the drawer has countermanded payment:

(*d*) As regards the indorser in the following cases, namely, (1) where the drawee is a fictitious person or a person not having capacity to contract and the indorser was aware of the fact at the time he indorsed the bill, (2) where the indorser is the person to whom the bill is presented for payment, (3) where the bill was accepted or made for his accommodation.

As the result of several decisions, it has been considered that in all cases where, in consequence of the dishonour of bills or notes, made or become payable to bearer, a remedy arises on the consideration, the transferor is entitled to notice of dishonour.

The amount which a holder may recover in an action on a dishonoured bill is prescribed in Section 57:

Where a bill is dishonoured, the measure of damages, which shall be deemed to be liquidated damages, shall be as follows—

(1) The holder may recover from any party liable on the bill, and the drawer who has been compelled to pay the bill may recover from the acceptor, and an indorser who has been compelled to pay the bill may recover from the acceptor or from the drawer, or from a prior indorser—

(*a*) The amount of the bill:

(*b*) Interest thereon from the time of presentment for payment if the bill is payable on demand, and from the maturity of the bill in any other case:

(*c*) The expenses of noting, or, when protest is necessary, and the protest has been extended, the expenses of protest.

(2) In the case of a bill which has been dishonoured abroad, in lieu of the above damages, the holder may recover from the drawer or an indorser, and the drawer or an indorser who has been compelled to pay the bill may recover from any party liable to him the amount of the re-exchange with interest thereon until the time of payment.

(3) Where by this Act interest may be recovered as damages, such interest may, if justice require it, be withheld wholly or in part, and where a bill is expressed to be payable with interest at a given rate, interest as damages may or may not be given at the same rate as interest proper.

The following is a specimen of a form which may be used in giving notice of dishonour:

British Bank plc
Leeds ...19

Please take notice that the bill for £100 upon John Brown, of King Street, Leeds, drawn (or indorsed) by you, dated ..., at ... months' date, due ... 19.., and payable at ..., upon which you are liable as drawer (or indorser), has been dishonoured by non-acceptance (or non-payment), and we request immediate payment thereof, with expenses.

To John Jones, ..., Manager
English Street, Leeds

Where an inland bill has been dishonoured it may, if the holder think fit, be noted for non-acceptance or non-payment, as the case may be, but it is not necessary to note such a bill in order to preserve recourse against the drawer or indorsers; neither is there any need to protest an inland bill, and it is not usually done. SEE *Noting*

Where a foreign bill, appearing on the face of it to be such, has been dishonoured by non-acceptance, it must be duly protested for non-acceptance, and where such a bill, which has not been previously dishonoured by non-acceptance, is dishonoured by non-payment, it must be duly protested for non-payment (SEE *Protest*). The bill may be noted on the day of dishonour and must be noted not later than the next succeeding business day (SEE *Bills of Exchange (Time of Noting) Act 1917*). The protest may be extended later. A bill drawn in the Republic of Ireland and payable in England is a foreign bill within the meaning of the Bills of Exchange Act, and if dishonoured by non-acceptance or non-payment, must therefore be noted or protested. SEE UNDER *Foreign Bill*

Protest is essential before presentment of a bill for acceptance for honour, or payment for honour.

Noting or protest does not do away with the necessity of giving the notices of dishonour to drawer and indorsers. As soon as payment is refused on the due date, a holder may give notice of dishonour. He need not necessarily wait till the end of the day before doing so. The holder of a dishonoured bill should give notice at once to all parties liable on the bill, otherwise, if he merely gives notice to the indorser from whom he received the bill and that indorser fails to give due notice to the person from whom he received it, that person and any persons prior to him would be discharged, and the holder would have only the indorser (to whom notice was given) and the acceptor (who does not require notice) from whom to recover the amount of the bill.

Where a bill is to be noted, there is nothing to prevent it being noted as soon as dishonoured. An action cannot be commenced till after the end of the due date. In *Kennedy* v *Thomas* [1894] 2 QB 759, where an action was brought by the holder of a dishonoured bill upon the last day of grace, it was dismissed as premature.

Where a bill, which a banker has discounted for a customer, is dishonoured, the banker should debit it to the customer's account and advise him at once (returning the bill to him), so that he may be in time to give the required notices to prevent the release of other parties. But if the account does not justify the dishonoured bill being charged to it, the banker should retain the bill and debit it to an account called 'dishonoured bills', or 'overdue bills', and at once send notice of dishonour, and request for payment, to all the parties to the bill.

If the bill was not indorsed by the customer for whom it was discounted, he is not liable on the bill in the event of its dishonour, unless by special agreement.

Where a bill which has been paid in for collection is dishonoured, the banker should at once give notice to his customer. In collecting a bill, the banker acts as agent for his customer (the principal), and by Section 49, subsection 13, an agent may either himself give notice to the parties liable on the bill or he may give notice to his principal.

If a banker wrongfully dishonours a bill or cheque he will be liable in an action by his customer for damages, and if he dishonours it because certain cheques paid to the credit of his customer have not been cleared, he may also be held liable in damages if it has been the banker's practice to allow the customer to treat uncleared cheques as cash.

A banker has no lien on a customer's credit balance for the contingent liability on any maturing bills except by agreement. SEE *Lien*

As it is a serious matter to damage a customer's credit by dishonouring a bill or cheque which ought to be paid, a banker will naturally make quite sure of the position before returning it. He should ascertain that everything has been credited to the account and that the balance is correct. When a cheque is returned simply from some irregularity in the document itself, such as an incorrect indorsement, an alteration, a difference in amount, or any other similar kind of cause, the banker should make the reason quite clear so that no reflection may be cast upon the customer's credit. A cheque returned for a technical irregularity should never be referred to as a 'dishonoured' cheque. A cheque marked 'refer to drawer' in practice means, as a rule, that the drawer has not sufficient funds in his account to meet it, although there is a decision that it means only what it says (*Flach* v *London & South Western Bank* (1915) 31 TLR 334). However, some doubt has been cast upon this contention because of the popular meaning that is attributed to 'R/D'. In the case of *Jayson* v *Midland Bank Ltd* [1967] 2 Lloyd's Rep 563, the jury found that 'refer to drawer' was likely 'to lower the plaintiff's reputation in the minds of right-thinking people'. However, they found that on the facts the dishonour was justified and the Court of Appeal dismissed the plaintiff's appeal on this point. It seems likely that the jury's view would be followed in any similar action on the words used.

It is customary (except where a special arrangement exists) to debit charges quarterly and until the usual time for debiting them has arrived, a cheque should not be dishonoured by anticipating the item for charges or debiting them at an unusual time. A delay in payment of a cheque is justified when there is a reasonable ground for suspicion that it has been tampered with. (See the reference to *London Joint Stock Bank Ltd* v *Macmillan and Arthur* under *Payment of Cheque*.)

Wrongful dishonour may, as stated above, render a banker liable to pay damages. In the case of *Rolin* v *Steward* (1854) 23 LJCP 148, it was said by Mr Justice Williams

> Although no evidence is given that the plaintiff has sustained any special damage, the jury ought not to limit their verdict to nominal damages, but should give such temperate damages as they may judge to be a reasonable compensation for the injury the plaintiff must have sustained from the dishonour of his cheque.

In *Marzetti* v *Williams* [1830] 1 B and Ad 415, where a sum of £40 had been paid to credit about one o'clock and a cheque was dishonoured shortly after three (although the banker had, after including the amount paid in at one, sufficient funds of the drawer with which to pay the cheque). Mr Justice Taunton said

The jury have found that when the cheque was presented for payment a reasonable time had elapsed to have enabled the bankers to enter the £40 to the credit of the plaintiff, and, therefore, that they must or ought to have known that they had funds belonging to him. That was sufficient to entitle the plaintiff to recover nominal damages, for he had a right to have his cheque paid at the time when it was presented, and the bankers were guilty of a wrong by refusing to pay it. Independently of other considerations, the credit of the plaintiff was likely to be injured by the refusal of the defendants to pay the cheque.... The case put in the course of the argument, of the holder of a cheque being refused payment, and called back within a few minutes and paid, is an extreme case, and a jury probably would consider that equivalent to instant payment.

In *Gibbons* v *Westminster Bank Ltd* [1939] 3 All ER 577, where a customer's rent cheque for £8 16s had been wrongfully dishonoured, nominal damages of £2 were awarded.

The judge said

The authorities which had been cited all laid down that a trader whose cheque was wrongfully dishonoured was entitled to recover substantial damages. It had never been held that the exception to the general rule with regard to the measure of damages for breach of contract extended to anyone who was not a trader.... A person who was not a trader was not entitled to recover substantial damages for the wrongful dishonour of his cheque unless he pleaded and proved special damage.

In *Baker* v *Australia and New Zealand Bank* [1958] NZLR 907, the bank had wrongly dishonoured three cheques drawn by the plaintiff for £23 6s 7d, £11 13s 1d, and £40 respectively, having in error posted a credit for £235 deposited by the plaintiff to another account. Each of the three cheques was returned unpaid with the answer 'present again'. The plaintiff claimed damages for breach of contract and libel. On the first ground she was held not to be a trader, and as she had not alleged or proved actual damage resulting from the dishonour of her cheques, she was entitled only to nominal damages, which were assessed at £2 per cheque. On the second ground the learned judge said

Whatever the answer 'present again' may imply as to prospects of future or later payment, it surely imports the clear intimation that the maker of the cheque so answered has defaulted as to time for performance of the legal and ethical obligation to provide for payment by the bank on presentation of a cheque issued for immediate payment. Written words which convey such meaning must, to my mind, tend to lower a person in the estimation of right-minded members of society generally.

The sum of £100 was awarded to the plaintiff by way of damages for libel. One of the factors taken into consideration by the Court in assessing this sum was that no retraction or apology had been made by the defendant bank to the payees of the cheques or otherwise. Being a Commonwealth decision it is persuasive but not binding in Britain.

Where libel is involved the customer may obtain general damages, that is, he does not have to prove specific loss, irrespective of whether or not he is a trader: he can, of course, increase his claim by such proof.

When a cheque which has been credited to a customer's account is returned unpaid, a banker debits it to that account if the balance permits of it, and gives him notice of dishonour. If the cheque is returned for an irregularity which the banker can confirm without reference to his customer, he should nevertheless give his customer notice of dishonour; otherwise if it is again returned on re-presentment, the customer may claim that he has treated it as paid. When a cheque which has been returned is recalled by telephone, it is advisable for a banker to advise his customer of the circumstance, in order that he may be on his guard.

Cheques paid to credit are often not indorsed by the customer, but the fact that the cheque was not indorsed by the customer when placed to his credit does not affect at all the banker's right to debit his account with it when returned dishonoured.

When it is desired to recall a dishonoured cheque by telephone, the words should be, say, 'cheque would be paid if in our hands now and in order'. These words would not render the banker liable to pay the cheque if there was some obstacle to its payment when received.

If the customer pays in, or 'earmarks', a sum specifically to meet the dishonoured cheque, the banker must retain that sum as instructed. SEE *Appropriation of Payments*

When a banker dishonours a customer's cheque, the balance on the drawer's account is available to pay any cheque, which may be presented subsequently, up to the amount of the balance or sum available, but in Scotland, when a cheque is dishonoured, any funds that there may be in the drawer's account are attached in favour of the person presenting the cheque, the amount being transferred by the banker to a suspense account (Bills of Exchange Act 1882, Section 53).

A cheque paid to the credit of a customer of the X & Y Bank, drawn by another customer of the same bank, may be returned on the following day. Even if the paying-in-slip counterfoil is initialed by the bank cashier, as it often is, it would not affect the banker's right to return the cheque. The banker is not obliged to inform the person paying in to credit a cheque drawn on the banker by another customer, that the cheque may not be paid. He may take the cheque without comment and, after he has looked into the position of the drawer's account, may return it dishonoured. The banker who receives such a cheque for collection does so merely as the agent of the customer paying it in and has the usual time of an agent in which to deal with it, as though it were a cheque on another banker (*Boyd* v *Emmerson* (1834) 2 A & E 184). SEE *Presentment for Payment*

Where a customer has two accounts, one in credit and one overdrawn, and the credit balance is regarded as a set-off to the debit, cheques on the credit account may be dishonoured if their payment would reduce the balance below the amount owing on the overdrawn account, unless there is some arrangement or custom to the contrary.

Where a customer has a deposit account and a current account, and cheques are drawn upon the account in excess of the balance, a banker usually pays such cheques so long as they do not exceed the amount of the deposit account. Should such cheques be inadvertently dishonoured, the banker would, probably, not be liable, seeing that deposit accounts are not intended to be drawn against by cheque.

See further information under *Acceptance for Honour; Payment of Bill; Payment of Cheque; Protest.*

SEE *Bill of Exchange*

DISSOLUTION OF COMPANY A company is dissolved when winding-up proceedings have come to an end (SEE *Winding Up*), or when the Registrar of Companies has struck the company's name off the Register as defunct. SEE *Defunct Company*

DISSOLUTION OF PARTNERSHIP The death, bankruptcy, or retirement of a partner dissolves the firm, and if the remaining partners continue in business a new partnership is created. A partnership may also be dissolved by mutual agreement or by order of the court. SEE *Partnerships*

DISTRIBUTION In general terms, a distribution made by a company may be a dividend declared on the share capital, it may be distribution of capital profits or it may be a return of capital. More precise definitions apply, however, in relation to income tax on distributions, advance corporation tax and company law generally.

Income tax is assessable under Schedule F (SEE *Income Tax*) on dividends and other distributions from companies resident in the UK and Section 232 of the Income and Corporation Taxes Act (1970 ICTA) provides that 'for purposes of Income Tax all such distributions shall be regarded as income, however they fall to be dealt with in the hands of the recipient'.

Section 233 of the ICTA defines 'distribution' as follows:

In relation to any company 'distribution' means—

(*a*) any dividend paid by the company, including a capital dividend—

(*b*) any other distribution out of assets of the company (whether in cash or otherwise) in respect of shares in the company, except so much of the distribution, if any, as represents a repayment of capital on the shares or is, when it is made, equal in amount or value to any new consideration given for the distribution—

(*c*) any redeemable share capital or any security issued by the company in respect of shares in the company otherwise than wholly for new consideration, or such part of any redeemable share capital or any security so issued as is not properly referable to new consideration—

(*d*) any interest or other distribution out of assets of the company in respect of securities of the company (except so much, if any, of any such distribution as represents the principal thereby secured), where the securities are either—

(i) securities issued as mentioned in paragraph (*c*) above, but excluding securities issued before 6th April 1965; or

(ii) securities convertible directly or indirectly into shares in the company and not securities quoted on a recognised stock exchange nor issued on terms which are reasonably comparable with the terms of issue of securities so quoted; or

(iii) securities under which the consideration given by the company for the use of the principal secured is to any extent dependent on the results of the company's business or any part of it, or under which the consideration so given represents more than a reasonable commercial return for the use of that principal; or

(iv) securities issued by the company and held by a company not resident in the United Kingdom, where the former is a 75 per cent subsidiary of the latter or both are 75 per cent subsidiaries of a third company; or

(v) securities which are connected with shares in the company, where 'connected with' means that in consequence of the nature of the rights attaching to the securities or shares, and in particular of any terms or conditions attaching to the right to transfer the shares or securities, it is necessary or advantageous for a person who has, or disposes of or acquires, any of the securities also to have, or to dispose of or to acquire, a proportionate holding of the shares;

(*e*) any such amount as is required to be treated as a distribution by subsection (3) below, or by section 234 below.

Subsection (3) of Section 233 provides

Where on a transfer of assets or liabilities by a company to its members or to a company by its members, the amount or value of the benefit received by a member (taken according to its market value) exceeds the amount or value (so taken) of any new consideration given by him, the company shall be treated as making a distribution to him of an amount equal to the difference:

Provided that, where the company and the member receiving the benefit are both resident in the United Kingdom and either the former is a subsidiary of the latter or both are subsidiaries of a third company also so resident, the said amount shall not be treated as a distribution.

Section 234 provides

(1) Where a company—

(*a*) repays any share capital, or has done so at any time after 6th April 1965; and

(*b*) at or after the time of that repayment issues as paid up or otherwise than by the receipt of new consideration any share capital, not being redeemable share capital; the amount so paid up shall be treated as a distribution made in respect of the shares on which it is paid up, except in so far as that amount exceeds the amount or aggregate amount of share capital so repaid less any amounts previously so paid up and treated by virtue of this subsection as distributions.

(2) Subsection (1) above shall not apply where the repaid share capital consists of fully paid preference shares—

(*a*) if those shares existed as issued and full paid preference shares on 6th April 1965 and throughout the period from that date until the repayment those shares continued to be fully paid preference shares, or

(*b*) if those shares were issued after 6th April 1965 as fully paid preference shares wholly for new consideration not derived from ordinary shares and throughout the period from their issue until the repayment those shares continued to be fully paid preference shares.

(3) In this section—

'ordinary shares' means shares other than preference shares;

'preference shares' means shares—

(*a*) which do not carry any right to dividends other than dividends at a rate per cent of the nominal value of the shares which is fixed, or fluctuates only with the standard rate of income tax, and

(*b*) which carry rights in respect of dividends and capital which are comparable with those general for fixed-dividend shares quoted on stock exchanges in the United Kingdom.

'New consideration not derived from ordinary shares' means new consideration other than consideration consisting of the surrender, transfer or cancellation of ordinary shares of the company or any other company or consisting of the variation of rights in ordinary shares of the company or any other company, and other than consideration derived from a repayment of share capital paid in respect of ordinary shares of the company or of any other company.

Under the Finance Act 1972, advance corporation tax (q.v.) is payable on all qualifying distributions made by a company. 'Qualifying distribution' is defined by Section 84(4) of that Act as any distribution other than—

(*a*) a distribution which, in relation to the company making it, is a distribution by virtue only of paragraph (c) of section 233(2) of the Taxes Act (bonus redeemable share capital and bonus securities); or

(*b*) a distribution consisting of any share capital or security which the company making the distribution has directly or indirectly received from the company by which the share capital or security was issued and which, in relation to the latter company, is a distribution by virtue only of that paragraph.

The Second Directive on Company Law of the EEC imposes on companies a number of conditions which they must satisfy before making distributions to their members. These requirements were implemented in the Companies Act, 1980, Section 45 of which now re-enacted in the 1985 Act Section 263 defines 'distribution' for the purpose of the Act

as any distribution of a company's assets to its members (whether or not it is made in cash) *other than* a distribution that is made by way of:

(*a*) The issue of either fully or partly paid bonus shares.

(*b*) The redemption of preference shares with the proceeds of a fresh issue of shares and the payment of any premium payable on redemption out of the share premium account.

(*c*) The reduction of share capital by

(i) Extinguishing or reducing liability in respect of share capital that is not paid up, or

(ii) Paying off paid up share capital.

(*d*) The distribution of assets to members on a winding up.

Section 263(1) of the 1985 Act provides

A company shall not make a distribution except out of profits available for the purpose.

and under Section 263(3) of the Act

... a company's profits available for distribution are its accumulated, realised profits, so far as not previously utilised by distribution or capitalisation, less its accumulated, realised losses, so far as not previously written off in a reduction or reorganisation of capital duly made.

The foregoing provisions apply to public and private companies. A *public* company, however, must satisfy the following further conditions before it makes a distribution to its members.

1. The amount of its net assets at the time of the proposed distribution must exceed the aggregate of its called-up share capital plus its undistributable reserves (Section 40(1)), and
2. the distribution must not reduce the amount of its net assets below the aggregate of its called-up share capital plus its undistributable reserves (Section 40(1)).

'Undistributable reserves' are defined as
(a) The share premium account.
(b) The Capital Redemption Reserve Fund.
(c) The excess of accumulated unrealized profits, not previously capitalized, over accumulated unrealized losses, not previously written off by reduction or reorganization of capital
(d) Any reserve which the company is prohibited from distributing by any enactment or by its memorandum or articles of association.

Perhaps the main point emerging from this legislation is that a company, public or private, may not make a distribution to its members except out of profits available for the purpose, i.e. as defined in Section 45 above.

DISTRINGAS Latin, that you distrain. The writ of distringas was abolished in 1883. In place thereof, the Rules of the Supreme Court (Order XLVI, Rules 2–11) provide that any person claiming an interest in stocks or shares may, on filing an affidavit in a specified form in the Central Office of the Supreme Court or in any District Registry, together with a notice also in specified form, procure an office copy of the affidavit and a duplicate of the filed notice authenticated by the seal of the Central Office or District Registry, and serve these documents on the company concerned. Thereafter, the company must give eight days' notice to the party serving the notice before passing a transfer of the stock or shares concerned or paying a dividend to the registered holder. This interval will give the interested party time to apply to the court for an injunction restraining the company from passing the transfer or paying the dividend. The method is not usually employed by a banker to protect himself in respect of untransferred shares held as security, but if money is lent on the mortgage of a reversionary interest in an estate comprising stocks and shares, a notice in lieu of distringas is sometimes served on the several companies as a precaution against the trustees dealing with the securities to the bank's detriment.

Notice in lieu of distringas must be distinguished from a Charging Order (q.v.).

DIVIDEND The share of profits distributed to the shareholder or stockholder of a company. The dividend may be payable at a fixed rate (as on preference shares), or the rate may be, as in the case of ordinary shares, dependent upon the profits that are made. It may also be cumulative. SEE *Cumulative Dividend*

The clauses in Table A of the Companies Act 1948, with respect to dividends are as follows.

Dividends and reserve

114. The company in general meeting may declare dividends, but no dividend shall exceed the amount recommended by the directors.

115. The directors may from time to time pay to the members such interim dividends as appear to the directors to be justified by the profits of the company.

116. No dividend shall be paid otherwise than out of profits. [Under the Companies Act 1980 this is amended to 'No dividend or interim dividend shall be paid otherwise than in accordance with the provision of Part III of the Companies Act 1980 which applies to the company'. SEE *Distribution*]

117. The directors may, before recommending any dividend, set aside out of the profits of the company such sums as they think proper as a reserve or reserves which shall, at the discretion of the directors, be applicable for any purpose to which the profits of the company may be properly applied, and pending such application may, at the like discretion, either be employed in the business of the company or be invested in such investments (other than shares of the company) as the directors may from time to time think fit. The directors may also without placing the same to reserve carry forward any profits which they may think prudent not to divide.

118. Subject to the rights of persons, if any, entitled to shares with special rights as to dividend, all dividends shall be declared and paid according to the amounts paid or credited as paid on the shares in respect whereof the dividend is paid, but no amount paid or credited as paid on a share in advance of calls shall be treated for the purposes of this regulation as paid on the share. All dividends shall be apportioned as paid proportionately to the amounts paid or credited as paid on the shares during any portion or portions of the period in respect of which the dividend is paid; but if any share is issued on terms providing that it shall rank for dividend as from a particular date such share shall rank for dividend accordingly.

119. The directors may deduct from any dividend payable to any member all sums of money (if any) presently payable by him to the company on account of calls or otherwise in relation to the shares of the company.

120. Any general meeting declaring a dividend or bonus may direct payment of such dividend or bonus wholly or partly by the distribution of specific assets and in particular of paid-up shares, debentures or debenture stock of any other company or in any one or more of such ways, and the directors shall give effect to such resolution, and where any difficulty arises in regard to such distribution, the directors may settle the same as they think expedient, and in particular may

issue fractional certificates and fix the value for distribution of such specific assets or any part thereof and may determine that cash payments shall be made to any members upon the footing of the value so fixed in order to adjust the rights of all parties, and may vest any such specific assets in trustees as may seem expedient to the directors.

121. Any dividend, interest or other moneys payable in cash in respect of shares may be paid by cheque or warrant sent through the post directed to the registered address of the holder, or, in the case of joint holders, to the registered address of that one of the joint holders who is first named on the register of members or to such person and to such address as the holder or joint holders may in writing direct. Every such cheque or warrant shall be made payable to the order of the person to whom it is sent. Any one of two or more joint holders may give effectual receipts for any dividends, bonuses or other moneys payable in respect of the shares held by them as joint holders.

122. No dividend shall bear interest against the company.

Dividends must be paid only out of profits, but a company has power, in certain special cases, to pay interest out of capital (Section 65 of the Companies Act 1948) but see also under *Distribution*.

Interest upon debentures is commonly regarded as a dividend, but it is really interest upon a loan, and must be paid by the company quite irrespective of any question of profits.

A dividend is also the name given to the amount which is paid to creditors from a bankrupt's estate. SEE *Company; Dividend Warrant; Dividends in Bankruptcy; Distribution; Income Tax*

DIVIDEND COVER This is the number of times the declared annual dividend on the shares of a company is covered by available profits. Available profits, in this context, means profits available for distribution out of the year's earnings, after payment of prior charges such as interest payments and preference dividends. Cover of 1 would mean that the company is paying out the full amount of its available earnings in dividends. The simplest calculation of 'cover' is earnings per share divided by dividend per share.

DIVIDEND MANDATE A written order from a shareholder requesting the company of which he is a member to send his dividends direct to his banker to be placed to the credit of his account. The advantages of having dividends and interest paid direct to a bank are: reduced risk of the warrants being lost or mislaid; saving of trouble in signing and dispatching warrants to a bank after receipt; and obtaining earlier credit in the account. Mandated dividends are now paid through Bankers' Automated Clearing System (q.v.).

DIVIDEND WARRANT An order, or warrant, issued by a company, and drawn upon its bankers, in favour of a member of the company, for payment of the dividend due to him upon his holding of shares or stock in the company.

Section 95 of the Bills of Exchange Act 1882, is 'the provisions of this Act as to crossed cheques shall apply to a warrant for payment of dividend'. SEE *Crossed Cheque*

In *Slingsby and Others* v *Westminster Bank Ltd* [1931] 1 KB 173, Finlay, J, in the course of his judgment said

> The point is whether 'dividend' in the Act of 1882 is used in the narrower sense as meaning that part of the profits of a company divisible among its shareholders, or in a broader sense as meaning that which is divided. I think that the broader construction is to be preferred. I arrive at this conclusion on the construction of Section 95 of the Act of 1882.

In that case the document before Finlay, J, was a warrant for interest on War Loan and he held that that document was a dividend warrant within Section 95. He pointed out that 'dividend' was the word used by the legislature to signify interest on Government stock. It cannot, however, be assumed from that decision that interest warrants issued by companies are dividend warrants within the meaning of Section 95.

Section 97(3) provides

> Nothing in this Act or in any repeal effected thereby shall affect—
>
> (a) The validity of any usage relating to dividend warrants, or the indorsements thereof.

It used to be common practice for a space to be left at the foot of dividend warrants for the proprietor's signature. Now, however, dividend warrants take the form of a standard cheque with no indorsement being required if credited to the proprietor's account.

Where a warrant is payable to, say, John Brown, with a note thereon 'A/c John Brown and John Jones', it should go to the credit of the joint account and not to J. Brown's private account.

Many dividend warrants are crossed and the effect is the same as when a cheque is crossed (Section 95 above). The banker on whom a crossed warrant is drawn should pay it only to another banker. As far as the collecting banker is concerned, these instruments, whether crossed or open, appear to be covered by Section 4 of the Cheques Act 1957.

There is often a note on a warrant that it must be presented within three months from date. If not so presented, it should be returned by the shareholder to the company for verification. (See the case of *Thairlwall* v *Great Northern Railway* under *Cheque*.)

The counterfoil of a dividend warrant shows the amount of the tax credit (SEE *Advance Corporation Tax*) and is retained by the shareholder as a certificate of the deduction of income tax and used, by those who are entitled, when claiming a return of tax from the Inland Revenue Commissioners.

The articles of association of a company may include a clause to the effect that 'the company shall not be responsible for the loss in transmission of any cheque or warrant sent through the post to the registered address of any member, whether at his request or otherwise'. The shareholder may protect himself from loss in post by having the dividend credited direct to his bank account. SEE *Dividend Mandate*

An ordinary dividend warrant is a cheque in a special form, but the dividend warrant of a bank, being drawn by a bank on a bank, is of the nature of a bank draft rather than a cheque. A dividend warrant by a bank in payment of the bank's own dividend should not be payable to bearer on demand as that would constitute an infringement of Section 11 of the Bank Charter Act 1844. SEE *Banker's Draft*

DIVIDEND YIELD This is the annual dividend on an ordinary share expressed as a percentage of the share price, namely,

$$\frac{\text{gross dividend per share}}{\text{market price of share}} \times 100$$

'Gross dividend' means the net amount of dividend grossed up for the amount of the tax credit. SEE *Advance Corporation Tax* The dividend yield on a share can normally only be expressed as an historic yield, i.e. in relation to dividends already paid or declared, future dividends being uncertain. The dividend yield obviously varies with each movement in the share price.

DIVIDENDS IN BANKRUPTCY The distribution of dividends among the creditors of a bankrupt's estate is governed by the Bankruptcy Act 1914, which provides

62.—(1) Subject to the retention of such sums as may be necessary for the costs of administration, or otherwise, the trustee shall, with all convenient speed, declare and distribute dividends amongst the creditors who have proved their debts.

(2) The first dividend, if any, shall be declared and distributed within four months after the conclusion of the first meeting of the creditors, unless the trustee satisfies the committee of inspection that there is sufficient reason for postponing the declaration to a later date.

(3) Subsequent dividends shall, in the absence of sufficient reason to the contrary, be declared and distributed at intervals of not more than six months.

(4) Before declaring a dividend, the trustee shall cause notice of his intention to do so to be gazetted in the prescribed manner, and shall also send reasonable notice thereof to each creditor mentioned in the bankrupt's statement who has not proved his debt.

(5) When the trustee has declared a dividend, he shall send to each creditor who has proved a notice showing the amount of the dividend and when and how it is payable, and a statement in the prescribed form as to the particulars of the estate.

Joint and separate dividends

63.—(1) Where one partner of a firm is adjudged bankrupt, a creditor to whom the bankrupt is indebted jointly with the other partners of the firm, or any of them, shall not receive any dividend out of the separate property of the bankrupt until all the separate creditors have received the full amount of their respective debts.

(2) Where joint and separate properties are being administered, dividends of the joint and separate properties shall, unless otherwise directed by the Board of Trade, on the application of any person interested, be declared together, and the expenses of an incidental to such dividends shall be fairly apportioned by the trustee between the joint and separate properties, regard being had to the work done for and the benefit received by each property.

Right of creditor who has not proved debt before declaration of a dividend

65. Any creditor who has not proved his debt before the declaration of any dividend or dividends shall be entitled to be paid out of any money for the time being in the hands of the trustee any dividend or dividends he may have failed to receive before that money is applied to the payment of any future dividend or dividends, but he shall not be entitled to disturb the distribution of any dividend declared before his debt was proved by reason that he has not participated therein.

Before declaring a final dividend, the trustee shall give notice to creditors whose claims have not been established to his satisfaction, that, if not established within a time limited by the notice, he will make the final dividend without regard to their claims (Section 67). SEE *Bankruptcy*

DIVORCE AND SEPARATION The financial consequences of divorce and separation are currently the subject of much debate (see below). The existing rules and procedures are, in some cases, anomalous and can result in hardship to one party or another. Divorce is, of course, the termination of marriage by order of the court. Separation is a matter for agreement between the parties. There is no strict rule on which the courts will fix the amount of any maintenance payments.

There is, however, what is known as the 'one-third rule' which is adopted quite frequently but not inevitably, i.e. that a wife will be awarded one-third of the total income of herself and her husband. Additional payments would be ordered for any dependent children.

Some Taxation Aspects

If the couple agree to separate permanently, the Inland Revenue will normally accept the separation date as agreed between the parties. If any maintenance payments are purely voluntary on the part of the husband, he will continue to be entitled to the married man's personal allowance but the payments will not be allowed for tax purposes. If, however, maintenance payments arise from a legally binding agreement, the party making the payments (usually the husband) will deduct tax at source from the payments and they will be part of the taxable income of the recipient.

From a tax planning point of view there is often some advantage in splitting maintenance payments between the wife and individual children in order to maximize the personal allowances in each case. Each child will be entitled to the single person's allowance so that in the absence of other income the full amount of tax deducted from the maintenance payments may be covered by the amount of the personal allowance.

Maintenance payments for children do, however, count as income of the child if and when he or she goes to university. Local education authorities regard maintenance payments as part of the investment income of the student.

Voluntary payments made by a parent for the maintenance of a chiild are disregarded for tax purposes. If in fact a fund is set aside on a voluntary basis for the child's maintenance, the income of the fund will still be deemed to be that of the parent until the child is 18, following the normal tax rule.

There is a statutory provision for 'small' maintenance payments to be paid without deduction of tax at the time of writing, in the case of payments not exceeding £33 per week or £143 per month to a husband or wife for their own maintenance, or payments not exceeding £18 per week or £78 per month to a husband or wife for the maintenance of children, the payments must be made without deduction of tax. From the passing of the 1982 Finance Act, however, the higher limits of £33 per week or £143 per month will apply to payments made direct to children under 21 years for their own maintenance, etc.

Such payments, whether made to the parent or to the child, are part of the recipient's income for tax purposes and are allowed as a deduction from the payer's income. These provisions apply only to payments under court orders.

Where school fees are paid direct to a school under a court maintenance order, the Inland Revenue have agreed that the spouse paying the fees will be allowed tax relief, provided it is a term of the court order that the fees be paid direct to the school. The fees will be part of the child's taxable income, but it is necessary for the contract under which the fees are paid to be between the school and the child and not between the school and the spouse making the payment.

The Matrimonial Home

The rights of a husband and wife to continue living in the matrimonial home is a legal matter rather than a financial one. Even if the home has been provided by the husband and, for example, all mortgage payments made by him, a divorced or separated wife cannot be turned out of the home. Indeed, neither party can be turned out of a matrimonial home except by a court order, which would take into account all the relevant circumstances, including the best interests of any children. If an order is made for the house to be sold, the court will have regard to all the circumstances, including the contribution by the parties over the years to the common purse, in determining the destination of the proceeds. Whenever possible it is best for the parties to come to an agreement as to the future of the matrimonial home. If, for example, the wife is to remain there with the children, this will be taken into account in assessing any maintenance payments to be made by the husband. The right to a future share of the sale proceeds of a home is registrable as a land charge.

The court has extensive powers to deal with the matrimonial home, but in general if the house is in joint names or in the husband's name solely, the house will normally have to be sold when any children come of age or cease full-time education. Until that time, the wife and dependent children will normally be able to remain in the home. If either party buys a separate house on mortgage, the maximum limit will still apply for tax relief. It is better, therefore, for a wife to take over the mortgage payments of the old matrimonial home and the husband to increase, under court order or legal agreement, the amount of maintenance to cover the mortgage costs. The wife will then qualify for tax relief on the mortgage interest payments and the husband will get tax relief on his maintenance payments.

The Financial Consequences of Divorce

A discussion paper on the financial consequences

of divorce was published by the Law Commission in 1980 (Cmnd 8041, HMSO). *Inter alia*, the paper included for discussion the following bases of dealing with the financial implications of divorce:

1. the limitation of financial support to cases of real need;
2. the division of property once and for all in the 'clean break' approach;
3. an inflexible mathematical formula to deal with all cases;
4. the restoration of the parties to their position had the marriage never happened.

In December 1981, the Law Commission published its recommendations *The Financial Consequences of Divorce* (Cmnd 112) and, in general, recommended that the Courts should no longer be obliged to put divorced parties into the financial position they would have enjoyed had the marriage not broken down. The aim should be that the divorced parties should seek to be self-sufficient in time and not continue to rely on maintenance from the other spouse. It was recognized, however, that it may be appropriate in some cases for a spouse to receive maintenance payments for life and, wherever there are children, their financial needs must be an overriding priority.

The Matrimonial and Family Proceedings Act 1984, gave effect to some of the recommendations of the Law Commission. The new Act, in particular on this subject, amends the Matrimonial Causes Act 1973, and requires the court to give consideration in all cases to the welfare during minority, of any child of the family under the age of 18. The court must also take into account any increase in the earning capacity which it would be reasonable to expect a party to the marriage to acquire and any contributions which either of the parties is likely to make to the welfare of the family in the foreseeable future.

The Act removes the earlier requirement that the parties be placed in the same financial position as they would have been had the marriage not broken down.

The Act also imposes an obligation on the court to consider whether or not to terminate the financial obligations of each spouse to the other whether to limit the period of any periodical payments order, and whether to dismiss an application for periodical payments and direct that no further application be made.

DOCUMENTARY BILL A documentary bill is a bill of exchange which is accompanied by various documents, such as bill of lading, dock warrant, delivery order, policy of insurance, invoice.

Insurance documents must be as specifically described in the instructions, and must be issued and/or signed by insurance companies or their agents, or by underwriters.

Cover notes issued by brokers will not be accepted, unless specifically authorized in the instructions.

When a banker receives a bill for acceptance, with documents attached, and he sends the bill to the drawee to be accepted, and informs the drawee that the bill of lading and invoice are in his possession, the banker is not thereby held responsible if the bill of lading should prove to be a forgery. And where a banker accepts a documentary bill at the request of a customer, and the bill of lading proves to be forged, the banker, having paid the bill, may recover the amount from the customer.

A forged date on a bill of lading does not necessarily render the bill null and void for all purposes.

In *Kwei Tek Chao* v *British Traders and Shippers Ltd*, [1954] 1 All ER 779, sellers in London agreed to sell Swedish bleaching chemical to buyers in Hong Kong. It was a condition of the contract that the buyer would provide a letter of credit in the seller's favour, payment against documents including a bill of lading to show shipment not later than 31st October, 1951. The goods were shipped in fact on 3rd November, but the bills of lading were forged as respects the date of shipment and purported to be within the terms of the credit. The buyers, who had pledged the documents of title to their bank, in due course took delivery of the goods on the bank's behalf. Subsequently the forgery was discovered and the buyers rejected the goods and sued the sellers for the return of the money paid on the grounds that the consideration had failed entirely. Alternatively, they claimed for damages for fraudulent misrepresentation or breach of duty and for loss of profit on an aborted contract of resale.

Devlin, J, refused to accept the argument that the forgery of the date on the bill of lading rendered that document null and void for all purposes. The true view, he held, was that the nature of the alteration must be examined and an opinion formed as to whether it went to the essence of the instrument. In this case it did not and the bill, although having a forged date, was an enforceable contract of affreightment.

He also held that the buyer had two distinct rights: the right to reject the documents and the right to reject the goods. The first right arose when the documents were tendered for payment, and the second when the goods were examined and found not to correspond with the terms of the contract.

Bankers opening documentary credits usually cover themselves by the terms on which they do business against payment against forged bills of lading or other forged documents as now provided in the Uniform Customs (q.v.).

The holder of a bill, by presenting it for acceptance or for payment, does not warrant the genuineness of the bill or of any of the signatures thereon, or that any accompanying documents are genuine or represent actual goods, and does not undertake to indemnify the acceptor in the event of the documents proving to be forgeries. (*Guaranty Trust Company of New York* v *A. Hannay & Co* (1918) 34 TLR 427). SEE *Presentment for Payment*

If documents are sent out along with the bill to the drawee in order that he may inspect them, they should not be left with him. A banker, however, may have received instructions, from the correspondent sending him the bill, to deliver up the documents to the drawee upon his acceptance of the bill; or he may have instructions to give up the documents on payment of the bill under rebate.

When a banker advances against shipments he sends the bill abroad, with the bills of lading attached, for payment. When the documents are given up against acceptance, the banker has then to rely upon the acceptor, regarding whom he should have satisfactory information.

Where a credit is opened abroad at a customer's request, against bills of lading, policy, etc., the foreign banker draws on the banker in the UK and sends the bill, with the documents attached, to the English banker. The documents may be taken by the customer and paid for at once; or the amount may be charged to the customer and the documents held as security until required. In some cases, the bills of lading may be handed to the customer and a letter taken from him hypothecating the goods to the bank, and undertaking to hand over to the bank the proceeds from the sale of the goods, and until that is done the customer agrees to hold the goods or the proceeds in trust for the bank. When this is done a separate account is usually opened for the operation. In such cases the banker really parts with his security and has to rely upon the honesty of his customer. In case of failure, trustees generally recognize these undertakings. There is the danger, however, that there may be a contra account due from the customer to a purchaser of the goods, in which case, as the latter has no notice of the hypothecation, he is entitled to deduct the contra account from the amount he is due to pay as the purchase price of the goods.

When documentary bills are discounted, the banker takes a note of hypothecation or memorandum of deposit from the customer, by which the bill of lading and the goods are pledged to the banker and under which he is given a right, if necessary, to sell the goods. SEE *Bill of Lading; Trust Letter or Receipt*

See the case of *Ladenburg & Co* v *Goodwin, Ferreira & Co Ltd (in Liquidation) and Garnett (the Liquidator)*, under *Registration of Charges*.

If a banker sells a documentary bill he indorses it and thus becomes liable thereon; the bills of lading, indorsed in blank by the shipper, and the insurance policy, accompany the bill.

A banker keeps a record of all his liabilities on acceptances and indorsements.

Where documents are given up against payment of a bill under rebate, the rate is usually ½ per cent above the London Clearing Bankers deposit rate, and is calculated from the date when the money (free of cost) will be in the hands of the person entitled to receive it, and at the place where it is payable. A receipt is indorsed upon the bill that the amount has been paid under rebate at . . . per cent. SEE *Bill of Exchange; Bill of Lading; Documentary Credit; Marine Insurance*

DOCUMENTARY CREDIT One method adopted to finance overseas trade is to insert in a contract for the sale of goods a provision that payment shall be made by a banker. The banker assumes liability for the payment of the price of the goods and receives in return a percentage commission and the security afforded by the pledge of the relative documents of title. Importers approach their bankers with the request that the latter should lend their names as drawees of bills covering goods sold to the importers. They do so at the instance of exporters who may not desire to ship goods to parties whose credit is unknown to them and who may wish to discount their drawings at a fine rate at their own bankers. The term at which a bill shall be drawn is a matter concerning the buyer and seller. If the bill is drawn at sight, it is called a bank sight credit; if the bill is drawn at a period after sight, it is called a bank acceptance credit. If the shipping documents are not attached to the bill, the credit is described as a 'clean' or 'open' credit. Such credits are only opened for customers of the highest standing. The more usual course is for the shipping documents to accompany the bills drawn under the credit.

When a banker pays a bill drawn under a sight credit he looks to his customer to provide him with the funds to do so. When he accepts a term bill drawn under a documentary credit it is customary for him to release the documents to the importer against a letter of hypothecation (q.v.) in order that the importer may be able to clear and market the goods. When the bill matures, the banker will expect his customers to put up the funds with which to meet it. In both cases a banker will expect all but his strongest customers to furnish at least partial security.

The banker granting the credit will either advise the exporter direct or through a correspondent banker in the exporter's country. The letter of advice will state the conditions governing the credit, such as its expiry date, its terms, what documents must be attached to the bill or bills, the nature and description of the goods, the date by which goods must be shipped, and the ports of loading and destination. The beneficiary (exporter, drawer) must mark all his drawings with the number and date of the letter of credit under which they are drawn. The granting banker is under no obligation to honour drafts which have not been drawn within the terms of the credit and he will be unable to debit his customer should he do so.

Where the credit calls for specified documents, it is not necessary that the bills of lading should describe the goods in full detail as they are described in the credit. It is enough if the documents are individually valid, are identifiable with the shipment, and as a set contain all the particulars given in the credit, and so long as those particulars in themselves do not show any conflict.

In *Midland Bank* v *Seymour* [1955] 2 Lloyd's Rep. 147, the bank were instructed to open a confirmed irrevocable letter of credit in favour of an exporter in Hong Kong, Mr Seymour being their customer and the importer of the goods. As this was the first occasion on which Mr Seymour had dealt with this particular firm of exporters in Hong Kong he asked his bank to obtain a report on them. The reply was brief and not very informative, but later when Mr Seymour opened further credits, the Chartered Bank in Hong Kong cabled back that, while nothing detrimental was known of the exporting concern, the credits had not yet been advised to them on the grounds that the total quantity of goods mentioned in the credits was not likely to be available in Hong Kong. Also they thought the price was much below current market price. They suggested that the goods should be examined after loading by a recognized surveyor. This information duly reached the Midland Bank and was passed on by them to their customer, who did not think there was anything in the points made. The credits were, therefore, duly opened.

About a fortnight later a further report reached the Midland Bank on the exporters, and this report, while repeating information already known, contained the phrase 'transactions should be on a marginal basis'. This report was apparently not passed on to the customer. When the cargo of goods was found to be of very poor quality and the exporters, having collected substantial sums under the credits, disappeared, the bank was alleged to have been negligent in that, on receipt of the first report, they had failed to make further enquiries, and in respect of the third report, they had failed to communicate it to their customer. Devlin, J, reviewed the bank's duty to its customer and on the first ground found no fault on the bank's part.

> The bank must take care not to supply misleading information.... Is there a duty upon the bank to prosecute its inquiries with due diligence? Having got the information, it must take care that it is not misleading information, and of course, if it makes what are obviously wholly inadequate inquiries, it may get information which it knows or ought to know is misleading; but, apart from that, has it got a duty to exercise due diligence in the prosecution of its inquiries? That arises on the first head chronologically of negligence that is claimed in this case. Mr Seymour's complaint is that the bank ought to have realised that the answer it got was not an adequate answer and that the bank was, therefore, negligent in not making further supplementary inquiries in order to get further information.
>
> I am not satisfied that the bank's duty goes as far as that. After all, a bank is not employed as a private inquiry agent.

On the second ground, the judge held that the bank was guilty of a breach of duty in failing to pass on a material communication.

> Once one grants that there is a duty not to give misleading information, then I think that that duty is a continuing one in this sense, that so long as the relationship exists, and so long as the matter to which the information was relevant is still, as it were, in hand, there is a duty to pass on any supplementary information which might alter the character of the original information.

It is no part of a banker's duty when paying under an irrevocable credit to scrutinize minutely the terms of a bill of lading, to consider their legal effect and, in the interests of the buyer, satisfy himself that any particular clause had been complied with. His duty is to satisfy himself that the correct documents have been presented to him, and that the bills of lading bear no indorsement or clausing by the shipowners or shippers which could reasonably mean that there was, or might be, some defect in the goods, or their packing (See

British Imex Industries Ltd v *Midland Bank* [1958] 1 All ER 264, where the bill of lading contained a printed clause relieving the shipowner from liability in respect of the insufficiency of packing and marking of steel bars and the bank called for an acknowledgment that the shippers had complied with the requirement. It was indicated in the Court of Appeal that only if clear evidence of fraud were available might the party establishing the credit be able to obtain an injunction delaying payment.)

In the case of *Gian Singh & Co Ltd* v *Banque de l'Indochine* [1974] 2 All ER 754, a company had instructed a bank to open an irrevocable documentary credit, payment to be made on presentation of a sight draft, accompanied by a certificate signed by a named person who was a director of the company. The bank made payment on the production of the certificate which turned out to be forged. The company claimed that payment had been made improperly because the terms of the documentary credit had not been complied with. The Privy Council, on appeal from the Court of Appeal of Singapore held that the bank had taken reasonable care to examine the certificate when presented. It bore the company's letter heading and had apparently been signed by the correct person beneath the words of a rubber stamp giving the name of the company. After the signature the word director had been rubber stamped. It was held that the bank had complied with the terms of the credit.

A number of points of law came before the court in the case of *Soproma Spa* v *Marine and Animal By-Products Corporation* [1966] 1 Lloyd's Rep 367. The main question was whether there had been good tender under a letter of credit established by Italian buyers in favour of New York sellers of fishmeal. On this point there were a number of decisions: that the bill of lading was marked 'Freight Collect' whereas the credit called for 'Freight Prepaid' caused the tender to be bad, and the fact that in practice objection was seldom raised to this point was irrelevant as to the legal position; that the bill of lading, although issued in Italy, was subject to English Law (as was the contract of sale) and was not good tender because it was not blank endorsed; that the difference of 0.5 per cent in the centigrade temperature of the shipment between the bill of lading and the terms of the credit could not be disregarded under the *de minimus* rule; that the tender was bad because of inconsistent protein statements described in the shipping documents. On a wider aspect it was held that, although the credit opened by its terms failed to accord with the contract, by tendering documents the sellers were precluded from taking the point and that where, by the terms of the contract, payment was to be made by a letter of credit, the seller could not tender documents direct to the buyer.

When advising the opening of a credit, the grantor banker will state whether the credit is to be revocable or irrevocable. A credit of the former type can be cancelled at any moment, but a banker must honour drafts drawn under an irrevocable credit even if his customer has failed in the meantime. Bankers therefore charge an additional commission when they open irrevocable credits on behalf of their customers. It is often said that an irrevocable credit is the same thing as a confirmed credit, but this is not accurate since there are credits which are both irrevocable and unconfirmed.

> For example, an American bank may ask its London correspondent to open a credit for an Indian beneficiary, the credit to be irrevocable on the part of the American bank and unconfirmed by the London bank.... Where more than one bank is concerned, whether or not the credit is irrevocable by all depends on the instructions each receives. [*Journal of the Institutue of Bankers*, May 1936]

Quite apart from whether a credit is revocable or irrevocable, it may be in one of several forms. There is the 'marginal' credit, so-called from the fact that the instrument in question consists of a blank form of bill of exchange, in the margin of which are contained the terms of issue of the credit. (Such credits are now rarely seen.)

A 'revolving' credit is one for a certain sum which is automatically renewed by 'putting on at the bottom what is taken off at the top' so that, as drawings are paid, the beneficiary's power of availment reverts *pari passu* to the original figure. In the Australian, New Zealand, and South African trades there is in use an 'anticipatory' letter of credit which contains a clause entitling the beneficiary to draw on the issuing bank before shipment. A 'reimbursement' credit is created when a banker in country X requests a banker in country Y to allow an exporter in Y to draw bills on the Y banker, the X banker undertaking to reimburse his correspondent as and when such drawings have to be honoured by the Y banker.

The 'anticipatory' or 'pre-shipment' type of credit may contain what is known as a 'red' clause, which authorizes the seller to obtain an advance before shipment of goods for which he has to pay in advance. This is common in the South Africa, Australia and New Zealand wool trade.

The so-called 'green' clause covers the same pre-shipment advance, but storage as well.

A 'negotiation' credit is one where a buyer opens a credit in favour of the seller, not in the seller's country, but in a third country, and the seller's bills on the bank opening the credit are negotiated in his own country. Thus, a German buyer from India might pay by means of an irrevocable credit in sterling opened with a London bank. The seller's bills drawn on the London bank are purchased with recourse by a bank in India.

A 'back-to-back' credit is one arranged in favour of the original supplier of the goods on the strength of a credit already opened in favour of the middleman by the ultimate purchaser. Both credits must be in identical terms and are placed 'back-to-back'. When the goods are first paid for in, say, London, the middleman substitutes his own invoices and the documents are presented for payment at the bank of the ultimate purchaser. The middleman's profit is the difference in price, less expenses.

A 'transferable' credit is one which specifically authorizes the beneficiary to transfer part or whole of the credit to someone else. Thus, a buying agent abroad can arrange the purchase of goods on behalf of his principal on the footing that the principal opens a transferable credit in favour of the agent and the agent transfers the benefit of the credit to the suppliers of the goods.

A 'refinance' credit is used where a buyer requires, say, three months' credit, but the seller wants his money at once. The difficulty is overcome by a provision in the credit that as soon as the seller's sight bill has been paid the advising bank will accept the buyer's bill at three months. This is then discounted by the advising bank and the proceeds remitted by that bank to the opening bank, who are thus reimbursed for the payment to the seller.

A standard international procedure for dealing with documentary credits was first published in 1933 by the International Chamber of Commerce under the title *The Uniform Customs and Practice for Documentary Credits.* Revised versions were issued in 1951, 1962, 1974 and 1983. The United Nations Commission on International Trade Law commended the use of the 1974 Revision in all transactions involving the establishment of documentary credits. SEE *Uniform Customs and Practice for Documentary Credits*

DOLLAR CERTIFICATES OF DEPOSITS SEE *London Dollar Certificates of Deposit*

DOMICILE This is the permanent home of an individual. Two factors are essential to establish domicile; one is the fact of residence in a particular place, and the other is the intention of remaining there, the *animus manendi.* Under English law, everyone is presumed to have a domicile and no one may have two domiciles. A person's domicile of origin is determined by the domicile at the time of birth, of the father or other person on whom the child is legally dependent. A foundling's domicile of origin is the country in which he is found. The domicile of origin of an illegitimate child is that of his mother. A person may change his or her domicile by adopting a domicile of choice, provided that the two requirements are satisfied, namely, the fact of residence and the intention to remain. If a domicile of choice is forsaken for any reason, the domicile of origin reverts unless another domicile of choice is immediately adopted.

An anomaly in the concept of domicile was introduced by the British Government in the Finance Act, 1975 (Section 45), when the Government sought to arrest the drain of personal wealth to the Channel Islands and the Isle of Man by decreeing that any person who left the UK and became domiciled in those islands after 10th December, 1974 was deemed (subject to certain exceptions) still to be domiciled in the UK. This provision was however repealed in the Finance (No. 7) Act 1983.

Domicile is important in certain financial matters, notably contracts, capital transfer tax (and some other aspects of taxation), marriage and testamentary dispositions.

DOLLAR PREMIUM In 1962 the Government introduced requirements (with a view to diminishing the flow of funds from the UK) that securities outside the Sterling Area could be bought only with currency arising from the sale of similar securities by other UK residents. Thus an 'investment dollar pool' was created which, because of the demand for investment currency, attracted premium rate. The premium varied over the years from approximately 10 per cent to nearly 100 per cent. On the sale of overseas securities the premium was recovered but in 1965 the Government introduced a rule requiring sellers of premium currency to sell a quarter thereof to the Bank of England at the normal rate of exchange. This effectively reduced the size of the dollar pool and increased the premiums. In 1972 the arrangements were extended to most of the countries which were formerly part of the old Schedules Territories.

DOMICILED BILL Where a bill of exchange is accepted payable at some place other than the acceptor's private or business address it is said to be domiciled at the place. A drawer may, if he wishes, name the domicile or place of payment in the body of the bill or below the drawee's name.

DONATIO MORTIS CAUSA This is a gift made in anticipation of and conditional upon the death of the donor. If the donor dies the gift takes effect, except in the case where the death contemplated is suicide (*re Dudman* [1925] Ch 553). Whilst the donor lives he may revoke the gift. If the donor dies it does not matter that he dies of a death other than that which was contemplated when he made the gift.

A donatio mortis causa is one of the very few ways in which property may pass from one person to another on death, other than under a will or intestacy. The general rule is that property which confers title on delivery (e.g. a gift of money or furniture) can be the subject matter of a donatio mortis causa but not property which requires some further legal act to complete the title (e.g. the transfer of freehold or leasehold property).

If a person, in anticipation of death, draws a cheque and hands it to, say, his son, unless the cheque is actually or constructively paid before death takes place, the gift is ineffectual. It cannot be paid by the banker after he has had notice of the drawer's death, and it does not form a charge upon the deceased's estate. But if the donee transfers the cheque to another party, for value, that party would have a claim upon the estate for the amount, though the banker would not pay it after notice of death.

There is, however, a difference between a cheque drawn by the donor, and one payable to the donor. In the former case 'his own cheque is not property, it is only a revocable order', but in the latter case it is the 'indicia of title to property which belonged to him' (Lord Justice Buckley). When it is payable to the donor, the person who receives it obtains a good donatio mortis causa, and is fully entitled to the amount. If not indorsed by the donor, it has been held that the recipient is entitled to require the indorsement of his legal representatives.

A bill, a promissory note and a bond and mortgage deed have also been held to form good subjects of gifts made in anticipation of death. A dying man's own promissory note is not a proper subject of a donatio mortis causa (*re Leaper, Blythe* v *Atkinson* [1916] 1 Ch 579).

Where a banker's deposit receipt was handed over by the donor immediately prior to his death, it was held to be a good donatio mortis causa (*re Dillon; Duffin* v *Duffin* (1892) 62 LT 614).

Where the certificate of registration of an Exchequer Bond (which certificate entitled the owner to delivery of the Bond on demand) was handed over as a dying gift, it was held to be a good donatio mortis causa of the Bond (*re Lee; Treasury Solicitor* v *Parrott* [1918] 2 Ch 320).

Deposit books of savings banks and clearing banks were held to be essential documents of title in *Birch and Another* v *Treasury Solicitor* [1950] 2 All ER 1198, where three questions indicating the tests to be imposed in such a case were answered affirmatively by the Court of Appeal.

The three questions are

1. Is there a sufficient delivery of the subject-matter of the alleged gift to support a donatio?
2. Is there the necessary intention to make the gift (*animus donandi*)?
3. Assuming the first two questions to be answered affirmatively, then where the subject-matter of the gift is a bank balance (a chose in action incapable itself of physical delivery) and a bank deposit book relating to the account is delivered, is this document such an essential indication of title as is necessary to constitute a valid donatio mortis causa of a chose in action?

Although a cheque payable to the donor or a deposit receipt, forms an effectual gift, a banker, with notice of a payee's death, would not pay such cheque or deposit receipt to the recipient of the gift (even if indorsed by the deceased donor), until indorsed by the legal representatives of the deceased. SEE *Gifts* Inter Vivos

DORMANT BALANCES These are the balances of banking accounts which have not been operated upon for a long period. They presumably include accounts of people who have died (without any claim by their executors), gone abroad, forgotten they had the account or, for some other reason, prefer to remain incognito. The amounts involved are believed to be very considerable in total and, in fact, were estimated to be as much as £8 million in 1920. The subject was discussed by a Select Committee of Parliament in 1919 and has been raised on various occasions since then. The question as to whether unclaimed dividends, dormant bank balances and other unclaimed assets could not be put to some use by the Government was answered in the House of Lords on 13th December, 1961 when a Government spokesman said that there was no valid justification for the course proposed, that the Government would have no moral title to dormant balances, the secrecy attaching to private bank accounts would be violated, and that difficulties would be raised in regard to the particular point in time at which any particular balance should be considered to be dormant.

In *Swiss Bank Corporation* v *Joachimson* (1921)

37 TLR 534, the Court of Appeal held that express demand by a customer for repayment of a current account balance is a condition precedent to the right to sue the banker for the amount. Atkin, LJ said

> The result of this decision will be that for the future bankers may have to face legal claims for balances of accounts which have remained dormant for more than six years. But seeing that bankers have not been in the habit as a matter of business of setting up the Statute of Limitations against their customers or their legal representatives. I do not suppose that such a change in what was supposed to be the law will have much practical effect.

DOUBLE TAXATION RELIEF The UK Government has entered into agreements with a number of other countries for reciprocal taxation arrangements designed to prevent double taxation. There are various categories of agreement resulting in differing treatment of a recipient's income. In some cases, it is agreed that the income will be taxed in the country of residence of the recipient and not in the other country which is a party to the agreement. More usually, there is provision for withholding tax of, say, 15 per cent in the country where the income originates with full set-off of any additional tax against the tax liability of the recipient in the UK. Even in those cases where there is no double taxation agreement with a particular country, and tax paid in that country on income arising from there will usually be allowed as a deduction from that income for the recipient's tax purposes in the UK.

General agreements on taxation have been entered into between the UK and the following countries (SEE Supplement):

Algeria
Antigua
Australia
Austria
Bangladesh
Barbados
Belgium
Belize
Botswana
Brunei
Burma
Canada
China
Cyprus
Denmark
Dominica
Egypt
Falkland Islands
Faroe Islands
Fiji
Finland
France
Gambia
German Federal Republic
Ghana
Gilbert Islands (Kiribati)
Greece
Grenada
Guernsey
Hungary
India
Indonesia
Irish Republic
Israel
Italy
Jamaica
Japan
Jersey
Kenya
Korea
Kuwait
Lesotho
Luxembourg
Malawi
Malaysia
Malta
Isle of Man
Mauritius
Montserrat
Netherlands
Netherlands Antilles
New Zealand
Nigeria (terminated)
Norway
Pakistan
Philippines
Poland
Portugal
Romania
St Christopher and Nevis
St Lucia
St Vincent
Seychelles
Sierra Leone
Singapore
Solomon Islands
South Africa
South West Africa (Namibia)
Spain
Sri Lanka
Sudan
Swaziland
Sweden
Switzerland
Tanzania (terminated)
Thailand
Trinidad and Tobago
Tunisia
Tuvalu
Uganda
USA
Yugoslavia
Zambia
Zimbabwe

DOW JONES INDUSTRIAL AVERAGE One of the market indicators, compiled by Charles H. Dow of Dow Jones & Company, New York. It is made up of the price movements of 30 major stocks traded on the New York Stock Exchange.

DRAFT From the verb to draw, formerly spelled 'draught' and 'drawght'. Bills of exchange on demand, or after sight, or after date, are called drafts, because they are drawn by one person on another. Cheques also are sometimes called drafts. But the word is used principally when referring to a banker's own draft, or instrument drawn upon another banker or upon one of his own branches, or to a draft drawn upon his London agents or London office, at seven, 14 or 21 days after date, or on demand, or to a foreign draft drawn by a banker in one country upon a banker in another. SEE *Banker's Draft*

DRAWEE The drawee of a bill is the person to whom it is addressed. By Section 6 of the Bills of Exchange Act 1882

> (1) The drawee must be named or otherwise indicated in a bill with reasonable certainty.
> (2) A bill may be addressed to two or more drawees whether they are partners or not, but an order addressed to two drawees in the alternative or to two or more drawees in succession is not a bill of exchange.

Where different parties to a bill are the same person, Section 5 provides

> (1) A bill may be drawn payable to, or to the order of, the drawer; or it may be drawn payable to, or to the order of, the drawee.
> (2) Where in a bill drawer and drawee are the same person, or where the drawee is a fictitious person or a person not having capacity to contract, the holder may treat the instrument, at his option, either as a bill of exchange or as a promissory note.

The drawee is the person who is expected to accept the bill and, at maturity, to pay it. If the drawee, on receiving a bill, agrees to pay the amount as indicated therein, he signifies his assent to the drawer's order by signing his name across the face of the bill. This is called accepting the bill. When the drawee has accepted a bill he is then called the acceptor and his written assent on the bill is his acceptance (q.v.).

With regard to funds in the hands of a drawee, Section 53 enacts

(1) A bill, of itself, does not operate as an assignment of funds in the hands of the drawee available for the payment thereof, and the drawee of a bill who does not accept as required by the Act is not liable on the instrument. This subsection shall not extend to Scotland.

(2) In Scotland, where the drawee of a bill has in his hands funds available for the payment thereof, the bill operates as an assignment of the sum for which it is drawn in favour of the holder from the time when the bill is presented to the drawee.

The drawee of a cheque is the banker on whom it is drawn. The banker is responsible only to the drawer and is under no liability to the person presenting the cheque for payment, except in Scotland, where the presentment of a cheque attaches any balance there may be in the drawer's account to the extent of the cheque. In Scotland, if the balance in an account does not admit of the payment of a cheque the cheque is returned and the balance of the account is transferred to a 'funds attached' account.

The drawee of a bank draft is the bank to which the order to pay is addressed. SEE *Acceptance; Bill of Exchange; Presentment for Acceptance*

DRAWER The drawer is the person who signs a bill of exchange giving an order to another person, the drawee, to pay the amount mentioned therein.

In the usual course, a drawer makes out the bill himself, signs it, and sends it to the drawee for acceptance. But a person may sign a bill as drawer which has already been made out and accepted, and even indorsed. When a simple signature on blank paper is delivered by the signer in order that it may be converted into a bill, it operates as a prima facie authority to fill it up as a complete bill, using the signature, if so authorized, as that of the drawer. SEE *Inchoate Instrument*

Section 55 of the Bills of Exchange Act 1882, provides

(1) The drawer of a bill by drawing it—
- (*a*) Engages that on due presentment it shall be accepted and paid according to its tenor, and that if it be dishonoured he will compensate the holder or any indorser who is compelled to pay it, provided that the requisite proceedings on dishonour be duly taken;
- (*b*) Is precluded from denying to a holder in due course the existence of the payee and his then capacity to indorse.

A drawer may, if he wish, limit his liability on the bill by such words as 'Pay John Brown or order without recourse', or 'sans recours'. Permission to do so is given in Section 16, as follows:

The drawer of a bill, and any indorser may insert therein an express stipulation—

(1) Negativing or limiting his own liability to the holder.

(2) Waiving as regards himself some or all of the holder's duties.

Where different parties to a bill are the same person, Section 5 provides

(1) A bill may be drawn payable to, or to the order of, the drawer; or it may be drawn payable to, or to the order of, the drawee.

(2) Where in a bill drawer and drawee are the same person, or where the drawee is a fictitious person or a person not having capacity to contract, the holder may treat the instrument, at his option, either as a bill of exchange or as a promissory note. [SEE *Parties to Bill of Exchange*]

Where a drawer is dead, notice of dishonour must be given to a personal representative; where he is bankrupt notice may be given either to the party himself or to the trustee. SEE *Dishonour of Bill of Exchange*

In applying the provisions of Part IV of the Bills of Exchange Act 1882, the first indorser of a promissory note is (by Section 89) deemed to correspond with the drawer of an accepted bill payable to the drawer's order. The drawer of a cheque is the person on whose account it is drawn and who must provide the funds to meet it.

If the drawer's signature is forged, the banker cannot charge the cheque to his customer's account. Even if the forgery is so perfectly done as to defy detection under the closest scrutiny, it does not affect the banker's liability. His customer cannot be debited with a cheque which he has not drawn unless the drawer has adopted it or is estopped from setting up the forgery. SEE *Forgery*

When a cheque is returned with the answer 'signature differs', the paying banker should advise the drawer. (See the case under *Signature*.)

The drawer of a cheque must take care to fill up the cheque in such a manner that, after it leaves his hands, it cannot readily be altered without giving reasonable ground for suspicion. (See *London Joint Stock Bank Ltd* v *Macmillan and Arthur*, under *Alterations to Bills of Exchange; Cheque*

When mandates or authorities are held regarding the signing of cheques, the instructions must be carefully observed. A difficulty sometimes arises where a banker is authorized by a limited company to pay cheques when signed by two directors and the secretary, and the secretary is also a director, his name appearing on cheques in both capacities. In such a case the banker should ascertain if the articles of association permit a director to act also as secretary. Even if they do so permit, it is better to have a clear understanding with the company on the point.

Where a person draws a cheque in a representative capacity, words should be added to show clearly that he signs for and on behalf of a principal. SEE *Agent; Per Pro*

Notice of a customer's death cancels the banker's authority to pay his cheques, and any cheques presented after receipt of such notice are returned 'drawer deceased', except in the case of a cheque which the banker has agreed to pay, by marking or certifying it, at the drawer's request for payment.

Where a person is too ill to sign his name, his mark should be witnessed by two persons, one of whom should be the doctor in attendance. It is usual for the doctor to certify that his patient clearly understood the nature of the transaction.

The drawer of a bill payable on demand is discharged if it is not presented for payment within a reasonable time.

The drawer of a cheque is, in an ordinary case, liable thereon for six years from the date of the cheque. SEE *Alterations to Bills of Exchange; Cheque; Joint Account*

DRAWING ACCOUNT A current account.

DRAWINGS The method by which some fixed interest stocks or bonds are redeemed. SEE *Drawn Bonds*

DRAWN BILL A bill drawn in the UK and payable abroad, if negotiated direct from the drawer to a foreign banker in London, is termed a drawn bill. SEE *Made Bill*

DRAWN BONDS Where a certain amount of bonds is to be repaid periodically, the method adopted, in order to determine which of the bonds should be paid, is to 'draw' numbers, on the lottery principle, up to the amount required. The numbers so drawn represent the bonds to be paid off, which are then called 'drawn bonds'.

Advertisements of such drawings are given in the press, and the Bondholders' Register gives complete lists of drawn bonds.

After a bond is drawn interest ceases. In the cases of some foreign government bonds, however, the coupons may continue to be paid after a bond is drawn for repayment, but the amounts so paid are treated as repayments on account of the principal.

DRIVE-IN BANK A service to motorists whereby cheques may be cashed or money paid in through a window between the car driver and the bank cashier. For security reasons there may be an armour plated glass window, conversation between customer and cashier being carried on through a two-way microphone and loudspeaker system. The cashier controls a steel drawer which slides through a hatch in the wall, by means of which money and documents are passed.

The first UK drive-in bank was opened in Liverpool at the end of January 1959.

DROPLOCK In the case of a loan agreement with a variable rate of interest, a provision is sometimes included to allow one of the parties, usually the borrower, to change to a fixed rate of interest at some point during the currency of the loan. This is known as a 'droplock' provision. If, therefore, the borrower takes the view that interest rates are likely to rise, he may elect to invoke the provision and convert the then variable rate into a fixed rate for the rest of the term. Such an arrangement will normally be subject to an agreed minimum.

DUE DATE OF BILL SEE *Time of Payment of Bill*

E

EARNED INCOME For income tax purposes, all income of private individuals is classified as earned or unearned. For many years different rates of tax have applied to each of these two main categories of income. The principal difference was that unearned income beyond a certain limit was subject to the investment income surcharge (q.v.).

Earned income for income tax purposes consists of the following:

1. Income from employment, including wages and salary, overtime pay and other emoluments of employment.
2. Pensions paid to a retired employee or his wife or widow under an approved occupational pension scheme.
3. Income from a trade or profession in which a person is engaged, either as a sole proprietor or as an active partner.
4. Retirement pensions and widows' pensions under the National Insurance Act.
5. Royalties and other income from copyrights, patents, etc.
6. Certain Social Security benefits.
7. Retirement annuities taken out by self-employed persons or by employed persons in augmentation of the State pension scheme.

EARNINGS The word is used in various contexts and in the case of a private individual may, for example, refer to earned income (q.v.). The word is also used in relation to the income of a company, e.g. the price/earnings ratio. In that context, the earnings of a company are the net profits available for distribution to shareholders (whether distributed or not) in any particular year.

EARNINGS LIMIT SEE *Lower Earnings Limit, National Insurance*

EARNINGS-RELATED BENEFITS Certain Social Security benefits are paid partly at a flat rate and partly as an earnings-related supplement, calculated according to the earnings on which the claimant has paid contributions in past years. Since January 1982, earnings-related supplement no longer applies to unemployment benefit (q.v.), sickness benefit (q.v.), maternity allowance (q.v.) or widows' allowance (q.v.). There is still an earnings-related supplement, however, on retirement pensions, invalidity pensions, widowed mothers' allowance and widows' pension.

EARNINGS-RELATED PENSIONS An earnings-related pension is one which is calculated according to the level of the recipient's earnings before retirement. All present-day occupational pension schemes provide pensions calculated by reference to wages or salaries, whether it be based on final wage or salary, the last three years, or some average over a number of years.

An earnings-related pension is also payable under the State pension schemes. This is known as 'additional pension' and is payable in addition to the basic State pension. It is payable only to a person who retired on or after 6th April, 1979 and who has paid the requisite level of Class I contributions. SEE *Pensions*

EARNINGS YIELD The term usually applied to the annual earnings per share of a company expressed as a percentage of the current share price. The earnings in this context means the residual profit of the company for the year, after meeting all prior charges and taxation.

EDITH PLC This company, formerly known as Estate Duties Investment Trust, was formed in 1953 with a capital of £1 million to provide funds to meet death duties where assets were held in shares in private companies. Four-fifths of the capital was provided by certain insurance companies and a number of investment trust companies, the remaining one-fifth being subscribed by the Industrial and Commerical Finance Corporation (q.v.). The company obtained a public quotation in 1962 but in 1984 the 3i Group (formerly Finance for Industry (q.v.)) made a bid for the 60 per cent or so shares of EDITH which it did not already own. EDITH plc is an approved investment trust and is managed by Investors in Industry (q.v.). Its purpose is to purchase minority interests in unlisted companies enabling shareholders to raise cash to meet tax and other obligations, without losing control. Investments are made either for cash or, in some cases, by the issue of quoted shares in EDITH. These are normally long-term investments and EDITH does not usually require a nominee director on the board.

EDUCATION, COSTS OF The cost of education at independent schools may be provided for, and to some extent alleviated, in one or more of the following ways.

Payments out of income This may be done in a way which spreads the cost over a longer period than the years of schooling and is usually coupled with a life insurance contract (see below).

Annuity purchase scheme See below.

Composition payments A number of schools will accept a capital sum payable in advance by way of commutation of the fees eventually payable. The composition may be made by parents or anyone else. The scheme has the advantage that if a capital sum is available now it may be used to secure the future education of a child at a given level of fees. Even if a degree of inflation is built into the composition payment, there is no certainty that the provision will be sufficient when the time comes. That applies, however, to any attempt to forecast the future level of fees.

A composition fee cannot be paid, of course, until the school has been selected for the child. Some schools will, however, accept a composition arrangement on the basis that it can be transferred to another school if the need arises.

If a parent makes a composition payment in this way, there is no charge for capital transfer tax (see below) but a charge may rise if the payment is made by any other person. The usual exemptions will apply, however (see below), so that it may be possible to mitigate the capital transfer tax liability.

Loans A number of financial institutions will lend money for school fees, or indeed for a composite fee as described above. Again, banks and insurance companies may help in this way and allow the burden of repayments to be spread over a reasonable number of years. Life assurance is usually a factor in any of these arrangements (see below).

Deeds of covenant For a deed of convenant to be tax effective, it must be entered into by someone other than the parent, otherwise the income arising from the covenant remains the parent's income for tax purposes. If, however, a grandparent, godparent or other friend or relative enters into a deed of covenant in favour of the child, the tax deducted from the covenanted sum will be recoverable on behalf of the child to the extent that the child's income does not attract tax at the basic rate. As in some cases the annual school fees may now far exceed the amount of a child's personal allowances, there is only a limited scope for the use of covenants in this way.

Income tax will not be recoverable on covenanted payments if there is any reciprocal arrangement, e.g. A covenants in favour of the child of B in consideration of B covenanting in favour of the child of A. Any suggestion or implication of a reciprocal benefit must therefore be avoided.

Company scholarships Over the years, a number of companies have offered schemes under which school fees have been paid for the children of their executive employees. In December 1982, in a case involving executives of ICI, the House of Lords ruled that the benefit of such scholarships was not taxable as the income of a parent. That decision was reversed, however, in the Finance Act 1983, so that new scholarships awarded on or after 15th March, 1983 will give rise to a taxable benefit in the case of those parents who are directors or higher-paid employees of the company concerned.

Scholarship awards made to students before 15th March, 1983 and taken up before 6th April, 1984, were exempted from tax under the Finance Act 1983, so long as the student remained at the same educational establishment. Under revised arrangements introduced in 1984, the exemption will continue regardless of a change of educational establishment, until the scholarship runs out or until 5th April, 1989, whichever is the sooner. If, however, a student remains on 6th April, 1989 at the same educational establishment as he was attending on Budget Day (15th March, 1983) or, in the case of a pre-Budget Day award, taken up after Budget Day but before 6th April, 1984, at the original educational establishment for which the award was made, the exemption will continue so long as he remains at that establishment receiving the award.

Under earlier legislation (Finance Act 1976) there is no charge for tax on a scholarship award if in the year in which the award is made, no more than 25 per cent of the payments from that fund are benefits in kind of directors or employees. Thus if 75 per cent of the awards in any one year from a particular scholarship fund were made to persons who had no connection with the employer company, no charge for tax would arise. This provision was, however, varied in the Finance Act 1984, to the extent that even in such cases, i.e. where 75 per cent of the fund goes to non-employees, there will be a charge to tax if it can be shown as a matter of fact that the payment to or for the benefit of a particular child was made because his parent was a director or higher paid employee of the company concerned and that the payment was 'by reason of' his employment.

Grants from charitable trusts There are a large number of charitable funds set up, in some cases many years ago, to assist with the education of children at independent schools. The trustees of such funds would normally have regard to the personal circumstances of the family. They may make a grant where, for example, the parent of the child has died or is ill. Other funds are for the purpose of educating a particular class of children, e.g. the children of Church of England clergymen.

Local authority grants Local education authorities have powers to make grants for the education of children at independent schools but generally these powers have been used only where special circumstances have applied, e.g. the absence of parents overseas or difficult home circumstances or in some cases, the special aptitude of a child requiring attendance at a boarding school.

Scholarships and exhibitions Many independent schools offer scholarships and exhibitions on a competitive basis and some provide bursaries where there is a special need.

In practical terms for most people, the provision of school fees means finding money out of capital (whether from the parents or from grandparents or other people) or out of current income. In some cases the right answer will be a combination of both. In any case, the sooner an arrangement is set up the better. This is not only because of the obvious benefit of spreading the cost over a longer period of years, but it also enables greater advantage to be taken of the available taxation benefits.

Capital Schemes

Any parent with the available capital resources may set aside at any time a sum of money to provide for the future education of his children. He will have to take certain decisions on how the money is to be invested and either manage it himself or pay someone to manage it. The income will be that of the parent and will be taxed at his marginal rate. The amount available when the time comes to pay school fees will of course depend on the investment performance of the fund. If the fund performs well, there will be a capital gains tax liability on realization.

The alternative is to purchase one or more single premium bonds, which offer the advantage of (1) special management, (2) tax paid by the life office at a lower rate, and (3) no capital gains tax payable when the bond is realized. There may, however, be a charge to higher-rate tax at that point and this could be a very real disadvantage.

Most capital schemes therefore involve an education trust enjoying charitable status for tax purposes. The capital sum is paid to the trust which then purchases a deferred annuity from a life office. Thus, a capital sum paid now produces an annuity for the child at some future date when schooling begins and covering the five or six years at an independent school.

Any quotation for the purchase of a deferred annuity will take into account the following factors:

1. The period which will elapse before the fees become payable (e.g. the investment may be made when the child is only a baby with a view to fees commencing at preparatory school age or at common entrance age).
2. The period for which fees are to be paid, e.g. six years.
3. The amount of capital to be invested.
4. Whether or not an escalation clause is to be included for increases in fees over the period.

Payments out of Income

The only satisfactory way to finance out of income school fees required in future years is by means of life assurance. This may be by endowment assurance or deferred annuity.

Endowment assurance This method of funding is more or less straightforward endowment assurance. It is important that the policy should be with profits in order to provide a degree of protection against inflation, and as the school fees will be required over a period of five or six years, it will usually be desirable to take out a series of policies maturing at yearly intervals.

This method of financing is not very appropriate if the parent has left matters a little late and school fees are to be required in the next few years. This is because a qualifying policy for tax purposes must be for at least a 10 year period. If fees are required in, say, seven years, a 10 year endowment policy may still be appropriate because it will normally be possible to take out a loan from the insurance company, but if fees are required in less than seven years, this method of financing is not appropriate because the burden of loans would be too expensive or, indeed, not available at all because of the low surrender value in the early years.

Most insurance brokers recommend conventional endowment policies for this method of financing. The same effect may be achieved with unit-linked policies, but because the maturity values depend on the value of the underlying securities, the amount payable in any particular year is unpredictable.

The one exception to these comments about

unit-linked policies is perhaps building-society-linked assurance. This form of investment is not subject to the vagaries of the stock market, and because of the proportionately higher yields in the early years such a policy may be appropriate where fees are required in a few years' time.

The quotations for this type of assurance, as with all endowment assurance, vary quite widely in the market, the variable factors being the age of the parent, the period of the assurance and the investment performance of the life office.

An essential feature of such endowment schemes is that in the event of the death of the parent the sum assured is payable so that sums continue to be available for school fees.

Deferred annuity The essence of this type of scheme is that monthly premiums are paid over the life of the policy in order to purchase guaranteed annuity payments during the years of schooling. Life assurance can also be included on the life of the parent or other benefactor so that in the event of his or her death the annuity will continue to be paid.

A scheme of this type may be set up even though a comparatively short period remains, e.g. as little as two years, before school fees become payable. The scheme also has the advantage that the annuity payments are guaranteed.

Capital Transfer Tax

Under Section 46, Finance Act 1975, payments by a parent for the education and maintenance of his or her child are exempt from capital transfer tax. The exemption does not apply to payments by other people, e.g. grandparents.

It follows that where a parent has entered into one of the capital schemes for the provisions of school fees there is no capital transfer tax on the amount paid. Under some of the capital schemes, however, there is an option for the parent or donor to elect to cancel the policy before the school fees became payable and recover the value of the policy. In other cases, however, the payment is irrevocable unless the child dies or for any other reason the fees are not required when the time comes to pay them.

In the first of these two cases, i.e. where the parent or donor retains the option to surrender, the gift is not complete until the contract becomes irrevocable, i.e. until the fees become payable. If the donor or settlor is the parent and he or she dies before the fees become payable, there is potential liability for capital transfer tax because the policy forms part of the parent's estate. There is no exemption from capital transfer tax on death in respect of payments for maintenance and education.

If, however, the donor or settlor is a third party and the right of revocation has been retained, there will not be any capital transfer tax during the donor's lifetime (because the gift is not complete) until the fees become payable. At that point there is a possible charge to capital transfer tax at a rate depending on whether or not the donor is then alive or deceased.

If the option to cancel the policy is not preserved and the parent is the donor, there is no liability for capital transfer tax because of the exemption under Section 46. If the donor is any other person, however, and the right to revoke or cancel the policy is not retained, there is a potential charge to capital transfer tax immediately, subject to the usual exemptions.

Even where the circumstances give rise to a possible charge to capital transfer tax, no tax will be payable if the capital payment falls within any of the statutory exemptions.

Payments made by a parent or guardian under an income scheme will similarly be exempt from tax under Section 46. If the payments, i.e. insurance premiums, are paid by another party, there will be a prima facie liability for capital transfer tax. The amount involved may well fall within the £3,000 per annum exemption limit or in some cases the exemption for 'normal expenditure'. SEE *Capital Transfer Tax*

University Education

The fees of UK residents for attending approved courses at universities, polytechnics, training colleges and certain other establishments of higher education are paid by the local education authority in the area where the student has his permanent home address. The fees are paid each term direct to the university or other establishment concerned.

Under the present system of university grants, the living costs of students, including accommodation, meals, books, etc., are intended to be covered by the system of student grants, also paid by the local education authority. Student grants are means-tested and are paid according to a sliding scale depending on the level of parental income. It is expected that where less than the maximum grant is payable to a student the balance will be made up by his or her parents.

Student grants are paid for the academic year commencing in October each year (usually taken as 1st September). Parental income is taken as the agreed income of the parent for tax purposes for the year ending the previous 5th April. If the final figures for the previous year's income are not available, the local education authority will make a provisional assessment, leaving the final term's grant to be adjusted when the parent's income is known. A parent who has a fluctuating income may elect to have the grant paid on the basis of the current year's income.

For the purpose of calculating parental income, personal allowances are not included, but mortgage interest payments and one-half of life assurance premiums on policies taken out before 14th March, 1984 are deducted and in the case of a person engaged in a trade or business the normal expenses allowed for income tax are also deducted, including capital allowances.

Independent students A student may claim independent status if:

1. he or she was aged over 25 at the beginning of the academic year, and
2. he or she has supported himself or herself out of earnings for the past three years (which may include period of sickness, invalidity or maternity benefit, or period spent at home by a married student looking after children).

Married students If a student is independent (see above) and married, the income of the husband or wife will be assessed in the same way as parental income for the purpose of determining the level of the grant.

EFFECTS NOT CLEARED This really means 'cheques not cleared' and refers to those items, usually cheques, which have been paid in by a customer and credited to the customer's account but for which the bank has not received payment from the paying banker. If a banker is not willing to pay a cheque which his customer has drawn against those uncleared items, he will return the cheque 'effects not cleared'.

In *Capital and Counties Bank* v *Gordon* [1903] AC 240, Lord Lindley said

> It must never be forgotten that the moment a banker places money to his customer's credit, the customer is entitled to draw upon it unless something occurs to deprive him of that right.

Bankers, however, caution their customers by a notice to the effect that the right is reserved to postpone payment of cheques drawn against uncleared effects which may have been credited to the account and presumably this precaution saves them from the above ruling.

If there is an agreement express or implied such as would arise out of a course of business to pay against uncleared effects, a banker would be bound to honour cheques drawn against such effects and he cannot arbitrarily and without notice withdraw such facilities.

A banker who expressly or impliedly agrees to drawings against uncleared effects is a holder for value of such effects. SEE UNDER *Collecting Banker*

As to the effect of a garnishee order on uncleared effects, see *Garnishee Order*.

ELECTION A technical term used in the law of wills. The doctrine of election comes into play when a testator leaves a gift to A and at the same time purports to give B something which he cannot give because in fact it belongs to A. In such a case, A cannot both take the gift under the will and retain his own property. He must elect either to take under the will, in which case he will receive the testator's gift, but at the same time transfer his property to B; or to take against the will, in which case he will keep his own property and abandon the legacy (or if its value exceeds the value of his own property, compensate B out of the legacy). The application of the doctrine of election depends not upon the intention of the testator, but upon his having purported to dispose of property of which he was unable validly to dispose. (See *Re Mengel's Will Trusts: Westminster Bank Ltd* v *Mengel and Others* [1962] All ER 490.)

ELECTRONIC FUNDS TRANSFER (EFT) This is the transfer of payments by electronic means. Nowadays very substantial payments are made in this way, whether by Post Office lines, radio telegraphy, the exchange of electronic tapes, video screens or even satellite communication. SEE *Bankers' Automated Clearing Services Limited; Clearing House Automated Payments System; Home Banking; Society for Worldwide Interbank Financial Telecommunications*

ELECTRONIC FUNDS TRANSFER, POINT OF SALE (EFTPOS) This is a system agreed to in principle by the major banks in 1982 to facilitate the settlement of transactions by electronic means (usually a keyboard) verified by a card bearing a personal identification number (PIN) at a retail point of sale, e.g. stores, supermarkets, airports and petrol stations. At the time of writing, most of these developments are at an experimental stage but will lead in time to very major transfers of customer funds by electronic means, rather than the traditional cheque.

ELIGIBLE BILLS Bills accepted by the leading banks and acceptance houses in London which have the special standing of rediscountability at the Bank of England. From time to time, the Bank of England adds to its list of eligible names. Traditionally, they have been the London and Scottish clearing banks, the members of the Accepting Houses Committee and the major

British, Overseas and Commonwealth banks. The criterion for inclusion was always that the acceptor should have a broadly-based and substantial acceptance business commanding the finest rates in the market. In more recent times the list has been extended to include a number of leading names among overseas banks and at the time of writing the number of eligible names is approximately 120.

ELIGIBLE LIABILITIES These are the sterling deposit liabilities of the monetary sector, other than those with an original maturity of over two years, plus any sterling resources resulting from the switching of foreign currency into sterling. For the purpose of monetary control, the Bank of England's calculation of an individual institution's eligible liabilities is arrived at as follows:

1. Sight deposits (except those of the institutions' overseas offices).
2. Time deposits of the UK monetary sector.
3. Time deposits (other than those in 2 above and those of the institutions' overseas offices) with an original maturity of two years or less.
4. Certificates of deposit, promissory notes, bills and other negotiable paper issued.
5. Items in suspense.
6. Sixty per cent of credit items in transit.
7. Net sterling liabilities to overseas offices.
8. Net liabilities in other currencies.

From the total of these items is deducted

1. Sixty per cent of debit items in transit.
2. All funds lent to the UK monetary sector.
3. Secured money at call placed with money brokers and gilt-edged jobbers in the Stock Exchange.
4. Certificates of deposit, promissory notes, bills and other negotiable paper issued by listed institutions.

EMIGRATION FROM UNITED KINGDOM The financial aspects of emigration are usually concerned with currency regulations, income tax, capital gains tax, and capital transfer tax.

Currency Regulations

With the abolition of exchange control in the UK, there is no limit on the value of goods and money which an emigrant may take out of the UK. The intending emigrant should remember, however, that other countries have their own regulations in the matter of exchange control and capital transfers. Should he or she contemplate returning to the UK at some future date, it may not be so easy to repatriate their personal fortune.

Income Tax

It will be necessary for the emigrant to satisfy the Inland Revenue that he or she is leaving this country permanently and will no longer be either resident or 'ordinarily resident' in the UK (SEE *Residence*). This may take a little time to establish, possibly up to three years. On the other hand, non-resident status may be granted almost immediately. Each case is considered on its merits, but if there is some delay in establishing non-residence, once it has been granted it will be back-dated to the date of departure from these shores.

There will almost certainly be difficulty and delay in establishing non-resident status if the emigrant retains a place of residence available for occupation in this country. The mere ownership of a property is not a bar to non-resident status, but the availability of even one room for occasional use by the emigrant will be so.

When non-residence has been established, the emigrant will cease to be liable to British income tax except on income arising in the UK. Thus, a pension earned in this country and dividends from ordinary shares will be taxed at source in the ordinary way. The emigrant will be able to set against such income that proportion of his personal allowances which his UK income bears to his worldwide income.

Capital Gains Tax

Capital gains tax is payable in this country on chargeable gains arising in a tax year for any part of which the taxpayer was resident or ordinarily resident in the UK. By concession, however, the Inland Revenue do not charge capital gains tax on gains arising after the date of departure. It should be borne in mind, however, that if the emigrant returns to this country having been non-resident for less than three consecutive years, he will be taxed on gains accruing in the year of return even though the disposals were before the date of return.

In view of this concessionary treatment, the intending emigrant may wish to defer until after his or her departure any sales of assets which are likely to result in a chargeable capital gain. Any losses incurred before the date of departure will, however, be available in the ordinary way to offset against any other chargeable gain.

Capital Transfer Tax

Capital transfer tax, like its forerunner estate duty, is based on the concept of domicile rather than that of residence. If the transferor of capital assets is domiciled in the UK, there is a prima facie charge to tax and this applies wheresoever in the world the transferred assets are situated.

Domicile in this context means permanent home. There are two essential ingredients of domicile: the *fact* of living in a particular country, and the *intention* of remaining there.

A person's domicile of origin is that which is acquired at birth; a domicile of choice is one which is acquired by intention at some future date. Under English law, a person can have but one domicile at any one time. SEE *Domicile*

It follows that if an emigrant intends to depart permanently from this country, he must establish that he has acquired a new domicile. Failing that, he will be deemed to have retained his UK domicile and will continue to be liable for capital transfer tax both on lifetime transfers of capital assets and on transfers on death. It is not easy to establish a change of domicile. The advice usually given to an intending emigrant is to sever completely his links with the UK, to sell up his home in this country, cancel club subscriptions and not even retain for himself a grave space.

If the emigrant can establish that he has forsaken his UK domicile (which means acquiring a foreign domicile or reverting to his domicile of origin), he and his estate will be free from British capital transfer tax. The tax will still be payable, however, on assets situated in the United Kingdom, notwithstanding that the owner may have acquired a domicile outside the UK.

Special rules applied under the Finance Act 1975, Section 45, to persons taking up residence in the Channel Islands or Isle of Man but these were repealed by the Finance Act 1983. Under that same section, however, a person who was resident in the United Kingdom on or after 10th December, 1974, and was so resident in not less than 17 of the previous 20 years, shall be deemed to be domiciled in the United Kingdom.

EMPLOYEE TRUSTS Paragraph 17(1) of Schedule 5 of the Finance Act 1975, contains certain exemptions from capital transfer tax in respect of settled property held on trust for the benefit of

1. persons of a class defined by reference to employment in a particular trade, profession or undertaking or employment by, or office with, a body carrying on a trade, profession or undertaking; or
2. persons of a class defined by reference to marriage or relationship to or dependent on persons of a class defined as mentioned in (1) above, or
3. charities.

Under the Finance Act 1976, Section 90, there is a considerable degree of exemption from capital transfer tax for such employee trusts, not only in relation to the transfer of funds for the provision of employees of a company, but also to dispositions thereafter made from such funds.

Under Section 90, a disposition by a close company (q.v.) to trustees for the benefit of the company's employees will be exempt from capital transfer tax provided

1. the persons entitled to benefit from the trust are all or most of the persons employed by or holding office with the company or its subsidiaries;
2. the terms of the trust exclude from benefit any participator in the company, or anyone who has been a participator at any time after, or during the ten years before, the transfer or anyone who is a connected person.

A 'participator' for this purpose has the same meaning as in Section 39, Finance Act 1975, which in turn adopts the definition in Chapter 3 of Part XI of the Income and Corporation Taxes Act 1970. In general terms, a participator in a company is any person having a share or interest in the capital or income of the company, including shareholders, loan creditors or any persons who possess or acquire a right to participate in a company' distributions. For the purpose of employee trusts, loan creditors are excluded by the 1975 Act and under the 1976 Act, Section 90, the definition excludes any participator who on a winding-up of the company would not be entitled to five per cent or more of its assets.

Under Section 90(2) of the 1976 Act, no capital transfer tax will be payable on a disposition to trustees by a person beneficially entitled to shares in a company whereby the shares are to be held on trust for the benefit of the employees. For the exemption to apply

1. the transfer must relate to all shares or other securities of the company to which the transferor is beneficially entitled,
2. immediately after the transfer there must be no shares or securities of the company to which the transferor or his or her spouse are beneficially entitled,
3. as a result of the transfer, the trustees must hold all or substantially all the ordinary shares of the company and have the exercise of the majority of the voting power.

As with transfers by a close company, the persons for whose benefit the trusts are declared must include all or most of the employees of the company.

In the case of such a transfer by a private individual, the exemption will only apply if the same considerations are observed in relation to participators and connected persons as described above.

Exemption from capital transfer tax will apply to any distributions by an employee trust during any period within which the settled property can be applied only for the benefit of employees, the relatives or dependants of employees, or charities.

The exemption is wider than that available in the case of transfers *to* employee trusts in that a trust itself enjoys exemption from tax if the beneficiaries are defined by reference to employment in a particular trade, profession or undertaking, or by reference to employment by or office with a body carrying on a trade, profession or undertaking. In this latter category, however, the class must comprise all or most of the persons employed by or holding office with that body.

ENDORSEMENT SEE *Indorsement*

ENDOWMENT ASSURANCE A policy of assurance which is payable on the assured surviving to a certain age, or payable at death if it occurs before that age. SEE *Life Assurance*

ENDOWMENT EFFECT A term which is sometimes applied to the benefit which accrues to banks from their current account balances at the time of high interest rates. When interest rates are high, the banks are able to deploy the current account balances at a high level of return without having to pay interest on those balances. Traditionally this has been a major factor in the cyclical nature of bank profits. In modern times, however, periods of very high interest rates have, understandably, coincided with high levels of inflation. Thus the costs to the banks of administering current accounts rose substantially and is currently believed to be of the order of eight to nine per cent of the balances. In times of lower interest rates, therefore, the endowment effect disappears entirely, and indeed becomes negative, unless the cost of operating the accounts is recouped in charges to customers.

ENDOWMENT MORTGAGE This is a method of repayment of a long-term mortgage loan, usually a loan for house purchase from a building society or a bank. Under this method, the amount of the loan remains fixed for the term of the mortgage and is repaid at the end of that time from the proceeds of an endowment assurance policy. There are three principal categories of endowment mortgage:

1. *Without-profits endowment mortgage* The sum assured will be the amount required to repay the loan at maturity.
2. *With-profits endowment mortgage* In this case also, the sum assured will be the amount required to repay the loan at maturity but at the end of the term the borrower will receive bonuses declared on the policy and thus will enjoy the benefit of this additional form of saving.
3. *Low cost endowment mortgage* This is a scheme available through most assurance companies, under which the sum assured is less than the amount of the loan but some allowance is made for a modest level of bonuses in order to bring the policy proceeds up to the amount of the loan at maturity. As the sum assured is less than the mortgage debt, the position would be uncovered in the event of the death of the borrower. The assurance company therefore combines in the package sufficient term assurance to make up the necessary cover. SEE ALSO *Mortgage Protection Policy*

ENDOWMENT POLICY This is a form of life assurance under which the sum assured is payable on the death of the life assured or at the end of an agreed term, whichever is the earlier date. Endowment assurance may be taken out with profits or without profits.

ENTAIL SEE *Estate Tail*

EQUALIZATION (UNIT TRUSTS) When an investor buys units in a Unit Trust (q.v.), the price he pays reflects not only the current market value of the underlying securities in the Unit Trust but also dividends received by the Unit Trust since the last distribution to unit holders. On the occasion of the next distribution, the new purchaser will receive the same distribution per unit as all other unit holders. In his case, however, that first distribution will represent partly a return of capital (i.e. the amount he paid for the dividends already in hand in the Unit Trust when he made his purchase) known as 'equalization' and partly his share of the dividends received since the date of his purchase. Only the latter part is income for tax purposes.

When a unit holder sells his units the sale price would include dividends received into the Unit Trust since the last distribution to unit holders. This is a capital item however, in the hands of the seller and although advance corporation tax will have been paid on the underlying securities in the Unit Trust, the seller will not receive a tax credit for those dividends included in the sale price.

EQUIPMENT LEASING SEE *Leasing*

EQUIPMENT LEASING ASSOCIATION This is the representative body for equipment leasing companies in the UK. It was formed in

1971 for the purpose of representing to the authorities the views of its members on proposed or existing legislation and 'to increase awareness of leasing and its role in helping the economic development of the country'.

The association maintains up-to-date statistics on equipment leasing activities in the UK. The Association has approximately 60 members who account for eighty per cent of all leasing business in Britain. SEE *Leasing*

EQUITABLE ASSIGNMENT This is an informal assignment of a chose in action (q.v.). An equitable assignment may be by word of mouth or even established from a course of dealing between the parties. However, some form of writing is desirable as a matter of evidence. An assignment is a form of contract and should, therefore, be supported by valuable consideration, unless it is an assignment by way of gift. Examples of equitable assignments are

1. A letter by a creditor to a debtor requesting the debtor to sign an undertaking to pay the debt to a third party, the documents then being transmitted to the third party.
2. A direction to a person holding funds belonging to the assignor, requiring that person to pay them over to a third party.
3. A transfer of an interest in a personal contract and of moneys receivable under the contract (but not in the case of a contract of personal service).
4. An undertaking to pay over to another person, moneys to be received from a particular source (but not merely a promise to pay when those funds are received).

Any equitable charge created by companies on their book debts must be registered under Section 395, Companies Act 1985.

EQUITABLE MORTGAGE Where a borrower gives to a lender, as security, the title deeds of his property, without any document of charge, or the deeds with a memorandum of deposit, or even a memorandum of charge without the deeds, it is an equitable mortgage. An equitable mortgage does not vest a legal estate in the lender, as does a legal mortgage, but in the memorandum which usually accompanies the deposit of deeds, the borrower, as a rule, promises to grant a legal mortgage when requested to do so. SEE *Memorandum of Deposit*

The expression is sometimes loosely used where any chose in action (e.g. shares, a life policy or a debt) is given as a security without the legal title being formally transferred to the lender—subject of course, to the right to redeem.

An equitable mortgagee, when he desires to realize his security, will have to apply to the court for power to sell, or to foreclose, or to enter into possession, or to appoint a receiver (unless the mortgage is by deed). If, however, he obtains a legal mortgage he has power to sell or put in a receiver without applying to the court, but, in the case of a mortgage deed executed after 1925, the mortgagee's power to sell or appoint a receiver shall not be exercised only on account of the mortgagor committing an act of bankruptcy or being adjudged a bankrupt, without the leave of the court. SEE UNDER *Mortgage*

By Section 91(7) of the Law of Property Act 1925, the court may, in the case of an equitable mortgage, create and vest a mortgage term in the mortgagee to enable him to carry out a sale as if the mortgage had been made by deed by way of legal mortgage.

This act does not affect the right to create an equitable mortgage by deposit of the deeds relating to a legal estate.

By Section 13, 'the Act shall not prejudicially affect the right or interest of any person arising out of or consequent on the possession by him of any documents relating to a legal estate in land'. If a person obtains a legal mortgage (subsequent to a banker's equitable mortgage with deeds) registration of that mortgage will not secure priority to the banker's charge if he continues to hold the deeds.

An equitable mortgage by deposit of deeds does not require to be registered under the Land Charges Act 1925, but an equitable charge without a deposit of deeds must be registered. SEE *Land Charges*

When an equitable mortgage is given by a company with or without the deeds, the charge must be registered within 21 days after the date of its creation. SEE *Registration of Charges*

When a limited company (which has power to give an equitable mortgage without using its common seal) authorizes one of the directors or an official of the company to sign a memorandum of deposit under hand the document should be accompanied by a properly certified copy of the resolution of the directors empowering him to deposit the deeds and sign the memorandum.

In Scotland, a deposit of title deeds, either with, or without, a memorandum of deposit does not create an equitable mortgage, as in England. If, therefore, a banker in England advances against real property in Scotland, the form of charge must conform to the law of Scotland.

EQUITIES The ordinary shares of companies. The use of the word in this context is a little obscure. It appears to have become synonymous with right or ownership: thus, a person will speak of the equity in his house, meaning that which is his after paying off a mortgage. That particular use of the word 'equity' almost certainly derives from 'equity of redemption' (see below) which in turn arose from the exercise of the courts 'equitable jurisdiction' (Latin *aequus* meaning fair). Thus the equity in the company is the proprietory ownership after paying off all prior charges etc., i.e. the ordinary shares or, in the USA, the common stock.

EQUITY CAPITAL FOR INDUSTRY (ECI) This institution was set up in 1976 under the guiding hand of the Bank of England for the purpose of providing equity capital for small and medium-sized businesses in circumstances where it might not otherwise be available from existing capital markets. A wide range of city institutions participated in the scheme and provided the initial capital of £41 million.

EQUITY LINKED A form of life assurance linked to the performance of equity stocks. SEE *Life Assurance*

EQUITY OF REDEMPTION Before 1926, a legal mortgage of a freehold was made by the mortgagor conveying to the mortgagee the whole of his interest in the fee simple, subject to a proviso that if he repaid the mortgage debt within a stipulated time (usually six months) the mortgagee would reconvey the property to him. Until such time the mortgagor had a legal right to recover his land, but after such time the mortgagee had a legal right to the land and the mortgagor had only an equitable right, called the equity of redemption. The Court of Chancery enforced this equitable right where non-payment was due to accident, etc., but later gave relief in *all* cases where default was made at the prescribed time for payment. Thereafter any stipulation in the mortgage deed which qualified the equity of redemption was of no effect, hence the phrase 'Once a mortgage, always a mortgage'.

Since 1925, a mortgage of freeholds is effected by a demise for a term of years absolute (SEE *Mortgage*). In this way, the legal estate remains in the mortgagor (previously he retained only an equity of redemption) and the mortgagee has a legal estate also in the shape of a term of years. They are both called estate owners. The equity of redemption is preserved by a provision in the mortgage for cesser of the term of years on redemption. The courts will not enforce a provision preventing the mortgagor from redeeming for an undue length of time or in circumstances considered unfair. When repayment of the money secured by the mortgage is made, a receipt for it is indorsed upon the mortgage (which receipt operates without any reconveyance), and the mortgage term becomes a satisfied term and shall cease (cesser of the mortgage term). The receipt must be stamped as a reconveyance.

Where a mortgagor is entitled to redeem, he is entitled to require the mortgagee, instead of reconveying or surrendering, to assign the mortgage debt and convey the mortgaged property to any third person, as the mortgagor directs. This provision does not apply in the case of a mortgagee being or having been in possession (Law of Property Act 1925, Section 95).

Subject to any contrary intention expressed in the mortgage deed, a mortgagor seeking to redeem any one mortgage is entitled to do so without paying any money due under any separate mortgage made by him, solely on property other than that comprised in the mortgage which he seeks to redeem (Section 93).

A mortgagor is entitled, as long as his right to redeem subsists, at his own cost, to inspect and make copies of, or extracts from, the documents of title relating to the mortgaged property (Section 96). SEE *Mortgage; Title Deeds*

A 'mortgage' of a chose in action such as a shareholding or a debt can still be created by a transfer of title coupled with a right to retransfer when the obligation secured is redeemed.

ESCALATOR BONDS A form of building society share account. The essence of this type of investment is that the rate of interest increases year by year over, say, a five-year period. Thus it is an inducement to the investor to leave his investment with the society.

ESCHEAT Where a tenant in fee simple died intestate and without heirs, his estate escheated or reverted to the superior lord, i.e. the Crown. Escheat was abolished by the Administration of Estates Act 1925, and if an estate owner dies intestate or without heirs, his property goes to the Crown as *bona vacantia*. SEE *Intestacy*

ESCROW Where a deed has been executed by one or more parties on a condition that some other party or parties shall execute the deed it is delivered as an escrow and does not take effect as a deed until that condition has been satisfied. The word is derived from scroll, indicating a written document, i.e. a simple form of writing which does not become a deed until some condition has been performed. If the condition does not take effect, the writing remains entirely inoperative.

It is usually said that an escrow must be delivered to some third party, e.g. a solicitor, to hold pending fulfilment of the condition. This, however, is not strictly necessary. The document may be delivered as an escrow even though it is retained in the possession of the grantor. It cannot be an escrow, however, if it is delivered to the other party to the document, i.e. the grantee, because the act of delivery to that party would complete the document as a deed (SEE *Deed*). It would appear, however, that in such circumstances the grantee would be restrained in equity from enforcing the deed until the condition had been fulfilled.

An assignment of property for the benefit of creditors is not an act of bankruptcy if the document is delivered as an escrow. No act of bankruptcy is committed unless or until delivery is complete and the deed becomes operative. SEE *Act of Bankruptcy; Assignment for Benefit of Creditors*

A bill of exchange may be delivered subject to a condition in the same way that a deed may be delivered in escrow but with the difference that a bill of exchange may be delivered to one of the parties to the bill which, as mentioned above, is not possible with a deed. SEE *Delivery of Bill*

ESTATE AGENTS ACT 1979 This Act, the major provisions of which came into effect on 3rd May, 1982, applies to 'estate agency work'. This is defined by Section 1 of the Act as

> things done by any person in the course of a business pursuant to instructions received from another person ('the client') who wishes to dispose of or acquire an interest in land—
> (*a*) for the purpose of, or with a view to, effecting the introduction to a client of a third person who wishes to acquire or dispose of such an interest, and
> (*b*) after such an introduction has been effected in the course of that business, for the purpose of securing the disposal or the acquisition of that interest.

One of the principal provisions of the Act (Section 3) is that the Director-General of Fair Trading may prohibit a person from doing estate agency work if he is satisfied that the person is unfit to do so.

Sections 12–17 of the Act deal with clients' moneys and require these to be kept in separate trust accounts. Section 18 requires information to be given to clients about their possible liabilities before entering into a contract with an estate agent. Section 19, which has not yet been brought into operation, enables the Secretary of State to prescribe the maximum amount which may be received from a prospective purchaser of land as a pre-contract deposit by a person engaged in estate agency work.

Section 21 relates to transactions in which an estate agent has a personal interest and Section 23 prohibits undischarged bankrupts from engaging in estate agency work.

ESTATE DUTIES INVESTMENT TRUST SEE *Edith PLC*

ESTATE DUTY A form of duty introduced by the Finance Act 1894, and imposed on the value of all real and personal property passing on the death of any person after 1st August, 1894. Over the next 80 years, there were numerous amendments in various Finance Acts and a considerable volume of case law was built up to such an extent that estate duty became one of the most complicated aspects of personal finance in this country. The estate duty legislation was repealed by the Finance Act 1975, which introduced capital transfer tax in lieu. This has done little, if anything, to simplify the subject because for the most part, the rules of estate duty have been imported into the capital transfer tax regime. The principal difference between capital transfer tax and estate duty is that the former applies to all transfers of capital (subject to statutory reliefs and exemptions), whether in life or on death. Estate duty applied only to the passing of property on death and gifts *inter vivos* within periods up to seven years prior to death. SEE *Capital Transfer Tax*

ESTATE PLANNING An American term introduced into Britain in the late 1960s. A similar expression previously in use in this country (but not quite synonymous) was 'estate duty planning'. Estate planning means the arrangement of one's affairs to the best advantage. It is concerned with the whole field of personal finance, including such matters as

1. minimizing the burden of taxation;
2. investment planning, e.g. for capital growth or to maximize income;
3. provision for the family (SEE *Education, Costs of*);
4. pension arrangements, (SEE *Pensions*);
5. testamentary arrangements.

A good estate plan will take into account the philosophy and temperament of the person concerned and advise upon the best arrangement of his financial affairs against the current fiscal and economic climate.

All the major banks and a number of other financial institutions offer estate planning services.

ESTATE TAIL An estate tail (or fee tail) is the opposite of fee simple. An estate tail is where land is granted to a person and the heirs of his body, so long as there are such heirs, whereas a fee simple is granted to his heirs, which need not necessarily be the heirs of his body. SEE *Intestacy*

The word 'tail' is from the French *taille*, a cutting, indicating that the land is cut or separated from any other estate and limited to the person and the actual descendants of the person to whom it is conveyed. If the man has been married more than once, the descendants of each marriage are included; but if the land is granted, or limited, to the descendants of one wife it is called a 'special estate tail'.

When an estate tail is converted into a fee simple, it is said to be disentailed, the entail being barred, and the tenant may then dispose of the estate at will.

On 1st January, 1926, any legal estate tail then existing was, by the Law of Property Act 1925, converted into an equitable interest. From that date an estate tail cannot exist as a legal estate (SEE *Legal Estates*). An equitable estate tail may, however, be created in any property, real or personal.

ESTOPPEL A rule of evidence whereby a man is not allowed to disprove facts in the truth of which he has by words or conduct induced others to believe, knowing that they might or would act on such belief. A man is not permitted to resist an inference which a reasonable person would necessarily draw from his words or conduct.

According to Halsbury

> Where one has either by words or conduct, made to another a representation of facts, either with knowledge or with falsehood, or with the intention that it should be acted upon, or has so conducted himself that another would, as a reasonable man, understand that a certain representation of fact was intended to be acted upon, and that the other has acted on the representation and thereby altered his position to his prejudice, an estoppel arises against the party who made the representation, and he is not allowed to aver that the fact is otherwise than he represented it to be.

Thus estoppel may arise from a person's conduct but it may arise also from the terms of a deed (estoppel by deed), or by the judgment of a court or other official body (estoppel by record).

A drawer of a cheque may be estopped from denying the genuineness of his signature, notwithstanding that it is forged, where his own conduct has led the banker into paying the cheque, i.e. by keeping silent when he should have warned the banker. Where a wife forged her husband's cheques which were paid by the bank and the husband subsequent to his wife's confession delayed advising the bank until after his wife's death, it was held that he was estopped from denying the genuineness of the signature on the ground that his stance had deprived the bank of its civil remedy against the forger, on account of her death (*Greenwood* v *Martins Bank Ltd* [1932] 1 KB 371).

In the case of *Brown* v *Westminster Bank* [1964] 2 Lloyd's Rep 187, the principle appears to have been extended. There the acknowledgment of the customer resulted in the bank being able to debit her account with earlier and later forgeries. However, the customer owes the bank no duty to check his bank statement and he is not estopped from action by his failure to realize that forged cheques have been paid on his account. (See *Kepitigalla Rubber Estates* v *National Bank of India Ltd* [1909] 2 KB 1010.)

The following estoppels arise on bills of exchange.

The acceptor cannot deny to a holder in due course the existence of the drawer, the genuineness of his signature, and his capacity and authority to draw the bill. Where a bill is payable to the drawer's order, the acceptor cannot deny the capacity of the drawer to indorse, but he can deny the genuineness or validity of his indorsement. Likewise, he cannot deny a payee's existence and capacity to indorse, but he can deny the genuineness or validity of his indorsement (Section 54, Bills of Exchange Act 1882).

The drawer cannot deny the existence of the payee and his capacity to indorse.

The indorser cannot deny the genuineness and regularity of the drawer's signature and all previous indorsements (Section 55, Bills of Exchange Act 1882).

EUROBONDS These are long-term loans issued in terms of US dollars, Deutsche marks, composite units of account and other currencies. They may be in the form of loans, debentures or convertible debentures and are issued by large companies of sound international repute at a fixed rate of interest. They change hands in the market at a price which varies mainly according to the rate of interest prevailing for Euro-dollar (q.v.) deposits.

The first clearing house to be set up for Eurobonds was Euroclear in Brussels, owned by Morgan Guaranty Trust. In 1972 the ownership was transferred to a new British registered company, Euroclear Clearance System, owned by 118 banks and financial institutions. In 1970 approximately 50 major international banks contributed over £330,000 to establish a new clearing house in Luxembourg known as CEDEL (Centre of Deliveries), of which they became shareholders, as it was desirable to have a clearing house completely independent of the market. CEDEL came into full operation in 1971. SEE Supplement

EUROCHEQUE SCHEME This is a scheme in which, at the time of writing, approximately 15,000 banks, with nearly 200,000 branches in 39 countries, participate. Most of the English banks are members of the scheme, which enables customers to draw cash in European countries at banks displaying the Eurocheque symbol (EC). Up to two cheques a day may be cashed for up to £75 each and may be written in local currency. They are acceptable in over 4½ million retail outlets in twenty countries. SEE *Cheque Card*

EURO-CURRENCY The Euro-currency market is the somewhat misleading name given to the participation of banks in the UK with banks in other centres in their foreign currency deposit business. Euro-currencies are those other than the domestic currency of the country in which the bank taking the deposit or lending the funds is located. For banks in the UK, both UK registered banks and the UK branches of overseas banks, Euro-currency business comprises taking deposits and lending in currencies other than sterling. The main currency traded is US dollars, hence the term Euro-dollars (q.v.), but the major west European currencies are deposited and lent, together with those of countries outside Europe. It is not possible to arrive at a precise definition as some foreign currency deposits held by residents outside the countries of the currencies concerned, are not necessarily lent in the Euro-currency market.

The most important reasons for the growth of this market are

1. The rates and the reserve requirements applicable to domestic banking do not apply in this market.
2. Large sums are dealt with and as the maturities of deposits—it is essentially a time-deposit market—and lending can be broadly matched, the rates can be finer than the domestic ones and the banks can operate on modest reserves.
3. The market itself is not subject to exchange or other controls, although suppliers and borrowers are in their own countries.
4. The nature of the market allows anonymity if a holder of a foreign currency does not place it directly with a bank of the country whose currency is involved.

EURO-DOLLARS These are US dollars deposited outside the USA. A large proportion of these deposits were originally in Europe, hence the name Euro-dollars but they can be deposited in any country other than the USA. The Euro-dollar market first evolved in the late 1950s following a period in which there had been a strong flow of dollars to Europe. With the clamp-down on capital movements by both Britain and the USA, the pool of US dollars in Europe was very much in demand and a new supply of credit was created. The so-called Euro-dollars would be taken in by banks and lent on to other banks and other customers. In more recent years, the build-up of dollars in the Far East has led to a pool of Asian-dollars but generally the term Euro-currency (q.v.) is applied to any expatriate currency, hence Euro-sterling, Euro-marks, Euro-lire, etc. SEE ALSO *Eurobonds*

EUROPEAN CURRENCY UNIT (ECU) The Ecu is the official unit of account of the European Economic Community. (It has continental associations with *l'ecu* introduced in France by Louis IX.) The Ecu was created in January 1979 but did not become the official unit of account until 1981. It is calculated by reference to the currencies of the member states and is the central feature of the European Monetary System (EMS) (q.v.). The accounts of the EEC are expressed in Ecus. Bank accounts and banking transactions are conducted in terms of the Ecu and its value in relation to other international currencies is published daily. With effect from 17th September, 1984, the Ecu is defined by the Council of the European Communities as the sum of the following amounts of the currencies of the Member States:

DM	0.719	Bfrs	3.71
£	0.0878	Lfrs	0.14
Ffrs	1.131	Dkr	0.219
Lit	140	Dr	1.15
Fl	0.256	Ir£	0.00871

EUROPEAN ECONOMIC COMMUNITY (EEC) The European Economic Community was formally established by the Treaty of Rome on 25th March, 1957 by the six member countries: Belgium, France, Germany, Italy, Luxembourg and the Netherlands. It was the culmination of 12 years or so of discussions, negotiations and other cooperative measures in post-war Europe. The principal milestones on the way to the Treaty of Rome were the setting-up in 1949 of the Organisation for European Economic Co-operation (OEEC), the European Payments Union (EPU) and the Council of Europe in Strasbourg, followed in 1951 by the signing of the European Coal and Steel Community Treaty and the creation of the European Court of Justice.

The United Kingdom, Ireland and Denmark, joined the EEC on 1st January, 1973. Greece joined on 1st January, 1981, bringing the number of members up to 10. SEE Supplement

The four principal institutions of the EEC are

The European Parliament consisting of 434 members elected by their respective countries, namely, France, Germany, Italy and the United Kingdom (81 members each), the Netherlands (25 members), Belgium and Greece (24 members each), Denmark (16 members), Ireland (15 members) and Luxembourg (6 members).
The Court of Justice consisting of 11 judges whose task is to enforce the body of law created by the various EEC treaties.
The Council of Europe consisting of representatives of the governments of the member states.
The European Commission consisting of four team members appointed by agreement among the member governments. The Commission, in turn, appoints the Court of Auditors, who audit the accounts of the Community, examine its revenue and expenditure and generally monitor the Community's financial management.

The aims of the EEC are primarily economic, e.g. the removal of tariff barriers between member countries, the free movement of labour, ultimately the free movement of capital and a better use of economic resources. The Community is now the world's largest trading group, accounting for over 40 per cent of all world trade.

Perhaps the major financial implications for the UK thus far are the Common Agricultural Policy (q.v.), the Directives on Company Law, which are dealt with under their respective headings, and the very considerable sums received in loans and grants from the Regional Development Fund and, more particularly, the European Investment Bank (q.v.).

EUROPEAN INVESTMENT BANK The European Investment Bank is designed to provide financial assistance to both public and private enterprises which serve the interests of member states of the EEC, promote industrial modernization or conversion, contribute to solution of regional problems or assist new ventures.

Loans may be granted by the Bank of up to 50 per cent of expenditure on fixed assets for approved schemes. The Bank will also guarantee repayment of guarantee funds raised commercially for approved projects. The Department of Trade and Industry acts as agents for the Bank, dealing with applications in the UK.

Since the UK joined the European Community in 1973, the European Investment Bank has provided loans totalling nearly £3,000 million to UK borrowers. Loans may be for periods of up to 20 years, rates of interest are normally fixed for the duration of the loan at the time of borrowing, and repayment is normally by equal half-yearly payments of capital and interest after a moratorium on capital repayments up to five years.

The role of the European Investment Bank has increased considerably over the years and, in 1983, its financing operations to help economic development in member states and in other countries linked to the EEC amounted to a total of approximately 6,000 million Ecus (q.v.).

EUROPEAN MONETARY SYSTEM (EMS) This is the bringing together of the currencies of the Common Market countries in a joint unit. All the member countries with the exception of the UK have accepted the concept of the EMS, which came into effect in April 1979.

The principal reasons for the UK not joining the EMS were

1. The rigidity of the system.
2. The belief that sterling's link with oil prices would be disturbing to the EMS.
3. The argument that a strict monetary policy and exchange rate stability are incompatible.
4. The sensitivity of sterling to movements in the dollar.

There is a view in some official quarters that some of these considerations are now of less importance than hitherto and, in 1983, the House of Lords' European Committee recommended that the UK should join the European Monetary System.

EX ALL Shares sold 'ex all' exclude the buyer from accrued dividends, and all rights which the seller may have as shareholder.

EXCEPTED ESTATES With effect from 1st August, 1981 and in respect of deaths on or after 1st April, 1981, it is no longer necessary to deliver an account (i.e. the Inland Revenue Affidavit) if the gross value of the deceased's estate does not exceed £40,000, provided

1. the estate consists only of property which has passed under the deceased's will or intestacy, or by nomination, or beneficially by survivorship, and
2. not more than 10 per cent of the gross value of the estate or £1,000, whichever is the higher, consists of property situated outside the UK, and
3. the deceased died domiciled in the UK and had made no lifetime gifts chargeable to capital transfer tax.

Such exempt cases are designated 'excepted estates', but the Inland Revenue reserves the right to call for an account by serving on the personal representatives a written notice within 35 days of the issue of the Grant of Probate. This is known as the 'prescribed period'. If the Inland Revenue do not issue such a notice, the personal representatives are automatically discharged from any further claim for capital transfer tax at the end of the prescribed period, except in cases where there has been fraud or failure to disclose material facts, or where it is subsequently discovered that there is further property in the estate taking it out of the excepted estate definition.

EX COUPON Without the coupon for interest just due. Bonds are usually quoted as ex coupon on the evening of the date when the coupon is due.

EX DIVIDEND Without the dividend. A purchaser buying shares so quoted will not get the benefit of a dividend in course of payment. British Government and corporation securities are quoted 'ex div' about one month before the interest date. Bearer bonds with sterling coupons and registered debentures are 'ex div' on the day the coupon or interest is payable.

US and Canadian shares are quoted 'ex div' on the day following that on which they are similarly quoted in New York or Montreal.

Securities transferable by deed (other than registered debentures) are generally quoted 'ex div' on the contango day (qv) following the date of which the dividend has been declared if the company's transfer books have been closed for the preparation of the dividend warrants.

It is possible for medium-dated and long-dated gilt-edged stocks to be bought 'special ex dividend' during the three weeks before the stock becomes officially ex dividend. This means that an investor may buy a government stock (other than short-term bonds) ex dividend and sell it a little over 12 months later cum dividend, having received only one half-yearly interest payment during the year. Thus a tax-free capital gain is secured because the stock has been held for more than 12 months. SEE *Capital Gains Tax*

EX DRAWING Without any benefit there may be from a drawing of bonds for payment which is due to be made.

EX INTEREST Without interest.

EX NEW Where new shares are being issued to the present shareholders of a company, a shareholder sometimes sells his old shares 'ex new', that is, he reserves to himself the right to receive the new shares.

EX RIGHTS Shares sold 'ex rights' are without any rights to a new issue of shares which the old shareholders are entitled to, the seller reserving such rights to himself.

EXCHANGE CLAUSE A clause placed by the drawer on a bill of exchange drawn in his own currency and payable in another country. Its purpose is to ensure that any exchange charges shall be paid by the drawee. There are many forms of exchange clause and in some countries the law will only recognize clauses worded in a particular manner.

A few examples follow, the bill in each case being drawn in sterling:

'Payable at the current rate of exchange for sight drafts on London'
'Payable by approved banker's cheque on London without loss in exchange'
'Payable at banker's selling rate of exchange for sight drafts on London'
'Payable in pounds sterling effective'
'Payable at banker's selling rate of exchange for 90 days' sight drafts on London' [in the South American trade]
'Exchange as per indorsement'

Exchange clauses are frequently referred to as sight clauses.

EXCHANGE CONTROL ACT 1947 This Act codified all Exchange Control Orders under what were previously known as the Defence Finance Regulations and was designed primarily to mobilize and control the country's liquid resources abroad and the international movement of currency owned by residents of the UK. Exchange Control was managed by the Bank of England as the Central Bank acting on behalf of HM Treasury, and the commercial banks known as Authorized Banks under the Act were appointed sub-agents of the Bank of England, to whom wide powers were delegated to approve, *inter alia*, the purchase of exchange for transfer abroad.

Exchange control restrictions were removed in the UK with effect from 24th October, 1979.

EXCHEQUER BILLS Promissory notes of the Government. They were first issued in 1696, and constituted the floating debt of the country for 160 or 170 years. There are no Exchequer Bills now in existence, Treasury Bills having superseded them. SEE *Treasury Bills*

EXCHEQUER TALLY A notched piece of wood, 8 or 9 inches in length, which, at one time, was given as a form of receipt to a person who deposited money with the Government. A similar notched stick was retained in the Exchequer Department, and when the depositer wanted his money he produced his portion of stick, and if the two sticks 'tallied', that is, the notches on the one agreed with the notches on the other, he was paid his money.

It is said that a notch of $1\frac{1}{2}$ inches represented £1,000, 1 inch £100, $\frac{3}{8}$ inch £10, half a notch of that size £1, $\frac{3}{16}$ inch 1s, smallest notch 1d, a small hole $\frac{1}{2}$d.

The use of tallies was abolished in 1782, but the old ones were preserved till 1834, when it was ordered that all the old tallies in the possession of the Government should be destroyed. They were burnt in stoves in the House of Lords, and it is supposed that they were the cause of the fire which destroyed both Houses of Parliament.

EXECUTOR An executor is the person appointed in the will of a testator to administer his estate, to pay his debts, and distribute his assets as instructed in the will.

The probate is the official evidence of an executor's title, but not the origin of his title, which is the will itself. His powers commence as from the death of the testator, when the latter's real and personal property vests in the executor. Strictly speaking, an executor can do everything appertaining to his office (except maintain an action) before he obtains probate. In practice, however, he confines his activities before probate to safeguarding the assets of the estate and taking the necessary steps to obtain probate. He can get in debts and collect rents, but third parties are not bound to pay him money or accept his title until he exhibits probate to them. An administrator's powers, on the other hand, flow from the grant of Letters of Administration and the deceased's assets vest in him only from that date.

A person named in a will as executor can decline to act, but if he wishes to do so he must clearly renounce before undertaking any executorial act. Once having obtained probate, he cannot renounce except in favour of the Public Trustee with the permission of the court. In Scotland, however, an executor may by a deed of renunciation resign his office after appointment. An executor who performs any act of administration in connection with the personal estate of the testator is personally liable to a penalty of twice the amount of capital transfer tax if he does not prove the will within six months of the testator's death. An infant cannot act as executor and, if he is named as sole executor, an administrator with the will annexed is appointed to act during his minority.

Notwithstanding that an executor possesses such wide powers before probate, it is the custom in the ordinary course not to permit an executor to deal with the credit balances in the deceased's name or with his securities until probate has been exhibited. It is possible that a later will may come to light revoking the previous one and appointing different executors, in which case the earlier will and the appointment of executors therein would be invalid. This general banking practice is supported by the case of *Tarn* v *Commercial Bank of Sydney* (1884) 12 QBD 294, where executors before probate sued the bank for the return of a bill lodged by the deceased for collection. The judge said

> Bankers are in a peculiar position and when asked to pay over large sums of money to persons claiming as executors of a deceased customer, I think they are justified in requiring to be made safe by production of probate.

But payments made to an executor after probate has been granted constitute a valid discharge even if the probate is afterwards revoked in favour of a later will.

When probate has been exhibited it is customary to transfer any credit balance on the deceased's account to the executor's account by means of a cheque or authority signed by all. If the deceased's account is in debit, it should not be transferred into the name of the executor, for the banker would then exchange a claim against the deceased's estate for a claim against the executor personally.

A debit balance on the deceased's account should not be liquidated from credit balances on the executor's account without the latter's consent, as there is no right of set-off.

Where two or more executors are appointed, they are in law regarded as one person, and the acts of any one are deemed to be the acts of all except that all proving executors must join in conveying real estate or in transferring stocks and shares. One executor may dispose of the testator's assets and so bind the others and a receipt by one for money received will be binding on his co-executors. Likewise, in the absence of a contrary mandate, payment to one of several executors will be a valid discharge to a banker, who cannot refuse to pay cheques drawn by any one executor. In practice, specific instructions are taken on the opening of an executorship account as to how it is to be conducted.

Executors can authorize one or more of their number to operate on the account, etc., but cannot delegate powers to outside parties.

In practice, it is expedient to arrange for *all* executors to sign, so that if and when the executorship merges into a trust, there will be no irregularity on account of one or more but not all of the trustees signing.

Where a sole executor dies, his powers and interest pass to *his* executor. If, however, a sole executor dies intestate, his powers and interest will not devolve on his administrator, and a new grant of administration must be obtained from the court, known as *de bonis non* (i.e. *de bonis non administratis*—of goods or assets not already administered). In the case of co-executors, on the death of one, his powers and interest vest in the survivor(s).

It is difficult to decide the point of time when executors become trustees. In the case of *In Re Smith, Henderson-Roe* v *Hitchins* (1889) 42 ChD 302, the judge said

> It is the duty of the executor to clear the estate, to pay the debts, funeral and testamentary expenses and the pecuniary legacies and to hand over the assets specifically bequeathed to the specific legatees. When all this has been done, a balance will be left in the executor's hands and I think it is plain that this balance will be held by him in trust.

Where an executorship bank account has been open for a period ordinarily incompatible with pure executorship, enquiries should be made as to whether a trust has commenced. If this be so, the style of the account should be altered and arrangements made for all to sign if this is not already the case.

An executor cannot purchase any asset of the estate either directly or through a nominee, whether he pays full value or not, unless the sanction of the court is obtained.

Executors have power to borrow before probate as well as after probate and such borrowings are their personal responsibility. They can in either case, however, give a specific charge over assets of the estate; they cannot charge the general estate.

Borrowing before probate is usually required for the payment of duty, probate fees, and funeral expenses.

Section 5 of thc Finance Act 1894 says

> A person authorised or required to pay estate duty in respect of any property, shall, for the purpose of paying the duty, have power, whether or not the property is vested in him, to raise the amount of the duty by the sale of or mortgage on that property.

Where an advance is required for probate purposes, it is usual, unless the executors are known to the bank, to require an introduction from a solicitor.

An undertaking is executed by all the proving executors whereby they undertake to apply the advance in payment of capital transfer tax, etc., and to repay the advance out of the first moneys received on account of the estate. They also give a charge on the balance of the deceased's account and any of his securities that may be in the banker's hands. Strictly speaking, such an advance should not be of a fluctuating nature.

Borrowings after probate are permissible for administration purposes, i.e. to pay the debts of the estate. Unless expressly given in the will, there is no power to borrow or give security for the purpose of paying legacies. Where any borrowing is allowed, the executors should charge assets of the estate—it is their personal liability and the bank cannot be a creditor of the deceased's estate.

The probate of a deceased trader or business man should be scrutinized to see if there are any directions for continuing the business. As a general rule, executors have no authority in law to carry on the business save for realization, a reasonable time being allowed to enable them to wind it up to the best advantage or to sell it as a going concern. Executors are personally responsible for all debts incurred in so trading, even though they make it plain that they are acting as executors, and the creditors' remedy is against them personally and not against the estate. They are, however, entitled to be indemnified out of the assets properly employed in carrying on the business.

Often, where an estate is undoubtedly solvent, a banker will lend with or without security, with the authority of the principal beneficiaries being of full age.

Executors may be empowered by the will to carry on a business for the benefit of the beneficiaries. In such a case, an executor can employ only such assets as were employed in the business at the time of the testator's decease, unless the will specifically authorizes otherwise.

Where the business is carried on, any creditors of the deceased can demand to be paid out of existing assets. If they assent to the carrying on of the business, however, they will rank after the creditors of the executors as regards business assets.

Personal representatives have authority to carry on a business for as long as necessary to wind it up (or sell it) and for that purpose it would appear that they can charge assets and borrow. SEE ALSO *Administrator; Personal Representatives; Probate*

EXECUTOR DE SON TORT A person who inter-meddles, without authority, with the estate of a deceased person, is called an executor *de son tort*, that is, an executor of his own wrong. By the Administration of Estates Act 1925, any person who fraudulently obtains any estate of a deceased person shall be charged as executor in his own wrong to the extent of the estate received, after deducting any debt due to him from the deceased and any payment made by him which might properly be made by a personal representative (Section 28).

EXEMPT FUND An investment fund which is exempt from all (or most) forms of taxation, sometimes known as 'gross' funds because there is no liability for tax on the income. All approved pension funds are exempt in this way as are a number of unit trusts set up as vehicles for investment by pension funds and charities. SEE *Unit Trusts*

EXEMPT PRIVATE COMPANY By the Companies Act 1948, the privilege of not filing, with the annual return to the Registrar, the annual accounts of a private company was restricted to a special type of such company known as an 'exempt' private company. The status of these exempt private companies was abolished as from 27th January, 1968, by the Companies Act 1967.

EXEMPT UNIT TRUST SEE *Exempt Fund; Unit Trusts*

EXEMPTED DEALER This is a dealer in securities enjoying the status of 'exempted' dealer, as distinct from 'licensed' dealer, under the Prevention of Fraud Investments Act 1958. There are believed to be approximately 400 such exempted dealers, consisting mainly of merchant banks, insurance companies, licensed deposit takers, and others engaged in issuing house or underwriting work. Once such exemption has been granted by the Department of Trade and Industry it can be revoked only on the ground that the prescribed conditions have not been fulfilled or that the circumstances in which the exemption was granted have materially changed. SEE *Gower Report; Licensed Dealer; Prevention of Fraud (Investments) Act 1958*

EXPECTATION OF LIFE A person's expectation of life may be calculated from so-called mortality tables. These tables were first devised by James Dodson, FRS, in or around the year 1750. Until then, subscribers to burial funds and life assurance schemes (see *Life Assurance*) paid the same contributions regardless of their age. However, James Dodson made a study of the ages of people on gravestones and by this means and by various other observations constructed the first mortality table. It was largely Dodson's ideas that set the pattern for modern life assurance.

Mortality tables show the average expected life-span of males and females of a particular age in a particular environment. the following is an expectation of life table for life assurance purposes, for males living in the UK, at the present time. Expectation of life for a female may be obtained by using the figure for a male four years younger.

Present age	Expectation of life in years	Present age	Expectation of life in years
0	73.8	51	25.17
1	72.86	52	24.3
2	71.91	53	23.44
3	70.95	54	22.6
4	69.99	55	21.77
5	69.03	56	20.95
6	68.06	57	20.14
7	67.09	58	19.35
8	66.12	59	18.57
9	65.15	60	17.81
10	64.17	61	17.07
11	63.2	62	16.33
12	62.22	63	15.62
13	61.24	64	14.92
14	60.27	65	14.24
15	59.3	66	13.58
16	58.33	67	12.94
17	57.38	68	12.31
18	56.44	69	11.71
19	55.49	70	11.12
20	54.55	71	10.55
21	53.59	72	10.0
22	52.64	73	9.47
23	51.68	74	8.96
24	50.72	75	8.47
25	49.76	76	8.0
26	48.79	77	7.55
27	47.82	78	7.12
28	46.85	79	6.71
29	45.88	80	6.32
30	44.91	81	5.94
31	43.94	82	5.58
32	42.97	83	5.24
33	42.0	84	4.92
34	41.03	85	4.62
35	40.06	86	4.33
36	39.1	87	4.06
37	38.13	88	3.8
38	37.17	89	3.56
39	36.21	90	3.34
40	35.26	91	3.12
41	34.31	92	2.92
42	33.37	93	2.74
43	32.43	94	2.56
44	31.49	95	2.4
45	30.56	96	2.25
46	29.64	97	2.11
47	28.73	98	1.97
48	27.83	99	1.85
49	26.93	100	1.74
50	26.04		

EXPORT CREDITS GUARANTEE DEPARTMENT (ECGD) This was set up in 1919 and was designed to provide cover for a variety of trade risks which were not otherwise insurable.

The scope of the Department's powers was widened considerably by Statute over the years, enabling the Department to cover up to 90 per cent of most commercial risks, e.g. the insolvency or default of the buyer and up to 95 per cent of risks of a political nature, e.g. Government action which prevents payment. Following the Radcliffe Report, a number of schemes were introduced under the aegis of the ECGD to support the banks in the provision of finance for export and provide credit protection for the exporter.

ECGD Insurance Cover

When the ECGD provides protection to an exporter against the risk of non-payment, the Department will usually require all that company's export business to be so insured in order to spread the risks. There are three main categories of policy, namely

Comprehensive short-term policy This covers contracts with credit terms up to six months. As mentioned above, the cover is for 90 per cent of loss due to insolvency or other default by the buyer and up to 95 per cent for political frustration of the contract. The cover will normally apply from the time the goods are shipped.

Supplemental extended terms policy This covers contracts in excess of six months and up to five years duration. Each contract must be separately approved by the ECGD (whereas the short-term policies operate under a blanket discretionary arrangement so that the exporter does not need to inform the ECGD of each contract unless some problem arises).

Capital goods and capital projects policy Major contracts for capital goods or construction work on credit terms extending over two years may be insured individually with the ECGD. It is necessary for the Department to be brought into the negotiations from the beginning and they will confirm the credit-worthiness of the buyer and whether or not cover is available for the country concerned. Cover is not normally given against the failure to take up the capital goods on the part of a non-government purchaser.

Other policies ECGD cover is also available in certain cases against escalation of UK manufacturing costs for contracts of £2 million or over, extending over at least two years. Cover is also available for the insolvency of subcontractors or consortium members. The Department is, in fact, willing to look at virtually any legitimate trading risk involving the export of goods or services from the UK, including losses on overseas investments through political intervention and failure to pay royalties on patented inventions.

ECGD Guarantees

Contracts which are insured an an ECGD policy may also be financed with the benefit of an ECGD guarantee. In that case, the British bank will provide the finance either directly to the exporter or, if it is a major capital contract overseas, direct to the overseas buyer (or other approved borrower) with the benefit of an ECGD guarantee. This may take the form of either

1. short-term supplier credit for
(a) contracts covered by bills of exchange or promissory notes for periods up to two years, or
(b) contracts on open account where the credit period does not exceed six months;
2. medium-term supplier credit, which is available to exporters of capital goods and services where the contract provides for credit of two years or more.

In the case of short-term supplier credits, the rate charged to the exporter by the bank for the export finance is at a very fine rate (currently $\frac{5}{8}$ per cent over base rate). In the case of medium-term supplier credits, the interest rate is fixed at the outset by the ECGD depending on the circumstances of each contract. When the interest received by a bank under medium- and long-term loans falls below current market rates, an interest adjustment in favour of the bank is received from the ECGD. An adjustment is made in favour of the Department if interest rates fall below the fixed rate under the guarantee.

The exporter must agree to indemnify the ECGD in respect of any sums which the Department has to pay to the financing bank under the guarantee. The exporter will then be able to claim correspondingly under his ECGD insurance policy up to 95 per cent of the amount involved depending on the circumstances.

ECGD Support Services

Where banks have entered into performance bonds (q.v.) for overseas contracts these may be covered by the ECGD if they are for amounts of £1 million or over.

Similarly, the Department will indemnify banks in respect of 'tender guarantees', i.e. where the bank has guaranteed to the overseas buyer that the UK exporter will comply with the conditions of his tender and enter into a contract if it be accepted, and 'advance payment guarantees' where the bank guarantees that if the exporter fails to complete his contract, any advance payments which the buyer has made may be recovered.

In all these cases, the indemnity support of the ECGD is available only if the contract value is £250,000 or more; payment under the contract is in cash or near cash, and ECGD credit insurance has been effected.

Buyer Credit Guarantees
In some cases, the ECGD will guarantee a bank loan to the overseas buyer of British goods in order that the UK exporter may be put in funds straight away. This is known as a 'buyer credit' and it is available only for high value goods and services, i.e. those where the contract value is in excess of £1 million. The amount of the loan and of the guarantee will be up to 85 per cent of the contract value. The ECGD will investigate the credit-worthiness of the buyer and may require a guarantee from an overseas bank or the parent company of the buyer.

Buyer credit may be (1) for single contracts; (2) for multiple contracts—general-purpose line of credit where there is a number of UK exporters as well as a number of overseas buyers (even though the individual contracts may be for quite small amounts); and (3) for a multiple contract—a project line of credit which is to cover purchases from a number of UK exporters to one overseas buyer provided it is in connection with a particular project.

In the case of a buyer credit, there is no liability of the UK supplier for the amount of the loan unless he fails to fulfil his part of the contract. It is not necessary, therefore, for the supplier to take out ECGD insurance because his only responsibilities are the fulfilment of the contract and payment of the premium for the guarantee.

In April 1984, a committee appointed by the Government, under the chairmanship of Sir Peter Matthews, recommended that the Export Credits Guarantee Department should cease to be a department of the Department of Trade and Industry, and be constituted as a public corporation. This report came at a time when the ECGD was in deficit for the first time in 30 years, a situation resulting in the main from the rescheduling of debts by a large number of countries. The Matthews Report suggested that the ECGD would be able to discriminate in relation to particular risks if it were a public corporation, rather than a Government department. Subsequently, a feasibility study within the Civil Service suggested that there would be little benefit in such a change.

EXPORT FINANCE COMPANIES Included in the membership of the British Export Houses Association are export finance companies who are not merchants but rather specialists in providing and arranging finance on a non-recourse basis for capital and semi-capital goods. These companies can offer to arrange ECGD (q.v.) cover themselves or they will take the assignment of the exporter's policy and, with the larger contracts, can arrange and manage the finance on behalf of a syndicate of banks in Britain. Finance can be provided for single transactions, or for a series of orders, or as a 'package deal' for a larger project, or through a credit line negotiated with a bank in the buyer's country. Their services are thus similar to, and extend beyond, those provided by merchant banks. The export finance companies can also usually arrange finance for non-sterling contracts raising a proportion of the required finance overseas.

Where these companies provide finance out of their own resources, it is usually on a non-recourse basis for 90 per cent or 100 per cent of the amount payable by the buyer over the credit period, thus relieving the exporter of the recourse liability to ECGD which is involved when the exporter arranges the finance through his bank on the basis of the special ECGD-backed facilities. The export finance companies under standard arrangements pay to the exporter any cash with order payment received from overseas buyers and the balance against presentation of shipping documents—this being without recourse to the exporter other than for technical performance of the sale contract. The traditional risks borne by these companies and the advisory and management services they provide naturally involve some additional expense to the exporter. The length of credit arranged will depend on the value of the contract, among other factors, but can be for as long as 10 years or more for larger projects.

EXPORT HOUSES Merchants, or more correctly export houses, play an important part in Britain's export trade, handling goods in practically every market in the world, serving all kinds of companies from the largest to the smallest and financing entrepot trade. They may be concerned at any stage in a transaction between a manufacturer and an overseas buyer, their activities ranging from the promotion of sales to the collection of debts. Among the many combinations of services, the main ones undertaken are to buy and sell on their own account as principals or to act as agent for the manufacturer or overseas buyer. Their financial services include paying the manufacturer immediately on shipment, making arrangements for credit facilities on behalf of their clients, where these are required, or, as factors (q.v.) assuming the full responsibility for the collection of the debts.

In the case of overseas firms engaged in importing direct from Britain, they will also act as 'confirming houses', financing and confirming contracts on behalf of the buyer, that is to say, in respect of documentary credits for which additional safeguards are required, they assume vis-a-vis a British manufacturer the responsibility for accepting delivery of and making payment for the goods ordered from him by an overseas buyer. The confirming house will send to the manufacturer or exporter written confirmation and the order will be regarded as having been placed for the account of the confirming house and not for the account of the overseas buyer. This function is also undertaken by accepting houses.

There are over 700 export houses in Britain, covering a very wide range of activities. It was estimated by the Committee on Invisible Exports that they have an annual turnover of over £1,000 million, while their overseas earnings arising from commission, profits, and interest on credits granted by them amount to some £26 million a year. Some 350 of these firms belong to the British Export Houses Association; they are thought to handle or finance some 10 per cent of Britain's export trade.

EXTERNAL ACCOUNTS The sterling accounts of non-residents maintained with authorized banks and with other banks in the UK which were specifically authorized by the Bank of England to maintain such accounts, during the years of exchange control (SEE *Exchange Control Act 1947*). They did not include accounts in respect of which restrictions had been imposed under Section 40 of the Exchange Control Act 1947. External accounts could be credited only in accordance with certain permissions given by the Bank of England to the banks concerned: a general permission had been given for these accounts to be debited.

EXTRAORDINARY GENERAL MEETINGS Meetings which are convened for the transaction of special business. The directors of a company shall, on the requisition of the holders of not less than one-tenth of such of the paid up capital of the company as carries the right of voting at general meetings, forthwith proceed to convene an extraordinary general meeting of the company. Directors may, whenever they think fit, convene an extraordinary general meeting (Table A, Clause 49). For further information see Section 368 *et seq.* of the Companies Act 1985.

EXTRAORDINARY RESOLUTION SEE *Resolutions*

F

FACSIMILE SIGNATURE A signature placed on a document by means of printing or by a rubber stamp. Banks were traditionally unwilling to deal with such instruments as there is no way of knowing whether the facsimile signature has been placed there with the authority of the person whose signature it purports to be. (See *Kepitigalla Rubber Estates Ltd* v *The National Bank of India Ltd* [1909] 2 KB 1010 under *Alterations*.) For this reason the banks invariably take indemnities from their customers if they agree to honour instruments so authenticated.

In *Goodman* v *J. Eban Ltd* [1954] 1 All ER 763, the Court of Appeal supported the validity of a signature other than in handwriting, but Denning, LJ, dissenting, did not think it right that in law a person could sign a document by using a rubber stamp with a facsimile signature. 'The validity of a signature lies in the fact that no two persons write exactly alike, so it carries on the face of it a guarantee that the person who signs has given his personal attention to the document.'

The point again arose in *Lazarus Estates Ltd* v *Beasley* [1956] 1 All ER 341, where the facsimile signature was that of a limited company. The validity of the signature was not contested, but the same judge referred to the previous decision and added 'but it has not yet been held that a company can sign by its printed name affixed with a rubber stamp'.

If it is for the purposes of indorsement that a facsimile signature is used, the drawee banker might well ask for the confirmation of the presenting banker (*Questions on Banking Practice*, 9th Edition, No. 641).

In *Meyappen* v *Manchanayake* [1961] Ceylon NLR 529, an indorsement by means of a rubber stamp bearing the name of a partnership was held invalid. The case was an appeal by the second and third defendants who, with the fourth defendant, were partners in business under the name of Nirchalananthan Company. Judgment had been entered against them on four cheques drawn by the first defendant payable to bearer and indorsed with a rubber stamp in the name Nirchalananthan Company. This name was stamped on the back of each cheque by an employee of the firm on instructions from the second defendant, before the plaintiff was handed the cheques.

The point at issue was whether the second and third defendants were liable on the cheques. The relevant sections of the Ceylon Bills of Exchange Ordinance are similar to those in the Bills of Exchange Act 1882.

Sansoni, J, said that he thought the correct view was that, unless there was added to the name so stamped a signature of a person verifying the so-called signature to show that it was placed there with the authority of the firm, the document could not be regarded as validly signed. No case had held that the mere stamping of the name of a company or a partnership on a document was a valid signature. He doubted whether in the case of a bill of exchange even a facsimile reproduction of a person's signature would be sufficient. (Goodman's case, above, concerned a solicitor's facsimile signature on his bill of costs, and was a decision under the Solicitors Act 1932.)

This observation of the learned judge was *obiter*, and the decision is, of course, of persuasive value only in the courts of this country, but nevertheless serves to emphasize the importance of the banker's idemnity referred to above, in what has now become a very widespread practice.

FACTORING The management and in some cases the purchase of business debts which, in the words of Mr Justice Mocatta, is 'the business nowadays somewhat confusingly called factoring' (*Hamilton Finance Co Ltd* v *Coverley, Westray, Walbaum & Tosetti Ltd and Portland Finance Co Ltd* [1969] 1 Lloyd's Rep 53 at p.58). The word in its modern form came to us from the USA, but almost certainly had its origin in the older concept of a factor as an agent. The word may owe something to the agency contracts *facio ut facias* of the later Roman Empire. Certainly the Romans employed agents to manage businesses, including the recovery of debts due under contracts, and to take charge of trading ships for the purpose of managing contracts entered into on the voyage. In parts of Europe in the thirteenth and fourteenth centuries, agents were employed on a commission basis to sell goods and in some cases undertook responsibility for the credit-worthiness of the buyer. This became the origin of the *del credere* agent who would receive an extra commission from his principal for guaranteeing the solvency of the customer to whom the goods were sold on credit.

Attempts have been made to show that modern factoring is related, perhaps a little tenuously, to the trading and financing operations of the Pilgrim Fathers on their arrival in America. What seems more certain is that with the upsurge of the textile industry in the USA at the turn of the last century, the trading aspect of factoring diminished and the term was applied to the method of financing some of the newer industries, particularly that of textiles. Henceforth, the factor would be more concerned with assessing the credit-worthiness of the buyer and in some cases would buy outright the debts receivable. Factoring remained a feature of the textile industry alone right through the years up to the Great Depression in the 1930s, and it was not until after the Second World War that factoring in the USA was extended to other industries.

Going back over 100 years or more, a number of US factoring companies provided factoring services for sales to the USA by a number of British companies in the Yorkshire woollen trade. This was, it seems, the first acquaintance with modern factoring in this country and it was not until 1960 that locally based factoring operations were set up here. In that year, Tozer Kemsley & Millbourn set up a factoring operation under the name of Towergate Securities later to become International Factors. In the same year, Meinhard & Co, one of the factoring houses in New York, commenced a factoring operation in the UK which, although not greatly successful in itself, sparked off considerable interest among other institutions. The National Provincial Bank, as it then was, became the first of the English clearing banks to enter the factoring field in 1968 and it was followed in turn by all the other major banks.

There are three main aspects of the factoring function. They are an administrative service, a system of credit protection and a method of financing.

Administrative Service

Under this service, the factor manages the trade debts of the client company. The factor will keep the sales ledger, issue the invoices, collect payment when due and generally relieve the client of the administrative burden of this side of the business. This is something more than the typical customer-billing service which a company might arrange through a computer bureau. Under a factoring contract, the sales ledger of the client company will be managed by the factor. Thus the client will be saved the administrative costs of bookkeeping, invoicing, credit control and debt collection.

The factoring company can usually handle these matters more economically because it will be organized on a large scale, it will be able to make more efficient use of computers and it will be trained in credit control. The client company fee would save the cost of the bookkeeping clerk (including social security contributions and pensions) and the not inconsiderable cost of stationery, postage and telephone charges. More particularly, management time would be saved, the company would be seen to have an efficient invoicing service and there could be sustantial savings from the more speedy collection of debts. The small- to medium-sized company is thus able, at a very modest cost, to import a degree of professionalism in the management of its debts far beyond that which it might otherwise achieve from its own resources.

Credit Protection

A system of credit protection can operate by which the factor assumes responsibility for the trade debts due to the client company and thereby relieves the client of the risk of loss. This is a central, but not essential, aspect of factoring. In effect, the factor purchases the debts from the client company so that in the client's books one debt due from the factor takes the place of all the various trade debts due from the company's customers. Just as the large factoring companies have the resources to manage sales ledgers in an efficient, large-scale operation, so they have the facilities for credit intelligence to enable them to assess credit risks and advise their clients accordingly. In the comparatively rare instances of 'with recourse' factoring (see below), the risk of bad debts remains with the client, but in a more typical 'without recourse' relationship the factor assumes the credit risk and therefore the entire responsibility for credit control. The extent of credit allowed by the client to individual customers will be approved by the factor and the monitoring of that customer's account will become part of the factor's day-to-day operations. The pursuit of outstanding debts may require careful handling, particularly if the customer is an important supplier of the factor's client. The factor is unlikely to take any precipitate action without consultation with the client and it may be in some cases that the client will assume the risk rather than see his customer sued. In the last resort, however, the decision to take legal action will be that of the factor to whom ownership of the debt has passed.

The assessment of credit risk is something at which the factoring company will normally be much more expert than the client. The staff of the factoring house is trained in the assessment of credit-worthiness and will have access to very extensive information on the financial standing and credit rating of individual customers and corporations. When taking on a new client, the factor will examine the sales ledger closely and will not take on the responsibility for any debts which look 'doubtful'. A factoring house is not a debt collection agency and it cannot turn bad debts into good ones. What the factor does offer is credit control conducted in a very professional way from the outset of the client–factor relationship.

Financing
There is financing in that the factor who takes over the client's trade debts will, in certain circumstances, advance a proportion of their value immediately and the balance on maturity of the debts. The client's liquidity is thus improved to the extent that a cash balance has been substituted for book debts. In earlier days, the discounting of one's debts was looked upon as the last resort of a bankrupt trader and it was this attitude perhaps which gave a bad name to factoring (or more correctly invoice discounting, because in many instances it was not a factoring operation). However, it is now generally recognized that book debts are as important an asset as any other and in some instances, such as where companies have a very large turnover but few tangible assets, the book debts will form the principal asset. As mentioned above, the essence of factoring is the purchase by the factor of the entire turnover of the trading operation. If payment is made by the factor to the client as and when the debts mature, there is no element of financing. The factor is providing a sales accounting and credit insurance facility, as explained above. In most cases, however, the factor will be willing to advance a proportion, say 80 per cent, of the outstanding debts ahead of the maturity dates. In such instances, the factoring operation becomes an additional source of finance for the client. The factor will charge interest on the funds advanced, probably at a rate of between two per cent and four per cent over bank base rate.

The suitability of this form of finance will depend, as with any financing operation, on the nature of the business and the purpose for which the money is used. For obvious reasons, it would be quite unsuitable to finance long-term capital needs from the factoring of trade debts. On the other hand, if an advance from a factor will permit substantial discounts to be obtained from trade creditors, this could be a profitable operation. In other cases, factor finance (because it increases the availability of working capital) might enable a company to make use of spare capacity or otherwise expand turnover. It is obvious that a company which receives immediate payment (assuming for the moment 100 per cent finance) from a factor instead of waiting, say three months, for customers to pay, is increasing its capital resources by a sum equal to 25 per cent of the annual turnover. Nor is this a once-for-all injection of capital because the product cycle is speeded up so long as the factoring operation continues. If in a typical case the cycle is six months from manufacture to the date of payment, including three months' credit, the immediate factoring of the debt can reduce the product cycle by one-half or, in effect, double the circulation of capital in the business.

There are other related aspects of factoring. They are

Invoice discounting This is the purchase of a debt or a number of debts from a client, usually in order to improve the client's cash flow, and under the title of 'receivables financing' it is a service which has existed in the United States alongside factoring for a long time. Strictly speaking it is not a factoring operation in the accepted sense because (1) the factor does not control the client company's sales ledger and (2) invoice discounting is usually a 'one off' operation and does not involve the purchase by the factor of the entire sales turnover of the client. It has certain attributes of factoring in that the client is put in funds and there is a degree of credit insurance. (At least one major factoring company undertakes invoice discounting on a 'total turnover' basis on the assumption that this gives the factor a stronger legal position than with individual transactions.)

With recourse factoring Although a full factoring service will usually include the full underwriting of the client's trade debts, the factor may in exceptional circumstances wish to retain recourse against the client in the event of the failure of a debtor to meet his obligations. Such 'with recourse' arrangements may apply to particular transactions, e.g. above an agreed level, or to certain customers where the credit risk is not acceptable to the factor.

Non-notification factoring It is doubtful whether this is strictly factoring at all because the client's debtors are not informed of the arrangement and the client continues to collect the debts himself, having sold them to the factor. It is similar to invoice discounting with the difference that it would normally apply to the entire sales turnover. Although it may have its usefulness in certain cases, it is not a form of factoring adopted by the clearing banks in this country. If a client company particularly wishes to conceal the factor's presence, an arrangement can be made for a company to be set up, owned by the factor, with a name similar to that of the client company. This is not non-notification factoring, but a normal full factoring service with a company interposed for cosmetic reasons.

Not all companies are suitable candidates for factoring and, in general, the following may not be appropriate:

Small companies which would normally find it more economical to run their own sales ledger.
Companies with large numbers of debtors for small amounts.
Companies with a speculative business.
Companies with an unusually high bad debt experience (although, if this arises from bad credit control, a factoring service may solve the problem).
Construction companies and others employing sub-contractors and requiring stage payments.
Companies selling a large range of small products to the general public.

Most factors would also exclude those companies where the management is patently inefficient and the supervision of the sales ledger could become a burden or even an embarrassment.

Some companies by nature lend themselves to the possibility of factoring. To quote one leading factor: 'Factoring is most suitable for goods which can be made, sold and forgotten.' In general terms, they are well-conducted, medium-sized companies selling not too diverse a range of products to a good spread of customers in a traditionally reliable sector.

As the business of factoring has grown in recent years, there has been a degree of specialization among and within the factoring houses themselves. Factoring houses and officials within those houses continue to build up a wealth of experience of particular industries. They are also able to build up from their own experience a considerable fund of data which, in addition to the normal commercial sources of information enables them to advise clients on specific credit risks.

In English law, factoring contracts and invoice discounting arrangements are essentially assignments of debt. The only other sphere of law — apart from bankruptcy and liquidation regulations — which relates to trade debts held for the benefit of a third party is that of a floating charge created under a debenture. Whereas a debenture is registrable, there is no provision in English law for the registration of debt assignments and it is, therefore, impossible to tell from any public source whether or not a company has entered into a factoring agreement. A factoring house which acquired the trade debts of a company after the company had given a duly registered debenture to its banker might be postponed to the bank in a receivership situation. The point is not entirely free from doubt because, in the ordinary way, a company which has given a floating charge may continue to dispose of its assets in the ordinary course of business and there is some legal authority for the view that the factoring of book debts is in the course of business. If, on the other hand, a floating charge (given, for example, in a debenture to a bank) prohibits the sale or factoring of debts subject to the charge, it is essential that the book debts be released from the floating charge by agreement with the debenture-holder if the factor is to have priority of title to the book debts. From the bank's point of view, the obligation of the factor to the client company under the factoring agreement will be caught under the debenture representing a single and implicitly safer debt than would have been the case if the debts had not been factored.

In 1971, the Crowther Committee on Consumer Credit (q.v.) recommended that all security interests should be the subject of public registration. This would enable the factoring houses to ascertain whether trade debts were in any way encumbered in priority to their own position as factors, and also to register their interest as assignees of the debts under the factoring agreement. However, the recommendation has not passed into law and in the meantime factors must continue to rely on their own investigations before entering into credit insurance arrangements.

There have been various developments of factoring business in overseas markets, referred to loosely as 'international factoring'. This includes the factoring of exports from, say, the UK, the better term for which is probably 'export factoring'. It is also used to refer to the opening of offices or affiliates in other countries to undertake the factoring of both domestic and export business from those countries. Lastly, the term is used to describe the international groupings of the factors to undertake import–export factoring among trading nations generally, and this is more correctly referred to as 'multinational factoring'.

The factoring of export sales is fundamentally the same as for domestic business. The exporter may have no adequate means of assessing the credit-worthiness of his customer, and the language and documentation may be completely unfamiliar to him. There may be import duties and other local requirements, and the terms of trade may be much longer than those to which he is accustomed in this country. The factor who can take care of those problems as well as provide, as the larger houses do, information in local markets and introductions to agents and distributors, is giving the client a service which he would be hard put to match from his own resources. Thus it is that even the largest companies, who would not have recourse to factoring for their domestic business, have arranged to factor their exports.

For the factoring house, the work of export factoring opens up a whole new dimension, calling as it does for knowledge of overseas customs and the credit appraisal of the overseas buyers. The bank-controlled houses have perhaps a special advantage in this respect, drawing as they do on the international connections of the major banks. It was a natural extension of export factoring that the principal UK factors should set up offices in countries abroad.

The comparatively recent development of factoring in the UK was followed rapidly in most European countries, notably Sweden and West Germany. Factoring developed under the umbrella of existing financial institutions and was soon extended to a wide range of industries and professions.

International factoring has become centred on a handful of major groupings and it seems that this will continue to be the pattern. Three of the main groupings are the International Factors Group, the UK end of which is controlled by Lloyds Bank; the Walter E. Heller Overseas Corporation, which is the largest factoring organization in America; and Credit Factoring International, controlled by National Westminster group and having its world centre of operations in the UK. There is, additionally, a network of other leading factoring houses operating in association with each other under the title Factors Chain International. This association of factors has members throughout the world and has a permanent secretariat in Amsterdam. The aim is to achieve uniformity of standards and to assist members with legal and other technical information about the countries of operation, Factors Chain International enjoy a 'correspondent relationship' among their members, so that they are able to assist each other from their knowledge of the law, practice and language in each place, and the collection and guaranteeing of debts on behalf of members. The Report of the Association of British Factors Limited for 1984 showed that in that year, 3,632 companies were using the factoring services of the Association's members. The total volume of business factored in that year was £3,808 million, an increase of 37 per cent on the previous year. Approximately one-half of the Association's clients were in manufacturing industries, while 28 per cent were in distributive industries and 23 per cent were in services. SEE *Association of British Factors Limited; Debts, Assignment of*

FACTORS ACT 1889 This Act deals with dispositions of goods by factors, or mercantile agents, and dispositions by sellers and buyers of goods. SEE *Bill of Lading; Warehouse-Keeper's Warrant*

The principal part of the Act is as follows.

Definitions

1. For the purposes of this Act—

(1) The expression 'mercantile agent' shall mean a mercantile agent having in the customary course of his business as such agent authority either to sell goods, or to consign goods for the purpose of sale, or to buy goods, or to raise money on the security of goods:

(2) A person be deemed to be in possession of goods or of the documents of title to goods, where the goods or documents are in his actual custody or are held by any other person subject to his control or for him or on his behalf:

(3) The expression 'goods' shall include wares and merchandise:

(4) The expression 'document of title' shall include any bill of lading, dock warrant, warehouse-keeper's certificate, and warrant or order for the delivery of goods, and any other document used in the ordinary course of business as proof of the possession or control of goods, or authorising or purporting to authorise, either by indorsement or by delivery, the possessor of the document to transfer or receive goods thereby represented:

(5) The expression 'pledge' shall include any contract pledging, or giving a lien or security on goods, whether in consideration of an original advance or of any further or continuing advance, or of any pecuniary liability:

(6) The expression 'person' shall include any body of persons, corporate or unincorporate.

DISPOSITION BY MERCANTILE AGENTS

Powers of mercantile agent with respect to disposition of goods.

2.—(1) Where a mercantile agent is, with the consent of the owner, in possession of goods or of the documents of title to goods, any sale, pledge, or other disposition of the goods, made by him when acting in the ordinary course of business of a mercantile agent, shall, subject to the provisions of this Act, be as valid as if he were expressly authorised by the owner of the goods to make the same; provided that the person taking under the disposition acts in good faith, and has not at the time of the disposition notice that the person making the disposition has not authority to make the same.

(2) Where a mercantile agent has, with the consent of the owner, been in possession of goods or of the documents of title to goods, any sale, pledge, or other disposition, which would have been valid if the consent had continued, shall be valid notwithstanding the determination of the consent; provided that the person taking under the disposition has not at the time thereof notice that the consent has been determined.

(3) Where a mercantile agent has obtained possession of any documents of title to goods by reason of his being or having been, with the consent of the owner, in possession of the goods represented thereby, or of any other documents of title to the goods, his possession of the first-mentioned documents shall, for the purposes of this Act, be deemed to be with the consent of the owner.

(4) For the purposes of this Act the consent of the owner shall be presumed in the absence of evidence to the contrary.

Effect of pledges of documents of title

3. A pledge of the documents of title to goods shall be deemed to be a pledge of the goods.

Pledge for antecedent debt

4. Where a mercantile agent pledges goods as security for a debt or liability due from the pledgor to the pledgee before the time of the pledge, the pledgee shall acquire no further right to the goods than could have been enforced by the pledgor at the time of the pledge.

Rights acquired by exchange of goods or documents

5. The consideration necessary for the validity of a sale, pledge, or other disposition of goods, in pursuance of this Act, may be either a payment in cash, or the delivery or transfer of other goods, or of a document of title to goods, or of a negotiable security, or any other valuable consideration; but where goods are pledged by a mercantile agent in consideration of the delivery or transfer of other goods, or of a document of title to goods, or of a negotiable security, the pledgee shall acquire no right or interest in the goods so pledged in excess of the value of the goods, documents, or security when so delivered or transferred in exchange.

Agreements through clerks, etc.

6. For the purposes of this Act an agreement made with a mercantile agent through a clerk or other person authorised in the ordinary course of business to make contracts of sale or pledge on his behalf shall be deemed to be an agreement with the agent.

Provisions as to consignors and consignees

7.—(1) Where the owner of goods has given possession of the goods to another person for the purpose of consignment or sale, or has shipped the goods in the name of another person, and the consignee of the goods has not had notice that such person is not the owner of the goods, the consignee shall, in respect of advances made to or for the use of such person, have the same lien on the goods as if such person were the owner of the goods, and may transfer any such lien to another person.

(2) Nothing in this Section shall limit or affect the validity of any sale, pledge, or disposition by a mercantile agent.

Dispositions by Sellers and Buyers of Goods

Disposition by seller remaining in possession

8. Where a person, having sold goods, continues, or is in possession of the goods or of the documents of title to the goods, the delivery or transfer by that person, or by a mercantile agent acting for him, of the goods or documents of title under any sale, pledge, or other disposition thereof, or under any agreement for sale, pledge, or other disposition thereof, to any person receiving the same in good faith and without notice of the previous sale, shall have the same effect as if the person making the delivery or transfer were expressly authorised by the owner of the goods to make the same.

Disposition by buyer obtaining possession

9. Where a person, having bought or agreed to buy goods, obtains with the consent of the seller possession of the goods or the documents of title to the goods, the delivery or transfer, by that person or by a mercantile agent acting for him, of the goods or documents of title, under any sale, pledge, or other disposition thereof, or under any agreement for sale, pledge, or other disposition thereof, to any person receiving the same in good faith and without notice of any lien or other right of the original seller in respect of the goods, shall have the same effect as if the person making the delivery or transfer were a mercantile agent in possession of the goods or documents of title with the consent of the owner.

Effect of transfer of documents on vendor's lien or right of stoppage in transitu

10. Where a document of title to goods has been lawfully transferred to a person as a buyer or owner of the goods, and that person transfers the document to a person who takes the document in good faith and for valuable consideration, the last-mentioned transfer shall have the same effect for defeating any vendor's lien or right of stoppage *in transitu* as the transfer of a bill of lading has for defeating the right of stoppage *in transitu*.

Supplemental

Mode of transferring documents

11. For the purposes of this Act, the transfer of a document may be by indorsement, or, where the document is by custom or by its express terms transferable by delivery, or makes the goods deliverable to the bearer, then by delivery.

Saving for right of true owner

12.—(1) Nothing in this Act shall authorise an agent to exceed or depart from his authority as between himself and his principal, or exempt him from any liability, civil or criminal, for so doing.

(2) Nothing in this Act shall prevent the owner of goods from recovering the goods from an agent or his trustee in bankruptcy at any time before the sale or pledge thereof, or shall prevent the owner of goods pledged by an agent from having the right to redeem the goods at any time before the sale thereof, on satisfying the claim for which the goods were pledged, and paying to the agent, if by him required, any money in respect of which the agent would by law be entitled to retain the goods or the documents of title thereto, or any of them, by way of lien as against the owner, or from recovering from any person with whom the goods have been pledged any balance of money remaining in his hands as the produce of the sale of the goods after deducting the amount of his lien.

(3) Nothing in this Act shall prevent the owner of goods sold by an agent from recovering from the buyer the price agreed to be paid for the same, or any part of that price, subject to any right of set-off on the part of the buyer against the agent.

A mercantile agent or factor is defined in Section 1 of the Act. He was put under penalty for dealing wrongfully for the goods or documents of title to goods under his control by the Larceny Act 1916, which provided that

Every person who, being an agent or factor entrusted either solely or jointly with any other person for the purpose of sale or otherwise, with the possession of any goods or of any document of title to goods contrary to or without the authority of his principal in that behalf for his own use or benefit, or the use or benefit of any person other than the person by whom he was so entrusted, and in violation of good faith—

(1) Consigns, deposits, transfers, or delivers any goods or document of title so entrusted to him as and by way of a pledge, lien or security for any money or valuable security borrowed or received, or intended to be borrowed or received by him; or

(2) Accepts any advance of any money or valuable security on the faith of any contract or agreement to consign, deposit, transfer, or deliver any such goods or documents of title; shall be guilty of a misdemeanour, etc.

The offence of larceny has now been replaced by that of theft under the Theft Act 1968 (q.v.).

FAIR TRADING ACT 1973 This Act relates more to matters of consumer protection and monopoly trading, than to the sphere of finance. Nevertheless, it has financial implications and is thus included here for reference purposes. The main provisions of the Act are as follows.

1. the appointment of a Director-General of Fair Trading, whose responsibility is to keep under review those commerical activities which may adversely affect the economic interests of consumers in connection with the supply of goods or services, or which may constitute monopoly situations or uncompetitive practices;
2. the establishing of a Consumer Protection Advisory Committee;
3. replacing the provisions of the Monopolies and Mergers Acts 1948 and 1965 and empowering the Director-General of Fair Trading to make references to the Monopolies Commission;
4. the abolition of the office of Registrar of Restrictive Trading Agreements and transferred his function to the Director-General of Fair Trading;
5. provisions relating to pyramid selling and similar trading activities.

The main provisions of the Act came into effect on 1st November, 1973.

FALSE PRETENCES Where a person obtains payment of a cheque by falsely representing himself to be the payee, he is liable to be prosecuted for obtaining money by false pretences. Also, if a person obtains goods and gives in payment thereof a cheque drawn upon a bank where he has no account, or gives a cheque which he knows is worthless and will not be honoured, he is likewise liable to prosecution.

The offence of obtaining property by deception is now contained in Section 15 of the Theft Act 1968 as amended by the Theft Act 1978. SEE *Theft Acts*

FAMILY INCOME BENEFIT Provision under a policy of life assurance (q.v.) for a regular income to be paid to the widow or widower or children of the life assured in the event of his or her death. This may be on a reducing term basis coupled with, for example, a mortgage protection policy (q.v.) or it may be attached to some other form of term assurance, e.g. until the children of the life assured have completed full-time education. In broad terms, family income assurance is a means of providing an annual income for dependents in addition to or in lieu of a capital sum on the death of the life assured.

FAMILY INCOME SUPPLEMENT This is a Social Security benefit designed to augment the earnings of poorer families. It differs from supplementary benefit in that it applies only to persons who are employed or self-employed, and who are bringing up children.

The amount of the benefit will vary according to the number of children, but there must be at least one child in the family.

In the case of a claim by a married couple, the man must be working for at least 30 hours a week. If the claim is by a single parent or other single person bringing up children, he or she must work 24 hours a week.

Family income supplement is payable if the total family income (see below) is below a qualifying level. In calculating the total family income, i.e. income from all sources including full-time and part-time employment, the following are omitted: (1) child benefit, (2) attendance or mobility allowance, (3) the first £4 of a war disablement pension, (4) rent allowance, (5) payment for children boarded with the family, (6) education maintenance allowance, and (7) income of children (unless the income is paid for a child's maintenance).

The qualifying level for family income supplement is published by the Department of Health and Social Security from time to time. The amount of the supplement is one-half of the difference between the family income and the qualifying level of income shown in the table.

Families in receipt of the family income supplement are automatically entitled to free school meals, free milk for the under-fives and expectant mothers, and free dental treatment, glasses and prescriptions (SEE *Appendix 2*).

FAMILY LAW REFORM ACT 1969 The principal provisions of this Act, which came into force on 1st January, 1970, are contained in Parts I and II and amend the law relating to the age of majority and the property rights of illegitimate children.

Part I

As from 1st January, a person attains full age on attaining the age of 18 (Section 1) and thereafter is able (*inter alia*) to make a valid will and to give receipts and discharges. A person over 18 but under 21 on 1st January, 1970 is deemed to have come of age on that date.

As a result, reference to 'full age', 'minority', 'infancy' or any similar expression in any statute (whenever enacted) or in any deed, will or other instrument *made on or after that date* is now construed as a reference to the age of 18 in the absence of a definition or of any indication of a contrary intention (Section 1(2)). A will (or codicil) is, of course, 'made' on the date on which it is executed and not on the date of the testator's death (when it comes into operation) and it is provided that, for the purpose of the Act, it shall not be treated as having been made after 1st January by reason only that it is confirmed by a codicil executed after that date.

In the case of intestacy, the statutory trusts (q.v.) established in Section 47(1) of the Administration of Estates Act 1925, will apply only up to the age of 18 in respect of a death on or after 1st January, 1970. However, this part of the Act does not affect the Inheritance (Family Provision) Act 1938 as amended, but it is specifically provided (Section 5(1)) that the term 'dependant' in that Act shall continue to include a son who has not attained 21. SEE *Inheritance (Provision for Family and Dependants) Act 1975*

The effect of Part I on will trusts already in existence on 1st January is mainly that

1. where a person under 21 has an *immediate vested interest* in capital, he may give a valid receipt and discharge for it on 1st January, 1970 or on his 18th birthday, whichever is the later; and
2. although Section 31 of the Trustee Act 1925 is unaltered in its application, payments made after 1st January, 1970, for the maintenance, education or benefit of any person then over 18 may, at the discretion of the trustees, be direct to the beneficiary instead of to his parent or guardian (Schedule 3, Section 5(1)).

Part II

The property rights given to illegitimate children , by this part affect only inter vivos documents made, wills coming into operation, and rights in the estate of a person dying intestate, after 1st January, 1970.

In any such deed, will or other instrument, any reference to children of any person shall include any illegitimate children of that person, and any reference to persons related in some other manner (e.g. nieces) shall include persons who would be so related if they or any persons through whom the relationship is deduced (e.g. their parents), had been born legitimate (Section 15(1)) unless, in either case, a contrary intention is shown. This provision applies only to determine if a person is to benefit under a disposition: it does not affect the construction of the words 'heir' or 'heirs' or any other expression used to create an entailed interest, nor the devolution of any property passing with a dignity or title or honour. References to illegitimate children in this Section include legitimated persons but are without prejudice to Sections 16 and 17 of the Adoption Act 1958 (which relates the construction of dispositions in cases of adoption). Furthermore, the rights of illegitimate children are imported into Section 33 of the Trustee Act 1925 (protective trusts) and Section 33 of the Wills Act 1837 (saving of gifts to predeceasing issue of a testator) (Sections 15(3) and 16) and it is declared that a disposition in favour of illegitimate children not in being at the date of the gift is no longer void as contrary to public policy.

On the subject of intestacy, Section 14 provides that where either parent of an illegitimate child dies intestate, that child or, if he is dead, his issue, shall be entitled to benefit as if the child had been born legitimate. In addition, on the death of an illegitimate child intestate, *each* parent, if surviving, shall be entitled to an interest in the estate, although, to avoid excessive difficulty, an illegitimate child is presumed not to have been survived by his father unless the contrary is shown. In this Section, the term 'illegitimate child' does not include a person who has been legitimated or adopted, as these are provided for in earlier legislation.

It is important to note also that Section 14 is concerned only to bring into benefit illegitimate *children* of an intestate: the parents of an intestate illegitimate child and all other persons entitled to benefit (including the issue of an illegitimate child who has predeceased) must themselves be legitimate and must be able to trace their title through legitimate descent (except for the inclusion of an illegitimate *child* of the intestate).

It will be appreciated that the office of personal representative or trustee becomes extremely onerous when it is necessary to have regard to the possibility of illegitimate children at all stages, and protection is accordingly provided in Section 17. Personal representatives and trustees may hereafter distribute trust property among the persons entitled thereto *without having ascertained* that there is no person entitled by virtue of Sections 14, 15 and 16 of the Act (except for the mother of an illegitimate child dying intestate) and shall not be liable to any such person of whose claim they have not had notice at the time of the distribution (without prejudice to the right of such person to follow the trust property). What constitutes 'notice' of such claim is probably to be decided under the normal rules, but it is suggested that it is more than ever necessary not to omit publication of the notice to claimants referred to in Section 27 of the Trustee Act 1925.

Finally, illegitimate children count as *dependants* under the Inheritance (Family Provision) Act 1938, as amended (Section 18), and as *children* in Section 11 of the Married Women's Property Act 1880 (Section 19).

FARMING PROFITS The general rule is that a person who farms land on a commercial basis with a reasonable expectation of profit will be taxed under Schedule D Case I as carrying on a trade.

The normal Schedule D rules apply in relation to the business of farming, but there are the following special factors:

1. The profits of farming may be averaged over any two consecutive years provided the farmer exercises this option within two years from the end of the second year. It is a condition of this concession, however, that profits of the 'lower' year be no more than 70 per cent of the profits of the better year.
2. If a farmer has more than one farm, both or all of his farms will be assessed as one business.
3. Farming losses may be set against other sources of income provided that the farming is conducted on a commercial basis with a reasonable expectation of profit. Any person who farms as a hobby, however, will not be able to set off farming losses against other sources of income, but will be able to carry forward his farming losses against future profits from his hobby.
4. A farmer who receives deficiency payments from the Government in respect of particular crops will, by concession, be taxed on these in the year in which the payments are received rather than when the crops are sold.
5. The owner of agricultural property let to a tenant may offset any losses from the agricultural letting against other income (contrary to the general rule relating to Schedule A assessments).

FARTHING The name is derived from feorth or fourth. A penny at one time was actually divided into four parts, called feorthlings or fourthings — hence farthings. Its standard weight is 43.75 grains troy. The coin is an alloy of copper, tin and zinc. The farthing has not been legal tender since 1st January 1961.

FEDERAL RESERVE SYSTEM SEE *Central Bank*

FEE SIMPLE The utmost interest in land a person can hold. Under the feudal system, grants of land were made as a reward for military service and the land was held 'in fee', i.e. as a reward for services rendered. Such grants in fee were originally for life only but later were extended to include the sons of the first grantee and the interest was then called a 'fee simple'.

A fee simple estate in land can only terminate upon the death of the owner intestate and leaving no persons entitled on intestacy, in which case it passes to the Crown.

A conveyance of a freehold to a purchaser in fee simple used to contain such words as 'to hold unto and to the use of the purchaser in fee simple', or, what has the same effect, 'to the use of the purchaser his heirs and assigns for ever'.

From 1st January, 1926, by the Law of Property Act 1925, the words 'heirs' or 'in fee simple' need not be used in a conveyance, as a conveyance of freehold land without words of limitation passes the fee simple, unless a contrary intention appears in the deed (Section 60).

By the same Act, the only legal estates which are capable of existing are

1. an estate in fee simple absolute in possession (freehold);
2. a term of years absolute (leasehold).

When an estate in fee simple is mortgaged, the mortgagor retains the fee simple and the mortgagee takes a term of years absolute or is given a charge by way of legal mortgage. In the former case, both are 'estate owners', as each has a legal estate. A legal charge, however, confers a legal interest not a legal estate.

A legal estate may subsist concurrently with or subject to any other legal estate in the same land. SEE *Legal Estates; Mortgage*

FEME COVERT A married woman. 'Covert' means literally sheltered, a wife being in former days sheltered by her husband from certain legal liabilities from which she would not have been exempt if unmarried.

FEME SOLE An unmarried woman.

FI. FA. A contraction of *fieri facias* (q.v.).

FICTITIOUS PAYEE Where the payee is a fictitious or non-existing person, a bill or cheque may be treated as payable to bearer. (Section 7(3), Bills of Exchange Act 1882.) In *Bank of England* v *Vagliano* [1891] AC 107, the meaning of a fictitious person was enlarged to include a real person who never had nor was intended to have any right to the bills. Lord Herschell said in the course of his judgment

> I have arrived at the conclusion that whenever the name is inserted as that of the payee is so inserted by way of pretence merely, without any intention that payment shall only be made in conformity therewith, the payee is a fictitious person within the meaning of the statute, whether the name be that of an existing person or of one who has no existence.

An instrument payable to 'wages' or 'cash', or some similar word is payable to an impersonal payee and does not come within the section. An impersonal payee is not the same as a fictitious person. SEE *Impersonal Payees*

FIDUCIARY CAPACITY From the Latin *fiducia*, confidence. A person who holds anything in trust for another is said to hold it in a fiduciary capacity. When a banker has notice that certain moneys deposited with him are of a fiduciary nature, he must not, knowingly, be a party to any wrongful use of such moneys, otherwise he will be responsible to the person entitled to the moneys. A banker cannot be held liable when he is unaware that they are trust moneys. SEE *Trustee*

FIDUCIARY ISSUE That part of the note issue of the Bank of England which is authorized to be made against the securities as opposed to a metallic backing. The fiduciary issue was instituted by the Bank Charter Act 1844 (q.v.) and its amount was fixed at £14,000,000. The securities which backed it comprised the Government debt to the Bank of £11,015,100, the balance, £2,984,900, being convertible securities.

The Bank of England was authorized to increase the fiduciary issue by taking up two-thirds of the issues of other note-issuing banks, as their issues lapsed in accordance with the Act on account of amalgamations and absorptions. By 1923, the fiduciary issue had thus grown to £19,750,000, by which time no other banks of issue remained in England and Wales.

In 1928 the Currency and Bank Notes Act transferred the currency note issue of the Treasury to the Bank of England, and consequently the latter's fiduciary issue was raised to £260,000,000 — a figure which approximated to the combined maximum fiduciary issue of the Bank of England and the Treasury for 1927. Provision was made in the Act for the Treasury to sanction a reduction in the fiduciary issue. By Section 8, on application by the Bank of England, the Treasury could permit an increase for an initial period of six months, renewable from time to time, provided that any increase beyond two years required parliamentary sanction. Moreover, the Treasury minute authorizing any increase had to be laid before both Houses of Parliament. Finally, the Act provided that the fiduciary issue must be backed by securities which could include £5,500,000 of silver. On the outbreak of war in 1939, the Currency (Defence) Act increased the fiduciary issue to £580,000,000, as a result of the transfer of £280,000,000 of gold backing to the Exchange Equalisation Account.

In August 1941, Defence (Finance) Regulation 7 AA extended the maximum period of increase without parliamentary sanction from two to four years; and in August 1943, an amendment to this Regulation further increased the period to six years. Finally, to avoid further legislation, in September 1945 (i.e. six years from September 1939), a further Defence (Finance) Regulation was made (SR & O, 1945/1001), enlarging the period of excess over the statutory figure of £260,000,000, without parliamentary sanction, to the life of the Emergency Powers (Defence) Act 1945.

The Currency and Bank Notes Act 1954 (q.v.) raised the fiduciary note issue of the Bank of England to £1,575 million, subject to variations by the Treasury, though an upward change lasting for over two years has to be confirmed by Parliament. On the same day the Defence Finance

Regulations, which had hitherto governed the note issue, were revoked.

FIERI FACIAS A writ of *fieri facias*, often abbreviated as fi. fa., takes its name from the words appearing in the document 'quod fieri facias de bonis', etc. The writ is issued on behalf of a creditor who has obtained judgment for a debt, ordering the sheriff to levy the amount on the goods of the debtor. Bank notes, money, cheques, and bills are included amongst the things which the sheriff may seize.

FINANCE CORPORATION FOR INDUSTRY (FCI) FCI was formed in 1945 to provide temporary or longer-period finance for industrial businesses with a view to their quick rehabilitation and development in the national interest, thereby assisting in the maintenance and increase of employment. This objective was to be achieved by supplementing but not replacing the activities of other lenders.

In 1973, FCI and the Industrial and Commerical Finance Corporation (ICFC) (q.v.) were brought within the umbrella of a new holding company Finance for Industry (FFI) (q.v.), which was renamed Investors in Industry Group plc (q.v.) when the group was reorganized in 1983.

FINANCE HOUSE It is doubtful whether 'finance house' has any precise legal meaning, although 'finance company' was defined in Schedule 7 to the Companies Act 1948 as a 'body corporate whose ordinary business includes the business of lending money or of subscribing to shares or debentures', although this appears to apply only to listed companies or to those designated as finance companies by the Department of Trade and Industry.

However, the essence of a finance house or finance company is the provision of credit and generally this means consumer credit, although the finance houses do conduct a very substantial business in industrial credit.

Historically, finance houses have been associated with hire purchase but nowadays the larger finance houses not only conduct hire purchase business in all its forms but a wide range of other credit operations including leasing and factoring. Some of the larger ones are recognized banks and most of them engage in deposit-taking activities to finance their lending business. A number of them grant personal loans as part of their consumer credit operations.

It was estimated by the Crowther Committee (q.v.) that there were as many as 1,900 finance houses in the UK but, of these, only 1,000 or so were thought to be in active operation. Apart from those finance houses which grew up independently as financial institutions there are those which were established as subsidiaries of manufacturing companies and retail stores. SEE *Finance Houses Association; Hire Purchase Finance; Leasing*

FINANCE HOUSES ASSOCIATION The Association was formed in 1949 and now consists of 43 members who together account for 90 per cent of the hire purchase business undertaken by finance houses in the UK, in addition to a considerable amount of leasing business. The aims of the Association are to promote the interests of its members; to act as a channel of communication between members and government departments, local and other public authorities, trade associations and the press; to establish and maintain good relations with the public; and to promote good business practice among members of the Association and disseminate information of interest to the credit industry.

FINANCE FOR INDUSTRY (FFI) This was established in 1973 as a holding company to bring together the Industrial and Commercial Finance Corporation (q.v.), the Finance Corporation for Industry (q.v.) — both of which had been in existence since 1945 — Finance for Shipping (FFS), and for other subsidiary companies involved in leasing and consultancy activities. In 1983 the group was reorganized as the Investors in Industry Group plc (q.v.).

FINANCE FOR SHIPPING LIMITED (FFS) A subsidiary of Finance for Industry (FFI) (q.v.).

FINANCIAL FUTURES SEE *London International Financial Futures Exchange (LIFFE)*

FINANCIAL TIMES ACTUARIES INDICES These include indices relating to various stockmarket groups, e.g. chemicals, heavy engineering. The constituent shares of each index are weighted according to the size of each company's market capitalization in the sector.

The most widely used of the Financial Times Actuaries Indices is the All-Shares Index made up of approximately 750 shares. Such a wide cross-section of shares is reasonably representative of the overall performance of the London Market, and most experts regard the All-Share Index as a better long-term indicator than the Ordinary Share Index. The movement in the All-Share Index over recent years is shown in the accompanying graph on page 274. SEE Supplement

FINANCIAL TIMES INDUSTRIAL ORDINARY SHARE INDEX This Index, sometimes known as the 30 share Index, was introduced in 1935 as a measurement of stockmarket performance. It is based on a limited number of shares (i.e. 30) in some of the largest companies, the theory being that such companies account for a large proportion of daily transactions in the stock market and are a good barometer of the market's overall performance. At present the constituent shares are

Allied-Lyons	Grand Metropolitan
Associated Dairies	GKN
Beecham Group	Hanson Trust
BICC	Hawker Siddeley
Blue Circle Industries	ICI
Boots	Imperial Group
BOC Group	Lucas Industries
British Petroleum	Marks & Spencer
British Telecom	National Westminster Bank
BTR	P & O
Cadbury Schweppes	Plessey
Courtaulds	Tate & Lyle
Distillers	Thorn–EMI
General Electric	Trust House Forte
Glaxo Holdings	Vickers

Equal weight is given to the performance of each share in the Index and each day the notional portfolio is adjusted to allow for rises and falls in individual shares in order to maintain the same proportion of each stock. The performance of the Financial Times Ordinary Share Index over recent years is shown in the accompanying graph.

FINANCIAL TIMES–STOCK EXCHANGE 100 INDEX This Index known in brief as the FTSE 100 Index, was introduced by the Stock Exchange and the *Financial Times* on 3rd January, 1984 with a base level of 1000 as at the close of business on 30th December, 1983. The Index is compiled from price movements minute by minute in the 100 shares with the largest capitalization on the London Stock Market. The Index was introduced primarily for the convenience of the London International Financial Futures Exchange (LIFFE) to facilitate the introduction of futures contracts in equity markets.

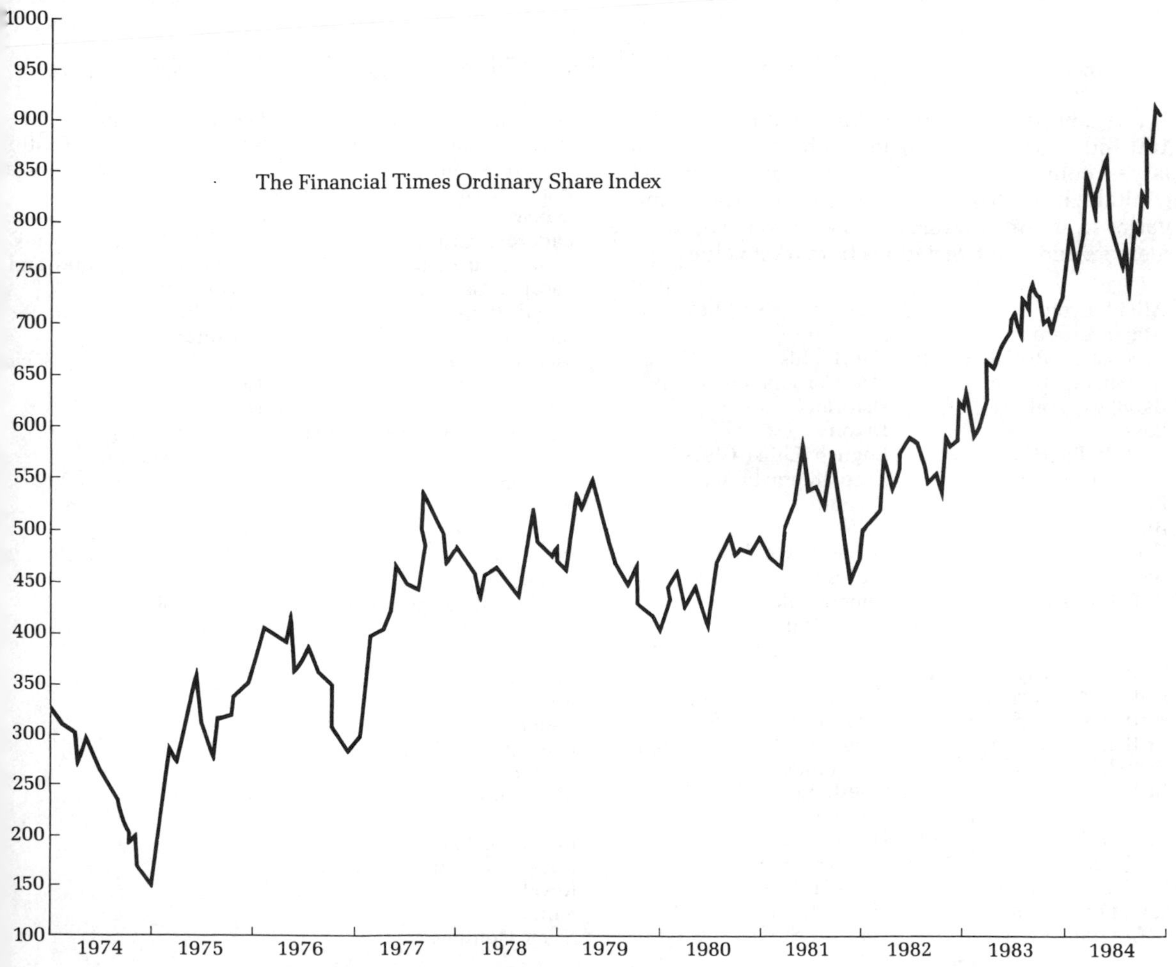

FINANCIAL TIMES–STOCK EXCHANGE 100 INDEX

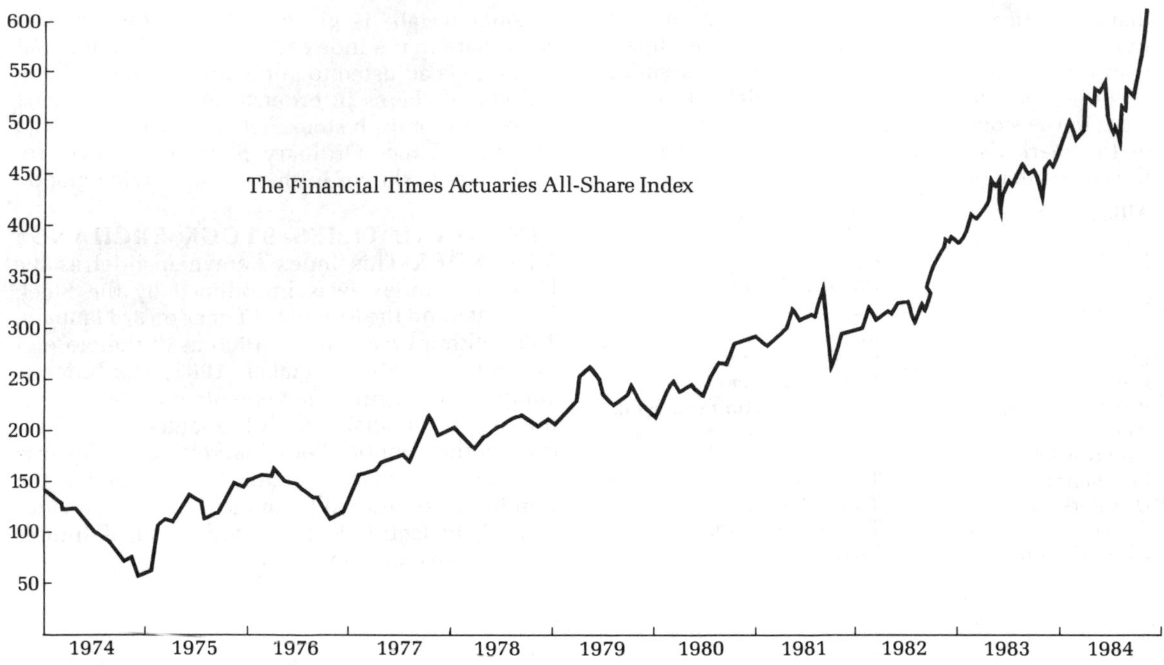

The companies currently included in the FTSE 100 Index are set out below. These are the 100 largest companies, calculated according to market capitalization. The list is revised quarterly and varies from time to time because of take-overs and mergers and other variations in market values.

Allied Lyons
Argyll Group
Associated British Foods
Associated Dairies Group
Barclays Bank
Bass
BAT Industries
Beecham Group
BICC
Blue Circle Industries
BOC Group
Boots
BPB Industries
British & Commonwealth Shipping Company
British Electric Traction
British Aerospace
British Home Stores
British Petroleum
British Telecom
Britoil
BTR
Burton Group
Cable and Wireless
Cadbury Schweppes
Commercial Union Assurance
Consolidated Gold Fields
Courtaulds
Dee Corporation
Distillers
Dixons
English China Clays
Exco International
Ferranti
Fisons
General Accident Fire & Life Assurance
General Electric
Glaxo Holdings
Globe Investment Trust
Granada Group
Grand Metropolitan
Great Universal Stores
Guardian Royal Exchange Assurance
Guest, Keen & Nettlefolds
Guinness
Hammerson Property and Investment Trust
Hanson Trust
Harrison and Crosfield
Hawker Siddeley Group
Imperial Chemical Industries
Imperial Continental Gas Association
Imperial Group
Jaguar
Ladbroke Group
Land Securities
Legal & General Group
Lloyds Bank
Lonrho
Marks & Spencer
MEPC
Midland Bank
National Westminster Bank
Northern Foods
Pearson (S) and Son
Peninsular & Oriental Steam Navigation
Pilkington
Plessey
Prudential Corporation
Racal Electronics
Rank Hovis
Rank Organization
Reckitt and Colman
Redland
Reed International
Reuters
Rio Tinto-Zinc
RMC Group
Rowntree Mackintosh
Royal Bank of Scotland Grou
Royal Insurance
Sainsbury (J)
Sears Holdings
Sedgwick Group
Shell Transport & Tradin
Smith & Nephew Associa Companies
Smiths Industries
Standard Chartered Bank
Standard Telephones and Cables
Sun Alliance & London Insurance
Sun Life Assurance Socie
Tarmac
Tesco
Thorn-EMI
Trafalgar House
Trusthosue Forte
Ultramar
Unilever
United Biscuits (Holdings
Whitbread
Willis Faber
Woolworths

FINE PAPER Bills which are drawn upon banks or first-class firms.

FINENESS OF COINS The 'fineness' is the amount of fine or pure metal in a coin. The standard fineness of gold and silver coins is specified in the first schedule to the Coinage Act 1870, as amended by the Acts of 1891 and 1920. SEE *Coinage*

FIRM Strictly speaking, a firm is a partnership carrying on a business or a group of persons working together (*Oxford English Dictionary*). Thus, it was customary to draw a distinction between a firm and a company. That distinction seems to have gone by the board in modern times. The word is used colloquially to apply to almost any business enterprise of more than one person: hence the Committee of Inquiry on Small *Firms*. In England and Wales a partnership, being an unincorporated association, is not a legal entity but in Scotland it is a legal person distinct from the individual partners.

Until 1981, firms carrying on business under a name other than the true surnames of the partners had to be registered under the Registration of Business Names Act 1916. That Act was repealed however, by the Companies Act 1981, which introduced new regulations in relation to the use of business names. SEE NOW The Business Names Act 1985. SEE *Partner; Registration of Business Names*

FIRST–CLASS PAPER Treasury Bills and bills which bear the names of banks and financial houses of the very highest standing.

FIRST OF EXCHANGE SEE *Bill in a Set*

FIRST MORTGAGE A charge upon property which takes priority to any other charges. SEE *Legal Mortgage; Mortgage*

FIRST NOTICE DAY The term used in the commodity markets to indicate the first day on which notice may be given or received of an intention to deliver commodities under a futures contract. SEE *Futures*

FIXED ASSETS Assets (such as land, buildings, plant, machinery), which are not turned into cash, but are used indirectly for the purposes of providing the income of a business. Assets which are fixed assets in connection with one business, may in another business be floating assets, e.g. the plant and machinery which are used by a company to produce certain goods are fixed assets but where the machines themselves are made in order to be sold they are circulating or floating assets. Under Paragraph 75 of Schedule 1 to the Companies Act 1981, the assets of a company shall be taken to be fixed assets if they are intended for use on a continuing basis in the company's activities. SEE NOW Sec. 4 Companies Act 1985. *Balance Sheet; Current Assets; Floating Assets*

FIXED CHARGE Debentures and debenture stock may be secured on the property of the company by a 'fixed' charge or by a 'floating' charge. In a fixed charge the property is, sometimes, by a trust deed, vested in trustees for the debenture holders or debenture stockholders, so that no other person may obtain a prior charge. The company cannot deal in any way with the property covered by a fixed charge without the consent of the chargees. The term is also used in respect of any fixed mortgage given by a company in contra-distinction to a floating charge — as, for example, a mortgage of the company's land. SEE *Debenture; Floating Charge*

FIXED DEPOSIT The deposit of a definite sum for a fixed period at a fixed rate.

FIXED INTEREST SECURITIES Stocks and bonds on which the rate of interest is fixed in the terms of issue, e.g. most government securities, company loan stocks and preference stocks, local authority bonds. Approximately 3,000 separate fixed interest securities are quoted on the London Stock Exchange, in addition to British Government stocks and local authority issues. SEE *Index Linked Securities; Variable Rate Stock*

FIXED TRUSTS SEE *Unit Trusts*

FIXTURES As a general rule, whatever is affixed to a freehold by a lessee or tenant becomes part of the freehold and cannot be removed without the permission of the landlord. But in the case of a lessee who has fixed plant or machinery for the purpose of his business, there is an exception, as he is entitled, as against the landlord, to remove the same during his tenancy, provided that it is not contrary to the terms in his contract of tenancy and that trade fixtures can be removed without causing material injury to the building.

A mortgagor, however, cannot remove fixtures from a property as against a mortgagee, even though they are of such a nature as to be removable as between landlord and tenant.

A deposit of title deeds, as well as a legal mortgage, carries with it the right of the mortgagee to any fixtures there may be on the property.

The Bills of Sale Act 1878 provides that the expression 'personal chattels' shall mean goods, furniture, and other articles capable of complete transfer by delivery, and (when separately assigned or charged) fixtures and growing crops, but shall not include chattel interests in real estate, nor fixtures (except trade machinery as hereinafter defined), when assigned together with a freehold or leasehold interest in any land or building to which they are affixed (Section 4). By Section 5

From and after the commencement of this Act trade machinery shall, for the purposes of this Act, be deemed to be personal chattels, and any mode of disposition of trade machinery by the owner thereof which would be a bill of sale as to any other personal chattels shall be deemed to be a bill of sale within the meaning of this Act.

For the purposes of this Act—

'Trade machinery' means the machinery used in or attached to any factory or workshop;

(1) Exclusive of the fixed motive powers such as the water-wheels and steam engines, and the steam boilers, donkey-engines, and other fixed appurtenances of the said motive-powers; and,

(2) Exclusive of the fixed power machinery, such as the shafts, wheels, drums, and their fixed appurtenances, which transmit the action of the motive-powers to the other machinery, fixed and loose; and,

(3) Exclusive of the pipes for steam, gas, and water in the factory or workshop.

The machinery or effects excluded by this section from the definition of trade machinery shall not be deemed to be personal chattels within the meaning of this Act.

A deed, therefore, by which fixtures (other than trade fixtures) are separately assigned must be registered as a bill of sale, as must also a deed which assigns fixed trade machinery, whether assigned separately or not. If, however, the trade machinery is assigned, not as chattels, but as part of the freehold to which it is affixed, the deed does not require registration under the Bills of Sale Act.

In *Batcheldor* v *Yates* (1888) 57 LJ Ch 697, there was a mortgage of freehold property on which there happened to be some trade machinery. Cotton, LJ, in his judgment said

The instrument is a conveyance of land, and although that does give a right to all fixtures on the land, including this trade machinery, yet it does so, not as an assurance of that trade machinery, or of those things which the Act says are to be considered as personal chattels, but merely as conveying and assigning all the land, and everything so fixed to the freehold as to be passed by a conveyance of the land. It does not enable the mortgagee, within the meaning of Section 3, to seize or take possession of these personal chattels. It enables him to take possession of the land, and he thereby has possession of the trade machinery as part of the land, but in no other way.

In this mortgage there is no right at all on the part of the mortgagee to sever these fixtures from the land. He could only do so if empowered by the terms of the power of sale so to do. The mortgage is a mere ordinary mortgage, referring, it is true, to the land, the workshop, and the yard, but not in any way dealing either with the house, or with the workshop, or the machinery as anything to be separated from, or severed, or capable of being severed, from the freehold to which it is affixed. .... In my opinion it would be wrong to say that such a mortgage as this was a bill of sale of the trade machinery, even although the Act does declare that trade machinery is to be considered for the purpose of the Act personal chattels.

The above case of *Batcheldor* v *Yates* does not apply where there is an express assignment of chattels, as chattels, and not as incident to the land. Where land was conveyed by a mortgage together with fixed and movable plant, machinery, fixtures, etc., the deed has been held to be a bill of sale as regards the trade machinery and to require registration as such (*Small* v *National Provincial Bank of England* [1894] 1 Ch 686).

FLEXIBLE TRUST SEE *Unit Trust*

FLOATING ASSETS Assets such as cash, stock, bills of exchange, which are continually changing as opposed to fixed assets (q.v.) such as premises, plant and machinery, etc.

FLOATING CAPITAL SEE *Capital*

FLOATING CHARGE A floating charge has been defined by Lord Macnaghten as

an equitable charge on the assets for the time being of a going concern. It attaches to the subject charged in the varying condition in which it happens to be from time to time. It is of the essence of such a charge that it remains dormant until the undertaking charged ceases to be a going concern, or until the person in whose favour the charge is created intervenes.

Debentures or debenture stock, in addition to being secured by a fixed charge upon the company's property, may also be secured by a floating charge, that is a charge upon the stock, book debts, etc., of the company, which permits the company to make use of those assets in any way in connection with its ordinary business. A charge of that description 'floats' until such time as default is made in payment of interest, or the company goes into liquidation, or breaks some other condition of the debenture. When such an event occurs, the charge becomes fixed, and the assets at that date become a fixed security for the debentures and may be realized for the benefit of the debenture holders. SEE *Debenture*

As well as being contained in a debenture trust deed, a floating charge to cover all moneys owing may be and often is given to a banker by a company.

If the debentures create a floating charge upon the land of the company, as well as upon the stock, book debts, and uncalled capital, the company is not precluded by that floating charge from selling or mortgaging the land. Some floating charges, however, contain a clause to the effect that the company will not mortgage the property so as to create an equal or prior charge, but even in that case if anyone grants the company a loan against the title deeds, without any notice of the condition, he may obtain priority under the doctrine that where the mortgagor has ostensible authority to deal with the property all dealings with a bona fide mortgagee are valid.

Likewise a lender, aware of the floating charge but unaware of such a clause therein, will get priority. Hence, when registering a floating charge, it is expedient to include in the details of registration any such clause, as this will be notice to subsequent lenders.

In *National Provincial Bank of England* v *United Electric Theatres Ltd* [1916] 1 Ch 132, Astbury, J, quoted with approval the words of Romer, LJ, in a case in the Court of Appeal, in which he stated that

> A mortgage or charge by a company which contains the three following characteristics is a floating charge: (1) If it is a charge on a class of assets of a company present and future; (2) if that class is one which, in the ordinary course of the business of the company, would be changing from time to time; and (3) if you find that by the charge it is contemplated that, until some future step is taken by or on behalf of those interested in the charge, the company may carry on its business in the ordinary way as far as concerns the particular class of assets I am dealing with.

The words of Lord Macnaghten in the House of Lords were also quoted with approval:

> A specific charge is one that without more fastens on ascertained and definite property, or property capable of being ascertained and defined; a floating charge, on the other hand, is ambulatory and shifting in its nature, hovering over and, so to speak, floating with the property which it is intended to affect until some event occurs or some act is done which causes it to settle and fasten on the subject of the charge within its reach and grasp.

Particulars of every floating charge on the undertaking and property of a company must be delivered to the Registrar of Companies for registration (SEE *Registration of Charges*). By the Companies Act 1985, all floating charges on the undertaking or on any property of the company must be entered in the company's register of mortgages (Section 407).

Where a company goes into liquidation within 12 months of the creation of a floating charge, such charge will be invalid except in respect of cash paid to the company subsequent to the creation of and in consideration of the charge, unless it can be shown that the company was solvent immediately after the creation of the charge (Companies Act 1985, Section 617).

Where there is a promise to give a floating charge and money is lent prior to the execution of the charge on the faith of the promise, the cash so provided is regarded as being made available at the time of the creation of the charge (*Re Columbia Fireproofing Company Ltd* [1910] 2 Ch 120).

But if, by the application of the Rule in Clayton's Case (q.v.), it can be shown that the balance due at the time of liquidation is money lent subsequent to the creation of the charge (i.e. where subsequent credits paid in equal or exceed the debt at the time the charge was given), the charge will not be invalid. (In *Re Thomas Mortimer Ltd* (1925), confirmed in *Re Yeovil Glove Company Ltd* [1962] 3 WLR 900.) SEE *Cork Committee*

FLOATING CURRENCY A currency is said to float when it is allowed to find its own level in relation to other world currencies. After the Second World War the major world currencies were fixed by international agreement (SEE *Bretton Woods*). This gave way to the 'crawling peg' (q.v.) to be followed ultimately by the acceptance of the floating rate principle by the major world trading countries.

The theory of floating rates is that when pressure builds up on a particular currency the exchange rate automatically moves downwards in relation to other stronger currencies. This in turn leads to lower export prices, higher import prices and, in theory at least, a return of confidence in the currency. Thus there is no need to use the country's reserves to support the exchange rate and the central bank of that country will intervene only to smooth out major movements. One argument advanced against floating rates is that it makes it difficult for international trade, in that merchants do not know the value of currencies at some future date unless they buy 'forward'. Another apparent disadvantage is that if rates are allowed to float freely, governments lose a degree of control over the national currency with the result that adverse movements can react unfavourably on the economy as a whole. SEE *Devaluation*

FLORIN A 10p piece, formerly a two-shilling piece. Derived from the Latin *flos, florem*, a flower. The Italian fiorino (a florin) was so called because there was the figure of a lily upon it. It is also stated that the coin is named from the City of Florence, where florins were first coined. It was introduced into the coinage in 1849 and became known as the 'Godless florin' owing to the omission (for that one year) of the words 'Dei Gratia' and 'Dei Defensor'.

The standard weight of a florin was 174.54545 grains troy and its standard fineness thirty-seven-fortieths fine silver, three-fortieths alloy; altered by the Coinage Act 1920, to one-half fine silver, one-half alloy. The florin was superseded in 1968 by the two-shilling piece. SEE *Coinage*

FLOTATION The bringing of an unlisted company to the stock market. SEE *Merchant Banking; Stock Exchange; Unlisted Securities Market*

FOR CASH A transaction on the Stock Exchange which is 'for cash' or 'for money' means that the security which has been sold, must, as soon as delivered, be paid for in cash. SEE *For the Account*

FOR THE ACCOUNT A transaction on the Stock Exchange may be 'for the account', that is, for settlement on the next 'account day' or 'settling day'. SEE *For Cash*

FORECLOSURE Where a mortgagor has failed, after due notice, to make repayment of the mortgage debt, the mortgagee has the right to apply to the court for an order for foreclosure, i.e. the banning of the mortgagor from any further rights in the mortgaged property.

Neither a legal mortgagee nor an equitable mortgagee can foreclose without sanction of the court. A legal mortgagee can, however, sell the property or put in a receiver under the power contained in his mortgage deed, but see Section 110 under *Mortage.*

The expression 'redeem up, foreclose down' applies when a mortgagee makes application to the court for foreclosure, as he forecloses any subsequent mortgagees, as well as the mortgagor, and redeems any prior mortgagee.

Application for foreclosure must be made within 12 years from the last payment of interest by the mortgagor or written acknowledgment of the debt.

Where a mortgagee remains in possession of the property and receives the rents for 12 years after default is made under the mortgage, and does not during that time acknowledge in writing the title of the mortgagor or his right to redeem, foreclosure takes place by the lapse of time and the mortgagor's right to redeem is extinguished at the end of the 12 years.

Where a mortgagee forecloses and thus becomes absolute owner of the property, he has no further claim upon the mortgagor. But if a mortgagee sells the property, instead of foreclosing, he may claim upon the mortgagor if the proceeds of the sale are not sufficient to repay the mortgage debt, and the mortgage — as is usual — contains a personal covenant on the mortgagor's part to repay the mortgage debt. SEE *Mortgage*

Nowadays, a mortgagee's right to foreclose is seldom exercised because the alternative rights of a legal mortgagee to sell the property or to appoint a receiver are more expeditious. Seldom, if ever, does a bank or building society have occasion to apply for foreclosure when acting under their standard forms of mortgage agreement.

FOREIGN BILL The Bills of Exchange Act 1882, Section 4, defines an inland bill as a bill which is or on the face of it purports to be (1) both drawn and payable within the British Islands, or (2) drawn within the British Islands upon some person resident therein. Any other bill is a foreign bill. The British Islands means any part of the United Kingdom of Great Britain and Ireland, the islands of Man, Guernsey, Jersey, Alderney and Sark, and the islands adjacent to any of them being part of the dominions of Her Majesty, and a bill drawn in any of those places is an inland bill.

A bill that is drawn in the Republic of Ireland and payable in England is a foreign bill within the meaning of the Bills of Exchange Act.

The regulations regarding bills are not the same in all countries and the Bills of Exchange Act in Section 72 sets forth the rules to be observed where laws conflict:

Where a bill drawn in one country is negotiated, accepted, or payable in another, the rights, duties and liabilities of the parties thereto are determined as follows:

(1) The validity of a bill as regards requisites in form is determined by the law of the place of issue, and the validity as regards requisites in the form of the supervening contracts, such as acceptance, or indorsement, or acceptance *supra* protest, is determined by the law of the place where such contract was made:
Provided that—

- (*a*) Where a bill is issued out of the United Kingdom it is not invalid by reason only that it is not stamped in accordance with the law of the place of issue:
- (*b*) Where a bill, issued out of the United Kingdom, conforms, as regards requisites in form, to the law of the United Kingdom, it may, for the purpose of enforcing payment thereof, be treated as valid as between all persons who negotiate, hold, or become parties to it in the United Kingdom.

(2) Subject to the provisions of this Act, the interpretation of the drawing, indorsement, acceptance, or acceptance *supra* protest of a bill is determined by the law of the place where such contract is made.
Provided that where an inland bill is indorsed in a foreign country the indorsement shall as regards the payer be interpreted according to the law of the United Kingdom.

(3) The duties of the holder with respect to presentment for acceptance or payment and the necessity for or sufficiency of a protest or notice of dishonour, or otherwise, are determined by the law of the place where the act is done or the bill is dishonoured.

(4) Where a bill is drawn out of but payable in the United Kingdom and the sum payable is not expressed in the currency of the United Kingdom, the amount shall, in the absence of some express stipulation, be calculated according to the rate of exchange for sight drafts at the place of payment on the day the bill is payable.

(5) Where a bill is drawn in one country and is payable in another, the due date thereof is determined according to the law of the place where it is payable.

A foreign bill may be drawn in this country and be payable abroad, e.g. where goods are exported from England to the USA the exporter may draw a bill upon his correspondent in the USA for the value of the goods.

Bills payable abroad are either collected by bankers for their customers or else bought (or discounted or negotiated).

A foreign bill drawn in this country in sterling may include the words 'exchange as per indorsement'. The rate is indorsed on the bill in London when first negotiated and constitutes the rate at which the bill is payable.

It is considered that a bill or promissory note which includes the words 'plus bank charges and stamps' is not a valid bill of exchange within the meaning of Sections 3 and 83 of the Bills of Exchange Act 1882, because the Act prescribes that a bill or note must be drawn for 'a sum certain in money'.

As to a bill which contains an interest clause, see under *Interest on Bill.*

Where a foreign bill, appearing on the face of it to be such, has been dishonoured by non-acceptance, it must be duly protested for non-acceptance, and where such a bill, which has not been previously dishonoured by non-acceptance is dishonoured by non-payment it must be duly protested for non-payment. If it be not so protested the drawer and indorsers are discharged (Section 51(2), Bills of Exchange Act) (SEE *Protest*). If a foreign bill is accepted as to a part only of the amount, it must be protested in respect of the balance (Section 44(2)).

A foreign bill may be payable at one or more 'usances'. A usance is the time which, by custom, is allowed between two countries for the currency of a bill.

Under the Uniform Law (q.v.), the countries which have signed the Convention undertake that no bill or promissory note drawn within their territories shall be invalidated for non-compliance with revenue laws. Penalties may be imposed, and all remedies on the bill may be suspended until the stamp laws are complied with. SEE *Bill of Exchange; Documentary Bill; In Case of Need; Inland Bill*

FORESTRY, INVESTMENT IN SEE *Woodlands, Investment In*

FOREX This is an abbreviation for the International Foreign Exchange Market. This is the largest market of any kind in the world and is believed to have a daily volume estimated of around $200,000 million. The market does not have a physical location as such but is made up of the banks and foreign exchange brokers dealing in currencies throughout the 24 hours of each day.

It is believed that only five per cent or so of total foreign exchange business relates to underlying commercial transactions. The remaining 95 per cent is made up of currency transactions among the various banks. About 60 per cent of foreign exchange dealings are 'spot', the remainder being 'forward'. SEE *Forward Exchange; Spot Price; Spot Rate*

FORFEITURE OF SHARES SEE *Lien; Share Capital*

FORGED TRANSFER Where a banker takes as security a transfer of stock or shares registered in the names of several holders, it is advisable that the transfer should be signed at the bank by each holder, because if one of the holders forges the signature of another holder to the transfer, the banker, even after registration and ultimate sale of the stock, may be compelled to make good the value of the stock to the true owner. This point was decided in the important case of *Sheffield Corporation* v *Barclay and Others* [1905] AC 392. The House of Lords (1905) reversed the decision of the Court of Appeal (1903) and restored that of the Lord Chief Justice (1902), where judgment for the plaintiffs was given for the amount claimed.

The Lord Chancellor (the Earl of Halsbury) said

> Two persons, Timbrell and Honnywill, were joint owners of corporation stock created under a local Act of Parliament. Timbrell, in fraud of Honnywill, forged a transfer of the stock, and borrowed money on the security of the stock which the transfer was supposed to have transferred. A bank which lent the money sent the transfer to the proper officer of the corporation, and demanded, as they were entitled to do, if the transfer was a genuine one, that they should be registered as holders of the stock. The corporation acted upon their demand; they transferred the stock into the names of the bank, and the bank in ordinary course transferred it to holders for value. The corporation also, in ordinary course, issued certificates, and the holders of these certificates were able to establish their title against the corporation, who were estopped from denying that

those whom they had registered were the stockholders entitled. Honnywill, after the death of Timbrell, discovered the forgery that had been committed, and compelled the corporation to restore the stock, and the question in the case is whether the corporation has any remedy against the bank who caused them to act upon a forged transfer, and so render themselves liable to the considerable loss which they have sustained. Now, apart from any decision upon the question (it being taken for granted that all the parties were honest), I should have thought that the bank were clearly liable. They have a private bargain with a customer. Upon his assurance they take a document from him as a security for a loan, which they assume to be genuine. I do not suggest there was any negligence — perhaps business could not go on if people were suspecting forgery in every transaction — but their position was obviously very different from that of the corporation. The corporation is simply ministerial in registering a valid transfer and issuing fresh certificates. They cannot refuse to register, and though for their own sake they will not and ought not to register or to issue certificates to a person who is not really the holder of the stock, yet they have no machinery, and they cannot inquire into the transaction out of which the transfer arises. The bank, on the other hand, is at liberty to lend their money or not. They can make any amount of inquiries they like. If they find that an intended borrower has a co-trustee, they may ask him or the co-trustee himself whether the co-trustee is a party to the loan, and a simple question to the co-trustee would have prevented the fraud. They take the risk of the transaction and lend the money. The security given happens to be in a form that requiries registration to make it available, and the bank 'demand,' as, if genuine transfers are bought, they are entitled to do, that the stock shall be registered in their name or that of their nominees, and are also entitled to have fresh certificates issued to themselves or nominees. This was done, and the corporation by acting on this 'demand' have incurred a considerable loss. As I have said, I think if it were *res integra* I should think the bank were liable; but I do not think it is *res integra*, but is covered by authority. In *Dugdale* v *Lovering* (1875) 10 CP 196, Mr Cave, arguing for the plaintiff, put the proposition thus: 'It is a general principle of law when an act is done by one person at the request of another, which act is not in itself manifestly tortious to the knowledge of the person doing it, and such act turns out to be injurious to the rights of a third party, the person doing it is entitled to an indemnity from him who requested that it should be done.' I think both upon principle and authority the corporation are entitled to recover.

The Forged Transfers Acts 1891 and 1892 were passed with the object of enabling purchasers of stock to be protected from losses through forged transfers. Companies, however, are not obliged to adopt them, and those which adopted them were chiefly railway companies. Section 1 of the 1891 Act is as follows:

(1) Where a company or local authority issue or have issued shares, stock, or securities transferable by any instrument in writing or by an entry in any books or register kept by or on behalf of the company or local authority, they shall have power to make compensation by a cash payment out of their funds for any loss arising from a transfer of any such shares, stock, or securities, in pursuance of a forged transfer or of a transfer under a forged power of attorney whether such loss arises, and whether the transfer or power of attorney was forged before of after the passing of this Act, and whether the person receiving such compensation, or any person through whom he claims, has or has not paid any fee or otherwise contributed to any fund out of which the compensation is paid. [The words 'whether such loss, etc,' were added by the 1892 Act.]

(2) Any company or local authority may, if they think fit, provide, either by fees not exceeding the rate of one shilling on every one hundred pounds transferred, with a minimum charge equal to that for twenty-five pounds, to be paid by the transferee upon the entry of the transfer in the books of the company or local authority, or by insurance, reservation of capital, accumulation of income, or in any other manner which they may resolve upon, a fund to meet claims for such compensation. [The words 'with a minimum charge equal to that for £25' were added by the 1892 Act.]

(3) For the purpose of providing such compensation any company may borrow on the security of their property, and any local authority may borrow with the like consent and on the like security and subject to the like conditions as to repayment by means of instalments or the provision of a sinking fund and otherwise as in the case of the securities in respect of which compensation is to be provided, but any money so borrowed by a local authority shall be repaid within a term not longer than five years. Any expenses incurred by a local authority in making compensation, or in the repayment of, or the payment of interest on, or otherwise in connection with, any loan raised as aforesaid, shall, except so far as they may be met by such fees as aforesaid, be paid out of the fund or rate on which the security in respect of which compensation is to be made is charged.

(4) Any such company or local authority may impose such reasonable restrictions on the transfer of their shares, stock, or securities, or with respect to powers of attorney for the transfer thereof, as they may consider requisite for guarding against losses arising from forgery.

(5) Where a company or local authority compensate a person under this Act for any loss arising from forgery, the company or local authority shall, without prejudice to any other rights or remedies, have the same rights and remedies against the person liable for the loss as the person compensated would have had.

Some companies, instead of adopting the Forged Transfers Acts, protect themselves against liability arising from forgery by a policy of insurance. SEE *Company (Companies)*; *Transfer of Shares*

FORGERY Until 1981, forgery was a crime at common law and in relation to certain documents, it was also a statutory offence under the

Forgery Act 1913. That Act was repealed by the Forgery and Counterfeiting Act 1981, which now defines the crime of forgery and which abolished forgery at common law, including the offence of uttering a forged instrument.

Under the 1981 Act, a person is guilty of forgery if he makes a false instrument with the intention that he or another shall use it to induce somebody to accept it as genuine and by reason of so accepting it, to do or not to do some act to the prejudice of himself or the other person (Section 1 of the Act).

It is also an offence (Section 2 of the Act) for a person to make a copy of an instrument which is, and which he knows or believes to be, a false instrument, with the intention that he or another shall use it to induce somebody to accept it as a copy of a genuine instrument, and by reason of so accepting it, to do or not to do some act to his own or any other person's prejudice.

Under Section 3 of the Act, it is an offence for a person to use an instrument which is, and which he knows or believes to be, false, with the intention of inducing somebody to accept it as genuine, and by reason of so accepting it to do or not to do some act to his own or other person's prejudice.

Under Section 4, it is an offence for a person to use a copy of an instrument which is, and which he knows or believes to be, a false instrument, with the intention of inducing somebody to accept it as a copy of a genuine instrument, and by reason of so accepting it to do or not to do some act to his own or any other person's prejudice.

Under Section 5, it is an offence for a person to have in his custody or under his control, a specified instrument (see below) which is and which he knows or believes to be, false, with the intention that he or another shall use it to induce somebody to accept it as genuine, and by reason of so accepting it to do or not to do some act to his own or any other person's prejudice. Under the Act, such instruments are: money orders, postal orders, UK postage stamps, Inland Revenue stamps, share certificates, passports and documents which can be used instead of passports, cheques, travellers' cheques, cheque cards and certified copies or certificates relating to an entry in a register of births, adoptions, marriages or deaths. Under this same Section, it is an offence for a person to have in his custody or under his control, without lawful authority or excuse, a specified instrument (as above) which is, and which he knows or believes to be, false.

Under Section 5, it is also an offence for a person to make or have in his custody or under his control a machine or implement, or paper or any other material, which to his knowledge is or has been specially designed or adapted for the making of a specified instrument (as above) with the intention that he or another shall make a specified instrument which is false and that he or another shall use the instrument to induce somebody to accept it as genuine, and by reason of so accepting it, to do or not to do some act to his own or any other person's prejudice. Further, under Section 5, it is an offence for a person to make or have in his custody or under his control any such machine, implement, paper, or material without lawful authority or excuse.

Under Section 9 of the Act, an instrument is false for the purposes listed above in the following circumstances:

1. if it purports to have been made in the form in which it is made by a person who did not in fact make it in that form; or
2. if it purports to have been made in the form in which it is made on the authority of a person who did not in fact authorize its making in that form; or
3. if it purports to have been made in the terms in which it is made by a person who did not in fact make it in those terms; or
4. if it purports to have been made in the terms in which it is made on the authority of a person who did not, in fact, authorize its making in those terms; or
5. if it purports to have been altered in any respect by a person who did not, in fact, alter it in that respect; or
6. if it purports to have been altered in any respect on the authority of a person who did not, in fact, authorize the alteration in that respect; or
7. if it purports to have been made or altered on a date, or at a place at which, or otherwise in circumstances in which, it was not in fact made or altered; or
8. if it purports to have been made or altered by an existing person but he did not, in fact, exist.

A currency note is not a specified instrument for the purpose of the offence of forgery, but comes within those provisions of the 1981 Act relating to counterfeiting. SEE *Coinage Offences*

Where the numbers on certain Bank of England notes had been altered, the intention being to prevent the notes (payment of which had been stopped) being traced, it was held in the case of *Suffell* v *Bank of England* (1882) 9 QBD 555, that the plaintiff, who was an innocent holder for value, could not recover from the Bank of England because the notes had been altered in a material part. The importance of the numbers on notes was pointed out by Jessel, MR, in the course of his judgment. SEE *Bank of England Notes*

If a banker, unknowingly, gives forged bank notes in payment of a cheque, they do not operate as a payment.

A transferor by delivery warrants to his immediate transferee, being a holder for value, that the note is what it purports to be, and therefore the person who receives a forged bank note can reclaim the money from the person who gave him the note, provided he makes the claim within a reasonable time.

It is not a statutory forgery if a genuine signature is affixed by a person who indicates on the face of the document that he signs 'per pro.' on behalf of another, notwithstanding that the authority so to sign has been misused and fraudulently used. The signature to a cheque cannot be a valid signature in the hands of one person and a forgery in the hands of another; it cannot be valid today and a forgery tomorrow. (The Lord Chief Justice in *Morison* v *London County and Westminster Bank Ltd* [1914] 3 KB 356.)

The Bills of Exchange Act, 1882, Section 24, enacts as follows.

Subject to the provisions of this Act, where a signature on a bill is forged or placed thereon without the authority of the person whose signature it purports to be, the forged or unauthorised signature is wholly inoperative, and no right to retain the bill or to give a discharge therefor or to enforce payment thereof against any party thereto can be acquired through or under that signature, unless the party against whom it is sought to retain or enforce payment of the bill is precluded from setting up the forgery or want of authority.

Provided that nothing in this Section shall affect the ratification of an unauthorised signature not amounting to a forgery.

The words 'through or under that signature' in the Section just quoted require particular attention. An innocent possessor for value cannot retain a bill, or give a discharge for it or sue upon it, where a signature on the bill is forged. The forged signature which is referred to is the signature which is necessary to transfer the bill to the holder, that is, the one through or under which he gets his title. If an indorsement which is necessary to pass the title of the bill is forged, the bill is valueless to the party acquiring it through that signature. But where an indorsement, which is not necessary for the transfer of the title, is forged, that forged indorsement may be ignored and the holder in due course can sue all the other parties to the bill. For example, where a bill is specially indorsed, say, to John Brown, the real signature of John Brown is required in order to make the bill valid and to pass the title to a succeeding holder. If John Brown's signature is forged, a subsequent holder gets no title. If John Brown's signature is genuine and the indorsement is in blank (the bill then passing by simple delivery), it does not matter to a subsequent holder whether a signature following that of John Brown is a genuine one or not, as that subsequent holder derives his title through John Brown and not through the person from whom he received the bill.

If a holder obtains payment of a bill which is affected with a forged signature he cannot retain the money. The rightful owner of the bill can demand to have the bill given up to him and can sue the acceptor thereon. The acceptor will have a right of action against the holder for the return of the money he paid to him. The holder will look to the person from whom he obtained the bill for repayment, and that person will then look to his transferor, but the person who actually took the bill through the forged indorsement will have no one to proceed against on the bill though he will have a personal remedy against the forger if he can be found. If the holder, in such a case as that referred to, to whom the acceptor paid the forged bill, cannot be found, the acceptor will lose the money, as he is liable to the true owner.

If a banker pays a bill bearing a forged acceptance or a forged indorsement (either of the payee or any indorsee) he cannot debit his customer with the amount. A banker ought to know whether his own customer's (the acceptor) signature is genuine, but the banker is not particularly concerned with the genuineness of the drawer's signature, as the acceptor by accepting the bill is precluded (Section 54) from denying to a holder in due course the genuineness of the drawer's signature.

If a banker has paid an acceptance and one of the indorsements is subsequently found to have been forged, the banker cannot hold the acceptor liable for the amount. The banker is liable to the true owner for conversion. SEE *Indorsement*

If there is an indorsement subsequent to the forged one the banker may be able to recover from the person to whom he paid the bill if it is not too late for that person to give notice of dishonour to the indorser subsequent to the forgery. That is the effect of the judgment in *Imperial Bank of Canada* v *Bank of Hamilton* [1903] AC 49. In *London & River Plate Bank* v *Bank of Liverpool* [1896] 1 QB 7, a case concerning a bill with forged indorsements, it was held that

if the mistake is discovered at once, it may be that the money can be recovered back; but if it be not, and the money is paid in good faith and is received in good faith, and there is an interval of time in which the position of the holder may be altered, the principle seems to apply that money once paid cannot be recovered back.

SEE *Payment of Bill*

When a bill is payable to bearer, either originally or by a genuine indorsement in blank, and the banker has paid it to a holder who has no title, the bill may be charged to the acceptor's account as it is an authority to pay it to the person who appears to be the holder.

Where a banker on whom a cheque is drawn pays it in good faith and in the ordinary course of business, he is not liable for the indorsement of the payee or any subsequent indorser, even though the indorsement is forged (Section 60, Bills of Exchange Act 1882). But if a banker gives cash for a cheque drawn upon another banker, he is not protected by Section 60, and is liable as any other person. Protection is afforded by Section 80, to a banker on whom a crossed cheque is drawn, if he pays it in accordance with the crossing.

Where a drawer's signature on a cheque is forged, the banker cannot charge his customer's account therewith (except as below), for he has not obeyed his customer's mandate; the question of negligence is immaterial. A forged signature cannot be ratified, for ratification implies agency. An unauthorized signature, however, can be ratified. A forged signature can be adopted, however, provided there is consideration for such adoption. 'The supposed signer might say, "I will recognize this signature as my own; you may debit my account with these cheques."' (Scrutton, LJ, in *Greenwood* v *Martins Bank* [1932] 1 KB 371) A drawer may be estopped from denying the genuineness of the signature where his conduct has been so negligent as to lead the bank into paying the cheque. For example, if the drawer was aware that forged cheques were in circulation and did not advise the banker, his silence might be regarded as the proximate cause of the payment and estop him from denying that the signatures were his own.

A banker must give notice of a drawer's forged signature on the day he receives such a cheque. SEE *Signature*

A banker collecting a cheque or an instrument to which Section 4 of the Cheques Act 1957 applies, is protected by that Section if the cheque or instrument has a forged indorsement, provided that collection is made in good faith, for a customer, and without negligence. SEE *Collecting Banker*

As to fraudulent alterations in amounts of bills and cheques, see the cases under *Alterations to Bills of Exchange*. The effect of the cases is that where a cheque, on which the amount has been fraudulently increased, has been paid, the loss falls upon the drawer if he drew the cheque negligently so as to facilitate the fraud; but if he was not negligent and exercised reasonable care in drawing the cheque, the loss falls upon the banker who paid the cheque.

A banker is protected in paying one of his own drafts bearing a forged indorsement by Section 80 of the Bills of Exchange Act (as extended by Section 5, Cheques Act 1957) as regards crossed drafts, and by Section 19 of the Stamp Act 1853, as regards open drafts (SEE *Banker's Draft*). It is suggested by some writers that Section 1 of the Cheques Act 1957 may have some relevance, but this is doubtful.

FORWARD EXCHANGE Foreign currency bought or sold for future delivery is known as forward exchange and its price, called the forward rate, is expressed as being at a premium (or discount) to the spot rate.

The facilities offered by the existence of a forward market are of particular use to importers and exporters who may have to receive or deliver foreign currencies at some future date and who wish to make sure of the sterling equivalent that they will then receive or have to pay. Thus, an English exporter (with sterling costs) who has invoiced goods to a French buyer for 50,000 Fr payment to be made in three months' time, will desire to know at the time of shipment the amount of pounds that he will be likely to obtain for the francs, since any depreciation in the value of the franc may wipe out his profit. By selling the expected francs forward to his banker, he can make sure of avoiding a loss, always provided his debtor makes payment at maturity.

Similarly, an English importer who has undertaken to pay francs at a future date may buy them forward to fit in with the day of payment.

Forward rates are quoted for one month, two months, and three months, transactions for intermediate periods being calculated therefrom.

It sometimes happens that the customer may be unable to fix a definite date for delivery. In such cases, the currency can be bought or sold forward 'option' such and such a date — option February, March; option end November, etc. This means that the customer can perform his part of the contract any time within the arranged period, while the banker fixes to the transaction that rate which will be most favourable to himself.

The question of whether a forward quotation shall stand at a premium or a discount will depend on such factors as comparative interest rates, the strength of the respective economies and, therefore, the strength of the respective currencies. A banker who does a forward deal with a customer immediately covers himself by doing a 'spot' (TT) deal in the opposite sense. Thus, a London banker selling Paris francs forward will at once buy them spot. He will then be 'out' of the sterling and be the possessor of francs. If the London interest rate is higher than that ruling in Paris, he will be subjected to a loss unless he so adjusts the forward rate as to compensate himself.

Operations consisting of a simultaneous sale or purchase of spot currency accompanied by a purchase or sale, respectively, of the forward are known as 'swaps', because the spot is 'swapped' against the forward. By these means short-term investors try to take advantage of differences in interest rates in two different centres (say London and New York) while at the same time safeguarding themselves against exchange rate fluctuations. The currency which is bought spot is left on deposit in the higher interest centre or else is invested in bills.

FORWARD PRICE The 'forward' price of a commodity is the quotation for delivery and payment at a future date. The 'spot' or 'cash' price is for immediate delivery and payment.

FORWARD RATE The rate of exchange at which currency may be bought or sold today for delivery at some future date SEE *Forward Exchange*

FORWARDATION An alternative term for contango (q.v.) and the opposite of backwardation (q.v.)

FOUNDERS' SHARES Shares created for the benefit of the original promotors of a business. Such shares usually carry some special rights to share in the future success of the enterprise. This may, for example, take the form of an enhanced share of the profits over and above a fixed dividend or the founders' shares may carry some beneficial options. Under Schedule 3, Companies Act 1985, a prospectus issued by a company must state *inter alia* the number of founders or management or deferred shares and the nature and extent of the interest of the holders in those shares.

FRACTIONAL CERTIFICATE A certificate for a fraction of a share. For example, in connection with the merger of two companies there may be an exchange of shares on the basis of, say, three shares of the old company for four shares of the new, and a shareholder with, say, five shares would receive in exchange six new shares and a fractional certificate for two-thirds of one share. He could then either sell the two-thirds, or purchase another one-third so as to make one whole share.

FRANKED INCOME The word 'franked' in this sense means free of further charge and the term is applied to income which has suffered tax and which is, in certain circumstances, deemed to be free from any further tax charge of a similar kind. In the case of a company *investing* in loan stock of another company, the interest on that stock would not be 'franked' income for corporation tax purposes, in the hands of the investing company. This is because the interests on the loan stock will have been allowed as a deduction for corporation tax purposes in the accounts of the paying company and thus will not have been paid out of profits which have suffered tax. If, on the other hand, a company invests in the ordinary shares or preference shares of another company, the dividend received is 'franked' income, i.e. it is paid out of profits which have borne corporation tax in the paying company. In the ordinary way therefore, no further corporation tax will be payable on such dividend income by the investing company.

FRAUDULENT CONVEYANCE One of the ten acts of bankruptcy. A conveyance, gift, delivery, or transfer of a debtor's property with the intention of defeating or delaying his creditors. A fraudulent conveyance is not necessarily a dishonest transaction, but one that defeats or delays a man's creditors; it does not necessarily imply a dishonest motive or a state of insolvency. Where a builder converted his business into a limited company which took over his assets and liabilities, without notifying his creditors, a receiving order was made on the petition of one of them, the act of bankruptcy relied on being a fraudulent conveyance in that the transfer of the debtor's assets to the company within the previous three months had defeated or delayed his creditors. The floating charge over such assets given by the new company was consequently set aside, as the trustee's titled related back to such transfer (In *Re Sims, ex parte A. E. Quaife* v *W. Sims and Lloyds Bank Ltd* [1930] WN 6). SEE *Act of Bankruptcy; Settlements, Settlor Bankrupt*

FRAUDULENT PREFERENCE The Bankruptcy Act 1914, Section 1 (1), includes as an act of bankruptcy any conveyance or transfer of a debtor's property or any charge thereon, which would be void under the Act as a fraudulent preference if he were adjudged bankrupt. SEE *Act of Bankruptcy*

Section 44 of the Act says

> (1) Every conveyance or transfer of property, or charge thereon made, every payment made, every obligation incurred, and every judicial proceeding taken or suffered by any person unable to pay his debts as they become due from his own money in favour of any creditor, or any person in trust for any creditor, with a view of giving such creditor or any surety or guarantor

for the debt due to such creditor, a preference over the other creditors, shall, if the person making, taking, paying, or suffering the same is adjudged bankrupt on a bankruptcy petition presented within three (now six) months after the date of making, taking, paying, or suffering the same, be deemed fraudulent and void as against the trustee in the bankruptcy.

(2) This Section shall not affect the rights of any person making title in good faith and for valuable consideration through or under a creditor of the bankrupt.

A preference to be fraudulent must be voluntary and not under duress and the debtor making it must be insolvent.

The burden of proving a fraudulent preference lies upon the trustee in bankruptcy and he must show that the dominant motive of the debtor was to prefer a particular creditor; inference is not necessarily sufficient. As Lord Tomlin said (*Peat* v *Gresham Trust* [1934] AC 252):

The onus is on those who claim to avoid the transaction to establish what the debtor really intended, and that the real intention was to prefer. The onus is only discharged when the Court upon a review of all the circumstances is satisfied that the dominant intent to prefer was present; that may be a matter of direct evidence or of inference, but where there is not direct evidence and there is room for more than one explanation it is not enough to say there being no direct evidence the intent to prefer must be inferred.

Where a trader had an overdraft guaranteed by his father, and ceased to pay his creditors, but collected moneys owing to him and paid them into his account, thereby reducing his father's guarantee liability by some £698, it was held that there was no fraudulent preference, as the debtor operated his account in exactly the same way as before. 'To say that the only inference possible from his conduct was that he intended to prefer his father ignored the essential nature of a fraudulent preference laid down by Lord Tomlin in *Peat* v *Gresham Trust*.' (*In Re Lyons, Times*, 13th October, 1934.)

In *Re T. W. Cutts (a Bankrupt), ex parte Bognor Mutual Building Society* v *Trustee in Bankruptcy* [1956] 2 All ER 537, the Master of the Rolls, Lord Evershed, reviewed the law relating to fraudulent preference. The following extract is taken from his judgment:

(1) The onus is on the person alleging a 'fraudulent preference' to prove to the satisfaction of the Court that the payment impugned was made by the debtor 'with a view of' preferring the payee over his other creditors; in other words, the onus is on the person alleging a fraudulent preference (normally, as here, the trustee in bankruptcy) to prove the fact of the debtor's requisite state of mind, that is, his intention.

(2) It is competent for the Court to draw the inference of intention to prefer from all the facts of the case, particularly when there is no direct evidence of intention before it; but the inference should not be drawn, having regard to the situation of the onus of proof, unless the inference is the true and proper inference from the facts proved. Thus, it will not be drawn if the inference from the facts is equivocal, and, in particular, it will not be drawn from the mere circumstances that the creditor paid was in fact 'preferred' in the sense that he was paid when other creditors were not paid and could not be paid.

(3) The words used in the Section are 'with a view of'. I have used the word 'intention' as synonymous with the word 'view'; and other words — e.g. 'object' — have also been used as synonyms in the cases. Whether the word used be 'intention' or some other word, since it is notorious that human beings are by no means always single-minded, the intention to prefer which must be proved is the principal or dominant intention. There may also be a valid distinction for present purposes between an intention to prefer and the reason for forming and executing that intention.

It is at this point that the greatest difficulty, as it seems to me, arises, the difficulty being as often as not one of definition of the words used. If a debtor, knowing himself to be insolvent and knowing, also, that bankruptcy is imminent, deliberately elects to pay his oldest friend or his closest relative, and to leave his other creditors unpaid or with little chance of being paid, it would appear to me to be irrelevant that he made the selection because of the love he bore for his friend or relative or because of his hopes for general but unspecified favours from them in the future. I am not, therefore, prepared to accept the submission of counsel for the Society that a deliberate choice in the present case by the debtor of the Society for payment because the Society was the most important of his clients could not for that reason constitute a fraudulent preference. For if a debtor deliberately selects for payment A in preference to all his other creditors, it cannot to my mind matter, in the absence of other relevant circumstances, whether A is the debtor's oldest friend, closest relative or best client. On the other hand, where a debtor, owing money in all directions, has also robbed his employer's till, he may, knowing himself to be insolvent, elect to reimburse the till in order that, when the crash comes, the damaging fact of his robbery may not be discovered. Or a debtor may elect to make a particular payment under pressure of some threat, or to obtain for himself some immediate and material benefit or to fulfil some particular obligation. In these cases, the reason for the payment affects, essentially, the intention in making it. In the instances given, the intention, that is the real or dominant intention, will no longer be 'to prefer' (i.e., to pay, as it were, out of turn) but will be to avoid the detection of a criminal act; to relieve the threat; to get the benefit and postpone the evil day; or to satisfy the particular obligation. Though the question of pressure in some form or another has, in the reported cases, often been the crux of the matter, it is plain that an inference of intention to prefer may be displaced in many other ways than by showing that the debtor acted under pressure.

Sections 92(4) and 115(4) of the Companies Act 1947, protected bankers where fraudulent preference of a guarantor was alleged, by empowering the court to grant relief and to give leave to bring in the guarantor as a third party in the action (SEE NOW Rules of the Supreme Court [Writ and Appearance] 1979 S.1. No. 1716). Winding up is covered in Section 616 of the Companies Act 1985.

By the Companies Act 1948, Section 320,

(1) Any conveyance, mortgage, delivery of goods, payment, execution or other act relating to property made or done by or against a company within six months before the commencement of its winding up which, had it been made or done by or against an individual within six months before the presentation of a bankruptcy petition on which he is adjudged bankrupt, would be deemed in his bankruptcy a fraudulent preference, shall in the event of the company being wound up be deemed a fraudulent preference of its creditors and be invalid accordingly:

Provided that, in relation to things made or done before the commencement of this Act, this subsection shall have effect with the substitution, for references to six months, of references to three months.

(2) Any conveyance or assignment by a company of all its property to trustees for the benefit of all its creditors shall be void to all intents.

(3) In the application to Scotland of this section, the expression 'fraudulent preference' includes any alienation or preference which is voidable by statute or at common law on the ground of insolvency or notour bankruptcy, the expression 'bankruptcy petition' means petition for sequestration and for the words 'three months' there shall be substituted the words 'sixty days'.

In the case of *Re T. W. Cutts* (above), the preference was established notwithstanding that the transaction implemented a pre-existing promise that itself was of a preferential character and the case of *Re M. Kushler Ltd* [1943] Ch 348 illustrates the vulnerability of a preference of a banker for the benefit of a guarantor. However, in the case of *Re F. L. E. Holdings Ltd* [1967] 1 WLR 1409, the intention to keep open a line of credit was held sufficient to negative the suggestion of a preference. In the case of *Osterreichische Landerbank* v *S'Elite Ltd* [1980] 2 All ER 651, Roskill, LJ, pointed out that 'fraudulent preference' may have no element of common law fraud. "It has often been pointed out that the phrase is an inept one and that a better phrase ... is voidable preference".

FREE MARKET The term may be used in relation to the purchase and sale of any commodity where there is complete freedom to deal. It is normally applied, however, to dealings on the Stock Exchange where there is said to be a free market if the shares of a particular company may be bought or sold freely in substantial amounts. This is in contrast to a limited market, where a share may be dealt with only in small amounts or where, at some particular time, it may be impossible to deal at all.

FREEHOLD A legal interest in land in the shape of an estate in fee simple absolute in possession (Law of Property Act 1925, Section 1). It is the highest interest a person can have in land, and the term dates back to feudal times when land was granted by a tenant-in-chief to A and his heirs in return for certain fixed services, such as supplying a number of soldiers or tilling a number of acres. Such services were *free* services as contrasted with the menial services of villeins who held their land under copyhold tenure. These free services were in time commuted for money payments which in time, for the most part, lapsed, although some rent charges still subsist. A freehold interest can exist subject to a chief rent or fee farm rent.

An owner of a freehold estate in land can grant a legal estate in the shape of a term of years absolute, i.e. a leasehold. This is the only other legal estate in land (Law of Property Act 1925, Section 1).

A freehold interest in land is *real* property, because formerly if a freeholder was ejected from his land, he could bring an action to recover the 'thing' (res) of which he had been deprived; a leaseholder, however, only had a right of action for damages against the person who had dispossessed him. SEE *Leasehold; Legal Estates; Personal Representatives; Real Estate; Title Deeds*

FRIENDLY SOCIETY Friendly societies are one of the six classes of unincorporated organizations which may be registered under the Friendly Societies Act 1896. These are friendly societies, benevolent societies, cattle insurance societies, working men's clubs, old people's home societies, and other specially authorized societies.

Within the first category of friendly societies there are friendly societies *per se*, building societies (q.v.) which are subject to separate statutory control, cooperative societies and trade unions.

To be registered as a friendly society, a society must be formed for the purpose of providing by voluntary subscription of its members, with or without the aid of donations, for any of the following:

1. The relief or maintenance of the members, their husbands, wives, children, fathers, mothers, brothers or sisters, etc., during sickness, old age or widowhood.

2. The provision of insurance on the life of a member or a member's husband or wife or child.
3. The provision of relief or maintenance of members who are unemployed or in other distressed circumstances.
4. The provision of endowment assurance for members or their wives or husbands.

Friendly societies are not charities, except in the case of those societies which provide *inter alia* for the relief of poverty. Registered friendly societies are, however, exempt from tax, i.e. both from income tax and corporation tax.

Within the fairly modest level of life assurance benefits permitted by statute, registered friendly societies are thus able to offer attractive tax-free insurance contracts for persons seeking to provide for dependants within the spirit of the Friendly Societies Acts.

The Friendly Societies Act 1984, ensures the enforceability of certain contracts entered into between friendly societies and their members since 3rd May, 1966, in cases where the validity of such contracts was in doubt. The Act also increases the tax exemption limits in relation to members' benefits to permit the investment linking of such benefits. Until the passing of the 1984 Act, the performance of investment linked contracts was having the effect of taking members' benefits beyond the permitted levels of tax exemption under the Friendly Societies Act 1974 and the Income and Corporation Taxes Act 1974. SEE Supplement

FUNDS A term applied loosely to Government securities (q.v.).

FUNERAL EXPENSES At the present time, funeral expenses vary between, say, £250 and £1,000, with an average of around £450. The cost of a funeral can be very much more if special services are required or the remains have to be transported a long way.

Reasonable funeral expenses and reasonable costs of mourning will be allowed as a deduction from the gross value of an estate for capital transfer tax purposes. No allowance will be made, however, for the cost of a memorial stone. In cases where a death grant is payable under the Social Security regulations, it will normally be paid to the person who is responsible for paying the funeral expenses. SEE *Death Grant*

FUNGIBLE ASSETS Fungible assets were defined by Paragraph 27(6) of Schedule 1 to the Companies Act 1981, as assets which are substantially indistinguishable one from another. It is a requirement of the Act that any material difference in the carrying value of stocks and fungible assets and their replacement cost be disclosed in the notes to a company's acounts. SEE NOW Schedule 4 of the 1985 Act.

FUTURES The concept of 'futures' is historically a feature of the commodity markets.

A futures contract arises when an investor agrees on, say, 1st January to buy cocoa for delivery nine months hence on 30th September at a predetermined price, believing that the spot price of cocoa on 30th September will be greater than the agreed price. On the 'terminal' date of the contract, he will take delivery and sell the cocoa immediately at the spot price. If prices have moved against him, he will make a loss. If he was right in his judgment, he will make a profit. In fact, he will not necessarily wait for the terminal date. If before 30th September he sees the opportunity for selling the cocoa 'future' at a profit, he may do so. A converse situation may arise in that an investor expecting a fall in commodity prices may agree to sell cocoa, or whatever, in nine months' time at an agreed price. Before the terminal date, he will hope to buy the commodity at a lower price for delivery on the same terminal date. He thus matches his book or is said to 'cancel' his contract. It is understood that about 90 per cent of all futures contracts are matched in this way, i.e. do not run through to the settlement date.

Trading in futures enables a large number of people to invest or speculate in commodity markets, without being involved as suppliers or users of the commodities. This helps to maintain an active and continuous market, so that prices for most commodities are always available. The clearing house for all trading in soft commodities on the London exchange is the International Commodities Clearing House Limited (q.v.). In the case of metals, there is no clearing house as such. The members of the London Metal Exchange deal as principals, albeit on behalf of other individual clients.

In recent years a market in financial futures has been established in London. SEE *London International Financial Futures Exchange*

G

GARNISHEE ORDER From the French *garnir*, to warn. The object of a garnishee order is the attachment by a judgment creditor of moneys of the judgment debtor in the hands of a third party—the garnishee. Bankers, as the depositees of other people's money, are perhaps the most usual recipients of garnishee orders.

An application with affidavit is made under Order 14 of the Rules of the Supreme Court by the judgment creditor's solicitor and an order *nisi* is thereupon made which, when served on the garnishee, restrains him from parting with any moneys due or accruing due to the judgment debtor and orders his appearance in court on a given date (usually eight or more days later) to show cause, if he can, why such moneys shall not be taken in satisfaction of the debt due to the judgment creditor.

A copy of the order is served by the creditor's solicitor on the head office of the bank concerned and usually on the branch as well. The original order should be exhibited and the copy should be compared with it. It is now the practice to specify the name of the branch on all orders served on a head office. Any ambiguity in the description of the judgment debtor must be cleared up before attaching the account, and cheques paid between the service of the order and such clearing up are in order (*Koch* v *Mineral Ore Syndicate* (1910) 54 Sol J 600). Service cannot be avoided, however, merely because the account is in the debtor's known trade name.

On the appointed day, the bank's solicitor will appear in court and also the judgment debtor if he wants to enter a defence. Failing the latter, the court will issue an Order Absolute, whereupon the garnishee (the bank) will pay over to the judgment creditor the amount of the order and costs or the available balance if less than the order. Such payment operates as a full discharge by the bank against his customer the judgment debtor.

All moneys due or accruing due are attached and thus all credit balances on current account in the customer's name come under the order, and the accounts should be stopped under advice to the customer, notwithstanding that the amount of the order is small and the balances are large. If circumstances make it expedient, a new account should be opened and an overdraft permitted if necessary. The attached balance should not be disturbed for there is the risk of service of a second garnishee order, or a receiving order may be made before the order is made absolute, or there may be trust funds in the account, in which case the court may rule that the customer's moneys were drawn out first. If the circumstances demand that cheques presented after service of the order should be returned, they should bear the answer 'Refer to Drawer'. Moneys paid in after the service of the order are not attached.

For some time past, a practice has been observed whereby limited orders are issued for the amount of the judgment debt and costs, plus a round sum for possible garnishee costs. In such cases, it is customary to transfer such sum to a suspense account to await the hearing and to permit the current account to be carried on.

Where an order is served and cheques have been received through the clearing earlier in the day it is the practice to pay them.

Where the credit balance includes uncleared effects, it is submitted that the amount of such items is not attached unless there is an agreement to allow drawings before clearance. It was so held in *Fern* v *Bishop Burns & Co Ltd* [1980] New LJ, 10th July, O'Connor, J, basing his finding on the Underwood and Zang decisions.

Where a cheque has been marked for payment (SEE *Marked Cheque*) a banker is entitled to reserve the amount of it from any attachable balance. Where payment of a cheque has been promised by telephone without any usual reservation, the banker could not deduct the amount thereof from any attachable balance. Where the account is overdrawn, it is usual to inform the judgment creditor's solicitor forthwith, who will arrange for the order to be withdrawn without waiting for the hearing in court.

All accounts in the customer's name must be taken into account and a debit balance may be set off against a credit balance before arriving at the attachable sum.

Where there is a loan payable on demand, any credit balance on a current account could presumably be set off and thus escape the operation of an order, but in practice the question would be put to the Master in Chambers. Where forms of charge give a lien on any credit balances and it is desired to exclude the operation of an order, the matter should likewise be mentioned to the Master.

Trust moneys are not attachable but cause must be shown to the Master in Chambers. Under Rule 5 of Order 45, where a garnishee suggests that the funds in question belong to a person other than the judgment debtor, the court may order the appearance of such party.

A solicitor's client account is attached by a garnishee order. In *Plunkett and Another* v *Barclays Bank* (1936) 52 TLR 353, it was held that a balance on the client account was money due by the bank to the solicitor and the bank could not be expected to adjudicate on conflicting equities.

A garnishee order citing a sole judgment debtor does not operate on a joint account in which such debtor is a party. But an order citing joint debtors will attach moneys standing to the credit of one of them. Probably, however, this does not apply to monies held in respect of a partnership where a partner is the subject of the garnishee proceedings. At all events it has been so held in Canada (*Hoon* v *Maloff* (*Yarus Construction Co Garnishees*) (1964) 42 DLR (2d) 770).

A garnishee order will not attach balances held abroad (*Richardson* v *Richardson and National Bank of India* (1927) 43 TLR 631).

Salaries of Crown servants are not attachable, not being due from the Crown as a debt (*Lucas* v *Lucas and High Commissioner for India* [1943] 2 All ER 110).

Moneys held by a bank in the name of the liquidator of a company cannot be attached on account of a debt due by the company in liquidation (*Lancaster Motor Co (London) Ltd* v *Bremith Ltd* [1941] 2 All ER 11).

In *Harrods Ltd* v *Tester* [1937] 2 All ER 236, where a married woman's account was the subject of a garnishee order, the husband brought evidence that all the moneys in the account were his and it was held that there was a resulting trust in favour of him and the account was not attached.

A banker is not entitled to deduct interest and commission charges accruing from any attachable balance.

Where a garnishee order *nisi* has been served and, before it is made absolute, notice of an act of bankruptcy or presentation of a petition is received, or if a receiving order has been made, the garnishee order fails (see Bankruptcy Act 1914, Section 40).

Where a company is being wound up by the court, any attachment after the commencement of the winding up is void (Companies Act 1948, Section 228; now Section 523, 1985 Act).

Likewise, where an order *nisi* is outstanding on a company's account and a petition for winding up is presented, the order will fail (Companies Act 1985, Section 621(1)). Where a company was being wound up voluntarily and a judgment creditor attached the banking account standing in the name of the liquidator, it was held that the mere fact that the company's account stood in the name of the liquidator made no difference to the judgment creditor's rights, and the Section 228, of the Companies Act 1948, only applied to a winding up by the court (*Gerard* v *Worth of Paris Ltd* [1936] 2 All ER 905, but this decision was overruled in the case of *Lancaster Motor Company (London) Ltd* v *Bremith Ltd* (above)).

A balance on a *deposit* account was not formerly attachable if a number of days' notice was required before repayment, or if it was a condition of repayment that the deposit book should be produced. The position was, however, altered by the Administration of Justice Act 1956, which provides (in Section 38) as follows.

> (1) A sum standing to the credit of a person in a deposit account in a bank shall, for the purposes of the jurisdiction of the High Court and the county court to attach debts for the purpose of satisfying judgment or orders for the payment of money, be deemed to be a sum due or accruing to that person and, subject to rules of court, shall be attachable accordingly, notwithstanding that any of the following conditions applicable to the account, that is to say:
>
> (*a*) any condition that notice is required before any money is withdrawn;
>
> (*b*) any condition that a personal application must be made before any money is withdrawn;
>
> (*c*) any condition that a deposit book must be produced before any money is withdrawn; or
>
> (*d*) any other condition prescribed by rules of court, has not been satisfied.
>
> (2) This section shall not apply to any account in the Post Office Savings Bank [now National Savings Bank] in any Trustee Savings Bank or in any Savings Bank maintained in pursuance of any enactment by any local authority or to any account in any bank with two or more places of business if the terms applicable to that account permit withdrawals on demand, on production of a deposit book, at more than one of those places of business, with or without restrictions as to the amount which may be withdrawn.

It would seem, therefore, that unless the banks contract to allow withdrawals on demand elsewhere than at the branch where the account is kept, all deposit balances will be attachable as sums due or accruing due to the depositors.

Although, as mentioned above, a garnishee order will not attach balances held abroad, foreign currency balances held in this country may be attached for the purpose of satisfying a sterling judgment debt, per the Court of Appeal in *Choice Investments Ltd* v *Jeromnimon; Midland Bank, Garnishee* [1981] 2 WLR 80. The question arose in that case, not only as to whether or not a currency balance could be so attached but how the sterling equivalent should be calculated. The court held that the order *nisi* should require the bank to put a stop on the account sufficient to realize the sterling debt, calculated at the buying rate for sterling at that date. On the order becoming absolute, the bank would be required to exchange the currency for sterling up to the amount of the judgment debt. If owing to exchange fluctuations, the amount so stopped was more than the amount of the debt, the surplus would not be attached and thus be made available to the customer on demand.

In *Brooks Associates Inc and Another* v *Basu and Another (Department for National Savings, Garnishee)* [1983] 2 WLR 141), it was held that a garnishee order could be made by the court attaching a bank balance with the National Savings Bank notwithstanding that the National Savings Bank is a Crown institute. Woolf, J, held that the Crown was always within the jurisdiction of the court in respect of its banking activities carried on in England. The fact that the head office of the National Savings Bank is in Glasgow did not affect the position.

Under the Attachment of Debts (Expenses) Order 1983, SI 1983 No. 1621, a deposit-taking institution on which a garnishee order is served, may deduct £30 towards clerical and administrative expenses incurred in complying with the order, from money held on a debtor's behalf which would otherwise be attached by the order.

In the case of *Alcom Limited* v *Republic of Colombia* [1983] 1 WLR 906, the Court of Appeal held that diplomatic immunity under the State Immunity Act 1978, S.13, does not extend to property which is in use or intended for use for commercial purposes. In that case, the bank account was used for goods and services in connection with the running of the embassy and thus was liable to be attached in satisfaction of a judgment debt.

GARNISHEE SUMMONS A garnishee summons is issued by a county court, is served by an officer of the court, and is returnable at the county court. The operation is the same as a garnishee order except that a summons may be settled as far as the bank is concerned by paying to the county court registrar, five days before the date of hearing of the summons, the amount due thereunder or the amount of the balance if less than this. The registrar's receipt will be a good discharge against the customer.

GEARING The gearing of a company is the relationship of its total debt, i.e. loan stocks, debentures, bank borrowings, etc., to the total equity, i.e. issued capital plus reserves. Alternatively, gearing may be expressed as the ratio of a company's loan capital to its total capital. The former is, in fact, the original way in which the term was used and is, it is suggested, to be preferred. Thus, if a company has ordinary capital of £1 million and its total loan capital and other debt is £1 million, its gearing is 1:1. The effect of gearing is analogous to mechanical gearing—hence the name. In times of profitable trading, increased gearing can increase substantially the return to the ordinary shareholders provided the borrowed money is earning more in the business than the amount of the interest charge. On the other hand, in bad times, the burden of the interest charge can be a serious incubus and the gearing has a reverse effect.

Gearing may also be an important factor in portfolio management. In such a case, the term is used in relation to the borrowing by the owner or the manager of a portfolio of investments in order to inflate the portfolio in anticipation of a market rise. In a Bull market the rewards of gearing can be very substantial. On the other hand, gearing can be disastrous on a falling market, as applied in the market recession of 1974 when a number of funds had borrowed money in order to invest abroad. Investment trusts in Britain may borrow for their portfolio management purposes but unit trusts may not do so.

The advantages and risks of gearing are not limited to dealings on the Stock Exchange but apply equally in any of the commodity markets. SEE ALSO *Options; Warrants (Stock)*

GEARING RATIOS There is no hard and fast rule for the desirable level of gearing (q.v.) for commercial and industrial companies. It will vary from industry to industry, from company to company and from time to time. Certain categories of business, notably property companies, have tended to be relatively highly geared. The average level of gearing, i.e. ratio of borrowing to capital employed, among commercial and industrial companies in the UK is thought to be of the order of 20 per cent although the figure was around 25 per cent in the mid-1960s.

From a banker's point of view, the level of gearing can be very important. The following is an extract from the evidence of the Committee of London Clearing Bankers to the Wilson Committee (q.v.).

Current and prospective gearing ratios are of concern to a bank when lending to any company, but particularly so when lending to smaller companies where the risks of overtrading can be acute. The main continuing requirement is that the proprietorship resources of the business should be sufficient to meet the normal trading risks and also to provide a buffer to meet any unexpected problems that could arise. This does not mean that bank lending can be risk-free; but it does seek to ensure that the total risks of a business are *appropriately shared* between its proprietors and its lenders, bearing in mind that the maximum return to a lender is the net margin between the cost of his funds and his lending rates; as the proprietors stand to benefit most from the success of an enterprise, it is quite reasonable that they should also bear the primary risk of failure. Generally speaking, the proprietorship resources should be at least equal to the level of facilities provided by a company's bankers and any other borrowings, but there will be many occasions when higher gearing ratios can be accepted. In calculating gearings ratios it is important to stress that a borrower's assets are given 'going concern' values based on their future earning potential, rather than the values that they might fetch in liquidation.

GENERAL ACCEPTANCE SEE *Acceptance, General*

GENERAL AGREEMENT ON TARIFFS AND TRADE (GATT) The General Agreement on Tariffs and Trade (GATT) was entered into in 1947 with a view to developing and liberalizing world trade. Originally there were 23 signatories but there are now 90 members of GATT. The essence of GATT is that the member countries will not seek to exclude imports by means of increased tariffs, although they may do so by import quotas.

From time to time the provisions of GATT are revised following a 'round' of negotiations among the member countries. The negotiations cover such matters as customs duties, import quotas, anti-dumping agreements, preferential dealings between countries and reciprocal concessions.

GENERAL AVERAGE A term used in connection with shipping. A clause usually found in a charter party is 'General average as per York–Antwerp rules'. The rules referred to are those which have been adopted at various times by international conferences: York in 1864, Antwerp in 1877, and Liverpool in 1890. Further revisions have taken place in more recent years. Where extraordinary sacrifices have been made, such as throwing cargo overboard or cutting away the masts or other parts of the ship, in order that the vessel and the rest of the cargo may be saved from destruction, the loss does not fall upon the owner of the ship or of the property thrown overboard, but is apportioned among all the parties; that is, the shipowner and the owners of the cargo (or the underwriters, if insured) according to their interest in the ship and cargo. The calculation of the amount payable by each part is usually made by persons called average adjusters. SEE *Bill of Lading; Charter Party; Particular Average*

GENERAL EQUITABLE CHARGE An equitable charge not secured by deposit of title deeds and which does not arise under or affect an interest under a settlement or trust for sale must be registered under the Land Charges Act 1925, as a Class C (iii) Land Charge. SEE *Land Charges, Mortgage*

GENERAL LEGACY A general legacy should be distinguished from a specific legacy (SEE *Legacy*) and a demonstrative legacy (q.v.). A general legacy is a gift by will out of the personal estate of the testator but is not necessarily any particular part of that estate. General legacies are usually, but not necessarily, pecuniary legacies. Thus A may give B a legacy of £1,000 even though A's estate does not actually include any cash assets. The legacy will be raised out of the other assets in the estate. On the other hand, a general legacy may be of a non-pecuniary nature. For example, A may give B 'a gold watch', not being any particular watch which A possesses: indeed A may not possess any gold watch. It would be necessary therefore, for the executors to buy a gold watch for B out of the estate. Alternatively he will be entitled to the value of the gold watch.

The distinction between general legacies and other legacies is important in relation to the doctrines of abatement (q.v.) and ademption (q.v.).

A general legacy carries interest from one year after the testator's death at the rate of 4 per cent per annum unless there is a clear indication that the legacy is to be paid at an earlier date, in which case interest accrues from that date. If a legacy is given in satisfaction of a debt, interest accrues from the date of death. A legacy expressed to be payable at some future date, i.e. more than a year from the testator's death, carries interest from that date. Thus legacies payable on the death of a life tenant carry interest from the date of that death.

GENERAL MEETING SEE *Meetings, Companies*

GIFTS INTER VIVOS Gifts between living persons. An *inter vivos* gift is a gift that takes effect in the lifetime of the donor. As the gift takes effect at one, it differs from a *donatio mortis causa* (q.v.) which takes effect only in the event of the donor dying from the illness from which he is suffering at the time the gift is made. SEE *Capital Transfer Tax*

GILT BOND Loose terminology for a single-premium life assurance policy invested in Government stocks. SEE *Bond; Managed Bond; Life Assurance*

GILT EDGED SECURITIES Generally synonymous with the securities of or guaranteed by the British Government, Commonwealth Governments, local authorities and public boards.

GIRO A system first used in continental Europe for the cheap and simple transfer of money either through a bank or through a postal agency. All accounts are numbered, and a transfer is effected on the receipt of the appropriate form duly completed. The recipient is advised of the transfer. Charges are kept as low as possible, and in some cases interest is allowed on credit balances. No overdrafts are permitted.

A National Giro was introduced in the UK in 1968 and the banks restyled their credit clearing, Bank Giro. SEE *Credit Clearing; National Girobank*

GOLD In ancient times, gold was not used as a base currency, i.e. it was not looked upon as a means of exchange or as a basis for other means of exchange. Some gold coins existed, but most coins were silver. The discovery of gold in large quantities in the nineteenth century in North America, Australia and South Africa made it possible for gold to acquire a monetary role until Britain went off the gold standard in 1931, followed by most of the trading countries of the world and by the USA in 1933. In that year, the USA fixed the price of gold at $35 per ounce and so it remained until 1971.

So long as gold had an official status in the monetary systems of the world, its value was stable even through the years of extreme slump. As a free market commodity, however, gold more than anything else is a barometer of worldwide political and economic expectations. Almost every political or economic crisis in a major area of the world will lead to a rush into gold. This is not necessarily logical because gold has no particular qualities other than for industrial and certain medical and dental purposes and its attraction for decorative purposes.

Nevertheless, it has the following features in its favour:

1. It is universally accepted as a store of value and as a means of exchange.
2. It is virtually indestructible and maintains its intrinsic condition indefinitely.
3. There are limited stocks of gold in the world.
4. In contrast to paper money, which governments can manufacture at will, gold is in reasonably constant supply.
5. Gold has a very good record of stability through times of crisis.

GOLD, INVESTMENT IN After many years of restriction, UK residents may now invest freely in gold as may residents of the USA. The choice open to the investor is gold jewellery, gold bullion or gold coins.

For investment purposes, there is little, if any, purpose in investing in new gold jewellery, particularly in the western world where jewellery pieces may cost as much as ten times the bullion value of the gold content.

Investment in bullion direct has the disadvantage that gold bars are difficult to carry around and have no artistic value. This is nevertheless the traditional form of gold hoarding in many parts of the world, particularly in times of political instability. The purchase of bullion is really only appropriate for large-scale investors, who would seldom have occasion to take deliver of the bullion, but would arrange for it to be held to their order in the vaults of a bank.

For investors in the UK, the most convenient way of acquiring gold is through the purchase of gold coins. Here again, however, a gold coin may command a price far in excess of the gold content, perhaps because of the rarity aspect, e.g. English sovereigns. The only gold coins of which the price relates entirely to the current price of gold are those coins currently issued by a number of countries at a price directly related to the price of gold. In this category, the leading gold coin is the Krugerrand of South Africa which contains exactly 1 oz of pure gold and is priced at exactly 3 per cent above the value of the gold content. There are a number of alternative bullion coins, including the Mexican peso, the Canadian Mapleleaf, the French Napoleon, the Austrian Crown of Crowns and the Russian chervonetz, but these are far less readily available and stand at a higher premium, i.e. the official price is relatively higher in relation to the price of the gold than is the case with Krugerrands.

Krugerrands and other gold bullion coins may be purchased from the members of the London Gold Market, namely, Rothschilds, Samuel Montagu & Co Ltd, Sharps Pixley, Johnson Matthey (*de facto* the Bank of England following the collapse of Johnson Matthey in 1984) and Mocatta & Goldsmid. Of these, Johnson Matthey trade in small quantities of coins, even single Krugerrands, and it is also possible to buy them through the clearing banks in the UK. The dealing margin on a Krugerrand is around £2. In addition to the dealing margin, a small charge is made for purchases through the clearing banks to cover commission, postage and packaging.

With effect from 23rd September, 1980, mini-Krugerrands were introduced. These are fractional Krugerrands containing half, quarter or one-tenth of an ounce of gold. The coins are issued at a premium slightly above that for Krugerrands, i.e. up to 10 per cent for the one-tenth coins.

With effect from 1st April, 1982, VAT became payable on gold coins. Prior to that date, no VAT was payable on Krugerrands and other gold coins currently in issue because they are regarded as currency. VAT was introduced on the discovery of a major tax fraud involving the melting down of gold coins and the sale of the gold as bullion, which has always attracted VAT.

In October 1980, the Royal Mint announced the limited issue of 10,000 sets of gold coins containing a gold £5, £2, sovereign and half-sovereign. These were the first sets of their kind to be issued since the coronation of King George VI. These are 'proof' coins produced with highly polished dies, carefully selected blanks and the closest possible quality control. At £1,100 per set they are priced at approximately 100 per cent over the meltdown value of the gold.

The Royal Mint also announced a limited issue of 100,000 1980 'proof' half-sovereigns at £65 each.

GOLD BULLION STANDARD A monetary system under which gold coins are not in circulation, the internal circulating medium being token paper money and silver and copper. The free import and export of unminted bulk gold is allowed for international payments and the central bank will buy or sell gold at current market rates.

GOLD COIN Since the late fifth century in Britain, gold coins have circulated intermittently, and during the reign of Edward III, probably about 1343 or 1344, a national gold currency was established. Gold florins and guineas were finally replaced by the gold £1 in 1816 as the legal standard unit. This new gold 'sovereign' was to weigh 123.27447 grains of standard gold, eleven-twelfths fine, and be supported by a token silver coinage. Gold coin is legal tender for any amount as long as it does not fall below 122.5 grains. In 1914, gold was called in from circulation, by means of notices and posters, but no compulsion was used and it was not until 1919, after the war was over, that it was forbidden to export 'gold coin, and bullion', although it had not actually been minted since 1917. The return to gold in 1925, in which year there was a mintage of gold, did not mean a return to the circulation of gold coin, but a return to gold coin reserve; this had a severe deflationary effect, and was finally abandoned in 1931 in favour of a gold bullion reserve.

GOLD EXCHANGE STANDARD This has been called the elastic gold standard by which the standard of value is still reckoned in so much fine gold, whether coin or bullion, but the actual value is preserved by the purchase and sale of foreign exchange by the central bank. The money in circulation is consequently token money.

GOLD RESERVES This term formerly denoted the stocks of gold coin and bullion held as cover for an issue of notes where the notes were convertible into gold on demand. In the 1930s, the principal countries abandoned the gold standard (q.v.); gold coins ceased to be used as currency and notes were no longer convertible into gold. Gold was still used, however, to make international payments. The term 'gold reserve' came to be used more generally to denote any stock of the metal held by a central authority for the purpose of making such payments. On the 7th September, 1939, the gold reserve of the Bank of England was transferred to the Exchange Equalisation Account, and as from that date the latter authority, among its other functions, holds the country's reserves of monetary gold.

GOLD STANDARD The system in force in this country before the First World War. There are three essential conditions to a gold standard proper:

1. There must be free mintage of gold into the standard legal coins.
2. There must be free and unfettered movement of gold into and out of the country.
3. The legal tender paper money of the country must be absolutely convertible into gold at will.

The export of gold was prohibited, except under licence of the Treasury, from the spring of 1919 until April 1925, when the gold standard in international matters with a free export of gold was resumed. The Gold Standard Act 1925 was passed to facilitate the return to a gold standard and for the purposes connected therewith. As explained by the Chancellor of the Exchequer, the Act provided, among other things, (1) that until otherwise provided by proclamation, the Bank of England and Treasury notes would be convertible into coin only at the option of the Bank of

England; and (2) that the right to tender bullion to the Mint to be coined should be confined in the future by law, as it had long been confined in practice, to the Bank of England.

The Act also provided that

> The Bank of England shall be bound to sell to any person who makes a demand in that behalf at the head office of the Bank during the office hours of the Bank and pays the purchase price in any legal tender, gold bullion at the price of £3 17s 10½d per ounce troy of gold of the standard of fineness prescribed for gold coin by the Coinage Act, 1870, but only in the form of bars containing approximately 400 ounces troy of fine gold.

This last provision was suspended by the Gold Standard (Amendment) Act 1931, and thus the public no longer had a legal right to demand gold bullion from the Bank of England in return for payment in legal tender.

GOLDSMITH'S NOTES The prototypes of the modern bank notes. Before banking became a separate business in Britain, goldsmiths received money on deposit and the receipts given for the money were called goldsmith's notes. The notes were payable on demand, and circulated instead of coins. We are told that

> It was not only the greater security of the goldsmiths' shops which attracted deposits but also the great convenience of their paper money. Their running cash notes originated as receipts for the deposit of gold and silver which were later endorsed when part of the deposit was withdrawn or when interest was added. As the use of these notes increased, the practice began of issuing the notes in standard units to facilitate the withdrawal of part of the deposit and its subsequent use to meet payments to other merchants. In this way, the banknote, which was a promise to pay on demand, came into existence. [*Four Centuries of Banking* by George Chandler, Batsford, 1964]

GOOD CONSIDERATION SEE *Consideration*

GOOD DELIVERY On the Stock Exchange a security is not a 'good delivery' if it is affected with some irregularity such as absence of coupons, or necessary stamps; or, in the case of a bearer security, if a holder has written his name on it. A certified transfer is accepted as a 'good delivery'.

GOOD FAITH By the Bills of Exchange Act 1882, Section 90

> A thing is deemed to be done in good faith, within the meaning of this Act, where it is in fact done honestly, whether it is done negligently or not.

The same definition is given in the Sale of Goods Act 1893.

In a case in 1892, Lord Herschell said

> If there is anything which excites the suspicion that there is something wrong in the transaction, the taker of the instrument is not acting in good faith, if he shuts his eyes to the facts presented to him and puts the suspicions aside without further inquiry.

SEE *Factors Act 1889; Holder in due Course; Uberrimae Fidei*

GOOD LEASEHOLD TITLE A lease may be registered under the Land Registration Act 1925, with a good leasehold title, if for 21 years or more unexpired. If the applicant for the first registration is the original lessee, a good leasehold title may be granted on his written statement that he has not created any incumbrances. A good leasehold title may be converted into an absolute title after 10 years, on proof that the proprietor or successive proprietors have been in possession for that time (Land Registration Act 1925, Section 77(4)). SEE *Land Registration*

GOOD NAMES (GOOD MARKING NAMES) These are accredited institutions in the UK which act as nominees for holders of US and Canadian shares. Although shares in US and Canadian companies are in registered form, the form of transfer is on the reverse of the certificate. Thus, if the registered holder signs the transfer in blank, the security is effectively in bearer form and passes by delivery. To facilitate the transfer of such North American securities in the UK, a number of institutions have been recognized by the Stock Exchange as good marking names. These 'names', which may be banks, stockbrokers or other nominee institutions, hold the shares on behalf of the beneficial owner, collect the dividends when due, deal with currency exchanges and effect any further transfers on behalf of the owner. Shares registered in good marking names normally command a better price in the market than those registered in unknown names because of the greater efficiency and security which the good marking name offers.

GOOD ROOT OF TITLE This is a term applicable to the ownership of freehold and leasehold property. The title under which ownership is claimed must have its origin in some document which deals with the entire legal and equitable estate and which does not depend for its validity upon any previous document and which contains nothing to cast any doubt on the title. In general, the best root of title for unregistered land is a conveyance on sale or a legal mortgage. In the absence of express stipulation or agreement in an open contract for the sale of land, the vendor is required under the Law Reform Act 1969, to show a title for at least fifteen years, commencing with a 'good' root of title. In the case of registered land, the root of title is the land certificate. SEE *Abstract of Title*

GOODS AND CHATTELS SEE *Chattels*

GOODWILL This has been the subject of many different definitions over the years but can most simply be described as the value placed on the profit-making capacity of a business. Thus, the goodwill of an enterprise may derive from such factors as market share, name and tradition, business connections, e.g. a good sales ledger, some special status or licence or the flair of a particular proprietor. Thus it is an intangible asset. There is no universal rule for the valuation of goodwill. It may, for example, be reflected by a purchase price of three to five years' pre-tax profits. On the other hand, an insurance agency may change hands at a price equivalent to one year's commissions. Practices vary from time to time and between trades.

It has for many years been regarded as a matter of good accounting practice to write off goodwill in the balance sheet of a business. This is no doubt because it has no separate saleable value, even in a successful business (except on the sale of the business itself) and has no value at all in an unsuccessful business.

The Companies Act 1981, implementing the Fourth Directive of the European Economic Community on company accounts, permitted the inclusion of goodwill in company balance sheets if the goodwill has been acquired for valuable consideration (SEE NOW Schedule 4, Companies Act 1985). The consideration must be depreciated systematically over a period chosen by the directors and the period must not exceed the useful economic life of the goodwill. The period in question and the reason for its choice must be disclosed in a note to the accounts. These rules do not apply to the valuation of goodwill arising on consolidation of balance sheets.

GOVERNMENT SECURITIES Securities issued by the British Government fall into two main categories: quoted securities and national savings (q.v.). Quoted securities are by far the major component of the National Debt (q.v.). In 1984 the National Debt was approximately £142,000 million, of which £108,000 million was represented by quoted Government securities. New Government stocks are issued from time to time (1) to replace existing securities on maturity, (2) to finance budget deficits, and (3) as an instrument of monetary policy in controlling the money supply.

All Government securities are quoted in nominal units of £100 but may be bought or sold in any amounts to the nearest 1p nominal stock. They are not necessarily issued at par, but may be at a discount or premium. Thereafter, their price reflects market conditions.

The names of Government stocks, e.g. Treasury, Exchequer, etc., have no particular significance other than in those cases, e.g. 3 per cent Transport Stock 1978–88 where a particular stock has been issued to finance the nationalization of an industry. All Government stocks are registered on the Bank of England Register and interest is payable half-yearly by the Bank. With very few exceptions, notably $3\frac{1}{2}$ per cent War Loan, interest is paid after deduction of tax at the basic rate. This does not apply however, to Government stocks purchased through the National Savings Stock Register (q.v.).

Government stocks are usually categorized as short, medium and long-dated. Stocks with less than five years to the date of redemption are sometimes referred to as 'bonds'. They do not necessarily perform in line with the rest of the gilt-edged market, partly because bonds are sought after by banks and building societies, and partly because their short-term nature keeps them much more in line with current interest rates in the money market. All gilt-edged stocks are likely to be affected by the expectations of investors and potential investors, but the longer-dated stocks will react more to long-term trends in the world economic situation and particularly inflation.

Government stocks also fall into the following categories:

1. Dated stocks, i.e. those which have a stated year of redemption, e.g. $12\frac{1}{4}$ per cent Exchequer Stock 1999, and those which have a bracket of earliest and latest redemption dates, e.g. $8\frac{1}{4}$ per cent Treasury Stock 1987–1990.
2. Undated stocks, e.g. $2\frac{1}{2}$ per cent Consols and $3\frac{1}{2}$ per cent War Stock, which are redeemable entirely at the discretion of Her Majesty's Government.
3. Variable-rate stocks (q.v.).
4. Index-linked stocks.

As a general rule new issues of Government stocks are made through the Bank of England. The issue may be at a fixed price or by tender. In some cases, the full amount is payable on application; in other instances payment is by instalments, a call or calls being made in the ensuing months. Stock not taken up by the public remain 'on tap' and is available through the Government broker until the issue is exhausted.

The quoted Government securities in issue as at 31st December, 1984, and the amounts of stock outstanding in each case are given in the following tables.

GOVERNMENT SECURITIES

Amount of stock outstanding £m Dec. 1984	Stock in order of latest redemption Short dated: up to five years to redemption	Dividend date (last date of redemption in heavy type)
997	Treasury Conv $8\frac{3}{4}$ per cent 1985	3 M **S**
1,300	Exchequer $12\frac{1}{4}$ per cent 1985	22 M **N**
1,150	Exchequer $11\frac{3}{4}$ per cent 1986	25 **F** A
690	Treasury 10 per cent Conv 1986	11 **A** O
800	Treasury 3 per cent 1986	19 **M** N
1,099	Exchequer Conv $10\frac{1}{2}$ per cent 1986	19 **M** N
1,150	Treasury 12 per cent 1986	12 **J** D
600	Treasury $8\frac{1}{2}$ per cent 1984–86	10 J **J**
1,000	Exchequer 14 per cent 1986	29 A **O**
650	Exchequer $2\frac{1}{2}$ per cent 1986	21 M **N**
1,250	Exchequer $13\frac{1}{4}$ per cent 1987	22 **J** J
998	Treasury Conv $10\frac{1}{4}$ per cent 1987	10 **F** A
900	Exchequer $2\frac{1}{2}$ per cent 1987	24 **F** A
1,550	Exchequer $12\frac{1}{2}$ per cent 1987	6 **A** O
559	Funding $6\frac{1}{2}$ per cent 1985–87	1 **M** N
1,500	Treasury 10 per cent 1987	12 **J** D
950	Treasury 3 per cent 1987	14 J **J**
1,950	Treasury 12 per cent 1987	3 M **N**
500	Treasury $7\frac{3}{4}$ per cent 1985–88	26 **J** J
1,450	Exchequer $10\frac{1}{2}$ per cent 1988	10 **M** N
1,150	Exchequer Conv $9\frac{3}{4}$ per cent 1988	14 **J** D
1,302	Transport 3 per cent 1978–88	1 J **J**
2,050	Treasury $9\frac{1}{2}$ per cent 1988	25 A **O**
2,250	Treasury $11\frac{1}{2}$ per cent 1989	22 **F** A
1,100	Treasury $9\frac{1}{2}$ per cent 1989	18 **A** O
1,200	Treasury $10\frac{1}{2}$ per cent 1989	14 **J** D
2,400	Exchequer 10 per cent 1989	1 F **A**
1,200	Exchequer 11 per cent 1989	29 M **S**
601	Treasury 5 per cent 1986–89	15 A **O**

Amount of stock outstanding £m Dec. 1984	Stock in order of latest redemption Medium dated: 5–15 years to redemption	Dividend date (last date of redemption in heavy type)
950	Treasury 13 per cent 1990	15 **J** J
1,100	Exchequer $12\frac{1}{2}$ per cent 1990	22 **M** S
600	Treasury $8\frac{1}{4}$ per cent 1987–90	15 **J** D
1,200	Treasury 10 per cent Conv 1990	25 A **O**
2,000	Treasury $11\frac{3}{4}$ per cent 1991	10 **J** J
400	Funding $5\frac{3}{4}$ per cent 1987–91	5 **A** O
1,150	Exchequer 11 per cent 1991	25 A **O**
850	Treasury $12\frac{3}{4}$ per cent 1992	15 **J** J
800	Treasury 10 per cent 1992	21 **F** A
950	Treasury $10\frac{1}{2}$ per cent Conv 1992	7 M **N**
1,350	Exchequer $12\frac{1}{4}$ per cent 1992	25 F **A**
1,757	Exchequer $13\frac{1}{4}$ per cent 1992	22 M **S**
1,100	Treasury $12\frac{1}{2}$ per cent 1993	14 J **J**
600	Funding 6 per cent 1993	15 M **S**
1,250	Treasury $13\frac{3}{4}$ per cent 1993	23 M **N**
600	Treasury $14\frac{1}{2}$ per cent 1994	1 **M** S
1,100	Exchequer $13\frac{1}{2}$ per cent 1994	27 **A** O
1,550	Exchequer $12\frac{1}{2}$ per cent 1994	22 **F** A
900	Treasury 9 per cent 1994	17 M **N**
2,100	Treasury 12 per cent 1995	25 **J** J
214	Gas 3 per cent 1990–95	1 **M** N

(continued next page)

Amount of stock outstanding £m Dec. 1984	Stock in order of latest redemption Medium dated: 5–15 years to redemption	Dividend date (last date of redemption in heavy type)		
1,800	Exchequer $10\frac{1}{4}$ per cent 1995	21	J	**J**
1,000	Treasury $12\frac{3}{4}$ per cent 1995	15	M	**N**
900	Treasury 14 per cent 1996	22	**J**	J
750	Treasury 9 per cent 1992–96	15	**M**	S
1,350	Treasury $15\frac{1}{4}$ per cent 1996	3	**M**	N
800	Exchequer $13\frac{1}{4}$ per cent 1996	15	**M**	N
41	Redemption 3 per cent 1986–96	1	A	**O**
1,500	Treasury $13\frac{1}{4}$ per cent 1997	22	**J**	J
1,600	Exchequer $10\frac{1}{2}$ per cent 1997	21	**F**	A
1,000	Treasury $8\frac{3}{4}$ per cent 1997	1	M	**S**
1,000	Exchequer 15 per cent 1997	27	A	**O**
1,100	Exchequer $9\frac{3}{4}$ per cent 1998	19	**J**	J
1,100	Exchequer $9\frac{3}{4}$ per cent 1998 'A'	19	**J**	J
1,000	Treasury $6\frac{3}{4}$ per cent 1995–98	1	**M**	N
1,100	Treasury $15\frac{1}{2}$ per cent 1998	30	M	**S**
2,500	Exchequer 12 per cent 1998	20	M	**N**
850	Treasury $9\frac{1}{2}$ per cent 1999	15	**J**	J
2,900	Exchequer $12\frac{1}{4}$ per cent 1999	26	**M**	S
1,051	Treasury $10\frac{1}{2}$ per cent 1999	19	**M**	N
1,098	Conversion $10\frac{1}{4}$ per cent 1990	22	M	**N**

Amount of stock outstanding £m Dec. 1984	Long dated: over 15 years to redemption	Dividend date (last date of redemption in heavy type)		
1,767	Treasury 13 per cent 2000	14	J	**J**
1,250	Treasury 14 per cent 1998–2001	22	**M**	N
1,550	Exchequer 12 per cent 1999–2002	22	**J**	J
516	Conversion 10 per cent 2002	11	**A**	O
1,800	Treasury $13\frac{3}{4}$ per cent 2000–03	25	J	**J**
1,550	Treasury $11\frac{1}{2}$ per cent 2001–04	19	**M**	S
443	Funding $3\frac{1}{2}$ per cent 1999–2004	14	J	**J**
2,200	Treasury $12\frac{1}{2}$ per cent 2003–05	21	M	**N**
600	Treasury 8 per cent 2002–06	5	A	**O**
2,900	Treasury $11\frac{3}{4}$ per cent 2003–07	22	**J**	J
1,250	Treasury $13\frac{1}{2}$ per cent 2004–08	26	**M**	S
1,000	Treasury $5\frac{1}{2}$ per cent 2008–12	10	**M**	S
600	Treasury $7\frac{3}{4}$ per cent 2012–17	26	**J**	J
1,000	Exchequer 12 per cent 2013–17	12	J	**D**

Amount of stock outstanding £m Dec. 1984	Index-linked	Dividend date (last date of redemption in heavy type)		
1,000	Treasury 2 per cent IL 1988	30	**M**	S
400	Treasury 2 per cent IL 1900	25	J	**J**
1,000	Treasury 2 per cent IL 1996	16	M	**S**
500	Treasury $2\frac{1}{2}$ per cent IL 2001	24	M	**S**
450	Treasury $2\frac{1}{2}$ per cent IL 2003	20	**M**	N
1,000	Treasury 2 per cent IL 2006	19	J	**J**
600	Treasury $2\frac{1}{2}$ per cent IL 2009	20	**M**	N
850	Treasury $2\frac{1}{2}$ per cent IL 2011	23	F	**A**
950	Treasury $2\frac{1}{2}$ per cent IL 2016	26	J	**J**
750	Treasury $2\frac{1}{2}$ per cent IL 2020	16	A	**O**

Amount of stock outstanding £m Dec. 1984	No final redemption date	Dividend date (last date of redemption in heavy type)
359	Consols 4 per cent 1957–aft	1 **F** A
1,909	War Loan $3\frac{1}{2}$ per cent 1952–aft	1 J **D**
165	Conversion $3\frac{1}{2}$ per cent 1961–aft	1 A **O**
56	Treasury 3 per cent 1966–aft	5 A **O**
276	Consols $2\frac{1}{2}$ per cent 1923–aft	5 JA JO
475	Treasury $2\frac{1}{2}$ per cent 1975–aft	1 A **O**

GOWER REPORT This discussion document, prepared by Professor L. C. Gower and entitled *Review of Investor Protection*, was published in January, 1982 had been commissioned by the Secretary of State for Trade to undertake the review with the following terms of reference:

1. To consider the statutory protection now required by (a) private and (b) business investors in securities and other property, including investors through unit trusts and open-ended investment companies operating in the UK.
2. To consider the need for statutory control of dealers in securities, investment consultants and investment managers.
3. To advise on the need for new legislation.

The report dealt with the existing system of regulation, both statutory and non-statutory; the changing face of the securities industry; the defects of the existing regulatory system; the relative advantages of self-regulation and Governmental regulation and possible lines of reform including a possible regulatory framework.

Professor Gower proposed as a basis for discussion a new regulatory framework based on a new Securities Act to replace the existing Prevention of Fraud (Investments) Act. All dealers in securities would be registered with the Department of Trade and Industry, who would be empowered to make regulations and to give directions under the Act. Self-regulatory agencies would undertake the day-to-day administration of the regulations and these agencies would be (1) the Stock Exchange, (2) an enlarged Panel on Takeovers, (3) a regulatory body for dealings outside the Stock Exchange, investment advice and investment management, and (4) unit trusts.

The document included *inter alia* the following particular observations.

On insurance:

Something clearly needs to be done to tackle the problems raised by the growing popularity of bonds linked to life policies. The life-cover is generally a negligible element in the investment package—indeed it is often described as being given away with the bond—which is generally sold for a single lump-sum premium and essentially, what are being sold are units in an authorised or unauthorised unit trust. Many new and relatively small 'insurance companies' have sprung up to take advantage of the greater freedom allowed than if the units themselves were being marketed.

On insurance brokers:

Unfortunately the Act (The Insurance Brokers (Registration) Act) is flawed in that it does not prevent anyone from carrying on business as an insurance broker unless he and his business are registered with, and thus subject to the discipline of, The Insurance Brokers' Registration Council; it merely prevents him from describing himself as an insurance broker. Hence, someone describing himself as, say, an insurance consultant or an investment broker, manager or consultant does not need to register. It appears that advantage is being taken of this loophole.

On commodities and financial futures:

The present weakness, as I see it, is that the self-regulation of the Exchanges and the surveillance of the Bank of England are directed towards the efficient running of the markets and the protection of the members in their dealings *inter se* on the Exchanges, and not towards the protection of investors—the ultimate clients on whose behalf they are dealing. Rules banning practices unfair or detrimental to the latter are hardly to be found; nor are compensation provisions for their protection.

On pension funds:

To most people the investment made by or for them in a pension fund is, apart from their home, the only substantial investment that they will have. That being so, one would have expected that it would be subject to strict regulation and that steps would be taken to ensure that beneficiaries had detailed information about it and an effective say in its operation. Such however is not the case. Of all investments it is, perhaps, the least regulated. There is no specific statutory regime for pension funds; they depend simply on the law of trusts. . . . Insofar as any form of official authorisation is required of pension schemes, it consists only of the need to obtain approval by the Inland Revenue if they are to benefit from certain tax concessions and to satisfy the Occupational Pension Board that its requirements are met if they are to be contracted-out of the State scheme. Neither scrutiny is directed primarily towards the protection of beneficiaries.

General:

A test of competence seems to me to be particularly needed in the field in which, at present, it is most conspicuously lacking—investment management and advice. More investors, I suspect, have suffered from the incompetence of their advisors, than their dishonesty ... I would have thought that the ability to read and write and, indeed, something considerably more, is needed and should be demonstrated.

The nature of the securities industry has changed and is still changing. The major tendencies are a movement from direct to indirect investment, distortions resulting from tax considerations and from different methods of remuneration, the growth of investment management and advice, the internationalisation of investment, the establishment of multi-purpose firms and multi-national groups providing a range of financial services, and increasing influence of EEC regulations.

The perceived defects of the present system are complication, uncertainty, irrationality, failure to treat like alike, inflexibility, excessive control in some areas and too little (or none) in others, the creation of an elite and a fringe, lax enforcement, delays, over-concentration on honesty rather than competence, undue diversity of regulations and regulators, and failure overall to achieve a proper balance between Governmental regulation and self-regulation.

The final version of Professor Gower's Report was published in January, 1984. To some extent his recommendations departed from the original proposals in the discussion document and, in particular, his original proposals for four regulatory agencies had been the subject of criticism in the City. The final report contains a number of major recommendations, the main one of which is a proposal for an Investor Protection Act to set up a network of self-regulatory agencies, supervised by the Department of Trade and Industry. It would be a criminal offence to carry on investment business unless registered either with one of the self-regulatory agencies or direct with the Department. There were further proposals for the Council for the Securities Industry to have a wider role, partly as co-ordinator of the self-regulatory agencies and partly for the purpose of approving all issues of securities other than those on the Stock Exchange. Other recommendations related to the power to approve the marketing of insurance contracts offered by companies outside the EEC, the permitting of 'cold calling' the sale of authorized unit trusts as well as for life policies, power for the Secretary of State to set maximum commissions for insurance intermediaries and various other recommendations concerning the method of trial, the level of fines and closer cooperation between the regulatory and prosecuting authorities in the event of breach of the regulations.

In January 1985, the Government issued a White Paper proposing the creation of two regulatory bodies, viz. a 'securities and investments board' and a 'marketing of investments board' to provide investor protection for the securities industry. SEE *Investor Protection*

GRADUATED PENSION A form of State pension which operated under the Graduated Pension Scheme between April, 1961 and April, 1975. The scheme was similar in part to the earnings-related pension (q.v.) in that higher contributions were paid on higher levels of earnings which, in turn, resulted in a higher pension entitlement. Thus, certain persons are entitled on retirement to this graduated pension in addition to the basic pension and additional pension payable under the State schemes (SEE *Pensions*). During the years the scheme operated, it applied only to employed persons earning over £9 per week. The amount of graduated pension received on retirement will depend on the level of graduated contributions paid during those years.

GRANNY BONDS SEE *Index-Linked Savings Certificates*

GRANT OF LETTERS OF ADMINISTRATION SEE *Administrator; Letters of Administration*

GRANT OF PROBATE SEE *Executor, Probate*

GREEN POUND The unit of account for the Common Agricultural Policy (q.v.) of the European Economic Community.

GRESHAM'S LAW 'Bad money drives out good.' Where new coins and old worn coins are current at the same time, the new coins gradually disappear and leave the old worn ones in circulation. The first person who discovered and explained the cause of the disappearance of good coins from circulation was Sir Thomas Gresham in the sixteenth century. The principle (now called Gresham's Law) which he stated is

If coins of the same metal, but of varying weight and quality, circulate together at the same nominal value, the worse coins will tend to drive the better from circulation, but the better will never drive out the worse.

The practice of picking out the gold coins of full weight and leaving the light ones in circulation (called garbling the coinage) was carried on principally by goldsmiths or other persons who melted the coins for jewellery, or exported them and sold them by weight. In the ordinary course of business, very little attention was paid to a coin, so long as the stamp upon it was visible, whether it was a light one or not. SEE *Coinage*

GROSS Apart from its numerical sense of 12 dozen (from the French *grosse*), the word has a varied and rather imprecise usage. For example, gross profit will normally mean profit before deduction of expenses; gross takings would normally mean total turnover, i.e. before deduction of the costs of the goods sold; gross pay normally means wages or salary before deduction of tax, social security and other stoppages; and gross dividend usually means the amount of a dividend before the deduction of tax.

It is in this last sense that the word probably has its widest financial usage. Thus it is usual to speak of gross income, gross interest etc., meaning the amount payable before tax is deducted. SEE *Gross Fund*

GROSS DOMESTIC PRODUCT (GDP) The total value of goods and services produced within a particular country. It differs from Gross National Product (GNP) in that the latter includes earnings from overseas. In calculating the GDP, there is a considerable volume of economic activity which goes unrecorded, e.g. the contribution of housewives and do-it-yourself enthusiasts. Also, the market value of goods and services in any particular year is confused by Government subsidies which find their way into the system and indirect taxes, notably VAT, imposed by the Government.

The following table shows the level of the GDP in the UK over the 10 years to 1984. The second column, GDP at Factor Cost, is adjusted to allow for subsidies, VAT and goods imported from overseas.

	Gross domestic product at market prices (£ million)	Gross domestic product at factor costs (£ million)
1975	104,413	93,954
1976	124,330	111,245
1977	143,064	126,111
1978	164,034	144,442
1979	190,440	064,385
1980	230,010	199,136
1981	253,759	217,578
1982	276,969	235,501
1983	300,812	257,181
1984	318,386	272,577

Source: Central Statistical Office.

GROSS FUND A term applied to charities and pension funds and any other funds which are exempt from UK tax, particularly income tax and capital gains tax. Because of the absence of taxation, it is usually a matter of no great consequence to a gross fund, whether its investment portfolio is enhanced by way of income or capital gains. In the case of charities, however, the distinction is sometimes still of importance, either because of some provision in the constitution, or as a matter of their own housekeeping.

GROUND RENTS Rents which are reserved to the owner of a freehold and which are payable by the person to whom the land has been leased. For example, if the owner of freehold land leases a portion to a person, called the lessee or leaseholder, he stipulates that he must receive, during the continuance of the lease (usually a term of 99 years), a certain yearly rent, that is, a ground rent. In the case of a building lease, the lessee is obliged to build upon the land, and as he erects houses he sub-leases them to other parties, who in their turn pay ground rents to him. If the lessee pays a ground rent to the freeholder or lessor, of, say, £100 a year, and the lessee builds houses and sub-leases, say, 20 houses at a ground rent of £10 each per annum, the lessee thus obtains £200 a year and, after paying the freeholder the £100, he has a profit left of £100 a year; this profit is termed the improved ground rent. At the termination of a lease, the buildings become the property of the lessor.

When ground rents are purchased, the purchaser usually acquires the rights of the freeholder, that is, the right to receive the ground rents during the continuance of the original lease and at the end of the lease to take possession of the land with the buildings thereon. As the end of the lease approaches, his investment will naturally increase much in value. An investment in such ground rents is therefore an increasing one year by year, but in the case of an investment in improved ground rents it is just the opposite, for the purchaser's rights to receive the rents continue only during the unexpired period of the lease. The value of his investment will accordingly depreciate in value year by year, and at the same time he will be required to pay the full ground rent to the owner of the freehold. The position of the owner of ground rents is a safe one, for the buildings on the land are an assurance that the rent will be punctually paid, and at the end of the lease he will, in an ordinary case, be able to let the property for more than the ground rent. If, during the continuance of the lease, the lessee failed to pay the ground rent, the lessor would have the right to re-enter into possession of the land with the buildings attached. If, however, ground rents alone are purchased, that is, *without* the rights to the freehold, then this investment will be a depreciating one and will become extinct at the termination of the lease.

Where ground rents are offered as a security, the banker should ascertain what buildings there are upon the land, otherwise he might find himself in possession of security with insufficient or even without any buildings to secure the rents. If he decides to accept them, he should have the counterpart leases deposited with or charged to him. SEE *Leasehold Reform Act 1967*

GUARANTEE From the French *garantir*, to warrant. A guarantee is an undertaking by one person (called the guarantor) given to another, usually a banker (the creditor), to be answerable for the debt of a third person (the debtor) to the creditor, upon default of the debtor.

In *Halsbury*, a guarantee is defined as

> an accessory contract whereby the promisor undertakes to be answerable to the promisee for the debt, default or miscarriage of another person whose primary liability to the promisee must exist or be contemplated.

A depositor of security to secure another's account is a guarantor or surety (q.v.) (*Re Conley* [1937] 4 All ER 438).

In order to be enforceable at law, a guarantee must be in writing. By the Statute of Frauds 1677 (29 Car II c 3), Section 4, it is enacted that

> No action shall be brought whereby to charge the defendant upon any special promise to answer for the debt, default or miscarriage of another person, unless the agreement upon which such action shall be brought, or some memorandum or note thereof shall be in writing and signed by the party to be charged therewith, or some other person thereunto by him lawfully authorised.

According to Lord Justice Farwell, in *Wauthier* v *Wilson* (1912) 28 TLR 239, 'There can be no surety without a principal.'

To be legally effective, a guarantee must be given for a debt which is enforceable. If the debt is not enforceable, the guarantee will not be enforceable. Thus, a guarantee to secure an account opened under an impersonal heading, such as 'Blackwall Parish Hall' is legally invalid, as a parish hall cannot, of course, be sued for a debt (SEE *Societies*). Likewise, a minor not being answerable for a debt he incurs, a guarantee for such debts is likewise void (*Coutts & Co* v *Brown Lecky and Others* [1946] 2 All ER 207).

Banks now normally include an indemnity clause in their forms of guarantee providing that where the debtor is under a legal disability, such as minority etc., the surety shall be liable as principal.

A guarantee is a very convenient form of security but it is one which the guarantor never expects to have to honour, and because of the ease with which it can be given, a banker should be careful to make it clear to a proposed surety the nature of the document which he has to sign, even though normally such a party cannot later plead ignorance of the contents of the guarantee.

It used to be the practice, when a woman gave a guarantee, to ensure that she was separately advised by a solicitor, so that she could not later plead that she had not understood the nature of the transaction. This often caused indignation in women obviously well capable of understanding business documents, and the Sex Discrimination Act 1975 merely reinforced a tendency already well-developed to leave to the discretion of managers the decision as to whether separate advice was necessary. Banks now seek to ensure that guarantors of either sex are separately advised where there is any doubt as to their understanding.

The point is of particular importance when a married woman guarantees the account of her husband, or of a business in which he is financially interested, when there is always a possibility that she may later seek to avoid liability with the plea that she acted under the influence of her husband. The 1975 Act does not in any way touch the continuing relevance of the decision in *Bank of Montreal* v *Stuart and Another* (1910) 103 LT 641.

In *Bank of Montreal* v *Stuart and Another*, a wife gave a guarantee to a bank in order to help her husband and a company in which he was interested and which was in pecuniary difficulties. She alleged that she acted of her own free will, without any pressure having been put upon her, but it appeared that she acted in passive obedience to her husband's directions and would have signed anything that he asked her to sign and had no means of forming an independent judgment even if she had desired to do so. It was held that the transaction could not stand. Lord Macnaghten said

> In the case of husband and wife the burden of proving undue influence lies upon those who allege it. It is difficult to determine in any case the point at which the influence of one mind upon another amounts to undue influence. It is especially so in the case of husband and wife. . . . It may well be argued that where there is evidence of overpowering influence and the transaction brought about is immoderate and irrational, as it was in the present case, proof of undue influence is complete.

In an ordinary case a banker is not obliged to give information, voluntarily, to a proposed surety, regarding the debtor's affairs. 'Unless questions are particularly put by the surety to gain this information, I hold that it is quite unnecessary for the creditor, to whom the suretyship is given, to make any such disclosure.' (Lord Campbell, in *Hamilton* v *Watson* (1845) 12 Cl & Fin 109.)

In *Royal Bank of Scotland* v *Greenshields* [1914] SC 259, it was held that

> The only circumstance in which a duty to disclose would emerge, and a failure to disclose would be fatal to the bank's case, would be where a customer put a question, or made an observation in the hearing of the bank agent, which would inevitably lead anyone to the conclusion that the intending guarantor was labouring under a misapprehension as to the state of the customer's indebtedness.

In *National Provincial Bank of England* v *Glanusk* [1913] 109 LT 103, the defendant guaranteed all moneys which might be due to the plaintiffs on any accounts whatever from one Coles, who was defendant's agent. The plaintiff's manager became aware that Coles was paying a debt due from him to another bank by an overdraft on the plaintiffs. He did not communicate this fact to the defendant, and it was contended that the latter was discharged from liability under the guarantee by reason of the failure of the plaintiffs to inform him of the above fact which might have indicated to him that his agent was behaving improperly towards him. It was held that there was no duty upon the plaintiffs to communicate to the defendant their suspicion that Coles was not acting properly towards him and consequently that the failure to make such communication did not discharge the defendant from liability under the guarantee.

In *Cooper* v *National Provincial Bank Ltd* [1945] 2 All ER 641, a guarantor sought to repudiate his liability on the grounds that the bank did not disclose to him that the husband of the principal debtor was an undischarged bankrupt, that he had power to sign on his wife's account, and that the account had been conducted irregularly. It was held that these were not such unusual features as to warrant voluntary disclosure by the bank, particularly as the husband was not using the account as a cloak for his own business activities.

If a guarantor inquires as to the extent of his liability upon the account for which he is surety, he is entitled to the information, but a banker should not exhibit the debtor's account to a surety or give details regarding it. If the debt to the bank is in excess of the amount of the guarantee, the guarantor should be told only that his guarantee is fully relied upon.

In the case of *O'Hara* v *Allied Irish Banks* (1984) *Times*, 7th February, it was held that where a bank seeks to take a guarantee from a prospective guarantor who is not that bank's customer, there is no duty of care on the bank to explain to the guarantor the legal effect and possible consequences of the guarantee.

In estimating the value of anyone as a surety the point is, as George Rae put it in *The Country Banker*:

> Not what you might be able to squeeze out of him by process of exhaustion, but what he could at any time pay, over and above his other engagements, without serious inconvenience or detriment to himself. That is the true meaning of his fitness as a surety; and if you take him for more than this, you may do him a fatal disservice, and possibly lay the foundation of a bad debt for yourselves.

A guarantee may take the form of a bond or a guarantee under seal. The usual form, however, is a guarantee under hand.

It is essential that a guarantee form should be most carefully drawn so as to create an effective security, and bankers have their own printed forms of guarantees drafted so as to meet, as far as possible, the various requirements of a good and complete guarantee.

The surety's signature should, as a rule, be witnessed by a bank official, and some bankers require it to be witnessed by two officials. Where the surety lives in another town, the document should be sent to a bank in that town and the surety be requested to call there to sign it.

The form of guarantee should never be entrusted to the principal debtor so that he may obtain the signature of the surety. (See the case of *Carlisle and Cumberland Bank* v *Bragg*, 1911, under *Signature*.)

The position of the banker is slightly improved if the guarantor has been negligent, as a result of the decision of *Saunders* v *The Anglia Building Society* [1970] 3 All ER 961. SEE ALSO UNDER *Signature*

If there are any alterations in the document, they should be initialled by the guarantor; and if the guarantee being given is in addition to one already signed by him for the same account, a clause should be added at the end of the guarantee, if not already contained therein, to the effect that 'this guarantee is in addition to and not in substitution of my guarantee dated . . . for £ . . . .,' and the clause should be signed by the guarantor, but no alteration in the bank's standard form of guarantee (or indeed of any other standard form) should be made without legal advice.

Where there are more guarantors than one, the guarantee should be 'joint and several'. The banker can then sue one, or all, of the guarantors as he may consider necessary. If he sues one surety and fails to obtain all that is required, he may then sue the others. This could not be done if the guarantee was 'joint' only. In a 'joint' guarantee, all the sureties must be sued together, and if one of them died his estate would not be liable. The banker in that case would have to look to the surviving guarantors; but if the guarantee is 'joint and several' the estate of a deceased surety would be liable. In a 'several' guarantee each one of the guarantors may be sued separately for the full amount. The most satisfactory guarantee for a banker to take is, therefore, a 'joint and several' one.

Consideration is not necessary in guarantee under seal, but in a guarantee under hand, i.e. a simple contract, there must be consideration. The consideration, as a general rule, is the granting of an advance to a customer against the guarantee, or it may be the granting of further time to a debtor. A banker's guarantee usually states the consideration, but the document is not invalid merely by reason that the consideration is not expressed therein. (Mercantile Law Amendment Act 1856, Section 3.) In a guarantee simply for a past debt, there would be no legal consideration, but that point is covered in the usual form of banker's guarantee, e.g. 'In consideration of the bank allowing . . . to keep or to continue an account with them or otherwise granting him banking facilities or accommodation upon the terms that the bank should be secured as hereinafter appears, I hereby guarantee, etc.'

The term 'banking facilities' customarily used in bank guarantee forms is sufficiently wide to include foreign exchange transactions. (*Bank of India* v *Trans Continental Commodity Merchants Ltd and Patel* [1983] 2 Lloyd's Rep 298.)

An important point in connection with a guarantee is that it should be a continuing guarantee, that is, a security which will continue, although the balance of the debtor's account may fluctuate from time to time. A guarantee should therefore expressly state that it 'shall be a continuing guarantee', otherwise it might be held to cover merely the debt which existed at the time the guarantee was given.

Upon the expiration of notice from a surety to determine his guarantee, the debtor's account or accounts should be broken, and the banker should communicate at once with his customer. Unless the account is broken all payments to credit will go to release the surety, and all debits will form a fresh unsecured advance. The customer's written consent to the opening of the new account should, if possible, be obtained.

But where a guarantee contained the following clause

> In the event of this guarantee being determined either by notice by me or my legal personal representatives, or by demand in writing by the bank, it shall be lawful for the bank to continue the account with the principal, notwithstanding such determination, and the liability of myself or my estate for the amount due from the principal at the date when the guarantee is so determined, shall remain, notwithstanding any subsequent payment into or out of the account by or on behalf of the principal.

it was held that the operation of the rule in *Clayton's* case was avoided notwithstanding that the account was not broken on determination of the guarantee and subsequent credits to the account were sufficient to extinguish the overdraft existing at the time of determination (*Westminster Bank Ltd* v *Cond* (1940) 46 Com Cas 60).

Where a guarantee contained the words 'to continue in force until three months after notice', it was held that notice to the bank of the death of the guarantor amounted to a determination of the guarantee so far as future advances were concerned. But some guarantee forms provide for three months' notice by the personal representatives of the deceased guarantor. In such a case the executors should be immediately advised of the existence of the liability and the terms of its determination.

If there is no question of notice arising, when the surety informs the banker that he withdraws from any further liability under his guarantee, it will be at the banker's own risk if he pays any further cheques after receipt of such notice; but if he has promised the debtor to pay certain specific cheques, those cheques must be paid. The banker should see his customer at once as to the withdrawal of the guarantee. Some guarantees expressly state that the guarantee shall continue

> until you shall receive notice in writing from me withdrawing the same, provided that the receipt of such notice shall not affect my liability hereunder in respect of any moneys that may then be due to you from the debtor, or subsequent interest thereon, nor in respect of any bills, notes, drafts, cheques or other instruments which may then be outstanding, or any transaction which may then be pending.

The limitation in a guarantee should always be in respect of the liability and not the agreed amount of the loan. Otherwise if the debt is allowed to exceed the specified amount, it might be contended that the guarantee was void. More important is the effect of limitation of the liability and not of the agreed advance as regards the debtor's bankruptcy, for it will give the creditor the right to prove on the debtor's estate for the whole debt and to use the sum paid by the surety for any deficiency; the creditor is not bound to deduct the amount paid under the guarantee before proving, and the guarantor cannot prove unless he pays, not the amount mentioned or the limit of his liability, but the entire debt.

In the case of *In Re Sass, ex parte National Provincial Bank of England* [1896] 2 QB 12, a surety guaranteed the payment of all sums of money which were or might from time to time become due or owing to the bank on the account of S and the guarantee was limited to the amount of £300. The guarantee gave the bank the right to receive dividends from the debtor's estate. On the bankruptcy of S the bank, after receiving the £300 from the surety, claimed to prove on the estate for the full amount due. It was held by Vaughan Williams, J, that although the surety's liability was limited, still 'his suretyship was in respect of the whole debt, and he, having paid only a part of that debt, has in my judgment no right of proof in preference or priority to the bank to whom he became guarantor'.

Under a banker's ordinary guarantee form, the banker can prove upon his customer's estate for the full amount of the debt (allowing for any securities held from the debtor himself) and require payment in full, if necessary, from the guarantor of the amount of his guarantee, but he cannot receive more than the total of his indebtedness.

Upon default of a debtor, a banker should require immediate payment by a surety of the amount of his guarantee. If payment by the guarantor does not clear the indebtedness, the amount should be placed to a separate account, and not go directly in reduction of the debtor's account, if the banker intends to claim upon the debtor's estate. In such a case, the guarantee should not be cancelled, nor an absolute discharge given to the guarantor. If the sum tendered by the guarantor is sufficient to clear off the debt, the amount is usually placed at once to credit of the debtor's account. Many guarantees specifically empower the banker to place any such moneys to a separate or suspense account.

When one of, say, two guarantors pays a part of the amount of the guarantee, the guarantors are released to the extent of the amount paid, but the banker can sue either or both the guarantors for the balance of the guarantee.

If after all dividends have been received from the bankrupt's estate, the guarantee money in the banker's hands should be more than sufficient to pay off the indebtedness, the balance remaining should be returned to the surety, or, if several sureties, to each one in proportion to the amount he paid.

When a banker has demanded payment from a surety, no further cheques should be debited to the debtor's account, unless notice was given to the surety, when the demand was made, of the existence of further claims by the bank upon the debtor.

Upon receiving notice of the death of a surety, the debtor's account or accounts should be stopped pending fresh arrangements, unless the guarantee expressly provides that the estate of the deceased surety is to continue liable.

Where there are several sureties and one of them dies, the account should be broken, until a fresh guarantee is signed or the surviving sureties have given a written request that the existing guarantee be continued.

If a deceased surety's estate is to be held liable, notice of the guarantee should be given to the legal representatives.

The mental illness of a guarantor operates in the same way as the death of a guarantor. In *Bradford Old Bank* v *Sutcliffe* (1918) 34 TLR 299, where it was argued for the plaintiffs that, as this was a continuing guarantee with a clause giving the guarantors, their executors and administrators, power to terminate it by three months' notice, it did not determine, but continued to be operative after the mental illness of the guarantor, it was held that

> this is wrong; the notice clause has nothing to do with lunacy. So far as lunacy is concerned, the guarantee makes no provision for that event; it was neither contemplated nor provided for in the document. The bank, when it had received notice of the lunacy, could no longer makes advances upon the faith of the guarantee. Lunacy operated upon this guarantee just as death operates upon a continuing guarantee, and it contains no provision requiring a notice to terminate it. The creditor then knows that the guarantor has no longer a contracting mind, and consequently cannot be fixed with a contractual liability by an act done by the creditor alone.

When a surety has paid off the full amount of the debt on the account for which he is guarantor, he is entitled to the rights of the banker, that is to sue the debtor and to receive the benefit of any securities held by the banker for the debt, whether the securities were held at the time the guarantee was given, or were subsequently received.

By the Mercantile Law Amendment Act 1856, Section 5,

> Every person who, being surety for the debt or duty of another, or being liable with another for any debt or duty, shall pay such debt or perform such duty, shall be entitled to have assigned to him, or to a trustee for him,

every judgment, specialty, or other security which shall be held by the creditor in respect of such debt, or duty, whether such judgment, specialty, or other security, shall or shall not be deemed at law to have been satisfied by the payment of the debt or performance of the duty, and such person shall be entitled to stand in the place of the creditor, and to use all the remedies, and, if need be, and upon a proper indemnity, to use the name of the creditor, in any action, or other proceeding, at law or in equity, in order to obtain from the principal debtor, or any co-surety, co-contractor, or co-debtor, as the case may be, indemnification for the advances made and loss sustained by the person who shall have so paid such debt or performed such duty, and such payment or performance so made by such surety shall not be pleadable in bar of any such action or other proceedings by him: provided always that no co-surety, co-contractor, or co-debtor, shall be entitled to recover from any other co-surety, co-contractor, or co-debtor, by the means aforesaid, more than the just proportion to which, as between those parties themselves, such last-mentioned person shall be justly liable. [SEE *Subrogation*]

When a surety pays off an account and requires any securities to be given up to him, the banker should, before parting with them, communicate with the debtor or any other parties concerned with the account. A surety is not entitled to any of the debtor's securities held for the account unless the whole debt is paid off, and this is provided for in the usual banker's guarantee form.

Where a guarantor has discharged his liability under a guarantee, a banker is frequently asked to supply a certificate stating that included in the payment was a certain sum for interest, the object being that the guarantor may claim repayment of income tax on the interest debited to the account. In *Commissioners of Inland Revenue* v *Holder* (*Times*, 12th March, 1931), where a guarantor paid off his liability to a bank and claimed repayment of the income tax on the interest debited to the account, the Master of the Rolls held that the interest debited to the overdrawn account each year had, in fact, been capitalized with the approval of the principal debtor, and that the sum paid by the guarantor was capital and not capital plus interest. A letter to be given to the Inspector of Taxes outlining the facts and leaving the decision to him would appear to be unobjectionable.

If, under a joint and several guarantee, a banker obtains payment of the full amount of the guarantee from one of the sureties, that surety can call upon his co-sureties to pay him their proportion of the amount. Unless specially provided against in the guarantee, if a banker releases one of several joint co-sureties that release may have the effect of releasing all the sureties. Before releasing one of several sureties a banker should, unless the guarantee provides for such a release, obtain the written assent of the other sureties, or take a fresh guarantee.

When a surety gives notice to terminate a guarantee, the banker should, if possible, obtain the notice in writing. If the surety subsequently withdraws his notice, a fresh guarantee should be signed.

A guarantee under hand is barred by the Limitation Act 1939, six years from the date when the right of action first accrued against the guarantor. In *Bradford Old Bank* v *Sutcliffe* [1918] 2 KB 833, where in a guarantee there was an undertaking to pay 'on demand', it was held that there was no cause of action till after the demand. Pickford, LJ, in the course of his judgment, said that in the case of what has been called a direct liability, for example a promissory note payable on demand, the liability exists as soon as the loan is made, and the words 'on demand' may be neglected.

It has, however, been held long ago that this doctrine does not apply to what has been called a collateral promise or collateral debt, and I think that a promise by a surety to pay the original debt is such a collateral promise or creates a collateral debt.

Where the guarantee does not expressly stipulate that demand shall precede payment by the guarantor, see the case *Parr's Banking Company* v *Yates* below.

If there is a clause in the guarantee that payment is to be made a stated number of days 'after demand', the statute in such a case will not begin to run until the demand has been made. It is advisable to get all guarantees under hand renewed before they are six years old, as it brings to the notice of the surety the fact that his liability still continues, and avoids any danger there may be of the operation of the Limitation Act 1939.

A guarantee under seal is not barred till twelve years from the date when the cause of action arose. And if the guarantee is in respect of a debt secured by a mortgage of land, the period is twelve years by the Real Property Limitation Act of 1874, whether the covenant of the surety is in the mortgage deed itself, or is contained in a collateral bond. Payments to the credit of an account by a debtor keep the debt alive as against the debtor, but they do not prevent the statute from running in favour of a surety. SEE *Limitation Act 1939*

When a surety guarantees the general balance of the customer's account, in order to ascertain that balance, all accounts between the customer and the banker at the time the guarantee comes to an end must be taken into account. (*In Re Sherry, London and County Banking Co* v *Terry* (1884) 25 ChD 692.) In such cases all the customer's accounts should be broken, including any account with a credit balance.

A guarantee for the general balance of all the accounts of a customer is to be distinguished from a guarantee for an advance on a specific account only. In the latter case, on the determination of the guarantee, the surety would be liable only for the balance of that specified account. When an account is broken, upon the determination of a guarantee, and a new and distinct account is opened for future receipts and payments, any credit balance on this new account does not go to release the surety's liability on the old account, and any overdraft on the new account is not covered by the old guarantee. As to the position when the account is not broken, see the case of *Bradford Old Bank* v *Sutcliffe* under *Clayton's Case*.

Upon the failure of a guarantor, unless the debtor supplies other security, the banker should call in his advance and, if repayment is not made, claim upon the surety's estate. The debtor's account should be broken on receipt of the notice.

Where there are several sureties and one of them dies, or becomes bankrupt, or gives notice to terminate his liability, the account of the debtor should be broken until fresh arrangements are made.

Any material variation of the original agreement between the debtor and creditor, unless provided for in the guarantee or made with the assent of the guarantor, will have the effect of releasing the guarantor from liability. In *Samuel* v *Howarth* (1817) 3 Mer 272, Lord Eldon said

> The surety is held to be discharged for this reason, because the creditor, by so giving time to the principal, has put it out of the power of the surety to consider whether he will have recourse to his remedy against the principal or not, and because he, in fact, cannot have the same remedy against the principal as he would have had under the original contract.

Where a guarantee has been given for a fixed period and at the end of that period it is arranged that it be continued for a further period, either a new guarantee should be taken or the old guarantee should be indorsed accordingly. Any such indorsement should, of course, be signed by the guarantor, or, if more than one, by all of them. If a new guarantee has not been obtained, or the old one extended, before the fixed period expires, the account should be stopped when the date arrives until a fresh arrangement is made.

In the case of a guarantee by a partnership, it should, in order to avoid the risk of any future uncertainty, be signed by each partner.

Where a change of partnership takes place and a guarantee is held for the account, unless the form provides for such change, the account should be broken until fresh arrangements are made. Even if the guarantee contains such provision, it is necessary to break the account if the banker intends to claim on the estate of the partner who has died, or retired, or become bankrupt.

By Section 18 of the Partnership Act 1890:

> A continuing guaranty or cautionary obligation given either to a firm or to a third person in respect of the transactions of a firm is, in the absence of agreement to the contrary, revoked as to future transactions by any change in the constitution of the firm to which, or of the firm in respect of the transactions of which, the guaranty or obligation was given.

Before accepting a guarantee by a company, a banker should see that the memorandum of association gives power to the company to give a guarantee.

In the case of *Yorkshire Wagon Co* v *Maclure* (1882) 19 ChD 478, where the directors had borrowed *ultra vires* and given their personal guarantee, and it was contended that as the transaction was *ultra vires* there was no liability on the guarantee, for where there was no principal there could be no surety, the Court held that the directors were nevertheless liable on their guarantee. In *Garrard* v *James* [1925] WN 99, the Court reaffirmed the judgment in the above case, drawing a distinction between the guarantee of a contract which was merely *ultra vires* the contractor, and one which was illegal as being contrary to public policy or the provisions of a public statute. A guarantee to carry out an illegal contract is not enforceable. The application of the *ultra vires* principle in relation to a general borrowing power (despite the existence of an independent object clause), where the purpose of the borrowing is beyond the objects of the company (established in the case of *National Provincial Bank Ltd* v *Introductions Ltd* SEE UNDER *Company*) is likely to have a similar effect on a general power of a company to give guarantees.

Where, subsequent to the giving of a guarantee by directors, security of the company is taken, the resolution authorizing the charging thereof should be passed in general meeting, unless the articles provide that the directors can vote on contracts in which they are personally interested. For the taking of security will lessen the guarantee liability of the directors, and to this extent they are personally interested (*Victors Ltd (in liquidation)* v *Lingard* [1927] 1 Ch 323).

The majority of articles of association now specifically cover this position and make unnecessary the passing of a resolution by the company in general meeting that would otherwise be required.

Under the Bankruptcy Act 1914, Section 44, and the Companies Act 1948, Section 320, a payment made to a creditor with the dominant motive of giving a surety or guarantor a preference over other creditors shall be void as against the trustee. SEE *Fraudulent Preference*

When a guarantee has been discharged, or is no longer required, it should be retained by the banker after being cancelled by, or in the presence of, the surety. A cancelled guarantee may be given up to the surety if he demands it.

If an account which has been closed be subsequently reopened, any guarantee held for the old account would not be available for the new account.

As soon as a surety's obligation to pay has become absolute, he has a right in equity to be indemnified by his principal. In *Ascherson* v *Tredegar Dry Dock and Wharf Co Ltd* [1909] 2 Ch 401, A and four other directors of a company gave a bank a joint and several guarantee to secure the overdraft on the company's current account. A died, and the bank then stopped the account on which a certain sum was owing and opened a new account. A's executors requested the company to discharge the liability, which was refused. It was held that the guarantors were entitled to be discharged by payment by the company of the sum owing. 'Where there is an actual accrued debt and the surety is liable and admits liability for the amount guaranteed, he has a right to compel the principal debtor to relieve him from his liability by paying off the debt.'

In the case of *Thomas* v *Notts Incorporated Football Club Ltd* [1972] 1 All ER 1176, it was held that a guarantor of a frozen debt could obtain a directive from the court for repayment of the debt in order that he be released.

Each of the above quoted cases, where the amount payable under the guarantee was definitely ascertained, is to be distinguished from the following case where the amount had not been ascertained. In *Morrison* v *Barking Chemicals Co Ltd* [1919] 122 LT 423, M gave a guarantee to a bank to secure an account current of the defendant company, and M sought to compel the company to give him relief from his liability to the bank under the guarantee. Sargant, J, in his judgment said that the guarantee was to continue until terminated on the initiative either of the bank or of the surety. The bank could close the account, ascertain the amount due and make demand on the surety. The surety could, by the terms of the guarantee, cause his liability to be definitely ascertained by giving the bank three months' notice to determine the guarantee.

> If and when this is done there will be an immediate enforceable liability on the part of the surety of the bank, and he will then be within the decision of *Ascherson* v *Tredegar Dry Dock and Wharf Co Ltd*. [See above.] There is no accrued or definite liability on the part of the surety until there has been some such termination or ascertainment as stated.

It was held that as neither of those steps had been taken M had no immediate right to compel the defendant company to relieve him from his liability.

GUARANTEED INCOME BONDS SEE *Income Bonds*

GUARANTEED STOCK Stock upon which the due payment of the interest is guaranteed either by the company issuing the stock or by another company or by a government. Sometimes payment of the principal also is guaranteed.

GUARANTOR A surety. A person who gives a guarantee to a banker (or other creditor), agreeing to be answerable for the debt of another person if he defaults. SEE *Guarantee*

GUARDIAN'S ALLOWANCE A person who provides a home for an orphan is entitled to receive a guardian's allowance in addition to child benefit (q.v.). As with child benefit, the guardian's allowance should normally be claimed by the wife if the child is being cared for by a married couple and, in general, the rules governing payment follow those for child benefit.

For guardian's allowance to be payable, the child must have been orphaned for one of the following reasons:

1. The death of both parents.
2. The death of one of divorced parents where the other parent did not have custody of the child, was not maintaining the child, and was not liable for maintenance under a court order.
3. One parent is dead and the other missing after genuine attempts to trace him or her.
4. One parent is dead and the other is in prison for a period of five years or more. (The allowance stops when the parent comes out of prison.)
5. The mother of an illegitimate child is dead and the father is unknown.

The guardian's allowance is not payable in the case of legal adoption because the adoptive parents are then treated as the parents of the child. The payment is tax-free and not means-tested.

No contribution record is necessary on the part of the person or persons caring for the child, but

1. one of the child's parents must have been born in the UK, or
2. one of the parents must have been in the UK for a total of 52 weeks in any period of two years since they were 16 years of age, or
3. the parent whose death gives rise to the claim must have died before 6th April, 1975, and been insured under the national insurance scheme (See Appendix 2).

GUINEA A gold coin at one time current in Great Britain at the value of 21 shillings. It was first coined in 1663 from gold brought from the coast of Guinea, whence its name. It was the custom in certain trades and professions to quote fees in guineas rather than in pounds but decimalization and VAT discouraged this practice.

H

HALF-CROWN Half-crowns were first coined in 1551. The standard weight of a half-crown was 218.18181 grains troy, and its standard fineness thirty-seven-fortieths fine silver, three fortieths alloy; altered by the Coinage Act 1920 to one-half fine silver, one-half alloy. By the Coinage Act 1946, these coins were made of cupro-nickel. They were demonetized from 1st January, 1970. SEE *Coinage*

HALFPENNY The old halfpenny was made of bronze—that is, a mixture of copper, tin and zinc. Its standard weight was 87.50000 grains troy and the diameter was exactly one inch. It was withdrawn from circulation in August, 1969.

The new halfpenny, which entered circulation on 15th February, 1971, had a standard weight of 1.78200 grams, a diameter of 1.7145 cm and was also made of bronze. The Royal Mint issued its last halfpenny on 29th March, 1984 and the halfpenny was withdrawn from circulation in October of that year. SEE *Coinage* and *Decimal Coinage*

HALF-SOVEREIGN Its standard weight is 61.63723 grains troy and its standard fineness eleven-twelfths fine gold, one-twelfth alloy. When its weight, from wear and tear, fell below 61.125 grains troy it ceased to be legal tender (SEE *Coinage*). In October, 1980, the Royal Mint announced a limited issue of 10,000 sets of gold coins, including half-sovereigns. These were the first sets of that kind to be issued since the coronation of King George VI. At the same time, the Royal Mint announced a limited issue of 100,000 'proof' sovereigns at £65 each.

HALLMARKS The impressed stamps on gold, silver and platinum under the authority of the Goldsmiths' Company and the various assay offices.

Hallmarking is of particular relevance to silver, partly because silver has traditionally been in more common use than gold, and also because of the facility for converting silver articles into coinage. There has always been a close link between silver and coinage, not least because either could be melted down and converted into the other (in the days when coins were silver). In 1238 in the reign of Henry III, it was decreed that the silver content of English silver plate should be the same as that of English silver coin, i.e. 11 oz and 2 pennyweights (dwt) of pure silver in every pound. This became known as the sterling standard, so named because the penny coins then in circulation bore the sign of a small star which became known as a starling, corrupted to sterling.

In 1300, the first hallmarks were introduced to protect the sterling standard and every piece of silver (or gold) had to be stamped with the leopard's head before leaving the smith's workshop. The leopard's head remains the hallmark of the London Assay Office to this day.

In 1363, it was required that in addition to the leopard's head, each piece of silver should bear a distinguishing mark of the particular smith. Those early marks have not survived and the names of silver-makers are not known prior to 1697 when they were all required to re-register their marks with the first two letters of their surname.

The third component of a hallmark is the 'date letter' in use in this country since 1478. There is a cycle of 20 letters laid down by the Goldsmiths' Company (I and J are treated as one letter, so are U and V and X, Y, Z are disregarded). Only the style of the letter distinguishes each 20 year cycle.

The next historical development was the introduction in 1544 of the lion passant guardant as a symbol of sterling standard. This was at first introduced by the Goldsmiths' Company for London, but became in 1719 the standard mark for the whole of England.

The last component of hallmarking was the sovereign's head showing that duty had been paid on the piece of silver bearing the mark. This appears on all silver made between 1st December, 1784 and 30th April, 1890 (with certain minor exceptions).

Thus, a piece of silver made in, say, Birmingham in 1889 would bear (in order of the hallmark):

1. a lion (known as the assay mark),
2. an anchor (the 'mark of origin' for Birmingham),

3. the sovereign's head—in this case Queen Victoria (known as the duty mark),
4. the letter 'q' indicating the year.

From 1696 until 1720, the existing hallmarking system was suspended and a new one introduced. This was because, with the shortage of silver, a number of silversmiths were converting silver coins into silver plate. The New Sterling Act 1697 raised the standard of purity of silver plate from 92.5 per cent (11 oz and 2 dwts) to 95.8 per cent to discourage the conversion of coins into plate. A new hallmarking system was introduced depicting the figure of Britannia and the lion's head 'erased', meaning a serrated neckline. This system of hallmarking was compulsory until 1720 and optional thereafter (and is still permitted). Silver pieces bearing this system of hallmarking are known as Britannia silver.

The assay offices which remain in existence at the present time are Birmingham, Dublin, Edinburgh, London and Sheffield. In the past there were assay offices at Chester, Exeter, Glasgow, Newcastle, Norwich and York, but all these have been closed.

It is illegal in Britain to forge or fake hallmarks, or to sell silver or gold knowing that it bears a false hallmark.

HAMMERED When a member of the Stock Exchange is unable to meet his liabilities, his failure is announced in the 'House' after attention has been obtained by one of the waiters giving three blows on his stand with a wooden hammer. A defaulter is thus said to be 'hammered'.

HANDYCARD The credit card of the Co-operative Bank. SEE *Credit Card*

HEIR The heir or heir-at-law was the person entitled, by law, to the real property of a deceased person who left no will. In ascertaining who was heir, the eldest son and his descendants came first, then the other sons in order and their descendants. If there were no sons, but only daughters, they succeeded to the property as coparceners, that is, they succeeded to it equally. Failing lineal descendants, the nearest lineal ancestor was the heir. Heirship was abolished after 1925. SEE UNDER *Intestacy*

HIGHER-PAID EMPLOYMENT This terminology is a feature of the income tax legislation in the UK and was originally introduced by the Finance Act 1976, Section 60. Originally, it meant 'employment with emoluments at the rate of £5,000 a year or more'. The corresponding figure is now (since 1980–81) £8,500.

The definition is applied for the purpose of taxing under Schedule E those expenses and other fringe benefits paid to higher-paid employees by virtue of their employment. Such an employee is sometimes known as a P11D employee, this being the number of the form used by employers to make a return of employee benefits to the Inland Revenue.

Higher-paid employees are taxed on the same basis as directors of companies, a director for this purpose meaning any director of a company except a director who owns no more than five per cent of the company's capital and works full-time in the company.

In general terms, directors and higher-paid employees are taxed on all benefits, whether in cash or in kind, which they receive from their employment (subject to certain minor exceptions). Lower-paid employees are not taxed on certain benefits, notably the free use of a motor car, interest-free loans and private medical cover. SEE *Income Tax*

HIGHER-RATE INCOME TAX This is part of the unified system of taxation which was introduced by Section 38, Finance Act 1971, and came into force on 6th April, 1973. Under this system, there are two levels of personal taxation on income, namely, income tax and higher-rate income tax, administered entirely by the offices of HM Inspectors of Taxes throughout the country. This replaced the former two-tier system of income tax and surtax, the latter being administered by the Special Commissioners.

For all practical purposes, there is now one graduated system of taxation on personal income. The threshold and rates of higher-rate income tax are varied from time to time and for the fiscal year 1985–86 are as follows.

Band of taxable income £	Rate per cent
16,201–19,200	40
19,201–24,400	45
24,401–32,300	50
32,301–40,200	55
over 40,200	60

SEE ALSO *Income Tax*

HIRE PURCHASE FINANCE This is a particular aspect of instalment credit. It is the provision of finance to be repaid by instalments over a period in accordance with a contractual arrangement. The term hire purchase had its origin in the 'hire and purchase' of goods, principally sewing machines and pianos, which developed in Britain in the 1840s. It seems to have had its roots in the practice which had arisen in both France and the USA, of hiring furniture, perhaps a whole houseful, on a temporary basis. The essence of 'hire and purchase' was that the hirer had the option to purchase the goods at the end of the hiring period. Because the hirer did not have title to the goods, he could not pass a good title, even to a purchaser in good faith, a principle established in the leading case of *Helby* v *Mathews* [1895] AC 471, which set the pattern for hire-purchase contracts through to the present day.

According to the Report of the Crowther Committee on Consumer Credit (q.v.) 'The system of hire purchase has been one of the chief contributory causes of the great rise in the material standard of living of the British people in the last generation.' Hire purchase has traditionally been the largest single category of instalment credit in Britain and is a good example of what the Crowther Report called 'vendor credit', i.e. an arrangement made with the vendor of goods whereby the purchase price is to remain outstanding over a period and repaid on an agreed basis.

There are two broad categories of hire purchase business: consumer hire purchase and industrial hire purchase. The first is the provision of hire purchase credit for private individuals; the latter is hire purchase for businesses. The distinction is somewhat blurred, however, because of the high proportion of private motor cars, approximately 60 per cent, which are purchased for business uses.

Consumer hire purchase is normally a three-cornered affair involving the vendor, the purchaser and a finance house. The finance house may be set up and owned by the manufacturer or supplier of the goods, or it may be one of the independent finance houses. The hire purchase agreement will be between the finance house and the purchaser, although the finance house must rely to a considerable extent on the experience and good sense of the supplier and the quality of his business generally.

Industrial hire purchase had its origin in the hiring of railway wagons during the last century. It was in 1861 that the North Central Wagon Company was formed in Rotherham for the 'purchasing, hiring and manufacturing of railway wagons, etc.' Such was the demand for coal, both for domestic and industrial purposes, in the late nineteenth century that neither the railway companies nor the colliery companies could afford to provide the necessary wagons and a number of wagon companies were formed to manufacture or purchase wagons and hire them to the railway companies and collieries. By 1900 North Central Wagon Company had 25,000 railway wagons on hire to its customers. It is believed to be the oldest hire purchase company in the world and lives on as Lombard North Central, part of the National Westminster Bank Group.

It is believed that industrial hire purchase now accounts for 70 per cent (and in some cases more) of the total business of the finance houses. A company with sufficient taxable profits may be attracted more to hire purchase than to, say, leasing (q.v.). The particular benefits of industrial hire purchase may be summarized as follows.

1. Capital allowances may be obtainable.
2. The company's working capital would not be strained.
3. Budgetting may be facilitated by the fixed and regular nature of the instalments.
4. Individual assets can be seen to earn their keep.
5. Hire purchase contracts generally have the advantage of simplicity and a degree of flexibility.

Nowadays, industrial hire purchase is commonly available for the purchase of all industrial and agricultural equipment, plant and machinery, and business assets generally. As with consumer finance (see above), the equipment is purchased by the finance house and hired to the business customer, to whom ownership passes on payment of the last instalment.

The motor industry is the largest single category of customer among the finance houses. Most of the major car distributors in the UK have an established link with one of the leading finance houses for point-of-sale financing of their cars.

SEE *Consumer Credit Act 1974; Consumer Credit; Crowther Committee on Consumer Credit; Finance Houses Association; Leasing*

HOLDER SEE *Holder of Bill of Exchange*

HOLDER OF BILL OF EXCHANGE The holder of a bill is the person who is in possession of it and may be either the payee, or an indorsee, or the bearer (Bills of Exchange Act 1882, Section 2).

There are three kinds of holder: a simple holder of a bill, a holder for value, and a holder in due course.

If the holder of a bill has not given value for it, he cannot sue any party subsequent to the last indorsement when value was given.

The holder of a bill, unless it is indorsed payable to him, need not indorse it, though, as a rule, any person taking a bill would require the person from whom he takes it to indorse it. The person receiving a bill has the right to demand the indorsement of the transferor if the bill was payable to his order.

If a bill is payable to the holder's order, he must indorse it, whether the transferee demands his indorsement or not, except that by Section 2 of the Cheques Act 1957 (q.v.), a holder is *deemed* to have indorsed a cheque.

Where the holder of a bill payable to bearer (SEE *Bearer*) negotiates it by delivery, without indorsing it, he is called a 'transferor by delivery' (q.v.) and warrants to his immediate transferee that the bill is what it purports to be.

No one can be a holder, holder for value, or holder in due course whose title has to be made through a forged signature.

Any holder may convert a blank indorsement into a special indorsement by writing above the indorser's signature a direction to pay the bill to the order of himself or some other person.

A holder may strike out any indorsement on a bill, and the person whose signature is struck out is thereby released from liability, and so are all subsequent indorsers. A banker usually cancels his indorsement on a dishonoured bill.

If a holder receives payment of a bill from an indorser, the bill must be given up to that indorser, who will then have all the rights of the holder from whom he received it. SEE *Payment for Honour*

The law regarding the indorsement of cheques was changed by the Cheques Act 1957 (q.v.).

A banker is under no liability on a cheque or bill to a holder, unless he has in some way given the holder to understand that the cheque or bill will be paid. SEE *Bill of Exchange; Holder for Value; Holder in Due Course; Transferor by Delivery*

HOLDER IN DUE COURSE The Bills of Exchange Act 1882, Section 29, defines a holder in due course as follows.

> (1) A holder in due course is a holder who has taken a bill, complete and regular on the face of it, under the following conditions, namely—
>
> (*a*) That he became the holder of it before it was overdue, and without notice that it had been previously dishonoured, if such was the fact:
>
> (*b*) That he took the bill in good faith and for value, and that at the time the bill was negotiated to him he had no notice of any defect in the title of the person who negotiated it.
>
> (2) In particular the title of a person who negotiates a bill is defective within the meaning of this Act when he obtained the bill, or the acceptance thereof, by fraud, duress, or force and fear, or other unlawful means, or for an illegal consideration, or when he negotiates it in breach of faith, or under such circumstances as amount to a fraud.
>
> (3) A holder (whether for value or not) who derives his title to a bill through a holder in due course, and who is not himself a party to any fraud or illegality affecting it, has all the rights of that holder in due course as regards the acceptor and all parties to the bill prior to that holder.

A bill does not require acceptance to make it 'complete and regular on the face of it'. (*National Park Bank of New York* v *Berggren & Co* (1914), 110 LT 907.)

The position of the collecting banker having a debit balance but not otherwise having given value for a cheque appears now to be stronger than previously thought. In the case of *Re Keever* [1966] 3 All ER 631, the banker collecting a cheque was held to be a 'holder in due course' merely because there was a debit balance. The debit balance was an 'antecedent debt and therefore "value" for the purpose of the Bills of Exchange Act, Section 27(1)'. The same point was followed in *Barclays Bank* v *Astley* [1970] All ER 85, for one particular cheque. This appears to be good law despite dicta in the House of Lords in the *Zang* case [1966] AC 211.

In *R. E. Jones Ltd* v *Waring & Gillow Ltd* [1926] AC 670, the House of Lords held that the expression 'holder in due course', as defined in Section 29, does not include the original payee of a bill or cheque. Before a person can be a holder in due course, the instrument must have been negotiated to him, and the original delivery of the bill or cheque to the payee is not such a negotiation.

By Section 30

> (1) Every party whose signature appears on a bill is *prima facie* deemed to have become a party thereto for value.
>
> (2) Every holder of a bill is *prima facie* deemed to be a holder in due course; but if in an action on a bill it is admitted or proved that the acceptance, issue, or subsequent negotiation of the bill is affected with fraud, duress, or force and fear, or illegality, the burden of proof is shifted, unless and until the holder proves that, subsequent to the alleged fraud or illegality, value has in good faith been given for the bill.

The meaning of 'good faith' is given in Section 90: 'A thing is deemed to be done in good faith, within the meaning of this Act, where it is in fact done honestly, whether it is done negligently or not.'

If, for example, Jones is the holder in due course, he has the right to sue any party to the bill, but if in an action it is proved that the bill is affected with some taint, as described in the above sections, it will be necessary for Jones, in order to preserve his rights, to show that he gave value for the bill subsequent to the alleged taint, and that he took it in good faith without knowledge of anything being wrong with the bill.

If Jones, the holder in due course, transfers the bill to Brown, but without any value being given therefor, Brown obtains the same rights that Jones had and can sue any party prior to Jones, but he cannot sue Jones because of the absence of consideration.

'No consideration' is a good defence between parties closely related on a bill, but a holder in due course is not affected by the fact of there having been 'no consideration' between any parties before it was transferred to him for value.

Section 38 deals with the rights of a holder:

> The rights and powers of the holder of a bill are as follows—
> (1) He may sue on the bill in his own name:
> (2) Where he is a holder in due course, he holds the bill free from any defect of title of prior parties, as well as from mere personal defences available to prior parties among themselves, and may enforce payment against all parties liable on the bill:
> (3) Where his title is defective (*a*) if he negotiates the bill to a holder in due course, that holder obtains a good and complete title to the bill, and (*b*) if he obtains payment of the bill the person who pays him in due course gets a valid discharge for the bill.

Where a signature on a bill is forged, no one can obtain any right to the bill through or under that signature. SEE *Bill of Exchange; Forgery; Holder for Value*

HOLDER FOR VALUE A holder for value of a bill of exchange is defined by Section 27 of the Bills of Exchange Act 1882:

> (2) Where value has at any time been given for a bill the holder is deemed to be a holder for value as regards the acceptor and all parties to the bill who became parties prior to such time.
> (3) Where the holder of a bill has a lien on it, arising either from contract or by implication of law, he is deemed to be a holder for value to the extent of the sum for which he has a lien.

By Section 30

> (1) Every party whose signature appears on a bill is prima facie deemed to have become a party thereto for value.

A holder for value is not liable upon a bill unless he endorses it, but may sue on the bill in his own name.

The holder for value of a bill may be the payee who is in possession of it, or an indorsee who is in possession of it, or the bearer of it.

A banker who merely collects a cheque is neither a holder for value nor a holder in due course (q.v.). If, however, he cashes a cheque drawn on another banker he may become, like any other party taking a transfer of a fully negotiable instrument, a holder in due course (or have equivalent rights). Some assistance is obtained from the case of *Barclays Bank Ltd* v *Harding* (1962), *Journal of the Institute of Bankers*, April, 1962, in differentiating between a holder for value and a holder in due course. In that case, the banker had paid against uncleared effects, and it appears that, if there has been a specific agreement or a course of dealing that this would be done, then the banker can claim to be a holder in due course. In *Midland Bank Ltd* v *Charles Simpson (Motors) Ltd* (1960), *Journal of the Institute of Bankers*, February, 1961, the banker had advanced to a new customer against a fully negotiable cheque. The cheque was stopped because the car for which it had been given did not belong to the vendor, but the banker was held to be a holder in due course, and recovered the amount that he had advanced. The position would be similar if he had received a cheque specifically in reduction of an overdraft. To make the banker a holder in due course there must be an express or implied agreement between banker and customer when the cheque is handed to the banker. (See *A. L. Underwood* v *Bank of Liverpool and Martins Ltd*; and v *Barclays Bank Ltd* under *Collecting Banker*.)

A banker is a holder for value if, without such pre-existing agreement, he receives a cheque for collection and finds upon its dishonour (not necessarily *because* of its dishonour) that his customer is overdrawn. His right to sue the drawer depends on whether the customer himself gave value; if the banker cannot prove this he may fail in his action against the drawer, in contradistinction to his position if he is a holder in due course. Since the passing of the Cheques Act 1957 (q.v.), by Section 2 of that Act the indorsement which the banker would have needed to show that he was a holder is deemed to have been made, although in fact there is no signature of the customer. This point is mentioned in *Barclays Bank Ltd* v *Harding* (above).

A banker who discounts a bill will be a holder in due course unless he is unable to bring himself within the statutory definition (see below).

Until value is given no party can sue upon a bill. If, for example, no value is given on a bill till it reaches the hands of a third indorser, none of the parties before that third indorser can sue upon the bill, but the third indorser, because he has given value, can sue all the prior parties. If that third indorser transfers to a fourth person, without any value being given, that person cannot sue the third indorser, seeing he did not give value to the third indorser for the bill, but he can sue all the parties to the bill that the third indorser had the right to sue.

The holder of a bill payable to his order must indorse it if he wishes to negotiate it. When the holder of a bill payable to bearer (SEE *Bearer*) negotiates it by delivery, without indorsing it, he is called a 'transferor by delivery' (q.v.) and warrants to his immediate transferee that the bill is what it purports to be.

If the title of a holder for value is defective, as where the bill was obtained by fraud, duress, or force and fear, or for an illegal consideration, he cannot recover the amount from the person defrauded or otherwise. But a holder in due course can sue any party to the bill. No title, however, can be obtained through a forged signature. (The rights of a banker who has given value appear to have been shown to be wider than previously thought as a result of two cases, *Re Keever Ltd* and *Barclays Bank* v *Astley* which see under *Holder in Due Course*). SEE *Bill of Exchange; Cheque; Consideration for Bill of Exchange.*

HOLDING COMPANY The definition of a holding company and a subsidiary company is given in Section 736, Companies Act 1985. For the purpose of the Act, a company is deemed to be the holding company of another company only if that other company is its subsidiary (SEE *Subsidiary Company*). If at the end of a company's financial year it has any subsidiaries, the accounts of those subsidiaries must be laid before the holding company in general meeting when the holding company's own balance sheet and profit and loss accounts are so laid. The 'group' accounts must be consolidated accounts, comprising a consolidated balance sheet dealing with the state of affairs of the company and all the subsidiaries to be dealt with in the group accounts, and a consolidated profit and loss account, dealing with a profit or loss of the company and those subsidiaries.

HOLDING OUT Words or conduct giving rise to the idea that definite relations exist such as those of agency or partnership. It is a special application of the principle of estoppel (q.v.). In the Partnership Act 1890, Section 14, it is enacted that everyone who by words spoken or written, or by conduct represents himself, or who knowingly suffers himself to be represented as a partner in a particular firm, is liable as a partner to anyone who has on the faith of any such representation given credit to the firm. SEE *Partnerships*

HOME BANKING This is the service by which bank customers are enabled to conduct money transfers and other basic banking transactions by means of a combination of a Post Office telephone line and a television set. A Viewdata service was first introduced by the Post Office in 1978 and this was followed in 1980 by the introduction by the Post Office of Prestel which was acclaimed as the world's first public Viewdata service. By means of a keyboard, the viewer could select any 'page' of information on a wide range of subjects and, for example, might book airline tickets, theatre tickets, obtain information on financial services and make retail purchases. The first application of this facility to retail banking in the UK was introduced in 1983 by the Nottingham Building Society and the Bank of Scotland, in cooperation with British Telecom. It became possible for an investor in the building society to obtain from his television screen, details of his account, make transfers of funds between the building society and the Bank of Scotland and to instruct the bank to make normal current account payments. In January 1985, the Bank of Scotland introduced home banking for its own customers. Earlier experiments in home banking had been conducted by Citibank and Chemical Bank in the USA, and by Verbraucher Bank in Germany. Since then, home banking services have been introduced in a number of banks in other countries and, at the time of writing, it seems extremely likely that some degree of home banking will become at least part of the normal banking scene in Britain.

HOME IMPROVEMENT GRANTS These are grants which may be obtained from local authorities, depending on the nature of the improvement and the location of the property. There are three main categories of grants: intermediate grants, repairs grants and improvement grants.

Intermediate Grants

These are for the purpose of providing the 'standard amenities' of bath, shower, washbasin, kitchen sink, hot and cold running water and an indoor WC. Local authorities have a legal obligation to make intermediate grants for these purposes provided

1. the owner lives in or proposes to live in the house or proposes to let it for at least five years (but see below),
2. all standard amenities are supplied, i.e. a grant will not be allowed for a bath if there is no kitchen sink (but see below),
3. the house, on completion of the work, is in a good state of repair and has an expected life of at least 15 years,
4. the work is not started before the grant is approved,
5. the work is completed within the time stipulated by the local authority (but at least a year must be allowed).

In Housing Action Areas the maximum grant will be 75 per cent of the approved cost. In other areas the maximum will normally be 60 per cent. Such grants are mandatory. The maximum total cost towards which a grant may be given is £6,000 in Greater London and £4,400 in other parts of the country. During 1982–83 the 75 per cent rate of grant was increased temporarily to 90 per cent of the eligible cost but reverted to 75 per cent maximum from 1984.

Repairs Grants
These are grants made towards the cost of work of a substantial or structural nature, e.g. replacing roofs, foundations, internal walls and staircases. The property must have been built before 1919 and have a rateable value of less than £400 in Greater London or £225 elsewhere. The total cost towards which the grant is made must not exceed £5,500 in Greater London or £4,000 elsewhere. Repairs grants are usually discretionary unless they relate to work which the local authority requires to be done. The level of grant is the same as for intermediate grants.

Improvement Grants
These may be available for a wide range of home improvements, including property conversions. These grants are entirely at the discretion of local authorities and their councils vary considerably in their attitudes to improvement grants. In general, if an improvement grant is allowed it will be up to 50 per cent of the agreed work.

Improvements for which an improvement grant may be given include rewiring, putting in a damp-proof course, additional toilet facilities, additional storage space, insulation of loft, installing additional windows, removing disused fireplaces, installing downstairs central heating, insulating walls.

Improvement grants will not be available for repairing damage caused by neglect or for interior decorations. Grants may be obtained, however, for a wide range of repairs except those which come in the category of normal maintenance.

Improvement grants will not normally be made unless, when the improvements have been completed, the following conditions apply:

1. the house will have a life expectation of at least 30 years,
2. in addition to the improvements, the house has all the standard amenities,
3. it must be free from damp,
4. all habitable rooms must have adequate lighting,
5. there must be adequate provision for preparing and cooking food,
6. provision for heating must be adequate,
7. provision for fuel storage and dustbins must be adequate,
8. thermal insulation of the roof must conform to building regulations,
9. the structure must be sound,
10. the lighting and electric installation must be safe and adequate,
11. there must be adequate drains.

Since the introduction of the Housing Act 1980, it is possible, however, to modernize individual amenities in a property without bringing the entire property up to the standard indicated above.

The purpose of intermediate grants and improvement grants is to increase the housing stock by bringing existing buildings up to a more satisfactory standard of habitation. At times of stringency in local government finance, however, many authorities are reluctant to make any more grants than absolutely necessary. Some councils give no improvement grants at all as a matter of general policy.

With effect from 27th October, 1980, new rules came into force under the Housing Act 1980. A local authority is no longer able to demand repayment of an improvement grant if an owner-occupier sells his property within five years of obtaining the grant. Grants will also be available on properties occupied by members of an applicant's family without the applicant having to be a resident of the property in question.

Rateable values no longer limit the possibility of a grant in Housing Action Areas, nor for improvements which are for disabled occupants.

HOME LOAN PLANS This is the title normally applied to schemes which enable older people to mortgage their houses, with the benefit of tax relief, and purchase an annuity. In this way, capital which would otherwise be locked up is turned into income during the lifetime of the owner. Under the Finance Act 1974 (paragraph 24 of Schedule 1) income tax relief may be obtained on mortgage loans for this purpose, i.e. for the purchase of annuities, provided that the annuitant, or each of the annuitants where there is more than one, have attained the age of 65 years at the time the loan is made.

HOMELOAN SCHEME (FIRST-TIME BUYERS) On 1st December, 1978 the Government introduced the Homeloan Scheme to give assistance to first-time house buyers. Under this scheme, a first-time house buyer may receive

1. a cash bonus of up to £110 in accordance with the following scale:

Minimum balance	*Cash bonus*
£300–£399	£40
£400–£499	£50
£500–£599	£60
£600–£699	£70
£700–£799	£80
£800–£899	£90
£900–£999	£100
£1,000 or more	£110

2. a loan of £600 which will be added to the house buyer's normal mortgage loan. To qualify for this assistance the house purchaser must

1. have saved for at least two years with a building society, bank, Trustee Savings Bank, friendly society, National Savings Bank, National Girobank or any other saving institution participating in the scheme,
2. have at least £300 in the saving scheme one year before applying for the benefits,
3. have kept at least £300 in the savings account during the year immediately prior to applying for the benefits.

The cash bonus is tax free and paid in addition to the normal interest allowed on the savings account with the institution concerned.

Applicants who have at least £600 in their savings account when applying for the benefits may also receive a loan of £600. This will be additional to the normal mortgage on the house and repayments of the £600 need not commence until five years from the date of the loan. Thereafter, the repayments of the £600 loan will be added to the normal mortgage repayments (including interest).

Savers who wish to take advantage of this scheme should give notice to that effect to the institution with whom they have opened, or intend to open, a savings account.

The benefits will only be paid

1. to a first-time purchaser,
2. if the total mortgage loan is at least £1,600 and equal to not less than 25 per cent of the purchase-price, and
3. if the applicant intends to occupy the home as a main residence within a year of purchase.

If there are joint purchasers, their *savings* may be added together for the purpose of the scheme, but only one bonus and one loan will be granted.

The scheme applies to most forms of house property, including flats and maisonettes, but not to mobile homes, caravans and houseboats.

HOME RESPONSIBILITIES PROTECTION With effect from 6th April, 1978, special provisions apply to protect the basic retirement pension of someone who is unable to work regularly through having to stay at home to look another another person.

A person will be able to qualify for home responsibilities protection in any tax year if for the whole of that year:

1. he or she had been receiving child benefit (q.v.) for a child under 16; or
2. he or she had been looking after another person on a regular basis for at least 35 hours every week without qualifying for invalid care allowance (q.v.) but the invalid is getting attendance allowance (q.v.) or constant attendance allowance (q.v.); or
3. he or she had been receiving supplementary benefit to enable an elderly or sick person to be looked after; or
4. a combination of these circumstances covers the whole tax year.

In the case of persons receiving child benefit or supplementary benefit as outlined above, the home responsibilities protection will automatically apply. In other cases, it will be necessary to make application to the local social security office.

The effect of home responsibilities protection is that the number of qualifying years for a full basic retirement pension will be reduced by the number of years for which home responsibilities protection has been granted. Thus, a person who required 39 contribution years to qualify for a full pension and who had been credited with home responsibilities protection for 10 years would need to qualify for only 29 years in order to obtain a full basic pension.

Home responsibilities protection does not affect additional earnings-related pension (q.v.). It is not normally possible by the operation of home responsibilities protection to reduce the number of qualifying years below 20.

Reduced rate contributions paid by a married woman or widow do not qualify for home responsibilities protection.

HOME SERVICE INSURANCE This is the category of life assurance, also called industrial branch insurance, for which the premiums are collected on a regular basis by an agent who calls at the insured's home. SEE *Industrial Life Assurance*

HOTCHPOT In law, the gathering together of property for the purpose of making an equal division. Thus, where a testator has during his lifetime advanced a sum of money to a beneficiary under his will, on his death such beneficiary must account for such sum as against other beneficiaries. While this presents no difficulty, the question of the division of the income arising (in the case of a will, from the date of death to the date of distribution of the estate) has been resolved in two ways. The first, known as the Hargreaves method, is based on the decision in *Re Hargreaves, Hargreaves* v *Hargreaves* [1903] 88 LT 100, and followed in *Re Mansel, Smith* v *Mansel* [1930] 1 Ch 352. This is to divide the income proportionately to the beneficiaries' net shares. The second, called the Poyser method, is based on the decision in *Re Poyser* [1908] and was followed in *Re Wills, Dulverton* v *Macleod* [1939] 2 All ER 775. In this case, each beneficiary is credited at the date of distribution with his full share of the estate and is then debited with interest at 4 per cent on any sums brought into hotchpot, for the period between date of distribution and date of payment. The interest is added to the estate income, the total income being finally paid over to the beneficiaries in proportion to their gross shares of the estate.

It was pointed out (in *Re Slee, Midland Bank, Executor and Trustee Company Ltd* v *Slee* [1962] 1 All ER 542) that while the Poyser method was to be preferred as being more accurate, nevertheless where there is a substantial fall in values between the relevant dates, the Hargreaves method might have to be followed. Thus, where the value of the property to be distributed has fallen considerably between the date on which the funds became distributable and the date on which they were actually distributed, the adoption of the Poyser method could result in any one beneficiary obtaining more than his fair share. This could arise as a result of advancements being brought into hotchpot which, because of the fall in value would exceed his share of the distributable funds. Before this became clear, the trustees might in all good faith have paid some income over to him.

HOUSE BILL A bill drawn by a company or firm upon itself, as between different branches.

HOUSE PURCHASE There are approximately 21 million houses in Britain, of which 55 per cent or so are owner-occupied, the remainder being rented from local authorities or private individuals. The proportion of owner-occupation is higher than in some other countries, e.g. Switzerland (28 per cent), Sweden (35 per cent), West Germany (34 per cent), Netherlands (36 per cent). The UK percentage is not as high, however, as Bulgaria and Yugoslavia (each 71 per cent), New Zealand (68 per cent), Australia (67 per cent) and the USA (64 per cent).

Approximately 31 per cent of the housing stock in England is privately owned with the aid of some sort of mortgage finance.

The sources of finance for house purchase in Britain are building societies, the clearing banks, insurance companies, local authorities, overseas banks, and private persons.

Until 1978 approximately 94 per cent of all mortgage loans then outstanding in Britain were building society loans. However, with the upsurge of bank lending for house purchase purposes in the early 1980s, the proportion of building society loans fell to approximately 80 per cent and in the case of new loans (as distinct from outstanding loans) the bank proportion of total lending for house purchase reached as high as 40 per cent. Thus, the market for house purchase finance is dominated by the building societies and the clearing banks.

Mortgage loans for house purchase are normally repaid by one of two methods: the annuity method or the endowment method. These are discussed in more detail under the entry *Building Society Mortgage Loans*. SEE ALSO *Mortgage Interest Relief at Source; Option Mortgage*

HOUSEHOLD INSURANCE This is a convenient heading under which to discuss house insurance and contents insurance. Both are, in fact, aspects of property insurance in the wider sense of that term.

Nowadays, both house insurance policies and contents policies normally cover what are sometimes referred to as 'the standard perils' (see below).

In general, house insurance covers the structure of the property plus all fixtures and fittings, such as sinks, baths, fitted wardrobes. Internal decorations such as paintwork and wallpaper are regarded as part of the structure, but not soft furnishings. Everything within the curtilage of the main property is also covered, e.g. gates, drives, greenhouses, garages, swimming pools and fences. Similarly, the main services to the property, e.g. gas, electricity and water pipes, are also covered to the extent that they are within the property boundary.

Most house insurance policies provide cover against fire, flood, theft, explosion, lightning storm and earthquake, riots and malicious damage, subsidence and landslip, aircraft and items falling from aircraft, escape of water from tanks, pipes and domestic appliances, escape of oil from heating installations, damage by impact of vehicles or animals, and damage caused by falling trees.

In the case of a contents policy, the same 'standard perils' are covered but usually the cover would not extend to articles which are lost, articles which are accidentally damaged, e.g. wine or pet marks on a carpet, normal wear and tear, articles in transit, cars, boats and other vehicles, money in excess of a stated sum, e.g. £50, breakages of china and glass, and electrical or mechanical failures, e.g. television sets and hi-fi equipment. Most policies will include, however, articles temporarily removed from a house, damage to mirrors and glass in furniture and various aspects of liability to other people, e.g. injury to tradesmen or domestic staff.

Damage or loss caused by rebellion, sonic boom, nuclear fall-out and acts of war are normally excluded from cover under both house and contents policy.

A policy of insurance is a contract of indemnity and it was normal in former days to cover houses and their contents on a straightforward indemnity basis, i.e. in the event of loss or damage the insurance company would pay the owner the value of the goods at the time of the damage, after making a deduction for wear and tear. In times of inflation, however, the strict indemnity value might not go very far towards replacement of the insured property. Nowadays, therefore, insurance companies offer cover on the 'new for old' basis, under which they will pay the full replacement cost in the event of loss or damage. A number of companies offer index-linked policies which automatically increase the cover in line with the index of retail prices. SEE ALSO *All Risks Insurance*

HOUSEHOLDER'S PROTEST Where the services of a notary cannot be obtained at the place where a bill is dishonoured, any householder or substantial resident may, in the presence of two witnesses, give a certificate attesting the dishonour of the bill, and the certificate shall in all respects operate as if it were a formal protest of the bill (Section 94, Bills of Exchange Act 1882). SEE ALSO *Protest*

HOUSEKEEPER ALLOWANCE This is an income tax allowance which a widower or widow may claim in respect of any person, whether a relative or an employee, who lives in the home and acts as a housekeeper. If, however, the housekeeper is a relative and is married, the allowance will not be available if the husband of the housekeeper is claiming the married man's personal allowance. At the present time, the allowance is £100 per annum and if there are children in the home it is more advantageous to claim instead the additional personal allowance for children. SEE *Income Tax* (See Appendix 2).

HOUSING ASSOCIATION A housing association is defined by the Housing Act 1957, Section 189(1), as a society, body of trustees, or company, which does not trade for profit or whose constitution or rules prohibit the issue of any capital with interest or dividend exceeding a prescribed rate, whether with or without differential as between share and loan capital, which is established for the purpose of, or among whose objects or powers are included those of, constructing, improving or managing or facilitating or encouraging the construction or improvement of houses.

In general, housing associations come under the control of the Housing Corporation which was established under the Housing Act 1964, for the purpose, *inter alia*, of promoting and assisting the development of registered housing associations. A register of housing associations is now established and maintained by the Housing Corporation and the Corporation may register any housing association which is a registered charity or which is a society registered under the Industrial and Provident Societies Act 1965, provided it fulfills certain conditions. The principal conditions are that it must not trade for profit and it must be established for the purpose of providing, constructing, improving or managing (1) houses to be kept available for letting; or (2) houses for its members to occupy, whether as tenants or otherwise; or (3) hostels; and that any additional purposes must be related to these primary purposes, e.g. the provision of amenities for the benefit of the occupants of the houses or hostels.

A housing association which is registered under the Act may be entitled to loans, grants and guarantees from the Public Works Loan Commissioners or the Secretary of State or, in certain circumstances, the Housing Corporation.

The Commission for New Towns, or approved development corporations, the Church of England Pensions Board and a number of associations set up by churches or other charities throughout the country or promoted by local authorities or county councils are registered as housing associations.

Some housing associations are 'unregistered' associations in that they are not registered under the 1974 Act and are not, therefore, eligible for the housing association grants under that Act. Otherwise the main differences between unregistered and registered associations are

1. Unregistered associations are not supervised by the Housing Corporation under the 1974 Act: they are nevertheless registered as friendly societies and come under the supervision of the Registrar.
2. Unregistered associations do not require the

approval of the Housing Corporation to the sale or other disposal of land.
3. Unregistered associations have greater freedom in the form of their accounts (on the grounds that they have not received housing association grants).
4. Unregistered associations may undertake new house construction for sale, whereas registered associations may not.
5. Unregistered associations may change their rules without the formal approval of the Housing Corporation.

HOUSING BENEFIT Housing benefit was introduced by the Housing Benefits Regulations 1982, and came into operation (apart from certain transitional arrangements) in April, 1983.

Housing benefit replaced the earlier system of rent relief, rent rebate and rates rebate. It is administered by local authorities who receive grants for the purpose from the Department of Health and Social Security.

There are two broad categories of persons entitled to housing benefit, namely

1. *Certificated claimants*, i.e. householders who are in receipt of supplementary benefit. Such a person would normally be entitled to 100 per cent relief for rent and general rates. Not every person entitled to supplementary benefit is entitled to housing benefit—he or she must be a householder.
2. *Standard claimants*, i.e. a person who may be entitled to benefit in respect of a proportion of his or her rent or rates depending on personal circumstances.

In the case of both certificated and standard claimants, the amount of housing benefit is reduced if the dwelling in question is shared by other persons who are not dependent on the householder and who are over the age of 21 years (See Appendix 2).

In the case of a standard claimant, the amount of the benefit will depend on their personal financial circumstances. The amount payable will be 60 per cent of the rent or rates paid by the claimant (known as the 'starting figure'), less a deduction (see Appendix 2), in respect of non-dependants who share the accommodation, plus or minus a further figure depending on the claimant's financial circumstances (called 'needs allowance').

There is no maximum benefit as with the former system of rent relief and rate rebate but no claimant can receive more than the actual amount of rent or rates paid.

The amount of a claimant's 'needs allowance' will vary according to the number of dependants and whether or not the claimant or his or her partner is disabled (See Appendix 2).

The amount of housing benefit payable will depend on whether the dependant's actual income exceeds or is less than the 'needs allowance'. In this context, the claimant's weekly income includes the earnings of the claimant and his partner (before tax and National Insurance contributions) and all other income of the claimant and his partner, excluding in particular the following items:

1. The first £18 per week of the claimant's earnings, and the first £5 per week of his partner's earnings.
2. Any supplementary benefit received.
3. Any mobility allowance or attendance allowance.
4. Interest on National Savings Certificates.
5. Any rent or rates received from a sub-tenant to the extent that this has been taken into account in calculating the eligible rate for rent.

Where the claimant's income *is less than* his or her 'needs allowance' the amount of the benefit will depend on whether or not either claimant has reached pensionable age. If one of them is of pensionable age, the amount of benefit will be

1. in the case of rent benefit, the starting figure (as explained above) less any non-dependant deductions plus 50 per cent of the shortfall of income below the 'needs allowance'; and
2. in the case of rate benefit, the starting figure less any non-dependant deductions plus 20 per cent of the shortfall of income below the claimant's 'needs allowance'.

If, however, both claimants are under pensionable age, the benefit will be

1. in the case of rent benefit, the starting figure less any non-dependant deductions plus 25 per cent of the shortfall; and
2. in the case of rate benefit, the starting figure less any dependant deductions plus eight per cent of the shortfall.

In a case where the claimant's income is *higher than* the needs allowance, there is no distinction between those above or below pensionable age. The amount of benefit will be

1. in the case of rent benefit, the starting figure less any dependant deductions, less 21 per cent of the excess amount of income over the needs allowance; and
2. in the case of rate benefit, the starting figure less any non-dependant deductions, less seven per cent

of the excess amount of income above the needs allowance.

Claimants seeking to obtain housing benefit should apply in writing to their local authority or, in the case of those receiving supplementary benefit, should apply to the Department of Health and Social Security.

A form of supplementary benefit known as housing benefit supplement may be payable in certain cases where an applicant has had a claim for supplementary benefit declined. Housing benefit supplement was introduced in April, 1983 and applies to cases where a person

1. has claimed supplementary benefit but the claim has been declined only on the grounds that his or her income was sufficient to meet their living requirements (as defined for supplementary benefit purposes);
2. he or she has claimed and been allowed housing benefit;
3. he or she has insufficient excess income to cover the amount of the rent or rates.

The normal supplementary benefit regulations will apply in assessing whether housing benefit supplement is payable.

HYPOTHECATION In maritime law, the term refers to the charging of a ship or its cargo or its freight as security for a debt without possession or ownership thereof passing to the creditor.

In banking matters, the term is sometimes used to denote an agreement to give a charge over goods or documents of title thereto without conferring possession, but undertaking to give a pledge when the goods or documents are to hand.

A letter of hypothecation is sometimes used to describe a trust letter.

The expression is also sometimes used where a credit balance on the account of A is charged as security for the liabilities of B. SEE *Trust Letter or Receipt*

I

ILLEGAL CONSIDERATION SEE *Consideration*

IMMEDIATE ANNUITY An immediate annuity is payable commencing with a payment usually six months after the purchase is completed and ending at death. SEE *Annuity*

IMPACT DAY The day on which a new issue is announced on the Stock Exchange. In times when the new issue market is active, an impact day will have to be agreed with the Quotations Committee of the Stock Exchange in order that the 'impact' of new issues may be reasonably spread.

IMPERSONAL PAYEES Cheques payable to 'cash or order', 'wages or order', etc., are not payable to bearer under the Bills of Exchange Act 1882, Section 7, subsection 3, being payable to impersonal payees. In some cases, such cheques are payable on the drawer's indorsement. They are not bills of exchange, however. In *North and South Insurance Corporation Ltd* v *National Provincial Bank Ltd* [1936] 1 KB 328, the liquidator of the company claimed that the bank, in paying a cheque payable to 'cash or order' had wrongly paid an order instrument without indorsement. It was held, however, that an instrument payable to 'cash or order' was not a cheque for it did not conform to the definition of a bill, in that 'cash' was not a specified person. The document merely directed the payment of cash to some impersonal account which could not indorse, and the printed words 'or order' were overridden by the written word 'cash'. The document was thus a good direction to pay money to bearer and the bank was not held liable. In this case, however, the money had reached the party whom the drawer intended, and the judgment was influenced by this fact. It is doubtful as to what would happen if the money got into wrong hands. Hence, a paying banker would probably be justified in returning a document drawn in such terms as an irregular document if he was not satisfied that it had reached the proper party.

However, in the case of *Orbit Mining Company Ltd* v *Westminster Bank Ltd*, [1962] 3 WLR 1256, the Court confirmed that a draft payable to 'cash' was not a cheque although its collection was protected by Section 4 of the Cheques Act 1957. It was also held upon the evidence that the fact that such an instrument was crossed and tendered for collection was not so unusual as alone to put the collecting banker on enquiry.

IMPORT FINANCE The commercial banks in the UK offer facilities to finance the import of goods from overseas, whether by the acceptance of bills of exchange drawn by the foreign exporters or by the setting up of documentary credit facilities for the UK buyer. A traditional aspect of import finance is the 'produce' loan designed to finance the purchase of goods on the sea. This normally involves the pledging of the produce to the bank, against payment in due course.

IMPROVEMENT GRANTS SEE *Home Improvement Grants*

IN CASE OF NEED A referee 'in case of need' is the person whose name a drawer or any indorser may insert in a bill, to whom a holder may resort in case the bill is dishonoured, by non-acceptance or by non-payment (Bills of Exchange Act 1882, Section 15). The words are usually placed in the left-hand bottom corner of the bill, as 'In case of need with the English Bank Ltd, London'. A holder may please himself whether or not he resorts to the referee.

Where a dishonoured bill contains a reference in case of need, it must be protested for non-payment before it is presented for payment to the referee in case of need (Section 67, Bills of Exchange Act 1882). SEE *Acceptance for Honour; Referee in Case of Need*

INCHOATE INSTRUMENT An incomplete document, as, for example, a bill form, signed by a person and handed to another person to fill up and make into a complete bill.

By Section 20 of the Bills of Exchange Act 1882

(1) Where a simple signature on a blank stamped paper is delivered by the signer in order that it may be converted into a bill, it operates as a prima facie authority to fill it up as a complete bill for any amount the stamp will cover, using the signature for that of the drawer or the acceptor, or an indorser; and, in like manner, when a bill is wanting in any material particu-

lar the person in possession of it has a prima facie authority to fill up the omission in any way he thinks fit.

(2) In order that any such instrument when completed may be enforceable against any person who became a party thereto prior to its completion, it must be filled up within a reasonable time, and strictly in accordance with the authority given. Reasonable time for this purpose is a question of fact.

Provided that if any such instrument after completion is negotiated to a holder in due course it shall be valid and effectual for all purposes in his hands, and he may enforce it as if it had been filled up within a reasonable time and strictly in accordance with the authority given.

By Schedule 5 of the Finance Act 1970, the words, 'stamped' and 'the stamp will cover' are deleted from subsection (1) above.

It is important to note that an incomplete bill must be filled up strictly in accordance with the authority given. If a person signs a form as an acceptor and hands it to another person to fill up in a certain specified manner and sign it as drawer, and the drawer exceeds his authority, the acceptor will not be liable thereon to the drawer, but if the bill is negotiated to a holder in due course, he will be liable to such a holder. By accepting a bill in blank an acceptor may thus find himself in the awkward position of having to pay a very much larger sum than he intended to pay when he placed his name on the paper.

The Court of Appeal said in *France* v *Clark* (1884) 26 ChD 257

The person who has signed a negotiable instrument in blank or with blank spaces is, on account of the negotiable character of that instrument, estopped by the law merchant from disputing any alteration made in the document after it has left his hands by filling up blanks (or otherwise in a way not *ex facie* fraudulent) as against a bona fide holder for value without notice, but it has been repeatedly explained that this estoppel is in favour only of such a bona fide holder, and a man who, after taking it in blank, has himself filled up the blanks in his own favour without the consent or knowledge of the person to be bound, has never been treated in English Courts as entitled to the benefit of that doctrine.

[SEE *Bill of Exchange*]

If a bill is stolen before it is completed although it may be signed by an acceptor, a party who would normally have the rights of a holder in due course cannot enforce the bill (*Baxendale* v *Bennett* [1878] 3 QBD 525). It is otherwise if the bill has been completed before it is stolen (*Ingham* v *Primrose* (1859) 7 CBNS 82).

If a customer draws a cheque with blank spaces, so that it is put into the power of a dishonest person to increase the amount by forgery, the customer must bear the loss as between himself and the banker. SEE *London Joint Stock Bank Ltd* v *Macmillan and Arthur* under *Alterations to Bills of Exchange.*

INCOME BONDS These are fixed interest single-premium policies issued by a life assurance company. Some of these bonds are known as guaranteed income bonds because they provide a fixed return guaranteed by the life office during the currency of the policy. There are a number of different types of income bond, but there are two main categories:

1. A single premium endowment policy for a fixed term, the annual bonuses on which are used to provide an income for the life assured.
2. A bond comprising a series of single-premium policies, one of which is automatically cashed each year to provide an income for the life assured and to pay the premium on a separate 'qualifying' life policy (SEE *Income Tax*). The qualifying policy operates to replace the original sum invested at the end of the bond term.

The income from such bonds is free of income tax at the basic rate (the funds already having borne income tax at the life assurance rate of tax) but may be subject to higher-rate tax if taken out by higher-rate taxpayers.

INCOME AND CORPORATION TAXES ACT 1970 (ICTA) This Act was a consolidating Act dealing with all the main legislation on income tax and corporation tax as at 1970. This was the third occasion on which income tax legislation had been consolidated in the UK, the two previous occasions being 1918 and 1952. Since the 1970 Act was passed, it has been amended extensively by later Acts, principally successive Finance Acts. The Act itself runs to nearly 700 pages and up to 1983, the amended legislation had taken up a further 700 pages.

In July 1983, the Solicitor General announced that work on a new consolidation of income tax and corporation tax law would commence in the autumn of that year and that it was hoped a new consolidation Bill would be introduced in the 1987–88 session of Parliament.

INCOME TAX Income tax was introduced by William Pitt in 1799. There were various taxes on income which came and went in the ensuing years but when income tax was introduced again by Sir Robert Peel in 1842, it came to stay, despite Gladstone's observation in 1852 that it was 'a temporary device' and his promise in 1874 to 'abolish the income tax'. No-one has improved on Lord Macnaghten's definition that 'Income tax . . . is a tax on income' (*London County Council* v *Attorney General* [1901] AC 26).

For the most part, the income tax law in the UK is now codified in the Income and Corporation Taxes Act 1970, and the Taxes Management Act 1970, as amended by successive Finance Acts. The general effect of the income tax legislation is to impose a charge for income tax on any person residing in the UK, who is in receipt of income, from whatsoever source, and also to charge to income tax any person not resident in the UK in respect of any income which he or she receives from the UK. The individual liability to tax depends, of course, on various exemptions and reliefs as discussed below.

There is no comprehensive statutory definition of 'income'. There must normally be a receipt of money or money's worth and it is the quality of that money in the hands of the recipient which determines whether or not it is income for tax purposes. Thus a payment may be made from some capital source at regular intervals and yet be income in the hands of the recipient. Whether or not a particular benefit is income and whether or not it is taxable will depend on whether it falls within one of the Schedules and Cases of the Income Tax Acts. These Schedules and Cases have their origin in the Income Tax Act 1952, and are as follows.

Schedule A Income arising from land and buildings.
Schedule B Income arising from certain categories of land, notably woodlands.
Schedule C Income from Government stocks and other funds payable out of any public revenue in the UK, and certain overseas public stocks.
Schedule D
  Case I Income from trade.
  Case II Income from professions or vocations.
  Case III Interest and other payments of an annual nature such as annuities.
  Case IV Income from foreign securities not covered in Schedule C.
  Case V Income from foreign possessions.
  Case VI Miscellaneous sources of income not falling within Cases I–V above.
Schedule E
  Case I Wages, salaries, directors' fees and other remuneration received from any 'office or employment' in the UK.
  Case II Emoluments paid to a non-resident for work done in the UK.
  Case III Emoluments remitted to this country by a UK resident for work done wholly abroad.
Schedule F Dividends from companies

Income tax and higher-rate income tax are part of the unified taxation system introduced with effect from 6th April, 1973 (SEE *Higher-Rate Income Tax*). The main aspects of income tax in relation to various categories of income are set out below in the order of the Income Tax Schedules, although, as indicated, it may be a matter of definition or even choice as to whether particular income is dealt with under one schedule or another:

Income from Land and Property (Schedules A and D)
Income from land and property takes various forms, including, for example, the following: rent from land or buildings, ground rents and chief rents, rent from furnished lettings, royalties from mines and quarries, shooting and fishing rights, premiums on leases, farming, sale of timber, dealing in land.

As a general rule, income of an annual nature arising from the ownership of land and buildings is assessable for tax under Schedule A. There is a number of exceptions to this rule. Income from furnished lettings may, for example, be assessable under Schedule D Case VI. Income from woodlands will generally be assessable under Schedule B and farm profits will normally be assessable under Schedule D Case I. Dealers in property will be deemed to be carrying on a business and will be assessable under Schedule D Case I and, in certain cases, capital gains tax and development land tax may be payable on the proceeds of the sale of land.

Income assessable under Schedule A This category of income includes most rents under leases, chief rents, rent charges, feu duties in Scotland, wayleaves and easements.

Such rents or other income, less expenses (see below), are assessable to income tax in the fiscal year in which the income arises. As Schedule A tax is payable on 1st January each year, it has to be paid before the amount of the assessable income (for the year to the following 5th April) is known. The assessment is made, therefore, on the basis of the previous year's income and then adjusted after the end of the fiscal year.

Income assessable under Schedule A is investment income and was, until 1983–84, subject to the investment income surcharge. Expenses which may be deducted for tax purposes under Schedule A are set out in Sections 71–79 of the Income and Corporation Taxes Act 1970 and may be summarized as follows.

1. any rents, ground rents, chief rents, etc., which the owner is liable to pay;
2. general rates and water rates and any other local authority charges for which the owner is responsible;

3. insurance of the fabric of the building;
4. costs of rent collection, advertising and related professional charges;
5. the cost of any services, e.g. security, cleaning, gardening, for which the owner may be responsible;
6. maintenance and repairs attributable to deterioration or dilapidation during the period of the lease.

If, after the deduction of expenses, there is a loss in any year, this may be carried forward against future income assessable under Schedule A, but may not be set off against other sources of income.

Income from furnished lettings Income from furnished lettings is normally taxed under Schedule D, Case VI, but the taxpayer may elect for assessment under Schedule A at any time within two years from the end of the tax year.

The expenses allowable in the case of furnished lettings are approximately the same as those which would be allowed under a Schedule A assessment (see above). Insurance premiums on the contents will, however, be allowed and an additional allowance will be made to cover wear and tear of furniture. This may be an actual cost of replacements each year, or a deduction of 10 per cent from the gross rents.

Losses from furnished lettings can be set off against other Schedule D Case VI income or may be carried forward against other Schedule D Case VI income.

Where services are provided, e.g. cleaning, laundry, meals in connection with furnished lettings, the Inland Revenue will normally allow the income to be treated as earned income.

Where a house owner lets part of his or her principal residence, whether furnished or unfurnished, there is a prima facie possibility that capital gains tax relief will be lost on the sale of the house to the extent that part of it has been let. However, under the Finance Act 1980, as amended, any chargeable gain which arises because of the letting of part of a principal residence will be reduced by either £20,000 or the amount of the gain that qualifies for exemption, whichever is the less.

With effect from 6th April, 1982, income from the letting of furnished holiday accommodation may be treated as earned income provided that the property (a) is available for letting commercially to the public as holiday accommodation for at least 140 days in the year, (b) is actually let for at least 70 days, and (c) is not normally occupied by the same tenant for more than 31 consecutive days during a period of at least seven months. This need not be a continuous period but must include the time in which the property is let under (b). Assets used in such business lettings will qualify for capital gains tax relief applicable to business assets, including retirement relief. SEE *Capital Gains Tax*

The assets used in the business of holiday lettings may be eligible for capital gains tax retirement relief and relief on replacement of business assets. SEE *Capital Gains Tax*

Premiums on a lease If a premium is received on the granting of a lease for a term not exceeding 50 years, the amount of the premium is assessable to income tax under Schedule A. From the amount of the premium a deduction is allowed equivalent to 2 per cent of the total premium for each full 12-month period which the lease has to run, excluding the first year. As a heavy burden could fall on a taxpayer in a year in which he sold a lease at a premium, there is a statutory provision for top-slicing relief. This is achieved by dividing the total premium by the number of years of the lease and this amount, less any unrelieved expenses, is used to determine the appropriate rate of tax, which is then applied to the total amount of the premium.

Income from Woodlands (Schedules B and C)

The owner of woodlands will be taxed on them only if he occupies them, i.e. has the use of them, and manages them on a commercial basis. The owner-occupier will be taxed in one of two ways:

Under Schedule B In this case, tax will be paid on the 'assessable value' of the woodlands, which is one third of the annual rental value of the land in its unimproved condition. No tax is payable on the proceeds of timber sales and no expenditure is allowed for tax relief. With effect from 13th March, 1984, an occupier of woodlands may not be assessed under Schedule B if he uses his woodlands for the purpose of a timber trade.

Under Schedule D The occupier may elect to pay tax under Schedule D, Case I as a business venture. Income tax will then be payable on the net profits and the net losses may be offset against other income.

Once an occupier has made an election to be taxed under Schedule D he cannot revert to a Schedule B basis. SEE *Woodlands, Investment In*

Income from Farming SEE *Farming Profits*

Interest on Government Securities, etc.
(Schedule C)

Interest on most Government securities in the UK is paid after deduction of income tax at the basic rate in force at the time. Interest is paid gross, however, on

1. 3½ per cent War Stock
2. Smallholdings of Government securities where the gross half-yearly interest is less than £2.50, and
3. Certain Government stocks purchased on the Register of the Department for National Savings.

Interest on National Savings Certificates (q.v.) and Index-Linked Savings Certificates (q.v.) is free of income tax.

Income from Trade, Professions and Vocations (Schedule D Case I and Case II)

The nature of trading A person who is engaged in a trading activity is assessed for income tax under Schedule D Case I, and a person who is engaged in a profession or vocation is assessed under Schedule D Case II. Here the word 'trading' is used to apply to the activities of traders as such and professional people.

Whether a person is trading or not will depend on the facts of each case. A person who lives by buying and selling or manufacturing will clearly be engaged in trade. A person who makes a living from buying and selling property will be deemed to be trading, whereas a person who buys a particular property with a view to securing a particular return will be taxed as an investor. Similarly, a person who invests in stocks and shares will normally be liable to income tax on the dividends and interests and capital gains tax on any capital profits. If, however, he or she is actively engaged in stock-market operations as a business, tax will be payable on the trading profits. This will mean normally that income tax, rather than capital gains tax, is paid on capital profits.

In some cases, the taxpayer will be engaged in neither trading nor investing, but merely pursuing a hobby. It may, for example, be very profitable to indulge in home wine-making, but no tax liability arises unless and until the home producer starts to sell his wine for gain. In many cases it is a question of degree and will depend, as mentioned above, on the facts of each case.

There is a number of factors which will be relevant in determining whether or not a taxpayer is trading. These include, for example, the repetition of transactions of the same kind, the particular skills and experience of the taxpayer, and the nature of the goods or services which the taxpayer is providing.

It is not necessarily a disadvantage to be deemed to be 'trading' for tax purposes. Although normally it will involve the payment of income tax at the appropriate rate on all the gains or profits of the business activity, the taxpayer may nevertheless be entitled to claim expenses and allowances which would not otherwise have been deductible.

Allowable business expenses An employed person (see below) may claim a deduction for tax purposes in respect of those expenses incurred 'wholly, exclusively and necessarily' in the performance of his employment. In the case, however, of someone who is engaged in a trade or business (i.e. self employed) a deduction will be allowed for tax purposes on those expenses which are incurred 'wholly and exclusively' for business purposes, i.e. it is not necessary in the case of a self-employed person to show that the expenses were *necessarily* incurred in the business.

The following are examples of expenses which will be allowed as deductions for income tax purposes provided they satisfy the 'wholly and exclusively' test.

Normal trading costs, e.g. cost of goods for resale, advertising and marketing costs, storage, carriage and delivery costs, trademarks and patent fees, etc.
Normal office costs, such as rent, rates, insurance, stationery, postage, heating, lighting, cleaning, telephone charges and repairs and renewals.
Employee costs, including the salaries, wages, national insurance, pensions, redundancy payments and welfare expenses of employees.
Costs of finance, including bank interest on business overdrafts, hire purchase and leasing charges.
Travel and hotel expenses incurred for business purposes by the proprietor or his employees.
Bad debts incurred in connection with the business and provision for doubtful debts.
Professional charges, including solicitors' fees, accountants' fees and charges for debt collection.
Entertainment of overseas customers or potential customers.
Trade and professional subscriptions, and the cost of relevant books, magazines and other periodicals.
Gifts not exceeding £10 per person per annum. made for advertisement purposes and gifts of any amount made to employees.

Non-allowable expenses The following are examples of expenses which, notwithstanding that they may have been paid out of the business profits, will not be allowed for tax purposes.

Expenses which do not relate wholly and exclusively to the business.
Drawings by the proprietor.

Entertainment other than entertainment of overseas customers or potential customers.
Initial costs of plant and machinery (but see capital allowances below).
Setting-up costs.
Costs of buildings, and any capital used for improvements to buildings.
Payments of tax.
Charitable and political donations (other than small gifts to local charities, which may be allowed).
Travel between home and business.
Expenses incurred for private or domestic purposes.

Basis of assessment The normal basis of assessment for trades and professions under Schedule D is that tax is paid in the year of assessment on the profits of the accounting year ending in the preceding tax year. Special rules apply, however, for the opening and closing years of a business. In those years the basis of assessment is as follows.

The first year	Tax is payable on the actual profit of that year.
The second tax year	Tax is payable on the actual profit in the first 12 months of the business.
The third tax year	Tax is payable on the profits of the accounting year ending in the preceding tax year (but if the first accounting year has not come to an end in the preceding tax year, tax will be based on the first 12 months' profit).

In the second and third tax years, the taxpayer may choose to pay tax on the actual profit for each of those tax years. The taxpayer may elect in this way at any time within seven years of the end of the second tax year.

The fourth tax year and thereafter	Tax is payable on the profit for the accounting year ending in the preceding tax year.
The last tax year	Tax is payable on the *actual* profit in that tax year.

On the conclusion of a business, the Inland Revenue has the option to assess the tax for the two years prior to the closing year on an *actual* basis, i.e. on the profits of those years, and will normally do so if this results in a higher charge for tax. He may do so, however, only for both the years in question and not for one year only.

Capital expenditure In the ordinary way, expenditure of a capital nature on, for example, plant and machinery, furniture and commercial vehicles, is not a deductible expense for income tax. In recent years, however, there have been various statutory provisions for grants or allowances in respect of capital expenditure in order to encourage business investment. From October 1970, these provisions took the form of capital allowances, which could be set off against Schedule D tax assessment in the year in which the capital expenditure was incurred and the assets brought into use in the business. From March 1972, the full amount of the capital expenditure, i.e. 100 per cent allowance, could be taken in the first year, i.e. the year in which the expenditure was incurred if the taxpayer so wished. With effect from March 1984, however, the Chancellor introduced a staged reduction in the amount of these first year allowances:

1. to 75 per cent in respect of expenditure incurred on or after 14th March, 1984,
2. to 50 per cent in respect of expenditure incurred on or after 1st April, 1985, and
3. to nil in respect of expenditure incurred on or after 1st April, 1986. SEE *Capital Allowances*

To the extent that a first-year allowance is not available or not used, the balance of expenditure is carried forward in a 'pool'—the pool may be one asset or the residual value of a number of assets—and a 'writing-down balance' is available each year up to 25 per cent of the outstanding balance of the pool. If an asset is sold the proceeds are brought in as a deduction from the pool balance. If the proceeds exceed the balance of the pool, there is a balancing charge in favour of the Inland Revenue, i.e. the excess sale price is brought into account for tax purposes in that year.

Capital allowances may be claimed in respect of virtually all legitimate capital expenditure on equipment used 'wholly and exclusively' for business purposes. Different rules apply for motor cars, however (see below).

The normal 'preceding year' basis of assessment of income tax is that the tax assessment for the current year is based on the accounting period ending the previous fiscal year. This is usually known as the base period. Capital allowances are similarly computed, i.e. are calculated according to the expenditure incurred in the base period provided the assets in question had been brought into use. It has been announced, however, that with effect from 1st April, 1985, writing down allowances will commence to run from the date the expenditure is incurred, whether or not the asset concerned has been brought into use.

Motor car depreciation Initial, i.e. first-year allowances are not available for private motor vehicles, but they apply to commercial vehicles or motor cars which are used for hire to the public. Under the Finance Act 1979, however, a vehicle purchased after 12th June in that year will not qualify for the first-year allowance as a car available for public hire if it is leased to any one person for more than 30 consecutive days or for more than 90 days in any total period of 12 months.

Motor cars used for business purposes qualify for writing-down allowances along with other capital assets used in the business. If, however, the purchase price of the car exceeds £8,000, the maximum allowance available each year is 25 per cent of £8,000, i.e. £2,000.

Industrial and agricultural buildings allowances Special allowances apply to buildings of an industrial nature used in a business. From April, 1981, an initial capital allowance of 75 per cent was allowed in respect of industrial buildings (lower rates of allowance applied before that date) but with effect from March, 1984, the initial allowance is reduced to 50 per cent in respect of expenditure incurred on or after 14th March, 1984; to 25 per cent in respect of expenditure incurred on or after 1st April, 1985; and to nil in respect of expenditure incurred on or after 1st April, 1986. A writing-down allowance of four per cent is available however, each year in respect of industrial building costs including additions and improvements.

Expenditure incurred before 1st April, 1987 under a binding contract entered into on or before 13th March, 1984, qualifies for the 'old' 75 per cent rate of initial allowance.

Under the Small Workshops Scheme introduced in the Finance Act 1980, 100 per cent capital allowances were available for the period from 26 March, 1980 to 27th March, 1983 in respect of capital expenditure on the construction, improvement, alteration or extension of industrial buildings providing working space of 2,500 ft^2 or less. In such cases, this is in lieu of the industrial buildings allowance mentioned above. Under the 1982 Finance Act, 100 per cent initial allowances under the Small Workshops Scheme were available until March, 1985 in relation to industrial workshops not exceeding 1,250 ft^2. Also under the Act, the definition of industrial building is widened to include premises used for maintenance and repair purposes in connection with an industrial business, or in certain circumstances, in connection with a retail business.

In the case of all buildings relating to a business of an agricultural nature, i.e. farming, forestry, smallholdings, etc., an initial capital allowance of 20 per cent of the cost may be claimed in the first year and thereafter an annual writing-down allowance of 10 per cent is available. With effect from 1st April, 1986, however, the initial allowance is reduced to nil and the writing-down allowance reduced to four per cent.

Hotel buildings Since the Finance Act 1978, capital allowances up to 20 per cent in the first year and thereafter a writing-down allowance of four per cent of the original cost are available in respect of the construction or improvement of hotel buildings, provided the hotel has at least 10 bedrooms available for letting for at least four months in the period from April to October and provided the service includes breakfast and an evening meal. From 1st April, 1986, this initial allowance is reduced to nil and the writing-down allowance to four per cent.

Stock relief To ameliorate the burden of maintaining stock levels in times of inflation, the Government introduced a system of stock relief in the Finance Act 1975 (originally for companies, but then for all trades and professions). In essence, relief was available in the year of assessment to the extent that stocks increased in value during the year, less a deduction equal to 10 per cent of the taxable profits of the trade or business after deducting all allowable expenses and capital allowances. New provisions were introduced, however, in the Finance Act 1981 and relate to all accounting periods ending on or after 14th November, 1980. Under these arrangements, the increase in the value of stocks over the accounting period is measured by reference to an *all stocks* index published by the Department of Trade and Industry. The increase in the amount of the index is applied to the value of stocks held at the beginning of the accounting period, regardless of any actual movement in the amount of stock held. Stock relief will be allowed against profits up to the amount of the increase in the index expressed as a percentage of stocks held at the beginning of the period. No relief is given for periods of account beginning on or after 13th March, 1984, i.e. stock relief now only applies to accounting periods ending on or including 13th March, 1984.

The first £2,000 of stock held in a business did not qualify for relief. Where there is a subsequent fall in stock values, there will be no clawback of relief (as was the case under the earlier regulations) except in cases where a business ceases, or the scale of its operations become negligible in comparison with the recent past.

Losses in new businesses The Finance Act 1978, Section 30, out of a desire on the part of the Government to encourage new business ventures, provides that with effect from the fiscal year 1978–79 any loss made from a trade or profession in the first year of assessment, or in any of the following three years, may be set off against income earned in the three years of assessment prior to the year in which the losses arise. If this option is exercised, the losses must be set against the income of the earliest year first. The taxpayer must exercise this option, if he wishes to do so, within two years of the end of the year of assessment.

Losses on unquoted shares Under the provisions of the 1980 Finance Act, Section 37, where an investor has subscribed for shares in an unquoted trading company and disposes of them at a loss after 5th April, 1980, he will be able to set that loss against his taxable income for that tax year. Any loss unrelieved may be carried forward to the following year. The taxpayer must claim relief within two years of the tax year in respect of which he seeks relief.

The relief applies only to ordinary shares, i.e. not fixed interest investments. The relief extends only to shares which the investor acquired as a subscriber and not to those acquired by inheritance or gift. The relief is, however, available between husband and wife, e.g. if a husband subscribes for shares which he gives to his wife, which she subsequently disposes of at a loss.

The disposal must (1) arise from an arm's-length sale, or (2) result from the liquidation of the company, or (3) be a notional disposal in the case of shares which have no saleable or a negligible value.

The shares of the company must never have been quoted on a recognized Stock Exchange and at the time of the disposal the company must be a trading company in the UK or have ceased trading and carried on no other business within the previous three years. The company must have traded continuously for the preceding six years, or for such lesser period of its existence other than the first year.

Interest and Other Payments of an Annual Nature (Schedule D Case III)

This heading covers such items as annuity payments, bank interest, building society interest, income from trusts and deeds of covenant.

Interest on National Savings Bank Ordinary Accounts up to £70 per annum is free of income tax.

Interest on building society shares and deposits is paid without deduction of tax but building societies are themselves charged a composite rate of tax based on the total income of the society. The rate of tax is calculated for the building society movement as a whole by the Inland Revenue each year and is intended to reflect approximately the average level of tax liability of building society shareholders. In the taxpayer's income tax return, the amount of building society interest must be grossed up at the basic rate of tax. If the taxpayer is not liable for higher-rate tax, there will be no further tax to pay. If, however, the taxpayer is not liable to even the basic rate of tax, he will not be able to recover any tax on the building society interest. If the taxpayer is liable to higher rates of income tax, such higher rate will be payable on the grossed-up interest.

With effect from the fiscal year 1985/86, banks and licensed deposit-takers were brought within the same system of taxation on personal accounts as described above in relation to building societies. For the year 1985/86 and the three subsequent years, the composite rate of tax is arrived at by reference to the data which applies to building societies and the account holder is taxed on the bank interest in the same way as described above.

Income from Overseas (Schedule D, Cases IV and V)

Income from investments overseas will normally be charged for tax under Case IV of Schedule D.

Overseas income from companies will normally have suffered withholding tax before the dividend is received in the UK. UK tax will also be payable on the amount of the distribution, but in most cases where there is a double taxation agreement in force between the UK and the other country concerned, the total amount of tax payable will be that for which the shareholder is liable as a UK resident. In certain other cases where there is no double taxation agreement in force, the British Government will allow unilateral relief in order to avoid double payment of tax. In other cases, the amount of the overseas tax will be deducted from the gross dividend and UK tax charged on the net sum received in the UK.

The UK taxpayer should show the gross amount of the dividend on his or her tax return and the amounts of any overseas or UK tax deducted at source.

Distributions from companies and unit trusts located in certain tax-free or low-tax centres in various parts of the world, e.g. the Channel Islands and Bermuda, will normally be paid to non-residents of those places without deduction of tax. Such distributions are taxable in the hands of the UK resident and the gross sum should therefore be shown in his or her income tax return in the UK.

In addition to liability under Case IV of Schedule D on income from securities (see above), residents of the UK are charged to tax under Case V of Schedule D on 'possessions' outside the UK. This applies in certain cases to businesses conducted abroad as well as to physical possessions.

If, for example, the UK resident hires out a caravan, a house or a boat on the continent, he must show the gross amount of the hire charges in his UK tax return. A deduction will be allowed, however, for the expenses of managing the asset in question in very much the same way as would apply to the earnings from property in this country but mortgage interest is not deductible.

The normal basis of assessment is that tax will be paid in the UK on the income for the previous year, i.e. the preceding year basis.

Miscellaneous Sources of Income (Schedule D Case VI)

This covers various categories of income not covered by Cases I to V of Schedule D including, for example, patent rights, authors' copyright and certain transactions in securities.

Patent rights The sum received for the sale of patent rights in the UK is chargeable to tax under Case VI of Schedule D. For the purpose of calculating the tax liability, however, the payment may be spread over the following six years or over past years if the payment is for patent rights already enjoyed.

Where a patent right is not sold, but the holder of the right receives royalties from the patent user, the royalties will be subject to tax under Case VI of Schedule D. In the ordinary way, tax at the basic rate will be deducted at source and the patent-holder will receive a tax credit for that amount. Whether tax is deducted at source or not, the gross amount of the royalties will be part of the patent-holder's Schedule D income.

Authors' copyright Royalties paid to authors are paid without deduction of income tax at source. The treatment of the tax in the hands of the author will depend on whether or not he or she is an author by profession or whether he or she writes as a sideline. Professional authors, journalists and composers are taxed under Case II of Schedule D as 'earnings of a profession', whereas the occasional earnings of a part-time author would normally be taxed under Case VI of Schedule D. The difference in practice is that any loss made by a professional author will be available to be offset against other income, whereas losses incurred in the course of activities taxed under Case VI cannot be offset against other earnings except other Case VI earnings.

If an author or composer sells all or part of the copyright in his work, income tax will prima facie be payable in the year in which the payment is received. It may be possible, however, to spread the proceeds over a two- or three-year period, i.e. the year of receipt and the preceding year or years, depending on the time taken to prepare the work. If it took over a year to write the book or compose the music, the copyright proceeds may be spread over two years. If it took over two years to complete the work, the proceeds may be spread over three years, i.e. the year of receipt and the two preceding years.

If the copyright of an established work is sold 10 years or more after publication, the sum so received may be spread over the following six-year period for tax purposes. Similarly, if an interest in the copyright is granted to a licensee for two years or more, the sum received may be spread over the period of the licence.

Transactions in securities The Inland Revenue have wide powers under Sections 460–468 of the Taxes Act and Schedule 11 of the Finance Act 1973 to tax as income any financial advantage gained from transactions in securities. The legislation covers, for example, schemes involving the purchase or formation of companies with a view to their sale or liquidation and the stripping of the company's assets for the benefit of the temporary owner. These and similar schemes may attract capital gains tax liability, but would not have given rise to a charge to income tax without these statutory provisions.

If the proposed transactions are for good commercial reasons, there is a statutory right to place the circumstances before the Inland Revenue, who must indicate within a period of a month whether or not a clearance from income tax will be granted. SEE ALSO Supplement under *Bond-washing*.

Transfer of assets abroad Section 478 *et seq.* of the Taxes Act contains far-reaching provisions to prevent UK residents transferring their assets abroad for tax avoidance purposes while still retaining some benefit of those assets. In general, if a person transfers assets abroad and retains a power to enjoy the income of those assets, either now or in the future, directly or indirectly, there will be a charge to income tax under Schedule D Case VI. The provisions apply to any transfers abroad, whether to a person, a company or to a trust.

With effect from 10th March, 1981, the provisions of Section 478, Taxes Act, were widened to include any person who *benefits*, directly or indirectly, from the transfer of property abroad.

Income from Office or Employment (Schedule E Case I)
This category of income includes all the earnings of employed persons. It includes virtually all payments made by an employer in return for the employee's services and therefore includes salary, wages, overtime payments, cost of living allowances, gratuities, bonus schemes, compensation for loss of office and a wide range of fringe benefits. A director of a company is taxed under this heading in respect of his director's fees and other emoluments of his office.

Payments made to an employee in respect of wages, salaries, overtime payments or fees paid to a director are made after deduction of tax under PAYE (q.v.) and at the end of the year an income tax certificate is issued to the employee (Form P60) showing the gross earnings and the amount of tax deducted. Certain fringe benefits, which are not susceptible to tax deduction at source, e.g. the provision of a company car, are not the subject of deduction under PAYE and will be separately assessed after the employee's tax return has been submitted.

Under the heading of 'earnings', therefore, it is the actual money paid to the employee which will be shown in the tax return and which will normally coincide with the figure on the Form P60.

Benefits and expense allowances The treatment of expenses and benefits in kind depends on whether or not the individual is classified as being an employee in higher-paid employment (q.v.).

For the most part, an employee is not taxed on benefits in kind if

1. he earns less than £8,500 per annum, and
2. he is not a director of a company (or, being a director, he does not own more than 5 per cent of the shares in a company for which he works full-time).

If, however, the employee

1. is paid more than £8,500 per year, or
2. is a director of a company (other than a director who does not own more than 5 per cent of the shares in the company for which he works full-time) all benefits in kind will be taxed along with the employee's other income. A director, whether full time or part-time, of a charitable or non-profit-making company may be exempted from this rule.

There are certain categories of benefit on which *all* employees and directors must pay tax. These include profit-sharing schemes and share options, luncheon vouchers in excess of 15p per day, company houses occupied rent free, virtually any payments in cash. A higher-paid employee or director will pay tax on all the foregoing benefits in addition to a company car and fuel for private motoring, interest-free loans, expense allowances (see below), assets made available for the employee's use, e.g. furniture. A number of these items call for separate consideration.

Expenses An employee taxed under Schedule E may claim a deduction for tax purposes in respect of those expenses which he incurs *wholly, exclusively and necessarily* in the performance of his employment. Typical examples of such allowable expenses are

Tools of a workman's trade.
Protective clothing and overalls (an office worker may not, however, claim for his suits no matter how well 'turned out' his employer may expect him to be).
Home expenses, e.g. telephone and heating, where the employee is required to work from home.
Subscriptions to professional associations, e.g. a bank clerk may claim for his Institute of Bankers subscription.
Books and stationery provided they are *necessary* to the job, and not merely an aid to the job.
Travelling and hotel expenses.
Use of private car on company business.
Expense of entertaining overseas customers if necessary to the company's business.
Contributions to the company pension scheme. (This is one of the more important allowable expenses. An employee may claim as an expense not only the contributions paid to the main company scheme, but also any additional voluntary contributions made under a company scheme to the extent of 15 per cent in total of his taxable earnings, including overtime, bonuses, etc.).

To the extent that an employee is reimbursed expenses by his employer, the employee will not be taxed on the amounts so paid if the expenses are wholly, exclusively and necessarily related to the employment. If, therefore, an employee incurs travelling expenses in the course of his employment and receives no reimbursement from his employer, he may claim those expenses as an allowable deduction for tax purposes. If the employee receives reimbursement from his employer (which more often than not will be the case), the employee will not have to pay tax on the sum received, provided the 'wholly, exclusively and necessarily' rule is satisfied.

If, for example, an employed person pays a golf club subscription, he will not be able to deduct this as an expense in his tax return because it is not wholly, exclusively and necessarily related to his duties. If, therefore, the employer reimburses the amount of a golf club subscription paid by an employee, the employee will have to pay tax on it as an emolument of his employment. Similarly, because travel between home and work is not allowed as a deductible expense, if the employer pays an employee's travelling expenses to work, the amount reimbursed will be taxable in the employee's hands. Under the Finance Act 1981, the cost of season tickets purchases by employers on behalf of their employees became chargeable to tax under Schedule E with effect from 6th April, 1982.

A particular area of difficulty is that of entertainment expenses. Where an employee bears these himself, he cannot claim tax relief unless they are for the entertainment of overseas customers or potential customers and are wholly, exclusively and necessarily in the course of his duties. Where the employer reimburses entertainment expenses to the employee, the employee will not be taxed on the amount of the reimbursement, but the employer will not be able to claim tax relief unless, again, the entertainment was of an overseas visitor. In general, therefore, we may say that an employee will not be taxed on reasonable entertainment expenses incurred in the course of his duties. Where, however, he receives an *entertainment allowance* from his employer, the position is not so clear. The Inland Revenue do not look with great favour on lump sum allowances and certainly any excess of the allowance over and above the entertainment expenses actually incurred will be taxable in the employee's hands.

There is a number of benefits in kind and expenses which are the subject of special rules and these are dealt with below. In the case of straightforward reimbursement of expenses for such items as travel and entertainment, a number of employers, particularly the larger companies, have a dispensation from the Inland Revenue from making returns of the reimbursed expenses up to an agreed figure provided they are incurred wholly, exclusively and necessarily in the course of the employees' duties. The Inland Revenue retain the right, however, to call for the detailed figures at any time.

Under the 1981 Finance Act, as amended by the 1982 Act, employees are taxable on vouchers provided by their employers if they can be exchanged for money, goods or services. The tax charge arises when the employee uses a voucher and it is the cost so incurred by the employer which is taxable. A 'voucher' for this purpose includes payments by cheque. Relief from tax will be available, as already described, to the extent that such payments are for allowable business expenses.

A charge for tax also arises on benefits provided for an employee under a credit card or similar voucher provided by the employer. The amount chargeable to tax is the cost to the employer of the goods or services so provided.

Motor cars SEE *Company Cars*

Living accommodation for employees The general rule is that an employee is taxed on the value of any living accommodation made available by the employer, and that the employee pays tax on the gross annual value (the figure from which the rateable value is derived) plus any expenses, e.g. heating and cleaning, paid by the employer. The employee will be exempt from tax on this presumed benefit, however, if

1. he has to live in the accommodation in order to carry out his duties properly, e.g. the caretaker of a property, or
2. it is customary in that class of employment to have accommodation provided and it helps the employee to do his job better, e.g. a resident nurse at an old people's home, or
3. the employment involves a security risk and the accommodation is provided for the employee's safety.

In the case of a higher-paid employee or director, only this last category will entitle him to exemption from tax. Additionally, a higher paid employee or director will be assessed for tax on any expenses paid by the employer in connection with the accommodation (up to 10 per cent of the employee's net emoluments from that company excluding the expenditure in question).

Interest-free or low-rate loans Only higher-paid employees and directors are required to pay tax on loans at preferential rates of interest. In such cases, the employee will be charged tax on the difference between the rate of interest, if any, which he pays on the loan and the 'official rate' published from time to time by the Inland Revenue. The same situation applies in the case of loans to a near relative of the employee, which means parent, grandparent, child, grandchild, brother or sister as well as the wife or husband of the employee and of any of these relatives. No tax is payable, however, if the loan in question is a 'qualifying' loan for tax purposes, e.g. for house purchase. No tax is payable if the value of the 'benefit' is no more than £200. Loans made before 26th March, 1974 will normally qualify for tax relief as qualifying loans and thus no tax will be payable on any interest benefit.

Medical insurance Under the Finance Act 1976, medical insurance premiums paid by employers on behalf of their employees became taxable in the hands of the employees. Since the Finance Act 1981, only higher-paid employees and directors are now taxable on the amount of premiums paid by employers for private sickness insurance. The cost of medical cover for overseas service is not taxable. Any payments made under such a scheme, e.g. for hospital care, are not taxable benefits.

Premiums paid by employers under medical benefit schemes for the protection of their pensioners are not taxed in the hands of the pensioner, presumably because they are not at that point an emolument of an office or employment.

In those cases where employers pay National Insurance contributions on behalf of their employees, i.e. the employees' contributions, the amount so paid is taxed as a benefit in the hands of the employees.

Loss of office or employment SEE *Compensation for Loss of Office or Employment*

Duties performed abroad The 1977 Finance Act introduced a measure of tax relief for employees resident in the UK who undertook overseas duties for at least 30 days in any tax year. The rules for calculating the number of days spent abroad were as follows:

1. The day of departure counted as a day spent overseas, but not the day of return. The general rule was that days on which the employee was in the UK at midnight were excluded.
2. Days spent travelling overseas may be counted as working days (again provided the employee had not returned to this country by midnight on that day).
3. Weekends and other holidays spent overseas may be counted as working days provided they were part of a period of seven or more consecutive days spent working abroad.

The effect of the deduction was that employees working abroad for a qualifying period received free of tax a quarter of their salary relating to the days worked abroad. With effect from 6th April, 1984, the relief was reduced to $12\frac{1}{2}$ per cent and from 6th April, 1985, abolished altogether.

Longer periods overseas With effect from April, 1974 employees are exempt from tax in the UK on overseas earnings provided 365 days or more are spent working abroad. The following rules apply.

1. The 365-day qualifying period does not need to be a tax year from April to April. Any 365-day period will suffice.
2. Occasional work in the UK in connection with the overseas employment will not break the qualifying period. This, however, is a matter of degree and a lengthy visit to this country might be held not to be incidental to the overseas employment.
3. The qualifying period will be broken if a visit to the UK exceeds 62 days or if the total number of days spent in the UK, including business visits, exceeds a sixth of the total period abroad. This rule is applied in a cumulative way, so that in calculating a sixth the number of days spent in this country are related to the period to date. In other words, the employee cannot spend, say, a month in the UK after only one month abroad because he will have spent a half of the total period to date in the UK and the qualifying period would have been broken.
4. The employee may take holidays in the UK during the qualifying period provided he returns overseas at the end of the holiday. He may not, for example, spend 11 months abroad ending up with a month's holiday in this country.

If for any reason the qualifying period is broken other than in accordance with these rules, the 100 per cent tax relief is lost and the period cannot be used again.

If an employee leaves the UK during the tax year and returns during a subsequent tax year, he will be able to set off the usual income tax allowances, e.g. personal allowance and mortgage interest, against his earnings in the UK for the time that he was in the UK. It may therefore benefit the employee to postpone his departure until a little later in the tax year or to return a little earlier before the end of the following year. An employee who coincided his overseas work with the tax year in the UK would not feel the benefit of the tax allowances in the UK for that year. Expenses incurred by an employee overseas in the course of his employment will not be taxable as a benefit. If the employer pays for the employee's wife to accompany him, this expense would normally be taxable except to the extent that it could be shown that the wife was assisting the husband in his business duties, or if there was some health reasons why the wife should assist him.

Under the Finance Act 1977, if an employee is working abroad for at least 60 continuous days, the employee will not be assessed for tax purposes if the employer pays for up to two visits by the employee's wife (or husband) and children under the age of 18 years, i.e. two visits in any tax year.

State retirement pensions All pensions payable under the state pension scheme, i.e. either the basic pension or earnings-related pension, are taxable in the hands of the recipient as earned income. This applies to a wife's pension, for which she may qualify in respect of her contributions, and to a widow's pension.

National Insurance contributions are not allowed as a deductible expense from employees' earnings for tax purposes, nor are contributions under the earnings-related state pension scheme paid by those employees who are not contracted out of the state scheme.

No tax is payable on supplementary pensions, the £10 Christmas bonus payable to state retirement pensioners, pensions paid for war injury, pensions paid for industrial injury, pensions awarded to holders of certain medals (VC, GC, Albert Medal, Edward Medal, MC, DFC, CGM, DSM, MM, and DFM) and war widows' pensions.

Occupational pensions and other pensions Pensions payable under employers' pension schemes are taxable as earned income. Widows' pensions payable under such occupational schemes are also taxable as earned income.

Capital payments received under pension schemes up to one and a half times final salary (as calculated under the rules of the schemes) are tax free. SEE *Profit-Sharing Schemes; Share Option Scheme*

Emoluments Paid to a Non-resident for Work Done in the United Kingdom (Schedule E Case II)

In the ordinary way, a person who is not resident in the UK is liable to its income tax only on income arising in the UK. In many cases where a non-resident is entitled to income arising in the UK, there will be a double taxation agreement in force between the two countries concerned so that double-taxation will be avoided and, in some cases, the UK income will be paid without deduction of tax.

To clarify the position regarding the resident status of visitors to the UK, the Inland Revenue issued guidelines on the subject in April, 1981.

In general, a person who comes to the UK is not regarded as having been ordinarily resident until he has been in the country for at least three years, unless it is clear before then that he intends to be here for three years or more. It is the practice of the Inland Revenue to regard someone who comes to the UK, whether to work here or not, as ordinarily resident for tax purposes

1. from the date of arrival if the visitor has, or acquires during the year of arrival, accommodation for his use in the UK which he occupies on a basis that implies a stay in this country of three years or more, or
2. from the beginning of the tax year in which such accommodation becomes available.

This does not apply in the case of hotel accommodation or the use of a company flat, nor to accommodation rented and furnished for less than a year, nor to furnished accommodation taken for less than two years.

If a visitor, who has been regarded as ordinarily resident solely because he has accommodation here, disposes of the accommodation and leaves the UK within three years of his arrival, he would normally be treated as not ordinarily resident for the duration of his stay. SEE *Residence*

Dividends from Companies (Schedule F)

When a company pays a dividend to its shareholders, it does not deduct tax from the dividend but it pays to the Inland Revenue an amount of Advance Corporation Tax currently calculated at the rate of three sevenths of the amount of the dividend paid.

Similarly, a company is required to pay Advance Corporation Tax on other benefits to shareholders if they are deemed to be 'qualifying distributions', which in general means those cases where the distribution confers some claim on the profits of the company. Thus, dividends on preference shares or other special categories of shares and distributions of capital profits would all attract Advance Corporation Tax.

Tax so paid is shown as a tax credit on the voucher to the shareholder and for his or her tax purposes the total dividend or other distribution is the net amount received plus the amount of the tax credit.

In the case of interest payments from companies, e.g. on debenture stock or loan stock, income tax will be deducted by the company at the basic rate of tax in force at the time of the payment and the payment will be accompanied by an income tax certificate showing the amount of tax so deducted. In the hands of the taxpayer, the amount to be shown in his or her income tax return is the gross amount before deduction of tax. The tax so deducted will be taken into account in the overall calculation of any remaining tax liability or repayment.

Personal Allowances

All persons are entitled to one or other of the personal allowances, i.e. the initial allowance which is deductible from what would otherwise be taxable income, before the tax liability is calculated. The amount of the personal allowances will vary according to the fiscal policy of the Government and to some extent with inflation. In recent years, personal allowances have been adjusted to take account of any rise in the Retail Price Index, in the 12 months ending at the

December prior to the year of assessment. This practice was not adopted, however, in the 1981 Finance Act.

Single personal allowance For the purpose of claiming the personal allowance, the following persons are deemed to be single:

1. a bachelor or spinster,
2. a widow or widower,
3. a divorced person,
4. a separated husband or wife (but not a husband who wholly and voluntarily maintains his wife, who is entitled to the married man's allowance, see below),
5. a married man and woman who have chosen to have the wife's earnings taxed separately (see below)—in such a case, they both receive the single personal allowance,
6. a single woman who receives the personal allowance in the year she gets married (See Appendix 1).

Married man's personal allowance A married man is entitled to this allowance if he is married at the commencement of the tax year, i.e. 6th April. He is also entitled to the full allowance if he became married between 6th April and 5th May in the tax year.

A man who marries after 5th May in the tax year will suffer a deduction of one-twelfth of the difference between the married man's allowance and single person's allowance for each month in which he is a single person during the tax year. For example, a man who marries on 6th August will suffer a deduction of four months, i.e. one-third, of the difference between the two allowances. If, before marriage, a man is receiving a housekeeper allowance (see below) or an allowance for other purposes special to single persons, e.g. additional personal relief for children, these allowances will cease on marriage. In the year of marriage, however, a man may retain these allowances in lieu of the married man's allowance if it is to his advantage to do so (See Appendix 1).

Wife's earned income allowances If a wife is in receipt of *earned* income, she may claim against that income the equivalent of a single person's allowance. In that event, a couple will receive a married man's personal allowance for the husband and the wife's earnings allowance in respect of the wife's earned income.

If a husband and wife have elected for separate earnings assessment, they will each receive the single person's allowance, but the wife will be separately taxed on her earned income instead of being taxed at the rate appropriate to the combined income. Whether or not it is advantageous to elect for separate assessment in this way will depend on the relative levels of the husband's total income and the wife's earned income.

Age allowance In lieu of the personal allowance for single or married persons, an age allowance may be claimed by any person who, or whose wife, is over age 64 at the commencement of the income tax year on 6th April.

The full age allowance is paid only to those persons whose total income for tax purposes does not exceed a statutory limit (see Appendix 1). If the income exceeds that amount, the age allowance is reduced by two-thirds of the excess over that amount until the relief is entirely absorbed and the normal personal allowance applies (See Appendix 1).

Widow's bereavement allowance With effect from the tax year 1980–81 a widow is entitled to an additional personal allowance in the year of her husband's death if he is entitled to the married man's personal allowance or would have been so entitled but for any election he had made to the contrary (See Appendix 1).

Additional personal allowance for children This is an additional personal allowance for persons who have the care of children but do not have a husband or wife to assist them. There are two categories of person who may claim:

1. a single person, e.g. a widow or widower, a separated or divorced parent, and a single step-parent or adoptive parent;
2. a married man whose wife is totally incapacitated throughout the tax year.

Such a person may claim the additional allowance if a child or children live(s) with him or her for all or part of the tax year and is maintained at his or her expense.

In the case of a child over 16 years of age, the additional allowance will continue provided the child is continuing further education or undergoing full-time training for at least a two-year period. In the case of an illegitimate child, the allowance may not be claimed beyond the age of 18.

The allowance cannot be claimed in the same year as a married man's personal allowance is claimed (see above). The allowance is the same regardless of the number of children (See Appendix 1).

Allowance for son's or daughter's services If a person is aged 64 years or over at the commencement of the tax year, or infirm and had to depend on the services of a son or daughter, there is a tax allowance (see Appendix 1). The son or daughter must live with the claimant and must be maintained by the claimant. As a general rule, a married man who is aged or infirm will not be able to claim this allowance if his wife is under the age of 64 and is in good health. The allowance cannot be claimed if a housekeeper's allowance or blind person's allowance is being received. SEE ALSO *Blind Person's Allowance; Dependent Relative Allowance; Housekeeper Allowance; Pensions—Personal pension schemes*

Loan Interest

Interest on loans is allowed as a deduction for tax purposes only in the following circumstances:

(1) Loans taken out for the purchase or improvement of the taxpayer's main or only residence. In November 1980, the High Court ruled that a taxpayer's residence could be the 'main' residence, notwithstanding that he spent only two or three days a month there. Depending on the circumstances of each case, the taxpayer was entitled to determine which was the main residence.

(2) Loans taken out for the purchase or improvement of property which is available for letting throughout the year and is actually let at a commercial rent for at least 26 weeks in the year.

(3) Loans taken out for business purposes.

(4) Loans, overdrafts and other credit facilities which were incurred on or before 26th March, 1974, but which might not necessarily come within the above categories.

Under (1) above, interest is allowed for tax purposes only on loans up to £30,000 in amount. Two or more people living together and separately taxed (but not husband and wife) are each entitled to £30,000 tax relief for loan interest on the principal residence.

On a change of house, interest will normally be allowed on a bridging loan of up to £30,000 for a period of one year and any outstanding loan on the old house will continue to qualify for relief for up to twelve months from the time the new loan is taken, even though the borrower has moved into a new house and made it his only or main residence.

From 6th April, 1983, where interest is added to the amount of a qualifying loan (perhaps through failure to keep up to date with mortgage instalments), the first £1,000 of such interest does not count towards the £30,000 permitted maximum for tax purposes. The effect of this, therefore, is that the permitted maximum is now £31,000 provided £1,000 is 'rolled-up' interest.

Where one party leaves a house and goes to live with another party on marriage, the Inland Revenue have agreed by extra-statutory concession that mortgage interest relief will continue on the vacated property for a period of twelve months provided the property is being sold. This will not affect the total relief available on the new joint home. If both parties of the marriage leave their houses and set up a third home, the tax relief will be available on all three properties.

Under (3) above, the interest on loans for business purposes will be allowed without limit as to the amount of the loan, provided that it is incurred wholly and exclusively for the purpose of the business. A person who borrows money to invest in a close company, of which he has more than five per cent of the capital, may obtain income tax relief on the interest on the loan. With effect from 9th March, 1982, the income tax relief also applies to an investor who does not have five per cent of the share capital, but who, from the time of making the investment to the time of payment of the interest, has worked for the 'greater part of his time' in the management or the conduct of the company or an associated company. The Inland Revenue have confirmed that this means that 'more than half' the shareholders' time should be taken up in the business of the company.

Under the Finance Act 1983, relief for income tax is allowed on loans incurred for the purchase of shares in an employee controlled company, which means in this context a company where more than 50 per cent of the ordinary capital, or the voting power, is beneficially owned by persons who, or whose spouses, are full-time employees of the company, full-time employee meaning a person who works for the greater part of his time as an employee or a director. Where an employee owns more than 10 per cent of the shares or voting power, the excess is to be left out of account in determining whether the employee-control test is satisfied. The 10 per cent limit applies separately to a husband and wife, both of whom are full-time employees. During the period between the acquisition of the shares and the payment of the interest, the company must be unquoted and must be a trading company or a holding company of a trading group and during the year of assessment in which the interest is paid, the company must either have become an employee-controlled company, or have been such a company throughout a period of at least nine months.

INCOME TAX ON LIFE ASSURANCE POLICIES SEE *Qualifying Policy*

The Assessment of Income Tax

Schedule E income tax, i.e. on the income of an office or employment, is normally deducted under the PAYE system (see below). In all other cases, the Inspector of Taxes will issue a Notice of Assessment when he receives the completed income tax return and claim for allowances.

The normal date for payment of tax, other than under Schedule E, is 1st January in the year of assessment. Schedule D assessments on business profits normally require payment in two instalments on 1st January in the year of assessment and on the following 1st July.

Higher-rate income tax on any income not taxed at source is payable on 1st January in the year of assessment. Higher-rate income tax on income which has suffered basic rate of tax at source is normally payable on 1st December in the year following the year of assessment.

Appeal against assessments A taxpayer may appeal against an assessment within 30 days of the date of the Notice of Assessment. An extension of this period will normally be allowed for good reasons, such as absence from home. The appeal must be in writing.

If it still proves impossible to reach agreement between the taxpayer and the Inland Revenue, the appeal will go either to the General Commissioners of Inland Revenue or Special Commissioners of Inland Revenue. The General Commissioners are local lay people, but the Special Commissioners are full-time civil servants with taxation experience.

In the ordinary way, an appeal will go to the General Commissioners, but the taxpayer has a degree of choice whether he wishes the appeal to be heard by the General Commissioners or the Special Commissioners. As a general rule, the more routine matters and straightforward matters of fact will be dealt with by the General Commissioners. Some of the more technical and sophisticated aspects of income tax, e.g. transactions in securities and transfers of assets abroad, will automatically go to the Special Commissioners as will any major point of law. If the taxpayer is relying on a legal point in support of his appeal, he may well be advised to elect for it to be heard by the Special Commissioners.

There is no appeal from the Commissioners on questions of fact, but on questions of law the taxpayer or the Commissioners may appeal to the High Court and, from there, to the Court of Appeal and the House of Lords.

An assessment may be made any time within six years after the end of the chargeable period to which the assessment relates. If, however, there has been any fraud or wilful default on the part of the taxpayer, the Inland Revenue may go back over as many years as they please. If a taxpayer wishes to re-open past assessments, he may go over the last six completed years.

Interest on overdue tax Interest is payable by the taxpayer from the date the tax becomes due and payable (see above). Under the Finance Act 1982, the Inland Revenue is enabled to charge interest on unpaid tax, notwithstanding that the tax has not previously been assessed. Thus, if an additional amount of tax is payable as a result of an appeal, interest is payable on the additional sum from the date of the original assessment, notwithstanding that the Inland Revenue may have agreed to a deferment of payment of tax or to a provisional payment.

Repayment supplement If there is a repayment of tax due to the taxpayer of £25 or above, interest known as a repayment supplement is payable on the outstanding tax from either the end of the year of assessment in which the tax was paid or, if later, 5th April, following the year in respect of which the repayment is made. The repayment supplement is not subject to income tax.

Interest and penalties Where there is an underpayment of tax through fraud, wilful default or neglect, interest is charged on the outstanding tax from the date it should have been paid. Severe penalties may also be payable depending on the circumstances of the case and extending to twice the additional tax payable.

The PAYE system Most Schedule E earnings, i.e. those arising from an office or employment in the UK, are taxable under the Pay-As-You-Earn system, i.e. tax will be deducted at source by the employer. Since 1973, when the unified system of tax was introduced, the higher rates of tax have also been included in the PAYE system.

The essence of the system is that each employee, including directors, is issued with a code number relating to his or her earnings from that particular source. The code number reflects the various allowances and other deductible items to be taken into account in calculating the employee's tax liability. The code is calculated by dividing the total allowances, etc. by 10 and rounding down to the nearest whole number. An employee who has allowances of, say, £3,046, would thus have a code number of 304. If the employee has a number of sources of employment his principal code number will be calculated according to his main source of employment, thereby using up his allowances. The other sources of income will then be taxed according to differing code numbers, reflecting any higher rates of tax for which he may be liable.

The code number may be prefaced by a letter indicating the employee's status, namely

L Single person or working wife
H Married man
P Single pensioner*
V Married pensioner*

*Pensioner in this context means a taxpayer entitled to the age allowance.

T Taxpayer with no personal allowances to be set against pay or where the liability to tax is dealt with under other arrangements
D Taxpayer on higher rate of tax
F Employee where each payment is taxed in isolation
BR Taxpayer with other employment but not on higher rates of tax

Each employer is issued with tables by the Inland Revenue showing the tax calculation weekly or monthly for different codes.

At any one point the tax tables will show the appropriate level of tax in relation to the total earnings of the employee during that fiscal year. If, therefore, there is a reduction in earnings for any reason, e.g. the employee is on strike or becomes unemployed, he may have paid more tax during the working weeks than would be appropriate to the whole time in which he was employed. He will thus be able to receive an appropriate repayment of tax.

At the end of each tax year the employer must complete a form P35 to be sent to the Inland Revenue showing the gross pay and tax deducted in relation to each employee during the year and each employee will receive a form P60, also showing the gross pay and income tax deducted.

On a change of employment, the employee will receive form P45 from his old employer and this he must hand to this new employer who will set up an appropriate tax record.

Any underpayment or overpayment of tax at the end of the fiscal year may be dealt with as it arises or carried forward in the coding calculation of the following year.

In the case of a tax repayment due to a working wife, this will now be paid direct to her and not to her husband.

INCOME TAX RATES See Appendix 1

INCOMPLETE BILL SEE *Inchoate Instrument*

INCONVERTIBLE PAPER CURRENCY A bank note which cannot be exchanged for gold on demand, at the bank which issued it, for the full value as shown upon the face of the note is called inconvertible paper. When it can be exchanged for its full value, it is convertible paper.

INCORPORATED COMPANY SEE *Company (Companies)*

INCUMBRANCE A liability, such as a mortgage upon an estate or property (SEE *Mortgage*). A property is unincumbered when it is free from any charge.

INDEMNITY An undertaking to hold harmless; usually a promise to make a monetary compensation for loss sustained. Fire insurance and marine insurance are contracts of indemnity.

An indemnity must be distinguished from a guarantee; the former need not be in writing, the latter must; an indemnity is a primary liability, whilst a guarantee is a collateral liability. Bankers take indemnities in respect of lost drafts and deposit receipts, and are frequently asked to give indemnities on behalf of customers in respect of lost share certificates, dividend warrants and bank notes, and missing bills of lading. In such cases, counter indemnities are usually taken from the customer. An advantage of an indemnity, as against a guarantee, is that it is not vulnerable to the lack of capacity of the principal debtor.

An indorser of a bill of exchange is entitled to an indemnity from the acceptor. Partners are also entitled to be indemnified out of the partnership assets in respect of liabilities property incurred in the course of the partnership business. In general, an agent acting in the course of his agency is entitled to be indemnified by his principal: thus a broker has the right to be indemnified by his client and the servant or employee is entitled to the indemnity of his employer in respect of liabilities incurred in the proper performance of his employment. Trustees and personal representatives are entitled to be indemnified out of the trust fund or estate in respect of costs properly incurred in the course of their duties.

INDENTURE From the Latin *in* and *dens*, a tooth. A deed to which there are two parties or sets of parties.

Its name dates from the time when a deed was indented along one of the margins. It was the custom to write a deed in two parts on the one parchment, and between each part a blank space was left; along the blank space a word, often the word 'chirographum', was written and the parchment was then cut into two by dividing it with an indented or wavy line through that word. Each of the two parties to the deed received a part, and when at any time the two parts were brought together again it showed that they were the correct documents when the indents agreed and the divided word was completed.

The writing of the word 'chirographum' or other words or letters in the blank space was in later times omitted, and the parchment was merely divided with an indented line. Finally an Act was passed (8 & 9 Vict c 106, Section 5) providing 'that a deed executed after the first day October, 1845, purporting to be an indenture, shall have the effect of an indenture although not actually indented'.

Instead of starting a deed with the words 'This Indenture', the words 'This Conveyance', 'This Deed', 'This Legal Charge', etc., are now used according to the nature of the transaction.

INDEX LINKING As the term implies, this is the linking of a particular value or benefit to an index. For most purposes, however, the term is used in relation to the General Index of Retail Prices, colloquially known as 'the cost of living' (SEE *Cost of Living*). Index linking is a feature of recent years and, for the most part, is confined to certain National Savings Certificates and to certain Government securities (although at least one building society issues an index-linked bond). The purpose of indexation or index linking is to give the investor a hedge against inflation by maintaining the purchasing power of his investment up to the date of redemption. Certain pensions, principally those in the public sector, are also index linked.

INDEX-LINKED SAVINGS CERTIFICATES There are three categories of index-linked certificates currently in issue: the Retirement Issue, the Second Index-Linked Issue and Save-As-You-Earn contracts.

Retirement Issue

These certificates were on sale from 2nd June, 1975 to 15th November, 1980 and were in units of £10 each. No person could hold more than 120 units. They were available only to men who had attained the age of 65 years and women who had attained the age of 60 years.

Second Index-Linked Issue

These certificates became available from November, 1980 to all persons over the age of 60 years and from April, 1981 to all persons over 50 years. From 7th September, 1981, the issue was made available to persons of any age.

Both the Retirement Issue and the Second Index-Linked Issue do not increase in value during the first year but thereafter the repayment value is calculated according to the growth in the General Index of Retail Prices since the date of purchase. The current values of certificates are displayed in post offices. A bonus of four per cent of the purchase price is added to certificates of the Retirement Issue and the Second Index-Linked Issue when repaid on or after the fifth anniversary of the purchase date. The treasury may pay an additional amount over and above the Retail Price Index increase if they consider it appropriate to do so. In October, 1983 a supplement of 2.4 per cent per annum was announced to take affect from 31st October, 1982 for holders of the certificates on that date, provided the certificates were still held on 1st November, 1983. A further supplement of 2.4 per cent was added for the year to 31st October, 1984, and a supplement of three per cent for the year to 1st November, 1985. There are to be at least three further annual supplements, the amounts of which will be announced each year. Savers who retain their certificates for a full 10 years from the date of purchase receive a four per cent bonus on the tenth anniversary, in addition to the fifth anniversary bonus of four per cent mentioned above.

All bonuses and supplements are index-linked.

Certificates of the Retirement Issue may be held indefinitely and the index linking continues after the original five-year term.

Save-As-You-Earn

This service was introduced from 1st October, 1969 and at the time of writing there have been three issues. The third issue was introduced on 1st July, 1975 and is linked to the General Index of Retail Prices. Participation in the third issue is by monthly payments from £4 minimum to £50 maximum per person. The payments continue for a five-year period, at the end of which time, each monthly payment is revalued in accordance with the General Index of Retail Prices and the saver receives either the total of his contributions or the revalued total in accordance with the Index, whichever is the greater. If a saver ceases payment altogether or omits to make more than six payments during a five-year period, the contract is terminated. If repayment is then taken by the saver at any time between the first and seventh anniversary of the contract date, the contract will not be index linked but interest will be paid at the rate of six per cent per annum. At the end of five years, a saver may cease contributions under his contract but may allow the total contributions to remain for a further two years on the same index linked basis. At the end of the additional two-year period a bonus equal to two monthly payments will be added. After the seventh anniversary the third issue contracts continue to be index linked at three-monthly intervals.

The 3rd issue of the Save-As-You-Earn service ceased to be on sale after 31st May, 1984 but contributions to existing contracts may continue until 1989.

The proceeds of all categories of index linked certificates are free from UK income tax.

INDEX-LINKED SECURITIES The first index-linked quoted security in the UK was two per cent Treasury Stock 1996, introduced by the Government in March, 1981. This was at first available for investment only by pension funds and insurance companies and friendly societies, to the extent that they were engaged in pension fund business. Since then a number of index-linked stocks have been issued and, at the time of writing, they are

Treasury 2 per cent 1988
Treasury 2 per cent 1990
Treasury 2 per cent 1996
Treasury 2½ per cent (Convertible) 1999
Treasury 2½ per cent 2001
Treasury 2½ per cent 2003
Treasury 2 per cent 2006
Treasury 2½ per cent 2009
Treasury 2½ per cent 2011
Treasury 2½ per cent 2016
Treasury 2½ per cent 2020

All the index-linked stocks are now available to private investors as well as to institutions.

The essential feature of the index-linked stocks is that the capital sum and the half-yearly interest are linked to the General Index of Retail Prices. As indicated above, there is a low rate of interest payable on the stocks over and above the element of index linking. The index linked element of both capital and interest is free of all taxes.

Such stocks are particularly attractive to investors when a high rate of inflation is expected. As with all quoted securities, the price of the stock in the market reflects investor demand.

INDEXATION See *Index Linking*

INDORSEMENT From the Latin *in dorsum*, on the back. A writing upon the back of a document. Spelled also 'endorsement'. In Scotland the word used is often 'indorsation'.

The indorsement of a bill (or cheque) is the writing, signed by the holder upon the back, by which a bill (or cheque) payable to order is transferred from one person to another. The simple signature of the indorser is a valid indorsement, and it is not invalid by reason of its being written in pencil. 'It was held as long ago as 1826 that a pencil indorsement was valid and effective.' (MacKinnon, J, in *Importers Company Ltd* v. *Westminster Bank Ltd* (1927) 43 TLR 325).

'Indorsement' means an indorsement completed by delivery.

The requisites of a valid indorsement are given in Section 32 of the Bills of Exchange Act 1882:

An indorsement in order to operate as a negotiation must comply with the following conditions, namely—

(1) It must be written on the bill itself and be signed by the indorser. The simple signature of the indorser on the bill without additional words, is sufficient. An indorsement written on an allonge, or on a 'copy' of a bill issued or negotiated in the country where 'copies' are recognised, is deemed to be written on the bill itself.

(2) It must be an indorsement of the entire bill. A partial indorsement, that is to say, an indorsement which purports to transfer to the indorsee a part only of the amount payable, or which purports to transfer the bill to two or more indorsees severally, does not operate as a negotiation of the bill.

(3) Where a bill is payable to the order of two or more payees or indorsees who are not partners all must indorse, unless the one indorsing has authority to indorse for the others.

(4) Where, in a bill payable to order, the payee or indorsee is wrongly designated, or his name is misspelt, he may indorse the bill as therein described, adding, if he think fit, his proper signature.

(5) Where there are two or more indorsements on a bill, each indorsement is deemed to have been made in the order in which it appears on the bill, until the contrary is proved.

(6) An indorsement may be made in blank or special. It may also contain terms making it restrictive.

There are four kinds of indorsement: a conditional indorsement, an indorsement in blank, a special indorsement, and a restrictive indorsement.

A conditional indorsement is referred to in Section 33:

Where a bill purports to be indorsed conditionally the condition may be disregarded by the payer, and payment to the indorsee is valid whether the condition has been fulfilled or not.'

The condition would be operative as between the indorser and the indorsee. See *Conditional Indorsement*

An indorsement in blank and a special indorsement are explained in Section 34:

(1) An indorsement in blank specifies no indorsee, and a bill so indorsed becomes payable to bearer.

(2) A special indorsement specifies the person to whom, or to whose order, the bill is to be payable.

(3) The provisions of this Act relating to a payee apply with the necessary modifications to an indorsee under a special indorsement.

(4) When a bill has been indorsed in blank, any holder may convert the blank indorsement into a special indorsement by writing above the indorser's signature a direction to pay the bill to or to the order of himself or some other person.

A restrictive indorsement is defined in Section 35:

(1) An indorsement is restrictive which prohibits the further negotiation of the bill or which expresses that it is a mere authority to deal with the bill as thereby directed and not a transfer of the ownership thereof, as, for example, if a bill be indorsed 'Pay D only,' or 'Pay D for the account of X,' or 'Pay D or order for collection'.

(2) A restrictive indorsement gives the indorsee the right to receive payment of the bill and to sue any party thereto that his indorser could have sued, but gives him no power to transfer his rights as indorsee unless it expressly authorise him to do so.

(3) Where a restrictive indorsement authorises further transfer, all subsequent indorsees take the bill with the same rights and subject to the same liabilities as the first indorsee under the restrictive indorsement.

No person is liable as indorser who has not signed the instrument as such (Section 23). The liability of an indorser is defined by Section 55(2). SEE UNDER *Indorser*

The indorsement of cheques and analogous instruments was to a great extent rendered unnecessary by the passing of the Cheques Act 1957 (q.v.). Indorsements are now required as a matter of banking practice only in the following cases.

(1) Where cheques are cashed or exchanged across the counter. The Mocatta Committee set up by the Government to examine the whole question of indorsement attached importance to indorsement of such cheques as possibly affording some evidence of identity of the recipient and some measure of protection for the public.

(2) Where cheques are negotiated, i.e. where cheques are tendered for the credit of an account other than that of the ostensible payee. In such cases the indorsement of the payee, and any subsequent indorsee, will be required, but not the endorsement of the customer for whose account the cheque is collected.

(3) Where cheques payable to joint payees are tendered for the credit of an account to which all are not parties.

(4) In the case of combined cheque and receipt forms, where a bold letter "R" on the face of the cheque is an indication to the payee that there is a receipt which he is required to complete.

(5) In the case of bills of exchange (other than cheques) and promissory notes, which are unaffected by the Cheques Act.

It is to be noted that items (1) and (4) instance indorsements which, while not required by law, are taken as a matter of practice. The indorsement required at the counter is intended to make the cashing of a stolen cheque as difficult as possible for a thief, who is thus obliged to leave a specimen of his handwriting, while the combined cheque and receipt forms are used to accommodate customers who do not rely on Section 3 of the Cheques Act 1957 (q.v.), but require a specific receipt.

In relation to item (2) above, the decision of the House of Lords (upholding the Court of Appeal) in the case of *Zang* v *Westminster Bank* [1966] AC 211, appears to have confirmed that the law rather than the practice of bankers will prevail.

Foreign cheques continue to require indorsement according to the laws of the particular country, and travellers' cheques continue to require a signature, in the presence of the cashing agent, by the person cashing them.

An indorser may insert an express stipulation (1) negative or limiting his own liability to the holder, (2) waiving as regards himself some or all of the holder's duties (Section 16). An example of an indorsement so qualified is where an indorser adds after his signature the words 'without recourse' or the French equivalent 'sans recours'. This stipulation releases the indorser from liability in the event of the cheque being dishonoured, but does not release him from liability with respect to any forgery on the cheque before he indorsed it.

By Section 31(3), 'A bill payable to order is negotiated by the indorsement of the holder completed by delivery'.

A transferee for value acquires the right to have the indorsement of the transferor, where the bill was payable to the transferor's order (Section 31(4)).

A bill payable to 'John Brown or order' may be indorsed simply 'John Brown'. He may then transfer the bill by simple delivery to another person. By John Brown's indorsement in blank the bill becomes payable to bearer, and may pass from hand to hand without any further indorsement, though, as a rule, any one taking a bill will require the transferor to indorse it, so that he may thereby become a party to the bill and be liable thereon. If, however, John Brown indorsed the bill 'Pay John Jones or order, John Brown' (or 'John Brown, pay to the order of John Jones'), the bill is specially indorsed, and requires the signature of John Jones before he can transfer it to anyone else. Any holder may convert an indorsement in blank into a special one to himself, or to any other person. If a bill with John Brown's indorsement in blank passes through the hands of certain holders who do not indorse it, and then comes into the possession of William Robinson, he may write above John Brown's signature the words 'Pay William Robinson'. Before further negotiation, the bill requires William Robinson's indorsement. If John Brown indorses the bill 'Pay John Jones only', the indorsement of John Jones is required, but John Jones cannot transfer the bill to anyone else, as John Brown by his restrictive word prohibits the further negotiation of the bill. Payment must be made only to John Jones himself. If presented through another bank, the indorsement should be confirmed.

A cheque or bill payable 'to order' should be indorsed in any of the cases listed above. But see under *Payee* as the case of a payee refusing to indorse a cheque when presented by himself. A cheque payable to bearer does not require to be indorsed. A cheque indorsed in blank is payable without further indorsement.

An indorsement, as the name implies, should be upon the back of a bill or cheque, but it has been held that an indorsement of the face is valid.

An indorsement should be spelled exactly in the same way as the person's name appears on the face of the bill (or cheque) as payee, or in the special indorsement as indorsee. If the person's name has been misspelt by the drawer or the prior indorser, his indorsement should also be misspelt, but he may indorse it below with his name spelled correctly. All necessary indorsements must be examined, even if they are in a foreign language.

If a holder strikes out, intentionally, the indorsement of any indorser, that indorser and all indorsers subsequent to him are discharged from liability on the bill. (Section 63(2) see under *Cancellation of Bill of Exchange*.)

Where a bill is negotiated back to a prior indorser, he is not entitled to enforce payment of the bill against any intervening party to whom he was previously liable. (See Section 37 under *Negotiation of Bill of Exchange*.)

A minor may indorse a bill or cheque and pass on to an indorsee a good title, but he is under no liability with regard to it. Section 22(2) provides that where a bill is indorsed by a minor or corporation having no capacity or power to incur liability on a bill, the indorsement entitles the holder to receive payment of the bill, and to enforce it against any other party thereto.

Where the signature of any person is required, under the Bills of Exchange Act, it is not necessary that he should sign it with his own hand. It is sufficient if his signature is written thereon by some other person by or under his authority (Section 91). A banker, however, would require undoubted evidence of authority before accepting an indorsement written by some other person. If an indorsement is impressed by a stamp, a banker should confirm it, when he is satisfied that it has been made by a duly authorized person.

In the case of a corporation, an indorsement sealed with the corporate seal is sufficient (Section 91(2)).

Where a banker on whom a cheque is drawn, pays it in good faith and in the ordinary course of business, the banker is protected by Section 60, even though the indorsement of the payee or a subsequent indorser has been forged or made without authority. He must, however, exercise reasonable care, and see that the cheque he is asked to pay appears to be in order and that any essential indorsements thereon are apparently correct.

A cheque drawn in the form 'Pay A B per X' should be indorsed 'A B per X'. In *Slingsby and Others* v *The District Bank Ltd* [1932] 1 KB 544, Wright, J, in the course of his judgment said (referring to a cheque in the above form)

> It seems clear that if X has no right to receive the money except in a representative capacity, his signature should show that he is acting in accordance with that, and he ought to sign in a representative capacity: he is not authorised to receive the money as his own, or to deal with it except for his principals. That is the intention.

If a banker pays a customer's acceptance to a person appearing to be the holder, but claiming through or under a forged indorsement, he cannot charge such an acceptance to the customer's account (Sections 24 and 59. SEE *Forgery*). If he has paid such an acceptance to a banker who sent it for collection he cannot claim the amount back from that banker.

The paying banker thus incurs liability in paying a bill under a forged indorsement, but in paying a cheque with a forged indorsement he is protected.

The banker who collects for a customer a cheque crossed generally, or specially to himself, is not liable for a forged indorsement, provided he receives payment of the cheque for his customer in good faith and without negligence. A collecting banker should see that the necessary indorsements on all order cheques which appear to have been negotiated are apparently correct. If he fails to observe that an indorsement does not correspond with the name of the indorsee, or that the last or only indorsement negotiates the cheque to a person other than the person for whom he is collecting the cheque, that would be negligence sufficient to deprive him of his protection under Section 4 of the Cheques Act 1957 (q.v.).

The banker paying a draft or order drawn upon him, payable to order on demand, which purports to be indorsed by the person to whom the same shall be drawn payable, is not liable if the indorsement proves to have been forged. It shall not be incumbent on such banker to prove that such indorsement, or any subsequent indorsement, was made by or under the direction or authority of the person to whom the said draft or order was or is made payable, either by the drawer or any indorser thereof (Section 19, Stamp Act 1853). A banker paying a crossed draft or order drawn on him is protected by Section 80, Bills of Exchange Act 1882, as extended by Section 5 of the Cheques Act 1957 (q.v.).

It is a well-recognized custom to pay a dividend

warrant, payable to several persons, when discharged by one of those persons (SEE *Dividend Warrant*). As to whether all interest warrants are dividend warrants within the meaning of Section 95, see the case under *Dividend Warrant*.

Where a bill has been seized in execution, a sheriff can give a good discharge when payment is made to him.

Where a bill drawn by a firm is payable to their order, one partner may draw the bill and, probably, another partner may indorse it. Thus, though the signatures of the firm on the bill differ, it may be in accordance with the practice of the firm to treat bills in that way.

The signature of the name of a firm is equivalent to the signature by the person so signing of the names of all persons liable as partners in that firm (Section 23(2)).

Where a person indorses a bill in a trade or assumed name, he is liable thereon as if he had signed it in his own name (Section 23(1)).

Where payable to a fictitious or non-existing person no indorsement is required, as the instrument may be treated as payable to bearer (Section 7(3)). SEE *Fictitious Payee*

Instruments payable to 'Cash or order', 'Wages or order', etc., are sometimes paid on the indorsement of the drawer. See, however, *Impersonal Payees*.

'Per pro' indorsements are usually accepted by bankers, but some companies put a note upon their cheques to the effect that a 'per pro' discharge will not be accepted, unless guaranteed by the payee's banker. A banker is not obliged to accept a 'per pro' indorsement if there are suspicious circumstances demanding inquiry as to the person's authority to indorse. A 'per pro' discharge is not accepted on a dividend warrant.

An indorsement which is not strictly in order is frequently confirmed by a banker as 'Indorsement confirmed. Per pro X & Y Bank plc, T. Brown, Manager'. This is better than 'Indorsement guaranteed', as it precludes any chance of liability to stamp duty as a guarantee.

Where a person is under obligation to indorse in a representative capacity as treasurer or executor, he may indorse in such terms as to negative personal liability (Section 31(5)).

Section 33 of the Companies Act 1948 enacts that

> a bill of exchange or promissory note shall be deemed to have been made, accepted, or indorsed on behalf of a company if made, accepted, or indorsed in the name of, or by or on behalf or on account of, the company by any person acting under its authority.

Although this Section makes an indorsement of simply the name of a joint stock company (if made by a person acting under authority) legally correct, it is the practice of bankers always to require that it be signed by some person on behalf of the company, e.g. 'For and on behalf of John Brown & Co Ltd, J. Jones, Secretary', or 'Per pro John Brown & Co Ltd, J. Jones', or 'John Brown & Co Ltd, J. Jones, Secretary'.

Although an indorsement in the last mentioned form is frequently accepted as sufficient, it is very desirable that it should be preceded by the words 'per pro' or 'for' or 'for and on behalf of'. In the case of *Elliot* v *Bax-Ironside* (1925) 41 TLR 631, where an indorsement on a bill was

Fashions Fair Exhibition Limited.

H. O. Bax-Ironside
Ronald A. Mason } *Directors.*

The name of the company having been impressed by a rubber stamp, the Court of Appeal held that there was nothing in the form of the signature on the back of the bill which was conclusive as a matter of law that it was the signature of the company, and that the directors were personally liable. In this case, however, the indorsement was not a discharge of a payee but an indorsement by way of security as the facts showed that it was the intention that the directors should incur personal liability by indorsing the bill. In applying Section 26(2) of the Bills of Exchange Act 1882 (SEE UNDER *Agent*), the construction that the signatures on the back of the bill were the personal signatures of the directors was held to be the construction most favourable to the validity of the bill.

In the case of *Rolfe Lubell & Co (a firm)* v *Keith and Another* [1979] 1 All ER 860, it was held that extrinsic evidence was admissible where a dispute arose as regards the capacity of an indorser. In that case, the plaintiffs who were the holders of two bills accepted by the company, had made it clear to the managing director of the company that the bills were to be indorsed personally by the managing director and the company secretary and that they would accept personal liability. In the result, the signatures were prefaced by the words 'for and on behalf of the company'. The defendant maintained that this indicated that he had signed in a representative capacity and that he was not personally liable as the indorser. It was held that he was liable because there was a clear agreement among the parties to that effect.

It was to be noted also that the bills were accepted and indorsed by the company. The essence of an indorsement however, is a transfer of liability to the indorser and said Kilner-Brown, J, 'No-one can transfer liability from himself to himself'. The bill was, as counsel for the plaintiffs remarked, 'a mercantile nonsense'.

Where a cheque payable to John Brown is indorsed 'Place to credit of my account, J. Brown', it is not necessary that the cheque should be indorsed by the bank in any way. The paying banker is not concerned with the instruction to the collecting banker.

A bearer cheque does not require indorsement and any indorsements which may have been placed thereon need not be examined. A bearer cheque cannot be turned into one payable to order by indorsement.

In the case of a cheque payable to order which has been indorsed in blank, thus making it payable to bearer, a subsequent holder may again make it payable to order by writing a direction above the last indorsement to pay to the order of a further party.

If an indorsement has been altered, it should, if correct, be confirmed. An indorsement by means of an impressed stamp should be confirmed by a collecting banker, if he is in a position to do so.

Words of courtesy should not appear in an indorsement, but indorsements are occasionally met with having Mr or Esq added to the name. If the name has been written by the right party, the indorsement is sufficient, but a collecting banker should confirm it.

In the case of cheques which are provided with a form of receipt, there is frequently an intimation printed thereon that the signature of the receipt is intended to be also an indorsement of the cheque.

In Scotland, when the payee is a married woman, the cheque is frequently drawn as 'Pay Mrs Mary Young or Campbell', Young being her maiden name and Campbell the married name. The indorsement is accepted whether signed 'Mary Young' or 'Mary Campbell'.

If a payee presents an 'order' cheque himself, it is the custom to require him to indorse it, but if he declines to indorse it see *Payee*. The payee's indorsement need not necessarily be the first signature on the back of the cheque, though, of course, it usually is.

There is no authorized form of indorsement, and in consequence the variations in indorsements are very numerous and often puzzling to decide upon. Below is a list of specimens; in one column are included indorsements which, as a rule, would be passed, either because they are strictly correct or sufficiently accurate to justify their acceptance; in the other column are shown indorsements which are not generally accepted, either because they are quite wrong or so doubtful as to cause the cheques bearing them to be returned 'indorsement irregular' or 'confirmation of indorsement required'. A banker is entitled to confirmation of any indorsement about which he has any doubt.

Payee	Correct or usually accepted	Wrong or not usually accepted
John Brown	John Brown	J. Brown, p.p. J. Jones
	J. Brown	John Brown, per J. Jones. (Proof of authority required)
	per pro John Brown, J. Jones	John Brown, pro J. Jones
	p.p. John Brown, J. Jones	John Brown by J. Jones
	per pro Mr John Brown, J. Jones	For John Brown, J. Jones. (Proof of authority required)
	pro (or for) John Brown, J. Jones, Agent	For J. Brown & Co., J. Brown
	J. Jones, Agent, for (or pro) John Brown	J. Brown for Self and Co-Executors of W. Brown
	J. Jones, per pro John Brown	J. Jones, Solicitor to J. Brown
	per pro. John Brown, J. Jones & Coy	John Brown, J. J.
	John Brown by J. Jones, his Attorney	John Browne
	J. Jones, W. Brown, Executors of the late John Brown	John J. Brown
	J. Brown, per J. Jones, Agent	pro John Brown, J. Jones. (Proof of authority required)
	J. Brown, without recourse	Mary Brown, widow of late John Brown
		J. Jones, Agent to J. Brown
		For J. Brown, J. Jones, Trustee. (Proof of authority required)
J. Brown	Received cash, J. Brown.	J. J. Brown
	J. Brown	
	John Brown	
	James Brown	

INDORSEMENT

Payee	Correct or usually accepted	Wrong or not usually accepted
Dr John Brown	John Brown, MD John Brown	Dr J. Brown
Captain John Brown	J. Brown, Captain J. Brown	Capt J. Brown
Mr John Brown	John Brown	Mr John Brown
Mr Brown	J. Brown J. Brown, Junior per pro Mr Brown. J. Jones	Brown Mr Brown
Mrs John Brown	Mary Brown, wife of John Brown Mary Brown, widow of John Brown Mary Brown (Mrs John Brown)	Mary Brown John Brown Mrs John Brown
Mrs Brown	Mary Brown M. Brown (Mrs) Mary Brown	Mrs Brown Mrs Mary Brown
John Brown, Senr	John Brown, Senr John Brown	
John Brown, Junr	John Brown, Junior	John Brown
Rev John Brown	John Brown John Brown, Vicar of All Saints', Oldtown (Rev) John Brown	Rev John Brown
Mr & Mrs Brown	John Brown. Mary Brown	J. & M. Brown
John Brown per A. Smith	John Brown per A. Smith	John Brown
George Brown (a minor)	George Brown	John Brown, father of George Brown
Misses Brown	Jane Brown. Mary Brown	J. & M. Brown For Self and Jane Brown, Mary Brown. (Confirmation required)
John Brown & another	For Self & another, J. Brown	J. Brown
John Brown (now deceased)	For Self & Co-Executors of late John Brown, J. Jones For the Executors of J. Brown, deceased, J. J. Jones, an Executor John Jones, Executor to the late John Brown J. Jones, R. Smith } Administrators of the late John Brown	John Brown. J. Jones Mary Brown, widow of John Brown Jones & Co., Solicitors to the Estate of John Brown, decd
Mrs John Brown (now deceased)	J. Jones, Executor of the late Mary Brown, wife of John Brown (or widow of the late John Brown)	
John Brown (who cannot write)	his John **x** Brown mark Witness, J. Jones, 13 King St, Leeds	John Brown, J. Jones John Brown **x**
John Brown (Indorsed 'Credit my Account, John Brown')	Indorsement by Bank not necessary	
John Brown (Indorsed 'Credit *a/c* J. Jones, John Brown')	Indorsement by Bank not necessary	
John Joseph Simpson Brown	J. J. S. Brown	J. J. Brown
Mr Fitz-Brown	John Fitz-Brown	Fitz-Brown
Brown Brothers	Brown Brothers	J. Brown & Bros J. Brown. T. Brown J. & T. Brown
W. Brown, J. Jones, R. Smith	W. Brown. J. Jones. R. Smith	Brown, Jones & Smith For Self, Jones & Smith, W. Brown
W. Brown & J. Jones	W. Brown. J. Jones J. Jones. W. Brown W. Brown per pro J. Jones, W. Brown. (If one is dead, the cheque is payable to the survivor on proof of death of the other)	Brown & Jones

Payee	Correct or usually accepted	Wrong or not usually accepted
William & Thomas Brown	William Brown. Thomas Brown	For William Brown & Self, Thomas Brown
W. or T. Brown	(Either may indorse)	
Messrs. Brown	J. & T. Brown Brown & Son J. Brown & Sons per pro Messrs Brown, J. Jones Brown Bros Brown & Brown Browns	Brown Brown & Coy Messrs Brown
Messrs J. & T. Brown	J. & T. Brown per pro Messrs J. & T. Brown, J. Jones John & Thomas Brown John Brown. Thomas Brown	J. & T. Brown, per J. Jones J. & T. Brown, J. Jones
Messrs W. Brown	W. Brown, W. Brown W. & W. Brown	Messrs W. Brown W. Brown W. Brown & Son. (Confirmation required) J. & W. Brown
Messrs Browns	Browns	Brown & Coy
Brown & Co	Brown & Coy per pro Brown & Co, J. Jones, Manr per pro Brown & Co, J. Jones Brown & Co, by J. Jones, Agent	For Brown & Co, J. Jones Brown & Co, J. J. Brown, Smith & Jones Jas Brown & Co per pro Brown & Co, pro J. Jones. R. Smith
Thomas Brown & Coy	T. Brown & Coy	Brown & Co
T. Brown & Coy	Thomas Brown & Coy	Brown & Co
Messrs Brown & Co	Brown & Coy per pro Messrs Brown & Co, J. Jones Brown & Co, John Brown, Partner	Messrs Brown & Co
Messrs Brown & Jones	J. Brown. J. Jones Brown & Jones	Jones & Brown
T. Brown & Coy Ltd	per pro T. Brown & Coy Ltd, J. Jones, Secretary (An indorsement with the correct title may be added: a limited company's name is fixed)	per pro Thomas Brown & Co Ltd, J. Jones, Secretary (The correct title of the company)
Brown & Jones Ltd	per pro Brown & Jones Ltd, J. Smith, Secretary	Brown & Jones Ltd per pro Brown & Jones Ltd, J. Smith, Clerk
The British Coy plc, per John Brown	per pro The British Co plc John Brown, Secretary	John Brown
The British Coy plc	Indorsed by order of the British Company plc, and placed to the credit of their account per pro the X & Y Bank plc, J. Brown, Manager per pro The British Coy plc, J. Brown, Secretary per pro The British Coy plc, J. Brown	per pro The British Coy plc, J. Brown, pro Manager per pro The British Company, J. Brown, Secy The British Coy plc, per pro J. Brown, Secy (This form is not accepted by bankers)
The British Coy plc	pro, or For, The British Coy plc, J. Brown, Manager For the British Coy plc, J. Brown, Director The British Coy plc, J. Brown, Secretary	per pro The British Coy plc, per pro John Brown, Secy J. Jones For the British Co plc, J. Brown, Representative

INDORSEMENT

Payee	Correct or usually accepted	Wrong or not usually accepted
The British Coy plc	The British Coy plc, per J. Brown, Secy	The British Coy plc (But see Section 37, Companies Act 1985, under *Companies*)
	Received in payment of call & passed to credit of payees. per pro The X & Y Bank plc, J. Brown, Manager	
	For the British Coy plc in Liquidation J. Brown J. Jones } Liquidators	For the British Coy plc, in Liquidation For J. Brown, Liquidator, J. Jones
	For or on behalf of the British Coy plc, J. Brown, Secy	
	per pro The British Coy plc, Brown & Co	
The British Baking Coy	per pro The British Baking Coy, J. Brown, Secretary	The British Baking Co, p.p. J. Brown, Secy
	per pro The British Baking Coy, Brown & Jones	
	For the British Baking Coy, J. Brown, Agent	John Brown, Manager, British Baking Coy
	per pro The British & Universal Baking Coy (Formerly the British Baking Co), J. Brown, Secy	per pro The Baking Coy, J. Brown, Secy The British Baking Coy per pro The British Baking Co plc, J. Brown, Secy
	p.p. The British Baking Coy, J. Brown, Proprietor	
	The British Baking Coy, J. Brown, cashier authorised to sign	
	The British Baking Coy, J. Brown, Manager (It is better that Brown should sign per pro, For, or On Behalf of)	
The British Shipping Coy, J. Brown & Co, Agents	For the British Shipping Coy, J. Brown & Co, Agents	The British Shipping Coy, per pro J. Brown & Co, Agents, J. Jones
John Brown, Secretary, British Coy plc	John Brown, Secretary, British Coy plc	per pro J. Brown, Secy, British Co plc, J. Jones John Brown
The British Banking Co plc	For the British Banking Co plc J. Brown Manager	
	per pro The British Banking Co plc J. Jones, Pro Manager (Not strictly correct but very common in banks)	
John Brown, Executor	John Brown, Executor	John Brown
John Brown, Treasurer, Redby Cricket Club	John Brown, Treasurer, Redby Cricket Club	John Brown
John Brown, Treasurer, Redby District Council	John Brown, Treasurer, Redby District Council	John Brown John Brown, Treasurer
Redby Urban District Council	For Redby Urban District Council, J. Brown, Treasurer	(If indorsed by a rate collector, confirmation is desired)
Official Receiver of J. Brown & Co	J. Jones, Official Receiver of J. Brown & Co	per pro J. Jones, Official Receiver of J. Brown & Co R. Smith
The Collector of Customs and Excise	J. Brown, Collector of Customs and Excise	per pro J. Brown, Collector of Customs and Excise J. Jones
Earl of Redby	per pro Earl of Redby, J. Brown	J. Brown, agent to the Earl of Redby
Lord Brown	Brown	

Payee	Correct or usually accepted	Wrong or not usually accepted
Lady Brown	Mary Brown	Brown
The Mayor of Oldtown	John Jones, Mayor of Oldtown per pro The Mayor of Oldtown, John Brown	Mayor of Oldtown
The Oldtown Corporation	per pro The Oldtown Corporation, John Brown, Treasurer	per pro The Oldtown Corporation, J. Jones, Rate Collector
Managers of Redby School	J. Brown } Managers of Redby School J. Jones } For the Managers of Redby School, J. Brown, Chairman	J. Jones, Manager J. Brown. J. Jones
Redby Vestry	per pro Redby Vestry, J. Brown, Clerk	J. Brown, clerk to Redby Vestry
Brown frères	Brown Bros. Brown frères	
Owners of Redby Estate per W. Brown	For Owners of Redby Estate, W. Brown	W. Brown
Self or order (drawn by J. Brown)	J. Brown per pro J. Brown, J. Jones. (But evidence of authority required)	
Self or bearer	No indorsement required	
Administrators of Wm Brown (the same remarks apply as in the case of executors)		
Executors of Wm Brown	J. Jones for self & Co-Exor of Wm Brown For Exors of Wm Brown, J. Jones, Exor	per pro Exors of Wm Brown, R. Smith, Solicitor to the Estate per pro Exors of Wm Brown, R. Smith For J. Jones, Executor of Wm Brown, R. Robinson J. Jones for self and Co-executors J. Jones, Exor of Wm Brown J. Jones, Executors of late W. Brown
Executors of the late Wm Brown	J. Jones } Exors of the late Wm J. Brown } Brown	
J. Brown & J. Jones, Executors of the late J. Smith	For Self and Co-Executor of the late J. Smith, J. Brown	J. Brown. J. Jones
Representatives of the late W. W. Brown	For self & Co-Executor of the late W. Brown, J. Smith	J. Smith
Trustees of Wm Brown	J. Brown } Trustees of Wm Brown J. Jones } Trustees of Wm Brown, J. Brown J. Jones	per pro Trustees of Wm Brown, J. Brown For Self & Co-Trustee of Wm Brown, J. Brown o/a Wm Brown's Trust, J. Jones J. Brown
John Brown & J. Jones, Trustees of R. Smith	John Brown } Trustees of R. Smith J. Jones }	John Brown, J. Jones
Liquidators of the X & Y Coy plc	The X & Y Coy plc, in Liquidation, J. Brown } Liquidators J. Jones }	The X & Y Coy plc, For Self & Co-Liquidator J. Brown J. Brown (SEE *Liquidator*) J. Jones
IRREGULAR, ETC, PAYEES		
order	Requires drawer's indorsement	
or order	Return cheque for payee's name	
W. Brown or	Requires W. Brown's indorsement	
Cash or order Wages or Order Estate *a/c* or order	Sometimes indorsed by the drawer, but see under *Impersonal Payees*	
Wages or Bearer	No indorsement required	
King Charles the First or Order	No indorsement required	

INDORSEMENT

Payee	Correct or usually accepted	Wrong or not usually accepted
Dick Swiveller or Order (a fictitious person)	No indorsement required	
s.s. *Britannia* or order	Requires indorsement by an authorized official	
Corporation Stock or Order	Requires City Treasurer's indorsement	
Bearer or Order	Usually treated as payable to bearer	
Income Tax or Order	Requires indorsement of Collector of Inland Revenue	
My son the bearer	Requires son's indorsement	
My son, the bearer or Order	Requires son's indorsement	
Bearer (J. Brown) or order	J. Brown	
J. Brown *a/c* J. Jones	J. Brown *a/c* J. Jones	J. Brown
W. B.	W. B., W. Brown	
a/c of John Brown	Placed to credit of Payee's Account per pro British Banking Co Ltd, J. Jones, Manager	
Brown & Jones (names transposed)	per pro Brown & Jones, T. Smith, Manr per pro Jones & Brown, T. Smith, Manr	
Ann Brown (spelled wrongly)	Ann Brown, Anne Browne (Both in same writing)	Anne Browne
Robert MacIntyre (spelled wrongly)	Robert MacIntyre, Robt MacIntyre (Both in same writing)	Robert McIntyre
W. Brown	Requires payee's indorsement	
Brown	J. Brown	Brown
John Brown & Another	For Self & Another, J. Brown	John Brown
Representatives of John Brown	For Self and Co-Executors of the late John Brown, J. Jones	
John Brown per J. Jones	For John Brown, J. Jones John Brown per J. Jones	J. Brown (confirmation should be obtained)
John Brown for J. Jones	John Brown for John Jones	per pro J. Brown, R. Smith
Miss Brown (now married)	M. Jones *née* Brown	
Brown & Co (correct title R. Brown & Co Ltd)	per pro Brown & Co per pro J. R. Brown & Co Ltd, J. Jones, Secy per pro Brown & Co, J. Jones, Secretary per pro J. R. Brown & Co Ltd, J. Jones, Secretary	
The Secretary (drawn by a Company)	J. Jones, Secretary	
Roseworth Estate per J. Brown	For Roseworth Estate, J. Brown	J. Brown
J. Brown in full settlement	(If indorsed 'J. Brown in part Settlement' a banker would be justified, in the interests of his customer in returning the cheque)	
DIVIDEND WARRANT		
John Brown, John Jones and R. Smith	John Brown (or John Jones or R. Smith may sign alone)	
John Brown & Another	John Brown	Jas Smith (the other referred to)
John Brown	John Brown	per pro John Brown, J. Jones
John Brown, or Bearer	John Brown should sign	
John Brown per British Banking Co Ltd	per pro British Banking Co Ltd, J. Jones, Manager	

INDORSEMENT CONFIRMED An indorsement made by a stamp ought, if the banker knows it to have been placed thereon by an authorized person, to be confirmed. An indorsement may be confirmed where, on the face of it, the signature appears to be incorrect or the situation is not clear and the banker is able to confirm that it is in order.

INDORSEMENT GUARANTEED SEE *Indorsement Confirmed*

INDORSER When a payee writes his name upon the back of a bill or cheque, he is called an 'indorser', and when the instrument is negotiated to other persons, each person may indorse it in turn and become an indorser. Each indorser of a bill (or cheque) is liable thereon.

Any indorser, however, may add after his signature such words as 'without recourse to me', or 'sans recours'. The sanction is given by Section 16 of the Bills of Exchange Act 1882, which provides that any indorser may insert an express stipulation

(1) Negative or limiting his own liability to the holder;
(2) Waiving as regards himself some or all of the holder's duties.

The use of the words 'sans recours' releases the indorser from liability in the event of the cheque being dishonoured, but does not release him from liability with respect to any forgery before his indorsement.

The liability of an indorser is defined by the Bills of Exchange Act, Section 55:

(2) The indorser of a bill by indorsing it—
- (a) Engages that on due presentment it shall be accepted and paid according to its tenor, and that if it be dishonoured he will compensate the holder or a subsequent indorser who is compelled to pay it, provided that the requisite proceedings on dishonour be duly taken;
- (b) Is precluded from denying to a holder in due course the genuineness and regularity in all respects of the drawer's signature and all previous indorsements;
- (c) Is precluded from denying to his immediate or a subsequent indorsee that the bill was at the time of his indorsement, a valid and subsisting bill, and that he had then a good title thereto.

From the above Section it is seen that an indorser engages to compensate a subsequent indorser if the bill is dishonoured. When a bank is the holder of a bill payable to its own order and obtains an indorsement (after its own) by a third party to strengthen its security, the third party is not liable to the bank, as the bank is a prior indorser. If the third party's indorsement is obtained, before the bank has indorsed, the bank would not be a holder in due course (q.v.). When a bank obtains an indorsement to strengthen its security the bank 'should either get, at the same time, a letter acknowledging the indorser's liability to the bank in case of the dishonour of the bill, or should have a statement to this effect written on the bill and signed by the surety'. SEE *Backing a Bill*

Section 56 provides 'Where a person signs a bill otherwise than as drawer or acceptor, he thereby incurs the liabilities of an indorser to a holder in due course'.

Where a person is under obligation to indorse a bill in a representative capacity as treasurer or executor, he may indorse the bill in such terms as to negative personal liability (Section 31(5)).

Where an indorser is dead and the party giving notice knows it, notice of dishonour must be given to his personal representative if such there be, and with the exercise of reasonable diligence he can be found (Section 49(9)).

Where an indorser is bankrupt, notice may be given either to the party himself or to the trustee (Section 49(10)). SEE *Bill of Exchange; Dishonour of Bill of Exchange; Indorsement; Negotiation of Bill of Exchange*

INDUSTRIAL BUILDINGS ALLOWANCE An allowance for tax purposes applicable to industrial buildings used in a business. From April, 1981, an initial capital allowance of 75 per cent of cost was allowed in respect of industrial buildings and thereafter, an allowance of 4 per cent of the original cost was available each year. With effect from 14th March, 1984, the allowance was reduced to 50 per cent and thereafter to 25 per cent in respect of expenditure incurred on or after 1st April, 1985, and to nil in respect of expenditure incurred on or after 1st April, 1986. The annual writing down allowance remains at 4 per cent. All additions and improvements to industrial buildings also qualify for the initial industrial buildings allowance. SEE ALSO *Income Tax; Small Workshop Scheme; Capital Allowances*

INDUSTRIAL AND COMMERCIAL FINANCE CORPORATION (ICFC) The Corporation was formed in 1945 at the instance of the Government and under the aegis of the Bank of England. It was designed to fill the so-called 'Macmillan gap' by providing capital for those smaller companies which were not yet of a size to obtain a Stock Exchange quotation. ICFC has become the major provider of equity finance to smaller and medium-sized companies in this country and is now a subsidiary of Investors in Industry (q.v.).

INDUSTRIAL DEATH BENEFIT Where a man or woman has died as a result of an industrial injury or certain prescribed industrial diseases, the following benefits may be payable to his or her dependants.

Widow's Benefit

Industrial widow's benefit will be paid only to the lawful widow of the deceased. If the widow remarries, the pension will end but she will receive a gratuity equal to one year's pension.

There are three rates of pension:

1. The maximum rate of pension will be paid for the first 26 weeks following the husband's death. Thereafter, one of two permanent rates will be paid:
2. The higher permanent rate will be paid if the widow was over 50 when the husband died or if she was permanently incapable of supporting herself or if she was expecting a child by her late husband or has a child or children for whom child benefit is payable.
3. In other cases, the lower permanent rate will apply.

Benefit for Dependants

In general, benefit will be paid for dependent children for whom child benefit is payable.

A widower may be entitled to benefit if his wife died as a result of an industrial injury or disease and at the time of her death he was permanently incapable of supporting himself and his wife had been contributing more than half the cost of his maintenance.

Parents and other relatives may also receive industrial death benefit if they were receiving 25p or more a week from the deceased towards the cost of their maintenance at the time of the death. If, however, the deceased did not contribute more than half the cost of maintenance of the relative, the relative must be incapable of supporting himself or herself. Thus the benefit will vary according to the extent of maintenance by the deceased and the degree to which the relative is permanently incapable of self-support (See Appendix 2).

INDUSTRIAL DISABLEMENT BENEFIT SEE *Disablement Benefit*

INDUSTRIAL INJURY BENEFIT This used to be one of the two main categories of payment for injuries at work, namely industrial injury benefit and industrial disablement benefit (SEE *Disablement Benefit*). With effect from 6th April, 1983, however, industrial injury benefit was abolished. It was a fixed weekly payment paid to persons incapable of work because of an accident at work. It applied to persons gainfully employed under a contract of service who

1. suffered injury caused by an accident on or after 5th July, 1948; and
2. sustained that injury in the course of employment.

With effect from 6th April, 1983, industrial injury benefit has been replaced by statutory sick pay (q.v.) up to the first eight weeks of disability and thereafter, sickness benefit (q.v.). SEE ALSO *Industrial Diseases*

INDUSTRIAL DISEASES Industrial injury benefit and industrial disablement benefit are payable not only as a result of a direct injury; they may be payable where the employee is suffering from a disease contracted in the course of his employment. There are three main conditions which must be satisfied:

1. The employee must be suffering from one of the prescribed diseases.
2. It must have been contracted in one of the occupations listed under the industrial injuries scheme as conducive to a prescribed disease.
3. The disease must have arisen from employment since 4th July, 1948 (something which will, in many cases, be assumed if the first two conditions are satisfied).

The prescribed diseases embrace a considerable number of occupational hazards including, for example, poisoning from the use of chemicals, anthrax from handling animal hides, malignancies due to electromagnetic radiation, and illnesses such as pneumoconiosis, silicosis and asbestosis from industrial dusts.

INDUSTRIAL LIFE ASSURANCE This is the business of effecting life assurance, the premiums on which are received by house-to-house collection. The life assurance may take various forms such as whole life, endowment, term assurance or, in earlier days, provision for the payment of funeral expenses. However, the essence of industrial insurance, under the terms of the Industrial Assurance Act 1923, is that the premiums or contributions are collected by house-to-house visits—hence the more modern term, home service insurance. If the premiums on a life policy are payable at fixed intervals of more than two calendar months, the policy is not within the Industrial Assurance Acts. The term appears to have arisen from the growth of this type of business in industrial towns, where the population had very little opportunity of paying regular insurance premiums unless someone called at their homes. Most industrial policies were for small amounts and had little or no surrender values. However, the total business was very considerable and formed the basis of the early growth of some of our major life offices of today. The following table shows the total numbers of industrial life policies and the levels of premiums in recent years. SEE ALSO *Life Assurance* and Supplement

In force at end of year	1978	1979	1980	1981	1982
Number of paying policies	58.8m	57.4m	54.5m	52.2m	49.7m
Number of free policies	23.3m	22.9m	22.6m	22.5m	22.2m
Total number of policies	82.1m	80.3m	77.1m	74.7m	71.9m
	£m	£m	£m	£m	£m
Yearly premiums	621	843	938	992	1,070
Sums insured and bonuses	11,700	14,500	16,200	17,400	18,800

INDUSTRIAL PROPERTY A term usually applied to factories and warehouses and other buildings put to an industrial use in contrast to commercial property (usually shops and offices), residential property and agricultural land. SEE ALSO *Industrial Buildings Allowance; Small Workshop Scheme*

INDUSTRIAL AND PROVIDENT SOCIETIES These are societies which are registered under the Industrial and Provident Societies Act 1893, as amended. They are incorporated bodies owned by their members and may be formed for the purpose of carrying on any industry, trade or business. Special rules apply if they wish to carry on the business of banking. The name was originally applied to societies formed for the purpose of making profits which were to be distributed in a provident and frugal way to their members. It is of the essence of industrial and provident societies that they should be co-operative in nature and Co-operative Societies, as known in the UK, are usually incorporated under the Industrial and Provident Societies Acts 1893 to 1965. The principal benefits attaching to membership of these Societies, at least historically, were incorporation with limited liability, power to hold land, the right of members to dispose of their interest in the Society on death by nomination, and provisions for a simple method of settlement of disputes.

Societies which contain provisions in their rules permitting the withdrawal of share capital are not allowed to carry on the business of banking.

INFANTS All persons below the age of 18 are, by English law, called minors. The generally accepted legal opinion appears now to be that a banker may, without risk, allow a minor to open an account and draw cheques upon it, but that the account must not be overdrawn, for money lent to a minor cannot be recovered, even if he gave security. All contracts entered into by a minor for the repayment of money lent are absolutely void (Infants' Relief Act 1874, Section 1). Nor can such contracts effectively be ratified after the minor attains full age.

The opening of a credit account, it is suggested, should be subject to the banker having no reason to believe that the minor operating the account does not understand the simple nature of the transaction.

By the Infants' Relief Act 1874, Section 2,

> no action shall be brought whereby to charge any person upon any promise made after full age to pay any debt contracted during infancy or upon any ratification made after full age, of any promise or contract made during infancy whether there shall or shall not be any new consideration for such promise or ratification after full age.

The holder of a minor's cheque, which has been dishonoured, cannot sue the minor upon it; and where a cheque has been exchanged for a minor and is subsequently dishonoured, the money cannot be recovered by law from the minor.

In savings banks, receipts are given by minors and accepted, but in those cases special provision is made under the Savings Bank Acts that the receipt of a person of the age of seven years or upwards shall be a sufficient discharge.

A minor cannot be sued on a bill of exchange or promissory note, even though it be given for necessaries (*In re Soltykoff* [1981] 1 QB 413).

Section 22(2) of the Bills of Exchange Act 1882, provides

> Where a bill is drawn or indorsed by an infant, minor, or corporation having no capacity or power to incur liability on a bill, the drawing or indorsement entitles the holder to receive payment of the bill, and to enforce it against any other party thereto.

The signature of a minor upon a bill does not in any way affect its negotiability. He may pass on a good title to others, and though he cannot be sued himself he may 'by his next friend' sue other parties to the bill. Even if a minor accepts a bill in payment of necessaries, he cannot be sued upon it.

A minor cannot sue in his own name, except in a county court for wages due to him. In an action by a minor he must sue by his 'next friend', and in an action against a minor a guardian is appointed.

But if a minor has made a false representation as to his age and thereby induced a banker or anyone to enter into a contract with him, he cannot afterwards obtain relief by proving that he is below the age of 18. On the other hand, a banker cannot enforce such a contract.

The Limitation Act 1939 does not begin to run until the minor has reached the age of 18.

Shares with a liability should not be registered in the name of a minor, as he may repudiate any liability thereon, either before he comes of age or within a reasonable time afterwards.

A minor may sign as a witness; he may also act as an agent and sign cheques, and draw, accept, or indorse bills, and the liability rests with the person who gave him the authority to do so. He may sign cheques upon an overdrawn account if that power is included in the authority. There is nothing to prevent a minor being a partner in any business, but in any action against the firm the minor would be excluded. A minor cannot undertake the duties of an administrator or executor nor act as a proxy in bankruptcy proceedings. He cannot make a will except on active service and in the event of his death, letters of administration require to be taken out by his father or mother or nearest of kin. A minor cannot be made liable on a guarantee.

A legal estate in land cannot be conveyed to a minor (Law of Property Act 1925, Section 1(6)). A minor cannot be appointed a trustee (Section 20).

An account is sometimes opened with a banker in joint names of a parent or guardian and a minor: such an account should be treated by the banker like an ordinary joint account as to authority for signing of cheques, etc., but he will, of course, bear in mind the non-liability of the minor for an overdraft, as before mentioned. If the minor is a very young child, the better plan is for the account to be opened in the parent's or guardian's name for the child, thus, 'John Brown, in re Timothy Brown', in which case no mandate is required, and the adult has full control.

A deposit receipt may be issued in the name of a minor. On withdrawal he is able to give a good discharge for the money.

In the case of stock in public funds, by the National Debt Act 1870, Section 19,

Where stock is standing in the name of an infant or person of unsound mind, jointly with any person not under legal disability, a letter of attorney for the receipt of the dividends on the stock shall be sufficient authority in that behalf, if given under the hand and seal of the person not under disability, attested by two or more credible witnesses.

By the National Debt (Stockholders Relief) Act 1892, Section 3,

(a) Where an infant is the sole survivor in an account; and
(b) where an infant holds stock jointly with a person under legal disability; and
(c) where stock has by mistake been bought in or transferred into the sole name of an infant, the Bank may, at the request in writing of the parent, guardian, or next friend of the infant, receive the dividends and apply them to the purchase of like stock, and the stock so purchased shall be added to the original investment.

By the Family Law Reform Act 1969, in documents executed after 31st December, 1969, full age is attained on the eighteenth birthday. In the case of documents executed before 1st January, 1970, full age is attained on the twenty-first birthday.

In 1984, the Law Commission published a Report on 'The Law of Contract—Minors' Contracts'. The Commission considered that there was little need for radical change in the law on this subject and that the general rule should remain, that a minor's contract is unenforceable against a minor, subject to a number of specific exceptions. The Commission did recommend, however, that Section 1 of the Infants' Relief Act 1874, should be repealed to the intent that a minor, on attaining majority, would then be able to ratify a contract made during minority. Also, the Commission recommended that provision should be made to allow a guarantee given for a loan to a minor to be enforceable against the guarantor in the same way as should be the case if the minor had been an adult. A further recommendation was that where a minor acquires goods under a contract which is unenforceable against him because he is a minor and he refuses to pay for the goods, the Court should be able to require the minor to return the goods or the equivalent property to the other party.

INFLATION It may be said of inflation as Lord Denning said of bankers—'It is easier to recognize than to define'. It may be expressed in terms of rising prices or, conversely, the fall in the purchasing power of a monetary unit. A modest level of inflation is not necessarily a harmful thing if its effects are spread evenly throughout the community (which is seldom the case). Serious inflation is harmful to society, in that it destroys confidence in the currency and inhibits the conduct of business. Its impact is felt particularly on those sections of society who are on fixed incomes. There is little agreement as to the causes of inflation. In its simplest terms, it is the increase of money (cash and credit) in a community without any corresponding increase in goods and services. Thus, the money supply is an important factor in the control of inflation and this is the main plank of the so-called monetarist view. There would appear to be little doubt that lavish Government expenditure can be inflationary and, equally, that firmness in controlling the money supply in the western world in recent times has helped to reduce inflation. Other factors can, however, be inflationary, certainly in the short term. Prices may rise because of excess demand or because of rising costs (so-called cost push inflation).

The accepted measurement of prices in the UK is the General Index of Retail Prices. SEE *Cost of Living*

The following table shows the purchasing power of £1 in domestic terms since 1914, taking its value as equivalent to 100p in various years.

	Year in which purchasing power was 100p									
	1914	**1920**	**1930**	**1938**	**1946**	**1950**	**1960**	**1970**	**1980**	**1983**
1914	100	250	160	160	260	320	450	660	2,400	3,000
1920	40	100	60	60	110	130	180	260	1,000	1,200
1930	60	160	100	100	170	200	280	420	1,500	1,900
1938	60	160	100	100	170	200	280	420	1,500	1,900
1946	40	90	60	60	100	120	170	250	900	1,100
1950	30	80	50	50	80	100	140	210	740	940
1960	20	60	40	40	60	70	100	150	530	680
1970	15	40	20	20	40	50	70	100	360	460
1980	5	10	5	5	10	15	20	30	100	130
1983	5	10	5	5	10	10	15	20	80	100

Source: Government Statistical Service.

Reading off the left-hand scale of years, the individual columns show the corresponding purchasing power of 100p in the years from 1914 to 1983, e.g. reading across from 1946 it will be seen that £1 in that year had the corresponding purchasing power of 40p in 1914, and 1,100p, i.e. £11.00 in 1983.

INFLATION ACCOUNTING The term applied to the various techniques adopted in modern times to adjust business accounts, principally those of public companies, to correct the impact of inflation. It became apparent during the 1970s that the historic cost methods of accounting were not realistic in times of high inflation and that, to some extent, the profits of some companies were illusory. The traditional methods of financial accounting did not reflect the changes in the purchasing power of money, nor the true replacement costs of stock in trade and depreciating assets. The method of accounting eventually proposed for public companies was set out in *Statement of Standard Accounting Practice* 16 (SSAP 16) of the Institute of Chartered Accountants in England and Wales. This was based on the concept of current cost accounting and has been the subject of much discussion and some amendment. SEE *Current Cost Accounting*

INGOT A bar of gold or silver.

INHERITANCE (PROVISION FOR FAMILY AND DEPENDANTS) ACT 1975 This Act, which is concerned with provision for dependants of a deceased person, repealed and replaced the Inheritance (Family Provision) Act 1938, the Family Provision Act 1966 and certain sections of the Matrimonial Causes Act 1965.

The principal provision of the Act is that where a person dies domiciled in England or Wales, leaving

1. a wife or husband; or
2. a former wife or husband who has not remarried; or
3. a child; or
4. 'a child of the family' in respect of any marriage of the deceased; or
5. any other person who was being maintained wholly or partly by the deceased at the time of his or her death,

and if the deceased's will or the provisions arising on intestacy do not make 'reasonable provision' for the maintenance of those persons, the court may order appropriate provision to be made out of the estate. A surviving husband or wife may apply for provision to be made under the Act even though he or she may not be financially in need of maintenance.

Unless the court agrees otherwise, an application under the Act may not be brought after the expiry of six months from the date on which a Grant of Probate or Grant of Letters of Administration has been taken out.

The court has wide powers to make an order for a lump sum or for periodic payments to be made to the applicant and may do so out of the estate or out of settled property or *donationes mortis causa* or out of property which has been nominated.

If an asset has been transferred for less than its full value within six years before the death, with the intent to defeat a claim under the Act, the court has power to order the recipient to set aside all or part of that property for the purpose of making provision for the deceased's dependants.

If a party to a marriage dies within 12 months of a decree of divorce, nullity, or judicial separation, and no order has been settled (for maintenance etc.) under the Matrimonial Causes Act 1973, the court may, on the application of the survivor to the marriage, make an order under the Inheritance (Provisions for Family and Dependants) Act, as if the decree, etc., had not been granted. The Act further provides, however, that on the granting of a decree of divorce, nullity or judicial separation, the Court may with the agreement of the parties, order that either party shall not be entitled on the death of the other to apply for an order under the Inheritance (Provision for Family and Dependants) Act.

A personal representative who has distributed all or part of an estate after the end of the six months period incurs no liability for not having taken into account the possibility that the court might grant an application under the Act after the end of the statutory period.

In considering an application under the Act, the court has to determine whether, under the will or intestacy (or a combination of both), 'reasonable provision' has been made for the applicant. In determining whether reasonable provision has been made, the court is required under the Act to have regard to

1. the financial resources and the financial needs which the applicant has or is likely to have in the foreseeable future;
2. the financial resources and financial needs which any other applicant for such an order has or is likely to have in the foreseeable future;
3. the financial resources and the financial needs which any beneficiary of the estate of the deceased has or is likely to have in the foreseeable future;
4. any obligations and responsibilities which the deceased had towards any applicant for such an order or towards any beneficiary of his estate;
5. the size and nature of the deceased's estate;
6. any physical or mental disability of any applicant for such an order or any beneficiary of the deceased's estate; and
7. any other matter, including the conduct of the applicant or any other person, which in the circumstances of the case, the court may consider relevant.

In the case of an application by a deceased's wife or husband, or former wife or husband who has not remarried, the court must have regard to the applicant's age, the duration of the marriage and the contribution made by the applicant to the welfare of the deceased's family, including any contribution made by looking after the home or caring for the family.

On an application by the child of the deceased or a person who has been treated by the deceased as a 'child of the family' the court must have regard to the manner in which the applicant was being, or in which he might expect to be, educated or trained.

Provision is made for the admissibility of statements made by the deceased but the court is no longer required to place itself in the position of the deceased in the circumstances foreseeable at the time of death (as used to be the case under the earlier legislation and resulting decisions). The court must now take into account the facts as they are known to exist at the date of the hearing. SEE *Administration of Estates; Intestacy; Will*

INJURY BENEFIT SEE *Industrial Injury Benefit*

INLAND BILL The Bills of Exchange Act 1882, Section 4, defines an inland bill as follows.

> (1) An inland bill is a bill which is or on the face of it purports to be (a) both drawn and payable within the British Islands, or (b) drawn within the British Islands upon some person resident therein. Any other bill is a foreign bill.
>
> For the purpose of this Act, 'British Islands' mean any part of the United Kingdom of Great Britain and Ireland, the islands of Man, Guernsey, Jersey, Alderney, and Sark, and the islands adjacent to any of them being part of the dominions of Her Majesty.
>
> (2) Unless the contrary appear on the face of the bill the holder may treat it as an inland bill.

The definition of 'British Islands' has, since the establishment of the Irish Free State, been modified by Section 2 of Statutory Rules and Orders 1923, to exclude the Irish Free State. A bill, therefore, that is drawn in the Irish Free State (now known as the Republic of Ireland) and is payable in England is a foreign bill within the meaning of the Bills of Exchange Act. SEE UNDER *Foreign Bill*

Where an inland bill is dishonoured, it is not necessary that it should be noted or protested for non-acceptance or non-payment in order to preserve recourse against the drawer or indorser. It is only necessary when proceedings for dishonour are going to be taken. The sections of the Act with regard to noting and protest are given in the entry *Protest*.

Where an inland bill is indorsed in a foreign country, the indorsement shall as regards the payer be interpreted according to the UK law. As to the other rules laid down in the Bills of Exchange Act with regard to bills drawn in one country and negotiated, accepted or payable in another, see Section 72 under *Foreign Bill*.

INLAND REVENUE ACCOUNT The document delivered to the Capital Taxes Office by an executor or an administrator of a deceased person, setting out the details of the assets and liabilities of the deceased's estate. It is required for the purpose of determining any capital transfer tax liability and must be delivered notwithstanding that there may be no such liability. The Grant of Probate or Grant of Letters of Administration will not be issued by the Probate Court until the Inland Revenue Account has been delivered and any duty assessed and paid.

In the case of deaths on or after 1st April, 1983, it is not necessary to deliver an Inland Revenue Account if the gross value of a deceased's estate does not exceed £40,000, provided

1. the estate consists only of property which has passed under the deceased's will or intestacy, or by nomination, or beneficiary by survivorship, and
2. not more than 10 per cent of the gross value of the estate or £1,000, whichever is the higher, consists of property situated outside the UK, and
3. the deceased died domiciled in the UK, and had made no lifetime gifts chargeable to capital transfer tax.

Such exempt cases are known as 'excepted estates'. The Inland Revenue reserves the right to call for an account by serving on the personal representatives a written notice within 35 days of the issue of the Grant of Probate. If the Inland Revenue do not issue such a Notice the personal representatives are discharged from any further claim for capital transfer tax at the end of the 35 days (provided there has been no fraud or failure to disclose material facts). If, however, further property is discovered in the estate, taking it above the 'excepted estate' level, an account will then be required.

INSCRIBED STOCK No certificates are issued to the holders of inscribed stock, but their names and the amount of the stock they hold are inscribed in the registers kept for the purpose at the registrars who have the management of the stocks.

Originally, Government stocks were issued only in inscribed form, but later, stock certificates to bearer and registered stock with a stock certificate were permitted. SEE *National Debt*

As from 1st January, 1943, inscribed stock for Government securities was abolished in favour of stock entailing the issue of certificates either registered or to bearer, the former type prevailing. Other inscribed stocks domiciled at the Bank of England, such as Metropolitan Water Board issues were similarly converted to registered form and inscribed stock has now virtually disappeared.

INSIDER DEALING It is provided by Section 1 of the Company Securities (Insider Dealing) Act 1985 that

> an individual who is, or at any time in the preceding six months has been, knowingly connected with a company shall not deal on a recognised stock exchange in securities of that company if he has information which:
>
> (*a*) he holds by virtue of being connected with the company;
> (*b*) it would be reasonable to expect a person so connected and in the position by virtue of which he is so connected not to disclose except for the proper performance of the functions attaching to the position; and
> (*c*) he knows is unpublished price sensitive information in relation to those securities.

Subsection (2) provides that, subject to certain exceptions (see below)

> an individual who is, or at any time in the preceding six months has been knowingly connected with a company shall not deal on a recognised stock exchange in securities of any other company if he has information which
>
> (*a*) he holds by virtue of being connected with the first company;
> (*b*) it would be reasonable to expect a person so connected and in the position by virtue of which he is so connected not to disclose except for the proper performance of the functions attaching to that position;
> (*c*) he knows is unpublished price sensitive information in relation to those securities of that other company; and
> (*d*) relates to any transaction (actual or contemplated) involving both the first company and that other company or involving one of them and securities of the other or to the fact that any transaction is no longer contemplated.

Subsections (3) and (4) provide (subject to the same exception, see below) that where

(a) any individual has information which he knowingly obtained (directly or indirectly) from another individual who is connected with a particular company, or was at any time in the six months preceding the obtaining of the information so connected and who the former individual knows or has reasonable cause to believe held the information by virtue of being so connected; and

(b) the former individual knows or has reasonable cause to believe that, because of the latter's connection and position, it would be reasonable to expect him not to disclose the information except for the proper performance of the functions attaching to that position;

then, the former individual:

(i) shall not himself deal on a recognised stock exchange in securities of that company if he knows that the information is unpublished price sensitive information in relation to those securities; and

(ii) shall not himself deal on a recognised stock exchange in securities of any other company if he knows that the information is unpublished price sensitive information in relation to those securities and it relates to any transaction (actual or contemplated) involving the first company and the other company or involving one of them and securities of the other or to the fact that any such transaction is no longer contemplated.

Subsection (5) provides that

where an individual is contemplating, or has contemplated, making, whether with or without another person, a take-over offer for a company in a particular capacity, that individual shall not deal on a recognised stock exchange in securities of that company in another capacity if he knows that information that the offer is contemplated or is no longer contemplated is unpublished price sensitive information in relation to those securities.

Subsection (6) provides that

where an individual has knowingly obtained (directly or indirectly), from an individual to whom subsection (4) above applied, information that the offer referred to in subsection (4) is being contemplated or is no longer contemplated, the former individual shall not himself deal on a recognised stock exchange in securities of that company if he knows that the information is unpublished price sensitive information in relation to those securities.

Subsection (7) provides that

an individual who is for the time being prohibited by any provision of this section from dealing on a recognised stock exchange in any securities shall not counsel or procure any other person to deal in those securities, knowing or having reasonable cause to believe that that person would deal in them on a recognised stock exchange.

Subsection (8) provides that

an individual who is for the time being prohibited as aforesaid from dealing on a recognised stock exchange in any securities by reason of his having any information, shall not communicate that information to any other person if he knows or has reasonable cause to believe that that or some other person will make use of the information for the purpose of dealing, or of counselling or procuring any other person to deal, on a recognised stock exchange in those securities.

These provisions do not prohibit a person by reason of his having any information from

(a) doing any particular thing otherwise than with a view to the making of a profit or the avoidance of a loss (whether for himself or another person) by the use of that information;

(b) entering into a transaction in the course of the exercise in good faith of his functions as liquidator, receiver or trustee in bankruptcy; or

(c) doing any particular thing if the information:

(i) was obtained by him in the course of a business of a jobber in which he was engaged or employed; and

(ii) was of a description which it would be reasonable to expect him to obtain in the ordinary course of that business.

Thus, 'insider dealing' means dealing in the securities of a company whilst in possession of unpublished price-sensitive information. For this purpose, the following are deemed to be 'connected with a company':

1. Individuals who are, or at any time in the preceding six months have been, knowingly connected with a company.
2. Individuals who are contemplating, or have contemplated, making a takeover offer for a company in a particular capacity.
3. Individuals who have knowingly obtained, either directly or indirectly, certain information from an individual in one of the first two categories above.

Thus, connected persons not only include directors and senior officials of companies, but also their auditors, solicitors, merchant bankers and other professional persons acting on the companies' behalf. Whilst a bank acting as a merchant bank is certainly in the first category above, it is perfectly possible that a banker acting as banker could be in that same category. In any case, the banker could certainly be in the third category, i.e. that of receiving information from another person such as one of the company officials. One of the apparent anomalies of the legislation is that a connected person is free to deal in the securities concerned six months after his connection has terminated (although normally the price-sensitivity of his information would have passed by that time), whereas someone who receives information from a connected person appears to remain disqualified for so long as the information remains price-sensitive. The meaning of 'unpublished price-sensitive information' is defined in the Act. It must relate to *specific* matters concerning the company whose securities are in question, it must not be generally known to those persons who are accustomed to, or are likely to, deal in those securities and it must be such that, if it were generally known, it would be likely materially to affect the price.

INSOLVENCY A person is insolvent who is unable to pay his debts, and he is said to be in a state of insolvency.

An insolvent debtor is not necessarily a bankrupt (see below) and a bankrupt is not necessarily insolvent (e.g. a partner in a bankrupt firm).

An insolvent person may have a receiving order made against him and suffer proceedings under the Bankruptcy Acts (SEE *Bankruptcy; Receiving Order*) or he may call his creditors together and endeavour to come to an agreement with them (apart from the Bankruptcy Acts), usually either by offering to pay a composition—that is, to pay so much in the pound in full discharge of what he is owing to them (SEE *Composition with Creditors*)—or by offering to transfer his property to a trustee in order that it may be realized and the proceeds divided amongst his creditors according to the amounts of their respective claims. SEE *Assignment for Benefit of Creditors*

If a person becomes bankrupt, having continued to trade with knowledge of his insolvency, he cannot be granted an immediate unconditional discharge by the court (Section 26, Bankruptcy Act 1914).

The term 'corporate insolvency' is used to apply to a company which is in an insolvent state.

The whole question of insolvency law and practice in relation both to individuals and companies, was the subject of a Report in April, 1981 of a review committee under the chairmanship of Sir Kenneth Cork (SEE *Cork Committee*). This was followed in February, 1984 by a White Paper entitled *A Revised Framework for Insolvency Law* (Cmnd 9175, HMSO). The main proposals contained in the White Paper and listed below, were intended as the basis for a new Insolvency Bill to be introduced in the Parliamentary Session 1984–85. The main provisions of the White Paper under the principal headings are as follows.

Professional Standards for Insolvency Practitioners

The present law which allows persons with no practical experience or relevant professional qualification to act as trustee or liquidator, or as receiver for a debenture-holder, is unsatisfactory.

To give creditors confidence in the persons they appoint to administer insolvent estates and to reduce the amount of supervision required by the Department of Trade and Industry, insolvency practitioners will normally have to be practising solicitors or members of accountancy bodies recognized for the purpose by the Secretary of State. They will also be obliged to obtain an insurance bond against all types of dishonesty and negligence. The Review Committee on Insolvency Law and Practice proposed that there should be transitional arrangements to cater for experienced but unqualified practitioners. The Secretary of State will have powers to authorize any person who has regularly acted as an insolvency practitioner over a period of five years before the issue of this White Paper.

Steps will be taken to extend the power of the court to enforce the duties that liquidators, administrators or trustees have to those entitled to participate in the distribution of funds which they administer. It is for consideration as to how far parallel duties should be extended to receivers.

Disqualification and Personal Liability of Company Directors

Directors who allow their companies to arrive at a state of affairs where they are wound up compulsorily by the court have demonstrated that they are not fit to be in control of a company and the proposed legislation will therefore provide (with limited exceptions) for the automatic disqualification for three years from the management of a company of the directors of insolvent companies wound up by the court.

The Government will also amend Section 9 of the Insolvency Act 1976 (under which persons involved in two insolvent liquidations can now be disqualified for up to 15 years) to enable it to operate after one liquidation and to allow a voluntary liquidator to make an application.

Disqualified persons will, however, be able to seek the leave of the court to act in the management of a company, as they can at present.

Disqualified persons who take part in the management of a company without the leave of the court or those who act on their behalf, will be personally liable for the debts incurred by that company while they were acting.

The Review Committee's concept of wrongful

trading will be introduced in a modified form, to enable a civil liability to be imposed upon a director (including a shadow director) who allows a company to continue to trade when he knew, or should have known that there was no prospect of it being able to meet its liabilities. Only a liquidator will be able to pursue a personal liability claim.

Procedural Changes in Corporate and Personal Insolvency

Once the court has made an order, matters should proceed much as at present, although the compulsory winding-up and bankruptcy procedures should be modernized, improved and harmonized wherever this is possible. The major changes proposed are as follows.

1. *Public examinations* The public interest will be better served by the revived use of such examinations in compulsory winding-up proceedings in cases where this will assist the Official Receiver's investigation.
2. *Bankruptcy orders* A single bankruptcy order will replace the present sequential receiving and adjudication orders for personal debtors.
3. *Small cases* Where a debtor with assets presents his own petition and his liabilities do not exceed £15,000, a modified procedure will apply with a view to diverting away from the Official Receiver a number of cases where his investigative skills are not required.
4. *Acts of bankruptcy* The concept of acts of bankruptcy will be abolished and petitions for bankruptcy will be put on much the same basis as those for compulsory winding up.
5. *Deposits on petitions* To offset the Official Receiver's costs and expenses in company cases where there is a paucity of assets, a petition deposit equivalent to that for creditors' petitions in bankruptcy will be introduced for compulsory winding up.
6. *Petition debts* The minimum debt capable of supporting a creditor's petition for both compulsory winding up and bankruptcy will be increased from £200 to £750. (Now done.)
7. *Discharge of debtors* Debtors will be automatically discharged from a first bankruptcy three years after the date of the bankruptcy order, introducing uniformity of treatment for debtors and avoiding the involvement of the Official Receiver and the court in complex discharge procedures. Automatic discharge will not apply in relation to second or subsequent bankruptcies.
8. *Interest on claims* Interest rates applicable in insolvencies will be brought up to date and the various winding-up and bankruptcy provisions will be harmonized.

Voluntary Procedures

Corporate debtors Voluntary winding up is a valuable procedure enabling insolvent companies and their creditors to settle their affairs privately without official involvement, strict standards for insolvency practitioners, improved disqualifying measures and new provisions imposing personal liability on directors will go a long way towards protecting creditors' interests. However, the Government feels that further measures are necessary, in particular to deal with the practice of an insolvent company acting in breach of the present provisions by appointing a liquidator to realize its assets before the creditors have met and had a chance to appoint their own nominee.

This effectively wrests control from the creditors and provides scope for the disposal of assets at below their true value, possibly involving collusion between the liquidator and the company's directors. Provisions have been designed to remedy this abuse and to provide creditors in a voluntary winding up with better and more detailed information.

Personal debtors Personal debtors who wish to make a voluntary settlement with their creditors by using a deed of arrangement are often advised not to do so, since a deed, even if the majority of creditors accept the proposals, does not bind the minority and any non-assenting creditor can still petition for bankruptcy. Provisions will, therefore, be introduced to make it easier for debtors to make binding private arrangements with their creditors without unnecessary official involvement. The new small case procedure is specificially aimed at assisting debtors with assets to avoid bankruptcy by entering into an arrangement.

The Floating Charge and Company Receivership

The gradual development this century of the law relating to the appointment of receivers and managers under a floating charge as a result of decisions of the courts has given rise to uncertainty as to the exact nature of the powers and obligations of receivers and managers.

The Insolvency Bill will, therefore, contain provisions which will establish more clearly in the legislation these powers and obligations. In addition, the opportunity will be taken to impose additional obligations on the receiver to grant unsecured creditors of a company in receivership the opportunity to form a committee and to provide such committees with information.

The committee of unsecured creditors will be

empowered to seek redress from the court if dissatisfied with the information provided by a receiver.

The Administrator

Receivership is not necessarily the complete remedy where a concern is confronted by serious financial problems but where there is a reasonable prospect of rehabilitation in whole or in part.

The Government agrees with the Review Committee's recommendation that an alternative insolvency mechanism, to be known as the administrator procedure, should be established. This new procedure will facilitate the rehabilitation or reorganization of a company in difficulties with a view to restoring it to profitability or will encourage the preservation of viable elements of a company as going concerns.

The court will be empowered to appoint an administrator to a company on the application of the company or a creditor of the company, where the company is insolvent or close to insolvency but where there is a reasonable prospect of rehabilitation or reorganization of the company in whole or in part.

No administrator will be appointed, however, where the holder of a floating charge wishes to exercise his right to appoint a receiver and manager.

The task of the administrator will be in two stages. On appointment, he will assume the management of the company and undertake the preparation of a rescue or rehabilitation policy, or failing that, a policy for the most profitable realization of assets in the interest of the company's creditors and shareholders.

The administrator will then be required to submit his proposed policy to the company's unsecured creditors. If, in the light of his proposals, they vote in favour of his continued appointment, the administrator will so report to the court, which will have the power to confirm his appointment subject to hearing views expressed by other interested parties.

During the currency of an administrator's appointment, no petition for winding up may be made without the leave of the court. The appointment of the administrator will bring about a stay on all proceedings and actions and on the creditors' rights to enforce security or payment, or to levy execution, except where proceedings to levy distress commence prior to the appointment.

The administrator will be under a duty to act at all times in the interest of the creditors and shareholders as a whole.

The introduction of wrongful trading will encourage directors to consider at an earlier stage the financial position and prospects of their companies. The availability of the administrator procedure will ensure that an alternative to receivership or liquidation will be available where there are reasonable grounds for supposing that rehabilitation or reorganization of a company is achievable.

The Role of the Insolvency Service

The Government considers it essential, both in the public interest and that of the creditors, that the Official Receiver should continue to become actively involved in compulsory windings up and bankruptcies immediately an order is made by the court and that his present role as regards the protection and preservation of assets should continue.

This function also has the advantage from an investigative point of view of enabling the Official Receiver at a very early stage to obtain an essential insight into how the affairs of the company or debtor have been conducted.

The Official Receiver's investigative role is of paramount importance. The reforms to insolvency procedures will have the effect of freeing the Official Receiver from time-consuming and demanding tasks which have no direct bearing on investigation. The Government wishes to see insolvency-related offences prosecuted wherever possible, thus enhancing commercial morality and acting as a deterrent to those who might otherwise engage in illegal activities.

The Department of Trade and Industry will have the power to appoint liquidators in compulsory windings up where none has otherwise been appointed, as it does for trustees in bankruptcy.

At the time of writing, the Government's proposals have been embodied in an Insolvency Bill, at present before Parliament. It has given rise to a considerable amount of debate, principally on the subject of automatic disqualification of directors of companies which have been put into compulsory liquidation (See Supplement).

INSOLVENCY ACT 1976 This Act (*inter alia*) increased certain monetary limits in connection with bankruptcy and liquidation. In particular, it raised to £800 the maximum sum in respect of wages or salary ranking as preferential debt, it increased to £2,000 the maximum amount for jurisdiction in the County Court in bankruptcy proceedings and the maximum share capital (now £120,000) for winding-up proceedings of a company in the County Court, and increased to £6,000 the maximum unsecured liabilities for exemption of a bankrupt person from criminal liability where he has failed to keep books of account, in those cases where he has not previously been made bankrupt or made a composition or arrangement with his creditors. In all other cases, the maximum is £1,200.

The Act also extends the time for compliance with a Bankruptcy Notice (q.v.) from seven days to ten days.

Section 7 of the Act enables the court to make an order for the automatic discharge of a bankrupt person five years after his adjudication.

Section 9 enables the court to order that a person shall not be a director of a company, without leave of the court, for a maximum period of five years in cases where

1. that person is or has been the director of a company which has gone into liquidation at a time when it was insolvent;
2. has been a director of another company which has similarly gone into liquidation within five years of the date on which the first company went into liquidation; and
3. the court is satisfied that his conduct as a director of any other companies makes him unfit to be concerned in the management of a company.

INSTALMENT CREDIT The term may be applied to virtually any credit arrangement where the amount involved is to be repaid over a period. Thus, hire purchase, credit sales, credit card finance, and budget accounts in stores are all examples of instalment credit. Leasing is also categorized sometimes as instalment credit but is not strictly so because a leasing contract provides for the payment of rent, rather than repayment of money. SEE *Credit Card; Crowther Committee on Consumer Credit; Hire Purchase Finance; Leasing*

INSTITUTE OF BANKERS This was founded in 1879 and is a professional association of men and women engaged in banking. The objects of the Institute are

1. to afford opportunities for the acquisition of a knowledge of the theory of banking;
2. to facilitate the consideration and discussion of matters of interest to bankers;
3. to take any measures which may be desirable to further the interests of banking.

As at 1st January, 1985, the Institute had 111,135 members, made up of 2,968 Fellows, 40,885 Associates and 67,282 other members.

The Institute is primarily an educational body and is the examining body for the Institute's Diploma. These are the Banking Diploma, the Trustee Diploma and, from 1985, an International Banking Diploma. There are also a number of diplomas in specialist subjects.

The Institute provides comprehensive library and information facilities in Lombard Street and is also the publisher of a number of works on banking and related subjects. It operates through local centres in the UK and overseas.

The Institute publishes monthly, jointly with Waterlow Publishers Limited, *Banking World*, which now combines the former *Journal of the Institute of Bankers* and the former *Bankers' Magazine*.

The history of the Institute is told in *Debtors to the Profession* by Edwin Green, published to mark the centenary of the Institute in 1979.

The Institute works closely with the Institute of Bankers in Scotland and the Institute of Bankers in Ireland, which operate similarly in their respective countries. The Scottish Institute was, in fact, the first Institute of Bankers to be established in the British Isles, having been founded in 1875.

INSTITUTE OF CHARTERED ACCOUNTANTS IN ENGLAND AND WALES The Institute was incorporated by Royal Charter on 11th May, 1880. The charter was granted on the petition of the presidents of five societies of accountants then existing in London, Liverpool, Manchester and Sheffield, together with two public accountants in Manchester. Rules of professional conduct were established and a required standard of skill was set. Membership totalled 587.

The Institute developed rapidly and by 1890, with 1678 members, it was important commercially and held in respect by government officials. A fundamental reason for the increase in the importance of chartered accountants was the growth in the number of limited liability companies. The 1900 Companies Act required that all limited companies must produce an audited balance sheet.

During the First World War, some members looked after enemy alien-owned banks and companies. Others assisted in controlling the production of the vast quantities of munitions required for the war effort. Wartime taxation was another important area of work. By 1930, with a membership of approximately 9,000, the Institute's position had been greatly strengthened in all parts of the country by the growth of the provincial societies.

The Institute continued to perfect its techniques and expand its functions. In many directions there was fresh scope for the chartered accountant's knowledge and experience. The rise in the number, and the increase in the size, of joint stock companies resulted in a growing demand for more scientific management and a greater knowledge of costing. Members of the Institute acted as consultants and economic advisors, considering the individual problems of clients in the light of the general economic situation.

A supplemental Royal Charter was granted on 21st December, 1948. This redrafted the constitution and simplified the administration of the Institute's affairs by removing many difficulties and obscurities.

In 1957 the Society of Incorporated Accountants was integrated with the Institute. Over 10,000 members of the Society became members of the Institute under the scheme of integration.

A further scheme for integration of the various accountancy bodies to create three geographical Institutes for England and Wales, Scotland and Ireland was turned down by members in 1970. However, in 1974, the Consultative Committee of Accountancy Bodies was set up to enable the six bodies concerned to work closely together and to issue joint statements.

The Institute celebrated its Centenary in 1980 and it continues to play a leading part in the development of the accountancy profession, and of accounting policies, in this country and overseas. At December, 1983, the Institute had over 78,000 members in the UK and overseas. Of these, approximately 22,000 held practising certificates.

INSURABLE INTEREST Before a person can effect an insurance on the life of another person, or can insure a ship or cargo, or a house against fire, or any other thing, he must have an insurable, that is, a pecuniary, interest in the person or thing to be insured. In every insurance contract, the assured must have an insurable interest in the sense that 'the event must be one which is prima facie adverse to the interest of the assured' (*Prudential Insurance Co* v *Inland Revenue Commissioners* [1904] 2 KB 658). Under the Marine Insurance Act 1906, every person has an insurable interest who is interested in a marine adventure and its proceeds. A person is deemed to be 'interested' in an event if, on the happening of the event, he will gain an advantage or suffer a loss. The basic principle of 'insurable interest' applies to all categories of insurance. Thus, in life assurance the assured person must have an insurable interest in the life of the person insured and cannot, for example, capriciously take out a life policy on the life of some public person, e.g. soldier or statesman, because that would be a wager, rather than a contract of insurance. SEE *Life Assurance*

INSURANCE The concept of insurance in its modern commercial sense arose out of the practice in earlier times of insuring ships and their cargoes in the course of their mercantile adventures. The sums involved were considerable in relation to other forms of wealth and personal fortunes would often depend on the safe arrival of a ship and its cargo. It would appear that modern insurance, in all its forms, thus had its origin in marine insurance (q.v.) which in itself continues to be a major part of the world-wide insurance market. The underwriting of marine insurance risks in a collective way had its origin in the practice of merchants and shippers to meet in the coffee house of Edward Lloyd in the City of London, commencing in 1688 and Lloyds of London (q.v.) was to become the world centre for shipping insurance.

The earliest categories of non-marine insurance were life assurance and fire insurance. Until approximately 100 years ago, these three categories formed almost the entire insurance market.

There are today four main aspects of insurance: (1) personal insurance, including life and accident assurance, sickness and permanent health insurance, etc.; (2) property insurance, including household insurance, and the insurance of motor cars, aeroplanes, and small boats and livestock; (3) liability insurance, usually covering third-party risks, whether arising from some aspect of public liability or professional liability or the liability of employers; and (4) contingency insurance covering events which could cause financial loss, e.g. loss of profits insurance and the insurance of debts.

An insurance contract is basically a contract of indemnity, i.e. the liability of the insurer is to cover the actual loss sustained by the person insured. Contracts of life assurance, personal accident, and health insurance are to some extent an exception to the general rule because no loss needs to have been incurred by the insured. In theory, he is putting a value on the loss of his own life, or the loss of a limb or the loss of his capacity to work and so to that extent he is being indemnified for loss, although in practice there may not be a pecuniary loss. Many contracts of life assurance, notably endowment policies, are taken out entirely for investment purposes rather than for any sort of 'indemnity': thus the savings and investment concept has grown out of or been attached to the basic insurance concept.

At common law any two persons may enter into a contract of insurance and the insurer may be a private individual or a company or other incorporated body. Nowadays, however, most categories of insurance can be entered into only by those bodies authorized or approved by the Insurance Companies Acts (see below).

Only the following may carry on insurance business in the UK at the present day:

1. a body authorized to do so by the Secretary of State under the Insurance Companies Act 1981;
2. a body previously authorized under the Insurance Companies Act 1974;
3. a member of Lloyd's;
4. a registered Friendly Society;
5. a trade union employers' association, in relation to the provision for its members of provident benefits or strike benefits; and
6. a bank carrying on the business of credit insurance, suretyship and similar cover against financial loss.

The principal Acts are the Insurance Companies Act 1974 (itself a consolidating Act) and the Insurance Companies Act 1981, which amended the 1974 Act. Under the Acts, insurance business is classified (as it had been previously) into long-term and general. There are two classes of long-term business: ordinary long-term and industrial life assurance (q.v.).

Under the 1981 Act, long-term business embraces (1) all life and annuity business; (2) contracts of insurance to provide sums of money on marriage or birth; (3) linked long-term business (SEE *Linked Life Assurance*); (4) permanent health assurance; (5) pension fund management contracts, and certain other minor categories.

Under the 1974 Act, general business is divided into 17 classes which, where relevant, are dealt with under their respective headings throughout this work, namely, accident, sickness, vehicles, railway rolling stock, aircraft, ships, goods in transit, fire and natural forces, damage to property, motor-vehicle liability, aircraft liability, ships liability, general liability, credit insurance, suretyship, miscellaneous financial loss and legal expenses.

In most respects, the business of insurance companies is now regulated by the Insurance Companies Act 1974, the Act of 1981 and various Regulations issued from time to time under the Acts. The main areas governed by the Regulations are contents of advertisements; fraudulent inducements to do business; the conduct of intermediaries; the issue of statutory notices in relation to long-term business; the right of a proposer for long-term insurance to withdraw from the transaction before the expiration of the tenth day after he receives the statutory notice or the earliest day on which he knows both that the contract has been entered into and that the first or only premium has been paid, whichever is the later; the conduct of *linked* long-term business in relation, for example, to the categories of property to which benefits under the contract may be linked, rules regarding valuation and the provision of information to the insured; the allocation of funds to policy holders; the appointment of an actuary; the approval by the Secretary of State of the proposed managing director or chief executive and of any proposed controller of an insurance company; the duty of the insurance company to notify changes of director, controller or manager; the separation of assets and liabilities attributable to long-term business; the publication of annual and periodic statements and the deposit of accounts with the Secretary of State, and extensive powers of intervention by the Secretary of State, including power to require a company not to effect any category of business.

The individual regulations are too extensive to include in a work of this nature but reference may be made to the Insurance Companies (Accounts and Statements) Regulations 1980, the Insurance Companies Regulations 1980, the Insurance Companies (Accounts and Statements) (Amendment) Regulations 1982, and the Insurance Companies (Amendment) Regulations 1982. SEE *Aviation Insurance; British Insurance Association; Credit Insurance; Household Insurance; Life Assurance; Life Offices Association; Life Assurance; Motor Vehicle Insurance*

The worldwide premium income of the 340 or so insurance companies which are members of the British Insurance Association is shown in the table below:

	1979 (£m)	1980 (£m)	1981 (£m)	1982 (£m)	1983 (£m)
Fire & Accident (non-motor)	4,449	4,833	5,687	6,605	7,359
Motor	2,545	2,782	3,281	3,642	3,964
Marine, Aviation and Transport	515	532	686	806	876
Total General Business	7,509	8,147	9,654	11,053	12,199
Ordinary Long-Term (i.e. life, annuity and permanent health)	5,085	6,012	7,384	8,446	10,542
Industrial Long-Term	746	883	950	1,000	1,080
Total Long-Term Business	5,831	6,895	8,334	9,446	11,622
Total	13,340	15,042	17,988	20,499	23,821

Source: British Insurance Association.

INSURANCE BROKERS' (REGISTRATION) ACT (1977) This Act became law on 29th July, 1977. It provided for the establishment of self-regulatory arrangements in the insurance-broking profession under the Insurance Brokers' Registration Council. The Council was formed by the four major insurance-broking organizations in the UK, and now constitutes the British Insurance Brokers' Association. Under the Act, the Association maintains a Register of Insurance Brokers, establishes the criteria for registration and, through a disciplinary committee, regulates the conduct of registered members. The Act confers on the Association wide powers to regulate the educational requirements and qualifying examinations of insurance brokers but also makes provision for registration of those who are qualified by experience.

The Act provides for two categories of registration, namely, insurance brokers as individuals and insurance brokers as businesses. Any person of the right experience and integrity may register as a broker and thus enjoy that professional status. For a *business* to be registered, it must be run by a registered broker or brokers, it must satisfy the regulations regarding capital requirements, it must separate the firm's money from its clients' money and it must take out the statutory minimum indemnity insurance, currently £250,000, or three times the commission income of the business in the last accounting period, up to a maximum of £7.5 million, whichever is the greater.

Under the Act, it is an offence for anyone not registered as an insurance broker to use the style, title or description of 'insurance broker' or other related descriptions. Thus, the term 'insurance consultants' came into wider use.

The Act is a good example of the situation in which a professional body is permitted to regulate its own affairs within a statutory framework laid down by Parliament.

INSURANCE BROKING A directive issued by the European Economic Commission defines insurance brokers as

> persons who, acting with complete freedom as to their choice of undertaking, bring together, with a view to the insurance or re-insurance of risks, persons seeking insurance or re-insurance and insurance and re-insurance undertakings, carry out work preparatory to the conclusion of contracts of insurance or re-insurance and, where appropriate, assist in the administration and performance of such contracts, in particular in the event of a claim.

In a consultative document issued by the British Insurance Brokers' Council in August, 1976, the business of insurance broking was classified into three broad areas:

1. International insurance broking, in which brokers play a leading part in maintaining London's importance as the largest international insurance centre.
2. Commercial insurance broking, which consists mainly of servicing the insurance needs of industry and commerce.
3. Personal insurance broking, which embraces the great majority of smaller insurance broking firms, who seek to meet the insurance needs of private individuals.

The insurance broking world may be further divided between Lloyd's of London (q.v.) and the rest of the insurance brokers in the UK. Prior to the introduction of the Insurance Brokers' Registration Act 1977 (see above), there were approximately 9,000 companies, partnerships or sole operators using the title 'insurance broker'. Of these, approximately 280 were members of Lloyd's Insurance Brokers' Association.

In broad terms, it is the broker's task to meet the insurance needs of his client by obtaining cover in the market, having first researched the market to ascertain the most appropriate contract for the purpose. This is not necessarily the cheapest contract, although cost may well be a major factor. Other considerations will be the standing of the insurance company, past performance, flexibility, and the customer's own preferences.

Only a person or business registered under the Insurance Brokers' (Registration) Act 1977 (q.v.) may use the description 'insurance broker'.

It is believed that insurance brokers deal with approximately one-half of all non-life insurance business in the UK, between 30 per cent and 50 per cent of life business and up to 90 per cent of pensions business. In the late 1970s it was estimated that the total premium income of all the insurers in the UK, including Lloyd's, was approximately £15,000,000,000, of which insurance brokers accounted for approximately one-half.

INSURANCE CERTIFICATE Insurance certificates are issued by insurance brokers as evidence that marine insurances have been effected. Such certificates are sometimes accepted in lieu of actual policies, but they have one great disadvantage in that the rights of the insured cannot be passed on by indorsement and delivery, as in the case of a policy. Consequently, insurance certificates are not accepted by buyers under ci or cif contracts, since in the event of partial or total loss of the goods insured, the buyers could not claim against the insurance company on the strength of any document other than a policy. Insurance certificates must be distinguished from cover notes (q.v.); these are merely brief memoranda issued in all classes of insurance to accepted proposers on payment of the first premium stating that the latter are held covered pending the preparation of the relative policy.

The Uniform Customs and Practice for Documentary Credits (1983 Revision) (q.v.) provides that insurance documents must be as specifically described in the credit. Cover notes issued by brokers will not be accepted, unless specifically authorized in the credit. Unless otherwise specified in the credit, the insurance documents must be expressed in the same currency as the credit. SEE *Marine Insurance*

INTANGIBLE ASSETS A term sometimes applied to those assets of a business which, although invisible in themselves, may nevertheless play a major part in the success of the enterprise. These include, for example, goodwill (q.v.), trade marks and patent rights. Under the Companies Act 1981, special rules applied to intangible assets. In particular, such assets as concessions, licences, trade marks and patent rights could be included in a company's balance sheet only if (1) the assets were acquired for valuable consideration, or (2) the assets were created by the company itself. Separate rules apply to goodwill. These types of intangible asset may well have a commercial value, particularly whilst the company is a going concern. Other intangible assets, such as preliminary expenses, research costs, etc., which do not have a commercial value in themselves, may not be shown as assets in the balance sheet (see Companies Act 1981, Schedule 1) and Companies Act 1985 Schedule 4

INTER-BANK RESEARCH ORGANISATION (IBRO) This is the policy research and advisory unit of the London and Scottish Clearing Banks. It was set up in 1968 and provides advice and information on most policy issues which are of a collective interest to the clearing banks. From its inception, IBRO has taken a major role in a number of matters of common interest to its sponsoring banks. It assisted the banks in the preparation of evidence for the Wilson Committee (q.v.) and has advised on a number of public affairs aspects of British banking. IBRO has had a special role in relation to the new technologies affecting banking, as well as research into consumer attitudes and other aspects of the changing legal and economic environment. It has been very much involved with the application of information technology to banking, the development of money transmission systems (including the development of Bankers' Automated Clearing Services (BACS) (q.v.)) and the encouragement of payment of wages through banking accounts. IBRO also maintains the Inter-Bank Standards Unit, dealing with standards for bank documentation, including for example, machine-readable credit vouchers.

INTER-BANK MARKET Until the early 1960s, nearly all clearing bank deposits were held on either current accounts or seven-day notice accounts. Over the last 20 years, however, the banks have increasingly accepted 'wholesale' deposits from large corporations or other financial institutions. At the present time, such 'wholesale' deposits account for approximately 50 per cent of the clearing banks' total sterling deposits. Part of the wholesale market is the inter-bank market consisting of virtually all the banks, domestic and overseas, operating in London. The banks operate as both borrowers and lenders in the market, both in sterling and in Euro-currencies, depending on the banks' respective positions. The principal factors affecting both the volume and interest levels in the inter-bank market are the demand for commercial loans within each bank, their respective liquidity situations, movements between the private and public sectors, and the operations of the Bank of England itself. Movements in the inter-bank sterling market are considerable but are essentially short-term, a large part being overnight money.

INTER VIVOS SEE *Gifts Inter Vivos*

INTEREST Interest is the cost of money: it is the money which is paid for the use of money. Throughout the Middle Ages in England, the lending of money at interest was considered to be unchristian and was forbidden to Englishmen, some of whom were hanged for the offence. The taking of interest was stigmatized with the name of usury and appears to have been based on a rather strict interpretation of the Mosaic Law: 'Thou shalt not lend upon usury to thy brother'. The Jews, however, took a more relaxed view of their law, in that 'unto a stranger thou mayest lend upon usury'. Thus, the lending of money was monopolized by the Jews in England until their expulsion by Edward I in 1290. The Lombards then became the principal money lenders in England, operating from a site granted to them by Edward II in what is now Lombard Street. Despite the odium attaching to the business of money lending and its illegality, the practice continued to thrive, largely because successive monarchs were among the principal customers of first the Jews and then the Lombards. The usury laws were partly abolished by Henry VIII in 1545 and the taking of interest on loans was made legal. The rate was fixed at 10 per cent per annum, to be reduced over the next 150 years or so to 8 per cent, then 6 per cent and then 5 per cent. It was not until 1900 in the Moneylenders' Act, that legislation was again introduced to regulate the lending of money and the charging of interest. Under that Act, however, bankers were excluded from the definition of 'moneylenders'.

The allowing of interest on deposit accounts was apparently not known until the second half of the sixteenth century. Then we are told that Sir Thomas Gresham 'the father of English banking' was the goldsmiths' banker in Lombard Street from 1549 onwards, and that he was not only a lender of money, but was also paying interest on deposits (*Four Centuries of Banking*, by George Chandler, Batsford, 1964).

The calculation of interest may be 'simple' or 'compound'. Simple interest is the application of a percentage rate to the principal sum for the period in question, as is expressed in the equation

$$i = \frac{p \times t \times r}{100}$$

where i is the actual interest, p is the principal sum, t is the time or period of the loan in years and r is the percentage rate of interest. Compound interest is interest on the principal sum, plus the accruing interest, as expressed in the equation

$$i = p\left(1 + \frac{r}{100}\right)^{t} - p$$

for interest compounded annually, or

$$i = p\left(1 + \frac{r}{100q}\right)^{tq} - p$$

for interest compounded q times per year.

Interest on bank accounts is 'simple' interest but is compounded in the case of a deposit account to the extent that interest is allowed on interest previously credited to the account. The 'rests' between interest dates are critical. Clearly, the compounding effect of interest allowed yearly in arrears is not so good as the compounding on interest allowed, say, quarterly.

Generally in the UK, current accounts do not bear interest, but an overdraft on current account bears interest on a day-to-day basis. This is the principal reason why borrowing on overdraft is cheaper than most other forms of credit, i.e. interest is charged from day to day on the actual balance so that credit is given for amounts paid into the account.

In the case of an overdrawn current account, interest is calculated from the actual date when a customer's cheque is paid (not from the date of the cheque), and from the actual date when money is credited to the account (usually at the computer centre), not necessarily the day it is paid in at a branch. Where a cheque is paid at another bank or branch under advice, the banker is entitled to charge interest from the date when so paid. The calculations are in most banks effected by means of 'products' by which the balance of an account, on the occasion of each change, is multiplied by the number of days it has remained undisturbed, the product, say, 2,650, being simply £2,650 for one day, or put in another form £1 for 2,650 days. The total of all the products on an account by the end of a half-year is therefore that number of pounds for one day at the rate of interest to be allowed or charged. With the aid of a product table the amount of interest is very quickly ascertained.

On an account secured by an ordinary banker's mortgage for a fluctuating balance, compound interest may be charged. But where a banker takes a mortgage for a fixed sum, unless there is a special agreement to charge compound interest, he can charge only simple interest, because the position is no longer that of banker and customer but that of mortgagee and mortgagor. For this reason, a loan account which is secured by a mortgage for a fixed sum must be kept distinct from the working account. The usual method in such a case is to obtain a cheque from the debtor upon the working account for the interest upon the loan account as it falls due.

A ready way of telling approximately the number of years in which an amount at compound interest will double itself, is to divide 70 by the rate per cent.

At compound interest, an amount doubles itself:

At	per cent in	years	days
7		10	89
6		11	327
5		14	75
4½		15	273
4		17	246
3½		20	54
3		23	164
2½		28	26
2		35	1 day

At simple interest, an amount doubles itself:

At	per cent in	years	days
7		14	104
6		16	239
5		20	—
4½		22	81
4		25	—
3½		28	208
3		33	121
2½		40	—
2		50	—

Under the Consumer Credit Act 1974 (q.v.), a lender under a 'consumer credit agreement' (namely, a personal credit agreement, by which the creditor provides the debtor with credit not exceeding £15,000 is required to make known to the borrower the true cost of the credit provided. In the case of a bank overdraft, the true cost is the same as the quoted rate per cent because, as mentioned above, it is calculated on a day-to-day basis. In the case, however, of personal loans, hire purchase and credit sales etc., the rate of interest is expressed and charged in relation to the initial amount of the credit and does not take into account the reduction in that credit by instalments over the period of the loan. In such cases the true rate of interest is substantially greater than the 'quoted' rate and, generally in relation to credit spread over a 12-month period, the true rate of interest is approximately double the quoted rate. The following table shows the true rates of interest for varying quoted rates with monthly reductions over 12 months, 24 months and 36 months.

Quoted rate percentage on initial loan	True rates percentage over varying repayment periods with monthly reductions		
	12 months	24 months	36 months
5	9.5	9.7	9.7
6	11.5	11.7	11.7
7	13.4	13.7	13.6
8	15.4	15.7	15.6
9	17.5	17.7	17.5
10	19.5	19.7	19.5
11	21.6	21.8	21.4
12	23.7	23.8	23.4
13	25.8	25.9	25.4
14	28.0	28.0	27.3
15	30.1	30.1	29.3
16	32.3	32.2	31.3
17	34.5	34.3	33.3
18	36.8	36.4	35.3
19	39.0	38.6	37.3
20	41.3	40.7	39.3

INTEREST BEARING ELIGIBLE LIABILITIES (IBELS) SEE *Corset*

INTEREST ON BILL 'Where a bill is expressed to be payable with interest, unless the instrument otherwise provides, interest runs from the date of the bill, and if the bill is undated from the issue thereof.' (Section 9, subsection (3), Bills of Exchange Act 1882).

In an action on a dishonoured bill, interest as damages can be claimed from the time of presentment for payment, if the bill is payable on demand, and from the maturity of the bill in any other case; but such interest may, if justice require it, be withheld, and where a bill is expressed on the face to be payable with interest at a given rate, interest as damages may or may not be given at the same rate as the interest proper (Section 57). The usual rate of interest allowed is 5 per cent, but a higher rate would be allowable if it is expressed in the bill, but the court has power to set aside an agreement as to the rate of interest if it is considered excessive.

In practice, a clause as to interest is seldom inserted in an inland bill of exchange, although this is frequently done in a promissory note, the wording then being: 'On demand (or six months after date) I promised to pay to CD or order one hundred pounds with interest at the rate of five per centum per annum, for value received. AB.' If the note does not contain the interest clause, interest is not legally enforceable.

In the case of *Commonwealth Bank of Australia* v *Rosenhain* (1922), the High Court of Australia held (though the judgment does not bind an English court) that a document drawn in New York on Melbourne, 60 days after sight pay, etc. 'with interest at the rate of 8 per cent per annum until arrival of payment in London to cover value received' was not a bill of exchange. To conform to the provisions of the Bills of Exchange Act, the sum payable must be certain at the fixed time for payment.

But clearly the sum was not certain on that date from anything appearing on the face of the document, for interest was to run on from the time fixed for payment, namely sixty days after sight, until arrival of payment in London, and it was quite uncertain, both on the face of the document and in fact, when this event would happen, or indeed whether it would happen at all.

INTEREST CERTIFICATE A certificate issued by a bank, building society or other lender of money, showing the interest charged on a particular loan in a given period, usually the income tax year from April to April. Such certificates are accepted by the Inland Revenue as evidence of the payment of interest in those cases where income tax relief may be relevant, e.g. a qualifying loan for house purchase. SEE *Income Tax*

INTEREST-FREE LOANS SEE *Income Tax—Interest-free or low-rate loans*

INTEREST ON INCOME TAX SEE UNDER *Income tax*

INTEREST WARRANT An order or warrant for payment of interest on Government stocks, debenture and loan stocks and other fixed-interest securities. SEE *Dividend Warrant*

The Bills of Exchange Act 1882 recognizes 'any usage relating to dividend warrants or the indorsements thereof' (Section 97(3),(*d*)), but no reference is made to interest warrants. See, however, *Slingsby and Others* v *Westminster Bank Ltd*, under *Dividend Warrant*

INTERIM DIVIDEND The dividend of a joint stock company is declared by the company in general meeting; but power is given, in most articles of association, to the directors to pay to the members such interim dividends as appear to them to be justified by the profits which have been earned. An interim dividend is therefore one which is paid in the meantime, and which comes forward for confirmation when the general meeting is held.

INTERNATIONAL BANK FOR RECONSTRUCTION AND DEVELOPMENT This was set up together with the International Monetary Fund as a result of the United Nations Monetary Conference at Bretton Woods, USA, in 1944. It is colloquially known as the World Bank.

The membership of the Bank is open to all the United Nations and the function of the Bank is to encourage international trade by financing productive projects for reconstruction and development.

The Bank can make or guarantee loans for programmes of economic reconstruction and reconstruction of monetary systems, including long-term stabilization loans. Loans and guarantees must not exceed the subscribed capital of the Bank plus its reserves and surplus.

Part of the World Bank is the International Development Association (IDA). The purpose of IDA is to channel aid from rich countries to poor countries. From time to time IDA is replenished by the richer countries and it then dispenses aid to the poorest nations to help them to build up their own self-sustaining economies.

INTERNATIONAL COMMODITIES CLEARING HOUSE LIMITED (ICCH) The clearing house for 'soft' (i.e. non-metallic) commodities traded on the London futures market, other than wheat and barley. Its role is concerned with the orderly conduct of the market, which includes the registration of contracts between brokers (who will be members of the clearing house) and the guaranteeing of the due fulfilment of the contract. Settlement of contracts is done through the clearing house, thus eliminating, or at least reducing, the risk of insolvency by the other contracting party.

INTERNATIONAL MONETARY FUND (IMF) Set up together with the International Bank for Reconstruction and Development (q.v.) as a result of the United Nations Monetary Conference at Bretton Woods, USA, in 1944, its object is to establish stable relations between currencies, thus cushioning member states against temporary dislocations in foreign trade. An initial fund of £2,190,000,000 was to be subscribed by member nations according to an arranged quota. Twenty-five per cent of the quota must be contributed in gold and the balance in the particular currency of each member at a prescribed rate of exchange. There were three main provisions for operating the Fund:

1. There must be no devaluation of currencies except by agreement.
2. The proceeds of international transactions must be freely and rapidly convertible into other currencies.
3. Members are to be able to buy with their own currencies limited amounts from the pool of foreign currencies for paying off legitimate trade balances.

At the end of 1946, it was announced that the Fund would be open for exchange operations as from 1st March, 1947. The Fund commenced with 39 members and the initial parities were based on the rates of exchange ruling at the end of 1946.

It was the object of the Fund to evolve some method of economizing the use of gold and currency reserves, and one of its chief defects has been the failure to provide for any multilateral clearing system of debit and credit balances. The aim of achieving convertibility between its members' currencies has not as yet been fully realized, and in practice there have been few effective measures which the Fund could take to force its member countries to institute appropriate internal action to correct disequilibrium in the international balance of payments, except that such countries, if they wished to look to the Fund for financial assistance, were expected to have regard for its principles. In this way it has at least been possible to establish and maintain a code of international behaviour.

In 1961 it was realized that the resources of the Fund needed to be strengthened in currencies other than sterling and dollars, which are national as well as international currencies and as such are always vulnerable to changes in the balance of payments of their respective countries. This need was emphasized in August of that year when Britain secured from the Fund in the largest single operation in its history credits equivalent to $2,000 million, $1,500 million being taken in the form of an immediate drawing and the remaining $500 million being left as a reserve to be drawn upon if required in the succeeding 12 months. This reserve was in fact never utilized, and the $1,500 million was repaid in six instalments, commencing in October, 1961, the last being made on 31st July, 1962. At this time the International Monetary Fund entered into a stand-by arrangement with the UK authorizing drawing up to the equivalent of $1,000 million over the 12-month period from August, 1962.

There are now 146 members of the IMF, each of whom is assigned a quota based on the relative significance of the member country's economy and its share of world trade. The quota determines the members' subscriptions to the Fund, establishes their voting rights, limits their borrowing rights and determines their share of allocations from the Fund. Transactions with the Fund are in units of account known as Special Drawing Rights (SDRs).

With the introduction of floating exchange rates in the 1970s, it was not possible to uphold the concepts of Bretton Woods as mentioned above, but the IMF continued to have an expanding role, particularly in relation to the less-developed countries (LDCs). These countries, usually operating in a serious deficit situation, have little access to private international finance and have to draw heavily on support from the IMF. Lending by the IMF in 1983 accounted for approximately 20 per cent of the current account deficts of the LDCs. In that year, many of the LDCs ran into financial difficulties and as many as 30 countries had to reschedule their loan agreements in respect of their outstanding debt. Their problems were aggravated by the recession in the industrial countries and the high levels of interest rates world-wide.

The original purpose of the IMF was to bridge short-term or cyclical movements in members' balance of payments, but in more recent years the imbalances of the financial structure of many countries has required longer-term financing. This led to the introduction of the Extended Fund Facility, which provides medium-term assistance and the Supplementary Financing Facility and Enlarged Access Policy, under which larger amounts for longer periods can be provided.

Generally, in order to have help from the IMF, a borrowing country must agree on an economic and financial programme designed to reduce that country's balance of payments deficit. As a rule, the more indebted a country becomes to the Fund, the higher the level of conditions imposed on that country.

Although the IMF is basically supported by members' subscriptions, the claims on the Fund have been so enormous in recent years that quota subscriptions have had to be augmented by borrowing to a level of nearly one-third of quotas. Supplementary arrangements also exist, under which ten industrial nations and Switzerland agree to support the Fund to 'forestall or cope with an impairment of the international monetary system'.

INTERPLEAD To interplead is to bring before the court the claims of two persons to the same object and to obtain the decision of the court. A banker might have occasion to interplead, for example, if two persons each laid claim to a security deposited with him.

INTESTACY, INTESTATE An intestacy arises when a person dies without leaving a valid will. The deceased person is referred to as an intestate. In the UK approximately one-third of those cases where a grant of representation is required on death, are cases of intestacy. The person or persons entitled to apply for a Grant of Letters of Administration on Intestacy will normally be those who are entitled to the intestate's estate. SEE ALSO *Administrator*

The rules governing the distribution of an estate on intestacy are contained in the Administration of Estates Act 1925, as amended by the Intestates Act 1952 and subsequent Acts. The rules are summarized in the table opposite.

Under the Inheritance (Provision for Family and Dependants) Act 1975, a testator may not dispose of his estate in a way which excludes those persons who were financially dependent on him at the time of his death. Even a woman with whom a testator has been cohabitating may have a claim under the Act if she was financially dependent on him, and this may be so even in the case of intestacy where under the statutory rules the woman would receive no benefit.

Under the Family Law Reform Act 1969, the position of an illegitimate child is equated with that of a legitimate child, in respect of all deaths occurring after 1st January, 1970.

INTRODUCTION (TO THE STOCK EXCHANGE) This is one of the various methods of obtaining a Stock Exchange quotation for a company. It is normally appropriate only where there is a fairly large number of shareholders already in the company and where it is desired to obtain a wider market for the shares. The introduction is achieved by application to the Quotations Committee of the Stock Exchange. No prospectus need be published because no capital is being raised but the Stock Exchange will require all the usual documentation in relation to the company's history, its business, its prospects and management.

Surviving relatives	Benefits
Husband or wife but no issue	Whole estate absolutely.
Husband or wife and issue	1. *Surviving spouse takes* (a) £40,000 (or whole estate if less than this) free of capital transfer tax and costs, plus: (b) personal chattels, plus (c) a life interest in one-half of the remaining estate. 2. *Child or children take(s)* (a) one-half of the remaining estate on the 'statutory trusts' [The 'statutory trusts' are set out in the Administration of Estates Act 1925, as amended. The term means that children attain a vested interest in the estate when they attain the age of 18 or marry under that age.], and (b) the other half of the estate on the statutory trusts on the death of the surviving wife or husband.
Husband or wife and no issue, but parent(s) or brother(s) or sister(s) of the whole blood or their issue	1. *Surviving spouse takes* (a) £85,000 (or whole estate if less than this) free of capital transfer tax and costs, plus: (b) personal chattels, plus: (c) one-half of the remaining estate. 2. *The parent(s) (if alive) take(s)* the other half of the remaining estate absolutely. 3. *(If no parent(s) alive) the brothers and sisters and issue of deceased brothers and sisters take* the other half of the remaining estate in equal shares absolutely.
Issue but no husband or wife	*The child or children take(s)* the whole estate on the statutory trusts.
No husband or wife or issue	The whole estate passes to the following in order of priority Parent(s), failing whom Brothers and sisters of the whole blood and issue of deceased brothers or sisters of the whole blood, failing whom Brothers and sisters of the half blood and issue of deceased brothers or sisters of the half blood, failing whom Grandparent(s), failing whom Uncles and aunts of the whole blood, failing whom Uncles and aunts of the half blood, failing whom The Crown.

INVALID CARE ALLOWANCE This allowance is payable to certain persons who cannot undertake employment because they have to look after a sick or disabled relative. For invalid care allowance to be payable, the following requirements must be satisfied:

1. The claimant must be 'regularly and substantially' engaged in caring for a severely disabled relative. This will normally mean spending at least 35 hours a week caring for the relative. A severely disabled person is one who is receiving either attendance allowance, or constant attendance allowance, together in the latter case with a war pension, industrial injuries pension, workmen's compensation or disablement allowance for an industrial disease.
2. The relative must be either the wife of the claimant or other near relative of the claimant, such as parents, grandparents or children or grandchildren; aunts, uncles, nephews or nieces; step-parents, half-brothers and half-sisters or the 'in-laws' of the claimant.
3. If the claimant is a woman, she must be either single or living apart from her husband and receiving towards her maintenance less than the amount of the invalid care allowance. A woman living with a man as his wife may not claim the allowance for a disabled relative.
4. The claimant must not be 'gainfully employed', which means in this instance not in receipt of earnings of more than £6 a week. 'Earnings' includes all remuneration, i.e. commission, overtime, etc. and earnings from self-employment as well as from employment. Meal vouchers, free meals and free accommodation provided by the employer are not included as earnings.
5. The claimant must not be in receipt of sickness

or unemployment benefit, or other social security benefits, but if the amount of any such benefit is less than the invalid care allowance, the claimant may receive the difference up to the amount of the invalid care allowance.

Allowance for Dependants
A man who is entitled to invalid care allowance may claim an additional allowance for his wife if she is living with him (but if, for example, she is entitled to any social security benefit in her own right, excluding attendance allowance or mobility allowance, this will be taken into account in calculating the additional invalid care allowance).

Either a man or woman may claim additional allowance in respect of dependent children, the normal test being whether or not child benefit (q.v.) is payable. Any increase in the allowance will be additional to child benefit.

In certain cases, a man may also be entitled to an increase in respect of a housekeeper who looks after a child (but not in addition to an increase for the claimant's wife and not if the housekeeper has earnings higher than the appropriate increase).

Attainment of Retirement Age
When a person in receipt of invalid care allowance reaches the normal retirement age of 60 in the case of a woman or 65 in the case of a man, the allowance will normally end and the state retirement pension will become payable. If, however, the pension is less than the amount of the invalid care allowance, the allowance may continue provided the entitlement conditions apply. A person who continues to draw invalid care allowance in this way may continue to do so beyond the age of 65 in the case of a woman and 70 in the case of a man, notwithstanding that they are no longer 'regularly and substantially' engaged in caring for a severely disabled relative.

National Insurance Contributions and Taxation
The payment of invalid care allowance does not depend on a contribution record. The recipient of the invalid care allowance is not required to pay National Insurance contributions, but during the currency of the allowance will be credited with Class 1 contributions.

The allowance is payable without regard to the claimant's means, but is subject to income tax (See Appendix 2).

INVALIDITY BENEFIT There are three categories of invalidity benefit. They are invalidity pension, non-contributory invalidity pension (renamed severe disablement allowance from November, 1984), and invalidity allowance.

Invalidity Pension
This form of pension is designed to cover long-term illness. In the ordinary way, sickness benefit is not payable beyond a period of 168 days from the date of illness (SEE *Sickness Benefit*). A person may claim invalidity benefit if he or she has been incapable of work for 168 days and is unable to work. The period of 168 days does not have to be a continuous one. Separate spells of illness of two days or more may be added together and treated as one period of interruption of employment provided the gap between the separate spells of illness does not exceed 13 weeks. The period of 168 days must be made up of days for which the claimant was entitled to sickness benefit (including any period for which maternity allowance was payable).

In certain cases (see below), widows and widowers may qualify for invalidity pension, notwithstanding that they may not have qualified for sickness benefit (see below).

The medical requirements relating to the claiming of invalidity pension are broadly those which apply to sickness benefit. Sickness statements will be required from a doctor on a continuing basis, but this will normally be less frequently than in the case of claims for sickness benefit.

The amount of invalidity pension is announced each year. Additional pension is payable for a wife or adult dependant and for each dependent child.

The fact that the claimant was a member of a contracted-out occupational pension scheme does not affect the calculation of invalidity benefit, as the rules governing increases in pension for dependent adults and children are similar to those applicable to sickness benefit (q.v.).

Severe Disablement Allowance
Until November, 1984, this was called the non-contributory invalidity pension. It may be claimed by persons under the normal retirement age of 65 for men and 60 for women notwithstanding that they may not have sufficient national insurance contributions to qualify in the ordinary way.

The following conditions must be satisfied:

1. The claimant must be at least 16 years of age (or at least 19 years of age if undergoing full-time education, unless that education is of a kind specially designed for physically or mentally handicapped people).
2. The claimant must be resident in the UK or the Isle of Man.
3. The claimant must have been present in the UK or the Isle of Man for at least 26 weeks in the 12 months prior to payment of the allowance.

4. The claimant must have lived in the UK or the Isle of Man for a total of 10 years out of the past 20 (or 10 years since birth in the case of persons under the age of 20).
5. The claimant must have been continuously incapable of work for at least 28 weeks (including any absence abroad for not more than 28 days in that period).

Severe disablement allowance will not be paid if the claimant is receiving an equivalent sum in other forms of sickness or invalidity benefit, widow's benefit or training allowance. If the claimant is receiving any such benefits at a rate lower than the severe disablement allowance, the invalidity pension will be correspondingly reduced.

Severe disablement allowance will be payable to a married woman who

1. has been continuously incapable of paid work for at least 28 weeks, and
2. has been continuously incapable of performing normal household duties for that same period.

In other respects, the claim by a married woman is subject to the same requirements as those relating to a man.

Invalidity Allowance

This is an allowance paid in addition to invalidity pension (or severe disablement allowance) and is designed to benefit persons who are incapable of work but have what would otherwise have been a large part of their working life in front of them. The allowance is therefore graduated to take into account the age of the claimant. The highest rate of allowance is payable for claimants under the age of 40 on the first day of their incapacity, the middle level of rate is payable for claimants between the age of 40 and 49 and the lowest rate for men between the age of 50 and 59 and women between 50 and 54.

All the foregoing categories of pension and allowances are known collectively as invalidity benefit.

Widows and Widowers

Special rules apply to enable widows and widowers to claim invalidity benefit even though they may not have qualified for sickness benefit.

Widows A widow may qualify for invalidity pension if

1. her widow's allowance or widowed mother's allowance has ended, and
2. she is incapable of work, and
3. she is not entitled to a widow's pension at the full rate either because she was under 50 when her husband died or when her widowed mother's allowance ended.

The invalidity pension will be payable at the level at which the widow's pension would have been paid on her husband's contributions had she been over 50 when he died or when the widowed mother's allowance ended.

If, however, the widow is entitled to an invalidity pension on her own contributions, the pension will be paid at the higher of these two rates.

In other respects the rules relating to invalidity pension payable to widows correspond to the general rules set out above.

Widowers If a man is incapable of work at the time of his wife's death or becomes so within 13 weeks after her death, he may qualify for invalidity pension after his incapacity has lasted for 168 days, notwithstanding that the widower may not have been entitled to sickness benefit.

In the case of widows and widowers, invalidity allowance will be paid in addition to the invalidity pension at the rate appropriate to the claimant at the time of the incapacity.

Persons over Retirement Age

Men over 65 and women over 60 who postpone taking their retirement pensions may continue to receive invalidity pensions for periods when they are incapable of working. Periods during which invalidity pension is paid, however, after the normal retirement age do not count towards extra pension.

In such cases invalidity pension is paid at the rate which the retirement pension would have been paid if it had been taken at the normal retirement age.

If the claimant was in receipt of invalidity allowance within the 13 weeks before normal retirement age, this will continue to be paid.

After the age of 70 in the case of men and 65 in the case of women, or in the event of final retirement before those ages, invalidity pension ceases to be payable. Where, however, an invalidity allowance has been paid, the retirement pension will be increased permanently by this sum if, as mentioned above, invalidity allowance was payable not more than 13 weeks before the normal retirement date and the claimant is entitled to a retirement pension based on his own contributions or as a replacement for invalidity pension under the widow and widower rules (see above).

Invalidity benefit in general is not taxable, nor subject to any means test. Where, however, a retirement pension has been augmented by invalidity allowance, as mentioned in the previous paragraph, the enlarged pension is taxable as a whole (See Appendix 2).

INVESTMENT COMPANY Investment companies are subject to special rules regarding distributions and also enjoy special taxation status provided they satisfy the statutory requirements of an investment company. A company is an investment company under Section 266, Companies Act 1985, provided

1. it is a listed public company,
2. it has given notice in the prescribed form to the Registrar of its intention to carry on business as an investment company and, since then
3. its business has consisted of investing its funds principally in securities with the aim of spreading the investment risk and giving its members the benefit of the results of its management of funds, and
4. none of its holdings in companies (other than investment companies) represents more than 15 per cent of its total investment, and
5. its memorandum or articles of association prohibit the distribution of capital profits, and
6. it has not retained more than 15 per cent of its income from securities in any accounting reference period.

An investment company may make distributions to members on the same basis as applies to all public companies (SEE *Distribution*), or on the basis of an asset ratio test, which means, under Section 265 that the company's assets must be at least 50 per cent greater than the total of its liabilities and remain so after the distribution has been made.

Before an investment company may make a distribution under Section 265, two main conditions must be satisfied, namely, that the company's shares were listed on a recognized stock exchange during the whole of that year and, during the year and the previous accounting reference period, it had not distributed any capital profits nor applied any capital profits or unrealized profits in paying up debentures or any amounts unpaid on any of its issued shares.

In the UK, the term 'investment company' is usually synonymous with 'investment trust' (see below). Provided an investment company satisfies the statutory requirements listed above, it will usually be granted 'approved' investment trust status by the Inland Revenue and will be exempt from capital gains tax on capital gains within the portfolio (Section 81, Finance Act 1980).

INVESTMENT CURRENCY This was the name given to foreign currency which, during the period of Exchange Control, the Bank of England permitted to be used for investment purposes outside the Scheduled Territories (q.v.). Such currency usually accrued to residents of the Scheduled Territories from the sale or redemption of foreign currency securities or the realization of direct investments in areas outside the Scheduled Territories. SEE *Dollar Premium*

INVESTMENT INCOME SURCHARGE This was an additional form of income tax, first introduced under the Finance Act 1971, and abolished in the Finance Act 1984. It applied to *all unearned income* above a certain level and was charged at the rate of 15 per cent. This was in addition to basic-rate income tax and any higher-rate income tax which was payable. At one point, it took the maximum rate of personal income tax to 98 per cent for those taxpayers who had unearned income above the threshold.

The equivalent of investment income surcharge continues to be payable on the income of discretionary trusts and accumulation settlements. It is calculated according to the difference between the basic rate of income tax and the rate applicable to the second higher rate band for personal income tax purposes, i.e. currently 15 per cent.

INVESTMENT MANAGEMENT SERVICES These services usually entail the management of an investment portfolio on behalf of a private client or an institution, the receipt and distribution of dividend and all other administrative work in connection with the portfolio. These investment 'accounts', as they are usually called, may be conducted on either a discretionary basis (in which case the investment manager acts at his own discretion in the management of a portfolio, without referring to the client) or non-discretionary (in which case the manager will recommend investment sales and purchases to the client and await the latter's approval). The tendency nowadays is for investment management to be on a discretionary basis in order that the manager may act quickly.

Those engaged in investment management are principally merchant banks, clearing banks and stockbrokers. There is, however, a large number of independent houses offering investment management services (SEE *National Association of Share Dealers and Investment Managers*). The charges for investment management range from approximately 60p per cent up to one pound per cent on the current market value of the portfolio.

At the end of 1981, the clearing banks in the UK had an investment management responsibility for approximately 37,500 private client portfolios, with a total value of approximately £2,000 million, and about 550 institutional portfolios, with a total value of nearly £7,000 million. Figures are not available for the total portfolios managed by merchant banks and stockbrokers but they are believed to be considerably in excess of those managed by the clearing banks and must, therefore, be very substantial indeed.

Most merchant banks will not accept a management responsibility for portfolios worth less than, say, £100,000 in value, but the clearing banks will usually accept smaller portfolios, of, say, £50,000.

In his *Review of Investor Protection*, Professor L. C. N. Gower said on the subject of investment management:

> Fifty years ago there were few firms which specialised in managing and advising on investments for individual investors. Insofar as this role was performed it was as a minor offshoot of the provision of stockbroking, legal or banking services. Now it is an important service in its own right; and one which the existing regulatory legislation—primary or secondary—still fails to place under any control unless the way the business is conducted requires the firm to obtain a licence as a dealer or deposit-taker (or both) rather than a manager or advisor. SEE *Gower Report*

INVESTMENT TRUSTS The term 'investment trust' is a misnomer. An investment trust, as now known in the UK, is not a trust as such but is an investment company (q.v.).

The first investment trust company was the South American Investment Company incorporated in 1860 in Glasgow—the beginning of a long tradition of investment trust management in Scotland. Although that first investment trust was an incorporated company, there appeared in the following years a number of trusts, e.g. Foreign & Colonial Government Trust and Government & Guaranteed Securities Permanent Trust, which were established as trusts and not as companies. There followed a period of uncertainty as to whether or not such trusts infringed the then companies legislation that unincorporated associations carried on for gain may not have more than 20 members. The point was resolved in the courts of 1880 in the case of *Smith* v *Anderson* [1880] 15 ChD 247, which cleared the way for investment trusts to operate as trusts rather than as companies. This, in the event, was to permit the later development of unit trusts, but investment trusts chose to go via the company route. Thus, all investment trusts, as now known in the UK are incorporated companies.

An investment trust is essentially a company formed for the purpose of investing in other companies. They may have a specialist investment philosophy or may be incorporated for the purpose of investing worldwide. Investment trusts may be quoted (there are some hundreds listed on the Stock Exchange) or unquoted.

An investment trust will normally take powers to borrow and thus may raise loan finance in order to increase its portfolio investment. Thus gearing (q.v.) is a characteristic of many investment trusts, i.e. a given level of loan finance will have a disproportionate effect on the value of the investment portfolio in a rising market. The reverse is equally true—on a falling market the trust's portfolio assets will diminish, leaving a fixed loan liability still to be met. Much of the skill of investment trust management, therefore, lies in the judgment of its gearing.

As with all shares, the price will vary according to the demand for shares and their availability. This will be true whether the investment trust is quoted or not. The demand will increase (and therefore the price) when a particular investment trust offers the investor some particular attraction or facility which is not available to the investor himself. For example, during the period of restraint on investment by institutions in overseas shares, those investment trusts which already had an overseas—and particularly an American—content were much in demand. Similarly, the ability to gear an investment may offer a facility which the private investor may not have, e.g. trustees of a private trust would not normally have power to borrow for the purpose of increasing the portfolio in anticipation of a market rise, but an investment in an investment trust would give them, at one remove, that facility. Most of all, however, the characteristic which will determine the share price of an investment trust is the success or otherwise of the investment trust manager.

Some of these characteristics of investment trusts may result in the share price being greater than the total value of the underlying portfolio, i.e. the share will stand at a premium on asset values but more usually investment trusts stand at a discount on the market value of the underlying investments.

The advantages of investment in investment trusts are

1. the spread which the portfolio offers,
2. professional management,
3. the 'gearing' facility,
4. the favourable taxation treatment for capital gains (SEE *Investment Company*), and
5. the opportunity, in some cases, of buying at a discount on asset values.

INVESTOR PROTECTION There is no one body of law and no single institution relating universally in the UK to the protection of investors. Protection lies in a number of diffused areas.

INVESTOR PROTECTION

The Companies Acts afford considerable protection to investors in the matter of disclosure by directors of public and private limited companies, The Prevention of Fraud (Investments) Act 1958 (q.v.), deals with the licensing of dealers in securities and provides an umbrella legislation for unit trusts. The Insurance Companies Acts (SEE *Insurance*) and the Policyholders' Protection Act (q.v.) and the Insurance Brokers (Registration) Act (q.v.) all provide a degree of protection for those who take out policies of insurance. Building societies are governed in the conduct of their affairs by the Building Society Act 1962 (q.v.), and banks and deposit-takers are recognized or licensed under the Banking Act 1979. There are certain other non-statutory regulatory bodies, notably the Stock Exchange (q.v.) which imposes stringent requirements on listed companies, the Panel on Takeovers and Mergers (q.v.) and the Council for the Securities Industry (q.v.). There is also an investors' protection scheme introduced by the Building Societies Association. SEE *Investors' Protection Scheme (Building Societies)*

Despite this extensive, albeit fragmented, framework of protection, there have been a number of investment losses in recent years, which prompted the appointment of Professor Gower to review the whole field of investor protection. SEE *Gower Report*

Consequent upon the Gower Report and the ensuing debate, the Government issued, in January 1985, a White Paper entitled 'Financial Services in the United Kingdom: A New Framework for Investor Protection'. At the time of writing, it is envisaged that the Government will introduce legislation along the lines of the White Paper in the 1985/86 Parliamentary Session. The White Paper contemplates the setting up of two authorities, viz. a Securities and Investments Board, covering the regulation of securities and investments and a Marketing of Investments Board, covering in particular, life assurance and unit trusts. The following are some of the main aspects of the White Paper:

A principle of fair dealing: specific rules would prohibit unfair practices and require investment businesses to be conducted in accordance with good market practice.

A duty of skill, care and diligence in the provision of investment advice and the transaction of investment business: this would mean, for example, that those holding themselves out as being qualified to give investment advice and who would stand to profit when their advice is followed would be held to owe a duty of care commensurate with their responsibilities.

A duty to disclose: this would require an investment business to disclose in advance any material interest in the proposed transaction, including the capacity in which it would act, the fees it would charge, the remuneration it might receive from other parties, and any connection which it might have with other parties interested in the transaction.

Fraud, etc.: it would be a criminal offence for any person knowingly or recklessly to engage in any act, device, scheme, practice or course of conduct in relation to investment business which was likely to defraud, deceive or mislead.

A 'best execution' principle: all instructions from clients must be executed to the client's best advantage.

A 'subordination of interest' requirement: this would ensure that clients' interests are paramount and that clients would be given priority in the execution of orders when an investment business is also dealing on its own account.

Clients' accounts: investment businesses will be required to hold funds on behalf of a client in segregated trust accounts.

Compensation for investors: compensation would be available for investors in the event of loss arising from fraud, negligence or failure to comply with statutory requirements for the protection of clients' assets.

Pension schemes: there would be a requirement to disclose to members of pension schemes, comprehensive information about the manner in which the scheme's assets are invested. Any investment manager or adviser involved in the administration of pensions schemes as a business would require authorization.

Advertisements: only authorized investment businesses would have the statutory right to issue advertisements or circulars likely to lead to the sale or purchase of investments.

Unit trusts: the authorization of unit trusts (q.v.) would become the responsibility of the Securities and Investments Board.

Insider dealings: the new legislation would extend the provisions of the Companies Act 1980, in relation to insider dealings (q.v.) to cover all securities, including options and future contracts.

Self-regulation: the proposed Boards would have power to recognize self-regulatory organizations such as the Stock Exchange (q.v.), the National Association of Security Dealers and Investment

Managers (q.v.) and the Insurance Brokers Registration Council. SEE *Insurance Broking*

INVESTORS IN INDUSTRY GROUP PLC Formerly Finance for Industry plc (q.v.), this Group was reorganized from 1st July, 1983 under this new name. Eighty-five per cent of the capital is owned by the nine English and Scottish clearing banks, the balance of 15 per cent being owned by the Bank of England. The balance of the Group's very substantial resources is raised in the UK and international money markets. The Group consists of three divisions which are broadly investment, advisory and overseas. The largest single component is ICFC (q.v.) which is claimed to be the 'world's largest source of private venture capital'. The ICFC Division is the successor to the Industrial and Commercial Finance Corporation Limited, which was formed in 1945 to provide long-term capital for smaller and medium-sized business, since when it has invested in over 7,000 companies. The Division's outstanding investments in 1983 amounted to approximately £500 million. The investment divisions also include Property Division (formerly ICFC Co-operative Limited and Anglia Commercial Properties (Investments) Limited), Shipping and Energy Division (formerly Finance for Shipping Limited (q.v.)) and Ventures Division (formerly Technical Development Capital Limited).

The Group also provides extensive consultancy services and leasing and hire purchase finance, and manages EDITH plc (q.v.).

INVESTORS' PROTECTION SCHEME (BUILDING SOCIETIES) In April, 1982, the Building Societies Association announced an investors' protection scheme by which share investors in building societies are now protected up to 90 per cent of their investment in the event of the failure of the society. Protection up to this level applies to investment with those societies which contribute to the scheme. To be a contributing member, a society must comply with certain prudential requirements which are approximately the same as those which qualify for trustee status. Share accounts with other societies, i.e. those not contributing to the scheme, are protected to the extent of 75 per cent of the investor's capital.

INVISIBLE EARNINGS The name applied to the export of services as distinct from the export of tangible goods. The invisible earnings of the UK include banking, insurance, shipping, tourism, air transport, royalties, copyrights and patent rights.

Invisible earnings make a very substantial contribution to the UK balance of payments. For the five years to 1983, the respective figures for invisible net earnings and the visible balance of trade are given in the table below.

	Visible trade (net) £m	Invisible earnings (net) £m
1980	1,361	2,116
1981	3,360	3,569
1982	2,055	2,879
1983	−1,165	3,708
1984	−4,255	4,306

Source: Financial Statistics.

IRREDEEMABLE A stock for which there is no provision for redemption in the terms of issue. Thus, an irredeemable debenture stock continues into perpetuity as a loan to the company, secured by a debenture over the company's assets. The term is also applied incorrectly to stocks, notably certain Government stocks, which have no fixed date of redemption.

IRREVOCABLE CREDIT A credit which, once opened and advised to the beneficiary, cannot be cancelled by the bank by which it is established. An irrevocable credit is not the same thing as a confirmed credit (q.v.) since a credit may be both irrevocable and unconfirmed. Dutch banks, for example, may open credits through a London bank in favour of, say, an Asiatic beneficiary, such credits to be irrevocable so far as the Dutch banks are concerned, but unconfirmed on the part of the London bank. Thus where more than one bank is concerned, whether or not the credit is irrevocable by all depends on the instructions each receives. SEE *Documentary Credit; Uniform Customs and Practice for Documentary Credits*

ISSUE OF BILL The 'issue' of a bill of exchange is defined by Section 2 of the Bills of Exchange Act 1882, as 'the first delivery of a bill or note, complete in form, to a person who takes it as a holder'. This definition is particularly relevant to Section 9(3), which provides

> Where a bill is expressed to be payable with interest, unless the instrument otherwise provides, interest runs from the date of the bill, and if the bill is undated, from the issue thereof,

and Section 12, which is as follows:

> Where a bill is expressed to be payable at a fixed period after date is issued undated, or where the acceptance of a bill payable at a fixed period after sight is undated, any holder may insert therein the true date of issue or acceptance, and the bill shall be payable accordingly.

SEE *Delivery of Bill*

ISSUE OF CHEQUE The Bills of Exchange Act 1882, provides that, except as otherwise stated, the rules applicable to bills of exchange are also applicable to cheques. The definition of the 'issue of a cheque', therefore, is the same as that given for a bill in the preceding entry. SEE *Delivery of Bill*

ISSUED CAPITAL That part of the nominal or authorized capital of a company which has been issued by the directors and been taken up or subscribed by the shareholders. The issued capital may be fully paid up, or it may be only partly paid up, the remainder being the 'uncalled' capital. SEE *Capital*

ISSUING HOUSES The work of an issuing house is to supervise the issue of a company's stock or shares. This may be the first public issue of a hitherto private company which is seeking a stock exchange quotation or it may be a further issue of stock (a rights issue) to existing shareholders. It may be an issue of ordinary stock or of loan stock, or a variation of either. It may be a public issue or a private placing.

The issuing house which brings a company to the market has a great responsibility. It must be satisfied that the company is one for which a public quotation would be appropriate. This is partly a matter of assets, size, turnover, past profitability and profit forecasts, but it is more than that. The issuing house is putting its name to a venture in which the public at large are being invited to participate. The issuing house must therefore satisfy itself as to the standing and business integrity of the company, the nature and value of its contracts, the quality of the management, the adequacy of its records, its labour relations record, its marketing strength and virtually every aspect of the business relevant to its long-term stability. In all this, the issuing house will work closely with the firm of accountants—usually known as the reporting accountants, whose report will accompany the offer documents—and with the firm of solicitors responsible for the documentation of the issue. The issuing house will also work closely with the stockbrokers to the issue and one of the major decisions will be that of the issue price. This will be fixed at the last moment and will reflect the general state of, and expectation in, the market, and indeed the economy at large; the size and standing of the company in question; the market view of that particular sector; the level of interest rates; dividend expectations and the dividend cover of the company concerned; and every factor large or small which may affect the price of the shares when issued.

ISSUING HOUSES ASSOCIATION The majority of the houses interested in new-issue business are members of the Issuing Houses Association, which was founded in 1945. Its objects are to act as a consultative and advisory body representing the interests of banking houses and other institutions in respect of their activities as issuing houses and, in particular, to provide a medium for placing before the Government, the Bank of England, the Council of the Stock Exchange, and other public bodies, authorities and individuals the views of the association on matters affecting such activities. The membership at present totals 56 houses, including the 16 members of the Accepting Houses Committee. SEE *Accepting Houses*

J

JENKINS COMMITTEE A Committee of Inquiry under the chairmanship of Lord Jenkins to

review and report upon the provisions and workings of the Companies Act, 1948, the Prevention of Fraud (Investments) Act, 1958, except in so far as it relates to industrial and provident societies and building societies, and the Registration of Business Names Act, 1916, as amended; to consider in the light of modern conditions and practices, including the practice of take-over bids, what should be the duties of directors and the rights of shareholders; and generally to recommend what changes in the law are desirable.

The Committee reported in June, 1962. Among the main proposals were: exempt private companies should no longer be excused from filing accounts and should publish profit and balance sheet details; control of take-over bids should be tightened by making them subject to the statutory regulations which govern prospectuses for the issue of shares; restrictions should be placed on the extent to which an owner of shares may conceal his identity behind a nominee company; beneficial owners of 10 per cent or more of the equity capital of a company whose shares are quoted on the Stock Exchange should reveal their identity and report their transactions in such shares.

A majority of the Committee did not agree that voteless shares should be legally abolished. The Board of Trade (now Department of Trade and Industry) should seek help from the Stock Exchange and other bodies to ensure that, in future, buyers of such shares should clearly realize their implications. Notice of general meetings should be given to holders of voteless shares, and they should be entitled to receive a copy of any chairman's statement sent out with the accounts.

A minority of three thought that future issues of non-voting and restricted voting ordinary shares should be banned, and that all shareholders, regardless of whether they have voting rights or not, should be entitled to attend and speak at all general meetings.

The Committee laid down a code of conduct for company directors, who should furnish full details of their deals in the shares of their company. Directors should be barred from option deals in their own shares and should be made personally responsible in the court if they bought or sold shares on the strength of their inside knowledge.

A completely new system of control for unit trusts was proposed, allowing more discretion than formerly to the managers. All companies should make their accounts more informative. Turnover figures should be given. The accounts should describe shareholdings in other companies, the breakdown value of property assets, and rent and overdraft charges. Directors should comment when assets are worth much more than the balance sheet valuations, and should reveal the true value of trade investments. Shares of no par value should be permitted. With regard to hidden reserves, a majority recommended that the exemption from full disclosure for banking and discount houses should continue. Insurance companies should remain partly exempted; that is, they should give more information, particularly about investment income. There was no case for exemption of shipping companies. A Minority Report recommended that the existing exemption should be withdrawn from banks and discount houses but that the Board of Trade (now Department of Trade and Industry) should be empowered to grant individual exemptions.

Many recommendations were made to tighten up the control on soliciting for money. Advertisements on radio and television and investment circulars were instanced.

Reference to the Jenkins Committee is included here because of its particular historical significance. Most of the recommendations passed into law via subsequent Companies Acts including such matters as disclosure of beneficial holdings in nominee companies, more informative company accounts, disclosure of the true value of company assets, the disclosure of bank profits, the degree of control over advertisements for financial products and the filing of accounts by private companies. Similarly, the problem of insider dealing (q.v.) has been dealt with. On the other hand, new unit trust legislation contemplated by the Committee has not been introduced and the unit trust industry still operates under the Prevention of Fraud (Investments) Act 1958, and the Department of Trade and Industry Regulations.

JOBBER SEE *Stock Exchange; Stock Jobber*

JOINT ACCOUNT (Other than a partnership, executor, or trustee account.) Unless otherwise provided for, all the parties to a joint account must operate on the account jointly. Likewise, if powers are given to an outside party to sign, all the joint account holders must concur. And if either or any one or more of the joint account holders are authorized to operate on the account, one of them cannot give a power of attorney to an outside party to act on his behalf without the consent of the others.

A garnishee order (q.v.) citing a sole judgment debtor will not attach a joint account in which such debtor is a constituent.

An authority for either to sign on a joint account of two parties does not extend to other operations, such as withdrawal of items left for safe custody, etc., nor will it make one party liable for an overdraft created by the other party.

On the death of one party to a joint account, the benefit of any credit balance passes to the survivor(s) and the executors of the deceased party must look to such survivor(s) for any interest of the deceased in the balance. They cannot prevent the banker paying the survivor(s) unless they get a court order. In practice, a banker would act warily in the case of a dispute. Where the joint account is of husband and wife, however, whether the wife can appropriate the balance on the death of her husband is a question of intention when the account was opened. Where the account was opened for a matter of convenience, the balance belongs to the husband's estate (*Marshal* v *Crutwell* [1875] 20 LR Eq 328); but where the account was opened to provide for the wife on the death of the husband, the balance belongs to the wife (*Foley* v *Foley* [1911] 1 IR 281).

These rights of husband and wife do not prevent the survivor from giving a good discharge to the banker whose mandate has been suitably worded.

On the death of a joint account holder, his estate is not liable for any debit balance unless he was severally liable. SEE *Joint and Several Liability*

On notice of the death of one joint account holder, any cheques drawn by the deceased alone under authority should be returned. Cheques signed by the survivor(s) may safely be paid.

The bankruptcy of a joint account holder severs the joint relationship; any mandate lapses and operations on the account must be jointly transacted by the trustee and the solvent party. Cheques drawn alone by the bankrupt must be returned; so likewise must cheques drawn by the solvent party under mandate, but care must be taken not to damage his credit and the answer should be 'Joint account holder "A" in bankruptcy' or in similar terms.

The mental incapacity of a party to a joint account cancels any mandate held, and the balance must be held to the order of the sane party and the Receiver. Failing such appointment, application should be made to the Court of Protection for directions.

One party to a joint account may stop payment of a cheque drawn by another party to the account.

The form of the mandate taken on the opening of a joint account differs; some banks use a comprehensive form covering all transactions on credit and debit accounts; other banks use a special form for debit accounts. Both types establish joint and several liability.

The following matters are usually provided for in one form or the other. Clear instructions will be given as to whether both or either or all or some of the joint account holders may draw on the account. Mention will be made that the account is with benefit to survivor; this is not a covenant (save in the case of husband and wife) but a reminder of the law on the subject. Where one party can sign alone, it will be arranged that any overdraft created by him is the responsibility also of the other party. Joint and several liability will also be arranged, for the reasons given under *Joint and Several Liability*. Power to negotiate advances and to lodge security therefor will be provided for and arrangements made as to the withdrawal of items lodged for safe custody or security not only during the lifetime of the parties but also on the death of one of them.

The nature of a bank's liability to customers on a joint account was a matter of controversy following the decision in *Brewer* v *Westminster Bank Ltd* [1952] 2 All ER 650, where the plaintiff was an executrix of her father's will. Her co-executor forged her signature on cheques to a total of £3,000, and when she brought this action against the bank for payment of cheques bearing only one authorized signature, it was held that action on a joint account could only be brought by the account holders jointly, and as one of them here could not, because of his forgeries, sue the bank, the other was also debarred.

The decision was much criticized, and in *Jackson* v *White and Midland Bank Ltd* [1967] 2 Lloyd's Rep 68 and a succession of cases other judges either distinguished the decision or refused to follow it. The most recent example is *Catlin* v *Cyprus Corporation* (*London*) *Ltd* [1983] 1 All ER 809, where Bingham, J, analysed the reasoning in *Brewer* and said that the bank's agreement to honour instructions signed by both account holders imported a negative agreement not to honour instructions not signed by both.

A duty on the defendants which could only be enforced jointly with the party against the possibility of whose misconduct a safeguard was sought, and where the occurrence of such misconduct through the negligent breach of mandate by the defendants would deprive the innocent party of any remedy, would be worthless.

The question has not been to the Court of Appeal, all the decisions being at first instance (in the case of *Brewer* the appeal was withdrawn on the payment by the bank of a substantial sum to the plaintiff); but it is unlikely that any bank will again raise the defence.

JOINT AND SEVERAL LIABILITY With *joint* liability, a creditor can only bring one action and not several. If he sues one or some, but not all, of the joint debtors, and obtains judgment which is unsatisfied, his right of action against the remainder is barred. But with *joint and several* liability, a creditor has as many rights of action as there are debtors; he can sue them jointly or severally until he has recouped himself, and an unsatisfied judgment against one debtor leaves the creditor with recourse against the survivor(s) or solvent parties. With joint and several liability, the estate of a deceased or bankrupt debtor can be held liable for the amount of the debt due at the time of his decease or failure, provided such amount is determined by breaking the account.

With joint liability no right of set-off obtains in respect of any credit balances on private accounts of the parties, but with joint and several liability, credit balances on any private account of the parties may be set off against the debt on the joint account.

Partners are only jointly liable in England and Wales, but severally liable in Scotland. But in England and Wales recourse can be had to a deceased partner's estate for the firm's debts after all his private creditors have been satisfied; however, if the joint and several liability has been established, the firm's creditors are not postponed to the deceased partner's private creditors, but stand on equal footing.

Where a note runs 'I promise to pay' and is signed by more than one person, it is deemed to be their joint and several note (Bills of Exchange Act 1882, Section 85(2)).

In *Re a Debtor* [1971] 1 All ER 504, where there was joint property charged by debtors who were jointly and severally liable, on the bankruptcy of one of the debtors, half the value of the property had to be treated as direct security and deducted from the proof.

In the case of *National Westminster Bank Ltd* v *Allen and Another* [1971] 3 All ER 201, the husband and wife, who owned a house as joint tenants, had joint banking accounts, both of which were overdrawn. It was held in that case that as the defendants were joint tenants holding on trust for sale and jointly entitled to the beneficial interest in the house, a charging order could be made in respect of their joint liability.

JOINT ANNUITY An annuity payable during the lives of two or more persons and during the life or lives of the survivor or survivors.

JOINT CREDIT CARD COMPANY A company set up in 1972 by National Westminster Bank, Midland Bank and Lloyds Bank, to promote the credit card Access (q.v.). Before the actual launching of the card the scheme was joined by Williams and Glyn's Bank, Clydesdale Bank, Northern Bank, Ulster Bank and Royal Bank of Scotland. SEE *Credit Card*

JOINT LIFE POLICY A policy of insurance under which the sum assured is payable on the death of the first of two or more lives.

JOINT STOCK COMPANY A company, or association of individuals, having a joint or common stock or capital. SEE *Company*

JOINT TENANTS Prior to 1926, property could be conveyed to two or more persons as joint tenants, each person having an equal interest in the whole of the property, and when one died his interest passed to the surviving joint tenant or tenants; or it could be conveyed to two or more persons as tenants in common, who had a unity of possession in the property, but each tenant had a separate and distinct share (the share being either equal or unequal). When one died, his share did not pass to the surviving tenant or tenants in common but could be disposed of by will.

Trustees and personal representatives, such as executors, were always joint tenants.

After 1925, tenancy in common could no longer be created as a legal estate. By the Law of Property Act 1925, the interest of joint tenants and tenants in common is in shares in the proceeds of the sale of the property and not in shares in the property itself. The conveyance vests the property in the grantees as joint tenants upon trust for sale (with power to postpone the sale), and to divide the proceeds of the sale between the persons who, in equity, are interested in the property. The legal estate is thus vested in trustees for sale, and these trustees may also be the persons who are, in equity, entitled to the proceeds of sale.

Where land is conveyed to more than four persons, the legal estate vests in the first four named in the conveyance as joint tenants upon trust for sale.

In some cases, the trustees for sale may not be the persons, or the only persons, who are entitled to the proceeds of a sale.

If the trustees for sale are, in equity, joint tenants, on the death of one before a sale of the property, the representatives of the deceased joint tenant have no claim upon the proceeds of a subsequent sale. The legal estate passes to the survivors.

But a sole surviving trustee cannot give a receipt for capital moneys other than a trust corporation; he must co-opt another trustee.

If the trustees for sale are, in equity, tenants in common, on the death of one the legal estate passes to the surviving trustees for sale, who continue to hold in trust for sale and to divide the proceeds of a sale between themselves and the representatives of the deceased tenant in common.

If the trustees are the same persons as the beneficiaries under the trust for sale, the trustees can mortgage as beneficial owners. If the trustees for sale are not the beneficiaries, or not all the beneficiaries under the trust, it will be necessary to ascertain who are the persons entitled to the proceeds of sale and get them all to join in the creation of a mortgage. In many cases where land has been conveyed since 1925 to joint owners, a provision has been inserted in the conveyance authorizing them to mortgage for any purpose.

It is, however, advisable, before taking a mortgage from co-owners, to obtain the advice of a solicitor.

A survivor of joint tenants who is solely and beneficially interested can deal with his legal estate as if it were not held on trust for sale (Law of Property (Amendment) Act 1926).

JUDGMENT CREDITOR Where a creditor has obtained judgment against a debtor for the payment of a debt, he may enforce the judgment in various ways:

1. By writ of *fieri facias* (q.v.), by which the sheriff can seize the debtor's *goods*.
2. By a charging order (q.v.), by which the sheriff can take possession of the debtor's *lands*.
3. By a garnishee order (q.v.), by which debts due to the debtor from a third person, e.g. a banker, can be attached.
4. By a charging order (q.v.), by which shares or stocks belonging to the debtor can be charged with the payment of the judgment debt.
5. If the debt is £50 or more, by issuing a bankruptcy notice (SEE *Act of Bankruptcy*), a non-compliance with the terms of which will constitute an act of bankruptcy and enable the judgment creditor to have the judgment debtor's assets administered in bankruptcy.
6. By equitable execution by means of the appointment of a receiver.
7. By a writ of attachment for contempt of court.

K

KAFFIRS A Stock Exchange term for South African gold mining shares.

KEEPING HOUSE The Bankruptcy Act 1914, Section 1(1)(*d*), enacts that a debtor commits an act of bankruptcy if, with intent to defeat or delay his creditors, be begins to 'keep house'. A debtor keeps house when he confines himself to the house and refuses to see a creditor who calls to see him for payment of the debt. Refusal to see a creditor who called at an unreasonable hour would not be keeping house within the meaning of the Act.

KRUGERRANDS A gold South African coin containing exactly one ounce of pure gold and priced at 3 per cent above the value of the gold content. Krugerrands may be purchased from members of the London Gold Market or through the clearing banks in the UK. Fractional krugerrands also exist: these contain one-half, one-quarter or one-tenth of an ounce of gold. SEE ALSO *Gold Coins*

L

LAND CERTIFICATE A certificate issued under the seal of the Land Registry to the owner of a registered title; it takes the place of title deeds as prima facie evidence of ownership. It contains an exact copy of the Property and Proprietorship parts of the Land Register and also comprises a Charges section which can at any time be written up to date without fee to correspond with the Charges Register by forwarding the land certificate to the Registry. A copy of that portion of the General Map in which the land in question is included is also provided. Where the certificate becomes overloaded with entries, a new one will be issued free of the cancelled entries.

In the case of an absolute title, no deeds or documents are necessary in addition to the land certificate; in the case of a good leasehold title the original lease should accompany the land certificate; and in the case of a possessory title all title deeds and documents up to the date of first registration are required in addition to the land certificate. SEE ALSO *Land Registration*

LAND CHARGES The Land Charges Act 1925 consolidated the various enactments relating to the registration of land charges and also provided for the registration of other charges and encumbrances previously incapable of registration.

This Act deals with unregistered land. Land with a registered title is dealt with in the Land Registration Act 1925.

Registration of any instrument or matter under the provisions of this Act in any register kept at the Land Registry, or elsewhere, is deemed to constitute actual notice of such instrument or matter to all persons and for all purposes connected with the land affected, as from the date of registration (Law of Property Act 1925, Section 198, subsection (1)). This Section operates without prejudice to the provisions respecting the making of further advances by a mortgagee, and applies only to instruments to be registered under the Land Charges Act 1925 (subsection (2)). SEE *Mortgage*

There are kept at the Land Registry registers of pending actions, annuities, writs and orders affecting land, deeds of arrangement affecting land, and land charges.

Pending Actions

By the Land Charges Act 1925, a pending action, that is any action or proceeding pending in court relating to land or any interest in or charge on land, and a petition in bankruptcy filed after the end of 1925, may be registered in the Register of pending actions. The registration of a pending action ceases to have effect at the end of five years, but may be renewed from time to time (Section 2).

A pending action shall not bind a purchaser without express notice thereof unless it is registered. If there has been a petition in bankruptcy, this protection applies only in favour of a purchaser of a legal estate in good faith for money, without notice of an available act of bankruptcy (Section 3).

Annuities

An annuity or rent charge created and registered under Acts prior to 1926 may be registered here, but not an annuity or rent charge devolving from a marriage settlement or will. The Register will be closed when existing entries on 13th January, 1926, are vacated. Annuities created before 1926 but unregistered are found in Class E of the Land Charges section. Annuities created after 1925 are registered in the Land Charges section, Class C (iii).

Writs and Orders Affecting Land

There may be registered (and re-registered every five years)

1. any writ or order affecting land;
2. any order appointing a receiver or sequestrator of land;
3. any receiving order in bankruptcy whether or not it is known to affect land (Section 6).

An unregistered writ or order is void as against a purchaser of the land. As regards an unregistered receiving order in bankruptcy, the protection only applies in favour of a purchaser of a legal estate in good faith and for money, without notice of an available act of bankruptcy (Section 7).

Deeds of Arrangement

A deed of arrangement may be registered (and re-registered every five years) (Section 8).

If not registered it shall be void as against a purchaser of any land comprised therein (Section 9).

Land Charges
The following classes of charges on land may (and should) be registered as land charges in the Register.
Class A A rent, annuity, or principal money, being a charge (otherwise than by deed) upon land, created pursuant to the application of some person under the provisions of various Acts.
Class B A charge on land (not being a local land charge) of any of the kinds in Class A created otherwise than pursuant to the application of any person.
Class C A mortgage, charge of obligation affecting land of any of the following kinds:

1. A puisne mortgage, that is a legal mortgage not being a mortgage protected by a deposit of documents relating to the legal estate affected, and (where the whole of the land is within the jurisdiction of a local deeds registry) not being registered in the local deeds register.
   In the case of a land charge, created by a company, registration under the Companies Act, is sufficient in place of registration under this Act (Section 10(5)).
2. Any equitable charge acquired by a tenant for life or statutory owner under the Finance Act 1894, or any other statute, by reason of the discharge by him of any death duties or other liabilities, and to which special priority is given by the statute (in the Act called 'a limited owner's charge').
3. Any other equitable charge, which is not secured by a deposit of documents, and does not arise under a trust for sale or a settlement and is not included in any other class of land charge (in the Act called 'a general equitable charge'). This includes an annuity created after 1925.
4. Any contract by an estate owner to convey or create a legal estate, including a contract conferring a valid option of purchase, a right of preemption or any other right (in the Act called 'an estate contract').

Class D A charge or obligation affecting land of the following kinds:

1. Any charge acquired by the Commissioners of Inland Revenue for death duties payable on any death which occurs after 1925.
   This provision applies only where the duty has become a charge on the land (Section 10(4)).
2. A covenant or agreement (not being between a lessor and lessee) restrictive of the user of land (in the Act called 'a restrictive covenant').
3. Any easement, right, or privilege over or affecting land, being merely an equitable interest (in the Act called 'an equitable easement') (Section 10).

Class E An annuity created before 1926 but not hitherto registered.
Class F A charge affecting any land by virtue of the Matrimonial Homes Act 1967. SEE *Married Woman*

Unregistered Land Charges
If the land charges in the above classes are not registered, they shall be void, as follows:

Class A, as against a purchaser (which includes a mortgagee or lessee) of the land.
Classes B and C, when created after 1925, as against a purchaser (mortgagee or lessee) of the land.
Class D, when created after 1925, and an estate contract (Class C, 4) only as against a purchaser of legal estate for money (Section 13).

A purchaser (mortgagee or lessee) shall not be prejudicially affected by notice of any instrument or matter capable of registration under the Land Charges Act 1925, which is void by reason of non-registration (Law of Property Act 1925, Section 199).

Priority Notice
Any person intending to make an application for the registration of any contemplated charge, in pursuance of the Land Charges Act 1925, may give a priority notice in the prescribed manner at least 14 days before the registration is to take effect. Where such a notice is given, it shall be entered in the register to which the intended application, when made, will relate, and if the application is presented within 14 days thereafter and refers in the prescribed manner to the notice, the registration shall take effect as if the registration had been made at the time when the charge was created. (Law of Property (Amendment) Act 1926, Section 4(1), and SR & O, 1940, No. 1998).

Local Land Charges
Any charge (called a local land charge) acquired by the council of any administrative county, metropolitan borough, or urban or rural district, or by the corporation of any municipal borough or by other local authorities, which takes effect by virtue of statute, shall be registered by the proper officer of the local authority in the register of the authority. Such registration shall take the place of registration in the Land Registry.

This Section applies to local land charges

affecting registered as well as unregistered land (Section 15).

A Local Land Charges Register consists of four parts:

Part I consists of general financial charges where a local authority has expended money on land for any purpose, and the work in question is not completed or the amount of the charge ascertainable.

Part II comprises specific financial charges where expenditure on completed work is ascertained and allocated. The charge contemplated by Part I or II is in respect of road and drainage charges.

Part III relates to town-planning schemes containing prohibitions or restrictions on the use of buildings or land.

Part IV relates to prohibitions and restrictions not arising under town-planning schemes.

Searches and Official Searches

Any person may search in any register kept in pursuance of this Act on paying the prescribed fee.

Any person may, on payment of a fee, require the Registrar to make a search, and the Registrar shall make the search and issue a certificate setting forth the result of his search (Section 17).

By the Law of Property (Amendment) Act 1926, Section 4(2), and the Land Charges Rules 1940:

> Where a purchaser has obtained an official certificate of the result of search, any entry which is made in the Register after the date of the certificate and before the completion of the purchase, and is not made pursuant to a priority notice entered on the Register before the certificate is issued, shall not, if the purchase is completed before the expiration of the fourteenth day after the date of the certificate, affect the purchaser .... In reckoning the number of days under this Section, Sundays and other days when the registry is not open to the public shall be excluded. [Subsection (3)]

Registered Land

With the exception of local land charges, the provisions of this Act requiring registration of charges shall not apply to registered land if and so far as they can be protected under the Land Registration Act 1925, Section 23. SEE UNDER *Land Registration*

Mortgages by Companies

The provisions respecting the registration of mortgages and charges under the Companies Act, are given in *Registration of Charges*. SEE ALSO UNDER *Mortgage* for registrations and searches necessary when taking charges over land.

LAND REGISTRATION The Land Registration Act 1925, repealed the whole of the Land Transfer Act 1875, and most of the Land Transfer Act 1897.

The Act provided for (1) voluntary registration of title to land in England and Wales, and (2) the gradual introduction, by Order in Council, of compulsory registration of title to land in England and Wales. HM Land Registry will supply details of all those areas of the country to which compulsory registration has been applied. This does not mean that all land must automatically be registered in those areas, but only that whenever there is a disposition on sale of a freehold estate or the grant of a lease of not less than 40 years, registration is compulsory.

The extension of compulsory registration is accomplished:

1. by Order in Council following a petition of a county authority ;
2. by Order in Council without petition from a county authority. By Section 120, Land Registration Act, this method could not operate until the expiration of ten years from 1st January, 1926, and during the first available year (1936) only one Order was to be made. Accordingly, an Order in Council was made on 3rd July, 1936, whereby registration of title to land was to be compulsory on sale in the administrative County of Middlesex on and after 1st January, 1937.

By the Land Registration Act 1966—which came into force 13th January, 1967—voluntary first registration of title in a non-compulsory area was suspended. It is possible in a voluntary area to have a registered title removed from the register and for the land to revert to the unregistered system of conveyancing.

At the present time the areas subject to compulsory registration are shown on pages 385–388.

The Land Register

This consists of three parts: (1) the Property Register giving the title number, a short description of the property, and a reference to the General Map; (2) the Proprietorship Register, giving the name, address, and description of the proprietor, the date of his registration, and the consideration that passed; (3) the Charges Register, whereon are placed details of charges, leases, covenants, etc. The Land Register is private and can be inspected only by permission of the registered proprietor (Section 112).

The Land Certificate when issued is a copy of the Land Register with the addition of a scale plan of the registered property. Certain items can be enrolled on the register after issue of the certi-

County or administrative area	Areas subject to compulsory registration	District land registry
Avon	Bath Bristol Kingswood	Plymouth
Bedfordshire	Luton North Bedfordshire South Bedfordshire	Stevenage
Berkshire	wholly compulsory	Gloucester
Buckinghamshire	South Bucks	Stevenage
Cambridgeshire	Cambridge Peterborough	Peterborough
Cheshire	wholly compulsory	Birkenhead
Cleveland	wholly compulsory	Durham
Clwyd	wholly non-compulsory	Swansea
Cornwall	wholly non-compulsory	Plymouth
Cumbria	Barrow-in-Furness	Durham
Derbyshire	Bolsover Chesterfield Derby Erewash South Derbyshire	Nottingham
Devon	East Devon Exeter Plymouth South Hams Teignbridge Torbay	Plymouth
Dorset	Bournemouth Christchurch Poole Weymouth and Portland Wimborne	Plymouth
Durham	Chester-le-Street Darlington Durham Easington Sedgefield	Durham
Dyfed	Llanelli	Swansea
East Sussex	wholly compulsory	Tunbridge Wells
Essex	Basildon Brentwood Epping Forest Harlow Southend-on-Sea Thurrock	Stevenage
Gloucestershire	Gloucester	Gloucester
Greater London	Bexley Bromley Croydon Greenwich Kingston upon Thames Lambeth	Croydon

County or administrative area	Areas subject to compulsory registration	District land registry
Greater London	Lewisham Merton Richmond upon Thames Southwark Sutton Wandsworth	Croydon
	Barnet Brent Camden City of London City of Westminster Ealing Enfield Hackney Hammersmith and Fulham Haringey Harrow Hillingdon Hounslow Inner Temple and the Middle Temple Islington Kensington and Chelsea Tower Hamlets	Harrow
	Barking and Dagenham Havering Newham Redbridge Waltham Forest	Stevenage
Greater Manchester	wholly compulsory	Lytham
Gwent	Islwyn Newport	Swansea
Gwynedd	wholly non-compulsory	Swansea
Hampshire	Eastleigh Fareham Gosport Havant New Forest Portsmouth Southampton	Weymouth
Hereford and Worcester	Bromsgrove Hereford Worcester	Swansea
Hertfordshire	wholly compulsory save for the districts of Dacorum and North Hertfordshire	Stevenage
Humberside	Cleethorpes East Yorkshire Great Grimsby Kingston upon Hull Scunthorpe	Durham
Isle of Wight	wholly non-compulsory	Weymouth
Isles of Scilly	wholly non-compulsory	Plymouth

County or administrative area	Areas subject to compulsory registration	District land registry
Kent	wholly compulsory	Tunbridge Wells
Lancashire	Blackburn Blackpool Burnley Fylde Preston Rossendale	Lytham
Leicestershire	Blaby Charnwood Hinckley and Bosworth Leicester North West Leicestershire Oadby and Wigston	Peterborough
Lincolnshire	Lincoln	Peterborough
Merseyside	wholly compulsory	Birkenhead
Mid Glamorgan	Ogwr Rhondda Taff-Ely	Swansea
Norfolk	Norwich	Peterborough
Northamptonshire	Kettering Northampton	Peterborough
Northumberland	Blyth Valley Wansbeck	Durham
North Yorkshire	Craven (Parish of Kildwick only) York	Durham
Nottinghamshire	wholly compulsory save for the districts of Bassetlaw and Newark	Nottingham
Oxfordshire	Oxford South Oxfordshire Vale of White Horse	Gloucester
Powys	wholly non-compulsory	Swansea
Shropshire	wholly non-compulsory	Swansea
Somerset	wholly non-compulsory	Plymouth
South Glamorgan	wholly compulsory	Swansea
South Yorkshire	wholly compulsory	Nottingham
Staffordshire	Cannock Chase Lichfield Newcastle-under-Lyme Stoke-on-Trent Tamworth	Nottingham
Suffolk	Ipswich	Peterborough
Surrey	wholly compulsory	Tunbridge Wells
Tyne and Wear	wholly compulsory	Durham
Warwickshire	wholly compulsory save for the district of Stratford-on-Avon	Gloucester

County or administrative area	Areas subject to compulsory registration	District land registry
West Glamorgan	wholly compulsory	Swansea
West Midlands	wholly compulsory	Gloucester
West Sussex	wholly compulsory save for the districts of Chichester and Horsham	Weymouth
West Yorkshire	wholly compulsory	Nottingham
Wiltshire	wholly non-compulsory	Plymouth

ficate, without production of the latter, but the certificate will always be written up to correspond with the Register without charge.

From 1st January, 1926, legal estates became the only interests in land in respect of which a registered title can be given (Section 2). SEE *Legal Estates*

In a compulsory area, every conveyance on sale of freehold land and every grant of a term of years absolute, not being less than 40 years, and every assignment on sale of leasehold land held for a term of years absolute having not less than 40 years to run, must be registered (Section 123). Leases under 21 years to run cannot be registered; leases over 21 but under 40 years may be registered. But where the freehold title, out of which the lease is granted, is registered, any lease with over 21 years to run must be registered, whether in a compulsory or voluntary area.

Trust interests are, as far as possible, kept off the Register (Section 74) but sometimes find a place in the Proprietorship section of the Register, e.g. where the registered proprietor is the tenant for life a restriction will be entered against a transfer on sale unless the consideration money is paid into court or to the trustees of the settlement. Likewise, where the registered proprietors are joint tenants, a note will be made that no transfer on sale will be registered unless the consideration money is paid to at least two trustees or a trust corporation.

Such matters as deeds of arrangement, receiving orders, and pending actions are protected by lodging a creditor's notice, or inhibition, or a caution respectively. These, with restrictive covenants and annuities, are registered in the Charges section.

Personal covenants are not entered on the Charges Register, but sometimes an office copy of the conveyance or grant of a lease wherein they are recited is stitched in the land certificate on first registration. Attention is drawn on the land certificate to the possible existence of easements and leases of less than 21 years, which can be ascertained by personal enquiry.

There are four classes of title granted: absolute, good leasehold, possessory, and qualified.

Absolute Title

This is granted in respect of a freehold estate after examination of the applicant's title by the Registrar and, in some cases, advertisement in the *London Gazette* and a local paper.

The grant of an absolute title gives the owner a State-guaranteed title against all the world and thereafter the land certificate is the one essential document of title, the former title deeds being redundant.

Absolute title in respect of leasehold land is granted only on first registration where there is evidence of the freehold title from which the lease has been granted—usually where the freehold interest is already registered with absolute title.

Good Leasehold Title

Usually a leaseholder cannot produce evidence of the freeholder's title to grant the lease (he cannot demand it of the freeholder—Law of Property Act, Section 44(2)) and hence a good leasehold title is granted on first registration. In such a case, the lease should accompany the land certificate. A good leasehold title may be converted into an absolute title after ten years on proof that the proprietor or successive proprietors have been in possession for that time (Land Registration Act 1925, Section 77(4)).

Possessory Title

Where a possessory title is granted, no official examination is made other than to establish that the applicant has a prima facie right to the land and no guarantee of title is given up to the point of registration. From that date, however, the title is guaranteed, and dealings can be made only by registered instruments. All the documents of title must accompany the land certificate, and the title up to the date of registration must be investigated in the ordinary way. Where land has been registered with a possessory title, if freehold for 15 years and if leasehold for ten years, the Registrar may grant an absolute title in the case of freehold land and a good leasehold title in the case of leasehold land.

The Registrar can refuse to register with possessory title and can grant an absolute or good leasehold title as the case may be, whether the applicant consents or not (Land Registration Act, Section 4(3) and 8(4)).

Possessory titles are consequently now quite exceptional.

Qualified Title

This is practically unknown and was devised to meet cases where the title can be established only for a limited period. A title so registered is subject to any rights or interests arising before a specified date or that are specifically described in the Land Register.

Mortgages of Registered Land

The counterpart of a legal mortgage of unregistered land is, in the case of registered land, a registered charge. This gives the owner of the charge the equivalent of a lease of 3,000 years if a freehold is concerned and a sub-lease for the term of the lease less one day if leasehold. The chargee also gets all the powers and remedies of a legal mortgagee of unregistered land. A registered charge must be by deed, but may be in any form provided that the land is identified by reference to its title number, or in any other manner not requiring reference to other documents. The Land Registry supply a form of charge (Form 45), but bankers usually use a form of charge under seal incorporating the special features of a banker's mortgage (q.v.). The form of charge with a copy must be lodged at the Registry, together with the land certificate and the relative search certificate. The Registry keep the last two documents, together with the duplicate of the charge, and issue a charge certificate in which is stitched the original charge branded with the Land Registry stamp.

Before 1914 charge certificates were not issued, but the land certificate was returned to the chargee with an office copy of the charge indorsed with a certificate of registration. Before 1926 the land certificate was not impounded by the Registry, and before 1936 the practice was to retain the original charge and stitch the office copy thereof in the charge certificate.

Before taking a registered charge, an official certificate of search should be obtained on Form 94 with the written authority of the registered proprietor—such certificate will be supplied free. An official search is to be preferred because any errors therein are the liability of the Registry, and, if the application to register the charge is lodged with the search certificate within 14 days of the date of the latter, no adverse entries in the interim will affect the charge, with the exception of a mortgage caution or a priority notice (see below). In cases of urgency a search may be requisitioned by telegram or telephone (Rule 293), but the reply will be limited to a statement that there is no subsisting entry or otherwise.

A priority notice may be given by an intending chargee on Form 18 accompanied by the land certificate. Provided the charge is delivered for registration within 14 days of the giving of the notice, it will have priority over any application or instrument delivered in the meantime.

The priority of a registered charge is regulated by the date of its registration and not by the date of its creation.

Where, as in the case of a registered charge given to a bank, the charge is drawn to secure further advances, the Registrar must advise the chargee before making any entry in the Register—such as a second charge—that would adversely affect the priority of any further advances by the first chargee (Section 30).

Where the security is vacated, Form 53 (Discharge of Registered Charge) together with the Charge Certificate is forwarded to the Registry. The form of discharge will require sealing by the bank.

There is an alternative form of effecting a legal mortgage of registered land provided by Section 106—by the execution of an ordinary legal mortgage and registering a special form of caution known as a mortgage caution at the Land Registry. This must be accompanied by the land certificate, the mortgage deed, and a certified copy thereof. The caution is entered on the Register and the original mortgage returned to the chargee. This method, however, is practically unknown.

Second Charge of Registered Land

This is done by lodging the charge in duplicate at the registry and getting a certificate of second charge stitched therein. Alternatively, the second charge may not be registered, but a caution lodged at the Registry.

Sub-charges

A sub-mortgage of registered land is obtained by lodging the charge certificate at the Registry with the sub-charge in duplicate and getting in exchange a certificate of sub-charge. Alternatively, an equitable sub-charge can be obtained by giving notice of deposit of the charge certificate to the Registry and getting the Registrar's acknowledgment thereof. In such a case, it is usual to take a sub-charge under seal, although it is not registered.

Equitable Mortgages of Registered Land
By Section 66 the deposit by the registered proprietor of the land certificate with a third party creates a lien equivalent to a lien created in the case of unregistered land by the deposit of documents of title (i.e. an equitable mortgage). Such a charge can be protected by lodging a special form of caution at the Land Registry called Notice of Deposit of Land Certificate (Form 85A). This should be signed on behalf of the bank by the manager or his deputy. It is sent with a duplicate which is returned to the cautioner as an acknowledgment. Lodgment of Notice of Deposit has been free since 1st June, 1970. On receipt of the Notice of Deposit, no dealings may take place in the land without prior warning to the party lodging the Notice.

Where a banker is content to take an equitable charge over registered land by such means he may also require a memorandum of deposit to be executed by his customer, or, more usually, the latter will complete a charge under seal which is capable of registration at a later date.

The certificate will be forwarded to be written up to date or searches made.

Where a title is being registered for the first time, or where a title is in course of transfer, and consequently the land certificate is not immediately available for deposit, Notice of Intended Deposit can be lodged at the Registry on Form 85C, signed by the prospective registered proprietor. When the land certificate is eventually deposited with the lender, there is no need to lodge an additional Notice of Deposit.

Where the land certificate is released on repayment of the advance, the Notice of Deposit should be withdrawn. The duplicate Notice of Deposit, which the Registry returns to the bank as an acknowledgment, contains on the reverse side a form of withdrawal for this purpose; it should be signed by the manager or his deputy. Any unregistered form of charge which has been held does not need a formal discharge, but may be cancelled.

No searches of, or registrations on, the Land Charges Register are necessary in the case of registered land; in the case of limited companies, however, searches should be made at Companies House and registration of the charge made there in addition to the Land Register.

LAST TRADING DAY The term used in the commodities markets for the day on which trading ceases for delivery in a particular month. Contracts which are open on that day, i.e. have not been matched or 'cancelled', will normally have to be settled by delivery of the actual commodity. SEE *Commodities*

LAW REFORM (ENFORCEMENT OF CONTRACTS) ACT 1954 Section 4 of the Statute of Frauds Act 1677 originally covered five types of contract which were unenforceable unless they, or some note or memorandum thereof, were in writing and signed by the party against whom it was sought to enforce them. The Law of Property Act 1925, had already amended Section 4 by eliminating the words 'or upon any contract for the sale of lands, etc.,' and substituting for it the present Section 40; and in later years two Law Reform Committees considered Section 4, the first recommending that the section be repealed altogether, the second recommending that the 'special promise to answer for the debt, default or miscarriage of another person' be saved. This latter recommendation received statutory approval in the 1954 Act which by Section 1 repeals in Section 4 of the Statute of Frauds Act the words 'whereby to charge any executor or administrator upon any special promise to answer damages out of his own estate', and the words 'or to charge any person upon any agreement made upon consideration of marriage' and the words 'or upon any agreement that is not to be performed within the space of one year from the making thereof' in relation to any promise or agreement, whether made before or after the commencement of the Act. Apart from the contracts relating to land, therefore, it is only the agreement in respect of a guarantee which now has to be evidenced in writing if it is to be enforceable.

Section 2 repealed Section 4 of the Sale of Goods Act 1893, which rendered unenforceable by action any contract for the sale of goods for £10 or upwards, unless the buyer should accept part of the goods and actually receive them or give something in earnest to bind the contract or in part payment, or unless some note or memorandum in writing be made and signed by the party to be charged. The Law Reform Committee saw no reason why the requirement as to writing and to signature should apply only to such contracts.

LAW REFORM (MARRIED WOMEN AND TORTFEASORS) ACT 1935 This Act enlarges a married woman's power to deal with property and to enter into contracts whilst extending her legal liability. By Section 1 a married woman can hold and dispose of property, be capable of rendering herself and being rendered liable on any tort, contract, debt, or obligation, can sue and be sued, and is subject to the law of bankruptcy, in all respects as if she were a feme-sole (q.v.). Section 2 abolished restraint on anticipation, but any restraint on anticipation existing before 1st January, 1936, or imposed in any instrument executed before that date, was to continue to be or would become effective. But this was qualified by Section 2(3), which provided that the will of any testator who dies after 31st December, 1945, shall be deemed to have been executed after 1st January, 1936, notwithstanding that it was executed before that date. This put a time limit on the possibility of any testamentary restraint on anticipation not yet in force.

The Married Women (Restraint on Anticipation) Act 1949, abolished all such restraints. A creditor can now get judgment against a married woman personally, and against her property notwithstanding it was subject to a restraint on anticipation imposed before 1936. Bankruptcy proceedings are now available whether a married woman is in trade or business or not. SEE *Married Woman*

The statute also established a right of contribution as between joint tortfeasors.

LEASEUROPE The European Federation of Equipment Leasing Company Associations. SEE *Equipment Leasing Association*

LEASEHOLD From the Saxon *leasum*, to enter lawfully. Where the owner of freehold land grants it to a person for a term of years, it is called a lease and the land is then leasehold. The person leasing it is the lessor (who is possessed of the reversion), and the party in whose favour the lease is given is the lessee. When a lease is granted for more than three years the land is 'demised' by deed to the lessee. When the lessee transfers his term to some one else he 'assigns' the lease. The consideration in a lease may be the payment of so much per annum, or a lump sum, called the premium, in addition to the annual payment together with covenants. When a lessee grants to another person a part only of his interest under a lease, it is termed a sub-lease, or under-lease.

The interest of a lessee may be a tenancy at will or for years, and is personal property. The subject-matter of a lease must be real estate or a chattel real.

In *Camberwell and South London Building Society* v *Holloway* [1879] 13 ChD 754, Jessel, MR, said

> The word 'lease' in law is a well-known legal term of well-defined import. No lawyer has ever suggested that the title of the lessor makes any difference in the description of the instrument, whether the lease is granted by a freeholder, or by a copyholder, with the licence of the lord, or by a man who himself is a leaseholder. It being well granted for a term of years it is called a lease. It is quite true that where the grantor of the lease holds for a term, the second instrument is called either an under-lease or a derivative lease, but it is still a lease.

In taking the deeds of leasehold property as security, it should be remembered that failure to fulfil the covenants contained in the lease may result in the forfeiture of the lease, and re-entry of the lessor. If the last receipt for the landlord's rent is produced, it is a waiver of any breach of covenant of which the landlord was aware before giving the receipt, but it is not a waiver with regard to any breach of which he was ignorant.

By the Law of Property Act 1925, a right of re-entry or forfeiture under any stipulation in a lease for a breach of any covenant in the lease shall not be enforceable unless the lessor serves on the lessee a notice

1. specifying the breach complained of; and
2. if the breach is capable of remedy, requiring the lessee to remedy it; and
3. in any case, requiring the lessee to make compensation for the breach,

and the lessee fails to remedy the breach or to make reasonable compensation in money to the lessor (Section 146). This section does not apply to a condition for forfeiture on the bankruptcy of the lessee.

Under a contract to grant a term of years to be derived out of a freehold estate, the intended lessee shall not be entitled to call for the title to the freehold; and on contract to grant a lease for a term of years to be derived out of a leasehold interest with a leasehold reversion, the intended lessee shall not have the right to call for the title to that reversion. These Sections, however, apply only where a contrary intention is not expressed in the contract (Section 44).

Where a lease is made under a power contained in a settlement, will, Act of Parliament, or other instrument, any preliminary contract for or relating to the lease shall not, for the purpose of the deduction of title to an intended assign, form part of the title, or evidence of the title, to the lease (Section 44).

Where land sold is held by lease (not including under-lease), the purchaser shall assume, unless the contrary appears, that the lease was duly granted; and, on production of the receipt for the last payment due for rent under the lease before the date of actual completion of the purchase, he shall assume, unless the contrary appears, that all the covenants and provisions of the lease have been duly performed and observed up to the date of the actual completion of purchase (Section 45).

Where land sold is held by under-lease, the purchaser shall assume, unless the contrary appears, that the under-lease and every superior lease were duly granted, and on production of the last receipt for rent he shall assume that all covenants and provisions of the under-lease and of every superior lease, as well as all rent due, have been duly performed and paid up to date (Section 45).

A mortgage of leasehold property, after 1925, is to be effected by a sub-demise for a term of years absolute, less by one day at least than the term vested in the mortgagor, subject to a provision for cesser on redemption (SEE UNDER *Mortgage*). The mortgagor retains a legal term of years absolute, and the mortgagee takes a legal term of years, so that they both have legal estates. SEE *Legal Estates*

A mortgage may also be effected by deed expressed to be a charge by way of legal mortgage. SEE *Mortgage*

Since 1925 a mortgage of leaseholds cannot be made by assignment.

Where any part of the property of a bankrupt consists of land of any tenure burdened with onerous covenants, the trustee may, with leave of the court, disclaim the property. Where a trustee disclaims leasehold property the court shall not make a vesting order in favour of any person claiming under the bankrupt, whether as under-lessee or as mortgagee by demise, except upon the terms of making that person subject to the same liabilities and obligations as the bankrupt was subject to under the lease in respect of the property at the date when the bankruptcy petition was filed, and any mortgagee or under-lessee declining to accept a vesting order upon such terms shall be excluded from all interest in and security upon the property (Section 54, Bankruptcy Act 1914).

A lessor cannot compel an equitable mortgagee by deposit of a lease to take a legal assignment, but if the mortgagee enters into possession of the property he is liable on the covenants of the lease.

If there is a covenant in the lease that the lessees cannot sub-demise without the consent of the lessor, the licence of the lessor should accompany the deeds where there is a mortgage by sub-demise, but if the deeds are held merely with a memorandum of deposit, the licence is not required. The lease should be perused to see whether the lessor's consent is required for a mortgage of the property, or whether he requires notice of a mortgage.

Upon the death of an owner of leasehold property, the estate becomes vested in the personal representatives (executors or administrators) of the deceased. When, therefore, the deeds of leasehold property are lodged by a borrower who has obtained the property, after the death of the previous owner, the assent in writing of the personal representatives should be deposited along with the title deeds. The assent operates to vest the legal estate in the person named therein.

In the case of *Re Owers* [1941] Ch 389, the contingent liability of personal representatives entering into possession of leaseholds was evident; for this reason executors frequently seek an indemnity from beneficiaries, or sometimes insurance cover. SEE *Personal Representatives*

Where the deeds of leasehold property are deposited as security, they should as a rule be accompanied by the original lease, but it may occur that the original lease included two properties, and is not along with the deeds given as security. There should, however, be an attested copy of the lease, or it should be abstracted, and an acknowledgment given for its production.

Where a sub-lease is deposited as security, it should be accompanied by an attested copy of the original lease.

If parts of a leasehold property have been sub-leased, the counterparts of the sub-leases should accompany a deposit of the lease or assignment thereof.

In Scotland, an assignment of a lease for thirty-one years and longer, when recorded in the Register of Sasines, forms a legal security; but, when the term is for a less period, it is necessary that the assignee enter into possession, otherwise the assignment does not hold good as against creditors. SEE *Leasehold Reform Act 1967; Shorthold Tenancy*

LEASEHOLD REFORM ACT 1967 This Act gives tenants of leasehold houses the right to acquire the freehold or an extended leasehold of their homes on fair terms in cases where

1. the tenancy is a long one (meaning in this context a tenancy granted for a term of years exceeding 21 years);
2. the rent is low (meaning for this purpose, rent which is not equal to or more than two-thirds of the rateable value of the property);
3. the rateable value of the house is below a prescribed amount; and
4. the tenant has occupied the house as his residence for the last three years or for periods amounting to three years in the last ten years.

Where the right applies, it extends to the entire

house and premises, including any garage, outbuildings, garden and other appurtenances let with the house. In the case of *Tandon* v *Trustees of Spurgeon's Homes* [1982] 1 All ER 1086 HL, it was held that whether a building may reasonably be called a house is a question of law, notwithstanding that the 'house' might quite reasonably be called something else.

The 'appropriate day' for determining whether the Act applies to a particular house is 23rd March, 1965, or such later date as may apply under the Rent Act 1977, which usually means 23rd March, 1965 or the date on which a rateable value for the house was first shown in the valuation list.

In the case of houses in Greater London, the right applies if

1. the appropriate day (see above) fell before 1st April, 1973, and the rateable value did not exceed on that day £400, or in cases where the tenancy was created on or before 18th February, 1966, and the rateable value on 1st April, 1973 did not exceed £1,500;
2. where the appropriate day falls on or after 1st April, 1973, the right exists, if the tenancy was created on or before 18th February, 1966, and the rateable value on the appropriate day was not more than £1,500, or if the tenancy was created after 18th February, 1966, the rateable value on that day was not more than £1,000.

The corresponding figures for houses outside Greater London are one-half of the above in each case.

In general, where the tenant of a house has died while occupying it as his or her residence, the right continues for the benefit of any member of the family who acquires the tenancy on death and for this purpose a member of the family means antecedents and descendants and their respective wives or husbands.

In order to acquire the freehold or an extended lease, the tenant must give written notice to the landlord, in which case the landlord is obliged to comply with the Act except in a limited number of circumstances, such as where the landlord requires the property for redevelopment after he has granted an extension of the tenant's lease.

In the event of disagreement over the price to be paid for the freehold or extended lease, the matter must be referred to a valuation tribunal. SEE ALSO *Ground Rents*

LEASING When the word 'leasing' is used on its own, it usually refers nowadays to the leasing of goods or equipment, rather than the leasing of land (SEE *Leasehold*). Leasing as a large-scale business operation is a comparatively modern phenomenon. Nevertheless, there have been instances down the ages of the goods of one person being used, by arrangement, in the business of another. A good example is the chartering of ships. Similarly, the hiring of railway wagons, which was a forerunner of industrial hire purchase finance (q.v.) was more truly a leasing operation.

The business of leasing as known today in the UK arose from the development of leasing in the USA after the Second World War. The opening of subsidiaries of US companies in the UK brought an awareness of leasing facilities, and thus leasing transactions were entered into by UK merchant banks and finance houses. Leasing is a contractual arrangement, under which one party, in return for an agreed rent, uses a capital asset owned by another party. Such leased assets are typically plant and equipment but may include a wide diversity of assets such as aircraft, ships, furniture, hospital beds and oil rigs. Thus, leasing is based on the fundamental aspect that one does not need to own an asset in order to enjoy the benefit of it in business.

From the hirer's point of view, a leasing contract has the advantage that it is, in effect, an additional source of finance. A company may be short of working capital, particularly in a growth situation, and the position would be aggravated by the additional purchase of fixed assets. The leasing of those assets will leave the working capital unimpaired and in effect the cost of the equipment is spread over a number of years. Indeed, if the investment appraisal has been done correctly, the leased assets should more than earn their keep and thus, the leasing contract becomes, as it were, self-liquidating. It may also be said that leasing contracts introduce a measure of stability into the budgeting process in that costs are spread more or less evenly over a number of years and can be precisely identified in relation to a particular area of the business. Also, leasing contracts are extremely flexible and the leasing company will normally structure the contract to suit the particular needs and characteristics of the hirer. In 1972, the taxation relief was increased to 100 per cent of the acquisition costs and remained at that level until 1984. In his Budget of that year, the Chancellor announced a staged reduction in the amount of first-year allowances. SEE *Capital Allowances*

It may be, however, that a company does not have sufficient taxable profits in a particular year to take advantage of the capital allowances and may not be sufficiently sure of future profits to take advantage of the carry forward provisions. If, however, a company acquires equipment under a leasing contract, the leasing company, being the purchaser and owner of the equipment, will obtain the capital allowances which, assuming that the leasing company has sufficient taxable profits, will enable some of the benefit of the allowances to be passed on to the hirer in the rental terms.

Although the capital allowances are a legitimate feature of leasing business, the Inland Revenue will not permit them to be claimed if the contract is not a bona fide leasing transaction, e.g. if it has been entered into merely for the purpose of securing allowances which would not otherwise be obtained. This will apply also if the vendor and the purchaser are connected with each other. Since 1979, leasing companies have been unable to claim capital allowances on equipment leased to local authorities and others who have no liability for corporation tax, although the normal 'writing down' allowances may be claimed in such cases.

The fact that a leasing contract does not appear in a company's balance sheet has been the subject of criticism. The Companies Act 1967 (Schedule 1 11(3)) required a company to show in its profit and loss account 'the amount, if material, charged to revenue in respect of sums payable in respect of the hire of plant and machinery'. It has been argued however, that finance leases (see below) should be capitalized in the balance sheet of the lessee company and recommendations were made on the subject in Exposure Draft 29 of the Accounting Standards Committee. In broad terms, the recommendations were to the effect that leased assets should be shown in the lessee's balance sheets under the heading 'leased property under finance leases', and that the outstanding liability for future rental instalments should be shown under 'obligations under finance leases'. These recommendations were put into effect in an *Accounting Standard* (SSAP 21) issued by the Accounting Standards Committee in August 1984. The principal requirement of SSAP 21 is that lessee companies should capitalize finance leases in their balance sheets which, in the words of the Standard involves 'reflecting in a balance sheet the leased asset and the obligation to pay future rentals'. The initial sum to be recorded in the balance sheet will be the present value of the minimum lease payments which will normally be close to the 'fair value' of the asset. The new requirement applies to old and new leases and comes into effect from July 1987.

A finance lease is a contract which virtually transfers all the risks and rewards of ownership of the asset in question from the lessor to the lessee. The entire outlay by the lessor and his profit are covered by the rentals received during the primary rental period. This is in contrast to an operating lease, under which the lessee has the use of an asset for which he pays a rental but which is expected to be returned to the lessor at the end of a period and which is expected to have retained some value by that date. Thus, operating leases are appropriate to technological equipment which the user may wish to enhance or upgrade or replace from time to time and other assets such as motor cars, which have a second-hand saleable value.

The Equipment Leasing Association (q.v.) gives the following examples of items which are leased by their members:

Computers
Office equipment, e.g. accounting machines and copying machines
Telecommunication equipment
Contractor's plant
Machine tools
Oil exploration and extraction equipment
Printing presses
Textile machinery
Aircraft
Business cars
Commercial vehicles
Containers
Locomotive and rolling stock
Ships
Agricultural equipment
Hotel equipment
Medical and dental equipment
Shop fittings
Vending machines

A typical finance lease will include:

1. a schedule of the equipment to be leased;
2. an undertaking by the lessee to pay when due the rent provided for in the agreement;
3. undertakings by the lessee to keep the equipment in good repair, to keep it insured to its full replacement value and to allow the lessor access for inspection of the equipment;
4. provision for termination of the agreement in the event of default;
5. provision that the equipment shall remain movable property in the ownership of the lessor, notwithstanding that it may be affixed to any land or buildings; and
6. an indemnity in favour of the lessor against any claim by a third party arising out of the condition or use of the equipment.

The decision, on behalf of a company whether or not to lease or buy new equipment will depend on a number of factors, including the following:

1. the opportunity cost of capital, i.e. what the purchase price of the equipment would earn if used elsewhere in the company's business; or
2. the current cost of borrowing elsewhere, discounted over the period in question; and
3. the current (discounted) value of future tax allowances; and
4. the discounted cost of meeting the annual or quarterly rental payments over the period of the lease.

In a situation where the capital allowances would be available equally to either the lessor or the company client and where there is equal access to finance at equivalent rates, leasing will be more costly than buying. The difference is the premium which one pays the lessor by way of his profit and administrative costs. Whether that premium is acceptable would be a matter of business judgment depending on the overall position of the company, other foreseeable calls on its resources, budgeting convenience, balance sheet considerations and even differing views of movements in interest and tax rates.

The volumes of business dealt with by the member companies of the Equipment Leasing Association are shown under that entry.

LEEMAN'S ACT Sale and Purchase of Bank Shares Act 1867, 30 Vict c 29. The name of an Act of Parliament (passed with the intention of preventing speculation in bank shares) by which it is provided that all contracts for sale or purchase of bank shares or stock except shares or stock of the Bank of England or Bank of Ireland must set forth the numbers of the shares or stock, or, if there are no distinguishing numbers, the name of the registered proprietor. Section 1 is as follows.

All contracts, agreements, and tokens of sale and purchase which shall be made or entered into for the sale or transfer, or purporting to be for the sale or transfer, of any share or shares, or of any stock or other interest, in any joint stock banking company in the United Kingdom of Great Britain and Ireland constituted under or regulated by the provisions of any Act of Parliament, Royal Charter, or letters patent, issuing shares or stock transferable by any deed or written instrument, shall be null and void to all intents and purposes whatsoever, unless such contract, agreement or other token shall set forth and designate in writing such shares, stock, or interest by the respective numbers by which the same are distinguished at the making of such contract, agreement, or token on the register or books of such banking company as aforesaid, or where there is not such register of shares or stock by distinguishing numbers, then unless such contract, agreement, or other token shall set forth the person or persons in whose name or names such shares, stock, or interest shall at the time of making such contract stand as the registered proprietor thereof in the books of such banking company; and every person, whether principal, broker, or agent, who shall wilfully insert in any such contract, agreement, or other token any false entry of such numbers, or any name or names other than that of the person or persons in whose names such shares, stock, or interest shall stand as aforesaid, shall be guilty of a misdemeanour, and be punished accordingly, and, if in Scotland, shall be guilty of an offence punishable by fine or imprisonment.

This Act is still in force, but its provisions are disregarded on the London Stock Exchange, as it is not the practice to specify the numbers of bank shares on the contract note. Where a person, in ignorance of that practice, instructed his brokers to purchase for him certain shares in a joint stock bank, and, before the settling day, repudiated the contract, it was held (*Perry* v *Barnett* [1885] 15 QBD 388) that the contract, which was made contrary to this Act, was not binding upon him. But where a person purchases bank shares and is aware of the practice of the Stock Exchange he cannot repudiate the contract.

Sections 2 and 3 of the Act are as follows.

2. Joint stock banking companies shall be bound to show their list of shareholders to any registered shareholder during business hours, from ten of the clock to four of the clock.
3. This Act shall not extend to shares or stock in the Bank of England or the Bank of Ireland.

LEGACY A gift of money or of a specific item bequeathed by will. SEE *Abatement; Ademption; General Legacy; Specific Legacy*

LEGACY DUTY The duty which was payable upon bequests of personalty (not including leaseholds) by a testator who was domiciled in the UK at the time of his death, or in respect of personal property received, in the case of intestacy, by the next of kin. Legacy Duty was abolished by the Finance Act 1949.

LEGAL ESTATES Since 1st January, 1926, there have been only two legal estates in land, fee simple (freehold) and a term of years absolute (leasehold). Interests or charges in or on land, such as easements, rent charges, etc. are called 'legal interests'. All other charges are equitable interests. This is enacted in the Law of Property Act 1925, as follows.

1.—(1) The only estates in land which are capable of subsisting or of being conveyed or created at law are:

(*a*) an estate in fee simple absolute in possession;
(*b*) a term of years absolute.

(2) The only interests or charges in or over land which are capable of subsisting or of being conveyed or created at law are:

(*a*) An easement, right, or privilege in or over land

for an interest equivalent to an estate in fee simple absolute in possession or a term of years absolute;

(b) A rentcharge in possession issuing out of or charged on land being either perpetual or for a term of years absolute;

(c) A charge by way of legal mortgage;

(d) Land tax, tithe rentcharge, and any other similar charge on land which is not created by an instrument;

(e) Rights of entry exercisable over or in respect of a legal term of years absolute, or annexed, for any purpose, to a legal rentcharge.

(3) All other estates, interests, and charges in or over land take effect as equitable interests.

A legal estate may subsist concurrently with or subject to any other legal estate in the same land (Section 1(5)). For example, a mortgagor of freeholds retains the legal fee simple and the mortgagee also has a legal estate, if he takes by demise a term of years absolute. They are both called 'estate owners'. In a mortgage of leaseholds, the mortgagor retains a term of years absolute and the mortgagee takes by sub-demise a legal term of years absolute. SEE *Joint Tenants; Mortgage; Settled Land; Tenancy in Common*

LEGAL MORTGAGE This is accomplished in the case of a freehold by the demise of a term of years absolute, subject to cesser on redemption, or by a charge by deed expressed to be by way of legal mortgage (Section 85, Law of Property Act 1925). A legal mortgage of a leasehold is made by the grant of a sub-lease less by at least one day than the unexpired term of the borrower, subject to cesser on redemption, or by a charge by way of legal mortgage. Before 1926, a legal mortgage of a freehold was made by the conveyance of the fee simple to the mortgagee, the mortgagor being left with the equity of redemption. Thus only one legal mortgage could be subsisting at one time and second and subsequent mortgages were equitable only, for the fee simple was in the hands of the first mortgagee. By the Law of Property Act, 1925, it is possible for there to be any number of legal mortgages subsisting at the same time on the same property, for the fee simple remains in the mortgagor who grants legal estates in the shape of terms of years to successive mortgagees. Thus, a first mortgagee may get a lease of 3,000 years, and a second mortgagee a lease of 3,000 years and one day, and so on. SEE *Equity of Redemption; Mortgage*

LEGAL TENDER Coins issued in the UK by the Royal Mint (q.v.) are legal tender as follows:

1. gold coins, for payment up to any amount, provided they are of statutory weight;
2. silver or cupro-nickel coins of denominations of more than 10p for payment of any amount not exceeding £10;
3. cupro-nickel coins of denominations of not more than 10p, for payment up to any amount not exceeding £5;
4. bronze coins for payment of any amount not exceeding 20p.

All notes of the Bank of England are legal tender in England and Wales. Notes of the Bank of England for less than £5 are legal tender in Scotland and Northern Ireland. Scottish and Irish notes are not legal tender in England and Wales.

LEGATEE The person to whom 'personal' property (SEE *Personal Estate*) is left, or bequeathed, in a will. The person who takes all the personal property remaining after all legatees have received their shares is called the residuary legatee.

LEGITIMACY ACT 1959 This Act, which came into force at the end of October, 1959, remedied certain deficiencies in the Legitimacy Act of 1926. In the earlier Act, inheritance rights in the estates of parents were given to children legitimated by the Act, and, similarly, parents were given rights in the estates of such children. These rights, however, did not extend to the cases of illegitimate children who could not be legitimated under the Act, for example, where although the parents married at a later date, there was at the time of the birth a legal obstacle to marriage. Nor was any provision made for the case of a child born to parents whose marriage was subsequently annulled.

The Legitimacy Act 1959 provides in Section 1 that an illegitimate person whose father or mother was married to a third person at the time of the birth shall be placed in the same position as an illegitimate person neither of whose parents was married at that time. By Section 2, the children of certain void marriages, whether born before or after the commencement of the Act, are to be treated as legitimate persons provided that the father was domiciled in England at the time of the birth or at the time of his death, whichever was the earlier. This Section does not affect any rights under the intestacy of any person who died before the commencement of the Act, nor, with some exceptions where a title of honour is concerned, does it affect the operation or construction of any disposition coming into operation before the commencement of the Act.

The rights of succession to an illegitimate person dying intestate after 1st January, 1970 are covered by the Family Law Reform Act 1969, which also deals with other aspects relating to their property.

LENDING BY BANKS Traditionally the lending business of the UK clearing banks has been based on the concept of the overdraft, which in itself arose from the development of the current account, the issuing of cheques and the banks' money transfer system.

The overdraft, i.e. a current account with an agreed lending limit, has been and, for the most part is still, the central feature of bank lending in the UK. Bank deposits in Britain have been traditionally short-term, being repayable on demand in the case of current accounts and on seven days notice in the case of deposit accounts. This obligation to repay on demand or short notice coloured the whole lending scene, with the result that bank overdrafts are generally still repayable on demand or, at least are subject to review within a comparatively short time. From the banker's point of view, an overdraft has the advantage that it is self-liquidating by the normal turnover of the current account, although in many instances this can be an illusion because of the tendency of accounts to develop a 'hard-core' of lending. From a customer's point of view, the overdraft has the advantage that interest is charged on a day-to-day basis and thus full credit is given for payments into the account.

To some extent the overdraft has been supplemented and perhaps, in some cases, supplanted by other forms of lending. In their evidence to the Wilson Committee (q.v.), the London clearing bankers said

> In addition to the traditional overdraft, a variety of other lending facilities for both corporate and personal customers is now available through the banks' branch networks, although several are provided by subsidiary and affiliated companies. In terms of the range of facilities available, from the very short-term advance to the occasional equity investment, the clearing banks are now much closer than they used to be to the traditionally continental concept of the 'universal bank'.

During the 1970s, UK banks moved into the business of contractual medium-term loans, principally for industrial and commercial concerns, and these now represent approximately 40 per cent of total bank lending to the business sector. Unlike an overdraft, such a loan is repayable only at the end of the term or in the event of breach of the arrangements by the borrower. The rate of interest may be fixed but, more usually, it would be expressed by reference to the inter-bank rates in force from time to time.

In addition to the provision of medium-term loans, the extent of which is limited because of the short-term nature of their deposit banking base, the banks provide extensive facilities, some of them of a long-term nature, either under special government schemes, e.g. for export credit and for shipbuilding or through specialist corporations, such as the Agricultural Mortgage Corporation (q.v.) and Finance for Industry (q.v.), in which the banks are shareholders. Also, through their subsidiary companies, the banks provide 'asset finance' in the form of hire purchase (q.v.), factoring (q.v.) and leasing (q.v.).

The personal sector has also seen a widening of the lending facilities on offer from the commercial banks. The 'personal loan' was first introduced in 1958 and was the banks' first real venture into personal instalment finance. Another major development in the personal lending sector has been that of the credit card (q.v.) and the offering of hire purchase facilities through the banks' subsidiaries.

At the end of 1984, the total sterling advances of the London and Scottish clearing banks to UK residents was approximately £72,000 million. The following table shows the growth in the total sterling advances of the clearing banks to UK residents over recent years.

Year	London clearing banks £m	Scottish clearing banks £m	Total £m
1975	14,088	1,505	15,593
1976	15,851	1,744	17,595
1977	17,383	1,930	19,313
1978	20,567	2,144	22,711
1979	25,492	2,738	28,230
1980	31,085	3,531	34,616
1981	40,102	4,295	44,397
1982	52,182	5,359	57,541
1983	58,882	6,278	65,160
1984	64,646	7,296	71,942

Source: CLCB Statistical Unit.

In their evidence to the Wilson Committee (q.v.), the London clearing bankers also said

> The pattern of clearing bank lending between the different sectors of the economy is determined largely by the demands of the bank's customers, reflected in the first instance in requests for facilities and then in the use actually made of the facilities agreed.

And again:

> The clearing banks themselves do not set out to strike a particular balance between different sectors of the economy in their lending activities.

There are times when qualitative and quantitative controls imposed by the Treasury through the Bank of England have affected the level of lending to particular sectors of the economy. For example, the banks have been encouraged on some occasions to give priority to export industries and on some occasions not to increase their lending to the property sector. There have been constraints from time to time on lending for speculative purposes and, during times of credit squeezes, the banks have been required to lend to the personal sector for consumer purposes only within the rules appertaining to hire purchase.

Figures are published quarterly showing the classification of bank advances by industry and the following table shows the analysis of total sterling and foreign currency lending by all banks in the United Kingdom to UK residents, as at February, 1985.

Type of borrower	£m
Manufacturing industry	
Extractive industries and mineral products	1,766
Metal manufacturing	1,730
Chemicals and allied industries	2,495
Mechanical engineering	1,926
Electrical and electronic engineering	3,575
Motor vehicles and parts	1,185
Other transport equipment	1,381
Other engineering and metal goods	1,939
Food, drink and tobacco	5,046
Textiles, leather, footwear and clothing	1,744
Other manufacturing	5,541
Other production	
Agriculture, forestry and fishing	5,386
Oil and extraction of natural gas	4,525
Other energy industries and water	2,849
Construction	4,957
Services	
Wholesale distribution	10,385
Retail motor trades	2,097
Other retail distribution	5,709
Hotels and catering	3,336
Transport and communications	4,001
Central and local government	2,203
Property companies	5,849
Business and other services	12,758
Financial	
Building societies	1,516
Investment and unit trusts	3,056
Insurance companies and pension funds	2,578
Leasing companies	4,961
Other financial	21,791
Persons	
House purchase	17,516
Other purposes	17,758
Total	161,559

Source: Bank of England.

LETTER OF ALLOTMENT The letter which is sent by a company to an applicant for shares, stocks, or bonds which are being offered to the public, stating what has been allotted to him and requesting payment of the amount due to be paid thereon. SEE *Application for Shares*

In 1960 a new type of allotment letter was introduced with the object of avoiding the necessity for exchanging an allotment letter for a definitive certificate. Basically, it is a certificate which is renounceable up to a certain date. The printing relating to the renunciations and registrations is put on the back of the certificate, and the instructions which are normally found in the body of an allotment letter are contained on a perforated slip, which may later be torn off, attached to one side of the certificate.

Allotment letters do not form a security for an advance, though they may in some cases be held temporarily and exchanged for the certificates when ready, when a transfer of the shares can be taken in the usual way. When an underwriter takes up shares which have not been subscribed for by the public, he may receive allotment letters in blank. These are sometimes lodged with a bank as a temporary security, and when the underwriter obtains purchasers their names are filled in and the allotment letters released against payment.

In the case of an issue of new shares, a shareholder may agree to accept the number of new shares provisionally allotted to him, by signing a form of acceptance, or he may renounce his rights to the shares by signing a form of renunciation. He may renounce in favour of another person, who should sign the form of acceptance, or he may sell his rights through a broker (SEE *Letter of Renunciation*). A stamp is not required on the form of acceptance.

An allotment of stock or shares or bearer bonds may be payable by instalment.

LETTER OF APPLICATION When an issue of shares is offered to the public, a person who wishes to subscribe for some of them sends in a letter of application stating how many he requires and enclosing at the same time a cheque for the amount payable on application. If his application is not successful, the money is returned, but if successful he receives in due course a letter of allotment. SEE *Application for Shares; Letter of Allotment*

LETTER OF CREDIT A letter of credit is a document issued by a banker authorizing the banker to whom it is addressed to honour the cheques of the person named to the extent of a certain amount and to charge the sums to the account of the grantor; or it may be worded so as to authorize the person to whom it is addressed to draw on demand or, over a dated period, upon the banker issuing the letter, and the grantor undertakes, in the letter, to honour all drafts drawn in accordance with the terms of the credit. The letter states the period for which the credit is to remain in force, and it should be indorsed with particulars of all drafts drawn under the credit. When a letter of credit is issued, the amount is debited to the customer's account and credited to a 'Letters of Credit' account. If not debited to his current account on issue it may be necessary, if the customer's account is overdrawn, to require security in order to protect the bank against its undertaking in the letter of credit to honour drafts drawn thereunder. The amount of the letter of credit is passed to two contra accounts in the general ledger and reversing entries are made whenever a payment is made under the credit, so as to enable the banker at any time to ascertain his total liability under letters of credit.

A circular credit is addressed to all correspondents of a bank, and a direct credit is addressed to a specified correspondent.

Where a banker is authorized to pay cheques under a letter of credit, he must see that the signature of the drawer is correct and that the terms of the letter are strictly observed. He should be furnished with a specimen of the signature of the person who is entitled to draw the money, and will be responsible for any loss if he pays on a forged signature.

A letter of credit is not a negotiable instrument.

Of recent years, the letter of credit has become largely superseded by travellers' cheques. SEE *Circular Letter of Credit; Documentary Credit*

LETTER OF LIEN A debtor frequently gives a banker, as security for an advance, a letter of lien or charge upon goods in the hands of a third party. In the case of *In Re Hamilton, Young & Co* [1905] 2 KB 772, where a letter of lien over goods in the hands of certain bleachers, accompanied by their receipt, was given, it was held that the letter was a document used in the ordinary course of business as a proof of the control of goods. The letter should empower the banker to sell, in default of payment of the debt.

LETTER OF RENUNCIATION Where shares have been allotted to a person and he does not wish to keep them, he may renounce them in favour of another person. The document by which this is effected is called the Letter of Renunciation. SEE *Renunciation*

LETTERS OF ADMINISTRATION Where a person dies and leaves no will, the Probate Registry will, on application, appoint a person, the administrator, to wind up the estate, and will grant to him Letters of Administration, that is, a document empowering him to administer the estate of the deceased. If the deceased person left a will but did not nominate any person to act as executor, or if the persons nominated are dead or incapable of acting, e.g. infants or mentally ill, or if the persons nominated renounce probate, that is, they decline to act as executors, Letters of Administration with the Will annexed will be granted by the Probate Registry. The administrator in such a case (called an administrator *cum testamento annexo*) must carry out the terms of the will just like an executor.

If the balance of a deceased's account is small, some bankers pay it, on receiving a satisfactory indemnity, without production of Letters of Administration.

Where Letters of Administration are revoked, the banker is protected in any payments he may have made upon the Letters. The sections of the Act relating to this point are quoted under *Probate*. *In Hewson* v *Shelley* [1914] 110 LT 785, where real property had been sold by an administrator and a will was subsequently found, the Master of the Rolls said

> The person for the time being clothed by the Court of Probate with the character of legal personal representative is the legal personal representative and enjoys all the powers of a legal personal representative unless and until the grant of administration is revoked or has determined. If this view is not right no person could safely deal with, or accept a title from, an administrator, for it is impossible to prove that there may be no will.

See the provisions of the Administration of Estates Act 1925, under *Personal Representative*. SEE *Administrator; Administrator De Bonis Non*

LEVERAGE An American term meaning the same as gearing (q.v.) in the UK.

LICENSED DEALER Under the Prevention of Fraud (Investments) Act 1958, it is an offence for any person to carry on the business of dealing in securities unless he is licensed by the Department of Trade and Industry, or is an exempted dealer (q.v.), or exempted from the requirements of the Act (see below). There are two categories of licence: a principal's licence and a representative's licence. Licences are granted annually on application to the Department of Trade and Industry and once granted will be renewed annually unless the holder ceases to carry on business or fails to give the required information to the Department, or for some reasons is thought not to be a fit and proper person to hold a licence. This last disqualification would arise only if the licence-holder or his employees or associates are convicted of an offence involving fraud or dishonesty, or a breach of the Act, or if he has failed to comply with the Conduct of Business Rules made under the Act. At the present time there are approximately 350 licensed dealers.

An exempted dealer should be distinguished from dealers who are exempted from the need to obtain a licence under the Act. Those who are exempt from the need to obtain a licence include members of the Stock Exchange, the Bank of England, statutory or municipal corporations, industrial and provident societies, building societies, exempted dealers or persons acting as managers or trustees of authorized unit trusts and members of recognized associations of dealers in securities. Such associations are expected to have their own rules of conduct and include the London Discount Market Association, the Association of Stock and Share Dealers, the National Association of Security Dealers and Investment Managers, the Law Society of Scotland, the United Kingdom Association of New York Stock Exchange Members, the Association of Canadian Investment Dealers and members of the Toronto and Montreal Stock Exchanges in Great Britain and, lastly, the United Kingdom Association of Tokyo Stock Exchange Members. The Law Society of Scotland is included, but not the English Law Society, because Scottish lawyers deal more in securities than do their English counterparts.

In 1983, new rules came into operation under The Licensed Dealers Conduct of Business (Rules) 1983 and the Dealers in Securities (Licencing) Regulations 1983. The principal features of these rules are

1. A licensed dealer is required to keep client moneys and investments separate from his own moneys and investments.
2. Clients must be informed of the insurance or other arrangements made by licensed dealers to safeguard the clients' interests.
3. A licensed dealer must disclose to his clients any material interest he may have in a transaction and in certain cases where there is an inherent conflict of interest, the client's agreement must be obtained.
4. The licensed dealer must keep detailed books and records of all transactions involving his clients' money and investments and clients are entitled to see extracts from such records.
5. Licensed dealers are required to keep the Department of Trade and Industry advised of certain relevant changes in their organization, e.g. changes in directors.
6. New clients, with effect from September, 1983, must be advised how their money and investment is to be dealt with and dealers undertaking investment management operations must enter into formal contracts with their clients.

At the time of writing there are approximately 500 licensed dealers in the UK.

LIEN This is the right to retain property belonging to another until a debt due from the latter is paid. This is a possessory lien as opposed to a maritime lien (q.v.).

A possessory lien is of two kinds: particular and general. A particular lien is the right to retain goods in respect of which the debt was incurred. For example, a carrier has a lien on goods entrusted to him for transport; a watchmaker has a lien on articles left for repair in respect of the cost thereof. A general lien is a right of retainer not only for a debt incurred for particular goods but for the general balance due. Thus bankers, solicitors, stockbrokers, in certain circumstances may have a lien on clients' securities, etc., for all moneys due.

A banker's lien is a special form of general lien, for it includes a right of sale after reasonable notice. It is the right of a banker to retain such of his customer's property as comes into his hands in the ordinary course of business as a banker; it is an implied pledge.

In *Brandao* v *Barnett* [1846] 3 CB 519, Lord Campbell stated 'bankers have a general lien on all securities deposited with them as bankers by a customer, unless there be an express contract, or circumstances that show an implied contract, inconsistent with lien'.

A lien does not attach to any instrument which the banker knows is not the property of his customer.

The lien is not affected by reason that negotiable securities do not belong to the person depositing them, if the banker is unaware of the fact.

A banker has no lien on securities which are deposited for some particular purpose. For example, it has been held that where a conveyance of two separate properties was deposited, with a memorandum of charge upon only one of the properties, the banker had not a general lien upon the other property (*Wylde* v *Radford* [1863] 33 LJ Ch 51).

Bills and documents left for collection are part of a banker's ordinary business, and he has a lien upon them, but he may also be a holder in due course (q.v.), if he satisfies that definition.

Section 27(3) of the Bills of Exchange Act 1882, provides

Where the holder of a bill has a lien on it, arising either from contract or by implication of law, he is deemed to be a holder for value to the extent of the sum for which he has a lien.

If a bill has been transferred absolutely to a banker he is entitled to the full amount of it, but if he has merely a lien upon it his interest is limited to the extent of that lien.

In the case of cheques, bills, or promissory notes subject to the lien, it is the duty of the banker to present them in due course, and, in case of dishonour, to give the appropriate notice.

Where a banker negotiates a bill with shipping documents attached he has probably the right, should the occasion arise, to realize the goods to the extent of the amount of the draft, but such action might lead to tedious and costly legal proceedings. The proper course is to insist upon a letter of hypothecation (q.v.) in every case.

When a banker has discounted bills for a customer, the banker has no lien on any credit balance on the account with respect of the contingent liability on the bills not yet due. 'There would be no use in discounting the bills' if the banker had a lien on the cash balance (*Bower* v *Foreign and Colonial Gas Co* [1874] 22 WR 740). But a contingent debt is provable in bankruptcy, and a lien on a credit balance can then be claimed. It is, of course, otherwise if the discounted bill is dishonoured on maturity. SEE *Proof of Debts; Set-Off*

The securities over which a banker has a lien are understood to be principally negotiable securities. In *Wylde* v *Radford* [1863] 33 LJ Ch 51, Kindersley, VC, held

What is intended is such securities as promissory notes, bills of exchange, exchequer bills, coupons, bonds of foreign governments, etc.; and the Courts have held that if such securities are deposited by a customer with his banker, and there is nothing to show the intention of such deposit one way or the other, the banker has, by custom, a lien thereon for the balance due from the customer.

In *Davis* v *Bowsher* [1794] 5 TR 488, Lord Kenyon said

Whenever a banker has advanced money to another, he has a lien on all the paper securities which come into his hands for the amount of his general balance.

In *Re United Service Company* [1870] 6 Ch App 212, where railway share certificates were deposited with a bank and a commission was charged for collection of the dividends, it was held that the certificates came into the bank's custody in the ordinary course of their business as bankers, that they were deposited with the bank by a customer of the bank, and that such deposit was made under such circumstances as would have entitled the bank to a lien upon them for their general banking account. Several authorities, however, express doubts as to certificates being the subject of a banker's lien.

A conveyance of land is not subject to a banker's general lien, but where deeds are deposited with the intention of creating a security, without any memorandum of charge, they form an equitable mortgage by deposit.

A banker has no lien upon articles left for safe custody, as the circumstances of the deposit are inconsistent with lien. A customer may, however, sign an agreement giving the banker a lien on securities left for safe custody.

A banker has no lien upon a security handed to him for the purpose of selling it through a stockbroker (*Symons* v *Mulkern* [1882] 46 LT 763).

In *Re Bowes; Earl of Strathmore* v *Vane* [1886] 33 ChD 586, where a customer deposited a life policy for £5,000, with a memorandum stating that it was to form a security to the extent of £4,000 with interest, commission, and other charges, it was held that the banker could not claim more on the policy than the £4,000 and charges, as limited in the charge. Mr Justice North said

It is said that the bankers have a banker's lien; that Bowes was their customer, and handed over to them the policy as security, that they had it in their hands and were entitled to hold it, not only for the £4,000, interest and commission, for which they had a written agreement, but that in addition they had a further right as bankers to hold it in respect of the rest of his debt to them; or in other words they claim a right under the special contract in writing and also under an implied contract. It appears to me that that is inconsistent with the terms of the agreement, which is for a security for a sum not exceeding £4,000 principal and no more, with interest and commission, and that when the contract says in so many words that the charge is for a sum not exceeding £4,000, the charge is limited to that amount .... It has not been suggested that the sale was wrong in any way; and it may well be that bankers who have a power of selling securities deposited, when they have sold, and have clear money in their hands after satisfying the charge, may be entitled to say they will set off that money against further sums due to them; but that seems to me a totally different case from the present, where the security is of a wholly different nature, and the bank had no power of sale. It is quite true that, after a demand for payment had been made, the bank might have insisted on having a mortgage with a power of sale. No such demand was made or mortgage given, the bank never had a power to sell and convert the policy into money. ... It seems to me that the express terms of this deposit were that sums not exceeding £4,000 were to be paid out of the policy moneys, and it would be inconsistent with that, in the absence of any additional agreement, to allow the bank to hold the policy for something more.

Where a customer has a credit balance on one account and is owing money on another, the banker may, in the absence of contrary agreement, express or implied, set off one balance against the other. This right, which is subject to limitations, is sometimes referred to as a banker's lien, but the more exact term is set off. SEE *Set-Off*

The deed of settlement, or articles of association, of a banking company may provide that the partly-paid shares of the members shall be subject to a lien in favour of the bank for all moneys due to the bank in respect of any call or debt due from the shareholder, whether alone or jointly with any other person, to the bank. It has been held that such a power gives the bank a lien upon the dividends, as well as upon the shares.

A company's articles of association may give a lien on a member's shares for any debt due by him to the company, and a lien on shares held jointly for debts due by the separate holders. In companies, however, which have adopted Table A of the Companies Act, the lien is restricted to partly-paid shares.

Table A does not provide for a lien on fully-paid shares, and a condition precedent to a quotation in the London Stock Exchange Official List is that fully-paid shares shall be free from lien.

In *Hopkinson* v *Mortimer, Harley & Co Ltd* [1917] 1 Ch 646, where the articles of association of the defendant company provided that it should have a lien on its shares for debts due by the registered holders of such shares to the company, and that the board might by resolution forfeit the shares, it was held that such power of forfeiture was *ultra vires* and invalid on the grounds that its exercise would amount to a reduction of capital, which would be illegal unless sanctioned by the court, and would operate as a clog on the equity of redemption. In view of this decision, articles of association should prescribe a sale of the shares as the method of enforcing such a lien. Although shares cannot be forfeited for failure to pay a debt due (otherwise than in respect of the shares themselves) by a shareholder to the company, a company's articles of association may give power to forfeit shares if a shareholder fail to pay any call or instalment due on the shares. A provision to this effect is included in Table A.

In *Mackereth* v *Wigan Coal and Iron Co Ltd* [1916] 2 Ch 293, it was held that where partly-paid shares of a company, whose articles of association contain a lien clause, are held by trustees upon a trust of which the company has had notice, the company cannot exercise its lien by retaining dividends or selling the shares in order to recover a debt due to it by one of the trustees.

When a bank's partly-paid shares have been transferred into the names of the personal representatives of a deceased shareholder in such circumstances as to constitute notice to the bank that the shares are held in a fiduciary capacity, it follows, from the above case, that the bank could not exercise its lien on the shares in order to recover money advanced to the representatives for purposes not authorized by the trust.

A vendor has a lien upon the land for any unpaid part of the purchase money as against a subsequent purchaser with notice; but

> a receipt for consideration money or other consideration in the body of a deed, or indorsed thereon, shall, in favour of a subsequent purchaser, not having notice that the money or other consideration thereby acknowledged to be received was not in fact paid or given, wholly or in part, be sufficient evidence of the payment or giving of the whole amount thereof. [Law of Property Act 1925, Section 68(1)]

Since 1957 the position of a banker who has a lien on a cheque is safeguarded by Section 2 of the Cheques Act of that year which provides

> A banker who gives value for, or has a lien on, a cheque payable to order which the holder delivers to him for collection without indorsing it has such (if any) rights as he would have had if, upon delivery, the holder had indorsed it in blank.

The banker's position as a holder for value or in due course depended before 1957 on the indorsement of his customer, which when in blank made the cheque a bearer cheque and thus brought the banker within the definition of a holder as a person in possession of a bearer cheque. With the ending of the requirement of indorsement the banker could no longer claim to be a holder, but by this Section he is placed in the same position as if he were a holder.

The working of this Section was well illustrated by a decision of the Mayor's and City of London Court, *Midland Bank Ltd* v *Charles Simpson Motors Ltd* [1960] 7 Legal Decisions affecting Bankers 251, where the payee of a cheque for £465, drawn by Charles Simpson Motors Ltd, called at the Midland Bank, Park Lane, and said he wished to open a current account with the cheque and to borrow £165 against it to meet a deposit on a flat which he wished to rent. The Midland Bank enquired by telephone of the drawee bank as to the probable fate of the cheque and was informed that if at that moment the cheque was in the hands of the drawee bank and was in order, it would be paid. The Midland Bank was able to verify, also over the telephone, the introduction of the payee, and then proceeded to advance £165 to its new customer as requested, subsequently collecting the cheque through the usual channels. The cheque was returned unpaid with the answer 'Orders not to pay'. Thereupon, the Midland Bank brought an action against the drawers, Charles Simpson Motors Ltd, claiming £165 with interest on the ground that it was a holder in due course of the cheque. The court held that the bank had established its claim to be a holder in due course, and was entitled to judgment for £165 with interest and costs.

In *Re Keevor* [1966] 3 All ER 1961, a bank was held to be protected by Section 45 of the Bankruptcy Act 1914 in respect of a cheque collected for their customer, the cheque having been paid in before the making of a receiving order, although the proceeds were not received until the day the order was made.

In the case of *National Westminster Bank Ltd* v *Halesowen Presswork and Assemblies Ltd* [1972] AC 785, the House of Lords found in favour of the bank where there had been an arrangement prior to liquidation that an existing loan account would be frozen for four months and the company permitted to operate a current account in credit. Liquidation ensued well before the four months expired and there was a substantial credit balance on the active account at the time. The decision was based on the ground that the agreement had not survived the liquidation. It is true that the construction was helped by the provision that it was not to apply in materially changed circumstances *if the bank* gave notice. No such notice was given and the decision sustains the principle that an agreement is terminated by the liquidation. Furthermore, the majority of the court considered that Section 31 of the Bankruptcy Act 1914, providing for balances resulting from mutual dealings to be set off and applying also to liquidations, could not be the subject of specific exclusion by the parties. This may be an embarrassment where parties wish to agree to a moratorium since the opening of a separate account at another bank may not be acceptable to the first bankers. A possible solution may be the opening of an account with a subsidiary of the first bankers which would preclude set-off but enable the first bankers to know what credit moneys exist. To avoid remotely possible controversy an authority to disclose could be taken from the customers.
SEE *Lien Letter; Set-off*

LIEN LETTER When an arrangement is made by which a certain amount in a customer's credit account is to be regarded as a security for an advance to him on another account, an agreement not to reduce the balance below the amount agreed upon, should be signed by the customer. The document should also authorize the banker to refuse payment of any cheques which would reduce the balance on the credit account below the stipulated amount and to combine the two accounts at any time without notice. A similar agreement should be signed when a customer's credit balance, or part of it, is to be held as a security for an advance to another customer.

LIFE ASSURANCE So far as is known, the earliest form of life assurance was that practised by the Greeks in connection with their burial societies. The Romans, too, had a system of payment on death for the benefit of dependants and they are also credited with the development of marine insurance (q.v.). It seems that life assurance had its origins not so much in the desire to provide for dependants but more particularly in other areas of human concern—the fear of not having a decent burial and the wish to protect personal fortunes. The desire to provide for burial found expression in the mutual societies of the mediaeval guilds and, to some extent, this contributed in modern times to the development of industrial life assurance (q.v.). The commercial insurance of life, i.e. the beginning of modern life assurance, appears to have originated in the practice of insuring the life of a ship's captain along with his ship and its cargo. The assurance would last for the period of the voyage. By the end of the seventeenth century, a number of societies had developed life assurance and annuity schemes. These early societies functioned without the benefit of mortality tables or actuarial calculations and this operated unfairly on younger members. Also, the benefits fluctuated widely depending on the sums available in the fund. In the mid-eighteenth century, James Dodson formulated the basis of modern life assurance by devising mortality tables, compound interest formulae and tables of annual premiums. As a result of Dodson's work, the Society for Equitable Assurances on Lives and Survivorships was founded in 1762, forerunner of The Equitable Life Assurance Society of the present day, which thus claims to be the oldest life assurance company in the country.

In the early days of life assurance, it was difficult at times to distinguish a genuine life assurance contract from a mere wager on the life of a particular person. Thus, the practice grew of taking out 'bets' on the lives of well-known personalities, such as soldiers and statesmen. However, under the Life Assurance Act of 1774, it became necessary that the proposer for life assurance should have an insurable interest (q.v.) in the life of the assured. That interest must be a pecuniary one. Thus, a man may have an insurable interest in his own life, a wife has an insurable interest in her husband and a husband in his wife. A creditor may insure his debtor for the amount of the debt and the company has an insurable interest in a director on whose good health the prosperity of the company depends. Where, however, a life policy is assigned, the assignee does not need to have an insurable interest in the life assured.

Categories of Life Assurance

The following are some of the principal types of life policy met with in practice.

Whole life assurance The sum assured is paid only on the death of the life assured.

Endowment assurance The sum assured is payable on the death of the life assured or at the end of an agreed term, whichever is the earlier date.

With-profits assurance In return for a higher premium, the amount payable under the policy, whether of the whole life or endowment kind, will be augmented by a share of the profits of the life office over and above the stated sum assured.

Term assurance The sum assured is payable only in the event of death within the period stated in the policy. Such a policy has no surrender value.

Convertible term assurance This is a term assurance policy, carrying the option to convert to an endowment policy or whole life policy or to extend the term of the policy without, in each case, the need for further medical examination.

Decreasing term assurance A form of term assurance, under which the life cover decreases over a stated period.

Mortgage protection assurance A form of decreasing term assurance, under which the sum assured reduces in line with the capital sum outstanding on a mortgage.

Family income assurance A means of providing an annual income for dependants in addition to or in lieu of a capital sum on the death of the life assured.

Joint whole-life assurance The sum assured is payable on the first death of two or more lives

Last survivor assurance The sum assured is payable on the death of the last survivor of two or more lives.

Accident insurance This is designed to provide a capital sum and usually, an income benefit on death or injury through accident.

Health insurance Sometimes known as permanent health insurance, this is a form of life assurance which guarantees payment of a regular income for a stated period or up to a stated age in the event of disability

SEE ALSO *Annuity; Deferred Annuity*

The premiums on a life assurance policy may be payable annually, quarterly, monthly or, in the case of industrial insurance (q.v.), even weekly. They may be payable throughout the entire life of the policy or for a given number of years. Alternatively, a premium may be a single payment on what would then usually be called a single premium policy. SEE *Qualifying Life Policies*

Life assurance policies may also be 'conventional' or 'linked' (see below).

The Purposes of Life Assurance

Life assurance is taken out for two basic purposes: protection or as a means of saving, or to achieve a combination of the two.

Historically, life assurance is a matter of protection—protection against the costs of death (as in the case of burial policies) or provision for the financial losses occasioned by death, i.e. for the protection of dependants. This is still a fundamental and very important aspect of life assurance and for the most part the life offices still emphasize the element of 'cover' in their products.

In the last 50 years or so, the public have recognized the value of life assurance as a means of saving, while still valuing the protection aspect. It was a natural development. If a sum of money is to be payable on the death of the assured, it is a small step for him to contract that it should be payable to him at the end of a fixed period of years if he is still alive.

In very broad terms, the protection aspect is emphasized in the early and middle years of marriage and family responsibilities. The savings aspect is often related in people's minds to the provision of a nest egg for the later years. A term assurance policy (see above) or a mortgage protection policy (see above) are essentially for protection whereas a personal pension plan, for example, is essentially a method of saving for the future.

Conventional and Linked Life Assurance

In the last quarter of a century, there has emerged a form of life assurance, known as linked life assurance, which differs in certain material respects from what is now usually called 'conventional' life assurance.

With conventional life assurance the amount

payable on a policy on death or maturity will be the predetermined sum assured plus, in the case of a with-profits policy, any bonuses declared by the directors of the company at their discretion. The assured person has no right or claim to any recognizable part of the assets of the life office and there will be no predetermined formula by which the benefits under the policy may vary by reference to the underlying assets.

In the case of linked life assurance, however, the benefits payable under the policy are calculated by reference to a formula which 'links' the benefits either to relevant assets or index or some other variable but identifiable factor. Linked life assurance was well defined by the Scott Committee (*Linked Life Assurance: Report of the Committee on Property Bonds and Equity Linked Life Assurance.* (Chairman: Sir Hilary Scott) Cmnd 5281, HMSO, 1973):

> All life assurance and annuity contracts, the benefits of which are calculated in whole or in part by reference to the value of, or the income from, specified assets or groups of assets or by reference to movements in a share price or other index, whether or not subject to deductions in respect of tax or expenses.

The London & Edinburgh Insurance Company is usually credited with the introduction of the first linked life assurance policies in 1957, in co-operation with the Unicorn Unit Trust Group. In fact, the London & Manchester Assurance and the M & G Group introduced variations on the linked life assurance theme more or less contemporaneously. Initially, these schemes met with little success, but in time the linked life movement gathered momentum. Nowadays, approximately a third of new life assurance annual premiums for new sums assured are related to policies which are linked in one way or another.

The principal differences between conventional and linked life assurance are

1. In the case of a linked life policy, the value at any one time will depend on the value of the assets (or index) to which the policy is linked; the value of a conventional policy will depend on the amount of profits allocated by the company to the policy, taking into account the experience of the life fund.
2. The value of a linked policy may be subject to very wide fluctuations, depending on the values of the underlying assets; the benefits of a conventional with-profits policy will always be a fixed predetermined sum (or in the case of surrender a sum calculated according to a predetermined formula) plus any bonuses which have been declared.
3. Holders of linked policies will receive details, usually on an annual basis, of the assets to which their policies are linked, including current valuations; holders of conventional policies do not receive such details because there are no specific assets to which their policies are related (although they do of course receive details of bonuses added to the policies).

Over the last 20 years an increasing number of conventional life offices have issued linked life assurance policies (in addition to their normal range of policies) for those customers who prefer to have a linked policy.

On the whole, conventional life assurance places greater emphasis on the 'protection' aspect of their policies (while still offering very attractive investment returns in some cases). The linked life policy, however, having its origin in the unit trust movement, tends to emphasize the investment aspect. In some cases the life assurance content of a linked life policy may be quite modest and this enables the medical requirements to be reduced to a minimum.

In linked life assurance there is an element of customer choice and quite a wide range of products have been devised to meet differing preferences. Some of these are set out below.

Types of Linked Life Policy

Equity link The policy is linked to ordinary stocks and shares, usually through a particular unit fund, which may have a particular investment emphasis, e.g. high income, international stocks, commodities.

Property link These are policies linked to units in a property fund, usually of a commercial and industrial nature, but may in some cases include agricultural land.

Fixed interest link Policies invested in a fund of fixed interest securities with in some cases a particular emphasis, e.g. British Government stocks, international bonds.

Building society link Policies linked to shares or deposits in building societies.

Money linked Policies linked to liquid or short-term assets, e.g. deposits with banks, finance houses and local authorities, but sometimes including short-term government securities such as Treasury Bills.

Managed fund A policy linked to a variety of assets, the insurance company giving greater or less emphasis to a particular category of asset as a matter of investment policy or in some cases to conform to a policy-holder's wishes.

There are two broad categories of linked life policies:

1. Single-premium policies, normally known as

bonds. These are lump sum investments in a life policy linked to one of the above-mentioned types of fund, e.g. property bond, gilt bond. The life cover is minimal probably little more than the amount of the premium and such policies are not taken out for protection purposes—they are strictly of an investment nature.
2. Multiple-premium policies, taken out for a period of years with premiums payable monthly or at other regular intervals. Such policies are more akin to conventional life policies in that they are sold on their merits as life assurance as well as for investment purposes.

These policies may be either whole life or endowment, as with conventional life policies.

The performance of life offices is nowadays the subject of comment by the press and other professional observers. Such performance and, therefore, the value of the life policies of particular companies will depend on

1. their mortality experience (SEE *Expectation of Life*),
2. their expense ratios which can be high in the early years of a life office's development because of the promotional cost of new business, and
3. investment performance.

Of these three factors, the mortality experience is perhaps the least critical in that the mortality tables, based as they are on actual experience, are a reasonably accurate guide to future mortality trends. The expenses of a life office however, are a major factor in determining overall performance and perhaps the most important factor of all is the investment competence. The 'bonuses' paid by life offices over the years show wide variations, reflecting the degree of success of individual companies in the management of the life funds.

Medical Considerations
As mentioned above, life assurance premiums are based on the current expectation of life tables. These are, of course, for normal lives or health risks and premiums will be loaded, i.e. increased, for sub-normal lives.

Life offices vary in the evidence they require on the proposer's health. The very least that a life office will require (even in the case of a single premium policy where the life cover is little more than the premium) is a declaration by the proposer that he is in good health. More usually it will be necessary for the proposer to complete a fairly detailed health questionnaire and authorize the life office to communicate, if they so wish, with his medical attendant. For larger sums assured, depending on the regulations of each life office, a medical examination will normally be necessary.

In the UK, the main cause of death among males under 35 is accident, but above that age the main cause is heart disease. In the case of women, the main cause of death in the middle years is cancer, but above the age of 65 or so heart disease is more common.

As smoking, high blood pressure and obesity are regarded as contributory factors in heart disease, these are all matters on which the insurance doctor will report. A record of alcoholism or drug dependency will also be a critical factor. In other instances, a disease in early life, e.g. tuberculosis, may be of diminishing significance with the passing of the years so that in only the early years will the premiums be loaded or the sum assured reduced.

Life assurance contracts are among those which are said to be *uberrimae fidei*, i.e. of the utmost good faith, so that the non-disclosure by the proposer of some material fact at the time of the contract may result in the contract being set aside by the insurer at some future date. If there is a health problem, the standard premium level will normally be increased and the effect is the same as if the proposer were taking out life assurance at a slightly higher age. In some instances, a life office may decline altogether to insure a life and a proposer will need to look elsewhere in the life assurance market.

A proposer who has been refused life assurance at the normal premium rates will be required to disclose this in any future proposal to any company for life assurance. If he fails to do so, it will probably come to light from the insurance company's own enquiries.

In the case of lives over 50, medical examination will normally be necessary except for quite modest sums assured. There is a small number of schemes on the market, however, under which the over-50s can obtain life assurance without medical examination.

Surrender Values
The surrender value of a policy is the amount payable to the policy-holder if he wishes to terminate his policy. In the first three years of a whole life policy and the first two years of an endowment policy, there is unlikely to be any significant surrender value. Thereafter, the surrender value will increase with the life of the policy and with successive declarations of bonuses.

The actuarial calculation of life assurance premiums is based on the assumption that policies will continue until maturity or prior death. The surrender of a policy therefore distorts to some extent the life fund calculations. Also, one may assume that surrenders are more likely to be requested by healthy people, so that a spate of surrenders would leave a balance of unhealthy lives on the books and upset the claims experience. For these reasons, there is an element of penalty in the surrender of a policy.

There are, however, two more tangible reasons why a life policy has little, if any, value if surrendered in the early years. The first is that the costs of setting up a policy, including the promotional and administrative costs, bear most heavily at the outset. If, for example, a 2 per cent commission is paid to an agent, the expense is borne out of the first two years' premiums. The second reason is that however young the policy at the date of surrender, the company has been at risk from its inception. The life assured has had the benefit of the full life cover up to the date of surrender. This must be paid for.

A policy taken out for investment reasons, possibly with the minimum of life cover, will tend to acquire a surrender value more quickly than a policy taken out for protection reasons. This is because of the low life assurance content. Even so, an investment policy will have to bear the 'front load' of expenses, as mentioned above, and in the first year or two only a modest proportion of the premiums will be invested in the life fund.

The same considerations apply to unit linked policies, but the surrender value of a linked policy will depend at any one time primarily on the value of the underlying assets. Thus, at a time of favourable stock market or property market performance, even a young policy may acquire an attractive surrender value.

Loans Against Life Policies

A life policy is usually an acceptable form of security for a loan up to the amount of the surrender value. From the lender's point of view a life policy has the advantage that a surrender value can only increase so long as the premiums are paid and will not reduce even if, for any reason, the policy-holder ceases to pay the premiums.

Life policies will normally be accepted by banks as security for overdrafts or for separate loan accounts.

For short-term purposes, a bank loan is usually the ideal arrangement. If, however, a loan is required for a longer period, e.g. more than two years, it will normally be to the policy-holder's advantage to borrow from the life office who issued the policy. A loan taken on a policy in this way may remain outstanding until the policy-holder dies or the policy matures. The rate of interest charged by the life offices will usually be less than for bank loans and will usually remain fixed over the years unless there is an agreement for a variable rate of interest. At a time of high interest rates, a loan from an insurance company can therefore be a disadvantage if the rate is to remain at that level throughout the life of the loan. SEE *Life Policies as Security*

LIFE ASSURANCE RELIEF SEE *Qualifying Life Policies*

LIFE FUND That part of an insurance company's assets or liabilities which relates to its life assurance and annuity business. It receives the company's premium income and it holds the investments which relate to its commitments under the life policies which have been issued. It is the subject of annual actuarial valuation and must be maintained in a solvent state. Any surplus on valuation, i.e. over and above the life fund's commitments, may be transferred to the general account of the insurance company, in which case it becomes part of the life office's own funds held to the benefit of the shareholders.

LIFE OFFICES ASSOCIATION The Life Offices Association, together with the Associated Scottish Life Offices, the Industrial Life Offices Association and Linked Life Assurance Group transact over 95 per cent of all life assurance business written in the UK. These associations publish annual statistics showing the level of life assurance business and generally co-operate in the best interests of their members and their policy-holders.

The following are the principal figures published by the combined associations for long-term business in the UK for 1983:

Total premium income	£11,050 million
Investment income	£6,751 million
Total life assurance funds	£80,700 million
New yearly premiums on individual life and annuity business	£1,540 million
New single premiums	£2,400 million
New yearly premiums and single premiums for linked life assurance (included in the above)	£1,700 million

At the end of 1983, 2,970,000 policies were in force in respect of personal pension plans, with total yearly premiums of £666 million.

At the end of the year there were 68.8 million industrial life insurances in force for sums assured (and bonuses) of £20,300 million with yearly premiums of £1,150 million.

LIFE POLICIES AS SECURITY Before accepting a life policy as security, a bank or other lender will wish to peruse it to see if any onerous restrictions are imposed on the assured, relating to such matters as foreign residence, air travel, etc. Sometimes there is a suicide clause, providing that the policy shall be void if the assured dies by his own hand within six months of the contract of assurance. It is usual to provide in such cases, however, that the rights of assignees for value shall not be affected. If a life is accepted without medical examination, sometimes only a partial amount of the sum assured is payable if death occurs within a specified period.

It is necessary to see that the policy-holder has power to deal with his interest. Industrial policies are usually unassignable without the consent of the company.

The age of the assured should be admitted on the policy, for otherwise if the age has been understated on the proposal form, the company would be entitled to deduct from the policy moneys due to the difference, with interest, between the premiums paid and the premiums which ought to have been paid. An insurance company before indorsing a policy 'age admitted' will require production of the birth certificate or certificate of baptism giving the date of birth. Where these are not available, a certified extract from a family bible or a statutory declaration will be required.

The policy should be examined to see that all interested parties join in the security. Where a policy is not payable to the assured or his personal representatives but to a third party who is alive on the maturity of the policy or who survives the assured, such party, if of full age, must join in the charge. Under the Married Women's Property Act 1882, Section 11, a policy on the life of a husband for the benefit of his wife and/or issue creates a trust in favour of the beneficiaries. Where no trustees are appointed, the husband is trustee. Where a husband insured his life for the benefit of his wife under the above Act and his wife predeceased him, it was held on appeal that the wife had a vested interest in the policy and that therefore on her predecease the policy moneys passed under her will (*Cousins* v *Sun Life Assurance Society* [1932] WN 198). Therefore, where a wife is named as a beneficiary in a policy, she should be joined in the assignment of the policy. Where a policy merely mentions that the contract is in favour of the wife of the life assured without mention of her name or using any expression that would limit 'my wife' to 'my present wife', a second wife would be entitled to the benefit of the policy (*Re Browne's Policy* [1903] 1 Ch 188). Such a policy cannot become a banking security owing the the impossibility of ensuring that possible future beneficiaries join in the charge. Where a wife takes out a policy on her husband's life, provided she pays the premiums, no trust is involved and she can validly charge the policy in her own right.

Where the beneficiaries include children, the latter, if of full age, must join in the security. If there are minors, a good security cannot be obtained.

Where a policy is taken out by a parent as agent for an infant, any charge given by the former would be effective only if the child died before his majority; the policy becomes his absolute property on his attaining full age. Insurance companies lend on policies of this type only for the purpose of paying the premiums. But where a policy is taken out by a parent for the benefit of his child on attaining a certain age, no absolute interest accrues to the child and on the death of the parent before maturity of the policy, the benefit of the policy passes to the deceased's estate. Where a father in a proposal form declared he was making the proposal for his child, it was held that he was not acting as an agent for the latter but entering into the contract for the benefit of the child (*Tibbetts* v *Englebach* [1924] 2 Ch 348). Most modern children's 'deferred' policies are in fact assignable by the parent.

A life policy is a chose in action, and a mortgage thereof is accomplished by an assignment of the policy-holder's rights with a proviso for redemption. The form of assignment will be by deed and will contain the usual provisions as to continuing security for all moneys etc. It will cover any bonuses and additions to the policy and contain an undertaking of the assignor to pay the premiums or for the bank to charge his account therewith in default. Authority will be given for the bank to give a discharge on behalf of the assured's personal representatives to avoid joining them in if the policy becomes a claim, and power will be taken to sell or surrender the policy.

By the Policies of Assurance Act 1867, Section 3, no assignment shall confer on the assignee any right to sue for the amount of the policy until written notice of the assignment is given to the company. The date of receipt of such notice regulates priority of conflicting interests in the policy. But an assignee having notice of a previous assignment, notice of which has not been given to the company, cannot get priority over such previous assignment by registering his notice first (*Newman* v *Newman* [1885] 28 ChD 674).

Occasionally, a banker is asked to lend against the assignment of a policy that has been lost. Apart from the necessity of providing an indemnity to the company before it will pay over the policy moneys, there is the risk that the policy is in the hands of a prior assignee, and non-production of the policy might be held to be constructive notice of his interest.

A statutory acknowledgment of notice of assignment must be given on request by the company. When giving notice, it is usual to ask the company if any prior notice of dealings with the policy has been received. If such is the case all prior assignments and re-assignments should be obtained and kept with the security, as they form part of the chain of title, and the company will not discharge the policy moneys without their production.

Where the security is withdrawn, a re-assignment must be executed under seal and handed to the assignor with the policy, the assignment, and any other relative documents. Notice of re-assignment should be sent to the company.

Where a policy becomes a claim by reason of death or maturity, a form of receipt by the assignee supplied by the insurance company must be completed. Most companies require such receipt to be under the seal of the bank.

Where surrender of the policy is contemplated, the company should be asked for how long the policy can be held without loss of surrender value or without incurring liability for premiums. When a policy is being surrendered on account of the assignor's bankruptcy, his trustee should first be given an opportunity of redeeming it. Occasionally it profits an assignee to pay the premium, inasmuch as sometimes the surrender value increases by more than the premium paid. Occasionally a legal mortgage by way of assignment is not taken, but the policy is deposited with a bank with or without a written memorandum of deposit. A company is under no duty to recognize such as equitable interest, but in practice it usually accepts notice of an equitable charge. An equitable charge by deposit is good against a trustee in bankruptcy, even without a written memorandum, provided nothing has been done to nullify the charge, such as entering the policy in the bank's safe custody records. When enforcing security in this form, it is necessary to get the cooperation of the policy-holder or his personal representatives.

LIFE TENANT A life tenant is strictly the person who has a right or interest in landed property for life or during the life of some other person (called an estate *pur autre vie*). For many years, however, the terms, life tenant and tenant for life, have been used in relation to settlements of personalty. Thus, any person who receives the income of a settled fund for his or her life or during the life of another person is said to be a tenant for life. If on the death of the life tenant the settled property returns to the grantor of the life interest, the grantor is said to hold the reversion to the property, but if it does not revert to him but passes to another person, that person is said to hold the 'remainder' and is called the remainderman. Here again, however, the term reversionary interest is now used synonymously with interests in remainder.

A life tenant has power to raise money on mortgage of the settled land for the purposes set out in Section 71 of the Settled Land Act 1925. These include payment off of encumbrances and payment for any improvement authorized by the Act. SEE *Settled Land*

LIFEBOAT 'The Lifeboat' was the term used colloquially to describe the support operation mounted by the Bank of England and the London and Scottish Clearing Banks to meet the secondary banking crisis in 1973–74, and the subsequent effects of that crisis. This was essentially a crisis of confidence, leading to the withdrawal of deposits of a number of secondary or fringe banks and this in turn led to major liquidity problems among the secondary banks and some of their principal customers, notably in the property sector. A total of 26 financial institutions received support from 'The Lifeboat' and most of these institutions were able to resume trading from their own resources in due time, although eight of them went into liquidation. The support took the form of the placing of deposits with the troubled institutions by the clearing banks to match those deposits which were being withdrawn for want of confidence. The exercise was entirely successful in that it prevented serious damage to the reputation of the banking system in the UK, which could have led to serious balance of payments problems and a major impact on the economy. It may, in fact, be argued that the smooth working and success of 'The Lifeboat' operation served to enhance the reputation of London as a banking centre. Nevertheless, the crisis was very real. The amounts involved approached at one time £1,200 million and support of that order imposed a serious strain on the banking system as a whole.

LIFETIME GIFTS A term applied to transfers of property during life. SEE *Capital Transfer Tax*

LIMITATION ACT 1939 This Act came into force on 1st July, 1940, and consolidated with sundry amendments the law governing the time limits for instituting actions on contracts. Such law had been generically known as the Statutes of Limitation, which included the Limitation of Actions Act 1623, the Civil Procedure Act 1835, the Mercantile Law Amendment Act 1856, and the Real Property Limitation Act 1874. The idea that rights created and recognized by law can be nullified or cancelled by the passage of time is founded on reasons of expediency and convenience, for it is unreasonable that a party should be subject to the risk of a law action based on an old claim of which he may be entirely ignorant or to which he can give no answer owing to the destruction of the relative evidence. Accordingly, the Limitation of Actions Act 1623, provided that all actions on contracts not under seal and all actions for arrears of rent must be brought within six years of the cause of action accruing. Contracts under seal were dealt with in the Civil Procedure Act 1835, which provided that actions on such contracts must be brought within 20 years after the cause of action first accrued. A later statute, known as the Real Property Limitation Act 1874, limited the period to 12 years in respect of land and any interests therein and, in addition, not only thereafter barred the remedy by action, but also the remedy against the land itself.

The Limitation Act of 1939 is a comparatively short measure of 34 sections, and consolidates and amends some half-a-dozen statutes of various dates, including those mentioned above, with all the beneficent results that attend a consolidating Act.

The time limit for simple contract actions was left at six years, which means, for example, that six years from the date on which a creditor is entitled to sue for the recovery of a debt, his legal remedy in the Courts will be barred, unless there has been in the period an acknowledgment in writing by the debtor of his liability or he has made payment of interest or principal thereon. It is only the *remedy by action* that is lost—the debt still remains, although not enforceable at law. Any security, other than land which the creditor holds, will be enforceable in discharge of the debt.

The Act reduced the limitation period of 20 years in respect of contracts under seal to 12 years. The other amendment of outstanding interest was that which put a limitation period of 12 years on mortgages of personalty, such as charges on stocks and shares and assignments of life policies. Prior to the 1939 Act, there was a limitation of 12 years in respect of recovery of a debt covered by a charge on leasehold or freehold property, but there was no such limitation in respect of mortgages of personal property. But an important difference between charges on realty and on personalty still obtains, namely, that, after the expiration of the prescribed period of 12 years, the lender's right against mortgaged freehold or leasehold property is barred, in addition to his right to recover on the personal covenant to repay. In the case of a charge on personalty, however, although the right to sue on the underlying debt is lost at the expiration of 12 years, the right over against the security is not disturbed.

When part payment of a debt is made, or interest is paid thereon, or an acknowledgment of the debt is given in writing by the debtor, the debt is thereby kept alive and the six years or 12 years then begin to run from the date of the last payment or acknowledgment. For example, if Brown signed in 1983 a promissory note payable on demand in favour of Jones, and neither pays interest nor repays any part of the principal nor gives any further written acknowledgment of the debt for a period of six years, at the end of that time Brown may plead the statute and be entirely released from his liability on the note to Jones. But if Brown, in say, the year 1986 repays part of the money owing, the six years will begin again to run from the year 1986, and so on, the six years commencing afresh at each payment or acknowledgment. But a payment by a debtor does not keep the debt alive as against a surety.

(But see Limitation Amendment Act 1980 below.)

By the Statute of Frauds Amendment Act 1828 (Lord Tenterden's Act), Section 1, in actions of simple contract debts, no acknowledgment or promise by words only shall be sufficient evidence to take the case out of the statute, unless such acknowledgment or promise be made in writing and signed by the party chargeable, or (by 19 & 20 Vict c 97, s 13) by his agent duly authorized.

In *Jones* v *Bellegrove Properties Ltd* (1949), it was held that the production of a company's balance sheet, at its annual general meeting, showing an item 'Sundry creditors' was sufficient acknowledgment in writing of a debt due by the company, and included in such items, as to prevent such debt being statute-barred.

In the case of a minor or a mentally ill person, no action can be brought personally either by or against either of them until the minor attains his majority or the mentally ill person recovers. A minor or person of unsound mind may recover any land or rent within six years from the ceasing of the disability. The utmost allowance for disability is 30 years from the right accruing. If a defendant is beyond the seas or out of the jurisdiction, when the cause of action arises, an action may be brought within six years from his return; but where the defendant goes out of the jurisdiction after the cause of action arises, the running of the statute is not affected. If a plaintiff is beyond the seas when a cause of action arises, no additional time is allowed—the statute runs against him.

Where there are several debtors (except in the case of a mortgage of land), the debt must be acknowledged by each one in order to keep it alive against each, and anyone who has not acknowledged it may plead the statute. Where there are two or more joint contractors, no such joint contractor shall be chargeable in respect of the written acknowledgment only of the other. Where there are two or more co-contractors or co-debtors, none of them shall lose the benefit of the limitation, by reason only of payment of any principal or interest by any of the others.

A debt of a deceased person which is statute-barred may legally be paid by his executor, as in an ordinary contract the statute does not bar the right but only the remedy.

Where a loan is granted against security and the debt has become statute-barred, the banker is unable to sue the customer for the debt, but the fact of the banker's claim against the debtor personally having been barred does not affect his claim upon the security other than land, nor does it affect his claim upon any securities or money belonging to the debtor which may come into his possession as a banker after his right to sue the debtor is statute-barred.

In *Lloyds Bank* v *Margolis and Others* [1954] 1 All ER 734, the bank held as security for an advance a mortgage over land dated 16th September, 1936, under which it gave notice demanding repayment on 19th December, 1938. The bank issued a summons on 29th November, 1950, claiming to enforce their mortgage by foreclosure or sale. The defendants claimed that the legal charge was no longer enforceable because the remedy was statute-barred, more than 12 years having elapsed since the granting of the advance. However, Upjohn, J., held that time did not begin to run until demand was made: the bank was thus within the 12 year period.

A defendant must, if he intends to plead the statute, set up a special plea before the hearing of the action or he will not be allowed to advance it against the plaintiff's claim.

Certain amendments to the Limitation Act 1939 were made by the Limitation Amendment Act 1980. In particular, Section 1 of the 1980 Act provides that where no arrangements have been made as to when repayment of a loan shall be made the limitation period shall begin to run on the day that a written demand for repayment is made by or on behalf of the creditor. Section 6 of the 1980 Act renders it impossible to re-open an expired limitation period by acknowledgment of a debt or part payment thereof (although as indicated above an acknowledgment or part-payment during a limitation period will have the effect of extending the time).

Effect of the Limitation Act

The effect of the Limitation Act may be considered briefly in relation to the following subjects:

Administrator SEE *Trustee* below.

Bank notes The Limitation Act 1939 does not apply to bank notes.

Bill of exchange An action on a bill of exchange must be commenced within six years from the time when the cause of action arose; that is, from the date when the bill was due to be paid as regards the acceptor, and from the date when notice of dishonour is received as against the drawer or an indorser.

Bond A bond continues for 12 years from the date on which the right to bring an action first accrues. SEE *Debt* below

Breach of trust The Limitation Act cannot be pleaded to a breach of trust. SEE *Trustee* below

Calls A call is a specialty debt, and may be sued for in England at any time within twelve years. See Section 20(2), Companies Act 1948, under *Articles of Association*.

Composition with creditors If a debtor fails to pay a composition as provided in the deed of arrangement, the statute begins to run from the date of the failure to keep his promise.

Current accounts In *Swiss Bank Corporation* v *Joachimson* [1921] 37 TLR 534, the Court of Appeal held that express demand by a customer for repayment of a current account balance is a condition precedent to the right to sue the banker for the amount. Atkin, LJ, said

> The result of this decision will be that for the future bankers may have to face legal claims for balances of accounts which have remained dormant for more than six years. But seeing that bankers have not been in the habit as a matter of business of setting up the Statute of Limitations against their customers or their legal representatives, I do not suppose that such a change in what was supposed to be the law will have much practical effect. SEE *Dormant Balances*

Where a debit balance has remained standing without payment, either of principal or interest, or without any written acknowledgment, the debtor may plead the statute at the end of six years and the banker will be unable to recover the money, unless demand for payment has to be made (as is provided in most forms of charge) when the time runs from the date of demand. A mere debit to the account by the banker for interest does not keep the debt alive.

If the account is in several names the debt is kept alive only against those who have acknowledged it; a payment by one does not prevent the others from pleading the statute.

If a customer has several accounts they must all be considered as really one account; that is, if a loan account has been absolutely dormant for six years the customer cannot plead that the loan is statute-barred if he has also other accounts which have been operated upon.

In an ordinary loan account the statute runs from the date when the money was paid and not necessarily from the date of the cheque.

If a loan is statute-barred it does not follow that the interest on the loan is also barred. SEE *Interest* below

Debt A person cannot be sued for a debt after six years from the date when it was incurred. If part payment has been made or formal acknowledgment given, the six years begin to run from the date of the payment or acknowledgment. The acknowledgment must be in writing, and be signed by the party chargeable (or his duly authorized agent). (Lord Tenterden's Act 9 Geo IV c 14 s 1 and 19 & 20 Vict c 97 s 13.)

In the case of a debt which is more than six years old, in respect of which no payment or acknowledgment has been made, if the debtor then makes a payment on account of the debt, the payment does not bring the debt to life again, unless a promise, express or implied, is made to pay the debt. In order to take a statute-barred debt out of the statute, there may be an acknowledgment of the debt from which a promise to pay it must be implied; or an unconditional promise to pay it; or a conditional promise to pay the debt in writing and evidence that that condition has been performed. In *Philips* v *Philips* 13 LJ Ch 445, Wigram, VC, said

> The new promise and not the old debt is the measure of the creditor's right. If the debtor simply acknowledges an old debt, the law implies from that simple acknowledgment a promise to pay it, for which promise the old debt is a sufficient consideration. But if the debtor promises to pay the old debt when he is able, or by instalments, or in two years, or out of a particular fund, the creditor can claim nothing more than the promise gives him.

Where a debt is statute-barred and the debtor makes any promise or acknowledgment, he has always the right to couple any terms with his promise or acknowledgment, and unless these are satisfied, the creditor cannot sue with success. The acknowledgment or promise to pay a statute-barred debt must be in writing, but see Limitation Amendment Act 1980 above.

In the case of a specialty debt—that is, where the debt is acknowledged in a document under seal—the period is 12 years from the date on which the right to bring an action first accrues.

Deposit accounts The six years being to run when demand for payment has been made.

If the deposit is repayable after expiration of a specified notice, then the years commence from the date on which the deposit is due to be paid. If repayable at the end of a fixed period, the years commence from that date.

Dividend A dividend being a payment under a company's articles of association is a specialty debt, and is not barred until after 12 years.

Drawer of cheque The drawer of a cheque is liable to pay it any time within six years from its date or the date of its issue, whichever is the later, except where through delay in presentation he suffers damage by the banker's failure.

Where a loan has been made on an account, the six years run from the date the money was paid, not necessarily from the date of the cheque, though in most cases the dates will actually be the same.

Executor SEE *Trustee* below

Guarantee under hand The banker's right against a guarantor is barred in six years from the date when the right to bring an action against the guarantor first accrued. Where the guarantee does not contain an express covenant to pay 'on demand' (SEE *Parr's Banking Co* v *Yates* under *Guarantee*) if has been held that the right of action on each item of the account arose as soon as that item became due and was not paid. Acknowledgments by a debtor do not keep the debt alive as against a guarantor.

If a guarantee does not contain a covenant to pay on demand, it should be renewed before the expiration of six years from its date, as this avoids any danger of the operation of the statute. Instead of a fresh guarantee being taken, a written acknowledgment upon the old guarantee by the surety, or sureties, that the guarantee is still in force is sometimes taken.

If the guarantee is drawn as payable on demand or several days after demand, the six years would not begin to run until demand had been made. In *Bradford Old Bank* v *Sutcliffe* [1918] 2 KB 833, where in a guarantee there was an undertaking to pay 'on demand' it was held that there was no cause of action till after demand. SEE *Guarantee*

When repayment is demanded from the guarantor, the statute beings to run in his favour.

Guarantee under seal The period is 12 years, otherwise the same remarks apply as in a guarantee under hand.

But if it is in respect of a debt secured by a mortgage of land the limitation is 12 years both as to the remedy on the covenant and the remedy against the land, whether the covenant of the surety is in the mortgage deed itself or in a collateral bond (*Sutton* v *Sutton* [1882] 22 ChD 511).

Income tax The Limitation Act is not binding on the Crown (*Lamber* v *Taylor* [1825] B & C 138; *Rustomjee* v *The Queen* [1876] 1 QBD 487).

Interest It has been held (*Parr's Banking Co* v *Yates* [1898] 2 QB 460) that where certain advances were barred by the statute, the interest did not fall to the ground at the same time. In this case, principal and interest were guaranteed, and, though the banker's right against the surety was barred, it was held that the payment of interest, commission and other banking charges which had accrued against the guaranteed party within six years before the commencement of the action were as much guaranteed as the payment of the advances, and that the statute did not affect those items.

Judgment A judgment is statute-barred after 12 years.

Minor The statute does not begin to run until he has reached the age of 18. (See above.)

Promissory note If on demand, the six years begin to run in favour of the maker from the date of the note or the date of its issue, whichever is the later, or from the last instalment paid or acknowledgment given. If there are several makers of the note there must be an acknowledgment from each one, otherwise the debt will be kept alive only against the maker who has acknowledged the debt or made the payment, and the others will be released. It is advisable always to have a note renewed before the six years expire, so as to avoid any question of release being raised. Where a promissory note on demand is given as collateral security, with a memorandum of deposit, it is also advisable to have it renewed before the six years expire, though in such a case it is possible that the statute might be held to run from the date of demand for payment and not from the date of the note.

If the note is payable at a specified period after demand, or after date, the six years do not commence to run till the day on which the note is due to be paid.

In *Fettes* v *Robertson* [1920] KB 37 TLR 80, an action in which the defendant pleaded the statute with respect to a promissory note indorsed by him and dishonoured, Bailhache, J, said

> If there was an unqualified admission of a debt without anything further, the law implied a promise to pay, but if the admission was accompanied by words of hope or expectancy that the defendant would be able to pay, those words might render the admission not unqualified.

The Court of Appeal [1921] 37 TLR 581 held that in the defendant's letters there was no unqualified promise to pay.

Property Section 18 of the Limitation Act 1939 provides

> (1) No action shall be brought to recover any principal sum of money secured by a mortgage or other charge on property, whether real or personal, or to recover proceeds of sale of land, after the expiration of twelve years from the date when the right to receive the money accrued.
>
> (2) No foreclosure action in respect of mortgaged personal property shall be brought after the expiration of twelve years from the date on which the right to foreclose accrued:
>
> Provided that if, after that date, the mortgagee was in possession of the mortgaged property, the right to foreclose on the property which was in his possession shall not, for the purposes of this subsection, be deemed to have accrued until the date on which his possession discontinued.

An acknowledgment from one mortgagor of land is sufficient to keep the debt alive.

Rent No arrears of rent can be recovered by distress, action, or suit, but within six years after the same shall have become due, or after an acknowledgment in writing. Actions of debt for rent on an indenture of demise and all actions of covenant shall be brought within 12 years after the cause of action.

Specialty debt SEE *Debt* above

Stocks and shares There is no period of limitation with regard to a mortgage of stocks and shares. If the debt is statute-barred, that does not affect the banker's claim upon the security.

In *London and Midland Bank Ltd* v *Mitchell* [1899] 2 Ch 161, where shares had been given as security, with a blank transfer, it was held that, although the personal action on the debt was barred, the bank's right of property in the shares was not destroyed. Mr Justice Stirling said

> Though the debt is barred in the sense that a personal action can no longer be brought to recover it, the debt is not gone; nor is the right of property destroyed, for there is no provision in any statute of limitations with reference to personal property similar to that contained in 3 & 4 William IV, c 27, Section 34, whereby the title to land is extinguished after a lapse of a certain period.

Trustee By the Trustee Act 1888, Section 8, trustees are placed on the same footing as other persons, provided that, in any proceeding against a trustee in which the statute is pleaded, the claim is not founded upon any fraud or fraudulent breach of trust to which the trustee was a party or was privy, or to recover trust property, or the proceeds thereof, which is still retained by the trustee or which has been previously received by him and converted to his own use (see Limitation Act, Section 19). For the purposes of the Trustee Act, the expression 'trustee' shall be deemed to include an executor or administrator. (Section 1(3).) The Limitation Amendment Act 1980 gives relief to a trustee who may have retained trust property for this own use, in those cases where the trustee is also a beneficiary. Section 10 of that Act also amends Section 21, Administration of Estates Act 1925, and gives a debtor the protection of the Limitation Act, notwithstanding that he may become his creditor's administrator.

LIMITED CHEQUE A cheque limited to a certain amount as, for example, where the written amount must not exceed the amount printed in the margin. A limited cheque drawn by a bank upon a foreign correspondent may have in the left-hand margin columns for £5, £10, £20, £30, £40, £50, and underneath each such amount the equivalents in foreign currencies. If a cheque for, say, £8 or its equivalent in foreign money is drawn, the columns £20 and upwards are cut off so that the left-hand remaining column will then be for £10 and its equivalents, thus indicating that the cheque is limited to an amount not exceeding £10 or its equivalents.

LIMITED COMPANY SEE *Close Company; Company Limited by Guarantee; Company Limited by Shares; Company Unlimited; Limited Partnership; Private Company; Public Company*

LIMITED PARTNERSHIP Limited partnerships were established by the Limited Partnerships Act 1907, which came into operation on 1st January, 1908. The idea of the limited partnership has not appealed to the business world and since the passing of the Act comparatively few such partnerships have been registered.

The Act does not provide for the formation of partnerships with limited liability, but merely for the creation of one or more partners with limited liability, the other partner, or partners, being responsible to an unlimited extent for the debts of the firm.

As limited partnerships are a comparative rarity, the full provisions of the Act are not included here. It may be noted, however, that under Section 6 of the Act, a limited partner shall not take part in the management of the partnership business, and shall not have the power to bind the firm. The Section does not definitely say that he must not draw cheques upon the banking account of the firm, but it is probably safer to infer that he has no power to operate upon the account. At any rate bankers are not likely to regard a limited partner as having such authority.

The same Section says that a limited partner may at any time inspect the books of the firm, but before allowing a limited partner to receive the firm's statement, or to inspect the firm's account, the authority of the other partners should be obtained.

There is no provision in the Act that a distinctive name should be used to indicate when a firm is a limited partnership.

It may be difficult, in some cases, for a banker to know whether a person is a limited or general partner. If he cannot obtain reliable information from the partners themselves, he may inspect the register or obtain extracts therefrom (see Section 16). The provisions of the Bankruptcy Act 1914 shall 'apply to limited partnerships in like manner as if limited partnerships were ordinary partnerships, and, on all the general partners of a limited partnership being adjudged bankrupt, the assets of the limited partnership shall vest in the trustee', (Section 127). SEE *Company; Partnerships*

The death, mental incapacity, or bankruptcy of a limited partner does not dissolve the firm.

LINK ORGANISATION, THE This is an organization launched in January 1985 to provide a shared network of automated teller machines (ATM) (q.v.) throughout Britain. The members of LINK are National Girobank, the Abbey National Building Society, the Co-operative Bank plc, Nationwide Building Society, and a consortium of 17 other institutions operating under the name Funds Transfer Sharing Limited. The aim of the organization is to provide the customers of the member organizations with electronic banking services.

LIQUID ASSETS These, sometimes called floating assets, consist of cash and other assets continually undergoing conversion into cash, such as stock, sundry debtors, bills receivable. They are to be distinguished from fixed assets which are acquired for use in the business, such as premises, plant, and machinery. It is the function of an asset, not its nature, which determines into which category it goes. For example, machinery is a fixed asset in a factory—it is what a business trades *with*; in a business concerned with the manufacture of machinery, it will be a liquid asset—it is what the business trades *in*. SEE ALSO *Liquidity Ratio*

LIQUIDATED DAMAGES A sum payable as damages for breach of contract the amount of which is not left to assessment by a jury, but is previously agreed by the parties to the contract. In an action for breach of contract, neither more nor less than the agreed sum can be awarded, as opposed to a penalty, where a plaintiff can get such damages as he can prove which may be more or less than the penalty. The measure of damages on a dishonoured bill is deemed to be liquidated damages. It is also used in relation to damages given where the action is in tort.

LIQUIDATION A winding up, or closing of business. A company which is being wound up, is said to be 'in liquidation'. SEE *Liquidator; Winding up*

LIQUIDATOR A person appointed by the court (in a compulsory liquidation) or by the creditors of a company (in a creditors' voluntary winding up) or by members of a company (in a members' voluntary winding up) to get in what may be owing to the company from its debtors, to realize other assets, to collect what may be due from its members, and after payment of the company's debts to distribute any balance to the members in proportion to their share holding.

The liquidator in a compulsory winding up must use the Insolvency Services Account at the Bank of England, unless the Department of Trade and Industry authorizes him to use a local bank (Section 542, Companies Act 1985). When asked to open an account for a liquidator in a compulsory winding up, a banker should therefore ask for exhibition of the Order of the Court appointing him, and also for the Department of Trade and Industry's sanction for opening the account.

A liquidator appointed under a voluntary winding up may open a bank account where he pleases, subject to the consent of the committee of inspection, if any, and need only produce a certified copy of the resolution of the creditors or members of the company appointing him.

A liquidator's account should be opened in the name of the company in compulsory (or voluntary) liquidation.

In a compulsory winding up, cheques drawn on the banking account must be payable to order, and bear on their face the name of the company. They must be signed by the liquidator and countersigned by at least one member of the committee of inspection. In the absence of a committee of inspection, the Official Receiver may, at the direction of the Department of Trade and Industry, exercise the functions of a committee with regard to the bank account.

Where two or more liquidators are appointed, all must sign cheques unless the Order of the Court, in a compulsory winding up, provides for less than all to act or, in a voluntary winding up, the resolution to wind up provides for less than all to sign, or makes no provision, in which case not less than two may sign. Where a voluntary winding up is placed under supervision of the court, the signing powers of the liquidators are not affected.

There are no statutory powers for a liquidator to delegate signing powers to an outside party. In practice, bankers are frequently asked to accept such delegation for the convenience of the liquidator (e.g. in a heavy liquidation involving the drawing of large numbers of cheques), and in cases where the standing of the liquidator is high, such delegation will be permitted with or without an indemnity from the liquidator according to the circumstances.

A liquidator in a compulsory winding up has power to raise money on the assets of the company for liquidation purposes, without the leave of the court.

In cases where the borrowing is required to bring or defend an action on behalf of the company, or to carry on the business, the sanction of the court or the committee of inspection is necessary.

In a voluntary winding up of either type, a liquidator does not require sanction to borrow, but if there is a committee of inspection, it may be advisable to get its permission. In practice, where the liquidation proceedings are likely to be involved, or where considerable sums are required, the consent of the court will in many cases be sought if it is a creditors' voluntary winding up. In similar circumstances in a members' voluntary winding up, the approval of the company in general meeting is often sought.

A charge over any assets of the company given by a liquidator will have priority over all creditors of the company, save those already secured at the time the winding up is commenced.

A liquidator is not personally liable for a borrowing on behalf of a company, unless he specially covenants to that end. SEE ALSO *Winding Up; Cork Report; Insolvency*

LIQUIDITY That proportion of a person's or institution's assets which is held in cash or near-cash, i.e. assets which are immediately realizable at their current market value.

LIQUIDITY RATIO Prior to September, 1971, control of credit operated through official controls on the liquidity of the banks and a series of quantitative and qualitative restraints on the lending activities of the banks and finance houses. In particular, banks maintained a ratio of 8 per cent between cash held in tills and at the Bank of England and their gross deposits. The total of cash and other liquid assets, including money at call and short notice, Treasury Bills, other commercial bills, and refinanceable credits, was maintained at a minimum level of 28 per cent of each bank's gross deposits.

The Liquidity Ratio was replaced by a Reserve Asset Ratio in 1971, when quantitative ceilings were abolished and the Reserve Asset Ratio applied uniformly to all banks at a minimum of $12\frac{1}{2}$ per cent of total eligible liabilities, i.e. sterling deposits other than those with a maturity of over two years. SEE *Competition* and *Credit Control*

In more recent times, the system of Reserve Asset Ratios has been abandoned and in its place a system of prudential controls has been introduced by the Bank of England for the guidance of individual banks whose figures are monitored on a regular basis.

Different rules apply to building societies. Under the Building Societies Act 1962 (paragraph 3 of Schedule 2), it is provided that

At the end of the last financial year ending before the date of the application, the value of the liquid funds of the building society must have been seven and a half per cent or more of the value of the assets of the society. For the purposes of this paragraph—

(*a*) 'Liquid funds' means the funds of the building society (however represented by investments or on loan to a bank or held in cash) which were not immediately required for its purposes, less any amount due from the society (whether immediately payable or not) otherwise and in respect of shares in, or deposits with, the society; and

(*b*) the value of such of the funds of the society as were represented by investments shall be the value at which they were taken into account in the balance sheet for the last financial year ending before the date of the application, and not any alternative value shown in that balance sheet.

LITHOGRAPHED SIGNATURE SEE *Facsimile Signature*

LLOYD'S LIST AND SHIPPING GAZETTE A daily newspaper printed and published by the Corporation of Lloyd's. Established in 1734, it gives news of interest to those engaged in shipping and details of the movements of ships and marine casualties. This information is subdivided under overseas movements, coastwise shipping, and ships in British ports.

LLOYD'S OF LONDON The Corporation of Lloyd's had its origin in Mr Lloyd's coffee house in 1688 and became, over the next 300 years, the world centre of shipping insurance. It became possible in time for virtually any category of insurance, other than life assurance, to be transacted through Lloyd's. Membership of Lloyd's includes the underwriters (who carry personally the individual insurance risks) and the brokers who make the market. There are also brokers who are not members of Lloyd's as such but are subscribers to Lloyd's. The underwriters operate in syndicates specializing in one or other sector of the insurance market. All the major insurance brokers in the UK are represented at Lloyd's and there are nearly 300 Lloyd's brokers, i.e. members of the Lloyd's Insurance Brokers' Association.

LOAN BACKS A term used to describe loans made by a life assurance company to a subscriber under a personal pension plan, usually a self-employed person, the loan being made out of the assets which are backing the plan. Thus, the person concerned is borrowing back a proportion of the funds which he has himself subscribed towards the pension plan. SEE *Pensions*

LOANS SEE *Lending by Banks*

LOAN CAPITAL A term applied a little loosely to long-term loans to companies. They may, for example, take the form of loan stocks or debenture stocks. It may be a single loan, e.g. from a merchant bank or pension fund, or a public issue to a number of subscribers. Such loans are not 'capital' in the equity sense but represent funded debt repayable by the company under the terms of issue and in priority to any distribution of equity capital.

LOANS TO DIRECTORS Loans by a company to its directors and the provision of guarantees or security in respect of loans by a company, to its directors were prohibited by Section 190, Companies Act 1948. This rule was subject, however to a number of exceptions, notably those companies whose normal business was the lending of money, and this led to fairly widespread abuse within the secondary banking system. Section 190 of the 1948 Act was repealed by the Companies Act 1980, and the law on the subject is now governed by Section 331 *et seq* of the 1985 Act.

Section 331 of the 1985 Act provides that

(*a*) a company shall not—

(i) make a loan to a director of the company or of its holding company;

(ii) enter into any guarantee or provide any security in connection with a loan made by any person to such a director. (Provision (*a*) relates to all companies, whether public or private but is qualified by Section 334 of the 1985 Companies Act which provides that loans up to £2,500 per director may be permitted.); and

(*b*) a relevant company (see below) shall not—

(i) make a quasi-loan to a director of the company or of its holding company;

(ii) make a loan or a quasi-loan to a person connected with such a director;

(iii) enter into a guarantee or provide any security in connection with a loan or quasi-loan made by any other person for such a director or a person so connected.

For this purpose a 'relevant company' is

1. a company that is not a private company; or
2. a company that belongs to a group in which any of the member companies is not a private company.

Under the provisions of the Act, a 'quasi-loan' is a transaction under which one party (the creditor) agrees to pay, or pays otherwise than in pursuance of an agreement, a sum for another (the borrower), or agrees to reimburse or reimburses otherwise than in pursuance of an agreement, expenditure incurred by another party for another (the borrower)

1. on terms that the borrower or a person on his behalf will reimburse a creditor; or
2. in circumstances giving rise to a liability on the borrower to reimburse the creditor.

A typical example of a quasi-loan would be the use of a company credit card.

For the purpose of the 1985 Act, a person is 'connected' with a director of a company if he or she is

1. that director's spouse, child or step-child; or
2. a body corporate with which the director is associated; or
3. a person acting in his capacity as the trustee (other than as trustee under an employees' share scheme or a pension scheme) of any trust, the beneficiaries of which include the director, his spouse or any of his children or step-children or a body corporate with which he is associated, or the terms of which confer a power on the trustees that may be exercised for the benefit of the director, his spouse, etc.

Under Section 330, a 'relevant company' is also prohibited from entering into a 'credit transaction' for a director or connected person. For this purpose, a credit transaction means any transaction where a creditor

1. supplies any goods or sells any land under a hire purchase agreement or conditional sale agreement;
2. leases or hires any land or goods in return for periodical payments;
3. otherwise disposes of land or supplies goods or services on the understanding that payment (whether in a lump sum or instalments or by way of periodical payments or otherwise) is to be deferred.

The broad effect of the foregoing provisions is that a private company may not make loans in excess of £2,500 to a director and that public companies may not make loans to a director in excess of that figure nor enter into any credit transaction or arrangement for the director's benefit, nor for the benefit of his family.

The Act contains certain notable exceptions to these provisions:

1. A quasi-loan is not prohibited if there is provision that the director reimburses the company within two months of the quasi-loan being incurred and the aggregate amount outstanding does not exceed £1,000.
2. Credit transactions (see above) are exempted provided that they do not exceed in aggregate £5,000, or they are entered into on an arm's-length basis, which means in this context that the transactions were in the ordinary course of a company's business and the transaction is not greater nor its terms more favourable than it would be reasonable to expect the company to have offered in respect of a person unconnected with the company, but who has the same financial standing as the director or connected person concerned.
3. The provisions of funds for a director to meet expenses incurred for the purposes of the company.
4. Loans or quasi-loans made by money-lending companies to a director or connected person (a) in the ordinary course of the company's business and (b) the amount must not be greater, nor the terms more favourable than those which would be offered to a person unconnected with the company but of the same financial standing of the director or connected person, and (c) the amounts in question do not exceed in aggregate £50,000, unless the company is a recognized bank under the Banking Act 1979, in which case there is no limit.

Loans by recognized banks to their directors are not subject to any limit (except in the case of house mortgage loans (see below), provided that they are on normal commercial terms and are disclosed to shareholders. Loans made by money-lending companies, including recognized banks, for house purchase and house improvement purposes to their directors or connected persons must not exceed £50,000 in aggregate per director. It does not matter that such loans are on terms more favourable than would normally apply in the ordinary course of business, provided that (1) the loan is for the purpose of a purchase or improvement of a director's only or principal residence, and (2) the company makes loans on similar terms for similar purposes to its employees.

Under Section 341 of the 1985 Act, a transaction entered into by a company in contravention of Section 330 is voidable at the instance of the company and the company will be able to recover the money or other assets which are the subject matter of the arrangement, unless this is no longer possible or any rights which have been acquired bona fide and for value by other persons would be affected.

LOCAL AUTHORITIES, INVESTMENT IN There is a number of ways in which local authorities raise money and these include the issue of securities for participation by the public. Only in a limited number of cases are these securities quoted on the Stock Exchange.

The main source of finance for local authorities is by way of declaration of the general rate on domestic and business premises within the authorities' boundaries. Local authorities may also borrow from their banks for short-term needs and they may raise short-term loans from members of the public. They may also issue mortgage loans, i.e. by way of mortgage of the general rate.

Long-term borrowing by local authorities requires the approval of the Ministry of the Environment, although a few authorities—notably the Greater London Council—have statutory powers to raise funds, including the issue of short-term bills. A number of authorities have raised long-term loans through the stock market.

Thus, the investor has the following avenues for investment in local authorities:

Long-term Loan Stock

Local authority issues which may not exceed 60 years to redemption are Stock Exchange securities and a selection of them are quoted in the daily press. The final redemption yield of the stock is effected by means of a sinking fund. The general principles governing price, running yield and redemption yield apply for corporation stocks as for Government securities. The yields are, however, a little higher, reflecting the lower status of the security. The leading stocks are freely marketable.

Mortgage Loans and Bonds

These are fixed-rate securities for periods from two to 15 years, sometimes carrying a small capital bonus at maturity. Interest is paid half yearly after deduction of income tax except in the case of bonds issued for a year or less, in which case the interest is normally paid on maturity. Local authority bonds are not quoted on the Stock Exchange, but a number of stockbrokers maintain a market in the bonds. They tend to be sold in the market at a discount and thus can offer an attractive running yield to the buyer who is prepared to wait for them to become available.

Local Authority Deposits

Local authorities accept deposits through the money market for amounts of £5,000 upwards, and for periods from two days to two years. The rate paid will reflect general money rates in the market, but will normally be very competitive with other rates.

Investors may acquire local authority mortgage loans and bonds in response to advertisements in the press or, as mentioned above, may purchase existing bonds through a stockbroker.

Quoted local authorities' stocks may be purchased direct in accordance with details advertised in the press at the time of issue. Thereafter, they may only be purchased on the Stock Exchange.

Local authority deposits may only normally be made through the money market via a money broker, or with the assistance of a stockbroker or bank.

LOCAL LAND CHARGE See *Land Charges*

LONDON CLEARING BANKS See *Clearing Banks*

LONDON DISCOUNT MARKET See *Bill Broker*

LONDON DISCOUNT MARKET ASSOCIATION The self-regulatory association of members of the London Discount Market. The Association is one of the recognized associations of dealers in securities under the Prevention of Fraud (Investments) Act 1958.

LONDON DOLLAR CERTIFICATES OF DEPOSIT The market in these certificates came into being in May, 1966, following a similar introduction in New York in 1961 and the establishment of a secondary market in them there. By 1970 over 30 banks—international subsidiaries of clearing banks, merchant banks and British overseas banks—were issuing dollar certificates of deposits in London. They are issued in multiples of $1,000 with, generally, a minimum amount of $25,000, for, normally, maturities of 30, 60, 90, 120, 150, 180 days, 12 months and for several years, although certificates have been issued for odd dates.

The certificates are issued by London branches of US banks against the payment of their dollar amounts to their offices in New York. Upon receiving advice from their New York offices that payment has been effected, the London branches issue the certificates to banks nominated by the depositors. Maturing certificates are repaid with interest at the New York office of the issuing bank concerned, upon the surrender of the certificates by the depositor to the London branch. Payments are made through the medium of a bank representing the depositor.

Nearly all certificates are payable to bearer and are negotiable. The obligations of the issuing bank are subject to the laws of the UK.

Interest rates are based on the current Euro-dollar (q.v.) rates and are about $\frac{1}{8}$ per cent lower.

The secondary market for these certificates comprises mainly bill brokers (q.v.).

LONDON INTERNATIONAL FINANCIAL FUTURES EXCHANGE (LIFFE) This Exchange known as LIFFE (pronounced *life*) was set up in London on 30th September, 1982. It was a result of a discussion paper published two years earlier by a working party set up by the International Commodities Clearing House (ICCH) (q.v.). To some extent it was modelled on the Chicago International Monetary Market (IMM), which was set up in 1971 and began trading the following year.

The principles underlying a financial futures market are in essence the same as apply to the futures markets in commodities (q.v.). It is the trading in contracts related to the future value of money and that value may be expressed either in terms of exchange rates or rates of interest.

The market was set up to trade in seven categories of contracts, namely gilt-edged stocks (initially long-term gilts), three-month sterling, three-month Euro-dollars, and four international currencies (yen, sterling, Deutschmarks and Swiss francs) all against the US dollar. The market developed steadily and modestly exceeded its initial expectations. One million contracts were entered into during the first 10 months and by the end of the first year, trading was at an average level of approximately 6,500 contracts per day. Since then business has increased rapidly and on one day in July 1984 a new record of 20,800 contracts was achieved. New categories of contract are added from time to time and in 1984 the Exchange introduced an equity index contract based on the FTSE 100 Share Index (q.v.) and a US Treasury bond contract.

The Exchange was set up with 261 members, who owned 373 'seats'. Approximately one-third of the seats were taken by British and overseas banks, the remainder being taken by money and commodity brokers, discount houses, stockbrokers, jobbers and other financial institutions. There are also a number of trading companies and private individuals who have seats on the Exchange. The seats were available in two branches at £20,000 and £30,000 each and now change hands at a premium.

As in any futures market, the members or their clients may use the market to 'hedge' or 'trade'. Hedging is designed to protect a known future commitment. Thus, for example, a company which knows that it would have to borrow sterling in, say, six months time may hedge against the possibility of a rise in interest rates; it may enter into a futures contract to sell a six month deposit maturing at around the time the borrowing will be required. If interest rates rise, the company will be able to close the contract at a profit, thus offsetting the high cost of borrowing. If interest rates fall, the contract will make a loss but the intended borrowing can be entered into more cheaply. Similarly, a fund manager who knows that money will be available for the purchase of gilts later in the year, may guard against a rise in the price of gilts by the purchase of gilt contracts through LIFFE for delivery at the time he would normally be making the gilt purchase. If gilts fall, he will make a loss on the contract, but will be able to complete his cash purchase of gilts at a lower price. Generally, the cost of hedging in this way will be less than borrowing the money in advance in order to buy the gilts earlier. Almost any institution or a person with a known future commitment of a financial nature can hedge the attendant risks by an appropriate contract through LIFFE.

The other principal activity is 'trading'. Traders (or speculators) are the other main participants. They make up the major part of the Chicago market but, at the present time, LIFFE is predominantly a market for hedging. Trading is based on the forecasting of future movements in money markets, whether in exchange rates or interest rates. It is therefore a risk-taking activity and a trading position which is left 'open' (see below) can result in considerable risks.

A contract is said to be 'open' when it has not been matched by an equal (but reverse) contract in the market and the 'commodity' has not yet been delivered. It is, thus, an open position. The trader may, however, at any time, conclude an open contract by covering it with an equal but opposite contract for delivery on the same date.

When a contract is entered into, both the buyer and seller pay the 'initial margin' which is a nominal percentage, e.g. 3 per cent of the contract sum on gilt-edged stock, 4 per cent of the contract on short-sterling deposits and 2 per cent on short Euro-dollars. It is paid to the clearing house (see below) and may be deposited in cash or negotiable securities. If at the close of business each day a loss on a contract exceeds the margin, the trader must either close the contract immediately, or make up the loss by payment of a 'variation margin'.

Financial settlement is through the International Commodities Clearing House (ICCH), which receives the margin payments, monitors the financial stability of the members and guarantees the contracts.

Trading on the floor of LIFFE is by 'open outcry', a noisy oral process of communication between the trading members, a process with a language of its own, based on the Chicago Pit.

All LIFFE contracts are in fixed unit amounts, e.g. £250,000 for sterling three-month deposits, $1 million for Euro-dollar three-month deposits, £50,000 nominal for long-dated gilts. Foreign currency contracts are in units of £25,000 sterling, 125,000 Swiss francs, 125,000 Deutsche mark and 12½ million Japanese yen.

At the time of writing, a degree of uncertainty surrounds the tax treatment of LIFFE contracts but, in general, financial institutions will be taxed under Case I of Schedule D (SEE UNDER *Income Tax*) but it is thought that private individuals will be taxed under Case VI of Schedule D. The 1984 Finance Act contains provision for financial futures transactions by pension funds to be brought in line with the general tax treatment of pension funds.

LONDON METAL EXCHANGE (LME) This is an international commodity exchange, trading in London in six of the non-ferrous metals, namely, aluminium, copper, lead, nickel, tin and zinc and, to a degree, in silver. It is a self-regulatory body and has existed for the last 100 years or so. Unlike many commodity exchanges, it trades not only in futures (q.v.) but in the physical commodities which are thus moved into or out of the Exchange's registered warehouses. The exchange is managed by a Committee of Subscribers who are elected by the members. Subscribers may be personal, i.e. on their own account, or representatives of institutions. The members, of whom there are 30 or so principal ring members, trade as principals and must, therefore, be able to meet themselves their market obligations.

LONDON STOCK EXCHANGE SEE *Stock Exchange*

LONG-DATED PAPER A term applied to bills of exchange which have more than three months to run.

LONG-DATED STOCK Not a precise term but in the case of British Government securities would normally apply to stocks with more than 15 years to run to maturity.

LOST BILL OF EXCHANGE The Bills of Exchange Act 1882, Section 69, provides

> Where a bill has been lost before it is overdue, the person who was the holder of it may apply to the drawer to give him another bill of the same tenor, giving security to the drawer if required to indemnify him against all persons whatever in case the bill alleged to have been lost shall be found again.
>
> If the drawer on request as aforesaid refuses to give such duplicate bill, he may be compelled to do so.

By Section 70

> In any action or proceeding upon a bill, the Court or a judge may order that the loss of the instrument shall not be set up, provided an indemnity be given to the satisfaction of the Court or judge against the claims of any other person upon the instrument in question.

By Section 51(8), 'where a bill is lost or destroyed, or is wrongly detained from the person entitled to hold it, protest may be made on a copy or written particulars thereof'.

Where a cheque has been lost, the loser of it should at once request the drawer to give notice to the banker on whom it is drawn to stop payment, and the banker should notify any branches, where it might be presented, of the loss. A record of the loss should be made in the customer's account in the ledger.

If a banker pays a bill or cheque where he has received instructions from the drawer not to do so, he is liable to lose the money, for he cannot debit the amount to his customer's account. The utmost care, therefore, is necessary in dealing with 'stop orders', as such notices from customers are called, and copies of all stop orders should be supplied to each cashier, day book clerk, and ledger keeper, through whose hands the cheque may pass, so that all may keep a sharp look-out in case the lost cheque should be presented.

Before giving a duplicate cheque, it is advisable

for the drawer to obtain a satisfactory indemnity, otherwise he may have to pay the original cheque (unless it was a crossed cheque marked 'not negotiable') to a bona fide holder for value, as well as the duplicate. As to a banker collecting a lost cheque, SEE *Collecting Banker*

Where a cheque has been lost and a necessary indorsement has been forged, an innocent person who has given value for the cheque has no recourse against the drawer. The true owner can demand payment from the drawer. If the person in possession of the cheque has obtained payment from the drawer, he is liable to the true owner.

If the cheque was payable to bearer and crossed 'not negotiable', the position is the same, the holder cannot recover.

If the cheque was payable to bearer, either uncrossed or crossed without the words 'not negotiable', an innocent holder for value can enforce payment of it from the drawer. The loser of the cheque must suffer the loss.

Where the cheque was duly indorsed before being lost and was not 'not negotiable', a subsequent holder for value without knowledge that it had been lost could sue the drawer and indorsers.

As to a cheque lost or stolen before delivery, SEE *Delivery of Bill*

Where a banker pays a cheque with a forged indorsement, SEE *Collecting Banker; Paying Banker*. SEE ALSO *Payment Stopped*

Where a banker's draft is lost, a duplicate will only be issued against a satisfactory indemnity. If it was lost before indorsement the drawee banker would be in order in requiring confirmation of the indorsement if presented by another banker, ostensibly duly indorsed. If presented uncrossed by a non-banker, in such circumstances he would be in order in demanding proof of the presenter's title. It must be remembered, however, that by the laws of some continental countries, a title can be made through a forgery.

If the draft were lost after indorsement, the drawee banker would have no answer against an innocent holder for value.

LOST DIVIDEND WARRANT In the case of *Thairlwall* v *Great Northern Railway Company* [1910] 2 KB 509, where certain dividend warrants sent by the defendants to the plaintiff were lost in the post, the defendants, upon being informed of the loss, sent to the plaintiff a form of indemnity, and stated that on its being signed by the plaintiff, they would give him a duplicate dividend warrant. The plaintiff declined to sign the indemnity, and brought an action to recover the amount of the dividends. The Divisional Court (reversing a judgment of the County Court in favour of the plaintiff) held that the stockholders of the company having by resolution determined the method in which the dividends were to be paid, i.e. by the sending of dividend warrants, the only obligation of the company was to pay by means of a dividend warrant, and that, having sent such a document by post, they had discharged their duty even although the warrant was lost in the post and never reached the plaintiff. The plaintiff could get payment only by giving a proper indemnity to the company.

The articles of association of a company may include a clause that the company shall not be responsible for the loss of a dividend warrant sent by post. A shareholder may protect himself against such a risk by instructing the company to pay the dividend direct to his bankers. SEE *Dividend Warrant*

LOST SHARE CERTIFICATE The articles of association of a company usually provide that a shareholder who has lost his certificate may obtain a fresh one, on giving such an indemnity as the directors require. A company should exercise great care in issuing a new certificate as the old certificate may have been deposited elsewhere as security for a loan.

Likewise, a banker should only give an indemnity on behalf of a customer for this purpose when the latter's counter indemnity is undoubted, for if the lost certificate came to light in the hands of a party with a charge on it, the company may have to recognize the latter's claim and must do so if the shares have been transferred to a third party on a forged transfer.

If, however, the *registered owner* has deposited the first certificate as security and obtained a duplicate on a false assertion of loss of the earlier certificate, it appears that no claim can be made under the indemnity. This is because there is no claim against the company since it does not warrant that the person named on a certificate is entitled to the benefit of the shares. The company may effect a new registration on a genuine signature and duplicate the certificate.

LOT A unit of goods offered for sale by auction (q.v.).

LOW-COST ENDOWMENT MORTGAGE This is a form of house purchase loan, where the amount of the mortgage is repaid by means of an endowment policy. Generally, with a with-profits endowment mortgage, the lender will lend only against the sum assured under the policy, because future bonuses are uncertain. In the result, the borrower may well receive a total sum under the policy far in excess of his mortgage debt and although this may be an attractive method of saving, it can be an expensive way of buying a house. Accordingly, most insurance companies have introduced low-cost endowment policies, under which the sum assured is less than the amount of the loan, but some allowance is made for a modest level of bonuses in order to bring the policy proceeds up to the amount of the loan at maturity. As the sum assured is less than the mortgage debt, the position would be uncovered in the event of the borrower's death and thus the assurance company includes in the total package sufficient term assurance to meet any shortfall. SEE *Life Assurance*

LOWER EARNINGS LIMIT A term used in the social security legislation to denote that level of earnings below which National Insurance contributions are not payable, either by the employer or the employee. The lower earnings limit is applied to each particular job so that if, for example, an employee has two or more jobs, each paying below the lower earnings limit, no contributions will be payable by him or by his employers in relation to any of those jobs.

The lower earnings limit for the year 1985–86 was £35.50 per week; the equivalent figures for previous years were

1978–79	£17.50
1979–80	£19.50
1980–81	£23.00
1981–82	£27.00
1982–83	£29.50
1983–84	£32.50
1984–85	£34.00

SEE ALSO *National Insurance Contributions; Upper Earnings Limit*

M

M0, M1, M2 AND M3 These are the terms used to describe the varying forms of measurement of the money supply or of monetary aggregates in the UK.

M0 was introduced as a monetary target by the Chancellor of the Exchequer in October 1983. It is the 'monetary base' of the money supply and consists of all notes and coin in circulation with the public, money in the tills of the banks and balances held by the banks with the Bank of England. It is the equivalent of what was previously known as the 'wide monetary base' although it is the narrowest of the various aggregates used in relation to the total supply of money.

M1 refers to notes and coins in circulation with the public plus private sector holdings of 'sight' bank deposits, i.e. personal current accounts.

M2 is made up of bank current accounts plus retail bank deposits, i.e. those which are available on short notice, retail building society deposits and ordinary accounts with the National Savings Bank.

M3 is sometimes expressed as Sterling M3 (£M3) which is made up of M1 (see above) plus private sector time deposits with banks and sterling bank certificates of deposit. M3 equals £M3, together with private sector bank deposits in foreign currency.

Further monetary aggregates are expressed as PSL1 (Private Sector Liquidity) which is equivalent to Sterling M3, less bank time deposits of more than two years, plus private sector money market instruments and certificates of tax deposits. PSL2 equates with PSL1 less building society holdings of money market instruments and bank deposits, plus private sector holdings of building society deposits and National Savings Certificates etc.

MACMILLAN GAP The term applied to the lack of provision for longer-term equity capital in the UK for smaller and medium-sized companies. This was first emphasized in the Macmillan Report (see below) in 1931 and has been a continuing theme since then in all discussions concerning capital for industry and was referred to in the Radcliffe Report of 1959 and the Wilson Report of 1980 (q.v.). In the intervening years, much has been done in the financial sector to establish vehicles to provide finance for smaller companies, including in particular the Industrial and Commercial Finance Corporation (ICFC) (q.v.) and Finance Corporation for Industry (FCI) (q.v.) and Equity Capital for Industry (ECI) (q.v.).

MACMILLAN REPORT The Committee on Finance and Industry was set up in 1929 under the chairmanship of Lord Macmillan and published its report in 1931. Among other matters, the Report supported the use of tariffs, the raising of international wholesale commodity prices, the maintenance of the gold standard in the UK and a reduction of the value of gold in terms of commodities. It sought closer cooperation between the Bank of England and the clearing banks and condemned the practice of 'window dressing' the published figures of the banks. The Report also drew attention to the shortage of capital for those companies which were not large enough to seek a stock market quotation. SEE *Macmillan Gap*

MADE BILL A bill drawn in England and payable abroad, if negotiated and indorsed in England by a correspondent of the drawer, is called a made bill. Such a bill thus bears the name of an indorser as well as that of the drawer and drawee. SEE *Drawn Bill*

MAIL TRANSFER The transfer by mail of an amount of currency or sterling to another country. The remitter signs an order requesting the banker to transfer the amount by mail, giving the name and address of the payee and stating whether the payment is to be made (1) under advice, (2) on application and identification (a specimen signature of the payee should, if possible, be supplied), (3) to credit of payee's account at ... bank.

MAINTENANCE PAYMENTS A term usually applied to the financial provision made for a party to a marriage or the children of a marriage on divorce or separation. Such payments may be made on a voluntary basis or may be ordered by the court. There is no strict rule by which the courts fix the amount of maintenance payments. There is, however, what is known as the 'one-third rule', which is adopted quite frequently but not invariably, i.e. that a wife will be awarded one-third of the total income of herself and her husband and additional payments ordered for any dependent children.

A discussion paper on the financial consequences of divorce was published by the Law Commission in 1980 (Cmnd 8041, HMSO). Amongst other things, the paper includes for discussion the following bases of dealing with the financial implications of divorce:

1. the limitation of financial support to cases of real need,
2. the division of property once and for all in the 'clean break' approach,
3. an inflexible mathematical formula to deal with all cases.
4. the restoration of the parties to their position had the marriage never happened.

In December 1981, the Law Commission published its recommendations *The Financial Consequences of Divorce* (Cmnd 112) and, in general, recommended that the courts should no longer be obliged to put divorced parties into the financial position they would have enjoyed had the marriage not broken down. The aim should be that the divorced parties should seek to be self-sufficient in time and not continue to rely on maintenance from the other spouse. It was recognized, however, that it may be appropriate in some cases for a spouse to receive maintenance payments for life and, wherever there are children, their financial needs must be an overriding priority. SEE *Divorce*

MAKER OF PROMISSORY NOTE The person who signs a promissory note promising to pay another person is called 'the maker'. By Section 88 of the Bills of Exchange Act 1882

> The maker of a promissory note by making it:
> (1) Engages that he will pay it according to its tenor;
> (2) Is precluded from denying to a holder in due course the existence of the payee and his then capacity to indorse.

There may be two or more makers, and they may be liable jointly, or jointly and severally, according to the tenor of the note (Section 85).

Where a promissory note is in the body of it made payable at a particular place, it must be presented for payment at that place in order to render the maker liable. In any other case, presentment for payment is not necessary in order to render the maker liable (Section 87(1)).

The maker of a note is deemed to correspond with the acceptor of a bill. SEE *Presentment for Payment; Promissory Note*

MAKING-UP DAY The first day of the settlement on the Stock Exchange.

MANAGED BOND A single-premium life assurance policy taken out for investment purposes, the underlying portfolio consisting of equities, gilt-edged stocks, property etc., the proportions varying at the discretion of the insurance company. Such a bond is said to be 'managed' in that the managers seek to vary the proportions in each category of security, depending on their view of the markets. SEE *Bonds*

MANAGED FUND A fairly loose expression which may apply to any investment portfolio which is 'managed' in the sense that it receives continuous professional supervision. The term is more usually applied, however, to those funds which are managed by insurance companies on behalf of pension schemes. Thus, the trustees of a pension scheme who do not wish to manage the investment within their organization, nor employ an outside organization to do so may, if they wish, apply the pension funds contributions in the purchase of units in an insurance company's managed fund. Such a fund enjoys the taxation reliefs common to all approved pension schemes and, to that extent, is like an exempt unit trust (q.v.). The insurance company will deal with all the necessary administration on behalf of the employer and the performance of the fund will be evident for the trustees of the pension scheme to follow.

MANAGEMENT BUY-OUT This is in essence the purchase of a business enterprise by its managers. Usually a management buy-out takes one of three forms:

1. the sale by a company of its entire business or, more usually, the sale of one of its subsidiaries to the management team;
2. the sale of a company or a subsidiary to a consortium, e.g. of financial institutions, the management team taking a significant proportion of the equity; and
3. the sale from the public sector of a company to its employees, as in the case of National Freight Consortium.

Management buy-outs have been a feature of the years of recession, particularly in cases where a trading group wished to dispose of a subsidiary, or perhaps peripheral activity and the management agree to take it over. In appropriate cases, the banks will usually assist with finance to facilitate a management buy-out provided there is a good management team and reasonable prospects for the future.

There can be taxation complications in connection with a management buy-out and it is essential to have good professional advice.

MANDATE An authority in writing by which one person (the mandator) empowers another person (the mandatory) to act on his behalf. If John Brown authorizes T. Jones to sign cheques upon his account, the usual form of signature is 'per pro [or p.p.] John Brown, T. Jones'. The mandate should state that Jones may sign whether the account is in credit or in debit (if that is the wish of Brown) and a specimen of the signature of Jones should be given on the mandate in the form in which he will sign. In cases where the principal has arranged for an overdraft on the account, a mandate would cover the cheques drawn by the agent within that arrangement, in the event of the mandate not including such words as 'whether the account is in credit or is overdrawn', but it is usual practice and it is advisable to include those words in the authority. In the absence of such, or similar words in the mandate, the principal would not be liable for an overdraft created by the agent without the principal's sanction or knowledge. A mandate by Brown may authorize Jones to sign Brown's name, but the preferable way is, as given above, for Jones to sign 'per pro'.

In *Kepitigalla Rubber Estates Ltd* v *The National Bank of India Ltd* [1909] 2 KB 1010, it was held that it is 'clearly the duty of a person giving a mandate to take reasonable care that he does not mislead the person to whom the mandate is given'.

A mandate is terminated by the death, bankruptcy, or mental incapacity of the person, or one of the persons in the case of a joint account, who gave the authority. SEE *Joint Account*

A person who has authority to sign for another has not, as a rule, any power to delegate that authority.

In the case of joint accounts, the joint and several liability established by the mandate permits the banker, in the event of death, mental incapacity or bankruptcy of one of the joint account-holders, to claim on his or her estate for an overdrawn balance. Such an agreement also gives the banker the right, after reasonable notice, to set off a credit balance on any of their private accounts against an overdraft on the joint account.

The cases of *Selangor United Rubber Estates Ltd* v *Cradock* [1968] 2 All ER 1073, and *Karak Rubbers Co. Ltd* v *Burden and Others* (No. 2) [1972] 1 All ER 1210—see under *Paying Banker*—appear to have reduced the extent to which a banker can rely on his mandate alone. SEE *Agent Company; Delegation of Authority, Executor; Partnerships*

MARGINAL COSTING This is one of the various methods of arriving at the cost of a product as a constituent of a pricing policy. The marginal cost of a product is strictly the cost of producing one more unit. It is sometimes known as direct costing because it disregards any element of overhead costs. In a direct or marginal costing system, the difference between the costs and the market price contributes to the unallocated overhead costs and ultimately, therefore, to profit.

MARGINS In the commodity markets, a margin is the amount which an investor has to pay to the broker at the outset in relation to a particular transaction. It is thus in the nature of a deposit and on the successful conclusion of a contract he may make a very considerable profit without having to make any further payment beyond the original margin, which would probably be of the order of 10 per cent. On the other hand, the capital investment could be eliminated completely by a fall in the commodity market. Over a period of unfavourable trading the margin would have to be topped-up to maintain the level of the original margin. This is known as a 'margin call'.

Margin trading is also a Stock Exchange term which is more common in other countries, notably the USA and Japan, than in the UK. It usually refers to trading in the Stock Market with short-term borrowed funds.

MARINE INSURANCE Marine insurance is a contract whereby one party, in consideration of a premium paid, undertakes to indemnify the other party against loss from certain perils or sea risks to which his ship or cargo may be exposed.

A policy of marine insurance is usually effected with insurers, called 'underwriters'. The term 'underwriter' is applied because each person who acts as an insurer signs his name at the foot of the policy and states the amount for which he is to be liable. The ship or the goods may be insured either for a certain voyage or during some period of time, and the underwriters by the contract agree to indemnify the insurer against loss in accordance with the terms of the policy.

A person wishing to insure usually employs an insurance broker to arrange the terms of the policy with the underwriters.

The person insured must have an insurable interest in the ship or its cargo, otherwise the contract is not legally binding.

There are several kinds of marine policies, the principal being

1. A *valued policy*, where the value of the ship or subject insured is stated in the policy. Ships and freights are usually insured under a valued policy.

2. An *open policy*, where the value of the subject insured is not stated in the policy. When a loss occurs, the value has to be proved. Goods are usually included in an open policy. The description in the policy should agree with that in the bill of lading.
3. There are also a *time policy*, that is a policy for a fixed time, a *voyage policy*, that is for a particular voyage, a *floating policy*, which insures the subject-matter in whatever ship it may be; and other varieties.

The underwriters are liable for the full amount of the insurance in the event of the ship being totally lost, but in the case of a partial loss the underwriters are usually liable only for two-thirds, the remaining one-third of the loss falling upon the owner of the ship.

As from 1st February, 1938, what is known as the Waterborne Agreement came into force among London underwriters, whereby war risk is covered only whilst goods are actually on ship, except that 15 days are allowed for loading and unloading, and 15 days for transhipment where such is necessary as from an up-river vessel to an ocean-going boat.

An insurance certificate is sometimes attached to a bill, and is a declaration by an insurance company that the goods are insured under a policy which also covers other goods.

A document of insurance is not a good tender in England under an ordinary cif contract unless it be an actual policy (*Scott* v *Barclays Bank Ltd* (1923) 39 TLR 198). SEE *Documentary Credit*

In *F. W. Berk and Company Ltd* v *Style* [1955] 3 All ER 625, it was held that marine policies expressed to cover 'all risks of loss and for damage from whatsoever cause arising' did not cover loss from inherent vice. The policies embodied the Institute Cargo Clauses (Wartime Extension), in particular the provision that 'this insurance shall in no case be deemed to extend to cover loss, damage or expense proximately caused by delay or inherent vice or nature of the subject-matter insured'. The Marine Insurance Act 1906, Section 55(2)(c), is to much the same effect, 'unless the policy otherwise provides'.

The cargo consisted of kieselguhr packed in paper bags and the learned judge found as a fact that the subject-matter of the insurance was kieselguhr in paper bags, not kieselguhr alone, and that owing to defective packing there was at the time of shipment inherent vice, against which the plaintiffs were not insured. The policies covered a risk and not a certainty, and in this case it was virtually certain that the bags would not hold their contents.

MARITIME LIEN A lien which attaches to a vessel and/or its cargo as a result of some liability incurred in respect of a voyage. It is not necessarily a possessory lien and is enforced by a legal process in the Admiralty Court. Examples are a lien of seamen for wages, a lien of a master of a ship for wages and disbursement, lien in respect of salvage.

MARKED CHEQUE Marking cheques, a rare procedure, can take one of two forms—marking for clearing purposes and marking at the request of the drawer. Before the abolition of local clearings (or exchanges) in country towns, cheques were presented by one banker to another in the same town to be 'marked' as good. If the cheque were all right, the banker on whom it was drawn would initial it and hand it back to the presenting banker. The banker holding the cheque could then rest satisfied that it would be paid when presented through the clearing later on in the day, or, if too late for that day's clearing, through the clearing on the following day, or as would happen nowadays, through the London Clearing House, being received at the paying bank on say, the third working day. The arrangement is one between the two bankers and has nothing to do with the drawer, payee or holder. If further cheques should be presented for payment before the marked cheque arrives through the clearing, and the balance of the customer's account, taking the amount of the marked cheque into consideration, will not permit of their payment, the banker is justified in refusing payment of those subsequent cheques. When the banker marked the cheque, he virtually paid it, and is entitled to regard it as paid, although, for the convenience of the two bankers, the cheque itself is permitted to be passed through the clearing with other cheques. The marked cheque will, of course, be debited to the drawer's account when it comes in, even though the drawer in the interval has died or become mentally incapable or bankrupt. The drawer cannot stop payment of the cheque after it has been marked.

Instead of marking a cheque, some bankers pay it, if in order, and give in exchange a clearing voucher to be passed through the clearing.

Bankers were occasionally requested by the drawer of a cheque to mark or certify it as good for the amount, as, for example, when the customer desired to settle for the purchase of property or to pay customs duties. In 1920, the Committee of London Clearing Bankers recommended that such marking should be discontinued in favour of the issue of a banker's draft. Where very exceptionally a cheque is marked for a customer, it is the practice to take his authority to debit his account forthwith and to credit a suspense account to which the marked cheque is debited on presentation. The drawer cannot stop payment of a cheque marked at his request.

In the Privy Council case of *Bank of Baroda Ltd v Punjab National Bank Ltd* [1944] 2 All ER 83, it was held that marking or certification is neither in form nor effect an acceptance of which the holder or payee can avail himself. It was said that 'it would certainly require strong and unmistakable words to amount to the acceptance of a cheque'.

In the USA, cheques are freely certified by bankers, and such certification is held by law to be equivalent to acceptance. SEE *Certification of Cheques; Cheque*

MARKET OVERT An open or public market. By custom, shops in the City of London are market overt for the purposes of their own trades, and outside the limits of the city the name is applied to particular places which are set apart for a market by grant or by prescription. When a person buys, in market overt, goods which have been stolen he obtains a good title, unless the thief is afterwards prosecuted and convicted, when the property in the goods revests in the original owner. Sale in market overt is the chief exception to the rule that a purchaser obtains no property in goods of which his transferor was not the owner.

MARKING NAMES Certain international securities—generally those of the 'American' type—may be registered in the names of nominees, such as a member of the Stock Exchange or a banker. The certificates are discharged in blank by the nominee on the reverse side and are then transferable by delivery as with a security payable to bearer. Accordingly, the transfer need not be registered with the company.

The London Stock Exchange has compiled a list of firms recognized by the Market as 'good marking names' for this purpose of nominee holdings. Shares so registered usually command a slightly better price than those not in a good marking name.

Dividends and other cash or stock distributions and rights to new issues must be collected from the marking name. These duties are usually undertaken on behalf of the owner by his banker.

The marking name makes a charge for its services generally by quoting a rate of exchange for cash distributions which is less favourable than that actually received.

The collecting agent also makes a charge for his services in collecting dividends, etc. The relative certificates are marked on the back with a rubber stamp by the marking name to indicate that dividends, etc., have been claimed.

MARRIAGE, GIFTS ON SEE *Capital Transfer Tax*

MARRIAGE, TAXATION ASPECT SEE *Capital Transfer Tax; Income Tax*

MARRIAGE SETTLEMENT A settlement of property, provided by either or both of the parties to the contract of marriage, and made either before or after the marriage. In the former case it is called an ante-nuptial settlement, and in the latter, post-nuptial. Except in the case of fraud, an ante-nuptial settlement is one made for valuable consideration, the marriage being the consideration. But in the case of a post-nuptial settlement, there is only what is known in law as 'good consideration', and the settlement may be avoided in certain cases if the settlor becomes bankrupt within a certain period after the settlement is made. SEE *Settlements—Settlor Bankrupt*

See the provisions of the Settled Land Act 1925 under *Settled Land*

MARRIED WOMAN The Married Women's Property Act 1882 permitted a married woman to hold property as her separate estate and to dispose of such separate estate subject to any restraint on anticipation. Restraint on anticipation occurred where a married woman was prohibited from anticipating the income of settled funds or from charging or alienating the capital. A creditor's remedy was thus confined to a married woman's separate property free from restraint on anticipation, except that by the Bankrupty Act 1914, Section 125, a married woman could be made bankrupt if she were in trade or business, whether separately from her husband or not.

A husband was fully liable for his wife's civil wrongs during marriage.

But by the Law Reform (Married Women and Tortfeasors) Act 1935, Section 1, a married woman became

1. capable of acquiring, holding, and disposing of any property; and
2. capable of rendering herself, and being rendered, liable in respect of any tort, contract, debt, or obligation; and
3. capable of suing and being sued, either in tort or in contract or otherwise; and
4. subject to the law relating to bankruptcy and to the enforcement of judgments and orders.

in all respects as if she were a feme-sole.

Section 2 says that all property which

1. immediately before the passing of this Act was

the separate property of a married woman or held for her separate use in equity; or
2. belongs at the time of her marriage to a woman married after the passing of this Act; or
3. after the passing of this Act is acquired by or devolves upon a married woman, shall belong to her in all respects as if she were a feme-sole and may be disposed of accordingly.

Existing restraints on anticipation or those imposed in any instrument executed before 1st January, 1936 continued to be, or should in due course become effective (Section 2). By Section 3 it was provided that the will of a testator who died after 31st December, 1935 should be deemed to have been executed after 1st January, 1936, notwithstanding its actual date of execution. Thus a statutory limit was put to a testator's imposition of a restraint on anticipation in an instrument executed before 1st January, 1936.

However the Married Women (Restraint on Anticipation) Act 1949, abolished all such restraints.

Hence, a married woman can hold property in all respects as if she were unmarried and she can enter into any contract and be sued for any debt or tort. A creditor can obtain judgment against her personally and has his rights against her property notwithstanding it was subject to a restraint on anticipation imposed before 1936. Section 125 of the Bankruptcy Act 1914 is repealed and a married woman is subject to bankruptcy law whether in trade or business or not. A husband is no longer liable for his wife's civil wrongs but a husband's liability remains for debts incurred by his wife for necessaries for herself and his household is however left untouched.

Where a married woman is adjudged bankrupt, her husband is postponed as to dividend as her creditor until the claims of the other creditors have been met. Where a husband is bankrupt, his wife cannot claim any dividend as a creditor until the claims of the other creditors have been satisfied (Bankruptcy Act 1924, Section 36(1) and (2)).

A banker should take care to see that the account of a wife of an undischarged bankrupt is not used for collecting her husband's cheques.

Where a married woman has a joint account with her husband, her right to any credit balance on his decease is a question of intention on the husband's part. Where the express intention of opening the account in joint names was to make provision for his wife, she can deal with the balance (*Foley* v *Foley* [1911] 1 IR 281). But where the account was opened by the husband for his convenience, the balance cannot be claimed by the wife (*Marshal* v *Crutwell* (1875) 20 LR Eq 328). In practice, a mandate is taken on opening the account wherein it is acknowledged that the account is with benefit to survivor, thus avoiding any doubt as to intention. The effect of this mandate is to protect the banker from involvement in any dispute between the survivor and another party. The common law presumption that sole ownership of the joint property passes to the survivor on the death of the other party may be displaced by a number of factors, particularly the intention of the parties, as mentioned above, and disputes may arise, for example, between a widow and the personal representative of the deceased husband. Nevertheless, the banker will be safe in relying on his mandate, unless he has direct notice that to do so will be to further a fraudulent transaction. Where a married woman gives a guarantee for her husband's account she should be separately advised by her solicitor and should acknowledge in writing that she understands the terms of the document and enters into the contract freely and voluntarily. SEE *Guarantee*

The Married Women's Property Act 1964 was intended to clarify the position relating to a wife's savings out of her housekeeping allowance. Section 1 provides that such savings, or any property acquired out of such savings, shall, in the absence of any agreement to the contrary, be treated as belonging to the husband and wife in equal shares.

The right of a deserted wife to occupy the matrimonial home against a bank to whom the home has been mortgaged as security was discussed in *National Provincial Bank Ltd* v *Hastings Car Mart Ltd and Others* [1963] 2 WLR 1015, where the bank, not having notice at the time of the mortgage of the desertion, later took out a summons for possession, which was resisted by the wife. The bank was held to be entitled to an order for possession, and the wife appealed. The appeal was allowed by a majority of the Court of Appeal. The majority held ([1964] 2 WLR 751):

1. that the husband was conclusively presumed to have authorized his wife to remain in the matrimonial home,
2. that it was settled law that a deserted wife's right to remain in the matrimonial home was a licence coupled with an equity and binding on the husband's successors in title so long as the wife remained in actual occupation of the home; and
3. that, so far as registered land is concerned, the right of a deserted wife to remain in occupation was an overriding interest within Section 70(1)(g) of the Land Registration Act 1925, available

against all the husband's successors in title save where enquiry was made of the wife and her interest was not disclosed.

The decision of the Court of Appeal was however reversed in the House of Lords. The position is now covered by the Matrimonial Homes Act 1967, by which a Land Charge, Class F, may be registered to cover the contingency of a married woman being deserted.

In the case of *Williams & Glyn's Bank Ltd* v *Boland* (and a similar case of *Williams & Glyn's Bank Ltd* v *Brown*) [1979] 2 WLR 550, it was held that a wife who had made a contribution to the purchase of the matrimonial home, the house being in the sole name of the husband, had an overriding interest in the property which took priority to the legal charge which had been given to the bank to secure the husband's debt. It was held that, in such circumstances, a wife who had contributed to the purchase of the home was an equitable tenant in common and thus had a proprietory interest in the matrimonial home. This was a Court of Appeal judgment which was confirmed in the House of Lords [1983] WLR 138, their lordships suggesting that a practice of more careful enquiry into the circumstances of the occupation of the mortgagee's property could not be considered unacceptable. There the matter rests, although the Law Commission in a report on the case (Cmnd 8638, HMSO) took the view that the situation was far from satisfactory. The Commission recommended that the interest of any co-owner should be registrable whether or not that owner was in occupation and that a purchaser or mortgagee should not be postponed to that interest unless it was protected by an entry on the register of title or by registration as a land charge. In the meantime it would appear that a mortgagee, whether bank or building society, must have due regard to the possible rights of a party to a marriage, notwithstanding that the property is in the other party's name. Thus, appropriate enquiries should be made in each case and, depending on the circumstances, both parties to the marriage be required to enter into the mortgage deed.

The Boland principle applies only to registered land but it expressly covers any third party, not merely a spouse, who can prove an interest: and it may affect companies as well as individuals.

MARRIED WOMEN'S PROPERTY ACTS SEE *Life Policies as Security; Married Women*

MARSHALLING OF SECURITIES The equitable doctrine which provides that a creditor who has recourse to more than one security of the debtor shall not in exercising his rights prejudice another creditor who is covered by one of the same securities.

Thus where A mortgages two properties X and Y to B and later gives a second mortgage on Y to C, C may demand that the securities be marshalled, i.e. that B's claim shall be satisfied as far as possible from property X, that property Y or as much as is not required to satisfy B's claim be left to satisfy C's mortgage.

The doctrine of marshalling will not be allowed to prejudice a third mortgagee, however.

MATERIAL ALTERATION Section 64 of the Bills of Exchange Act 1882, provides that where a bill or acceptance is materially altered without the assent of all parties liable on the bill, the bill is avoided except as against a party who has himself made, authorized, or assented to the alteration, and subsequent indorsers.

Where the alteration is not apparent, however, a holder in due course may enforce payment of the bill according to its original tenor, e.g. a cheque raised from eight pounds to 80 pounds, so that the alteration cannot be detected with reasonable care, would give a holder in due course the right to enforce payment against the drawer for the original sum of eight pounds. Section 64 says that, in particular, alteration of the date, the sum payable, the time of payment, the place of payment and the addition of a place of payment without the acceptor's consent where the bill has been accepted generally, are material alterations. Where a bill was accepted bearing neither date nor drawer's name, and bearing on the top the word 'London', the substitution by the drawer when he signed it of 'Lausanne' was held not to be an alteration of an existing instrument (*Foster* v *Driscoll* [1929] 1 KB 470). But where, subsequent to completion and execution of a bill, an alteration was made of the place where the bill purported to be drawn so as to make it a foreign bill, it was held to be a material alteration as it altered the rights and liabilities of parties (*Koch* v *Dicks* [1933] 1 KB 307).

Where a solicitor prepared a cheque for signature by executors as drawers, payable to 'John Prust & Co', and after the cheque was returned to him duly signed by the drawers, added to the payee's name the words 'per Cumberbirch & Potts', the name of his firm, it was held to be a material alteration. The drawee banker, notwithstanding that the alteration was not apparent, was liable for having paid the cheque *Slingsby* v *District Bank* [1932] 1 KB 544).

The trial judge, whilst holding, in this case, that the leaving of space after the payee's name was not contributory negligence on the part of the drawer, hinted, however, that if such cases of loss thereby became common, the drawer might be held to be liable. SEE *Alterations to Bill of Exchange*

MATERNITY ALLOWANCE This is a Social Security benefit designed to assist mothers and mothers-to-be with financial support during the weeks in which they will not be able to work because of the confinement and subsequent birth. The allowance is payable for 18 weeks, starting with the 11th week before the week in which the baby is expected. If, however, the mother does not claim until the confinement, the allowance is payable only for the week of the confinement and the following six weeks. The allowance is not payable for any week in which the mother or mother-to-be is working. The allowance is not payable if, during the period in question, the mother or mother-to-be is receiving, at the same or higher rate, sickness benefit, unemployment benefit or certain other Social Security benefits.

The allowance is payable on the mother's own contributions and she must therefore, have paid or have been credited with the requisite number of either Class I or Class II contributions. As with sickness benefit (q.v.), the mother may be able to obtain an additional allowance for dependent adults and her own dependent children. A divorced woman may receive maternity allowance provided she satisfies the contribution conditions. A widow may receive maternity allowance and the contribution requirements will be modified or waived if she has been receiving a widow's or widowed mother's allowance. Maternity allowance is tax-free.

MATERNITY GRANT This is a lump sum payable to a mother to assist with the expenses of having a baby. It is payable on the contribution record of either the mother or her husband. The grant is payable to the mother and may be paid notwithstanding the baby is still-born, if the pregnancy has lasted at least 28 weeks.

In the case of the birth of twins, triplets, etc., the grant is payable for each child who lives for more than 12 hours. One grant is payable if one or all children fail to survive for that period. The claim for maternity grant may be made at any time from the beginning of the 14th week before the baby is due and up to three months after the birth.

A single mother may claim maternity grant on her own contributions provided she satisfies the contribution requirements. A widow may claim in respect of her late husband's child, either on his contributions or her own. A divorced mother cannot claim the grant unless she does so before the baby is born and she was married for 11 weeks preceding the date of confinement to the man on whose contribution record she is claiming.

MATERNITY PAY This is a payment which an employer is required to make, under the Employment Protection (Consolidation) Act 1978, to a woman employee who becomes pregnant. In order to qualify, the woman must have been continuously employed for two years or more by the time her pregnancy has reached a point when only 11 weeks remain before the date the baby is expected, and provided she has worked for at least 16 hours per week for that employer. If a woman has been employed continuously for five years or more, she will qualify for maternity pay if she worked only eight hours per week.

Maternity pay is payable for the first six weeks after the woman leaves work in preparation for her confinement.

Maternity allowance (q.v.) (whether or not the claimant is entitled to it) is deducted from maternity pay, and the pay is calculated at the rate of 9/10 of the employee's normal week's pay. Maternity pay is taxable.

MATE'S RECEIPT A document acknowledging receipt of goods on board ship, and signed by the mate. It states that the goods are received in good order and condition and gives their description and distinguishing marks, and the name of the shipper, but not usually the name of the consignee.

The mate's receipt is exchanged later for the bill of lading. It is not a document of title and it is not necessary for a shipping company to demand the mate's receipt before issuing the bill of lading, but it is the invariable practice of English companies to issue bills of lading only against production of the relative mate's receipt.

Lord Wright in the Privy Council case of *Nippon Yusen Kaisha* v *Ramjibon Serowjee* (1938) said

> The mate's receipt is not a document of title to the goods shipped. Its transfer does not pass property in the goods nor is its possession equivalent to possession of the goods. It is not conclusive and its statements do not bind the shipowner as do the statements in a bill of lading signed within the master's authority. It is however, prima facie evidence of the quantity and condition of the goods received and prima facie it is the recipient or possessor who is entitled to have the bill of lading issued to him. But if the mate's receipt acknowledges receipt from a shipper other than the person who actually receives the mate's receipt and, in particular, if the property is in that shipper and the shipper has contracted for the freight, the shipowner will prima facie be entitled and indeed bound to deliver the bill of lading to that person.

In *Kum and Another* v *Wah Tet Bank Limited* [1971] 1 Lloyd's Rep 439, where it was claimed that mate's receipts were documents of title by local custom in Sarawak and Singapore, the Privy Council said that there is no reason why local custom should not create a document of title, Lord Devlin remarking that 'It was by the custom of merchants that the bill of lading became such a document'. To establish the claim, there must be evidence that the custom is generally accepted by traders in the market concerned and is so generally known that anyone making reasonable enquiry would become aware of it. However, in the present case, the fact that the mate's receipts were marked 'not negotiable' was fatal to their negotiability even though the words had been ignored by everyone concerned in the trade.

MATURITY The maturity of a bill of exchange or promissory note is the date upon which it matures or falls due to be paid. SEE *Presentment for Payment*

MAUNDY MONEY The money which the sovereign causes to be distributed on Maundy Thursday—that is, the Thursday in Holy Week—to as many poor men and women as he or she is years old. The money, which is of the same number of pence as the sovereign's age, consists of four silver coins, a fourpenny piece, a threepenny piece, a twopenny piece, and a penny piece. The coins are not of much use to the recipients, except to sell to anyone who is interested in coins. Originally, the bestowal of the Royal Maundy gifts was preceded by a service during which the king in person washed the feet of poor persons in token of humility, but since the reign of James II this part of the ceremony has not been observed. The origin of the word Maundy is, by some persons, said to be derived from the Latin *mandatum novim* (a new commandment) as those were the first words of the anthem which used to be sung when the king performed the ceremony of washing the feet of the poor people. Another explanation of the origin of the word is that it is derived from the 'maunds' or baskets, which contained the bread for distribution to the poor.

By the Decimal Currency Act 1969, Section 1(6), the silver coins of the Queen's Maundy money made in accordance with Section 3 of the Coinage Act 1870, shall be treated as made in accordance with Section 2 of the Decimal Currency Act 1967.

MEETING OF CREDITORS After a receiving order has been made against a debtor, he is not immediately adjudged a bankrupt, but a meeting of creditors is held shortly afterwards to consider whether a proposal for a composition or a scheme of arrangement shall be entertained or whether he shall be adjudged bankrupt.

The following are some of the rules in Schedule 1 of the Bankruptcy Act 1914, with respect to meetings of creditors.

1. The first meeting of creditors shall be summoned for a day not later than fourteen days after the date of the receiving order, unless the Court for any special reason deem it expedient that the meeting be summoned for a later day.

2. The official receiver shall summon the meeting by giving not less than six clear days' notice of the time and place thereof in the Gazette and in a local paper.

3. The official receiver shall also, as soon as practicable, send to each creditor mentioned in the debtor's statement of affairs, a notice of the time and place of the first meeting of creditors, accompanied by a summary of the debtor's statement of affairs, including the cause of his failure, and any observations thereon which the official receiver may think fit to make; but the proceedings at the first meeting shall not be invalidated by reason of any such notice or summary not having been sent or received before the meeting.

8. A person shall not be entitled to vote as a creditor at the first or any other meeting of creditors unless he has duly proved a debt provable in bankruptcy to be due to him from the debtor, and the proof has been duly lodged before the time appointed for the meeting.

9. A creditor shall not vote at any such meeting in respect of any unliquidated or contingent debt, or any debt the value of which is not ascertained.

10. For the purpose of voting, a secured creditor shall, unless he surrenders his security, state in his proof the particulars of his security, the date when it was given, and the value at which he assesses it, and shall be entitled to vote only in respect of the balance (if any) due to him, after deducting the value of his security. If he votes in respect of his whole debt he shall be deemed to have surrendered his security unless the Court on application is satisfied that the omission to value the security has arisen from inadvertence.

11. A creditor shall not vote in respect of any debt on or secured by a current bill of exchange or promissory note held by him, unless he is willing to treat the liability to him thereon of every person who is liable thereon antecedently to the debtor, and against whom a receiving order has not been made, as a security in his hands, and to estimate the value thereof, and for the purposes of voting, but not for the purposes of dividend, to deduct it from his proof.

12. It shall be competent to the trustee or to the official receiver, within twenty-eight days after a proof estimating the value of a security as aforesaid has been made use of in voting at any meeting, to require the creditor to give up the security for the benefit of the creditors generally on payment of the value so estimated, with an addition thereto of twenty per centum. Provided, that where a creditor has put a value on such security, he may, at any time before he has been required to give up such security as aforesaid, correct

such valuation by a new proof, and deduct such new value from his debt, but in that case such addition of twenty per centum shall not be made if the trustee requires the security to be given up.

13. If a receiving order is made against one partner of a firm, any creditor to whom that partner is indebted jointly with the other partner of the firm, or any of them, may prove his debt for the purpose of voting at any meeting of creditors, and shall be entitled to vote thereat.

14. The chairman of a meeting shall have power to admit or reject a proof for the purpose of voting, but his decision shall be subject to appeal to the Court. If he is in doubt whether the proof of a creditor should be admitted or rejected he shall mark the proof as objected to and shall allow the creditor to vote, subject to the vote being declared invalid in the event of the objection being sustained.

15. A creditor may vote either in person or by proxy.

18. A creditor may give a general proxy to his manager or clerk, or any other person in his regular employment. In such case the instrument of proxy shall state the relation in which the person to act thereunder stands to the creditor.

20. A proxy shall not be used unless it is deposited with the official receiver or trustee before the meeting at which it is to be used.

27. No person acting either under a general or special proxy shall vote in favour of any resolution which would directly or indirectly place himself, his partner or employer, in a position to receive any remuneration out of the estate of the debtor otherwise than as a creditor rateably with the other creditors of the debtor. Provided that where any person holds special proxies to vote for the appointment of himself as trustee he may use the said proxies and vote accordingly.

The official receiver, or some person nominated by him, shall be the chairman at the first meeting (Rule 7). SEE *Act of Bankruptcy; Bankruptcy; Public Examination of Debtor; Receiving Order*

The term 'meeting of creditors' also refers to the meeting called by a debtor who is in financial straits, sometimes with a view to getting such creditors to accept a composition. If the debtor at the meeting gives notice of suspension of payment of his debts, he commits an act of bankruptcy. As to what constitutes such a notice, see the case of the *Anglo-South American Bank Ltd* v *Urban District Council of Withernsea* under *Act of Bankruptcy*.

The term is also applicable to company liquidation, whether compulsory or voluntary. The Companies Act 1985, provides as follows.

533. The following provisions with respect to liquidators shall have effect on a winding-up order being made in England—

(*a*) the official receiver by virtue of his office becomes the provisional liquidator and shall continue to act as such until he or another person becomes liquidator and is capable of acting as such.

(*b*) the official receiver shall summon separate meetings of the creditors and contributories for the purpose of determining whether or not an application is to be made to the court for appointing a liquidator in place of the official receiver.

(*c*) the court may make any appointment and order required to give effect to any such determination and, if there is a difference between the determinations of the meetings of the creditors and contributories in respect of the matter aforesaid, the court shall decide the difference and make such order thereon as the court may think fit.

246.—(1) Subject to the provisions of this Act, the liquidator of a company which is being wound up by the court in England and Wales shall, in the administration of the company's assets and in their distribution amongst its creditors, have regard to any directions that may be given by resolution of the creditors or contributories at any general meeting or by the committee of inspection, and (2) directions given by the creditors or contributories at any general meeting are in case of conflict deemed to override any directions given by the committee of inspection.

(3) The liquidator may summon general meetings of the creditors or contributories for the purpose of ascertaining their wishes, and it shall be his duty to summon meetings at such times as the creditors or contributories, by resolution, (either at the meeting appointing the liquidator or otherwise,) may direct, or whenever requested in writing to do so by one-tenth in value of the creditors or contributories (as the case may be).

Section 588 of the Companies Act, 1985, is also relevant in that it provides for a meeting of creditors to take place with a view to voluntary liquidation. SEE *Winding up*

MEETINGS, COMPANIES The Companies Act, 1985 contains the following provisions relating to the meetings of companies. The section numbers are from the 1985 Act which re-enacts with some variations the relevant provisions of the 1948 Act, as amended by the 1980 Act.

Annual general meeting

366.—(1) Every company shall in each year hold a general meeting as its annual general meeting in addition to any other meetings in that year, and shall specify the meeting as such in the notices calling it.

(2) However, so long as a company holds its first annual general meeting within 18 months of its incorporation, it need not hold it in the year of its incorporation or in the following year.

(3) Not more than 15 months shall elapse between the date of one annual general meeting of a company and that of the next.

(4) If default is made in holding a meeting in accordance with this section, the company and every officer of it who is in default is liable to a fine.

Secretary of State's power to call meeting in default

367.—(1) If default is made in holding a meeting in accordance with section 366, the Secretary of State may, on the application of any member of the company, call, or direct the calling of, a general meeting of the company and give such ancillary or consequential directions as he thinks expedient, including directions modifying or supplementing, in relation to the calling, holding and conduct of the meeting, the operation of the company's articles.

(2) The directions that may be given under subsection (1) include a direction that one member of the company present in person or by proxy shall be deemed to constitute a meeting.

(3) If default is made in complying with directions of the Secretary of State under subsection (1), the company and every officer of it who is in default is liable to a fine.

(4) A general meeting held under this section shall, subject to any directions of the Secretary of State, be deemed to be an annual general meeting of the company; but, where a meeting so held is not held in the year in which the default in holding the company's annual general meeting occurred, the meeting so held shall not be treated as the annual general meeting for the year in which it is held unless at that meeting the company resolves that it be so treated.

(5) Where a company so resolves, a copy of the resolution shall, within 15 days after its passing, be forwarded to the registrar of companies and recorded by him; and if default is made in complying with this subsection, the company and every officer of it who is in default is liable to a fine and, for continued contravention, to a daily default fine.

Extraordinary general meeting on members' requisition

368.—(1) The directors of a company shall, on a members' requisition, forthwith proceed duly to convene an extraordinary general meeting of the company.

This applies notwithstanding anything in the company's articles.

(2) A members' requisition is a requisition of—

(*a*) members of the company holding at the date of the deposit of the requisition not less than one-tenth of such of the paid-up capital of the company as at that date carries the right of voting at general meetings of the company; or

(*b*) in the case of a company not having a share capital, members of it representing not less than one-tenth of the total voting rights of all the members having at the date of deposit of the requisition a right to vote at general meetings.

(3) The requisition must state the objects of the meeting, and must be signed by the requisitionists and deposited at the registered office of the company, and may consist of several documents in like form each signed by one or more requisitionists.

(4) If the directors do not within 21 days from the date of the deposit of the requisition proceed duly to convene a meeting, the requisitionists, or any of them representing more than one half of the total voting rights of all of them, may themselves convene a meeting, but any meeting so convened shall not be held after the expiration of 3 months from that date.

(5) A meeting convened under this section by requisitionists shall be convened in the same manner, as nearly as possible, as that in which meetings are to be convened by directors.

(6) Any reasonable expenses incurred by the requisitionists by reason of the failure of the directors duly to convene a meeting shall be repaid to the requisitionists by the company, and any sum so repaid shall be retained by the company out of any sums due or to become due from the company by way of fees or other remuneration in respect of their services to such of the directors as were in default.

(7) In the case of a meeting at which a resolution is to be proposed as a special resolution, the directors are deemed not to have duly convened the meeting if they do not give the notice required for special resolutions by section 378(2).

Length of notice of calling meetings

369.—(1) A provision of a company's articles is void in so far as it provides for the calling of a meeting of the company (other than an adjourned meeting) by a shorter notice than—

(*a*) in the case of the annual general meeting, 21 days' notice in writing; and

(*b*) in the case of a meeting other than an annual general meeting or a meeting for the passing of a special resolution—

(i) 7 days' notice in writing in the case of an unlimited company, and

(ii) otherwise, 14 days' notice in writing.

(2) Save in so far as the articles of a company make other provision in that behalf (not being a provision avoided by subsection (1)), a meeting of the company (other than an adjourned meeting) may be called—

(*a*) in the case of the annual general meeting, by 21 days' notice in writing; and

(*b*) in the case of a meeting other than an annual general meeting or a meeting for the passing of a special resolution—

(i) by 7 days' notice in writing in the case of an unlimited company, and

(ii) otherwise, 14 days' notice in writing.

(3) Notwithstanding that a meeting is called by shorter notice than that specified in subsection (2) or in the company's articles (as the case may be), it is deemed to have been duly called if it is so agreed—

(*a*) in the case of a meeting called as the annual general meeting, by all the members entitled to attend and vote at it; and

(*b*) otherwise, by the requisite majority.

(4) The requisite majority for this purpose is a majority in number of the members having a right to attend and vote at the meeting, being a majority—

(*a*) together holding not less than 95 per cent in nominal value of the shares giving a right to attend and vote at the meeting; or

(*b*) in the case of a company not having a share capital, together representing not less than 95 per cent of the total voting rights at that meeting of all the members.

General provisions as to meetings and votes

370.—(1) The following provisions have effect in so far as the articles of the company do not make other provision in that behalf.

(2) Notice of the meeting of a company shall be served on every member of it in the manner in which notices are required to be served by Table A (as for the time being in force).

(3) Two or more members holding not less than one-tenth of the issued share capital or, if the company does not have a share capital, not less than 5 per cent in number of the members of the company may call a meeting.

(4) Two members personally present are a quorum.

(5) Any member elected by the members present at a meeting may be chairman of it.

(6) In the case of a company originally having a share capital, every member has one vote in respect of each share or each £10 of stock held by him; and in any other case every member has one vote.

Power of court to order meeting

371.—(1) If for any reason it is impracticable to call a meeting of a company in any manner in which meetings of that company may be called, or to conduct the meeting in manner prescribed by the articles or this Act, the court may, either of its own motion or on the application—

(a) of any director of the company, or
(b) of any member of the company who would be entitled to vote at the meeting,

order a meeting to be called, held and conducted in any manner the court thinks fit.

(2) Where such an order is made, the court may give such ancillary or consequential directions as it thinks expedient; and these may include a direction that one member of the company present in person or by proxy be deemed to constitute a meeting.

(3) A meeting called, held and conducted in accordance with an order under subsection (1) is deemed for all purposes a meeting of the company duly called, held and conducted.

Proxies

372.—(1) Any member of a company entitled to attend and vote at a meeting of it is entitled to appoint another person (whether a member of not) as his proxy to attend and vote insted of him; and in the case of a private company a proxy appointed to attend and vote instead of a member has also the same right as the member to speak at the meeting.

(2) But, unless the articles otherwise provide—

(a) subsection (1) does not apply in the case of a company not having a share capital; and
(b) a member of a private company is not entitled to appoint more than one proxy to attend on the same occasion; and
(c) a proxy is not entitled to vote except on a poll.

(3) In the case of a company having a share capital, in every notice calling a meeting of the company there shall appear with reasonable prominence a statement that a member entitled to attend and vote is entitled to appoint a proxy or, where that is allowed, one or more proxies to attend and vote instead of him, and that a proxy need not also be a member.

(4) If default is made in complying with subsection (3) as respects any meeting, every officer of the company who is in default is liable to a fine.

(5) A provision contained in a company's articles is void in so far as it would have the effect of requiring the instrument appointing a proxy, or any other document necessary to show the validity of, or otherwise relating to, the appointment of a proxy, to be received by the company or any other person more than 48 hours before a meeting or adjourned meeting in order that the appointment may be effective.

(6) If for the purpose of any meeting of a company invitations to appoint as proxy a person or one of a number of persons specified in the invitations are issued at the company's expense to some only of the members entitled to be sent a notice of the meeting and to vote at it by proxy, then every officer of the company who knowingly and wilfully authorizes or permits their issue in that manner is liable to a fine.

However, an officer is not so liable by reason only of the issue to a member at his request in writing of a form of appointment naming the poxy, or of a list of persons willing to act as proxy, if the form or list is available on request in writing to every member entitled to vote at the meeting by proxy.

(7) This section applies to meetings of any class of members of a company as it applies to general meetings of the company.

Right to demand a poll

373.—(1) A provision contained in a company's articles is void in so far as it would have the effect either—

(a) of excluding the right to demand a poll at a general meeting on any question other than the election of the chairman of the meeting or the adjournment of the meeting; or
(b) of making ineffective a demand for a poll on any such question which is made either—
    (i) by not less than 5 members having the right to vote at the meeting; or
    (ii) by a member or members representing not less than one-tenth of the total voting rights of all the members having the right to vote at the meeting; or
    (iii) by a member or members holding shares in the company conferring a right to vote at the meeting, being shares on which an aggregate sum has been paid up equal to not less than one-tenth of the total sum paid up on all the shares conferring that right.

(2) The instrument appointing a proxy to vote at a meeting of a company is deemed also to confer authority to demand or join in demanding a poll; and for the purposes of subsection (1) a demand by a person as proxy for a member is the same as a demand by the member.

Voting on a poll

374. On a poll taken at a meeting of a company or a meeting of any class of members of a company, a member entitled to more than one vote need not, if he votes, use all his votes or cast all the votes he uses in the same way.

Representation of corporations at meetings

375.—(1) A corporation, whether or not a company within the meaning of this Act, may—

(a) if it is a member of another corporation, being such a company, by resolution of its directors or other governing body authorise such person as it thinks fit to act as its representative at any meeting of the company or at any meeting of any class of members of the company;

(b) if it is a creditor (including a holder of debentures) of another corporation, being such a company, by resolution of its directors or other governing body authorise such person as it thinks fit to act as its representative at any meeting of creditors of the company held in pursuance of this Act or of rules made under it, or in pursuance of the provisions contained in any debenture or trust deed, as the case may be.

(2) A person so authorized is entitled to exercise the same powers on behalf of the corporation which he represents as that corporation could exercise if it were an individual shareholder, creditor or debenture-holder of the other company.

MEMORANDUM OF ASSOCIATION This is the principal document of incorporation by which a company is brought into existence. It is normally read together with the articles of association and in broad terms the memorandum governs the relationship of the company with the outside world, whereas the articles govern the internal management of the company and the powers of its officers, etc. SEE *Articles of Association*

The main statutory provisions regarding a company's memorandum of association are now contained in Sections 2–6 of the Companies Act, 1985, as follow:

2.—(1) The memorandum of every company must state—

(a) the name of the company;

(b) whether the registered office of the company is to be situated in England and Wales, or in Scotland;

(c) the objects of the company.

(2) Alternatively to subsection (1)(b), the memorandum may contain a statement that the company's registered office is to be situated in Wales; and a company whose registered office is situated in Wales may by special resolution alter its memorandum so as to provide that its registered office is to be so situated.

(3) The memorandum of a company limited by shares or by guarantee must also state that the liability of its members is limited.

(4) The memorandum of a company limited by guarantee must also state that each member undertakes to contribute to the assets of the company if it should be wound up while he is a member, or within one year after he ceases to be a member, for payment of the debts and liabilities of the company contracted before he ceases to be a member, and of the costs, charges and expenses of winding up, and for adjustment of the rights of the contributories among themselves, such amount as may be required, not exceeding a specified amount.

(5) In the case of a company having a share capital—

(a) the memorandum must also (unless it is an unlimited company) state the amount of the share capital with which the company proposes to be registered and the division of the share capital into shares of a fixed amount;

(b) no subscriber of the memorandum may take less than one share; and

(c) there must be shown in the memorandum against the name of each subscriber the number of shares he takes.

(6) The memorandum must be signed by each subscriber in the presence of at least one witness, who must attest the signature; and that attestation is sufficient in Scotland as well as in England and Wales.

(7) A company may not alter the conditions contained in its memorandum except in the cases, in the mode and to the extent, for which express provision is made by this Act.

3.—(1) Subject to the provisions of sections 1 and 2, the form of the memorandum of association of—

(a) a public company, being a company limited by shares,

(b) a public company, being a company limited by guarantee and having a share capital,

(c) a private company limited by shares,

(d) a private company limited by guarantee and not having a share capital,

(e) a private company limited by guarantee and having a share capital, and

(f) an unlimited company having a share capital,

shall be as specified respectively for such companies by regulations made by the Secretary of State, or as near to that form as circumstances admit.

(2) Regulations under this section shall be made by statutory instrument subject to annulment in pursuance of a resolution of either House of Parliament.

4. A company may by special resolution alter its memorandum with respect to the objects of the company, so far as may be required to enable it—

(a) to carry on its business more economically or more efficiently; or

(b) to attain its main purpose by new or improved means; or

(c) to enlarge or change the local area of its operations; or

(d) to carry on some business which under existing circumstances may conveniently or advantageously be combined with the business of the company; or

(e) to restrict or abandon any of the objects specified in the memorandum; or

(f) to sell or dispose of the whole or any part of the undertaking of the company; or

(g) to amalgamate with any other company or body of persons;

but if an application is made under the following section, the alteration does not have effect except in so far as it is confirmed by the court.

5.—(1) Where a company's memorandum has been altered by special resolution under section 4, application may be made to the court for the alteration to be cancelled.

(2) Such an application may be made—

(a) by the holders of not less in the aggregate than 15 per cent in nominal value of the company's issued share capital or any class of it or, if the company is not limited by shares, not less than 15 per cent of the company's members; or

(*b*) by the holders of not less than 15 per cent of the company's debentures entitling the holders to object to an alteration of its objects;

but an application shall not be made by any person who has consented to or voted in favour of the alteration.

(3) The application must be made within 21 days after the date on which the resolution altering the company's objects was passed, and may be made on behalf of the persons entitled to make the application by such one or more of their number as they may appoint in writing for the purpose.

(4) The court may on such an application make an order confirming the alteration either wholly or in part and on such terms and conditions as it thinks fit, and may—

(*a*) if it thinks fit, adjourn the proceedings in order that an arrangement may be made to its satisfaction for the purchase of the interests of dissentient members, and

(*b*) give such directions and make such orders as it thinks expedient for facilitating or carrying into effect any such arrangement.

(5) The court's order may (if the court thinks fit) provide for the purchase by the company of the shares of any members of the company, and for the reduction accordingly of its capital, and may make such alterations in the company's memorandum and articles as may be required in consequence of that provision.

(6) If the court's order requires the company not to make any, or any specified, alteration in its memorandum or articles, the company does not then have power without the leave of the court to make any such alteration in breach of that requirement.

(7) An alteration in the memorandum or articles of a company made by virtue of an order under this section, other than one made by resolution of the company, is of the same effect as if duly made by resolution; and this Act applies accordingly to the memorandum or articles as so altered.

(8) The debentures entitling the holders to object to an alteration of a company's objects are any debentures secured by a floating charge which were issued or first issued before 1st December 1947 or form part of the same series as any debentures so issued; and a special resolution altering a company's objects requires the same notice to the holders of any such debentures as to member of the company.

In the absence of provisions, regulating the giving of notice to any such debenture holdings, the provisions of the company's articles regulating the giving of notice to members apply.

6.—(1) Where a company passes a resolution altering its objects, then—

(*a*) if with respect to the resolution no application is made under section 5, the company shall within 15 days from the end of the period for making such an application deliver to the registrar of companies a printed copy of its memorandum as altered; and

(*b*) if such an application is made, the company shall—

(i) forthwith give notice (in the prescribed form) of that fact to the registrar, and

(ii) within 15 days from the date of any order cancelling or confirming the alteration, deliver to the registrar an office copy of the order and, in the case of an order confirming the alteration, a printed copy of the memorandum as altered.

(2) The court may by order at any time extend the time for the delivery of documents to the registrar under subsection (1)(*b*) for such period as the court may think proper.

(3) If a company makes default in giving notice or delivering any document to the registrar of companies as required by subsection (1), the company and every officer of it who is in default is liable to a fine and, for continued contravention, to a daily default fine.

(4) The validity of an alteration of a company's memorandum with respect to the objects of the company shall not be questioned on the ground that it was not authorized by section 4, except in proceedings taken for the purpose (whether under section 5 or otherwise) before the expiration of 21 days after the date of the resolution in that behalf.

(5) Where such proceedings are taken otherwise than under section 5, subsections (1) to (3) above apply in relation to the proceedings as if they had been taken under that section, and as if an order declaring the alteration invalid were an order cancelling it, and as if an order dismissing the proceedings were an order confirming the alteration.

With regard to the objects clause in the memorandum, the decision in *Cotman* v *Brougham* [1918] AC 514, to the effect that a clause was valid enabling every object stated to be treated itself as a principal object, has been widely adopted. Nevertheless, in 1970 in *Introductions Ltd* v *National Provincial Bank Ltd* [1970] Ch 199, the Court of Appeal ruled that a clause empowering the company to borrow, even though backed by a further clause making 'the object set out in each sub-clause ... independent objects of the company' did not legitimize borrowing not set out in the company's memorandum. Harman, LJ, said, 'Borrowing is not an end in itself and must be for some purpose of the company ... you cannot convert a power into an object merely by saying so.'

Sanction is given by the 1985 Act to alter the memorandum of association in certain ways as indicated below.

A company limited by shares, if authorized by its articles, may alter its memorandum to increase its share capital, consolidate its share capital into shares of larger amount, convert paid-up shares into stock and reconvert stock into shares, subdivide its shares, and cancel certain shares. (For particulars see Section 121 under heading *Share Capital*.) The conditions in the memorandum may, under certain circumstances, be modified so as to reorganize the share capital.

The amount of the share capital and of the shares may be reduced. See the provisions in Section 135, under *Reduction of Share Capital*.

Any company may, by special resolution, and with the approval of the Department of Trade and Industry change its name. SEE *Names of Companies*.

A company may provide that a specified portion of the uncalled capital shall not be capable of being called up except in the event and for the purposes of the company being wound up. See Section 124 under *Company Unlimited*.

A limited company, if so authorized by its articles, may, by special resolution, alter its memorandum so as to render unlimited the liability of its directors, or managers (Section 307).

By the Companies Act 1985, alterations in the memorandum or articles of a company increasing liability to contribute to share capital shall not bind existing members without their consent (Section 16). SEE ALSO *Company Purchase of Own Shares; Private Company; Public Company; Ultra Vires*.

MEMORANDUM OF DEPOSIT (LETTER OF DEPOSIT) A document setting forth the terms under which a deposit of security is made. It may be the written evidence of a pledge (as where bearer bonds are deposited as security); it may accompany a deposit of share certificates, constituting an equitable mortgage as where the shares are left in the depositor's name, or a legal mortgage as where the shares are put into the name of the bank's nominee; it may be given where title deeds are deposited with intent to give a charge over them, as evidence of the equitable mortgage.

The memorandum of deposit taken in respect of Stock Exchange securities usually contains the following features: a declaration that the securities listed in the schedule at the foot have been deposited as security. This settles the question of the depositor's intention and avoids the possibility of a later claim that the items were lodged for safe custody. The debt which the security covers is defined to cover existing and future advances so as to get a continuing security not adversely affected by the operation of the Rule in Clayton's Case (q.v.). The debt will also be phrased to cover all possible liabilities on current account, guarantees, etc. An agreement follows to maintain a specified margin of cover and an admission of the bank's power of sale is given. Reasonable notice of the bank's intention to exercise this power will have to be given unless it is expressed as immediate. If the shares are left in the depositor's name and no transfers have been signed, the power of sale will be ineffectual without recourse to the court. In some cases, an agreement follows to accept back, not necessarily the identical shares lodged, but shares of the same class and denomination. Otherwise it would appear that where shares are transferred to the bank's nominees, the depositor could demand the return of the identical shares lodged. The schedule of security lodged should be signed by the depositor. Many banks also use a memorandum of deposit without a schedule of specific items, which is phrased to cover all items at any time held by the bank for any purpose whatsoever. A company can execute the form under the hand of duly authorized officials, and in such a case a certified copy of the authorizing resolution should be filed attached to the memorandum.

A memorandum of deposit accompanying a deposit of title deeds will begin with the aforementioned declaration as to the purpose of the deposit—for security and not for safe custody—and will follow with a charge on the property detailed in the schedule to the memorandum. A continuing security will be given with an undertaking to repay on demand all existing moneys owing and all future sums borrowed so as to avoid the operation of the Rule in Clayton's Case diminishing the security. Provision for adequate insurance will be made and immediate powers of sale will be taken. There will also be convenants to execute a legal mortgage if the bank desires to perfect its security, and to execute any necessary documents to convey the property to a purchaser if the bank exercises its power of sale. Enforcement of these convenants, however, may require resort to the court. Some banks incorporate in the memorandum of deposit an irrevocable power of attorney in favour of an official of the bank to enable a sale to be effected; for the same purpose there may be a declaration of trust by the depositor of the security in favour of the bank with power to the bank to appoint fresh trustees. A limited company may execute a memorandum under hand as beforementioned. The depositor's execution of the form should be witnessed and the schedule of deeds and documents should be signed by the depositor.

No registration of an equitable mortgage is required where the deeds are deposited, except in the case of a limited company, where registration on the company's register of charges at Companies House is required. SEE ALSO *Mortgage*

MEMORANDUM OF SATISFACTION A notice addressed to the Registrar of Companies, which has to be entered on the register pursuant to Section 403 of the Companies Act 1985 (SEE *Registration of Charges*), that a mortgage or charge has been satisfied in whole or in part. The document requires to be impressed with a 25p Companies Registration Fee Stamp.

The form of the document is

The ... Limited hereby gives notice that the [insert here 'mortgage' or 'charge', 'debentures' or 'debenture stock' as the case may be] dated the ... day of .... One thousand nine hundred and ..., and created by the Company for securing the sum of £... was satisfied to the extent of £... on the ... of ... 19....

In witness whereof the common seal of the Company was hereunto affixed the ... day of ..., One thousand nine hundred and ... in the presence of

.... } *Directors*
....

.... *Secretary*

Accompanying the memorandum of satisfaction is a statutory declaration (no stamp) verifying the same:

'We ..., of ..., a director of the above-named Company, and ... of ... the Secretary of the above-named Company, solemnly and sincerely declare that the particulars contained in the Memorandum of Satisfaction dated ... now produced to us, are true to the best of our knowledge, information and belief. And we make this solemn Declaration, conscientiously believing the same to be true, and by virtue of the provisions of the Statutory Declarations Act 1835.

Declared by the said, etc.

The party in whose favour the charge is given has no part in agreeing to the filing of the memorandum of satisfaction, but before the Registrar will enter it on the file, he will address a warning notice to the owner of the charge giving him the opportunity of objecting.

By Section 403 the Registrar is empowered to register a memorandum of satisfaction of part of a debt or part of the property or undertaking charged.

MENTAL INCAPACITY Where a banker receives notice of a customer's mental disorder, his authority to pay the latter's cheques is countermanded; likewise, all other authorities and mandates given by the customer are in abeyance.

The Mental Health Act 1959 was a comprehensive enactment aimed at removing the stigma of lunacy from a person of unsound mind, who is now recognized as suffering from mental illness. This may be acknowledged in a number of ways.

1. A person may be compulsorily admitted to a hospital or a recognized nursing home on the grounds of mental disorder, for observation or treatment. A patient admitted for observation may be kept there for 28 days only, unless he or she has become liable to be detained for a further period as a result of a subsequent application or direction. The application for the admission should be made by the nearest relative or by a mental welfare officer to the managers of the hospital concerned, and must be supported by the recommendations of two medical practitioners who have recently examined the patient.
2. An application supported by two medical recommendations may be made to the local health authority for the appointment of a guardian. The authority may itself undertake the duty or may appoint the applicant, or any other suitable person. The acceptance of an application by the authority confers on the guardian the same powers in relation to the patient as those which may be exercised by a father in respect of his child who is under 14 years of age.
3. A hospital order may be made by a court for the compulsory admission and detention in a hospital of a person convicted in criminal proceedings, or already serving a prison sentence.
4. A person may voluntarily obtain hospital mental treatment.

Notice that a customer is suffering from mental disorder should be verified as soon as possible, but prima facie a person detained in a hospital or elsewhere, or subject to guardianship, may be regarded as mentally incapable. The entry of a patient into a hospital is not of itself a sufficient ground for the banker to stop his customer's account, for the entry may be a voluntary act. The managers of the hospital should be consulted as to whether the patient is capable of handling business matters. His state of health may vary from time to time and the managers should be asked to keep the bank advised. If the customer is not a full-time patient, other evidence may be necessary, preferably a medical certificate signed by two doctors. The appointment of a guardian would preclude the patient acting for himself.

Pending the appointment of a receiver, a banker may safely arrange for payments for necessaries. Although the expression is somewhat narrowly defined in practice, the cost of maintaining the patient can usually be covered. If in doubt the banker sometimes seeks an indemnity from a third party against the risk he is taking.

Once the customer is proved mentally incapable, all operations on his account must be suspended except to the extent mentioned above. The Court of Protection will make an order for the administration of the property and affairs of a person suffering from mental illness, such order usually providing for the appointment of a receiver and defining his powers and duties.

A receiver is authorized by the Court to receive and administer the assets of the estate according to the directions of the Court and must produce evidence of his appointment in the shape of the Order of Appointment, and the banker should ask for and retain an office copy of the Order bearing the stamp of the High Court. The Order has a threefold purpose: it is evidence of the receiver's authority, it provides for the disposition of the patient's estate, and it provides a Lodgment Schedule detailing what moneys and securities are to be delivered to the Accountant-General of the High Court. The main part of the Order provides for payment of the patient's debts and for the maintenance of the patient and any dependants. Surplus assets are usually directed in the Lodgment Schedule to be handed over to the Accountant-General. Sometimes there is no definite order in the Lodgment Schedule for this to be done, and then a separate Lodgment Order is supplied to the banker.

The terms of an Order of Appointment of a receiver should be strictly followed and, if moneys or securities are held which are not covered by its terms, reference should be made to the judge of the Court of Protection. Where a customer is known to be mentally incapable, a banker may safely give particulars of the account, etc., to a solicitor, who states that he is applying to the High Court for the appointment of a receiver.

A receiver should open a separate account suitably earmarked as to the patient's estate. The powers of a receiver cease immediately on the death of a patient in favour of the latter's personal representative (*Re Walker* [1907] 2 Ch 120).

The Personal Application Division of the Court of Protection facilitates the administration of the estates of mental patients, especially where the estate is small. The next-of-kin or best friend can by this means be appointed receiver cheaply and expeditiously.

On notice of the mental incapacity of a guarantor the principal debtor's account must be stopped (*Bradford Old Bank* v *Sutcliffe* [1918] 34 TLR 619).

The mental incapacity of a partner does not operate as a dissolution of the firm, but by Section 35 of the Partnership Act 1890, is ground for petitioning the court for a dissolution at the instance of a co-partner of the incapable partner's receiver. By Section 103 of the Mental Health Act 1959, the court may dissolve a partnership if a partner becomes of unsound mind.

Mental incapacity may be set up as a defence in an action on a bill as between immediate parties if the plaintiff was aware of the incapacity when he took the bill, but it is of no avail against a holder in due course (*Imperial Loan Co* v *Stone* [1892] 1 QB 599 CA).

Subject to certain provisos to be found in Section 22 of the Limitation Act 1939, any right of action accruing to a person under a disability (such as unsoundness of mind) may be brought at any time before the expiration of six years from the date when the person ceased to be under a disability, notwithstanding that the period of limitation has expired.

MENTALLY DISABLED, TRUSTS FOR A trust set up for the benefit of a mentally disabled person will enjoy exemption from capital transfer tax, provided the trust was set up during the lifetime of the mentally disabled person and at least one-half of the settled funds are held for the benefit of that person during his or her life. Such trusts are usually in discretionary form but will be exempt from the periodic charge (SEE *Capital Transfer Tax*) and distributions may be made for the benefit of the mentally disabled person without incurring a charge to tax.

The transfer of funds to such a settlement when it is set up will also be exempt from capital transfer tax if the disabled person is the settlor. He or she will be deemed to be the settlor if the Court has made the settlement on his or her behalf.

Trustees of trusts for the mentally disabled are entitled to the full small gains exemption for the purpose of capital gains tax, rather than the one-half exemption which applies to other trusts.

MERCANTILE AGENT SEE UNDER *Factors Act 1889*

MERCHANT BANKING The late Sir Edward Reid in his Presidential Address to the Institute of Bankers in May 1963, said that the term 'merchant bank' 'is sometimes applied to banks who are not merchants, sometimes to merchants who are not banks, and sometimes to houses who are neither merchants or banks'. The term has its origin in the merchanting activities of the late 18th and early 19th centuries when trade between countries would be financed by bills of exchange drawn on the principal merchanting houses. At that point, the merchants were merely financing their own trading activities. As international trade grew and other lesser-known names wished to import goods from abroad, the established merchants 'lent their names' to the newcomers by agreeing to accept bills of exchange on their behalf. The 'accepting house' would charge a commission for this service and thus there grew up the business of accepting bills to finance the trade not merely of themselves, but of others. Acceptance business thus became and to a degree always has been the hallmark of the true merchant bank. The acceptance 'credit' was primarily a means of financing international trade until the 1930s, but the use of acceptance credits for domestic business was given an impetus in 1931 by the Macmillan Report (q.v.). The Macmillan Committee recommended that commercial bills be used more widely as a means of financing domestic trade and either for this reason or because of the falling-off in foreign trade and the difficulties of a number of countries, bills of exchange became more widely used as a means of financing domestic trade. Although bank overdrafts were comparatively cheap by present-day standards, it was cheaper still to finance current transactions by means of acceptance credits. Thus bill finance became and still remains a valuable alternative source of finance for the shorter-term transactions of industry in the UK. Seventeen of the leading merchant banks constitute the Accepting Houses Committee, which acts as the regulatory and disciplinary body and also the principal mouthpiece of the UK merchant banks.

The second historical characteristic of the merchant banks was the raising of capital for foreign governments. In many cases, the merchants had been trading in the countries concerned and had gained the confidence of the governments and other authorities in those countries. So it was that they were entrusted with the issuing of bonds in the London market. Originally, the interest on such bond issues would be payable in foreign currency, but in 1818 Nathan Rothschild, the founder of N.M. Rothschild & Sons, floated the first foreign loans carrying interest in sterling and in the next 100 years or so, despite the interruption of the First World War, loan after loan was to be raised in London for foreign governments. Hambros Bank made 13 issues of loans for continental governments in the three years 1926–28; Morgan Grenfell & Co, handled six issues in those years; and Barings dealt with 12, all of them for various countries around the world.

As with acceptance credits, it was international business which preceded the developments in the domestic market. During the spate of foreign government loans, there had been very few issues for industry in the UK. The foreign bond business ceased with the failure of international currencies and the lack of international confidence. Those years—the 1930s—were to see the gradual move of British industry into a new dimension partly from growth within and partly from mergers. New capital was required and the merchant banks with their vast experience were on hand, both with expert advice and the machinery for capital issues. Thus the second principal ingredient of merchant banking became and still is the raising of capital through the issue of stock or bonds. This business, however, was not by any means the preserve of the merchant banks. Some of the leading stockbrokers have a long tradition of issuing work, and there are many firms with no tradition of commercial credit business which have undertaken capital issues. The regulatory body is the Issuing Houses Association (q.v.).

Thus there are accepting houses and issuing houses, and most of the leading merchant banks are in both categories. Together they make up the merchant banking scene. Some retain their original merchanting activities and all have moved into new financial activities. The scope of those activities was well summed up in the evidence of the Accepting Houses Committee to the Radcliffe Committee, which may be paraphrased as follows.

The granting of acceptance credits is a business which all have in common.
Many of the members act as issuing houses.
All conduct banking accounts in one form or another for customers at home and abroad.
All handle stock exchange business on their customers' behalf.
Most of them manage investments for private customers, pension funds, colleges and charities.
Several members have an active trustee business.
Several conduct registration work for companies.
Three are prominent in the bullion market.
Several are active dealers in foreign exchange.
Several handle insurance business.
Two run merchanting companies.
One owns subsidiary companies in the production and marketing of timber and one trades in rubber.
One is prominent in the London Coffee Market.

In addition, accepting houses and issuing houses manage investment trust companies, unit trusts, life assurance companies, pensions, consultancy services and almost every other form of financial activity.

Two particular characteristics are usually attributed to merchant bankers. They are (1) their entrepreneurial instinct, which is borne out in many ways—at one time by their merchanting activities and their handling of government loans, which in the early days they would take on to their own books in full before placing them with the public; and (2) their adaptability, borne out not only by the widespread nature of their present-day activities, but by their ability to adjust to changing circumstances over the years. A good example is their approach to the Euro-dollar (or Euro-currency)—the making of a market which enabled the principal currencies of the world to be used outside their countries of origin.

The principal activities of the present-day merchant banks tend now to be medium-term lending, corporate finance advice, new capital issues, equity participation in developing companies and various forms of investment management. Nowadays, most of the clearing banks participate, either directly or indirectly in merchant banking activities, e.g. Barclays Bank through Barclays Merchant Bank, Midland Bank through Samuel Montagu & Co, National Westminster Bank through County Bank, Bank of Scotland through the British Linen Bank and Royal Bank Group through Charterhouse Japhet.

MERGERS SEE *Take-overs and Mergers*

MIDDLE PRICE On the Stock Exchanges a dealer buys at one price (the offer price) and sells at another (the bid price). The middle price for a particular security is half way between the offer and bid prices.

MILLING The indented or ridged edge of a coin. In former times, the edges of coins were frequently clipped or filed by dishonest persons and the clippings or filings sold by weight. In order to prevent that practice, milling was invented. The edge of a coin is also turned up in order that the raised flanges may afford a certain amount of protection to the figures on both sides of the coin. SEE *Coinage*

MINIMUM LENDING RATE (MLR) The minimum rate quoted by the Bank of England for lending money to the money markets. It was in 1972 that the former Bank Rate (q.v.) was replaced by Minimum Lending Rate on the basis that MLR would more truly reflect the supply of and demand for money in the market. The intention was that MLR would be $\frac{1}{2}$ per cent above the average of each Friday's Treasury Bill tender rate, but in practice it was found that the Bank of England had to intervene to influence the levels of rates in the market.

From 20th August, 1981, MLR was suspended and the Bank of England no longer publishes a Minimum Lending Rate on a continuous basis. It may from time to time, however, announce a minimum rate which, for a period ahead, it would apply to loans to the market. In fact, the Bank did revert to announcing it's Minimum Lending Rate on 14th January, 1985, in order to exercise a degree of authority over interest rates in the particular turmoil of that time.

MINT The Mint, or more correctly the Royal Mint, is the place where the official coinage of the UK is made. The name appears to have been derived from the Anglo-Saxon *mynet*, meaning a coin, or the latin *moneta*, surname of Juno, whose temple was used by the Romans as a mint.

Coins have been minted in the British Isles since the first century BC, usually in various places around the country, under the authority of various rulers. It is known that the London Mint was producing coins as early as 825 but it is reasonably certain that London, as the capital of Mercia, minted coins even before this date. From earliest times, coins could be minted only with the authority of the Crown, although the Archbishops of Canterbury and York issued their own personal coins until the end of the tenth century and ecclesiastical mints at Canterbury, York and Durham, continued until they were abolished by Henry VIII.

In early times, it was the practice to establish a mint in each sizeable town because of the difficulty of transporting large quantities of coin. At the time of Aethelstan in the early tenth century, there were apparently 36 mints around the country but after another 300 years, nearly all the coin in the country was minted by London or Canterbury.

The London Mint was originally established in Westminster but moved in 1300 to a building erected in the Tower of London, between the inner and outer walls. It remained there for 500 years but then, with the need for greater space, moved to Tower Hill, where the first coins were struck in 1810.

The Royal Mint is not only responsible for the provision of coins for circulation in the UK but also conducts a very substantial export business in the provision of coins for other countries. By the 1960s the Mint was producing over 1,000 million coins a year, compared with a figure of only about 25 million 100 years earlier. The growth of the business and the anticipation of decimalization led to the move of the Royal Mint in 1968 from London to Llantrisant, near Cardiff. The production of coins was gradually transferred from London to Llantrisant until the last coin, a gold sovereign was struck in London in 1975.

Historically, the Master of the Mint was under contract to the Crown and out of his remuneration he paid for all the necessary tools and he paid the workforce. He had powers to obtain labour, if necessary, by press-gangs. Nowadays, the Chancellor of the Exchequer is ex officio Master of the

Mint. In addition to the production of coins, the Royal Mint strikes military medals and decorations, the Great Seals of the UK and the seals of office of Ministers of the Crown. A Royal Mint advisory committee advises the Deputy Master and Comptroller on all matters connected with the designing and preparation of seals, coins, medals and decorations.

MIRAS (MORTGAGE INTEREST RELIEF AT SOURCE) This is a system of income tax relief on mortgage interest, introduced with effect from 6th April, 1983. Prior to that date, interest on mortgage loans was paid gross and if the loan interest qualified for income tax relief this was taken into account in the PAYE coding (SEE *Pay-As-You-Earn*). The MIRAS system applies only to qualifying loans, principally those for house purchase and house improvement, up to the present limit of £30,000. The system applies only to basic rate tax—higher rates of tax are taken into account as hitherto in the PAYE coding in the case of employed persons. Mortgage interest relief at source applies to loans from banks and building societies and other lenders approved by the Treasury for the purpose of the scheme. SEE Supplement

MOBILITY ALLOWANCE This is a Social Security benefit which may be claimed by any person from age 5 up to age 65 if they are unable or almost unable to walk because of physical disablement. If the allowance is granted it may continue to the age of 75. It is a cash benefit paid at a flat weekly rate. It is non-contributory and is not means-tested. The claimant must however, produce satisfactory medical evidence. With effect from the 1982 Finance Act, mobility allowance is not taxable.

MONETARY POLICY This is a term of economics, rather than finance, but it nevertheless has considerable financial implications. Monetary policy is that aspect of a government's management of the economy which is concerned with the supply of and demand for money in the economy. It may be compared with fiscal policy, which is concerned with that aspect of economic management achieved by taxation. There are many instruments of monetary policy. They have included over the years (and in some instances still include) the enforcement of liquidity ratios (q.v.) and reserve asset ratios (q.v.); open market policy (q.v.); qualitative constraints on bank lending; quantitative constraints on bank lending; hire purchase controls; movement of Bank Rate (q.v.) and Minimum Lending Rate (q.v.); the 'corset' (q.v.); special deposits (q.v.); temporary ceilings on deposit interest rates and selective credit controls, e.g. emphasis on exports but constraint on property development. SEE *Lending by Banks; M0, M1, M2 and M3*

MONEY The standard by which the value of commodities is measured, and the medium by which they are bought and sold. Money, and credit, to which it gave birth, form the basis on which the business of banking has been built up. There is probably nothing which is of greater material importance in the civilized world than money, and nothing which comes more closely in contact with mankind in every department of life. Not only have all conceivable commodities a monetary value attached to them, but it is customary to ascribe a financial reason as the prime moving cause (either directly or indirectly) in almost every action in which a man is concerned.

In the primitive ages, there was no money, and when anyone wished to obtain food which belonged to another person, possession had to be obtained by barter; that is, some article considered of equal value, and of which the person who owned the food was in need, had to be offered in exchange. If one man was rich in food possessions and another in skins, there would be much inconvenience in always arranging a suitable exchange, as the food owner might not be in need of skins. This difficulty led most communities at a very early date, after experience with various substitutes, to adopt metals, particularly gold and silver, as a circulating medium. In the case supposed, the owner of food was then able to exchange his goods for a certain quantity of metal, which metal he could use for the purpose of obtaining from other persons articles which were more useful to him than skins.

In the Iliad, Homer says that the armour of Diomede was worth only nine oxen, and the armour of Glaucus was worth 100 oxen, which indicates that in those days oxen were regarded as a standard of value. Cattle were of great importance in the early states of civilization, and in several languages the name for money is identical with that of some kind of cattle or domesticated animal. *Pecunia*, the latin word for money, is derived from *pecus*, cattle; our word fee is derived from the Anglo-Saxon *feoh*, meaning alike money and cattle; and the words capital, chattel, and cattle are derived from the word *capitale*. Kine were called *capitale* because they were counted by the *caput*, or head.

At different periods and in various countries, many articles have been used to meet the necessity, which was felt by all, of having something to act as a measure of value. In India, certain parts of Southern Asia, and in Africa, shells, called cowries, are still used as a currency. Money is represented in Tibet and parts of China by small blocks of compressed tea; in Ethiopia by blocks of rock salt; and in some districts of Africa by dates. Sugar, tobacco, dried cod, dressed leather, furs, pieces of cloth, elephants' teeth, carved wood, and many other objects have been used for the same purpose. Carved pebbles were used by the Ethiopians, and Adam Smith relates that, even in his day (1776), there was a village in Scotland where it was not uncommon for a workman to carry nails instead of money to the baker's shop or the ale house. In more recent times, cigarettes have been used as a medium of exchange and a store of value, and postage stamps are still used as such in some countries, notably in the Middle East.

All that is necessary for the use of a commodity as money is that it should be accepted as such by a community. The use of metallic tokens or coins became particularly acceptable because they have the advantages of durability, portability, homogeneity and the ability for the supply to be controlled. Silver was used by the Hebrews and the first mention of money as a medium of exchange is found in Genesis, where Abraham purchased the cave of Machpelah from Ephron the Hittite, and weighed to Ephron 'four hundred shekels of silver, current money with the merchant'. It would appear that when first the metals, whether iron, copper, gold, or silver, were used they were in rude ingots or bars without any stamp or designation upon them, and when being paid over they had, as in the case of Abraham's famous purchase, to be weighed in scales. The inconvenience of always having to weigh the metals, and the difficulty also of knowing whether the quality of the metal was really what is was supposed to be, ultimately brought about the invention of coins. The Chinese are reported to have made coins as early as 2250 BC. The ingots, which had hitherto been so troublesome, were, by the invention of coins, divided up into pieces of different values so that they could be available for the smallest of purchases and operate as the medium of commerce without the process of weighing, a process which, in the case of the precious metals, was unreliable and open to misuse. The trouble of assaying the metals was done away with, for the coins at length came to bear upon their faces the government stamp, which, as a rule, assured the holder that they were of a certain quality of metal. The true nature or function of money is the right or title to demand something from others. John Stuart Mill says

> The pounds or shillings which a person receives weekly or yearly are not what constitute his income; they are a sort of tickets or orders which he can present for payment at any shop he pleases, and which entitle him to receive a certain value of any commodity that he makes choice of.

The word 'money' is derived from the temple of Juno Moneta, which was used by the Romans as a mint. SEE *Coinage; Gold Coin; Mint*

MONEY BOND A single premium life policy taken out for investment purposes, the premium being invested by the insurance company in short-dated deposits in the money markets. SEE *Bonds*

MONEY BROKER A person who operates in the money markets, placing funds on behalf of clients. He may, for example, deal with substantial sums on behalf of pension funds, building societies and other institutions which may not necessarily have the facilities for dealing direct in the market. The term is also applied to certain stockbroking firms who are authorized to borrow gilts and equities from various City institutions, including banks, and to lend them to jobbers.

MONEY AT CALL AND SHORT NOTICE This is one of the main items of liquidity in a bank's balance sheet. It comprises advances to stockbrokers and jobbers and, more particularly, loans to the money market. Such moneys are payable, either on demand or on a few days notice. Money lent to the market in this way is fully secured by Treasury bills, commercial bills, certificates of deposit and other forms of short-term paper. Traditionally, money at call was the safety net by which banks met certain outflows of funds. To a considerable extent, this role has now been taken over by inter-bank transfers in what is sometimes called the 'parallel' markets. If a bank experiences a major withdrawal of deposits or an upsurge in demand for its lending, the necessary movement is achieved in the inter-bank market and, in fact, only quite minor outflows of funds could be met from money at call through the discount market.

MONEY FUNDS A money fund is a vehicle which enables comparatively small amounts of money to be subscribed by the public and invested in the money market at rates of interest which are attractive by comparison with normal bank deposit rates. The minimum deposit may be quite high, e.g. £10,000, but in most cases, the minimum is £2,500 or even less. At the time of writing, money funds earn approximately three per cent per annum more than a seven-day deposit account with a clearing bank.

There are two types of money fund: those which are said to be 'off balance sheet' and those which are included in the balance sheet.

The off-balance-sheet type of fund is in some respects similar to a unit trust. It is a separate fund managed for the benefit of the subscribers with assets and liabilities exactly matched in order to minimize the risk. Because the fund is kept separate from the main balance sheet of the promoters, there is no risk arising from any pressures which may affect that balance sheet. On the other hand, deposits in such off-balance-sheet funds are not covered by the deposit protection fund under the Banking Act. The other category of funds, i.e. those which are 'on balance sheet' are perhaps more common. They are more truly a banking operation in that the deposits are held in the main balance sheet of the deposit-taking concern. The deposits are not necessarily matched in the balance sheet but they are covered by the guarantee of a 75 per cent return of the deposited money to a maximum of £10,000 in the event of the insolvency or other failure of the deposit taker.

In most cases, money fund deposits may be withdrawn on demand or on seven days notice. Some of the institutions offering money funds also provide a cheque book service.

MONEYLENDERS' ACTS 1900–1927 SEE *Moneylender*

MONEYLENDER Under the Moneylenders' Acts 1900 to 1927, the term 'moneylender' includes every person whose business is that of moneylending or who advertises or announces himself or holds himself out in any way as carrying on that business, subject, however, to a number of exceptions, the most important of which were registered friendly societies, banking and insurance businesses and building societies. The Board of Trade (now the Department of Trade and Industry) also had power under Section 123, Companies Act 1967, to issue certificates to the effect that a party was bona fide engaged in the business of banking and thus exempted from the Moneylenders' Acts. The Moneylenders' Acts were repealed by the Consumer Credit Act 1974, (q.v.) and Section 123, Companies Act 1967 became of little significance because of the Combined effect of the Consumer Credit Act (q.v.) and the Banking Act 1979 (q.v.).

MONEY MARKET The money market is not a particular place in a geographical sense, although most of its transactions take place in the 'square mile' of the City of London. The term is used to embrace the Bank of England, the clearing banks, the discount houses, the Stock Exchange and all who deal in money or who have significant balances to borrow or lend. There are, in fact, a number of markets and thus it is usual to refer to the 'money markets'. They include a number of integrated financial institutions which deal almost entirely by telephone and telex. The principal markets are the discount market, the inter-bank market (q.v.), the certificate of deposit (q.v.) market, the local authority market, the finance house (q.v.) market, the inter-company market and the Euro-currency market. SEE *Euro-currency; Local Authorities, Investment in*

MONEY ORDER Money orders are issued at any money-order office in the UK and in Eire for sums not exceeding £50, and are valid for 12 months. They can be effectively crossed and are not negotiable instruments. The Post Office is entitled to return money orders at any time after their collection by a bank on the ground of irregularity. There is no statutory protection for banks in respect of the collection of money orders for customers who have no title or a defective title to such orders.

MONEY PAID UNDER MISTAKE OF FACT SEE *Payments under Mistake of Fact*

MONEY SHOPS These are retail outlets for basic financial services offered by a number of UK institutions, but having their origin to some extent in the USA. They are not banks as such, but usually have a deposit-taking licence under the Banking Act 1979 and thus accept deposits from the public as well as providing personal loan facilities. In some cases, they provide other basic financial services, to private individuals, such as acting as insurance intermediaries. At the time of writing, the principal operators in this field are Citibank, Western Savings & Trust, HFC (Household Finance Corporation of Illinois), and Chartered Trust, which is a subsidiary of Standard Chartered Bank. There are approximately 1,000 money shops in the UK and the number is increasing.

MONEY TRANSFER (MONEY TRANSMISSION) It is believed that the number of payments made in Britain each year exceed 50,000 million (on average four per day for every adult person). Anyone in the UK wishing to make a money transfer to another person will normally do so by one of the following methods, which are dealt with under their respective headings, in other parts of this work; cash, cheques, bankers draft, bills of exchange, standing orders, direct debits, credit card, traveller's cheque, National Giro Credit, postal order or money order.

Anyone wishing to make a payment to someone overseas will normally do so by international money orders (q.v.), telegraphic transfers (q.v.), travellers cheques (q.v.) and, in the case of urgent business transfers, SWIFT (q.v.).

All money transfer falls into one of three main categories: cash, paper transfer (cheques and other vouchers), or transfer by electronic means.

Payment by *cash*, i.e. coin or notes, still accounts for 95 per cent by number of all monetary payments in the UK and this situation is not likely to change. The distribution of cash for both the private and public sectors is handled on behalf of the Bank of England by the clearing banks. All cash users, including the Post Office and the building societies, depend on the bank network for the availability of cash. SEE *Cash*

Payment by *voucher* includes bills of exchange, cheques, standing orders and other paper transfers listed above. Again, almost entirely, the system depends on the banks clearing system (SEE *Clearing Banks; Clearing House*) although some vouchers, e.g. bills of exchange, are presented direct and others, e.g. credit card vouchers, do not go through the clearing system as such. Approximately 3,500 million cheques and other vouchers are handled by the British banks each year and still account for the largest proportion, by value, of everyday money transfers. The system is, however, becoming increasingly automated. SEE *Bankers' Automated Clearing Services Limited; Clearing House Automated Payments System*

The third method, which is comparatively new, and which would appear to be the way for the future, is the transfer of money by electronic means. This has already been achieved to a considerable extent, partly by the use of magnetic tapes (SEE *Bankers' Automated Clearing Services Limited*) and partly by the electronic transfer system of the Town Clearing (SEE *Clearing House Automated Payments System*). Under a fully-automated electronic system (SEE *Electronic Funds Transfer*), there will not even be the need for a paper voucher to initiate a transfer. Existing schemes depend on the use of a plastic card, accompanied by a personal identification number (PIN) (q.v.), the payments being transmitted by a keyboard. This would appear to be the pattern for the future. This has opened up considerable scope for point of sale (POS) transactions in stores, filling stations and other retail outlets and the instantaneous logging of transactions by the use of British Telecom lines. SEE ALSO *Home Banking*

There would appear to be little doubt that the impact of electronic methods of transfer on banks, building societies and stores, will have a considerable impact on banking habits, cash circulation and the role of banking branches as known hitherto but the full nature and extent of that impact still remains to be seen.

MONTHLY INCOME SHARES A term applied to that category of building society shares which provide the investors with a monthly income, rather than the application of interest twice-yearly as applies traditionally to building society ordinary shares.

MORATORIUM From the Latin *mora*, delay. An extension of time which is sometimes granted by the government of a country during a financial emergency, postponing the due date for the payment of bills of exchange or other debts.

Where a bill falls due in a foreign country during the period of a moratorium, the rights of a drawer or an indorser in England are probably subject to the same law as the acceptor. (See the case of *Roquette* v *Overman* (1875) 10 QBD 525.)

The expression is also used in relation to the arrangement made by creditors with a debtor that they will not take action to enforce payment within a particular period.

MORTALITY SEE *Expectation of Life*

MORTGAGE From the French *mort*, dead, and *gage*, a pledge—a 'dead pledge'. A mortgage is a charge which a borrower gives to a lender upon part or the whole of his property. There are two kinds of mortgages: legal mortgage and equitable mortgage (q.v.).

With a legal mortgage, a banker has control of the property if the borrower fails to repay the advance made to him. But with an equitable mortgage—that is, a deposit of the title deeds with, as a rule, a memorandum of deposit—the banker will, unless the borrower gives a legal mortgage when requested, or unless a power of attorney or a declaration of trust is incoporated in the memorandum, have a certain amount of expense before he obtains the sanction of the court to dispose of the property.

If a banker takes a mortgage for a fixed amount, it terminates the relation of banker and customer in relation to that transaction, and the banker's position is that of an ordinary mortgagee. The advance must be made on a separate loan account, and not on a working account. The only entries in the account must be credits in reduction of the loan. As each credit reduces the amount due under the mortgage, any fresh withdrawal would not be covered by the mortgage. As to interest, see under *Interest*.

The form of mortgage usually taken by a banker is to secure all moneys at any time owing with a covenant that his right to sell the property shall arise immediately on default, after demand, or after, say, one month following demand. In such a mortgage, the relation of banker and customer continues.

In the event of a mortgagor's bankruptcy, if the property is not sufficient to cover the debt, the mortgagee should value the security and claim upon the bankrupt's estate for the difference. SEE *Proof of Debts*

Since 1925 only two legal estates in land are possible:

1. An estate in fee simple absolute in possession (that is freehold).
2. A term of years absolute (that is leasehold).

The owner of a legal estate is called an 'estate owner', and, under the law which came into force on 1st January, 1926, he remains an estate owner although he creates a mortgage on his land. The mortgagee also obtains a legal estate in the same land (or a legal *interest* in the case of a legal charge (see below). In freeholds, the mortgagor retains the legal fee simple and the mortgagee obtains by demise a term of years absolute. In leaseholds, the mortgagor retains the term of years absolute and the mortgagee obtains by sub-demise a term of years absolute.

By the Law of Property Act 1925:

Legal Mortgage of Freeholds

A mortgage of an estate in fee simple shall only be capable of being effected at law either by

1. a demise for a term of years absolute, subject to a provision for cesser on redemption, or by
2. a charge by deed expressed to be by way of legal mortgage

A first mortgagee has the same right to the possession of documents as if his security included the fee simple (Section 85(1)).

A purported conveyance of an estate in fee simple by way of mortgage, made after 1925, operates as a demise of the land to the mortgagee for a term of years absolute, but subject to cesser on redemption, namely:

1. A first or only mortgagee shall take a term of 3,000 years from the date of the mortgage.
2. A second or subsequent mortgagee shall take a term one day longer than the term vested in the first or other mortgagee whose security ranks immediately before that of such second or subsequent mortgagee.

This Section applies whether or not the land is registered under the Land Registration Act 1925, or the mortgage is expressed to be made by way of trust or otherwise (subsection (3)).

As stated in subsection (1), a mortgage must be by demise for a term of years, but any length of time may be selected when making a mortgage, the usual term being 3,000 years.

Second and Subsequent Legal Mortgages of Freeholds

A second mortgage is made by the grant to the mortgagee of a term of 3,000 years and one day or for a term one day longer than the term held by the first mortgagee. Subsequent mortgagees get grants of terms one day longer than their predecessors.

Thus, first, second, and subsequent legal mortgagees all get legal estates in the shape of long leases and there can be an infinite number of legal mortgages subsisting at the same time on the same parcel of land. Before 1926, this necessarily was not so, for a legal mortgage took the form of the conveyance of the fee simple to the mortgagee who alone possessed a legal estate. The mortgagor was left with an equitable interest in the shape of his right to redeem his mortgage (his equity of redemption) and second and subsequent mortgagees only got equitable mortgages in the shape of a right to any surplus proceeds of sale. This was so notwithstanding that their mortgages were drawn as legal mortgages.

Legal Mortgage of Leaseholds

A mortgage of a term of years absolute (leasehold) shall only be capable of being effected at law either by

1. a sub-demise for a term of years absolute, less by one day at least than the term vested in the mortgagor, subject to a provision for cesser on redemption, or by
2. a charge by deed expressed to be by way of legal mortgage (see below as to this form of charge).

Where a licence to sub-demise by way of mortgage is required such licence shall not be unreasonably refused. A first mortgagee shall have the same right to the possession of documents as if his security had been effected by assignment.

A mortgage of leaseholds must not be made by assignment.

Any purported assignment of a term of years absolute by way of mortgage, after 1925, shall (to the extent of the estate of the mortgagor) operate as a sub-demise of the leasehold land to the mortgagee for a term of years absolute, subject to cesser on redemption, as follows:

1. The term to be taken by a first and only mortgagee shall be 10 days less than the term expressed to be assigned.
2. The term to be taken by a second or subsequent mortgagee shall be one day longer than the term vested in the mortgagee whose security ranks immediately before that of the second or subsequent mortgagee, if the length of the last-mentioned term permits, and in any case for a term less by one day at least than the term expressed to be assigned.

This Section applies whether or not the land is registered under the Land Registration Act 1925, or the mortgage is made by way of sub-mortgage (Section 86).

Second and Subsequent Mortgages of Leaseholds
A second mortgage takes the form of a sub-lease one day longer than the first mortgagee's term and a third mortgage of a sub-lease one day longer than the second mortgagee's term and so on (Law of Property Act 1925, Section 86 (2)).

Puisne Mortgage
A legal mortgage which is not protected by the deposit of the relative title deeds. A second mortgage is usually, but not necessarily, a puisne mortgage. A puisne mortgage may be protected as to priority by registration as such as a Class C(i) charge on the Land Charges Register. (See later in this entry under *Registration of Mortgages* and also under *Land Registration*.)

A mortgage affecting a legal estate, made before 1926, which is not protected by a deposit of documents of title, or by registration as a land charge, shall not as against a purchaser without notice thereof, obtain any benefit by reason of being converted into a legal mortgage by the Act, but shall, in favour of such purchaser, be deemed to remain an equitable interest (Schedule 1, Part VII (6) and Part VIII (5)).

Charge by way of Legal Mortgage
The Law of Property Act, 1925, provides for an alternative form of mortgage of freeholds or leaseholds by deed expressed to be a charge by way of legal mortgage. The mortgagee thereby gets the same protection, powers, and remedies as if a mortgage term for 3,000 years had been created. The advantage of this method are brevity and simplicity; a common form can be used for freeholds or leaseholds and a statutory form is given in the Fifth Schedule to the Act. By Section 206 there is statutory authority as to the sufficiency of such an instrument in respect of form and expression. This has become the common form of mortgage in current usage.

Transfer of Mortgage
This is made by deed declaring that the mortgagee transfers the benefit of the mortgage and operates to transfer the right to recover the mortgage debt and interest, all securities held for the mortgage debt, and all the estate in the land vested in the transferor (Section 114, Law of Property Act 1925).

There is a second method available under Section 115(2), which provides that where the mortgage debt is repaid by someone other than the owner of the equity of redemption, the statutory receipt will operate as a transfer by deed of the benefit of the mortgage.

Sub-Mortgage
This is a mortgage of a mortgage as where a mortgagee raises money on his mortgage deeds. It is effected by a grant by the mortgagee to his lender of a term a few days shorter than his own term. SEE *Sub-mortgage*

Equitable Mortgage
An equitable mortgage gives no legal estate to the mortgagee; it gives him a charge on the land, an equity in the shape of a right to enforce his right by the aid of the courts. It is in effect an agreement to give a legal mortgage and the courts will so interpret it.

An equitable mortgage can be effected by

1. A mere deposit of deeds with intent to charge them as security. Whilst Section 53(1), of the Law of Property Act 1925, states that no interest in land can be created except by writing signed by the party creating the same or by his agent or by will or by operation of law, Section 55 provides that this does not affect the operation of law relating to part performance. The courts have always held that on the ground of part performance a mere deposit of deeds as security creates an equitable charge.
2. Writing under hand expressed to charge the land unaccompanied by the relative deeds. Such a mortgage will require registration as a general equitable charge Class C. iii on the Land Charges Register. (See under Registration in this entry.)
3. A memorandum in writing creating a charge on the land accompanied by the deeds.

If the mortgagor will not keep the covenants to convey on request or to give a legal mortgage, the mortgagee's only remedy is in the Courts.

In some bank forms of equitable charge, an irrevocable power of attorney is given appointing an official of the bank to sell on behalf of the mortgagor. This power is not revoked by the death, disability, or bankruptcy of the donor, *in favour of a purchaser* (Section 126(1)).

An equitable charge incorporating power of attorney must be under seal.

In some cases, a declaration of trust is contained in an equitable charge whereby the mortgagor acknowledges that he holds the property in trust for the bank and empowers the bank to remove him from the trust and appoint one of its officials in his place. SEE *Equitable Mortgage; Memorandum of Deposit*

Consolidation of Mortgages
The right to consolidate is not affected by the Act if the right to do so is reserved in one of the mortgages.

Tacking and Further Advances
Except in regard to further advances, tacking is abolished by the Act. In future, therefore, a third mortgagee cannot, by obtaining a transfer of a first mortgage, secure priority over a second mortgagee. SEE *Tacking*

With regard to tacking further advances to a prior mortgage, the Act provides as follows.

(1) A prior mortgagee shall have a right to make further advances to rank in priority to subsequent mortgages (whether legal or equitable)—

(*a*) If an arrangement has been made to that effect with the subsequent mortgagees; or
(*b*) If he had no notice of such subsequent mortgages at the time when the further advance was made by him; or
(*c*) Whether or not he had such notice as aforesaid, where the mortgage imposes an obligation on him to make such further advances.

This subsection applies whether or not the prior mortgage was made expressly for securing further advances.

(2) In relation to the making of further advances after 1925, a mortgagee shall not be deemed to have notice of a mortgage merely by reason that it was registered as a land charge or in a local deeds registry, if it was not so registered at the *time when the original mortgage was created*, or when the last search (if any) by the mortgagee was made, whichever last happened.

This subsection applies only where the prior mortgage was made expressly for securing a current account or other further advances.

[The words in italics were substituted by the Law of Property (Amendment) Act 1926, for the words 'date of the original advance' in the 1925 Act.]

(3) Save in regard to the making of further advances as aforesaid, the right to tack is hereby abolished.

(4) This Section does not apply to charges registered under the Land Registration Act. (Section 94.)

Mortgagee Taking Possession
The Act does not affect prejudicially the right of a mortgagee to take possession of the land, whether or not his charge is secured by a legal term of years absolute, but the taking of possession does not convert any legal estate of the mortgagor into an equitable interest (Section 95(4)). SEE *Mortgagee in Possession*

Priority of Mortgages
Before 1926 a legal mortgagee (there could only be one) had priority over all other interests which of necessity were of an equitable nature only, provided that when he took his mortgage he had no notice of earlier interests. (Non-production of the relative deeds without a reasonable explanation would have been construed as notice.) Equitable mortgagees took priority according to the date order of their mortgages. Since 1926 these rules are no longer applicable owing to the possibility of several legal mortgages existing at one and the same time. Priority now is accorded to the mortgagee—*legal or equitable*—who takes with his mortgage the relative title deeds, provided he has no notice of earlier interests. The only notice that can affect him in this respect is a registration on the Land Charges Register. Section 199 of the Law of Property Act 1925, makes this clear in subsection (1) which says

A purchaser shall not be prejudicially affected by notice of any instrument or matter capable of registration under the provisions of the Land Charges Act, 1925, ... which is void or not enforceable against him under that Act by reason of the non-registration thereof.

By Section 205(1), 'purchaser' includes a mortgagee.

Priority of mortgagees who do not obtain the relative title deeds (e.g. because they are in the hands of an earlier mortgagee) is determined not by date order of their mortgage but by date order of registration on the Land Charges Register as a puisne mortgage (legal mortage) or general equitable charge (equitable mortgage).

It should be added, however, that the position of a later mortgagee obtaining a registration earlier than an earlier mortgagee, where the former had notice of the earlier mortgage, has been the subject of controversy.

Remedies of Legal Mortgagee
1. He can sue the mortgagor on his personal covenant, incorporated in the mortgage deed, to repay the debt. This is a useful remedy where the security has depreciated.
2. He can enter into possession. A mortgagee in possession must account to the mortgagor not

only for all rents and profits arising from occupation of the land, but also for all revenues which he might have received if he had used all possible care in the administration of the property. Consent of the court is now necessary before physical possession can be obtained.

3. He can foreclose the mortgage. An order for foreclosure *nisi* will be made by the court, after default by the mortgagor, fixing a date (usually six months ahead) for repayment. If this does not materialize, an order for foreclosure 'absolute' will be made whereby the fee simple is vested in the mortgagee subject to any prior mortgage. Any subsequent mortgage is extinguished (Law of Property Act 1925, Section 88(2)). In the case of a leasehold, a foreclosure order absolute vests the leasehold reversion and any subsequent mortgage term in the mortgagee, subject to any prior mortgage (Section 89(2)). By Section 91, the court may make an order for sale in place of a foreclosure order. A mortgagee who gets a foreclosure order is not accountable to the mortgagor for any profits or surplus from a resulting sale.

4. He may sell under his statutory or express power of sale. Any conveyance thereunder vests the fee simple in the purchaser subject to any prior charge. If leasehold property is concerned, the assignment by the mortgagee vests in the purchaser the leasehold reversion.

Under Section 101(1), a power of sale arises where the mortgagor is three months in arrear with principal repayments or two months in arrear with interest payments or has broken any convenant in the mortgage. A bank form of mortgage, however, usually provides for an immediate power of sale on default (or on default for one month). The proceeds of sale must be applied as follows:

(a) In payment of any prior mortgages.
(b) In payment of the costs of sale.
(c) In payment of the mortgage debt and interest.
(d) In payment of any surplus to the mortgagor *or any subsequent mortgagees*. Hence a search on the Land Charges Register must be made before parting with any surplus proceeds of sale. (See under *Searches* in this entry.)

5. He may appoint a Receiver of Rents. Power to appoint a receiver only arises if a power of sale has arisen. The appointment of a receiver must be in writing but need not be by deed. A receiver is deemed to be the agent of the mortgagor.

A receiver must apply the income from the property as follows:

(a) In payment of rent, rates, and taxes, etc., for which the mortgagor is liable.
(b) In payment of interest on prior mortgages.
(c) In payment of fire insurance premiums, repairs, and receiver's remuneration.
(d) In payment of interest on the mortgage debt.
(e) In reduction of the mortgage debt.

A bank usually appoints a receiver where the property is let and it is not possible to effect an immediate sale.

Bankruptcy of Mortgagor

The mortgagee's power to sell or appoint a receiver shall not be exercised only on account of the mortgagor committing an act of bankruptcy or being adjudged a bankrupt, without the leave of the Court.

Discharge of Legal Mortgage

A receipt indorsed on, written at the foot of, or annexed to, a mortgage for all money secured, which states the name of the person who pays the money and is executed by the mortgagee shall operate, without any reconveyance, as a discharge of the mortgage (Section 115(1)).

This Section does not affect the right of any person to require a re-assignment, surrender, release, or transfer to be executed in lieu of a receipt (Section 115(4)).

A banker's mortgage is usually worded so as to form a security for 'all moneys' owing to the bank by the mortgagor. If the mortgagor's advance is being totally repaid, a receipt, indorsed by the bank on the mortgage, for 'all money thereby secured' would be in order; but a receipt for 'all money thereby secured' would not be appropriate if the bank was merely releasing a part of its security, or exchanging one security for another, and the account continued to be overdrawn. Instead of the receipt, some banks indorse on the mortgage a reconveyance, by which the premises vested in the bank by the mortgage are surrendered and conveyed unto the mortgagor 'freed and discharged from all moneys secured by the mortgage'.

Where by the receipt the money appears to have been paid by a person who is not entitled to the immediate equity of redemption, the receipt shall operate as if the benefit of the mortgage had by deed been transferred to him, unless—

(*a*) it is otherwise expressly provided; or
(*b*) the mortgage is paid off out of capital money, or other money in the hands of a personal representative or trustee properly applicable for the discharge of the mortgage, and it is not expressly provided that the receipt is to operate as a transfer. [Section 115(2))]

For example, if a mortgage by Brown to Jones is discharged by Robinson, the mortgage deed may be indorsed as follows:

The within named Jones hereby acknowledges that all money secured by the within written mortgage, including interest and costs, has been paid. The said money has been paid by Robinson of ....

Such a receipt operates as if the benefit of the mortgage has by deed been transferred to Robinson.

When an overdrawn account is transferred from one bank to another, if the security held is a mortgage, the mortgage should be reconveyed by the old bank to the customer and a fresh mortgage given to the new bank. If the old mortgage is discharged by a receipt showing that the money was paid by the new bank, it would, as stated above, operate as a transfer of the mortgage to the new bank, but the new bank could hold the mortgage merely for the specific amount which was paid to the old bank. That amount would require to be debited to a loan account, and the only transactions that could be made would be repayments in permanent reduction of the loan. If the amount were debited to a current account, each credit would go to reduce the amount of the mortgage, and each withdrawal would form an unsecured overdraft. SEE *Clayton's Case*

This Section does not apply to the discharge of a charge registered under the Land Registration Act 1925 (Section 115(10)).

Cesser of Mortgage Terms

When the money secured by a mortgage has been discharged, the mortgage term becomes a satisfied term and ceases (Section 116).

When a mortgage is discharged the deeds are returned to the mortgagor. By Section 96(2), a mortgagee shall not be liable if he delivers the deeds to the person not having the best right thereto unless he has notice of the claim of a person having a better right. To this subsection the following words were added by the Law of Property (Amendment) Act 1926: 'In this subsection 'notice' does not include notice implied by reason of registration under the Land Charges Act, 1925, or in a local deeds register'. 'Notice', therefore, in that subsection means actual notice, and the mortgagee (without any notice from a second mortgagee), need not require a search to be made in the Land Charges Register, or a local deeds registry, to ascertain if a second mortgage has been registered, before he returns the deeds to the mortgagor. A second mortgagee should give the prior mortgagee notice of his charge in writing.

Possession of Title Deeds

Where a banker or other lender is in possession of the title deeds either with a legal mortgage or a memorandum of deposit he is, as a general rule, in a safe position, as before any person can deal with the legal estate he must first ascertain where the title deeds are. The banker should, however, search the Land Charges Register. The effect of the possession of title deeds is given in Section 13:

This Act shall not prejudicially affect the right or interest of any person arising out of or consequent on the possession by him of any documents relating to a legal estate in land, nor affect any question arising out of or consequent upon any omission to obtain or any absence of possession by any person of any documents relating to a legal estate in land.

In connection with a banker's safe position, see also Section 94.

Statutory Mortgages

Short forms of mortgages are set out in the Act and certain provisions are deemed to be included in such mortgage deeds.

Registration of Mortgages

Legal and equitable mortgages by deposit of title deeds do not require registration as land charges.

Legal and equitable mortgages without a deposit of deeds, or all the material deeds, require to be registered as land charges, and they rank according to the date of registration (Section 97).

The registration as a land charge constitutes actual notice of such instrument to all persons and for all purposes connected with the land affected from the date of registration and so long as the registration continues in force. This Section applies without prejudice to the provisions (see Section 97 with respect to the making of further advances by a mortgagee). (Section 198)

The above provisions do not apply to registered land. SEE *Land Registration*

Mortgages and charges created by companies must be registered under the Companies Act 1948; and if it is registered land also under the Land Registration Act 1925.

By the Land Charges Act 1925, in the case of a charge on land (not registered land) created by a company, registration under the Companies Act 1948, was formerly sufficient. However, pursuant to the Law Reform Act 1969, since 1st January, 1970, mortgages of unregistered land, not supported by the deeds given by companies, must be registered at the Land Charges Registry as well as on the Companies Register. But if the company's land was within the jurisdiction of the Yorkshire Deeds Registries, a legal mortgage had also to be registered in the Registry of the particular Riding.

As these registries are now closed, both old and new charges on land in this area should be re-registered or registered at the Land Charges Registry.

Summary of Registrations
The mortgages and charges in which a banker is particularly interested are
Legal mortgage, protected by a deposit of all the material title deeds.
Puisne mortgage, that is, a legal mortgage not protected by a deposit of the title deeds or of all the material title deeds.
Equitable charge, that is, a deposit of all the material title deeds with or without a memorandum of deposit.
General equitable charge, that is, an equitable charge which is not protected by a deposit of all the material title deeds.

In the case of an equitable charge, a memorandum of deposit usually contains an undertaking to give a legal mortgage when required. This undertaking constitutes an 'estate contract' and, as such, is registrable as a land charge under the Land Charges Act 1925, but so long as a banker retains possession of the deeds he should be safe without registration. SEE *Land Charges*

Registration of a land charge must be made on Form LC4. If not made by a solicitor, it must be supported by a statutory declaration by the owner of the charge on Form LC9.
Charges by companies. All mortgages and charges (legal or equitable) whether accompanied by the deeds or not on any land, wherever situated, should be registered within 21 days from the date of creation of the mortgage. Such registration of a land charge takes the place of registration under the land Charges Act 1925.
Industrial and Provident Societies Act
Friendly Societies Act, Societies registered under these Acts do not come within the scope of the Companies Act, 1948, and therefore a charge does not require registration with the Registrar of Companies.

As to a charge on farming stock by an Industrial and Provident Society, see Agricultural Credits Act 1928, Section 14.
Registered land, that is, land registered under the Land Registration Act 1925 is not within the provisions of the Land Charges Act 1925. A charge must be registered at the Land Registry. Where a land certificate, or a certificate of charge, is deposited as security, and it is not proposed to take a registered charge, notice of deposit should be given to the Land Registry. Where a mortgage is effected as though the land were unregistered land, the mortgage must be protected on the register by a caution. A charge by a company must, in addition, be registered with the Registrar of Companies. SEE *Land Registration*
Priority notice A priority notice of the registration of a contemplated charge under the Land Charges Act, 1925, may be given at least 14 days before the registration is to take effect. SEE UNDER *Land Charges*

Summary of Searches
In taking a security on land, it is subject to any mortgage or charge which has been registered. Search should, therefore, always be made at the Land Charges Registry, London, to ascertain if there is any existing registered charge against a borrower.

The Local Land Charges Registers should be searched for road charges and town-planning schemes, the register of the county authority as well as the rural, urban, or municipal authority's register.

Where a limited company is concerned, a search must also be made on the company's file kept by the Registrar of Companies at Companies House.

Searches on the Land Charges Register should be made against the names of all persons through whom a title is being made. In searching against the name of a married woman, search should also be made against her maiden name, if she owned the land prior to her marriage. Where a person has changed his address, or has two addresses, search should be made against his name at each address. A search against a firm should be made against the name of each partner.

Where a mortgage is taken from executors, administrators, or trustees, a search should be made against each executor, administrator, or trustee, as well as against the deceased or the creator of the settlement. The deceased may have charged the property before his death; subsequent dealings by executors, etc., are registered under their own names as they are 'estate owners'. A search, however, under one executor's name should normally disclose any charges.

A search is made in the alphabetical index at the registry against the owner of the land. If that search shows that something is registered against his name, then an application should be made for an office copy of the entry in the register.

A search may be made personally, but the better way is to apply on Form LC 11 for a certificate of official search. Anyone obtaining an official certificate is protected against any loss that may arise from error in the certificate (Land Charges Act 1925, Section 17). By the Law of Property (Amendment) Act 1926, when a purchaser (which includes a mortgagee) has obtained an official certificate, any entry made in the register after the date of the purchase shall not, if the purchase is completed before the expiration of the 14th day after the date of the certificate, affect the purchaser.

In taking the title deeds as security, there should, strictly, be a certificate of an official search along with the deeds against each person who has been interested in the land since 1925. The absence of a certificate may mean that some purchaser failed to make a search and, possibly, to discover a registered charge.

When deeds are no longer required as security, they may be given up to the person who deposited them without searching the register. A banker or other mortgagee however, must not disregard any express notice that he may have received from a second mortgagee, and he should obtain written instructions from the mortgagor to hand the deeds to the second mortgagee.

Title deeds may be returned to a company without making a search on the company's file at Companies House.

When a bank or other mortgagee sells mortgaged property under its power of sale, a search should be made before paying over any surplus proceeds to the mortgagor, because, if the search reveals another interested person, the surplus must be held in trust for that person.

In the case of registered land, a search should be made at the Land Registry. Unless the land certificate is produced at the time of the search, the written authority of the registered proprietor is necessary.

Stamp duty on mortgages, bonds, debentures and covenants was abolished by the Finance Act 1971, Section 64.

It should be appreciated that there can be a legal or equitable mortgage of a 'chose in action' such as a life policy or shares. For a legal mortgage there has to be a transfer of title to the mortgagee with a re-transfer on redemption. An equitable mortgage can be treated informally by mere deposit so long as there is evidence of intent to create a security.

SEE *Attornment; Debts, Assignment of; Equitable Mortgage; Equity of Redemption; Foreclosure; Legal Mortgage; Married Woman; Mortgagee in Possession; Notice of Second Mortgage; Priorities; Receiver; Second Mortgage; Ship; Tacking*

MORTGAGE CAUTION An alternative form of mortgage of registered land is provided in Section 106 of the Land Registration Act 1925, to the method of registering a charge and getting a charge certificate. A registered title can be charged by an ordinary mortgage deed as if it were unregistered land, and the mortgagee can protect himself by lodging a special form of caution at the Land Registry called a 'mortgage caution'. This caution, when lodged, must be accompanied by the land certificate, the mortgage instrument, and a certified copy thereof. The caution is entered on the Proprietorship Register, the certified copy of the mortgage filed, and the original returned to the mortgagee. This system is, however, rarely used.

MORTGAGE DEBENTURE A debenture which not only provides for repayment of a certain sum but also charges some or all of the property of the company with the payment of the money. SEE *Debenture*

MORTGAGE OF EQUITABLE INTEREST A party may borrow by way of legal mortgage on his equitable interest in an estate. Thus a beneficiary under a trust for sale, the owner of a reversionary interest, a joint owner who is a tenant in common in equity, has an interest on which he can raise money. In these cases, there is no legal estate to charge; a beneficiary under a trust for sale has rights solely against the proceeds of sale, a remainderman has only his equitable interest, and a joint tenant, although he may hold the legal estate jointly as trustee, can only charge his beneficial interest in the proceeds of sale.

A mortgage of any such equitable interest in land will not be accompanied by the relative title deeds, which are vested in the trustees. Such a mortgage cannot be protected by registration on the Land Charges Register for it is not a charge on land but on the proceeds of sale thereof.

Protection is obtained by giving written notice of the mortgage to the trustees or to a trust corporation appointed for the purpose. An acknowledgment should be obtained and inquiry made of the trustees as to any prior notice received. Priority is determined by date order of the receipt of notice by the trustees. If a joint tenant mortgages his equitable interest, additional protection can be obtained by having a memorandum of the mortgage indorsed on the holding deed.

Where registered land is concerned, a mortgage of an equitable interest therein can be protected by registration on the Minor Interests Index.

Where stocks and shares are concerned, a notice in lieu of distringas (q.v.) can be served on the respective registrars.

It is important to see that a reversionary interest is absolute and not contingent. If the latter, the security should be supported by a life policy to cover the mortgagor's decease.

A mortgage of a reversionary interest in not an

ideal security, as the mortgagee cannot foreclose the assets of the estate, he can only sell the reversionary interest to another party. SEE *Reversion*

MORTGAGE OF SHIP SEE *Ship*

MORTGAGE PROTECTION POLICY A form of decreasing term life assurance, under which the sum assured reduces in line with the capital sum outstanding on a mortgage. SEE ALSO *Life Assurance*

MORTGAGEE The person is whose favour a mortgage is given.

MORTGAGEE IN POSSESSION Where a mortgagor has failed to repay the money due under his mortgage, and the mortgagee has taken into his own hands the collection of the rents and management of the property, he is a mortgagee in possession. A mortgagee, however, usually puts in a receiver to manage the estate and collect rents, as the mortgagee thereby avoids the liabilities to which he would be exposed by being a mortgagee in possession.

A bank's mortgage may include a clause by which the mortgagor attorns tenant to the bank, and provides that neither the tenancy created by the attornment nor any receipt of rent shall constitute the bank mortgagees in possession or render them liable to account as such. SEE *Attornment*

An equitable mortgagee by deposit of title deeds can take possession only after he has received the sanction of the court.

By the Law of Property Act 1925, Section 99, a mortgagee in possession shall have, if and as far as a contrary intention is not expressed in the mortgage deed, or otherwise in writing, power to make from time to time an agricultural or occupation lease for any term not exceeding 21 years, or in the case of a mortgage made after 1925, 50 years; a building lease for any term not exceeding 90 years, or in the case of a mortgage made after 1925, 999 years; and every such lease shall be made to take effect in possession not later than 12 months after its date. Every such lease shall reserve the best rent that can reasonably be obtained, and shall contain a covenant by the lessee for payment of the rent and a condition of re-entry on the rent not being paid within a time therein specified not exceeding 30 days. Every such building lease shall be made in consideration of the lessee, or some person by whose direction the lease is granted, having erected, or agreeing to erect within not more than five years from the date of the lease, buildings, new or additional, or having improved or repaired buildings, or agreeing to improve or repair buildings within that time, or having executed, or agreeing to execute within that time, on the land leased, an improvement for or in connection with building purposes. A peppercorn rent, or nominal rent, may be made payable for the first five years, or any less part of the term. Nothing in the Law of Property Act 1925, affects prejudicially the right of a mortgagee to take possession, but the taking of possession does not convert any legal estate of the mortgagor into an equitable interest (Section 95(4). SEE *Mortgage*

MORTGAGOR The person who mortgages or charges his property in favour of a party who has lent him money.

MOTOR VEHICLE INSURANCE There are four broad categories of motor insurance:

1. insurance under the Road Traffic Acts
2. third party insurance,
3. third party, fire and theft insurance,
4. comprehensive insurance.

These are considered in turn.

Road Traffic Acts Insurance

This is the minimum insurance required by law before anybody may venture on the public highway with a licensed vehicle. Anyone who takes on a public road a vehicle covered by the Acts without the basic insurance required under the Acts commits a criminal offence, as well as incurring a civil liability to any person injured by the uninsured vehicle.

Road Traffic Acts insurance covers (1) the owner or (2) any person driving the car with the owner's permission (provided they are authorized to do so under the policy) against claims for death or injury to any other persons, including passengers in the car.

This basic insurance covers no more than that. It does not, for example, cover damage or injury caused by some act of a passenger in the car. It does not cover any damage or injury caused by the driver when driving the car elsewhere than on a public highway. It does not cover any damage to a car or other property belonging to any other person in any circumstances whatever. The risk of taking a car on the road in modern conditions are so great that this basic insurance for the purpose of the Road Traffic Acts is quite inadequate and few, if any, insurance companies would encourage drivers to take out this minimum insurance *per se*.

Third Party Insurance

This type of cover includes the minimum insurance required under the Acts but provides also for injury to other parties and damage to other people's property. It protects the owner and any driver who is driving with the owner's permission within the terms of the policy against any claim by another party, but it does not enable the owner or driver to claim against the insurance company for any injury or damage to himself, his car or his other property.

Third Party, Fire and Theft Insurance
This is a combination of the two foregoing categories plus cover for damage or loss occasioned by fire or theft.

Many car owners regard this last category of insurance as sufficient for their purpose. It does not enable the insured to claim against the insurance company for any damage to the car or its contents as a result of an accident and it does not cover loss or damage to the contents of the car as a result of fire or theft.

Comprehensive Insurance
This embraces the first three categories of insurance stated above, together with cover for the owner in the event of damage to his car and damage to or loss of any of the contents. The extent of the cover will depend in each case on the wording of the policy but, in the case of the contents of the car, would not normally extend to items carried in the course of business. These should therefore be separately covered.

Although the aforementioned four categories of motor insurance are common to all insurers, there is a degree of variation in the extent of cover which they provide in each category. The following are the principal areas of difference:

1. Some companies will not insure drivers under the age of 25 years for driving high-powered cars.
2. The cover for theft may be restricted if the car is not kept in a locked garage.
3. Most insurers will not cover anyone driving a car for business purposes other than the insured person named in or covered by the policy.
4. Many companies will not cover the contents of a car above a stipulated figure.
5. Money and jewellery will not normally be covered if lost from a motor car.

In broad terms the level of motor car premiums will depend on quantitative, geographical and subjective considerations.

Quantitative Considerations
The financial risks borne by a motor insurer will vary not only according to the total value of a car at any point in time, but according to the characteristics of the car and the attendant costs. Thus, a sports car constitutes a higher risk factor than a family saloon. The cost of repairing certain cars will be much higher than repairing similar units in other cars. Generally, the more highly powered a car is, the greater the cost of damage ensuing from an accident. The leading companies categorize these risks into seven groups. These groupings are a major factor in determining the basic premium applied to each class of motor car, but within each group the amount of premium payable for comprehensive cover will of course vary according to the value of the car.

Geographical Considerations
The second major factor in determining the basic level of car premiums is the location where the car is normally kept and used. Statistically, a car is less likely to be involved in an accident in the country than in the centre of London. The seven areas into which the UK is divided for car insurance purposes are

Area 1 Scottish Islands, West Country, rural counties such as Lincolnshire and Shropshire.
Area 2 Most of Wales, much of Scotland, semi-rural counties such as Avon, Hampshire, North Yorkshire
Area 3 Medium-sized towns like Luton and Oxford, averagely populated counties such as Surrey and Kent
Area 4 Birmingham, Cardiff, Edinburgh, Greater London (except postal districts), Greater Manchester, Merseyside
Area 5 Liverpool, Manchester, outer Glasgow
Area 6 Central Glasgow, outer London postal
Area 7 Central London, Northern Ireland

Subjective Considerations
Although the foregoing factors will normally determine the basic level of premium for a particular motor car in a particular part of the country, there will be considerable further variation depending on the characteristics of the driver to be insured. The principal factors are

Inexperience A newly qualified driver may expect to pay a higher premium.
Youth Drivers under 25 years of age may have to pay higher premiums, particularly for higher-powered cars.
Age Some companies require medical evidence of fitness for drivers over 65 years of age and may load the premiums.
Driving record A series of accidents, and particularly a series of convictions, will usually lead to a loading of the premium.

Occupation Civil Servants, bank clerks and professional people tend to be regarded favourably; students, bookmakers, journalists and professional sportsmen may be considered more risky.
Business purposes Sales representatives and others using a car for extensive business use may have to pay a higher premium.
Named driver Most companies will allow a 15 per cent reduction in premium for a car to be driven by one named driver or a 10 per cent reduction for the car to be driven by the insured and perhaps his wife or one or two other named drivers.
Voluntary excess The insured may agree to pay, say, £50 of any damage, in which case there will be a corresponding reduction in the premium.
No claims The absence of claims under a motor policy will normally result in a build-up of discount in the premium over a period of years. After four years, many companies will allow a 60 per cent reduction in the premium.

No Claims Discount

The premium discount allowed by insurers in the event of there being no claim over a given period (colloquially referred to as a no claims bonus) may be lost if the insurer is called upon to make any contribution to a particular claim, notwithstanding that the insured may not have been in any way responsible for the loss or damage. This may arise, for example, where the person causing the loss or damage is not known, e.g. another driver who did not stop.

The same situation may arise where the insurer has a so-called 'knock for knock' agreement with the other party's insurer. Such an agreement, under which each insurance company pays for the damage incurred by its own insured party regardless of blame, can result in the loss to an innocent party of a no claims discount. This can be avoided by (1) taking out a policy which some companies offer whereby a no claims discount can be preserved on payment of a higher basic premium, but even here there is usually a limit on the number of claims which may be made without the loss of a discount, or (b) getting the other party and/or their insurers to admit liability and meet the whole of the claim.

Any insured person who does not wish to lose his no claims discount may in any case commence proceedings against any party whom he considers to be to blame for the accident. Such proceedings may be somewhat drawn out but, if successful, the other party and/or his insurers will pay the damages.

Certificate of Insurance

No vehicle may lawfully be driven on the road unless the driver is in possession of a valid certificate of insurance. A 'cover note' issued by the insurer pending the issue of the certificate of insurance will serve as a temporary certificate for the period named in the cover note. The possession of a motor car policy does not of itself authorize the insured to take a vehicle on the road. The certificate of insurance will indicate who is covered by the policy in question, e.g. the owner and one named driver.

The possession of a valid certificate of insurance will cover a driver while driving someone else's car (if this is within the terms of the policy, as would normally be the case), but such cover only extends to that required under the Road Traffic Act plus third party cover. It does not cover the driver for any damage done to the car he is driving.

MUTILATED CHEQUE OR BILL If a cheque is presented for payment and has been torn to such an extent as to suggest that it has been so torn with the object of cancelling it, the banker may be liable if he pays, and it is subsequently found that the drawer had torn up the cheque on purpose.

It is customary for the banker to return such a cheque (unless confirmed by the drawer) marked 'cheque mutilated' or 'cheque torn', but if a note is written upon the cheque by the collecting banker that the cheque was accidentally torn by him, or that he guarantees it, the paying banker usually accepts such an explanation or guarantee, as sufficient. An unconfirmed explanation by a payee is not as a rule accepted.

MUTILATED NOTES Mutilated Bank of England notes should be presented at the Bank of England. Where a fragment consists of more than half a note and contains the whole of the sentence 'I promise to pay the bearer on demand the sum of ...' together with some portion of the signature and one complete print of the series index and of the serial number, together with some portion of the other series index or the other serial number, such note will ordinarily be paid forthwith. Any notes not fulfilling these requirements will be dealt with according to the fragments presented and the nature of the evidence forthcoming regarding the destruction of the missing parts.

MUTUAL FUND The US counterpart of the English unit trust. A mutual fund is, however, a company, whereas a unit trust (q.v.) in the UK is a trust.

In the USA and certain other countries, it is possible for the capital of such a company to be increased or reduced consequent upon the issue or redemption of shares. Thus, the shares can be on sale to the public on a continuing basis, rather like the units of a unit trust. 'Open-ended' companies of this nature are not possible under UK company law.

MUTUAL ASSURANCE COMPANIES These are life offices in which the members, i.e. owners of the company, are the policy holders, as distinct from those insurance companies established in joint stock form whose owners are the shareholders, as distinct from the policy holders. In a mutual company, the profits accrue for the benefit of the members by way of bonus additions to their policies.

N

NAKED DEBENTURE A debenture which is a mere acknowledgment of a debt and which is not secured by a mortgage or charge upon the company's property in any way, is sometimes called a 'naked' debenture. SEE *Debenture*

NAMES OF COMPANIES The Companies Act 1981 introduced new provisions relating to the registration of company names. The Registration of Business Names Act 1916 was repealed as was Section 17 of the Companies Act 1948, which prohibited companies from being registered with the name which, in the opinion of the Board of Trade was undesirable. Under the 1985 Act, a company may not be registered with a name

1. which includes the words 'limited', 'unlimited' or 'public limited company' other than at the end of the name;
2. which is the same, apart from minor aspects, as a name already in the Index of Company Names (see below);
3. which would in the opinion of the Secretary of State, constitute a criminal offence or which, in the opinion of the Secretary of State, is offensive.

The Registrar of Companies is required to keep an index of the names of all limited and unlimited companies registered under the Companies Acts, limited partnerships registered under the Limited Partnership Act 1907, societies registered under the Industrial and Provident Societies Act 1965, and certain other corporate bodies which are required to comply with the provision of the Companies Acts.

A company may not, without the approval of the Secretary of State, register a name which gives the impression that the company is in any way connected with the Government, or with a local authority, or which includes any word or expression which may be specified in regulations made under Statutory Instruments under the Act.

As under the old legislation, a company may change its name by a Special Resolution and the Registrar will issue a revised Certificate of Incorporation.

The following categories of companies may be registered with a name which does not include the word 'limited':

1. private companies limited by guarantee, and
2. companies which, prior to the Act coming into force, were private companies, limited by shares, which were exempted from using the word 'limited' under a licence granted under the 1948 Act.

These exemptions apply, however, only to companies

1. whose objects are the promotion of commerce, art, science, education, religion, charity or any profession, and anything incidental or conducive to any of these objects, and
2. its memorandum or articles of association
(a) requires its profits or other income to be applied in promoting its objects,
(b) prohibits the payment of dividends to its members, and
(c) requires all the assets which would otherwise be available to its members generally to be transferred on a winding-up, either to another body with similar objects or to another body whose objects are the promotion of charity and anything incidental or conducive thereto.

NARROWER RANGE One of the categories of investment permitted for trustees under the Trustee Investments Act 1961 and consisting principally of Government securities, fixed interest stocks and deposits in banks and building societies. SEE *Trustee Investments*

NATIONAL ASSOCIATION OF PENSION FUNDS This is the principal forum for discussion concerning all matters relating to occupational pension schemes in both the public and the private sectors in the UK. Its membership is made up of nearly all self-administered funds and a large number of insured schemes. Although the Association is not a self-regulatory body, it is the mouth-piece on behalf of occupational pension fund matters generally in this country and the principal channel of communication on pension matters with the Government. In 1980, the Association submitted to its members a draft code of practice, on the provision of information to pension scheme members.

NATIONAL ASSOCIATION OF SECURITY DEALERS AND INVESTMENT MANAGERS (NASDIM) This Association was incorporated in May 1979 with the following objects:

1. To provide a forum for the examination and discussion of all relevant questions relating to dealings in securities and the management of and investment in securities in Great Britain, with a view to the promotion and maintenance of high standards of business conduct and professional competence.
2. To represent the interests and views of members of the Association on matters affecting their activities generally, and in particular before HM Government, the Bank of England, the Council for the Securities Industry, all governmental or public commissions and other inquiries, and for that purpose to make submissions and recommendations to, and give evidence before, such authorities, bodies, commissions and inquiries.
3. To develop the contribution of dealers in securities and investment managers to the efficient functioning of markets in securities in Great Britain.

Any corporation, firm or person who, in the opinion of the Council, carries on the business of dealing in securities and who satisfies the Council on certain major points may be accepted as a member of the Association. In particular, the Council must be satisfied that every person who is a director, controller or manager of the applicant is a fit and proper person to hold that position, that the applicant conducts its business in a prudent manner and that the applicant will support the objects of the Association and not take any action which is prejudicial to the interests of the Association.

In 1983, the Association made application to the Secretary of State for Trade and Industry for recognition of the Association under Section 15, Prevention of Fraud (Investments) Act 1958, so that individual members of NASDIM would not need in future to be individually licensed. This application was approved by the Secretary of State and NASDIM became a recognized association with effect from 31st December, 1983. Members of NASDIM therefore do not need to hold individual licences from the Department of Trade and Industry but come under the umbrella of Association. By December 1984 the Association had 566 members.

NATIONAL DEBT The total debt of the UK includes at any one time the External Debt, made up of loans from other countries, and the International Monetary Fund (q.v.) and the like, and the Internal Debt, made up of sums borrowed within the UK. The internal borrowings of the Government include the Floating Debt, consisting of the short-term borrowing of the Government for revenue purposes pending the receipt of taxation or other arrangements, and the Funded National Debt. The Funded National Debt is that part of the Government's borrowing for which Government securities have been issued. The total National Debt in March 1984 was £142 billion, of which approximately £109 billion was funded by the issue of securities. The main Funded Debt of the British Government is raised through the stock market. The securities issued were traditionally all of a fixed-interest nature but, in recent years variable rate stocks (q.v.) and index-linked securities have been issued.

NATIONAL ECONOMIC DEVELOPMENT COUNCIL (NEDC) This Council, generally known as 'Neddy', was set up in 1961, to bring together representatives of the Government, industry and trade unions, to achieve a measure of economic planning. Under the umbrella of the National Economic Development Office (NEDO) there are a number of little 'Neddies' and working parties relating to various sectors of industry and the economy.

NATIONAL ENTERPRISE BOARD A statutory body set up under the Industry Act 1975 to hold investments on behalf of the Government in a number of state-owned or semi-state-owned companies. The general aims of the Board are to develop the economy, encourage competitiveness in international markets, promote efficiency in industry and maintain employment in the UK.

In recent times, new investments by the National Enterprise Board have been severely restricted and the policy of the Board has been to concentrate for the most part on its existing investments, particularly in the areas of high technology. It has placed a particular emphasis on industrial investment in the north of England and in Scotland and among smaller firms.

In the years from 1980 to 1983, most of the National Enterprise Board's investments were disposed of, either by the sale of shares or, in some cases, the liquidation of the companies. The Board is now known as the British Technology Group.

NATIONAL GIROBANK The National Girobank, formerly the National Giro, was set up in October 1968 to provide a money transmission service on a national basis as an alternative to the cheque-clearing service provided by the commercial banks. This, in turn, necessitated offering account facilities to customers and, up to the present time, National Girobank has attracted approximately 1¾ million accounts. Like the National Savings Bank, it operates through offices of the Post Office. The bank has developed a number of financial services, including the provision of cheque account facilities and personal loans. It is a member of the Bankers' Clearing House.

The Wilson Committee (q.v.) agreed that, on the surface, 'it does seem irrational for there to be two separate public sector banks both operating across Post Office counters' (i.e. National Girobank and National Savings Bank) but, on balance, could not see any great advantage flowing from a merger.

NATIONAL HOUSE BUILDING COUNCIL (NHBC) A form of self-regulation for the building industry. In 1966 the Building Societies Association recommended that its members should make loans on security of *new* houses only if they had been constructed by a builder registered under the National House Building Council (NHBC), excepting cases where the building had been supervised by the purchaser's architect or surveyor. Nearly all new houses in the UK are now constructed to NHBC standards in matters of insulation, wood preservation, electrical safety, etc., and if the owner enters into the House Purchaser's Agreement of the NHBC, he is covered in certain material respects, namely:

1. protection up to £5,000 against the possibility of the builder going bankrupt,
2. the builder is obliged, at his own expense, to put right any defects through his failure to meet the NHBC's minimum standards of workmanship and material, and this protection extends for two years after the Notice of Insurance has been issued, and
3. from the end of the second year until the end of the tenth year, cover is provided under the NHBC's insurance policy against major damage due to any defect in the load-bearing structure.

NATIONAL INSURANCE CONTRIBUTIONS These are paid by employers, employees and self-employed persons within, in each case, certain prescribed limits (see below). The bulk of contributions go to finance the National Insurance Fund (q.v.), but part of the contributions are allocated to the National Health Service. Part of the employers' contributions are also allocated to the Redundancy Fund and Maternity Pay Fund. Subject to some fairly minor exceptions, National Insurance contributions are payable in respect of every employed or self-employed person in Great Britain who is 16 years of age or over and whose earnings are equal to or exceed the lower earnings limit (q.v.).

The contributions fall into four classes:

Class I Contributions payable by employees (who are above the minimum earnings limit) and their employers during the working years from age 16 to 65 in the case of men and 60 in the case of women. The contributions are calculated at a percentage rate which is varied from time to time and which is applied to earnings between the lower earnings limit (q.v.) and the upper earnings limit (q.v.). The contributions are payable on gross pay including salary or wages, commissions, overtime pay, holiday pay and other taxable earnings. The employee's contribution is deducted at source by the employer and accounted for to the Government, together with the employer's contribution. SEE Supplement

Class II Contributions payable by self-employed persons. Contributions are payable at a flat weekly rate and are not payable by a self-employed person earning less than the lower earnings limit.

Class III These contributions are voluntary. They may be paid by persons whose Class I or Class II contributions are insufficient or where their earnings are below the lower earnings limit. Class III contributions enable the contributor to qualify for basic State pension but do not count for unemployment pay, sickness benefit, maternity allowance or earnings-related pension.

Class IV This is in effect an additional form of taxation on self-employed persons. It is collected with Schedule D income tax and does not confer any social security benefits which would not otherwise be payable (See Appendix 2).

In the case of Class I contributions, the level of contribution for both employers and employees varies according to whether or not the employee is contracted out of the State pension scheme.

NATIONAL INSURANCE FUND Social Security benefits are financed to a great extent by contributions from employers and employees and self-employed persons to the National Insurance Fund. This had its origin in the national insurance scheme introduced in 1948 which, in turn, was based on the report of Sir William Beveridge in November 1942. The Beveridge Report is generally accepted as the foundation of the welfare state. It was implemented in the National Insurance Act 1946, and other contemporary Acts, but substantial reforms were introduced in later years, notably with the Social Security Act 1975, and the Social Security Pensions Act 1975.

Social Security benefits today cover almost every form of financial adversity in the UK, but are not all met out of the National Insurance Fund. Some Social Security benefits such as child benefit (q.v.), attendance allowance (q.v.), invalid care allowance (q.v.), etc., are provided for separately by Parliament. Some of these, such as supplementary benefit and family income supplement are means-tested. The benefits payable out of the National Insurance Fund, however, are paid as of right and include, in particular, unemployment pay (q.v.), sickness benefit (q.v.), retirement pension, maternity benefits (q.v.), death grant (q.v.) and widow's benefits (q.v.). All these are contributory but there are certain non-contributory benefits payable from the Fund, including guardian's allowance (q.v.) and disablement benefit (q.v.).

NATIONAL SAVINGS The Department for National Savings was established on 1st October, 1969. Prior to that it was the Post Office Savings Department and was part of the Post Office. National Savings are strictly those forms of savings for which the Department for National Savings has a responsibility. They are National Savings Bank (q.v.), National Savings Certificates (q.v.), National Savings Deposit Bonds (q.v.), National Savings Income Bonds (q.v.), National Savings Yearly Plan (q.v.), British Savings Bonds (q.v.), Premium Savings Bonds (q.v.), certain Government stocks (SEE *National Savings Stock Register*), the Save-As-You-Earn Service.

At the time of writing, National Savings account for approximately one-sixth of all personal sector liquid assets. For example, at the end of 1983, National Savings amounted to nearly £25,000 million out of total personal sector liquid assets of £157,000 million. The funds administered by the Department for National Savings at the end of 1984 are given in the table below.

	£ million
National Savings Certificates	16,947
British Savings Bonds	52
Premium Savings Bonds	1,743
Income Bonds and Deposit Bonds	2,758
National Savings Bank—ordinary accounts	1,757
National Savings Bank—investment accounts	4,962
Other securities on the National Savings Register	880
Total	29,099

NATIONAL SAVINGS BANK The National Savings Bank is administered by the Department for National Savings. It operates two categories of savings accounts;

Ordinary accounts, on which interest is paid at two levels, depending on the balance in the account, the rates of interest being announced by the Department from time to time, and

Investment accounts, offering a higher rate of interest which, again, is announced from time to time.

At the end of 1983, there were approximately 15,000,000 ordinary account holders with the National Savings Bank; total deposits with the Bank were approximately £1,700 million on ordinary accounts and £4,400 million on investment accounts.

The National Savings Bank has no branches but operates through the 20,000 or so Post Offices in the UK.

The following are the principal characteristics of ordinary and investment accounts;

Ordinary Accounts

1. Entries are recorded in a bank book, which is retained by the customer. Deposits and withdrawals may be made at any Post Office.
2. Accounts may be opened by any person over seven years of age and may be in sole or joint names. In the latter case, withdrawal applications must be signed by all the parties.
3. Accounts may be opened on behalf of or in the name of children under seven years of age, and they will be able to sign on the account when they reach that age.
4. Trustees wishing to open a National Savings Bank account may do so on application to the Director, National Savings Bank, Glasgow, G58 1SB.
5. An account holder may have a number of accounts in the same name, but the balance or the aggregate of the balances must not exceed £10,000. There are exceptions to this rule in the case of certain trust accounts, societies, clubs and the like.
6. Deposits may be accepted in the form of cash, savings stamps, transfers from a National Girobank account, cheques, dividend warrants and similar negotiable instruments payable on demand.
7. A depositor may withdraw up to £100 on demand at any Post Office. If the withdrawal exceeds £50, the bank book will be retained by the Post Office for examination at Savings Bank headquarters. Under a service introduced in May 1982, a customer may operate a Regular Customer Account at a Post Office of his or her choice with the facility of withdrawing up to £250 in cash on demand without surrendering the bank book. To qualify for this service, a customer must have used the Ordinary Account at the nominated Post Office for a period of six months.
8. Withdrawals up to any amount may be obtained by warrant on application to the Director

of Savings, using Form SB5 obtainable from any Post Office. An application for withdrawal from joint accounts or trust accounts must be signed by all the parties to the account.
9. Periodic payments for the purpose of insurance premiums, mortgage payments, etc. may be made by standing orders provided that payments are not more frequent than once a month and that a reasonable balance is maintained in the account.
10. Since August 1981, a 'Paybill' facility has operated on ordinary accounts. Under this scheme, customers may pay bills at the Post Office counter by making a single withdrawal from their accounts up to a total of £250 on any one day. This scheme extends to telephone accounts, television licences and all bills which are normally payable over a Post Office counter. It also applies to the payment of bills issued by any business which has a National Girobank account.
11. Interest on an ordinary account is paid without deduction of tax and the first £70 of interest each year is free of income tax.

Investment Accounts
1. An investment account may be opened on application to any Post Office. An application form has to be completed and lodged with the amount of the initial deposit. A receipt is issued by the Post Office and the official bank book is despatched to the depositor by the Savings Bank headquarters within 14 days.
2. Accounts may be similarly opened in joint names, but accounts in the names of clubs, societies or trusts may only be opened on direct application to the Director, National Savings Bank, Glasgow G58 1SB. As from October 1981, it also became possible for registered companies and other corporate bodies to open an investment account with the National Savings Bank on direct application to Glasgow.
3. A depositor may have a number of accounts in the same name, but the balance or aggregate balances must not exceed the current maximum of £50,000 (except in the case of balances held before 15th March, 1984, which may remain at the then maximum of £200,000, but if reduced may not be increased above the current maximum, apart from the addition of interest).
4. Withdrawal on demand is not possible. Application for withdrawal must be made to the Director, National Savings Bank, Glasgow G58 1SB, in writing and will be subject to one month's notice from the date the application is received there.
5. Interest at the appropriate rate is earned on each whole pound on deposit for a complete calendar month and is credited to accounts on 31st December each year. It is entered in the bank book when next received at the Savings Bank headquarters.
6. Interest on an investment account is paid without deduction of income tax, but is wholly subject to income tax, i.e. there is no exemption for the first £70 as with interest on an ordinary account.

NATIONAL SAVINGS CERTIFICATES

Savings certificates issued by the Department for National Savings (usually known as National Savings Certificates) are a form of Government security, redeemable at the original purchase price plus a previously stated amount of interest.

The earliest certificates, originally known as War Savings Certificates, were issued from February 1916 to March 1922.

The principal characteristics of National Savings Certificates are

1. They may be purchased at any Post Office or bank in the UK with the exception of Northern Ireland, where there are separate and comparable issues of Ulster Savings Certificates.
2. National Savings Certificates may be purchased only in the names of private individuals and not by corporate bodies or unincorporated associations.
3. Any person of seven years of age and upwards may purchase National Savings Certificates in his or her own name up to the maximum amount prescribed in the terms of each issue.
4. Certificates may be purchased in the name of children under the age of seven years, but will not be repayable until the child has reached that age unless the parents or guardians can show that the proceeds are required for some urgent purpose. Once a child has reached the age of seven years, repayment will not normally be made except on the child's signature.
5. Certificates may be purchased in joint names, in which case the number of units so purchased is attributed to each of the joint holders for the purpose of determining whether his or her total holding is within the permitted maximum.
6. Certificates may be held by trustees in their own names or in the names of the trustees and beneficiaries jointly.
7. For the purpose of determining the maximum permitted holding, trust holdings are not aggregated with private holdings. Where the maximum holding is exceeded owing to the inheritance of additional certificates, permission may be given by the Director of Savings for these to be retained, but no further certificates of that issue may be purchased while the total holding remains at or above the maximum.

8. National Savings Certificates may not be sold by one person to another. The transfer of certificates may be allowed with the permission of the Director of Savings.
9. The repayment of National Savings Certificates with accumulated interest may be obtained on written application to the Director, Savings Certificate and SAYE Office, Durham DH99 1NS. A minimum of eight working days' notice is necessary. The relevant application form P576 MA is available at Post Offices.
10. Interest payable on National Savings Certificates is exempt from UK income tax and capital gains tax.

At the time of writing, there have been 30 issues of savings certificates (other than index-linked certificates) and including the seventeenth issue which was announced but not introduced. Details of the interest currently payable on these earlier issues may be obtained from the Post Office. Since June 1982, a common rate of interest is earned by the certificates of those issues which have come to the end of their initial term. This common rate of interest is announced from time to time. Other issues are already subject to fixed terms or have not yet reached their maturity dates. SEE ALSO *Index-linked Savings Certificates*

NATIONAL SAVINGS DEPOSIT BONDS These were introduced on 17th October, 1983.

The bonds are sold in multiples of £50 with a minimum purchase of £100 and a maximum holding of £50,000. The Department for National Savings announced that the interest rate will be kept competitive.

A particular feature of the bonds is that interest, which is calculated on a daily basis, is accumulated and added to the capital value of the bond on each anniversary of the purchase date. The interest is taxable but is credited to the bond without deduction of tax at source.

Holders may obtain repayment of the bonds at any time on giving three months' notice. There are no penalties if repayment is taken on or after the first anniversary of purchase but the rate of interest on a bond (or part thereof) which is repaid during the first year will be at half the published rate. The minimum amount of repayment is £50.

The bonds may be held by individuals, alone or jointly, or by trustees, registered companies or other corporate bodies.

NATIONAL SAVINGS INCOME BONDS These were introduced on 2nd August, 1982.

Income Bonds are sold in multiples of £1,000 with a minimum holding of £2,000 and, prior to 15th March, 1984, a maximum of £200,000. The permitted maximum is now £50,000 but investments standing above that limit at the date it came into force may continue at the higher level.

Income on the bonds is calculated on a day-to-day basis and is paid to bond-holders monthly. The rate of interest is announced from time to time. The interest is taxable but is paid without deduction of tax at source.

Holders may obtain repayment of the bonds at any time on giving three months' notice. Full interest is paid during the notice period if the bond is repaid more than a year after purchase. If repayment is taken in the first year, interest on the amount repaid is at half-rate from the date of purchase.

Trustees, corporate bodies and clubs may buy income bonds.

On the death of an investor, withdrawal is allowed without notices.

Partial encashments are permitted in multiples of £1,000, provided the minimum balance of £2,000 is maintained.

NATIONAL SAVINGS YEARLY PLAN This scheme was introduced with effect from 21st July, 1984 to replace the index-linked SAYE scheme (q.v.).

Under this plan, savers may make monthly contributions by means of a bank standing order. The minimum monthly contribution is £20 and the maximum £100. Under the plan, contributions must be made for one year but may then be repeated for a year at a time for a total five-year period. During this five years, a fixed rate of interest is guaranteed and the interest is tax-free.

Varying rates are announced from time to time for new plans. The rate which applies when a plan is commenced is guaranteed for the five-year period.

The increase arising from indexation is exempt from UK income tax and capital gains tax.

NATIONAL SAVINGS STOCK REGISTER Many Government securities quoted on the Stock Exchange may also be purchased through the Department for National Savings. Application to purchase Government securities on the National Savings Stock Register should be made on Form GS1, obtainable at Post Offices.

The following are the main points to be noted:

1. Not more than £10,000 value of stock may be purchased on one application, but there is no limit to the total amount of stock which may be held.
2. The price of stock will be that quoted on the Stock Exchange at the time the Department for

National Savings deals with the application. It may thus vary from the price quoted in the daily press at the time the application is despatched.
3. The payment covering the application should cover the estimated amount of the stock and commission. Any excess will be returned by the Department after the purchase.
4. A certificate will be issued to the stockholder, showing the amount of stock inscribed in the holder's name on the National Savings Stock Register.
5. The stock may be sold by application to the Department (Form GS3). The certificate should accompany the application.
6. The commission charges for purchases and sales are

Purchases:	
for amounts not exceeding £250	£1
for amounts not exceeding £250	£1 and a further 50p for every additional £125 or part thereof
Sales:	
for amounts less than £100	10p for every £10 or part thereof
for amounts from £100 to £250	£1
for amounts exceeding £250	£1 and a further 50p for every £125 or part thereof

7. Stocks on the National Savings Stock Register may be transferred from one person to another. There is no charge for the registration of transfers.
8. Interest on Government stocks on the National Savings Stock Register is paid without deduction of income tax, but the interest is not exempt from tax.

The list of stocks available for purchase on the National Savings Stock Register varies from time to time, and is available from General Post Offices.

NEGOTIABLE INSTRUMENT A negotiable instrument is one which conforms to the following three tests:

1. It must be such and in such a state that the property in it (i.e. the legal ownership) passes by mere delivery or in some cases by indorsement and delivery.
2. A person taking it in good faith and for value and without notice of defect of title gets an indefeasible title against all the world. Such a person is called a bona fide holder for value without notice or, in the case of a bill or a cheque, a holder in due course.
3. It must contain a right of action in itself and entitle the holder to sue in his own name.

A negotiable instrument is an exception to the general rule of law that *nemo dat quod non habet* (no one can give what he has not), for a transferee under the conditions mentioned in (2) can obtain a good title from a thief even against the true owner. To affect a transferee with notice of defect of title there must be something more than negligence, and the doctrine of constructive notice is not applicable to negotiable instruments.

Where a stockbroker pledged clients' bearer bonds to a bank who advanced money against them in good faith and without notice, the bank was held to be entitled to hold them against the true owner (*London Joint Stock Bank* v *Simmons* [1892] AC 201). In the course of the judgment Lord Herschell said

> It is surely of the very essence of a negotiable instrument that you may treat the person in possession of it as having authority to deal with it, be he agent or otherwise, unless you know to the contrary, and are not compelled, in order to secure a good title to yourself, to inquire into the nature of his title, or the extent of his authority. . . . I should be very sorry to see the doctrine of constructive notice introduced into the law of negotiable instruments. But regard to the facts of which the taker of such instruments had notice is most material in considering whether he took it in good faith. If there is anything wanting which excites the suspicion that there is something wrong in the transaction, the taker of the instrument is not acting in good faith if he shuts his eyes to the facts presented to him and puts the suspicions aside without further inquiry. ... It is easy enough to make an elaborate presentation after the event of the speculations with which the bank managers might have occupied themselves in reference to the capacity in which the broker who offered the bonds as security for an advance held them. I think, however, they were not bound to occupy their minds with any such speculations. I apprehend that when a person whose honesty there is no reason to doubt offers negotiable securities to a banker or any other person, the only consideration likely to engage his attention is whether the security is sufficient to justify the advance required. And I do not think the law lays upon him the obligation of making any inquiry into the title of the person whom he finds in possession of them: of course, if there is anything to arouse suspicion, to lead to a doubt whether the person purporting to transfer them is justified in entering into the contemplated transaction, the case would be different, the existence of such suspicion or doubt would be inconsistent with good faith. And if no inquiry were made, or if on inquiry the doubt were not removed and the suspicion dissipated, I should have no hesitation in holding that good faith was wanting in a person thus acting.

The following are negotiable instruments: bank notes, bearer bonds, Treasury bills, share warrants and share certificates to bearer, debentures payable to bearer, bills of exchange, promissory notes, and cheques. The list of negotiable instruments is not closed and the courts will give judicial recognition to the custom of merchants to treat mercantile instruments as negotiable. A foreign instrument that is negotiable in the country of its origin is not necessarily negotiable in the UK. Share certificates in the US form, where a form of transfer is placed on the back, are treated as bearer instruments when duly indorsed by the registered holder, but they are not negotiable, for a transferee is unable to sue in his own name until he presents the instrument for registration. Bills of exchange (including cheques) are the most common example of negotiable instruments. They can lose their negotiable quality, however. A bill expressed to be payable to a particular person 'only' or 'not transferable', is neither transferable nor negotiable (Bills of Exchange Act 1882, Section 8). A bill that has been restrictively indorsed can only be negotiated subject to defects of title, i.e. it is not negotiable (Sections 35 and 36). An overdue bill can only be negotiated subject to any defect of title affecting it at maturity and thenceforward no person who takes it can acquire or give a better title than that which the person from whom he took it had; in other words, it is not negotiable (Section 36(2)). Where a bill was payable to the order of a specified payee 'only' and further bore on it the words 'not negotiable', it was held to be limited as to its effect as between the drawer and the acceptor, and to be neither negotiable nor transferable. There cannot be a holder, let alone a holder in due course capable of suing on it (*Hibernian Bank Ltd* v *Gysin & Hanson* [1939] 1 All ER 165). Where a crossed cheque bears on it the words 'not negotiable', he shall not have and shall not be capable of giving a better title to a cheque than that which the person from whom he took it had (Section 81). Such a cheque has lost its negotiability.

'Negotiability by estoppel' is a phrase mistakenly used for title by estoppel and in *Easton* v *London Joint Stock Bank* (1887) 34 ChD 95, it was made plain that no sort of negotiability can be infused into non-negotiable instruments, but that the estoppel is a personal matter of conduct, holding out, etc., wherein the instrument is evidence.

The Committee of London Clearing Bankers agreed in 1958 that the drawing of non-transferable cheques would create serious practical difficulties for the banks and might expose them to unacceptable risks; for example, a paying banker would have no statutory protection in respect of non-transferable cheques cashed at the counter and would in each case be obliged positively to identify the payee, while the collecting banker could not become a holder for value of a non-transferable cheque and would not be able to enforce payment in his own name. For these and other reasons, therefore, it recommended that in appropriate cases customers should be approached with a request that the practice should be discontinued.

SEE ALSO *Holder in Due Course; Not Negotiable Crossing; Overdue Cheque; Quasi-negotiable Instruments*

NEGOTIATED BACK See Section 37, Bills of Exchange Act 1882 under *Negotiation of Bill of Exchange*

NEGOTIATION OF BILL OF EXCHANGE The Bills of Exchange Act 1882, Section 8(2), provides that 'A negotiable bill may be payable either to order or to bearer'. The negotiation of a bill is defined in Section 31:

(1) A bill is negotiated when it is transferred from one person to another in such a manner as to constitute the transferee the holder of the bill.
(2) A bill payable to bearer is negotiated by delivery.
(3) A bill payable to order is negotiated by the indorsement of the holder completed by delivery.
(4) Where the holder of a bill payable to his order transfers it for value without indorsing it, the transfer gives the transferee such title as the transferor had in the bill, and the transferee in addition acquires the right to have the indorsement of the transferor.
(5) Where any person is under obligation to indorse a bill in a representative capacity, he may indorse the bill in such terms as to negative personal liability.

By Section 36

(1) Where a bill is negotiable in its origin it continues to be negotiable until it has been (*a*) restrictively indorsed, or (*b*) discharged by payment or otherwise.
(2) Where an overdue bill is negotiated, it can only be negotiated subject to any defect of title affecting it at its maturity, and thenceforward no person who takes it can acquire or give a better title than that which the person from whom he took it had.
(3) A bill payable on demand is deemed to be overdue within the meaning, and for the purposes of this Section, when it appears on the face of it to have been in circulation for an unreasonable length of time. What is an unreasonable length of time for this purpose is a question of fact.
(4) Except where an indorsement bears date after the maturity of the bill, every negotiation is *prima facie* deemed to have been effected before the bill was overdue.
(5) Where a bill which is not overdue has been dishonoured, any person who takes it with notice of the dishonour takes it subject to any defect of title attaching thereto at the time of dishonour, but nothing in this subsection shall affect the rights of a holder in due course.

With regard to the words 'unreasonable length of time' in the above Section, see *Presentment for Payment.*

A bill may, in the ordinary course of business, be negotiated back to a party already liable thereon. By Section 37

> Where a bill is negotiated back to the drawer, or to a prior indorser or to the acceptor, such party may, subject to the provisions of this Act, re-issue and further negotiate the bill, but he is not entitled to enforce payment of the bill against any intervening party to whom he was previously liable.

Where a bill has been transferred by indorsement to, say, four different persons and the fourth indorser indorses it back to the first, indorser number one cannot enforce payment against the second, third, or fourth indorsers, because each of those three indorsers has a claim against him as the first indorser. But if the first indorser negatived his liability when indorsing the bill, by the addition of the words 'without recourse' to his signature, he can enforce payment, when the bill is indorsed back to him, against the said second, third, or fourth indorsers because they have, in that case, no claim against him.

By Section 8(1) 'When a bill contains words prohibiting transfer, or indicating an intention that it should not be transferable, it is valid as between the parties thereto, but is not negotiable'. SEE *Bill of Exchange; Delivery of Bill; Indorsement; Transferor by Delivery*

NET REDEMPTION YIELD The yield to redemption after deducting all relevant taxation. SEE ALSO *Redemption Yield*

NEW ISSUES The term is applied to the issue of any new capital by a company, a public authority or the Government itself. New issues may be in the form of fixed interest securities, e.g. Government stocks, company debentures and other forms of loan finance or may be in the form of new ordinary stock or 'equity' (q.v.). Also, new issues may take the form of preference shares (q.v.) or convertible securities (q.v.).

The tables opposite show the proceeds of new issues on the London market for both the public sector and the UK company sector for the years from 1973 onwards.

SEE ALSO *Capital; Issuing House; Merchant Banking*

NEW TIME A Stock Exchange expression relating to dealings in the last two days of a Stock Exchange account when bargains may be done for the following account, i.e. for settlement on the Settlement Day for the following account. SEE *Settlement, Stock Exchange*

New Issue Proceeds (Public Sector)

Year	Total (£m)	British Government Securities (£m)	Corporation, County and Public Board (£m)	Irish Government and Overseas Public Sector (£m)
1973	3,766	3,504	262	—
1974	3,343	2,692	651	—
1975	7,260	6,225	1,022	13
1976	9,164	7,968	1,054	142
1977	15,283	13,300	1,289	694
1978	9,459	8,281	1,025	153
1979	16,510	14,119	646	1,745
1980	18,003	15,853	803	1,347
1981	14,499	12,016	841	1,642
1982	15,902	10,313	1,014	4,575
1983	19,879	14,077	1,033	4,769
1984	23,637	14,096	777	8,764

New Issue Proceeds (UK Company Sector)

Year	Total (£m)	Equities (£m)	Other Securities (£m)
1973	335	276	59
1974	214	175	39
1975	1,783	1,521	262
1976	1,269	1,157	112
1977	1,204	1,083	121
1978	1,396	1,324	72
1979	1,376	1,170	206
1980	1,620	1,098	522
1981	2,909	2,493	416
1982	3,020	1,776	1,244
1983	4,511	2,569	1,942
1984	8,790	7,228	1,562

Source: The Stock Exchange.

NEXT OF KIN This is not nowadays a very precise expression and it is probably better not to use the term unless the legal intention is absolutely clear. There is some authority for the view that a gift to 'next of kin' in a will includes the nearest blood relations, including relations of the half-blood, and that they would take the gift as joint tenants (q.v.). On the other hand, a reference to 'statutory next of kin' clearly means those persons entitled to benefit under the rules of intestacy (q.v.). The term 'next of kin' in relation to Social Security benefits is defined in the National Insurance Act 1946, as those persons who would take beneficially on intestacy.

NIGHT SAFES In order that customers may deposit cash or cheques after a bank has closed for the day or for the week-end, night safes were introduced in 1928. The entrance to these safes is in the outside wall of the bank, the opening being fitted with a locked cover to which customers who wish to use the safe are supplied with a key. The cash and cheques are placed in a locked wallet, which is put into the opening, and a chute conveys the wallet inside the bank. The customer calls at the bank in business hours and is given the wallet, which he unlocks, and he pays the contents into his account.

Alternatively, the bank may open the wallet, credit the customer's account with the proceeds, and return the empty wallet to him when he calls for it. Two officers will normally be present to vouch for the amount of cash found in the wallet.

NIL PAID A term applied to an issue of shares, usually a rights issue, where no payment has so far been made for the shares. Thus, the rights to new shares may be taken up by the shareholder and then sold or retained or the rights may be sold 'nil paid' by the shareholder for their market value.

NO PAR VALUE The Companies Acts in the UK require companies to issue shares with a stated nominal or par value, e.g. one pound per share. This inevitably means that after the company has been trading for a while, the true value of the shares will be more or less than the par value (depending on whether the company's position has improved or deteriorated) and in time the par value becomes meaningless in relation to the market value.

In 1920, US corporations began to issue shares with no par value. One object of this procedure was to enable business concerns to give a stated value for their common shares more in keeping with the real value of their assets than the nominal amount in which they were previously expressed. It also enabled corporations to issue new shares at any time at any price. The system has been of considerable advantage to issuing houses in the matter of new finance. For example, a new corporation would issue debentures to which were attached a certain number of shares of no par value. These shares were an incentive to subscribe, for if the new business prospered the debentures would be repaid and the equity of the business would rest in the holders of the shares.

In March 1954, the report was issued of the committee appointed by the President of the Board of Trade, with Mr M. L. Gedge, QC, as chairman, to consider the desirability of amending the Companies Act 1948, so as to permit the issue of shares of no par value. A majority of the committee felt that the present system of issuing shares of nominal value was misleading and hence, although such shares and shares of no par value were alike in that both represented simply a fraction or aliquot part of the equity, nevertheless sound reasons for reform existed. They strongly recommended that companies should be allowed to issue shares of no par value if they wished to do so, but that they should not be obliged to adopt the system. Shares of no par value should be confined to ordinary share capital and a company should not be permitted to arrange its ordinary capital on a mixed basis, consisting partly of shares with a nominal value and partly of no par shares. If shares of no par value are partly paid, and to this no objection was raised, then the fact should be indicated clearly on the share certificate and other appropriate documents.

Although a number of countries have adopted the US practice and permitted the issue of no par value shares, this is not so in the UK, where it is still not legally possible.

NOMINAL CAPITAL The amount authorized as the capital in the memorandum of association of a company, limited by shares, called also the 'authorized' or 'registered' capital. SEE *Capital*

NOMINAL CONSIDERATION Where shares are transferred for other than a monetary consideration, a nominal consideration, usually, say, £1, is inserted in the instrument of transfer. Such instruments attract a fixed stamp duty of 50p where the transfer occurs in the following circumstances:

1. On the appointment of a new trustee of a pre-existing trust, or on the retirement of a trustee.
2. To a mere nominee of the transferor where no beneficial interest in the property passes. The circumstances giving rise to the transfer should be stated.
3. As security for a loan, or a re-transfer to the original transferor on repayment of a loan. (A transfer from a vendor, made by direction of a purchaser to a person who is to hold the shares as security for a loan made to the purchaser, is liable to *ad valorem* duty.)
4. To a residuary legatee; stock, etc., which forms part of the residue divisible under a will.
5. To a beneficiary under a will who is entitled to the shares as a specific legacy.
6. To transfer to the party or parties entitled, shares, etc., forming part of the property of a person dying intestate.
7. To a beneficiary under a settlement on distribution of the trust funds, of shares, etc., forming the share, or part of the share, of those funds to which the beneficiary is entitled in accordance with the terms of the settlement.

In order to get a transfer stamped with the fixed duty of 50p, the transfer must be produced to the marking officer at a stamp office with a certificate on Inland Revenue Form 19 or on the back of the transfer, stating the circumstances under which the transfer is made. The certificate must be signed by both transferor and transferee or a member of the Stock Exchange or a solicitor acting for one of the parties or an accredited representative of a bank. Where a bank or its nominee is a party to the transfer, the certificate may be to the effect that 'the transfer is excepted from the provisions of Section 74, Finance (1909–10) Act, 1910'.

The certificate signed by the marking officer will be accepted by a company registrar as authority to register the transfer with the fixed duty of 50p.

Ad valorem duty is payable whatever be the consideration shown on the transfer where the transfer is made in satisfaction of a pecuniary bequest, or in liquidation of a debt or in exchange for other securities but not, from March 1985, by way of gift.

NOMINEE COMPANIES Instead of placing stocks and shares in the names of personal nominees for security and other purposes, it is the practice of banks to incorporate nominee companies whose sole function is to hold stocks and shares transferred to them by the owners for the purpose of forming security for advances or for purposes of convenience, e.g. to avoid the execution of transfers when the customer is resident abroad. Nominee companies having perpetual succession avoid the difficulty and trouble arising on the retirement or death of personal nominees. Dividends and interest are credited in due course by the nominee company to the customer to whom are passed on notices of meetings and other communications relating to the stocks or shares. It is advisable to take an indemnity from the depositors of shares who are domiciled abroad against any losses arising from notices, etc., not reaching them.

Where instructions are received from a transferor to hold shares already in the name of the nominee company to the order of a third party, the Inland Revenue consider that stamp duty is exigible, but legal opinion is to the opposite effect. Where shares are held on account of joint depositors, who hold as joint tenants, the nominee company is jointly responsible with the survivor(s) for payment of death duty; if the parties are tenants in common, however, the liability rests on the executors of the deceased. A bank must make a return to the Inland Revenue of holdings of 3½ per cent War Loan and of other British Government Stocks on the Post Office Register held in the names of any of its nominees on which untaxed interest of £15 or more is paid. This is a result of the decision in *Attorney-General* v *National Provincial Bank* (1928) 44 TLR 701.

The UK clearing banks will not knowingly allow their nominee services to be used for tax avoidance or any other abuse of fiscal legislation.

It was estimated by the Royal Commission on the Distribution of Income and Wealth (Report No. 2, Cmnd 6172, HMSO, 1975) that 25 per cent by value of ordinary shares in the leading UK companies were held in nominee names. Until comparatively recent times, it was possible to build up anonymously a substantial shareholding in a company by the use of nominee companies. Under Sections 198–220, Companies Act 1985, however, a person acquiring a five per cent interest in the voting capital of a company or reducing or increasing such an interest must notify the company of the details within five days of the transaction. That applies to all public companies.

Changes of more than one per cent in a notifiable interest (the percentages being rounded down to the nearest whole number) must be notified to the company as must the acquisition or cessation of such an interest. This applies not only when shares are acquired or disposed of but when other circumstances, e.g. a change in the capital structure of the company, affect the shareholders' percentage interest. The obligation to notify such a change depends however, on the shareholders' *knowledge* of the circumstances giving rise to the change.

The notification must be in writing and must specify the share capital to which it relates. It must also:

1. state the number of shares the person making the notification is interested in immediately after the change giving rise to the notification or, where he has ceased to have a notifiable interest, the fact that he no longer has such an interest;
2. state the name and address of the person making the notification;
3. identify each registered shareholder to which the notification relates, and the number of shares included in the notification held by each such holder, and
4. where a notification is being made by a person acting together with others, it must state that the person making the notification is a party to an agreement to which the Act applies, notify the names and addresses of the other parties to that agreement, state the numbers of shares to which the notification relates and state the name and address of any person ceasing to be a party to the agreement.

Section 208 of the Act defines in very wide terms

the interests in shares which are notifiable. The Section includes, in particular, the following instances:

1. where the shareholder's spouse or child (or stepchild) under the age of 18 has an interest, or
2. a corporate body has an interest and that body or its directors are accustomed to act in accordance with the notifying shareholders' instructions, or he is entitled to exercise or control one-third or more of the voting power of that body in general meeting, or
3. another person is interested in the shares and the notifying shareholder is acting together with that person, or
4. he is a beneficiary of a trust which includes an interest in the shares, or
5. he enters into a contract to buy the shares, or
6. not being the registered holder of the shares he is entitled to exercise control or control the exercise of any right conferred by the holding of those shares, or
7. he has, other than by virtue of an interest under a trust, the right to call for delivery of the shares or a right to acquire them or is under an obligation to take an interest in them.

NON-BUSINESS DAYS Section 92 of the Bills of Exchange Act, 1882 as amended by Section 3(1) of the Banking and Financial Dealings Act 1971, now reads:

> Where by this Act, the time limited for doing any act or thing is less than three days, in reckoning time, non-business days are excluded.
> Non-business days for the purpose of this Act mean:
> (*a*) Saturday, Sunday, Good Friday, Christmas Day;
> (*b*) A bank holiday under the Banking and Financial Dealings Act, 1971;
> (*c*) A day appointed by Royal proclamation as a public fast or thanksgiving day;
> (*d*) A day declared by an order under Section 2 of the Banking and Financial Dealings Act, 1971, to be a non-business day.

Any other day is a business day. SEE *Bank Holidays*

NON-CUMULATIVE DIVIDEND Where the dividend upon preference shares is payable only out of the profits of each separate year, it is a non-cumulative dividend. On the other hand, if the profits of succeeding years may be employed to pay up all dividends which have accrued on the preference shares, before the ordinary shares get anything, the dividend is said to be cumulative. SEE *Preference Stock or Shares*

NON-PAYMENT OF BILL OR CHEQUE When a bill or cheque, for any reason, is returned unpaid, the answer given by the banker, as the reason of its return, must not be at variance with the actual fact. The answer is usually written upon the bill or cheque. There is no legal obligation to give a written answer on an unpaid cheque, but if presented under Clearing House Rules, it must bear a written reason for non-payment. There is a danger in not putting a written answer on a cheque presented over the counter, for a subsequent holder would not know of its dishonour. A banker might be held liable in damages if he returned a cheque marked 'refer to drawer' when the correct answer should have been 'post-dated', or 'figures and words differ', or some similar answer.

It should be noted that a careless use of an abbreviated answer may render a banker liable. In an action on a returned bill which had been marked 'NA', it was suggested that those letters meant 'no assets' or 'no account', as well as 'no advice', which was the answer the banker intended to give.

The Committee of the Bankers' Clearing House, having observed that answers on unpaid cheques and bills are frequently indicated by initials which in some cases would convey little meaning to a bank's customer and are not always intelligible to the collecting bank, resolved that from 15th October, 1928, the general rule with regard to answers on returns be altered to read as follows:

> No return can be received without an answer in writing on the return why payment is refused, such answer in every case to be written in words without abbreviation and not indicated by initials.

A banker is sometimes able to get a technical mistake in a cheque corrected by the drawer, and where this can be conveniently done it is much better than returning the cheque.

Where there are not sufficient funds to meet a cheque, and there is also a technical irregularity in it, when the cheque is returned, the answer given often refers only to the irregularity and not to the want of funds, particularly if it is expected that by the time the irregularity has been put right the banker will be in a position to pay it.

The words 'will pay on banker's confirmation' are occasionally added to an answer, when the sole reason for the return of the cheque is a technical one, such as 'Discharge irregular'. If the drawer dies before the cheque arrives back, or the account changes so as not to admit of the cheque being debited, the banker is not liable, by reason of the words used, to pay the cheque. The words have reference only to the technical irregularity and not to the payment of the amount.

With regard to the answer to be given when a telephone request is received asking if a certain cheque will be paid, SEE *Advise Fate*

The following are some of the 'answers' which are given on cheques and bills (the answer being generally written in ink on the left-hand top corner):

Acceptor bankrupt
Acceptor dead SEE *Death of Acceptor*
Account attached SEE *Garnishee Order*
Account closed (More often 'No account')
Alteration in ... requires drawer's confirmation
Amounts differ
Crossed to two bankers (q.v.)
Date incomplete
Discharge irregular
Discharge required
Discharge requires confirmation
Drawer bankrupt
Drawer dead SEE *Death of Drawer*
Effects not cleared (q.v.)
Incompletely signed (Or 'Further signature required')
Insufficient funds
Irregularly drawn
Mutilated cheque (q.v.)
No account
No advice
No effects
No orders
Not provided for
Not sufficient (Also written 'Not sufficient funds')
Orders not to pay
Out of date SEE *Stale Cheque*
Post-dated
Present again (An insufficient answer in itself)
Refer to acceptor
Refer to drawer
Re-present
Requires banker's crossing SEE *Crossed Cheque*
Requires stamp of banker to whom crossed
Signature differs (That is, differs from the customer's usual hand or method of signing)
Stale SEE *Stale Cheque*
Words and figures differ

NOSTRO ACCOUNT London bankers keep accounts in currency with agents in many foreign centres. In any communication with the agents regarding the account, the London bank would refer to it as *nostro* account (meaning, our account with you), and the agents, in any communication with the London bank, would refer to it as *vostro* account, (meaning, your account with us). The London bank keeps records in its own books of its foreign *nostro* accounts, the items and balances being agreed from time to time.

Foreign agents also keep accounts in sterling with London banks. The agents would refer to the account, in any communication with the London bank, as *nostro* account, whilst the London bank would refer to it as *vostro* account. These accounts are similarly agreed from time to time.

The account which a London bank may keep with a foreign agent is, of course, quite distinct from the account which a foreign agent may keep with the London bank.

Loro account means their account. The expression is used when dealing with third parties. If two foreign banks have sterling accounts at the same London bank, one of them might, for example, instruct the London bank to transfer a sum from its *nostro* account to the *loro* account of the other bank.

NOT NEGOTIABLE CROSSING 'Where a person takes a crossed cheque which bears on it the words 'not negotiable', he shall not have and shall not be capable of giving a better title to the cheque than that which the person from whom he took it had.' (Bills of Exchange Act 1882, Section 81) The words need not be written between the lines of a general crossing but must be in some proximity to the crossing. The words on an open cheque have no significance but such a cheque presented over the counter by a non-banker would be referred back as an ambiguous document. The phrase in no way limits the transferability of a cheque; it merely removes it from the category of negotiable instruments so that any transferee takes it subject to any previous defects of title; it is a warning that the drawer and other prior parties may set up against a holder a claim of theft at an earlier stage in the cheque's history. There cannot be a holder in due course of a cheque crossed 'not negotiable'.

It is expedient to advise customers when drawing cheques to cross them 'not negotiable'; otherwise, although they may countermand payment, they may have nevertheless to pay a holder in due course (q.v.).

The words do not affect a collecting banker in the absence of other circumstances; neither do they concern a paying banker, who may safely pay a cheque so crossed bearing a series of indorsements. A banker exchanging a cheque so crossed drawn on another bank is in precisely the same position as any other transferee of such a cheque and cannot set up as a holder in due course.

A conditional form of cheque (i.e. one with a form of receipt, the completion of which is a condition of payment) is not negotiable. Such instruments are within the ambit of the Cheques Act 1957, and both paying and collecting bankers are protected when dealing with them but Section 6(2) of the Act expressly provides that the provisions of the Act do not make negotiable any instrument which, apart from them, is not negotiable.

NOTARY PUBLIC Originally a notary was a person who only took notes or minutes and made drafts of writings. He was called by the Romans *notarius*. The duty of a notary, so far as a banker is concerned, is to present dishonoured bills and 'note' them for non-acceptance or non-payment, and, if necessary, afterwards to extend the noting into a protest. SEE *Noting*

NOTE ISSUE Certain banks had the privilege of issuing their own notes, but the amount of the note issue of an English bank was strictly limited to the amount certified by the Commissioners of Inland Revenue as being the average amount of the notes of the bank in circulation during a period of 12 weeks preceding 27th April, 1844. The Bank Charter Act of 1844 regulated the note issues in England.

Through amalgamations, the last note issue of a joint stock bank in England disappeared in 1919, and of a private bank in 1921. SEE *Bank of Issue*

The Bank of England is now the sole bank of issue in England. In 1928, the currency note issue of the Treasury was transferred to the Bank of England and the Bank was empowered to issue notes for £1 and for 10s. SEE *Currency and Bank Notes Act 1954; Fiduciary Issue*

The issue of bank notes in Scotland is regulated by 8 & 9 Vict c 38, and in Northern Ireland by 8 & 9 Vict c 37. Both Acts were passed in 1845, and the regulations are somewhat similar to the Bank Charter Act 1844 (SEE *Bank of Issue*). Notes in Scotland and Northern Ireland may be for £1 and upwards.

Banks in Scotland and Northern Ireland may have an office in London without losing the right to issue own notes, though the right cannot be exercised by the London offices.

The 'note issue' of a bank means the total amount of own notes which the bank is legally authorized to issue. The expression 'note circulation' is generally used to mean the total of the bank's own notes which are actually in the hands of the public. SEE *Bank Notes*

NOTICE IN LIEU OF DISTRINGAS Rule 4 of Order 46 of the Supreme Court provides that a party claiming to be interested in shares or stock registered in the name of another may file a notice to that effect together with an affidavit in the Central Office of the Supreme Court or at a District Registry. An office copy of the affidavit and a sealed duplicate of the notice will be supplied to the applicant for service on the registered office of the company concerned. The company will then be under the necessity of giving the server of the notice eight clear days' warning of its intention to pass a transfer of the shares. This will give the interested party time to protect his interest by applying for an injunction. The notice in lieu of distringas can also be drawn to restrain the payment of dividends without first of all advising the server of the notice.

This method of safeguarding interests in stocks and shares is rarely used by English banks in the case of advances against untransferred securities. It is used in the case of a mortgage of an equitable interest in an estate comprising stocks and shares, where, in addition to serving the trustees with notice of the mortgage, a distringas notice is served on the companies concerned. SEE *Distringas*

NOTICE OF DISHONOUR Where a bill has been dishonoured by non-acceptance or non-payment, notice of dishonour must be given to the drawer, and each indorser and ordinarily any such party not receiving such a notice is discharged. (Section 48, Bills of Exchange Act 1882.) A collecting banker receiving back an unpaid cheque, forwarded for collection on behalf of his customer, must give such customer notice of dishonour. This is usually done by returning the article to him with a covering memorandum. If, however, the banker re-presents the cheque (as, for example, where he confirms an irregular indorsement), he must nevertheless send his customer notice of dishonour, otherwise in the event of the second dishonour of the cheque, the customer might refuse to be debited therewith on the grounds that not having received notice of dishonour in the first instance, he assumed the cheque was paid. For rules as to giving notice and as to when notice is excused, see under *Dishonour of Bill of Exchange*.

The practical importance of this is illustrated by the case of *Yeoman Credit Ltd* v *Gregory* [1963] 1 WLR 343, in which an indorser was held not to be liable because the holder had taken a day longer than permitted (despite the fact, incidentally, that the presenting banker had given notice to the holder a day earlier than was necessary). See also under *Dishonour* and case quoted therein.

In the case of *Eaglehill Ltd* v *J. Needham Builders Ltd* [1972] 2 QB 8, it was held in the House of Lords that a Notice of Dishonour is not invalid merely because it is posted before the due date of payment of the bill: it is a good notice unless it is received before the bill itself is dishonoured.

NOTICE OF LIEN A notice served on the secretary or registrar of a company, where stock or shares are held as security untransferred, advising him of the charge given by the borrower. It is usually served in duplicate with a request for the duplicate to be returned receipted as an acknowledgment. Some statutory companies require a registration fee.

Usually such a notice is ignored or a disavowal of the notice is sent by the company drawing attention to Section 117 of the Companies Act 1948, whereby a company is forbidden to take notice of any trust, express, implied, or constructive. It may be noted however, that in *Bradford Banking Co Ltd* v *Henry Briggs Son & Co Ltd* (1886) 12 APP Cas 29, the House of Lords held that the Notice of Deposit which the bank had sent to the company was not a matter of trust within Section 30 of the Companies Act 1862, the section now replaced by Section 117. It is understood that many companies keep an unofficial register of such notices which is useful where a shareholder attempts to obtain a duplicate certificate.

Some companies provide in their articles that they shall have a first and paramount lien on their shares for any moneys owing by a shareholder.

Notice of lien is sent to a company, not in its function as a registering body but in its trading capacity, whereby the shareholder may from time to time become indebted to it. The object of the notice is to warn the company against allowing its shareholder to become indebted to it subsequent to the notice. Thus a notice of lien given by a bank as mortgagee of a company's shares effectively warns the company that it cannot enforce its lien over the shares in question in respect of after-incurred debts of the particular shareholder. In the case of *Bradford Banking Co Ltd* v *Henry Briggs Son & Co* (1886) 12 App Cas 29, it was held that the words in the company's articles 'first and permanent lien' merely made the company first mortgagee of the shares of any shareholder indebted to it. As first mortgagee the company was at liberty to make further advances to its shareholder until it received notice of second mortgage, after which it could not make further advances to rank in front of the interest of which it had received notice. The notice of lien given by the bank was not notice of a trust, but was an effectual warning that the remanent interest in the shares had been charged to the bank. The Bank of England is prohibited by statute from receiving notice of lien in respect of Government stocks.

A condition of an official quotation on the Stock Exchange is that stock and fully paid shares shall not be subject to the company's lien, and hence many banks refrain from sending notice of lien in such cases, for there is no risk of the company raising a lien on its shares on account of a debt due to it from the shareholder.

Notice of lien is particularly necessary in the case of private companies where it is not uncommon for members to be indebted to the company. Likewise it is desirable to serve notice when lending against shares of another bank as it is conceivable that the shareholder may also become a borrower from such bank on the strength of his shareholding.

Notice in lieu of distringas (q.v.) is a method of giving notice of an interest in stocks or shares which a company or registrar must recognise. A charging order (q.v.) is another method, but is only available to a judgment creditor. SEE UNDER *Lien*

NOTICE OF SECOND MORTGAGE Where a second mortgage is taken, notice thereof should be given to the first mortgagee in order to fix the sum for which his mortgage shall be available as security. The first mortgagee should be asked to acknowledge in writing receipt of the notice, confirming the amount outstanding, and to state if he has received notice of any other mortgages and whether he is bound by the terms of his mortgage to make further advances. If the latter is the case, such further advances will rank in front of the second mortgage. This would be the case where the mortgagee was advancing a stated sum by instalments. Unless his mortgage contains such a covenant, a mortgagee, before making additional advances, must search the Land Charges Register to ascertain if any subsequent mortgages have been registered since he made his original advance.

In the case of a mortgage to secure a current account or other further advances, however, registration of a second mortgage will not affect the original lender with notice unless and until he searches. (Law of Property Act 1925, Section 94, as amended by the Law of Property (Amendment) Act 1926.) Receipt of direct notice, however, would affect him.

In the case of land with a registered title where a charge to secure further advances is registered, the Registrar must advise the first chargee before making any entry on the Register adversely affecting the priority of any further advances.

If a banker receives notice of a second mortgage and does not break the account, the operation of the Rule in Clayton's Case will mean that all subsequent credits to the account will go to reduce the advance as at the date of receipt of the notice, whilst all payments out of the account will be in the nature of fresh advances ranking behind the second mortgage. SEE *Deeley* v *Lloyds Bank Ltd* [1912] AC 756.

Frequently a banker receives notice of a second mortgage which expressly mentions that it is subject to an advance of a named amount by the banker. A banker will in such a case be safe in lending up to such sum by way of a non-fluctuating loan, but if the advance is by way of overdraft, the notice of second mortgage should specifically state that the banker is free to make advances by way of fluctuating overdraft to an amount not exceeding at any one time the named sum.

Where notice of second mortgage is received in respect of an advance on loan account, the borrower is free to deal with any credit balance on his current account, until such time as the banker calls for repayment of the loan and is thus in a position to appropriate any credit balance towards repayment of the loan.

In the case of a limited company, registration of a charge at Companies House is deemed to be notice to all the world. There is no duty on the part of a second mortgagee to give direct notice of his charge to a first mortgagee, and hence *Stubb's Weekly Gazette* (q.v.) should be closely searched for notice by way of debenture or otherwise. It is very doubtful if the exception in favour of bankers in Section 94 of the Law of Property Act 1925, regarding registration at the Land Charges Registry quoted above, applies similarly to registration of a company's charge at Companies House.

Where an account has been broken on receipt of notice of second charge, future interest charges will have priority to the second charge. Such interest should not be merged into the debt outstanding at the time of breaking the account, however, but debited to a suspense account pending provision by the borrower. SEE ALSO *Second Mortgage*

NOTING Where a bill has been dishonoured by non-acceptance or by non-payment it may be handed by the holder to a notary public to be noted. The notary presents the bill again to the drawee for acceptance, or to the acceptor for payment, or to the bank where accepted payable, and if acceptance or payment is still not obtained the bill is noted.

The noting consists of the notary's initials, the date, the noting charges, and a mark referring to the notary's register, written on the bill itself. The notarial registers bear certain letters upon them and a corresponding letter is put upon the bill as a mark. A ticket or label is also attached to the bill on which is written the answer given to the notary's clerk who makes the notarial presentment, e.g. 'no orders', 'no advice', 'no effects', 'office closed'. Before sending out the bill, the notary makes a full copy of it in his register and then subsequently adds the answer given, if any. From these records the notary will draw up the protest, if such is required. A nominal fee is charged by notaries.

In the case of an inland bill, it is not necessary to note or protest any such bill in order to preserve the recourse against the drawer or indorsers. (Section 51(1). Bills of Exchange Act 1882.) When an inland bill is noted, it is generally with the idea of getting someone to accept the bill for the honour of one of the parties to it. A banker does not usually note a dishonoured inland bill which he has received for collection, unless instructed to do so by his customer or correspondent.

In the case of a foreign bill, however, which has been dishonoured by non-acceptance or non-payment, it must, in order to charge the drawer and indorsers, be duly protested for non-acceptance or non-payment (Section 51(2)), unless instructions are received from the remitter of the bill that it is not to be noted or protested. Noting is a preparatory step to the protest (SEE *Protest*). Bills to be noted are, in some country banks, sent to the notary before the close of business, but in London it is the practice of bankers to send them after the close of business, thus giving the acceptor up till that hour the opportunity to meet them. A bill may be noted on the day of its dishonour, and must be noted not later than the next succeeding business day (SEE *Bills of Exchange (Time of Noting) Act 1917*); the protest may be subsequently extended as of the date of the noting (Section 51(4)). Delay in noting is excused when the delay is caused by circumstances beyond the control of the holder and not imputable to his default, misconduct, or negligence (Section 51(9)).

A holder of a dishonoured bill is entitled to recover the expenses of noting from any party liable on the bill. (SEE SECTION 57, UNDER *Dishonour of Bill of Exchange*)

If the services of a notary cannot be obtained at the place where a bill is dishonoured, the Bills of Exchange Act 1882 provides that any householder or substantial resident of the place may, in the presence of two witnesses, give a certificate attesting the dishonour of the bill, which shall operate as if it were a formal protest of the bill. SEE *Bill of Exchange; Householder's Protest; Protest*

NOVATION Novation is the substitution of a new obligation for an old one, or of a new debtor for an old one. In *Scarfe* v *Jardine* (1882) 7 App Cas 345, Lord Selborne gave the following definition:

There being a contract in existence, some new contract is substituted for it, either between the same parties (for that might be) or between different parties, the consideration mutually being the discharge of the old contract.

Where one bank amalgamates with another, the debtors of the old bank, as well as those who have given security in any form, are required to sign a form of assent agreeing to the transfer of their obligations from the one bank to the other. Until the form of assent is signed, the debt, or security, should not be transferred from the one bank to the other.

If the amalgamation is by private Act of Parliament, this point is covered in the Act.

Where a creditor of the old bank has received notice of the amalgamation, Mr Justice Buckley said (in his work *Company Law*)

Although he do not by an express agreement assent to the novation, yet if he acts upon it, and takes the benefits which he could only be entitled to upon the assumption that he has assented to it, there will be evidence on which the Court may find, and, unless there is something to contradict it, ought to find, that he has agreed to take the liability of the new company in substitution for that of the old one.

In *Bradford Old Bank* v *Sutcliffe* [1918] 2 KB 833, where it was argued that a surety was discharged by a novation of the debt, by which another bank (with whom the plaintiffs had amalgamated) became the creditor, Pickford, LJ, in the Court of Appeal, in the course of his judgment, said there can be no doubt that a novation by which the original debtor is released from his debt discharges the surety, but a transfer of an existing and ascertained debt to another creditor stands on a different footing. In order to discharge the surety, it must effect a material alteration in his position. Here the debt was ascertained as long ago as 1899, and the alleged novation did not take place until 1907, the original debtor still remaining liable for the debt. It has been clearly decided that an assignment of the debt does not discharge the surety. For all purposes, so far as the interests of the surety are concerned, a novation by which the original creditor releases the debtor has no greater effect than an assignment of the debt with notice to the surety. In either case, the transferee of the debt, whether by novation or assignment, is the person with whom the surety has to deal; and as the liability is already ascertained, it is a matter of no consequence as to whom he has to pay it.

O

OCCUPATIONAL PENSION SCHEMES SEE *Pensions, Pension Schemes*

OCCUPATIONAL PENSIONS BOARD The Occupational Pensions Board was set up in 1973 and under the Social Security Pensions Act 1975, which came into effect in April 1978, the Board assumed responsibility for approving those occupational pension schemes which were contracted out of the State scheme. Contracting out certificates were issued by the Board to those schemes which were approved which, in general, meant those which provided benefits at least equivalent to the minimum benefits under the State scheme.

The Board has a general supervisory role in relation to occupational pension schemes and has conducted a number of studies and surveys at the request of the Government of the day. In a report prepared for the Government in 1975, the Board made the following recommendations.

1. Trustees or managers of funded schemes in which the benefits were not fully secured by insurance policies should be expressly required to prepare annual reports and accounts, to secure an auditor's report on the accounts and to obtain an actuarial report when the scheme was set up and at least triennially thereafter. For schemes with benefits fully secured by insurance policies, there should be an annual statement signed on behalf of the life office concerned showing that the benefits were fully secured and that the premiums required in the previous year had been paid.
2. There should be a clear legal requirement on trustees and managers of pension schemes to make certain financial and other information available to scheme members on request.
3. Members and beneficiaries should be explicitly entitled to pass this information on to their trade unions or other representatives.
4. All schemes, whether contracted-out or not, should be obliged to register with a central authority to ensure that the scheme rules made proper provision for disclosure of information.
5. Consideration should be given to legislation to allow suitable cases involving breach of trust to be heard in the county courts so as to make it easier for beneficiaries and members to obtain redress.
6. Member participation in occupational pension schemes should be encouraged by publication of a code of good practice. There should be a long-term study over a five-year period to check that the proposed code was having the desired effect.

At the time of writing, none of these recommendations has been adopted as a matter of law but further study and debate continues into the matter of the regulation of occupational schemes.

OFFER PRICE The price at which the jobber offers to sell stocks or shares and at which therefore, the broker may buy. Hence, from the standpoint of the public, the offer price is the purchase price. The term is also used in relation to unit trusts (q.v.), the offer price being that at which the public may purchase units from the managers. SEE *Bid Price*

OFFER FOR SALE An invitation to the public to buy the shares of a new issue from the issuing house to whom the issue has been sold outright by the company concerned. The document whereby the invitation is made is deemed to be a prospectus (q.v.) issued by the company, subject to all the requirements of the Companies Acts. The issuing house which is sponsoring the offer may be remunerated, wholly or in part, by a differential between the price which the company and/or the vendors receive, and the price at which the shares are offered to the public. SEE *Merchant Banking*

OFFICIAL CUSTODIAN FOR CHARITIES This office was set up under the Charities Act 1960 for the purpose of holding property in trust for charities. The Charity Commissioners designate one of their officers as the Official Custodian and he works from the Commissioners' office.

Under the Charities Act the Official Custodian may hold in trust for charities:

1. any land or other property vested in him by an order of the Court or of the Charity Commissioners for England and Wales, and
2. any personal property, e.g. stocks and shares

held by or in trust for a charity, or comprised in any testamentary gift to a charity, which the Official Custodian agrees may be transferred to him, his receipt for property so comprised being a complete discharge to the person administering the will.

The Official Custodian provides two particular services: he keeps in safe custody charity funds transferred to him and he remits the gross income from those funds to the charity trustees.

The Official Custodian makes no charge for his services and, indeed, has no power to charge fees. He is prohibited by statute from exercising any powers of management and the responsibility of management remains with the charity trustees. He has the same powers, duties and liabilities as a custodian trustee under Section 4, Public Trustee Act 1906. SEE *Public Trustee*

In summary, the advantages of appointing the Official Custodian are

1. The trust funds are held in safe custody.
2. The Official Custodian has perpetual succession and thus the need to transfer investments on the death or retirement of trustees is avoided.
3. The Official Custodian reclaims all recoverable tax deducted from dividends and interest, arising from the investments held by him, and thus remits the income gross to the trustees.
4. The Official Custodian deals with all administrative matters in connection with the investment.
5. The Official Custodian will assist the charity trustees with information or advice in relation to investment matters. The address of the Official Custodian is at the office of the Charity Commissioners, 14 Ryder Street, St James's, London SW1Y 6AH.

OFFICIAL LIST SEE *Stock Exchange Daily Official List*

OFFICIAL RECEIVER An official receiver is a person appointed by the Department of Trade and Industry to administer the estates of bankrupt persons. He acts under the directions of the Department and is also an officer of the court to which he is attached. There may be more than one official receiver attached to a court (Section 70 of the Bankruptcy Act 1914).

The duties of an official receiver are set forth in the following Sections of the Bankruptcy Act 1914.

Status of Official Receiver

72.—(1) The duties of the official receiver shall have relation both to the conduct of the debtor and to the administration of his estate.

(2) An official receiver may, for the purpose of affidavits verifying proofs, petitions, or other proceedings under this Act, administer oaths.

(3) All provisions in this or any other Act referring to the trustee in a bankruptcy shall, unless the context otherwise requires, or the Act otherwise provides, include the official receiver when acting as trustee.

(4) The trustee shall supply the official receiver with such information, and give him such access to and facilities for inspecting the bankrupt's books and documents, and generally shall give him such aid, as may be requisite for enabling the official receiver to perform his duties under this Act.

Duties of Official Receiver as regards the Debtor's Conduct

73. As regards the debtor, it shall be the duty of the official receiver—

(a) To investigate the conduct of the debtor and to report to the court, stating whether there is reason to believe that the debtor has committed any act which constitutes a misdemeanour under this Act, or any enactment repealed by this Act, or which would justify the Court in refusing, suspending, or qualifying an order for his discharge;

(b) To make such other reports concerning the conduct of the debtor as the Board of Trade may direct;

(c) To take such part as may be directed by the Board of Trade in the public examination of the debtor;

(d) To take such part and give such assistance in relation to the prosecution of any fraudulent debtor as the Board of Trade may direct.

Duties of Official Receiver as to Debtor's Estate

74.—(1) As regards the estate of a debtor it shall be the duty of the official receiver—

(a) Pending the appointment of a trustee, to act as interim receiver of the debtor's estate, and where a special manager is not appointed, as manager thereof:

(b) To authorise the special manager to raise money or make advances for the purposes of the estate in any case where, in the interests of the creditors, it appears necessary so to do:

(c) To summon and preside at the first meeting of creditors:

(d) To issue forms of proxy for use at the meetings of creditors:

(e) To report to the creditors as to any proposal which the debtor may have made with respect to the mode of liquidating his affairs:

(f) To advertise the receiving order, the date of the creditors' first meeting and of the debtor's public examination, and such other matters as it may be necessary to advertise:

(g) To act as trustee during any vacancy in the office of trustee.

The powers and duties of the official receiver with regard to the winding up of companies are defined in Sections 526–530, Companies Act 1985, which are as follows.

526.—(1) For the purposes of this Act as it relates to the winding up of companies by the court in England and Wales, the term "official receiver" means the official receiver (if any) attached to the court for bankruptcy purposes or, if there is more than one such official receiver, then such one of them as the Secretary of State may appoint or, if there is no such official receiver, then an officer appointed for the purpose by the Secretary of State.

(2) Any such officer shall, for the purpose of his duties under this Act, be styled "the official receiver".

527.—(1) If in the case of the winding up of a company by the court in England and Wales it appears to the court desirable, with a view to securing the more convenient and economical conduct of the winding up, that some officer other than the person who would under section 526 be the official receiver should be the official receiver for the purposes of that winding up, the court may appoint that other officer to act.

(2) The officer so appointed is then deemed, for all purposes of this Act, to be the official receiver in that winding up.

528.—(1) Where the court in England and Wales has made a winding-up order or appointed a provisional liquidator, there shall (unless the court otherwise orders) be made out and submitted to the official receiver a statement as to the affairs of the company in the prescribed form.

(2) The statement shall be verified by affidavit and show particulars of the company's assets, its debts and liabilities, the names, residences and occupations of its creditors, the securities held by them respectively, the dates when the securities were respectively given, and such further or other information as may be prescribed or as the official receiver may require.

(3) The statement shall be submitted and verified by one or more of the persons who are at the relevant date the directors and by the person who at that date is the secretary of the company, or by such of the persons mentioned in the following subsection as the official receiver (subject to the direction of the court) may require to submit and verify the statement.

(4) The persons referred to above are—

(*a*) those who are or have been officers of the company,

(*b*) those who have taken part in the formation of the company at any time within one year before the relevant date,

(*c*) those who are in the employment of the company, or have been in its employment within the year just mentioned, and are in the opinion of the official receiver capable of giving the information required, and

(*d*) those who are or have been within that year officers of or in the employment of a company which is, or within that year was, an officer of the company to which the statement relates.

(5) For purposes of this section, "the relevant date" is—

(*a*) in a case where a provisional liquidator is appointed the date of his appointment, and

(*b*) in a case where no such appointment is made, the date of the winding-up order.

(6) The statement of affairs required by this section shall be submitted within 14 days from the relevant date, or within such extended time as the official receiver or the court may for special reasons appoint.

(7) If a person, without reasonable excuse, makes default in complying with the requirements of this section, he is liable to a fine and, for continued contravention, to a daily default fine.

529.—(1) A person making or concurring in the making of the statement and affidavit required by section 528 shall be allowed, and shall be paid by the official receiver or provisional liquidator (as the case may be) out of the company's assets such costs and expenses incurred in and about the preparation and making of the statement and affidavit as the official receiver may consider reasonable, subject to an appeal to the court.

(2) A person stating himself in writing to be a creditor or contributory of the company is entitled by himself or by his agent at all reasonable times, on payment of the prescribed fee, to inspect the statement submitted under section 528, and to a copy of or extract from it.

(3) A person untruthfully so stating himself to be a creditor or contributory is guilty of a contempt of court and, on the application of the official receiver or the liquidator, punishable accordingly.

(4) The statement required by section 528 may be used in evidence against any person making or concurring in making it.

530.—(1) When a winding-up order is made, the official receiver shall, as soon as practicable after the receipt of the statement to be submitted under section 528 (or, in a case where the court orders that no statement shall be submitted, as soon as practicable after the date of the order) submit a preliminary report to the court—

(*a*) as to the amount of capital issued, subscribed and paid up, and the estimated amount of assets and liabilities, and

(*b*) if the company has failed, as to the causes of the failure, and

(*c*) whether in his opinion further enquiry is desirable as to any matter relating to the promotion, formation or failure of the company or the conduct of its business.

(2) The official receiver may also, if he thinks fit, make further reports (one or more) stating the manner in which the company was formed and whether in his opinion any fraud has been committed by any person in its promotion or formation, or by any officer of the company in relation to it since its formation, and any other matter which in his opinion it is desirable to bring to the notice of the court.

(3) If the official receiver states in any such further report that in his opinion a fraud has been committed as above-mentioned, the court has the further powers provided in sections 563 and 564 (public examination of promoters and officers).

SEE *Bankruptcy; Company*

OFF–SHORE FINANCIAL CENTRES The expression 'off-shore' has acquired its own special meaning in the financial world. Naturally enough it was of geographical origin. People who moved their residence or their business affairs from some political land mass to a nearby tax-efficient base were usually moving to the nearest convenient haven within reach. It was literally off-shore — the British to the Channel Islands, the Americans to the Bahamas, the Chinese to Hong Kong and the Australians to the New Hebrides. In time, however, the term acquired a wider significance and was used to apply to any centre where international business may be done in a favourable tax climate. This may be an on-shore independent state, e.g. Panama, Liberia, Liechtenstein, but it may also be a state within a state — usually a situation where a country allows international business to be conducted free from the burden of its own tax laws. For example, non-resident companies may operate in Jersey free from Jersey's own income tax and in a number of countries it is possible for overseas nationals whether personal or corporate, to conduct business in a way which is reasonably free from the local fiscal legislation. Indeed, it is argued by some that the UK is one of the best 'off-shore' centres in the world because there is more international business conducted there, untrammelled by British taxation or other restrictions, than in any other place.

The services offered by off-shore centres include investment management (SEE *Off-Shore Funds*), the management of private trusts, company registration services, captive insurance companies, cash management on behalf of international companies and the 'booking' of bank loans, whether for reasons of tax efficiency or in order to take advantage of the freedom from regulatory provisions in a bank's home country.

The factors which affect the choice of an off-shore centre include (1) local exchange control regulations, if any, (2) freedom of foreign banks to operate, (3) freedom to operate in non-local currencies, (4) freedom from onerous local taxes, (5) local expertise, (6) political stability, (7) complete confidentiality and (8) (for the benefit of visitors) an agreeable climate.

OFF–SHORE FUNDS These are unit trusts (q.v.) or mutual funds (q.v.) or sometimes open-ended investment companies established in off-shore financial centres (q.v.) for the reasons stated under that heading. The particular reasons will usually be (1) freedom from local taxes, (2) freedom from exchange control regulations, and in some cases (3) freedom from the regulatory provisions of the home country. From the standpoint of British unit trust regulations, there are only modest advantages in an off-shore location, particularly since the abolition of Exchange Control. There are, however, the advantages that (1) there is little, if any, tax deducted from the fund at source, (2) funds may be marketed internationally without the disadvantage of UK taxation, (3) bearer securities may be issued in some centres, and (4) unit trusts may invest in assets other than securities within the meaning of Prevention of Fraud (Investments) Act 1958. (Unit trusts may indeed invest in such assets in the UK but they would not be authorized by the Department of Trade and Industry and thus would not enjoy the tax exemptions which apply to authorized unit trusts.)

Because off-shore funds are by definition not located in the UK they may not be authorized under the Prevention of Fraud (Investments) Act (regardless of the investment portfolio) and thus may not be marketed freely in the UK.

OLD LADY OF THREADNEEDLE STREET The term has been applied to the Bank of England and the directors of the Bank. In Brewer's *Dictionary of Phrase and Fable*, it is stated that the directors 'were so called by William Cobbett because, like Mrs Partington, they tried with their broom to sweep back the Atlantic waves of national progress'.

OPEN CHEQUE An uncrossed cheque. It can be presented for payment at the counter of the drawee banker, who is protected under certain conditions in the payment thereof against forged indorsements by Section 60 of the Bills of Exchange Act 1882. An open cheque payable to a limited company can safely be paid without inquiry as to the presenter's authority in the absence of suspicious circumstances, and provided the indorsement, in the case of an order cheque, purports to be correct.

As to suspicious circumstances, suggestions were made in *Vagliano* v *Bank of England* [1891] AC 107, and in *Auchteroni* v *Midland Bank* [1928] 2 KB 294, to the effect that presentment by a party unlikely to be trusted with an instrument convertible into cash, might put a bank on inquiry. In the latter case concerning the payment of a domiciled bill over the counter to a firm's cashier, it was implied that presentment by an office boy or tramp might amount to notice of defect of title under Bills of Exchange Act 1882, Section 59.

A banker collecting an open cheque is since 1957 protected from liability for conversion by the Cheques Act, Section 4, which covers both open and crossed instruments.

OPEN CREDITS A customer may, as a rule, arrange to have his cheques cashed at another bank or at some other branch. The request should be in writing and be signed by the customer. The letter advising the bank or branch to honour his cheques should be signed by the manager and state precisely what cheques are to be paid, to what extent and for how long the credit is to continue, and a specimen signature should accompany the advice. Such cheques should not be crossed.

A common form of advice is to honour cheques drawn by John Brown to the extent of £10 in any one day. An advice to honour cheques to the extent of £60 in any one week is not a good form, if the customer giving the order intends the money to be drawn at the rate of so much per day, as it is clear that the full amount may be drawn on one day and still comply with the letter of advice.

When a bank receives from another bank or branch a request to pay certain cheques, the greatest care should be taken to ascertain that the letter of advice is genuine. If there is any doubt, confirmation should be obtained.

Credits opened between different banks are, as a rule, arranged through the head offices of the respective banks.

Particulars of all credits opened should be recorded. The amount of such credits should be justified by the nature of the account. The banker having opened a credit cannot refuse to pay a cheque cashed thereunder, in the event of there being no funds to meet it in the customer's account.

The customer is sometimes given a special form of cheque book, the cheques being drawn upon the banker who is to pay the cheques and an indication is given upon the cheques of the name of the bank where the drawer's account is kept.

The mere fact that a banker pays a cheque drawn upon another bank, under a standing credit, does not release him from liability if he pays one bearing a forged indorsement. He should make certain that the party presenting a cheque is the person entitled to receive payment. If payment is made to the wrong person, the banker who cashes the cheque is liable for any loss. It is reasonable, however, to expect that a customer wishing his cheques so paid should state in writing that the banker shall not incur any greater liability than if the cheques were paid by the bank on which they are drawn. With regard to the liability of a bank which pays, under advice, a cheque drawn upon another bank, or upon another branch of the same bank, see under *Payment of Cheque*.

When a customer gives an order to stop payment of a cheque, notice should be given to each branch or bank which has authority to cash his cheques.

With increased use of credit cards, there is less need nowadays for open credit facilities.

OPEN MARKET OPERATIONS The purchase or sale of securities in the stock exchange or money market by the central bank to expand or contract the volume of credit. For example, when formerly the Bank of England found it necessary to raise the Bank Rate (q.v.), this measure would not be effective unless market rates of interest were raised in sympathy; and if the supply of money seeking investment was abundant, market rates might lag behind. In those circumstances, the Bank would sell Government securities (including Treasury bills) in the open market, thereby reducing the supply of funds in the money market and forcing up market rates. The reverse process, involving the purchase of securities, would be associated with a *reduction* in the Bank Rate. Of recent years, this technique has been completely overshadowed by the use of Treasury bills and Treasury deposit receipts, the issues of which have been adjusted in amount to absorb or release sufficient funds to produce the desired conditions in the money market. SEE *Monetary Policy*

OPENING A CROSSING Where a cheque is crossed and the drawer cancels the crossing by writing upon the cheque 'Pay Cash' and adding his signature, the operation is called 'opening the crossing'.

The effect of opening a crossed cheque is that the banker is thereby requested to pay cash over the counter instead of paying the cheque, in accordance with the crossing, to another banker if it was crossed generally or to the banker specified in the crossing if it was crossed specially. The Bills of Exchange Act does not make any provision for the cancellation of a crossing, and the use of the words 'pay cash' has arisen from custom.

Where the words 'pay cash' have been actually written by the drawer upon a crossed cheque payable to order and signed by him, and the banker pays the cheque to the payee, the banker does not, apparently, incur any liability. If, however, the signature to an opening is forged, the cheque remains a crossed cheque and the banker will incur liability if he cashes such a cheque over the counter to a person not entitled to the money.

When a drawer has issued a crossed cheque he cannot subsequently cancel the crossing to the injury of anyone who took it as a crossed cheque.

Owing to the losses which banks have suffered through the fraudulent opening of crossed cheques, the Committee of London Clearing Bankers in November 1912 passed the following resolution:

That no opening of cheques be recognised unless the full signature of the drawer be appended to the alteration, and then only when presented for payment by the drawer or by his known agent.

Adherence to this rule by bankers should provide protection against the risks from frauds of this nature.

OPTION The right to buy or sell a particular asset, usually at a stated price, and within a particular period, e.g. an option to buy or sell stocks and shares, commodities, property or land or whatever at some date in the future, at a price or according to a formula determined at the outset. The option is itself a contract, and must be therefore, accompanied by consideration (unless it is by deed), i.e. a price, however modest, must be paid for the option itself.

On the Stock Exchange, three-month options on leading shares cost approximately five to ten per cent of the current share price. Thus, there must be a movement of more than that amount in the share price to produce any profit on the deal. Shorter options can, however, be purchased through the Stock Exchange and these are usually cheaper, e.g. of the order of three per cent of the share price. It is possible to take out '16-day' options which run from the second Tuesday of one account to the second Thursday of the next. SEE *Account; Stock Exchange; Call Option; Option Mortgage; Traded Options*

OPTION MORTGAGE Any person who borrowed on mortgage but who did not pay tax or whose taxable income was less than the mortgage interest payment was at a disadvantage in relation to other borrowers. The Government therefore introduced in 1968, the Option Mortgage Scheme, which enabled a borrower, instead of obtaining tax relief to receive a subsidized rate of interest. The subsidy was paid by the Government to the building society and passed on to the borrower by way of a lower interest rate. The extent of the subsidy was approximately equivalent to the tax relief which would be available at the basic rate of tax. The borrower had to decide whether to avail himself of the Option Mortgage Scheme at the time he made application for his mortgage. In later years, if his income increased and he paid more tax he could elect to change to the normal tax relief basis. Under the Housing Act 1980, if a borrower commenced his mortgage on the basis of normal tax relief, he could switch to an option mortgage at some future date but the right to switch either way could only be exercised once, except in cases of hardship.

With effect from April 1983, the Option Mortgage Scheme was absorbed into the new system of Mortgage Interest Relief at Source (MIRAS) (q.v.).

ORDER (CHEQUE OR BILL OF EXCHANGE) The Bills of Exchange Act 1882, Section 8, provides as follows:

(4) A bill is payable to order which is expressed to be so payable, or which is expressed to be payable to a particular person, and does not contain words prohibiting transfer or indicating an intention that it should not be transferable.

(5) Where a bill, either originally or by indorsement, is expressed to be payable to the order of a specified person, and not to him or his order, it is nevertheless payable to him or his order at his option.

The word bill in these subsections includes a cheque.

If it is to be negotiated, a cheque payable to order should be indorsed by the person to whom it is payable (Section 31(3)). As to a payee's right to refuse to indorse a cheque when presented by himself for payment, see *Payee*

The drawer may strike out the word 'order' and insert the word 'bearer', thus making the cheque payable to 'bearer', which alteration must be initialled by him. If there are more drawers than one, each drawer must initial the alteration.

A bearer cheque may be converted into an order cheque by the word 'bearer' being crossed out; and this may be done by the payee as well as by the drawer. It is not essential to write the word 'order'.

Where the payee of an order cheque indorses it merely with his signature, it is an indorsement in blank, and the cheque may be transferred as a cheque payable to bearer. Any subsequent holder, however, may again make the cheque payable to order by indorsing it, e.g. 'Pay John Brown or order, T. Jones', or by writing above the last indorser's signature a direction to pay the bill or cheque to or to the order of himself or some other person (Section 34(4)).

A cheque drawn 'pay self or order' is equivalent to 'pay to my order' and requires the drawer's indorsement unless it is to be paid in for the credit of another account in the drawer's name. The indorsement required where the cheque is to be cashed over the counter is not required by law but is a result of a decision of the Committee of London Clearing Bankers. SEE UNDER *Cheque*

As between banker and customer, a cheque drawn 'pay order' is an incomplete document and should not be paid as no payee is specified.

An instrument payable to an impersonal payee, such as 'cash', 'wages', 'house', is not payable to a specified person or to bearer and is not a cheque as it does not satisfy Section 7, Bills of Exchange Act 1882. It is an order to pay money to bearer and whether a banker gets a good discharge in paying may depend on whether the money represented by the instrument reaches the right person (*North and South Insurance Corporation Ltd* v *National Provincial Bank Ltd* [1936] 1 KB 328, and *Orbit Mining Company Ltd* v *Westminster Bank Ltd* [1962] 3 WLR 1256.) SEE *Bill of Exchange; Cheque; Indorsement*

ORDERS NOT TO PAY SEE *Payment Stopped*

ORDINARILY RESIDENT Residence in the UK is in many cases a major factor in determining whether or not there is a liability to income tax. In the ordinary way, a person who is not resident here is liable to UK income tax only on income arising in this country. He is not liable to UK tax on income arising elsewhere in the world. In many cases, where a non-resident is entitled to income arising in the UK, there will be a double taxation agreement in force between the two countries so that double taxation will be avoided and in some cases the UK income will be paid without deduction of tax.

Residence is something different from domicile. A person visiting the UK temporarily with no intention of remaining here would not normally be deemed to have UK residence if he spent less than six months in the UK during a tax year. If a UK resident made a series of visits abroad, he would not lose his UK residence unless he was absent for at least an entire tax year.

Residence therefore may vary from year to year. It is not a permanent state and it will depend on the facts of each case, including the intention of the person concerned, the fact of his actual residence in a particular place and the time he spends there.

The fact of being *ordinarily resident* in a particular country has a longer term significance. A person who has lived in the UK all his life or for many years will be treated as ordinarily resident in the UK. A person who comes to the UK with the intention of staying here permanently will be regarded as ordinarily resident.

In view of the confusion which has arisen from time to time regarding the residence status of visitors to the UK for some temporary purpose, particularly for employment, the Inland Revenue issued some guidelines on the subject in April 1981, as follows.

In general, a person who comes to the UK is not regarded as having been ordinarily resident until he has been in the country for at least three years, unless it is clear before then that he intends to be here for three years or more. It is the practice of the Inland Revenue to regard someone who comes to the UK, whether to work here or not, as ordinarily resident for tax purposes:

1. from the date of arrival if the visitor has, or acquires during the year of arrival, accommodation for his use in the UK, which he occupies on a basis that implies a stay in this country of three years or more, or
2. from the beginning of the tax year in which such accommodation becomes available.

This does not apply in the case of hotel accommodation or the use of a company flat, nor to accommodation rented and furnished for less than a year, nor to furnished accommodation taken for less than two years.

If a visitor who has been regarded as ordinarily resident solely because he has accommodation here, disposes of the accommodation and leaves the UK within three years of his arrival, he would normally be treated as not ordinarily resident for the duration of his stay.

ORDINARY SHARE INDEX SEE *Financial Times Industrial Share Index*

ORDINARY SHARES The principal category of shares into which the capital of the company is divided, as distinguished from preference shares which in certain specified respects rank in front of the ordinary, and deferred shares which rank after. They may be for different nominal amounts, for example, 10p, 25p, 50p, £1, £5, £10, £100 each, and may be either fully paid up or only partly paid. In some companies, the ordinary shares consist of two kinds, preferred ordinary and deferred ordinary.

If a company limited by shares is authorized by its articles, it may convert its paid-up shares into stock. The company cannot issue original stock. It must first issue shares and then, when fully paid, convert them into stock.

For all practical purposes, ordinary shares represent the ownership of a company limited by shares (SEE *Equities*). There is some doubt as to the exact proportion of ordinary shares held by (1) institutions, and (2) private individuals. The Wilson Committee reported that

> Over the period between 1957 and 1975, the proportion of ordinary shares beneficially owned by persons fell from 66 per cent to 38 per cent and it is estimated to have fallen further to 32 per cent by the end of 1978.

This calculation has, to some extent, been challenged by a Stock Exchange survey published in September 1981 which suggested that 36 per cent of shares quoted on the Stock Exchange were still owned by private investors. The following table shows the totals, by value, of ordinary shareholdings of private persons over the years 1975–1982.

Year	Value of ordinary shares (including Unit Trusts) in personal ownership £m
1975	25,294
1976	22,946
1977	31,443
1978	32,181
1979	33,784
1980	39,474
1981	41,497
1982	49,605

Source: Financial Statistics.

ORGANIZATION FOR ECONOMIC COOPERATION AND DEVELOPMENT (OECD) This organization was set up under a convention signed in Paris on 14th December, 1960 by the member countries of the Organization for European Economic Cooperation and by Canada and the USA This convention provides that the OECD shall promote policies designed

1. to achieve the highest sustainable economic growth and employment and a rising standard of living in member countries, while maintaining financial stability, and thus to contribute to the world economy;
2. to contribute to sound economic expansion in member as well as non-member countries in the process of economic development;
3. to contribute to the expansion of world trade on a multilateral, non-discriminatory basis in accordance with international obligations.

The legal personality possessed by the Organization for European Economic Cooperation continues in the OECD which came into being on 30th September, 1961.

The present members of OECD are Australia, Austria, Belgium, Canada, Denmark, Finland, France, West Germany, Greece, Iceland, Ireland, Italy, Japan, Luxembourg, Netherlands, New Zealand, Norway, Portugal, Spain, Sweden, Switzerland, Turkey, the UK and the USA.

OECD conducts extensive study and research into the economies and industries of the member countries, and produces a wealth of literature containing information and forecasts of economic trends within the member states.

OUT OF DATE SEE *Stale Cheque*

OVERDRAFT SEE *Advances; Lending by Banks*

OVERDUE BILL A bill of exchange is overdue which has not been paid at maturity. A bill payable on demand is deemed to be overdue within the meaning, and for the purposes of Section 36 of the Bills of Exchange Act 1882, when it appears on the face of it to have been in circulation for an unreasonable length of time (SEE *Negotiation of Bill of Exchange; Presentment for Payment*). Where an overdue bill is negotiated, it can only be negotiated subject to any defect of title affecting it at its maturity, and thence-forward no person who takes it can acquire or give a better title than that which the person from whom he took it had, i.e. it is not negotiable (Section 36(2)).

Except where an indorsement is dated subsequent to the date of maturity of a bill, every negotiation is prima facie deemed to have been effected before the bill was overdue (Section 36(4)).

If an overdue bill is presented to the bank where it is domiciled, it is advisable, in such a case, to obtain a cheque from the acceptor or a written authority to pay it. SEE *Bill of Exchange*

Where a discounted bill is dishonoured, the banker who receives it back unpaid will debit it to his customer's account and send him notice of dishonour, together with the bill. If, however, the state of the customer's account does not permit of the debit, the bill is debited to Overdue Bills of Past Due Bills Account. SEE *Bill of Exchange; Dishonour of Bill of Exchange*

OVERDUE CHEQUE A cheque, being a bill of exchange payable on demand, is overdue *for the purpose of negotiation* when it has been in circulation for an unreasonable time (Section 36(3), Bills of Exchange Act 1882). By subsection (2) an overdue cheque can only be negotiated subject to any defect of title and is thus not a negotiable instrument. Any person taking such a cheque is, therefore, in the same position as if the cheque had been crossed 'not negotiable'. What is an unreasonable length of time is a question of fact. In a Cardiff County Court case reported in *Legal Decisions Affecting Bankers*, Vol. III, p. 226, it was held that a cheque dated 12 days previously was overdue when negotiated by a thief. In an earlier case *London & County Banking Company v Groome* (1881) 8 QBD 288, it was held that a period of eight days between the date of a cheque and its negotiation to a bank was a circumstance to be taken into account when considering if the transaction should have aroused suspicion. Sir John Paget considers that in the absence of special circumstances, 10 days or so would probably be held to be the limit of time before a cheque becomes overdue. It must be remembered, however, that it is a question of fact in each case, e.g. a cheque coming from abroad might conceivably not be overdue for considerably longer than 10 days after issue.

The foregoing has nothing to do with the practice of paying bankers in returning, as stale or out of date, cheques drawn six months or 12 months previously. SEE *Stale Cheque*

Nor does the foregoing mean that the drawer of a cheque is free from liability to a bona fide holder if the cheque is not presented within a reasonable time; his liability is governed by the Limitation Act 1939, whereby he is liable on the instrument for six years from its issue, except where the cheque is not presented within a reasonable time and the drawee bank fails before presentation. In such a case, if the drawer has lost money by such failure to present he is discharged to the extent of such loss (Section 74(1), Bills of Exchange Act 1882). SEE *Limitation Act* 1939; *Presentment for Payment*

OVERRIDING INTERESTS Interests in land which are not disclosed in the documents of title. An intending purchaser will not find them in an abstract of title and they are generally dealt with in the requisitions on title. Overriding interests comprise easements such as rights of way, light, drainage, etc. These may be ascertained by inspection of the land itself or by searching the Land Charges Registry, where they would be registered as a Class D (iii) charge. Then there are short leases which can be ascertained by inquiry of the occupier. There are also certain statutory interests arising under Acts of Parliament — land tax, redemption annuities, and restrictions arising from the various Building Acts and Public Health Acts. Local land charges (q.v.) are also overriding interests. These statutory interests can be ascertained from inquiry of the respective authorities who administer the Acts under which they are created. Overriding interests do not appear on the Register in the case of registered titles, and the position is the same as in the case of unregistered land.

In *Webb* v *Pollmount* [1966] 1 All ER 481, an option to purchase contained in a lease was held to be an overriding interest.

OVERSEAS EMPLOYMENT SEE *Income Tax*

OVER-THE-COUNTER MARKET (OTC) This is a term which originated in the USA, where there is a substantial volume of dealing in stocks and shares outside the stock exchanges. To a limited extent there is an over-the-counter market in London, where a small number of investment houses 'makes' a market in a limited number of unquoted shares, the prices being listed in the daily press. At the time of writing, the market value of shares quoted OTC is approximately £400 million.

P

PAGE COMMITTEE SEE *Committee to Review National Savings*

PAID CHEQUES SEE *Cancelled Cheques and Bills*

PAID-UP CAPITAL That part of the subscribed or issued capital of a company which has been paid, the other part being termed the 'uncalled' capital. The capital is fully paid if there are no further calls to be made, that is, no 'uncalled' capital, and no calls in arrears. SEE *Capital*

PAID-UP POLICY A life policy is said to be paid up when there are no further premiums payable. This may arise because the premiums are payable for a given number of years, even though the cover extends beyond that period. More usually, however, it arises because the life assured (or the proposer if this is a different person) does not wish to continue payment of the premiums but wishes the policy to remain in force. Generally, this will be more advantageous than the surrender of a policy because (1) the policy will continue to provide a degree of life cover, although not as much as would be so if payment of the premiums had continued, and (2) the reduced level of life cover will continue to earn bonuses.

PAID-UP SHARES Shares are 'paid up' when there is nothing further to be paid thereon. If calls are still to be made, the shares are only 'partly paid' (q.v.).

PANEL ON TAKE-OVERS AND MERGERS SEE *Take-overs and Mergers*

PAPER CURRENCY The paper instruments such as bank notes, cheques, bills, and other forms which take the place of money and act as a currency or circulating medium.

PAR, PAR VALUE The nominal value of stocks and shares. SEE *No Par Value*

PARI PASSU The Latin for 'at the same rate'. Where new shares or debentures, or some other form of security, are issued ranking *pari passu* with existing shares, etc., the rights attaching to the new shares will rank equally with the existing ones. Perhaps the most common example is the issue of a debenture ranking *pari passu* with an existing debenture. This can be done only with the consent of the existing debenture holder or holders as it would normally involve some diluting of their rights in the event of the security being enforceable.

PART PAYMENT

Inland Bill A part payment may be made by the acceptor at the maturity of a bill in which case the bill should be indorsed 'Received £... in part payment without prejudice to the rights of the other parties.' The holder can sue for the balance. Notice that full payment has not been made should be given to the drawer and indorsers. The bill itself is, of course, retained by the holder. The bill should be noted for the unpaid balance.

Foreign Bill Where a part payment is made, a foreign bill must be protested as to the balance.

Cheque Cheques are either paid in full or they are not paid at all. A part payment is not made. In Scotland, however, when a cheque is presented, if payment cannot be made in full, any balance in the drawer's account is attached in favour of the presenter. The banker transfers such amount to a special account.

Cash Order Part payment of a cash order is not accepted, unless under instructions to do so from the correspondent who sent the document for collection.

PARTIAL ACCEPTANCE SEE *Acceptance, Qualified*

PARTIAL INDORSEMENT An indorsement of a bill of exchange which purports to transfer a part only of the amount payable, or purports to transfer the bill to two or more indorsees severally, does not operate as a negotiation of the bill. SEE *Indorsement*

PARTICIPATING PREFERENCE SHARES SEE *Preference Stock or Shares*

PARTICULAR AVERAGE A term used in connection with shipping. In the case of a general average, a loss incurred for the common safety of the ship and cargo is borne by all the parties interested in the ship and cargo in proportion to their interests; but a particular average or loss is borne entirely by the owner (or his insurer) of the property which has been lost or damaged. His property may have become damaged by accident as by the sea, or may have got washed overboard, and in such cases (the loss or damage not having been incurred intentionally to save the ship), the owner alone is responsible. SEE *General Average*

PARTIES TO BILL OF EXCHANGE The parties to a bill of exchange are the drawer, the acceptor (called the drawee before he accepts it), the payee (who is often the same person as the drawer) and the indorsers. The parties may be either 'immediate' or 'remote'. They are 'immediate parties' when they are immediately connected with each other as the drawer and acceptor, the drawer and payee, and an indorsee and the indorser immediately in front of him. They are 'remote parties' when they are not closely related to each other, as the acceptor and an indorsee.

As to the capacity and authority of parties to a bill, the Bills of Exchange Act 1882, provides

22.—(1) Capacity to incur liability as a part to a bill is co-extensive with capacity to contract.
Provided that nothing in this Section shall enable a corporation to make itself liable as drawer, acceptor, or indorser of a bill unless it is competent to it so to do under the law for the time being in force relating to corporations.

(2) Where a bill is drawn or indorsed by an infant, minor, or corporation having no capacity or power to incur liability on a bill, the drawing or indorsement entitles the holder to receive payment of the bill, and to enforce it against any other party thereto.

23. No person is liable as drawer, indorser, or acceptor of a bill who has not signed it as such: Provided that—

(1) Where a person signs a bill in a trade or assumed name, he is liable thereon as if he had signed it in his own name:

(2) The signature of the name of a firm is equivalent to the signature by the person so signing of the names of all persons liable as partners in that firm. [SEE *Bill of Exchange*]

PARTLY PAID A term applied to stock and shares on which the full issue price has not been paid, usually because it is not due until some later date. This may arise because a particular stock, typically a Government stock or an issue of loan stock, is payable in, say, two instalments, perhaps a few months apart. Until the final instalment is paid, the stock is 'partly paid'.

It is comparatively unusual nowadays, however, to issue stocks with a long-term uncalled liability. At one time it was more common to issue partly-paid shares, particularly bank shares, where it was not contemplated that the 'uncalled' proportion of the nominal value would ever be required but it was there, as it were, in reserve in case of need. The holder of partly-paid shares may be called upon to pay the balance in accordance with the terms of issue of the shares and, in the event of the winding-up of a company, the liquidator will call up the capital on the partly-paid shares if this is necessary to meet the company's liabilities.

PARTNER Where several persons join to carry on a business, the combination is called a firm or partnership, and the individual members are the partners. A partner who takes an active interest in the management of the business is called an active partner, as a distinction from a dormant or sleeping partner who merely supplies funds for the business. A nominal partner is one who simply lends his name and has no real interest in the partnership. A partner (whether active or sleeping) is liable for all the debts and obligations of the firm. A limited partner, however, is not liable beyond the amount contributed at the time of entering into the partnership (SEE *Limited Partnership*). A general partner is the same as an ordinary partner. Everyone who has held himself out to be a partner in a particular firm is liable as a partner to anyone who has, on the faith of any such representation, given credit to the firm. SEE *Death of Partner; Partnerships*

Because partners are liable only jointly, bank mandates now invariably incorporate joint *and several* liability of the partners.

PARTNERSHIPS The bulk of the law relating to partnership is codified in the Partnership Act of 1890, which defines a partnership as 'the relation which subsists between persons carrying on a business in common with a view of profit'. The law prescribes the minimum of formality in the setting up of this relationship; no registration is necessary, no written agreement or deed of partnership is requisite, though highly desirable; all that is necessary is some sort of agreement—written, verbal, or implied—between the parties. The limitation as to the number of partners in a partnership contained in the Companies Act 1948, was enlarged by the Companies Act 1967. The maximum number of partners in a banking firm is 20 (Section 119), and for solicitors, members of a recognized stock exchange and accountants, there is now no limit (Section 120).

The following are the principal Sections of the Partnership Act 1890 (53 & 54 Vict c 39) from the point of view of persons dealing with partnerships.

NATURE OF PARTNERSHIP

Definition of partnership

1.—(1) Partnership is the relation which subsists

between persons carrying on a business in common with a view of profit.

(2) But the relation between members of any company or association which is—

(a) Registered as a company under the Companies Act, 1862, or any other Act of Parliament for the time being in force and relating to the registration of joint stock companies; or

(b) Formed or incorporated by or in pursuance of any other Act of Parliament or letters patent, or Royal Charter; or

(c) A company engaged in working mines within and subject to the jurisdiction of the stannaries:

is not a partnership within the meaning of this Act.

Rules for determing existence of partnership

2. In determining whether a partnership does or does not exist, regard shall be had to the following rules—

(1) Joint tenancy, tenancy in common, joint property, common property, or part ownership does not of itself create a partnership as to anything so held or owned, whether the tenants or owners do or do not share any profits made by the use thereof.

(2) The sharing of gross returns does not of itself create a partnership, whether the persons sharing such returns have or have not a joint or common right or interest in any property from which or from the use of which the returns are derived.

(3) The receipt by a person of a share of the profits of a business is *prima facie* evidence that he is a partner in the business, but the receipt of such a share, or of a payment contingent on or varying with the profits of a business, does not of itself make him a partner in the business; and in particular—

(a) The receipt by a person of a debt or other liquidated amount by instalments or otherwise out of the accruing profits of a business does not of itself make him a partner in the business or liable as such:

(b) A contract for the remuneration of a servant or agent of a person engaged in a business by a share of the profits of the business does not of itself make the servant or agent a partner in the business or liable as such:

(c) A person being the widow or child of a deceased partner, and receiving by way of annuity a portion of the profits made in the business in which the deceased person was a partner, is not by reason only of such receipt a partner in the business or liable as such:

(d) The advance of money by way of loan to a person engaged or about to engage in any business on a contract with that person that the lender shall receive a rate of interest varying with the profits, or shall receive a share of the profits arising from carrying on the business, does not of itself make the lender a partner with the person or persons carrying on the business or liable as such. Provided that the contract is in writing, and signed by or on behalf of all the parties thereto:

(e) A person receiving by way of annuity or otherwise a portion of the profits of a business in consideration of the sale by him of the goodwill of the business is not by reason only of such receipt a partner in the business or liable as such.

Postponement of rights of person lending or selling in consideration of share of profits in case of insolvency

3. In the event of any person to whom money has been advanced by way of loan upon such a contract as is mentioned in the last foregoing Section, or of any buyer of a goodwill in consideration of a share of the profits of the business, being adjudged a bankrupt, entering into an arrangement to pay his creditors less than 20/- in the pound, or dying in insolvent circumstances the lender of the loan shall not be entitled to recover anything in respect of his loan, and the seller of the goodwill shall not be entitled to recover anything in respect of the share of profits contracted for, until the claims of the other creditors of the borrower or buyer for valuable consideration in money or money's worth have been satisfied.

Meaning of firm

4.—(1) Persons who have entered into partnership with one another are for the purposes of this Act called collectively a firm, and the name under which their business is carried on is called the firm-name.

(2) In Scotland a firm is a legal person distinct from the partners of whom it is composed, but an individual partner may be charged on a decree or diligence directed against the firm, and on payment of the debts is entitled to relief *pro rata* from the firm and other members.

Relations of Partners to Persons Dealing with Them

Power of partner to bind the firm

5. Every partner is an agent of the firm and his other partners for the purpose of the business of the partnership; and the acts of every partner who does any act for carrying on in the usual way business of the kind carried on by the firm of which he is a member bind the firm and his partners, unless the partner so acting has in fact no authority to act for the firm in the particular matter, and the person with whom he is dealing either knows that he has no authority or does not know or believe him to be a partner.

Partners bound by acts on behalf of firm

6. An act or instrument relating to the business of the firm and done or executed in the firm-name, or in any other manner showing an intention to bind the firm, by any person thereto authorised, whether a partner or not, is binding on the firm and all the partners.

Provided that this Section shall not affect any general rule of law relating to the execution of deeds or negotiable instruments.

Partner using credit of firm for private purposes

7. Where one partner pledges the credit of the firm for a purpose apparently not connected with the firm's ordinary course of business, the firm is not bound,

unless he is in fact specially authorised by the other partners; but this Section does not affect any personal liability incurred by an individual partner.

Effect of notice that firm will not be bound by acts of partner

8. If it has been agreed between the partners that any restriction shall be placed on the power of any one or more of them to bind the firm, no act done in contravention of the agreement is binding on the firm with respect to persons having notice of the agreement.

Liability of partners

9. Every partner in a firm is liable jointly with the other partners, and in Scotland severally also, for all debts and obligations of the firm incurred while he is a partner; and after his death his estate is also severally liable in a due course of administration for such debts and obligations, so far as they remain unsatisfied, but subject in England or Ireland to the prior payment of his separate debts.

With respect to the joint liability referred to in Section 9, a creditor bringing an action should sue all the partners jointly, and having obtained judgment the creditor is then at liberty to levy execution against the partnership property or against all, or any, of the separate estates of the partners, each partner being liable to the full extent of his fortune for the debts of the firm. It is to be noted that this joint liability is also several in Scotland. The same Section provides that the estate of a deceased partner is also severally liable for the firm's debts, but, in England or Ireland, subject to the prior payment of the deceased's separate debts. When an advance is made to a firm, it is desirable for a banker to hold an undertaking signed by all the partners agreeing to be jointly and severally liable for any debt on the partnership account, because the partners may then be sued either jointly or severally, and the banker will have the right to set off any credit balances on the partners' separate accounts against a debt on the firm's account. In the absence of such an undertaking this right of set-off does not exist. When the partners have made themselves jointly and severally liable, the banker has further advantages, as upon the death of a partner his claim against the deceased's estate for a debt upon the firm's account would not be postponed to the payment of the deceased's separate debts, and in the event of bankruptcy the banker would be entitled to prove against the estate of the firm and at the same time against the separate estates of the partners. [SEE *Bankrupt Person*]

Liability of the firm for wrongs

10. Where, by any wrongful act or omission of any partner acting in the ordinary course of the business of the firm, or with the authority of his co-partners, loss or injury is caused to any person not being a partner in the firm, or any penalty is incurred, the firm is liable therefor to the same extent as the partner so acting or omitting to act.

Misapplication of money or property received for or in custody of the firm

11. In the following cases: namely—

(*a*) Where one partner acting within the scope of his apparent authority receives the money or property of a third person and misapplies it; and

(*b*) Where a firm in the course of its business receives money or property of a third person, and the money or property so received is misapplied by one or more of the partners while it is in the custody of the firm;

the firm is liable to make good the loss.

Liability for wrong joint and several

12. Every partner is liable jointly with his co-partners and also severally for everything for which the firm while he is a partner therein becomes liable under either of the two last preceding sections.

Improper employment of trust-property for partnership purposes

13. If a partner, being a trustee, improperly employs trust-property in the business or on the account of the partnership, no other partner is liable for the trust-property to the persons beneficially interested therein:

Provided as follows—

(1) This Section shall not affect any liability incurred by any partner by reason of his having notice of a breach of trust: and

(2) Nothing in this Section shall prevent trust money from being followed and recovered from the firm if still in its possession or under its control.

Persons liable by 'Holding Out'

14.—(1) Everyone who by words spoken or written or by conduct represents himself, or who knowingly suffers himself to be represented, as a partner in a particular firm, is liable as a partner to anyone who has on the faith of any such representation given credit to the firm, whether the representation has or has not been made or communicated to the person so giving credit by or with the knowledge of the apparent partner making the representation or suffering it to be made.

(2) Provided that where after a partner's death the partnership business is continued in the old firm-name, the continued use of that name or of the deceased partner's name as part thereof shall not of itself make his executors' or administrators' estate or effects liable for any partnership debts contracted after his death.

Admissions and representations of partners

15. An admission or representation made by any partner concerning the partnership affairs, and in the ordinary course of its business, is evidence against the firm.

Notice to acting partner to be notice to the firm

16. Notice to any partner who habitually acts in the partnership business of any matter relating to partnership affairs operates as notice to the firm, except in the case of a fraud on the firm committed by or with the consent of that partner.

Liabilities of incoming and outgoing partners

17.—(1) A person who is admitted as a partner into an existing firm does not thereby become liable to the creditors of the firm for anything done before he became a partner.

(2) A partner who retires from a firm does not thereby cease to be liable for partnership debts or obligations incurred before his retirement.

(3) A retiring partner may be discharged from any existing liabilities, by an agreement to that effect between himself and the members of the firm as newly constituted and the creditors, and this agreement may be either express or inferred as a fact from the course of dealing between the creditors and the firm as newly constituted.

Revocation of continuing guaranty by change in firm

18. A continuing guaranty or cautionary obligation given either to a firm or to a third person in respect of the transactions of a firm is, in the absence of agreement to the contrary, revoked as to future transactions by any change in the constitution of the firm to which, or of the firm in respect of the transactions of which, the guaranty or obligation was given.

Dissolution by bankrupty, death, or charge

33.—(1) Subject to any agreement between the partners, every partnership is dissolved as regards all the partners by the death or bankruptcy of any partner.

(2) A partnership may, at the option of the other partners, be dissolved if any partner suffers his share of the partnership property to be charged under this Act for his separate debt.

Rights of persons dealing with firm against apparent members of firm

36.—(1) Where a person deals with a firm after a change in its constitution he is entitled to treat all apparent members of the old firm as still being members of the firm until he has notice of the change.

(2) An advertisement in the *London Gazette* as to a firm whose principal place of business is in England or Wales, in the *Edinburgh Gazette* as to a firm whose principal place of business is in Scotland, and in the *Dublin Gazette* as to a firm whose principal place of business is in Ireland, shall be notice as to persons who had any dealings with the firm before the date of the dissolution or change so advertised.

(3) The estate of a partner who dies, or who becomes bankrupt, or of a partner who, not having been known to the person dealing with the firm to be a partner, retires from the firm, is not liable, for partnership debts contracted after the date of the death, bankruptcy, or retirement respectively.

Continuing authority of partners for purposes of winding up

38. After the dissolution of a partnership the authority of each partner to bind the firm, and the other rights and obligations of the partners, continue notwithstanding the dissolution so far as may be necessary to wind up the affairs of the partnership, and to complete transactions begun but unfinished at the time of the dissolution, but not otherwise.

Provided that the firm is in no case bound by the acts of a partner who has become bankrupt; but this proviso does not affect the liability of any person who has after the bankruptcy represented himself or knowingly suffered himself to be represented as a partner of the bankrupt. [SEE *Company; Death of Partner; Limited Partnership; Mental Incapacity*]

A partnership, although it may have a firm name, is not an entity existing apart from its members. In Scotland this is so, for Section 4(2) of the Partnership Act 1890 provides that a Scottish firm is a legal person distinct from the partners of whom it is composed, but in England and Wales there is no such conception of a partnership, and the firm name is but a convenient abbreviation for the names of all the members of the firm.

There is a distinction between co-ownership and partnership, and the rights and liabilities attaching to the latter differ from those belonging to the former. Joint tenancy, part ownership, the sharing of gross returns, do not necessarily connote partnership: the receipt of profits is prima facie but not conclusive evidence of the relationship. It is a question of intention. There are three broad distinctions between co-ownership and partnership. Firstly, co-ownership is not necessarily the result of agreement, whilst partnership is; secondly, co-ownership does not necessarily involve working for a profit, whilst partnership does; thirdly, a co-owner has the right of free disposition over his property, whilst one partner cannot replace himself by another without the consent of his co-partners.

There are two dominant principles underlying the relationship of the partners in a firm: first, the unlimited liability of each and every member of the firm for the firm's debts, and secondly, the power of any partner to bind his co-partners in the ordinary course of partnership business, subject to any restrictions in the articles of partnership of which outside parties may be aware.

Every partner is liable for the firm's debts to the full extent of his private resources in addition to his partnership capital; every secret partner is fully liable, whether the creditor was originally aware of his existence or not; any person who in any way holds himself out as a partner is fully liable for the firm's debts to the creditor who is thus misled.

The liability of partners in England and Wales for debts and contracts is joint only, whilst in Scotland it is joint and several. Thus in England and Wales care must be taken to join all partners in an action, preferably by suing the firm in the firm's name; if this is not done, any unsatisfied judgment against those who are sued will effectively bar an action against any uncited partners.

There is a modification of the principle of joint liability in that on the death or bankruptcy of a partner, his responsibility for the partnership debts is not extinguished and his estate is liable. But in the absence of several liability, partnership creditors are postponed to the creditors of the private estate, who must be paid in full before any distribution is made in respect of the firm's debts.

On the opening of a partnership banking account, if articles of partnership exist, they may be scrutinized to find out, amongst other things, if any of the implied rights of the partners are restricted or modified, and if arrangements are made regarding operations on the banking account. If nothing is said about these matters, any partner is entitled to draw cheques in the firm name, and by so doing he will bind the firm. 'The signature of the name of the firm is equivalent to the signature by the person so signing of the names of all persons liable as partners in the firm.' (Bills of Exchange Act 1882, Section 23(2)) It is usual, however, to take express instructions as to who may draw on the account and the form of signature to be employed. Some banks have a special form of mandate for the opening of partnership accounts, whilst others make use of the form of authority devised for joint accounts. But if no form of mandate is taken, a cheque signed in the firm name by any partner will be a good discharge to the bank against the firm, in the absence of abnormal circumstances.

One partner has power to countermand the payment of cheques drawn by another. The question of the payment of cheques presented after notice of the death of a partner does not depend on whether the cheque was drawn by the deceased partner, for his signature in the firm name is equivalent to the signatures of all members of the firm. On the one hand, as the decease of a partner puts an end to the partnership as such, the authority of any one partner as agent for the firm is revoked, and on these grounds it would seem that such cheques should not be paid. On the other hand, the surviving partners can deal with the account for the purpose of winding up the firm, and could consequently confirm any cheques outstanding at the time of decease.

This second view is considered the better and is generally accepted and acted upon by bankers.

Transactions on the private account of a partner require scrutiny in certain circumstances. Cheques payable to the firm should not be accepted for the private account of a partner without inquiry being made of the other partners. In the absence of inquiry, such a transaction would deprive a banker of the protection of Section 4 of the Cheques Act on the ground of negligence. If, however, a partner pays to the credit, of his private account a cheque drawn by him on the firm's account, there is no prima facie case for enquiry—the transaction may represent repayment of a loan to the firm or a share of partnership profits. In *Backhouse* v *Charlton* (1878) 8 ChD 444, transfers of this description were held to be regular on the face of them. The particular circumstances, however, such as the standing of the partner and the amount of the cheque, would influence a banker in dealing with such a situation. Where a banker has been pressing for reduction or repayment of a private overdraft, however, and the partner responds by offering for his credit a cheque drawn by him on the partnership account, inquiries are called for.

One partner is entitled to open an account for the firm's business provided that he opens it in the firm name (*Alliance Bank* v *Kearsley* (1871) LR 6 CP 433).

As regards borrowing and bill transactions, a partner's authority depends on whether the firm is a trading or non-trading partnership. A trading business has been defined as one which depends on the buying and selling of goods (*Higgins* v *Beauchamp* [1914] 3 KB 1192). Thus professional partnerships, such as doctors, solicitors, and accountants, are non-trading firms, and in decided cases, the businesses of farmers and innkeepers have been held to be non-trading partnerships.

In a trading firm, any partner, unless prohibited by the terms of the partnership agreement, has actual authority to pledge and sell the assets of the firm, to contract debts, to borrow, and to draw, accept, indorse, and discount bills of exchange. In a non-trading firm, however, no such authority exists. It is well settled, however, that a partner in a non-trading firm has implied power to bind the firm by drawing cheques (*Backhouse* v *Charlton*). In practice, express authority is taken from the members of a firm—whether trading or non-trading—as to the method by which advances are to be negotiated, partnership assets pledged, and bill transactions effected.

In England and Wales partnership liability is joint only, and it is desirable to get the members of a borrowing firm to covenant for joint and several liability. Amongst other advantages it will mean that a banker's position in the administration of a deceased partner's estate will be improved, for he will not have to wait until the private creditors of the deceased have been satisfied, but can claim side by side with them for any debt due by the firm. Furthermore, such a provision will give a banker a right of set-off on any private account of a partner in respect of the firm's debt, and in the event of bankruptcy he will have a right of double proof, for a joint and separate creditor may prove concurrently on the joint estate and the separate estate, his redress being limited, of course, to 100 pence in the pound.

As regards the pledging or mortgaging of security for advances, it is the usual practice to get all members of the firm to execute the necessary documents. One partner could, in a trading firm, validly pledge negotiable instruments and also execute a memorandum of deposit over the deeds of partnership property. He could not, however, give a legal mortgage over such property, for one partner cannot bind the firm by deed, unless authorized so to act, in which case the authority itself would have to be by deed. A legal mortgage given by one partner in the absence of proper authority would not be wholly void, however—it could be treated as an equitable charge, for in transactions where a deed is not necessary the seal may be disregarded and the signature considered as applying to a document under hand. Thus in *Marchant v Morton Down & Co* [1901] 2 KB 829, one partner sought to make a legal assignment of the firm's debts, under seal. It was held that whilst he had no power to bind the firm by deed, his signature to the document would be construed as the execution of an equitable assignment under hand.

When title deeds of property are offered as security, they may be in the sole name of one partner or in the names of all partners jointly. In the first instance, the property in question may belong to one partner in his own right, the firm having a tenancy thereof, or it may be held by him in trust for the partnership, in which case all partners should join in the execution of any charge, or give an authority for him to mortgage it. Where the property is vested in all the partners jointly, if there are more than four partners, such property cannot now be vested in more than four of them; it may be partnership property or not, according to whether it has been treated as part of the firm's assets or not. In either case, however, the mortgage of the property will require to be executed by all, for it will be vested in the several parties on trust for sale specifying that they hold the property for themselves as tenants in common in equity or jointly as partners.

When searching the Land Charges Register or other appropriate register in respect of partnership property, searches should be made against the names of all the partners, as well as against the name of the firm, for it is probable that any registration will have been made against the individual names of the partners.

Sometimes a guarantee of one partner or a joint and several guarantee of all the partners is taken in respect of a borrowing by the firm. Inasmuch, however, as all the partners are already unlimitedly liable for the firm's debts, such a guarantee appears at first sight to be superfluous, but it has the merit of giving the banker a right of proof against the private estate of each partner without waiting until the private creditors are satisfied. If, however, joint and several liability has been established on the opening of the account, the same right of proof accrues, so that in such a case a guarantee has no practical advantage. It is considered by some bankers that the taking of a guarantee brings home to the partners a sense of their personal liability for the firm's debts; on the other hand it is as well to inform them that the amount of the guarantee is not the limit of their responsibility and does not free them from liability for any borrowing in excess of the amount specified in the document.

Occasionally the guarantee of a firm is offered to secure the debt of a third party, and in such a case the signatures of all the partners should be taken to a joint and several guarantee, for one partner cannot, in the absence of specific authority, bind his co-partners by executing a guarantee in the firm name.

The partnership relation is severed on the retirement, death, or bankruptcy of one partner as well as in those cases where a dissolution of the firm takes place by agreement or order of the court or the bankruptcy of the firm itself, or by the terms of the partnership deed.

If the members of a firm decide to wind up the business, or if the court decrees a dissolution, the partners' authority to bind the firm continues in so far as its exercise is necessary to wind up the affairs of the business; if, however, the members of the firm are in disagreement and resort is made to the courts, it is not infrequent for the winding-up to be put into the hands of a receiver. In such a case, a credit balance on the firm's account can safely be paid over to the receiver, after due confirmation of his appointment. A partner's unlimited powers as agent for the firm then cease, for the trading activities of the firm are terminated and the receiver's function is to realize the partnership assets, pay out the firm's creditors and distribute any surplus amongst the partners, in accordance with the terms of the articles, if any. Occasionally a manager is appointed by the court, and his powers are wider than those of a receiver for he is empowered to carry on the business for the time being, to fulfil existing contracts and to enter into such new contracts as are essential to the ordinary conduct of the business. In this case also the court appointment of a manager will be sufficient mandate to the banker to recognize his authority to deal with the firm's balance. Any borrowings that may be allowed on the account of a manager or receiver are his personal responsibility, and he cannot validly charge any assets of the firm as security without the leave of the court. In such cases the bank should inspect the terms of the court order.

Such examples of dissolution are comparatively infrequent, as compared with the cases where dissolution automatically takes place by the retirement, death, or bankruptcy of one partner. Any change in the membership of a firm occasioned by withdrawal, decease, or insolvency of a partner, virtually puts an end to the firm; the surviving or remaining partners may continue to trade under the firm name, but in fact a new firm is created if they carry on for any purpose other than to wind up the affairs of the old firm.

In the case of the retirement of a partner, he will be liable for advances subsequently made to the firm unless the firm's bankers are notified of the severance of his relations with his co-partners, for Section 36 of the Partnership Act decrees that 'where a person deals with a firm after a change in its constitution, he is entitled to treat all apparent members of the old firm as still being members of the firm until he has notice of the change'. A secret partner, however, could not be saddled with any liability for the firm's indebtedness after his retirement, even though he omitted to notify the bank, for the equitable reason that credit was given to the firm without knowledge of, or reliance on, his membership thereof.

On notification of the retirement of a partner, the banker's action will depend on several circumstances.

If the account is in debit and security of the retiring partner is held, the accounts should be broken in order to establish the banker's rights over the security for the debt existing at the date of notification of retirement.

If the security consists of partnership assets, such as the deeds of property jointly charged, the banker can continue the account for the time being, as the presumption is that the remaining partners are carrying on the business for the purpose of winding it up. If the retirement of one partner is accompanied by the admission of a new partner, a conveyance of the property is sometimes executed by the old firm in favour of the new firm and this will entail the charging of the security anew. In such a case it is advisable to break the old account and start afresh, a cheque being drawn on the new account for the amount of the old debt by all members of the firm including the new partner, for an incoming partner is not necessarily liable for the debts of the old firm. If a separate conveyance of the partnership property is not made, the incoming partner should indorse the old form of charge to the effect that he agrees that the security covered thereby shall be available for the debts of the new firm as well as the old.

The death of a partner likewise has the legal effect of dissolving the firm. The personal representatives of the deceased have no power to step into the dead partner's shoes—they cannot take any part in the management of the firm, and their sole concern is to see that a proper account is taken of amounts due to the estate they are administering.

In the case of a credit account, there appears to be no reason why the account should not be continued unbroken by the surviving partners. In *Backhouse* v *Charlton* (1878) 8 ChD 444, it was held that where a banker had no notice of the state of accounts between the deceased partner and the survivor, he was under no duty to inquire. The banker is entitled to presume, in the absence of anything to the contrary, that the survivors will account to the representatives of the deceased for his share of the assets. In the case where the firm is indebted to the bank, any action will depend on the nature of the security lodged. If it was charged by the deceased as his private property the account must be stopped in order to fix the liability of his estate, for otherwise all sums credited after the crucial date will go to the reduction of the liability whilst all fresh debits will not be covered by the security held. If, however, the security held is partnership property, the account can be continued unbroken for the time being, for the surviving partners are entitled to deal with the firm's assets so far as may be necessary to wind up the partnership business.

The power of the surviving partners in a firm to continue the partnership business so far as it is compatible with the winding up of the firm, is illustrated as far as banking operations are concerned by the case of *In re Bourne, Bourne* v *Bourne* [1906] 2 Ch 427. Here an overdrawn banking account of a firm was continued unbroken after the death of one of the two partners, named Grove, and the survivor, Bourne, at a later date gave the bank an equitable charge on the deeds of real estate which formed part of the partnership assets. On the death of Bourne, the mortgaged property was sold and the bank's right to appropriate as much of the proceeds of sale as was necessary to satisfy its debt was disputed by the executors of the partner first deceased. In the lower court, the bank's claim was upheld, and the decision was confirmed on appeal. The executors of Grove claimed that Bourne had no right to mortgage the partnership property after the death of Grove, and contended that the payments into the account after his decease and before the mortgage of the property was given had extinguished the original debt and that by the working of the Rule in Clayton's Case (q.v.) the debt remaining at the time of Bourne's death was a subsequent creation, which could not be effectively secured by the mortgage of partnership property. The Appeal Court held, however, that it is both the right and duty of a surviving partner to realize the firm's assets, and in giving effect to this duty he can validly mortgage partnership property. In this case, the bank was entitled to assume that the overdraft was a partnership matter in the absence of anything showing to the contrary, and hence the account was properly continued on an unbroken basis, and payments in could be appropriated to payments out right up to the time when matters were crystallized by the death of the surviving partner.

If, however, a banker is fixed with notice that a surviving partner is continuing the business for his own ends and not for the purpose of winding up the firm, any charge given by him over partnership assets would be subject to the rights of the estate of the deceased partner.

A third cause of dissolution of a firm is found in the bankruptcy of one of the partners. In such a case his authority to act on behalf of the firm, including powers to operate on the banking account, at once ceases and his estate will not be liable for the debts contracted thereafter by the solvent partners. Such partners are entitled to continue the business for the purpose of winding up, to get in the assets and to complete transactions unfinished at the time of dissolution. They may continue to operate on the banking account to this end and payment of cheques drawn by them will be a good discharge against the firm and the trustee. Neither the trustee in bankruptcy nor the insolvent partner has any powers, however, to deal with the partnership affairs, and the trustee's interest in the business lies in getting an account of the partnership business taken with a view to receiving the bankrupt's share therein.

A cheque presented signed by a partner known to have committed an act of bankruptcy should not be paid until confirmation of the other partners is obtained.

If there is a credit balance on the account of a firm, a member of which has become bankrupt, it can safely be paid to the solvent partners. If, however, the firm is in debt to the bank, and it is desired to retain any rights on the bankrupt's estate, it is necessary to break the firm's accounts.

If joint and several liability is not established, the bank will be postponed in proving on the partner's private estate until all his separate creditors have been paid in full, which may mean that there will be nothing to come by way of dividend. If, however, joint and several liability has been stipulated for on the firm's account, the banker can prove as a creditor on equal footing with the partner's private creditors. In either case there is no need to deduct the value of any partnership security before proving against the private estate of the bankrupt partner.

The last case of dissolution to be considered is where the partnership itself becomes bankrupt. On such a happening the authority of the several partners to act for the firm ceases and the business vests in the trustee in bankruptcy in order to be wound up. Inasmuch as the title of the trustee relates back to the earliest of the acts of bankruptcy committed during the three months preceding the presentation of the bankruptcy petition, any transactions with the firm since that time are void as against the trustee unless covered by Sections 45 or 46 of the Bankruptcy Act 1914. SEE *Bankruptcy*

The bankruptcy of the firm involves the bankruptcy of the individual partners, and any steps taken with regard to the firm's account are equally applicable to the private accounts of the partners.

The principle in the administration of the respective estates is that the firm's debts are payable in the first instance out of the partnership assets and the private debts of the partners from their private assets. If a surplus results from any of the separate estates of the partners, it must be brought into the joint estate of the firm; and if a surplus accrues on the joint estate it is appropriated to the respective separate estates of the partners in due proportion.

There is an exception, however, to the rule of keeping the joint and the separate estates distinct in the first instance, namely—if there is no joint estate, on account of a *total* lack of assets or because all the firm's assets are mortgaged with no available equity, the partnership creditors can prove on equal footing with the creditors of the partners' separate private estates.

If partnership securities are held, which it is not proposed to renounce or realise forthwith, their value must be assessed before proving; if the security is collateral in the sense that it is lodged by a partner as a private asset, a banker is entitled to prove for the entire debt of the firm, and to realise the partner's security without diminishing his claim against the firm's estate. If joint and several liability has been established and thus a right of double proof obtained, and the security is partnership property, proof should be made against the private estates for the whole debt without regard to the security and against the firm's estate after allowing for the value of the security. If, on the other hand, the security is the private property of a partner, i.e. collateral, proof for the full amount can be made against the firm's estate, ignoring the security, the proof against the particular partner's estate being decreased by the assessed value of the security.

Security may be held available for the debt not only of the firm but of an individual partner. In such a case this security can be appropriated to whichever of the two estates the banker chooses and then he can proceed on the lines just indicated. Before making any allocation, however, the statement of affairs of the respective estates should be studied in order to see the prospects of dividends. As a general principle, it will be of advantage to allocate the security (which may be partnership property lodged to secure both the firm's and the partner's debts or the partner's own property covering the firm's advance as well as his own) to the estate to which it does not belong, because such a course will mean that a banker will not have to account for the value of the security in respect of either debt, treating it simply on a collateral basis.

In the absence of provision in the partnership deed, the mental incapacity of a partner in a firm does not operate like death as a dissolution of the firm, but by Section 35 of the Partnership Act it is a ground for petitioning the court for a dissolution. The court's intervention may be sought by a co-partner or by the receiver if one has been appointed, or by his next friend, or by anyone having a title to move in the matter. It is necessary, of course, for the partner to have been proved to be of unsound mind to the satisfaction of the court. Apart from these steps, by the Mental Health Act 1959, power is given to a judge of the Court of Protection to dissolve a partnership when a partner becomes of unsound mind. SEE ALSO *Limited Partnership*

PATENT RIGHTS An open letter, hence *lettres patentes*, usually from the sovereign power granting the exclusive right to make, use or sell a new invention. For the most part, matters concerning patent rights are the subject of patent law and are outside the scope of this work. There are, however, certain financial aspects, principally in relation to taxation.

The cost of acquiring a patent right for business purposes, will normally qualify for writing down allowances which, under Section 378, Income and Corporation Taxes Act 1970, will be spread over 17 years, commencing with the year of acquisition. On the other hand, the cost of establishing one's own patent rights, i.e. the payment of fees etc., are allowed as a deductible expense in the current year for income tax purposes.

Royalties received in respect of the use of a patent right are assessable under Case VI of Schedule D. If patent rights are sold in this country the sum received is chargeable to tax under Case VI but, for the purpose of calculating the tax liability, the sum received may be spread over the following six years or over past years if the payment is for patent rights already enjoyed.

PAY-AS-YOU-EARN (PAYE) SEE *Income Tax—The PAYE system*

PAY DAY Also known as settling day. The fifth day of the semi-monthly settlement on the London Stock Exchange, when the cash for a stock transaction is handed over by the purchaser, through his broker, to the seller and differences are settled.

PAYEE The payee in a bill, or cheque, is the person named therein to whom, or to whose order, payment is directed to be made.

If the bill is payable to 'John Brown or order', John Brown is the payee, and he should indorse it before the bill can be negotiated. When he has indorsed it—that is, has written his name upon the back—he is called an indorser.

Bills are frequently drawn 'pay to me or my order'. In such bills, the drawer and the payee are the same person, and the drawer must indorse the bill before negotiation. By Section 5(1) of the Bills of Exchange Act 1882, 'A bill may be drawn payable to, or to the order of, the drawer; or it may be drawn payable to, or to the order of, the drawee'.

Until a payee indorses a bill, he is not liable thereon, but when he indorses it he incurs the liabilities of an indorser. SEE *Indorser*

The Bills of Exchange Act 1882, Section 7, provides as follows:

(1) Where a bill is not payable to bearer, the payee must be named or otherwise indicated therein with reasonable certainty.

(2) A bill may be made payable to two or more payees jointly, or it may be made payable in the alternative to one of two, or one or some of several payees. A bill may also be made payable to the holder of an office for the time being.

(3) Where the payee is a fictitious or non-existing person the bill may be treated as payable to bearer.

When a person accepts a bill, he is precluded from denying to a holder in due course the existence of the payee and his then capacity to indorse. The acceptor is not, however, responsible for the genuineness or validity of the payee's indorsement.

Where a bill or cheque is payable to two or more payees who are not partners, all must indorse, unless there is an authority for one of them to sign for the others. If one of them is dead, payment may be made to the survivor on satisfactory proof of death.

Where a cheque payable to John Brown is presented over the counter by a stranger who represents himself to be the executor of Brown, the banker is entitled to ask for exhibition of the probate of Brown's will.

If a payee's name is misspelt, he should indorse the bill or cheque in precisely the same way, and add his proper signature below.

A cheque which is payable to 'John Brown only' is not capable of being transferred to anyone else, as the word 'only' cancels the negotiability of the instrument. A bill payable to 'John Brown only' should not be discounted as, in the event of the bill being dishonoured, the banker could not sue upon it.

Where there are several payees and the bill is payable in the alternative to one or some, only those who actually indorse the bill are liable thereon.

If the payee is a minor, or corporation having no power to contract, the payee can indorse and effectually transfer the bill to another party, but such a payee will not be liable on the bill.

In the case of a cheque drawn 'pay [blank] order', it has been held as being payable to the order of the drawer and, therefore, requiring his indorsement (*Chamberlain* v *Young* [1893] 2 QB 206). It is not a banker's duty to advise a holder to insert his own name in the blank. If not indorsed by the drawer, the best course is to get the incomplete cheque completed by the drawer. If payable to '... or order' the cheque should be returned for the drawer to insert the payee's name.

Where a payee is dead, his executors, or administrators may indorse and negotiate the cheque, and the indorsement should show the capacity in which they sign.

A payee is a 'holder for value' but is not a 'holder in due course'. The instrument has not been negotiated to him (although on the terms of Section 29 of the Bills of Exchange Act it has been otherwise contended in that he has taken the bill. See *Byles on Bills*, 25th edition, p. 203 *et seq*). The point was decided in *R. E. Jones* v *Waring and Gillow* [1926] AC 670.

As provided in Section 7(3) a bill payable to a fictitious or non-existing payee may be treated as being payable to 'bearer'. In *Bank of England* v *Vagliano Brothers* [1891] AC 107, it was held that a fictitious or non-existing person included a *real* person who never had nor was intended to have any right to the bills. SEE *Fictitious Payee*

In Scotland, when the payee is a married woman, cheques are frequently made payable to, e.g. Mrs Mary Burns or Scott, Burns being the maiden name and Scott the married name. The cheque may be indorsed either 'Mary Burns' or 'Mary Scott'.

Where a cheque is payable to 'wages or order', 'cash or order', or 'house account or order', it is sometimes treated as a cheque payable to the order of the drawer and indorsed by him. Such words as 'wages', 'cash', etc., cannot be regarded as coming under Section 7(3), which refers only to a fictitious or non-existing *person*.

In *North & South Insurance Corporation* v *National Provincial Bank Ltd* [1936] 1 KB 328, it was held that an instrument drawn payable to 'cash or order' was not a cheque, for it merely directed the payment of cash to some impersonal account which could not indorse and the printed words 'or order' must give place to the written word 'cash'. The document was a good direction to pay money to bearer and was not a bill of exchange. In this case, the money had got into the hands of the person contemplated by the drawer and the decision must not be taken to mean that a banker gets a good discharge in paying such an instrument if it has got into wrong hands. See also the case of *Orbit Mining Company Ltd* v *Westminster Bank Ltd* [1962] 3 WLR 1256. SEE *Impersonal Payees*

Where a cheque is payable to 'John Brown or order', and John Brown himself presents it at the counter for payment, it is the practice of bankers always to require it to be indorsed by Brown before payment can be made.

This practice was approved by the Mocatta Committee (Cheques Act 1957) which attached importance to indorsement in such cases as possibly affording some evidence of identity of the recipient and some measure of protection for the public. The Committee's recommendation on this point was accepted by the banks, and indorsement of cheques paid over the counter continues to be required.

If a cheque payable to, say, the British Baking Company Ltd is paid to credit of the manager's or secretary's private account, it should put the banker on enquiry at once, as he may be held liable if the cheque has been misappropriated. If it is necessary for agents, as, for instance, in the case of insurance companies, to place to the credit of their private accounts cheques which are payable to their principals, the banker should be duly authorized in writing by the principals to permit of cheques being dealt with in that way. (See the case of *A. L. Underwood Ltd* v *Bank of Liverpool and Martins Ltd* v *Barclays Bank Ltd*, and other cases under *Collecting Banker*.)

With regard to a cheque payable to one limited company and paid into credit of another limited company, see the case under *Collecting Banker*.

Where the payee of a cheque pays it into his own account, no indorsement is necessary since 1957, and the collecting banker handling such a cheque or instrument is protected by Section 4 of the Cheques Act 1957.

Where a cheque is payable to the bank on which it is drawn it is merely a direction to the bank to hold the amount as a trustee for its customers, the drawers, and to await further instructions from the drawers as to the disposal of the amount.

Where a payee's name was altered and the alteration was not authenticated by the initials of both the directors who had drawn the cheque, see the case of *Souchette Ltd* v *London County Westminster & Parr's Bank Ltd*, under *Alteration to Bill of Exchange*.

Where an addition was fraudulently made to the name of the payee of a cheque, after it was drawn, such alteration of the order to pay being facilitated by the leaving of a space after the payee's name, it was held not to be such negligence on the drawer's part as to absolve the banker from liability in paying the cheque in its altered state, although the addition was not apparent. The trial judge hinted, however, that if the practice of carelessly drawing cheques increased it might be held to be negligence on the drawer's part (*Slingsby and Others* v *District Bank Ltd* [1932] 1 KB 544).

In the case of a dividend warrant where several payees are named, it is the custom to pay upon the indorsement of one of them; but an interest warrant should, strictly, be indorsed by all the payees, though this is not always done in practice. SEE *Bill of Exchange; Cheque; Indorsement*

PAYING BANKER It is the duty of a paying banker to pay the cheques of his customer so long as he has sufficient funds belonging to his customer to enable him to do so. Before paying a cheque, a banker must, of course, examine it to see that it is properly signed, that any necessary indorsements are correct and, generally, that the cheque is in order.

In the case of bills domiciled with a banker, it is part of his duty, either from a course of dealing or by instructions of his customer, to pay them, though he is otherwise not legally bound to do so as in the case of a cheque. The paying banker is the drawee of a cheque, and therefore a party to it, but he is not a party to a bill which is merely domiciled with him.

If a drawer's or an acceptor's signature is forged, a banker cannot debit his customer's account with the cheque or bill.

With regard to indorsements, the position of the paying banker is as follows.

Bills

He cannot debit his customer's account with a bill bearing a forged indorsement. The Bills of Exchange Act does not give him any relief from a forged indorsement on a bill.

Cheques

If a banker pays an open cheque in good faith and in the ordinary course of business, he is protected against a forged indorsement by Section 60 of the Bills of Exchange Act 1882. A banker paying a crossed cheque in good faith and without negligence is protected by Section 80.

A banker paying a cheque, whether crossed or open, which is not indorsed or is irregularly indorsed, is protected by Section 1 of the Cheques Act 1957.

Cheque payable on condition that a form of receipt is signed The banker is protected by Section 1 of the Cheques Act 1957. It is not considered a transferable document. SEE *Receipt on Cheque*

Cheque crossed 'account payee' The words 'account payee' do not concern the paying banker so long as he pays to a banker in accordance with the crossing. SEE *Account Payee*

Cheque crossed 'not negotiable' The words 'not negotiable' do not affect the paying banker. The cheque is treated as an ordinary crossed cheque, and the banker is protected accordingly.

Crossed cheque The banker is protected by Section 80 of the Bills of Exchange Act (SEE *Crossed Cheque*), when he pays a cheque, crossed generally, to a banker, or crossed specially to the banker to whom it is crossed or his agent for collection being a banker. He also has the protection contained in the Cheques Act 1957.

Cheques paid under advice When drawn upon another branch of the same bank, or upon another bank. SEE *Payment of Cheque*

Cheque drawn in payment of banker's draft See the case quoted under *Banker's Draft*

Drafts (which are not cheques)

The banker is protected against a forged indorsement on an uncrossed banker's draft by Section 19 of the Stamp Act 1853. Crossed banker's drafts are protected by Section 80 of the Bills of Exchange Act 1882 (as extended by Section 5 of the Cheques Act 1957), and whether crossed or uncrossed Sections 1(2)(*b*) and 4(2)(*d*) of the Cheques Act protect the paying and collecting bankers respectively.

In the case of *Selangor United Rubber Estates Ltd* v *Cradock* [1968] 2 All ER 1073, a bank had paid a cheque, drawn by a company customer in circumstances where the amount of the cheque was being used to finance the company's purchase of its own shares in contravention of Section 54, Companies Act 1948. It was claimed that the bank was liable for the amount of the cheque because (1) it was in the position of constructive trustee for the company whose funds were being wrongly used, and (2) that they were in breach in contract with the plaintiff company for negligently paying their cheque. Ungoed-Thomas, J, found against the bank on both counts and observed

I can see no substantial difficulty in banks providing against such exceptional circumstances, involving substantial amounts, as in this case, being carried through by officials completely inexperienced in such transactions and unqualified to deal with them.

The decision in the Selangor case was followed in *Karak Rubber Co Ltd* v *Burden* (No. 2) [1972] 1 WLR 602, where the circumstances were similar. The judge, Brightman, J, appeared to draw a distinction between what he called 'a normal cheque transaction' and the type of transaction which was before the court. He said

The proper question in my view which should be supposedly put to the paying banker and customer, in a case such as the present, is whether the banker is to exercise reasonable care and skill in transacting the customer's banking business, including the making of such inquiries as may, in given circumstances, be appropriate and practical if the banker has, or a reasonable banker would have, grounds for believing that the authorized signatories are misusing their authority for the purpose of defrauding their principal or otherwise defeating his true intentions. The answer to that question is so obvious that I forebear to give it.

The constructive trust aspect of the Selangor and Karak Rubber cases was not followed in the cases of *Belmont Finance Corporation* v *Williams Furniture* [1979] Ch 250 and *Belmont Finance Corporation* v *Williams Furniture* (No. 2) [1980] 1 All ER 393. In the first of these cases, the Court of Appeal unanimously disagreed with the Selangor ruling upon the constructive trust aspect and in the second Belmont case the Court clearly adopted the principle that actual knowledge is to be proved in order to establish liability as a constructive trustee.

The contractual aspects of the Selangor and Karak Rubber cases remain and impose a considerable burden on a banker who pays a cheque where, with reasonable inquiries, he might have uncovered some illegal or unauthorized transaction underlying the issue of the cheque. SEE *Banker's Draft; Cheque; Collecting Banker; Payment of Cheque*

PAYMENT OF BILL A bill of exchange is, in the usual course of events, paid by the acceptor, and when so paid it is discharged and the bill delivered up to him. The Bills of Exchange Act 1882 provides

59.—(1) A bill is discharged by payment in due course by or on behalf of the drawee or acceptor. 'Payment in due course' means payment made at or after the maturity of the bill to the holder thereof in good faith and without notice that his title to the bill is defective.

(2) Subject to the provisions hereinafter contained, when a bill is paid by the drawer or an indorser it is not discharged; but

(*a*) Where a bill payable to, or to the order of a third party is paid by the drawer, the drawer may enforce payment thereof against the acceptor, but may not re-issue the bill.

(*b*) Where a bill is paid by an indorser, or where a bill payable to drawer's order is paid by the drawer, the party paying it is remitted to his former rights as regards the acceptor or antecedent parties, and he may, if he thinks fit, strike out his own and subsequent indorsements, and again negotiate the bill.

(3) Where an accommodation bill is paid in due course by the party accommodated the bill is discharged.

In *Auchteroni & Co* v *Midland Bank Ltd* [1928] KB 44 TLR 441, the plaintiffs drew a bill payable to themselves on the N. P. Company, who accepted the bill and gave their bankers, the defendants, instructions to pay it at maturity. When the bill became due, the plaintiffs handed it to their cashier to take it to their own bank and have it collected, but the cashier, instead of carrying out his duty, went to the defendant bank and obtained payment for it over the counter, and absconded with the money. The plaintiffs had indorsed the bill in blank before handing it to their cashier. The defendants held that, as the bill was a negotiable instrument, they were protected by Section 59. The plaintiffs held that Section 59 could not protect the defendants because the circumstances of the payment were so unusual that the defendants could not say that they had made the payment without notice of irregularity. Wright, J, in the course of his judgment, said

Was the demand for payment over the counter in this case so unusual that the defendant's suspicions ought to have been aroused? The evidence showed that though such a course was unusual, it was not unknown. If the contention of the plaintiffs was right, no banker could ever safely pay a bill over the counter without first making inquiries. If there were special circumstances as, for instance, if a bill for a large sum was presented by a tramp or by an office boy, the bank might properly wait to make inquiries, but if it did so in other cases it risked dishonouring the bill under Section 47 and committing a breach of its duty to its customer, the acceptor. The plaintiffs had entrusted the *indicia* of title to their servant and he had defrauded them, but for that the defendants were not responsible.

61. When the acceptor of a bill is or becomes the holder of it at or after its maturity, in his own right, the bill is discharged.

62.—(1). When the holder of a bill at or after its maturity absolutely and unconditionally renounces his rights against the acceptor the bill is discharged.

The renunciation must be in writing, unless the bill is delivered up to the acceptor.

(2) The liabilities of any party to a bill may in like manner be renounced by the holder before, at, or after its maturity; but nothing in this Section shall affect the rights of a holder in due course without notice of the renunciation.

If an acceptor pays the amount of a bill before it arrives at maturity, he may, should he wish to do so, re-issue the bill, because, being paid before it is due, it is not discharged. If he does not wish to re-issue the bill, he should cancel or destroy it, for if, by any means, the bill should come into the hands of a holder in due course before it matures, that holder will have a right of action against the acceptor and all other parties to the bill.

When a bill payable on demand is paid, it is discharged and cannot be re-issued; and when a bill payable after date is paid at or after maturity it also is discharged and cannot be re-issued.

No right of action can be maintained on a discharged bill, though the right to sue upon the consideration may still continue.

If an acceptor pays only a part of the amount of a bill at maturity, the part payment is a discharge to that extent, and the banker should place a receipt for the amount paid upon the back of the bill and qualify the receipt by adding that the part payment is accepted by him without prejudice to the rights of any of the other parties to the bill. Notice of the part payment should be given to the other parties. The bill itself is not, of course, given up against a part payment. The bill should be noted for the unpaid balance.

In the case of part payment of a foreign bill, the bill must be protested for the balance.

A bill should not, as a rule, be given up to an acceptor when, on presenting the bill to him for payment, he offers anything except cash or notes. If a cheque, which can be collected the same day, is offered, the bill should be retained until cash has been received for the cheque, or the bill may be pinned to the cheque so that the drawer can obtain it from his bankers when the cheque has been paid; but a cheque which cannot be cashed the same day should not be taken. It is necessary to bear in mind that if a cheque is taken in payment of a bill and the cheque is subsequently returned unpaid, the banker will have lost recourse against the various parties to the bill and will have only the acceptor to look to for the money. London bankers accept cheques upon clearing bankers in payment of bills, the cheques being attached to the bills and passed at once through the Clearing House.

A banker is not obliged to pay a bill after his usual hours of business.

Before paying a bill, the banker should see that it is in order in all respects. He must be satisfied that it bears the acceptor's signature and he should verify the due date. (See remarks under *Payment of Cheque*.)

A banker does not get a good discharge in paying bills (other than cheques) where there is a forged indorsement, for he has not paid the holder as required by Section 59 and hence has not paid the bill in due course, being consequently liable to his customer, the acceptor. In the case of cheques, statutory protection against this liability is given by Section 60. SEE *Payment of Cheque*

In *Bank of England* v *Vagliano Brothers* [1891] AC 107, Lord Macnaghten said

In paying their customers' acceptances in the usual way bankers incur a risk perfectly understood, and in practice disregarded. Bankers have no recourse against their customers if they pay on a genuine bill to a person appearing to be the holder, but claiming through or under a forged indorsement. The bill is not discharged; the acceptor remains liable; the banker has simply thrown his money away. [SEE *Forgery*]

When a promissory note is made payable at a bank, the banker is liable if he pays it in the event of a forged indorsement.

If the acceptor fails to pay a trade bill at maturity and an indorser or the drawer pays it, the bill is not discharged by such payment, and the drawer can sue the acceptor for the amount plus expenses and interest, and the indorser can sue the acceptor or any prior parties.

But if a bill is an accommodation bill and is not met by the acceptor when due, it is, if paid by the drawer or indorser, discharged when the party paying it is the person for whose accommodation the bill was drawn or accepted.

Between immediate parties the giving of a bill or cheque shifts the burden of proof. The drawer has to prove the absence of consideration; if there were no cheque, the onus would lie on the payee who would be suing for the money.

If an acceptor or any other person pays to a banker an amount for the special purpose of providing for a bill falling due, that amount is earmarked for that purpose and cannot be used by the banker for any other purpose, such as to reduce an overdraft which the acceptor may have.

Where a person accepts a bill payable at a bank where he has no account, the banker is under no obligation to receive money from the acceptor with which to pay the bill.

Where a bill is intentionally cancelled by the holder or his agent, and the cancellation is apparent thereon, the bill is discharged.

It is not necessary, on payment of a bill by the acceptor, to give a receipt for the money, as the delivering up of the bill to the acceptor is sufficient to cancel his liability upon it, but sometimes a receipt is indorsed upon the bill by the holder.

Where the holder of a bill is bankrupt, payment of the bill requires to be made to the trustee and not to the bankrupt.

Where the holder is dead, payment must be made to the executor or administrator.

If, instead of payment, a holder accepts a fresh bill from the acceptor, the drawer and indorsers of the old bill will be discharged, unless they are parties to the new bill.

When a banker is employed to collect a bill, he should not, unless under instructions from his correspondent, accept payment subject to any conditions, otherwise he may render himself liable for the amount of the bill.

With respect to a bill paid under rebate, see *Documentary Bill.*

If a banker wrongly dishonours an acceptance of his customer he will be liable in damages (SEE *Dishonour of Bill of Exchange*). He should, therefore, be careful to see that everything has been credited to the account and that the balance is correctly stated, before returning a bill.

If a banker pays a bill across the counter, and, as soon as he has done so, finds that he should not have paid it, he cannot compel the person to whom he paid the money to return it, though if a mistake is made by handing too much money to the customer the mistake may be rectified. SEE *Bill of Exchange; Cancellation of Bill of Exchange; Overdue Bill; Payment for Honour; Payment of Cheque; Payments under Mistake of Fact; Presentment for Payment; Time of Payment of Bill*

PAYMENT OF CHEQUE When an open cheque is presented for payment it requires to be carefully scrutinized to see that everything is in order. If the account upon which the cheque is drawn will admit of its payment, the banker, before paying it, must be satisfied that it bears the signature of his customer, or of the person who may have been authorized by his customer to sign, and that payment of the cheque has not been stopped by the drawer. If it is a cheque payable to order, any necessary indorsements must be scanned to see that they are apparently correct. It should also be noticed whether the cheque is post-dated or is stale dated, whether the amount in writing agrees with the amount in figures, and whether, if any alteration has been made in the cheque, such alteration is duly initialed by the drawer or drawers. On being satisfied that all these various points are in order, and that there is no other reason why the cheque should not be paid, the banker may, if the person presenting the cheque appears, so far as he can tell, to be entitled to it, pay the cheque.

Since 1957 a banker paying a cheque, whether crossed or open, which is not indorsed or which is irregularly indorsed, is protected by Section 1 of the Cheques Act, provided that he pays in good faith and in the ordinary course of business.

If a cheque has been marked for payment it must be taken into account in ascertaining the balance, as the banker must pay that cheque.

If a banker dishonours a cheque which ought to be paid he will be liable in damages.

In *London Joint Stock Bank Ltd* v *Macmillan and Arthur* [1918] AC 777, Lord Shaw said

> If the cheque does not contain on its face any reasonable occasion for suspicion as to the wording and figuring of its contents, the banker, under the contract of mandate which exists between him and his customer, is bound to pay. He dare not, without liability at law, fail in this obligation and the consequences to both parties of the dishonour of a duly signed and *ex facie* valid cheque are serious and obvious. In the second place, if there be on the face of the cheque any reasonable ground for suspecting that it has been tampered with, then that, in the usual case is met by the marking 'refer to drawer', and by a delay in payment, until that reference clears away the doubt. Always granted that the doubt was reasonable, the refusal to pay is warranted.

In practice, however, a banker would refer such a cheque marked with some other form of answer than the words 'refer to drawer', as those words are commonly used when returning a cheque for lack of funds.

When paying a crossed cheque to another banker practically the same points require to be observed and, in addition, the nature of the crossing. SEE *Crossed Cheque*

When a cheque is presented for payment, a

banker is required either to pay it or dishonour it. If everything is in order he is obliged to pay it, or stand the consequences of wrongly refusing to pay, apart from the exceptions coming under *Payments under Mistake of Fact*.

It is possible for everything connected with a cheque to be absolutely correct and yet the cashier who has to pay it may have a strong suspicion that the person presenting it is not entitled to it. Lord Halsbury in *Vagliano Bros v Bank of England* [1891] AC 107, said

> I can well imagine that on a person presenting himself, whose appearance and demeanour was calculated to raise a suspicion that he was not likely to be entrusted with a valuable document for which he was to receive payment in cash, I should think it would be extremely probable that, whether the document were a cheque payable to bearer for a large amount, or a bill, the counter clerk and banker alike would hesitate very much before making payment.

An open cheque payable to a company, purporting to bear any necessary indorsement, can, it is thought, safely be paid to a stranger without inquiry, unless any suspicious circumstances were present that would amount to notice of defective title.

When a cheque has a notice upon it that it must be presented for payment within a certain fixed time from the date of the cheque, the banker must see that the time has not expired before paying the cheque.

Where a customer has two accounts with the same bank, one at Branch A and another at Branch B, and both are credit accounts, the banker at Branch A, when a cheque drawn upon his branch is presented, is not obliged to take into consideration a balance at any other branch than his own. If, however, the account at Branch B is overdrawn and at Branch A is in credit, a banker may, if necessary, regard them as one account. SEE *Set-off*

The drawer of a crossed cheque is not entitled to a longer time to provide for it than in the case of an open cheque. A crossed cheque received from another bank by post or through the local exchange or by special presentation, may be dishonoured forthwith if there are no funds and need not be held until the close of business to see if it is provided for or if the drawer desires to stop it.

A banker at Branch A is not obliged, before dishonouring a cheque to ascertain if the customer has paid in at Branch B on that day for his credit at A, even though the customer is in the habit of paying in at B.

It is very necessary, before paying a cheque, that the banker should be fully satisfied that it ought to be paid, because, as soon as he hands the money across the counter, the ownership in that money passes from the banker to the person presenting the cheque, and, unless the presenter is willing to repay, the banker cannot obtain it back, even if he discovers immediately that the money should not have been handed over.

Where a banker has given his agent orders to pay certain cheques, or cheques up to a fixed amount, on behalf of a customer, the cheques, when paid, are debited to the customer's account on the day they are received by the banker, but any interest on the account is reckoned as though the cheques had been debited on the actual date when they were paid by the banker's agent.

When a branch pays, under advice, a cheque drawn upon another branch of the same bank, payment at the substituted branch is a payment by the bank on which the cheque is drawn, and the bank obtains the protection of Section 60 of the Bills of Exchange Act 1882. (See *Questions in Banking Practice*, 11th Edn, p. 354.)

When a banker learns that a customer is dead, or has become mentally incapable, or he receives notice of the presentation of a bankruptcy petition, or ascertains that a receiving order has been made, he must not pay any further cheques on the account, but return them to the presenter with an answer written upon them.

After notice of commission of an act of bankruptcy, cheques should only be paid to the drawer or his assignee, and cheques payable to third parties should be dishonoured. SEE *Act of Bankruptcy*

As to payments to undischarged bankrupts, see under *Bankrupt Person*.

Where a banker has been served with a garnishee order, see *Garnishee Order*.

In cases where a cheque has a bill attached, if the cheque specifically refers to the bill, the banker must see that the bill, as well as the cheque, is in order, but if the cheque does not allude to the bill the cheque must be dealt with, without regard to the bill.

It is desirable that cheques should, as far as possible, be paid in the order in which they are presented. A cheque which arrives in the morning's clearing must be paid, if the account will admit of it, and must not be dishonoured in order to admit of a cheque presented across the counter later in the day being paid.

If a cheque is dishonoured because of insufficient funds, a cheque presented subsequently should be paid if the funds are sufficient for it.

A cheque does not operate as an assignment of the drawer's funds in the hands of the drawee, but in Scotland it is otherwise. (See Section 53, Bills of Exchange Act 1882, under *Drawee*.)

Before returning a cheque a banker should make certain that everything has been credited to the account and that the balance is stated correctly, for if he wrongfully dishonours a cheque of his customer he will be liable in damages. Bank charges should not be debited to an account at an unusual time unless by agreement with the customer. SEE *Dishonour of Bill of Exchange*

As regard cheques which a customer has paid in, but which the banker has not yet cleared, it is a matter of arrangement between the banker and the customer as to whether or not they are to be considered as definitely placed to the customer's credit and so available as funds in hand with which to meet any of the customer's own cheques which may be presented, and it is very advisable to have a definite understanding on the point. Subject to whatever arrangement has been made between himself and his customer, the banker will either pay such cheques or return them unpaid with answer marked thereon 'effects not cleared'. SEE *Effects not Cleared*

A banker who, in good faith and in the ordinary course of business, pays a cheque drawn on himself, is protected by Section 60 of the Bills of Exchange Act 1882, if an endorsement proves to have been forged or made without authority. A banker who pays a crossed cheque, in accordance with Section 80, is protected against a forged indorsement. (See the Section under *Crossed Cheque*.)

A banker is not obliged to pay a cheque out of bank hours. If he does so, he may lose the protection of Section 60, and runs the risk of paying a cheque, payment of which may be 'stopped' by the drawer as soon as the bank doors are opened for business.

As to a cheque presented through the post by a stranger, see under *Presentment for Payment*. It is, of course, in order for a customer to send a cheque by post so that cash may be remitted to him.

Cheques received through the clearing must be paid or dishonoured on the day of receipt; cheques paid to credit which are drawn upon the same branch may be returned unpaid on the following day, but in practice all cheques are either paid or dishonoured on the day they are received, except that where the system of deferred posting is in force, or the accounts of the branch are attached to a computer which only produces an 'out of order' list the following day, the clearing bankers have agreed that returns may be made within 48 hours of presentation, provided that notice of dishonour is advised to the presenting bank by midday on the second day. SEE *Dishonour of Bill of Exchange*

Where a cheque was paid in at the same branch upon which it was drawn for the credit of the account of an employee of the drawer and payable to a third party, it was held that it was paid in the ordinary course of business notwithstanding that negligence was present. Nevertheless, the bank in its other function as collecting agent was liable for conversion on the grounds of such negligence (*Worshipful Company of Carpenters* v *British Mutual Banking Co* [1937] 3 All ER 811).

When a banker is requested by telephone to state if a certain cheque will be paid when presented, a guarded reply such as that recommended by the Institute of Bankers, 'Would pay if in our hands and in order', should be given. A reply such as 'Yes, if in order', would render the banker liable if, before the cheque is actually presented, the customer's balance is altered so as not to admit of its payment, or if the cheque is 'stopped' by the drawer, or if the balance is legally attached. SEE *Advise Fate*

By Section 75 of Bills of Exchange Act 1882

> The duty and authority of a banker to pay a cheque drawn on him by his customer are determined by:
> (1) Countermand of payment;
> (2) Notice of the customer's death.

It is desirable that a countermand of payment of a cheque should be in writing and be signed by the drawer, and if the countermand is subsequently cancelled it also should be in writing. SEE *Payment Stopped*

PAYMENT COUNTERMANDED SEE *Payment Stopped*

PAYMENT FOR HONOUR When an acceptor fails to pay a bill at maturity, any person may, after the bill has been protested, pay it *supra protest* for the honour of some party to the bill.

The regulations regarding payment for honour *supra protest* are contained in Section 68 of the Bills of Exchange Act, 1882 which is as follows.

> (1) Where a bill has been protested for non-payment any person may intervene and pay it *supra protest* for the honour of any party liable thereon, or for the honour of the person for whose account the bill is drawn.
>
> (2) Where two or more persons offer to pay a bill for the honour of different parties, the person whose payment will discharge most parties to the bill shall have the preference.
>
> (3) Payment for honour *supra protest*, in order to operate as such and not as a mere voluntary payment, must be attested by a notarial act of honour, which may be appended to the protest or form an extension of it.
>
> (4) The notarial act of honour must be founded on a declaration made by the payer for honour, or his agent in that behalf, declaring his intention to pay the bill for honour, and for whose honour he pays.
>
> (5) Where a bill has been paid for honour, all parties

subsequent to the party for whose honour it is paid are discharged, but the payer for honour is subrogated for, and succeeds to both the right and duties of, the holder as regards the party for whose honour he pays, and all parties liable to that party.

(6) The payer for honour on paying to the holder the amount of the bill and the notarial expenses incidental to its dishonour is entitled to receive both the bill itself and the protest. If the holder does not on demand deliver them up he shall be liable to the payer for honour in damages.

(7) Where the holder of a bill refuses to receive payment *supra protest* he shall lose his right of recourse against any party who would have been discharged by such payment.

The drawer or any indorser may insert on a bill the name of a person to whom the holder may resort on dishonour of the bill by non-acceptance or non-payment. Such person is called a 'referee in case of need', and, if so disposed, will accept or pay the bill for the honour of the drawer or indorser as the case may be (Section 15, Bills of Exchange Act 1882). SEE *Acceptance for Honour; Bill of Exchange*

It was held in the case of *Momm* v *Barclays Bank International Ltd* [1976] 3 All ER 588 that in these days of computerized banking, payment by a banker is made when the computer process has been set in motion and that thereafter countermanding instructions would not normally be accepted. That particular case concerned, not the payment of a cheque, but the time of payment of a transfer between two customers in the books of the same banking branch. The bank had received instructions to transfer £120,000 from the account of their customer H to another customer M. In accordance with the bank's usual practice, the instructions were put into effect when received. In the days before computerization, if it transpired that the balance of the account was insufficient to meet the transfer, it would be reversed before the close of business that day. With computerized accounting, however, the balance of H's account was not known until the following day when, in view of the insufficiency of funds in H's account, the bank reversed the entries. Later that day, H went into liquidation. Customer M claimed repayment of the sum of £120,000. The bank maintained that the transfer between the accounts had been only on a conditional basis, pending receipt of the computer print-out the following day. The judge held, however, that in accordance with usual banking practice, a day ended at the close of working hours and it had to be known by the end of that day whether a payment due that day had been made or not. The bank could not hold over the decision until the following morning.

PAYMENT STOPPED A customer has the right to give notice to his banker to stop payment of a cheque which he has issued. The notice should be in writing, give accurate particulars of the cheque and be signed by the drawer.

If a banker pays a cheque after a 'stop order' has been received, he will be liable for so doing. It is necessary, therefore, to warn each branch where the cheque may be presented of the notice which has been received. A notice should be placed in the customer's account, so that anyone referring to the account may at once observe particulars of the 'stop'. A list of all orders to stop payment should be kept in some convenient form for ready reference by those officials who are concerned with the payment of cheques. In these days of computerization, details of the stopped cheque are fed into the computer which prints out a list of possible stopped cheques on a daily basis.

In *London Provincial and South-Western Bank Ltd* v *Frank Buszard* (1918) 35 TLR 142, Lawrence, J, held that notice of the stopping of a cheque at one branch of a bank was not notice to the other branches. He said that it appeared from *Clode* v *Bayley* (1843) 12 M and W 231, that there was a right to a separate notice of dishonour as between the different branches of a bank.

The drawer of a cheque is the only person who can stop payment of it, but bankers often receive notice from the payee of a cheque that it has been lost or stolen. Where notice is received from a payee, he should be requested to inform the drawer at once so that the latter may instruct the banker to stop payment. If the cheque is presented before such instructions are to hand, a banker will exercise great discretion before honouring it.

If the cheque which is lost is signed by several persons, a notice from one of them, e.g. one executor, one trustee, a secretary, etc., is usually acted upon by a banker. Where the account is in several names and the lost cheque is signed by, say, only one of the account holders, or by one partner, a notice from any of the other holders or partners is sufficient authority to a banker to justify him in stopping payment of the cheque.

When the drawer wishes to cancel his order to stop payment, it should be done in writing and be signed by him.

When a drawer wishes to stop payment of a cheque, he is entitled to do so during the usual business hours, and if a banker pays a cheque before the commencement of business, or after the doors are closed, he incurs the risk of paying a cheque which may be 'stopped' as soon as the drawer has the opportunity.

When an order to stop payment is received at the moment the cheque is presented and before the banker has paid over the money, the cheque should not be paid.

In the case of a cheque received through the clearing, the drawer has the right to stop payment of it up till the close of business, as the banker has that time in which to decide whether to pay or return a cheque. If the cheque has been cancelled, before the countermand of payment, it may be marked 'cancelled in error'.

An order to a banker to pay money is revocable until something definite has been done by the banker binding him to the person to be benefited, as by crediting him or admitting that he holds the money to his use.

Where payment of a cheque is countermanded by telephone or telegram, the written confirmation of the drawer should be obtained without delay. In *Hilton* v *Westminster Bank Ltd* (1927), 43 TLR 124, a drawer stopped payment of a cheque by telemessage, quoting the number as 117283 and later confirmed this by telephone. A cheque was later presented and paid for the same amount and identical in detail except the number was 117285. It transpired that this was in fact the cheque the drawer intended to stop, its number having been wrongly quoted. The drawer sued the bank for having paid contrary to instructions, contending that the bank was not entitled to assume that the cheque that was paid was a duplicate of the stopped cheque, especially as an examination of the drawer's paid cheques would have shown that the cheque bearing the number given in mistake by the drawer has already been paid and did not correspond with the stopped cheque. It was held in the House of Lords that the bank was entitled to assume that the cheque actually paid was a duplicate cheque as there could be only one cheque bearing a printed number, whilst there might be many cheques in favour of the same payee and for the same amount.

In *Curtice* v *London City & Midland Bank* [1908] 1 KB 293, a telegram from a drawer stopping payment of a cheque was delivered after hours in the bank letterbox and overlooked the next morning when the box was cleared. Before it was discovered, the cheque was presented and paid. The Appeal Court held that the cheque was not in fact stopped, as notification of the countermand did not actually come to the bank's notice and there could be no constructive countermand of payment. A verdict was given for the bank but the Court suggested that there might have been a ground of action for negligence in respect of the careless clearing of the letter-box.

Pending confirmation of a countermand by telemessage or telephone, a bank should not refuse payment but postpone it pending corroboration. Any answer put on a cheque in these circumstances should make this clear.

If, exceptionally, a banker has accepted a cheque in the same manner as a drawee might accept a bill of exchange, or if, in answer to a telegram from another bank, he unqualifiedly replies that the cheque will be paid, he must pay the cheque when presented. But if, in the meantime, the drawer has stopped payment of it, the banker cannot charge it to the drawer's account. (See further information under *Marked Cheque*.)

Although a drawer has the right to stop payment of a cheque drawn by him, yet if the payee has negotiated the cheque, any subsequent bona fide holder for value can sue the drawer, provided that the cheque was not crossed 'not negotiable'. SEE *Countermand of Payment; Lost Bill of Exchange*

In *Burnett* v *Westminster Bank Ltd* [1965] 3 All ER 817, the plaintiff had accounts at two branches. Contrary to advice circulated to customers, the plaintiff altered the address on one of the cheques which he then stopped. It was not noticed, partly because the magnetic ink characters were those of the other branch. It was held, however, that insufficient notice had been given to the customers of the prohibition against using the cheque of one branch, duly amended, for the account of the other customer. Inability to establish specific notice caused the bank to lose the case.

When returning a cheque, payment of which has been countermanded by the drawer, the answer written on the cheque should be 'payment countermanded by the drawer', or 'orders not to pay'. The answer 'payment stopped' should not be used, as it might be interpreted to mean that the drawer has stopped payment of his debts.

Where a banker pays a cheque countermanded by the customer and recredits the latter's account, he is subrogated to the rights of the person receiving the money, and may also prevent the customer from becoming 'unjustly enriched'; that is to say that the customer may not keep the money recredited and also reap the benefit he obtained from the party to whom the banker paid the stopped cheque in error. This subject is a difficult one and has rarely been before the Courts. (See also *Momm* v *Barclays Bank International Ltd* under *Payment of Cheque*.)

PAYMENT OF WAGES ACT 1960 The legal obligation in the UK to pay a workman in cash has its origin in the Truck Acts, principally the Truck Act of 1831. Under that Act, the amount of wages earned by, or payable to, any workman in respect of any labour done by him, must be actually paid to him in the 'current coin of the realm'. Any payment made by the employer in respect of wages by the delivery of goods, or otherwise than in current coin of the realm, is illegal. The original Act of 1831 applied only to 'artificers', but over the years the definition has been widened to include almost all workers or persons engaged in any manual work under a contract of service. Under the Payment of Wages by Cheque Act 1960, wages of a workman may be paid into his bank account or be paid by money order, postal order or cheque if the workman so requests and the employer agrees. Despite the enabling provisions of this Act, comparatively little progress has been made in the payment of wages other than in cash. This is partly because of traditional attitudes, but also because of the difficulty of obtaining the consents of those concerned. Any worker who withholds consent is still entitled to be paid in cash. For the most part, trade unions have been opposed to the payment of wages other than in cash, but their attitude has modified considerably over the years. On the whole, employers favour the move towards payment of wages through banking accounts, principally on the grounds of cost and security. There are, however, many problems to be overcome and, at the time of writing, the banks have set up a working party to explore the whole problem of payment of wages.

In 1983, the Secretary of State for Employment announced that the Government had decided to invite Parliament to repeal the Truck Acts and associated legislation. In the first instance, however, it would be necessary to renounce International Labour Organisation Convention 95, dealing with the protection of wages.

PAYMENTS UNDER MISTAKE OF FACT

Money paid away under mistake of fact can, in certain circumstances, be recovered. The mistake must be one of fact, not of law. Assuming that the receiver of the money took it in good faith—without which he would not be allowed to keep it—it is a general, though not an absolute, rule that he cannot be made to refund where he has changed his position and it would accordingly be prejudicial to him to repay. Money paid on a negotiable instrument can probably not be recovered. Paget (*Law of Banking*, 9th Edition, p. 356) on *Jones* v *Waring & Gillow* [1926] AC 670, says

> Money paid to someone under a mistake of fact can be recovered from him, although he has detrimentally altered his position, if he did so merely in consequence of the payment and not in reliance on some independent act or representation of the payer's or by some breach of duty on the payer's part, or unless the mistake of fact directly touches a negotiable instrument by virtue of which he received the money, and his position has been or might have been prejudiced in the interval between payment and reclamation.

In the case of *United Overseas Bank* v *Jiwani* (1976) 1 WLR 964, a bank in Switzerland had erroneously credited J's account twice over with the sum of $11,000 and advised J of his new, incorrect, balance. J made a number of withdrawals and reduced his balance to approximately $1,100. When the bank discovered the mistake, they reversed the second entry resulting in the account being overdrawn by approximately $9,900. MacKenna, J, held that J was liable to repay the amount of the incorrect credit. The judge held that in order to avoid the obligation to repay, J would have had to show that the bank was under a duty to give him accurate information, that they had failed in such duty, that the inaccurate information misled J and that in consequence, he changed his position to a degreee which would make it inequitable to require him to pay the money. In the circumstances of the case, J had not shown that he had honestly believed that both the transfers of $11,000 were correct. Even if he had been misled by the bank, he had not changed his position to a degree which would have made it inequitable to require him to repay the money.

The conditions governing recovery are

1. The mistake must be between the payer and receiver (*Chambers* v *Miller* (1862) 13 CBNS 125).

The payer must be under mistake as between himself and the receiver. It is not sufficient, for example, for the payer to be labouring under a mistake of fact relative to a third party— a banker paying a cheque in the belief that the drawer was alive, when he was in fact dead, would not be entitled to recover from the payee.

2. That the money has not been paid to an agent who has paid over to his principal.

The position depends on whether the agent has paid his principal. In *Kleinwort Sons & Co* v *Dunlop Rubber Company Ltd* (1907) 23 TLR 696, the defendants paid the plaintiffs in error, and it was held that the money could be recovered as the plaintiffs had not changed their position—they had made further advances to the customers for whom the payment was received, but the court held that they would have made such advances in any event and were not induced to do só by the payment in question. *Kerrison* v *Glyn, Mills & Co* (1911) 28 TLR 106, was on similar lines, the plaintiff having paid the defendants for a purpose which had failed. The defendants were not allowed to argue that, having credited their clients, they could not refund. The case of *Admiralty Commissioners* v *National Provincial Bank Ltd* [1922] 38 TLR 492, decided against the bank's argument that money admittedly paid to it in the belief that the intended payee was alive, when he was dead, could not be repaid without the consent of the deceased's personal representatives. *Gower* v *Lloyds & National Provincial Foreign Bank Ltd* [1938] All ER, decided that where a bank received money under mistake of fact and paid over to a principal, the fact that it was under a misapprehension as to the identity of the principal did not deprive it of its defence that it had altered its position, the money being irrecoverable from the persons to whom it had in error been paid away.

3. That the money has not been paid to a principal who would suffer if forced to repay.

He must, however, have been induced to change his position by some representation on the part of the payer (see Lord Cave in *Jones* v *Waring & Gillow* above) and not merely as a consequence of the payment.

4. That the money has not been paid on a negotiable instrument.

Money paid on a negotiable instrument can be recovered where the mistake is one as to the instrument itself, not to anything extraneous to it. Payment of a cheque over the counter cannot be recovered where the payer discovers that he has made a mistake in regard to the position of the account, provided the receiver took in good faith (*London & River Plate Bank* v *Bank of Liverpool* [1896] 1 QB 7). If, however, the instrument was a forgery, it might be that the money could be recovered, though Sir John Paget rather doubted if this is so. There would usually be an indorsement bringing the instrument within the general rule, and if there were not, as in the case of a bearer bill on which the drawer's signature was forged, the payee would probably not be worth proceeding against.

The holder of a bill has the right to know immediately on presentation whether it will be paid or not (*London & River Plate case* above), this, in the words of Sir John Paget, being an element essential to the negotiability of the instrument and imperatively demanded by the exigencies of business.

In *Imperial Bank of Canada* v *Bank of Hamilton* [1903] AC 49, it was suggested that the test was the loss of opportunity of giving notice of dishonour, but it is hard to conceive any case of payment by mistake when such opportunity would be lost.

PAY-OUT RATIO The proportion of a company's earnings paid out as dividend. Apart from investment companies (q.v.) there is no statutory requirement as to the proportion of a company's earnings which must be paid as dividend to the shareholders. On the whole, there has been a UK tradition of financing future growth by the retention of earnings, rather than the seeking of new capital in the market. Thus it has not been unusual over the years for as much as two-thirds of new resources in the industrial sector to come from retained earnings. The proportion of distributed earnings, i.e. the pay-out ratio has varied among the leading industrial companies from as little as, say, 25 per cent up to (in the 1960s) 66 per cent.

PENNY A silver penny is now issued only as Maundy money (q.v.). Its standard weight is 7.27272 grains troy. At one time silver pennies were frequently cut into halves and quarters to act as halfpence and farthings. A bronze penny is a mixed metal of copper, tin, and zinc. Its standard weight is 3.56400 grams. The old bronze coinage was first issued in 1860, and the new on 15th February, 1971. SEE *Coinage*

PENSIONEER TRUSTEE SEE *Pensions, Pension Schemes*

PENSIONS, PENSION SCHEMES There are three main sources from which pensions are paid in the UK. They are the State pension schemes, occupational pension schemes, and personal pension plans.

State Pension Schemes

There are two State schemes. There is the basic pension which everyone receives, provided the necessary contributions have been paid over the years, and there is an earnings-related pension introduced under the Social Security Pensions Act 1975, which came into force in April 1978, and which applied to all employees above the lower earnings limit (q.v.) who have not been contracted out of this part of the State scheme. Under the Act, contracting out was permitted only if the employee was a member of an occupational pension scheme (see below) approved by the Occupational Pensions Board (q.v.), which means in effect that the employer's scheme provided benefits at least comparable under the State scheme. Thus any employed person receiving more than the lower earnings limit and who has not been contracted out of the State scheme is automatically covered by the earnings-related State scheme. To the extent that an employee's earnings fall between the lower earnings limit and the upper earnings limit, each year of earnings qualifies for the earnings-related pension, equivalent to $1\frac{1}{4}$ per cent of those earnings up to a maximum of 20 years. Thus, an employee who has contributed for 20 years will receive a pension equal to 25 per cent of his earnings within the prescribed limits in addition to the basic State pension. The calculation of earnings for this purpose will be revalued at the date of retirement in order to bring the actual earnings figure in line with the growth in earnings generally.

The State scheme provides for retirement at age 65 for men and at age 60 for women. There is also provision for a widow to receive a pension based on her husband's earnings or, if she has been a contributing employee, on her own earnings. There are approximately $8\frac{1}{4}$ million people receiving State pensions, of whom 5 million are women. It is estimated that out of the total UK workforce of approximately 23 million, approximately 11 million are contracted out of the Government scheme. SEE Supplement

As mentioned above, an employee who is contracted out of the Government scheme must be entitled to receive from his employer's occupational scheme a pension at least equivalent to the State pension he would receive if he were not contracted out. This is known as the Guaranteed Minimum Pension (GMP). Whatever rules may apply to a particular occupational pension scheme (and these would in any case have to be approved by the Occupational Pensions Board), the employer cannot override the right of the employee to the Guaranteed Minimum Pension and indeed the occupational scheme must make provision for it. Furthermore, the occupational scheme must protect the employees GMP, notwithstanding that he may change his employment and move to another scheme. The amount of GMP which an employee is entitled to will be $1\frac{1}{4}$ per cent (one-eightieth) of his earnings in each year between the lower earnings limit and the upper earnings limit, revalued in line with inflation (as with the State scheme) up to retirement age.

All occupational pension schemes must also provide a guaranteed minimum pension for the widow of an employee or former employee. As with the State scheme, the GMP for a widow is one-half of the man's pension.

Under the State pension scheme, an employee may also be entitled to a graduated pension which applied to persons in employment from April 1961 until April 1975. Under that graduated pension scheme (q.v.), an employer could contract out those employees who were covered by an occupational scheme and contracted out employees receive less benefit under the graduated pension scheme. Those entitled under this scheme receive a small additional weekly amount of pension, in addition to the basic State pension and the earnings-related pension to which they may be entitled under the 1975 Act.

Extra Pension for dependents In addition to basic pension a man may receive extra pension for a wife, dependent children, and a woman looking after his children.

Extra Pension for a wife A pension will be payable for a wife on the man's own contributions provided

1. the man receives a basic pension (even if a reduced one, in which case the extra pension for his wife will be proportionately reduced),
2. the wife is living with her husband, or
3. he is paying towards her upkeep at least the amount of the standard increase in pension for a wife.

No pension is payable for a wife, however, if she receives a retirement pension or other National Insurance benefits on her own contributions, or if the husband is receiving benefit for her under the various industrial injuries and war pension schemes.

Extra pension for a dependent child A pension will be payable for the child of the pensioner provided

1. the husband receives a basic pension (even though this may be at a reduced rate, in which case the extra pension for the child is *not* proportionately reduced).
2. the parent is entitled to child benefit.

Extra pension for a woman looking after a child A pensioner who is not receiving extra pension for a wife may receive extra pension in respect of a woman looking after his child (provided the pensioner's wife is not receiving a pension on her own contributions).

Deferment or cancellation of retirement Men or women entitled to retirement pension at the normal retirement ages may

1. postpone their retirement, or
2. having commenced retirement and being in receipt of pension, cancel their retirement until a later date.

Either event will enable the pensioner to receive a higher pension on eventual retirement, or when they reach age 70 in the case of a man or 65 in the case of a woman.

Also, since April 1979, a pensioner may postpone receipt of his or her graduated pension in order to obtain extra pension on eventual retirement.

If a pensioner continues to work after pension

age, he or she pays no further National Insurance contributions, but the employer's contributions continue to be payable.

Any person who falls sick or becomes unemployed after deferring or cancelling his or her retirement will be entitled to sickness, unemployment or invalidity benefit. The benefit will be paid at the rate of basic retirement pension plus any graduated pension or earnings-related pension to which the recipient would have been entitled at pension age, but any extra pension earned by deferring or cancelling retirement will be excluded.

Pensioners' earnings If a person in receipt of a State retirement pension is under 70 in the case of a man or 65 in the case of a woman and has weekly earnings in excess of a certain level (see Appendix 2), he or she will incur a reduction in (1) basic pension, (2) invalidity pension, (3) extra pension for dependants other than children, (4) extra pension or invalidity addition arising from the deferment or cancellation of retirement.

Earnings in excess of the permitted level do not affect (1) additional pension (i.e. earnings-related pension), (2) graduated pension, (3) guaranteed minimum pension, (4) extra pension obtained by deferment or cancellation of retirement, (5) extra pension for children.

Earnings for this purpose include all wages or salary, overtime payments, commissions and gratuities (other than Christmas bonuses not exceeding £10) but certain expenses may be deducted. These include the cost of travelling to work, the cost of protective clothing, meals taken during working hours up to 15p per day, and the cost of having a member of the pensioner's household looked after during his or her absence at work.

The earnings rule applies only to the first five years above normal retirement age.

Married women A married woman may benefit from retirement pension in one or other of three distinct ways:

1. She may receive a retirement pension based on her own full-rate contribution record. In other words, she may receive a full single-person's retirement pension in the same way as a man, provided she has satisfied the contribution conditions which are the same for women as for men.
2. She may receive a retirement pension based on her husband's contributions if she is over 60 and retired and if her husband is receiving a basic retirement pension. A married woman who is entitled to a maximum pension on her own contributions cannot also receive a pension on her husband's contributions. If, however, she receives less than the maximum pension on her own contributions (perhaps because her contributions have not been sufficient for a full pension) and if the pension based on her own contributions is less than the maximum which she could obtain on her husband's contributions, she may combine the two sources of pension in order to make up the permitted maximum.
3. If she is under 60, she will not be entitled to a pension in her own right, but her husband may be entitled to an increase in pension for his dependent wife, as described above.

A retired married woman over 60 who for any reason does not qualify for a basic pension on her own or her husband's contributions may nevertheless be entitled to an additional pension or graduated pension on her own contributions.

A married woman will in any case be entitled to a non-contributory pension if she is aged 80 or over.

The general rules concerning graduated pension, additional pension and extra pension earned by deferred or cancelled retirement apply to married women as to men.

Under the earnings rule, a married woman who is in receipt of retirement pension, whether on her own contributions or those of her husband, will suffer a reduction in pension if her earnings exceed the earnings limit.

Widows The retirement pension payable to a widow will depend on whether (a) she was widowed before the normal retirement age of 60 or (b) she was widowed after the age of 60.

Widowed before the age of 60 When reaching 60 a widow may

1. claim retirement pension (see below) if she has retired from work, or
2. continue to claim widow's benefit until she retires or reaches age 65, or
3. give up any widow's benefit to which she may be entitled and defer her retirement pension in order to receive extra pension at age 65 or earlier retirement.

A widow who claims retirement pension at age 60 may do so on either her own contributions or those of her late husband.

If a widow is claiming on her own contributions, she must satisfy the normal contribution conditions, but special rules apply to enable credits to be given for weeks during which a widow has been receiving widow's allowance or certain other benefits.

A widow may qualify for retirement pension on the strength of her late husband's contributions if she has been receiving national insurance widow's pension. Her retirement pension will then be at the same rate as the widow's pension.

A widow may claim partly on her own contributions and partly on those of her late husband, but the combined pension cannot be more than the standard rate of basic pension paid to a single person. Any additional (earnings-related) pension calculated on both her own and her husband's contributions cannot be more than the maximum payable to a single person who had contributed from the inception of the state pension scheme on earnings at the upper limit.

If, even after combining the widow's contribution record with that of her late husband, her basic pension still does not reach the standard rate for a single person, special regulations may be applied with more favourable effect. This is to calculate the pension on the widow's own contribution record but with the husband's contribution record substituted either for the tax years of the wife's working life prior to widowhood or the tax years for the whole of their married life prior to widowhood.

As mentioned above, a retirement pension based on a late husband's contributions is at the same rate as widow's pension. If in fact, the husband was entitled to retirement pension at the time of his death, the widow will 'inherit' the basic pension, additional pension and one half of any graduated pension to which the husband may have been entitled. If the husband had deferred or cancelled his retirement, the widow would be able to inherit the extra basic and additional pensions plus half of the extra graduated pension and half of any extra guaranteed minimum pension to which the husband may have been entitled through his occupational pension scheme.

Widowed after the age of 60 The general rule is that a widow will qualify for retirement pension at the single person's rate on her husband's contributions whether or not she has in fact retired from work.

If, however, the husband was not in receipt of retirement pension at the time of his death because he was under 65 or had deferred his retirement, a widow will receive widow's allowance for the first 26 weeks after his death together with any earnings-related addition to widow's allowance. Widow's allowance is payable at a higher rate than widow's pension but it lasts only for the 26 weeks of widowhood. At the end of that period the widow will qualify for retirement pension as if her husband had been receiving it prior to his death.

Widowers If for any reason a widower's basic pension does not amount to the full standard rate, there are special rules which enable it to be calculated by reference to the late wife's contribution record in order to bring the basic pension up to, but not exceeding, the standard rate for a single person.

Income tax Income tax is payable on all State pensions, i.e. basic pension, earnings-related pension, graduated pension, extra pension for deferred or cancelled retirement and extra pension for dependants.

Contribution conditions The following conditions must be satisfied for a State basic pension to be payable:

1. that in any one tax year since 6th April, 1975 contributions equivalent to 50 times the lower earnings limit (q.v.) have been paid *or* at least 50 flat-rate contributions were paid before 6th April, 1975, and
2. contributions must have been paid, *or credited* over most (approximately nine-tenths) of the working life of the person concerned. 'Working life' normally means 49 years for a man and 44 years for a woman, i.e. running from the age of 16 years to normal retirement age. Persons whose working life started before 5th July, 1948 will be credited with a contribution for each week up to that date.

For the purpose of this second condition, a year's contributions will qualify in the following circumstances:

1. Flat-rate contributions paid, or credited, before *6th April, 1975* will be divided by 50 and rounded up to the nearest whole number in order to give the number of qualifying years (provided it is no more than the actual working life up to that date).
2. From 6th April, 1975 to 5th April, 1978, a year will be a qualifying year if contributions equal to 50 times the lower earnings limit for each year were paid or credited.
3. From 6th April, 1978 onwards a qualifying year is any tax year in which contributions on earnings of at least 52 times the lower earnings limit have been paid or credited.

For a working life of 31–40 years, the number of qualifying years necessary is the length of that working life minus four, e.g. someone who has worked for 36 years must have 32 years qualifying in order to be paid a full basic pension. In the case of a working life in excess of 41 years, the qualifying years are the length of that working life minus five. Thus for a man working from age 16 to age 65 (49 years) the number of qualifying years required is 44.

In the case of the second condition, it is sufficient that contributions have been 'credited', i.e. periods of sickness and unemployment will qualify. This does not apply, however, to the first condition.

Although most employed persons will have paid only Class 1 contributions, Class 2 contributions (self-employed persons) and Class 3 contributions (voluntary contributions) also qualify for both the first and second contributions conditions above.

A person who does not have the full number of qualifying years under the second condition will not be able to receive a full basic pension, but will be entitled to one proportionately reduced.

Old person's pension A person who does not satisfy the contributions requirements for a full or reduced State pension may nevertheless receive an Old Person's Pension from age 80 onwards. A person will qualify for an old person's pension if

1. he or she is not receiving a State retirement pension or other Social Security benefit at or above the rate of the old person's pension (but this does not apply to earnings-related pension, graduated pension (see above) or a guaranteed minimum pension under an occupational scheme (see above)), and
2. he or she is living in Great Britain and has done so for at least 10 of the 20 years immediately prior to his or her 80th birthday.

For further details of State retirement pensions, it is necessary to refer to the leaflets issued from time to time by the Department of Health and Social Security.

Occupational Pension Schemes
As mentioned above, an occupational pension scheme must satisfy the requirements of the Occupational Pensions Board, which was set up under the Social Security Act 1973 and whose functions were defined in the Social Security Pensions Act 1975. In essence, an occupational scheme must provide benefits at least comparable to those available under the State pension schemes and, in particular, there is a statutory obligation to provide a guaranteed minimum pension.

There is a great variation among occupational pension schemes. For example:

1. Some schemes are contributory on the part of members, others non-contributory.
2. Some schemes provide for pension units to be 1/60 of salary multiplied by the number of years' service, others use a less generous factor, e.g. 1/80.
3. In some cases, pensions are based on final salary. In other cases, the average of the last three years'salary, or some other basis, is taken.
4. Some schemes provide for retirement for men at 65 and women at 60, others provide for lower retirement ages.
5. Some schemes provide for dependants, others do not.
6. Some schemes provide for early retirement, others do not.
7. Some schemes provide for 'topping-up' by members on a voluntary basis, others do not.
8. Some schemes provide for the commutation of pension in return for a capital sum. Some schemes do not include this provision.
9. Some schemes provide a capital sum for dependants in the event of death in active service. Others have no such provision.

In addition to satisfying the requirements of the Occupational Pensions Board, a pension scheme must be approved by the Superannuations Funds Office of the Inland Revenue under the New Code under the Finance Act 1970, which came into effect for all new occupational schemes from that year, and has applied to all schemes, new and old, from 1980 onwards. The main provisions of the Code are set out below.

1. Retirement ages will normally be between 60 and 70 for men and 55 and 70 for women.
2. The maximum pension will normally be 40/60 of final salary subject to a minimum of 10 years' service.
3. Maximum lump salary benefits will be equivalent to 1½ times final salary provided 20 years' service has been completed.
4. The maximum pension payable to widows will be two-thirds of the employee's maximum pension.
5. The maximum lump sum payable in the event of death in active service will be four times the employee's salary, plus a refund of any contributions he has made.
6. Pensions may be guaranteed for a period of five years and in the event of death during this period a lump sum may be paid free of tax in commutation of the outstanding guaranteed instalments.
7. The maximum pensions payable under the Code may be increased after they become payable to the extent that there has been an increase in the Index of Retail Prices (or similar index). Such increase may be promised and funded in advance on a reasonable basis on the understanding that any increases actually paid are limited to the actual increase in the cost of living.

Under a scheme which is approved for Inland Revenue purposes (1) contributions of both employer and employee are allowed for tax purposes, (2) the pension fund itself is exempt from tax, (3) the permitted capital sum by way of commutation of pension is free of tax, and (4) the pension itself is deemed to be earned income for tax purposes.

An occupational pension scheme may be contributory or non-contributory. There is no statutory limit on the amount of an employer's contribution (although it must be realistic in relation to the funding requirements of the scheme) but there is a limit of 15 per cent on the amount which an employee may contribute to a scheme out of his total remuneration.

Prior to 1973 it was not possible for a director who held more than five per cent of the voting shares of a company that was director-controlled, i.e. where the director held more than 50 per cent of the voting rights, to be a member of the company's pension scheme, nor was it possible for the company to take out a separate scheme on such a director's behalf. With the passing of the Finance Act 1973, however, this rule was changed and it is possible now for a controlling director to join the company scheme or to benefit from a separate individual pension arrangement.

In the case of such controlling director schemes, substantial sums may be built up outside the company with complete freedom from capital transfer tax. Such schemes are very flexible and the company make make larger transfers in the more profitable years, thereby reducing corporation tax liability. Indeed, the funds built up under such a scheme need not be separately invested; they may be used in the company's business provided they are under the control of acceptable trustees and up to one half of the contributions may be put out on loan to the company. The Inland Revenue will require an undertaking from the trustees that they will not agree to the winding-up of the pension scheme other than in accordance with the terms of the trust deed. As an added safeguard to ensure that the trustees (who will in some cases be the directors of the company) do not wind up the fund and distribute the assets among themselves or their families, the Superannuation Funds Office requires that one of the trustees be what is now known as a 'pensioneer trustee'. This is a person or institution with professional experience of pension trusts who must be approved by the Superannuation Funds Office as a suitable trustee. This rule applies to all smaller pension schemes, which are defined as those with fewer than 12 members.

The following points are relevant to these 'controlling director' schemes.

1. There does not have to be a main scheme, e.g. the employees may be covered by the State scheme.
2. If it is a family business, the directors may wish to retain control of the pension scheme assets and thus will choose a self-administered scheme rather than an insurance company scheme.
3. There must be a pensioneer trustee (see above).
4. Transfers to the pension fund (which may be proportionately larger than with a large company) may result in substantial savings in corporation tax.
5. The pension fund assets may be used in the business, e.g. in the purchase of property or plant leased to the company.
6. In due time considerable sums may pass to the pension scheme beneficiaries with no liability to tax (other than income tax on normal pension payments).
7. Directors of private companies tend to retire much later than executives of large companies and quite often the capital sum on death, free of capital transfer tax, assumes a greater importance than the amount of pension payable.

Apart from such provision for director-controlled companies, it is possible for a company to introduce an 'executive' scheme for senior employees, sometimes referred to as AVC schemes because they involve additional voluntary contributions. The following are some of the principal characteristics of such schemes.

1. An executive may pay an additional contribution to bring his total contributions up to 15 per cent in total of his total remuneration, including bonuses, etc.
2. The company may pay up to any amount provided it is related to permissible benefits for the executives.
3. The executives may thus obtain additional benefits not otherwise available under the main company scheme, e.g. credit for additional years service, early retirement, higher death in service payments (see above). There is much more flexibility than in the main company scheme.
4. The additional benefits will usually be arranged through an insurance company in order that they may be guaranteed.

Pension preservation is a matter of importance in these days when there is perhaps a greater tendency for employees to change jobs. Under the Social Security Act 1973, which came into force in April 1975, a member of an occupational pension scheme who changes his job after five years' service and is then aged 26 or more is entitled to have his pension rights preserved in the scheme which he is leaving, or have the benefit of an equivalent transfer value to the scheme which he is joining. Although the employee is entitled to preservation of his pension benefits, he is not entitled to transferability as such, but his former employer may offer this. The transfer of pension benefits would not be to the advantage of the employee if the terms of his former scheme are more beneficial, particularly in relation to the escalation of pension in line with the cost of living.

In general, an employee who changes his employment a number of times will jeopardize his ultimate pension benefits. This is largely because his final pension will be paid by his last employer, with whom he may have had only a limited number of years' service. On the whole, there is no loss to the employee, however, if he moves to a scheme offering comparable benefits and his new employer gives him the benefit of past service in exchange for the transfer value of his existing pension rights.

Under the Finance Act 1981, the Inland Revenue may exercise their discretion to give tax approval to pension schemes which permit their members, on leaving their employment, to secure the paid-up pension benefits by the purchase of an annuity with an insurance company. There is no objection to a provision in the rules of a pension scheme that such an annuity may be taken out with an insurance company of the individual's choice.

In 1983 the Department of Health and Social Security issued a consultative document *On improved protection for the occupational pension rights and expectations of early leavers from occupational pension schemes*. This contained proposals for dealing with deferred pensions for early leavers. The principal recommendations were that in those occupational schemes based on final salary, the amount of deferred pensions would have to be revalued up to the date of commencement of the pension by at least five per cent per annum compound or, if less, by the amount of any rise in the Retail Price Index. In the case of those schemes with pensions based on average salary, it would be necessary to revalue pensions of early leavers at the same time as the benefits were revalued for those members remaining in the scheme, i.e. up to the minimum required for a final salary scheme. Discussion was invited on these and other related proposals.

At the time of writing, a bill, The Social Security Bill, is before Parliament. It embodies the principal recommendations contained in the consultative document on the subject of early leavers (SEE Supplement).

The Secretary of State also set up an inquiry to look at the whole question of provision for retirement. The report of that inquiry is still awaited but in the meantime, the Secretary of State has issued a consultative document on the subject of the 'portability' of pensions. This is based on the concept that 'personal pensions should be available as of right to all employees' and the document contains proposals to enable employees to opt out of the occupational scheme provided by his employer and to arrange his own 'personal pension'. Such a personal pension would also entitle the employee to contract out of the State earnings-related scheme. At present, many questions remain unanswered and the outcome of the consultative document is awaited.

Such personal pensions would be similar in some respects to those personal pension schemes available to self-employed persons, as discussed below.

Personal Pension Schemes

These schemes, more often known as personal pension plans, are those taken out by an individual for his own benefit rather than by or through an employer.

Personal pension plans are associated primarily with self-employed persons, but they are equally relevant to some categories of employed people. Accordingly, personal pension plans may be taken out by the following.

Self-employed persons There are approximately 2.4 million self-employed people in the UK and of these 1.5 million earn sufficient to pay National Insurance contributions at the self-employed rate. Self-employed persons do not, however, qualify for an earnings-related pension under the State scheme—they receive merely the basic State retirement pension. Since the passing of the Finance Act 1956, however, self-employed persons have been able to secure significant tax exemptions on amounts put by for pension purposes (see below).

Employed persons not contracted out of the State scheme There are approximately 11 million employed persons who were not contracted out of the State scheme and in the ordinary way will have no pension on retirement other than the basic State pension and the earnings-related State pension. Such persons may, if they wish, take out a personal pension plan in order to augment the State benefit.

Employed persons who have other earnings An employed person who is a member of an occupational pension scheme (or who has not been contracted out of the State scheme) may have earnings from an independent source of employment. For example, a medical consultant may have private fees in addition to his pensionable earnings under the National Health Service. Such a person may contribute to a personal pension plan in respect of these non-pensionable earnings.

For all practical purposes, these three categories of persons may be considered together in relation to personal pension plans.

The essence of a personal pension plan is that the earner can set aside so much of his earnings each year to be paid to an insurance company, who will invest the premiums in order to provide a capital sum at the date of the earner's retirement. That capital sum will then be used partly to pay a cash amount to the retired earner, but mostly for the purchase of an annuity to provide a pension for life.

Personal pension schemes enjoy the following taxation advantages.

1. The premiums paid (up to the permitted maximum) are wholly deducted for tax purposes and thus the earner saves tax at his marginal rate.
2. The premiums are invested by the insurance company in an 'exempt' fund on which no tax is payable.
3. No tax is payable on the capital sum which the earner receives at retirement.
4. The pension is treated as earned income for tax purposes, not as investment income, e.g. a husband does not have to pay tax on his wife's occupational pension as he would if it were investment income.

At the present time, the normal maximum contributions which may be paid annually for personal pension plan purposes if the taxation relief is to be obtained is 17½ per cent of earnings, but higher percentages apply, on a graduated scale, to persons born in or before 1933.

In the ordinary way, premiums paid on a personal pension plan will be allowed as a deduction for tax in the year in which they are paid. In many cases, however, a person engaged in a trade or profession will not know the amount of his taxable income until some time after the end of his financial year, and also there may be considerable fluctuations in the amount of his annual income. In general terms, a taxpayer may elect to have a premium paid before the expiry of six months after a previous year's tax assessment becomes final treated as having been paid in that previous tax year.

Under the Finance Act 1980, the following changes were introduced in relation to retirement annuities.

1. The previous limit of £1,000 on life assurance premiums (paid as part of the 17½ per cent overall limit) was removed. The limit for the life assurance content is five per cent of relevant earnings (as hitherto) but there is no absolute ceiling.
2. In calculating net relevant earnings for the purpose of determining the contribution level, it is no longer necessary to deduct mortgage interest or alimony payments.
3. Payments on death under retirement annuity schemes may now be paid to anyone. Hitherto such payments had to be made to the personal representatives.
4. From 1980–81 onwards an individual who pays more than the qualifying level of retirement annuity premiums in any year may bring forward any unused relief from the previous six years. The amount of the unused relief will be calculated according to the earnings of the past year(s) and the limit of relief then applying.
5. A person who pays a qualifying premium in any year of assessment may elect before the end of that year to have the premium treated as though paid in a previous year.

The following are some of the principal features of personal pension schemes:

1. The retirement pension may become payable any time from age 60 to 75, regardless of the actual date of retirement. In special circumstances, the Inland Revenue may agree to payment of the pension at an age earlier than 60, but payment may not commence at an age later than 75.
2. The contract may provide for part of the retirement annuity to be commuted for a cash sum which will be paid free of tax. The maximum permitted sum is three times the amount of the retirement annuity which will remain after commutation.
3. Provision may be made for a widow or widower or other dependant.
4. Term life assurance and provision for dependants may be taken out under Section 226 of the Taxes Act (see above).
5. The retirement annuity and any payments to dependants will be treated as earned income.
6. A guaranteed annuity may be paid for a period of five or ten years, which means that there would be a residual payment to the annuitant's estate in the event of death during that period.
7. A plan may be taken out on a 'guaranteed' or 'linked' basis.
8. When the retirement annuity becomes payable, the annuitant may, under the provisions of the Finance Act 1978, apply the cash value of the annuity in the purchase of an annuity from another life company. In other words, he may obtain the best annuity rates then available in the market and does not necessarily have to take the annuity from the company with whom he has until then conducted his pension plan. The annuitant cannot of course in any circumstances

receive the cash sum for his own use (other than the amount of the permitted commutation).

As with normal life assurance (q.v.), a personal pension plan may be taken out via a 'conventional' with-profits endowment scheme or through a 'linked' annuity scheme.

The advantage of the conventional type of policy is that there will be a guaranteed annuity at the end of the savings period. The life company may indeed improve on the amount of the guarantee if the policy is with-profits. The amount of the annuity and therefore the amount of the related cash sum which may be taken by commutation of part of the annuity will not be known until the end of the contract period, but at least the annuitant will know that the basic pension is guaranteed.

A linked pension plan will be linked to the performance of a particular fund and if, for example, there were a major fall in the stock market at the time the annuity were to commence, the cash available and therefore the amount of the annuity would be less than expected. On the other hand, a linked fund provides maximum flexibility in that it may be linked to gilt edged stocks, equities, building societies, property or, say, overseas stocks by an arrangement with the prospective annuitant and thus, in theory, take advantage of movements in the various markets. Also, the contributor can see at any time (or at least on an annual basis) how his investment is progressing.

The distinction between the two forms of contract tends to be a subjective matter. For some people a retirement annuity is too important to risk the hazards of the stock market. On the other hand, a personal pension plan may be merely to top-up the benefits from some other scheme and it may be reasonable to take the risk of a linked plan in return for the possibility of higher benefits. Many people do not wish to be involved with the investment aspects of their pension plan and prefer a straightforward conventional guaranteed scheme. Others prefer to take an active part in the choice of fund to which their scheme will be linked and to monitor its progress year by year.

In any case, a personal pension plan need not be confined to one contract with one life office. To achieve maximum flexibility, there is some advantage in taking out a number of plans, whether 'guaranteed' or 'linked' either with one office or a number of offices. It is not necessary for the annual premium to be a fixed sum. This may be determined year by year. The contributions may be a series of annual premiums on a policy, or may be a series of single premiums on separate policies. One particular advantage of having a number of policies is that they may be arranged with differing retirement dates spread over a number of years.

Following the introduction by the Government of index-linked stocks, it is now possible for a private pension plan to be invested in such stocks, thus achieving index-linking of the pension benefits.

In recent years 'loan back' facilities have been introduced in connection with personal pension plans. There is a number of variations in these schemes but they all have the common ingredient that a self-employed person under a private pension plan may borrow from his own accumulated pension fund. The loan is made, not against the value of the accumulated units, but against separate security, e.g. a house or portfolio of investments. There is usually a minimum level of loan and the maximum is the amount of the value of the units in the pension scheme. The advantage from the self-employed person's point of view is that if, for example, contributions to a scheme have totalled £10,000, costing say, £4,000, after tax relief, the total sum of £10,000 may be borrowed from the life office and tax relief, depending on the purpose of the loan, will normally be available on the interest. The loan to the self-employed person becomes an asset of his own pension plan and the interest he pays becomes part of the income of that plan.

PEPPERCORN RENT A purely nominal rent, e.g. nil. Provision for a peppercorn rental was often found in old deeds, the purpose being to establish a virtually rent-free tenancy, whilst still creating in law a landlord and tenant relationship.

PER CAPITA Per head. An indication that beneficiaries are to share in a fund equally, i.e. so much per head, in contrast to *per stirpes* (q.v.).

PER STIRPES Short for *per stirpes et non per capita*, meaning by the roots and not by the heads. An example of the use of the phrase is where John Brown leaves a sum of money to be equally divided amongst his, say, four sons, and if any son dies before the testator the share of that deceased son to be equally divided amongst the children of that deceased son. The children divide, therefore, merely the share of their deceased parent, or *per stirpes*; and do not each take an equal share of the full sum of money left by John Brown—that is, not per capita. SEE *Intestacy*

PERFORMANCE BOND A contract may be awarded by a government department or a public authority at home or abroad, subject to the provision on behalf of the contractor of a performance bond or guarantee of five to ten per cent or more of the value of the contract, to be completed by a bank or similar financially-acceptable institution. Perhaps the most common type of performance bond is that given on behalf of a customer who is entering upon a building contract for a local authority. In the case of a performance bond required abroad, e.g. for major repairs to a ship, the banker will normally instruct a correspondent to issue the required undertaking, counter-indemnifying him for doing so. A counter-indemnity must be taken from the customer in all cases. Once the bond or guarantee is delivered to the authority awarding the contract, that authority may claim under the bond in the event of non-fulfilment of contract. While the figure of five to ten per cent quoted above is the usual one, higher figures may be required in certain foreign countries, particularly the USA, where 50 per cent or even 100 per cent may be stipulated.

It follows, therefore, that the banker must feel quite satisfied as to the financial standing of his customer, and also as to his technical ability to carry through the proposed contract to a satisfactory conclusion. In some cases, it is possible to support a bond with an indemnity from the Export Credits Guarantee Department (q.v.). The liability of a bank under a performance bond can be a very real one. It is an independent obligation entered into by the bank with the institution or authority concerned and must be honoured regardless of any dispute between the other parties. To that extent, the liability under a performance bond may be likened to that under a guarantee (q.v.) or documentary credit (q.v.) (*State Trading of India Ltd* v *E.D. and F. Man (Sugar) Ltd*, TLR, 22 July, 1981).

PERMANENT BUILDING SOCIETY A society which has not, by its rules, any fixed date or specified result at which it shall terminate. SEE *Building Society*

PERMANENT HEALTH INSURANCE This is insurance against the possibility of long-term illness or disablement. Until comparatively recent years, permanent health insurance was not common in the UK but was widely available in the USA. It is not unusual for employers to provide a degree of cover for their employees in the event of long-term illness or disablement, either in the form of a salary continuation plan, the company's own sickness scheme or possibly, early retirement under the pension scheme. A self-employed person is, however, at some disadvantage, in that income tax relief is not *per se* obtainable on premiums paid for this purpose. It is possible however, to attach permanent health insurance cover to a self-employed pension plan (SEE *Pensions*). This has the advantage that the cost of the cover will enjoy income tax relief within the permitted maximum contributions to the scheme. The following regulations apply, however.

1. The self-employed person must be under age 60 at the time the cover is taken out.
2. Benefits must be payable only in the event of illness or disablement before age 60 (although the payments may continue until age 65).
3. Not more than one-quarter of the pension plan premiums may be applied for permanent health cover.
4. The maximum income benefit under the scheme must be limited to one-half of earnings at the time of disablement with an overall maximum limit of £25,000.

A disadvantage of this scheme is that the permanent health insurance is in lieu of the permitted degree of life cover under personal pension plans. If, therefore, any permanent health benefits become payable, the life cover under the scheme must cease and thus has to be replaced at normal rates for term cover with limited life assurance tax relief instead of the higher relief available under the pension plan. Furthermore, the insured person loses the right, which is normal under a self-employed pension scheme, to waive further payment of premiums.

PERPETUAL DEBENTURE Section 193 of the Companies Act 1985 states that a condition contained in any debentures, or in any deed for securing any debentures, shall not be invalid by reason only that the debentures are made irredeemable, or redeemable only on the happening of a contingency, however remote, or on the expiration of a period, however long, any rule of equity to the contrary notwithstanding.

Although the debentures may be called irredeemable or perpetual they are nevertheless redeemable when the company goes into liquidation. The effect of a debenture of this nature is to grant an annuity for the life of the company to the holder thereof. SEE *Debenture*

PERSONAL ACCIDENT INSURANCE The statutory definitions of personal accident insurance are contained in the Stamp Act 1891, and the Assurance Companies Act 1909. In essence, it is the provision for payment of a sum of money in the event of the insured's sustaining personal injury. Personal accident insurance was originally an aspect of life insurance, but has long been regarded as an insurance category of its own. It differs from other forms of insurance in that it is not strictly a contract of indemnity, but rather to pay a particular sum of money on the happening of a specified event. As in the case of life assurance, it is necessary for the proposer to have an insurable interest in the person assured, i.e. he must be exposed to some pecuniary loss in the event of the injury of the assured person.

In general, personal accident policies cover all cases of accidental injury or death, notwithstanding that the circumstances do not amount to 'an accident' as such. Thus, injury sustained as a result of a deliberate and unlawful act of another, e.g. a bank robber, are accidental for the purpose of this category of insurance. Similarly, injury or death caused by lightning, earthquake, excessive atmospheric conditions, negligence in hospitals or sporting injuries, have all been held to be accidental, although not necessarily arising from 'accidents' as such. The fact that the assured is susceptible to a particular type of injury, perhaps through some existing physiological defect will not, depending on the terms of the policy, invalidate a claim arising from accidental causes, notwithstanding that the assured may himself have been careless.

Nowadays, a large volume of personal accident insurance business is negotiated on special terms with affinity groups covering their members, or users of particular services, e.g. the Royal Automobile Club and users, for travel purposes, of American Express cards.

PERSONAL ALLOWANCES SEE *Income Tax*

PERSONAL CHATTELS SEE *Chattels*

PERSONAL ESTATE, PERSONALTY These terms are applied to assets such as bank balances, personal chattels, stocks and shares, etc., and leasehold property. Indeed, anything which is capable of ownership is personal estate, other than real estate, which in the UK means freehold property or an interest in freehold property. The difference lies historically in the type of action which could be brought at law for being dispossessed of land or chattels. A *real* action was for recovery of the property itself, whereas *personal* actions were for the payment of damages. As land was the only property which could be recovered at law *in specie*, real actions or actions *in rem* were restricted to freehold property which thus became known as real property. Leasehold property was different in that a leasehold interest was normally undertaken for personal, or indeed financial, purposes and thus, in this country, real property has never included leaseholds. They are sometimes referred to a chattels real, in that they are personal property but have their roots in freehold or real property.

The distinction has had little significance since 1925, when the laws governing the distribution and inheritance of real and personal estate were unified (SEE *Administration of Estates; Intestacy*). The distinction remains to some extent in the terminology used, namely, personal estate which is said to be 'bequeathed' whereas real property is 'devised'. Perhaps the major remaining distinction is that a charge or mortgage or other encumbrance on freehold property remains a primary charge on that property on the death of the owner, whereas other depts and obligations are a charge on the general residue of the estate. Thus a devisee of a freehold property, in the absence of a contrary intention, will take the property subject to any outstanding mortgage or other charge. SEE ALSO *Capital Transfer Tax; Personal Representatives.*

PERSONAL IDENTIFICATION NUMBER (PIN) A confidential number used by a customer of a bank for identification purposes when using cash dispensers or automated teller machines.

PERSONAL LOANS SEE *Lending by Banks*

PERSONAL PENSION PLAN SEE *Pensions*

PERSONAL REPRESENTATIVES The executors or administrators of a deceased person. Prior to 1926, real estate (q.v.) passed on death to the heirs and not to the representatives of the personal estate (SEE *Personal Estate*). The Administration of Estates Act 1925 provided that real estate to which a deceased person was entitled should on his death devolve on the personal representatives of the deceased 'in like manner as before 1926 chattels real devolved on the personal representative'. Under Section 1 of that Act, the personal representatives are deemed in law to be his heir and assigns 'within the meaning of all trusts and powers' and shall be the representatives in regard to the real estate as well as in regard to his personal estate. The act provides that, where there are two or more personal representatives, they must all join in any conveyance of the real estate, whereas one representative may deal with pure personal property.

Under Section 12 of the Act, it is provided that representations shall not be granted to more than four persons in regard to the same property and if any beneficiary is an infant or if a life interest arises under a will or in testacy, representation shall be granted either to a trust corporation or to not less than two individuals.

Assent or Conveyance by Personal Representatives
A personal representative may assent to the vesting in any person who may be entitled thereto of any estate or interest in real property to which the testator was entitled. The assent shall operate to vest the legal estate to which it relates in that person. An assent to the vesting of a legal estate shall be in writing, signed by the personal representative, and shall name the person in whose favour it is given. An assent not in writing or not in favour of a named person shall not be effectual to pass a legal estate.

The convenants for title implied by the use of certain words in unregistered conveyancing are set out in the Second Schedule to the Law of Property Act 1925, so that if the vendor conveys as personal representative he convenants only that he himself has not incumbered the property.

The case of *Re King; Robinson* v *Gray* [1962] 2 All ER 66 draws attention to the fact that, in registered conveyancing, unless Section 24(1) of the Land Registration Act 1925 is specifically limited, it automatically applies to all transfers of registered leasehold land. This section implies covenants as to payment of rent and performance and observance of convenants and conditions in the lease such as would be expected only of a person assigning as 'beneficial owner'. Consequently, a personal representative transferring a registered leasehold title should make sure that Section 24(1) is suitably restricted or negatived.

Where an advance is to be made on real property to the person entitled to such property consequent upon a death, the banker should see that he holds the assent or conveyance of the personal representative.

Power to Mortgage
In dealing with the real and personal estate, the personal representatives shall, for purposes of administration, or during a minority of any beneficiary or the subsistence of any life interest, or until the period of distribution arrives, have power to raise money by mortgage or charge (whether or not by deposit of documents) and such power may in the case of land be exercised by legal mortgage (Section 39).

Power to Postpone Distribution
A personal representative is not bound to distribute the estate before the expiration of one year from the death (Section 44).

Power To Employ Agents
Personal representatives have power, under Section 23 of the Trustee Act 1925, to employ agents in the administration of a testator's or intestate's estate. SEE UNDER *Trustee*

Insolvent Estate
SEE *Death of Insolvent person*
SEE ALSO *Administrator; Executor; Intestacy; Letters of Administration; Probate*

PERSONAL SECTOR BALANCE SHEETS
SEE *Balance Sheets of the Personal Sector*

PETITION SEE *Bankruptcy; Receiving Order; Winding Up*

PLACING A term applied to the process whereby a new issue of shares by a company is allotted to a stockbroker or syndicate, who then 'places' the shares with clients or the public through the medium of the Stock Exchange, or the placing of shares with institutions or other investors. SEE *Merchant Banking; Capital; Stock Exchange*

PLEDGE A pledge or pawn is a delivery of chattels or choses in action by a debtor to his creditor as security for his debt, or any other obligation. It is to be distinguished from a mortgage in that, whilst possession of the thing passes to the pledgee, the property in the thing (i.e. the legal ownership) remains with the pledgor. With a mortgage of things other than land, the property in the thing passes to the mortgagee whilst the possession of it may remain with the mortgagor.

POLICYHOLDERS' PROTECTION ACT 1975 An Act which established the Policyholders' Protection Board with power to impose a levy on insurance companies and others involved in the insurance industry, in order to protect policyholders in the event of the failure of a company or a broker or intermediaries. In general, policyholders are protected up to 90 per cent of their interests under policies of insurance, in the event of the failure of the insurer. The levy payable by insurance companies is calculated on premium income and is subject to a maximum figure of one per cent in any one year.

The scheme is administered by the Policyholders' Protection Board appointed by the Secretary of State for Trade and Industry.

POSSESSORY TITLE Where a person has been in the undisturbed possession of real property for 12 years and has not paid any rent or acknowledged any person's right to the property, he acquires a possessory title to the property. But if the rightful owner was under a disability, such an infancy or mental incapacity, an action may be brought against the person claiming a possessory title within six years after the disability has ceased, but in no case can the land be recovered after 30 years from the time when the right of action first accrued, although the person under disability may have remained under disability during the whole of the 30 years.

In the case of leasehold land, however, it has been held by a majority of the House of Lords (in *Fairweather* v *St Marylebone Property Company Ltd* [1962] 2 All ER 288) that the acquisition by adverse possession merely deprives the person against whom the right is acquired of the possibility of recovering possession and does not operate to transfer the title of the dispossessed owner to the squatter. Any other decision would result in the conclusion that a freeholder's right of recovery of his land would be barred by 12 years adverse possession against a tenant of the property, even though during this period the freeholder, not being in possession, might have no means of knowing that dispossession had taken place.

Where a mortgagee acquires a title against the mortgagor by undisturbed possession for 12 years of freeholds, he may enlarge the mortgage term into a fee simple (Law of Property Act 1925, Section 88(3)). In the case of leaseholds, he may by deed declare that the leasehold reversion shall vest in him (Section 89(3)).

POSSESSORY TITLE (LAND REGISTRY) Where a possessory title is granted, no official examination is made other than to establish that the applicant has a prima facie right to the land and no guarantee of title is given up to the point of registration. From that date, however, the title is guaranteed and dealings can only be made by registered instruments. All the documents of title must accompany the land certificate, and the title up to the date of registration must be investigated in the ordinary way. Where land has been registered with a possessory title, if freehold for 15 years and if leasehold for ten years, the Registrar may grant an absolute title in the case of freehold land and a good leasehold title in the case of leasehold land.

The Registrar can refuse to register with possessory title and can grant an absolute or good leasehold title as the case may be whether the applicant consents or not (Land Registration Act, Sections 4(3) and 8(4)).

Possessory titles are consequently now quite exceptional. SEE *Land Registration*

POST OFFICE MONEY ORDER SEE *Money Order*

POST OFFICE SAVINGS BANK SEE *National Savings Bank*

POSTAL ORDER A postal order is not a negotiable instrument, and therefore a holder does not obtain any better title to it than the person had from whom he received it. If a postal order is crossed, payment by the Post Office will only be made through a banker and, if the name of the banker is added, payment will only be made through that banker. The Post Office pay postal orders to a banker, without the signature of the payee, provided the banker's name is stamped upon them, but the banker should see that his customer always writes or stamps his name on all orders, in case they are returned from the Post Office. The crossing does not bring the orders within the crossed cheques sections of the Bills of Exchange Act.

By an arrangement with the Postmaster-General banks must furnish Post Office officials on demand with the name and address of the party who paid in a postal order which is the subject of inquiry.

A postal order may be collected either at the office where it is made payable, or at the General Post Office, London.

The banker's position, with regard to postal orders, is safeguarded by the Post Office Act 1953 (Section 21), which provides that a banker who, in collecting for any principal, shall have received payment or been allowed by the Postmaster-General in account, in respect of any postal order or of any document purporting to be a postal order, shall not incur liability to anyone except such principal by reason of having received such payment or allowance, or having held or presented such order or document for payment.

At the outbreak of war in 1914, postal orders were made legal tender for a short period. On 1st September, 1939, in anticipation of war, they were again made legal tender to ease the currency situation. They ceased to be legal tender in May 1940.

POSTCHEQUES These are issued, on application, in books of five, to holders of National Girobank (q.v.) current accounts for the purpose of obtaining money abroad. Postcheques may be cashed at any of the 90,000 or so post offices in 34 foreign countries and may be for a fixed amount of foreign currency or for the equivalent of £50. The postcheques themselves are issued free and there is no charge in the countries where they are used but an administration charge of 50p is made when a postcheque is debited to the customer's account in the UK.

POUND A sovereign (q.v.). In the time of William the Conqueror, a pound of silver was coined into 240 silver pence, each equal to a pennyweight, whence the origin of the word pound. The current pound coin was first introduced in April 1983. SEE *Coinage*

POUND COST AVERAGING This is the investment of a fixed sum at regular intervals over a given period in a particular investment. When the price of the investment is high, the fixed sum buys fewer units or shares; when the price is low the fixed sum buys more units or shares. The effect, arithmetically, is that the average cost per share over the period is lower than the average share price over the period. The system is particularly suitable for the regular purchase of units in unit trusts but equally valid in relation to any quoted security. The greater the volatility of the unit or stock, the more pronounced the advantage of pound cost averaging.

POWER OF ATTORNEY This is an instrument by which one person is empowered to act for another. It begins with the recitals—statements of the names, addresses, and descriptions of the donor and donee, the reason, perhaps, for the giving of the authority, and the expression of the authority itself. The body of the instrument gives the actual terms and limits of the authority, and the instrument closes with the signature of the donor and witnesses.

The law relating to powers of attorney was revised by the Powers of Attorney Act 1971, of which the following are the major provisions.

1.—(1) An instrument creating a power of attorney shall be signed and sealed by, or by direction and in the presence of, the donor of the power.

(2) Where such an instrument is signed and sealed by a person by direction and in the presence of the donor of the power, two other persons shall be present as witnesses and shall attest the instrument.

(3) This Section is without prejudice to any requirement in, or having effect under, any other Act as to the witnessing of instruments creating powers of attorney and does not affect the rules relating to the execution of instruments by bodies corporate.

2.—(1) As from the commencement of this Act no instrument creating a power of attorney, and no copy of any such instrument, shall be deposited or filed at the central office of the Supreme Court or at the Land Registry under Section 25 of the Trustee Act, 1925, Section 125 of the Law of Property Act, 1925, or Section 219, of the Supreme Court of Judicature (Consolidation) Act, 1925.

(2) This Section does not affect any right to search for, inspect or copy, or to obtain an office copy of, any such document which has been deposited or filed as aforesaid before the commencement of the Act.

3.—(1) The contents of an instrument creating a power of attorney may be proved by means of a copy which—

(*a*) is a reproduction of the original made with a photographic or other device for reproducing documents in facsimile;

(*b*) contains the following certificate or certificates signed by the donor of the power or by a solicitor or stockbroker, that is to say:

(i) a certificate at the end to the effect that the copy is a true and complete copy of the original; and

(ii) if the original consists of two or more pages, a certificate at the end of each page of the copy to the effect that it is a true and complete copy of the corresponding page of the original.

(2) Where a copy of an instrument creating a power of attorney has been made which complies with subsection (1) of this Section, the contents of the instrument may also be proved by means of a copy of that copy if the further copy itself complies with that subsection, taking references in it to the original as references to the copy from which the further copy is made.

4.—(1) Where a power of attorney is expressed to be irrevocable and is given to secure—

(*a*) a proprietary interest of the donee of the power; or

(*b*) the performance of an obligation owed to the donee, then, so long as the donee has that interest or the obligation remains undischarged, the power *shall not be revoked*:

(i) by the donor without the consent of the donee; or

(ii) by the death, incapacity of bankruptcy of the donor or, if the donor is a body corporate, by its winding up or dissolution.

(2) A power of attorney given to secure a proprietary interest may be given to the person entitled to the interest and persons deriving title under him to that interest, and those persons shall be duly constituted donees of the power for all purposes of the power but without prejudice to any right to appoint substitutes given by the power.

5.—(1) A donee of a power of attorney who acts in pursuance of the power at a time when it has been revoked shall not, by reasons of the revocation, incur any liability (either to the donor or to any other person) if at that time he did not know that the power had been revoked.

(2) Where a power of attorney has been revoked and a person, without knowledge of the revocation, deals with the donee of the power, the transaction between them shall, in favour of that person, be as valid as if the power had then been in existence.

(3) Where the power is expressed in the instrument creating it to be irrevocable and to be given by way of security, then, unless the person dealing with the donee knows that it was not in fact given by way of security, he shall be entitled to assume that the power is incapable of revocation except by the donor acting with the consent of the donee and shall accordingly be treated for the purposes of subsection (2) of this Section as having knowledge of the revocation only if he knows that it has been revoked in that manner.

(4) Where the interest of a purchaser depends on

whether a transaction between the donee of a power of attorney and another person was valid by virtue of subsection (2) of this Section, it shall be conclusively presumed in favour of the purchaser that that person did not at the material time know of the revocation of the power if—

(a) the transaction between that person and the donee was completed within 12 months of the date on which the power came into operation; or

(b) that person makes a statutory declaration, before or within three months after the completion of the purchase, that he did not at the material time know of the revocation of the power.

(5) Without prejudice to subsection (3) of this Section, for the purposes of this Section knowledge of the revocation of a power of attorney includes knowledge of the occurrence of any event (such as the death of the donor) which has the effect of revoking the power.

(6) In this Section 'purchaser' and 'purchase' have the meanings specified in Section 205(1) of the Law of Property Act, 1925.

(7) This Section applies whenever the power of attorney was created but only to acts and transactions after the commencement of this Act.

6.—(1) Without prejudice to Section 5 of this Act, where—

(a) the donee of a power of attorney executes, as transferor, an instrument transferring registered securities; and

(b) the instrument is executed for the purposes of a stock exchange transaction,

it shall be conclusively presumed in favour of the transferee that the power had not been revoked at the date of the instrument if a statutory declaration to that effect is made by the donee of the power on or within three months after that date.

(2) In this Section 'registered securities' and 'stock exchange transaction' have the same meanings as in the Stock Transfer Act, 1963.

7.—(1) The donee of a power of attorney may, if he thinks fit—

(a) execute any instrument with his own signature and, where sealing is required, with his own seal, and

(b) do any other thing in his own name,

by the authority of the donor of the power; and any document executed or thing done in that manner shall be as effective as if executed or done by the donee with the signature and seal, or, as the case may be, in the name, of the donor of the power.

(2) For the avoidance of doubt it is hereby declared that an instrument to which subsection (3) or (4) of Section 74 of the Law of Property Act, 1925, applies may be executed either as provided in those subsections or as provided in this Section.

(3) This Section is without prejudice to any statutory direction requiring an instrument to be executed in the name of an estate owner within the meaning of the said Act of 1925.

(4) This Section applies whenever the power of attorney was created.

8. Section 129 of the Law of Property Act, 1925 (which contains provisions, now unnecessary, in respect of powers of attorney granted by married women), shall cease to have effect.

9.—(1) Section 25 of the Trustee Act, 1925 (power to delegate trusts, etc., during absence abroad), shall be amended as follows.

(2) For subsections (1) to (8) of that Section there shall be substituted the following subsections—

(1) Notwithstanding any rule of law or equity to the contrary, a trustee may, by power of attorney, delegate for *a period not exceeding twelve months* the execution or exercise of all or any of the trusts, powers and discretions vested in him as trustee either alone or jointly with any other person or persons.

(2) The persons who may be donees of a power of attorney under this Section include a trust corporation but not (unless a trust corporation) the only other co-trustee of the donor of the power.

(3) An instrument creating a power of attorney under this Section shall be attested by at least one witness.

(4) Before or within seven days after giving a power of attorney under this Section the donor shall give written notice thereof (specifying the date on which the power comes into operation and its duration, the donee of the power, the reason why the power is given and, where some only are delegated, the trusts, powers and discretions delegated) to—

(a) each person (other than himself), if any, who under any instrument creating the trust has power (whether alone or jointly) to appoint a new trustee; and

(b) each of the other trustees, if any;

but failure to comply with this subsection shall not, in favour of a person dealing with the donee of the power, invalidate any act done or instrument executed by the donee.

(5) The donor of a power of attorney given under this Section shall be liable for the acts or defaults of the donee in the same manner as if they were the acts or defaults of the donor.

(3) Subsections (9) and (10) of the said Section 25 shall stand as subsections (6) and (7) and for subsection (11) of that Section there shall be substituted the following subsection—

(8) This Section applies to personal representative, tenant for life and statutory owner as it applies to a trustee except that subsection (4) shall apply as if it required the notice there mentioned to be given—

(a) in the case of a personal representative, to each of the other personal representatives, if any, except any executor who has renounced probate;

(b) in the case of a tenant for life, to the trustees of the settlement and to each person, if any, who together with the person giving the notice constitutes the tenant for life;

(c) in the case of a statutory owner, to each of the persons, if any, who together with the person giving the notice constitute the statutory owner and, in the case of a statutory owner by virtue of Section 23(1)(*a*) of the Settled Land Act, 1925, to the trustees of the settlement.

(4) This Section applies whenever the trusts, powers or discretions in question arose but does not invalidate anything done by virtue of the said Section 25 as in force at the commencement of this Act.

10.—(1) Subject to subsection (2) of this Section, a general power of attorney in the form set out in Schedule 1 to this Act, or in a form to the like effect but expressed to be made under this Act, shall operate to confer:

(*a*) on the donee of the power; or

(*b*) if there is more than one donee, on the donees acting jointly or acting jointly or severally, as the case may be, authority to do on behalf of the donor anything which he can lawfully do by an attorney.

(2) This Section does not apply to functions which the donor has as a trustee or personal representative or as a tenant for life or statutory owner within the meaning of the Settled Land Act, 1925.

As is evident from the statute, the donee cannot do more than the donor himself could have done. Someone of mental incapacity cannot grant a power of attorney and notice of the mental incapacity of the donor operates as the cancellation of the power except in the instance mentioned above of the irrevocable power.

Section 38 of the Companies Act 1985 also gives specific authority for an attorney to execute deeds on its behalf. The general law regarding a banker operating an account under a power of attorney, or by an agent, is unaffected.

If, for instance, a cheque drawn by X as attorney for Y is to be credited to the account of X, then there is an obligation to enquire, as will be evident from the case of *Midland Bank Ltd* v *Reckitt* [1933] AC 1, and also the case of *Reckitt* v *Barnett Pembroke & Slater Ltd* [1929] AC 176.

PREFERENCE STOCK OR SHARES Stock or shares entitling the holder to preferential rights as to dividend over other classes of shareholder and, in some cases, as to return of capital in addition. They bear a stated rate of dividend. In the case of cumulative preference shares, if such dividend is not earned in any one year, the profits of succeeding years must be used to pay the arrears before any dividend is paid on other classes of shares. In the case of non-cumulative preference shares, the dividend may only be paid for a year if distributable profits have been made in that year sufficient for the purpose. Participating preference shares entitle the holder to a fixed dividend and, in addition, to a share in any surplus profits after the ordinary shareholders have received a maximum stated percentage.

There may be first preference shares and second preference shares, etc., one class ranking behind the other as to priority of dividend or capital. Voting powers are often limited and, in many cases, are only exercisable after the company has passed its preference dividend.

By the Companies Act 1948, Section 58 (replaced by Sections 159–161, Companies Act 1985), a company may, if the articles so provide, issue redeemable preference shares. SEE *Redeemable Preference Shares; Share Capital, Shares*

PREFERENTIAL PAYMENTS The Bankruptcy Act 1914, Section 33, as amended, provides that in the distribution of property of a bankrupt there shall be paid in priority to all other debts

1. general rates due and payable within 12 months next before the relevant date;
2. income tax, corporation tax, capital gains tax and development land tax assessed on or before the 5th April next before the relevant date but not exceeding the whole of one year's assessment (the Crown may choose the year in question and may choose different years for different taxes);
3. PAYE deductions (including deductions on account of tax from payments made to certain independent sub-contractors, particularly in the construction industry) which were made or ought to have been made in the 12 months next before the relevant date;
4. value added tax and car tax for the 12 months next before the relevant date.
5. sums due in respect of general betting duty, gaming licence duty or bingo duty within 12 months next before the relevant date;
6. wages or salaries of employees due within four months next before the relevant date up to a maximum of £800 for each employee;
7. all accrued holiday remuneration of employees; and
8. earnings-related Social Security contributions and redundancy fund contributions in the 12 months next before the relevant date.

The relevant date in bankruptcy is the date of the receiving order, or in the case of a deceased debtor, the date of his death. In a compulsory liquidation, it is normally the date of the winding-up order, unless a provisional liquidator has already been appointed, when it is the date of his appointment. In a voluntary liquidation, it is the date of the resolution to wind up the company. In a receivership the relevant date is normally the date on which the receiver was appointed.

The foregoing debts shall, in the case of a company registered in England, so far as the assets of the company available for payment of general creditors are insufficient to meet them, have priority over the claims of holders of debentures under any floating charge created by the company, and be paid accordingly out of any property comprised in or subject to that charge (Section 614 Companies Act 1985). As to preferential rights with regard to a company's wages cheque, see *Wages Cheques of a Company*.

In the event of a landlord or other person distraining or having distrained on any goods or effects of a bankrupt, or a company being wound up, within three months next before the date of the receiving order, or winding-up order, the foregoing debts to which priority is given shall be a first charge on the good or effects so distrained, on, or the proceeds of the sale thereof; provided that in respect of any money paid under any such charge the landlord or other person shall have the same rights of priority as the person to whom the payment is made (Bankruptcy Act 1914, Section 33(4); and Companies Act 1985, Section 614 and Schedule 19).

Where a receiver is appointed on behalf of the holders of a company's debentures secured by a floating charge, then, if the company is not at the time in course of being wound up, preferential payments having priority to all other debts shall be paid out of any assets coming to the hands of the receiver in priority to any claim for principal or interest in respect of the debentures (Companies Act 1948, Section 94). In *Re Lewis Merthyr Consolidated Colleries Co Ltd, Lloyds Bank* v *The Company* (1928) *Weekly Notes*, p. 247, CA, the Court of Appeal held that Section 94 did not on its true construction apply so as to give priority in respect of assets secured by a fixed charge, but only of assets secured by a floating charge.

If a landlord distrains after the commencement of the bankruptcy, it shall be available only for the six months' rent accrued prior to the order of adjudication, but he may prove under the bankruptcy for the surplus due for which the distress may not have been available (Bankruptcy Act 1914, Section 35).

By the Friendly Societies Act 1896, Section 35, upon the bankruptcy of any officer of a registered society having in its possession by virtue of his office any money belonging to the society, the trustee shall pay the money to the society in preference to any other debts against the estate of the officer.

Preferential debts rank equally between themselves, and, if the assets are insufficient to meet them, they abate in equal proportions. Payment of these debts is subject to the retention of such sums as may be necessary for the costs of the administration or winding up. SEE *Fraudulent Preference*

PREFERRED SHARE A share having some preferred rights over the ordinary shares of the company. If the priority extends to dividend rights, the share is essentially the same as a preference share (q.v.).

PREMIUM A term used rather loosely to denote any margin over the issue price of a share. Thus, shares issued on the Stock Exchange may move to a premium above the issue price. Similarly, where shares are issued at a price in excess of their par value they are said to be issued at a premium (SEE *Share Premium Account*). The term is also used in commodity markets, where it is used to denote the price paid by the purchaser of an option.

A premium for a lease is that part of the consideration for a leasehold interest which is paid as a lump sum.

PREMIUM, INSURANCE The amount payable at regular intervals, or in some instances, as a single amount, in return for the particular cover provided by a policy of insurance. SEE *Insurance*

PREMIUM BOND Premium Bonds were first introduced on 1st November, 1956. They are a UK Government security. No interest is payable on the Bonds, but after a three-month qualifying period each Bond is eligible to be included in the draw for weekly and monthly prizes.

The principal characteristics of Premium Bonds are

1. Bonds which are in units of £1 but sold only in multiples of £5 are issued in denominations of £5, £10, £20, £25, £30, £40, £50, £60, £100, and in multiples of £100 up to £500. Each 1 unit gives the holder a chance of winning a prize. Thus, a £500 unit carries 500 chances.
2. Bonds may be bought by anyone of 16 years or above, or by a parent, grandparent or guardian puchasing Bonds in the name of a child under that age. Bonds may not be purchased by corporate bodies, or by individuals in joint names, or by unincorporated associations.
3. Bonds may be purchased through Post Offices and banks in the UK, the Channel Islands and the Isle of Man on completion of the appropriate application form P2436B.
4. The maximum holding per individual is £10,000.
5. The amount of the prize money for each draw is the notional amount of interest on the outstanding Bonds. This is calculated at present at the rate of seven per cent per annum.
6. *Each week;* one prize of £100,000; one prize of £50,000 one prize of £25,000. *Each month*: the

number of prizes varies according to the number of bonds in the draw.
7. Winners of prizes are notified by post and the winning Bond numbers (but not the names of prizewinners) are published in the *London Gazette Supplement*, copies of which are available at certain Post Offices.
8. All prizes on Premium Bonds are free of UK income tax and capital gains tax.
9. A holder may apply for repayment of his/her Bonds at any time through a Post Office or bank (Form P99MA).
10. On the death of a Bond holder, his or her Bonds will remain eligible for all prize draws for the month of death and for the following 12 months or until they are repaid during that period. Thereafter, they will be excluded from the draw.

PREMIUM CURRENCY SEE *Investment Currency*

PREMIUM DOLLAR SEE *Investment Currency*

PRESENTMENT FOR ACCEPTANCE When a bill of exchange is presented to a drawee in order that it may be accepted by him, it is a presentment for acceptance.

By Section 39 of the Bills of Exchange Act 1882

(1) Where a bill is payable after sight, presentment for acceptance is necessary in order to fix the maturity of the instrument.

(2) Where a bill expressly stipulates that it shall be presented for acceptance, or where a bill is drawn payable elsewhere than at the residence or place of business of the drawee it must be presented for acceptance before it can be presented for payment.

(3) In no other case is presentment for acceptance necessary in order to render liable any party to the bill.

(4) Where the holder of a bill, drawn payable elsewhere than at the place of business or residence of the drawee, has not time, with the exercise of reasonable diligence, to present the bill for acceptance before presenting it for payment on the day that it falls due, the delay caused by presenting the bill for acceptance before presenting it for payment is excused, and does not discharge the drawer and indorsers.

With regard to the time for presenting a bill payable after sight, Section 40 provides as follows:

(1) Subject to the provisions of this Act, when a bill payable after sight is negotiated, the holder must either present it for acceptance or negotiate it within a reasonable time.

(2) If he does not do so, the drawer and all indorsers prior to that holder are discharged.

(3) In determining what is a reasonable time within the meaning of this Section, regard shall be had to the nature of the bill, the usage of trade with respect to similar bills, and the facts of the particular case.

The rules as to presentment for acceptance and the excuses for non-presentment are given in Section 41:

(1) A bill is duly presented for acceptance which is presented in accordance with the following rules—

(*a*) The presentment must be made by or on behalf of the holder to the drawee or to some person authorised to accept or refuse acceptance on his behalf at a reasonable hour on a business day and before the bill is overdue:

(*b*) Where a bill is addressed to two or more drawees, who are not partners, presentment must be made to them all, unless one has authority to accept for all, then presentment may be made to him only:

(*c*) Where the drawee is dead, presentment may be made to his personal representative:

(*d*) Where the drawee is bankrupt, presentment may be made to him or to his trustee:

(*e*) Where authorised by agreement or usage, a presentment through the post office is sufficient.

(2) Presentment in accordance with these rules is excused, and a bill may be treated as dishonoured by non-acceptance—

(*a*) Where the drawee is dead or bankrupt, or is a fictitious person or a person not having capacity to contract by bill:

(*b*) Where, after the exercise of reasonable diligence, such presentment cannot be effected:

(*c*) Where, although the presentment has been irregular, acceptance has been refused on some other ground.

(3) The fact that the holder has reason to believe that the bill, on presentment, will be dishonoured does not excuse presentment.

In practice a bill is presented for acceptance as soon as possible after it has been drawn, and until it has been accepted the drawee is under no liability whatever with regard to it. An after-date bill having more than three days to run before maturity is, in London, presented for acceptance. The sooner the holder of an unaccepted bill procures the drawee's acceptance the better, for he then obtains the further security in the liability of the acceptor. When bills are received by a banker in order that he may get them accepted, they are presented to the drawee on the day of receipt, and if the drawee does not accept when they are presented it is customary to leave the bills with him for 24 hours (exclusive of Saturdays, Sundays and holidays), or until close of business on a half-holiday if the 24 hours are not completed, in which he has to decide whether or not he will accept them. When a bill is left for acceptance a banker marks it so that he may know that he gets the same bill back again. If a banker is negligent in obtaining an acceptance he may render himself liable thereon, especially in the case of a bill drawn payable at so many days 'after sight', as the drawer and indorsers may thereby be discharged. The law does not lay down any absolute rule as to what time is reasonable or unreasonable in which to carry out an instruction to obtain an acceptance, but in most cases a banker would present a bill for acceptance on the day that he receives it. Having left the bill with a drawee, it is part of the banker's duty to call again for it and not to wait till the drawee returns it to him, though an arrangement may be made with the drawee to return it. The holder of a bill may refuse to take a qualified acceptance (SEE *Acceptance, Qualified*), and a banker should therefore get instructions from his correspondent if a qualified acceptance is offered.

A banker should not give up a bill, sent to him to obtain acceptance, against the drawee's cheque as that would release the drawer and indorsers of the bill. If a cheque is offered, the banker should obtain instructions from his correspondent.

Where bills of lading and other documents are attached to a bill, they are exhibited to the drawee at the same time as the bill is presented for acceptance, but if the bill is left with the drawee until the next day the documents are retained by the banker and not left with the drawee. The banker, however, may have instructions to deliver up the documents to the drawee after he has accepted the bill. In the case of a foreign bill sent for acceptance, instructions usually accompany the bill as to what has to be done in the event of non-acceptance, such as 'protest if not accepted' or 'if not accepted do not protest but send an advice by wire' or 'no expense to be incurred'.

The holder of a bill, by presenting it for acceptance, does not warrant the genuineness of the bill, or of any of the signatures thereon, or that any accompanying documents are genuine or represent actual goods (*Guaranty Trust Company of New York* v *A. Hannay & Co* (1918) 34 TLR 427).

Where a bill is received from a correspondent in order to obtain the acceptance of the drawee, and the drawee lives at such a distance as to necessitate either sending the bill to him or asking him to call at the bank to accept it, the correspondent should be advised of what is being done so that he may understand the delay. SEE *Bill of Exchange*

PRESENTMENT FOR PAYMENT It is of the utmost importance that a bill of exchange be presented for payment on the date it falls due. The following rules are laid down by the Bills of Exchange Act 1882:

45. Subject to the provisions of this Act a bill must be duly presented for payment. If it be not so presented the drawer and indorsers shall be discharged.

A bill is duly presented for payment which is presented in accordance with the following rules—

(1) Where the bill is not payable on demand, presentment must be made on the day it falls due.

(2) Where the bill is payable on demand, then, subject to the provisions of this Act, presentment must be made within a reasonable time after its issue in order to render the drawer liable, and within a reasonable time after its indorsement, in order to render the indorser liable.

In determining what is a reasonable time, regard shall be had to the nature of the bill, the usage of trade with regard to similar bills, and the facts of the particular case.

(3) Presentment must be made by the holder or by some person authorised to receive payment on his behalf at a reasonable hour on a business day, at the proper place as hereinafter defined either to the person designated by the bill as payer, or to some person authorised to pay or refuse payment on his behalf if with the exercise of reasonable diligence such person can there be found.

(4) A bill is presented at the proper place—

(*a*) Where a place of payment is specified in the bill and the bill is there presented.

(*b*) Where no place of payment is specified, but the address of the drawee or acceptor is given in the bill, and the bill is there presented.

(*c*) Where no place of payment is specified and no address given, and the bill is presented at the drawee's or acceptor's place of business if known, and, if not, at his ordinary residence, if known.

(*d*) In any other case if presented to the drawee or acceptor wherever he can be found, or if presented at his last known place of business or residence.

(5) Where a bill is presented at the proper place, and after the exercise of reasonable diligence, no person authorised to pay or refuse payment can be found there, no further presentment to the drawee or acceptor is required.

(6) Where a bill is drawn upon, or accepted by two or more persons who are not partners, and no place of payment is specified, presentment must be made to them all.

(7) Where the drawee or acceptor of a bill is dead, and no place of payment is specified, presentment must be made to a personal representative, if such there be, and with the exercise of reasonable diligence he can be found.

(8) Where authorised by agreement or usage a presentment through the post office is sufficient.

Note that presentment through the post office (subsection 8) is in order only where authorized by agreement or usage. If, therefore, a bill accepted at the X & Y Bank, Leeds, is presented by post to that bank by a stranger, the bank would return it to the stranger with the answer that it must, according to custom, be presented through a banker.

Presentment to the acceptor of an accommodation bill must be made just as in the case of an ordinary bill.

It should be particularly noted that, if these rules are not properly attended to, the drawer and indorsers shall be discharged, both with respect to the bill and to the consideration for which the bill was given. The bill itself should be presented, and if the acceptor has left the address shown on the bill, reasonable diligence must be used to find his new address and present it there. An acceptor is not discharged if the bill is not presented to him.

Section 52 provides

(1) When a bill is accepted generally presentment for payment is not necessary in order to render the acceptor liable.

(2) When by the terms of a qualified acceptance presentment for payment is required, the acceptor, in the absence of an express stipulation to that effect, is not discharged by the omission to present the bill for payment on the day that it matures.

(3) In order to render the acceptor of a bill liable, it is not necessary to protest it, or that notice of dishonour should be given to him.

(4) Where the holder of a bill presents it for payment, he shall exhibit the bill to the person from whom he demands payment, and when a bill is paid the holder shall forthwith deliver it up to the party paying it.

Though non-presentment, or delay in presentment, of a bill releases the drawer and indorsers, there are certain cases where the Bills of Exchange Act excuses delay or non-presentment. They are given in Section 46:

(1) Delay in making presentment for payment is excused when the delay is caused by circumstances beyond the control of the holder, and not imputable to his default, misconduct, or negligence. When the cause of delay ceases to operate presentment must be made with reasonable diligence.

(2) Presentment for payment is dispensed with—

- (a) Where, after the exercise of reasonable diligence, presentment, as required by this Act, cannot be effected. The fact that the holder has reason to believe that the bill will, on presentment, be dishonoured, does not dispense with the necessity for presentment.
- (b) Where the drawee is a fictitious person.
- (c) As regards the drawer, where the drawee or acceptor is not bound, as between himself and the drawer, to accept or pay the bill, and the drawer has no reason to believe that the bill would be paid if presented.
- (d) As regards an indorser, where the bill was accepted or made for the accommodation of that indorser, and he has no reason to expect that the bill would be paid if presented.
- (e) By waiver of presentment, express or implied.

In the case of a bill after date, it is necessary, in order to prevent the discharge of the other parties, that the bill be presented to the acceptor, at the place where payable, even if he said before the bill was due that he would not pay it at maturity, or if he called at the bank on the due date and said he could not pay it. If it is accepted payable at a bank, and the acceptor says he has nothing in his account to meet the bill, it is still necessary formally to present the bill at the bank indicated. It must be presented within the usual business hours.

Presentment before the actual due date does not preserve recourse against the other parties.

Where a separate guarantee has been given by anyone on behalf of the drawer on an indorser, the guarantor is discharged by such delay or non-presentment as would discharge the drawer or indorser, but the liability of a guarantor for an acceptor continues in the same way as an acceptor's liability.

It has been decided that where a bill is held by a banker which is accepted at that banker's, he need not present it to the acceptor but merely refer to his own books containing the acceptor's account to ascertain whether or not it may be paid.

If a bill is drawn payable in one place, and accepted payable in another, it should be presented at the place where accepted payable.

If an acceptor does not pay a bill when it is presented to him a notice may be left at his address informing him that the bill lies at the bank, and that it requires his attention before closing time.

Lord Tenterden, in *Wilkins* v *Jadis* (1831), 2 B & Ad 188, said:

> A presentment to bankers out of the hours of their business is not sufficient; but in other cases the rule of law is that the bill must be presented at a reasonable hour; a presentment at twelve o'clock at night, when a person has retired to rest, would be unreasonable; but I cannot say that a presentment between seven and eight in the evening is not a presentment at a reasonable time.

When a banker requires to send bills to another banker for collection, they are usually forwarded a day or two before maturity, if domiciled at a bank; but, if not payable at a bank, they should be sent earlier, in case the collecting banker requires to write for instructions if he finds that expense will be incurred in presenting the bills at the place where made payable.

As to payment of a bill, SEE *Payment of Bill*.

A bill of itself does not operate as an assignment of funds in the hands of the drawee, but in Scotland where the drawee of a bill has in his hands funds available for the payment thereof, the bill operates as an assignment of the sum for which it is drawn in favour of the holder, from the time when the bill is presented to the drawee (Section 53). SEE *Drawee*

With respect to presentment to an acceptor for honour, the Bills of Exchange Act provides

67.—(1) Where a dishonoured bill has been accepted for honour supra protest, or contains a reference in case of need, it must be protested for non-payment before it is presented for payment to the acceptor for honour, or referee in case of need.

(2) Where the address of the acceptor for honour is in the same place where the bill is protested for non-payment, the bill must be presented to him not later than the day following its maturity; and where the address of the acceptor for honour is in some place other than the place where it was protested for non-payment, the bill must be forwarded not later than the day following its maturity for presentment to him.

(3) Delay in presentment or non-presentment is excused by any circumstances which would excuse delay in presentment for payment or non-presentment for payment.

(4) When a bill of exchange is dishonoured by the acceptor for honour it must be protested for non-payment by him.

A cheque must be presented for payment within a reasonable time. Section 74 of the Bills of Exchange Act provides

Subject to the provisions of this Act—

(1) Where a cheque is not presented for payment within a reasonable time of its issue, and the drawer or the person on whose account it is drawn had the right at the time of such presentment as between him and the banker to have the cheque paid and suffers actual damage through the delay, he is discharged to the extent of such damage, that is to say, to the extent to which such drawer or person is a creditor of such banker to a larger amount than he would have been had such cheque been paid.

(2) In determining what is a reasonable time regard shall be had to the nature of the instrument, the usage of trade and of bankers, and the facts of the particular case.

(3) The holder of such cheque as to which such drawer or person is discharged shall be a creditor, in lieu of such drawer or person, of such banker to the extent of such discharge, and entitled to recover the amount from him.

A person receiving a cheque should present it for payment as soon as possible; unless presented within a reasonable time after its indorsement, the indorsers will be discharged (see Section 45, above). If a drawer suffers actual loss, as where a banker fails, through a cheque of his not having been presented within a reasonable time after its issue, the drawer, as stated in Section 74, is discharged to the amount of such loss. There has not been any definite decision as to what is a 'reasonable time'; but it has been suggested that, in the absence of special circumstances, 10 days or so would probably be held the limit. After the 'reasonable time' has elapsed, no person who takes the cheque can acquire or give a better title than that which the person from whom he took it had (SEE *Overdue Cheque*). It is to be noted that the effect of Section 74 is to exclude cheques, so far as the drawer is concerned, from the operation of Section 45.

An instance of release of an indorser by failure to present on the due date can be seen in *Yeoman Credit Ltd* v *Gregory* [1963] 1 All ER 115.

There the acceptor telephoned requesting presentation at Bank B rather than Bank A, as indicated on the bill. Presentation was made at Bank B on the due date and at Bank A the day after. In neither case was it paid, but the indorser escaped liability because presentation at the place indicated on the bill was not made on the due date.

The drawer of a cheque is liable (except under the conditions defined in Section 74) to the holder for six years from the date of the cheque, and a banker would be justified in paying a cheque within that period, but, in practice, a banker does not pay a cheque which is six (in some banks twelve) months old, unless it is confirmed by the drawer. SEE *Stale Cheque*

When a cheque is paid to credit of an account at the same office as it is drawn upon, it is thought that the banker may legally hold the cheque until the close of business of the following day before returning it unpaid, and he need not inform the customer at the time of receiving the cheque that there are insufficient funds to meet it. In practice, however,a banker pays or returns such a cheque on the day of receipt whenever possible. However, with modern bookkeeping systems he has until midday on the following business day to notify the presenting banker that a cheque is being returned unpaid.

Where it is important to know as soon as possible whether a certain cheque will be paid or not, it is customary to send it direct, instead of through the Clearing House, and a stamped telemessage may be enclosed with a request to the banker on whom it is drawn to 'advise fate' (q.v.) of the cheque.

It has been held that, where a foreign cheque is drawn upon a place where the banker has no agent, the custom in London of presenting the cheque by post is a due presentment (*Heywood* v *Pickering* (1874) LR 9 QB 428), but if payment is not received by return of post, the customer from whom the bank received the cheque should be advised of the fact.

If a cheque is presented by post by a stranger, it should be returned with a request that it be presented, according to custom, through a banker.

The presentment of a cheque in England does not operate as an assignment of funds in the drawer's account. Part payment of a cheque is never made; it is either paid fully or dishonoured. In Scotland, however, where a cheque is returned unpaid for 'insufficient funds', any money in the drawer's account is transferred to a separate account, such as a suspense account, where it remains until the banker has evidence that the matter has been arranged. If the payee desires, the cheque may be retained by the banker in exchange for the amount attaching to it. (See Section 53 under *Drawee*.)

If there is a reasonable ground for suspecting that a cheque has been tampered with, a delay in payment may be made until a reference to the drawer clears away the doubt. (See *London Joint Stock Bank Ltd* v *Macmillan and Arthur*, under *Payment of Cheque*.)

The presentment for payment of a promissory note is dealt with by Sections 86 and 87 as follows.

86.—(1) Where a note payable on demand has been indorsed, it must be presented for payment within a reasonable time of the indorsement. If it be not so presented the indorser is discharged.

(2) In determining what is a reasonable time, regard shall be had to the nature of the instrument, the usage of trade, and the facts of the particular case.

(3) Where a note payable on demand is negotiated, it is not deemed to be overdue, for the purpose of affecting the holder with defects of title of which he had no notice, by reason that it appears that a reasonable time for presenting it for payment has elapsed since its issue.

87.—(1) Where a promissory note is in the body of it made payable at a particular place, it must be presented for payment at that place in order to render the maker liable. In any other case, presentment for payment is not necessary in order to render the maker liable.

(2) Presentment for payment is necessary in order to render the indorser of a bill liable.

(3) Where a note is in the body of it made payable at a particular place, presentment at that place is necessary in order to render an indorser liable; but when a place of payment is indicated by way of memorandum only, presentment at that place is sufficient to render the indorser liable, but a presentment to the maker elsewhere, if sufficient in other respects, shall also suffice.

When a promissory note is made payable at a bank, the banker will be liable if he pays it in the event of the note bearing a forged indorsement. SEE *Forgery; Payment of Bill*

The presentment of a bill or cheque through a Clearing House has the same effect as presenting it direct to the banker on whom the cheque is drawn or where the bill is payable. SEE *Bill of Exchange*

The holder of a bill, by presenting it for payment, does not warrant the genuineness of the bill or of any of the signatures thereon, or of any accompanying documents. In *Guaranty Trust Company of New York* v *A. Hannay & Co* (1918) 34 TLR 427, Pickford LJ said that the position of the holder of a bill of exchange who presents it for payment was well expressed in a lecture by Dean Ames, of Harvard, when he said:

The attitude of the holder of a bill who presents it for payment is altogether different from that of a vendor. The holder is not a bargainer. By presentment for payment he does not assert, expressly or by implication, that the bill is his or is genuine. He, in effect, says, 'Here is a bill which has come to me calling, by its tenor, for payment by you. I accordingly present it to you for payment, that I may either get the money or protest it for non-payment'.

In *Yeoman Credit Co Ltd* v *Gregory* [1963] 1 All ER 115, failure to present for payment on the due date resulted in an indorser being released.

In *Hamilton Finance Co Ltd* v *Coverly Westbay Ltd and Others* [1969] 1 Lloyds Rep 53, it was held that a bill due on 1st January, 1966 (a Saturday), presented on 31st December, 1965, and, on that day, returned dishonoured, was not duly presented for payment. In the same case, a bill, also due on 1st January, 1966, sent to a collecting banker for presentation so as to reach the branch on 31st December and being then sent on to the bank's head office but not being presented in fact until 4th January, was not duly presented for payment. This was despite the intervention of the New Year.

PREVENTION OF FRAUD (INVESTMENTS) ACT 1958 This Act made general provision for preventing fraud in connection with dealings in investments; regulates dealings in securities; restricts registration under the Industrial and Provident Societies Act 1893; and defines the powers of the Board of Trade in this field.

By Section 1(1), no person shall carry on the business of dealing in securities except under the authority of a principal's licence issued by the Board through the Department of Trade and Industry. The same requirements apply to a servant or agent of any person carrying on such business, such agent receiving a representative's licence. SEE *Licensed Dealer*

By Section 2(1), exemptions from this requirement as to licences are given to members of recognized stock exchanges or recognized associations of dealers in securities, the Bank of England, statutory and municipal corporations, industrial, provident and building societies, and managers or trustees of any authorized unit trust scheme. SEE *Exempted Dealers*

By Section 4, a principal's licence will be granted only against the deposit of £500 or the provision of an approved guarantee for that amount.

By Section 12, the Board of Trade may appoint an inspector to investigate and report on the administration of any unit trust scheme.

By Section 13, penalties are prescribed for fraudulently inducing persons to invest money.

By Section 14, it is a criminal offence for any person to distribute, cause to be distributed or have in his possession for the purpose of distribution, any documents which to his knowledge are circulars containing invitations to participate in any agreement or arrangement defined in the Act. In broad terms, this means 'dealing in securities', or entering into any arrangements with respect to property other than securities.

By Section 16, certain persons or bodies may be exempted from the necessity for obtaining licences.

The Act is administered by the Department of Trade and Industry in accordance with regulations made by the Board and sanctioned by Parliament.

The particular wording of the Act and the powers given to the Department of Trade and Industry have led to some quite remarkable results. It was not intended that the Act should provide a regulatory framework for the unit trust movement but, in fact, this is what has happened. The entire process of 'authorization' and regulation of the unit trust movement now rests with the Department of Trade and Industry. The result is that the very considerable unit trust business in the UK is now regulated in an administrative fashion by the Department without any meaningful legislative framework or canon of case law. Nevertheless, most people would probably agree that the system has worked very well. SEE *Exempted Dealers; Licensed Dealer; Unit Trusts; Gower Report; Scott Committee on Linked Life Assurance*

PRICE EARNINGS RATIO This is a simple measurement of the quoted price of a share in relation to the earnings attributable to it. It is the current share price divided by the earnings per share. Normally the price earnings ratio of a share is calculated by reference to the published earnings for the last accounting period, i.e. it is on an historical basis. Alternatively, a prospective price earnings ratio may be calculated on forecast earnings.

If, for example, the price of a share is 100p and the earnings per share is 25p, the price earnings ratio is 4.

PRIMARY SECURITY SEE *Mortgage*

PRIORITIES Since 1925 (except in the case of mortgages and charges of registered land), every mortgage affecting a legal estate in land, whether legal or equitable (not being a mortgage protected by the deposit of documents relating to the estate) ranks according to its date of registration as a land charge pursuant to the Land Charges Act 1925 (Law of Property Act 1925, Section 97). SEE *Land Charges*

The effect of that Section is that a legal or equitable mortgage which is supported by a deposit of the deeds of the land does not require to be registered; hence the importance of holding the deeds. A mortgage not accompanied by the relative deeds requires to be registered, and ranks according to the date of its registration.

In the case of registered land, charges registered under the Land Registration Act 1925 rank according to the order in which they are entered on the register and not according to the order in which they are created. Mortgages (other than registered charges) may, if made by deed, be protected by a caution in the register, and they will rank according to the date of the entry of the caution. SEE *Land Registration*

Prior to 1926 it was possible for a third mortgagee to obtain a transfer of the first mortgage and tack it to his third and thus obtain priority over the second mortgagee. Tacking, however, was abolished by the Law of Property Act 1925, except as follows.

By Section 94, a prior mortgagee has the right to make further advances to rank in priority to subsequent mortgages (whether legal or equitable):

(*a*) if an arrangement has been made to that effect with the subsequent mortgagees; or
(*b*) if he had no notice of the subsequent mortgage at the time he made the further advance; or
(*c*) whether or not he had such notice, where the mortgage imposes an obligation on him to make such further advances.

This provision applies whether or not the prior mortgage was made expressly for securing further advances.

Where the prior mortgage was made expressly for securing a current account or other further advances, the mortgagee shall not be deemed to have notice of a mortgage merely because it was registered as a land charge, if it was not registered at the time when the original mortgage was created or when the last search (if any) was made by the mortgagee, whichever last happened.

This Section does not apply to charges registered under the Land Registration Act 1925.

The Section is an important one to bankers. No person can proceed to deal with the legal estate in land without first ascertaining where the title deeds are, and so long as they are in the possession of a banker either with a legal mortgage or a memorandum of deposit or without a formal charge, no one will be able in ordinary cases to secure priority to the banker.

Where, however, there are a number of mortgages (without the deposit of deeds) difficulties may arise if the order of registration is different from the date order of the mortgages. This is because registration is notice, and notice of any kind, actual or otherwise, may affect the position. The matter is not free from doubt.

The effect of being in posession of the documents of title is given in Section 13. (See that Section under *Mortgage*.)

A mortgage of a ship takes priority from the date of production for registration, not from the date of the instrument. SEE UNDER *Ship*

The priority of claims under any assignment of a life policy is regulated by the date on which notice is received by the insurance company. SEE *Life Policy; Debts, Assignment of; Second Mortgage; Tacking*

PRIORITY NOTICE The Law of Property (Amendment) Act 1926, Section 4, as amended by the Land Charges Rules 1940, provides that a priority notice may be lodged not later than 14 days before a contemplated registration is to take effect. If formal application for registration is lodged within 14 days of the date of the priority notice, the registration will date back and take effect as from the date the charge was given.

A priority notice may also be registered at the office of a local authority where a local land charge is contemplated. Where such a notice relates to a town-planning scheme requiring the approval of the Department of the Environment the time limit for following up the priority notice with the registration of the actual charge is 14 days after the sanction by the Department.

In the case of land with a registered title, a party proposing to take a charge over a title may give a priority notice on Form 18, accompanied by the land certificate.

If the charge is delivered for registration within 14 days of the giving of the notice, it will take priority over any application or instrument that may have been delivered meanwhile.

PRIVATE COMPANY Under Section 28, Companies Act 1948, a private company was defined as one which by its Articles

1. Restricted the right to transfer its shares.
2. Limited the number of its members to 50, not including persons who are in the employment of the company, and persons who, having been formerly in the employment of the company, were while in that employment, and have continued after the determination of that employment to be, members of the company.
3. Prohibited any invitation to the public to subscribe for any shares or debentures of the company.

This definition was, however, repealed by the Companies Act 1980, which brought public companies within the requirements of the Second Directive of the European Economic Community (SEE *Companys*) and expressly defined a private company as a company that is not a public company. Under the 1980 Act unlimited companies and companies limited by guarantee but not having a share capital could not be public companies and, in all cases, must be private companies. Under the Act, all private limited companies must include as the last part of their name the word 'limited' or the abbreviation 'ltd'.

The relevant provisions of the 1948 Act as amended by the 1980 Act have been substantially re-enacted in the 1985 Act. The following are some of the principal characteristics of a private company:

1. It is any company other than a public company (see above).
2. It may be an unlimited company.
3. It may be a company limited by guarantee without having a share capital.
4. The articles need not contain the restrictions required previously by Section 28, Companies Act 1948 (see above).
5. A private limited company commits a criminal offence if it offers its shares or debentures to the public or allots shares or debentures (e.g. to an issuing house) for sale to the public. (Save that a company limited by guarantee without a share capital may allot debentures to the public.)
6. A new issue of shares need not be offered pro rata to existing shareholders (as in the case of a public company) if there is a contrary provision in the articles or, for example, in a resolution setting out the terms of issue of a class of shares, provided the contrary intention existed prior to the coming into force of the 1980 Act.
7. The restrictions on the charging by a public company of its own shares does not apply to a private company.
8. The restrictions which apply to the distributions by public companies (SEE *Distribution*) does not apply to private companies.

9. The restrictions which apply in the case of a public company to loans to directors do not apply to private companies, as regards quasi loans, connected persons and 'credit transactions' (except in the case of a private company which belongs to a group which includes a public company). SEE *Loans to Directors*
10. A private company may have only one director.
11. A proxy has the right to speak at meetings.
12. The accounts of a private company must be laid before the members within ten months after the end of the accounting period (seven months in the case of a public company).

SEE *Companies Acts; Limited Company*

PROBATE The document which is issued, with an official copy of a will, by the Probate Office to an executor. The principal registry of wills is at Somerset House, where the copy of a will may be seen on payment of 10p. There are also district registries where probate can be obtained of the wills of persons who were living in those districts at the time of their death, and a copy of a will which was provided in a district registry may be seen in that direct registry, as well as at Somerset House. A foreign or colonial probate does not govern the deceased's estate in the UK.

An official copy of the whole or any part of a will, or an official certificate or the grant of any letters of administration, may be obtained from the district registry where the will has been proved or the administration granted on the payment of certain fees.

Until probate is exhibited or, if no will, letters of administration are exhibited, a banker does not allow the balance of the deceased's account to be transferred, or any securities which he may have left with the banker to be removed. An executor must act or renounce within six months from the date of death.

In the event of a probate being lost, the court will issue a document called 'exemplification of probate', which has the same effect as the original document.

Where probate or letters of administration have been revoked, the banker is protected in any payments he may have bona fide made by reason of the probate or letters.

Protection is given to persons acting on probate or administration by the Administration of Estates Act 1925, Section 27:

(*i*) Every person making or permitting to be made any payment or disposition in good faith under a representation shall be indemnified and protected in so dealing, notwithstanding any defect or circumstance whatsoever affecting the validity of the representation.

(*ii*) Where a representation is revoked, all payments and dispositions made in good faith to a personal representative under the representation before the revocation thereof are a valid discharge to the person making the same; and the personal representative who acted under the revoked representation may retain and reimburse himself in respect of any payments or dispositions made by him which the person to whom representation is afterwards granted might have properly made.

All conveyances of any interest in real or personal estate made to a purchaser by a person to whom probate of letters of administration have been granted are valid notwithstanding any revocation of representation (Section 37(1)). 'Representation' means probate of a will or grant of administration. SEE *Executor, Letters of Administration; Personal Representatives; Transfer of Shares*

PRODUCTS The interest calculations in a current account, where the amount of the balance is multiplied by the number of days during which it continues undisturbed. The resulting products is the number of pounds for one day on which interest is to be allowed or charged.

PROFESSIONAL INDEMNITY INSURANCE This is a form of cover in respect of financial liabilities to third parties arising from acts or omissions in the course of a person's employment. Although this type of insurance is thought of in relation to the very substantial risks carried by professional people such as doctors, lawyers, accountants and merchant bankers, it is nevertheless possible for any person to insure against loss or damage to other persons occasioned by the insured in the course of his occupation. A number of professional people, e.g. lawyers, are covered by the group indemnity schemes of their own profession. Others, however, must make their own arrangements for insurance against possible liability for negligence and the market for this type of insurance in the UK is very limited. Only Lloyd's provide extensive cover of this kind. The sums involved are usually considerable and the premiums are not cheap. For example, a premium to cover a financial institution for corporate advisory services up to a limit of, say £500,000 for any one claim might be of the order of four per cent of the total fee income. Each case must be considered on its merits and the underwriters will wish to have detailed information on the business of the proposer and, in the case of a corporate body, the personal credentials of the directors and senior officials. The only satisfactory way to take out insurance of this nature is to do so through experienced insurance brokers who will obtain appropriate quotations from underwriters at Lloyd's.

PROFIT The surplus arising from a business enterprise in the course of a given accounting period. Profits may be calculated at different levels of operation, depending on the purpose of the calculation. Thus the trading profit, sometimes expressed as 'gross trading profit' will usually be the surplus arising from the basic activity of the business, e.g. the buying and selling of goods, before the allocation of 'overhead' costs, salaries, rent, pension contributions, etc.

Pre-tax profits in the case of a limited company will normally mean the net surplus for the year, before deducting the charge for corporation tax. Profit for tax purposes will normally be the operating surplus of the business, after deducting expenses, 'wholly and exclusively' incurred for the purpose of the business. SEE *Corporation Tax; Income Tax*

Measures of profitability include, for example, (1) the return on capital employed (which usually means shareholders funds, including preference shares, plus long-term finance such as debenture loans), (2) return on equity (usually meaning the ordinary shareholders capital, including reserves and accumulated profits), or (3) earnings per share (the gross or net earnings for the accounting period, divided by the number of ordinary shares in issue).

Profit is not a precise term and in any situation where the exact meaning is significant, e.g. in a profit-sharing agreement, or the calculation of a sale price by reference to annual profits, it is important that the intended meaning should be precisely defined.

PROFIT-SHARING SCHEMES These are schemes in which the employees of a business share in the profits of the enterprise, usually according to some predetermined formula. On the whole, such schemes have not been widespread in the UK, partly because of taxation disadvantages, and partly perhaps because the trade unions have favoured direct wage and salary payments, rather than any form of remuneration which might vary with profitability.

In general, any payment made by the employer to an employee calculated by reference to the profits of the company, whether paid in cash or as an allocation of shares, will be taxable in the employee's hands. The Finance Act 1978, however, made provision, with effect from 6th April, 1979, for a degree of tax relief for employees participating in a profit-sharing scheme.

Under the provision of the Finance Act 1978, as amended by the Finance Acts 1980 and 1985, tax relief is available under profit-sharing schemes if the following conditions are satisfied:

1. The scheme must be approved by the Inland Revenue.
2. Shares allocated under the scheme for the benefit of employees must be held by trustees.
3. The maximum value of shares allotted to any one participant in any one tax year was originally £1,000, then £1,250 (Finance Act 1982) and subsequently (Finance Act 1983) £1,250 or 10 per cent of the participant's salary, whichever is the greater up to a maximum benefit of £5,000.
4. The participant must agree to his shares being retained by the trustees for at least two years unless he dies, retires, or becomes redundant.

The shares may be released to the employee after two years. If the employee retains the shares for a further three years, there will be no income tax liability. If he sells the shares in that period income tax will be payable on the original value or the sale price, whichever is the greater, according to the scale in the table below.

Time of sale	Tax liability on
Years 3 and 4	100%
Year 5	75%

During the period in which the shares are held by the trustees, any dividends on the shares are paid to the participants and are taxable in their hands.

If the participant leaves the company on retirement or through redundancy before the sixth anniversary of the allocation of the shares, the percentage charge is 50 per cent.

PROMISSORY NOTE Part IV of the Bills of Exchange Act 1882 is devoted to promissory notes. Section 83 defines a promissory note as follows:

(1) A promissory note is an unconditional promise in writing made by one person to another, signed by the maker, engaging to pay, on demand or at a fixed or determinable future time, a sum certain in money, to, or to the order of, a specified person or to bearer.

(2) An instrument in the form of a note payable to maker's order is not a note within the meaning of this section unless and until it is indorsed by the maker.

(3) A note is not invalid by reason only that it contains also a pledge of collateral security with authority to sell or dispose thereof.

(4) A note which is, or on the face of it purports to be, both made and payable within the British Islands is an inland note. Any other note is a foreign note.

A promissory note is inchoate and incomplete until delivery thereof to the payee or bearer (Section 81).

The following are specimens of promissory notes signed by one person.

£100 Leeds, 1 June 19...
Three months after date I promise to pay to John Brown or order the sum of one hundred pounds for value received.

John Jones

John Jones is the maker of the note, and John Brown is the payee.

£100 Leeds, 1 June 19....
On demand I promise to pay to the X & Y Banking Company Limited, or order, at their Leeds office the sum of one hundred pounds with lawful interest for the same from the day of the date hereof.
Witness John Jones

A note which is written by John Brown in the form, 'I, John Brown, promise to pay', is valid, without his signature appearing at the foot, but variations from the usual forms should be discouraged.

If a note on demand does not include a promise to pay interest, interest cannot legally be enforced.

Section 85.—(1) A promissory note may be made by two or more makers, and they may be liable thereon jointly, or jointly and severally according to its tenor.

(2) Where a note runs, 'I promise to pay', and is signed by two or more persons, it is deemed to be their joint and several note.

The following is a specimen of a joint and several promissory note.

£100 Leeds, 1 June 19....
Three months after date we jointly and severally promise to pay to the X & Y Banking Company Limited, or order, at their Leeds office, the sum of one hundred pounds with lawful interest for the same from the date hereof.

John Brown
John Jones

Witness to both signatures

A note drawn at so many month's notice has been held to be in accordance with the Bills of Exchange Act.

A promissory note may be payable by instalments (*Kirkwood* v *Carroll* (1903) 88 LT 52).

When several persons sign a promissory note, the note is usually worded 'We jointly and severally promise to pay', and each person signing the note is liable for the full amount. If, however, the note is worded 'we jointly promise to pay', it is a promise by the combined parties and each person is not individually liable for the whole amount. In a joint note all the makers must be sued together; but in a joint and several note each may be sued separately or they may all be sued jointly.

The regulations of the Bills of Exchange Act regarding the presentment for payment of a promissory note are given in Section 86 and 87. SEE *Presentment for Payment*

To be valid, a promissory note must not be payable upon a contingency, such as the arrival of a ship.

Sections 88 and 89 provide as follows.

88. The maker of a promissory note by making it—

(1) Engages that he will pay it according to its tenor;

(2) Is precluded from denying to a holder in due course the existence of the payee and his then capacity to indorse.

89.—(1) Subject to the provisions in this Part and, except as by this Section provided, the provisions of this Act relating to bills of exchange apply, with the necessary modifications, to promissory notes.

(2) In applying those provisions the maker of a note shall be deemed to correspond with the acceptor of a bill, and the first indorser of a note shall be deemed to correspond with the drawer of an accepted bill payable to drawer's order.

(3) The following provisions as to bills do not apply to notes; namely, provisions relating to—

(*a*) Presentment for acceptance;
(*b*) Acceptance;
(*c*) Acceptance supra protest;
(*d*) Bills in a set.

(4) Where a foreign note is dishonoured, protest thereof is unnecessary.

A promissory note made by a banker, payable to bearer on demand, is a bank note. By the Currency and Bank Notes Act 1928, the Bank of England was empowered to issue notes for £1 and for 10s. Prior to that Act, bank notes under £5 were prohibited in England. In Scotland and Ireland bank notes for £1 and upwards are issued. There is no limit as to the amount of other promissory notes.

A promissory note (except a bank note) cannot be re-issued. Bank notes may be re-issued as often as desired.

If a person is induced by fraud to sign a promissory note, he may, unless negligence is shown, be held not to be liable thereon. This was the decision in the case of *Lewis* v *Clay* (1897) 14 TLR 149, where a person was induced to sign under the belief that he was witnessing a signature.

To some extent this view was modified in *Saunders* v *Anglia Building Society* [1970] 3 All ER 161, where it was held that a document should be considered void only where the element of consent to the document was totally lacking and for a person to succeed in setting aside a document, he must show that he took all reasonable care in the circumstances. The court considered that in determining whether or not there had been an exercise of all reasonable care it was not appropriate to draw any distinction between negotiable instruments and any other kind of document. SEE *Signature*

A banker is liable if he pays a promissory note, domiciled with him, bearing a forged indorsement.

It frequently happens where money is borrowed by way of a promissory note that another person also signs the note as surety for the borrower. If Brown borrows on a joint and several promissory note and Jones signs a surety for Brown, either of them is liable to pay the amount at maturity, or, if on demand, when the banker calls for repayment. If Brown does not pay the note at maturity Jones is not discharged from lack of notice of dishonour, but it is advisable to give such notice. If the note continues for more than six years and during that time the interest, as well as any instalments in reduction of the amount, is paid by Brown, the payments so made by Brown will not operate to keep the note alive as against Jones. If Jones has paid nothing and given no acknowledgment of the debt for six years from the date of the note, he will be discharged. It is necessary, therefore, before the six years are up, to obtain an acknowledgment from Jones (or from the maker who has not paid anything or confirmed the debt in any way). The best plan is to get a fresh note signed by both makers before the six years expire. Each time that a payment in reduction of a promissory note on demand is made, a paying-in slip should be signed in order to afford evidence of the payment. In the *Mutual Loan Fund Association* v *Sudlow* [1858] 5 CB NS p. 453, Mr Justice Byles said

> As between the makers and the payees of the note, at law both the makers are principals, and evidence would not be admissible to show that one of them signed the instrument as surety. But in equity, if it be made to appear that the lender was cognisant of the circumstances, you may show what the fact is. They become joint principals, or principal and surety according to the facts. [SEE *Limitation Act 1939*]

If a loan is made to a society or institution upon a promissory note signed, say, by the members of the committee, the members should sign as private individuals, without any reference to the name of the society or institution.

Where an advance is obtained from a banker upon a promissory note payable on demand, signed by the borrower and one or more makers (as sureties), the amount is usually debited to a separate loan account and the proceeds credited to the borrower's current account; if payable at so many months after date it is discounted. It frequently happens that when an afterdate promissory note is about due, it is arranged to renew it for a further period on the same signatures, and sometimes, for various reasons, it is impossible to obtain all the signatures to the new note before the old one is due. In such a case the old note should not be cancelled but should be pinned to the new note till all the makers have signed, as in the event of any signature not being obtained the old note may be sued upon.

Where a promissory note signed, say, by Brown in favour of Jones is lodged as security for an overdraft to Jones, the note should be indorsed by Jones and a memorandum should be signed by him to show the purpose for which the note is given; and where a note is signed, say, by J. Brown and J. Jones, payable to the bank and is given as security for Brown's account, a memorandum should be signed by the two makers. The memorandum of deposit should state that the note is given for securing the sum and sums of money which shall from time to time be due or owing from the customer on whose behalf it is given, either alone or with any other person or persons either on the balance of his current account or otherwise, and that the moneys intended to be secured by the promissory note shall be recoverable thereupon, although the bank may have taken or may hereafter take any further security, or may have given time for the payment thereof.

The period of limitation begins to run on a promissory note payable on demand from the date of the note or the date of its issue, whichever is later.

A promissory note payable at a fixed period after date is not regarded as a continuing security for an account and, to establish the contrary, evidence is required. In the case of In *Re Boys, Eedes* v *Boys* (1870) 10 LR Eq 467, where a note payable eight months after date was given as security, Lord Romilly said:

> I think that the burden of proof should lie upon those who seek to establish that it was intended to be a running security for the balance of the account from time to time.

In the case of a promissory note payable on demand, the liability exists as soon as the loan is made, and the words 'on demand' may be neglected. 'Express demand is not necessary in the case of a promissory note payable on demand; but it is otherwise when the debt is not present but to accrue as in the case of a note payable three months after demand.' (*Bradford Old Bank* v *Sutcliffe* [1918] 2 KB 833)

In *Williamson and Others* v *Rider* [1962] 3 WLR 119, the Court of Appeal decided by a majority that an instrument promising the payment of a sum of money 'on or before' 31st December, 1956, was not a promissory note. It was held that the option reserved by the instrument to pay at an earlier date than 31st December created an uncertainty and a contingency in the time for payment.

Stamp duty on promissory notes was abolished by the Finance Act 1970. SEE *Limitation Act 1939, Presentment for Payment*

PROOF OF DEBTS A proof of debt is the form which is filled up by a creditor setting forth the amount of his claim against the estate of a bankrupt.

When securities are held from a third party, proof may be made for the whole debt without any deduction for these securities. If third party securities are realized before the proof is made, the proceeds should be placed to a suspense account and proof be made for the full debt; but if the proceeds are placed to the credit of the bankrupt's account, then proof can be made only for the balance of the account.

A banker often delays proving for a debt until the trustee advertises the payment of a first dividend, up to which time a creditor has a right of proof.

The Bankruptcy Act 1914, provides as follows.

Description of debts provable in bankruptcy

30.—(1) Demands in the nature of unliquidated damages arising otherwise than by reason of a contract promise, or breach of trust, shall not be provable in bankruptcy.

(2) A person having notice of any act of bankruptcy available against the debtor shall not prove under the order for any debt or liability contracted by the debtor subsequently to the date of his so having notice.

(3) Save as aforesaid, all debts and liabilities, present or future, certain or contingent, to which the debtor is subject at the date of the receiving order, or to which he may become subject before his discharge by reason of any obligation incurred before the date of the receiving order, shall be deemed to be debts provable in bankruptcy.

(4) An estimate shall be made by the trustee of the value of any debt or liability provable as aforesaid, which by reason of its being subject to any contingency or contingencies, or for any other reason, does not bear a certain value.

A sum due from one party shall be set off (q.v.) against any sum due from the other party and the balance only shall be claimed or paid on either side respectively (Section 31).

In the case of partners the joint estate shall be applicable in the first instance in payment of their joint debts, and the separate estate of each partner shall be applicable in the first instance in payment of his separate debts. If there is a surplus of the separate estates it shall be dealt with as part of the joint estate. If there is a surplus of the joint estate it shall be dealt with as part of the respective separate estates in proportion to the right and interest of each partner in the joint estate (Section 33(6)). Joint creditors may receive dividends out of separate estates *pari passu* with separate creditors if there is no joint estate and if there is no solvent partner. Where a joint creditor is the petitioning creditor in a separate adjudication he may receive dividends out of the separate estate.

A proof of debt is limited to the amount of principal and interest due at the date of the receiving order. Interest subsequent to the receiving order cannot be added. SEE *Interest*

If the proof is in respect of a bill of exchange, promissory note, or other negotiable instrument, on which the debtor is liable, such instrument, subject to any special order of the court to the contrary, must be produced before the proof can be admitted either for voting or for dividend.

It should be noted (see Rule 13 below) that the trustee in bankruptcy may at any time redeem a security on payment to the creditor of the assessed value, but the secured creditor has the right to give the trustee notice, in writing, to elect whether he will, or will not, redeem the security at the assessed value. If the trustee fails to redeem it within six months, the security vests in the creditor, and he can thereafter sell the security and retain the proceeds even if it realizes more than the debt. If notice be not given, the trustee's right to redeem continues.

The rules in the second Schedule of the Bankruptcy Act, 1914, with respect to proof of debts are as follows.

Proof in ordinary cases

1. Every creditor shall prove his debt as soon as may be after the making of a receiving order.

2. A debt may be proved by delivering or sending through the post in a prepaid letter to the official receiver, or, if a trustee has been appointed, to the trustee, an affidavit verifying the debt.

3. The affidavit may be made by the creditor himself, or by some person authorised by or on behalf of the creditor. If made by a person so authorised it shall state his authority and means of knowledge.

4. The affidavit shall contain or refer to a statement of account showing the particulars of the debt, and shall specify the vouchers, if any, by which the same can be substantiated. The official receiver or trustee may at any time call for the production of the vouchers.

5. The affidavit shall state whether the creditor is or is not a secured creditor.

PROOF OF DEBTS

The following provision was inserted at the end of Rule 5 by the Bankruptcy (Amendment) Act 1926:

And if it is found at any time that the affidavit made by or on behalf of a secured creditor has omitted to state that he is a secured creditor, the secured creditor shall surrender his security to the official receiver or trustee for the general benefit of the creditors unless the Court on application is satisfied that the omission has arisen from inadvertence, and in that case the Court may allow the affidavit to be amended upon such terms as to the repayment of any dividends or otherwise as the Court may consider to be just.

6. A creditor shall bear the cost of proving his debt, unless the Court otherwise specially orders.

7. Every creditor who has lodged a proof shall be entitled to see and examine the proofs of other creditors before the first meeting, and at all reasonable times.

8. A creditor proving his debt shall deduct therefrom all trade discounts, but he shall not be compelled to deduct any discount, not exceeding five per centum on the net amount of his claim, which he may have agreed to allow for payment in cash.

9. Formal proof of debts in respect of contributions payable under the National Insurance Act, 1911, to which priority is given by this Act, shall not be required except in cases where it may otherwise be provided by rules under this Act.

Proof by secured creditors

10. If a secured creditor realises his security he may prove for the balance due to him, after deducting the net amount realised.

11. If a secured creditor surrenders his security to the official receiver or trustee for the general benefit of the creditors, he may prove for his whole debt.

12. If a secured creditor does not either realise or surrender his security, he shall, before ranking for dividend, state in his proof the particulars of his security, the date when it was given, and the value at which he assess it, and shall be entitled to receive a dividend only in respect of the balance due to him after deducting the value so assessed.

13.(a) Where a security is so valued the trustee may at any time redeem it on payment to the creditor of the assessed value.

(b) If the trustee is dissatisfied with the value at which a security is assessed, he may require that the property comprised in any security so valued be offered for sale at such times and on such terms and conditions as may be agreed on between the creditor and the trustee, or as, in default of such agreement, the Court may direct. If the sale be by public auction the creditor, or the trustee on behalf of the estate, may bid or purchase.

(c) Provided that the creditor may at any time, by notice in writing, require the trustee to elect whether he will or will not exercise his power of redeeming the security or requiring it to be realised, and if the trustee does not, within six months after receiving the notice, signify in writing to the creditor his election to exercise the power, he shall not be entitled to exercise it; and the equity of redemption, or any other interest in the property comprised in the security which is vested in the trustee, shall vest in the creditor, and the amount of his debt shall be reduced by the amount at which the security has been valued.

14. Where a creditor has so valued his security, he may at any time amend the valuation and proof on showing to the satisfaction of the trustee, or the Court, that the valuation and proof were made *bona fide* on a mistaken estimate, or that the security has diminished or increased in value since its previous valuation; but every such amendment shall be made at the cost of the creditor, and upon such terms as the Court shall order, unless the trustee shall allow the amendment without application to the Court.

15. Where a valuation has been amended in accordance with the foregoing rule, the creditor shall forthwith repay any surplus dividend which he may have received in excess of that which he would have been entitled on the amended valuation, or, as the case may be, shall be entitled to be paid out of any money, for the time being available for dividend, any dividend or share of dividend which he may have failed to receive by reason of the inaccuracy of the original valuation, before that money is made applicable to the payment of any future dividend, but he shall not be entitled to disturb the distribution of any dividend declared before the date of the amendment.

16. If a creditor after having valued his security subsequently realises it, or if it is realised under the provisions of rule 13, the net amount realised shall be substituted for the amount of any valuation previously made by the creditor, and shall be treated in all respects as an amended valuation made by the creditor.

17. If a secured creditor does not comply with the foregoing rules he shall be excluded from all share in any dividend.

18. Subject to the provisions of Rule 13, a creditor shall in no case receive more than twenty shillings in the pound, and interest as provided by this Act.

Proof in respect of distinct contracts

19. If a debtor was, at the date of the receiving order, liable in respect of distinct contracts as a member of two or more distinct firms, or as a sole contractor, and also as member of a firm, the circumstances that the firms are in whole or in part composed of the same individuals, or that the sole contractor is also one of the joint contractors, shall not prevent proof in respect of the contracts, against the parties respectively liable on the contracts.

Periodical payments

20. When any rent or other payment falls due at stated periods, and the receiving order is made at any time other than one of those periods, the person entitled to the rent or payment may prove for a proportionate part thereof up to the date of the order as if the rent or payment grew due from day to day.

Interest

21. On any debt or sum certain, payable at a certain time or otherwise, whereon interest is not reserved or agreed for, and which is overdue at the date of the receiving order and provable in bankruptcy the creditor may prove for interest at a rate not exceeding four per centum per annum to the date of the order from the time when the debt or sum was payable, if the debt or sum is payable by virtue of a written instrument at a certain time, and if payable otherwise, then from the time when a demand in writing has been made giving the debtor notice that interest will be claimed from the date of the demand until the time of payment.

Debt payable at a future time

22. A creditor may prove for a debt not payable when the debtor committed an act of bankruptcy as if it were payable presently, and may receive dividends equally with the other creditors, deducting only thereout a rebate of interest at the rate of five pounds per centum per annum computed from the declaration of a dividend to the time when the debt would have become payable, according to the terms on which it was contracted.

Admission or rejection of proofs

23. The trustee shall examine every proof and the grounds of the debt, and in writing admit or reject it, in whole or in part, or require further evidence in support of it. If he rejects a proof he shall state in writing to the creditor the grounds of the rejection.

24. If the trustee thinks that a proof has been improperly admitted, the Court may, on the application of the trustee, after notice to the creditor who made the proof, expunge the proof or reduce its amount.

25. If a creditor is dissatisfied with the decision of the trustee in respect of a proof, the Court may, on the application of the creditor, reverse or vary the decision.

26. The Court may also expunge or reduce a proof upon the application of a creditor if the trustee declines to interfere in the matter, or, in the case of a composition or scheme, upon the application of the debtor.

27. For the purpose of any of his duties in relation to proofs, the trustee may administer oaths and take affidavits.

28. The official receiver, before the appointment of a trustee, shall have all the powers of a trustee with respect to the examination, admission, and rejection of proofs, and any act or decision of his in relation thereto shall be subject to the like appeal.

Where a banker is a holder of a bill and the acceptor and drawer become bankrupt, he may claim upon both estates for the full amount of the bill, but he must not retain more than the amount of the bill. If a dividend has already been declared on one of the estates before sending in a proof of debt on the other estate, the banker's claim on the second estate will be only for the balance after crediting the dividend declared. If there is any balance standing to the customer's credit it will be retained by the banker against the bill.

PROPERTY SEE *Freehold; Leasehold; Personal Estate, Personalty*

PROPERTY, INVESTMENT IN The avenues of property investment available in the UK are direct purchase, investment in property bonds (q.v.), investment in property shares (q.v.).

The principal areas of property investment are domestic property, and commercial and industrial property. SEE *Agricultural Land, Investment in; Woodlands, Investment in*

Investment in Domestic Property

Approximately 55 per cent of householders in this country are owner-occupiers (SEE *House Purchase*). Their ownership is, of course, a matter of residence rather than one of investment but, nevertheless, for many people investment in their own houses has been rewarding. Beyond that, a number of people have purchased 'investment properties', i.e. rented house and flats, but from the First World War onwards there has been a degree of rent control in the UK and statutory protection for tenants of rented property. On the death of a tenant, certain close relatives have been able to succeed to a statutory tenancy, so that in some cases it has not been possible to sell rented property with vacant possession for two generations or so. To some extent this situation was modified by the Housing Act 1980, which introduced shorthold tenancies (q.v.). In general, therefore, investment in rented domestic property in the UK has been limited because of the difficulty of increasing controlled rents, the difficulty of obtaining vacant possession and the costs of repairs and maintenance which generally could not be recovered in rental income.

Investment in Commercial and Industrial Property

Not all commercial and industrial occupiers wish to finance and own their own accommodation and there is a widespread market for institutional and private investors to provide offices, shops, factories and warehouses for leasing. Generally, the term commercial investment is applied to shops and offices and industrial investment means factories and warehouses.

Some advantages of investment in commercial and industrial property are (1) the market in the UK is highly developed and operates efficiently and professionally; (2) an investment in commercial and industrial property is an investment in the business life of the country; (3) rents, and therefore capital values, tend to move with money values and thus provide a hedge against inflation; (4) there is no shortage of professional management: the leading firms are of the highest standard and integrity, often with world-wide reputations; (5) the investment is a tangible one which the investor may visit and inspect; and (6) property is a highly acceptable form of security for borrowing purposes.

Some disadvantages of this category of investment are (1) speculative property investment carries the attendant risk of finding suitable tenants; (2) location is of paramount importance and a badly sited development may become a white elephant; (3) the property market is affected by the overall economic climate: in times of recession, lettings may be difficult, tenants may suffer liquidations and bankruptcies and property values generally may slump; (4) an investment in property is less readily marketable than some other forms of investment; and (5) the cost of investment tends to be high—legal charges, stamp duty and management fees can amount to substantial sums.

It is difficult for investors of modest means to invest directly in commercial and industrial property, particularly with any degree of spread. Many investors turn, therefore, to the alternatives of property bonds (q.v.) and property shares (q.v.).

PROPERTY BOND A property bond is a contract of life assurance (q.v.). Investment may be by a single, i.e. lump sum premium, or by regular premiums over the life of the policy. A property bond is in the nature of a property unit trust. Because, however, a unit trust investing in property cannot be 'authorized' under the Prevention of Fraud (Investments) Act 1958 (q.v.), this particular form of investment has followed the alternative route of the life assurance contract.

Some of the advantages of investment in property bonds are

1. A much wider spread is obtained than would otherwise be possible for a small investor.
2. Units are easily available and readily saleable on the subscription day.
3. An investor gains the benefit of continuing professional management.
4. Costs are modest and kept so by competition.
5. The valuation of the portfolio is undertaken by independent audit valuers.
6. There may be certain taxation advantages to some investors.

Some disadvantages are

1. The price of the bonds is subject to the vagaries of the property market and all investors may not appreciate this.
2. Owing to the difficulty of accurate valuation of properties, the independent valuation of the portfolio at any one time may not necessarily reflect the price which the properties would fetch on a forced sale.
3. On a rapidly falling market, it may not be possible for the managers to move quickly enough to realize properties to the best advantage.
4. By the nature of property investment, there can be delays in selling the underlying properties and meeting the unit-holder's request for the redemption of units.

Although, in general, the performance of property bonds will follow movements in the property market, there will be differences reflecting (1) the composition of the portfolio, and (2) the degree of liquidity in the fund.

PROPERTY INSURANCE SEE *Household Insurance*

PROPERTY SHARES, INVESTMENT IN This is investment in the shares of property companies. It may take the form of a shareholding in a private and unlisted company or, more usually in the case of the larger companies, an investment in shares which are quoted on the Stock Exchange. The property companies may themselves be engaged in the development of properties, whether for sale or retention, or in the management of a property portfolio, or in some cases a combination of both.

Some advantages of investment in property shares are (1) the availability of experienced management, (2) the marketability of shares through the Stock Exchange (in the case of listed companies), and (3) the fact that most property companies resort to loan capital so that the gearing (q.v.) operates to the advantage of the ordinary shareholders on a rising market.

Some disadvantages are (1) the share price does not necessarily reflect directly the value of the underlying portfolio but, in the short term, the mood and fashion of property shares on the Stock Market, (2) highly geared companies may suffer badly during periods of high interest rates and during times of severe falls in property values, and (3) the yield on property shares tends historically to be below that of other listed companies.

PROPERTY UNIT TRUSTS These are unit trusts investing in property. They are 'unauthorized' unit trusts in that property does not satisfy the definition of 'securities' in the Prevention of Fraud (Investments) Act 1958 (q.v.) and thus it would be an offence under that Act to invite public subscription for the units or to issue circulars, or even to hold circulars calculated to induce investment in the unit trust. Over the years, however, a number of property unit trusts have been set up with the approval of the Department of Trade and Industry for investment exclusively by pension funds and charities and the Department have permitted the issue of prospectuses to these categories of investors. At the time of writing, there are 17 pension-fund property unit trusts in existence managing portfolios to an approximate value of £2,500 million.

PROSPECTUS Section 58 of the Companies Act 1985 provides 'If a company allots or agrees to allot its shares or debentures with a view to all or any of them being offered for sale to the public, any document by which the offer for sale to the public is made is deemed for all purposes a prospectus issued by the company'.

Any invitation to the public to subscribe for shares, even the issue of a simple form of application, must be accompanied by a full prospectus, except in the following cases: (1) bona-fide underwriting, (2) issues of shares not offered to the public, (3) issues of shares or debentures by way of rights to existing holders, and (4) issues of capital which are uniform with existing quoted capital.

The information required by the Companies Act 1985 to be included in a prospectus is set out in Schedule 3 to the Act. If, however, the shares are to be quoted on the Stock Exchange, the requirements of the Rules and Regulations of the Stock Exchange must also be satisfied. For the most part these follow the requirements of the Companies Acts, and the following is a summary of the contents of a prospectus as required respectively by company law and the Stock Exchange regulations.

1. Statement that a copy of prospectus and supporting documents has been sent to the Registrar of Companies.
2. Statement that application has been made to the Stock Exchange for permission to deal in the shares and for a quotation for the issue.
3. Date and time of opening of application lists.
4. Company's full name, date and country of incorporation and authority under which it was incorporated.
5. Authorized and issued or agreed to be issued share capital, amount paid up, description and nominal value of shares. Where 25 per cent, or more, of the voting capital (including unclassified shares) is unissued a statement that no issue will knowingly be made which could effectively alter the control of the company without prior approval of the shareholders in general meeting.
6. Loan capital and outstanding indebtedness of company and subsidiaries, including bank overdrafts, guarantees, and contingent liabilities.
7. Voting rights of single class capital, and, in cases where there is more than one class of share, voting rights of shareholders and rights to dividend, capital, redemption and issue of further shares, with consents to variation of rights.
8. Terms of offer for sale, followed by instructions for application and conditions of allotment including a statement that the shares which are on renouncable document will be free of stamp and that the allotment letters are renounced.
9. Full name, address and description of all directors including nationality if not British.
10. Name, address and professional qualification of auditors (and reporting accountants).
11. Name and address of bankers, solicitors, brokers, registrars and trustees (if any).
12. Full name and qualification of secretary, and address of registered office and transfer office.
13. *History and Business*
The general nature of the business, including the date business commenced, the relative importance of different activities (if applicable) and details of existing and projected subsidiaries.
14. *Management*
Statement usually including age and length of service of directors, service contracts.
15. *Employees*
Number of employees and other details covering continuity of management and labour relations, including pension arrangements.
16. *Plant and premises*
Situation, area of factories and other main buildings, with details of tenure, freeholds, leaseholds etc. (in the case of property companies a special layout is required).
17. *Working capital*
A statement that, in the opinion of the directors, working capital is sufficient, and if not, proposals to provide for same. Where new money is being raised by this issue of ordinary shares, or has been so raised during the past two years, an estimate of the proceeds of the issue and an indication of their application.
18. *Accountants report*
A report signed by the auditors, including
(a) *Profits* Five-year profits record (or less if incorporated more recently) both for parent company and (if applicable) group; notes to this paragraph usually include (i) the aggregate directors emoluments during the last year and the amount payable under the arrangements in force at the date of the prospectus, (ii) details of overseas interests (where material) with the basis on which foreign currencies and taxation have been dealt with, and any restrictions on remittance of funds.
(b) *Assets and liabilities* Figures at the date of last balance sheet for both parent company and group.

(c) *Intended purchase* If proceeds of issue to be used in purchase of business or shares in a company, a separate report on the profits of the business or company for the last five years, and of its assets and liabilities.
(d) *Dividends* Dividend record for five years (or less as in (a) above).
(e) *Accounts* If date of last accounts earlier than three months before the date of the prospectus, a statement that no subsequent accounts have been made up.
19. *Profits, prospects and dividends*
A statement of current trading with an indication, in the absence of unforeseen circumstances, of the outlook for profits and dividends. Where possible, a statement showing sales, turnover figures or group trading income over the last three years, including a reasonable breakdown between the more important trading activities.
20. *General information*
(a) Particulars of any issue or change of capital of the company or its subsidiaries within past two years.
(b) Particulars of acquisitions within past two years by means of issuance of shares or for cash, with details of directors' interest and goodwill element.
(c) Names and shareholdings of substantial or controlling shareholders together with details of directors' and their families' interests in the share capital of the company, differentiating between beneficial and other interests.
(d) Particulars of present promotion, with consideration of any benefit paid to promoter currently and within past two years.
(e) Particulars of preliminary expenses and expenses of issue.
(f) Statement that no part of proceeds of issue is payable to company, if applicable.
(g) Particulars of capital under option and any commissions, discounts, brokerages or other special terms granted.
(h) Statement of surtax clearance and indemnity as to surtax and estate duties, shortfall and special charge where applicable.
(i) *Articles of association*
Details of relevant provisions including those governing

(i) power of directors to vote remuneration to themselves,
(ii) retirement of Directors under an age limit,
(iii) borrowing powers,
(iv) prohibition of distribution of capital profits (investment trusts).

(j) *Contracts* (not being contracts entered into in the ordinary course of business). All material contracts entered into during the past two years, by company and subsidiaries.
(k) Statement that a Certificate of Exemption has been given by Stock Exchange, where applicable. (This allows certain variations from the full provisions of Schedule 4 of the Act where it may prove unduly burdensome due to the size of the issue, number of possible applicants, etc.)
(l) Details of any claim or litigation pending, or a statement that there is none.
(m) Statement that no long service agreements will prevent disposal of management.
(n) Declaration, where applicable, that no other capital issues have been made; options granted; commissions, brokerages, or other special terms granted within past two years.
(o) Statement that any experts contributing to the prospectus (normally accountants and surveyors) have given and have not withdrawn their consent to the issue of the prospectus and to the inclusion of their report.
(p) A statement that copies of all relevant documents supporting the prospectus may be examined during a period of not less than 14 days at a place within the City of London.
(q) The address(es) at which copies of the prospectus may be obtained.
21. The date.

Section 67 of the Companies Act 1985, provides

67.—(1) Where a prospectus invites persons to subscribe for a company's shares or debentures, compensation is payable to all those who subscribe for any shares or debentures on the faith of the prospectus for the loss or damage which they may have sustained by reason of any untrue statement included in it.
(2) The persons liable to pay the compensation are—
(*a*) every person who is a director of the company at the time of the issue of the prospectus,
(*b*) every person who authorised himself to be named, and is named, in the prospectus as a director or as having agreed to become a director (either immediately or after an interval of time),
(*c*) every person being a promoter of the company, and
(*d*) every person who has authorised the issue of the prospectus.

Section 68 of the Act contains certain exemptions from liability if a person can show that

(i) having consented to become a director he withdrew his consent before the issue of the prospectus and that it was issued without his authority or consent, or
(ii) that the prospectus was issued without his knowledge, etc., and on becoming aware of its issue he forthwith gave reasonable public notice that it was issued without his knowledge, etc., or
(iii) that after issue of the prospectus and before allotment under it he, on becoming aware of any untrue state-

ment in it, withdrew his consent to its issue and gave reasonable public notice of the withdrawal and of the reason for it.

The Section also includes exemptions if a person can show that he has reasonable grounds to believe that the statements in the prospectus were true and that in the case of incorrect statements made by experts, that he, the director or the promoter, believes that the expert was competent to make the statement and had given consent for its issue and had not withdrawn that consent, etc.

The term 'prospectus' is used not only in relation to companies registered under the Companies Acts, whether listed on the Stock Exchange or not, but also to issues of Government and public authority stocks. SEE ALSO *Prospectus Issue*

PROSPECTUS ISSUE This is the offer of securities direct to the public by means of a full prospectus. It may, for example, apply to an issue of Government stock or public authority stocks and, at one time, it was fairly common for companies registered under the Companies Acts to issue shares in this way. A prospectus issue has the disadvantage that, until the applications are received, it is not known whether all the shares have been taken up unless the issue has been underwritten. A more usual method of offering shares to the public is through an offer for sale (q.v.).

PROTECTION OF DEPOSITORS ACT 1963 The purpose of this Act was to introduce a measure of control over the practice of advertising for deposits. Companies seeking to advertise in this way had to satisfy regulations laid down by the Department of Trade and Industry. Advertisements had to be acceptable to the Department and up-to-date accounts had to be supplied for the Department and for the information of depositors. The Act did not apply to building societies, friendly societies, industrial and provident societies, local authorities, savings banks and banks exempted under the Companies Act 1948.

The Protection of Depositors Act was repealed by the Banking Act 1979 (q.v.), which introduced a new system for the licencing of deposit-taking institutions.

PROTECTIVE TRUSTS Protective trusts may arise under Section 33 of the Trustee Act 1925, or under some more specific provision in a trust instrument. Under a protective trust, whether statutory or otherwise, the beneficiary has an interest in the income of a settled fund during his life, subject to the proviso that if he becomes bankrupt or charges his interest in any way, or in the event of a number of other similar circumstances, his right to the income ceases and certain discretionary trusts come into operation. The purpose of such trusts is to protect a beneficiary from the consequences of his own bankruptcy. Because the income in question would cease to be payable as of right in the event of bankruptcy, the funds do not pass to the trustee in bankruptcy (q.v.), the interest of the beneficiary from that point, becoming merely at the discretion of the settlement trustees.

PROTEST A protest is the official certificate given by a notary public respecting the dishonour of a bill of exchange by non-acceptance or non-payment. When a bill is dishonoured, a holder may hand it to a notary public to be protested. The notary presents it again to the drawee or to the acceptor, and if acceptance of payment is still not obtained, a note of the facts is made upon the bill, or upon a slip attached to the bill, which act constitutes a 'noting' of the bill. SEE *Noting*. The official certificate, or protest, may be extended subsequently, as of the date of the noting. The bill may be noted on the day of its dishonour, and must be noted not later than the next succeeding business day.

It is not necessary to note or protest inland bills in order to preserve the recourse against the drawer or indorsers, although they are sometimes noted. However, in the case of foreign bills, it is necessary to have them noted and protested, unless the remitter of the bills sends instructions that they are not to be noted or protested. A bill drawn in Eire and payable in England is a foreign bill within the meaning of the Bills of Exchange Act, and if dishonoured by non-acceptance or non-payment must be noted or protested. SEE UNDER *Foreign Bill*

Bills must first be protested if they are to be accepted for honour or paid for honour. SEE *Acceptance for Honour; Payment for Honour*

Where an acceptor has become bankrupt or has disappeared, a bill is sometimes protested 'for better security'. In such a case, the bill would be presented at the address of the acceptor (not at the bank where it may have been accepted payable) and better security asked for, and be protested accordingly.

The rules regarding the noting of protest of a bill are contained in Section 51 of the Bills of Exchange Act 1882:

(1) Where an inland bill has been dishonoured it may, if the holder think fit, be noted for non-acceptance or non-payment, as the case may be; but it shall not be necessary to note or protest any such bill in order to preserve the recourse against the drawer or indorser.

(2) Where a foreign bill, appearing on the face of it to be such, has been dishonoured by non-acceptance it

must be duly protested for non-acceptance, and where such a bill, which has not been previously dishonoured by non-acceptance, is dishonoured by non-payment it must be duly protested for non-payment. If it be not so protested the drawers and indorsers are discharged. Where a bill does not appear on the face of it to be a foreign bill, protest thereof in case of dishonour is unnecessary.

(3) A bill which has been protested for non-acceptance may be subsequently protested for non-payment.

(4) Subject to the provisions of this Act, when a bill is noted or protested, *it may be noted on the day of its dishonour, and must be noted not later than the next succeeding business day*. (As amended by the Bills of Exchange (Time of Noting) Act, 1917.) When a bill has been duly noted, the protest may be subsequently extended as of the date of the noting.

(5) Where the acceptor of a bill becomes bankrupt or insolvent or suspends payment before it matures, the holder may cause the bill to be protested for better security against the drawer and indorsers.

(6) A bill must be protested at the place where it is dishonoured: Provided that—

(*a*) When a bill is presented through the post office, and returned by post dishonoured, it may be protested at the place to which it is returned and on the day of its return if received during business hours, and if not received during business hours, then not later than the next business day:

(*b*) When a bill drawn payable at the place of business or residence of some person other than the drawee, has been dishonoured by non-acceptance, it must be protested for non-payment at the place where it is expressed to be payable, and no further presentment for payment to, or demand on, the drawee is necessary.

(7) A protest must contain a copy of the bill, and must be signed by the notary making it, and must specify—

(*a*) The person at whose request the bill is protested:

(*b*) The place and date of protest, the cause or reason for protesting the bill, the demand made, and the answer given, if any, or the fact that the drawee or acceptor could not be found.

(8) When a bill is lost or destroyed, or is wrongly detained from the person entitled to hold it, protest may be made on a copy or written particulars thereof.

(9) Protest is dispensed with by any circumstance which would dispense with notice of dishonour. Delay in noting or protesting is excused when the day is caused by circumstances beyond the control of the holder, and not imputable to his default, misconduct, or negligence. When the cause of delay ceases to operate the bill must be noted or protested with reasonable diligence.

Section 93 of the Act defines when noting is equivalent to protest:

For the purposes of this Act, where a bill or note is required to be protested within a specified time or before some further proceeding is taken, it is sufficient that the bill has been noted for protest before the expiration of the specified time or the taking of the proceeding; and the formal protest may be extended at any time thereafter as of the date of the noting.

Where a notary public is not accessible, Section 94 of the Act makes provision for a bill to be protested by a householder or substantial resident of the place, in the presence of two witnesses. The words of the Section are

Where a dishonoured bill or note is authorised or required to be protested, and the services of a notary cannot be obtained at the place where the bill is dishonoured, any householder or substantial resident of the place may, in the presence of two witnesses, give a certificate, signed by them, attesting the dishonour of the bill, and the certificate shall in all respects operate as if it were a formal protest of the bill.

The form given in Schedule 1 to this Act may be used with necessary modifications, and if used shall be sufficient.

SCHEDULE 1

Form of protest which may be used when the services of a notary cannot be obtained.

Know all men that I, A B (householder, of in the county of , in the United Kingdom, at the request of C D, there being no notary public available, did on the day of , I . . ., at , demand payment (or acceptance) of the bill of exchange hereunder written, from E F, to which demand he made answer (state answer, if any) wherefore I now, in the presence of G H and J K, do protest the said bill of exchange.

Signed A B

G H }
J K } Witnesses

N.B.—The bill itself should be annexed, or a copy of the bill and all that is written thereon should be underwritten.

It is to be observed that G H and J K are merely witnesses to A B's signature, not witnesses to the presentment of the bill.

When this form of protest is used it is not preceded by 'noting'. The Act does not specifically refer to 'noting', but the above Section enacts that the certificate shall in all respects operate as if it were a formal protest of the bill. No stamp duty is payable on a householder's protest (see below).

A holder of a dishonoured bill may recover from any party liable on the bill the expenses of noting, or, when protest is necessary, and the protest has been extended, the expenses of protest (Section 57(1)(*c*)). Where payment is made to a notary when he presents the bill, the acceptor should pay the notary's charges, though it has been decided that, in such a case, the notary's charges cannot be enforced by law against the acceptor.

Where a foreign bill has been accepted or paid as to part, it must be protested as to the balance.

Where a foreign promissory note is dishonoured protest thereof is unnecessary (Section 89(4)).

The date on which bills are to be protested in foreign countries depends upon the laws of those countries.

Stamp duty on protests was abolished by the Finance Act 1949. SEE *Bill of Exchange; Noting*

Sometimes as between a collecting banker and his foreign principal there will be a specific instruction to protest. This of course should be obeyed. It may well be because it is better evidence, or perhaps the only acceptable evidence abroad, of dishonour.

PROVABLE DEBTS Those debts which a creditor is entitled to prove against a bankrupt's estate. SEE *Proof of Debts*

PUBLIC COMPANY Under the Companies Act 1985, a public company means a company limited by shares or limited by guarantee and having a share capital being a company

1. the memorandum of which states that the company is to be a public company, and
2. in relation to which the provisions of the Companies Acts as to the registration or re-registration of the company as a public company have been complied with on or after 22nd December 1980.

Those provisions are

1. The names as stated in the memorandum must include the words 'public limited company' or the abbreviation 'plc'.
2. The memorandum must state that it is to be a public company and the memorandum must be in the form required by the Act (see below).
3. There must be at least *two* subscribers (under the 1948 Companies Act, seven subscribers were necessary for registration as a public company).
4. The amount of the share capital stated in the memorandum must not be less than £50,000.

The requirements as to the memorandum (see (2) above) are

1. that the memorandum must state that the company is to be a public company, and
2. the company memorandum shall be in such form as shall be specified by regulations made by the Secretary of State or as near thereto as circumstances permit. SEE *Memorandum of Association*

PUBLIC EXAMINATION OF DEBTOR When a receiving order has been made, the debtor must within three days, if the order is made on the debtor's petition, or within seven days if made upon the petition of a creditor, submit a statement of his affairs to the official receiver. SEE *Receiving Order*

Section 15 of the Bankruptcy Act, which deals with the public examination of a debtor, is as follows.

(1) Where the Court makes a receiving order, it shall, save as in this Act provided, hold a public sitting on a day to be appointed by the Court, for the examination of the debtor, and the debtor shall attend thereat and shall be examined as to his conduct, dealings, and property.

(2) The examination shall be held as soon as conveniently may be after the expiration of the time for the submission of the debtor's statement of affairs.

(3) The Court may adjourn the examination from time to time.

(4) Any creditor who has tendered a proof, or his representative authorised in writing, may question the debtor concerning his affairs and the causes of his failure.

(5) The official receiver shall take part in the examination of the debtor; and for the purpose thereof, if specially authorised by the Board of Trade, may employ a solicitor with or without counsel.

(6) If a trustee is appointed before the conclusion of the examination, he may take part therein.

(7) The Court may put such questions to the debtor as it may think expedient.

(8) The debtor shall be examined upon oath, and it shall be his duty to answer all such questions as the Court may put or allow to be put to him. Such notes of the examination as the Court thinks proper shall be taken down in writing, and shall be read over either to or by the debtor and signed by him, and may thereafter, save as in this Act provided, be used in evidence against him; they shall also be open to the inspection of any creditor at all reasonable times.

(9) When the Court is of opinion that the affairs of the debtor have been sufficiently investigated, it shall by order declare that his examination is concluded, but such order shall not be made until after the day appointed for the first meeting of creditors.

SEE *Bankruptcy*

PUBLIC TRUSTEE The office of Public Trustee was created by the Public Trustee Act 1906, which came into operation on 1st January, 1908. The Act was passed with the express object of enabling the public to guard against the risks and inconveniences which are incidental to the employment of private individuals in trust matters. The Act was the culmination of 20 years of campaigning and sponsorship of various bills by Sir Howard Vincent, MP. The Act not only created the office of Public Trustee with power to charge for his services but also empowered banks and insurance companies and the like to act as Custodian Trustees (with power to charge fees) where the active management of a trust remained with private individuals.

The Public Trustee is authorized, if duly appointed, to act in any of the following capacities.

1. Executor or administrator of estates
(a) as executor and/or trustee (and guardian of infants);
(b) as administrator in place of executors appointed by will or where there is no executor;
(c) as administrator of intestates' estates, i.e. where there is no will.

2. Trustee
(a) as trustee of a new settlement;
(b) as trustee under a Declaration of Trust;
(c) as trustee of an old settlement, e.g. marriage settlement or settlement made by will;
(d) as custodian trustee;
(e) as trustee by appointment in a will.

3. Administrator of estates of small value.

4. Investigator and auditor of the accounts of trusts not administered by the Public Trustee.

The Public Trustee has, in addition to certain privileges conferred upon him by the Act, all the same powers, duties, and liabilities, and is entitled to the same rights and immunities, and is subject to the control and orders of the court, as a private trustee acting in the same capacity. The Public Trustee may, however, decline either absolutely or except on conditions prescribed by the rules, to accept any trust but he cannot decline on the ground only of the small value of the property. He may not accept any trust under a deed of arrangement for the benefit of creditors, nor for the administration of any estate known or believed by him to be insolvent, nor made solely by way of security for money, nor exclusively for religious or charitable purposes.

Wills

The Public Trustee may be appointed either alone or jointly with any other person or persons as executor, or as trustee, or as executor and trustee of a will, and either as ordinary trustee or custodian trustee.

The substitution of the name of the Public Trustee in a will already in existence for the names of the executors and trustees named therein, or the addition of his name, can be effected by a simple codicil. The Public Trustee's acceptance of the office need not be invited at the time the will or codicil is made, although it is desirable that this course should be adopted when the trust is of an unusual nature.

On the death of the testator it is the duty of the co-executor, if any, to enquire of the Public Trustee if he is prepared to act. On acceptance of office, he executes an instrument of consent.

Even after probate has been obtained an executor may, with the sanction of the court, renounce in favour of the Public Trustee.

The Public Trustee may be appointed either as an original trustee of a settlement, or as a new trustee in an existing settlement when a vacancy arises in the trusteeship by death, or by one or more of the trustees desiring to retire. In the case of an existing settlement, the persons entitled to appoint the Public Trustee are the person or persons having power to do so under the settlement, or if there are no such persons, then the continuing or surviving trustees or their executors or administrators. Enquiry should first be made if he will accept office, and notice should be sent to all persons beneficially interested to ascertain if they are aggreeable to the appointment.

Private trustees may retire, either singly or together, in favour of the Public Trustee.

The Public Trustee may be appointed custodian trustee. On appointment, all securities and documents of title relating to the trust property, which would otherwise have remained in the custody of the ordinary trustees, are to be transferred to the Public Trustee; but the management of the trust property, as distinct from the custody of the securities, is to remain in the hands of the ordinary or managing trustees.

Under the Public Trustee Act, a trustee or beneficiary can obtain an audit of trust accounts without applying to the court. Formal application must be made to the Public Trustee for the audit.

As a rule, the Public Trustee may not aggree to act as ordinary trustee where the trust involves the carrying on of a business, except where the carrying on of the business has for its ultimate object the sale or winding up of the business. But if he is to act merely as custodian trustee the carrying on of the business is immaterial, but he must not act in the management of the business, or hold any property which will expose the holder to any liability unless fully secured against loss.

The Public Trustee may employ such bankers and other persons as he may consider necessary, and in determining who is to be employed he is to have regard to the interests of the trust, and when practicable to take into consideration the wishes of the creator of the trust and of the other trustees, if any, either expressed or as implied by the practice of the creator of the trust or in the previous management of the trust.

Fees
The Public Trustee's fees are revised from time to time by Order in Council. The current fees (with effect from 1st April, 1985) are as follows:

Executorship fees

On the first £50,000	5½%
On the excess over £50,000 up to £75,000	4 %
On the excess over £75,000 up to £100,000	2 %
On the excess over £100,000	1%

Minimum fee £550

Acceptance fee (other than executorships)
One-half of the fees shown for executorships 2%

Acceptance fee (Declarations of Trust)

On the first £50,000	1¼%
On any excess over £50,000	½%

Minimum fee £175

Administration fee
This is a fee payable at the commencement of each financial year other than the first year and excluding cases where the Public Trustee acts as executor.

The fee is payable annually on the net capital value of the estate according to the following scale:

On the first £5,000	2½%
On the excess over £5,000, up to £10,000	2%
On the excess over £10,000, up to £50,000	1½%
On the excess over £50,000, up to £100,000	1%
On the excess over £100,000, up to £1,000,000	¾%
On any excess over £1,000,000	¼%

On Declarations of Trust, the administration fee is charged at the rate of three eighths of the rates shown above.

Withdrawal fee A withdrawal fee is payable when the Public Trustee ceases to act in any estate or trust or upon the withdrawal or distribution of part of an estate or trust, except where an executorship fee is payable or where trust property is held under a declaration of trust, in favour of one beneficiary and the property is transferred to a new executorship or a new trust accepted by the Public Trustee.

A withdrawal fee is charged at the rate of 4½ times the effective rate of the administration fee on the value of property withdrawn or distributed.

Fees for special services These include fees for tax work, investment sales and purchases, income collection and fees for additional work and duties of an unusual, complex or exacting nature.

PUISNE MORTGAGE A legal mortgage not protected by the deposit of the relative title deeds. It can be protected by registration as a Class C(i) charge on the Land Charges Register. Priority of puisne mortgages depends not on the date of their creation, but on the date of their registration. SEE *Land Charges Act; Mortgage*

PUT SEE *Option*

PUT AND CALL SEE *Option*

Q

QUALIFICATION SHARES The number of shares which is required to be held by a director of a company to qualify him for the office. The Companies Act does not provide for any special qualification, but in many companies a qualification is fixed by the Articles of Association. SEE *Directors*

QUALIFIED ACCEPTANCE SEE *Acceptance, Qualified*

QUALIFIED INDORSEMENT SEE *Indorsement*

QUALIFIED TITLE A type of title registered under the Land Registration Act 1925. It was devised to meet cases where the title can only be established for a limited period and is practically unknown. SEE *Land Registration*

QUALIFYING LIFE POLICY A policy which qualifies for relief for income tax purposes, both on the amount of the premiums if the policy was taken out before 14th March, 1984 and on the eventual proceeds. It must be a policy on which regular preimums are paid, whether annually or, more frequently, for a period of ten years or more. Premiums must be fairly evenly spread over the life of the policy. The policy will cease to qualify if the premiums payable in any one year are more than twice the premiums paid in any other year. In the first ten years, the premiums paid in any one year must not exceed one-eighth of the total premiums paid in the ten years. Thus, single premium policies and certain variations of single-premium policies are not 'qualifying' policies for tax purposes.

In the case of policies taken out after 1st April, 1976, the sum assured on a whole life policy must be not less than 75 per cent of the total premiums payable if death occurred at the age of 75 years.

In the case of an endowment policy taken out since 1st April, 1976, the sum assured must be not less than 75 per cent of the toal premiums paid during the term of the policy. There is an exception to this in the case of policies taken out by a person aged 55 or more, the stipulated proportion of 75 per cent, being reduced by two per cent for each year by which the proposer's age exceeds 55.

Qualifying policies include most forms of life policy, e.g. whole life, term assurance, endowment assurance, mortgage protection and family income policies.

Income tax relief arises in two respects: on premiums and on the proceeds of the policy, as explained below.

Income Tax Relief on Premiums

With effect from 5th April, 1979, new rules came into operation in relation to tax relief on life assurance premiums. Previously, it was necessary for taxpayers to claim relief for life assurance premiums in their annual claim for allowances. From April 1979 onwards, however, the relief is automatically deducted from all qualifying life assurance premiums. The rate of relief for 1979–80 and 1980–81 was $17\frac{1}{2}$ per cent. Under the 1980 Finance Act, this was reduced to 15 per cent with effect from 6th April, 1981.

The total relief available to each taxpayer is on £1,500 per annum or one-sixth of his or her total taxable income, whichever is the larger.

If the amount deducted from premiums exceeds the total available relief, the income tax assessment for that year will be correspondingly adjusted; or if it is a continuing situation, the Inland Revenue may require some or all of the premiums to be paid without deduction of the tax subsidy. In the case of married couples, the total tax relief available is on £1,500 or one-sixth of their total combined incomes, whichever is the greater, regardless of whether or not they are separately assessed. In order to qualify for relief, the life policy or policies must be on the life of the claimant or that of his or her wife or husband.

A taxpayer may, if he so wishes, elect to pay his life assurance premiums gross and claim from the Revenue any tax allowance to which he may be entitled.

If a qualifying policy is surrendered or converted to a paid-up policy during the first four years of the policy's life, the Inland Revenue will 'claw-back' some or all of the relief already allowed. In the event of surrender in (1) the first two years, (2) the third year, or (3) the fourth year, the Inland Revenue will 'claw-back'

1. 15%,
2. 15% × $\frac{2}{3}$ = 10% and
3. 15% × $\frac{1}{3}$ = 5%, respectively of the premiums paid.

The insurance company will be required to deduct this claw-back from the amount of the policy surrender proceeds.

The same rules apply to the converting of a policy to a paid-up policy or to the surrender of a bonus.

Tax relief on life assurance premiums does not apply to policies taken out after 13th March, 1984, nor does it apply to policies taken out on or before that date if such policies are varied or enhanced after that date. The relief continues, however, for all other life policies taken out before 14th March, 1984.

Freedom from Tax on Policy Proceeds
No basic rate income tax or capital gains tax is payable on the proceeds of a life policy whether it be a qualifying policy or not (other than the possibility of claw-back referred to above).

Under the provisions of the Finance Act 1975, however, higher-rate income tax may be payable on some part of the proceeds of a non-qualifying policy (e.g. a single premium policy) on the happening of a chargeable event, namely, (1) the death of the life assured; (2) the maturity of the policy; (3) the surrender or partial surrender of the policy; or (4) any assignment of the policy for money or money's worth.

As mentioned above, no income tax is payable on the policy proceeds (income tax having been paid by the life assurance company during the life of the policy). Any charge to higher-rate tax is calculated in the following way on the happening of any of the chargeable events:

1. The gain on the policy, i.e. the proceeds, less the amount of any premiums paid is divided by the number of full years for which the policy has been in force.
2. The amount so calculated is added to the taxpayer's other taxable income for the year in which the chargeable event occurs in order to determine the rate of higher-rate tax appropriate to the chargeable gain.
3. The whole gain is then charged to higher-rate tax at the rate so calculated.

By virtue of the Finance Act 1975 a policy-holder of a non-qualifying policy may surrender up to five per cent of the total premium or premiums paid without giving rise in that year to a chargeable event. Partial surrenders may continue up to the same amount in subsequent years to a total level of 100 per cent of the premiums paid. Thus, a policy-holder may surrender five per cent per annum for 20 years without a charge for tax arising in those years.

On the happening of a chargeable event, however, e.g. the death of the policy-holder or complete surrender of the policy, the charge to higher-rate tax is calculated as described above, the total gain on the policy being brought into account, including the amount of partial surrenders over the years.

QUARTER DAYS The English Quarter Days are

Lady Day	25 March
Midsummer Day	24 June
Michaelmas	29 September
Christmas Day	25 December

The Scottish Quarter Days are

Candlemas	2 February
Whitsunday	15 May
Lammas	1 August
Martinmas	11 November

QUARTER-UP A basis of valuation of quoted securities, so named because it is based on the quoted bid price (q.v.) plus one-quarter of the difference between the bid price and the offer price. This is a standard basis of valuation of quoted securities for probate purposes.

QUASI-NEGOTIABLE INSTRUMENTS Certain mercantile documents possess some, but not all, of the qualities of negotiable instruments and are thus called quasi-negotiable or semi-negotiable instruments.

The outstanding example of this type is the bill of lading (q.v.). It is capable of transfer or assignment by indorsement and delivery, and the assignee will acquire a right to the goods and a right to sue on the contract in his own name. Thus far the bill of lading is comparable to a fully negotiable instrument: but it ordinarily lacks the remaining quality of conferring a good title on an innocent transferee for valuable consideration, irrespective of prior absence or defect of title. There is, however, an exception to this rule in that an innocent sub-buyer can retain the goods represented by the bill against the unpaid seller in certain circumstances. Thus if the bill has been lawfully transferred to any person as buyer or owner of the goods, and that person transfers the bill to an innocent sub-buyer by way of sale, the unpaid seller's rights of lien of stoppage in transitu are defeated. SEE *Negotiable Instrument; Sale of Goods*

QUICK SUCCESSION RELIEF This provides a graduated relief from capital transfer tax, where there are two or more chargeable events, e.g. two deaths affecting the same property in a short period. If that happens, the tax on the second event will be reduced by a percentage of the tax paid on that property on the previous chargeable event. If the successive events arise within one year, relief is 100 per cent. It is reduced to 80 per cent, 60 per cent, 40 per cent and 20 per cent respectively, depending on whether the event occurs in the second, third, fourth or fifth years.

QUORUM Latin for 'of whom'. For example, there may be ten directors 'of whom' three may act. A quorum is the number of persons which must be present at a meeting of the directors or members of a company, before any business can be done. In companies governed by Table A of the Companies Act 1948, a quorum for a general meeting was three members. Under the Companies Act 1980, however, two members constitute a quorum for any company, public or private, unless the articles stipulate otherwise.

QUOTATION This is the price of a stock or share usually giving both the bid price (q.v.) and offer price (q.v.). The granting of a quotation means that the security concerned and the current price will be listed in the Official List of the Stock Exchange. SEE *Stock Exchange*

R

RACK RENT A rent which, as its name implies, has been stretched or raised to the full annual value of the property.

RANDOM WALK HYPOTHESIS A theory of stock market performance, principally developed in the USA, which holds the view that, particularly in the short term, stock market prices do not behave according to any rational or identifiable pattern—in other words, that markets behave in a random fashion, more attributable to chance than any scientific factors. This is in contrast to the efficient market hypothesis which contends that stock markets react in an efficient or near-perfect fashion in relation to all available data which may affect the performance of a particular share price at a particular time. SEE ALSO *Charts, Chartists*

RATE OF EXCHANGE The price of money in one country stated in the currency of another country. SEE *Bill of Exchange; Currency*

The following table shows the average daily telegraphic transfer rates for some of the world's principal currencies for the years 1979 to 1984:

	United States dollar	*Canadian dollar*	*Belgian franc*	*Swiss franc*	*French franc*	*Italian lira*	*Netherlands guilder*
1979	2.1225	2.4863	62.20	3.5266	9.0253	1,763	4.2558
1980	2.3281	2.7206	67.97	3.8938	9.8250	1,992	4.6211
1981	2.0254	2.4267	74.81	3.9690	10.9356	2,287	5.0289
1982	1.7489	2.1573	79.84	3.5467	11.4846	2,364	4.6675
1983	1.5158	1.8680	77.47	3.1822	11.5471	2,302	4.3251
1984	1.3364	1.7290	76.96	3.1301	11.6349	2,339	4.2738

	Deutsche mark	*Swedish krona*	*Norwegian kroner*	*Danish kroner*	*Austrian schilling*	*Spanish peseta*	*Irish pound*	*Japanese yen*
1979	3.888	9.0919	10.7364	11.165	28.36	142.38		465.55
1980	4.227	9.8387	11.4847	13.104	30.07	167.10	1.1319	525.59
1981	4.556	10.1919	11.5704	14.351	32.11	185.92	1.2520	444.63
1982	4.243	10.9627	11.2629	14.568	29.83	191.81	1.2313	435.20
1983	3.870	11.6217	11.0471	13.862	27.22	217.49	1.2195	359.93
1984	3.791	11.0269	10.8454	13.794	26.40	214.30	1.2320	316.80

RE-ACCEPTANCE SEE *Acceptance*

REAL ESTATE, REALTY SEE *Personal Estate, Personalty*

RECEIPT A receipt is a written acknowledgment of having received a sum of money. 'A receipt is not required to be given in a ready-money transaction' (*Bussey* v *Barnett* 9 M&W 312).

The Stamp Act 1891 required all receipts given for, or upon the payment of, money amounting to £2 or upwards, with certain specified exceptions, to be stamped 1d. This was increased to 2d by the Finance Act 1920, and abolished as from 1st February 1971 by the Finance Act 1970.

Where a debt is paid by cheque, it is not necessary to state on the receipt that payment was made by cheque, as the person taking the cheque, can, in the event of the cheque being dishonoured, sue the debtor for the amount.

By Section 3 of the Cheques Act 1957, 'an un-indorsed cheque which appears to have been paid by the banker on whom it is drawn is evidence of the receipt by the payee of the sum payable by the cheque'. This is thought to be declaratory of the earlier law. It is, of course, evidence of the receipt of money but not, as sometimes is the case with other receipts, evidence of the transaction to which the payment relates. The only exceptional instance is if there is a narrative preceding the wording of the receipt on the back of the cheque.

RECEIPT ON CHEQUE In some cases, customers use cheques with a form of receipt upon the face or upon the back, such receipt being, in most cases, the only one which the drawer of the cheque requires from the person to whom the cheque is payable. A document of this description is sometimes worded

Pay ... or order the sum of ... when the receipt on the back hereof has been duly signed and dated.

The printed form on the back may be

Received from ... the amount named on the face hereof. Date ... 19...

Below the receipt the following words are sometimes printed: 'The receipt as above is also the indorsement of the cheque and is the only acknowledgement required.'

The receipt, instead of being on the back, is, as mentioned, sometimes on the face, below the drawer's signature, and in addition to the receipt being signed the document may require to be indorsed.

Such a document does not agree with the definition of a cheque in the Bills of Exchange Act 1882. To comply with that Act a cheque must be an unconditional order in writing. In the form above given, the order to pay is conditional upon the receipt being duly completed.

The paying banker is protected as far as such instruments are concerned by Section 1 of the Cheques Act 1957, which provides (in subsection (2))

> Where a banker in good faith and in the ordinary course of business pays any such instrument as the following, namely—
>
> (a) a document issued by a customer of his which, though not a bill of exchange, is intended to enable a person to obtain payment from him of the sum mentioned in the document; he does not, in doing so, incur any liability by reason only of the absence of, or irregularity in, indorsement, and the payment discharges the instrument.

A banker might, of course, be liable to his customer for breach of duty if he paid such an instrument with an uncompleted form of receipt.

As regards a forged indorsement or receipt the banker is protected by Section 80 of the Bills of Exchange Act 1882, but not by Section 60. The latter Section is not included in those sections made applicable to instruments of this nature by Section 5 of the Cheques Act. A conditional order to pay is not negotiable and not apparently even transferable, and therefore Section 19 of the Stamp Act does not afford protection, because that Section refers to 'any draft or order drawn on a banker payable to order on demand'. The paying banker should therefore protect himself by taking an indemnity from his customer who desires to use conditional orders of this kind.

The collecting banker is protected against collecting unindorsed or wrongly indorsed conditional orders by Section 4(3) of the Cheques Act 1957, which is as follows:

> A banker is not to be treated for the purposes of this Section as having been negligent by reason only of his failure to concern himself with absence of, or irregularity in, indorsement of an instrument.

The Committee of London Clearing Bankers issued a circular dated 23rd September, 1957, indicating the cases where indorsement would continue to be required. The following is an extract.

> *Combined cheque and receipt forms*
>
> A bold letter 'R' on the face of a cheque is to be the indication to the payee that there is a receipt which he is required to complete.
>
> Section 3 of the Act, supported by the authoritative opinion of the Mocatta Committee, should render an indorsed receipt unnecessary unless the circumstances are exceptional. This Section provides that 'an unindorsed cheque which appears to have been paid by the banker on whom it is drawn is evidence of the receipt by the payee of the sum payable by the cheque.'
>
> The Mocatta Committee expressed the opinion 'that in law a simple receipt for a payment by cheque not linking the payment with the relative transaction has no greater value as evidence of payment than the paid cheque itself. This is so whether the receipt is printed on the cheque or is issued separately.'
>
> In order that the maximum saving of labour by all concerned may be obtained as a result of the new legislation, it is hoped that it will be found possible to dispense with the use of receipt forms on cheques in all but a very limited number of cases.
>
> In this Notice references to 'cheques' include dividend and interest warrants and other analogous instruments and the term 'indorsement' includes discharge where applicable.
>
> The Clearing Banks are anxious that customers should from the outset derive every possible benefit from the new legislation, and it is hoped that it will not prove necessary in the light of experience to modify the procedure outlined above which has been designed with this object in view.

Orders issued by local authorities are frequently payable upon condition that a form of receipt is signed, and in addition they are drawn upon the treasurer, and not upon a bank, and are therefore, again, not cheques. If the treasurer pays such orders to a wrong person, he is liable to the true owner. If a banker collects one of these orders bearing a forged indorsement, he also is liable to the true owner (See further under *Local Authorities*).

In addition to the form of document given above, some cheques have a note at the foot that 'the receipt on the back hereof must be signed and dated.' In other cases no reference at all to a receipt appears on the face of the cheque, but on the back may be found a receipt such as 'Received from ... the amount named on the face hereof'.

In the cases where there is no condition attached to the order to pay, the cheque is not excluded from the definition given in the Act. A mere note at the foot, or on the back, of a cheque with respect to a receipt, and the presence of a form of receipt on the cheque, so long as the order to pay is unconditional, does not, apparently, affect the nature of the instrument. In *Nathan* v *Ogden* (1905) 21 TLR 775, where a cheque had printed at the foot the words 'the receipt at back hereof must be signed, which signature will be taken as an indorsement of the cheque', it was held that the instrument was a cheque, and that the words at the foot were not addressed to the banker and did not affect him. In practice, bankers do regard such a note on a cheque as a condition which must be fulfilled before payment of the cheque.

The practice of taking receipts on cheques diminished substantially following the passing of the Cheques Act. Where the practice continues, it is still usual for banks to require an indemnity from the customer issuing this type of cheque notwithstanding the legislative protection referred to above.

RECEIVER (COURT OF PROTECTION) A person authorized by the court to receive and administer the assets of a person certified to be mentally incapable, under the direction of the court. He must give security to the satisfaction of a judge of the court, but there is no onus on a banker to satisfy himself that this formality has been completed. A receiver's authority is found in the document known as an Order of the Court of Protection, an official copy of which should be obtained and filed. Where the Order authorizes a receiver to deal with funds or securities in a banker's hands, the receiver's receipt therefor will be a good discharge for the banker.

A receiver has no power to borrow unless authorized by the Court. His account should be earmarked with the name of the patient's estate and it is in effect a trust account. On the death of the patient, the receiver's powers cease and the deceased's assets are administered by his personal representatives. In such a case a receiver would be entitled to complete any transactions entered into before the patient's decease.

Application for the appointment of a receiver where the estate is small can be made to the Personal Application Branch of the Management and Administration Department Royal Courts of Justice, London WC2. The procedure is neither expensive nor lengthy. SEE *Mental Incapacity*

RECEIVER FOR DEBENTURE HOLDERS A debenture holder or other creditor of a company who considers that the assets of the company are in jeopardy may apply to the court for the appointment of a receiver. By Section 491 of the Companies Act 1985, the Official Receiver may be so appointed. A receiver appointed by the court will, on the application of the liquidator of a company, have his remuneration fixed by the court (Section 494).

The appointment of a receiver for debenture holders usually arises, however, where, consequent upon default in principal or interest payment or on the happening of other event mentioned in the debenture or trust deed, the stipulated number of debenture holders execute a document under hand appointing a nominee as receiver.

The appointment of a receiver must be notified by the person making the application to the court, or by the person appointing the receiver under the powers contained in the debenture, to the Registrar of Companies within seven days under a penalty of £5 for each day of default (Section 102).

A receiver must lodge six-monthly statements of accounts with the Registrar of Companies (Section 498).

Where a receiver is appointed in respect of a debenture containing a floating charge, he must be supplied within 14 days with a statement of the company's affairs in prescribed form. Within two months of the receipt of such statement, the receiver must send to the Registrar of Companies and to the bank a copy of such statement with his comments thereon. Any trustees for the debenture holders must be supplied with a summary of the statement.

Thereafter the receiver must supply the Registrar of Companies, and any trustees for the debenture holders with a summary of receipts and payments for each 12 months within two months of the expiration of such period (Section 495).

The appointment of a receiver puts into his hands all the assets which were the subject of a fixed charge in the debenture, and also 'crystallizes' any floating charge, so that he is also entitled to any assets that were covered by such floating charge.

A banker should require evidence of appointment in the shape of the Court Order or the document of appointment by the debenture holders. In the latter case, he should see a copy of the debenture to confirm that the receiver has been duly appointed and also to ascertain if the debenture gives a floating charge on the company's assets. For the receiver will ask for any credit balance to be paid over to him and this should only be done where there is such a floating charge (which will have become 'fixed' by the receiver's appointment). A debenture usually contains a provision that any receiver appointed shall be deemed to be the agent of the company in order that the company shall be liable for his remuneration, default, etc. The appointment is usually phrased 'to act as Receiver and Manager' so as to enable the receiver to run the business if so desired. On notice that a receiver has been appointed the account(s) of the company should be stopped and any cheques thereafter presented returned marked 'Receiver appointed'.

In the absence of the earlier commencement of a winding up, a credit balance cannot be retained against a receiver in respect of unmatured discounted bills, but it can be retained in respects of discounted bills overdue and unpaid, and in respect of a loan. In the latter case, this is so even if no demand for repayment has been made, for a loan payable on demand (as all bank advances are) is presently payable although no demand has been made (*Re J. Brown's Estate* [1893] 2 Ch 300).

Where a receiver appointed by the court wishes to borrow, a Court Order authorizing the borrowing and the giving of security over the company's assets must be exhibited. In the absence of a personal covenant for repayment by the receiver or the giving of priority by the court to the bank advances over the receiver's right to be indemnified out of the assets of the estate in respect of his costs and charges, etc., the receiver will have first claim against the security in respect of his expenses, etc.

In the case of a receiver appointed out of court, he has power to borrow if the debenture conferred a power to carry on the business of the company, but if practicable the debenture holders should postpone their claims on the company's assets in favour of the bank.

By Section 492 of the Companies Act 1985, a receiver appointed out of court is personally liable for any contract he enters into (e.g. for any borrowing of money). Previously he was only personally liable if he had in some explicit way admitted liability. He is, of course, entitled to be indemnified from the assets.

A receiver appointed out of court may apply to the court for directions as in the case of a receiver appointed by the court (Section 492).

It appears that a receiver may sell and that so long as the price that he obtains is, as in the case of any other mortgage, a fair price he does not have to consider any prejudice suffered by the general creditors as a result (*Re B. Johnson and Co (Builders) Ltd* [1955] Ch 634). A course that may inhibit the receiver in practice although not in law is the appointment of an inspector from the Department of Trade and Industry following a special resolution of the company pursuant to Section 432 of the Companies Act 1985 (See *R v Board of Trade Ex parte St Martins Preserving Co Ltd*, [1965] 1 QB 603).

In the case of *Standard Chartered Bank Ltd* v *Walker and Another* [1982] 3 All ER 938, it was held that where a company's banking account had been secured by guarantees, the receiver appointed under the bank's debenture owed a duty to the guarantors to use reasonable care to obtain the best possible price for the company's assets. This case also rather suggests that where a receiver has been appointed as agent for a company (as is usual in the case of bank debenture forms), the bank must not interfere unduly in the sale of the company's assets by the receiver, e.g. by pressurizing the receiver to sell the assets quickly: such interference might constitute the receiver as agent for the bank and therefore, fix the bank with liability for any negligence on the receiver's part. SEE *Companies; Mortgage; Official Receiver; Trustee for Debenture Holders; Winding Up*

RECEIVER FOR PARTNERSHIP Where the members of a firm are in disagreement, application may be made to the Court for dissolution of the firm. The Court will appoint a receiver for the purpose of winding up the business of the firm. His function is to complete existing contracts, to get in the debts owing to the firm, to realize the partnership assets, discharge the firm's debts, and distribute any surplus to the partners in accordance with the articles of partnership, if any. On the appointment of a receiver, the partners' powers to bind the firm cease, and a credit balance on the firm's account can safely be paid over to the receiver after exhibition of his appointment and identification.

In some cases, a receiver and manager is appointed by the court, who will have power not only to fulfil existing contracts, but to enter into such new contracts as are necessary for the ordinary conduct of the business.

A receiver or receiver and manager cannot validly charge any of the firm's assets as security for an advance without the court's leave. Failing a Court Order, the receiver should assume personal liability for any borrowing.

RECEIVER OF RENTS When a mortgagee by deed, through default of the mortgagor, is in a position to exercise his power of sale, he may, if he choose, appoint a receiver to collect the rents and manage the estate or business. By so doing, the mortgagee avoids the risks to which he would be liable if he entered into possession himself, as a receiver is deemed to be the agent of the mortgagor.

The Law of Property Act 1925, Section 109, defines the appointment, powers, remuneration and duties of a receiver as follows.

(1) A mortgagee entitled to appoint a receiver under the power in that behalf conferred by this Act shall not appoint a receiver until he has become entitled to exercise the power of sale conferred by this Act, but may then, by writing under his hand, appoint such person as he thinks fit to be receiver.

(2) The receiver shall be deemed to be the agent of the mortgagor; and the mortgagor shall be solely responsible for the receiver's acts or defaults, unless the mortgage deed otherwise provides.

(3) The receiver shall have power to demand and recover all the income of the property of which he is appointed receiver, by action, distress, or otherwise, in the name either of the mortgagor or of the mortgagee, to the full extent of the estate or interest which the mortgagor could dispose of, and to give effectual receipts, accordingly, for the same.

(4) A person paying money to the receiver shall not be concerned to inquire whether any case has happened to authorise the receiver to act.

(5) The receiver may be removed, and a new receiver may be appointed, from time to time by the mortgagee by writing under his hand.

(6) The receiver shall be entitled to retain out of any money received by him, for his remuneration, and in satisfaction of all costs, charges, and expenses incurred by him as receiver, a commission at such rate, not exceeding five per centum on the gross amount of all money received, as is specified in his appointment, and if no rate is so specified, then at the rate of five per centum on that gross amount, or at such higher rate as the Court thinks fit to allow, on application made by him for that purpose.

(7) The receiver shall, if so directed in writing by the mortgagee, insure and keep insured against loss or damage by fire, out of the money received by him, any building, effects, or property comprised in the mortgage, whether affixed to the freehold or not, being of an insurable nature.

(8) The receiver shall apply all money received by him as follows, namely:

(*a*) In discharge of all rents, taxes, rates, and outgoings whatever affecting the mortgaged property; and

(*b*) In keeping down all annual sums or other payments, and the interest on all principal sums, having priority to the mortgage in right whereof he is receiver; and

(*c*) In payment of his commission, and of the premiums on fire, life, or other insurances, if any, properly payable under the mortgage deed or under this Act, and the cost of executing necessary or proper repairs directed in writing by the mortgagee; and

(*d*) In payment of the interest accruing due in respect of any principal money due under the mortgage: and

(*e*) In or towards discharge of the principal money if so directed in writing by the mortgagee;

and shall pay the residue of the money received by him to the person who, but for the possession of the receiver, would have been entitled to receive the income of the mortgaged property, or who is otherwise entitled to that property.

Any order appointing a receiver or sequestrator of land may be registered under the Land Charges Act 1925. SEE *Land Charges*

Where the power of a mortgagee either to sell or appoint a receiver is made exercisable by reason of the mortgagor committing an act of bankruptcy or being adjudged a bankrupt, such power shall not be exercised only on account of the act of bankruptcy or adjudication, without the leave of the Court. This applies only to a mortgage executed after 1925 (Section 110).

If a receiver is appointed in respect of land charged by a limited company, notice of the appointment must be lodged with the Registrar of Companies, otherwise a fine for each day of default will be incurred (Companies Act 1985, Section 405).

A receiver of rents is appointed by a bank where its power of sale has arisen over property held as security, and the property has been leased by the borrower and a sale is not immediately practicable.

RECEIVING ORDER Where a debtor has committed an act of bankruptcy (q.v.), a creditor, wishing to have the estate realized under the bankruptcy law for the benefit of the creditors, may petition the court to make a receiving order. The petition may be presented either by a creditor or by the debtor himself. When a receiving order is made, it means that the court appoints the official receiver to take charge of the debtor's estate as interim trustee. The debtor is not immediately adjudged a bankrupt, but as soon as may be after making a receiving order, a meeting of creditors is held to consider whether a proposal for a composition or scheme of arrangement shall be entertained, or whether he shall be adjudged bankrupt (SEE *Meeting of Creditors*). After a receiving order has been made, a creditor cannot bring any action against the debtor unless under sanction of the court, but a creditor's power to deal with any securities he may have is not affected by the receiving order. A receiving order may be made even if there is only one creditor. As soon as convenient after the expiration of the time for the submission of a debtor's statement of affairs (see Section 14 below), the court shall hold a public sitting for the examination of the debtor (SEE *Public Examination of Debtor*). As to the validity of certain payments made before a receiving order is made or notice of the presentation of a bankruptcy petition is received, see under *Act of Bankruptcy*.

A receiving order is operative as from the beginning of the day on which it is made. The making of the order, and not notice thereof, is the determinant factor in affecting the validity of transactions with the debtor concerned. To avoid the hardships that would arise where the gazetting of a receiving order is postponed, and a banker in ignorance thereof pays the debtor's cheques, the Bankruptcy (Amendment) Act 1926, provides that where any money or property of a bankrupt has, on or after the date of the receiving order, but before notice thereof has been gazetted in the prescribed manner, been paid or transferred by a person having possession of it to some other person, and the payment or the transfer is, under the provisions of the Bankruptcy Act 1914, void as against the trustee in bankruptcy, then, if the person by whom the payment or transfer was made proves that when it was made he had not had notice of the receiving order, any right of recovery which the trustee may have against him in respect of the money or property shall not be enforced by any legal proceedings except where the court is satisfied that it is not reasonably practicable for the trustee to recover from the person to whom it was paid or transferred (Section 4). In practice, a trustee is unable to refuse to sue the person concerned if the bank offers an indemnity as to costs. This section, however, does not give any protection against payments to the debtor personally in such circumstances.

The following sections of the Bankruptcy Act 1914, deal with a bankruptcy petition and the making of a receiving order.

Jurisdiction to make receiving order

3. Subject to the provisions hereinafter specified, if a debtor commits an act of bankruptcy the Court may, on a bankruptcy petition being presented either by a creditor or by the debtor, make an order, in this Act called a receiving order, for the protection of the estate.

Conditions on which creditor may petition

4.—(1) A creditor shall not be entitled to present a bankruptcy petition against a debtor unless—

(*a*) The debt owing by the debtor to the petitioning creditor, or, if two or more creditors join in the petition, the aggregate amount of debts owing to the several petitioning creditors amounts to fifty pounds, and

(*b*) The debt is a liquidated sum payable either immediately or at some certain future time, and

(*c*) The act of bankruptcy on which the petition is grounded has occurred within three months before the presentation of the petition, and

(*d*) The debtor is domiciled in England, or, within a year before the date of the presentation of the petition has ordinarily resided, or had a dwelling-house or place of business in England, or (except in the case of a person domiciled in Scotland or Ireland or a firm or partnership having its principal place of business in Scotland or Ireland) has carried on business in England, personally or by means of an agent or manager or (except as aforesaid) is or within the said period has been a member of a firm or partnership of persons which has carried on business in England by means of a partner or partners, or an agent or manager,

nor, where a deed of arrangement has been executed, shall a creditor be entitled to present a bankruptcy petition founded on the execution of the deed, or on any other act committed by the debtor in the course or for the purpose of the proceedings preliminary to the execution of the deed, in cases where he is prohibited from so doing by the law for the time being in force relating to deeds of arrangement.

(2) If the petitioning creditor is a secured creditor, he must in his petition either state that he is willing to give up his security for the benefit of the creditors in the event of the debtor being adjudged bankrupt, or give an estimate of the value of his security. In the latter case, he may be admitted as a petitioning creditor to the extent of the balance of the debt due to him, after deducting the value so estimated in the same manner as if he were an unsecured creditor.

Proceedings and order on creditors' petition

5.—(1) A creditor's petition shall be verified by affidavit of the creditor, or of some person on his behalf having knowledge of the facts, and served in the prescribed manner.

(2) At the hearing the Court shall require proof of the debt of the petitioning creditor, of the service of the petition, and of the act of bankruptcy, or, if more than one act of bankruptcy is alleged in the petition, of some one of the alleged acts of bankruptcy, and, if satisfied with the proof, may make a receiving order in pursuance of the petition.

(3) If the Court is not satisfied with the proof of the petitioning creditor's debt, or of the act of bankruptcy, or of the service of the petition, or is satisfied by the debtor that he is able to pay his debts, or that for other sufficient cause no order ought to be made, the Court may dismiss the petition.

Debtor's petition and order thereon

6.—(1) A debtor's petition shall allege that the debtor is unable to pay his debts, and the presentation thereof shall be deemed an act of bankruptcy without the previous filing by the debtor of any declaration of inability to pay his debts, and the Court shall thereupon make a receiving order.

(2) A debtor's petition shall not, after presentment, be withdrawn without the leave of the Court.

Effect of receiving order

7.—(1) On the making of a receiving order an official receiver shall be thereby constituted receiver of the property of the debtor, and thereafter, except as directed by this Act, no creditor to whom the debtor is indebted in respect of any debt provable in bankruptcy shall have any remedy against the property or person of the debtor in respect of the debt, or shall commence any action or other legal proceedings, unless with the leave of the Court and on such terms as the Court may impose.

(2) But this Section shall not affect the power of any secured creditor to realise or otherwise deal with his security in the same manner as he would have been entitled to realise or deal with it if this Section had not been passed.

Power to appoint interim receiver

8. The Court may, if it is shown to be necessary for the protection of the estate, at any time after the presentation of a bankruptcy petition, and before a receiving order is made, appoint the official receiver to be interim receiver of the property of the debtor, or of any part thereof, and direct him to take immediate possession thereof or of any part thereof.

The official receiver may, if necessary, appoint a special manager of a debtor's estate to act until a trustee is appointed (Section 10). Every receiving order must be gazetted, and advertised in a local paper (Section 11).

Debtor's statement of affairs

14.—(1) Where a receiving order is made against a debtor, he shall make out and submit to the official receiver a statement of and in relation to his affairs in the prescribed form, verified by affidavit, and showing the particulars of the debtor's assets, debts, and liabilities, the names, residences and occupations of his creditors, the securities held by them respectively, the dates when the securities were respectively given, and such further or other information as may be prescribed or as the official receiver may require.

(2) The statement shall be so submitted within the following times, namely:

(i) If the order is made on the petition of the debtor, within three days from the date of the order:

(ii) If the order is made on the petition of a creditor, within seven days from the date of the order:

but the Court may, in either case for special reasons, extend the time.

(3) If the debtor fails without reasonable excuse to comply with the requirements of this Section, the Court may, on the application of the official receiver, or of any creditor, adjudge him bankrupt.

(4) Any person stating himself in writing to be a creditor of the bankrupt may, personally or by agent, inspect the statement at all reasonable times, and take any copy thereof or extract therefrom, but any person untruthfully so stating himself to be a creditor shall be guilty of a contempt of Court, and shall be punishable accordingly on the application of the trustee or official receiver. [SEE *Bankruptcy*]

A petition in bankruptcy and any receiving order in bankruptcy made after 1925, whether or not it is known to affect land, may be registered under the Land Charges Act 1925. SEE *Land Charges*

RECOGNIZED BANK A bank recognized as such under Section 3, Banking Act 1979 (q.v.). At the end of the 1984, there were approximately 290 banks recognized as such for the purpose of the Act.

RECOURSE Literally, a running back. In the event of a bill of exchange being dishonoured at maturity, the holder has a right of recourse against, that is a right to fall back upon, the other parties to the bill. A holder, however, has no recourse against a drawer or an indorser who qualifies his signature with the words 'without recourse', or the French equivalent *sans recours*.

REDEEMABLE DEBENTURE SEE *Debenture*

REDEEMABLE PREFERENCE SHARES By Section 58 of the Companies Act 1948, a company limited by shares could, in certain circumstances and if authorized by its articles, issue preference shares which were liable at the option of the company to be redeemed. One of the provisos in the section was that the premium, if any, payable on redemption had to be provided for out of the profits of the company or out of the company's share premium account which, in the latter case, effectively meant reduction of capital.

The Section was repealed by the Companies Act 1981, which introduced new provisions for redemption of shares. Under these provisions, companies could issue redeemable equity shares, as well as redeemable preference shares. The following are the main provisions governing the issue of redeemable shares under the 1981 Act as now re-enacted in the 1985 Act.

1. The Articles must provide for the issue of redeemable shares.
2. They may not be issued unless there are shares in issue which are not redeemable.
3. Shares redeemed must be cancelled on redemption.
4. Only fully-paid shares must be redeemed.
5. They may be redeemed only out of distributable profits or the proceeds of a new issue of shares.

6. Any premium payable on redemption must be paid out of distributable profits (except that if the shares to be redeemed were issued at a premium, the premium on redemption may be paid out of the share premium account to the extent that it does not exceed the premium originally received on the shares to be redeemed or the balance of the share premium account, whichever is the lesser).

REDEMPTION YIELD This is the anticipated total return on a fixed interest dated stock to the date of redemption. If the stock was purchased at a discount on par value, there will be a capital gain in addition to the remaining interest payment. If the stock was purchased at a premium, there will be a capital loss which must be offset against the remaining interest payments. Thus a Government stock purchased at 90 in 1985, redeemable at par in the year 2000 will have a capital gain of ten points spread over 15 years, i.e. a return of 0.66 per cent per annum, in addition to the income return. The total return is the redemption yield. Thus, the redemption yield consists of two factors: the gain or loss if the stock is held to maturity and the running interest yield. In fact the true redemption yield can be obtained only by a complicated mathematical formula because the interest yield payable, say, half-yearly, must be calculated on a compound interest basis and the capital gain or loss, which does not occur until the redemption date, must be discounted over the life of the investment. A gross redemption yield takes no account of tax. There may, therefore, be wide disparities in the redemption yield available to different classes of investors, e.g. the gross-up yield on a heavily discounted Government stock for a higher income tax paying investor is very much higher than for a basic-rate taxpayer, taking into account the tax-free capital gain in the redemption yield.

REDISCOUNT A person who has discounted a bill may, if he wish, discount it afresh with another person (SEE *Discounting a Bill*). In some countries it is usual for commercial banks to rediscount bills with the central bank, a turn being obtained in the difference between the fine rate charged by the central bank and the rate applied in the first instance.

REDUCTION OF SHARE CAPITAL The principal provisions regarding a reduction of share capital in a company limited by shares are contained in the following Sections of the Companies Act 1985

135.—(1) Subject to confirmation by the court, a company limited by shares or a company limited by guarantee and having a share capital may, if so authorised by its articles, by special resolution reduce its share capital in any way.

(2) In particular, and without prejudice to subsection (1), the company may—

(*a*) extinguish or reduce the liability on any of its shares in respect of share capital not paid up; or

(*b*) either with or without extinguishing or reducing liability on any of its shares, cancel any paid-up share capital which is lost or unrepresented by available assets; or

(*c*) either with or without extinguishing or reducing liability on any of its shares, pay off any paid-up share capital which is in excess of the company's wants;

and the company may, if and so far as is necessary, alter its memorandum by reducing the amount of its share capital and of its shares accordingly.

(3) A special resolution under this section is in this Act referred to as "a resolution for reducing share capital".

136.—(1) Where a company has passed a resolution for reducing share capital, it may apply to the court for an order confirming the reduction.

(2) If the proposed reduction of share capital involves either (*a*) diminution of liability in respect of unpaid share capital; or (*b*) the payment to a shareholder of any paid up share capital, and in any other case if the court so directs, the next three subsections have effect, but subject throughout to subsection (6).

(3) Every creditor of the company who at the date fixed by the court is entitled to any debt or claim which, if that date were the commencement of the winding up of the company, would be admissible in proof against the company is entitled to object to the reduction of capital.

(4) The court shall settle a list of creditors entitled to object, and for that purpose—

(*a*) shall ascertain, as far as possible without requiring an application from any creditor, the names of those creditors and the nature and amount of their debts or claims; and

(*b*) may publish notices fixing a day or days within which creditors not entered on the list are to claim to be so entered or are to be excluded from the right of objecting to the reduction of capital.

(5) If a creditor entered on the list whose debt or claim is not discharged or has not determined does not consent to the reduction, the court may, if it thinks fit, dispense with the consent of that creditor, on the company securing payment of his debt or claim by appropriating (as the court may direct) the following amount—

(*a*) if the company admits the full amount of the debt or claim or, though not admitting it, is willing to provide for it, then the full amount of the debt or claim;

(*b*) if the company does not admit, and is not willing to provide for, the full amount of the debt or claim, or if the amount is contingent or not ascertained, then an amount fixed by the court after the like enquiry and adjudication as if the company were being wound up by the court.

(6) If a proposed reduction of share capital involves either the diminution of any liability in respect of unpaid share capital or the payment to any shareholder of any paid-up share capital, the court may, if having regard to any special circumstances of the case it thinks proper to do so, direct that subsections (3) to (5) of this section shall not apply as regards any class or any classes of creditors.

137.—(1) The court, if satisfied with respect to every creditor of the company who under section 136 is entitled to object to the reduction of capital that either (*a*) his consent to the reduction has been obtained; or (*b*) his debt or claim has been discharged or has determined, or has been secured, may make an order confirming the reduction on such terms and conditions as it thinks fit.

(2) Where the court so orders, it may also—

(*a*) if for any special reason it thinks proper to do so, make an order directing that the company shall, during such period (commencing on or at any time after the date of the order) as is specified in the order, add to its name as its last words the words "and reduced"; and

(*b*) make an order requiring the company to publish (as the court directs) the reasons for reduction of capital or such other information in regard to it as the court thinks expedient with a view to giving proper information to the public and (if the court thinks fit) the causes which led to the reduction.

The resolution for reduction, when registered, must be embodied in every copy of the memorandum issued after its registration (Section 138).

The reason for such a reduction would usually be that through bad management, adverse trading conditions or misfortune the shares of the company have fallen so far below their nominal figure that the company decides that the capital has been irretrievably lost and should be written off the profit and loss account by reducing the nominal value of the issued share capital. After such reduction the reduced shares may then be consolidated into shares of larger amounts. For example, an issue of 100,000 25p shares may be reduced in value to 5p per share, every 20 shares then being consolidated into one £1 share.

Alternatively, the reduction may be a consequence of a period of exceptional prosperity for the company, as a result of which the shares of the company have risen far beyond their nominal value, and it is thought desirable to pay out a proportion of the reserves to the shareholders. In the latter case, the court will stipulate for a bond for the purpose of securing the rights of the creditors of the company, and it is a recognized function of bankers to give such a bond in approved cases. SEE *Company Purchase of Own Shares; Company; Share Capital*

REDUNDANCY PAYMENTS When a person is dismissed from employment because of redundancy, i.e. the job ceases to exist, he or she may be entitled to

1. a statutory redundancy payment under the Employment Protection (Consolidation) Act 1978, or
2. a payment which has been negotiated between the employer and the employee's union, or
3. an ex-gratia payment made by the employer in return for voluntary redundancy. SEE *Compensation for Loss of Office*

Statutory redundancy pay is payable by employers but may be recoverable in part from the State. It will be paid to

1. an employee (and not to a self-employed person or independent contractor),
2. a person who has been continuously employed by the same employer for at least two years since the age of 18,
3. a person who is under the normal State retirement age, and
4. a person who is 'dismissed' (e.g. has not voluntarily resigned) for redundancy (and not, for example, for misconduct).

The basis for calculation of statutory redundancy pay is:

$1\frac{1}{2}$ week's pay for each year's service between age 41 and retirement age, plus

1 week's pay for each year's service between age 22 and age 41 plus

$\frac{1}{2}$ week's pay for each year's service between age 18 and 22.

Twenty years service is the maximum which may be brought into the calculation and there is a weekly earnings limit.

SEE Supplement

REFER TO DRAWER The answer put upon a cheque by the drawee banker when dishonouring a cheque in certain circumstances. The most usual circumstance is where the drawer has no available funds for payment or has exceeded any arrangement for accommodation. The use of the phrase is not confined to this case, however, it is the proper answer to put on a cheque which is being returned on account of the service of a garnishee order; it is likewise properly used where a cheque is returned on account of the drawer being involved in bankruptcy proceedings.

Although in *London Joint Stock Bank* v *Macmillan and Arthur* [1918] AC 777, it was suggested by Lord Shaw that 'refer to drawer' could be used in cases where there were any reasonable grounds for suspecting that the cheque had been tampered with, such an answer would rarely be given in practice for any reasons other than those given above.

In *Flach* v *London & South Western Bank Ltd* [1915], 31 TLR 334, Mr Justice Scrutton said that the words 'refer to drawer' in their ordinary meaning amounted to a statement by the bank 'We are not paying; go back to the drawer and ask why' or else 'go back to the drawer and ask him to pay'.

It is doubtful whether the unjustified use of the phrase, however, will involve a banker in an action for libel, in addition to that for breach of contract. Where a non-trading customer is concerned he has to prove loss to get more than nominal damages for breach of contract, but not for libel. A trading customer can obtain substantial damages without proving specific damages, although by doing so he can increase the amount awarded.

In *Frost* v *London Joint Stock Bank* [1906] 22 TLR 760, the general rule was laid down that where words are not obviously defamatory, it is not what they might convey to a particular class of persons that is the test but what they would naturally suggest to a person of average intelligence. The better view is that the words 'refer to drawer' are not libellous. This is still the law although doubts have been expressed in the light of evidence likely to be rendered. (See, however, *Dishonour of Bill of Exchange* and cases therein quoted including *Jayson* v *Midland Bank Ltd*.)

The abbreviation 'R/D' is not permitted on cheques presented through the Clearing House; the words must be written in full. SEE *Non-payment of Bill or Cheque*

REFEREE IN CASE OF NEED The person to whom a holder of a bill of exchange may apply, in case of the bill being dishonoured by non-acceptance or non-payment. The name of a referee may be inserted in a bill by the drawer or any indorser, and is usually put in the left-hand bottom corner of the bill, as 'In case of need apply to A & B Bank, London' or 'In case of need with the English Bank Ltd, London' or 'In need with X & Y Bank'.

By Section 15 of the Bills of Exchange Act 1882

> The drawer of a bill and any indorser may insert therein the name of a person to whom the holder may resort in case of need, that is to say, in case the bill is dishonoured by non-acceptance or non-payment. Such person is called the referee in case of need. It is in the option of the holder to resort to the referee in case of need or not as he may think fit.

No liability attaches to the referee in case of need until he has accepted for honour. SEE *Acceptance for Honour; Bill of Exchange*

REFERENCE In the absence of a satisfactory introduction, a banker will normally require a reference for opening an account for a new customer. If the referee is not known to the bank, steps should be taken to follow up his reliability and trustworthiness (by banker's enquiry, for example). Apart from the desirability of confirming that the new customer is reputable, the banker who does not obtain a satisfactory reference may get no protection from liability for conversion in respect of any stolen cheques paid in by the new customer, on the grounds of negligence. SEE *Banker's Opinions; Banker and Customer*

REGISTER OF CHARGES The Registrar of Companies keeps with respect to each company a register of all charges requiring registration under Section 395 of the Companies Act 1985. The register is kept at Companies House and may be inspected by any person on payment of the prescribed fee. (See *Registration of Charges* for charges and mortgages requiring registration.)

In addition to the register at Companies House, under Section 407 every limited company must keep at its registered office a register of charges and enter therein all charges specifically affecting property of the company and all floating charges on the undertaking or any property of the company.

The register is open to inspection by any creditor or member of the company without fee and to any other person on payment of a fee.

It will be noted that the register kept at the company's own office contains all charges given by the company, whereas the register kept at Companies House is reserved for the nine specified types of charge mentioned in Section 395. SEE *Registration of Charges*

REGISTER OF COMPANIES SEE *Registrar of Companies*

REGISTER OF DIRECTORS The Companies Act 1985 (Sections 288/290) requires that every company shall keep a register containing the names, any former Christian name or surname, the nationality, addresses and occupations of its directors or managers, particulars of any other directorships held and dates of birth (where the age limit of 70 applies). Under Section 289, Companies Act 1985, the register of directors must contain details of other directorships held in the last five years but this does not need to include dormant companies. A copy of the register must be sent to the Registrar of Companies, and from time to time he must be notified of any change therein.

REGISTER OF MEMBERS OF COMPANY Section 352, Companies Act 1985, provides *inter alia*:

352.—(1) Every company shall keep a register of its members and enter in it the particulars required by this section.

(2) There shall be entered in the register—

(*a*) the names and addresses of the members;

(*b*) the date on which each person was registered as a member; and

(*c*) the date at which any person ceased to be a member.

(3) The following applies in the case of a company having a share capital—

(*a*) with the names and addresses of the members there shall be entered a statement—

(i) of the shares held by each member, distinguishing each share by its number (so long as the share has a number) and, where the company has more than one class of issued shares, by its class, and

(ii) of the amount paid or agreed to be considered as paid on the shares of each member;

(*b*) where the company has converted any of its shares into stock and given notice of the conversion to the registrar of companies, the register shall show the amount and class of stock held by each member, instead of the amount of shares and the particulars relating to shares specified in paragraph (*a*).

The following are some of the principal requirements of the Act:

Trusts not to be entered on register

No notice of any trust, expressed, implied, or constructive, shall be entered on the register, or be receivable by the registrar, in the case of companies registered in England (Section 360).

Registration of transfer at request of transferor

On the application of the transferor of any share or interest in a company, the company shall enter in its register of members the name of the transferee in the same manner and subject to the same conditions as if the application for the entry were made by the transferee (Section 183(4)).

Transfer by personal representative

A transfer of the share or other interest of a deceased member of a company made by his personal representative shall, although the personal representative is not himself a member of the company, be as valid as if he had been such a member at the time of the execution of the instrument of transfer (Section 183(3)).

Inspection of register

The register must be open, for not less than two hours each day, to the inspection of any member gratis and of any other person on payment of the appropriate charge (Section 356).

Any member or other person may obtain a copy of the register, or any part, on payment of the appropriate charge (Section 356).

Power to close register

A company may, on giving notice by advertisement in some newspaper circulating in the district in which the registered office of the company is situate, close the register of members for any time or times not exceeding in the whole thirty days in each year (Section 358).

REGISTER OF SHIPS SEE *Ship*

REGISTERED CHARGE A legal mortgage of registered land is made by the execution of a charge by deed, which is lodged at the Land Registry with a duplicate and the relative land certificate. A charge certificate is issued in which is stitched the original charge. SEE *Land Registration—mortgages of registered land*

REGISTERED LAND SEE *Land Registration*

REGISTERED OFFICE Section 287, Companies Act 1985, provides:

(1) A company shall at all times have a registered office to which all communications and notices may be addressed.

(2) Notice (in the prescribed form) of any change in the situation of a company's registered office shall be given within 14 days of the change to the registrar of companies, who shall record the new situation.

(3) If default is made in complying with subsection (1) or (2), the company and every officer of it who is in default is liable to a fine and, for continued contravention, to a daily default fine.

Section 348 provides:

(1) Every company shall paint or affix, and keep painted or affixed, its name on the outside of every office or place in which its business is carried on, in a conspicuous position and in letters easily legible.

Section 351 provides that every company shall mention the company's place of registration and the number with which it is registered in all business letters and order forms of the company.

Section 725 provides that a document may be served on a company by leaving it at or sending it by post to the company's registered office.

REGISTRAR OF COMPANIES Section 704, Companies Act 1985, provides *inter alia*:

(1) For the purposes of the registration of companies under the Companies Acts, there shall continue to be offices in England and Wales and in Scotland, at such places as the Secretary of State thinks fit.

(2) The Secretary of State may appoint such registrars, assistant registrars, clerks and servants as he thinks necessary for that purpose, and may make regulations with respect to their duties, and may remove any persons so appointed.

Section 709 provides *inter alia* that

Subject to the provisions of this section, any person may:

(*a*) Inspect a copy of any document kept by the registrar of companies or, if the copy is illegible or unavailable, the document itself,

(*b*) Require a certificate of the incorporation of any company, or a certified copy or extract of any other document or any part of any other document.

When a certificate of incorporation is given by the Registrar in respect of any association, it is conclusive evidence that all the requirements in respect of the registration of the company have been complied with.

When a certificate of the registration of any mortgage or charge is given by the Registrar, it is conclusive evidence that all the requirements of the Companies Act have been complied with.

A register of mortgages is kept by the Registrar. The register is open to inspection by any person on payment of a fee. SEE *Company; Registration of Charges*

According to the report of the Department of Trade and Industry for 1983, there were 855,710 companies in Great Britain at the end of that year and during the year a record number of 96,188 new companies were registered.

REGISTRARS IN BANKRUPTCY Section 102 of the Bankruptcy Act 1914, provides as follows:

102—(1) The registrars in bankruptcy of the High Court, and the registrars of County Courts having jurisdiction in bankruptcy, shall have the powers and jurisdiction in this Section mentioned, and any order made or act done by such registrars in the exercise of the said powers and jurisdiction shall be deemed the order or act of the Court.

(2) Subject to general rules limiting the powers conferred by this Section, a registrar shall have power—

(*a*) To hear bankruptcy petitions, and to make receiving orders and adjudications thereon:

(*b*) To hold the public examination of debtors:

(*c*) To grant orders of discharge where the application is not opposed:

(*d*) To approve compositions or schemes of arrangement where they are not opposed:

(*e*) To make interim orders in any cases of urgency:

(*f*) To make any order or exercise any jurisdiction which by any rule in that behalf is prescribed as proper to be made or exercised in chambers:

(*g*) To hear and determine any unopposed or ex *parte* application:

(*h*) To summon and examine any person known or suspected to have in his possession effects of the debtor or to be indebted to him, or capable of giving information respecting the debtor, his dealings or property.

(3) The registrars in bankruptcy of the High Court shall also have power to grant orders of discharge and certificates of removal of disqualifications, and to approve compositions and schemes of arrangement.

(4) A registrar shall not have power to commit for contempt of Court.

(5) The Lord Chancellor may by order direct that any specified registrar of a County Court shall have and exercise all the powers of a registrar in bankruptcy of the High Court. [SEE *Bankruptcy*]

REGISTRATION OF BUSINESS NAMES This subject was governed by the Registration of Business Names Act 1916 until that Act was repealed by the Companies Act 1981. In summary, the effect of the Registration of Business Names Act was that a person or firm having a place of business in the UK and carrying on business under a business name were required to register that name with the Registrar of Business Names if

1. in the case of a firm the name did not consist of the true surnames of all the partners who were individuals and the corporate names of any partners who were incorporated without any addition other than the true Christian names of individual partners or the initials of those Christian names, and

2. in the case of an individual a business name which did not consist of his true surname without any addition, other than his true Christian names or the initials of those Christian names.

Any individual or firm had to register any change of name (other than the case of a woman in consequence of marriage).

Under Section 17, the Companies Act 1948 provided that the power conferred on the Registrar of Business Names under the Registration of Business Names Act 1916, to refuse registration of a business name, should be extended to any name which was in his opinion undesirable.

The requirements for registration and notification of change, etc., were not well observed and would probably have been less so but for the practice of the banks to call for the production of certificates of business names. The possible risk to a bank of not calling for a certificate was illustrated in the case of *Smith & Baldwin* v *Barclays Bank* (1944) *Journal of the Institute of*

Bankers, vol. 65, p.171, where crossed cheques payable to the Argus Press were fraudulently paid into the account with the defendant bank of B, who had been accepted as a partner in the Argus Press.

B had been satisfactorily introduced to the Bank, who entertained no doubts as to his honesty, but asked as a routine matter to see the Business Names Certificate. B was prepared for this, having already fraudulently registered himself as sole proprietor of the business. He was, therefore, able to produce it to substantiate his story of having bought the business from the Argus Press, and the bank was satisfied.

The real owners later sued the bank in conversion, and the bank relied on Section 82 of the Bills of Exchange Act 1882. It was held that there was no evidence of negligence, for the bank had discharged the onus by their enquiry as to the certificate. Although they had, even so, been deceived, they had nevertheless done all that they could reasonably be expected to do in the circumstances, and were accordingly entitled to the benefit of the Section.

As mentioned above, non-compliance with the registration requirements did much to weaken the effect of the Act but the Register did provide a useful means of tracing the ownership of unincorporated firms. However, the Act was repealed by the 1981 Companies Act and the Register of Business Names abolished.

Under the Companies Act 1981, new regulations were introduced in relation to companies and unincorporated businesses. In the case of *companies*, the Act provides that the Registrar of Companies must keep an index of limited and unlimited companies registered under the Companies Acts and of limited partnerships registered under the Limited Partnership Act 1907, and societies registered under the Industrial and Provident Societies Act 1965, and certain other corporate bodies. A company may not be registered with a name

1. which includes the name 'limited' or 'unlimited' or 'public limited company' except where such words appear at the end of the company's name, or
2. which is the same, or nearly so, as a name already registered on the index, or
3. which would in the opinion of the Secretary of State, amount to a criminal offence, or
4. which in the opinion of the Secretary of State is offensive.

In the case of *all* businesses, whether carried on by private individuals, partnerships or companies, certain rules apply under the 1981 Act if the business is carried on in a name other than

1. in the case of an individual, his or her surname;
2. in the case of a partnership, the surnames of all individual partners and the corporate names of all partners which are incorporated; and
3. in the case of a company, its corporate name.

In the case of an individual, his forenames or initials may be used and in the case of a partnership where two or more partners have the same name, the name may be used in the plural.

Any business not trading under the name of the proprietor, the partners or the company (as indicated above) are required to observe the following rules:

1. All business correspondence, all invoices, orders to suppliers, requests for payment and receipts must state legibly
(a) in the case of a partnership, the name of each partner (but see below);
(b) in the case of an individual, his own name;
(c) in the case of a company, the company's corporate name; and
(d) in all cases, an address in Great Britain, at which service of documents relating to the business will be effective.
2. On all business premises to which customers or suppliers have access, a notice containing the names and addresses referred to in (1) above must be prominently displayed.
3. Any person with whom anything is done or discussed in the way of business must be supplied, on request, with the names and addresses referred to in (1) above.

A particular exception to these rules applies to partnerships of more than 20 persons, in which case names and addresses of individual partners may be omitted but a list of the names of the partners must be kept at the principal place of business. Also in those cases, business letters, etc., must state the address of the partnership's principal place of business and indicate that the list of partners' names may be open to inspection at that address.

The Act also provides that a business to which the rules apply, i.e. one not carried on under the owners names as indicated above, may not, without the written approval of the Secretary of State, use a name which

1. would be likely to give the impression that the business is connected with the Government or a local authority, or
2. includes any word or expression which may be specified in regulations made from time to time under Statutory Instruments.

Special rules apply to those businesses which were carried on under a lawful business name prior to the coming into force of the 1981 Companies Act. In particular, a business may continue to use a name which was lawful under the old Act, notwithstanding that approval for that name would otherwise have been required under the 1981 Act. SEE ALSO *Private Company; Public Company*; Supplement

REGISTRATION OF CHARGES The provisions respecting the registration of mortgages and charges under the Land Charges Act 1925 are contained in the entries *Land Charges* and *Mortgage* and mortgages on ships in the entry *Ship*. A summary of registration of mortgages and charges and of searches in the appropriate registers is given under *Mortgage*. The provisions respecting the registration of mortgages and charges by companies are contained in this entry.

The Companies Act 1985, substantially re-enacting the provisions of the 1948 Act, provides as follows:

Registration of charges (England and Wales)

395.—(1) Subject to the provisions of this Chapter, a charge created by a company registered in England and Wales and being a charge to which this section applies is, so far as any security on the company's property or undertaking is conferred by the charge, void against the liquidator and any creditor of the company, unless the prescribed particulars of the charge together with the instrument (if any) by which the charge is created or evidenced, are delivered to or received by the registrar of companies for registration in the manner required by this Chapter within 21 days after the date of the charge's creation.

(2) Subsection (1) is without prejudice to any contract or obligation for repayment of the money secured by the charge; and when a charge becomes void under this section, the money secured by it immediately becomes payable.

396.—(1) Section 395 applies to the following charges—

(*a*) a charge for the purpose of securing any issue of debentures,

(*b*) a charge on uncalled share capital of the company,

(*c*) a charge created or evidenced by an instrument which, if executed by an individual, would require registration as a bill of sale,

(*d*) a charge on land (wherever situated) or any interest in it, but not including a charge for any rent or other periodical sum issuing out of the land,

(*e*) a charge on book debts of the company,

(*f*) a floating charge on the company's undertaking or property,

(*g*) a charge on calls made but not paid,

(*h*) a charge on a ship or aircraft, or any share in a ship,

(*j*) a charge on goodwill, on a patent or a licence under a patent, on a trademark or on a copyright or a licence under a copyright.

(2) Where a negotiable instrument has been given to secure the payment of any book debts of a company, the deposit of the instrument for the purpose of securing an advance to the company is not, for purposes of section 395, to be treated as a charge on those book debts.

(3) The holding of debentures entitling the holder to a charge on land is not for purposes of this section deemed to be an interest in land.

(4) In this Chapter, 'charge' includes mortgage.

397.—(1) Where a series of debentures containing, or giving by reference to another instrument, any charge to the benefit of which the debenture holders of that series are entitled pari passu is created by a company, it is for purposes of section 395 sufficient if there are delivered to or received by the registrar, within 21 days after the execution of the deed containing the charge (or, if there is no such deed, after the execution of any debentures of the series), the following particulars in the prescribed form—

(*a*) the total amount secured by the whole series, and

(*b*) the dates of the resolutions authorising the issue of the series and the date of the covering deed (if any) by which the security is created or defined, and

(*c*) a general description of the property charged, and

(*d*) the names of the trustees (if any) for the debenture holders,

together with the deed containing the charge or, if there is no such deed, one of the debentures of the series:

Provided that there shall be sent to the registrar of companies, for entry in the register, particulars in the prescribed form of the date and amount of each issue of debentures of the series, but any omission to do this does not affect the validity of any of those debentures.

(2) Where any commission, allowance or discount has been paid or made either directly or indirectly by a company to a person in consideration of his—

(*a*) subscribing or agreeing to subscribe, whether absolutely or conditionally, for debentures of the company, or

(*b*) procuring or agreeing to procure subscriptions, whether absolute or conditional, for such debentures,

the particulars required to be sent for registration under section 395 shall include particulars as to the amount or rate per cent of the commission, discount or allowance so paid or made, but omission to do this does not affect the validity of the debentures issued.

(3) The deposit of debentures as security for a debt of the company is not, for the purposes of subsection (2), treated as the issue of the debentures at a discount.

398.—(1) In the case of a charge created out of the United Kingdom comprising property situated outside the United Kingdom, the delivery to and the receipt by the registrar of companies of a copy (verified in the prescribed manner) of the instrument by which the charge is created or evidenced has the same effect for purposes of sections 395 to 398 as the delivery and receipt of the instrument itself.

(2) In that case, 21 days after the date on which the

instrument or copy could, in due course of post (and if despatched with due diligence), have been received in the United Kingdom are substituted for the 21 days mentioned in section 395(1) (or as the case may be, section 397(1)) as the time within which the particulars and instrument or copy are to be delivered to the registrar.

(3) Where a charge is created in the United Kingdom but comprises property outside the United Kingdom, the instrument creating or purporting to create the charge may be sent for registration under section 395 notwithstanding that further proceedings may be necessary to make the charge valid or effectual according to the law of the country in which the property is situated.

(4) Where a charge comprises property situated in Scotland or Northern Ireland and registration in the country where the property is situated is necessary to make the charge valid or effectual according to the law of that country, the delivery to and the receipt by the registrar of a copy (verified in the prescribed manner) of the instrument by which the charge is created or evidenced, together with a certificate in the prescribed form stating that the charge was presented for registration in Scotland or Northern Ireland (as the case may be) on the date on which it was so presented has, for purposes of sections 395 to 398, the same effect as the delivery and receipt of the instrument itself.

399.—(1) It is a company's duty to send to the registrar of companies for registration the particulars of every charge created by the company and of the issues of debentures of a series requiring registration under sections 395 to 398; but registration of any such charge may be effected on the application of any person interested in it.

(2) Where registration is effected on the application of some person other than the company, that person is entitled to recover from the company the amount of any fees properly paid by him to the registrar on the registration.

(3) If a company fails to comply with subsection (1), then, unless the registration has been effected on the application of some other person, the company and every officer of it who is in default is liable to a fine and, for continued contravention, to a daily default fine.

Where a company registered in England acquires any property which is subject to a charge, the company shall cause particulars of the charge to be delivered to the Registrar within 21 days after the date on which the acquisition is completed.

The Registrar of Companies shall keep, with respect to each company, a register of all the charges requiring registration. The Registrar shall give a certificate of the registration of any charge, and the certificate shall be conclusive evidence that the requirements as to registration have been complied with. The register shall be open to inspection by any person on payment of a fee.

Section 402 of the 1985 Act provides:

(1) The company shall cause a copy of every certificate of registration given under section 401 to be endorsed on every debenture or certificate of debenture stock which is issued by the company, and the payment of which is secured by the charge so registered.

(2) But this does not require a company to cause a certificate of registration of any charge so given to be endorsed on any debenture or certificate of debenture stock issued by the company before the charge was created.

(3) If a person knowingly and wilfully authorises or permits the delivery of a debenture or certificate of debenture stock which under this section is required to have endorsed on it a copy of a certificate of registration, without the copy being so endorsed upon it, he is liable (without prejudice to any other liability) to a fine.

Section 404 provides:

(1) The following applies if the court is satisfied that the omission to register a charge within the time required by this Chapter or that the omission or mis-statement of any particular with respect to any such charge or in a memorandum of satisfaction was accidental, or due to inadvertence or to some other sufficient cause, or is not of a nature to prejudice the position of creditors or shareholders of the company, or that on other grounds it is just and equitable to grant relief.

(2) The court may, on the application of the company or a person interested, and on such terms and conditions as seem to the court just and expedient, order that the time for registration shall be extended or, as the case may be, that the omission or mis-statement shall be rectified.

Every company shall keep a copy of every instrument creating any charge requiring registration to be kept at the registered office of the company: provided that in the case of a series of uniform debentures, a copy of one debenture of the series shall be sufficient (Section 406).

In *Ladenburg & Co v Goodwin, Ferreira & Co Ltd (in Liquidation), and Garnett (the Liquidator)* [1912] 3 KB 275, the plaintiffs made advances to the defendant company on the company's drafts. The company gave the plaintiffs copies of the bills of lading and invoices of goods shipped by them and a letter stating that the company hypothecated the goods or the proceeds thereof to the plaintiffs. The goods were sold by the defendant company to their customers on the terms that all charges on the goods after they left the warehouse were paid by the customers, to whom a six months' credit was given. The bills of lading were made out to the customers' orders. The company having gone into liquidation the plaintiffs claimed the proceeds of the shipments received by the defendant company or the liquidator. Pickford, J, in the course of his judgment said

It is difficult to see how any valid charge or mortgage on the goods could have been given to the plaintiffs, for there was no interest in the goods remaining in the defendant company (except in the possible case of stoppage *in transitu*). Therefore the only thing remaining which could be the subject of the hypothecation was the proceeds of the goods. ... That constitutes a book debt owing by the customer to the defendant company. ... Was it a charge on the book debts of the defendant company within the meaning of Section 93(1)(e) of the Companies (Consolidation) Act, 1908? ... I come to the conclusion that they were in this case charges on the book debts of the defendant company, and as they were not registered they are void against the liquidator, and there must be judgment for the defendants.

Where a company wrote to a Government department authorizing it to remit all moneys due under a contract direct to the company's bankers, and stating that such instructions were to be regarded as irrevocable unless the bank should consent to their cancellation, it was held that the letter amounted to an equitable assignment by way of security for the bank overdraft. It constituted a charge on book debts of the company under the Act, and not having been registered it was void as against the liquidator (*Re Kent and Sussex Sawmills Ltd* [1946] 2 All ER 638).

See also *Independent Automatic Sales Ltd and Another* v *Knowles & Foster* [1962] 1 WLR 974, in which a similar decision was given. In the course of his judgment Buckley, J, said that a book debt was one that 'would or could' be recorded in the books of the company. Whilst this is only a *dictum* and not part of the decision, it is an indication of the wide interpretation that may be given to the description.

In *Paul and Frank Ltd and Another* v *Discount Bank (Overseas) Ltd and Another* [1967] Ch 348, the assignment of money payable under an ECGD policy was held not to be a book-debt. The judgment was controversial but the law does not now appear to be in doubt.

Vacation of Registration

Section 403 provides for the vacation of the registration of a charge. SEE UNDER *Memorandum of Satisfaction*

The Act imposes heavy penalties on the company and officials for neglect to register mortgages and charges (Section 399).

The Registrar's certificate of registration should be deposited when a charge is given on the company's property.

Every company must keep at its registered office a register of mortgages and charges and enter therein

> all charges specifically affecting property of the company and all floating charges on the undertaking or any property of the company, giving in each case a short description of the property charged, the amount of the charge, and (except in the case of securities to bearer) the names of the persons entitled thereto. [Section 407]

The register shall be open to the inspection of any creditor or member, without fee, and to any other person on payment of a fee (Section 408).

By Section 709 (SEE UNDER *Registrar of Companies*) any person may inspect the documents kept by the Registrar on payment of a fee.

When the title deeds of a company are given as security, either with or without a memorandum of deposit, it is a charge, and must be registered at the date of the deposit or within 21 days therefrom.

An agreement by a company to create a charge or issue debentures at some future date or in certain circumstances *whenever called upon to do so* does not create a present right to any security and hence does not require registration under Section 395 (*In re Gregory Love & Co, Francis* v *The Company* [1916] 1 Ch 203. But where money is advanced to a company on the understanding that debentures charged on any asset of the company shall be issued as security, the lender at once gets a charge in equity, and accordingly such an agreement confers a present equitable right in equity and should be registered.

It is to be noted that, by Section 395, a charge must be registered within 21 days after the date of its creation. In *Esberger & Sons Ltd* v *Capital and Counties Bank Ltd* (1913), 109 LT 140, the company deposited deeds with the bank, with a formal document of charge, on 17th September, 1910, duly executed but without a date. On 14th June, 1911, the date was filled in by the bank manager as 14th June, 1911. It was contended that the security was void by reason of non-registration within 21 days from 17th September, 1910. For the bank it was argued that if a document is dated on a certain day and is to secure future advances and future advances are not made until a later date the creation of the charge is the date when the future advances are made, and when, therefore, the document becomes an effective docu-the future advances are made, and when, therefore, the document becomes ann effective document to secure actual money, and is not the date when the actual charge was executed. Sargant, J, in the course of his judgment said that

> where there is an instrument creating or evidencing a mortgage or charge I feel clear that, on the true meaning of Section 9 of the Companies (Consolidation) Act, 1908, the date of the creation of the mortgage or charge is the date when that instrument was executed, and is not the date when any money is subsequently advanced so as to make an effective charge for the amount of that money.

However, in the case of *Re Nye* [1970] 3 WLR 158, it was held on appeal, that despite the incorrect insertion of a date of charge by a solicitor, the certificate of registration of the charge was binding and that the registrar's certificate, once issued, was conclusive evidence that all the formalities had been correctly completed. The decision might be different, however, in a case where the rights of third parties were prejudiced.

A preliminary to making an advance to a company is to make a search of the company's file at Companies House to see if any charges by way of debenture or otherwise affect the security offered. An inspection can also be made, if desired, of the company's own register of charges kept at its registered office, to ascertain if any charges are outstanding of a type not requiring registration at Companies House.

It should be particularly noted that if a mortgage or charge, as above specified, is not registered within 21 days, it is void against a liquidator and any creditor, so far as security on the company's property is concerned, and the money payable under the charge will then rank only as an unsecured debt.

The fact that the holder of a mortgage debenture, issued by a company and registered in accordance with Section 395, had express notice of the prior creation and non-registration within the required period by that Section of a first mortgage does not prevent the unregistered first mortgage from being declared void as against the subsequent registered mortgage debenture, having regard to the provisions of the Section, notice not being material in the case of a creditor, it not being fraud to take advantage of legal rights the existence of which might be assumed to be known to the parties interested (*In re Monolithic Building Co Ltd; Tacon* v *The Company* (1915) 112 TLR 619).

In the case of *Re Mechanisations (Eaglescliffe) Ltd*, [1966] Ch 20, other creditors were held subject to the priority of a charge, which although indicating an amount extended to other items that arose after the registration and increased the total obligation. In the case of *Re Eric Holmes Ltd* [1965] 2 All ER 333, charges in fulfilment of earlier unregistered undertakings were considered. The certificate of registration was good but the charge was vulnerable as a voidable preference.

When certificates for stocks and shares, life policies, warrants for goods, or negotiable instruments belonging to a company are given as security, the charge does not require registration with the Registrar of Companies.

A mortgage or charge on a ship or any share in a ship given by a company must be registered with the Registrar of Companies (Section 395, Companies Act 1985). It must also be registered under the Merchant Shipping Act 1894. Registration under the latter Act has the effect of fixing the priority of mortgages. SEE *Ship*

By the Land Registration Act 1925 (Section 60), where a company is proprietor of any registered land, any mortgage, debenture, or other incumbrance created by the company must be registered or protected by caution under this Act, in addition to the required registration under the Companies Act.

This may be relevant to an undertaking by solicitors to hold the deeds of a company on behalf of a bank, when the deeds have not previously been in the hands of the bank and their deposit is not therefore already duly registered (see below). In practice registration is a matter of discretion because, whilst vulnerable against a liquidator or a competing mortgagee, an unregistered charge is, of course, good against the company. In practice, it is only in exceptional instances that a banker would effect registration.

By the Land Charges Act 1925, in the case of a charge on land (not registered land) for securing money, created by a company, registration under Section 395 of the Companies Act 1985, shall be sufficient in place of registration under this Act (Section 10(5)).

A mortgage by a society registered under the Industrial and Provident Societies Act 1893, does not require registration as the society does not come within the scope of the Companies Act. A charge by such a society over 'personal chattels' requires registration as a bill of sale. A debenture given by such a society creating in favour of a bank a floating charge on farming stock, may be registered as an agricultural charge (Section 14, Agricultural Credits Act 1928).

RE-ISSUE OF BILL OF EXCHANGE SEE *Negotiation of Bill of Exchange*

RELATED COMPANY Under the Companies Act 1981, Schedule 1, a related company is any corporate body (other than one in the same group as the company) in which that company holds on a long-term basis a 'qualifying capital interest' for the purpose of securing a contribution to its own activities by the exercise of any control or influence arising from that interest. 'Qualifying capital interest' means an interest in the equity capital of the corporate body in question carrying full voting rights at general meetings of that body.

There is a presumption that a company is a related company if

1. a company holds a qualifying capital interest in a corporate body, and
2. the nominal value of shares comprised in that

interest is equal to 20 per cent or more of the nominal value of all equity shares of that corporate body, carrying the rights to vote at general meetings.

RELATION BACK See Section 37, Bankruptcy Act 1914, under *Adjudication in Bankruptcy.*

REMAINDER After the death of a person who has a life interest in a property, if the property does not revert to the grantor of the life interest, or his heirs, but passes to some other person, the interest of that person in the land is called a 'remainder'.

A remainder is sometimes erroneously referred to as a reversion, or reversionary interest.

It is a contingent remainder if the vesting of the remainder is dependent upon an uncertainty, as for example where the interest has to pass, after the death of the life tenant, to a child after attaining a certain age. When the child has attained that age it becomes a vested remainder. SEE *Reversion*

The expression is also used more generally in relation to the person ultimately entitled absolutely to an interest under a trust.

REMAINDERMAN The person entitled to a remainder (q.v.).

REMEDY ALLOWANCE This is the name given to an allowance made in connection with the making of coins. The Coinage Act 1971 defines the standard weight and fineness of each coin, but as in the making of coins it is impossible to produce them absolutely in accordance with the prescribed figures, the Act allows certain variations, the 'remedy allowance', from that standard weight and fineness. In gold coins the remedy for fineness was two parts in 1,000, and in silver coins it was four, altered by the Coinage Act 1920 to five parts in 1,000. For the remedy allowed in weight per piece, see Schedule 1 to the Coinage Act, and Schedule 1 to the Decimal Currency Act 1967, under *Coinage.*

RENEWAL OF BILL By arrangement amongst the parties to a bill of exchange, the bill may be renewed, that is, a new bill may be accepted in place of the old one to run for a further period of time. If the second bill is dishonoured the rights of the parties on the first bill (if the bill was left with the holder) are revived, but those parties who did not assent to the renewal are discharged.

The practice of extending an existing bill, common in some countries, is dependent upon the concurrence of all parties, and in the UK it seems that there must be an issue of a new bill in place of the original.

RENT ALLOWANCE SEE *Housing Benefit*

RENT CHARGE An annual payment arising out of real estate. SEE UNDER *Legal Estates*

RENT REBATE SEE *Housing Benefit*

RENT RELIEF SEE *Housing Benefit*

RENUNCIATION The giving up of a right. In the case of an issue of new shares, a shareholder may accept the number of shares provisionally allotted to him, or he may renounce by signing a form of renunciation. In *Re Pool Shipping Co Ltd* [1919] 122 LT 338, where directors had power, under the articles of association, to refuse any transfer of shares of which they might not approve, and a shareholder renounced his rights to certain new shares in favour of C, the directors refusing to register C, it was held that the renunciation of rights to shares was not a transfer of shares within the meaning of the articles of association and that the directors were not entitled to refuse to register C, as holder of the shares.

When the holder of a bill at or after its maturity renounces his rights against the acceptor, the bill is discharged, but the renunciation must be in writing, unless the bill is delivered up to the acceptor. SEE *Payment of Bill*

RE-PRESENT SEE *Present Again*

REPRESENTATION SEE UNDER *Personal Representatives*

REPUTED OWNER The person who is, from the situation in which goods are found, reputed to be the owner thereof. The Bankruptcy Act 1914 includes amongst the property which is divisible amongst the creditors of a bankrupt,

> all goods being, at the commencement of the bankruptcy, in the possession, order, or disposition of the bankrupt, in his trade or business by the consent and permission of the true owner, under such circumstances that he is the reputed owner thereof; provided that things in action other than debts due or growing due to the bankrupt in the course of his trade or business shall not be deemed goods within the meaning of this Section. [Section 38(2)(c)]

In most cases the effect of this Section is in practice negatived by the custom of the trade.

RESERVE ASSET RATIO Under the Bank of England's paper *Competition and Credit Control* (q.v.), which came into effect from 16th

September, 1971, British banks were required to maintain 'eligible reserve assets' of an amount equal to not less than 12½ per cent of their 'eligible deposits'. Hitherto, the clearing banks (and not other banks) had been required to hold assets in the form of cash in hand and at the Bank of England, money at call and short notice, and bills to cover not less than 28 per cent of their deposits (30 per cent prior to 1963) with cash covering not less than eight per cent of deposits.

Eligible reserve assets were defined as balances with the Bank of England (other than Special Deposits (q.v.)), British Government and Northern Ireland Government Treasury Bills, company tax reserve certificates, money at call with the London money market, British Government stocks with one year or less to final maturity, local authority bills eligible for re-discount at the Bank of England and (up to a maximum of two per cent of eligible liabilities) commercial bills eligible for rediscount at the Bank of England.

'Eligible liabilities' were defined as the sterling deposit liabilities of the banking system as a whole, excluding deposits having an original maturity of over two years, plus any sterling resources obtained by switching foreign currencies into sterling. Interbank transactions and sterling certificates of deposits (q.v.) (both held and issued) were taken into the calculation of individual banks' liabilities on a net basis.

RESERVES Sums set aside out of the profits of a company and not distributed as dividends. They are created for the purpose of meeting contingencies, for equalizing dividends, etc.

Article 117 of Table A of the Companies Act 1948 provided:

The directors may, before recommending any dividend, set aside out of the profits of the company such sums as they think proper as a reserve or reserves which shall, at the discretion of the directors, be applicable for any purpose to which the profits of the company may be properly applied, and pending such application may, at the like discretion, either be employed in the business of the company or be invested in such investments (other than shares of the company) as the directors may from time to time think fit. The directors may also, without placing the same to reserve, carry forward any profits which they may think prudent not to divide.

The Schedule 8 to the Companies Act 1948 provided as regards a company's balance sheet:

6.—The aggregate amounts respectively of capital reserves, revenue reserves and provisions (other than provisions for depreciation, renewals or diminution in value of assets) shall be stated under separate headings: Provided that:

(a) this paragraph shall not require a separate statement of any of the said three amounts which is not material; and

(b) The Department of Trade and Industry may direct that it shall not require a separate statement of the amount of provisions where they are satisfied that that is not required in the public interest and would prejudice the company, but subject to the condition that any heading stating an amount arrived at after taking into account a provision (other than as aforesaid) shall be so framed or marked as to indicate that fact.

7.—(1) There shall be also shown unless it is shown in the profit and loss account or a statement or report annexed thereto, or the amount involved is not material:

(a) where the amount of the capital reserves, of the revenue reserves or of the provisions (other than provisions for depreciation, renewals or diminution in value of assets) shows an increase as compared with the amount at the end of the immediately preceding financial year, the source from which the amount of the increase has been derived; and

(b) where:

(i) the amount of the capital reserves or of the revenue reserves shows a decrease as compared with the amount at the end of the immediately preceding financial year; or

(ii) the amount at the end of the immediately preceding financial year of the provisions (other than provisions for depreciation, renewals or diminution in value of assets) exceeded the aggregate of the sums since applied and amounts still retained for the purposes thereof, the application of the amounts derived from the difference.

(2) Where the heading showing any of the reserves or provisions aforesaid is divided into subheadings, this paragraph shall apply to each of the separate amounts shown in the subheadings instead of applying to the aggregate amount thereof.

Under the Companies Act 1981, where there has been a revaluation of assets, any adjustments to the company reserves, whether an increase or reduction, must be shown as a revaluation reserve (although not necessarily under that name) and an amount may be transferred from revaluation reserve to profit and loss account only if (1) it was previously charged to that account, or (2) it represents realized profit. See Sch. 4, 1985 Act.

RESIDENCE The term 'residence' is not defined in the Income Tax Acts. Section 49 of the Income and Corporation Taxes Act 1970 provides for assessment if a British subject or citizen has his ordinary residence in the UK. This is in contradistinction to occasional residence. Whilst time or duration is an important factor in determining ordinary residence, it is not conclusive. It was said by Lord Warrington in the case of *Levene v The Inland Revenue Commissioners* [1928] AC 217, to mean 'residence according to the way in which a man's life is usually ordered'. SEE *Ordinarily Resident*

If a person is to be 'resident' in the UK for a tax year, he must be physically present in the country for part of that year. If he is physically present for six months or more in the tax year, he will be deemed to be resident in all cases. For this purpose, six months mean 183 days, and travelling days are ignored.

A person may be resident in the UK but not 'ordinarily resident' (q.v.), ordinary residence meaning habitual residence. If, for example, a person normally lives abroad but spends six months of a year in the UK, he will be resident for that year, even though he is not ordinarily resident here.

If a person is deemed to be resident in the UK in a tax year, he is deemed to be resident for the whole year: it is not possible to be resident for part only of a tax year. There are some exceptions to this rule, however, where, by concession, the Inland Revenue will allow a year to be apportioned, e.g. where a person who has not been ordinarily resident in the UK, comes here to live permanently, or where a person leaves the UK to take up permanent residence abroad, and ceases to be ordinarily resident here.

The question of residence and ordinary residence of a wife is determined by her own circumstances and not by that of her husband.

If a person leaves the UK to take up permanent residence abroad, he is still regarded as resident and ordinarily resident here if he returns for periods amounting to an average of three months or more in the tax year and this is so regardless of whether or not he or she has accommodation available in the UK. Generally, if a person is intending to take up residence abroad, he should produce evidence that he has set up a permanent home overseas and given up his home, e.g. sold his house in the UK. In such circumstances, he will normally be allowed to claim that he is not resident and not ordinarily resident with effect from the date of leaving the UK. When he or she has been abroad for a period which includes a complete tax year, and in that time visits to the UK have not exceeded, on average, three months or more a year, the status of being non-resident and not ordinarily resident will be confirmed.

A person who has lived abroad and comes to the UK to take up permanent residence will normally be regarded as resident and ordinarily resident in the UK from the date of his arrival. If a person comes to the UK to work for a period of three years or more, he too will be treated as a resident, from the date of arrival to the date of departure. Other persons coming to the UK in the course of their employment will not normally be treated as resident, unless they spend six months or more here in a tax year, or unless they have accommodation available for their use. If accommodation is 'available' it does not matter that the visitor owns or rents the accommodation. He may indeed own property which is let to another person so that he does not *de facto* have accommodation available for his use. Generally, the availability of accommodation is ignored if the person is working full-time on behalf of a business, profession, or other employment carried on *wholly* abroad.

The general rule for determining the residence of a company was laid down in the case of *De Beers Consolidated Mines Ltd* v *Howe (Surveyor of Taxes)* [1906] AC 455, HL. It is that a company is deemed to be resident for tax purposes where its central management and control is found. In a press release dated 27th July, 1983, however, the Inland Revenue indicated that they would not apply this test where the appearance of a company's management and control had been created in a particular place if in reality the management and control was somewhere else.

RESIDUARY REVISEE Under a will, the person who takes all the real property which remains after the devisees (q.v.) have received their shares. SEE *Personal Estate, Personalty*

RESIDUARY LEGATEE Under a will, the person who takes all the personal property which remains after the legatees (q.v.) have received their shares. SEE *Personal Estate, Personalty*

RESIDUE That which remains of a deceased person's estate after all the debts, expenses and legacies have been paid.

RESOLUTIONS Resolutions passed by the members of a company in general meeting may be (1) ordinary resolutions (which may be passed by a bare majority of those voting), (2) extraordinary resolutions (see below), or (3) special resolutions (see below).

A company's articles of association often provide that certain acts shall be done only by extraordinary resolution.

The provisions of the Companies Act 1985 with regard to extraordinary and special resolutions are as follows.

378.—(1) A resolution is an extraordinary resolution when it has been passed by a majority of not less than three-fourths of such members as (being entitled to do so) vote in person or, where proxies are allowed, by proxy, at a general meeting of which notice specifying the intention to propose the resolution as an extraordinary resolution has been duly given.

(2) A resolution is a special resolution when it has been passed by such a majority as is required for the passing of an extraordinary resolution and at a general meeting of which not less than 21 days' notice, specifying the intention to propose the resolution as a special resolution, has been duly given.

(3) If it is so agreed by a majority in number of the members having the right to attend and vote at such a meeting, being a majority—

(*a*) together holding not less than 95 per cent in nominal value of the shares giving that right; or

(*b*) in the case of a company not having a share capital, together representing not less than 95 per cent of the total voting rights at that meeting of all the members,

a resolution may be proposed and passed as a special resolution at a meeting of which less than 21 days' notice has been given.

(4) At any meeting at which an extraordinary resolution or a special resolution is submitted to be passed, a declaration by the chairman that the resolution is carried is, unless a poll is demanded, conclusive evidence of the fact without proof of the number or proportion of the votes recorded in favour of or against the resolution.

(5) In computing the majority on a poll demanded on the question that an extraordinary resolution or a special resolution be passed, reference is to be had to the number of votes case for and against the resolution.

(6) For purposes of this section, notice of a meeting is deemed duly given, and the meeting duly held, when the notice is given and the meeting held in the manner provided by this Act or the company's articles.

Section 380 provides:

(1) A copy of every resolution or agreement to which this section applies shall, within 15 days after it is passed or made, by forwarded to the registrar of companies and recorded by him; and it must be either a printed copy or else a copy in some other form approved by the registrar.

(2) Where articles have been registered, a copy of every such resolution or agreement for the time being in force shall be embodied in or annexed to every copy of the articles issued after the passing of the resolution or the making of the agreement.

The cases in which special resolutions are necessary, as provided by the Act, are referred to under the following entries:

Names of Companies
Memorandum of Association
Articles of Association
Reduction of Share Capital
Winding Up, compulsory
Winding Up, voluntary

SEE *Company (Companies)*

RESTRAINT ON ANTICIPATION Where property was settled on a married woman in order that she might receive the income as it became due, it was usual for the deed to include a restraint on anticipation, by which she was prevented from mortgaging or giving a charge of any kind upon the future income. By the Law Reform (Married Women and Tortfeasors) Act 1935, restraint on anticipation was abolished. Existing restraints, or those imposed in any instrument executed before 1st January, 1936, continued to be or would in due course become effective. The will of a testator who died after 31st December, 1945, would be deemed to have been executed after 1st January, 1936, whatever its actual date. Thus a time limit was put on a testator's imposition of restraint on anticipation. SEE *Married Woman*

By the Married Women (Restraint on Anticipation) Act 1949, all such restraints were abolished.

RESTRICTIVE INDORSEMENT An indorsement is restrictive which prohibits the further negotiation of a bill or cheque, or which expresses that it is a mere authority to deal with the bill as thereby directed, as 'Pay John Brown only'. SEE *Indorsement*

RESTRICTIVE TRADE PRACTICES ACT 1956 An Act to control in the public interest agreements placing restrictions on the prices, supply or manufacture of goods. The Act lays down rules as to the matters to be taken into account in determining the public interest, and set up the Restrictive Practices Court to hear and decide such cases. The members of the Court are drawn from three judges of the English High Court, one judge each of the courts of Scotland and Northern Ireland, and ten persons experienced in industry, commerce or public affairs, appointed by the Lord Chancellor. The result of a finding that an agreement is against the public interest is to render it void. There are provisions in the Fair Trading Act 1973 for an extension to 'services' to be made by order.

RETAINED PROFITS Sometimes referred to as retained earnings, the term is applied to that part of a company's profits which relates to the equity share capital but which has not been distributed as divided. SEE *Distributions*

RETIREMENT, RETIREMENT AGE For the purpose of the State pension scheme, the age of retirement is 65 for men and 60 for women (SEE *Pensions*). Either a man or a woman may, however, secure the benefit of extra pension by deferring retirement, whether actually working or not, until a later date but not beyond the age of 70 for a man and 65 for a woman.

A retirement pension under a personal plan may be payable at any time from age 60 to age 75, regardless of the actual date of retirement from work. In special circumstances (perhaps because of the nature of the employment), the Inland Revenue may agree to payment of such a pension at an earlier age but it may not commence later than 75. In general, the benefits available to retired persons (assuming that State retirement age has been reached) include (1) basic pension, (2) additional or earnings-related pension, (3) graduated pension, (4) extra pension for deferred retirement, (5) invalidity allowance (SEE UNDER *Invalidity Benefit*), (6) age addition (for persons who have reached the age of 80) (7) Christmas bonus, (8) reduced fares on public transport, and (9) non-contributory retirement pension for persons who have reached the age of 80. SEE *Pensions, Pension Schemes*

Age allowance (q.v.) is the higher amount of personal allowance available to persons aged 65 and over.

RETIREMENT ANNUITY SEE *Pensions — personal pension plans*

RETIRING A BILL Strictly speaking, to retire a bill is to pay it at or before maturity. More usually the phrase is used to denote the redemption of the bill by the drawer or acceptor from the holder before maturity. A banker holding a discounted bill will use discrimination in permitting it to be retired before its due date, and will usually advise the acceptor if the drawer or an indorser retires it. There are obvious possibilities of raising money on forged acceptances, if discounted bills can be withdrawn before maturity, and the practice also lends itself to accommodation acceptances.

RETIRING A BILL UNDER REBATE Where a documentary bill has been discounted, the acceptor may wish to obtain the attached documents of title before maturity, and if the bill is marked 'documents against payment', he must arrange with the holder to retire it, i.e. pay it before it is due. In consideration of so doing, a rebate is allowed by the holder, usually calculated at ½ per cent above the London Clearing Bankers' Deposit Rate on the amount of the bill. SEE *Documentary Bill*

RETURNED CHEQUE OR BILL A cheque may be returned unpaid for many reasons. The drawer may not have sufficient funds to meet it; he may be dead or bankrupt; he may have instructed his banker not to pay it; the banker may have received some legal notice preventing him from paying any further cheques upon the drawer's account; or the cheque itself may not be in order, the date or the amount, or other material part may have been altered, and not have been initialled by the drawer; the amount in words and figures may differ; the drawer's signature may not be recognized; an indorsement may be wrong; it may be post-dated; or crossed to two bankers; or it may be stale through having been issued so long. These are the typical reasons necessitating the return of a cheque.

If there be on the face of a cheque any reasonable ground for suspecting that it has been tampered with, a refusal to pay is warranted. (See *London Joint Stock Bank Ltd* v *Macmillan and Arthur* under *Payment of Cheque*.)

When the cheque is returned, an 'answer' is marked upon it by the drawee banker, usually in the top left-hand corner.

Cheques received otherwise than through the Clearing House may be returned on the day following the receipt, but in practice they are usually returned on the same day. When a bill is to be noted, it may be noted on the day of its dishonour and must be noted not later than the next succeeding business day (SEE *Noting; Protest*). A cheque or bill cashed over the counter by the paying banker cannot subsequently be returned.

The customer for whom a bill payable to order was discounted is not liable, in the event of its dishonour, unless by special agreement, if the bill was not indorsed by him.

REVERSE YIELD GAP In broad terms, this is the return on British Government stocks compared with the return on ordinary stocks and shares. More precisely, it is the difference between the yield on 2½ per cent Consols and the dividend yield on the Financial Times Actuaries All Share Index (q.v.).

Historically, the yield on Government securities was low, principally because they were in demand as safe income-bearing investments, the capital value of which was returned intact on the redemption date. The acute inflation of the 1960s and 1970s, however, resulted in serious erosion of the capital values of gilt-edged stocks in real terms with consequent disenchantment on the part of investors. Thus institutions and private investors turned increasingly to equity investment. Historically, equity yields had been high, reflecting the traditional risk. With the 'cult of the equity' which began in the late 1950s, ordinary stocks became more popular and yields fell. In 1959, the yield on leading equities fell for the first time below the yield on 2½ per cent Consols. Since then, the 'reverse yield gap' has persisted, so-called because it is the reverse of that which was expected historically in terms of comparative risks.

REVERSION Where a lease of land is granted for a number of years, the lessor remains possessed of the reversion, that is the interest in the estate remaining to the lessor after the lease has been granted. For example, if John Brown grants a lease to John Jones for a certain number of years, at the end of that period, that is at the expiration of the lease, the property reverts to John Brown, or to his representatives. The person to whom the property reverts is called the reversioner.

This term is used loosely to indicate the rights of a beneficiary under a trust who is entitled absolutely on the death of a life tenant. Reversionary interest societies and some insurance companies will lend money against such an interest.

REVERSIONARY ANNUITY An annuity which commences on the death of one person and becomes payable during the life of another person, e.g. an annuity to be paid to a wife on the death of her husband.

REVERSIONER SEE *Reversion*

REVOCABLE CREDIT SEE *Documentary Credit*

REVOLVING CREDIT A credit under which an indefinite amount may be drawn as opposed to a fixed credit, which permits of drawings by one or more drafts up to a fixed sum, the reaching of which means the exhaustion of the credit. In *Nordsko* v *National Bank* [1922] 10 Ll LR 652, an expert witness defined the term as follows: 'A revolving credit is one for a certain sum which is automatically renewed by putting on at the bottom that which is taken off at the top'. It may be a blank credit—a rare variety—where an unlimited amount may be drawn at any time; or it may be for an unlimited amount in total but with a stated limit to the amounts of drafts that may be outstanding at any one time. Sometimes it is for an unlimited sum, but with a limit on the amount which may be drawn at any one time. Another type provides for a limited amount to be drawn within a given period, and once the limit has been utilized in the given period, no further drawings can be made until the new period commences.

A number of retail stores offer revolving credit to their customers, usually repaid by fixed monthly amounts. Similarly, the amount of credit available to credit card holder (SEE *Credit Card*) is on a revolving basis.

RIGHTS ISSUE This is an issue of shares to existing shareholders of a company on a proportionate basis, usually on preferential terms. Those who do not wish to take up the new shares may sell their 'rights' or the company may do this for them. Clearly, the issue of additional shares to other parties without giving the existing shareholders the opportunity to subscribe would reduce the existing shareholders' proportion of the total capital, i.e. it would 'water' their equity. The Stock Exchange would not allow a listed company to issue new shares without giving pre-emption rights to the existing shareholders but this was not required as a matter of company law in the UK until the Companies Act 1980, brought the UK law in line with the Second Directive of the EEC.

Under Section 17 of the 1980 Act, a company may not allot equity securities for cash until it has first made an offer of those securities to the equity shareholders. Under Section 17, the pre-emption rights apply to persons who hold either 'relevant shares' or 'relevant employee shares'. For this purpose, 'relevant shares' means any shares in a company, other than

1. shares which carry rights to anticipate in distributions by way of dividend and capital but are limited to a specified amount, and
2. shares which are held or are to be held under an employees' share scheme.

'Relevant employee shares' are shares that would be relevant shares but for the fact that they are held under an employees' share scheme.

Convertible loan stocks are not relevant shares within the meaning of the Section. A person who holds one class of shares may, however, be entitled to pre-empt on rights in respect of the issue of a different class of shares.

Pre-emption rights do not apply under the 1980 Act to

1. bonus shares or other shares which do not satisfy the test of 'equity securities';
2. shares which are to be paid up wholly or partly otherwise than for cash;
3. shares issued by a private company in cases where the memorandum or articles of association are inconsistent with pre-emption rights;
4. shares issued by the directors of a company under an express authority for that purpose; the authority must be renewed by special resolution when it has expired;
5. a shareholder who has entered into a binding renunciation of his pre-emptive rights.

In general, an offer must be made to each person who holds relevant shares or relevant employee shares on either the same terms as those which the company proposes to allot shares to other persons or on more favourable terms. The pre-emptive offer must be for the same proportion of securities, as nearly as practicable, as the existing shareholder holds of the existing relevant shares.

In general, the Act applies to private companies although a private company may expressly exclude the pre-emption requirement by its memorandum or articles. SEE Sections 89–94, 1985 Act.

ROLL-OVER LOANS These are usually medium-term loans, where the interest rate is reviewed in accordance with market conditions at the end of each 'roll-over' period, usually every six months. The advantage to the bank making such a loan is that it can match it with deposits for each successive roll-over period, thus avoiding the need to take a long-term view of interest rates.

ROLL-OVER RELIEF This applies to capital gains tax (q.v.). Where business assets are sold there is a *prima facie* charge to capital gains tax on any resulting profit. If, however, the proceeds of the business assets are reinvested in the replacement of those assets within one year before the sale, or within three years afterwards, any capital gains tax liability is rolled-over to the extent that any gain on the disposal is deducted from the cost of the new assets.

ROOT OF TITLE A purchaser of land can, unless there is an agreement to the contrary, require the title to be deduced for fifteen years. Previous to 1st January, 1926, the period was 40 years, and until the passing of the Law Reform Act 1969, it was 30 years on contracts before the 1st January, 1970. It may be necessary to go back further than 15 years to obtain a good root of title. The deed which is taken as the beginning of the title is called the root of title.

If it is stipulated in a contract for sale of a property, or in the printed 'conditions of sale', that the title shall commence with a certain deed or will, then that deed or will becomes the root of title for the purposes of that contract.

A mortgage deed or purchase deed is a good root of title, but a general devise of property in a will is not a good root of title, as the will does not identify the property.

Section 45(6) of the Law of Property Act 1925 provides as follows.

> Recitals, statement, and description of facts, matters and parties contained in deeds, instruments, Acts of Parliament or statutory declarations, twenty years old at the date of the contract, shall, unless and except so far as they may be proved to be inaccurate, be taken to be sufficient evidence of the truth of such facts, matters and descriptions.

By the Law of Property Act 1925, Section 45(1),

> A purchaser of any property shall not require the production, or any abstract or copy, of any deed, will or other document, dated or made before the time prescribed by law, or stipulated, for commencement of the title . . . .

ROYAL MINT SEE *Mint*

ROYALTY A rent, payable to the landlord, of a certain percentage of the profits derived from the working of a mine upon his estate, or from the minerals reserved to him, or so much per ton from the minerals raised.

The term is also used loosely in relation to payment received in respect of a copyright. SEE ALSO *Income Tax*

RULE IN CLAYTON'S CASE SEE *Clayton's Case*

RULE IN TURQUAND'S CASE SEE *Turquand's Case*

S

SAFE CUSTODY It is the custom of bankers to receive and take charge of deed boxes, securities and all manner of articles of value belonging to their customers. When articles are deposited for safe custody, some banks give a form of receipt.

The customer depositing the articles for safe custody may be required to sign the counterfoil bearing the same number as the receipt which he obtains.

This acts as a confirmation from the customer of the articles which he has left in the bank's custody.

Where a locked box, or sealed packet is received for safe custody, any receipt given therefor should state 'contents unknown'.

Some bankers, however, do not give any receipts for articles left with them for safe keeping, unless specially requested so to do. They merely keep particulars of them in the safe custody register, and when the customer receives the articles back again he signs an acknowledgment for them in the register. Some bankers, who give no acknowledgments, permit the customer to see the entry of the deposit in the safe custody register.

When articles have been deposited in joint names they should not be given up except on the written authority of all the parties. If one of the depositors has died, the authority of his legal representatives should be obtained before delivery to the survivor or survivors.

The modern form of mandate for a joint account provides, however, for the delivery of safe custody items to either or both of two depositors, and in some cases for a good discharge by delivery to the survivor(s) in the case of decease of one of the depositors.

All the executors of a deceased person should join in an authority to give up safe custody articles which were deposited in the name of the deceased.

Where articles are deposited in the names of executors, the signatures of all, or the survivors, should be required before delivery.

Where the lodgment is in the names of trustees, it is particularly necessary to obtain all their signatures before delivery. In *Mendes* v *Guedalla* (1862) 2 J & H 259, where a box containing bearer bonds was lodged for safe custody by three trustees and one of them held the key in order to cut off the coupons half-yearly, it was held that the bankers 'ought not to have parted with the box, or allowed more than the coupons to be taken out, without the authority of all the three trustees'.

If the customer becomes bankrupt, the directions of his trustees should be obtained.

If a banker receives an authority from a depositor to allow another person to remove a certain article from a box or parcel, the banker must see that only the specified article is taken out.

By the Trustee Act 1925, a trustee must deposit bearer bonds held by him with a bank for safe custody and collection of income. (See Section 7 under *Trustee Investments*.)

By Section 21 a trustee may deposit with a bank any documents relating to the trust. SEE UNDER *Trustee*

The acceptance of articles for safe custody makes the banker a bailee, and the extent of his liability as such depends on whether he is a gratuitous bailee or a bailee for reward. A gratuitous bailee 'is bound to take the same care of the property entrusted to him as a reasonably prudent and careful man may fairly be expected to take of his own property of the like description' (*Giblin* v *McMullen* (1868) LR 2 PC 339). In the Privy Council case of *Port Swettenham Authority* v *T. W. Wu & Co* [1979] AC 580, their lordships concluded that the standard required of gratuitous bailee at common law, although high, may be less exacting than that required of a bailee for reward 'but the line between the two is very fine, very difficult to discern and impossible to define'. They went on to say

> There is some authority at common law that in the case of a gratuitous bailee, the onus of proving that the loss of goods bailed was caused by the negligence or misconduct of the bailee rests on the bailor. Their lordships think that authority is not compelling and gravely doubt the correctness of *Giblin* v *McMullen*.

It is clear, however, a bailee for reward must use the highest degree of care and use all precautions and devices available in taking care of valuables deposited with him. Some English banks do not make a practice of making a specific and express charge for safe custody facilities and are consequently gratuitous bailees.

In some quarters it is contended that there is valuable consideration in the keeping of the customer's account and that consequently a banker is a bailee for reward. The distinction tends to be academic, however, for a banker gives the same care to the custody of his customer's property as he does to his own valuables. If a banker delivers articles left for safe custody to other than the customer or his authorized agent, or if he fails to deliver them to the right party on demand, he will be liable for conversion quite apart from negligence. A banker is not liable for the theft of his employees provided he has exercised care in his choice of them.

In the case of *Haughland* v *R. R. Low (Luxury Coaches) Ltd* [1962] 2 All ER 159 at p. 161, Ormerod, LJ, expressed the view that to try to put a bailment into a watertight compartment such as 'gratuitous bailee' and 'bailee for reward' was to overlook the infinite variety of cases that could arise. The question that always had to be considered was whether a sufficient standard of care had been observed in a particular case.

If a banker has doubt as to the genuineness of a signature upon an order for delivery of a safe custody article, or any suspicion as to the authority of the person who presents the order, he is justified in having the signature confirmed by the customer. In the case of *Mrs Langtry* v *The Union Bank of London* (which was settled by judgment for the plaintiff by consent for £10,000), the plaintiff's property was obtained from the bank by a person presenting a forged order purporting to be signed by Mrs Langtry, requesting the bank to hand her box to the bearer.

In the opinion of most authorities, a banker has no lien (q.v.) upon securities or articles left with him for safe custody. If a safe custody article is to be taken as a security at any time the customer should sign the necessary document of charge.

SALE AND LEASEBACK The term is normally applied to the type of property transaction in which an owner-occupier of commercial or industrial property, sells the property to a buyer and takes a lease of it for the vendor's continued occupation. Typical buyers in a leaseback transaction are insurance companies, pension funds and property unit trusts which thus acquire an investment whilst the vendor is able to release funds otherwise locked up in property and make use of them in his business.

SALE OF GOODS In common with most UK commercial law, the law relating to the sale of goods arose out of the 'law merchant' but for the most part was codified in the Sale of Goods Act 1893, and recodified in the Sale of Goods Act 1979. With a few exceptions, the 1979 Act repealed the Act of 1893.

The Act governs contracts for the sale of goods and forms part, therefore, of the wider law of contract. It does not, for example, apply to other contractual relationships, such as bailment (q.v.), agency (SEE *Agent*) and mortgages (q.v.). Similarly, the Act does not affect the general laws of bankruptcy (q.v.) and liquidation (q.v.). Certain contracts of sales, e.g. hire purchase (q.v.) are subject to separate legislation (SEE *Consumer Credit Act 1974*) and in certain respects the Sale of Goods Act is subject to and must be read alongside other legislation, e.g. the Unfair Contract Terms Act 1977.

The law relating to the sale of goods applies only to contracts of sale and not, for example, to contracts of bailment, mortgage, pawn or pledge. It applies only to 'goods' and not, for example, to land, choses in action (q.v.) or contracts for work and labour.

The Sale of Goods Act deals with many matters which are not primarily of a financial nature and are, therefore, outside the scope of this work. They include, for example, the rules relating to conditions and warranties, sale by sample, undertakings as to title, the transfer of title, delivery and acceptance. From a financial point of view, the principal considerations are the rules relating to payment, the rights of an unpaid seller, the remedies of sellers and buyers and the special rules relating to overseas contracts (see below).

Subject to agreement to the contrary, payment for goods is due when the property in the goods has passed to the buyer. If, however, it is part of the bargain that the goods will be delivered before payment, then payment is due when the goods are delivered. The question whether or not the property in goods has passed to a buyer is subject to some extensive legal rules but the basic rule is that the property passes when, under the terms of the contract, the parties intend that it should pass. Whether parties have agreed that payment should be made by a bill of exchange or promissory note, this is prima facie conditional on the bill or note being honoured at maturity. If the bill or note is not honoured at maturity, there is an implied agreement on the part of the buyer to pay interest on the outstanding price from the date of maturity of the bill or note.

If, in a particular contract, there is no provision for the time or method of payment, reference may be made to the general usage in the trade or the course of dealings previously between the parties.

No interest is payable on the outstanding

purchase price under a sale of goods contract unless this has been agreed as a term of the contract or if, again, there has been a course of dealing between the parties to that effect. (But see the case of a dishonoured bill or note above.)

An unpaid seller of goods has a lien (q.v.) on those goods if he has possession of them until the price is paid or tendered and, if the buyer is insolvent, the unpaid seller has the right to stop the goods in transit and both remedies arise, whether or not the property in the goods has passed to the seller. A seller may be deemed to be an unpaid seller and may therefore, exercise this latter right, notwithstanding that the goods were to be paid for at some future date if, in the meantime, the buyer becomes insolvent.

An unpaid seller may exercise his right of stoppage in transit, either by resuming possession of the goods or by giving instructions to the carrier or other person who has possession of the goods. Goods are deemed to be in transit from the time they are delivered to a carrier or other bailee for the purpose of transmission to the buyer, until the point where the buyer or his agent takes delivery from the carrier or bailee.

An unpaid seller's lien and right of stoppage in transit is not affected by any sale or other transfer of the goods by the buyer to another person, unless the seller has agreed to that sale or transfer. Where, however, the documents of title to goods have been transferred by the buyer to another person, who takes the documents in good faith and for valuable consideration, the unpaid seller's right of lien or stoppage in transit is defeated if the transfer was by way of sale and if it was by way of pledge, the unpaid seller's rights may only be exercised subject to the rights of the transferee.

An unpaid seller would usually have (1) the right to bring an action against the buyer for the price of the goods whether the property in the goods have passed to the buyer or not, and (2) a right to bring an action against the buyer for damages for non-acceptance if the buyer wrongfully refuses to accept and pay for the goods. In this latter case, the normal rules of contract will apply and the measure of damages will be the loss resulting directly in the ordinary course from the buyer's breach.

If the seller of goods fails to deliver the goods, the buyer may bring an action for damages for non-delivery (which generally will be the difference between the contract price of the goods and the market value at the time they ought to have been delivered). Alternatively, the buyer may apply to the court for specific performance of the contract, but this will not normally be possible where damages would be an adequate remedy. Alternatively, where there has been a breach of warranty by the seller, the buyer may seek a reduction in the purchase price or bring an action against the seller for damages for breach of warranty. A 'warranty' is an agreement with reference to goods which are the subject of a contract of sale but collateral to the main purpose of such a contract, the breach of which gives rise to a claim for damages but not to a right to reject the goods and treat the contract as repudiated (Section 61, Sale of Goods Act 1979).

As to contracts of overseas trade, SEE *Bill of Lading*

SANS RECOURS These words, the French term for 'without recourse', may be added by the drawer of a bill or an indorser to his signature to negative his own liability to the holder in the event of the bill being dishonoured, but the words would not free an indorser from liability for any forged signature prior to his indorsement. SEE *Drawer; Indorser; Without Recourse*

SAVE-AS-YOU-EARN SEE *National Savings*

SAVINGS (PERSONAL) The total level of personal savings in the UK represents the difference between total disposable incomes and total consumer expenditure. The following graph shows the level of personal savings over the years

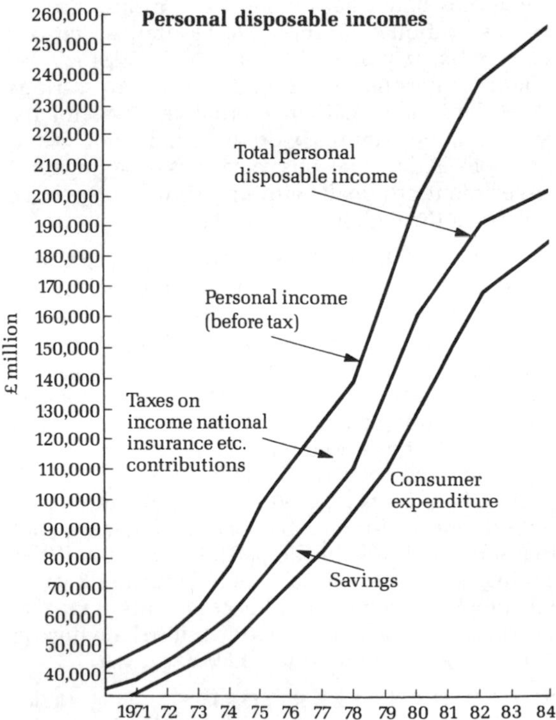

Source: Financial Statistics.

to December 1984. In recent years, the level of savings has fluctuated from approximately 16 per cent in the second quarter of 1980, to approximately $4\frac{1}{2}$ per cent at the end of 1982. Annually, however, the savings ratio varies between approximately eight per cent and 14 per cent.

SAVINGS ACCOUNT An account, usually with a bank or a building society, designed to encourage the savings habit and to lead to a long-term banking or investment relationship. Bank savings accounts are in the nature of deposit accounts (q.v.) and are not normally available for drawings. Rates of interest are typically ahead, by a small margin, of seven day deposit rates. Similarly, building society savings accounts normally attract a rate of interest slightly ahead of the ordinary share account rate.

Savings accounts with the banking sector represent a very small proportion of total deposits.

SAVINGS BANKS SEE *National Savings Bank; Trustee Savings Bank*

SAVINGS CERTIFICATES SEE *National Savings Certificates*

SAVINGS MARKET This is not a very precise term. It applies loosely to all repositories for personal savings. There is in the UK a very wide choice for savers and investors, the principal categories being bank deposits, building society shares, national savings, life assurance, various categories of pension schemes, direct stock exchange investments or unit trusts and various categories of so-called alternative investments, such as coins, stamps, works of art, diamonds and antiques. All the various categories of savings and investment are dealt with under their respective headings throughout this work.

SAVINGS RELATED SHARE OPTION SCHEMES These are schemes approved by the Inland Revenue under the Finance Act 1980, whereby savers may set aside a monthly sum (currently the maximum is £100 a month) to take up shares in their employer companies. This may be done through Save-As-You-Earn contracts or through savings accounts with building societies.

Under such contracts the maximum savings period is 5 years, i.e. 60 months, at the end of which time a 14-month bonus is added, taking the maximum savings in the period to £7,400. If the savings are left in the scheme for a further 2 years (although no further monthly contribution may be made) a further bonus of 14 months' savings is added, taking the total to £8,800.

SCHEDULED TERRITORIES The Scheduled Territories as defined by the Exchange Control Act 1947, as amended, comprised the British Commonwealth (except Canada and Rhodesia), Bahrain, Bangladesh, Iceland, the Irish Republic, the Hashemite Kingdom of Jordan, Kuwait, Pakistan, Qatar, South Africa and South West Africa, United Arab Emirates, the People's Democratic Republic of Yemen.

With effect from 23rd June, 1972, the Scheduled Territories comprised only the UK (including the Isle of Man and the Channel Islands) and Eire and became known as the New Sterling Area. With the removal of Exchange Control in 1979 the New Sterling Area was suspended.

SCHEME OF ARRANGEMENT Section 16(1) of the Bankruptcy Act 1914 provides

> Where a debtor intends to make a proposal for a composition in satisfaction of his debts, or a proposal for a scheme of arrangement of his affairs, he shall within four days of submitting his statement of affairs, or within such time thereafter as the official receiver may fix, lodge with the official receiver a proposal in writing, signed by him, embodying the terms of the composition or scheme ... and setting out particulars of any sureties or securities proposed.

Such a composition or scheme requires the acceptance of a majority in number and three-quarters in value of all proving creditors, as well as the approval of the court, which will not be given unless it provides reasonable security for the payment of not less than 25p in the pound on all unsecured debts in cases where an unconditional discharge would be refused. Acceptance by the creditors and approval by the court means the discharge of the receiving order. The debtor or any trustee appointed under the scheme is revested with his property and thereupon put into the same position as if he had got his discharge in bankruptcy save for the provision of the scheme or composition.

A scheme of arrangement (made after a receiving order) must not be confused with a deed of arrangement made to avoid bankruptcy proceedings. SEE *Deed of Arrangement*

SCHOOL FEES SEE *Education, Costs of*

SCOTT COMMITTEE This was the Committee on Property Bonds and Equity-Linked Life Assurance, under the chairmanship of Sir Hilary Scott, which reported in April 1973. The terms of reference of the Committee were

> To consider the working of the Insurance Companies Acts, 1958–67, and of the Prevention of Fraud (Investments) Act, 1958, insofar as the latter is relevant in the light of life assurance schemes involving the issue of equity-linked policies, unit-linked policies, property bonds and similar schemes, and to advise on the ade-

quacy of the protection afforded by these Acts to policy holders in these Schemes.

The Committee made a number of far-reaching recommendations on the subject of the solvency of linked-life assurance companies, the conduct of their business and their selling methods, most of which recommendations were incorporated in subsequent legislation. SEE ALSO *Gower Report; Life Assurance*

SCOTTISH CLEARING BANKS There are three Scottish clearing banks; Bank of Scotland, Royal Bank of Scotland and Clydesdale Bank. Bank of Scotland is owned as to 35 per cent by The Standard Life Assurance Company, the remaining 65 per cent being in public hands. Royal Bank of Scotland is also a public company, in which Lloyds Bank has 16 per cent of the equity. Clydesdale Bank is wholly owned by Midland Bank.

SCRIP, SCRIP CERTIFICATE Scrip is a contraction of 'subscription'. Ordinary certificates are very commonly referred to as 'scrip'; but scrip or a scrip certificate is really the document or provisional certificate which is given to a person who has, for example, agreed to take up bonds in connection with a Government loan and has paid the first instalment. Scrip is principally associated with the issue of debentures, or bonds. The term is also used loosely in 'scrip issue', meaning a capitalization issue (q.v.).

SCRIPOPHILY The name given to the collecting of old scrip certificates, sometimes known as 'busted bonds'. Many of the earlier bonds issued by Japan, Russia, other European countries and some South American countries, which long since ceased to have any value as bonds, have acquired value among collectors.

SEAL As impression in wax, or other soft substance, made by an engraved stamp. Also the engraved stamp itself. At one time the seal was usually attached to the document by a strip of parchment or a cord. As deeds now require to be signed by the parties thereto, the use of the seal has become a mere formality and a simple wafer is frequently used instead of an impression in wax.

The letters LS inside a circle, thus (L.S), which are seen on transfer forms, stand for *locus sigilli*, and mean the place of the seal. They do not, however, act instead of a seal or wafer.

The seal of a company is called its common seal. Every company 'shall have its name engraven in legible characters on its seal'. If an officer of a company, or any person on its behalf uses or authorizes the use of any seal purporting to be a seal of the company, whereupon its name is not engraven as aforesaid, he shall be liable to a fine. (Section 350 of the Companies Act 1985.) The seal of a company is usually affixed in the presence of two directors, who sign the document, which is also counter-signed by the secretary or such other person as the directors may appoint for the purpose. A record is kept of each document which is sealed, the entry being initialled by the persons who witnessed the affixing of the seal. The seal is usually kept in a box or case secured by two locks, the keys of which are held by different persons.

Sections 38 and 39 of the Companies Act 1985 give powers to a company to empower any person, as its attorney, to execute deeds abroad and to have an official seal for use abroad, as follows:

38.—(1) A company may, by writing under its common seal, empower any person, either generally or in respect of any specified matters, as its attorney, to execute deeds on its behalf in any place elsewhere than the United Kingdom.

(2) A deed signed by such an attorney on behalf of the company, and under his seal, binds the company, and has the same effect as if it were under the company's common seal.

39.—(1) A company whose objects require or comprise the transaction of business in foreign countries may, if authorised by its articles, have for use in any territory, district or place elsewhere than in the United Kingdom, an official seal, which shall be a facsimile of the common seal of the company, with the addition on its face of the name of every territory, district or place where it is to be used.

(2) A deed or other document to which the official seal is duly affixed binds the company as if it had been sealed with the company's common seal.

(3) A company having an official seal for use in any such territory, district or place may, by writing under its common seal, authorise any person appointed for the purpose in that territory, district or place to affix the official seal to any deed or other document to which the company is party in that territory, district or place.

(4) As between the company and a person dealing with such an agent, the agent's authority continues during the period (if any) mentioned in the instrument conferring the authority, or if no period is there mentioned, then until notice of the revocation or determination of the agent's authority has been given to the person dealing with him.

(5) The person affixing the official seal shall certify in writing on the deed or other instrument to which the seal is affixed the date on which and the place at which it is affixed.

Section 41 provides for the authentication of documents as follows.

A document or proceeding requiring authentication by a company may be signed by a director, secretary, or other authorised officer of the company, and need not be under the company's common seal. [SEE *Company*]

SEARCHES SEE *Mortgage—summary of registrations; Mortgage—summary of searches*

SECOND-CLASS PAPER First-class paper includes bank bills and bills bearing names of the highest standing. Where the position is not so good, the bills fall into a second or a third-class position, or even into a still lower class, according to circumstances.

SECOND OF EXCHANGE SEE *Bill in a Set*

SECOND MORTGAGE Where a mortgagor has given a first mortgage, he can thereafter create a second and subsequent mortgages on the same property. Moreover the fact that the first mortgage is a legal one will not now debar him from creating subsequent legal mortgages. Before the Law of Property Act 1925, second mortgages were of necessity equitable ones, for the legal estate was conveyed to the first mortgagee assuming that he took a legal mortgage. A second mortgage will now take the form of a grant of a term of years longer (usually by one day) than the first mortgagee's term (usually 3,000 years).

It is desirable to take a second mortgage in legal and not equitable form, for it is possible in some circumstances for an equitable mortgage to be overriden even if registered.

If a second mortgage is taken as security, notice should be given to the first mortgagee and his acknowledgment obtained, together with confirmation of the amount due to him. He should be asked if he is under any obligation to make further advances, for if so, such further advances will rank in front of the second mortgage. No right of consolidation should be claimed by the first mortgagee. The usual searches should be made to see if any prior incumbrances exist. Usually the relative deeds will be with the first mortgagee, in which case the second mortgage must be registered as a Class C(i) charge (puisne mortgage) if a legal mortgage, or C(iii) Charge (general equitable charge) if an equitable mortgage. Such registration will protect the second mortgagee against subsequent mortgages.

In the case of registered land, a second charge can be taken and registered at the Land Registry, who will issue a certificate of second charge. SEE *Land Registration*

A second mortgage is not a desirable banking security; the paper margin between the value of the property and the first mortgage tends to shrink on realization; a first mortgagee is not bound to consider a second mortgagee in realizing the security, and although a second mortgagee is entitled to sell without obtaining the first mortgagee's permission, he must redeem the first mortgage before applying the proceeds of sale to his mortgage. Frequently, a second mortgagee has perforce to take over the first mortgage in order to deal effectively with the security. SEE *Mortgage*

SECRECY One of the terms of the relationship between banker and customer is that the former will keep the latter's affairs secret, and every member of a bank's staff is required to sign a declaration of secrecy as regards the business of the bank.

The occasions when a banker is discharged from his duty of secrecy were summed up in the case of *Tournier* v *National Provincial Bank Ltd* [1924] 1 KB 461. They are

1. Where disclosure is under compulsion of law (e.g. an order made under the Bankers' Books Evidence Act 1879 or information given to the Director of Public Prosecutions concerning a company's account, under Sections 169(2) and 334(5) of the Companies Act 1948).

Under this head the most important reasons for disclosure are connected with the working of the revenue laws. Amongst others, the Taxes Management Act 1970 contained several sections compelling disclosure for the purpose of defeating tax evasion. Section 13 enables the revenue authorities to call for information as to the names and addresses of all persons whose securities are being held (banks are, of course, only one of a class of persons to whom this Section applies). Section 17 obliges a borrower to make a return of interest paid by him on the money in his hands belonging to a lender, and banks are here expressly named. The Section is mainly applicable to Deposit Interest Paid. Cases where the annual amount involved is less than £15 (now increased to £25) are excepted. Under the same provision banks must, if asked, prepare lists of customers in certain cases, and in Section 234 power is given to the Special Commissioners to obtain information as to income from securities. These provisions are of less importance with the deduction of tax from bank interest at source on private accounts from the year 1985/86.

2. Where there is a duty to the public to disclose.
3. Where the interests of the bank require disclosure (e.g. where a bank issues a writ for repayment of an advance stating thereon the amount due or where demand is made on a guarantor for the amount owing by the customer).
4. Where the disclosure is made with the express or implied consent of the customer.

The duty of secrecy does not cease with the closing of the customer's account. SEE *Banker's Opinions; Banker and Customer*

SECURED CREDITOR 'A person holding a mortgage charge or lien on the property of the debtor, or any part thereof, as a security for a debt due to him from the debtor.' (Bankruptcy Act 1914, Section 167) SEE *Proof of Debts*

SECURITIES In *Re Douglas's Will Trusts, Lloyd's Bank* v *Nelson and Others* [1959] 2 All ER 620, the court had to consider the meaning to be given to the word 'securities' in the investment clause of a will. The primary meaning is a 'a debt or claim the payment of which is in some way secured', but there is no doubt that in modern business and legal usage the word has acquired a meaning synonymous with investments generally. In this case, Vaizey, J, decided in favour of the wider meaning and held that the word meant investments and was not confined to secured investments. He declared that 'securities' in the clause before him included any stock or shares or bonds by way of investment.

SECURITY Although the word 'security' may be used in common parlance to denote an investment (see above), it usually denotes an asset which has been charged, whether formally or informally, to 'secure' repayment of a debt. The various categories of security are dealt with under various entries throughout this work, for example *Bill as Security; Charge by Way of Legal Mortgage; Documentary Credit; Guarantee; Life Policies as Security; Mortgage; Share Capital, Shares.*

SEIGNIORAGE, SEIGNEURAGE Originally, the word was applied to that part of the income of the king or seigneur which was derived from the coinage of metal by the Mint. Since 1666, the coinage of gold has been free of charge. The word is now commonly used to apply to the profit which the Government makes on the manufacture of cupro-nickel and bronze coins. These coins are token money, and the value which is affixed to them by law is greater than the value of the metal of which they are composed, and it is from that difference that the profit is obtained.

SELF-EMPLOYED For the purpose of National Insurance, a self-employed person is a person gainfully occupied in employment, who is not an employed person (National Insurance Act 1946). The words 'gainfully occupied' have been construed as being independent of the commercial result of a person's activities (*Vandyk* v *Minister of Pensions and National Insurance* [1955] 1 QB 29). For the purpose of the Income Tax Acts, a person is deemed to be employed if he is under the general control and management of another person and the common law relationship of master and servant, as evidenced in a long line of cases, stems from the fact that the master directs the servant, not only as to the nature of the work to be done, but also the manner in which the work is to be done. Generally, therefore, it may be said that a person is self-employed if he is gainfully occupied but are not under the control of another person as to the way his work is carried out. It is essentially an area of employment law, rather than one of finance and reference should be made to the leading cases. Whether or not a person is self-employed has financial implications, however, (1) for income tax purposes, (2) for the purpose of National Insurance contributions and (3) in relation to any claim for wrongful dismissal. At the present time, there are believed to be approximately 1.6 million self-employed people in the UK. SEE *Income Tax; National Insurance Contributions*

SEPON SEE *Talisman*

SEQUESTRATION In Scotland, a decree of sequestration is equivalent to an adjudication of bankruptcy in England. The word is also applied to the placing of a property, about which there is a dispute, in the hands of a third party until the dispute is settled. SEE ALSO *Writ of Sequestration*

SEQUESTRATION OF A BENEFICE When a benefice is vacant and before a new incumbent is appointed, the finances of the living are administered by a sequestrator, appointed by the diocesan bishop. The parochial church council has nothing to do with the duties of sequestration, nor has the sequestrator anything to do with the parochial church council. The income of the benefice is entirely distinct from the church funds. A sequestrator's duties are to receive the income of the benefice, to make such payments therefrom as are necessary for the services of the church, and to protect the property of the benefice. A special banking account should be opened by the sequestrator entitled 'Sequestration Account of the Benefice of X', and if more than one sequestrator is appointed, both or all must sign cheques, etc. The sequestration document should be produced when the account is opened and overdrafts are usually permitted in anticipation of income; interest on such overdraft is a lawful charge upon the account.

SET-OFF In law, set-off consists of the total or partial merging of a claim of one person against another in a counter-claim by the latter against the former. Whilst set-off may be given by agreement, it is essentially a statutory right or a right created by Rules of Court. The first statute giving a defendant a right to plead a set-off was passed in 1729 and re-enacted in 1735. These statutes are now repealed and their substance is found in the Rules of the Supreme Court. Where no right of set-off exists in law, it may be created by agreement express or implied, such as a course of mutual dealing.

A banker has a right of set-off in respect of different accounts of his customer which are in the same right and provided there is no agreement to the contrary. Thus there is no right of set-off against the credit balance on the account of a trustee or executor in respect of a debt on his private account. A credit balance on an executor's account cannot be set off against a debit balance on the decreased's account, neither can a credit balance on the deceased's account be set off against a debit balance on the executor's account, for set-off may only be claimed if both debts have arisen either before or after death.

A partner's credit balance cannot be set off against a debit balance on the firm's account unless several liability has been established. A credit balance on a firm's account cannot be set off against a debit balance on a partner's private account.

Credit balances on a solicitor's client account cannot be set off against moneys owing on the solicitor's other accounts (Solicitor's Act 1957, Section 85).

In the old case of *Marten* v *Rocke Eyton and Co* (1885), an auctioneer habitually paid the proceeds of sale of livestock into his private account at the bank. The bank knew the nature of the credits and had sanctioned an overdraft limit of £2,500. The bank without notice withdrew the facility and applied the proceeds of a sale in reduction of the overdraft. The plaintiff brought the action against the bank on behalf of all the vendors concerned for the recovery of the sale proceeds less the auctioneer's commission. It was held that the auctioneer paid the proceeds of the sale into his private account in the ordinary course of business and was not guilty of a breach of trust in so doing. The bank was entitled to take the action which it did and the plaintiff had no remedy against the bank.

In respect of local authorities, a loan or overdraft in connection with one undertaking cannot be set off against moneys appropriated to another, for such sums are in the nature of trust moneys raised for a specific object.

The conditions under which a right of set-off may be exercised depend on whether the accounts are 'stopped' or 'running' accounts. In the case of stopped accounts, the right of set-off accrues automatically. That is to say, where accounts are broken by death of the customer they may be combined before paying over to the legal personal representatives of the deceased; where a garnishee order is served in respect of a customer having more than one account in his own right, any debit balances may be set off before accounting to the judgment creditor.

Where the accounts are still operative, however, opinions differ as to whether a right of set-off accrues without notice. The case of *Garnett* v *McKewan* (1872) 27 LT 560 is high legal authority for the proposition that a banker may set off different accounts of his customer without notice, whether such accounts are kept at the same or different branches. Here, where a credit balance at one branch was appropriated to meet a dormant overdraft at another branch, resulting in the dishonour of cheques at the first branch, it was held that there was no special contract or usage proved to keep the accounts separate and that while it might be proper and considerate to give notice to a customer of intention to combine accounts, there is no legal obligation on a bank to do so, arising either from express contract or course of dealing.

In practice, a banker would not arbitrarily and without notice exercise his right of set-off unless he had an agreement to that effect or the customer was in breach of contract or had been guilty of fraud. The custom of taking a 'set-off letter' is very prevalent, but such an agreement does not create a right of set-off—it is rather evidence that the banker has not waived it and it avoids awkward situations that might arise if cheques were dishonoured without notice.

A deposit account may be set off against an overdraft, for the dishonour of cheques does not arise but a credit balance on current account cannot be set off against a loan account without notice unless payment of the loan has been demanded or unless there is an agreement to combine without notice.

Section 31 of the Bankruptcy Act 1914 provides as follows.

> Where there have been mutual credits, mutual debts or other mutual dealings, between a debtor against whom a receiving order shall be made under this Act and any other person proving or claiming to prove a debt under the receiving order, an account shall be taken of what is due from the one party to the other in respect of such mutual dealings, and the sum due from the one party shall be set off against any sum due from the other party, and the balance of the account, and no more, shall be claimed or paid on either side respectively; but a person shall not be entitled under this Section to claim the benefit of any set-off against the property of a debtor in

any case where he had, at the time of giving credit to the debtor, notice of an act of bankruptcy committed by the debtor and available against him.

Under the above Section a banker may, in the event of his customer's bankruptcy, set off a credit balance on the account against the contingent liability on any bills he has discounted for the customer. The banker has the same right when a company is being wound up.

In *Re E. J. Morel (1934) Ltd* [1962] Ch 21, it was held *inter alia* that where there was a stopped account in debit, a wages account also in debit, and a current account in credit, the bank could not set off the current account credit balance against the stopped account but must reduce the wages account (which was preferential). The decision depends on the express or implied agreement of banker and customer in each case.

In the case of *National Westminster Bank Ltd* v *Halesowen Presswork and Assemblies Ltd* [1972] AC 785, the House of Lords found in favour of the Bank where there had been an arrangement prior to liquidation that an existing loan account would be frozen for four months and the company permitted to operate a current account in credit. Liquidation ensued well before the four months expired and there was a substantial credit balance in the active account at the time. The decision was based on the ground that the agreement had not survived the liquidation. It is true that the construction was helped by the provision that it was not to apply in materially changed circumstances *if the bank* gave notice. No such notice was given and the decision sustains the principle that an agreement is terminated by the liquidation. Furthermore, the majority of the court considered, that Section 31 of the Bankruptcy Act 1914, providing for balances resulting from mutual dealings to be set off and applying also to liquidations, could not be the subject of specific exclusion by the parties. This may be an embarrassment where parties wish to agree to a moratorium since the opening of a separate account at another bank may not be acceptable to the first bankers. A possible solution may be the opening of an account with a subsidiary of the first bankers which would preclude set-off but enable the first bankers to know the extent of credit monies in existence. To avoid remotely possible controversy an authority to disclose could be taken from the customers. SEE *Clients' Account; Garnishee; Joint Account; Lien; Lien Receiver Order; Set-off*

SETTLED LAND The Settled Land Act 1925 consolidated the enactments relating to settled land, including the amendments contained in the Law of Property Act 1922.

Since 1925 every settlement of a legal estate in land *inter vivos* has had to be effected by two deeds, a 'vesting deed' and a 'trust instrument'. The former vests the land in the tenant for life of the whole fee simple or the absolute interest in a lease; and the latter declares the trusts of the settled land.

Trust Instrument

The trust instrument shall

1. declare the trusts affecting the land;
2. appoint trustees of the settlement;
3. contain the power, if any, to appoint new trustees;
4. set out any powers intended to be conferred by the settlement in extension of those conferred by this Act;
5. bear any *ad valorem* stamp duty which may be payable (whether by virtue of the vesting deed or otherwise) (Section 4).

Where a settlement is created by a will, the will becomes the trust instrument, and the personal representatives shall hold the settled land on trust to convey it to the person who is the tenant for life (Section 6).

Vesting Deed

By the vesting deed the legal estate in the land is conveyed to the tenant for life. A vesting deed shall contain the following particulars:

1. A description of the settled land.
2. A statement that the land is vested in the person to whom it is conveyed upon the trusts from time to time affecting the settled land.
3. The names of the trustees of the settlement.
4. The name of the person entitled to appoint new trustees (Section 5).

Where a settlement is created by will the personal representatives of the testator hold the land in trust and, when required, convey it to the tenant for life. This conveyance is effected by a vesting assent, in which the representatives assent to the vesting of the property and supply the same particulars as in a vesting deed.

On the death of a tenant for life, if the land remains settled land, his representatives convey it to the next tenant for life (Section 7). See as to special executors for settled land under *Personal Representatives*

Deed of Discharge

On the termination of a settlement, the trustees must execute a deed of discharge declaring that they are discharged from the trust. A purchaser is then entitled to assume that the land has ceased to be settled land (Section 17).

Dispositions of Settled Land
'Disposition' includes a mortgage, charge by way of legal mortgage, lease, and every other assurance of property except a will.

Any disposition by a tenant for life, unless authorized by this Act or any other statute, or powers in the vesting deed, shall be void, except to convey such equitable interests as he has under the trust instrument.

If any capital money is payable in respect of a transaction, a conveyance to a purchaser of the land shall only take effect if the capital money is paid to or by the direction of the trustees or into court.

Notwithstanding anything to the contrary in the vesting instrument or the trust instrument, capital money shall not, except where the trustee is a trust corporation, be paid to or by the direction of fewer persons than two as trustees of the settlement (Section 18).

(In certain instances a tenant for life can sell or mortgage, and the purchaser or mortgagee is not concerned as to his capacity—see above.)

Tenant for Life
A tenant for life is the person of full age who is for the time being beneficially entitled under a settlement to possession of settled land (Section 19).

Various other limited owners have powers of a tenant for life under Section 20 of the Act.

Land vested in trustees for charitable, ecclesiastical, or public trusts is deemed to be settled land, and the trustees have the powers of a tenant for life and of trustees of a settlement. A purchaser (including a mortgagee) of such land is bound to see that any consents or orders requisite for authorizing the transaction have been obtained.

Part II of the Act defines the powers of a tenant for life, to sell, exchange and lease the settled land.

The tenant for life has power to borrow money for the various purposes as detailed in Section 71, which includes money required to discharge an incumbrance on the settled land, or to pay for any improvement authorized by this Act or by the settlement, or to extinguish any manorial incidents, etc. He may raise the money so required on the security of the settled land, or of any part thereof, by a legal mortgage, and the money so raised shall be capital money.

Capital money arising under this Act shall not be paid to fewer than two trustees, unless the trustee is a trust corporation (Section 94). See also the provisions of Section 18 referred to above.

A purchaser or mortgagee is not concerned with the trusts of a settlement, or whether the vendor or mortgagor is in fact a tenant for life, or a person having the powers of a tenant for life, or whether the trustees are properly constituted Settled Land Act trustees. He has practically a certified life tenant and certified trustees with whom he can safely deal so long as he observes the above provisions as to capital money.

Section 110 gives protection to a purchaser or mortgagee dealing in good faith with the tenant for life. The purchaser or mortgagee of a legal estate in settled land is not entitled to call for the production of the trust instrument, or any information concerning it, or any *ad valorem* stamp duty thereon. He is entitled, if the last or only principal vesting instrument contains the particulars required by this Act, to assume that

1. the person in whom the land is thereby declared to be vested is the tenant for life and has all the powers of a tenant for life;
2. the persons stated therein to be the trustees are the properly constituted trustees of the settlement;
3. the particulars required by the Act and contained in the instrument were correct at its date.

Existing Settlements on 1st January, 1926
The settlement is to be treated as the trust instrument, and the trustee may, and on request of the tenant for life shall, execute a vesting deed declaring that the legal estate is vested in him (Schedule 2).

SETTLEMENT A settlement is an instrument which limits real or personal property, or the enjoyment thereof, to several persons in succession. It may be made by deed or by will. An example is the deed of settlement made by parties who are about to marry. SEE *Married Woman; Restraint on Anticipation; Settled Land*

Settlement Duty was abolished from August 1962 by the Finance Act 1962.

There is also a definition of 'Settlement' in Para (2) Finance Act 1975 for the purpose of capital transfer tax (q.v.).

SETTLEMENTS (SETTLOR BANKRUPT) Voluntary settlements by a person who subsequently becomes bankrupt are dealt with by Section 42 of the Bankruptcy Act 1914:

Avoidance of certain settlements

(1) Any settlement of property, not being a settlement made before and in consideration of marriage, or made in favour of a purchaser or incumbrancer in good faith and for valuable consideration, or a settlement made on or for the wife or children of the settlor of property which has accrued to the settlor after marriage in right of his wife, shall, if the settlor becomes bankrupt within two years after the date of the settlement, be void against the trustee in the bankruptcy, and shall, if the settlor

becomes bankrupt at any subsequent time within ten years after the date of the settlement, be void against the trustee in the bankruptcy, unless the parties claiming under the settlement can prove that the settlor was, at the time of making the settlement, able to pay all his debts without the aid of the property comprised in the settlement, and that the interest of the settlor in such property passed to the trustee of such settlement on the execution thereof.

(2) Any covenant or contract made by any person (hereinafter called the settlor) in consideration of his or her marriage, either for the future payment of money for the benefit of the settlor's wife or husband, or children, or for the future settlement on or for the settlor's wife or husband or children, of property, wherein the settlor had not at the date of the marriage any estate or interest, whether vested or contingent, in possession or remainder, and not being money or property in right of the settlor's wife or husband, shall, if the settlor is adjudged bankrupt and the covenant or contract has not been executed at the date of the commencement of his bankruptcy, be void against the trustee in the bankruptcy, except so far as it enables the persons entitled under the covenant or contract to claim for dividend in the settlor's bankruptcy under or in respect of the covenant or contract, but any such claim to dividend shall be postponed until all claims of the other creditors for valuable consideration in money or money's worth have been satisfied.

(3) Any payment of money (not being payment of premiums on a policy of life assurance) or any transfer of property made by the settlor in pursuance of such a covenant or contract as aforesaid shall be void against the trustee in the settlor's bankruptcy, unless the persons to whom the payment or transfer was made prove either—

(*a*) that the payment or transfer was made more than two years before the date of the commencement of the bankruptcy; or

(*b*) that at the date of the payment or transfer the settlor was able to pay all his debts without the aid of the money so paid or the property so transferred; or

(*c*) that the payment or transfer was made in pursuance of a covenant or contract to pay or transfer money or property expected to come to the settlor from or on the death of a particular person named in the covenant or contract and was made within three months after the money or property came into the possession or under the control of the settlor:

but, in the event of any such payment or transfer being declared void the persons to whom it was made shall be entitled to claim for dividend under or in respect of the covenant or contract in like manner as if it had not been executed at the commencement of the bankruptcy.

(4) 'Settlement' shall, for the purposes of this Section, include any conveyance or transfer of property. [SEE *Bankruptcy*]

In *Re Hart; ex parte Green* v *Hart & Lomas* (1912) 107 LT 368, a bankrupt made a voluntary transfer of shares to his daughter within two years before his bankruptcy. After he had committed an available act of bankruptcy the daughter transferred the shares to a bona fide purchaser for value who had no notice of the act of bankruptcy. Cozens-Hardy, MR, in the course of his judgment, said

It has been decided that the word 'void' in Section 42 must be construed as meaning 'voidable,' and not 'absolutely void,' and that a bona fide purchaser for value from the voluntary donee who has derived title to the property before the date of the commencement of the bankruptcy has a good title against the trustee in bankruptcy.

In this connection reference may be made to Section 172 of the Law of Property Act 1925, which is as follows.

172.—(1) Save as provided in this section, every conveyance of property, whether made before or after the commencement of this Act, with intent to defraud creditors, shall be voidable, at the instance of any person thereby prejudiced.

(2) This section does not affect the operation of a disentailing assurance, or the law of bankruptcy for the time being in force.

(3) This section does not extend to any estate or interest in property conveyed for valuable consideration and in good faith or upon good consideration and in good faith to any person not having, at the time of the conveyance, notice of the intent to defraud creditors.

SETTLEMENT, STOCK EXCHANGE The London Stock Exchange has two Accounts in each month, the intervening period being ordinarily 14 days. The settlement for each account lasts five days. The first is Making-up Day (Wednesday), when arrangements for postponing a settlement or delivery until the next account are made. The second day is Name Day or Ticket Day (Thursday), when a ticket passes in respect of each transaction from broker to jobber, specifying details for the transfer deed. The third and fourth days are known as 'intermediate' days (Friday and Monday), when uncompleted business on the Name Day is settled. The fifth day (Tuesday) is called Account Day or Settling Day or Pay Day, when securities bought for the Account are delivered, payments for purchases made, and differences settled.

During the war of 1939–45, settlements were abolished and all dealings were for cash. On 7th October, 1946, the Council of the Stock Exchange announced the resumption of fortnightly settlements as on 10th January, 1947. The settlement period was extended from four to five days by the inclusion of a second intermediate day on Monday, thus making the settling day Tuesday.

Settlements for British Government stocks is for cash.

The settling (pay) day on which securities bought or sold are due to be settled for is usually shown on the broker's contract note.

Securities payable to bearer are handed over on the settling day. Ten days are allowed in which to complete the delivery of registered securities; but if not delivered within that time the stock or shares may be 'bought in' through the official buying-in department, and the loss must be borne by the seller. SEE *Account, Stock Exchange*

SEVERAL LIABILITY SEE *Joint and Several Liability*

SEVERE DISABLEMENT ALLOWANCE This category of Social Security benefit was introduced with effect from November 1984 to replace the then existing non-contributory invalidity pension and housewives' non-contributory invalidity pension. The benefit is payable to persons who have become incapacitated for work when under the age of 20. It is also payable to persons who become incapacitated for work late in life through being severely disabled, the normal criterion being that of 80 per cent disability. SEE *Invalidity Benefit*

SHARE CAPITAL, SHARES A share is the right which a member of a company has to a certain proportion of the capital, the capital being the total fund contributed by the members. On the other hand, he is liable for any unpaid balance there may be on the shares he holds. Directors usually have power to decline to register any transfer of shares, not being fully-paid shares, to a person of whom they do not approve, and also to decline to register any transfer of shares on which the company has a lien (SEE *Transfer of Shares*). A minor should not be registered as a shareholder, because he can at any time during his minority repudiate the shares. The memorandum of association (q.v.) of a company limited by shares must state the amount of share capital with which the company proposes to be registered, and the division thereof into shares of a fixed amount.

There are special provisions with regard to the sale and transfer of bank shares. SEE *Leeman's Act*

Shares are known by various names, such as preference, guaranteed, ordinary, deferred, founders' shares and other varieties. The rights of each class of share depend upon the provisions in the memorandum and articles of association, or in special resolutions of the company. The rights attaching to a certain class of shares in one company are not necessarily the same as those in another company. (See Section 119, Companies Act 1985, given below.)

If authorized by its articles, a company limited by shares may convert its paid-up shares into stock (see Section 61, below). This is the only way in which it can create stock. Shares are, practically, divisions of stock in fixed amounts, and a shareholder obtains so many of those divisions, but a stockholder may obtain any (usually not less than 5p and multiples thereof) amount of the stock; for example, a share may be for 5p, 10p, 50p, £1, £5, £10, £20, £100 and such-like amounts, each share bearing a distinct number; whereas a holding of stock may be for £70, or for any amount, and without any distinguishing number. In an ordinary limited company, transfers of stock are generally, for convenience, restricted to certain round sums. In Government stocks, a transfer may be for any odd amount, e.g. £33.69.

Before an official quotation on the London Stock Exchange can be obtained for stocks and shares, the certificates must conform to certain regulations of the Council. The articles of association must provide that none of the funds of the company shall be employed in loans upon the security of its own shares, and that fully-paid shares shall be free from all lien.

Shares are taken as security in a variety of ways. The mere deposit of the certificate with an intent to charge gives an equitable mortgage on the shares. In the ordinary course a memorandum of deposit (q.v.) is taken when the share certificate is deposited. If it is not proposed to take a legal mortgage but to leave the shares in the borrower's name, notice of lien may be given to the company, although in the case of fully-paid shares with an official quotation this is superfluous, for such shares cannot be the subject of a lien by the company (SEE *Notice of Lien*). Sometimes a blank transfer is taken in which the name of the bank's nominee may be inserted as transferee. More rarely, a completed transfer is taken and stamped but held unregistered (SEE *Blank Transfer*). All such methods do not give complete security and the only way of perfecting the security is to have the shares registered in the name of the bank or its nominee. Otherwise, if the registered holder of shares should prove to be merely a trustee, or a nominee of the true owner, the banker, who takes the certificate as security for an advance to the registered holder, may have to surrender the certificate if the true owner intervenes before the banker has had the shares registered in his own name. But when the banker, without notice of any prior equitable charge, has been registered he obtains the legal title to the shares. SEE *Transfer of Shares*

Where the shares are only partly paid, however,

they are not, save in exceptional circumstances, transferred, for not only would the bank be liable for calls, but such liability would continue until one year after they had been retransferred or sold.

In most cases, a certificate must be surrendered before a transfer of the shares can be effected, but this is not an absolute protection to a banker, as it has been held that a footnote upon a certificate to the effect that no transfer of the shares will be effected without production of the certificate does not constitute a contract and is not binding on the company. SEE *Certificate*

The Companies Act 1985, provides as follows:

182.—(1) The shares or other interest of any member in a company—

(*a*) are personal estate or, in Scotland, moveable property and are not in the nature of real estate or heritage,

(*b*) are transferable in manner provided by the company's articles, but subject to the Stock Transfer Act 1963 (which enables securities of certain descriptions to be transferred by a simplified process).

(2) Each share in a company having a share capital shall be distinguished by its appropriate number; except that, if at any time all the issued shares in a company, or all the issued shares in it of a particular class, are fully paid up and rank pari passu for all purposes, none of those shares need thereafter have a distinguishing number so long as it remains fully paid up and ranks pari passu for all purposes with all shares of the same class for the time being issued and fully paid up.

186. A certificate, under the common seal of the company or the seal kept by the company by virtue of Section 40, specifying any shares held by a member is prima facie evidence of his title to those shares.

Membership of a company is defined in Section 22 of the 1985 Act, re-enacting Section 26 of the 1948 Act as follows:

(1) The subscribers of a company's memorandum are deemed to have agreed to become members of the company, and on its registration shall be entered as such in its register of members.

(2) Every other person who agrees to become a member of a company, and whose name is entered in its register of members, is a member of the company.

Provision for different amounts to be paid on shares

119. A company, if so authorised by its articles, may do any one or more of the following things:

(*a*) make arrangements on the issue of shares for a difference between the shareholders in the amounts and times of payment of calls on their shares

(*b*) accept from any member the whole or a part of the amount remaining unpaid on any shares held by him, although no part of that amount has been called up;

(*c*) pay dividend in proportion to the amount paid up on each share where a larger amount is paid up on some shares than on others.

Alteration of share capital

121.—(1) A company limited by shares or a company limited by guarantee and having a share capital, if so authorised by its articles, may alter the conditions of its memorandum in any of the following ways.

(2) The company may—

(*a*) increase its share capital by new shares of such amount as it thinks expedient;

(*b*) consolidate and divide all or any of its share capital into shares of larger amount than its existing shares;

(*c*) convert all or any of its paid-up shares into stock, and re-convert that stock into paid-up shares of any denomination;

(*d*) sub-divide its shares, or any of them, into shares of smaller amount than is fixed by the memorandum (but subject to the following subsection);

(*e*) cancel shares which, at the date of the passing of the resolution to cancel them, have not been taken or agreed to be taken by any person, and diminish the amount of the company's share capital by the amount of the shares so cancelled.

(3) In any sub-division under subsection (2)(*d*) the proportion between the amount paid and the amount, if any, unpaid on each reduced share must be the same as it was in the case of the share from which the reduced share is derived.

(4) The powers conferred by this section must be exercised by the company in general meeting.

(5) A cancellation of shares under this section does not for purposes of this Act constitute a reduction of share capital.

Notice to the Registrar of Companies must be given of any increase of share capital, consolidation of share capital, conversion of shares into stock, etc (Sections 122 and 123).

Maintenance of Capital

The Companies Act 1980 introduced a number of measures concerning the maintenance of share capital. In particular, it enacted that if it becomes known to the directors of a public company that there has been a serious loss of capital, they must convene an extraordinary general meeting to inform the shareholders and to consider what measures, if any, should be taken to deal with the matter. In this context, a serious loss of capital is deemed to occur when a company's net assets represent 50 per cent or less of its called up capital.

Under Section 143 of the 1985 Act, a company which has a share capital may not acquire its own shares except as specifically provided for in the Act. All companies with a share capital may acquire their own fully paid shares by way of gift, and any company may acquire its own shares in a reduction of capital. SEE *Company's Purchase of Own Shares, Reduction of Share Capital*

Under the 1980 Act, re-enacted in the 1985 Act a company is not considered to have acquired its own shares where

1. it redeems preference shares under a power in the articles;
2. it purchases shares under a Court Order; or
3. shares have been forfeited or surrendered in accordance with the articles where there has been a failure to pay a sum of money due in respect of the shares.

A company may, if so authorized by its articles, issue redeemable preference shares, but the redemption of redeemable preference shares must be out of profits available for distribution (Companies Act 1980). SEE *Blank Transfer; Call; Company; Company Purchase of Own Shares; Holding Out; Leeman's Act; Reduction of Share Capital; Stock; Transfer of Shares*

SHARE CERTIFICATE SEE *Certificate*

SHARE EXCHANGE SCHEME A scheme operated by a number of unit trust groups to enable investors to exchange their existing portfolios for units in a unit trust. Those groups which operate such schemes will normally take privately owned shares into their portfolios at a price higher than the bid price which the investor would obtain in the market. Any holdings which the trust managers do not wish to retain will be sold but some groups pay the Stock Exchange commission on the sales. The exchange of shares for units in this way nevertheless constitutes a disposal for capital gains tax purposes.

SHARE OPTION SCHEMES These are schemes under which directors and employees of companies are given options to acquire shares in their company at a pre-determined price. Thus, if during the option term the market price of shares rise, the director or employee can exercise the option at the option price and thereby secure, in some cases, a considerable capital gain. The law and Inland Revenue practice relating to share option and profit-sharing schemes generally became somewhat obscure, partly because of the repeated legislation on the subject. To some extent however, the position has been clarified by the 1984 Finance Act. In broad terms, there are the following categories of profit-sharing and option schemes:

(1) Profit sharing schemes under the Finance Act 1978, as amended. SEE *Profit Sharing Schemes*

(2) Share option schemes under the Finance Act 1980 (see below).

(3) Savings related share option schemes under the Finance Act 1980. SEE *Savings Related Share Option Scheme*

(4) Share option schemes under the Finance Act 1984 (see below).

In the case of option schemes established prior to 6th April, 1984, the tax liability on a director or employee receiving and subsequently exercising an option could be very considerable. Under the Finance Act 1972, if an option was given for a period of more than seven years, tax would be payable at the time of the granting of the option on its notional value and, in all cases (prior to 6th April, 1984) there is a prima facie liability for tax at the time the option is taken up. Income tax is payable on the value of the shares at the time the option is exercised, less the price paid by the employee for the shares and any price he paid for the option itself. This latter liability to Schedule E income tax still applies to schemes approved under the Finance Act 1980.

However, under the Finance Act 1984, new share option schemes may be approved by the Inland Revenue provided that they satisfy certain requirements regarding the size of the options, their duration and the frequency of their exercise. In such cases, participants will not be subject to Schedule E income tax liability at the time the option is exercised on any increase in value of the shares between the date the option was granted and the date it is exercised. Any such gain will continue, however, to be subject to the normal rules of capital gains tax when the disposal of the shares takes place.

The principal conditions are for approval of share option schemes under the 1984 Act are:

(1) Participants under the scheme must be full-time directors or 'qualifying employees', viz. employees who are required, under the terms of their employment, to work for the company for at least 20 hours per week. A full-time director is one who is required to devote substantially the whole of his time to his duties as a director.

(2) Under the terms of the scheme, no person may acquire options which, at the time the options are granted, extend to a market value of shares exceeding the greater of (a) £100,000, or (b) four times the participants' emoluments for the current year or the preceding year of assessment (whichever is the greater).

(3) The scheme must not permit any participant to transfer his or her option to any other person (although if the scheme so provides, an option may be exercised up to one year after the date of a participant's death).

In order to secure the exemption from Schedule E income tax as mentioned above, the option must be exercised by the participant not less than three years, nor more than 10 years, from the date the option was granted, and an option may not be exercised within three years of the date on which the participant last exercised an option under the same scheme, or under any other scheme approved under the 1984 Act.

Schemes set up prior to 6th April, 1984, may be submitted to the Inland Revenue for approval under the 1984 legislation, provided that all necessary amendments to the scheme have been made in order to conform with the 1984 Act. Income tax relief under the 1984 Act cannot however, apply to options granted under such earlier schemes prior to 6th April, 1984.

SHARE PREMIUM ACCOUNT If shares in a company are issued at a price in excess of their nominal or par value, the difference is credited to a share premium account. This forms part of the reserves of the company and, being of a capital nature, is not available for the payment of dividends. The obligation to create a share premium account arose under Section 56 of the Companies Act 1948, and led to problems in some cases on the merger of two companies for a 'paper' consideration, i.e. where one company issued its shares to the members of another company in exchange for the transfer of shares in that company.

The Companies Act 1981, Sections 37 and 38 (Ss. 131–132, 1985 Act), provide relief from Section 56 of the 1948 Act in the following circumstances.

1. Where the company issuing the shares is a wholly-owned subsidiary of another company and allots shares either to the holding company or to another wholly-owned subsidiary in consideration for the transfer of shares of another subsidiary of the holding company, the amount to be transferred to the share premium account need not exceed the excess over the nominal value of the shares of the cost to the transferor company or the book value of those shares in the transferor company immediately before the transfer, whichever is the less.

2. Where a company issues shares in exchange for at least 90 per cent of the equity share capital of another company Section 56 of the 1948 Act (S. 130, 1985 Act) no longer applies to the extent that there is a premium in the price.

SHARE REGISTRATION It is a requirement of Section 352, Companies Act 1985, that every company shall keep a register of its members and that the register will contain the names and addresses of the members, a statement of the shares held by each member, distinguishing each share by its number, so long as it has one, and the amount paid or agreed to be considered as paid on the shares of each member. The register must also show the date on which each person was entered as a member and the date on which any person ceased to be a member. Section 722 of the Act also requires the register of a company to be kept either in a bound book or in such other form as may be adequate to guard against falsification. Under the Stock Exchange (Completion of Bargains) Act 1976, there is provision for company registers to be kept 'otherwise than in a legible form so long as the recording is capable of being reproduced in a legible form'. The purpose of the Act was to permit company registers to be stored on computers.

There are about eight major registration services operating in England, handling approximately 12 million shareholder accounts, out of a total market of about 20 million. Five of these are clearing bank registrars who handle seven million or so individual shareholder accounts. There is a continuing trend for company registration work to be centred in the hands of these service registrars, thereby saving the companies concerned a considerable amount of work in the control of the company registers. Company registrarship includes not only the maintenance of the members' registers, but also the preparation of share certificates, answering enquiries from shareholders and stockbrokers, making dividend or interest payments, convening meetings, issuing the statutory returns and dealing with a very considerable volume of stock transfers.

SHAREHOLDER BENEFITS In addition to normal dividend payments, some companies allow benefits in kind to their shareholders, the benefit usually relating to the particular type of business in which the company in engaged. Thus, some hotel companies offer their shareholders a reduction on room prices, tailors offer reduction on clothing, a cross-Channel ferry company offers reduction on fares to the Continent, a dry cleaning company offers a reduction on its cleaning charges and so on. There are now many such instances and, as the matter stands at present, such benefits are not taxed in the hands of shareholders.

SHAREHOLDERS' REGISTER SEE *Register of Members of Company*

SHILLING This coin has varied considerably in value at different times. A coin of that name was first issued in 1504. In 1560 a pound troy of silver was coined into 60 shillings. In 1600 it was coined into 62 shillings, and by the Act 56 George III it was ordered to be coined into 66 shillings out of a pound troy of silver of the fineness of 11 ounces two pennyweights of fine silver and 18 pennyweights of alloy in every pound weight troy. A shilling was later minted of three-quarter copper and one-quarter nickel. On decimalization it became a 5p piece. SEE *Coinage; Decimal Coinage*

SHIP Every British ship shall, unless exempted from registry, be registered under the Merchant Shipping Act 1894. Ships not exceeding 15 tons burden, employed solely in navigation on the rivers or coasts of the UK, are exempt from registry under the Act.

The chief officer of customs is the registrar of British ships at any port in the UK, or Isle of Man, approved by the Commissioners of Customs for the registry of ships.

When registered, the registrar shall grant a certificate of registry. The certificate of registry shall be used only for the lawful navigation of the ship, and shall not be subject to detention by reason of any title, lien, charge or interest by any owner, mortgagee or other person.

Most ships are also registered at Lloyd's Register of Shipping, and their names appear in Lloyd's Register with particulars of the registered tonnage, classification, survey, age, builders, owners, port of registry and engines. Registration with Lloyd's facilitates insurance and also charterings.

The property in a ship is divided into 64 shares.

A person is not entitled to be registered as owner of a fractional part of a share, but any number of persons not exceeding five may be registered as joint owners of a ship or of any share therein.

A corporation may be registered as owner by its corporate name.

A registered ship or a share therein (when disposed of to a person qualified to own a British ship) shall be transferred by bill of sale.

The bill of sale must be in the form as specified by the Merchant Shipping Act 1894.

A purchaser of a registered British vessel does not obtain a complete title until the bill of sale has been recorded at the port of registry of the ship; and neglect of this precaution may entail serious consequences.

A registrar shall indorse on the bill of sale the fact of the registration with the day and hour thereof.

The following Sections of the Merchant Shipping Act 1894, regulate mortgages of a ship or shares therein:

Mortgage of ship or share

31.—(1) A registered ship or a share therein may be made a security for a loan or other valuable consideration, and the instrument creating the security (in this Act called a mortgage) shall be in the form marked B in the first part of the first schedule to this Act, or as near thereto as circumstances permit, and on the production of such instrument the registrar of the ship's port of registry shall record it in the register book.

(2) Mortgages shall be recorded by the registrar in the order in time in which they are produced to him for that purpose, and the registrar shall by memorandum under his hand notify on each mortgage that it has been recorded by him, stating the day and hour of that record.

Entry of discharge of mortgage

32. Where a registered mortgage is discharged, the registrar shall, on the production of the mortgage deed, with a receipt for the mortgage money indorsed thereon, duly signed and attested, make an entry in the register book to the effect that the mortgage has been discharged, and on that entry being made the estate (if any) which passed to the mortgagee shall vest in the person in whom (having regard to intervening acts and circumstances, if any) it would have vested if the mortgage had not been made.

Priority of mortgages

33. If there are more mortgages than one registered in respect of the same ship or share, the mortgagees shall, notwithstanding any express, implied, or constructive notice, be entitled in priority, one over the other, according to the date at which each mortgage is recorded in the register book, and not according to the date of each mortgage itself.

Mortgagee not treated as owner

34. Except as far as may be necessary for making a mortgaged ship or share available as a security for the mortgage debt, the mortgagee shall not by reason of the mortgage be deemed the owner of the ship, or share, nor shall the mortgagor be deemed to have ceased to be the owner thereof.

Mortgagee to have power of sale

35. Every registered mortgagee shall have power absolutely to dispose of the ship or share in respect of which he is registered, and to give effectual receipts for the purchase money; but where there are more persons than one registered as mortgagees of the same ship or share, a subsequent mortgagee shall not, except under the order of a Court of competent jurisdiction, sell the ship or share without the concurrence of every prior mortgagee.

Mortgage not affected by bankruptcy

36. A registered mortgage of a ship or share shall not be affected by any act of bankruptcy committed by the mortgagor after the date of the record of the mortgage, notwithstanding that the mortgagor at the commencement of his bankruptcy had the ship or share in his possession, order or disposition, or was reputed owner thereof, and the mortgage shall be preferred to any right, claim or interest therein of the other creditors of the bankrupt or any trustee or assignee on their behalf.

Transfer of Mortgages

The main provisions of sections 37 and 38 are as follows:

A registered mortgage of a ship or share may be transferred to any person, and the instrument effecting the transfer shall be in the prescribed form, or as near thereto as circumstances permit. On production of such instrument, the registrar shall record it in the register and notify the fact on the instrument of transfer.

Where the interest of a mortgagee is transmitted on marriage, death, or bankruptcy, or by any lawful means, other than by a transfer under this Act, the transmission shall be authenticated by a declaration of the person to whom the interest is transmitted, containing a statement of the manner in which and the person to whom the property has been transmitted, and shall be accompanied by the like evidence as is by this Act required in case of a corresponding transmission of the ownership of a ship or share. On receipt of the declaration and the production of the evidence, the registrar shall register the person entitled as mortgagee.

Mortgage to Secure Current Account

The prompt registration of a mortgage deed at the port of registry of the ship is essential to the security of the mortgagee, as a mortgage takes its priority from the date of registration, not from the date of the instrument. A record of the registration is notified on the mortgage, e.g. 'Registered 4th day of April 19 ..., at 10 am, J. Brown, Registrar of Shipping, ...' Before advancing money on the mortgage of a ship, a banker should search the register to see if there is any prior registration outstanding. Unless the mortgage is in the special form to secure a current account, he should search again before increasing the loan.

Although the prescribed form of mortgage must be completed, it contains only general covenants, and it is usual for a banker to supplement this form of mortgage with a collateral deed imposing additional stipulations. Such a deed would provide for payment on demand and for the security to be available for all liabilities however they may arise. It would make clear the circumstances under which the security becomes enforceable, and would reserve to the banker power to insure, if the mortgagor failed to do so, the premiums being added to the principal sum due.

This collateral deed does not have to be registered.

Very occasionally a mortgage will extend to items not included as part of the ship, e.g. furniture or, perhaps, freights.

A transfer of mortgage, to be indorsed on the original mortgage, is as follows:

['I' or 'we'] the within-mentioned ... in consideration of ... this day paid to ['me' or 'us'] by ... hereby transfer to ['him' or 'them'] the benefit of the within-written security. In witness whereof [etc., as above].

When a mortgage is paid-off, the following memorandum of its discharge may be indorsed on the mortgage:

Received the sum of £... in discharge of the within-written security. Dated at ... this ... day of ... 19 ....

Witness ..... of ....

A banker may insert, as the sum received in discharge of the mortgage, a nominal amount of, say, £1. When the discharge is registered, the mortgage is marked: 'Discharge registered 10th day of May 19...., at 3 pm, J. Brown, Registrar of Shipping, ...'

The Commissioners of Customs may, with the consent of the Department of Trade and Industry, make such alterations in the prescribed forms as they may deem requisite (Section 65). The forms can be obtained from the registrar at any port of registry.

No notice of any trust, express, implied, or constructive shall be entered in the register book (Section 56).

Any register book may be inspected on payment of a fee not exceeding five pence (Section 64).

Any instruments used with regard to the registry ownership and mortgage of a British ship are exempt from stamp duty (Section 721). SEE *Stamp Duty*

When a banker takes a mortgage upon a ship, the policy of insurance should be left in his possession, and it is better that it should be in the bank's name. In some cases, however, it is sufficient if a letter is given by the customer stating that he holds the policy on behalf of the bank.

The insurance should cover not only the valuation of the vessel but also the statutory liability for salvage and personal injury.

When the premiums are payable quarterly, the brokers of the underwriters will require to hold the policy, and in that case a letter should be taken from the brokers stating that they hold the policy (subject to their claim for the amount of any quarterly premiums remaining unpaid), on behalf of the bank, and undertaking to advise the bank of any premiums which fall due and are not paid. The policy should not be in a mutual society if the banker is not prepared to accept liability for calls.

In a mutual insurance company 'no owner whose shares in a ship are mortgaged shall be insured by the company unless the mortgagee or other approved person shall give a written guarantee to the satisfaction of the directors for payment of all demands in respect of such ship'. In taking policies, the banker should inquire as to liabilities and, generally, as to the nature of the policies.

It is very essential that a ship should be entered by the owner in a protection club for the risks of protection, indemnity and defence, and be insured up to so much per ton on her gross registered tonnage against liability for damage that may be done by the boat to other vessels. A banker should satisfy himself that this important matter has been attended to by the owner.

The valuation of a ship as security may prove a difficult problem. It is, perhaps, possible to arrive at an approximate assessment on the basis of the age, type and size of the vessel, for the current values are usually ascertainable in the ports, and a valuation according to a sliding scale based on length, type and age may suffice. Otherwise, it will be necessary to have a professional valuation, which will add to the cost for the borrower.

The mortgage should, as stated above, be registered at once. If there is a bill of sale in the customer's possession, it is usual to have it lodged, as it is useful to supply the particulars required for the mortgage, but the banker's security is obtained by registration of the mortgage. There is no value in the bill of sale itself, as, upon a sale or mortgage, it is not required by the registrar.

By Section 395 of the Companies Act 1985, 'a charge on a ship or any share in a ship' given by a company must be registered with the Registrar of Companies (SEE UNDER *Registration of Charges*). It must also be registered under the Merchant Shipping Act 1894.

Registration of the statutory mortgages of ships under the Merchant Shipping Act has the effect of fixing the priority of mortgages.

When a banker receives notice of a second registered mortgage upon the ship over which he already holds a registered mortgage to secure a current account, the account should be broken. SEE *Notice of Second Mortgage*

If a banker has a mortgage on less than 33 shares, the management of the ship is in the hands of those who hold the majority of the shares, a position which may not prove satisfactory to the banker.

The register exists only for British ships, and if a vessel should be sold to a foreign flag, the registrar will give notice to any mortgagee whose charge is entered on the register that the transfer is taking place. If a reply of satisfaction is received the entry is expunged from the register; if the reply is otherwise, the entry remains, but the transfer of the vessel still takes place. The effect is that the registrar gives a mortgagee notice, and the mortgagee must then look out for himself. It is all-important that the mortgagors should be men of honour, or the security may, in the above way, suddenly disappear. SEE *Certificate of Mortgage of Ship*

A British ship is liable to be attached in a foreign port for a debt incurred in that country, and whenever that happens it is clear that the value of a banker's mortgage in this country may be seriously affected. A lien on the ship, in priority to a mortgage, may arise from a collision at sea, and from services with regard to salvage of the ship, a salvor having a maritime lien on the property salved. The master who has ordered necessaries and is personally liable to pay for them has a prior claim to a mortgagee. In the case of a foreign owned ship, a merchant who has supplied it with stores may sometimes enforce his claim in priority to a mortgagee. The claim of the crew for wages always ranks in front of a mortgage. SEE ALSO *Bottomry Bond; General Average; Particular Average*

SHIP MORTGAGE FINANCE COMPANY LIMITED This company was formed in 1951 to assist in financing shipbuilding in Britain. It makes loans to British and foreign shipowners normally on the security of a first mortgage on ships constructed in British shipyards. It will also subscribe share capital in shipping companies and will arrange ship leasing transactions when applicable. The share and loan capital have been subscribed by the Shipbuilders' and Repairers' National Association, ICFC and some 50 insurance companies and financial institutions. Since 1951 the company has assisted in financing the building of over 100 ships by the provision of finance totalling more than £30 million from its own funds and by finding participants for a further £19 million. The company's advances and investments are currently in excess of £13 million. In 1968 it began to provide post-delivery finance for hovercraft.

The company acts for the Government in the operation of the Guaranteed Loan Scheme which was introduced under the Shipbuilding Industry Act 1967. The operation of the scheme has affected the volume of the company's other business, since many of the loans made under the scheme at concessionary rates of interest would normally have been made by the company. Under an earlier scheme a loan of £17.6 million was made available in 1963 to the Cunard Steam-Ship Co Ltd to finance the construction of the liner Queen Elizabeth 2. The Company has also financed a number of sales of second-hand ships to foreign buyers.

SHIP'S HUSBAND The person to whom the

management of a ship is entrusted by or on behalf of the owner. Any person whose name is so registered at the custom house of the port of registry of the ship shall, for the purposes of the Merchant Shipping Act 1894, be under the same obligations and subject to the same liabilities as if he were the managing owner (Section 59 of the Act).

A ship's husband, unless authorized by the owners of the ship, has no power to borrow so as to bind the owners. SEE *Ship*

SHORTHOLD TENANCY This is a type of protected tenancy introduced under Section 51–55 of the Housing Act 1980. For a protected shorthold tenancy to exist, all the following conditions must apply.

1. It must be for a term of at least one year and not more than five years.
2. It must not be determinable by the landlord before the expiry of the term, except in the case of forfeiture.
3. Before the tenancy was granted the landlord must have given to the tenant a valid notice stating that the tenancy was to be a protected shorthold tenancy.
4. A fair rent for the dwelling house must have been registered at the time of the grant or application made for registration of a fair rent within 28 days.
5. Immediately before the tenancy was granted the tenant must not have been a protected or statutory tenant under the Rent Acts.

At the end of a protected shorthold tenancy, the landlord may recover possession after serving due notice on the tenant, in accordance with the terms of the Act.

SICKNESS BENEFIT This is a Social Security benefit applicable to persons who are normally employed or self-employed and who have paid the requisite number of Class I or Class II National Insurance contributions (SEE *National Insurance Contributions*). The benefit is payable for the first 28 weeks of illness, but see *Statutory Sick Pay*.

Sickness benefit is a flat-rate weekly payment with additions for adult dependents and children. It is not payable unless the claimant has been incapable of work for four consecutive days (excluding Sundays). Once the four qualifying days have passed, the benefit will continue for the period of the illness. If the claimant subsequently becomes ill again, a further minimum period of four qualifying days will apply. If the second period of incapacity occurs within eight weeks of the first period of illness, the two periods will be added together for the purpose of calculating the 28 weeks of benefit. If however, the second illness is more than eight weeks after the first, the twenty-eight week period will commence to run afresh.

Where Statutory Sick Pay is payable, sickness benefit is not payable during the period that Statutory Sick Pay is received.

Where an illness lasts for one week or less, claimants may issue their own sickness claims (self-certification) but for longer periods of illness a doctor's statement is necessary.

Sickness benefit cannot be paid at any time when the claimant is receiving unemployment pay, widow's benefit, maternity allowance, industrial injuries benefit, training allowance or retirement pension. It is not affected however, by attendance allowance, maternity grant or industrial disablement pension.

The payment of sickness benefit is not affected by the fact that an employer, a trade union, a friendly society, or other insurer may continue to pay remuneration or other allowances or benefits to the claimant.

Benefit may cease if the claimant, or a dependent for whom it is claimed, does any work during the period of sickness. A claimant who wishes to undertake any work during the benefit period must obtain consent from the local Social Security office, who will wish to know the views of the claimant's doctor on the subject and the amount which it is proposed to earn after deducting allowable expenses. In the ordinary way permission to work during the currency of sickness benefit will not be granted where the anticipated earnings exceed the lower earnings limit (q.v.).

Sickness benefit will normally be reduced after a claimant has been in hospital for more than eight weeks if he or she is receiving free in-patient treatment.

Sickness benefit may be discontinued for a period of up to six weeks if the claimant

1. becomes sick through his or her own misconduct,
2. does anything to retard his or her recovery,
3. fails to give notice to the local Social Security office on leaving the address which has been given to the office, or
4. refuses to see a doctor from the Regional Medical Service at the request of the local Social Security office.

SIGHT BILL A bill of exchange payable 'at sight' is payable on presentation. The due date of a bill payable at a period 'after sight' is calculated from the date of sighting. SEE *Sighting a Bill*

SIGHTING A BILL When a bill is drawn at

a fixed period after sight, it is sent to the drawee to be 'sighted'; that is, that he may accept the drawer's order for payment by signing his name across the face of the bill with the date of his acceptance. The date when the bill will be due can then be calculated from the date of the acceptance. If he omits to insert a date, the holder may put in what he considers the true date (SEE *Date on Bill of Exchange*). If the acceptor writes across the bill 'Sighted 1st June, accepted 2nd June', the currency is calculated from 1st June, as the holder is entitled to have the bill accepted with the date when first presented for acceptance.

A bill payable at sight is equivalent to one payable on demand. SEE *Bill of Exchange; Time of Payment of Bill*

SIGNATURE If a banker pays a cheque on which his customer's signature is forged, he cannot charge it to the latter's account unless the drawer is estopped from denying its genuineness (SEE *Forgery*). If a drawer's signature differs from his usual one and a banker is in doubt as to whether or not it is genuine, it is customary to return the cheque with the answer 'signature differs'.

When a cheque is returned with the answer 'signature differs', the paying banker should inform the drawer that the cheque has been returned. Failure to warn the drawer might, if the signature proved to be a forgery, involve the banker in a claim for damages. In *Greenwood* v *Martins Bank Ltd* [1932] 1 KB 371, Scrutton, LJ, in the course of his judgment said

> The banker, if a cheque was presented to him which he rejected as forged, would be under a duty to report that to the customer to enable him to inquire into and protect himself against the circumstances of forgery. That would involve a corresponding duty on the customer, if he became aware that forged cheques were being presented to his banker, to inform the banker in order that the banker might avoid loss in the future.

As to a bill of exchange made, accepted, or indorsed by a company, see Section 33, Companies Act 1948, under *Indorsement*.

Section 91 of the Bills of Exchange Act says

> Where, by this Act, any instrument or writing is required to be signed by any person, it is not necessary that he should sign it with his own hand, but it is sufficient if his signature is written thereon by some other person by or under his authority.

A banker, however, would require a proper authority from a customer before paying a cheque on which the drawer's signature was written by someone other than the drawer himself. In cases where a customer desires to give authority to another to draw cheques upon his account, it is much better that the usual method should be adopted and cheques be signed per pro. SEE *Mandate*

A signature may consist of a cross or similar mark and is occasionally met with in the case of persons unable to write or so ill that the labour of a full signature is beyond their strength. Such a mark is customarily witnessed by two persons, and a banker would normally honour a cheque so authenticated if he were satisfied of the standing of the witnesses or had cognisance of the circumstances. The use of a description or an assumed name will, in appropriate circumstances, constitute a signature. By way of comparison, *In the Estate of Cook, deceased* [1960] 1 All ER 689, the deceased had written a will which began in the usual form by identifying the testatrix by name and ended with a bequest to her son, followed by the words 'your loving mother'. It was held that these words were meant to represent the name of the testatrix and were a sufficient signature for the purposes of the Wills Act 1837.

The practice of signing with an ordinary pencil is not a desirable one, and it is advisable to discourage it as much as possible. A signature may be lithographed, as in the case of dividend warrants, or it may be placed on a cheque by means of a rubber stamp by the person whose signature it is, or by anyone duly authorized by him. A rubber stamp signature, however, is full of danger, and its use should be avoided. A cheque with a stamped signature should not be paid without verification, unless a written authority is held from the customer that such signatures are to be accepted. SEE *Facsimile Signature*

It is very imprudent for anyone to put his signature on a blank cheque, and a person so signing may be liable to a holder in due course, not for the amount which he authorized to be filled in above his signature, but for the amount which actually is filled in. SEE *Alterations to Bill of Exchange*

For many years it was understood that a person who signed a document in the mistaken belief that it was a different type of document could plead the defence *non est factum*, i.e. that the signature was null and void on the grounds that the mind of the party signing it 'did not go with his pen'. Thus, in *Carlisle and Cumberland Banking Company* v *Bragg* [1911] 1 KB 489, where Bragg had signed a bank guarantee, having been deliberately misled by the principal debtor into believing that it was a proposal for insurance, it was held that Bragg was not liable on the guarantee because he had no intention of entering into that particular contract. In more recent times, however, this was overruled in *Saunders* v *Anglia Building Society* [1970] 3 All ER 961. In that case, an elderly lady had assigned the leasehold interest in her property to a Mr Lee in the mistaken belief that she was, in fact, assigning it to her nephew, Mr Parkin. Subsequently, the property was charged to a bona fide third party, i.e. the building society. The House of Lords upheld the decision of the Court of Appeal that a person who signs a document without taking the trouble to read it and relies on the word of another person as to its character or contents or effect, cannot subsequently plead *non est factum*. Lord Reid said

I do not say that the remedy (*non est factum*) can never be available to a man of full capacity. But that could only be in very exceptional circumstances: certainly not where his reason for not scrutinising the document before signing it was that he was too busy or too lazy. In general, I do not think that he can be heard to say that he signed in reliance on someone he trusted. ... There must, I think, be a radical difference between what he signed and what he thought he was signing ... what amounts to a radical difference will depend on all the circumstances.

SILVER, INVESTMENT IN The advantages of silver as an investment are

1. It is virtually indestructible.
2. It is universally acceptable.
3. It is a rare metal.
4. Most silver pieces are functional.
5. There is a great variety of silverware.
6. The system of hallmarking ensures authenticity (see below).
7. Silverwork is an art form.
8. It has reflected movements in other art forms, notably architecture and painting.
9. It is pleasing to look at and to hold.

On the other hand, there are the disadvantages that (1) there is a security risk, (2) insurance premiums for a collection may be high, (3) values change with fashion, and (4) it needs cleaning (but can be treated to obviate this).

There is not much very old silver in existence. This is partly because of the ancient custom of melting down silver pieces to be refashioned in new designs (nobody kept old pieces for their own sake in those days), but more particularly because of the melting down of silver to pay for expensive wars and expensive tastes of successive monarchs. Silver was used to finance 'public expenditure' before the days when governments could print paper money. Thus, silver was used to pay the ransom for Richard I in 1194, it was used following the sacking of the monasteries by Henry VIII to pay for his expensive habits and it was used by both sides to pay for the Civil War. The Church lost most of its silver to the Tudors; the Oxford and Cambridge colleges lost most of their silver to Charles I. Only about 400 pieces of silver have survived from mediaeval times.

Silver came into its own again with the restoration of the monarchy in 1660 and by common consent that is the beginning of the age of English antique silver. That age gradually drew to a close in the mid-1800s with the advent of machinery to replace the craftsman in silver, but the accepted date for silver to be treated as 'antique' is 1880. This is by international agreement for the purpose of Customs' duties. From 1881 onwards, silver is 'modern'.

The collector or investor will encounter little or nothing prior to 1660 for the reasons mentioned. From that date onwards, however, there is an abundance of collectable items of English silver, whether antique or modern, in addition to which there are plenty of collectable pieces made in other countries. English old silver (it should perhaps be British old silver because all the four countries of the British Isles have produced superb silver pieces) did in fact follow the classical designs of other countries, but the quality of workmanship, the adaptability of the silversmith, the system of hallmarking and the love of the English upper classes for silver in their homes all combined to make English silver the most sought-after in the world.

Very old silver (the little which survives) tends to be formal and ceremonial in its use. Silver objects generally, however, are characterized by their usefulness and the list of pieces produced for use in the home was seemingly endless, e.g. knives, forks, spoons, salvers, cups and tankards, entree dishes, sugar dredgers, candlesticks, salt-cellars, teapots, toast and muffin racks, snuff-boxes, candelabra, tureens, sauce-boats, ink-stands, wine coasters and wine coolers. SEE *Hall Marks*

SILVER COINS The British silver coins were the crown, half-crown, florin, shilling, sixpence, groat, threepence, twopence, penny. The groat (four pennies), twopence and silver penny are now only coined in very small quantities as Maundy money (q.v.).

They were a legal tender only to the amount of 40 shillings. Silver coins were tokens, that is, the value of the silver in them was less than the legal value which was attached to the coin. There was no weight fixed below which silver coins ceased to be legally current.

Owing to the rise in the price of silver from its pre-First World War level, it was not possible to mint silver coins except at a loss and the Coinage Act 1920 was passed to reduce the fineness of the silver in the coins minted after that date (SEE *Coinage*). The issue of the new coinage commenced on 13th December, 1920. The new coins were similar to the old in design, size and weight and were somewhat harder, but did not possess quite such a white appearance and had not such a pronounced ring. The composition of the new coins was 500 parts silver, 400 parts copper, and 100 parts nickel.

SIMPLE CONTRACT SEE *Contract*

SIMPLE INTEREST SEE *Interest*

SIMULTANEOUS DEATHS SEE *Commorientes*

SINKING FUND A fund which is created for the purpose of redeeming debentures as they become due for payment, or of extinguishing a debt, or providing for the expiry of a lease. A certain annual sum is set aside out of profits, which, when invested, will produce at compound interest an amount equal to the sum which is required at a particular future date.

SIXPENCE Its standard weight was 43.63636 grains troy, and its standard fineness one-half fine silver, one-half alloy, until it was issued as a cupro-nickel coin under the Coinage Act 1946. It served as a 2½ pence piece in the early days of decimalization.

SMALL FIRMS LOAN GUARANTEE SCHEME This was introduced by the Government in June 1981, consequent upon a recommendation of the Wilson Committee (q.v.). The Scheme was set up for an experimental period of three years but has since been extended. Under the Scheme, the Government guaranteed 80 per cent of a loan up to a maximum of £75,000, the loan to be repayable over a period of two to seven years. The loans are made through the banks who joined the Scheme, but in each case the loan has to be approved by the Department of Trade and Industry. Also, the lending bank must sign a declaration that the loan would not have been made without the guarantee, i.e. the guarantee facility may not be used as a substitute for a loan which the bank would have been willing to make in any case.

The Treasury originally set aside £150 million under the Scheme for the first three years but the response was considerable and loans totalling £50 million were made in the first six months. By the end of 1983 loans made under the Scheme totalled £510 million. The Government makes a charge of five per cent per annum for guarantees under the Scheme, which is additional to the rate of interest charged by the banks themselves.

SMALL GIFTS EXEMPTION SEE *Capital Transfer Tax*

SOCIAL SECURITY The main Social Security benefits payable in the UK at the present time are listed under their respective headings throughout this work. They are *Age Addition, Attendance Allowance, Child Benefit, Child's Special Allowance, Death Grant, Disablement Benefit, Family Income Supplement, Guardian's Allowance, Industrial Death Benefit, Industrial Injury Benefit, Invalid Care Allowance, Invalidity Benefit, Maternity Allowance, Maternity Grant, Mobility Allowance, Non-contributory Invalidity Pension, Non-contributory Retirement Pension, One-Parent Benefit, Pensioners' Christmas Bonus, Retirement Pension, Sickness Benefit, Supplementary Benefits, Widowed Mothers' Allowance, Widows' Allowance, Widows' Pension.* SEE ALSO Appendix 2

SOLA BILL From the Latin *solus*, alone, solitary. A bill which consists simply of one document, as distinguished from foreign bills drawn in a set—that is, issued in duplicate or triplicate. The words 'sola bill' are sometimes used in the body of the bill, e.g. in a bill drawn by a branch of the Bank of England on London, the words may be 'seven days after date pay this sola bill of exchange', etc. SEE *Bill in a Set*

SOLICITORS' ACCOUNTS The Solicitors' Accounts Rules 1975, made by The Council of the Law Society under Section 32, Solicitors Act 1974 (following the pattern of previous Acts), require every solicitor (with certain exceptions such as those employed by local authorities) to open and keep accounts at a bank or banks for clients' money and to keep accounts containing particulars and information as to money received, held or paid by him for or on account of his clients.

Under the Solicitors' Accounts Rules 'client's money' means

> money held or received by a solicitor on account of a person for whom he is acting in relation to the holding or receipt of such money, either as a solicitor or, in connection with his practice as a solicitor, as agent, bailee, stakeholder or in any other capacity, but does not include (i) money held or received on account of the trustees of a trust, of which the solicitor is a solicitor trustee, or (ii) money to which the only person entitled is the solicitor himself or, in the case of a firm of solicitors, one or more of the partners.

Under the Solicitors' Accounts (Deposit Interest) Rules 1975, a solicitor who holds or receives client money on which, in all fairness, interest ought to be earned for the client, must either deposit the money in a separate designated account and accounts to the client for the interest thereon or pay to the client out of his own money, a sum equivalent to the interest which the client would have received if the money had been deposited in a separate account.

Under the Solicitors' Trust Accounts Rules 1975, every solicitor-trustee is required to open and keep an account at a bank for money of any trust of which he is a sole trustee or co-trustee (if he is a co-trustee only with a partner, clerk or servant of his or with more than one of such persons) and to keep accounts containing particulars and information as to money received, held or paid by him for or on account of any such trust.

Under the Solicitors' Act 1974, Section 85, a bank with whom a solicitor maintains an account for clients' money incurs no liability and is under no obligation to make any enquiry nor is deemed to have any knowledge of any person as to any money paid or credited to any such account which it would not incur or would not be under or be deemed to have in the case of an account kept by a person entitled absolutely to the money paid or credited to that account. In other words, the fact that the bank knows that the account holds clients' moneys does not impose any extra obligation on the bank. On the other hand, the bank has no right by way of set-off or counterclaim against money standing to the credit of such a client's account in respect of any liability which the solicitor may have to the bank, other than a liability in connection with the client's account.

The effect of the bankruptcy of a solicitor in relation to his client's account was considered in *Re A Solicitor* [1951] M No 234. The trustee in bankruptcy in that case applied for an order that the bankers should pay to him any moneys standing to the solicitor's credit with them. The court held that the client's moneys were held by the bankrupt solicitor on trust, within the meaning of Section 38(1) Bankruptcy Act 1914, and therefore did not vest in the trustee in bankruptcy. SEE *Clients' Accounts*

SOLICITOR'S UNDERTAKING When a customer desires any of his securities which are held by a banker to be lent to his solicitor for inspection, written instructions should be taken from the customer. When the securities are handed to the solicitor, the solicitor should sign an undertaking to return them in the same condition as he receives them and not to charge them or affect the banker's security in any way. Bankers have their own forms for use in these cases.

If the securities are to be given up to a solicitor, or anyone, against payment of a certain sum, the letter of authority should specifically state the amount. The undertaking will then be to pay the amount or return the securities.

It is thought that a solicitor's undertaking amounts to an equitable mortgage. Certainly if a solicitor in the course of his professional practice gives an undertaking on behalf of a client, the court will, if necessary, require the solicitor to perform his undertaking. This appears to be based on the fact that a solicitor in his professional conduct is an officer of the Supreme Court and must honour his undertakings. This applies even though the undertaking may be given to a third party, e.g. a bank (see, for example, *Re A Solicitor* [1966] 3 All ER 52).

SOURCES OF FINANCE There is a wide range of financial facilities available in the UK for both private individuals and businesses. For the most part, these sources are dealt with under their respective headings throughout this work.

For private individuals, finance is available from the clearing banks (SEE *Lending by Banks*), hire purchase or credit sales from finance houses (SEE *Hire Purchase Finance; Finance House; Instalment Credit*), credit cards (q.v.), budget accounts and similar revolving credit facilities from retail stores and for house purchase and related purchases, the building societies (SEE *Building Societies; Mortgage*).

For business purposes, the principal sources of finance are

Overdrafts
Short-term and medium term loans SEE *Lending by Banks; Merchant Banking*
Factoring and invoice discounting (q.v.)
Leasing (q.v.)
Industrial hire purchase SEE *Hire Purchase Finance*
Export finance SEE *Export Credit Guarantee Department*
Bill finance SEE *Discounting a Bill; Accepting Houses*
Medium-term and long-term loans from specialist institutions e.g. Industrial Commercial Finance Corporation (q.v.)
Sale and leaseback (q.v.)
Equity capital from merchant banks or specialist institutions or when companies are large enough and have an adequate record, a quotation on the Unlisted Securities Market (q.v.) or a full listing on the Stock Exchange (q.v.)

In recent times, the clearing banks have set up a number of subsidiary companies for provision of loan finance and equity capital for smaller and medium-sized businesses and there has been an increasing tendency for pension funds to provide long-term resources for particular ventures. SEE ALSO *Equity Capital for Industry*

In addition to these avenues of finance in the private sector, there is a number of Government agencies providing equity capital and cash grants of various kinds, either for particular areas of the country or particular types of enterprise. These Government sources include the National Enterprise Board, the Scottish Development Agency and Welsh Development Agency, the Highlands and Islands Development Board, the National Research Development Corporation, the Northern Ireland Development Agency and 'Selective Assistance' from the Industrial Development Unit of the Department of Trade and Industry for a limited range of major projects. Further information is available in all cases, from the agencies concerned.

The provision of risk capital and long-term loan finance for smaller businesses has been the subject of much discussion right back to the time of the Macmillan Report (q.v.) and the so-called Macmillan Gap (SEE ALSO *Bolton Committee*). In their evidence to the Wilson Committee (q.v.) the clearing banks said

> One of the most important features of the development of the clearing banks over the past 20 years has been the increasing range of facilities available through their branch outlets to meet the needs of smaller businesses at each successive stage of their development.

This perhaps, more than anything else, is what the growth of the concept of 'universal banking' has meant in practice.

The main conclusions of the Wilson Committee (q.v.) as regards the subject of finance for small businesses were summarized in their report as follows.

1. There is a widespread reluctance on the part of proprietors of small businesses to seek outside equity because of suspicions about possible interference in the firm's affairs and even eventual loss of control.
2. In any case, external equity is more difficult for small firms to find and may only be obtainable on relatively unfavourable terms, since the administrative costs of raising outside capital do not fall in proportion to the amount of capital raised.
3. Although in recent years a number of institutions have set up intermediaries specifically charged with investment in smaller businesses, for example, the Small Business Capital Fund and Moracrest, these tend to be mainly concerned with larger small firms, leaving the Industrial and Commercial Finance Corporation (ICFC) as effectively the only source of permanent long-term outside capital for the really small companies.
4. For a number of small firms, banks in effect supply some permanent capital through overdrafts which are continually extended; however, there is a possibility that banks exercise excessive caution in their assessment of the risks presented by lending to small firms, particularly in the case of customers with no capital of their own.
5. Other handicaps suffered by small companies are that venture capital is particularly hard to obtain, some Government support schemes specify minimum qualifying levels which small businesses cannot hope to attain, and some export credit facilities also exclude small firms.

In June 1981, the Government introduced the Small Firms Loan Guarantee Scheme (q.v.).

SOVEREIGN The standard of the British coinage. Its standard weight is 123.27447 grains troy and its standard fineness eleven-twelfths fine gold (113.0016 grains), one-twelfth alloy, chiefly copper (10.2728 grains).

By 56 Geo III (1816) it was provided that sovereigns coined weighing 20/21 parts of a guinea were to pass for 20s. They were issued in 1817. Coins of the same name but of different value were coined about 1489. SEE *Coinage; Pound*

SPECIAL CROSSING Where the name of a banker is written, or stamped, across the face of a cheque, either with or without the words 'not negotiable', that addition constitutes a crossing and the cheque is crossed specially and to that banker. The parallel lines which are necessary to constitute a general crossing are not necessary in a special crossing. SEE *Crossed Cheque*

SPECIAL DEPOSITS An instrument of monetary policy designed to restrict credit. The Bank of England may call for special deposits to be made with it by the banks, as appears necessary, to restrict liquidity and the ability of the banks to create credit. A similar system has been operative for many years in the USA, under which each member bank of the Federal Reserve system is required to hold a minimum percentage, in the form of a balance with its Reserve Bank, against its deposits, this minimum ratio being higher in respect of demand deposits than of deposits subject to notice of withdrawal. These minimum ratios are altered from time to time by the Federal Reserve Authorities, upward to put a check on credit expansion or downwards to encourage it, according to the needs of the current situation.

The system of special deposits took the place of the quantitative restrictions on the lending power of each bank such as had previously been imposed. The advantage over the preceding technique of 'requests' to banks not to allow their advances to rise above specific ceilings was said to lie mainly in the fact that the special deposit would leave banks free to compete against one another for new business, whereas the former quantitative controls 'froze' the scope for each bank's advances while the 'request' remained in force.

In May 1971, the Bank of England issued a consultative document, *Competition and Credit Control*. After discussions with the banks and other financial institutions the proposals were accepted as the basis of a new system of credit control. When the new system came into effect in September 1971, all Special Deposits were repaid to the banks on condition that the funds released were immediately invested in new issues of Government stocks.

Special Deposits at $1\frac{1}{2}$ per cent of sterling resources (eligible liabilities) were again called for in the autumn of 1972. SEE *Competition and Credit Control*

SPECIAL DRAWING RIGHTS (SDRs) A form of international money or credit created in 1969 to augment the dollar and gold as international means of payment, and thereby facilitate international trade. SDRs are issued by the International Monetary Fund (q.v.) and countries which hold them do so as part of their reserves as they might balances at a bank. Notwithstanding the general desire to move away from gold as the basis of international monetary settlements, the SDRs were fixed in terms of gold at a unit figure of 0.888671 grams. They are now expressed however, in terms of the principal world currencies.

SPECIAL INDORSEMENT A special indorsement specifies the person to whom or to whose order a bill or cheque is to be payable (Bills of Exchange Act 1882, Section 34(2)) as 'Pay John Brown or order, J. Jones'. The converse term is an 'indorsement in blank', where the indorser merely signs his name. SEE *Indorsement*

SPECIAL RESOLUTION SEE *Resolutions*

SPECIALITY DEBT A debt which is acknowledged in a document under seal. SEE *Limitation Act* 1939

SPECIE From the Latin *specio*, to look, to see. Visible money. Gold and silver coins and bullion, as distinguished from paper money.

SPECIFIC CHARGE A term used to describe a fixed charge as opposed to a floating charge (q.v.). A debenture given to a bank will usually give a specific charge on named assets and a floating charge on the remainder. The specific charge may be either by way of a legal mortgage or a mere equitable charge. SEE *Debenture*

SPECIFIC LEGACY This is a gift by will of a specific item of a testator's personal estate. This could, for example, be a gift of a piano, a desk or a horse, but it is not necessarily a gift of a tangible item. It may be a legacy of a particular investment, e.g. 'my holding of $3\frac{1}{2}$ per cent War Stock'. It must be clearly distinguishable from the rest of the testator's estate.

It is necessary to draw a distinction between specific legacies and (1) general legacies, and (2) demonstrative legacies. A general legacy is a gift by will not of an identifiable part of the estate, but of a more general nature and which the executors must provide, if there are sufficient assets, out of the general estate. Thus, a gift of £100 $3\frac{1}{2}$ per cent War Stock would be a general legacy which the executors would be obliged to appropriate or buy out of the estate for the beneficiary, whereas a gift of 'my £100 $3\frac{1}{2}$ per cent War Stock' would be a specific legacy. A demonstrative legacy has some of the attributes of general and specific legacies. It is a pecuniary legacy (and to that extent is 'general' in kind) which is directed to be paid out of a specific fund in the estate.

The distinction between these three categories of legacies is important under the Rules of Abatement (q.v.) and Ademption (q.v.).

SPLIT LEVEL TRUSTS These are investment trusts which issue shares of two or more categories with differing rights as to capital and income. In a typical case, the holders of the income shares will receive the income of the entire portfolio and the holders of the capital shares, will receive no income but will receive the benefit of capital growth on the whole portfolio. The advantage of such a trust is that investors in need of income will receive a larger than usual income with, in the ordinary way, the benefit of dividend increases over the years. The capital shares will normally appeal to high taxpayers who do not require the income but prefer to have capital appreciation.

SPOT PRICE The 'spot' price of silver or any commodity is another name for its 'cash' price for delivery at once. The 'forward' price is the quotation for delivery and payment at some future time.

SPOT RATE The rate at which foreign exchange dealers can buy or sell a telegraphic transfer in the foreign exchange market.

STAG The term used to describe a party who applies for a new issue of stocks or shares with the intention of selling, after allotment, at a profit.

STALE BULL A person who has invested in shares in anticipation of an increase in price which in the event has not materialized. SEE *Bear; Bull*

STALE CHEQUE A cheque is considered by bankers to be stale six (by some bankers, twelve) months after the date of the cheque, and such a cheque is usually returned marked 'out of date'. When the stale date is confirmed by the drawer the cheque is paid. The practice of not paying cheques which are out of date is one which may perhaps be upheld as part of the contractual arrangement; that is, the banker may have a right to return such cheques. If this is so, and a banker has previously returned such cheques, then he may well have a liability if he fails to do so on a subsequent occasion. The drawer as a party to the instrument is of course not released from liability until after six years.

By Section 45, Bills of Exchange Act 1882, presentment of a bill payable on demand 'must be made within a reasonable time after its issue in order to render the drawer liable, and within a reasonable time after its indorsement in order to render the indorser liable'. Cheques, so far as the drawer is concerned, are not included in this Section. The drawer remains liable, as above stated for six years from the date of the cheque, unless he suffers actual loss, as where a banker fails, through his cheque not having been presented for payment within a reasonable time when he is discharged to the extent of such loss (see Section 74 under *Presentment for Payment*).

By Section 36(3), Bills of Exchange Act 1882, a bill payable on demand is deemed to be overdue when it appears on the face of it to have been in circulation for an unreasonable length of time. Such an instrument is not negotiable (Section 36(2)). Unreasonable length of time is a question of fact. SEE UNDER *Overdue Cheque*

STAMP COLLECTING Systems of payment for delivery of messages have no doubt existed since earliest times, but right up to the last century it was the practice to pay for the delivery of a message on its arrival. It was in 1839 that Rowland Hill, having written a pamphlet on *Postal Reform*, was appointed to run the 'Penny Post' introduced in 1840. This was the first prepaid postal system introduced anywhere in the world, but by 1862 stamps had been issued by about 100 states and some stamps were already changing hands at 100 times their face value.

Stamps were not perforated until 1850 and thus had to be cut from the sheet with scissors. This was not always done with care and so today a stamp cut neatly from the sheet with even margins is worth far more than a carelessly cut one.

The first postage stamp was the Penny Black. There were in fact 68 million issued and even today a Penny Black can be purchased for the comparatively modest cost of about £30, although a good specimen might cost £2,000. In those early days, stamps were no more than a receipt for the amount of the postal charge and the first stamp to be issued for any commemorative purpose was to mark Queen Victoria's Golden Jubilee in 1887.

There is a certain similarity between the collecting of stamps and the collecting of coins. Indeed, in some countries at particular times stamps have been used freely as currency, as they are today in some parts of the Middle East.

Although postage stamps have been in use for only the last 140 years, compared with over 2,500 years in which coins have been struck, the range of choice facing the new collector or investor is indeed formidable. It is essential to specialize, as with coins, and many collectors find it more satisfying to collect in depth rather than over a wide field. It has long been the custom to collect stamps of a particular country or period, but much narrower themes based on design or purpose of the stamp are now common, e.g. stamps bearing designs of flowers or animals, or commemorative issues marking centenaries and similar occasions. Some very serious collectors confine themselves to a very narrow period or area or theme, and in some cases, only one particular stamp, i.e. one issue, is collected. This specialization enables the true collector or the investor to become very expert on the chosen theme and knowledgeable on such matters as the number of stamps issued, the current prices and forgeries. Damaged stamps are worthless and stamps which are stained or of which the colour has 'toned' may be of little, if any, value. Hinged stamps may be unsaleable because of the damage to the original gum. In the early days the gum was potato paste, but was soon replaced by gum arabic. Re-gumming is one of the deceptions resorted to by fakers (see below).

Some Advantages of Stamp Collecting

1. The 'classics', i.e. those issued in the nineteenth century, have an increasing rarity value as do some of the stamps issued up to the mid-1930s.
2. Stamps are miniature works of art.
3. They are readily transportable and transferable.
4. They are very marketable in most countries.

5. They have historical, geographical, commemorative and thematic interest.
6. The number of collectors and investors is growing. (In the UK, the number of devotees is said to be 'second only to fishing'.)

Some Drawbacks

1. Stamps are easily damaged.
2. They are affected by climatic conditions.
3. There are many fakes and forgeries.
4. Valuable collections present a security risk.
5. There may be insurance problems.
6. Dealing costs are higher than for some conventional investments.
7. The amateur is very much dependent on the expert.

The Faking of Stamps

The faking of a stamp is the altering of its condition in some way to upgrade its quality. This includes re-gumming as mentioned above, re-perforating, removing ink marks and even changing the colour of stamps by chemical means. Forgery, on the other hand, is the making of a counterfeit stamp either to defraud the postal authorities, as was more common years ago in some countries, or to defraud collectors. Both categories of forgery have become collectors' items in their own right if they are sufficiently old and interesting. Stamp forgery continues on a large scale around the world and usually the forged versions can be detected only by the experts.

It is a source of protection to collectors and investors that many dealers are now members of the Philatelic Traders Society, which has approximately 450 trading members in the UK and about 950 members world-wide. Members agree to accept the code of ethics of the Association and the Association also provides an arbitration service.

The Royal Philatelic Society, London, will give a certificate as to the authenticity of a stamp, but not a guarantee as to its value. The British Philatelic Association Expertising Limited will also pronounce on the authenticity and quality of a particular stamp or stamps.

STAMP DUTY This is the oldest form of Inland Revenue tax in the UK. It was first introduced in the reign of William and Mary in 1694. The principal enactment covering Stamp Duty in modern times is the Stamp Act 1891. This was a consolidating Act at that time but it still governs the main principles of Stamp Duty although there have, of course, been numerous amendments over the years.

Stamp Duty in its concept was a duty on documents rather than on the transaction as such. Thus there were duties payable on cheques and receipts, conveyances and assignments, indentures and the admission of students to the Inns of Court and such less likely documents as playing cards and labels on medicine bottles.

The principal modern duties are on transfers of freehold and leasehold property, transfers of securities, the issue of shares by companies (capital duty), policies of life assurance, unit trust instruments and sundry other documents on which there are fixed duties. Stamp Duty was abolished in 1970 on receipts and bills of exchange, including cheques.

The following are the principal categories and scales of stamp duties currently in force:

Transfers of freehold property Since 20th March, 1984, no stamp duty has been payable on the transfer of freehold and leasehold property, unless the price exceeds £30,000. Above that figure, stamp duty is payable at the flat rate of one per cent.

Transfers of stocks and shares Duty is payable at one per cent on the consideration, except in the case of Government stocks, loan stocks and transfers to charities. Stamp Duty, payable on contract notes for the purchase and sale of stocks and shares, was abolished by the Finance Act 1985. No Stamp Duty is payable on the transfer of shares on a take-over in exchange for shares or other marketable securities in the acquiring company. The exemption does not apply, however, where the shareholders of the company being taken over receive cash for their shares.

Leases Duty is payable on any premium for a lease, on the same scale as conveyances of freehold land. Duty is also payable on the annual rent on a sliding scale, depending on the amount of the rent and the period of the lease.

Life assurance policies Duty is payable at 0.05 per cent of the sum assured rounded up to the nearest 50p per thousand pounds over £1,000. On annuities duty is payable at 0.5 per cent on the amount of the annual payment. Duty on non-life insurance policies was abolished in 1970.

Unit trust instruments All property, i.e. assets brought into a unit trust are subject to $\frac{1}{4}$ per cent *ad valorem* duty.

Capital duty Under various directives of the EEC, duty is payable on the raising of capital in member countries. In the UK this was given effect in the Finance Act 1973. The rate of duty is one per cent on the issued capital. There is no duty on the issue of bonus shares. SEE Supplement

Fixed duties, usually 50p or a maximum of 50p, are payable on a range of documents, such as declarations of trust, deeds (other than those on which *ad valorem* duty is payable), powers of attorney, and various documents of release or surrender (but see Supplement).

At the time of writing, stamp duties in the UK raise approximately £1,000 million per annum in Government revenue. A discussion document on possible revision of stamp duties was published in 1983. SEE *Adjudication Stamps; Ad Valorem; Conveyance*

STANDING ORDER SEE *Banker's Order*

STATE RETIREMENT PENSIONS SEE *Pensions, Pensions Schemes*

STATEMENT IN LIEU OF PROSPECTUS A statement filed with the Registrar of Companies where a public company having a share capital does not issue a prospectus, or having issued a prospectus, has not proceeded to allot any of the shares offered to the public.

In such cases no allotment of shares or debentures can be made until a statement in lieu of prospectus is filed at least three days before the first allotment, signed by every named director or proposed director (Section 48, Companies Act 1948).

STATUS REPORT SEE *Banker's Opinions*

STATUTE-BARRED A debt is said to be statute-barred when it cannot be recovered in a court of law, because the time within which the creditor had the right to sue the debtor has expired. SEE *Limitation Act* 1939

STATUTORY BOOKS The books which are required to be kept by companies registered under the Companies Act 1985, namely

By Section 352: Register of Members
By Section 363. Annual List of Members and Summary SEE *Register of Members of Company*
By Section 382: Minute Book
By Sections 288–290: Register of Directors, or Managers SEE *Directors*
By Section 407: Register of Mortgages SEE *Registration of Charges*

STATUTORY MEETING OF COMPANY Under Section 130, Companies Act 1948, every public company limited by shares and every company limited by guarantee which had a share capital, was required within a period of not less than one month, nor more than three months, from the date on which the company was entitled to commence business, to hold a general meeting of the members which was to be called the statutory meeting. This provision was repealed by the Companies Act 1980.

STATUTORY OWNER In the Settled Land Act 1925, statutory owner means the trustees of the settlement or other persons who, during a minority, or at any other time when there is no tenant for life, have the powers of a tenant for life under this Act, but does not include the trustees where the trustees have power, under an order of the court or otherwise, to convey the settled land in the name of the tenant for life. SEE *Settled Land*

STATUTORY SICK PAY This was introduced with effect from 6th April, 1983. For the first twenty-eight weeks of any employee's illness, sick pay must be paid by the employer, who then recovers an equivalent amount from the Department of Health and Social Security. Statutory sick pay is payable in every case where there is a period of incapacitation for work of four or more qualifying days. What amounts to a qualifying day is a matter of arrangement between the employer and the employee. Normally, it will be four consecutive days but if, for example, an employee worked normally on Mondays, Wednesdays and Fridays, the qualifying days will be the days when he normally works. Evidence of ill-health is primarily a matter for the employer. There is no legal obligation on the employee to provide a medical certificate but he must give his employer such evidence as the employer may reasonably require to determine whether statutory sick pay is payable.

Statutory sick pay is based on an employee's average earnings in the eight weeks before the period of sickness and is paid according to a scale published from time to time. The scheme applies to all employees paying Class I National Insurance contributions (SEE *National Insurance Contributions*). Consequently, those under the lower-earnings limit (q.v.) do not qualify. SEE ALSO *Sickness Benefit*

STATUTORY TRUSTS For the purposes of the Law of Property Act 1925 land held upon trust to sell the same and to stand possessed of the net proceeds, after payment of costs, etc., and upon such trusts as may be requisite for giving effect to the rights of the persons interested in the land (Section 35). SEE *Intestacy; Joint Tenants*

STERLING When gold and silver are of the standard fineness they are called sterling metals. Various explanations are given as to the origin of the word 'sterling'. A coin called an easterling was introduced into the coinage during the reign of King Richard I, and as that coin was considered superior to other coins in circulation at that time, it has been suggested that the word 'sterling' had its origin in easterling. The preferred view is, however, that the word arose from the decree of Henry III in 1238, that the silver content of English silver plate should be the same as that of English silver coin, i.e. 11 ounces and 2 pennyweights of pure silver in every pound. This became known as the sterling standard, apparently because the penny coins then in circulation bore the sign of the small star, which became known as a 'starling', corrupted to 'sterling'. With the sovereign becoming the standard for all British currency, it is understandable that the word became less-identified with the metal coin as such and more synonymous with the British currency in general.

STERLING AREA When Great Britain abandoned the Gold Standard in 1931, certain other countries, both within and without the Empire, followed suit and ceased to tie their currency to gold, linking it instead to the pound sterling. At the time of the outbreak of war in September 1939, all the countries of the Empire (except Canada), Norway, Sweden, Denmark, Finland, Greece, Portugal and Bolivia had adopted this system.

Until the passing of the Exchange Control Act 1947, what was known as the Sterling Area comprised all countries in the British Empire—except Canada and Newfoundland—and the mandated territories of Egypt, Iraq, Anglo–Egyptian Sudan, and Iceland. France, Belgium, Holland and their respective colonies, Sweden and Denmark were not in the Sterling Area, but were the subjects of monetary agreements, thus facilitating trade within the Sterling Area. The dollar area covered the USA, Canada and Newfoundland.

Under the Exchange Control Act 1947, the term 'Scheduled Territories' (q.v.) was substituted for Sterling Area.

STERLING BONDS Bonds of a foreign country which are payable in British currency.

STERLING CERTIFICATES OF DEPOSIT These were first introduced in 1968. A certificate of deposit is a negotiable instrument issued in return for a deposit with a bank. It may be at a fixed or floating rate of interest and may be issued for periods of from three months to five years. Certificates of deposit are in multiples of £10,000 with a minimum of £50,000 up to a normal maximum of £500,000, although this figure may be exceeded. The certificates are issued at par and the interest is rolled-up in the maturity value. They are now issued by over 100 banks in London and by some building societies. For the most part, they are held by other banks and other financial institutions. The discount market (q.v.) operates a secondary market in certificates of deposit. SEE *Certificate of Deposit; London Dollar Certificates of Deposit*

STOCK The capital of a company contributed by the members may be formed into stock. A member may hold so much stock or so many shares in the company. Stock may be held and transferred in any amounts (without distinguishing numbers) whereas shares are for fixed amounts and all numbered, e.g. a person may hold £150 of stock if the capital is dealt with in that way; but if the capital is divided into shares of, say, £5 each, fully paid, then the person with the same holding would have 30 shares of £5 each. Stock, by its nature, is fully paid up, but upon shares there is sometimes a liability. In Government stocks, any odd amount (e.g. £33.69) may be transferred; but in the case of an ordinary limited company, transfers of stock are usually, for convenience, restricted to certain round sums.

There may be varieties of stock as guaranteed, preference, ordinary, deferred and other kinds, which entitle the holders to different rights in the matter of dividends and in a division upon a winding-up of the company.

A company cannot make an original issue of stock. It can only be done by a conversion of fully-paid shares into stock. As to the power of a company limited by shares to convert shares into stock, see Section 121, Companies Act 1985, under *Share Capital*.

STOCKBROKER One who purchases or sells stocks and shares for clients. His remuneration is the commission he receives from his clients on the purchases and sales he effects on their behalf; the rate varies in different classes of stocks.

The scale of minimum commissions laid down by the London Stock Exchange which may be shared with agents, including banks which have been included in the London Stock Exchange Register of Banks, is given below. SEE ALSO *Stock Exchange*

Scale of Stock Exchange Minimum Commission Charges

A British funds, etc., Irish Government funds

New commission scales on government stocks were introduced with effect from 9th April, 1984, as follows:

Under 10 years to redemption:	*Divisible with agents* %	*Non-divisible* %
On the first £2,500	1.0	0.8
On the next £15,500	0.16	0.125
On the next £232,000	0.08	0.0625

Under 10 years to redemption:	Divisible with agents %	Non-divisible %
On the next £750,000	0.0625	0.05
On the next £3,000,000	0.0575	0.045
On the next £6,000,000	0.025	0.02
On the excess	0.0125	0.01
Over 10 years to redemption:		
On the first £2,500	1.0	0.08
On the next £15,500	0.3	0.25
On the next £232,000	0.16	0.125
On the next £750,000	0.125	0.1
On the next £3,000,000	0.1125	0.09
On the next £6,000,000	0.05	0.04
On the excess	0.025	0.02

Securities having five years or less to final redemption are 'at discretion'.

B Debentures, loan stocks and registered bonds

	Divisible with agents %
On the first £10,000	0.9
On the next £90,000	0.45
On the next £130,000	0.375
On the next £670,000	0.35
On the next £1,100,000	0.25
On the excess	0.16

	Non-divisible %
On the first £5,000	0.9
On the next £5,000	0.45
On the next £40,000	0.35
On the next £80,000	0.325
On the next £770,000	0.25
On the next £1,100,000	0.175
On the excess	0.125

C Ordinary and preference shares

	Divisible with agents %	Non-divisible %
On the first £7,000	1.65	1.65
On the next £8,000	1.25	0.55
On the next £10,000	0.9	0.55
On the next £25,000	0.75	0.55
On the next £80,000	0.625	0.55
On the next £115,000	0.625	0.5
On the next £170,000	0.55	0.4
On the next £600,000	0.4	0.3
On the next £1,100,000	0.27	0.2
On the excess	0.17	0.125

SEE ALSO *Stock Exchange*

STOCKBROKERS' LOANS When a stockbroker lends money to a client who desires to purchase stocks and shares, the securities are usually deposited with the broker as cover for the advance, and the broker is often authorized to transfer them to a banker as security when it is necessary for the broker to obtain an advance from him. In such cases, the broker's interest in the securities is limited to the money he has lent to his client, and if they are given to a banker as security for the general indebtedness of the broker various questions arise. The results of several important cases which have become before the courts show

1. that if a banker has definite knowledge when he takes certain securities from a broker that the broker is dealing with them beyond his authority—that is, that they are being given to the banker to cover a greater sum than the amount lent by the broker to the client—the client will be entitled to redeem them from the banker, even if transferred into the banker's name, on paying the amount due by him to the broker;
2. that if the banker has no reason to suppose that the securities are not the broker's own property, the client will not be entitled to redeem them (if they have been registered in the banker's name) except by payment of the debt due from the broker to the banker.

In *Bentinck* v *London Joint Stock Bank* [1893] 2 Ch 120, a firm of stockbrokers deposited with their bankers, as security for a loan, various stocks, shares and bonds belonging to a client, the securities having been pledged with the brokers by the client. The stocks and shares were registered in the names of the bank's nominees. The client asserted that he had authorized the brokers to repledge his securities only for an amount not exceeding that which he owed to the brokers, and that on paying such amount to the bank he was entitled to redeem his securities. In the course of his judgment, Mr Justice North said that when money is borrowed by a client from a stockbroker on contango or continuation, whether the money is obtained from the dealer, or from other stockbrokers, or from bankers, the result is the same; the arrangement is one by which the broker becomes, as between himself and his client, the owner of the shares in question, although he is under a contract to provide an equal amount of similar shares at a future date. It was held that there was nothing to lead the bank to suppose that the stocks and shares which were transferred to their nominees were not the broker's own property, and that the bank must therefore be treated as bona fide holders for value without notice. It was also held that, as to the stocks and shares of which the client had himself executed transfers, he was estopped from denying that the brokers had authority to pledge them to the bank for their full value.

When negotiable securities are pledged by a broker, there is no obligation upon a banker to inquire whether they are the property of the broker or not. If there is anything to arouse suspicion the banker would be put upon inquiry, but, apart from that, any person taking a negotiable instrument in good faith and for value obtains a title valid against all the world.

The fact that bankers may sometimes seek specific authority from the owner of the security as to the validity of the pledging is mere caution which in most cases is quite unnecessary but which is sometimes requested as a matter of form.

When a banker has notice that a broker has power to pledge a client's securities only to a limited extent, the banker's advance to the broker upon any such securities should not, of course, exceed that limit. The banker should receive a letter or memorandum from the broker's client agreeing to the broker charging the securities to the extent of the client's indebtedness to the broker. SEE *Blank Transfer; Negotiable Instruments*

STOCK EXCHANGE The London Stock Exchange had its origins in the seventeenth century when dealers in stocks and shares met informally in the coffee houses in the City and the first Stock Exchange was set up in its own building in 1773. The first Rules of the Stock Exchange date back to 1812. The railway boom and the market in railway shares in the nineteenth century led to the rapid development of the Exchange and the opening of exchanges in the provinces.

Although prior to the Second World War there were 32 stock exchanges in the UK, London always exercised a dominant role and by 1963 there were only six provincial markets, which in that year constituted the Federation of Stock Exchanges. In 1973 all the exchanges merged with London to form 'the Stock Exchange', although trading 'floors' remain in a number of principal provincial centres.

There are over 7,000 securities quoted on the Stock Exchange. These include all the major financial, commercial and industrial concerns in the UK and many smaller ones, and a large number of overseas companies, including mines, oil exploration, plantations, and virtually every legitimate business activity.

The Stock Exchange also provides a market for British Government stocks and the stocks and bonds of a large number of foreign governments and corporations.

The table above shows the categories of stocks quoted on the London Stock Exchange in 1984 with a total market capitalization of nearly £1,090,000 million.

Categories of Stocks	Number of securities	Market value £m
Public sector and foreign stocks:		
British Government and Government guaranteed	116	114,434
UK local authorities and public boards	309	1,853
Overseas public authorities (including the Republic of Ireland)	273	8,237
Company securities	5,236	896,803
Eurobonds:		
UK companies	81	1,284
Overseas companies	1,045	67,238
Total	7,060	1,089,849

Source: The Stock Exchange.

There are approximately 4,100 Stock Exchange members, of whom 3,500 are in London. Of these, fewer than 500 are jobbers, the remaining members being brokers. The jobbers act as principals in buying and selling stocks. They deal in particular sectors of the market and become specialists in their own field. They quote two prices for the securities in which they deal, the lower price being that which they are prepared to pay, the higher price being that at which they will sell.

Brokers are the agents for the investing public. On behalf of their clients they buy and sell stock, mainly through the jobbers, and they deal with the settlement of their clients' transactions. They are remunerated by commissions, whereas the jobbers make their profit from the difference between the buying and selling prices of the securities in which they deal.

The London Stock Exchange is the second largest capital market in the world and is approximately equivalent in size to the combined markets of the other EEC countries. In the course of a single day, the number of transactions (known as bargains) may vary from, say 5,000 up to 30,000 and the total number of bargains in the year now exceeds six million, representing an annual turnover in money terms in 1984 of approximately £365,000 million.

The main categories of investments quoted on the London Stock Exchange are British funds (stocks issued by the British Government), corporation loans (issued by local authorities), Commonwealth loans, loans issued by public boards (e.g. Agricultural Mortgage Corporation), ordinary stocks and shares of British financial, commercial, and industrial companies, loan stocks of British companies, preference stocks and shares, and stocks and bonds of companies registered overseas.

The Stock Exchange also deals in special categories of stocks, e.g. convertibles, stock options and warrants (q.v.).

In the summer of 1983, the Stock Exchange agreed with the Government that minimum commissions on the Stock Exchange would be abolished and also that outside persons, other than members of the Stock Exchange, would be appointed to the Stock Exchange Council. In return for this undertaking, the Government agreed that the Stock Exchange should be exempted from the restrictive practices legislation under which an investigation was then taking place by the Office of Fair Trading. In the ensuing discussion, a number of interrelated matters were ventilated. These were

1. the abolition of minimum commissions;
2. the departure from 'single capacity', i.e. the existing separation of the roles of broker and jobber;
3. changes to the dealing system, particularly in gilt-edged securities; and
4. an awareness of the need for larger and financially stronger units to compete with international investment houses who, with modern technology, were able to deal, virtually round the clock, in very considerable sums of money.

In April 1984, a discussion document was issued by the Stock Exchange with certain recommendations. The document contemplated (1) the abolition of fixed commissions by late 1985, (2) the gradual abolition of single capacity, (3) a change in the British Government securities market on the lines of the market for Treasury Bonds in the USA, (4) the abolition of the rule limiting outside ownership of a Stock Exchange firm to 29.9 per cent, and a general restructuring of the Stock Market to take advantage of developing technology.

The new proposals for the Stock Exchange contemplate that a number of primary dealers to be known as market makers will make continuous markets in a wide range of securities. These market makers will deal as principals with one another and will not act in a dual capacity, i.e. as brokers and jobbers, as is intended to apply to other firms.

In August 1984 the Stock Exchange issued a paper outlining the structure of the gilt-edged market under the new arrangements. This would require market makers to conduct their trading in gilt-edged stocks through separately capitalized subsidiaries. These gilt traders would have direct contact with the Bank of England whose responsibility it is to manage the gilt market on behalf of the Government. SEE *Account, Stock Exchange; Backwardation; Bear; Bull; Carry Over; Contango; Contract Note (Stockbroker's); Options; Quotation; Stockbroker; Stock Jobber*

STOCK EXCHANGE COMPENSATION FUND A fund out of which the clients of a stockbroking firm are reimbursed in the event of loss occasioned by the failure of the firm or in the rare case of dishonesty on the broker's part. The fund is topped-up at around the £1 million mark by means of levies on the members of the Stock Exchange.

STOCK EXCHANGE DAILY OFFICIAL LIST This is published by the Stock Exchange on each working day. It includes virtually all stocks and shares quoted on the London Stock Exchange, the quoted price that day and a note of prices at which bargains were transacted. It does not include quotations for shares on the unlisted securities market (q.v.) but it does include a record of USM bargains.

STOCK EXCHANGE QUOTATION SEE *Quotation*. SEE *Settlement, Stock Exchange*

STOCK JOBBER A dealer in stocks and shares who conducts his business with the stockbrokers, acting as intermediary between those brokers who have securities for sale and those who wish to purchase. By the rules of the London Stock Exchange, a jobber may not deal with the public direct. The jobber's profit (called the jobber's 'turn') is the difference between his buying and selling prices. He is also called a dealer. SEE *Stock Exchange*

STOCK RELIEF To ameliorate the burden of maintaining stock levels in times of inflation, the Government introduced a system of stock relief in the Finance Act 1975 (originally for companies, but then for all trades and professions). In essence, relief was available in the year of assessment to the extent that stocks increased in value during the year, less a deduction equal to 10 per cent of the taxable profits of the trade or business after deducting all allowable expenses and capital allowances. New provisions were introduced, however, in the Finance Act 1981, and relate to all accounting periods ending on or after 14th November, 1980. Under these arrangements, the increase in the value of stocks over the accounting period is measured by reference to an *all stocks* index published by the Department of Trade and Industry. The increase in the amount of the index is applied to the value of stocks held at the beginning of the accounting period, regardless of any actual movement in the amount of stock held. Stock relief will be allowed against profits up to the amount of the increase in the index expressed as a percentage of stocks held at the beginning of the period.

The first £2,000 of stock held in a business does not qualify for relief. Where there is a subsequent fall in stock values, there will be no clawback of relief (as was the case under the earlier regulations) except in cases where a business ceases, or the scale of its operations become negligible in comparison with the recent past.

The abolition of stock relief was announced by the Chancellor of the Exchequer in March 1984. No relief is now given for periods of account beginning on or after 13th March, 1984. For periods of account which ended on or included 13th March, 1984, the relief is based on the increase in stock prices up to that month.

In the case of a new business special rules apply. If the business commenced on or after 13th March, 1984, there is no entitlement to stock relief. In the case, however, of a business which commenced before 13th March, 1984 but its first accounting period ended on or after that date, the relief will be based on the closing stock value, discounted by reference to the rise in the published all-stocks index between the commencement of the business and March 1984.

STOCK TRANSFER ACT 1963 SEE *Transfer of Shares*

STOCK TRANSFER FORM SEE *Transfer of Shares*

STOCKS AND SHARES, OWNERSHIP OF SEE *Ordinary Shares*

STOLEN BANK NOTES Where bank notes have been stolen, a holder for value, without notice that they have been stolen, is entitled to payment and the person who lost them cannot recover from him. But where it is proved that bank notes have been stolen, the burden of proof that they were taken in good faith and for value rests upon the holder.

The numbers, when known, of notes which have been stolen are usually notified to bankers and money-changers, but it has been held that the mere fact that a person has possession of a list of the numbers of stolen notes will not, if he has, in good faith, given value for one of them, prevent him from recovering upon any such note (*Raphael* v *Bank of England* (1855) 25 LJCP 33).

STOLEN BILL A bill of exchange can be the subject of theft like any other valuable document of title, but it is unnecessary to enquire into anything beyond the civil position as to liability in the matter.

By Section 20 of the Bills of Exchange Act 1882, very full authority is given to fill up an inchoate instrument (q.v.) and turn it into a complete bill. But this does not permit of the filling up and the conversion being effected by any other than the duly authorized person. If, therefore, an inchoate instrument is stolen before completion, no action can be brought upon it, for it would have to be signed by some person or other, and the signature would be either forged or unauthorized, having been made by some person other than the one entitled to complete the bill. The forged or unauthorized signature is wholly inoperative (Section 24). This is well established by the case of *Baxendale* v *Bennett* (1878) 3 QBD 525. B put his blank acceptance in a desk. It was stolen, filled up as a bill by C with his own name as drawer, and negotiated. It was held that even a holder in due course could not recover from B, as he had never delivered the inchoate instrument for the purpose of being converted into a bill by C. Whatever remedies there may be for those persons who have dealt in and with the instrument, they are independent of the document, which never became a bill at all. But if a person accepts a bill in blank and authorizes the person to whom he issues it to fill it up, and it is filled up by him for any amount, the acceptor is liable even if filled up for a greater amount than he intended.

> Where a man has signed a blank acceptance, and has issued it, and has authorised the holder to fill it up, he is liable on the bill, whatever the amount may be, though he has given secret instructions to the holder as to the amount for which he shall fill it up; he has enabled his agent to deceive an innocent party, and he is liable. [Brett, LJ, in *Baxendale* v *Bennett*]

Again, if a bill complete in form is stolen, the liability of the parties will depend upon the particular circumstances. Thus, C, the holder of a bill, specially indorsed it to D, and forwarded it in a letter to D. In the course of transmission the bill was stolen and D's indorsement forged. The bill was afterwards negotiated. Since the indorsement of D was necessary for negotiation, and this had not been obtained, the signature was, under Section 24, wholly inoperative, and C still retained the property in the bill. No liability rested on any person who was a party to the bill prior to the time of D's forged indorsement (*Arnold* v *Cheque Bank* (1876) 1 CPD 578, at p. 584). If, on the contrary, the bill is indorsed in blank and stolen, a holder in good faith and without notice that his title to the bill is defective is entitled to demand payment of the same. And if a bill indorsed in blank is stolen whilst in the course of negotiation for any person who was the holder of it, the payment at maturity by the acceptor, provided he acts in good faith, is a good discharge of the bill, even though the payment is made to the actual thief. (See *Smith* v *Sheppard* (1776), a case cited by Chitty in his *Bills of Exchange*, 10th edn, p. 180.)

When a bill is in the hands of a holder in due course a valid delivery of the bill by all parties prior to him so as to make them liable to him is conclusively presumed (Section 21), but no title can be obtained through or under a forged or unauthorized signature (see Section 24 under Forgery).

As to bills of exchange in general, that is, those bills which do not fall within the definition of a cheque (see Section 60), a banker is in no better position than a private individual, unless special arrangements are made by the banker when a bill is made payable at his bank.

STOLEN CHEQUE Although for most purposes a cheque is a bill of exchange (q.v.), there are certain differences affecting the position of a banker if a bill or a cheque has been stolen. The civil liability when a bill is stolen has been referred to in the last entry. In the case of a cheque, the position appears to be as follows.

If a banker on whom an *open* cheque is drawn pays it in good faith and in the ordinary course of business, the banker is protected by Section 60 of the Bills of Exchange Act and is entitled to debit his customer. There is no responsibility resting upon the banker if the indorsement has been forged and the cheque stolen. It appears possible that Section 1 of the Cheques Act 1957 may also afford some protection depending on whether a cheque bearing a forged indorsement is considered to be the equivalent of a cheque bearing no indorsement.

In the case of a crossed cheque which has been stolen, the banker on whom it is drawn is protected if he pays it in accordance with Section 80 of the Act and the collecting bank is protected under Section 4 of the Cheques Act which affords protection in respect of both cheques and certain instruments analagous to cheques, whether crossed or open. SEE *Crossed Cheque*

If a cheque is stolen whilst in the course of transmission, a holder in due course (q.v.) is entitled to the value of it and if payment has been stopped he may sue the drawer or any other parties to the cheque. In the case of a cheque which has been crossed with the addition of the words 'not negotiable', any person taking such a cheque shall not have, and shall not be capable of giving, a better title to the cheque than that which the person had from whom he took it (Section 81 of the Act). SEE ALSO *Theft Acts*

STOLEN POST OFFICE MONEY ORDER Postal orders and money orders are not negotiable instruments, and the Post Office has the right, if any irregularity should be found, of returning them, at any subsequent date, to the banker who presented them and received payment.

STOP-LOSS ORDER Generally, an order to a broker to buy or sell a particular stock or commodity if the price moves to a particular level.

STOP ORDER, STOP PAYMENT, STOPPED CHEQUE SEE *Payment Stopped*

STOPPAGE IN TRANSITU SEE *Sale of Goods*

STRIKING PRICE The price of stocks and shares or commodities at which an option may be exercised, also known in commodity dealing as the 'basis price'. The term is also used in relation to sales by tender, the striking price being that which is determined by the sellers when all the tenders are in. SEE *Tender Issue*

STUDENT GRANTS The fees of UK residents for attending approved courses at universities, polytechnics, training colleges and certain other establishments of higher education are paid by the local education authority in the area where the student has his permanent home address. The fees are paid each term direct to the university or other establishment concerned.

Under the present system of university grants, the living costs of students, including accommodation, meals, books, etc., are intended to be covered by the system of student grants, also paid by the local education authority. Student grants are means-tested and are paid according to a sliding scale depending on the level of parental income. It is expected that where less than the maximum grant is payable to a student the balance will be made up by his or her parents.

Additional maintenance grants are payable for each additional week of required attendance at the course in excess of 30 weeks and three days during the academic year (25 weeks and three days in the case of Oxford and Cambridge). If the required attendance at the course exceeds 45 weeks in the year, the additional grants are payable for the full year.

The local education authority will also pay necessary travelling expenses and the cost of special equipment up to a stated maximum.

Student grants are paid for the academic year commencing in October each year (usually taken as 1 September). Parental income is taken as the agreed income of the parent for tax purposes for the year ending the previous 5th April. If the final figures for the previous year's income are not available, the local education authority will make a provisional assessment, leaving the final term's grant to be adjusted when the parent's income is known. A parent who has a fluctuating income may elect to have the grant paid on the basis of the current year's income.

For the purpose of calculating parental income, personal allowances are not included, but mortgage interest payments and 50 per cent of life assurance premiums on policies taken out before 14th March, 1984 are deducted and in the case of a person engaged in a trade of business the normal expenses allowed for income tax are also deducted, including capital allowances.

Independent Students

A student may claim independent status if

1. he or she was aged over 25 at the beginning of the academic year, and
2. he or she has supported himself or herself out of earnings for the past three years (which may include periods of sickness, invalidity or maternity benefit, or periods spent at home by a married student looking after children).

Married Students

If a student is independent (see above) and married, the income of the husband or wife will be assessed in the same way as parental income for the purpose of determining the level of the grant.

SUB-CHARGE The owner of a charge on registered land may raise money on it by means of a sub-charge. This may be registered at the Land Registry in exchange for a certificate of sub-charge. An equitable sub-charge can be obtained by the lodgment of the charge certificate and giving notice of deposit of the charge certificate to the Land Registry. SEE *Land Registration*

SUB-MORTGAGE A mortgage of a mortgage. A party who is a mortgagee may raise money on the security of his mortgage by means of a sub-mortgage. A legal sub-mortgage takes the form of a grant by the mortgagee to the sub-mortgagee of a term of a few days shorter than his own term. A sub-mortgage existing before 1926 was converted by the Law of Property Act into a lease less by one day than the term vested in the mortgagee.

An equitable sub-mortgage can be taken by the deposit of the mortgage deeds with a memorandum.

When taking a sub-mortgage, notice should be given to the mortgagor and his acknowledgment obtained in order that any repayments by him shall be made to the sub-mortgagee. He should confirm the amount owing.

Searches should be made against the sub-mortgagor; they are not necessary against the mortgagor.

SUBORDINATED LOAN STOCK This is a loan stock, the repayment of which is postponed to the payment of other creditors. This is in contrast to a secured loan stock which would enjoy a prior charge on the company's assets ahead of the unsecured credits. On the winding up of a company, the holders of subordinated loan stock will receive nothing if the company is insolvent, i.e. cannot meet its other debts in full. On the other hand, if there is a surplus, the subordinated loan stock holders will be paid in priority to the equity shareholders. Because of their postponed rights, holders of subordinated stock would normally receive a higher rate of interest than would otherwise apply.

SUBROGATION The acquiring of another person's rights, usually as a result of assuming or discharging that person's liabilities. If, for example, a guarantor repays the full debt due to the banker on the account for which he is surety, he is subrogated to the rights of the banker—that is, he is thereby entitled, in the absence of agreement to the contrary, to the banker's right to sue the debtor, or to claim upon his estate, and to the benefit of any securities which the banker held (SEE *Guarantee*). The same remarks apply where securities have been given by a third party and he pays off the whole debt. Before giving up any such security, the banker should obtain the consent of the customer and of any other parties interested in the account.

The principle is also applicable to stopped cheques paid in error and payments for necessaries made on behalf of persons who are of unsound mind.

SUBSCRIBED CAPITAL That part of the nominal or authorized capital which has been issued by the directors of a company and subscribed or taken up by the shareholders. It may be fully paid up, or only partly paid, in which latter case the remainder is termed the 'uncalled' capital. SEE *Capital; Uncalled Capital*

SUBSIDIARY COMPANY The Companies Act 1985, Section 736, contains a definition of a subsidiary company as follows:

> (1) For the purposes of this Act, a company is deemed to be a subsidiary of another if (but only if)—
> (*a*) that other either—
> (i) is a member of it and controls the composition of its board of directors, or
> (ii) holds more than half in nominal value of its equity share capital, or
> (*b*) the first-mentioned company is a subsidiary of any company which is that other's subsidiary.

The above is subject to subsection (4) below in this section.

(2) For purposes of subsection (1), the composition of a company's board of directors is deemed to be controlled by another company if (but only if) that other company by the exercise of some power exercisable by it without the consent or concurrence of any other person can appoint or remove the holders of all or a majority of the directorships.

(3) For purposes of this last provision, the other company is deemed to have power to appoint to a directorship with respect to which any of the following conditions is satisfied—

(a) that a person cannot be appointed to it without the exercise in his favour by the other company of such a power as is mentioned above, or

(b) that a person's appointment to the directorship follows necessarily from his appointment as director of the other company, or

(c) that the directorship is held by the other company itself or by a subsidiary of it.

(4) In determining whether one company is a subsidiary of another—

(a) any shares held or power exercisable by the other in a fiduciary capacity are to be treated as not held or exercisable by it,

(b) subject to the two following paragraphs, any shares held or power exercisable—

(i) by any person as nominee for the other (except where the other is concerned only in a fiduciary capacity), or

(ii) by, or by a nominee for, a subsidiary of the other (not being a subsidiary which is concerned only in a fiduciary capacity),

are to be treated as held or exercisable by the other.

(c) any shares held or power exercisable by any person by virtue of the provisions of any debentures of the first-mentioned company or of a trust deed for securing any issue of such debentures are to be disregarded,

(d) any shares held or power exercisable by, or by a nominee for, the other or its subsidiary (not being held or exercisable as mentioned in paragraph (c)) are to be treated as not held or exercisable by the other if the ordinary business of the other or its subsidiary (as the case may be) includes the lending of money and the shares are held or the power is exercisable as above mentioned by way of security only for the purposes of a transaction entered into in the ordinary course of that business.

(5) For purposes of this Act—

(a) a company is deemd to be another's holding company if (but only if) the other is its subsidiary, and

(b) a body corporate is deemed the wholly-owned subsidiary of another if it has no members except that other and that other's wholly-owned subsidiaries and its or their nominees.

(6) In this section 'company' includes any body corporate.

SEE *Holding Company*

SUBSTITUTED SECURITY SEE *Mortgage*

SUPERANNUATION FUNDS OFFICE SEE *Pensions, Pension Schemes*

SUPERANNUATION SCHEMES SEE *Pensions, Pension Schemes*

SUPERVISION OF BANKS Historically, there has been little 'supervision' of British banks, except in the matter of liquidity ratios (q.v.) and the constraints imposed from time to time by the Bank of England at the request of the Government in the quantitative and qualitative control of lending. For the most part, as the London clearing banks themselves indicated in the evidence to the Wilson Committee (q.v.) 'the most important prudential constraints on the banks are self-imposed'. Nevertheless, the influence of the Bank of Englanl is very considerable, albeit exercised for the most part in an informal manner. As a consequence of the secondary banking crisis of 1973–74, the Government issued a White Paper in August 1976 entitled *The Licensing and Supervision of Deposit Taking Institutions.* This in turn, led to the introduction of the Banking Act 1979 (q.v.). As explained under that heading, the licensing and supervision of banks and deposit-taking institutions is now entirely in the hands of the Bank of England and although guidelines have been issued on such matters as capital ratios and liquidity requirements, supervision is maintained by continuous monitoring of recognized banks and licensed deposit-takers, depending on their individual sizes and circumstances. SEE ALSO Banking Supervision

SUPPLEMENTARY BENEFIT The framework of supplementary benefit is governed for the most part by the Social Security Act 1980, which replaced the Supplementary Benefit Act 1976. The system of supplementary benefit is designed to assist people who do not have enough to live on and who have no substantial capital resources on which to draw. It is a non-contributory benefit and thus may be payable whether or not the claimant has paid National Insurance contributions over the years.

Supplementary benefit may be payable to any of the following depending on their financial needs:

1. persons over pension age (and no longer in full-time employment),
2. persons unfit for work,
3. unemployed persons,
4. persons only able to obtain part-time work,
5. persons bringing up children on their own,

6. persons needed at home to look after a disabled relative.

Persons who have more than £3,000 capital will not be entitled to supplementary benefit. Capital for this purpose does not, however, include the value of a person's house nor of the furniture, household effects and other everyday possessions. Other house property is valued at its open market value, as are other assets owned by the claimant. The present value of a reversionary interest is included as capital and sums held in a discretionary trust for the benefit of a claimant may be included as part of his resources. This would normally be so if the capital value of the trust is more than £4,000 and it was set up for the support of a claimant. Assets of a business owned by the claimant or his wife may be disregarded for as long as the benefit officer thinks reasonable.

The income on amounts of capital up to £3,000 is also disregarded in calculating the amount of any supplementary benefit which may be payable.

The calculation of supplementary benefit is based in the first instance on a notional sum which is deemed to cover normal living expenses (See Appendix 2). To this is added an additional sum at current rate for each dependent, depending on age (See Appendix 2).

An additional sum is added for water rates, mortgage interest, insurance and repairs for persons living in their own homes. (An allowance for rent in the case of tenanted property and for rates in respect of both tenanted and owner occupied property is paid by the local authority under the Housing Benefit Scheme introduced in April 1983.)

From the combined total is deducted the amount received by the applicant by way of income. If the applicant has any earnings, the first £4 of net earnings per week will be ignored. In this case 'net' means earnings after income tax, National Insurance contributions, if any, and other absolutely essential payments such as the cost of a child-minder.

In the case of single parents, the initial £4 of net earnings will be ignored in addition to half the net earnings between £4 and £20 per week. Thus, a single parent earning, say, £14 will not need to count the first £9 (i.e. £4 plus one-half of £14 minus £4).

Occupational pensions are taken into account in the income receipts of the applicant and any sickness benefit from an employer will be taken into account in full. The first £4 of industrial widow's benefit, disablement pensions and war pensions will be disregarded.

Earnings received from certain categories of voluntary work, e.g. lifeboat men and part-time firemen and attendance at Territorial Army drills (but not weekend camps or longer periods) are completely ignored.

If the total receipts thus calculated amount to less than the needs of the applicant calculated as above, the difference is made up by supplementary benefit. In addition to weekly benefit so calculated, supplementary benefit may also be paid from time to time for 'exceptional needs'. This does not extend to normal living expenses such as clothing, footwear, etc., because these are covered by the weekly scale payments. A payment will be made where it is considered that the person concerned would face severe hardship if the payment were not made. These payments, known as 'exceptional circumstances additions' (ECAs), may cover such expenses as special diets, extra heating on health grounds, central heating (because of the additional costs this normally involves), laundry costs occasioned from disability or infirmity, essential domestic help, telephone rentals for house-bound persons living in isolated areas, hire purchase instalments to which the claimant is committed for essential furniture, and alcoholic drinks which have been recommended by a doctor.

The Supplementary Benefits Commission also has discretionary power to make 'exceptional needs payments' (ENPs) which are usually in addition to weekly supplementary benefit but may be paid to people who are not receiving regular supplementary benefit. The purpose of this discretionary power is to assist people who would otherwise fall below the standard of living provided by the supplementary benefit scheme. Examples of items which may be covered by ENPs are

1. footwear and clothing beyond normal replacement costs;
2. furniture and bedding, etc., principally the replacement cost for essential items, and in a limited number of circumstances for furnishing new accommodation;
3. minor improvements and new decorations;
4. removal costs where there is good reason to change accommodation;
5. essential fares; and
6. local disasters.

There are two scales of supplementary benefit: the ordinary rate which applies to most persons below the age of 60, and the 'long-term' rate which applies to pensioners and other long-term claimants such as single parents, invalids and others not registered for employment. After one year of ordinary rate benefit, persons in these categories will qualify for the long-term rate, which is at a higher level than the ordinary weekly rate (See Appendix 2).

Persons in receipt of weekly supplementary benefit are automatically entitled to other benefits for themselves or their dependants, including free school meals, free milk and vitamins and free national health dental treatment, glasses and prescriptions.

In general, supplementary benefit is *not* taxable, but under the Finance Act 1981, benefit paid to an unemployed person, or to a person on strike is taxable. This applies only to the standard rate of benefit, including any addition for a wife or adult dependant. Benefits payable for children, housing and exceptional circumstances are not taxable.

With effect from November 1980, persons in receipt of supplementary benefit are allowed to spend up to four weeks abroad without loss of the benefit. This does not apply, however, to persons who are unemployed or temporarily away from work owing to sickness.

When an unmarried couple are living together as husband and wife, they are treated as husband and wife for supplementary benefit purposes, i.e. they cannot claim supplementary benefit as two single persons. This usually means that only the man will be able to claim benefit, although the level of benefit will take into account the needs of the woman and of any children. As with a married man, he will not be able to claim benefit if he is in full-time employment.

Supplementary Benefit for Persons on Strike
A person who is on strike as a result of a trade dispute cannot receive any supplementary benefit for himself. Accordingly, a single man or a single woman cannot normally receive supplementary benefit. The only exception to this is that benefit may be paid in the case of urgent need, but only after taking into account all the striker's financial circumstances. In general, the striker will be expected to make last as long as possible, and not at a rate exceeding £16.50 per week, any amounts he receives from (1) final wages before the dispute, (2) any subsequent wages in hand, and (3) any other income including PAYE tax refund and strike pay.

If both husband and wife are involved in a trade dispute and have no dependent children, similar provisions will apply and they will be expected to manage on their strike pay, wages in hand, etc. at a rate of not more than £33 per week. In fact, the maximum normally allowed will be £24 per week.

In the case of married man involved in a trade dispute, he may claim benefit for his wife and family and for rent. But the following rules will apply:

1. Benefit will not be paid until the striker's last earnings have run out.
2. If the striker's earnings for the last week of work are more than twice the supplementary benefit guidelines the excess is regarded as available income for a further week.
3. The striker will get nothing for his personal requirements and the amount which he will be deemed to require for his wife will be £14.65 per week.
4. Any strike pay and income tax refunds and other types of income will be taken into account, disregarding the first £4.
5. Any part-time or other earnings of the striker in excess of £2 and his wife's earnings in excess of £4 will be taken fully into account.

Unlike the general rules for supplementary benefit, a person involved in a trade dispute cannot receive supplementary benefit for clothing, fuel bills, hire purchase debts or extra heating (unless in this last instance it is essential for the health of a dependant).

A married woman involved in a trade dispute cannot claim supplementary benefit for herself or her children.

SUPPLEMENTARY PENSION This is similar to supplementary allowance (see above) but becomes payable when a claimant is of State pensionable age, i.e. 65 for a man and 60 for a woman.

SUPRA PROTEST Where a bill of exchange has been protested for dishonour by non-acceptance, any person may, with the consent of the holder, accept the bill supra protest for the honour of any party liable thereon. SEE *Acceptance for Honour*

Also, where a bill has been protested for non-payment, any person may intervene and pay it supra protest for the honour of any party liable thereon. SEE *Bill of Exchange; Payment for Honour*

SURETY The terms 'surety' and 'guarantor' are used more or less synonymously but 'surety' has a wider connotation. A guarantor under a contract of guarantee is a surety but a person may stand as a surety without there being a contract of guarantee in the accepted sense. The mere deposit of security for another person's debt will constitute a contract of suretyship, although there will not be a guarantee as such. In such a case, the surety does not incur a personal liability for the whole of the principal debtor's obligation but the security he has given may be used to discharge that obligation.

A person who signs a bill of exchange as an accommodation party (q.v.) is a surety for the due payment of the bill, and it has been held that a retired partner is a surety for the continuing members of the firm in respect of the partnership debts existing at the time of his retirement. SEE *Guarantee*

SURRENDER VALUE The amount which, depending on the terms of a life policy, may be payable on the surrender of that policy before the date of maturity. In general, during the life of the assured person, a life policy is only worth its surrender value. This will normally be little or nothing in the early years of the policy's life.

In the case of linked life assurance, the surrender value of a policy will be the current market value of the underlying securities, less any charge to which the life company may be entitled on surrender. SEE *Life Assurance*

SUSPENSION OF PAYMENT A debtor commits an act of bankruptcy if he gives notice to any of his creditors that he has suspended, or that he is about to suspend payment of his debts (Bankruptcy Act 1914, Section 1(1)(*h*)). SEE *Act of Bankruptcy*

SWIFT Society for Worldwide Interbank Financial Telecommunications is a co-operative organization set up in 1972 by 73 banks, including the London and Scottish clearing banks, to provide a communications network for the speedy transmission of international payments and messages. The system became fully operative on a worldwide basis in 1977 and enables payments to be made between banks instantaneously by electronic means.

T

TABLE A This is contained in Schedule 1 of the Companies Act 1948, and supplies model articles of association for the management of a company limited by shares. It contains 136 clauses.

In the case of a company limited by shares and registered after 1st July, 1948 (that is, the commencement of the Act), if articles are not registered, or, if articles are registered, in so far as the articles do not exclude or modify the regulations in Table A, those regulations are to be the regulations of the company in the same manner and to the same extent as if they were contained in duly registered articles (Section 8).

The borrowing powers of the directors of a company which has adopted Table A are as follows: in the case of companies registered between 1862 and 30th September, 1906, unlimited; in the case of companies registered after 30th September, 1906 (when Table A was revised), limited to the amount of the company's issued capital unless the company sanctions a borrowing in excess. (This is now subject to Section 14, Companies Act 1980, regarding the issue of share capital.) Companies registered on or after 1st July, 1948, which adopt Table A, can exclude temporary loans obtained from their bankers in computing their total outstanding borrowings. Moreover, no lender or other person dealing with the company is bound to see or inquire if the limit is observed.

Companies registered between 1862 and 30th September, 1906 are governed by Table A of the Companies Act 1862, and those registered between 1st October, 1906 and 31st March, 1909 by the revised Table A of 1906.

The Companies Act 1980 contained a number of amendments to Table A (see paragraphs 35 and 36 of Schedule 3 to the 1980 Act) and where relevant, these have been dealt with under their respective headings. SEE ALSO *Articles of Association; Call; Certificate; Directors; Distribution; Dividend; Lien; Quorum; Stock; Transfer of Shares; Votes.* SEE Supplement

TACKING Before the Law of Property Act 1925, a first mortgagee might advance further sums on the same security and could add or tack such further sums to his first advance in priority to any second mortgagee, of whose existence he was unaware, who had lent money between the time that the first mortgagee had made his first advance and his second advance. Likewise, a third mortgagee, who lent money in ignorance of the second mortgage, could, on discovering such second mortgage, take over the first mortgage and tack his third mortgage on to it and thus get priority over the second mortgage.

Tacking, except by a first mortgagee, was abolished by the Law of Property Act, Section 94(3). The scheme of registration of mortgages unprotected by the relative deeds, made this practicable, for by searching the Land Charges Register a prospective mortgagee can ascertain if any prior encumbrances unprotected by deeds are outstanding. A first mortgagee can still tack if:

1. he has arranged to that effect with subsequent mortgagees; or
2. he was without notice of any subsequent mortgage at the time he made the further advance; or
3. by the terms of the mortgage deed he is bound to make further advances, in which case he can tack whether he has notice of subsequent mortgages or not.

SEE *Mortgage*

TAKE-OVERS AND MERGERS A take-over is a form of amalgamation of companies by share purchase. The taking-over company may wish only to gain control over the composition of the board of directors, for which a shareholding of 51 per cent will be sufficient. If it desires to control special or extraordinary resolutions it will need 75 per cent. If it aims at total ownership it must acquire every share. An offer to acquire a company's shares may be made direct to the shareholders, or by friendly agreement between the boards of the two companies. The consideration offered may be cash or loan notes or shares or loan stock in the bidding company, or a combination of both. In the case of a quoted company, the price offered will generally be in excess of the market value of the shares to secure acceptance. It will often be stipulated that acceptances in respect of a certain proportion of shares must be received by a certain date. Power to acquire the shares of dissentient shareholders is given by Ss. 428–430 of the Companies Act 1985. Where the holders of 90 per cent of the nominal value of the shares for which an offer has been made, have accepted it within four months of the offer, the bidding company may compulsorily acquire on the same terms the remaining 10 per cent, or any of them, within a further two months. There is a right of appeal to the court for an order of restraint, to be exercised not later than one month from the receipt of the notice of compulsory acquisition.

The term 'merger' is normally used when two companies of roughly equal size amalgamate to form one company, e.g. the National Provincial Bank Ltd, with its wholly owned subsidiary District Bank Ltd, and the Westminster Bank Ltd merged to form the National Westminster Bank Ltd. The shareholders in the 'old' companies are given shares in the 'new' company in exchange for their old shares in agreed proportions.

The theory behind take-overs and mergers is that a fuller use of assets and managerial skills results. The threat of such an operation has often caused an offeree company to revalue its assets more realistically, either as a defence to a take-over bid or to increase the consideration being offered to shareholders.

In many instances, take-overs and mergers have no doubt resulted in the better use of resources and the greater efficiency which can be achieved in larger units. On the other hand, in the 1960s and 1970s there was much concern over the activities of the 'asset-strippers' who acquired companies, not with a view to a continuing business activity but in order to take out valuable assets for the benefit of the proprietors of the take-over company.

It was felt for some time that a desirable code of behaviour for bids and mergers was called for, and in 1959 a working party was set up at the instigation of the Bank of England for this purpose. The participants were the London Clearing Bankers, the Acceptance and Issuing Houses, the Stock Exchange Council, the Association of Investment Trusts, and the British Insurance Association Investment Protection Committee. As a result of the report published by this body, *The City Code on Take-overs and Mergers* was published in March, 1968, since when there have been a number of amendments and the *Code* is now in its eighth edition. The *Code* enunciates general principles of conduct to be observed in bid situations and it lays down certain rules, some of which are precise, and others no more than examples of the application of principles. Adherence to the *Code* is voluntary as it was considered to be impracticable to devise rules in such detail to cover all the various circumstances which arise in takeover or merger situations. It is, however, expected that persons engaged in these activities will observe not only the rules and general principles but also the spirit thereof. The main principles of the *Code* are

1. that all shareholders of the same class should be treated equally and different classes of shareholders comparably;
2. that the shareholder should be given adequate information;
3. that directors of the company receiving the bid should act in the best interests of their shareholders, and obtain adequate advice; and
4. that the creation of false markets in the shares should be avoided.

If a company and its associates acquire more than 15 per cent of the shares of a particular class in the 12 months prior to its making a take-over bid, it must offer a cash alternative, when making the bid, to all shareholders of that class, at the highest price paid during the period. If a company has acquired more than 30 per cent of the shares in another company, it must make a general offer to all shareholders at the highest price paid for any of the shares in the last 12 months.

The *Code* is not a legal document and it lacks legal sanctions for its enforcement. Nevertheless, failure to observe the *Code* may lead to the suspension of a Stock Exchange quotation, the admonishing of an institution or advisor by their professional or disciplinary body or the withdrawal of a dealer's licence by the Department of Trade and Industry. SEE *Licensed Dealer*

In order to interpret and administer the *Code*, a Panel on Take-overs and Mergers was set up in 1968 by the leading City institutions on the initiative of the Governor of the Bank of England. The Panel has an independent chairman and consists of representatives of City institutions. It has a Director-General and a small staff. Appeal from the rulings of the Panel is to a Committee presided over by a former High Court judge. The Panel is now part of the Council for the Securities Industry (q.v.).

One of the areas of concern to the Panel was the use of 'insider information' in take-over situations, but the law has been much strengthened on the subject of insider dealing by the Companies Act 1980. SEE *Insider Dealing*

Consequent upon the reclassification of public and private companies under the Companies Act 1980 (q.v.), a number of public companies have re-registered as private companies and yet are still similar to public companies in that they may have a large number of shareholders. Accordingly, in

June, 1983, the City Code on Takeovers was amended to include private companies which have been public companies in 10 years prior to any event which would involve the Code. The Panel on Take-overs indicated that this provision would be applied with a degree of flexibility, depending on the circumstances of each case.

TAKING UP A BILL SEE *Retiring a Bill*

TALISMAN This is a code name of the Stock Exchange computerized system for settlements. The initials stand for Transfer Accounting Lodgement for Investors, Stock Management for Jobbers. The system covers nearly all dealings on the Stock Exchange, other than new issues, gilt-edged stocks and bearer securities. Talisman works in cooperation with SEPON which is short for Stock Exchange Pool Nominees Limited. SEPON is used as a nominee company within the Stock Exchange for the transfer of shares of those companies who participate in the scheme. On the sale of shares, a signed transfer is executed in favour of SEPON and the Stock Exchange then holds the Stock (through SEPON as nominee) as trustee for the seller until Account Day. It is then held to the order of the buyer and a transfer effected into the name of the buyer. Thus at any one time, SEPON is a nominee shareholder on behalf of sellers and buyers of stock in those companies who participate in the scheme. The whole purpose of the scheme is to facilitate stock transfers by computerized methods and avoid delays in the issue of certificates and delays in the registration of transfers which can result in dividends going to a seller after stock has been sold cum dividend.

TAP STOCK A term usually applied to British Government stocks which are still in course of issue on behalf of the Government, through the Bank of England. Such stocks are available 'on tap' to the market through the Government broker, the supply being matched to the demand and the price reflecting market conditions. Such stocks are part of the Government's open-market operations (q.v.) and are thus an instrument of monetary policy. When a particular issue of stock has been exhausted, it is no longer 'on tap' and may only be bought like any other listed security, through the Stock Exchange.

TAX DEPOSIT CERTIFICATES These are certificates which a taxpayer may purchase for the purpose of meeting a future tax liability or which he may subsequently withdraw for cash if the certificates are not needed to meet a tax liability. The rates of interest are published at frequent intervals and vary with current market rates. The rates also vary according to the size of the deposit and whether or not it is eventually used to meet a tax liability or is withdrawn for cash. Interest on tax deposit certificates is taxable.

TAXATION OF BILLS OF COSTS The examination by the Taxing Master (an officer of the High Court) of bills of costs rendered by solicitors to their clients, or their opponents, in litigation, unfair or incorrect charges being disallowed by the Taxing Master.

TECHNICAL DEVELOPMENT CAPITAL LTD (TDC) A company formed in 1962 with the object of providing finance for the commercial development and exploitation of technological innovation in the UK. The capital of £2 million is now owned by Industrial and Commercial Finance Corporation Limited (q.v.).

When TDC assists companies—mainly medium and small ones—it is normally by subscribing for equity capital and by providing long-term loans at current rates of interest, fixed for the whole of the term, charged only on the outstanding amount. Loan repayments commence when the projects reach the requisite stage of profitability. If an offer by TDC is accepted, a small negotiation fee is charged. No fee is payable if agreement is not reached.

TEL QUEL RATE Also known as an 'all in' rate. A banker often uses this rate when he is buying a currency bill on a foreign centre when the bill has some time to run before maturity. A tel quel rate is built up on the telegraphic transfer rate, allowance being made for the time taken in transmission, the days elapsing between arrival in the foreign centre and the maturity, and also for stamp and sundry charges arising from bill collecting expenses.

TELEGRAPHIC TRANSFER Often called TT. The payment of money in a foreign country may, when necessary, be effected by telegraph, the banker in London sending a cable, with the necessary particulars, to his foreign correspondent. The cost of the cable is charged to the customer at whose request the transfer is made, unless the banker is instructed that charges are to be borne by the payee. Payment may be made to the payee (1) under advice, (2) on application and identification, (3) to credit of payee's account at ... Bank, according to the directions given by the remitter. Cable transfers are transmitted in currency when practicable unless they are specially required in sterling, and the remitter has the choice of having the cable sent at urgent, ordinary, or deferred rate.

The form of request, which is signed by a customer when he requires his banker to cable money abroad, should contain a clause to the following effect: 'I request that you will (using your telegraphic code as required) transfer the amount by telegraph on the understanding that you do so at my risk in every respect'. SEE ALSO *Swift*

TELLER One who 'tells', i.e. counts, from the Anglo-Saxon *tellen*, to count. That is, a cashier. The term is still used in the USA but not so widely nowadays in Britain. It has been revived to some extent with the introduction of Automated Teller Machines (ATMs) (q.v.).

TENANCY IN COMMON Before the Law of Property Act 1925, a tenancy in common existed where land was held by two or more persons in undivided shares, the revenue therefrom being shared jointly. On the death of a tenant in common, his interest passed to his heir or devisee. This was the distinction between tenancy in common and joint tenancy, for in the latter case the interest of a deceased joint tenant passed to the survivor(s), and on the death of the last survivor the entire interest passed to the beneficiaries or heirs of each party.

Tenancy in common was a legal estate; by the Law of Property Act 1925, however, it was abolished as such but can exist in equity. That is to say, the legal estate in the property is vested in trustees for sale, who hold the legal estate for the beneficiaries, i.e. the tenants in common in equity. Thus if A and B jointly own property they have a dual role—they are trustees for sale jointly holding the legal estate and they are beneficiaries under the trust. If A dies, his interest in the proceeds of sale passes to his estate, but the legal estate remains in B who will have to co-opt another trustee if and when the property is sold in order to give a valid receipt for the capital moneys. The legal estate cannot be vested in more than four trustees for sale, and thus if six persons are jointly interested in a property, the first four will hold as trustees for themselves and the last two. SEE ALSO *Joint Tenants*

TENANT FOR LIFE SEE *Life Tenant; Settled Land*

TENDER ISSUE This is an issue of stock which may, for example, be a new Government stock or it may be a new issue of ordinary shares, for which prospective purchasers offer or 'tender' the price which they think appropriate. The advantage of an offer by tender from the standpoint of the issuers of the stock, is that they or their advisers do not have the difficulty of arriving at a particular fixed price. On the other hand, from the purchasers' point of view, tender offers are not very popular because the purchaser has the difficulty of arriving at a correct price, sometimes without the experience and knowledge of the issuing house. In recent times, there has been a number of Government stocks, including 'privatization' stocks offered for sale by tender in order to avoid the embarrassment of considerable over-subscription or under-subscription, which can arise from a fixed-price offer.

If, say, a million shares are offered for sale by tender and tenders are received at a variety of prices (as will be the case), the striking price (q.v.) will be the price at or *above* which tenders have been received for a million shares. In practice, at that level, the tenders could far exceed the shares available, in which case they will generally be allocated by ballot.

TERM ASSURANCE SEE *Life Assurance—categories*

TERM OF A BILL The period for which a bill of exchange is drawn.

TERM SHARES An expression usually applied to building society shares issued for a period of one to five years. Term shares do not offer a fixed rate of interest over a period but they usually carry a fixed margin of interest, e.g. $1\frac{1}{2}$ per cent over the ordinary share rate. Thus the rate on term shares will fluctuate with the ordinary share rate but the differential will be maintained. The purpose of the shares is to attract longer-term investment (SEE *Building Societies, Investment in*). Some term shares carry an escalating rate of interest, i.e. the margin over the ordinary share rate increases slightly for each year the investment is held up to a maximum, usually, of five years. Most term shares carry a provision for early redemption by the shareholder on payment of an interest penalty.

TERMINAL BONUS An additional bonus paid on a with-profits life policy at maturity of the policy depending on the investment performance of the society. There is no obligation to pay a terminal bonus and indeed they were withheld by some companies during the Stock Market crisis of 1974–75. In general, like annual bonuses on with-profits policies, they are a means of sharing in the profits of the life office.

TERMINATING BUILDING SOCIETY A society which, by its rules, is to terminate at a fixed date, or when a result specified in its rules is attained. With few, if any, exceptions, all building societies nowadays are permanent. SEE *Building Societies*

THEFT ACTS The Theft Act of 1968 and that of 1978 belong to the field of criminal law, but are included here because of the impact of the Acts on certain financial dealings. The 1968 Act rationalized much of the old law, part of which had been codified in the Larceny Act of 1916. The old distinctions between larceny, embezzlement, fraudulent conversion and false pretences, have largely disappeared, although they remain within the body of case law. The principal sections which might have financial implications are quoted below.

DEFINITION OF 'THEFT'

1. BASIC DEFINITION OF THEFT

(1) A person is guilty of theft if he dishonestly appropriates property belonging to another with the intention of permanently depriving the other of it; and 'thief' and 'steal' shall be construed accordingly.

(2) It is immaterial whether the appropriation is made with a view to gain, or is made for the thief's own benefit.

(3) The five following Sections of this Act shall have effect as regards the interpretation and operation of this Section (and, except as otherwise provided by this Act, shall apply only for purposes of this Section).

2. 'DISHONESTLY'

(1) A person's appropriation of property belonging to another is not to be regarded as dishonest—

(a) if he appropriates the property in the belief that he has in law the right to deprive the other of it, on behalf of himself or of a third person; or

(b) if he appropriates the property in the belief that he would have the other's consent if the other knew of the appropriation and the circumstances of it; or

(c) (except where the property came to him as trustee or personal representative) if he appropriates the property in the belief that the person to whom the property belongs cannot be discovered by taking reasonable steps.

(2) A person's appropriation of property belonging to another may be dishonest notwithstanding that he is willing to pay for the property.

3. 'APPROPRIATES'

(1) Any assumption by a person of the rights of an owner amounts to an appropriation, and this includes, where he has come by the property (innocently or not) without stealing it, any later assumption of a right to it by keeping or dealing with it as owner.

(2) Where property or a right or interest in property is or purports to be transferred for value to a person acting in good faith, no later assumption by him of rights which he believed himself to be acquiring shall, by reason of any defect in the transferor's title, amount to theft of the property.

4. 'PROPERTY'

(1) 'Property' includes money and all other property, real or personal, including things in action and other intangible property.

(2) A person cannot steal land, or things forming part of land and severed from it by him or by his directions, except in the following cases, that is to say—

(a) when he is a trustee or personal representative, or is authorised by power of attorney, or as liquidator of a company, or otherwise, to sell or dispose of land belonging to another, and he appropriates the land or anything forming part of it by dealing with it in breach of the confidence reposed in him; or

(b) when he is not in possession of the land and appropriates anything forming part of the land by severing it or causing it to be severed, or after it has been severed; or

(c) when, being in possession of the land under a tenancy, he appropriates the whole or part of any fixture or structure let to be used with the land.

For purposes of this subsection 'land' does not include incorporeal hereditaments; 'tenancy' means a tenancy for years or any less period and includes an agreement for such a tenancy, but a person who after the end of a tenancy remains in possession as statutory tenant or otherwise is to be treated as having possession under the tenancy, and 'let' shall be construed accordingly.

(3) A person who picks mushrooms growing wild on any land, or who picks flowers, fruit or foliage from a plant growing wild on any land, does not (although not in possession of the land) steal what he picks, unless he does it for reward or for sale or other commercial purpose.

For purposes of this subsection 'mushroom' includes any fungus, and 'plant' includes any shrub or tree.

(4) Wild creatures, tamed or untamed, shall be regarded as property; but a person cannot steal a wild creature not tamed nor ordinarily kept in captivity, or the carcase of any such creature, unless either it has been reduced into possession by or on behalf of another person and possession of it has not since been lost or abandoned, or another person is in course of reducing it into possession.

5. 'BELONGING TO ANOTHER'

(1) Property shall be regarded as belonging to any person having possession or control of it, or having in it any proprietary right or interest (not being an equitable interest arising only from an agreement to transfer or grant an interest).

(2) Where property is subject to a trust, the persons to whom it belongs shall be regarded as including any person having a right to enforce the trust, and an intention to defeat the trust shall be regarded accordingly as an intention to deprive of the property any person having that right.

(3) Where a person receives property from or on account of another, and is under an obligation to the other to retain and deal with that property or its proceeds in a particular way, the property or proceeds shall be regarded (as against him) as belonging to the other.

(4) Where a person gets property by another's mistake, and is under an obligation to make restoration (in whole or in part) of the property or its proceeds or of the value thereof, then to the extent of that obligation the property or proceeds shall be regarded (as against him) as belonging to the person entitled to restoration, and an

intention not to make restoration shall be regarded accordingly as an intention to deprive that person of the property or proceeds.

(5) Property of a corporation sole shall be regarded as belonging to the corporation notwithstanding a vacancy in the corporation.

6. 'With the Intention of Permanently Depriving the Other of it'

(1) A person appropriating property belonging to another without meaning the other permanently to lose the thing itself is nevertheless to be regarded as having the intention of permanently depriving the other of it if his intention is to treat the thing as his own to dispose of regardless of the other's rights; and a borrowing or lending of it may amount to so treating it if, but only if, the borrowing or lending is for a period and in circumstances making it equivalent to an outright taking or disposal.

(2) Without prejudice to the generality of subsection (1) above, where a person, having possession or control (lawfully or not) of property belonging to another, parts with the property under a condition as to its return which he may not be able to perform, this (if done for purposes of his own and without the other's authority) amounts to treating the property as his own to dispose of regardless of the other's rights.

Fraud and Blackmail

15. Obtaining Property by Deception

(1) A person who by any deception dishonestly obtains property belonging to another, with the intention of permanently depriving the other of it, shall on conviction on indictment be liable to imprisonment for a term not exceeding ten years.

(2) For purposes of this Section a person is to be treated as obtaining property if he obtains ownership, possession or control of it, and 'obtain' includes obtaining for another or enabling another to obtain or to retain.

(3) Section 6 above shall apply for purposes of this Section, with the necessary adaptation of the reference to appropriating, as it applies for purposes of Section 1.

(4) For purposes of this Section 'deception' means any deception (whether deliberate or reckless) by words or conduct as to fact or as to law, including a deception as to the present intentions of the person using the deception or any other person.

16. Obtaining Pecuniary Advantage by Deception

(1) A person who by any deception dishonestly obtains for himself or another any pecuniary advantage shall on conviction on indictment be liable to imprisonment for a term not exceeding five years.

(2) The cases in which a pecuniary advantage within the meaning of this section is to be regarded as obtained for a person are cases where—

(*a*) any debt or charge for which he makes himself liable or is or may become liable (including one not legally enforceable) is reduced or in whole or in part evaded or deferred; [repealed by the Theft Act 1978—see below] or

(*b*) he is allowed to borrow by way of overdraft, or to take out any policy of insurance or annuity contract, or obtains an improvement of the terms on which he is allowed to do so; or

(*c*) he is given the opportunity to earn remuneration or greater remuneration in an office or employment, or to win money by betting.

(3) For purposes of this Section 'deception' has the same meaning as in Section 15 of this Act.

17. False Accounting

(1) Where a person dishonestly, with a view to gain for himself or another or with intent to cause loss to another,—

(*a*) destroys, defaces, conceals or falsifies any account or any record or document made or required for any accounting purpose; or

(*b*) in furnishing information for any purpose produces or makes use of any account, or any such record or document as aforesaid, which to his knowledge is or may be misleading, false or deceptive in a material particular;

he shall, on conviction on indictment, be liable to imprisonment for a term not exceeding seven years.

(2) For purposes of this section a person who makes or concurs in making in an account or other document an entry which is or may be misleading, false or deceptive in a material particular, or who omits or concurs in omitting a material particular from an account or other document, is to be treated as falsifying the account or document.

18. Liability of Company Officers for Certain Offences by Company

(1) Where an offence committed by a body corporate under Section 15, 16 or 17 of this Act is proved to have been committed with the consent or connivance of any director, manager, secretary or other similar officer of the body corporate, or any person who was purporting to act in any such capacity, he as well as the body corporate shall be guilty of that offence, and shall be liable to be proceeded against and punished accordingly.

(2) Where the affairs of a body corporate are managed by its members, this section shall apply in relation to the acts and defaults of a member in connection with his functions of management as if he were a director of the body corporate.

19. False Statements by Company Directors, etc.

(1) Where an officer of a body corporate or unincorporated association (or person purporting to act as such), with intent to deceive members or creditors of the body corporate or association about its affairs, publishes or concurs in publishing a written statement or account which to his knowledge is or may be misleading, false or deceptive in a material particular, he shall on conviction on indictment be liable to imprisonment for a term not exceeding seven years.

(2) For purposes of this Section a person who has entered into a security for the benefit of a body corporate or association is to be treated as a creditor of it.

(3) Where the affairs of a body corporate or association are managed by its members, this Section shall apply to any statement which a member publishes or concurs in publishing in connection with his functions of management as if he were an officer of the body corporate or association.

The Theft Act 1978 repealed Section 16(2)(*a*)

(see above) of the Theft Act 1968, and contains the following provisions.

Section 1 renders it an offence for a person, by any deception, dishonestly to claim services from another, it being an obtaining of services where the other is induced to confer a benefit by doing some act, or causing or permitting some act to be done, on the understanding that the benefit has been or will be paid for.

Section 2 makes it an offence for a person by any deception dishonestly to evade liability to make a payment, either by

1. securing the remission of the whole or part of any existing liability, whether his own or another's; or
2. inducing a creditor or any person claiming payment on behalf of the creditor to wait for payment, (whether or not the due date for payment is deferred) or forego payment, with intent to make permanent default in whole or part on any existing liability; or
3. obtaining any exemption from or abatement of liability.

'Liability' means legally enforceable liability and does not apply to a liability that has not been accepted or established to pay compensation for a wrongful act or omission. A person induced to take a cheque or other security by way of conditional satisfaction of a pre-existing liability is to be treated as being induced to wait for payment. 'Obtains' includes obtaining for another or enabling another to obtain.

Section 3 makes it an offence for a person, knowing that payment on the spot for any goods supplied or service done is required or expected of him, dishonestly to make off without payment and with intent to avoid payment. 'Payment on the spot' includes payment at the time of collecting goods on which work has been done or in respect of which service has been provided. No offence is committed where the supply of goods or doing of the service is contrary to law or where payment of the service is not legally enforceable.

It has been held that the sole directors and shareholders of a company may commit an offence under the Theft Act 1968, against that company, where they appropriate for themselves the company's assets. It was held that for the purpose of Section 21(b) (see above), 'Belief that he would have the others' consent' had to be an honest belief in a true consent which had been honestly obtained. In this case the defendants could not show that and, in fact, the company could not be 'the other' for the purpose of the Section because the defendants were the only directors and shareholders (Attorney General's reference (no. 2 of 1982) (1983) *Times*, 25th November).

THREEPENCE Formerly a silver coin with a standard weight of 21.81818 grains troy (SEE *Coinage*). By an Order in Council dated 18th March, 1937, a new type of threepenny piece was made legal tender for sums not exceeding two shillings. This coin, duodecagonal in shape, weighed 105 grains, and was an admixture of copper, nickel and zinc. It has no place in the decimal coinage system.

TICKET DAY Also called Name Day. The second day in the semi-monthly settlement on the London Stock Exchange was ticket day, when the brokers passed the names of the purchasers of stocks since the last settlement, certain tickets being exchanged preparatory for the fifth day, or pay day. With effect from 1979, this system was replaced by Talisman (q.v.). SEE *Settlement (Stock Exchange)*

TIMBER SEE *Woodlands, Investment in*

TIME OF PAYMENT OF BILL Bill payable on demand. By Section 10 of the Bills of Exchange Act 1882

> (1) A bill is payable on demand—
> (*a*) Which is expressed to be payable on demand, or at sight, or on presentation; or
> (*b*) In which no time for payment is expressed.
> (2) Where a bill is accepted or indorsed when it is overdue, it shall, as regards the acceptor who so accepts, or any indorser who so indorses it, be deemed a bill payable on demand.

Bill payable at a future date. By Section 11

> A bill is payable at a determinable future time within the meaning of this Act which is expressed to be payable—
> (1) At a fixed period after date or sight.
> (2) On or at a fixed period after the occurrence of a specified event which is certain to happen, though the time of happening may be uncertain.
> An instrument expressed to be payable on a contingency is not a bill, and the happening of the event does not cure the defect.

A document expressed to be payable 'thirty days after the arrival of the ship *Swallow* at Calcutta', or 'ninety days after sight or when realized' could not be supported as a bill of exchange, for it is quite indefinite when these uncertain events would probably be reduced to a certainty (*Palmer* v *Pratt* (1824), 2 Bing 185).

Similarly in the modern case of *Korea Exchange Bank* v *Debenhams* (*Central Buying*)

[1979] 1 Lloyd's Rep 548, the Court of Appeal held that '90 days D/A' meaning '90 days after acceptance' was not a 'fixed or determinable future date' within the meaning of the Act because acceptance can never be certain and an instrument payable on a contingency is not a bill of exchange.

As to the computation of time of payment of a bill payable after date, the Act provides as follows:

14. Where a bill is not payable on demand the day on which it falls due is determined as follows—

(1) Three days, called days of grace, are, in every case where the bill itself does not otherwise provide, added to the time of payment as fixed by the bill, and the bill is due and payable on the last day of grace; provided that—

(a) When the last day of grace falls on Sunday, Christmas Day, Good Friday, or a day appointed by Royal Proclamation as a public fast or thanksgiving day, the bill is, except in the case hereinafter provided for, due and payable on the preceding business day;

(b) When the last day of grace is a bank holiday (other than Christmas Day or Good Friday) under the Bank Holidays Act, 1871, and Acts amending or extending it, or when the last day of grace is a Sunday and the second day of grace is a bank holiday, the bill is due and payable on the succeeding business day.

(2) Where a bill is payable at a fixed period after date, after sight, or after the happening of a specified event, the time of payment is determined by excluding the day from which the time is to begin to run and by including the day of payment.

(3) Where a bill is payable at a fixed period after sight, the time begins to run from the date of the acceptance if the bill be accepted, and from the date of noting or protest if the bill be noted or protested for non-acceptance, or for non-delivery.

(4) The term 'month' in a bill means a calendar month.

Note that Days of Grace were abolished by the Banking and Financial Dealings Act 1971, Section 3(2):

For Section 14(1) of the Bills of Exchange Act 1882 (under or by virtue of which the date of maturity of a bill or promissory note that does not say otherwise is arrived at by adding three days of grace to the time of payment as fixed by the bill or note, but is advanced or postponed if the last day of grace is a non-business day), there shall be substituted, except in its application to bills drawn and notes made before this subsection comes into force, the following paragraph—

(1) The bill is due and payable in all cases on the last day of the time of payment as fixed by the bill or, if that is a non-business day, on the succeeding business day.

92. (As amended by the Banking and Financial Dealings Act, 1971, Section 3(1)) Where, by this Act, the time limited for doing any act or thing is less than three days, in reckoning time, non-business days are excluded.

'Non-business days' for the purposes of this Act mean—

(a) Saturday, Sunday, Good Friday, Christmas Day;

(b) A bank holiday under the Bank Holidays Act, 1871 (now repealed by the Banking and Financial Dealings Act, 1971), or Acts amending it;

(c) A day appointed by Royal proclamation as a public fast or thanksgiving day.

Any other day is a business day.

In addition to the 'non-business days' mentioned in Section 92(a) above, by Schedule 1 of the Banking and Financial Dealings Act 1971

1. The following are to be bank holidays in England and Wales—

Easter Monday.
The last Monday in May.
The last Monday in August.
26th December, if it be not a Sunday.
27th December in a year in which 25th or 26th December is a Sunday.

2. The following are to be bank holidays in Scotland—

New Year's Day, if it be not a Sunday or, if it be a Sunday, 3rd January.
2nd January, if it be not a Sunday, or, if it be a Sunday, 3rd January.
Good Friday.
The first Monday in May.
The first Monday in August.
Christmas Day, if it be not a Sunday or, if it be a Sunday, 26th December.

3. The following are to be bank holidays in Northern Ireland—

17th March, if it be not a Sunday or, if it be a Sunday, 18th March.
Easter Monday.
The last Monday in May.
The last Monday in August.
26th December, if it be not a Sunday.
27th December in a year in which 25th or 26th December is a Sunday.

The due date of a bill—that is, the date when it becomes payable—is calculated, in the case of a bill drawn payable three months after date, by counting three calendar months from the date of the bill. When drawn payable at so many days or months after sight, the date is calculated in the same way, but from the date when the bill was sighted. If the acceptor writes on the bill 'sighted 1st February, accepted 2nd February', the currency is calculated from the date when it was sighted, 1st February.

A few examples of the calculation of the time of payment are shown below.

A bill dated (or sighted) 1st January, payable one month after date (or sight), is due and payable on 1st February.
A bill dated (or sighted) 1st February, payable one month after date (or sight), is due and payable on 1st March (if leap year it is still due 1st March).
A bill dated (or sighted) 1st February, payable 30 days after date (or sight), is due and payable on 3rd March (if leap year on 2nd March).
A bill dated (or sighted) 1st March, payable 30 days after date (or sight), is due and payable on 31st March.
A bill dated (or sighted) 1st April, payable 30 days after date (or sight), is due and payable on 1st May.
A bill dated (or sighted) 28th January, payable one month after date (or sight), is due and payable on 28th February.
A bill dated (or sighted) 29th January, payable one month after date (or sight), is due and payable on 28th February (if leap year 29th February).
A bill dated (or sighted) 30th January, payable one month after date (or sight), is due and payable on 28th February (if leap year 29th February).
A bill dated (or sighted) 31st January, payable one month after date (or sight), is due and payable on 28th February (if leap year 29th February).
A bill dated (or sighted) 1st January, payable three weeks (= 21 days) after date (or sight), is due and payable on 22nd January.
A bill dated (or sighted) 31st May, payable one month after date (or sight), is due and payable on 30th June.
A bill dated (or sighted) 29th February (leap year), payable 12 months after date (or sight), is due and payable on 28th February.
A bill dated 1st March, payable one month after date (if accepted 'Payable at X & Y Bank, Leeds. J. Brown, 25th February') is due and payable on 1st April.
A bill dated 1st March, payable one month after sight, and is 'accepted 2nd March, payable, etc.,' is due and payable on 2nd April.
A bill dated 1st March, payable one month after sight, and is 'sighted 2nd March, accepted 3rd March, payable, etc.,' is due on 2nd April.

TITHES Originally the tenth part of the annual crop or produce of stock given voluntarily in support of the Church, tithes were commuted (1836) into annual rent charges fluctuating with the price of corn and payable by the landlord. These charges were stabilized in 1925.

The Tithe Act 1936 provided for the extinguishment of tithe rent charges as such and for their replacement by redemption annuities running for a term of 60 years from 2nd October, 1936. For every £100 of tithe rent charge on agricultural land at 1st April, 1936, an annuity of £91 11s 2d was payable. In the case of non-agricultural land, the annuity was £105. Where the annuity would exceed one-third of the Schedule B Assessment, one-half of the excess was remitted. Tithe owners received Redemption Stock to take the place of extinguished tithes on the basis of £91.56 of Stock for £100 of ecclesiastical tithe or £105 of Stock for £100 of tithe payable to a lay tithe owner. The Tithe Redemption Commission was established to set the scheme in operation, to collect the annuity payments during the first years, and to prepare a public register and map relating to all such annuities.

Section 13(8) of the 1936 Act provides that an annuity is to be deemed an incumbrance for the purposes of Section 183 of the Law of Property Act 1925 (relating to concealment upon disposal). It is not capable of being registered as a Class A or B charge in the Land Charges Register under Section 10(1) of the Land Charges Act 1925, as are charges in respect of voluntary tithe redemption under Section 6(1) of the Tithe Act 1918.

Under Section 56, Finance Act 1977, all tithe redemption annuities were extinguished with effect from 2nd October that year, and the Tithe Redemption Office was closed on 31st December, 1978. Maps and records used by the Tithe Redemption Office are now preserved for inspection at the Tithe Records Office of the Inland Revenue at Thames Ditton, Surrey, where enquiries can be made if it is thought that any tithes, such as corn rent annuities, are still outstanding on particular land.

TOP SLICING A term applied to the calculation of higher-rate income tax and (formerly) investment income surcharge on lump sums treated as income. The method used to be applied to compensation for loss of office (q.v.) but new rules now apply. Top slicing is applied, however, to gains but are subject to higher-rate income tax, where appropriate (basic rate tax having been paid by the insurance company). The gain is divided by the number of years a policy has been in existence, and the resulting sum is added to the taxpayer's income in the year of payment as a top slice for the purpose of determining the rate of tax which is to apply. The rate is then applied to the total gain in the year of receipt. SEE *Income Tax*

TOPPING-UP LOANS A facility offered by many insurance companies in recent times to augment or 'top-up' the amount of a mortgage loan available from a building society for house purchase. This might apply, for example, where the borrower has not been able to obtain the full amount of a required loan from the building society because of the earnings formula applied by the society (SEE *Building Societies; Mortgage*). In such a case, an insurance company might lend the balance of the loan on an endowment assurance basis.

TRADE BILL A bill drawn in connection with actual trade operations. The term is used to distinguish the paper from a bank bill or from a 'kite' or accommodation bill (q.v.).

TRADED OPTIONS An option (q.v.) is the right to buy or sell a security or commodity at a predetermined price at some date in the future. A traded option is an option which is itself bought or sold during the option period. Trading in options was first introduced in Chicago some years ago and was introduced to the London Stock Exchange in April, 1978. In 1984, there were traded options dealt with on the Stock Exchange in 24 public companies, the options being in series of three, six or nine months. In the ordinary way, option contracts are for 1,000 shares.

The important aspect of a traded option is that it is the option itself which is bought or sold, quite independently of the underlying security. It is, however, the investor's view of the likely price of the underlying security over three, six or nine months, which will dictate the option price. Thus, if the price of a share in the market is 300p, an investor might buy a three-month option at an exercise price of, say, 330p, the price of the option being, say 15p. If the underlying share price rises to, say, 350p, at the end of the three months, the investor has made a profit of 5p, i.e. the difference between the market price of the shares (350p), less the exercise price of the option (330p), less the cost of the option (15p), i.e. a 5p per share profit on an outlay of 15p per share. If, however, the price of the underlying shares falls, the value of the option may be reduced to nil. The investor's total loss, however, can only be the amount paid for the option.

In practice, the investor in options will actually exercise his option to take up the shares if he requires them for a longer-term investment. Most options are, however, not exercised because the investors 'trade' their options before the expiry date.

In every option price there is what is known as the 'intrinsic value' and the 'time value'. For example, an option to buy (i.e. a 'call' option) at, say 160p, when the price is already 200p in the market, might cost, say, 50p. Of that option price, 40p is the intrinsic value because the shares can always be sold for 40p more than the exercise price. The remaining 10p in the option price in that example, is the time value—what one might call a hope value for the price of the shares over the period of the option. It follows, therefore, that a nine-month option has a larger 'time' content than, say, a three-month option.

At the time of writing, approximately 5,000 contracts might be written in the course of a day in the traded option market of the London Stock Exchange.

TRANSFER IN BLANK SEE *Blank Transfer*

TRANSFER OF MORTGAGE Where a mortgagor is entitled to redeem, he may require a mortgagee instead of reconveying the property to him, to assign the mortgage debt and convey the mortgaged property to a third party, and the mortgagee is bound to comply (Section 95, Law of Property Act 1925). On the other hand, a mortgagee has the right to dispose of the mortgage by transfer to a third party.

The old method of transfer of a mortgage by a mortgagee was by a conveyance of the fee simple (q.v.) vested in him to the transferee, coupled with an assignment of the mortgage debt. The mortgagor usually joined in the conveyance to evidence that he had notice of the transfer; the equity of redemption, of course, remained with him. The new method of transfer of a mortgage is by execution of a deed declaring that the mortgagee transfers the benefit of the mortgage.

By the Law of Property Act 1925, Section 114

> (1) A deed executed by a mortgagee purporting to transfer his mortgage or the benefit thereof shall, unless a contrary intention is therein expressed, and subject to any provisions therein contained, operate to transfer to the transferee—
> (*a*) the right to demand, sue for, recover and give receipts for, the mortgage money or the unpaid part thereof, and the interest then due, if any, and thenceforth to become due thereon; and
> (*b*) the benefit of all securities for the same, and the benefit of and the right to sue on all covenants with the mortgagee, and the right to exercise all powers of the mortgagee; and
> (*c*) all the estate and interest in the mortgaged property then vested in the mortgagee subject to redemption or cesser, but as to such estate and interest subject to the right of redemption then subsisting.

If the mortgagor does not join in the transfer, the transferee should ascertain from the mortgagor, in writing, what is actually due under the mortgage. Until the mortgagor has received notice of the transfer, he is entitled to make payments to the mortgagee, of either principal or interest, and to have credit for them as against the transferee;

but when the mortgagor is a party to the transfer, he enters into a covenant with the transferee for payment of the mortgage debt and interest.

An alternative method of transfer is available, namely where a statutory receipt is executed for the moneys due under the mortgage, and it expresses the money as having been paid by someone not immediately entitled to the equity of redemption, i.e. by someone other than the original mortgagor or his transferee, the receipt will operate as a transfer by deed of the benefit of the mortgage to him, unless it is expressly provided otherwise, or the mortgage is discharged out of money in the hands of a personal representative or trustee (Section 115(2) Law of Property Act 1925).

Where a banker takes a transfer of a mortgage (as is exceptionally done when taking over an advance from another bank, instead of getting a fresh charge executed), the advance so transferred must be taken by way of loan on which all reductions are permanent. Otherwise, by the operation of the Rule in Clayton's case, all credits to the account will reduce the amount covered by the mortgage and all debits will be in the nature of fresh advances not covered by the mortgage security. A transfer of mortgage, whereby the transferor absolutely makes over his interest to a third party, must not be confused with a sub-mortgage, where a mortgagee mortgages his interest but has the right to pay off the sub-mortgage and resume his former rights in the mortgage. SEE *Mortgage; Sub-mortgage*

TRANSFER OF SHARES The instrument of transfer of shares should be in accordance with the company's regulations. In companies formed under the Companies Clauses Consolidation Act 1845, the transfer must be by deed; in other companies the transfer may be under hand or under seal, according to the articles of the company. In practice, however, the tendency is for the common form of transfer deed to be used, irrespective of the company's articles, except in those cases where a special form of transfer is necessary. The common form of transfer requires execution under hand; nevertheless, transfers in the common form are usually sealed. In order to obtain an official quotation on the London Stock Exchange, one of the conditions is that the articles must stipulate that the common form of transfer shall be used.

Table A of the Companies Act 1948 provided

Transfer of Shares

22. The instrument of transfer of any share shall be executed by or on behalf of the transferor and transferee, and, except as provided by sub-paragraph (4) of paragraph 2 of the Seventh Schedule to the Act, the transferor shall be deemed to remain a holder of the share until the name of the transferee is entered in the register of members in respect thereof.

23. Subject to such of the restrictions of these regulations as may be applicable, any member may transfer all or any of his shares by instrument in writing in any usual or common form or any other form which the directors may approve.

24. The directors may decline to register the transfer of a share (not being a fully-paid share) to a person of whom they shall not approve, and they may also decline to register the transfer of a share on which the company has a lien.

25. The directors may also decline to recognise any instrument of transfer unless—

(*a*) a fee of 12½p or such lesser sum as the directors may from time to time require is paid to the company in respect thereof;

(*b*) the instrument of transfer is accompanied by the certificate of the shares to which it relates, and such other evidence as the directors may reasonably require to show the right of the transferor to make the transfer; and

(*c*) the instrument of transfer is in respect of only one class of share.

26. If the directors refuse to register a transfer they shall within two months after the date on which the transfer was lodged with the company send to the transferee notice of the refusal.

27. The registration of transfers may be suspended at such times and for such periods as the directors may from time to time determine, provided always that such registration shall not be suspended for more than thirty days in any year.

28. The company shall be entitled to charge a fee not exceeding 12½p on the registration of every probate, letters of administration, certificate of death or marriage, power of attorney, notice in lieu of distringas, or other instrument.

Shares should not be registered in the name of a minor, as he may subsequently repudiate the contract.

The consideration money set forth in a transfer may differ from that which the first seller will receive, owing to sub-sales by the original buyer. The amount which is entered in the transfer is the price given by the last purchaser.

Since 1963 most Stock Transfer Forms require only the signature of the transferor. When a transfer is received for registration it must be carefully scrutinized and the particulars of the shares should be compared with the share register. If the instrument is correctly stamped and properly filled up and executed, the company will, before issuing a new certificate, send a notice to the transferor advising him that a document of transfer purporting to be signed by him has been received and that the shares will, unless he replies by return (or within, say, three days) to the contrary, be registered in the name of the transferee. If there are two or more joint holders of the shares it is advisable to send a notification to each one. Such a notice helps to prevent a company registering a transferee upon a forged transfer. A company must, within two months after the registration of a transfer, have the new certificate ready for delivery.

In the case of shares which are not fully paid, the directors of a company should consider whether a proposed transferee is good for the liability upon the shares; that is, if the articles give the directors power to refuse to register an unsatisfactory person. If the articles do not give such power the directors cannot refuse to register a transfer.

In *Re Pool Shipping Co Ltd* [1919] 122 LT 338, where the articles of association gave the directors power to refuse any transfer of shares of which they might not approve, it was held that a renunciation of rights to new shares was not a transfer of shares within the meaning of the articles and that the directors were not entitled to refuse to register the person in whose favour the rights to certain shares had been renounced.

Shares are very frequently transferred into a banker's name, or the names of his nominees, or the name of a nominee company, as security for a loan or overdraft. It is to be noted that the person in whose name shares are registered may be merely a trustee, or a nominee of the true owner; and that, if the registered holder obtains a loan against a deposit of the certificate, the true owner may intervene at any time before the banker has registered the shares and compel the banker to surrender the certificate. When a banker, however, without notice of any prior equitable charge, obtains a transfer duly executed and gets it registered, he has a legal title to the shares or stock transferred by the instrument. When the banker is registered as the owner of shares which are not fully paid he becomes liable for any calls that may be made, which is not the case if he merely holds the certificate with a blank transfer, or does not register a completed transfer. Though registration is necessary to give a banker a legal title, he will, as a rule, be quite safe if he holds the certificate and a duly executed transfer, and gives notice to the company.

When giving notice, the banker should ask the company to state whether notice of any prior charge has been received. The company may probably not accept notice, or even acknowledge receipt of the letter sending it, and it is, therefore, advisable for a banker to be able to prove that the notice was sent to the company. The company should be advised when the banker ceases to have a lien on the shares.

A limited company is under no obligation to accept notice, as by the Companies Act 1985, Section 360, 'no notice of any trust, expressed, implied, or constructive, shall be entered on the register, or be receivable by the Registrar, in the case of companies registered in England and Wales. When notice is given it does not, therefore, perfect an equitable title or secure priority over a security of prior date of which no notice was given to the company.

But where a company has a lien upon its shares for all debts due from the holder thereof, the company is affected by notice of an equitable interest. In that case it was held that the notice was not notice of a trust as defined in Section 117, but affected the company in their capacity as traders to the extent of the interest of the bank, and that the company could not, in respect of moneys which became due from the shareholder to the company after receipt of the notice, claim priority over advances by the bank made after such notice.

Under the rules of the London Stock Exchange, one of the conditions precedent to application for an official quotation is that fully-paid shares shall be free from all lien.

With regard to a 'notice in lieu of distringas' served upon a company, SEE *Distringas*.

Before registering shares in the bank's name, or the names of its nominees, a banker naturally ascertains if there is any liability upon the shares. The certificate, however, does not always show how much has been paid up per share, and the information must be obtained from other sources. If shares are only partly paid up, they should not be registered in the bank's name; the certificates should merely be held with a blank or a completed transfer (SEE *Blank Transfer*). The registered holder of partly paid up shares, is as stated above, liable for any calls that are made (SEE *Call*).

The transfer can be sent in to the company at any subsequent date for registration, but it is doubtful if it will hold good if the transferor dies or becomes bankrupt before registration is effected. It should be noted that, though a surrender of the share certificate is necessary in nearly all cases, there are a few instances where a surrender is not necessary before a transfer can be effected.

Although a banker can dispose of shares which are registered in his name if he holds an authority to dispose of them, without further reference to the transferor, it is customary to give the transferor notice of an intention to sell. If the banker does not hold (and cannot obtain) a transfer of the shares, to enforce the security, application must be made to the court for an order for foreclosure or sale.

The various ways in which shares can be made available as security are

1. A simple deposit of the certificate, with or without notice to the company.
2. A deposit of the certificate, accompanied by a memorandum of deposit, with or without notice to the company.
3. A deposit of the certificate with a blank transfer and memorandum of deposit, with or without notice to the company.
4. A deposit of the certificate with a completed transfer and memorandum of deposit, with or without notice to the company.
5. Registration of the shares in the name of a nominee company, or the names of nominees. A memorandum of deposit should be held.

Methods 1, 2, and 3 are merely equitable charges, and may be postponed to a prior equitable charge.

Method 4 is only an equitable security, but the legal estate can usually be obtained at any moment by sending in the transfer for registration.

Method 5 is the best form in which to take the security.

Although shares may be registered in the names of a bank's nominees, and those nominees be regarded by the company as the actual owners of the shares and the persons to whom dividends will be paid and who will be held liable for any calls which are made, it is understood between the customer and the bank that the transfer has been effected merely for the purposes of security and that, as soon as the necessity for the security ceases, the shares will be retransferred to the customer. To make the position clear, a memorandum or agreement is signed by the customer, on the same date as the transfer is signed, qualifying the deed of transfer and stating that the shares are transferred to the bank as security for all moneys owing and that the bank may, when necessary, realize the shares for the purpose of repaying any advance (See *Memorandum of Deposit*). All dividends received by the bank on such shares belong, of course, to the customer and will be credited to his account. A record should be kept of all stocks and shares registered in the names of the bank's nominees, so that, when the dividends are received, the banker may know to whom they belong, and that, when notices are received from the companies with respect to an issue of new shares or anything likely to affect the interests of the shareholders, the notices may be forwarded at once to the customers.

When the security is no longer required the shares are retransferred to the persons entitled to them. The shares thus retransferred do not always bear the individual numbers of the shares originally deposited with the bank, and it should be noted that in the Scottish case of *Crerar* v *Bank of Scotland* (June, 1921), where a customer claimed to have the identical shares which had been originally deposited retransferred to her, the Court of Session held that the bank was bound to identify the shares deposited by particular customers, unless the customers acquiesced in the course followed by the bank, that is to retransfer the shares without regard to the original numbers.

Where shares are transferred to a nominee company or the nominees of a bank as security for a loan or overdraft, the consideration which is inserted in the document of transfer is generally 25p or 50p. Such a consideration is called a 'nominal consideration' (q.v.), and the transfer requires to be impressed with a 50p stamp. See *Forged Transfer*

It is important to note that if a transfer taken by a banker as security should eventually be proved to be forged, the banker may, even though the shares were transferred into his name and sold, be compelled to make good the value of the shares to the true owner. Transfers should therefore, when possible, be signed in the presence of an official of the bank, and particularly if the shares are in the names of several persons (See *Forged Transfer*). Where a banker's name is inserted in a transfer as the transferee, the banker should not sign as witness to the transferor's signature.

It frequently happens that part of the shares included in a transfer which is held by a banker is sold by the customer. In such cases a fresh transfer should be taken for the shares which still remain as security. It is not sufficient to alter and initial the old transfer. A fresh transfer should also be taken, e.g. where shares are split into smaller denominations than quoted in the transfer; and where a further instalment is paid on partly-paid shares if the amount paid up is quoted in the transfer.

Where a company is being wound up voluntarily, every transfer of shares, made after the commencement of the winding up, except transfers made with sanction of the liquidator, shall be void; and in the case of a winding up by the court, every such transfer shall, unless the court otherwise orders, be void (Sections 522 and 576, Companies Act 1985).

A stockbroker often gives a banker security over shares which have been given to him by a client as security. See *Blank Transfer; Stamp Duty; Stockbrokers' Loans*

Where the transfer is effected merely as security, with a nominal consideration of, say, 25p, the deed of transfer takes a stamp of 50p (SEE *Nominal Consideration*). The agreement under hand, which usually accompanies it, has not required stamping since August, 1970.

A transfer must be stamped within 30 days after its execution, or within 30 days from the date of its arrival in the UK.

Instruments of transfer are properly stamped with the fixed duty of 50p when the transaction falls within one of the following descriptions:

1. Vesting the property in trustees, on the appointment of a new trustee, or the retirement of a trustee.
2. A transfer, as for a nominal consideration, to a mere nominee of the transferor where no beneficial interest in the property passes.
3. A transfer by way of security for a loan; or a retransfer to the original transferor on repayment of a loan.
4. A transfer to a residuary legatee of stock, etc., which forms part of the residue divisible under a will.
5. A transfer to a beneficiary under a will of a *specific legacy* of stock, etc.
6. A transfer of stock, etc., being the property of a person dying intestate, to the party or parties entitled to it.

In cases (2) and (3) a certificate setting forth the facts of the transaction, signed by both the transferor and the transferee, should be required.

A new form of transfer, known as the Stock Transfer Form, introduced by the Stock Transfer Act 1963 (q.v.), came into force on 26th October, 1963. Under this Act only one signed Stock Transfer Form is required for a sale, any subsequent splits being arranged by the broker. The signature of the transferor is not required to be witnessed.

In the case of sales, the address must be given where there is only one holder, but where there is more than one holder no addresses are required, although all the joint names must be stated in full.

In the case of purchases, the form does not need to be signed by the transferee. Any stock purchased will automatically be registered in the name or names supplied by the bank to the broker at the time the order is placed. It is important, therefore, that the details of the buyer's name and address should be correctly specified on the Stock Order Form.

The Stock Transfer Act applies only to fully paid-up registered securities. It does not apply to

1. stock or bonds on the Post Office Register, for which Post Office Forms G.S.1(G) or G.S.3(H) will continue to be used;
2. stock issued by the UK Government on the Register of the Bank of Ireland in Dublin;
3. Australian Government and certain other stocks, for which special forms, supplied by the broker, will continue to be used;
4. South African companies;
5. building society securities; and
6. savings certificates.

Abbreviations must not be used on the Stock Transfer Form unless they are so stated on the respective certificate. SEE *Blank Transfer; Certificate; Company; Leeman's Act; Shares; Talisman; Transmission of Shares*

TRANSFEROR BY DELIVERY A transferor by delivery is defined by the Bills of Exchange Act, Section 58, as follows.

(1) Where the holder of a bill payable to bearer negotiates it by delivery without indorsing it, he is called a 'transferor by delivery'.

(2) A transferor by delivery is not liable on the instrument.

(3) A transferor by delivery who negotiates a bill thereby warrants to his immediate transferee being a holder for value that the bill is what it purports to be, that he has a right to transfer it, and that at the time of transfer he is not aware of any fact which renders it valueless.

A transferor by delivery does not warrant that the instrument will be paid and in fact is not liable to a transferee if the bill is dishonoured for want of funds, etc. If however, it transpires that there is a forgery on the bill, the transferor by delivery is liable for breach of warranty. SEE *Bearer (Cheque or Bill); Bill of Exchange; Negotiation of Bill of Exchange*

TRANSMISSION OF SHARES When a shareholder dies, his right to deal with the shares passes to the executors or administrators, who produce to the company for registration the probate of the will or the letters of administration. The date of the shareholder's death should be entered in the register with a note of the executors' or administrators' names and addresses. The probate or letters of administration should be indorsed with a note that they have been exhibited to the company.

Unless the executors or administrators request to be registered as the actual holders of the shares, they will not be liable personally for any calls which may be made. If their names are entered in the register of shareholders merely as the executors or administrators of the deceased, the estate remains liable for calls. Some companies, however, do not permit shares to stand in the names of executors or administrators. When shares are specifically left by will, it is nevertheless necessary for a transfer to be executed from the executors to the legatee.

When shares in a bank are transferred into the names of the personal representatives of a deceased under such circumstances as to constitute notice to the bank that the shares are held in a fiduciary capacity, the bank could not exercise its lien on the shares in order to recover money lent to the representatives for purposes not authorized by the trust. SEE UNDER *Lien*

When shares are transferred by the representatives to a person to whom the shares have been left, the consideration in the transfer is merely a nominal one, say, 25p. The stamp duty on such a transfer is 50p. But if they are transferred to a legatee, who agrees to accept them instead of his cash legacy, the stamp duty is *ad valorem* and the consideration will be the price agreed upon between the representatives and the legatee.

Where a company has power to refuse to register an unsuitable person as a shareholder, it cannot avoid registering a legatee to whom shares may have been specifically bequeathed by a deceased shareholder, even if that legatee is considered quite unreliable for the liability upon the shares, unless the company's articles of association give the directors express power to decline to register any such person becoming entitled to shares in consequence of the death of a member.

By Article 24 of Table A, directors may decline to register any transfer of shares, not being fullpaid shares, to a person of whom they do not approve. This clause does not apply to a person claiming shares by transmission, but Article 30 (see below) extends the directors' right to decline registration to a person entitled to shares by transmission.

In companies where Table A (q.v.) applies (see Section 8 under *Articles of Association*), the regulations are as follows.

Transmission of shares

29. In case of the death of a member the survivor or survivors where the deceased was a joint holder, and the legal personal representatives of the deceased where he was a sole holder, shall be the only persons recognised by the company, as having any title to his interest in the shares; but nothing herein contained shall release the estate of a deceased joint holder from any liability in respect of any share which had been jointly held by him with other persons.

30. Any person becoming entitled to a share in consequence of the death or bankruptcy of a member may, upon such evidence being produced as may from time to time properly be required by the directors and subject as hereinafter provided, elect either to be registered himself as holder of the share or to have some person nominated by him registered as the transferee thereof, but the directors shall, in either case, have the same right to decline or suspend registration as they would have had in the case of a transfer of the share by that member before his death or bankruptcy, as the case may be.

31. If the person so becoming entitled shall elect to be registered himself, he shall deliver or send to the company a notice in writing signed by him stating that he so elects. If he shall elect to have another person registered he shall testify his election by executing in favour of that person a transfer of the share. All the limitations, restrictions and provisions of these regulations relating to the right to transfer and the registration of transfers of shares shall be applicable to any such notice or transfer as aforesaid as if the death or bankruptcy of the member had not occurred and the notice or transfer were a transfer signed by that member.

32. A person becoming entitled to a share by reason of the death or bankruptcy of the holder shall be entitled to the same dividends and other advantages to which he would be entitled if he were the registered holder of the share, except that he shall not, before being registered as a member in respect of the share, be entitled in respect of it to exercise any right conferred by membership in relation to meetings of the company.

Provided always that the directors may at any time give notice requiring any such person to elect either to be registered himself or to transfer the share, and if the notice is not complied with within ninety days the directors may thereafter withhold payment of all dividends, bonuses, or other moneys payable in respect of the share until the requirements of the notice have been complied with.

Where a shareholder is domiciled abroad, probate or letters of administration should be obtained in England. But where a Court of Probate in a British possession, to which the Colonial Probates Act 1892 applies, has granted probate or letters of administration, they may, as provided by Section 2 of that Act, be produced to a Court of Probate in the UK to be sealed with the seal of the Court, and thereupon they shall have the like force and effect as if granted by the Court. SEE *Companies; Executor; Shares; Transfer of Shares*

TRAVEL AND ENTERTAINMENT CARDS

These are payment cards such as those issued by American Express and Diner's Club, used extensively for payment of hotel bills, air fares, etc., but now used for the purchase of a much wider range of goods and services. Although categorized generally as credit cards (q.v.), they do not provide the user with extended credit. They are payment cards and the user is expected to pay his account from the card company, when delivered, usually monthly. The principal travel and entertainment card companies usually charge an enrolment fee and thereafter an annual fee for the use of the card. SEE *American Express Card; Diner's Club*

TRAVEL INSURANCE The principal categories of insurance relevant to overseas travel are cancellation of visit, baggage and personal belongings, personal accident, medical and other expenses, personal liability and motor insurance.

Cancellation of Visit
Insurance may be taken out to cover the possible loss of a deposit or other charges and expenses consequent upon the cancellation, e.g. through ill-health or other emergency, of an overseas visit. The cover may be taken out (1) by separate insurance cover; or (2) as part of an inclusive travel policy; or (3) as part of the package arranged though a travel agency.

Typical cover would extend to the illness, injury or death of the proposed traveller, or of a close member of the family or business associate, or of any other person with whom the insured was proposing to travel. The cover may also extend to cases where a member of the party is called for jury service or other court proceedings.

The cover provided in a typical all-in policy is normally quite modest, up to, say, £250 per person, and a traveller wishing to take out more substantial cover will probably have to obtain a separate quotation. The typical premium for holiday cancellation insurance would be 1.50 per cent of the amount of the cover.

Baggage and Personal Belongings
The need or otherwise for this category of cover will depend on the traveller's own all-risks insurance (q.v.) if any. A person whose all-risks insurance covers world-wide travel, or at least the countries which it is proposed to visit, will not necessarily need additional cover for baggage and personal belongings.

Baggage insurance would normally cover loss or damage to all personal belongings, clothing, suitcases, sports gear, cameras and binoculars. The cover would also extend to loss of personal money and travellers' cheques, usually up to quite a low maximum of, say, £150. Separate cover taken out for baggage and personal belongings in this way will normally incur a premium of approximately 1–1¼ per cent of the amount of cover for a period of, say, a month.

Personal Accident
Most companies offer personal accident cover for overseas travel, including such eventualities as death, permanent or temporary disablement, loss of one or more limbs and the loss of one or more eyes. A typical premium would be £1 for cover of £1,000 in the event of death or major injury.

Medical and Other Expenses
The cost of medical treatment in other countries, particularly in the USA, can be very expensive. To cover the cost wholly or in part the traveller may

1. take out insurance cover as part of the holiday package (in which case the cover may be quite modest); or
2. take out separate health insurance (which in some cases will be the only way of ensuring adequate cover); or
3. take advantage of the reciprocal health-care arrangements with EEC countries; or
4. rely on membership of a health insurance scheme.

Medical cover for overseas travel, whether taken out as part of a holiday package or separately arranged, will normally cover

1. the cost of medical, surgical or hospital treatment arising from illness or injury occurring during the visit;
2. additional costs of accommodation and travel expenses in returning home as a result of illness, injury or death (including the cost of any one person required on medical advice to accompany the insured);
3. similar costs of accommodation and travel arising from the injury, illness or death of any close relative or business associate not travelling with the insured;
4. in the event of the death of the insured, the cost of transporting the remains to the UK or the cost of burial or cremation in the country where death occurred.

In all cases, however, there will be an absolute ceiling on the amount payable by the insurance company depending on the extent of the cover taken out. While in some countries cover of £2,000 per person might be sufficient, it would certainly be very inadequate in the USA where cover up to £20,000 per person would be more appropriate. Indeed, major illnesses of visitors to the USA have been known to involve costs of £30,000–£40,000.

The cost of medical cover for overseas visits varies considerably and may be from £5–£15 per £1,000 of worldwide cover for a fortnight.

Subscribers to health insurance schemes in the UK are normally covered for illness and injury on temporary visits overseas, e.g. for holiday or business, up to the amounts for which they would be covered in this country. Bearing in mind, however, that medical costs overseas are usually so much higher, health insurance schemes offer worldwide travel schemes which provide an additional degree of cover with no territorial limits.

Visitors to the EEC countries may be covered by the reciprocal health-care arrangements which apply throughout the EEC. Subject to the rather onerous regulations, it is possible for a temporary visitor to another EEC country to obtain urgent medical treatment either free or at reduced cost. The requirements are

1. the visitor must be currently insured (i.e. having paid sufficient national insurance contributions in respect of the current or previous tax year) as an employed person in the UK; or
2. having been insured at some time as an employed person in the UK, the visitor must be currently insured as a self-employed person, or be a person paying voluntary Class 3 contributions, or be in receipt of National Insurance benefit, or be receiving a state retirement, invalidity or disablement pension or, if no longer working, must have sufficient contributions to carry an entitlement to a full basic retirement pension at retirement age.

If a person is covered in this way, his dependants will also be covered whether or not the insured person travels with them.

A person seeking to take advantage of the EEC cover must apply to the local social security office for Form E.111. The application should be made as soon as possible, but not more than six months before the date of the visit. Once Form E.111 has been obtained, its validity can be extended for further visits of less than three months duration.

Form E.111, known as the Certificate of Entitlement, is not needed for visits to the Irish Republic, Denmark or Gibraltar.

Persons not covered by the EEC regulations can also obtain urgent treatment in West Germany if they make application to the Department of Health and Social Security, Overseas Branch, at Newcastle upon Tyne not more than six months before the visit.

Travellers wishing to take advantage of the reciprocal arrangements must take with them the Certificate of Entitlement (except in the case of Denmark, Ireland and Gibraltar). The following arrangements will apply in each of the relevant countries.

Belgium The traveller must pay in full for the medical treatment, but a refund of approximately 75 per cent is obtainable from the Belgian Sickness Insurance Fund.

Denmark Medical costs, part-dental costs and part-prescription costs will be refunded by the local council in Denmark on production of the visitor's passport and relevant receipts.

France The visitor must pay for medical and dental treatment in full, but may obtain a refund of approximately 70–75 per cent from the French Sickness Insurance Office.

West Germany Hospital and other medical and dental treatment is free, but there is a small charge for prescribed medicines.

Gibraltar A small charge is made for prescribed medicines and free hospital treatment is available. Normally, the full cost of dental treatment must be paid for.

Ireland Medical treatment, prescribed medicines and hospital treatment are free to persons treated under the EEC regulations.

Italy Medical, hospital and dental treatment is free, but a small charge is made for prescribed medicines.

Luxembourg Hospital treatment is free. Payment will have to be made for other treatment, but a partial refund will be made by the Luxembourg Sickness Insurance Office.

The Netherlands All treatment is free except for a contribution to the cost of dental treatment.

Visits to non-EEC countries The Government has reciprocal health-care agreements with a number of countries covering travellers abroad in the event of accident or sudden illness. These arrangements do not apply in the case of illness incurred before leaving the UK. The countries concerned and the extent of the medical arrangements may be ascertained from the Department of Health and Social Security, International Relations Division, 1A Alexander Fleming House, Elephant and Castle, London SE1 6BY.

Personal Liability

Travellers abroad may wish to take out an indemnity policy in respect of possible liability for injury to third parties or to their property. A typical level of cover would be £250,000 and would quite often be included with other travel insurance without extra cost.

Exclusions

In all the foregoing categories of insurance there are typical exclusions. Most of the all-in policies and those booked as part of a package would not cover, for example,

1. accident in the course of dangerous sports such as skiing, rock-climbing, potholing, motor racing;
2. pregnancy or childbirth unless the pregnancy commenced after the insurance was taken out;
3. seizure or confiscation of goods by customs officials;
4. loss of money not reported to the police within 24 hours;

5. any liability arising in connection with the insured's business.

Motor Insurance
Persons travelling abroad by motor car should obtain from their insurers in advance an International Motor Insurance Certificate (Green Card). Outside EEC countries, travellers without Green Cards will normally be required to take out local insurance when crossing frontiers. Although a motorist does not strictly need a Green Card in EEC countries, it is desirable to carry one as evidence of insurance.

TRAVELLERS' CHEQUES A form of travel currency giving the holder the security of a letter of credit and the convenience of a local currency.

In the UK, they are usually issued in denominations of £2, £5, £10, £20, £50 and £100, and are encashable at the correspondents—at home or abroad—of the issuing bank. In practice, they are usually acceptable in payment of accounts on board ship, at hotels and in stores.

They are in a form whereby the beneficiary signs as drawer of a draft on the head office of the issuing bank. They should be so signed immediately on issue and a place is provided on the cheque for the signature of the beneficiary on its presentation for encashment at the correspondent bank, hotel or store etc. but not beforehand. This provides a method of identification of the beneficiary.

If travel cheques are lost in the UK, then the customer may obtain reimbursement by filling in a declaration form at his branch. If they are lost abroad, the customer should write or cable to his bank, which will then remit funds either by mail transfer or telegraphic transfer depending on the urgency of the request, and provided that there is no undue negligence.

If the customer requires replacement travellers' cheques, then these will be forwarded to an overseas correspondent to be handed to the customer.

The main British banks and Thomas Cook and American Express all issue travellers' cheques, denominated in either sterling or US dollars. Most banks will also make available travellers' cheques in the denomination of the principal overseas countries. Whether or not a traveller takes sterling or dollar travellers' cheques will depend very much on the comparative strength of these two main currencies at the time.

The normal charge for the issue of travellers' cheques is 1 per cent of the amount of the cheques, plus a further 1 per cent when the cheques are cashed, but not when changed back into sterling.

A major factor in the growth of travellers' cheque business has been the development of credit cards with their highly automated international network. This led to an announcement by the Visa group in 1979, that it was to undertake the marketing of travellers' cheques for its member banks and this was followed by a similar move by Mastercard who introduced the Master's travellers' cheque in March, 1980. American Express still account, however, for approximately one-half of the world-wide travellers' cheque business.

TREASURE TROVE Where money, plate, or bullion is found hidden in the earth or other private place and the owner is unknown, it is termed 'treasure trove' and passes into the possession of the Crown.

If similar property is found on the surface of the ground, it is not treasure trove, and the finder has a title to it against the whole world except the true owner.

The essential feature of treasure trove is that it must have been hidden at some time in the earth with the intention, on the part of the owner, of recovering it. It is not treasure trove and cannot be claimed by the Crown unless that test is satisfied.

The finder of treasure trove should report it immediately to the local coroner. If it is retained by the Crown or passed to a museum, the finder will receive its full market value. If it is not retained, the treasure will be returned to the finder for him to dispose of as he pleases. If treasure is found by two or more persons, the proceeds will be apportioned between them. The owner of the land does not have any title to treasure trove.

The Crown's right to treasure trove extends only to articles which are gold or silver. In the case of *AG of the Duchy of Lancaster* v *Overton (Farms) Ltd* [1980] 3 All ER 503, concerning some third century Roman coins found in the earth in an earthenware urn, it was held that as the coins were a mixture of silver and base metals, they were not silver coins as such and were not treasure trove.

TREASURY BILLS These are negotiable instruments issued by the Treasury for money borrowed by the Government and form part of the floating debt of the country. It is believed that Mr Walter Bagehot was responsible for the introduction of Treasury Bills in 1877 when he advised the then Chancellor of the Exchequer that 'The English Treasury has the finest credit in the world and it must learn to use it to the best advantage. A security resembling as nearly as possible a commercial bill of exchange—that is a bill issued under discount and falling due at certain intervals, would probably be received with favour by the money market and would command good terms'. His advice was acted upon and the bills have been issued ever since. In the past they have been issued for periods of three, six, nine or twelve months but since 22nd April, 1950, the bills have had a currency of 91 days.

Treasury bills do not carry interest as such but are issued at a discount. They are in denominations ranging from £5,000 to £1 million. Tenders are received at the Bank of England each Friday for bills to be issued during the following week. The discount houses apply collectively and undertake to tender for all the Treasury bills on offer. Each of the 11 houses is obliged to subscribe for a minimum quota in relation to the size of all the houses. For the most part, the clearing banks buy their Treasury bills in the secondary market, as do other institutions, companies and private individuals.

TRIAL OF THE PYX The Pyx (Greek for box) is a box in which are preserved samples of the coins made at the Mint. A jury of the Goldsmiths Company, who are summoned by the Lord Chancellor, test the coins annually (called the Trial of the Pyx) to see that the legal weight and fineness of the coins are maintained.

TRUCK ACTS SEE *Payment of Wages Act 1960*

TRUST SEE *Trustee*

TRUST CORPORATION Under the Law of Property Act 1925, Trust Corporation means the Public Trustee or a corporation either appointed by the court to be a trustee, or entitled by rules made under the Public Trustee Act 1906, to act as custodian trustee. This includes a bank. SEE UNDER *Custodian Trustee*

By the Law of Property Act 1925, Section 27(2), in a disposition on trust for sale of land or in the settlement of the net proceeds, the proceeds of sale or other capital money arising under the disposition shall not be paid to fewer than two persons as trustees of the disposition, except where the trustee is a trust corporation.

Out of the concept of a Trust Corporation has arisen the rather loose terminology of 'corporate trustee', which means an incorporated body empowered to act as a trustee rather as banks and insurance companies act as trustees for private trusts, unit trusts, debenture trusts and indeed a great variety of trust situations.

By the Law of Property (Amendment) Act 1926, 'trust corporation' includes in relation to the property of a bankrupt and property subject to a deed of arrangement, the trustee in bankruptcy and the trustee under the deed respectively (Section 3).

TRUST LETTER OR RECEIPT OR LETTER OF HYPOTHECATION A document executed by the pledgor of goods or the documents of title thereto, when such are released to him by a banker, in order that the goods may be sold and the loan repaid, or that they may be warehoused or reshipped. As the essence of a pledge is possession of the thing pledged, the release of documents of title by the banker would deprive him of his rights as pledgee and in the absence of provisions otherwise would deprive him of his security altogether. Professor Gutteridge, in *Bankers' Commercial Credits*, says

> Viewed as a whole, the legal consequences of a letter of hypothecation may be defined as a bailment of the documents of title to the pledgor by the pledgee, coupled with an equitable assignment or charge by the pledgor of the proceeds of sale.

The usual form of letter of trust or hypothecation acknowledges receipt of the documents of title mentioned in the schedule, and that they are held by the customer as trustee for the banker. The customer further undertakes to deal with the goods as agent for the banker for the purpose of getting delivery of the goods and selling or warehousing them and binds himself to pay over the proceeds of sale to the banker or to deliver to him the relative documents of title, such as dock warrants, if, for example, bills of lading have been released under the trust letter. The customer also binds himself to effect any necessary insurance and to keep the transaction separate from others.

A purchaser of the goods or relative documents with notice of the trust created by such a document will be bound to pay the purchase price to the banker on demand, if it has not already been paid to the customer. But an innocent purchaser who pays the sale proceeds to the customer will not be liable to the banker if the customer has diverted such proceeds to his own ends. The precaution of indorsing the documents of title with notice of the trust is not practicable, and beyond confining trust releases to undoubted borrowers and closely watching for the proceeds of sale, there is no safeguard against a dishonest customer.

A banker is sometimes faced by a claim by third parties to sale proceeds in respect of goods subject to a trust letter. In *Re David Allester Ltd* [1922] 2 Ch 211, a liquidator of a company which had pledged bills of lading to a bank and later received them back under a trust letter for sale purposes, claimed that the bank's security was void through non-registration as 'a charge created, or evidenced by an instrument which, if executed by an individual, would require registration as a bill of sale', (see Companies Act 1985, Section 395). It was held that the letter of trust neither created nor evidenced the charge which was created by the pledge and that the pledge was prior to and quite distinct from the letter of trust. It was further held that if the Bills of Sale Act did apply, the trust letter did not require registration because it did not come within the definition of a bill of sale mentioned in Section 4 of the Bills of Sale Act 1878.

A trust letter is not a charge on book debts. In the above case it was held 'these letters of trust really create no mortgage or charge on book debts in any true sense of the word at all. The bank had its charge before these letters came into existence'.

A trust letter takes the relative goods out of the operation of the reputed ownership clause in bankruptcy (*Re Young Hamilton & Co* [1905] 2 KB 381).

In *Lloyds Bank Ltd* v *Bank of America National Trust & Savings Association* [1938] 2 All ER 63, a company pledged bills of lading to the plaintiff which were afterwards released under a trust letter. Instead of selling the goods and accounting to the plaintiffs for the proceeds, the company pledged the documents afresh to the defendants for other advances. The company failed and the plaintiffs claimed return of the documents of title in question. It was held and confirmed on appeal that the company were in possession of the goods with the consent of the owner under Section 2(1) Factors Act 1889, and hence free to deal with them. This is an example of the risks run with trust releases.

The system provides a protection against insolvency but not against fraud on the part of the recipient of the trust letter.

TRUST POLICY A policy of life assurance written in trust for certain beneficiaries. This arose out of the practice of taking out life assurance policies under the Married Women's Property Acts for the benefit of a man's wife and children (SEE *Married Women*). In fact, however, a trust policy can be taken out for any named beneficiaries and the proceeds will be held in trust for those so named. The advantage from the capital transfer tax standpoint is that the policy proceeds, although passing on the death of the life assured, do not form part of his free estate.

TRUSTEE A trustee is the person to whom property is entrusted in order that he may deal with it in accordance with the directions given by the creator of the trust. The person for whose benefit a trust is created is called the *cestui que trust* (plural, *cestuis que trustent*).

A trustee must take as much care of the trust property as a reasonable business man would of his own property, and he must not make a profit out of the trust. Thus, in *Re Brooke Bond & Company Limited's Trust Deed* [1963] 107 Sol J 94, the company had created a fund for payment of retirement pensions to its employees, the trustees of which appointed an insurance company to be the custodian trustee. In 1962, Brooke Bond & Company Limited, as managing trustees, decided to secure payment of the pensions by means of a group insurance policy which they proposed to take out with the insurance company which was already acting as custodian trustee. The question then arose as to whether the insurance company could lawfully enter into such a contract with the managing trustees and retain any profit it might make. It was held that the proposed contract would not be lawful in the absence of an express power in the trust deed or an order of the court.

If customers (who are, in fact, trustees) open an account in their joint names and the banker has no notice or knowledge that they are trustees, the account may be treated as an ordinary joint account. But if John Brown and John Jones come to a banker with a request to open an account as 'Trustees of R. Smith, J. Brown, J. Jones', and the banker recommends with the idea of avoiding notice of trust, that the account should be called, for example, 'John Brown and John Jones, S account', the banker could not maintain, in the event of any subsequent trouble, that he was unaware that it was a trust account. His position would be exactly the same as if the account had been opened with a direct reference to the trust. All trustees should operate on a trust account unless the trust instrument permits less than the full number to sign, or unless delegation is permitted under the terms of Section 25 of the Trustee Act 1925 (amended by Section 9 of the Powers of Attorney Act 1971). Under this section, a trustee may by power of attorney delegate for a period not exceeding 12 months the execution or exercise of all or any of the trusts, powers and discretions vested in him either alone, or jointly with another or others. Such delegation may not be made to his only other co-trustee (unless a trust corporation) (SEE UNDER *Power of Attorney*). Where a trustee has to carry on a business the better view is that he can delegate the power to operate an account for the business to a manager.

Where it is expedient to depart from this rule, it is customary to take an indemnity from the body of trustees and, in some cases, to arrange for copies of the account to be furnished periodically to the non-signing trustees. In *Re Flower* [1884] 27 ChD 592, Mr Justice Kay said

> The very reason why more than one trustee is appointed is that they shall take care that the trust property or moneys shall not get into the hands of one of them alone, and that they shall take care that the trust property or moneys are always under the power or control of every one of them.

The credit balance of an account in the name of 'John Brown in trust for J. Jones' (or any similar wording giving notice of a trust), could not be held by a banker as a set-off for an overdraft on John Brown's private account; neither could a banker successfully hold to an amount transferred wrongfully by John Brown from the trust account to satisfy any pressing demands of the banker for a reduction of John Brown's overdraft. A transaction of that nature would give such a plain indication of irregularity that no banker would be justified in accepting money from that source. But a banker could hold a balance on, say a No 2 account as a set-off to the customer's overdrawn No 1 account, even if the moneys in the No 2 account should ultimately be proved to be trust moneys, so long as the banker had no knowledge of the fact.

If a trustee transfers an amount from the trust account to his own private account, and there is no benefit designed for the bank, the bank is not under any liability to ascertain that the trustee is entitled to make such transfer. But a banker must not be a party to a breach of trust. It has been held that if it is shown that a personal benefit to the banker is stipulated for, it will most readily establish the fact that the banker is privy to the breach of trust (*Gray* v *Johnston* [1868] LR 3 HL 1).

In *Ex parte Kingston* [1871] 6 ChD 362, Lord Justice Mellish said

> We are not really doing any prejudice to bankers by establishing a rule that if an account is in plain terms headed in such a way that a banker cannot fail to know it to be a trust account, the balance standing to the credit of that account will, on the bankruptcy of the person who kept it, belong to the trust.

In the case of *Rowlandson* v *National Westminster Bank Ltd* [1978] 1 WLR 798, it was held that where a bank had opened a banking account with four cheques knowing that the balance was for the benefit of the donor's grandchildren, the bank knew that the account was a trust account and should have questioned the suspicious circumstances in which the uncle of the children, being one of the account-holders, fraudulently appropriated the balance.

In the *Selangor* case [1968] 2 All ER 1073, the District Bank were regarded as having notice of the trust element involved in the directors' control of the company's money. This appears to be a much heavier burden than previously in that the transaction did not appear unambiguously to evidence a breach of trust. However as the law stands, it would appear that bankers must beware of any transaction in which there is a reasonable suspicion of a breach of trust.

Where a trustee has mixed trust moneys with moneys in his private account. SEE UNDER *Clayton's Case*

Securities deposited by trustees must not be given up, except under the authority of all the trustees.

If bearer bonds are lodged by a customer as security for an overdraft, and it ultimately transpires that the bonds do not belong to the customer but to a trust, the banker's right to the security will not be affected, provided that when he took the bonds he was in complete ignorance that they belonged to a trust. If instead of a negotiable security, as bearer bonds, the customer deposited a certificate of shares registered in his own name, along with a memorandum of deposit or a blank transfer, and the shares are eventually proved to belong to a trust, the banker will not be able to retain the security. To avoid such an unfortunate position and to have a complete security, a banker should, when taking certificates, have the stock or shares registered in his own name or the names of his nominees.

By the Trustee Act 1925:

Power to Deposit Money in Bank

Trustees may, pending the negotiation and preparation of any mortgage or charge, or during any other time while an investment is being sought for, pay any trust money into a bank to a deposit or other account, and all interest, if any, payable in respect thereof shall be applied as income (Section 11(1)).

Deposit of Documents for Safe Custody

Trustees may deposit any documents held by them relating to the trust, or to the trust property, with any banker or banking company or any other company whose business includes the undertaking of the safe custody of documents, and any sum payable in respect of such deposit shall be paid out of the income of the trust property (Section 21).

Bearer bonds held by a trustee must be deposited by him with a bank for safe custody and collection of income (Section 7). SEE UNDER *Trustee Investments*

Power of Trustees to Give Receipts

The receipt in writing of a trustee for any money, securities, or other personal property shall be a sufficient discharge to the person paying, transferring, or delivering the same, and shall exonerate him from being answerable for any loss or misapplication thereof (Section 14(1)).

(2) This Section does not, except where the trustee is a trust corporation, enable a sole trustee to give a valid receipt for—

(a) the proceeds of sale or other capital money arising under a trust for sale of land; [as amended by the Law of Property (Amendment) Act, 1926]

(b) Capital money arising under the Settled Land Act, 1925. [SEE *Trust Corporation*]

Power to Employ Agents

Trustees or personal representatives may, instead of acting personally, employ and pay an agent, whether a solicitor, banker, stockbroker, or other person, to transact any business or do any act required to be transacted or done in the execution of the trust or the administration of the testator's or intestate's estate, including the receipt and payment of money, and shall be entitled to be allowed and paid all charges and expenses so incurred, and shall not be responsible for the default of any such agent if employed in good faith (Section 23(1)).

A banker would not be protected if he acted on the signatures of less than all the trustees, unless such signatures were justified under the above Section. In the *Journal of the Institute of Bankers* (vol. 48, p. 455), Sir John Paget says that Section 23(1)

must be confined to the employment of an outside agent, entitled to be paid for his services, appointed by the whole body of trustees, either a solicitor, banker, stockbroker, or someone holding an analogous position, to do some specific act or piece of business in relation to the trust property.

The words 'pay an agent' are inapplicable to trustees delegating any of their powers to one or more of themselves.

In *Green* v *Whitehead* (1929) 45 TLR 602, it was held that a statutory trustee for sale of land in the UK who contracts to sell the land and to convey it in pursuance of the trust for sale, cannot delegate to his attorney the execution of the conveyance. Eve, J., said

The operation of the power of attorney was to commit to the sole and absolute discretion of the grantee all those matters in which a trustee was bound to exercise his own judgment and to use his own discretion. ... Such a delegation was not permissible.

By Section 23(3)

A trustee may appoint a banker or solicitor to be his agent to receive and give a discharge for any money payable to the trustee under or by virtue of a policy of assurance, by permitting the banker or solicitor to have the custody of and to produce the policy of assurance with a receipt signed by the trustee, and a trustee shall not be chargeable with a breach of trust by reason only of his having made or concurred in making any such appointment.

Nothing in this subsection shall exempt a trustee from any liability which he would have incurred if this Act had not been passed, in case he permits any such money, valuable consideration, or property to remain in the hands or under the control of the banker or solicitor for a period longer than is reasonably necessary to enable the banker or solicitor (as the case may be) to pay or transfer the same to the trustee.

Power to Delegate Trusts During Absence Abroad

A trustee intending to remain out of the UK for more than one month may, by power of attorney, delegate to any person (including a trust corporation) the exercise during his absence of all or any of the trusts vested in him. A person being the only other co-trustee and not being a trust corporation cannot be appointed an attorney. The power of attorney shall not come into operation until the donor is out of the UK, and shall be revoked by his return (Section 25).

The Section was amended by Section 9 of the Powers of Attorney Act 1971, enabling a trustee to delegate for a period not exceeding 12 months.

Power to Raise Money by Mortgage

Where trustees are authorized by the instrument creating the trust, or by law, to apply capital money for any purpose, they shall have power to raise the money by sale or mortgage of all or any part of the trust property.

This Section applies notwithstanding anything to the contrary in the trust instrument, but does not apply to trustees of property held for charitable purposes, or to trustees of a settlement for the purposes of the Settled Land Act 1925, not being also the statutory owners (Section 16).

Death of Trustee

See Section 18 under *Death of Trustee*

Power of Appointing New Trustees

By Section 36(1)

Where a trustee is dead, or remains out of the United Kingdom for more than twelve months, or desires to be discharged, or refuses or is unfit to act therein, or is an infant—

(a) the person or persons nominated for the purpose of appointing new trustees by the instrument, if any, creating the trust; or (*b*) if there is no such person, or no such person able and willing to act, then the surviving or continuing trustees or trustee for the time being, or the personal representatives of the last surviving or continuing trustee;

may, by writing, appoint one or more other persons to be a trustee or trustees.

Limitation of Number of Trustees
The number of trustees of a settlement of land or holding land on trust for sale is limited to four. This limitation only applies to land, and does not apply to land vested in trustees for charitable, ecclesiastical, or public purposes (Section 34).

Bankrupt Trustee
See Section 41 under *Bankrupt Person*

Executors and Administrators
This Act, except where otherwise expressly provided, applies to trusts, including, so far as this Act applies thereto, executorships and administratorships (Section 69(1)).

Breach of Trust
SEE *Breach of Trust*

Payment into Court
Where money or securities are vested in trustees, and the majority are desirous of paying the same into court, but the concurrence of the other or others cannot be obtained, and the money or securities are deposited with a banker, the court may order payment or delivery of the money or securities to the majority of the trustees for the purpose of payment into court (Section 63).

Minors
By the Law of Property Act 1925, a minor cannot be appointed a trustee (Section 20).

Trustees for Sale
Trustees for sale mean the persons (including a personal representative) holding land on trust for sale. SEE *Joint Tenants*

By the Law of Property Act 1925, 'a power to postpone sale shall, in the case of every trust for sale of land, be implied unless a contrary intention appears' (Section 25(1)).

Section 27(2) as amended by the Law of Property (Amendment) Act 1926, provides

Notwithstanding anything to the contrary in the instrument (if any) creating a trust for sale of land or in the settlement of the net proceeds, the proceeds of sale or other capital money shall not be paid to or applied by the direction of fewer than two persons as trustees for sale, except where the trustee is a trust corporation, but this subsection does not affect the right of a sole personal representative as such to give valid receipts for, or direct the application of, proceeds of sale or other capital money, nor, except where capital money arises on the transaction, render it necessary to have more than one trustee.

Trustees for sale have all powers of a tenant for life under the Settled Land Act 1925 (Section 28(1)). SEE *Settled Land*

SEE *Advancement; Breach of Trust; Custodian Trustee; Public Trustee; Trust Corporation; Trustee Investments*

TRUSTEE IN BANKRUPTCY When a debtor is adjudicated bankrupt, his property shall become divisible amongst his creditors, and shall vest in a trustee (SEE *Adjudication in Bankruptcy*). Until a trustee is appointed the official receiver acts as trustee.

The trustee may be appointed by the creditors, or they may leave his appointment to the committee of inspection. The trustee must give security to the satisfaction of the Department of Trade and Industry, and the Department, when satisfied, certifies that his appointment has been duly made.

The trustee's title to the bankrupt's property relates back to the earliest act of bankruptcy within three months of the receiving order. See Section 37 under *Adjudication in Bankruptcy*. See also Section 45 under *Bankruptcy*, and Section 46 under *Act of Bankruptcy*

The Bankruptcy Act 1914 provides

Powers of trustee to deal with property

55. Subject to the provisions of this Act, the trustee may do all or any of the following things—

(1) Sell all or any part of the property of the bankrupt (including the goodwill of the business, if any, and the book debts due or growing due to the bankrupt), by public auction or private contract, with power to transfer the whole thereof to any person or company, or to sell the same in parcels:

(2) Give receipts for any money received by him, which receipts shall effectually discharge the person paying the money from all responsibility in respect of the application thereof:

(3) Prove, rank, claim, and draw a dividend in respect of any debt due to the bankrupt:

(4) Exercise any powers, the capacity to exercise which is vested in the trustee under this Act, and execute any powers of attorney, deeds and other instruments, for the purpose of carrying into effect the provisions of this Act:

(5) Deal with any property to which the bankrupt is beneficially entitled as tenant in tail in the same manner as the bankrupt might have dealt with it.

Powers exercisable by trustee with permission of committee of inspection

56. The trustee may, with the permission of the

committee of inspection, do all or any of the following things—

(1) Carry on the business of the bankrupt, so far as may be necessary for the beneficial winding up of the same:

(2) Bring, institute, or defend any action or other legal proceeding relating to the property of the bankrupt:

(3) Employ a solicitor or other agent to take any proceedings or do any business which may be sanctioned by the committee of inspection:

(4) Accept as the consideration for the sale of any property of the bankrupt a sum of money payable at a future time, subject to such stipulations as to security and otherwise as the committee think fit:

(5) Mortgage or pledge any part of the property of the bankrupt for the purpose of raising money for the payment of his debts:

(6) Refer any dispute to arbitration, compromise any debts, claims, and liabilities, whether present or future, certain or contingent, liquidated or unliquidated, subsisting or supposed to subsist between the bankrupt and any person who may have incurred any liability to the bankrupt, on the receipt of such sums, payable at such times, and generally on such terms as may be agreed on:

(7) Make such compromise or other arrangement as may be thought expedient with creditors, or persons claiming to be creditors, in respect of any debts provable under the bankruptcy:

(8) Make such compromise or other arrangement as may be thought expedient with respect to any claim arising out of or incidental to the property of the bankrupt, made or capable of being made on the trustee by any person or by the trustee on any person:

(9) Divide in its existing form amongst the creditors, according to its estimated value, any property which from its peculiar nature or other special circumstances cannot be readily or advantageously sold.

The permission given for the purposes of this Section shall not be a general permission to do all or any of the above-mentioned things, but shall only be a permission to do the particular thing or things for which permission is sought in the specified case or cases.

Power to allow bankrupt to manage property

57. The trustee, with the permission of the committee of inspection, may appoint the bankrupt himself to superintend the management of the property of the bankrupt or of any part thereof, or to carry on the trade (if any) of the bankrupt for the benefit of his creditors, and in any other respect to aid in administering the property, in such manner and on such terms as the trustee may direct.

Allowance to bankrupt for maintenance or service

58. The trustee may from time to time, with the permission of the committee of inspection, make such allowance as he may think just to the bankrupt out of his property for the support of the bankrupt and his family, or in consideration of his services if he is engaged in winding up his estate, but any such allowance may be reduced by the Court.

Right of bankrupt to surplus

69. The bankrupt shall be entitled to any surplus remaining after payment in full of his creditors, with interest, as by this Act provided, and of the costs, charges, and expenses of the proceedings under the bankruptcy petition.

Subject to the retention of such sums as may be necessary for the costs of administration, the trustee shall declare and distribute dividends amongst all creditors who have proved their debts. SEE *Dividends in Bankruptcy*

Payment of money into Bank of England

89.—(1) The Bankruptcy Estates Account shall continue to be kept by the Board of Trade with the Bank of England, and all moneys received by the Board of Trade in respect of proceedings under this Act shall be paid to that account.

(2) Every trustee in bankruptcy shall, in such manner and at such times as the Board of Trade with the concurrence of the Treasury direct, pay the money received by him to the Bankruptcy Estates Account at the Bank of England, and the Board of Trade shall furnish him with a certificate of receipt of the money so paid.

"Provided that—

(*a*) If it appears to the committee of inspection that, for the purpose of carrying on the debtor's business, or of obtaining advances, or because of the probable amount of the cash balance, or if the committee shall satisfy the Board of Trade that for any other reason it is for the advantage of the creditors that the trustee should have an account with a local bank, the Board of Trade shall, on the application of the committee of inspection, authorise the trustee to make his payments into and out of such local bank as the committee may select;

(*b*) in any bankruptcy composition or scheme of arrangement in which the official receiver is acting as trustee, or in which a trustee is acting without a committee of inspection, the Board of Trade may, if for special reasons they think fit to do so, upon the application of the official receiver or other trustee, authorise the trustee to make his payments into and out of such local bank as the Board may direct.

(3) Where the trustee opens an account in a local bank, he shall open and keep it in the name of the debtor's estate, and any interest receivable in respect of the account shall be part of the assets of the estate, and the trustee shall make his payments into and out of the local bank in the prescribed manner.

(4) Subject to any general rules relating to small bankruptcies under Section 129 of this Act, where the debtor at the date of the receiving order has an account at a bank, such account shall not be withdrawn until the expiration of seven days from the day appointed for the

first meeting of creditors, unless the Board of Trade, for the safety of the account, or other sufficient cause, order the withdrawal of the account.

(5) If a trustee at any time retains for more than ten days a sum exceeding fifty pounds, or such other amount as the Board of Trade in any particular case authorise him to retain, then, unless he explains the retention to the satisfaction of the Board of Trade, he shall pay interest on the amount so retained in excess at the rate of twenty per centum per annum, and shall have no claim for remuneration, and may be removed from his office by the Board of Trade, and shall be liable to pay any expenses occasioned by reason of his default.

(6) All payments out of money standing to the credit of the Board of Trade in the Bankruptcy Estates Account shall be made by the Bank of England in the prescribed manner."

Trustee not to pay into private account

88. No trustee in a bankruptcy or under any composition or scheme of arrangement shall pay any sums received by him as trustee into his private account.

Investment of surplus funds

90.—(1) Whenever the cash balance standing to the credit of the Bankruptcy Estates Account is in excess of the amount which in the opinion of the Board of Trade is required for the time being to answer demands in respect of bankrupts' estates, the Board of Trade shall notify the same to the Treasury, and shall pay over the same or any part thereof as the Treasury may require to the Treasury, to such account as the Treasury may direct, and the Treasury may invest the said sums or any part thereof in Government securities to be placed to the credit of the said account.

(2) Whenever any part of the money so invested is, in the opinion of the Board of Trade, required to answer any demands in respect of bankrupts' estates, the Board of Trade shall notify to the Treasury the amount so required, and the Treasury shall thereupon repay to the Board of Trade such sum as may be required to the credit of the Bankruptcy Estates Account, and for that purpose may direct the sale of such part of the said securities as may be necessary.

The dividends on investments under Section 90 shall be paid into an account to be called The Bankruptcy and Companies Winding-up (Fees) Account (Economy, Miscellaneous Provisions, Act 1926).

By the Bankruptcy Rules 1915

No. 342. Where the trustee is authorised to have an account at a local bank, he shall forthwith pay all moneys received by him in to the credit of the estate. All payments out shall be made by cheque payable to order, and every cheque shall have marked or written on the face of it the name of the estate, and shall be signed by the trustee. Every cheque shall be countersigned in cases where there is a committee of inspection by at least one member of the committee, and by such other person, if any, as the creditors or committee of inspection may appoint, and where there is no committee, by such person, if any, as the Board of Trade may direct.

The trustee shall, as soon as may be, take possession of the bankrupt's property. By Section 48(6)

6. Subject to the provisions of this Act with respect to property acquired by a bankrupt after adjudication, any treasurer or other officer, or any banker, attorney, or agent, of a bankrupt, shall pay and deliver to the trustee all moneys and securities in his possession or power, as such officer, banker, attorney, or agent, which he is not by law entitled to retain as against the bankrupt or the trustee. If he does not, he shall be guilty of a contempt of Court, and may be punished accordingly on the application of the trustee.

The trustee's title dates back to the earliest act of bankruptcy within three months of the receiving order (SEE *Act of Bankruptcy; Adjudication in Bankruptcy*). The property of a bankrupt shall vest in the trustee for the time being without any conveyance, assignment or transfer whatever (Section 53(3)).

The remuneration of a trustee shall be fixed by an ordinary resolution of the creditors, or if the creditors so resolve by the committee of inspection, and shall be in the nature of a commission or percentage (Section 82(1)).

When the trustee has realized all the property of a bankrupt, or as much as he can, and distributed a final dividend he obtains his release by an order of the Department of Trade and Industry (Section 93).

The creditors may, if they think fit, appoint more than one trustee. When more than one are appointed the creditors shall declare whether any act to be done by the trustees is to be done by all or any one or more of such persons (Section 77(1)).

The creditors may also appoint persons to act as trustees in succession in the event of one or more of the persons first named declining to accept the office of trustee, or failing to give security, or of the appointment of any such person not being certified by the Department of Trade and Industry (Section 77(2)).

See Section 56, above, as to a trustee's power to borrow on the property of the bankrupt. If the trustee's personal liability for an overdraft is required, a guarantee should be obtained.

TRUSTEE FOR DEBENTURE HOLDERS
When a company seeks to issue debentures or debenture stock, or even unsecured loan stock, it is customary to appoint a trustee to protect the interests of the debenture-holders or stockholders. The issue is normally constituted under a trust deed entered into between the company and the trustee. The powers and duties of the trustee will be set out in the deed. In general, it is the concern of the trustee to see that the obliga-

tions of the company are duly performed. The debentures or stock may carry a fixed charge over certain fixed assets, or a floating charge over the undertaking generally, or both. The trustee would normally hold the documents of title to any specifically charged assets and in some cases may be required to ensure that the floating assets of the undertaking are maintained at a stipulated level. If there is a sinking fund for the redemption of the debentures or stock, the trustee will be responsible for seeing that the fund is operated in accordance with the deed. The trustee may have a particularly active role where there are a number of dealings in the charged assets by way of sales, purchases, leases, etc. The security property can be released only with the consent of the trustee and such consent would also be necessary where, for any reason, it is proposed to reduce the value of the security property by the withdrawal of assets from behind the debentures or stock without replacement. The trustee will also be responsible for seeing that freehold and leasehold properties are properly insured and that all outgoings are duly met.

The trustee's role will be comparatively passive unless and until the security becomes enforceable, when some action will be necessary by the trustee, usually the appointment of a receiver, to protect the security property for the benefit of the debenture-holders or stockholders. The trust deed will specify the circumstances in which the security shall become enforceable and these will normally include default in payment of principal or interest on the debentures or stock, the winding-up of the company, the cessation of business or breaches of covenant by the company. It is fortunately rare that a trustee has occasion to appoint a receiver, but it does happen from time to time and the responsibility of the trustee can then become an onerous one.

Debenture trusts are usually of long duration and call for trustees of standing and business experience. The banks and insurance companies are therefore well equipped for the task and, in the ordinary way, the business is remunerative.

While the duties are normally of an undemanding nature, they cease to be so if the security becomes enforceable and it is usual to provide that in such circumstances the level of remuneration shall be doubled, or even trebled.

As far as the banks are concerned, the business of debenture trusteeships has had a chequered career. It was not uncommon for a bank to accept debenture trusts in the years before and immediately after the Second World War, but it became a matter for comment in the report of the Cohen Committee on Company Law Amendment in 1945, which suggested that a conflict of interest might arise in cases where a bank was both the creditor of a company and trustee for the debenture-holders. Following the Cohen Committee, the Rules of the Stock Exchange were amended to provide that the trustee for the debenture-holders of a listed company must not have an interest in relation to the company which might conflict with the trustee's role as such.

After the Stock Exchange ruling, it was therefore left to the banks to act as debenture trustees for each others' customers but in practice this did not happen. Some banks were reluctant to become trustees for debenture-holders in a large public company if it might inhibit the possibility of their becoming bankers to the company at some future date. Others felt that the conflict was more apparent than real and continued to take debenture trusteeships. In more recent times the Stock Exchange rule has been relaxed and the problem no longer remains.

A trust deed securing a debenture issue must be registered in the company's register of mortgages and particulars delivered to the Registrar of Companies. SEE *Debenture; Registration of Charges*

TRUSTEE INVESTMENTS A trustee must invest the trust funds in accordance with the terms of the trust deed. In the absence of such directions the Trustee Act 1925, formerly provided (in Section 1) a list of authorized investments to which trustees were confined. The Trustee Investments Act 1961, repealed the whole of this Section and references in the 1925 Act to that Section are now to be construed as referring to Section 1 of the 1961 Act. Various other sections of the 1925 Act were repealed or amended, and the two Acts must now be read together as far as investments are concerned. The most important of the Sections of the 1925 Act dealing with this subject which are still in force are as follows:

2.—(1) A trustee may under the powers of this Act invest in any of the securities mentioned or referred to in Section 1 of this Act, notwithstanding that the same may be redeemable, and that the price exceeds the redemption value.

(2) A trustee may retain until redemption any redeemable stock, fund, or security which may have been purchased in accordance with the powers of this Act, or any statute replaced by this Act.

3. Every power conferred by the preceding Sections shall be exercised according to the discretion of the trustee, but subject to any consent or direction required by the instrument, if any, creating the trust, or by statute with respect to the investment of the trust funds.

4. A trustee shall not be liable for breach of trust by reason only of his continuing to hold an investment which has ceased to be an investment authorised by the trust instrument or by the general law.

5.—(1) A trustee having power to invest in real securities may invest and shall be deemed always to have had power to invest—

(b) on any charge, or upon mortgage of any charge, made under the Improvement of Land Act, 1864.

7.—(1) A trustee may, unless expressly prohibited by the instrument creating the trust, retain or invest in securities payable to bearer which, if not so payable, would have been authorised investments:

'Provided that securities to bearer retained or taken as an investment by a trustee (not being a trust corporation) shall, until sold, be deposited by him for safe custody and collection of income with a banker or banking company.

A direction that investments shall be retained or made in the name of a trustee shall not, for the purposes of this subsection, be deemed to be such an express prohibition as aforesaid.

(2) A trustee shall not be responsible for any loss incurred by reason of such deposit, and any sum payable in respect of such deposit and collection shall be paid out of the income of the trust property.

8.—(1) A trustee lending money on the security of any property on which he can properly lend shall not be chargeable with breach of trust by reason only of the proportion borne by the amount of the loan to the value of the property, at the time when the loan was made, if it appears to the Court—

(a) that in making the loan the trustee was acting upon a report as to the value of the property made by a person whom he reasonably believed to be an able practical surveyor or valuer instructed and employed independently by the owner of the property, whether such surveyor or valuer carried on business in the locality where the property is situate or elsewhere,

(b) that the amount of the loan does not exceed two third parts of the value of the property as stated in the report, and

(c) that the loan was made under the advice of the surveyor or valuer expressed in the report.

The long run of inflation after the Second World War penalized trustees and, through them, trust beneficiaries, because under the 1925 Act trustees were confined to the list of then authorized securities, which were all of the gilt-edged type unable to share in the increased profits being made in equity shares. This resulted in much adverse criticism of the authorized list, and suggestions were made that trustees should be authorized, quite apart from any permission given in the instrument setting up the trust, to hold good-class equities.

The Trustee Investments Bill was accordingly introduced into Parliament in the autumn of 1960, and after a long and exceptionally difficult passage through both Houses became law in August, 1961. By this Act trustees are given power to invest up to one-half of a trust fund in a wide range of investments, including equities. As a result of criticism in debate in the House it was agreed that this proportion might be increased to 75 per cent, if the Treasury should so by Order direct.

Existing trusts have the 1925 investment powers replaced by those in the new Act. Any special powers of investment which the trustees enjoyed, however sanctioned, remain valid, but are supplemented by the new statutory powers, even though the original trust powers specified narrower limits than the new Act allows. Thus, a direction in a will made before the new Act that moneys are not to be invested in ordinary shares can now be overridden.

Future trusts are affected in the same way except that instruments made after the Act may restrict or exclude the operation of its Sections or give trustees overriding powers.

The Act sets out two main categories of securities in which trustees are authorized to invest. The first category is designated Narrower Range Investments (NR), which are only a little wider than the 1925 authorized list; and the Wider Range Investments (WR), which consist of ordinary and preference shares in substantial, quoted companies.

Before investing in any WR securities the trustee must make an up-to-date valuation of the whole fund and divide it into two parts of equal value. The NR part may be invested only in NR investments, and the WR part may be invested in either NR or WR investments, or both. Once the division has been made, it is final and does not have to be done again whatever happens to the value of the two parts as time progresses. Assets may generally be transferred between one fund and the other only if a compensating transfer in the reverse direction is also made (Section 2).

In choosing the investments, the trustee must have regard to the need for diversification and suitability to the trust. He must obtain written advice on these matters from an able and experienced financial adviser, and on such intervals as he considers desirable. Advice may be given by one co-trustee if qualified to advise, or by anyone, such as a trustee bank official, who is in a position of employment as an officer or a servant (Section 6). This valuation once obtained will be conclusive in determining whether the division or transfer of property between the NR and WR parts has been duly made (Section 5).

Where capital assets accrue, without payment, to the trustee as owner of a specific investment contained in one part, they are added to that part. Where a trustee has to take assets out of the funds he has complete discretion as to the part from which they are to be taken. An interest in expectancy is not included with the trust property for purposes of division until it falls into possession.

Where assets on several identical trusts are held, they are regarded for the purpose of dividing them into NR and WR parts as forming a single fund (Section 4).

In addition the Act provides for a third category, known as the Special Range (SR), into which fall any investments held under special powers of a trustee, however obtained. The SR part is to be completely segregated from the NR and WR parts. If the trustee wishes to exercise his special powers after the initial division of the fund has been made, he may do so at the expense of either the NR or WR parts, or both, but if an investment from the SR part is sold and the proceeds are not reinvested in investments authorized by the special powers, the proceeds must be reinvested equally between NR and WR investments (Section 3).

Such special powers may have been given by the instrument setting up the trust, by a Court Order, or by an Act of Parliament. If in either of the last two cases the special powers were given within the last ten years, the trustee may choose whether he will use the existing special powers, or the new WR powers conferred on him by the Act.

Two amendments of importance to trust corporations are made to Section 10 of the 1925 Act:

1. To subsection (3) (which enables trustees to concur in any scheme or arrangement for the amalgamation of a company in which they hold investments, with another company). This power is extended to cases where control of the company is gained by another company.
2. To subsection (4) (which gives trustees power to subscribe for securities). This power is defined to include the power to retain them for any period for which the original holding could be retained (Section 9).

The list of Authorized Investments is contained in Schedule 1 to the Act, as amended, viz.

Narrower-Range—Part I (not requiring advice)
Defence Bonds (later British Savings Bonds), Savings Certificates, Post Office Savings Bank (now National Savings Bank) Deposits, and Trustee Savings Bank Ordinary Deposits.

Narrower-Range—Part II (requiring advice)
Other fixed-interest securities issued by, or the interest on which is guaranteed by, the Governments of the UK, Northern Ireland or the Isle of Man.

Treasury Bills.

Fixed interest securities issued by overseas governments or local authorities within the Commonwealth, or by the International Bank, or by any public authority or nationalized industry or undertaking in the UK.

Debentures registered and issued in the UK by a company incorporated in the UK.

Stock of the Bank of Ireland.

Debentures of the Agricultural Mortgage or Scottish Agricultural Securities Corporations.

UK local authority loans (subject to certain conditions).

Debentures or guaranteed or preference stocks of UK statutory water companies which have paid at least five per cent ordinary dividends throughout the last ten years.

Special investment accounts of Trustee Savings Banks.

Deposits in a building society designated under Section 1 of the House Purchase and Housing Act 1959.

Mortgages or heritable property in Scotland and on freeholds or leaseholds of 60 years or more elsewhere in the UK.

Perpetual rent charges on land.

Gilt-edged unit trusts.

Wider-Range—Part III
Share capital of UK companies, not being their loan capital which is included in the NR list.

Shares in any building society designated under Section 1 of the House Purchase and Housing Act 1959.

Unit trusts.

No securities qualify unless payment can be required in sterling. Securities must be registered or issued in the UK and must be quoted on a recognized UK stock exchange. Shares or debentures must be fully paid up, except for new issues to be paid up in nine months.

In the case of debentures, etc., and share capital of UK companies referred to in Parts II and III above, the company must have a paid-up share capital of at least £1 million, be incorporated in the UK, and have paid dividends throughout the last five years on all its shares issued and ranking for dividend.

Investments can be made without advice in the securities listed in NR Investments—Part I; or where special powers are exercised (unless the powers so stipulate). Likewise, no advice is obligatory where it is intended to keep securities acquired before the date of the Act.

Securities acquired at a time when they were duly authorized, whether by the trust instrument or by law, but which have since lost their status (e.g. South African Government Stocks no longer ranking as Commonwealth securities) may be retained by the trustee, but only as part of his WR portfolio.

This Act influenced investment policy and the markets. The investment needs of the differing types of trust could now be realistically assessed by trustees responsible for maintaining a fair balance between the rival claims of the tenant for life and the remainderman, between the charity and the pension fund. A gradual swing into equities lent support to an upward tendency in prices in that sector, while over a period the sale of gilt-edged securities tended to produce a corresponding depression in their prices.

Experience of the working of the Act suggests that, paradoxically, the powers of trustees were in some cases reduced. All well-drawn trusts had for many years contained an investment clause expressly authorizing trustees to invest in equities and generally to assume far more discretion than was permitted to them under the 1925 Act. This placed the older trusts at a disadvantage, and this fact among others led to the passing of the Variation of Trusts Act 1958 (q.v.) under the terms of which the Chancery judges were empowered to enlarge the investment powers of trustees. They used this power quite liberally and frequently allowed both charities and private trustees to invest the whole of a fund in equities. The 1961 Act recognized this and provided that

> the enlargement of investment powers of trustees by this Act shall not lessen any power of a Court to confer wider powers of investment on trustees, or affect the extent to which any such power is to be exercised.

In *Re Cooper's Settlement* [1961] 3 WLR 1029, trustees were authorized to retain shares and bonds in a private investment trust company which were originally settled, with power to sell and invest the proceeds in a restricted class of investments. Application was made to the court to vary the trusts and to widen the investment powers. The court took the view that, although before the passing of the new Act very wide investment powers had frequently been sanctioned by the court, Parliament had now indicated the extent to which trustees ought to be free to invest otherwise than in gilt-edged investments. The court would therefore have to be satisfied henceforth that there were special grounds before going beyond the limits of the new powers. No such special grounds were found in the case then before the court and no extension of the trustee's powers was approved.

In *Re Kolb's Will Trusts* [1962] 3 WLR 1034, the testator expressly provided in his will dated 1958 that his residue should be wholly invested in 'blue-chips' and prohibited any investment in gilt-edged securities. Expert evidence established that 'blue chip' was not an exact term. Cross, J, in a reserved judgment therefore held that the investment clause was void for uncertainty. Relief under the 1958 Act was also refused on the ground that, despite the testator's manifest intention, there were no special circumstances. Although the Act of 1961 provided in Section 15 that the court's power to widen the investment powers of trustees should be preserved, that power ought to be exercised only if a very special case could be made out for doing so. The court doubted that the wishes of the testator by themselves constituted such special circumstances as would justify a widening of the investment powers, and it refused to make the order asked for, that the trustees should be given power to invest the residuary estate in fully-paid ordinary shares or convertible debentures of companies with a paid-up capital of at least £1 million. It was, however, a factor in this decision that the residuary legatee objected to the proposed extension of the trustees' powers.

It followed from these and other cases, that the court would entertain an application for an extension of trustees' investment powers only if there were special grounds for seeking such an extension. In a case before the courts in 1983 however, Sir Robert McGarry V-C, said that conditions had changed so much since the Act was passed in 1961 that it was no longer necessary to show special grounds or give special reasons for an extension of the investment powers contained in the Act. He considered that in determining whether or not extended powers of investment should be conferred on trustees, the following matters should be taken into consideration:

1. the weight and width of any provisions for advice and control;
2. where powers are of great width, it is better to have a scheme of fractional division, confining part of the fund to relatively safe investments. Where the powers are appreciably less wide, no division of funds into portions will be required, the only division being into investments which require advice and those which do not;
3. the size of the fund in question is material; a large fund may justify a latitude of investment which would be denied to a more modest fund;
4. the objects of the trust are also material; where an increase in capital value is desirable, greater risks may be taken to secure capital appreciation. (*Trustees of the British Museum* v *Attorney-General* [1983] *Times*, 25th October.)

In the case of *Re Mineworkers' Pension Scheme Trust, Cowan v Scargill* [1984] *Times*, 18th April, Sir Robert McGarry V-C, ruled that the principles which applied to private trusts, applied also to pension funds and, indeed the large size of some pension funds emphasized the need for diversification of investments. In that case, the defendants were pension fund trustees who refused to accept an investment strategy for the pension scheme unless it was amended to exclude overseas investments and investments in industries which competed with the National Coal Board. It was held that: (i) the trustees were under a duty to exercise their powers in the best interests of present and future beneficiaries and to act impartially between different classes of beneficiaries. A power of investment had to be exercised in a manner which yielded the best return after consideration of the risks and prospects of the investments; (ii) in exercising a power of investment, trustees had to put their own personal interests and views aside; (iii) in making investments a trustee was required to take the care of an ordinary prudent man, including the duty to seek advice on matters he did not understand. It followed that a trustee was not entitled to reject advice, merely because he disagreed with it, unless he was acting as an ordinary prudent man would have acted; (iv) trustees were required to consider the need for diversification imposed by the Trustee Investments Act 1961.

It was also held that although the benefit to the beneficiaries was the trustees' paramount concern, if the beneficiaries held strong views on certain moral and social issues, it might not be for their benefit to profit from investment in activities to which they were opposed, i.e. 'benefit' had a wide meaning and an arrangement which was not particularly beneficial financially might, nevertheless, be a benefit. That situation did not exist, however, in the present case.

TRUSTEE SAVINGS BANK The first Trustee Savings Bank was founded by Rev Henry Duncan in Dumfriesshire in 1810 to provide a haven for the savings of the poor. In the following year, a considerable number of savings banks were set up in Scotland, England and Wales.

The Trustee Savings Banks (or Savings Banks as they were originally known) were based on the principle that the depositors' money was held in trust for the depositors by a Board of Trustees. Thus, the basic relationship was not that of debtor and creditor as in commercial banking and it was not contemplated that the deposits of customers would be onward-lent to other customers.

The movement developed so rapidly that, in 1817, an Act of Parliament was passed, establishing a Fund for the Banks for Savings to serve as a repository for Trustee Savings Bank deposits. The number of Trustee Savings Banks increased to 465 by 1819, but a number were closed when the Post Office Savings Bank was established in 1861. The special investment departments were set up from 1870 onwards to take in funds which were subject to notice of withdrawal and which were invested not in the Fund for the Banks for Savings, but in other government securities. It was this development which was largely responsible for the substantial growth of the Trustee Savings Banks.

There were 73 Trustee Savings Banks in existence when the Page Committee reported in 1973 on its review of national savings (SEE *Committee to Review National Savings*). The Committee recommended that the Trustee Savings Banks should merge to form not more than 20 separate units and that they should become the basis of the 'third force' in banking in the UK. The general recommendations of the Page Committee were put into effect in the Trustee Savings Bank Act of 1976 which provided for the setting-up of the Trustee Savings Bank Central Board. Within a short space of time, the 73 banks were merged into 17 banks, providing a very wide range of financial services. More recently, there has been a reorganization into five regional banks and statutory provisions are in hand to provide for the incorporation of the Trustee Savings Bank as a public limited company and the offering of its shares to the public. SEE Supplement

Until September, 1979, the Trustee Savings Banks functioned as a part of the Department for National Savings. The central Trustee Savings Bank is now a separate statutory creation, however, and is a member of the Banker's Clearing House (although not a member of the Committee of London Clearing Bankers).

TRUSTEE STATUS The concept of trustee status for building societies was introduced by the House Purchase and Housing Act 1959, which permitted trustees to hold building society *deposits* in those cases designated by the Chief Registrar as having 'trustee status'. The Trustee Investments Act 1961 (see above) not only included deposits in designated building societies as narrower range investments, but also included *shares* in a designated building society in the wider range category.

Under the House Purchase and Housing Act 1959, the Chief Registrar could designate a building society as having trustee status, only if

1. it was a permanent building society;

2. its total assets were at least £1 million;
3. all its borrowings were unsecured;
4. not more than 10 per cent of its mortgages were 'special advances' (SEE *Building Societies; Mortgage*);
5. the Society's total liabilities were not more than twice the amount due to its shareholders;
6. its liquidity ratio was at least 7½ per cent of total assets;
7. its reserves were maintained in accordance with the Building Societies (Designation for Trustee Investment) Regulations 1964, which requires societies to maintain reserves according to a sliding scale starting at 2½ per cent on assets up to £100 million, down to 1¼ per cent on assets over £1,000 million; and
8. the last annual return of the society shows that the above-mentioned regulations regarding total assets, liquidity ratio and reserves were fulfilled.

The designation of societies for trustee status is a matter at the discretion of the Chief Registrar and he will have regard to the overall efficient management of a society, its compliance with the Building Societies Act 1962, the overall prudence with which its affairs are conducted and its independence from outside control or influence.

Any society which does not satisfy these criteria will not achieve trustee status, or as the case may be, may lose the status already acquired. It is a matter of some importance to societies to achieve and maintain trustee status in view of the considerable amount of funds available for investment in this country on behalf of trustees.

TRUSTEES FOR SALE SEE UNDER *Joint Tenants; Trustees*

TURNOVER In broad terms, the total sales of goods and/or services in a particular business. Under Section 17, Companies Act 1967, a company is required to show its turnover attributable to each class of business and the pre-tax profit or loss attributable thereto, to be disclosed in the directors' report, but under the Companies Act 1981, this disclosure must now be in the notes to the accounts, together with the turnover attributable to each market geographically defined, to which the company has supplied its goods or services. Turnover is defined in Schedule 1 to the 1981 Act, as the company's ordinary activities, after deduction of trade discounts, value added tax and any other taxes based on the amounts so derived. (See now S. 261(6) and Schedule 10 Companies Act 1985.)

TURQUAND'S CASE In *Royal British Bank* v *Turquand* [1856] 25 LJ QB 327, it was decided that, if on the constitution of the company, directors might have been authorized to do certain things (e.g. enter into contracts), an outsider was entitled to assume that the directors had been so authorized. In other words, if an official of a company is found doing acts on behalf of the company which the articles permit him to do when duly authorized, a party doing business with the company is entitled to assume that the authority which the articles say the official can use has actually been put in his hands by the company. Where the articles of a company provided for the drawing of bills by the managing director as and when authorized by the board, and he drew bills without such authority and in fraud of the company, it was held that the company could not repudiate the bills, as outside parties were entitled to assume that the managing director was actually vested with the authority which the articles provided could be put in his hands (*Dey* v *Pullinger* [1921] 37 TLR 10).

The rule is not capable of simple application, however, and has been severely modified by later decisions. Firstly, a party cannot benefit by the rule if at the time he entered into business contracts with the company he did not know of the delegation of powers, i.e. if he was not cognisant of the contents of the articles of the company. The benefit of the Rule cannot be taken where there is forgery. (*Kreditbank Kassel GmbH* v *Schenkers Ltd* [1927] 1 KB 826). Again, the rule will not operate in favour of a party dealing with a company where the transaction is unusual or abnormal or not one which the person engaging the company might be expected to be trusted with, unless he is so empowered specifically in the articles of association (*Houghton & Co* v *Nothard Lowe & Wills* [1928] AC 1).

In *Rama Corporation* v *Proved Tin and General Investments Ltd* [1952] 2 QB 147, it was held that a person who, at the time of making a contract with a company, has no knowledge of the company's articles of association, cannot rely on those articles as conferring ostensible or apparent authority on the agent with whom he dealt.

Clause 9 of the European Communities Act 1972, provides that, 'the powers of the directors to bind the company shall be deemed to be free of any limitation under the memorandum and articles of association', in favour of a person dealing with a company in good faith. Constructive notice is excluded and good faith presumed unless the contrary is proved. This provision goes further than the Rule in Turquand's case. SEE ALSO *Ultra Vires*

TWINS, INSURANCE AGAINST It is possible to insure against a multiple birth, although the amount of the insurance will be subject to a fairly low limit, probably £750. The purpose of the cover is to provide for the extra expense which the birth of twins, triplets or quadruplets would entail. The insurers will require details of multiple births on either side of the family for two generations back and will require to know whether any fertility drugs have been taken and whether or not a doctor has expressed an opinion on the likelihood of a multiple birth. The insurers will quote the amount of the premium only when they are in possession of the required information.

TWOPENCE A silver coin of that denomination is now issued only as Maundy money (q.v.). Its standard weight is 14.54545 grains troy. There is now a bronze two pence piece in circulation, issued as part of the decimal currency. SEE *Coinage*

U

UBERRIMAE FIDEI Latin for 'of the utmost good faith'. In the ordinary way, it is not the duty of a contracting party to disclose everything that might influence the other party in his decision to enter into the contract, always provided that such non-disclosure does not cause any statements made to be actually false. There are certain contracts, however, which are voidable unless every material fact within the knowledge of one party has been disclosed to the other party at the time the contract is made. Such contracts are called contracts *uberrimae fidei*. They include contracts of insurance, contracts to take shares in companies, and partnerships. Contracts of suretyship or guarantee are not of this class, but are closely akin to it however. 'Very little said that ought not to have been said, and very little not said which ought to have been said, would be sufficient to prevent the contract being valid.' (*Royal Bank of Scotland* v *Greenshields* [1914] SC 259)

In the case of *Woollcott* v *Sun Alliance & London Insurance Ltd* [1978] 1 WLR 493, it was held that on the destruction of a house by fire the insured could not recover under the fire policy because he had not disclosed that he had been convicted and sentenced for robbery. In that case, the policy had been issued in the name of Mr Woollcott and a building society for a total sum of £30,000, £12,000 of which was the amount of the building society mortgage. The building society received payment under the policy, being unaware of Mr Woollcott's criminal history but the court held that Mr Woollcott should have disclosed all relevant facts, notwithstanding that he was not asked any specific questions regarding previous convictions. In recent times the *uberrimae fidei* principle has been criticized by the National Consumers Council on the grounds that a private individual has no means of knowing what a prudent insurer might require to know and what, therefore, a private individual should disclose.

ULTRA VIRES Latin for, 'beyond the powers'. The doctrine of *ultra vires* in English law is concerned with the capacity of companies to enter into transactions. It was established in *Ashbury Railway Carriage & Iron Company* v *Riche* [1875] LR 7 HL 653, and confirmed by a long line of cases since then, that a company registered under the Companies Acts may do only those things which are authorized in its memorandum of association (q.v.). The purpose for which a company is incorporated is set out in the objects clause of this memorandum and any acts which are outside those objects are *ultra vires* the company and cannot subsequently be ratified. Under the Companies Act, the provisions of the memorandum of association may be altered by the members in general meeting, but not for the purpose of ratifying an act which was *ultra vires* the company.

If, for example, a debt has been incurred by a company for a purpose beyond the scope of its memorandum of association, it is not recoverable from the company, nor therefore from its liquidator. In the case of *Re Jon Beauforte (London) Ltd* [1953] 1 All ER 634, the company which was authorized to carry on business as costumiers also entered into the business of making veneered panels, notwithstanding that this was outside the provision of its memorandum. The company ordered fuel for the purpose of its panel-making business and it was held that the supplier of the fuel, who knew the purpose for which the fuel was to be used, was fixed with constructive notice that the transaction was *ultra vires* the company and could not prove for the cost of the fuel in the company's eventual liquidation.

In *Ball House* v *City Wall Properties Ltd* [1966] 2 QB 656, the objects included power 'to carry on any other trade or business whatsoever' that could 'in the opinion of the board of directors be advantageously carried on by the company in connection with or as ancillary to any of the above businesses or general businesses of the company'. This was held to cover any businesses that the directors thought bona fide could be so carried on.

On the other hand, the case of *Introductions Ltd* v *National Provincial Bank Ltd* [1969] 1 All ER 887, concerned *ultra vires* activities of the company, for which purpose it had borrowed from the bank, giving a floating draft as security. The bank contended that the existence of a power to borrow together with an independent objects clause enabled the company to borrow for any purpose, as if borrowing were the principal object of the company. The court, however, differentiated between powers and objects. The capacity to borrow was considered to be a power, not an object, and therefore the borrowing and security were held to be bad as the borrowing was for an *ultra vires* object. It was indicated that the position would have been different if the bank had not known of the utilization of the money.

In the more recent case of *Rolled Steel Products (Holdings) Ltd* v *British Steel Corporation and Others* [1982] 3 WLR 715, where there was a power in the memorandum of association to lend and advance money, it was held by Vinelott, J, that the power to lend money could be exercised only in furtherance of the objects of the company and was not an independent object in itself.

The impact of the *ultra vires* doctrine has been modified to some extent by Section 9(1) of the European Communities Act 1972, which provides that if a person dealing with a company acts in good faith, any transaction decided on by the directors shall be deemed to be one which is in the capacity of the company. The powers of the directors to bind the company shall be deemed to be free of any limitation under the memorandum and articles of association. A person about to transact with a company is not bound to enquire as to the capacity of the company or as to any of the limitations on the powers of the directors—such a person shall be presumed to have acted in good faith, the onus of proving otherwise resting on whoever seeks to set aside the transaction. Section 9 also provides that the powers of the directors to bind a company shall be deemed to be free of any limitation under the memorandum and articles of association as regards a person dealing with a company in good faith, which again is to be presumed until the contrary is proved.

Nothing in the Section disturbs the underlying doctrine of *ultra vires* as regards companies as such—its purpose is to protect third parties dealing with the company in good faith. It must be doubtful, however, whether a person dealing with a company in a transaction which he knows is *ultra vires* the company can be said to be acting in good faith. Thus, in the case of *Introductions Ltd* v *National Provincial Bank Ltd*, mentioned above, the bank would presumably be in no better position under Section 9, because it had actual knowledge of the memorandum of association. In the Jon Beauforte case (see above), however, it seems fairly certain that the position has been changed by Section 9, because a person acting in good faith would not be deemed to have constructive notice of the contents of the memorandum.

The protection provided by Section 9 relates to transactions 'decided on by the directors' and it would appear that this means those transactions approved by the directors acting as a board. It would not apparently extend to individual acts of the directors (except in the case of a sole director), nor to those of other officers of the company. SEE *Rule in Royal British Bank* v *Turquand*

To sum up: it would appear that under Section 9 a person dealing in good faith with a company will not be affected by any lack of capacity by the company under the *ultra vires* doctrine, provided he is not aware of that lack of capacity and providing the transaction has been authorized by or subsequently ratified by the board of directors acting as such.

A company acting outside its powers may still however, be restrained from doing so by an injunction obtained by an objecting shareholder. Also, Section 9 applies only to 'dealings' by a company and does not, for example, authorize a company to make charitable gifts if these were outside the power contained in the memorandum.

In 1984, in the case of *Simmonds* v *Heffer* (unreported), the High Court held that a gift of £50,000 by the League of Cruel Sports to the Labour Party was *ultra vires* the League, a company limited by guarantee, because it was outside the objects clause of its Memorandum of Association. A second gift which was made conditionally on its being used by the Labour Party to publicize its commitment to the abolition of blood sports, was held to be within the League's powers.

UNCALLED CAPITAL The subscribed capital of a company may be either fully, or only partly, called up. The part which has not been called up is the uncalled capital. The uncalled capital may consist of a portion which may be called up by the directors of the company, as required, and also, as in the case of a banking company which has adopted certain provisions of the Companies Acts, of a portion which constitutes a reserve liability and is not capable of being called up except in the event of and for the purposes of the company being wound up.

When debentures are issued by a company they usually include a floating charge upon the uncalled capital. Such a charge does not prevent the directors of the company making calls upon the shareholders as may be required for the purposes of the business.

In certain cases, uncalled capital may be specially assigned or hypothecated. When this is done each shareholder should be served with notice that the unpaid capital must be paid only to the person to whom it has been assigned (*See Capital*). A charge on a company's uncalled capital requires registration with the Registrar of Companies under Section 95 of the Companies Act 1948.

UNCLAIMED BALANCES SEE *Dormant Balances*

UNCLEARED EFFECTS SEE *Effects not Cleared*

UNDATED STOCK SEE *Government Securities*

UNDERWRITER An underwriter is a person who, when an issue of shares is being made by a company, agrees, in consideration for a certain commission, to apply for, or find someone else to apply for, a certain number or all of the shares which are not applied for by the public. An underwriter should be financially able to fulfil his agreement if necessary. If the shares are not favoured by the public, the underwriters may be saddled with a heavy weight of them, whereas if the issue is eagerly taken up, they may receive the commission without having to subscribe to any shares at all.

The provisions of the Companies Act 1985 are as follows.

97.—(1) It is lawful for a company to pay a commission to any person in consideration of his subscribing or agreeing to subscribe (whether absolutely or conditionally) for any shares in the company, or procuring or agreeing to procure subscriptions (whether absolute or conditional) for any shares in the company, if the following conditions are satisfied.

(2) The payment of the commission must be authorised by the company's articles; and—

(*a*) the commission paid or agreed to be paid must not exceed 10 per cent of the price at which the shares are issued or the amount or rate authorised by the articles, whichever is the less; and

(*b*) the amount or rate per cent of commission paid or agreed to be paid, and the number of shares which persons have agreed for a commission to subscribe absolutely, must be disclosed in the manner required by the following subsection.

(3) Those matters must, in the case of shares offered to the public for subscription, be disclosed in the prospectus; and in the case of shares not so offered—

(*a*) they must be disclosed in a statement in the prescribed form signed by every director of the company or by his agent authorised in writing, and delivered (before payment of the commission) to the registrar of companies for registration; and

(*b*) where a circular or notice (not being a prospectus) inviting subscription for the shares is issued, they must also be disclosed in that circular or notice.

(4) If default is made in complying with subsection (3)(*a*) as regards delivery to the registrar of the statement in prescribed form, the company and every officer of it who is in default is liable to a fine.

98.—(1) Except as permitted by section 97, no company shall apply any of its shares or capital money, either directly or indirectly in payment of any commission, discount or allowance to any person in consideration of his subscribing or agreeing to subscribe (whether absolutely or conditionally) for any shares in the company, or procuring or agreeing to procure subscriptions (whether absolute or conditional) for any shares in the company.

(2) This applies whether the shares or money be so applied by being added to the purchase money of any property acquired by the company or to the contract price of any work to be executed for the company, or the money be paid out of the nominal purchase money or contract price, or otherwise.

(3) Nothing in section 97 or this section affects the power of a company to pay such brokerage as has previously been lawful.

(4) A vendor to, or promoter of, or other person who receives payment in money or shares from, a company has, and is deemed always to have had, power to apply any part of the money or shares so received in payment of any commission, the payment of which, if made directly by the company, would have been lawful under section 97 and this section.

The total amounts of sums, if any, paid by way of commission in respect of any shares or debentures must be included in the summary to be sent to the Registrar. SEE *Company (Companies)*

UNDISCHARGED BANKRUPT Section 47(1) Bankruptcy Act 1914, says

All transactions by a bankrupt with any person dealing with him *bona fide* and for value in respect of property whether real or personal, acquired by the bankrupt after the adjudication, shall, if completed before any intervention by the trustee, be valid against the trustee . . . For the purposes of this subsection, the receipt of any money, security, or negotiable instrument from or by the order or direction of, a bankrupt by his banker, and any payment and any delivery of security or negotiable instrument made to or by the order or direction of, a bankrupt by his banker, shall be deemed to be a transaction by the bankrupt with such banker dealing with him for value.

The risk of opening an account with an undischarged bankrupt is that it is difficult to know if any balances represent after-acquired property or not. By Section 47(2), it is provided that where a banker finds that a customer is an undischarged bankrupt, he shall, unless satisfied that the account is a trust account, inform the trustee in bankruptcy or the Department of Trade and Industry and shall make no further payments out of the account except under an order of the court or with the permission of the trustee. If, however, the trustee does not intervene by the expiration of one month, the account may be continued. Care should be taken in opening an account with the wife of an undischarged bankrupt, for it may be used in connection with property belonging to the bankrupt before adjudication.

It is a punishable offence for an undischarged bankrupt to obtain credit for more than £50 (£10 prior to 1977) or to trade in an assumed name, without disclosing his bankruptcy. If a cheque is presented payable to an undischarged bankrupt, it should not be paid, for to get a good discharge by paying the cheque, a banker must have no notice of the holder's defective title (Section 59, Bills of Exchange Act 1882). The answer on a cheque so returned should cast no reflection on the drawer's credit. SEE *Bankrupt Person*

UNEMPLOYMENT PAY Unemployment benefit is available to persons who are out of work and who have paid the requisite number of Class 1 National Insurance contributions.

A self-employed person who becomes out of work may claim unemployment benefit only if he or she has paid sufficient Class 1 contributions.

Men and women are equally entitled to unemployment benefit, provided they satisfy the contribution conditions. A married woman who has paid the reduced rate of contributions cannot receive unemployment benefit.

There are two conditions which must be satisfied in order to qualify for unemployment benefit:

1. The claimant must have paid in any one tax year since 6th April, 1975 Class 1 contributions equivalent to a total of at least 25 times the contributions payable on earnings at the lower earnings limit. This condition is met if at least 26 flat-rate Class 1 contributions were paid under the old system of national insurance prior to 6th April, 1975.
2. The claimant must also have paid, *or been credited with*, in the tax year ending in the calendar year before the unemployment benefit began Class 1 contributions equivalent to at least 50 times the contributions payable on earnings at the lower earnings limit for that year. A person who does not have the full total of contributions but has paid, or been credited with, at least 25 times the level of contributions payable on the lower earnings limits for that year may receive a reduced benefit.

Credits given to the claimant during any time that he or she was unemployed or sick will count during the tax year for which the credits were given only in the following circumstances:

1. Class 1 contributions of at least 13 times the lower earnings limit for that year must have been paid, or
2. the person must have claimed and qualified for unemployment benefit, sickness benefit or maternity allowance, or
3. if unemployment or sickness benefit for the period covered by the credits would have been paid if the maximum period had not expired, or
4. if, during the period covered by the credits the person received invalidity pension, invalid care allowance, injury benefit or unemployability supplement (or would have received any of these but for their receiving some other benefit), or
5. if credit was given for a period of approved training.

The first three days of unemployment are known as 'waiting days' and no benefit is paid for them. Thereafter, benefit continues for up to a year in any period of interruption of employment. Different rules apply to earnings-related benefit.

When a person has been receiving unemployment benefit for a year, it ceases until he or she has worked again as an employee for at least 13 weeks. For this purpose, a week consists of at least 16 hours.

A claimant may obtain an increase for his wife, provided

1. she is earning less than the amount of the increase,
2. she is living with the claimant, or
3. if husband and wife are living apart he must have been in the habit of paying, when working, at least as much as the unemployment increase for a wife towards her support.

In general, a child increase will be payable if child benefit is payable, provided child benefit is payable to

1. the claimant,
2. the claimant's wife or husband, provided they are living together,
3. the woman who lives with the claimant who is the father of the child,
4. the parent of the child who lives with the claimant, provided the claimant meets more than half of the cost of providing for that child,
5. the claimant's divorced or separated wife, for whose children he is providing.

A married woman can claim child increase only if she lives with her husband and he is too ill to keep himself.

An increase in unemployment benefit may be obtained for an adult dependant provided no increase is being paid for a wife or husband. The rules are in general the same as for sickness benefit.

A married woman claiming unemployment pay on her own contributions may receive an increase for her husband if he cannot support himself owing to physical or mental infirmity. She must be living with her husband in those circumstances or contributing to his upkeep as much as the amount of the basic adult dependant's increase.

If a widow receives widow's allowance or widowed mother's allowance, she may be able to receive unemployment benefit when those payments end. If, however, the widow receives a widow's pension at a higher rate than unemployment benefit, no unemployment benefit can be paid. She may, however, be entitled to earnings-related supplement based on her own contributions.

Women who are divorced or whose marriages are annulled will be able to obtain unemployment benefit only if they satisfy certain contribution conditions (q.v.).

If the claimant is (1) aged 60 or over, and (2) receiving an occupational pension of more than £35 a week under the claimant's former employer's pension scheme, the unemployment benefit (including earnings-related supplement) will be reduced by 10p a week for every 10p by which the occupational pension exceeds £35.

Persons in receipt of State retirement pensions cannot receive unemployment benefit. If, however, a person of retirement age (65 for a man, 60 for a woman) chooses not to retire but to continue working, and if he or she is entitled on retirement to a retirement pension based on their own contributions, he or she will be entitled to unemployment benefit if unemployed.

Unemployment benefit cannot be paid at the same time as the person is receiving

1. any other National Insurance benefit on a weekly basis, namely, sickness or invalidity benefit, maternity allowance, widow's benefit or retirement pension,
2. industrial injuries benefit,
3. unemployability supplement,
4. training allowance from public funds.

Unemployment benefit may also be affected by payments received from an employer, either in lieu of notice or in lieu of wages or payments made under the Employment Protection Act 1975 or under an occupational pension scheme.

Payments of holiday pay, payments under the Redundancy Payments Act 1965 and refunds of contributions, e.g. for an occupational pension scheme, do not affect unemployment benefit.

If an unemployed person does any work, paid or unpaid, no unemployment benefit can be paid unless all the following conditions are satisfied:

1. the rate of pay must be no more than £2 a day,
2. the person concerned must be available for full-time work as an employee,
3. the work must be such that the person concerned could continue to do it even after taking up full-time work,
4. the work must not be the person's usual occupation.

If a person (1) leaves his or her job voluntarily without good reason, or (2) loses his or her job through misconduct (which in this context means conduct which a reasonable employer would consider rendered the employee no longer fit to hold the job), unemployment benefit will not be payable for a fixed period of six weeks from the date unemployment begins.

In the ordinary way, an unemployed person may be refused unemployment benefit for a period of six weeks if

1. he or she has failed to take a reasonable chance of a job, or
2. without good reason he or she has refused or failed to apply for a suitable job, or
3. without good reason he or she has refused or failed to carry out a reasonable recommendation in writing from the Department of Employment, the Manpower Services Commission or local education authority, or
4. without good reason he or she has refused or failed to accept a reasonable opportunity of receiving approved training in order to obtain regular work.

Suitable employment will normally be that of a kind in which the unemployed person was usually employed. After a reasonable time, however, other work may be regarded as suitable, but not if (1) the wages and conditions are not as good as those generally paid by good employers in a particular form of employment, or (2) the job is only vacant because of a trade dispute.

Unemployment benefit will not be payable for any period in which a person is on holiday from work, even if he or she is not paid by the employer during that period. The benefit may be payable, however, if a person has to take an unpaid holiday and since the period 1st March has already had as much holiday as would normally be given in that job (even if the holidays were taken in a previous job). No unemployment benefit will be payable, however, in respect of unpaid holidays abroad.

An unemployed person who is proposing to be away from home, on holiday or not, when receiving unemployment benefit should inform the unemployment benefit office.

Unemployment benefit is not generally payable, however, in respect of periods spent outside the UK and the Isle of Man. There are exceptions to this rule in the case of seafarers and persons seeking work in another country of the EEC.

If a person loses his job because of a trade dispute at his place of work, he will not be able to obtain unemployment benefit while the stoppage lasts unless he can show that he was not taking part in, nor directly interested in, the dispute which gave rise to the stoppage.

A person who normally works for an employer for only part of the year may be able to establish that he is a seasonal worker for the purpose of unemployment benefit. Generally, a seasonal worker is someone who, in the last three years, has had a regular break from work of more than seven weeks each year and who was not employed during those breaks. A seasonal worker seeking unemployment benefit must satisfy the general conditions set out above, but must also be able to show

1. that he or she was registered for work at a Job Centre or Careers Office, etc., if he or she has been unemployed and capable of work in the previous two years, or since becoming a seasonal worker if that is the shorter period, and
2. that he or she has already worked during at least a quarter of the current off season or can reasonably expect to work for that period.

In essence, the seasonal worker must be able to show a record of seasonal work plus a genuine effort to obtain work during the off season.

Persons in receipt of unemployment benefit will normally receive contribution credits for each week or benefit. A married woman cannot, however, obtain credits if she has chosen to pay reduced contributions. Credits count for a number of benefits in the future, e.g. basic retirement pension, but do not count towards earnings-related supplement. An unemployed person may still get the benefit of the contribution credits even though he is not receiving unemployment benefit. This would apply

1. where he is not getting the benefit because he was unable to satisfy the contribution conditions, or
2. where he has not qualified for further benefit after the initial period of one year, or
3. where he has not satisfied the special conditions relating to seasonal workers (see above).
4. where his occupational pension exceeds the limit for unemployment benefit.

The Finance Act 1981 provides for the taxation of unemployment benefit. Any increases in benefit for children or for exceptional circumstances are not taxable, but tax is payable on the standard rate of benefit and any addition for a wife or adult dependant. No deduction of tax is made until after the period of unemployment, nor will any refund of tax be payable until the end of the unemployment period or the end of the tax year, whichever is the earlier.

UNFRANKED INCOME SEE *Franked Income*

UNIFORM CUSTOMS AND PRACTICE FOR DOCUMENTARY CREDITS The Uniform Customs and Practice for Documentary Credits were first codified and published by the International Chamber of Commerce in 1933 and revised versions were published in 1951, 1962 and 1975. The latest revision is that which was issued in June, 1983 and came into effect 1st October, 1984. The Uniform Customs are largely based on and replace what was formerly known as 'London Practice'. The rules have been formally adopted by the British Bankers' Association. They are available from the International Chamber of Commerce (UK), Centre Point, 103 New Oxford St, London WC1A 1QD, or from a local Chamber of Commerce.

UNIFORM RULES FOR COLLECTIONS The International Chamber of Commerce first published its *Uniform Rules for the Collection of Commercial Paper* in 1956. The Rules were revised in 1967 with effect from 1st January, 1968, and again in June, 1978 with effect from 1st January, 1979. They are available from the International Chamber of Commerce (UK), Centre Point, 103 New Oxford St, London WC1A 1QD, or from a local Chamber of Commerce.

UNITIZATION The practice by which shares in an investment trust may be transferred to a unit trust in exchange for units in that trust. Such schemes have some appeal for shareholders in smaller, unquoted, or less marketable investment trusts and the exchange for units does not give rise to a charge to capital gains tax.

UNIT LINKED SEE *Life Assurance*

UNIT TRUST ASSOCIATION Most unit trust groups in the UK are members of the Unit Trust Association, set up in 1959 as the Association of Unit Trust Managers, to monitor standards throughout the movement. The objects of the association are

1. to uphold standards of unit trust practice, to protect the interests of unit-holders and to maintain the good name of the unit trust industry;
2. to provide on behalf of its members an agreed channel of communication and representation to government departments and other authorities on matters relating to unit trusts;
3. to act in co-operation with other organizations on matters connected with investment protection.

The Association acts as a watchdog on advertisements by its members and, in particular, stipulates that no advertisements must be allowed to mislead the public. It is a rule of the Association that advertisements by its members must state the aim of the trust as well as contain a warning in precise words that the price of units and the income from them can go down as well as up.

The Association deals with enquiries of a factual nature from the public or the media and is a valuable source of information on the entire unit trust movement. The members of the Unit Trust Association are accountable for over 95 per cent of the total unit trust funds under administration in this country.

UNIT TRUSTS Unit trusts are trust funds held in unit form for the benefit of the unit-holders (although a more comprehensive definition is attempted below). Unit trusts do not fall naturally within the scope of company law or the general body of trust law in the UK. It is true that they have their origin in the basic trust concept—particularly in the use made of trusts to hold property for unincorporated associations—but on the whole they owe little to the general body of trust law. Considering the growth of unit trusts business there is remarkably little statutory or case law on the subject. This is no doubt attributable to the good sense of those engaged in the business, whether as managers or trustees and to the shrewd control exercised by the Department of Trade and Industry.

Trust funds were set up in Victorian England for the purpose of spreading investors' risks, the equalization of income, the gradual reinvestment of capital and ultimate disbursement of capital profits. These foundered on the company law rule that an association 'formed for the purpose of carrying on a business that has as its object the acquisition of gain' may not have a membership exceeding 20. Although the decision was overruled in the later case of *Smith* v *Anderson* (1880) 15 ChD 247, and the way cleared for the development of investment trust funds, it was the investment company rather than the trust concept which was to be developed in England during the 1930s.

The subsequent development owes something to the experience of investment trusts in the USA, a large number of which were created in the 1920s, not all with satisfactory results. Some of them were very hazardous and became worthless when Wall Street collapsed in 1929. These early trusts (which were in fact companies) were 'fixed', in that the subscriptions from investors were committed to a stated portfolio which remained fixed throughout the life of the trust. When all the units of a trust had been issued, a second trust would be set up on identical terms with an identical portfolio, and so on with successive trusts. There was some confusion of terminology when these trusts were introduced into the UK because in the UK each separate trust was called a unit and the 'shares' held by the public were known as sub-units. The first British trust of this type was launched in 1931 by Municipal & General Securities Company Limited (now the M & G Group) under the name of First British Fixed Trust. In the ensuing years, a number of other similar trusts were launched, but it soon became apparent that fixed trusts were too inflexible and the managers could not vary the investments. Thus the flexible unit trust was introduced and the first of these was the Foreign Government Bond Trust, which was launched in 1934. By the beginning of 1938, 73 unit trusts were in existence in the UK with a total market value of approximately £80 million. All existing fixed trusts were either converted to flexible trusts or wound up, and all the newly-formed trusts were 'open ended' in that the number of units in issue could vary according to the level of purchases and sales. The term 'sub-unit' was dropped in this country and the individual shareholdings became known as units or shares.

The principal difference between the British and US pattern of development lay in the fact that, under UK company law, it was not possible for a company to buy its own shares (although it has since become possible in certain circumstances under the Companies Act 1981). This limitation did not apply in the USA with the result that their mutual funds, as they are known today, grew out of the concept of the investment company.

In December, 1935, the London Stock Exchange published a report on *Fixed Trusts* and recommended that legislation be introduced for the protection of the investing public. This was followed in August, 1936 by a Board of Trade report which in turn recommended that there should be legislation on the subject of fixed trusts. There was no statutory regulation of unit trusts, however, until some clauses were inserted at the Committee stage in the Prevention of Fraud (Investments) Bill 1939, which became law on 8th August, 1944. Those provisions were updated and re-enacted 14 years later in the Prevention of Fraud (Investments) Act 1958 (q.v.). Under the Act, the regulation of the unit trusts movement was brought under the then Board of Trade and is now the responsibility of the Department of Trade and Industry.

As to the nature of the modern unit trust, there is a number of descriptions used for the benefit of the general public which are adequate for that purpose, but are not always technically accurate. It is sometimes said that a unit trust is a joint investment venture. In common parlance it is, but it is not so in any legal sense. Sometimes the expression 'association' of investors is used, but this again would be legally unacceptable. The essential point is that a unit trust is a trust. It is established by a trust deed, the parties to which are the 'managers', who are the promoters of the trust and undertake certain obligations in the trust deed, and the 'trustees', who are responsible for holding the trust assets which are divided into units for the benefit of the 'beneficiaries' or 'unit-holders'. Under the trust deed, the managers may offer units in the trust fund to potential investors who thereby become unit-holders, and the managers are obliged under the trust deed to buy back such units from any unit-holders who wish to sell them. Thus we may say that a unit trust is a form of trust where the trust fund is divided into units and held for the benefit of the unit-holders, who become unit-holders by the purchase of units from the managers of the trust and who at any time may resell their units to the managers of the trust, at a price determined in each instance in accordance with the terms of the trust deed.

The basic value of a unit is always the value of he trust fund divided by the number of units in ssue. Thus, if the trust fund has a current value of 1 million and there are a million units in issue, ach unit will be worth £1. The price of a unit for he purpose of purchase or sale will, however, ake into account the dealing expenses. A purhaser of units will pay a price calculated accordng to the underlying value of the units plus ealing costs, on the basis that his investment ncreases the value of the trust fund and addition-l securities will therefore be purchased. The eller of units will receive a price based on the nderlying value of the units less dealing costs, n the basis that his sale of units results in a reduction of the trust fund and the corresponding sale of securities. Thus there is a margin between the 'offer' and 'bid' prices.

In calculating the offer and bid prices, the rules laid down by the Department of Trade and Industry must be strictly followed. Under these rules, the maximum price at which units may be offered to the public must be calculated by reference to (1) the lowest price at which the underlying securities may be purchased on the Stock Exchange at that time *plus* (2) stock exchange commissions, (3) stamp duties—1 per cent on purchases and $\frac{1}{4}$ per cent instrument stamp duty, (4) the managers' initial charge of, say, 5 per cent, (5) accrued income in the fund and (6) a 'rounding' adjustment in the final figure in order to avoid fractions (this must be limited to 1 per cent or 1.25p whichever is the lesser amount). Thus the maximum purchase price is arrived at.

On the sale of units by a unit-holder to the managers, the minimum price which must be paid by the managers under the Department of Trade and Industry rules is calculated by reference to (1) the highest price obtainable at that time on the Stock Exchange for the underlying securities *plus* (2) the accrued income in the fund *less* (3) stock exchange commissions and (4) the permitted 'rounding' figure.

The margin between the maximum purchase price and minimum sale price permitted by the Department of Trade and Industry rules will normally be of the order of 13 per cent and such a margin would quite rightly be unacceptable to the investing public. In practice, the managers of unit trusts operate on a dealing margin of 6–7$\frac{1}{2}$ per cent, subject to certain exceptions. This is primarily because at any one time the manager will be buying or selling existing units so that some of the costs of creating, or as the case may be liquidating, units can be avoided. The margin would be smaller but for the fact that it includes stamp duty currently at 1 per cent.

When a trust is expanding, i.e. when the managers are selling more units than they are repurchasing, the offer price will be pitched as high as the Department of Trade and Industry regulations permit because that reflects the price which would have to be paid for new securities on the market. When a trust is contracting, i.e. because more units are being sold back by unit-holders than new units are being bought, the bid price, i.e. the price which managers will pay for units, will be as low as the Department of Trade and Industry regulations permit reflecting the fact that securities will have to be sold on the market. One should visualize, therefore, the managers' buying and selling margin of, say, 7 per cent moving up or down the much wider scale of, say, 13 per cent permitted by the regulations. When a trust is expanding, the price will be nudging the top of the scale, usually referred to as being on the offer basis: when a trust is contracting, the price will move to the lower level, i.e. the bid basis. It is thus an advantage to existing unit-holders that their trust should be on the offer basis so that if they sell their units (at the bid price of course), the price will be nearer the top of the Department of Trade and Industry scale. For the purchaser of units, it would be an advantage to buy when the price is on the 'bid basis' because the price he pays (the offer price) is that much lower.

A large part of the profits of unit trust groups comes from dealing in existing units. Equally it can be a source of losses. A management company must of course have sufficient capital for the purpose of such dealing. It is part of the managers' skill to fix the unit prices at the right level within the permitted range. If, for example, investors are selling back more units than they purchase, a manager who kept the trust on the offer basis, i.e. at the top of the range, would make a loss because he would be paying unit-holders at the higher price and having to liquidate units in the market at the ruling bid prices.

Authorization of Trusts

For a unit trust to be 'authorized' by the Department of Trade and Industry, it must be invested in 'securities' as defined in the Prevention of Fraud (Investments) Act 1958, Section 26(1). The term, for all practical purposes, means stocks or shares or Government securities. It is impossible therefore for an authorized unit trust to be invested in freehold or leasehold property. Property bonds (q.v.) are not authorized unit trusts.

Within the definition of 'securities', it is permissible and quite usual to launch unit trusts with a special investment emphasis. Most of the early unit trusts were 'middle of the road' trusts. They sought the kind of performance which would give a mixture of capital growth and a medium level of income. They were designed for the every-day investor. It was the pattern to follow up with a 'growth' trust designed to seek capital gain—if necessary at the expense of income—and an 'income' trust to suit those investors who were looking for as much income as possible from their equity investment. In practice over the years, many of the income trusts have had good capital performance and some of the growth trusts have been disappointing. There then followed over the years a variety of 'specialist' trusts with investment policies geared to individual sectors such as financial institutions, small companies, commodities, gold shares, energy shares, recovery shares and so on. The management of unit trusts is very much a marketing operation and many groups launched new funds with popular labels attached to them, but which over the years bore little relation to their investment merit. In more recent years, as anxieties increased over the UK economy, a large number of 'international' funds have been launched designed for overseas investment.

Until 1980 a unit trust investing in fixed interest stocks was at a disadvantage from a taxation standpoint. This anomaly was removed in the 1980 Finance Act and a number of gilt-edged and fixed interest funds were introduced. Thus, unit trust investment was no longer exclusively an 'equity' matter and many investors were attracted to the newer 'gilt' funds.

To obtain Department of Trade and Industry authorization, it is necessary for the trust deed to contain a provision that no investment shall exceed 5 per cent of the total value of the fund with the proviso that this may be increased to 7½ per cent in respect of not more than six separate holdings, provided that the total number of separate holdings shall not be less than 20 and the aggregate value of the trust's holdings of investment in any 10 separate holdings shall not exceed 55 per cent of the total value.

The normal rule is that investments shall be made only in securities quoted on recognized stock exchanges. Some of the older trust deeds do contain power to invest in unquoted securities, but under the modern deeds a total of no more than 5 per cent of the fund may be invested in this way. Consequent upon the introduction of the Unlisted Securities Market under the umbrella of the Stock Exchange in November, 1980, the Department of Trade and Industry rules were relaxed to enable up to 25 per cent of the assets of a unit trust to be invested in shares traded on the Unlisted Securities Market.

Since 1980, unit trusts have also been able to invest in the traded options market. In April that year, the Department of Trade agreed that new trusts may write or purchase call options, provided that they are 'covered' i.e. that the managers can deliver the stocks on which they have written options. Existing unit trusts were empowered to invest in options only if the unit-holders agreed and then, only to the extent of 50 per cent of the total market value of the portfolio. There is no such limit for new trusts. Managers may invest only in options traded on recognized stock exchanges and may do so only for legitimate investment purposes, not as speculations.

Some Advantages of Unit Trust Investment

As a vehicle for investment, unit trusts offer the following advantages:

1. It is possible to get a greater spread of risk than is normally available to the private investor.
2. Unit trusts enjoy the advantage of day-to-day management by those who are knowledgeable in investment matters.
3. The annual management charges are effectively allowed for tax within the fund, which would not be possible if an investor paid someone to manage his own portfolio.
4. Dealing costs are proportionately lower.
5. The investor has one investment instead of many and thus the administrative problems of dealing with dividend counterfoils, income tax certificates and allotment letters, etc. are reduced.
6. All subjective considerations are removed—the choice of shares and the degree of liquidity is left to the much more objective decision of the investment manager.
7. Authorized unit trusts enjoy exemption from capital gains tax on investment switches within each trust.

Unit Trust Charges

The charges in each unit trust are laid down in the trust deed but until 1980 these could not exceed the maximum level authorized by the Department of Trade and Industry rules. Under those rules, the maximum charge exigible by the unit trust management company over a 20 year period was $13\frac{1}{4}$ per cent of the value of the units in issue. Only two categories of fees were permitted. The first of these, the Initial Charge, could not exceed 5 per cent of the new monies invested in a trust. The other fee, the Annual Charge, could not exceed $\frac{1}{2}$ per cent of the funds under management. Thus, in order not to exceed the permitted maximum of $13\frac{1}{4}$ per cent over 20 years, the combination of fees was mainly an Initial Fee of $3\frac{1}{4}$ per cent and Annual Fees of $\frac{1}{2}$ per cent or, alternatively, an Initial Fee of 5 per cent and Annual Fees of $\frac{3}{8}$ per cent. Out of those fees, the managers had to pay all costs including the charges of the trustees and the auditors.

In December, 1979, the Department of Trade relinquished its control over the level of unit trust managers' charges, leaving the management companies to fix their own level of fees. This meant that, in the case of all new trusts, the level of fees inserted in the trust deeds need no longer conform to the old regulations and, in the case of old trusts, the fees could be increased provided the unit-holders agreed. The basic system of charges, i.e. an Initial Fee and an Annual Fee still remains and the fees of the trustees, auditors, registrars, etc. are still payable by the management company, not out of the trust fund itself. The relaxation of the rules was in response to representations by the Unit Trust Association who, in return, gave an assurance to the Government that it would not attempt to replace the Department of Trade and Industry regulations by any price fixing agreement within the movement.

Linked Life Assurance

Perhaps the most important single development in the unit trust movement over the years has been the introduction of 'linked' life assurance schemes, which provide for the investment of life assurance premiums in unit trusts. The subject is dealt with under the heading of *Life Assurance*. The London and Edinburgh Insurance Company introduced the first equity-linked policy when, in 1957, that company brought out a scheme whereby life assurance premiums were invested, not actually but notionally, in the Unicorn Trust (then owned by the London and Edinburgh) and the policies were valued according to the value of the units. In the subsequent years, unit-linked life assurance grew considerably to a point where investment through linked life assurance accounted for over one-quarter of all unit trust sales. The special advantages of unit linked life assurance from the standpoint of the unit trust managers are

1. The contractual nature of most life assurance policies provides a continuing flow of funds for investment,
2. Unit linked life policies can be sold by normal life assurance methods, thereby circumventing the statutory restraints, under the Prevention of Fraud (Investments) Act 1958, on unit trust advertising and marketing methods.
3. The permitted level of unit trust charges can be augmented by fees chargeable in the life office as distinct from the management company.
4. The investor receives the benefit of income tax relief on premiums paid under long term life assurance contracts taken out before 14th March, 1984.

Unit Trust Trustees

The powers and duties of a unit trust trustee are laid down in each case in the unit trust deed but the trust will not be 'authorized' by the Department of Trade and Industry unless the deed complies with the requirements of the Schedule 1 of the Prevention of Fraud (Investments) Act 1958 (q.v.). Certain duties of a routine or procedural nature are also imposed on trustees by the Unit Trust Records Regulations (Statutory Rules and

Orders, 1946, No. 1586). The functions of a unit trust trustee may be summarized as follows.

1. To secure the vesting in the trustee or his nominee of the trust property prior to the issue of units.
2. To be given reasonable time to consider or propose advertisements and related documents and to prohibit their issue if he, the trustee, disapproves.
3. To require the managers to retire from the trust if he, the trustee, is satisfied that it is in the interests of the unit-holders that they should do so.
4. To hold the investments of the trust and any cash deposited by the managers, to collect and distribute the income from the trust assets, to sign and issue certificates to unit-holders and to supervise the maintenance of the register of unit-holders.
5. To ensure general compliance with the terms of the trust deed.

The trustee of a unit trust does not have any specific responsibility for the content or performance of the portfolio, but if, for example, an investment were purchased outside the investment powers of the trust, it would be proper for the trustee to draw attention to the matter and require its rectification.

It is a statutory requirement that the effective control of the management company is exercised independently of the corporation acting as trustee. Thus, a corporate body may not be a trustee of a unit trust of which it is manager (except in the case of an unauthorized unit trust). For the most part the role of trustee of unit trusts in the UK is undertaken by the banks and insurance companies.

The table set out below gives some indication of the growth of the unit trust movement over the years.

At the end of 1984, there were 687 unit trusts in the UK, managed by approximately 110 groups. SEE ALSO *Exempt Fund; Life Assurance; Share Exchange Scheme; Unitization*

Year	Value of funds (at year end) £m	Sales £m	Re-purchases £m	Net investment £m
1959	200.0	na	na	na
1960	201.4	26.88	13.37	13.51
1961	236.6	21.57	14.21	7.36
1962	272.5	45.01	11.07	33.94
1963	371.2	77.46	17.78	59.68
1964	428.9	99.64	22.60	77.04
1965	521.9	80.80	21.78	59.02
1966	581.8	129.69	24.26	105.43
1967	853.6	126.56	42.64	83.91
1968	1,482.4	328.93	70.45	258.48
1969	1,411.9	262.70	76.53	186.17
1970	1,397.7	171.15	73.35	97.80
1971	1,991.2	204.10	127.45	76.65
1972	2,647.5	436.86	195.59	241.27
1973	2,060.4	357.90	171.75	186.15
1974	1,310.8	194.87	110.17	84.70
1975	2,512.4	321.21	130.90	191.31
1976	2,543.0	333.40	165.88	167.52
1977	3,461.3	372.32	257.90	114.42
1978	3,873.4	529.68	294.08	235.60
1979	3,936.7	411.95	353.87	58.08
1980	4,968.0	531.47	423.90	107.56
1981	5,902.4	955.60	428.03	527.57
1982	7,768.0	1,157.51	567.23	590.28
1983	11,689.9	2,459.75	960.18	1,499.56
1984	15,099.1	2,918.20	1,476.70	1,441.50

Source: Unit Trust Association.

UNITARY TAXATION This is a method of taxation adopted by some of the states of the USA for taxing corporations resident in those states. It is based on the allocation of profits of multinational companies as a proportion of world profits, i.e. the ratio of a company's sales, payroll and fixed assets in the territory of the taxing state, to the group's world sales, etc. This method differs from that which is more usually adopted by the developed countries, including the United States Federal Government, and recommended by the OECD Model Double Taxation Convention of 1977 and the United Nations Model of 1980. The following is an extract from an Inland Revenue press release on the subject.

The Government has consistently urged that action be taken to prevent the application of unitary taxes to United Kingdom businesses. It first sought to do so when negotiating the current United Kingdom/United States Double Taxation Agreement, but the United States Senate attached a reservation against the provision in the draft agreement which would have prevented individual States from applying the method to United States subsidiaries of United Kingdom corporate groups. In agreeing to ratify the Double Taxation Agreement without this provision the United Kingdom Government was given to understand that the United States administration would take steps to resolve the matter.

The constitutionality of unitary taxation was subsequently considered by the United States Supreme Court in the case of Container Corporation of America v The California Franchise Tax Board. In June 1983, the Supreme Court delivered a judgement upholding the right of a State to use this method of taxation in relation to a United States parent corporation and its foreign subsidiaries. The Court reserved the question of the position of corporations with foreign parents. In the light of this judgement the Government again urged the United Nations Administration to take action to resolve the position. The Chancellor and the Prime Minister wrote letters to Treasury Secretary Regan and President Reagan. The Chancellor and the Prime Minister also raised the matter with Treasury Secretary Regan and the President personally in Washington in September.

The United States administration decided not to file for a rehearing of the Container case. In September the President established a Working Group, composed of representatives of the Federal Government, State governments and the United States business community and chaired by Treasury Secretary Regan to explore its use and 'to produce recommendations that will be conducive to harmonious international relations while respecting the fiscal rights and privileges of the individual states.

The UK Government is not alone in objecting to worldwide combined unitary taxation. The European Community and the governments of other major OECD countries have also submitted testimony for the consideration of the Working Group. In addition a number of international businesses and business organisations have given evidence to the Working Group setting out their objections to unitary tax on a worldwide reporting basis.

There the matter rests for the time being.

UNIVERSITY EDUCATION, COSTS OF SEE *Education, Cost of*

UNLIMITED COMPANY SEE *Company, Unlimited*

UNLISTED SECURITIES MARKET (USM) The Unlisted Securities Market provides the means by which smaller companies can widen their shareholding base and achieve a market in their shares without the formality and cost of a full stock exchange listing. Prior to November, 1980, this was possible to a degree under Rule 163(2) of the Stock Exchange, which enabled stockbrokers, with the permission of the Council, to carry out transactions in shares notwithstanding that they were not listed in the market.

The Unlisted Securities Market in its new form was introduced by the Stock Exchange on 10th November, 1980. In general terms, the following rules apply for a company to be admitted to the USM:

1. A minimum 10 per cent of the company's capital must be in public hands.
2. The company will normally have been trading for at least three years, for which audited accounts will be available.
3. The company must be able to produce a table for financial statistics in a prescribed form, covering a five-year period, or such lesser period for which the company has been trading.
4. In the ordinary way, at least two firms of jobbers will be expected to register as dealers in the shares of the particular company, but if no two jobbers wish to do this, the sponsoring stockbroker may apply to the Council to be registered in that particular security and to provide a matching market.
5. A list of all companies traded in the Unlisted Securities Market and a record of business in their shares is included in the *Stock Exchange Daily Official List*.

There is a number of other regulations concerning dealings in shares in the Unlisted Securities Market, but on the whole the aim is to provide a market for the shares of smaller companies under the umbrella of the Stock Exchange without the onerous obligations of a full listing. At the end of 1984 there were 268 companies trading on the Unlisted Securities Market with a total market value of £2,863 million. Since the Unlisted Securities Market was introduced a total of 42 USM companies had moved to a full listing.

UPPER EARNINGS LIMIT National Insurance contributions are paid on a band of earnings between what is known as the lower earnings limit (q.v.) and the upper earnings limit. If a person earns less than the lower earnings limit, no contributions are payable. If a person earns more than the upper earnings limit, no contributions are payable on the excess above that figure. The weekly earnings limits are published from time to time and are currently:

lower earnings limit £35.50
upper earnings limit £265.00

V

VALUABLE CONSIDERATION See *Consideration*

VALUE ADDED TAX (VAT) VAT was introduced in the UK in the Finance Act 1972, and came into operation on 1st April, 1973. The law on the subject is included in the 1972 Act and subsequent Finance Acts and in various Orders in Council and Regulations made under the Act.

In essence, VAT is a tax on the supply of goods and services in the UK (including Northern Ireland) and the Isle of Man and on the import of goods into the UK and the Isle of Man. It is a tax which is borne ultimately by the consumer. This is because a taxable person (see below), and there may be many in the chain of production of goods and services, may set off tax paid, e.g. on the supply of goods, against tax charged by him on his supplies to other persons.

For VAT to apply there must be a 'taxable supply' by a 'taxable person'. A taxable person is anyone who, in the course of business, makes or intends to make a taxable supply of goods or services while he is, or is required to be, registered under the provisions of the Acts. Whether or not a person is required to be registered will depend on the level of his business turnover, i.e. the total value of his taxable supplies. The threshold for registration for VAT purposes has been increased from time to time. From 20 March 1985, a person is required to be registered if at the end of any quarter, the value of his taxable supplies in that quarter has exceeded £6,500 or, in the four quarters then ending, has exceeded £19,500.

Prima facie all goods and services supplied by a taxable person in the course of business are subject to VAT but there is a large number of statutory exemptions. 'Business' includes any trade, profession or vocation; the provision of broadcasting services by the Independent Broadcasting Authority; the admission for a consideration of persons to any premises; the provision by a club or an association of facilities available to its members and the provision by certain organizations of the advantages of membership.

Under the provisions of the 1972 Act, as amended, the supply of certain goods and services is *exempt* from VAT and in other cases, the supply is *zero-rated*.

Exempt supplies are categorized under the following headings: land; insurance; postal services; betting, gaming and lotteries; finance; education; health; and burial and cremation. These are broad categories for reference purposes only and it would be beyond the scope of this work to deal with each category in turn. For example, however, the sale of land is exempt but the provision of accommodation on land, e.g. in a hotel or caravan, is not exempt. Under the heading of finance, the advancing of money or the operating of a banking account are exempt but not the management of securities. Under the heading of insurance, the provision of any insurance is exempt, as is the making of arrangements for insurance, including for example, the payment of commission.

In the financial field, the following are examples of supplies which are *not* exempt: portfolio management, financial advice, executor and trustee services, administration of estates, management of trust funds, consultancy services, nominee services, debt collection and sales ledger accounting services, e.g. factoring, company registration services, safe custody, equipment leasing, and underwriting.

Under Schedule 4 of the 1972 Act (as amended) certain categories of supplies are zero-rated. In such cases, no VAT is charged but the supply is treated in all other respects as a taxable supply. For example, a registered person will be able to recover input tax (see below) paid by him. There are 17 zero-rated categories under the Act, namely: food; water; books; talking books for the blind and handicapped and wireless sets for the blind; newspaper advertisements; news services; fuel and power; construction of buildings; services to overseas traders or for overseas purposes; transport; caravans and house-boats; gold; banknotes; drugs, medicines, medical and surgical appliances on prescription; imports and exports; charities; and clothing and footwear.

Under the heading of food, the supply of any food for human consumption and the supply of animal feeding stuffs are zero-rated, but not so food supplied in the course of catering.

Under the heading of construction of buildings, the supply of any building or civil engineering work in the course of the construction, alteration or demolition of a building was zero-rated, but not so work of repair or maintenance, a distinction which led to difficulties of interpretation.

From 1st June, 1984, however, zero rating only applies to the construction of new buildings and new civil engineering works or to the demolition of a complete building. Alterations no longer qualify for zero rating and, accordingly, all work that is done on existing buildings is now subject to VAT at the standard rate. The construction of most garden buildings, such as detached garages, greenhouses and sheds, are now standard rated, but the supply of a reconstructed building is exempt. It is understood that the Commissioners of Customs and Excise take the view that constructing a building on an existing foundation of a former building which has been demolished, or by making use of a single remaining wall, such as the facade of a former building, would involve the construction of a building and be zero-rated. On the other hand, where the outer walls of an existing building are used, even without floors or a roof, any building operations in or around that shell would involve reconstruction and constitute standard-rated work.

The fact that an organization is charitable does not alter the liability to be registered for VAT purposes. If therefore, a charity has taxable outputs of goods and services, such as the sale of Christmas cards, it is required to register as a taxable person (unless the value of supplies is below the registration limit). Supplies by charities of the following are, however, zero-rated:

1. The supply by a charity established primarily for the relief of distress in relation to any goods which have been donated for sale;
2. The export of any goods by a charity.
3. The supply for donation to a designated hospital or research institution of medical or scientific equipment, solely for use in medical research, diagnosis or treatment, where the equipment is purchased with funds provided by a charity or from voluntary contributions.

The rate of VAT is determined by Parliament from time to time, and is currently 15 per cent on all taxable items. When the tax was introduced in April, 1973, the standard rate of VAT was 10 per cent. This was reduced to 8 per cent from 29th July, 1974 and increased to 15 per cent in the Finance Act 1979. In November, 1974 a higher rate of 25 per cent came into operation in relation to petrol (but not derv) and in May, 1975 was extended to cover goods and services specified in the Higher Rate Schedule (domestic electrical appliances, radios, tvs, pleasure boats, and aircraft, photographic equipment, furs and jewellery). This rate was reduced to $12\frac{1}{2}$ per cent in April, 1976 and discontinued in June 1979.

For the purpose of VAT, the word 'output' means the supply of goods and services by a registered person in the course of business. 'Output tax' is the tax chargeable on those supplies by a taxable person.

The term 'input' refers to the goods and services received by a taxable person for the purpose of a business and 'input tax' is the VAT on those inputs.

At the end of each prescribed accounting period, if the output tax charged by a taxable person exceeds the input tax paid by him, he must account for the difference to the Commissioners of Customs and Excise. If the input tax paid by him exceeds the amount of output tax charged by him on the supply of goods and services, the amount of the excess must be paid to the taxable person by the Commissioners.

If a taxable person supplies goods or services, part of which are taxable and part exempt (see above), any recovery of input tax will be limited to those inputs which are attributable to the taxable supplies, which in most cases, will mean an apportionment of the input tax in relation to the taxable and exempt outputs.

At the time of writing, the UK regulations on allowable input tax are more generous than those of the EEC. For example, although VAT on motor vehicles is not allowed, i.e. is not recoverable against VAT on outputs, normal business expenses and entertainment costs of overseas customers are allowed. If the Directive of the EEC on this subject is adopted, the UK will have to come in line with other member states, which would mean that a high proportion of VAT on business expenses would not be recoverable.

For the purpose of VAT registration, two or more corporate bodies in the UK or the Isle of Man may be treated as a group, provided (1) one of them controls the other or others, or (2) one person or body controls all of them, or (3) two or more individuals carrying on a business in partnership, control all of them. When a group is so registered, one of the group is treated as the representative member. Thereafter, any supplies by any member of the group is treated as being made by that representative member and any supply of goods or services by one member of the group to another member of the group is disregarded for VAT purposes.

Partnerships are registered for VAT purposes in

the name of the firm, disregarding any subsequent changes in the constitution of the partnership.

VALUE RECEIVED The last words in the body of a bill were very frequently 'value received', but they are not necessary to the validity of an English bill, as it is always implied in a bill of exchange that value has been received. It is otherwise in France. By Section 30 of the Bills of Exchange Act 1882, 'Every party whose signature appears on a bill is prima facie deemed to have become a party thereto for value'.

VARIABLE RATE STOCKS These were first introduced in the gilt-edged market in 1977. The essential feature of a variable rate stock was that the rate of interest varied according to the general level of interest rates ruling in the market from time to time. Each half-yearly interest payment on a variable rate stock was equivalent to one-half of the daily average of Treasury Bill rate over the period from which the stock last went ex dividend (q.v.), up to the current ex dividend rate, plus a fixed margin of one-half per cent. The rate for each interest payment was announced by the Bank of England on the business day immediately preceding the relative ex dividend rate. There were provisions for the rate to become fixed should there be any change in the arrangements for the issuing of Treasury Bills in a way which might be detrimental to the stockholders. All such variable rate stock has now been redeemed.

VARIATION OF TRUSTS ACT 1958 An Act to enlarge the jurisdiction of the courts when considering any arrangement for varying or revoking trusts or enlarging the powers of trustees of managing or administering any property subject to a trust. Before 1958 the statutory powers available to enable the courts to sanction arrangements dealing with the management or administration of trust property were contained in Section 57 of the Trustee Act 1925 (which applies to personalty settlements) and Section 64 of the Settled Land Act (which is restricted to settlements of land). It was thought, however, that apart from its statutory powers the court also possessed an inherent jurisdiction to sanction on behalf of infants and unascertained and unborn persons compromises which were thought to be for the benefit of such classes of persons and which had the approval of all beneficiaries who were *sui juris*. The House of Lords, however, decided in *Chapman* v *Chapman* [1954] 1 All ER 795, that such inherent jurisdiction existed only in cases when a dispute had arisen and not where the compromise represented a rearrangement of the beneficial interests with the consent of all beneficiaries *sui juris*.

This decision left very few opportunities for the rearrangement of trusts which for one reason or another no longer represented the best interest of all the beneficiaries, and accordingly the Law Reform Committee considered the whole question of the powers of the courts to sanction the variation of trusts. The result was the passing of the 1958 Act, which is intended to supplement the jurisdiction of the courts and leaves untouched the existing statutory powers. It is to be noted that the courts are given no powers to vary trusts, but only to sanction proposed variations on behalf of certain specified classes of beneficiaries, namely, in cases where such beneficiaries cannot give their consent owing to infancy or some other incapacity, or where at the time of the application members of a class of beneficiary not then ascertained would be entitled, or where the interests of some person not yet in existence are concerned, or where there is a beneficiary whose consent cannot be given because his interest is subject to protective or discretionary trusts.

Any such arrangement proposed must have the approval of all beneficiaries *sui juris*, and there is no power to vary or revoke trusts against the wishes of such beneficiaries.

The scope of the Act is very wide, and the powers given have been used by the courts in a generous fashion in a wide range of cases where trusts no longer seem to be giving effect to the wishes of the settlor, whether owing to changed circumstances or unforeseen difficulties. However, the passing of the Trustee Investments Act 1961 limited somewhat the extent of the influence of the 1958 Act, notwithstanding that the later Act provided that 'the enlargement of investment power of trustees by this Act shall not lessen any power of a court to confer wider powers of investment on trustees, or affect the extent to which any such power is to be exercised'.

In a number of cases the courts have taken the view that since Parliament has now indicated the extent to which trustees ought to be free to invest otherwise than in gilt-edged investments, special grounds must now be adduced before the limits set by the 1961 Act can be exceeded. SEE *Trustee Investments*

VESTING ASSENT SEE *Personal Representatives; Settled Land*

VESTING DEED A settlement of a legal estate in land is effected by two deeds, a vesting deed and a trust instrument. By the vesting deed the legal estate in the land is conveyed to the tenant for life or statutory owner. SEE *Settled Land*

VISA SEE *Credit Cards*

VOLUNTARY CONVEYANCE A conveyance of property when there is no valuable consideration. A deed of gift is a voluntary conveyance; but a marriage settlement is not, because the marriage is valuable consideration. SEE *Conveyance; Estate Duty; Gifts Inter Vivos; Settlements, Settlor Bankrupt*

VOLUNTARY LIQUIDATION, VOLUNTARY WINDING UP SEE *Winding Up*

VOLUNTARY SETTLEMENTS SEE *Gifts Inter Vivos; Settlements, Settlor Bankrupt*

VOSTRO ACCOUNT SEE *Nostro account*

VOTES, VOTING It is necessary to examine the articles of association of a company to determine the voting rights of the members. In the case of a company to which Table A applies (SEE *Table A*) the following are the relevant regulations:

62. Subject to any rights or restrictions for the time being attached to any class or classes of shares, on a show of hands every member present in person shall have one vote. On a poll every member shall have one vote for each share of which he is the holder.
63. In the case of joint holders, the vote of the senior who tenders a vote, whether in person or by proxy, shall be accepted to the exclusion of the votes of the other joint holders; and for this purpose seniority shall be determined by the order in which the names stand in the register of members.
64. A member of unsound mind, or in respect of whom an order has been made by any Court having jurisdiction in cases of mental illness, may vote, whether on a show of hands, or on a poll, by his committee, receiver, *curator bonis*, or other person in the nature of a committee, receiver, *curator bonis* appointed by that Court, and any such committee, receiver, *curator bonis*, or other person may, on a poll, vote by proxy.
65. No member shall be entitled to vote at any general meeting unless all calls or other sums presently payable by him in respect of shares in the company have been paid.
67. On a poll votes may be given either personally or by proxy.
68. The instrument appointing a proxy shall be in writing under the hand of the appointer or of his attorney duly authorised in writing, or, if the appointer is a corporation, either under seal or under the hand of an officer or attorney duly authorised. A proxy need not be a member of the company.
69. The instrument appointing a proxy and the power of attorney or other authority, if any, under which it is signed or a notarially certified copy of that power of authority shall be deposited at the registered offices of the company, or at such other place within the United Kingdom as is specified for that purpose in the notice convening the meeting, no less than forty-eight hours before the time for holding the meeting, or adjourned meeting, at which the person named in the instrument proposes to vote, or in the case of a poll, not less than twenty-four hours before the time appointed for the taking of the poll, and in default, the instrument of proxy shall not be treated as valid.

SEE *Company (Companies); Resolutions*

W

WAGES CHEQUES OF A COMPANY Schedule 19, Companies Act 1985, provides that a lender of money to a company for the payment of salaries or wages shall have the same right of priority in a winding-up as the clerk, workman, etc., would have had if he had not been paid. In a winding-up, a clerk or servant, or workman or labourer, is entitled to payment in full of salary or wages for the preceding four months up to a sum not exceeding £800 per employee. Hence any advance by a bank for the express purpose of providing salaries and/or wages of a company can be regarded as a preferential claim up to the above limit in the event of the company's liquidation. It is advisable to charge such cheques, clearly marked and drawn as wages cheques, to a separate account designated 'wages account' and opened under a resolution of the company. The procedure is useful where a banker does not wish to increase the company's advance against the existing security and the company appears to have sufficient free assets to support the preferential claim if winding-up takes place. The practice has been approved by the courts, in particular in the case of *National Provincial Bank* v *Freedman & Rubens* (1934) 4 Legal Decisions affecting Bankers 444, and in *Re Primrose Builders Ltd* [1950] Ch 561, but note the limitation in the case of *Re E. J. Morel (1934) Ltd* [1962] Ch 21, where the existence of a stopped account prevented the bank from setting off three accounts in the most advantageous way. However, in the case of *Re William Hall (Contractors) Ltd* [1967] 2 All ER 1150, where there was a wages account and an overdrawn current account, the bank was allowed to apply the proceeds of its security in reduction of its current account, which was non-preferential, and did not have to deal proportionately with them as the liquidator demanded. In the case of *Re Rampgill Mill Ltd* [1967] Ch 1138, monies standing to the debit of an account used for paying wages through another bank were held to be preferential.

In *Re A.C.W. and A.L. Hughes Ltd* [1966] 1 WLR 1369, it was held that payments to a ganger who independently paid workers was not preferential.

WAREHOUSE-KEEPER'S CERTIFICATE, OR RECEIPT A document issued by a warehouse-keeper stating that certain goods are held in his warehouse at the disposal of the person named. Such a certificate or receipt is not transferable, and the goods are not deliverable upon its production. It is simply an acknowledgment of having received certain goods.

When the owner wishes to obtain the goods, he signs a delivery order (q.v.); or, if desired, he may obtain a warehouse *warrant* stating that the goods are deliverable to the person named therein or to his assigns by indorsement. SEE *Warehouse-Keeper's Warrant*

When warehouse-keeper's receipts are pledged with a bank, the customer should sign the bank's letter of lien. The receipts must be in the bank's name, and when delivery of the goods is required the bank will sign a delivery or transfer order. Normally, such a pledge of a warehouse-keeper's receipt is not a good security without acknowledgment from the warehouse of the right of the bank to call for possession.

A banker should be careful to see that a warehouse-keeper's receipt states that the goods mentioned in the receipt are subject to rent only in respect of those goods, otherwise he may find that they are subject, in addition to that rent, to a general lien for rent and charges due in respect of other goods from the party to whom the receipt was originally issued.

In the event of the customer's bankruptcy, unless the goods have been registered in the banker's name, the property will vest in the trustee in bankruptcy.

Although a receipt or certificate is usually regarded as a mere acknowledgment of the goods, the term 'warehouse-keeper's certificate' is sometimes used (see Factors Act 1889, Section 1(4)) to indicate a document which is evidence of the title of the person named therein or his assigns to the goods.

WAREHOUSE-KEEPER'S WARRANT, WAREHOUSE WARRANT A document issued by the keeper of a warehouse stating that the goods named therein are entered in the books and are deliverable to the person mentioned or to his assigns by indorsement.

The warrant must be presented at the office, regularly assigned by indorsement, and all charges paid, before delivery of the goods can take place.

The expression 'warehouse-keeper's certificate' in the Factors Act 1889 (q.v.) refers to such a document as is here described as a warrant.

The remarks made regarding a dock warrant apply equally to a warehouse-keeper's warrant.

WARRANTS (STOCK) A stock warrant is a certificate issued by a company giving the warrant-holder the right to subscribe for shares in that company at a pre-determined price on various dates in the future. Generally, share warrants have been attached to issues of loan stock and, to that extent, are similar to convertible securities (q.v.). Such warrants have, however, acquired an existence of their own and are dealt in and quoted in the market. The price paid for a warrant will reflect (1) the current price of the ordinary shares into which the warrant is convertible, (2) the future prospects of the company, (3) other factors affecting the future level of the share price, and (4) the unexpired time within which the option must be exercised.

Warrants can be attractive to high-rate tax-payers because they provide the prospect of capital gain and do not pay any income. Also, because of the 'gearing' effect of a warrant, a small percentage increase in the ordinary share price can result in a large percentage increase in the price paid for the warrant.

WASTING ASSETS Assets, such as mines or quarries, which become used up in course of time by working them. A mine, for example, which is being steadily worked will become less valuable year by year as the mineral is extracted. To meet this depreciation in the value of the property, a certain sum should be provided out of each year's profits. Although it is a prudent and usual course for a company to adopt, there is, however, no obligation upon the company to provide such a fund. In *Verner* v *General and Commercial Investment Trust* [1894] 2 Ch 239, the Court of Appeal held

> that there is no law to prevent a company from sinking its capital in the purchase of a property producing income, and dividing that income without making provision for keeping up the value of the capital, and that fixed capital may be sunk and lost and yet the excess of current receipts over current expenses may be applied in payment of a dividend, though where the income of a company arises from the turning over of circulating capital, no dividend can be paid unless the circulating capital is kept up to its original value, as otherwise there would be a payment out of capital.

Plant and machinery wear out and become obsolete. A liberal depreciation should therefore be written off each year and a reserve fund be established for the purpose of replacing such assets when necessary.

A patent worked by a company is a wasting asset, and as it can only, as a rule, be kept alive by payment of certain fees for 14 years; that period is called the life of the patent. SEE *Depreciation*

WEATHER INSURANCE It is possible to insure against the effect of bad weather on outdoor events, such as agricultural shows, sports days and gymkhanas, son et lumière events, barbecues, street processions, etc. Similarly, insurance can be taken out against the impact of bad weather on major sporting events, e.g. a cricketers' benefit match. In all cases, the essence of the indemnity is that the bad weather has occasioned financial loss. One type of policy, the 'abandonment' policy, is designed to provide reimbursement of expenses incurred in arranging an event that has to be abandoned through wet weather. If it is not a money-raising event, the insurance cover will normally be limited to 80 per cent of the expenses incurred. An alternative type of policy is the 'agreed value' policy which may be taken out to cover not only the net expenses incurred, but the anticipated receipts, excluding any receipts which are not dependent on the weather. Premiums will be quoted in each case, depending on the amount of cover required, the geographical locality, the type of event and the duration of the event.

WHOLE LIFE ASSURANCE SEE *Life Assurance*

WIDER RANGE SEE Trustee Investments Act under *Trustee Investments*

WIDOWED MOTHER'S ALLOWANCE This is payable on termination of the widow's allowance (q.v.) in cases where

1. the widow has a child living with her under the age of 19 for whom she receives child benefit,
2. the child is that of the widow and her late husband, or a child for whom the widow is entitled to child benefit provided, in this last case, that she and her husband were residing together at the time of his death.

Widowed mother's allowance is also payable to a widow who is expecting her late husband's baby at the time of his death. The allowance depends on the contribution record of her husband. SEE *Widow's Pension* and Appendix 2

WIDOW'S ALLOWANCE The allowance

payable to a widow for the first 26 weeks after her husband's death, provided

1. the widow was under the age of 60 when her husband died, *or*
2. the husband was not in receipt of a state retirement pension at the time of death.

For the allowance to be payable, the husband must have paid at least 25 Class 1, Class 2 or Class 3 contributions before 6th April, 1975 (and before age 65) or must have paid contributions in any one tax year since April 1975 on earnings of at least 25 times the lower earnings limit for the year in question. SEE Appendix 2

WIDOW'S BEREAVEMENT ALLOWANCE An allowance first introduced in 1980 to provide assistance to widows in the period following the death of their husbands. With effect from April 1983, the relief was extended to the second year following the husband's death and made available to those widows who were bereaved since 5th April, 1982. This is, in effect, an additional personal allowance for income tax purposes, and the amount is the difference between the single person's and the married person's allowance. SEE *Income Tax* and Appendix 1

WIDOW'S PENSION Widow's pension is payable to widows who were aged 40 or over when the husband died. If, however, the widow is in receipt of widowed mother's allowance (q.v.), widow's pension will not be payable until the widowed mother's allowance ceases.

Both widow's pension and widowed mother's allowance depend on the contribution record of the husband. The conditions to be met are similar to those which apply to a basic retirement pension. The level of allowance or pension payable to the widow will depend not only on the contribution record, but on the number of qualifying years in which the husband paid, or was credited with, contributions. The required number of qualifying years will vary according to the working life of the husband as given in the table below.

Length of working life	Number of qualifying years needed
10 years or less	Working life, minus 1
11–20 years	Working life, minus 2
21–30 years	Working life, minus 3
31–40 years	Working life, minus 4
41 years or more	Working life, minus 5

Unemployment benefit, sickness and invalidity benefits, and maternity allowances cannot normally be paid in addition to widow's benefit. A widow may retain her entitlement to widow's benefit until the age of 65, but cannot be paid a basic retirement pension at the same time. SEE Appendix 2

WILL A written declaration by which an owner of property states what is to be done with it after his death. The person making a will is called the testator or, if female, the testatrix. A minor cannot make a valid will.

A testator's signature should be witnessed by two persons. The following is a common attestation clause (but see below):

> Signed by the said . . . the testator in the presence of us, both present at the same time, who in his presence and at his request and in the presence of each other have hereunto set our names as witnesses.

The Administration of Justice Act 1982 introduced a number of changes in the law relating to the execution of wills. Under Section 17 of that Act, it is no longer necessary to comply with the old requirements of the Wills Act 1837, regarding the positioning of a signature to the will. It is sufficient that it appears from the face of the will that the testator intended by his signature to validate the will. Also, under the 1982 Act, it is no longer necessary for the witnesses to a will to sign or acknowledge their own signatures in the presence of each other, provided they each attest and sign the will or acknowledge their respective signatures in the presence of the testator. Under the 1982 Act, these provisions came into effect in relation to the wills of testators who died on or after 1st April, 1983.

A will is revoked by the marriage of the testator. From 1st January, 1926, by the Law of Property Act 1925, a will expressed to be made in contemplation of a marriage shall not be revoked by the marriage (Section 177). Here again, the law has been amended as regards wills made after 1st January, 1983. Under the 1982 Act, where a gift in a will is expressed to be in contemplation of a particular marriage, there is a rebuttable presumption under the Act that other gifts in the will are to take effect.

Another provision of the Administration of Justice Act 1982 (Section 18) is that where a marriage has been terminated, i.e. annulled or dissolved, the appointment of the former spouse as executor or executrix and any gift to the former spouse by the will, automatically lapses. This is, however, subject to any contrary intention appearing from the will.

A codicil is an addition to a will by which some change in the terms of the will is effected, and it must be dated and signed by the testator and attested by two witnesses in the same way as the former part of the document.

The testator and each witness must sign his name or initials against any alteration or interlineation that may be made in a will; but no alteration must be made after execution. The alterations should also be referred to in the attestation clause.

The persons who are appointed by the testator to carry out the provisions of his will are called the executors, and it is their duty to obtain probate (q.v.) of the will; that is, an official copy of the will issued by the registrar of the registry where the will is proved. If any trusts are created by the will, the persons whom the testator names to carry out the provisions of such trusts are called the trustees. A copy of a will may be seen, on payment of a fee, at the registry where it was proved; and a copy of any will may be seen or obtained at Somerset House on payment of a fee. No search fee is payable if the will was proved within the previous three years.

A professionally drawn will will be strictly construed by the courts, but in the case of a 'home-made' will a degree of latitude may be given in trying to arrive at the true intention of the testator. Thus, in *Perrin* v *Morgan* [1943] 1 All ER 187, the word 'money' sufficed to pass all the personal estate.

The Administration of Justice Act 1982 introducod the right to apply to the court for the rectification of a will on the grounds that it is expressed in terms which fail to carry out the testator's intentions. This must arise howovor, from one of two causes, namely, (1) there is a clerical error or (2) a failure to understand correctly the testator's instructions. An action for rectification must be brought within six months of the date of the Grant of Representation.

The Act, in Section 21, also permits the admission of evidence to assist in the interpretation of wills in the following three circumstances:

1. where any part of a will is meaningless;
2. where the language of the will is ambiguous on the face of it; and
3. where evidence (other than evidence of the testator's intention) shows that the language of the will is ambiguous in the light of surrounding circumstances. SEE Supplement

Other provisions of the Act which, at the time of writing, have not come into effect (because they do not take effect until a date to be appointed) are (1) provision for the registration of wills at the principal registry, (2) regulations regarding the deposit of wills, (3) regulations bringing into force in the UK, the Convention on International Wills under the Washington Convention of 1973, which provides for an internationally recognized form of will.

WILSON COMMITTEE The full name is the Committee to Review the Functioning of Financial Institutions; the chairman was the Rt Hon Sir Harold Wilson, KG, OBE, FRS, MP. It was published as Cmnd 7937.

This Committee, usually known as the Wilson Committee, was appointed on 5th January, 1977 and issued its report on 22nd May, 1980. The Committee's terms of reference were

1. to enquire into the role and functioning, at home and abroad, of financial institutions in the UK and their value to the economy;
2. to review in particular the provision of funds for industry and trade;
3. to consider what changes are required in the existing arrangements for the supervision of these institutions, including the possible extension of the public sector, and to make recommendations.

The role of the Committee was similar in many ways to that of the Macmillan Committee on Finance and Industry in 1931 and the Radcliffe Committee on the Working of the Monetary System in 1959. If anything, however, the Wilson Committee's sphere of enquiry was even wider than those of the earlier committees, not least because of the development and growth in the intervening years of the financial sector. The Committee received evidence, either written or oral, from approximately 375 institutions, trade or professional associations, companies, other representative bodies and private individuals. The Report runs to approximately 600 pages and covers virtually every aspect of the corporate financial life of the UK. The Committee pursued their enquiries in two stages: first, the provision of funds to industry and trade, and second, the functioning of financial institutions, the arrangement for their supervision and the question of public ownership. In addition to its main Report, the Committee published interim reports on the financing of industry and trade, the financing of small firms and some of the principal evidence on financial institutions. The complete evidence, whether published or not, has been placed with the Public Records Office where it is available for study. The voluminous evidence and the far-ranging report constitute an essential starting point for anyone embarking on a study of financial institutions in the UK.

The principal recommendations of the Wilson Committee have, for the most part, been referred to under their respective headings elsewhere in this work. It is impossible to do justice to such a comprehensive Report in the space available here but the principal comments and recommendations may be summarized as follows.

The capital markets Savings and investment has become increasingly institutionalized and the Committee considered that the effects of institutional behaviour on the markets should be the subject of further research. In particular, the Committee observed that there was no comprehensive framework for securing the accountability of pension funds.

The availability of finance The Committee found that in general it was the price of finance in relation to expected profitability which was the major financial constraint on real investment. A majority of the Committee considered that there was sufficient scope through the use of existing institutional arrangements to deal with foreseeable difficulties in the financial system. A minority viewpoint was that there was a need for a new public sector investment bank, very much on the lines proposed by the Trades Union Congress.

Inflation and indexation The Committee recommended experimentation with the use of index-linked industrial bonds and possible indexation of Government securities and the housing market.

Finance for small firms The Committee suggested the setting up of a loan guarantee scheme and the creation of an English Development Agency. It also proposed a new form of investment trust for investment in small firms with tax relief for the investors. Further recommendations were made on the market in unlisted securities.

Building societies The Committee considered that, for the time being, the building society movement should continue to be excluded from the established system of monetary control. The Committee recommended the abolition of the system of recommended rates operated by the Building Societies Association and looked for an increase in competition among building societies.

Regulation of financial institutions The Committee considered that the present system was not wholly satisfactory, particularly because of the extent to which non-statutory regulation takes the form of self-regulation. The Committee therefore recommended the appointment of outside members to the Council of the Stock Exchange and the strengthening of the Council for the Securities Industry by the appointment of outside representatives and by making its authority over the Stock Exchange more explicit. The Committee further recommended that the Joint Review Body which has the oversight of the securities markets should be replaced by a wider ranging body, composed of outside members as well as civil servants, with responsibility for reviewing the overall arrangement for the regulation of the financial system.

The Bank of England The Committee recommended that the non-executive directors of the Bank of England should be drawn from a wider range of backgrounds.

Public ownership in the financial sector The Committee advised against any extension of the public sector by the nationalization of existing institutions.

SEE ALSO *Banking Act 1979; Building Societies; Business Expansion Scheme; Council for the Securities Industry; Gower Report; Index-Linked Securities; Pensions; Pension Schemes; Small Firms Loan Guarantee Scheme; Stock Exchange; Take-overs and Mergers; Trustee Savings Bank; Unlisted Securities Market*

WINDING UP There are three types of winding up: compulsory, voluntary, and voluntary under the supervision of the court.

Compulsory Winding Up

Under Section 517 of the Companies Act 1985, a company may be wound up by the court if

1. the company has by special resolution resolved that the company be wound up by the court;
2. default is made in delivering the statutory report to the Registrar or in holding the statutory meeting;
3. the company does not commence its business within a year from its incorporation or suspends its business for a whole year;
4. the number of members is reduced in the case of a private company below two or in the case of any other company below seven;
5. the company is unable to pay it debts;
6. the court is of the opinion that it is just and equitable that the company shall be wound up.

As to 5, a company is deemed to be unable to pay its debts if a creditor for a sum exceeding £50 has served a demand for payment on the company and has had no satisfaction at the end of three weeks. Also if execution or other process issued on a judgment is returned unsatisfied in whole or in part, and also if it is proved to the satisfaction of the court that the company is unable to pay its debts (Section 518).

An application to the court for winding up is made by petition presented by the company or by any creditor or contributory. Where a company is being wound up voluntarily or subject to supervision, a winding up petition may be presented by the official receiver.

The effect of a winding up order is to make the

official receiver provisional liquidator until such time as the court appoints a liquidator. Where a liquidator is not so appointed, the official receiver continues as liquidator of the company. A statement of affairs must be submitted to the official receiver within 14 days.

On the making of a winding up order, separate meetings of creditors and contributories are held to determine if application shall be made to the court for the appointment of a liquidator in place of the official receiver and also to determine if a committee of inspection shall be appointed to act with the liquidator and if so, to elect members thereof.

The powers of a liquidator in a compulsory winding up are given in the Companies Act 1985, as follows:

539.—(1) The liquidator in a winding up by the court has power, with the sanction either of the court or of the committee of inspection—

(*a*) to bring or defend any action or other legal proceeding in the name and on behalf of the company,

(*b*) to carry on the business of the company so far as may be necessary for its beneficial winding up,

(*c*) to appoint a solicitor to assist him in the performance of his duties,

(*d*) to pay any class of creditors in full,

(*e*) to make any compromise or arrangement with creditors or persons claiming to be creditors, or having or alleging themselves to have any claim (present or future, certain or contingent, ascertained or sounding only in damages) against the company, or whereby the company may be rendered liable,

(*f*) to compromise all calls and liabilities to calls, debts and liabilities capable of resulting in debts, and all claims (present or future, certain or contingent, ascertained or sounding only in damages) subsisting or supposed to subsist between the company and a contributory or alleged contributory or other debtor or person apprehending liability to the company, and all questions in any way relating to or affecting the assets or the winding up of the company, on such terms as may be agreed, and take any security for the discharge of any such call, debt, liability or claim and give a complete discharge in respect of it.

(2) The liquidator in a winding up by the court has the power—

(*a*) to sell any of the company's property by public auction or private contract, with power to transfer the whole thereof to any person or to sell the same in parcels,

(*b*) to do all acts and to execute, in the name and on behalf of the company, all deeds, receipts and other documents and for that purpose to use, when necessary, the company's seal,

(*c*) to prove, rank and claim in the bankruptcy, insolvency or sequestration of any contributory for any balance against his estate, and to receive dividends in the bankruptcy, insolvency or sequestration in respect of that balance, as a separate debt due from the bankrupt or insolvent, and rateably with the other separate creditors,

(*d*) to draw, accept, make and indorse any bill of exchange or promissory note in the name and on behalf of the company, with the same effect with respect to the company's liability as if the bill or note had been drawn, accepted, made or indorsed by or on behalf of the company in the course of its business,

(*e*) to raise on the security of the assets of the company any money requisite,

(*f*) to take out in his official name letters of administration to any deceased contributory, and to do in his official name any other act necessary for obtaining payment of any money due from a contributory or his estate which cannot conveniently be done in the name of the company (and in all such cases the money due is deemed, for the purpose of enabling the liquidator to take out the letters of administration or recover the money, to be due to the liquidator himself),

(*g*) to appoint an agent to do any business which the liquidator is unable to do himself,

(*h*) to do all such other things as may be necessary for winding up the company's affairs and distributing its assets.

Payments by liquidator into bank

542.—(1) The following applies to a liquidator of a company which is being wound up by the court in England and Wales.

(2) Subject to the next subsection, the liquidator shall, in such manner and at such times as the Secretary of State (with the concurrence of the Treasury) directs, pay the money received by him to the Insolvency Services Account at the Bank of England; and the Secretary of State shall furnish him with a certificate of receipt of the money so paid.

(3) However, if the committee of inspection satisfies the Secretary of State that for the purpose of carrying on the company's business or of obtaining advances, or for any other reason, it is for the advantage of the creditors or contributories that the liquidator should have an account at any other bank, the Secretary of State shall, on the application of the committee of inspection, authorise the liquidator to make his payments into and out of such other bank as the committee may select, and thereupon those payments shall be made in the prescribed manner.

(4) If the liquidator at any time retains for more than 10 days a sum exceeding £100 or such other amount as the Secretary of State in any particular case authorises him to retain, then unless he explains the retention to the Secretary of State's satisfaction, he shall pay interest on the amount so retained in excess at the rate of 20 per cent per annum, and is liable to disallowance of all or such part of his remuneration as the Secretary of State thinks

just, and to be removed from his office by the Secretary of State, and is liable to pay any expenses occasioned by reason of his default.

(5) The liquidator shall not pay any sums received by him as liquidator into his private banking account.

(6) The money sum for the time being specified in subsection (4) is subject to increase or reduction by regulations under section 664.

By section 536

(4) If more than one liquidator is appointed by the Court, the Court shall declare whether any act required or authorised by this Act to be done by the liquidator is to be done by all or any one or more of the persons appointed.

Where a special account is opened, all payments out are to be made by cheque payable to order, bearing on its face the name of the company, to be signed by one member of the committee of inspection and by such other person, if any, as the committee may appoint. If there is no committee of inspection, the official receiver may, subject to the directions of the Department of Trade and Industry, exercise the functions of a committee with regard to a special bank account. See further under *Liquidator*.

Compulsory winding up commences from the date of the presentation of the petition unless a voluntary winding up was previously in progress, in which case the winding up dates from the passing of the resolution to wind up.

Cheques drawn after the presentation of the petition and before the making of the Order in favour of the company may be paid in cash. This is because Section 522 of the Companies Act 1985 provides that in a winding up by the court, any disposition of the property of the company made after the commencement of the winding up shall be void, unless the court otherwise orders. A payment in cash to the company's agent cannot be a 'disposition' by the bank, but any payment to a third party may prove to be within that category. Sometimes, especially where a petition is presented by a contributory (i.e. a shareholder) arising out of a dispute, the company being clearly solvent, a good indemnity from a third party who is undoubted for the amounts involved may be the solution.

Whether a bank might allow the continuation of an account between the presentation of a petition and the making of the Order, in reliance on the expectation that the court would allow, under Section 522, transactions in the ordinary course of business, has been the subject of considerable debate, and of differences in banking practice, and there have been a number of judicial decisions which have seemed to justify the expectation. However, in *Re Grays Inn Construction Co Ltd* [1980] 1 All ER 814, the Court of Appeal took a harder line than had been expected and set out general principles which are likely to restrict the number of cases in which the banks anticipate the courts' decision.

Buckley, LJ, said that the court's discretion should be exercised within the context of the liquidation provisions of the Companies Act 1948, so that the assets should be distributed rateably among the unsecured creditors. The trial judge had spoken of the dilemma of banks in this situation: but a bank can seek a validation order from the court, and if this is not done the bank is at risk of later refusal of validation. On the facts before him the trial judge had held that credits were not 'dispositions' within Section 227, and he validated the payments out: the decision to allow banking facilities had been made by a prudent bank manager, who had enforced proper safeguards. But the Court of Appeal found differently: credits as well as debits were dispositions, and the bank was liable to restore to the company the amount lost in post liquidation trading. Had the bank sought a prospected validation order the court might have authorized continued trading subject to precautions to ensure that the company was not supported in unprofitable trading, unless this was for the benefit of creditors. Having taken the risk of going on without such an order, they must make good the loss.

Voluntary Winding Up

By Section 572(1), a company may be wound up voluntarily

(*a*) When the period, if any, fixed for the duration of the company by the articles expires, or the event (if any) occurs, on the occurence of which the articles provide that the company is to be dissolved and the company in general meeting has passed a resolution requiring the company to be wound up voluntarily.

(*b*) If the company resolves by special resolution that the company be wound up voluntarily.

(*c*) If the company resolves by extraordinary resolution to the effect that it cannot by reason of its liabilities continue its business and that it is advisable to wind up.

There are two kinds of voluntary winding up: a creditors' voluntary winding up and a members' voluntary winding up. Both kinds are brought about by resolutions of the company which must be advertized in the *London Gazette* within seven days. Both types of winding up commence from the passing of the resolution, from which date the company must cease to carry on business except for the purpose of winding up. On notice of the passing of a winding-up resolution the account should be stopped.

Creditors' voluntary winding up (Sections 587–605) A meeting of creditors must be summoned for the day or the day following the day when the meeting of the company is to be held at which the resolution to wind up is to be proposed. The meeting of creditors must be advertised in the *London Gazette* and at least two local newspapers. The creditors and the company at their respective meetings may nominate a liquidator; if different persons are nominated, the creditors' nominee shall be liquidator, and if the creditors make no nominations, the company's choice shall be liquidator. The creditors may appoint a committee of inspection to act with the liquidator. On the appointment of a liquidator the powers of the directors cease except so far as the committee of inspection or, if there is no such committee, the creditors, sanction continuance thereof. If a vacancy occurs by death, resignation or otherwise in the office of liquidator, the creditors may fill the vacancy. If more than one liquidator is appointed, the resolution should state how many are to act; failing any such provision not less than two must act.

Members' voluntary winding up (Sections 579–86) This occurs where the directors of a company at a board meeting make a statutory declaration, within the five weeks immediately preceding the date of the passing of the winding-up resolution, to the effect that they have made a full inquiry into the affairs of the company and have formed the opinion that the company will be able to pay its debts in full within 12 months from the commencement of the winding up. The declaration must embody a statement of the company's assets and liabilities as at the latest practicable date before the making of the statutory declaration.

Any director making such a declaration, without having reasonable grounds for believing that the company will be able to pay its debts in full within the specified period, incurs heavy penalties.

If the company is duly wound up, but its debts are not paid or provided for in full within the stated period, it will be presumed until the contrary is shown that the director did not have reasonable grounds for his opinion.

The company in general meeting shall appoint one or more liquidators, and thereupon the powers of the directors cease except in so far as the company in general meeting or the liquidator sanctions the continuance thereof. Vacancies in the office of liquidator may be filled by the company in general meeting, subject to any arrangement with its creditors.

A members' voluntary winding up usually occurs where a reconstruction is to take place or where the company is being dissolved for reasons not connected with its solvency.

Winding Up Subject to Supervision of the Court (Sections 606–10)

Where a company has passed a resolution for voluntary winding up, the court may on petition make an order for the continuance of the voluntary winding up subject to the supervision of the court. For this purpose it may appoint an additional liquidator. The date of commencement of winding up is the date of the resolution to wind up voluntarily.

Proofs and Claims in Winding Up

In every type of winding up the bankruptcy rules apply to the respective rights of secured and unsecured creditors.

In a compulsory winding up proof of debt is required as in bankruptcy, but in a voluntary winding up a formal claim on the liquidator is all that is usually necessary.

For liquidators' accounts and borrowings by liquidators, see under *Liquidator*. SEE ALSO *Committee of Inspection, Company (Companies); Official Receiver*

WITH PROFITS POLICY SEE *Life Assurance*

WITHOUT RECOURSE If the drawer, or an indorser, of a bill adds these words (or the French equivalent 'sans recours' to his signature, he thereby cancels his own liability to any subsequent holder, in the event of non-payment of the bill. But an indorser who has added the words 'without recourse' does not clear himself from liability if any signature prior to his own should prove to be a forgery.

The Bills of Exchange Act 1882 provides that the drawer of a bill, and any indorser, may insert therein an express stipulation (1) negativing or limiting his own liability to the holder, (2) waiving as regards himself some or all of the holder's duties (Section 16). SEE *Drawer; Indorser*

WOODLANDS, INVESTMENT IN All investment in woodlands is essentially an investment in land and in the timber which grows on the land. The world-wide demand for domestic and industrial purposes is considerable and at least one source (Centre for Agricultural Strategy, Reading University) has suggested that by the year 2000 demand for timber will exceed the world supply. Already in the EEC countries, timber production accounts for less than a half of the requirements of the EEC and the proportion is declining. The production of timber is therefore widely encouraged in the EEC by grants and fiscal advantages. In the UK, investment in timber is treated favourably for tax purposes (see below).

Investment in woodlands is essentially long-term. It may be an investment in a new plantation or it may be the purchase of existing woodlands. The maximum benefit from the investment may not in some cases arise for perhaps three generations, but there are many more immediate advantages to be gained:

1. Investment in land has historically kept pace with inflation.
2. There is an increasing world demand for timber.
3. The taxation and other financial advantages are attractive.
4. Well-planned woodlands have environmental advantages.
5. The investment is a tangible one which an investor can inspect physically.
6. The business of investing in woodlands is well developed and expertly managed in the UK.
7. Even small amounts may be invested in joint investment schemes.

Some disadvantages are

1. It is not a suitable investment for current yield.
2. It is not a highly marketable investment, although given reasonable notice an investment in woodlands can usually be disposed of satisfactorily.
3. There are risks of fire and storm (although it would be usual to insure against these).

Investments in woodlands enjoy favourable tax treatment for purposes of income tax, capital gains tax and capital transfer tax. In essence, the owner will be taxed under Schedule B unless he elects to be assessed under Schedule D. Under Schedule B, income tax will be payable annually on a third of the rental value of the unimproved land. No relief will be allowed for expenditure, but no tax will be payable on the proceeds of sale of timber. Under Schedule D, income tax is payable on the profits of the woodlands as a business and any resulting losses may be set off against the taxpayer's other income. This is particularly advantageous in the early years when the costs of setting up and managing a plantation may be considerable. An election by an owner of woodlands to be taxed under Schedule D is irrevocable throughout the remainder of his ownership.

Since 13th March, 1984, it has not been possible for an occupier of woodlands to be assessed under Schedule B if in connection with any trade he may carry on, he has the use of the woodlands wholly or mainly for the purpose of felling, processing or removing timber or clearing or otherwise preparing the lands, or any part of them, for replanting.

No capital gains tax is payable on the disposal of growing timber. Capital gains tax may be payable, however, on the disposal of the land itself, subject to roll-over relief.

Special rules apply for capital transfer tax purposes in relation to woodlands. SEE *Capital Transfer Tax*.

There are certain major factors which affect the performance of an investment in woodlands. These are

1. The growth of trees which, even at constant prices, will normally show a continuing improvement in value.
2. Price increases stemming from increased demand.
3. The increased scarcity value of the land.
4. Increases through inflation in both the value of the land and the timber.
5. The available grants and taxation reliefs.

WORKING CAPITAL The term is used in slightly varying senses. Sometimes it denotes the difference between current assets and current liabilities, but more generally it indicates that part of the capital of a business which turns over, i.e. is put to work in the business, as distinct from capital which may be locked up in fixed assets such as premises and plant and machinery. It has traditionally been the role of the banks to provide, or assist in providing, working capital for businesses, leaving the long-term capital to come from the proprietors. In 1959, the Radcliffe Committee reported

> English bankers have traditionally regarded and continue to regard themselves as properly engaged in financing working capital, particularly of the 'seed-time to harvest' kind, 'bridging transactions' and (within cautious limits) the temporary financing of fixed capital development, pending the raising of long-term finance through other channels.

WORLD BANK SEE *International Bank for Reconstruction and Development*

WRIT OF DISTRINGAS SEE *Distringas*

WRIT OF SEQUESTRATION A process available where the person against whom it is issued is in contempt for disobedience of the court, and it is, therefore, necessary as a preliminary to its issue that the judgment or order should have been served upon such person, or at least that he should have knowledge of it and have intentionally evaded such service. The writ will issue, without leave, on proof of disobedience of the judgment or order sought to be enforced, in two cases, namely (1) when the judgment or order is for the recovery of any property other than land or money; and (2) when it directs payment of money into court or the doing of any other act in a limited time, and such judgment or order has been duly served. The second category includes an order for payment of money to a person in a limited time, as opposed to a judgment for recovery of money, but does not include a purely negative order, such as an injunction to restrain pollution. In the case of *Eikman* v *Midland Bank Ltd* [1973] 1 All ER 609, sequestration was ordered where there had been contempt of court relating to an unpaid fine.

In 1983 a sequestration order was similarly made against a trade union for non-payment of a fine for contempt of court (*Messenger Newspapers Group Ltd* v *National Graphical Association, Times*, 3rd December, 1983). When in that case the sequestrators sought information from the union's auditors regarding the assets of the union, the auditors declined to give the information as they could not obtain the union's authority to do so. In the Court of Appeal, however, it was held that a third party has a duty not knowingly to take any action which obstructs a sequestrator in the course of his complying with a writ of sequestration. The duty arises whether or not the third party holds assets on behalf of the party in contempt and thus it was the duty of the auditors to disclose the information (*Messenger Newspapers Group Ltd* v *National Graphical Association* [1984] 1 All ER 293).

WRITING DOWN ALLOWANCES Writing down allowances are those allowances which are allowed for income tax purposes under the Finance Act 1971 (Section 44) and Finance Act 1976 (Section 39) on the depreciation of capital assets once any first-year capital allowances (q.v.) have been taken up. SEE *Capital Expenditure*.

In July, 1984, the Inland Revenue announced that in respect of chargeable periods ending on or after 1st April, 1985, writing down allowances would be available when the expenditure was incurred, even if the equipment had not yet been brought into use. A provision to this effect was included in the 1985 Finance Act. It was also provided that an amount of capital expenditure is to be taken to be incurred on the date on which the obligation to pay that amount becomes unconditional (whether or not there is a later date on or before which the whole or any part of the amount is required to be paid). If however, the date so determined is more than three months before the date on which payment is actually required to be made, then the later date is taken as the date on which the expenditure is incurred.

It was also announced that, in future, companies would be able to disclaim writing down allowances, i.e. they could delay the full amount of depreciation of an asset in order to increase the 'pool' of unallowed expenditure.

Y

YEARLINGS, YEARLING BONDS These are bonds issued by local authorities, so-called because they are issued for a period of a year or less, which enables the interest to be paid without deduction of income tax (although, of course, the income is taxable in the hands of the investor).

YEARLY TENANCY A tenancy from year to year which, by a six months' prior notice to quit from the landlord or the tenant, terminates at the end of the first year or end of any succeeding year. For example, if the tenancy commenced on 1st July, the six months' notice must be given so that the tenancy may terminate on a 1st July.

YEARS' PURCHASE The value of property is frequently indicated as being equal to the rent for a certain number of years. For example, a house with a rental of £500 at 20 years' purchase equals £10,000. If £10,000 is paid for the house, the investment (with a rental of £500) thus yields 5 per cent. The percentage is ascertained by dividing 100 by the number of years' purchase which is given.

YIELD The dividend income of an investment expressed as a percentage of the current market value. SEE ALSO *Redemption Yield*

YIELD CURVE This is the name given to the graph of interest rates on government stocks, according to the date of redemption. Thus, short-term rates will be high in times of 'dear' money at home and abroad, usually because of measures to control the money supply. Yields on longer dated stocks are more likely to reflect inflation expectations and the long-term view of the economy. The longer the term, the greater the uncertainty and therefore the higher the rate, i.e. the investor will look for a high return on his money. If, however, short-term rates were higher, this would be an indication of a squeeze on liquidity in the domestic economy, leading to recession and probably a check in the rate of inflation. This in turn would tend to bring down yields at the longer end of the market. A yield curve can be produced by plotting on a graph the yields of any stocks with varying redemption rates, not necessarily Government stocks as such.

YORKSHIRE BANK This bank, formerly the Yorkshire Penny Bank, is owned by Barclays, Lloyds, National Westminster and Williams and Glyn's Banks. It has just over 200 branches in England and offers a range of banking services comparable to the main clearing banks.

YORKSHIRE REGISTRY OF DEEDS These were the Registries of the North, West and East Ridings of Yorkshire in which title to land and charges over land in the three Ridings were registered until the registries were phased out under the Law of Property Act 1969, giving place to compulsory registration (under the Land Registration Act 1925) of all land in Yorkshire.

SUPPLEMENT

SUPPLEMENT

(as at June 1985)

ACCESS (p. 5) The number of cardholders is now approximately 7½ million.

AUTOMATED TELLER MACHINE (ATM) (p. 38) At the end of 1984 there were approximately 5,750 ATMs in use among the English and Scottish clearing banks.

BANKER AND CUSTOMER See *Tai Hing Cotton Mill Ltd v Lin Chong Hing Bank Ltd and Others, Times*, 10 July 1985.

BANKERS' BOOKS (EVIDENCE) ACT 1879 (p. 57) In the case of *R. v Nottingham Justices, ex parte Lynn* (1984) 79 Cr. App. Rep. 238, it was held that the power under Section 7 of the Act could only be used if the prosecution could show that the bank accounts would be relevant to the offence in question. Thus, the order made by the magistrate could stand in relation to those accounts. There was no power however to use an order under the Act to investigate the bank accounts of the accused during any other period, even though this might result in the suspicion of other offences having been committed. Thus, the order would be quashed.

BANKING SUPERVISION (p. 62) In November 1984 the Bank of England suggested new regulations governing the raising of capital by British banks in the form of perpetual floating rate note issues. Although in some respects these are similar to equity capital in that they do not have any redemption date, it is the view of the Bank of England that such note issues be treated as equity, for the purpose of capital ratio requirements, and they are convertible into equity capital if the issuing bank runs into financial difficulties. Subject to that requirement, a bank would be permitted to have up to one-half of its capital in the form of perpetual notes.

BARCLAYCARD (p. 65) The number of Barclaycard holders is now approximately 7.4 million.

BOND WASHING (p. 83) The 1985 Finance Bill contains provisions to prevent the practice known as bond washing in relation to most fixed-interest securities. This was the practice of selling securities before they became ex-dividend, thus securing a capital gain instead of chargeable income. The Bill contains provisions for the accrued interest in such cases to be taxed as income in the hands of the transferor. These provisions take effect from 28th February, 1986.

BRITISH INSURANCE ASSOCIATION Now part of the Association of British Insurers.

BUILDING SOCIETIES (p. 89) At the end of 1984 the corresponding figures were:

	£m	%
National Savings	27,870	15.7
Banks and savings banks	58,641	33.1
Building societies	90,365	51.0
Others	422	0.2
	177,298	100.0

In June 1985, the Government announced that it was proposed to give building societies even wider powers than those envisaged in the Green Paper. It was contemplated that a Bill would be introduced in Parliament in November 1985 with the intention that the legislation would come into effect on 1st January 1987. In addition to the changes contemplated in the Green Paper, societies would be allowed to operate full insurance broking activities, not merely those related to housing, and also to offer full estate agency services. The criteria for allowing societies to undertake unsecured lending and land ownership would also be relaxed in that such powers would be related to the total level of a society's commercial assets (not free reserves of £3 million as proposed in the Green Paper).

BUSINESS RETIREMENT RELIEF (p. 95) See *Capital Gains Tax* (below)

CAPITAL ALLOWANCES (p. 98) The 1985 Finance Bill contains detailed provisions to ensure that where expenditure is incurred on machinery or plant which becomes a fixture or fitting, capital allowances may be claimed, e.g. by the lessor of that equipment, notwithstanding that the ownership vests in some other person, e.g. a landlord of the business premises.

SUPPLEMENT

CAPITAL GAINS TAX (p. 102)

Business Retirement Relief

Under the Finance Act, 1985, a person may retire at age 60 and obtain retirement relief or may obtain relief at an earlier age if he or she has to retire on health grounds and can produce medical evidence to the satisfaction of the Inland Revenue. The graduated scale of relief for retirements between ages 60 and 65 no longer applies.

Piecemeal Gifts (p. 103)

The Finance Act 1985 contained provisions to change the basis of valuation in relation to a series of linked disposals. With effect from 19th March 1985, where there is a series of disposals to connected persons within a six year period up to the date of the last disposal, a charge to capital gains tax may arise if the aggregate market value of the assets disposed of exceeds the market value of the individual assets. For example, the latest gift in a series of connected disposals may give the donee (or connected donees) control of a company when added to the previous disposals. There will be a re-valuation of the total assets disposed of in the linked transactions and an additional charge to tax will arise on the amount by which the appropriate proportion of the aggregate market value of the asset disposed of at the time of the latest disposal, exceeds the market value of the individual asset. Any disposal which took place on or before 19th March 1985, will be included in a series of transactions if they took place not more than two years before the first transaction after that date.

Pooled Assets (p. 103)

The Finance Act 1985 re-introduced provisions relating to the pooling of assets for capital gains tax purposes. The following is an extract from the text of an Inland Revenue press release on this subject:

Share pooling

Schedule 16 of the Bill contains provisions to reintroduce a form of share pooling. This is an arrangement for treating a person's holding of shares of the same class as a single asset which grows as further such shares are required and diminishes when part of the holding is disposed of.

Under this arrangement, when part of the shares in the holding is disposed of, the disposal is treated as a disposal of part of an asset and the acquisition cost of those shares for capital gains tax purposes is not their actual cost but a proportionate part of the cost of all the shares in the holding.

Prior to the introduction of the indexation provisions in 1982, this arrangement applied—with certain exceptions—to all shares of the same class. However, the introduction of the indexation provisions in 1982 meant that share pooling was no longer practical for individuals. As the Chancellor announced in his Budget Speech, the proposed changes to the tax now enable a form of pooling of shares to be reintroduced.

In outline, the new provisions treat a holding of shares of the same class at 6 April 1985 (1 April 1985 for companies) as one asset. Any further acquisitions of the shares after that date will form part of this holding. But this holding cannot include shares of the same class which were acquired prior to 6 April 1982 (1 April 1982 for companies). The reason for this is two-fold.

First, it is only for assets acquired prior to 6 April 1982 that a claim for the March 1982 market value to apply can be made. Second, since a March 1982 valuation applies only to determine the amount of the indexation relief, and not the amount of the gain, it is not possible to amalgamate the costs of pre and post 1982 acquisitions.

Thus, the legislation provides that pre 6 April 1982 shares which are held at 6 April 1985 shall also form a separate asset (for companies pre 1 April 1982 shares held at 1 April 1985). And, as now, shares acquired before 6 April 1965 which were excluded from pooling under the old provisions will continue to be treated as separate assets.

When there is a disposal of shares, the Bill provides a first in, first out ordering rule to determine the holding from which they have been made. Generally, the new rules for pooling follow closely those which applied prior to 1982; adaptations are of course necessary to provide the indexation relief. And an additional provision which applies to all assets is that indexation relief is not to be given in the case of certain short term transactions—within a period of ten days—which span the end of a month.

Under the Bill, share pooling is to be introduced for shares and securities acquired on or after 6 April 1982 (1 April 1982 for companies). This is to be called the 'new holding'. Securities within the accrued income provisions, deep discount securities, qualifying corporate bonds and certain securities in offshore funds will however be excluded.

In order to take the indexation allowance into account, an addition will be made to the pool of expenditure associated with the new holding, whenever there is a transaction in the relevant shares. In most cases this will mean an acquisition or disposal, but it may also apply in the case of rights issues etc. This addition will be determined by multiplying the value of the pool immediately before the transaction by the increase in the Retail Prices Index over the period from the date of the last transaction to the present one.

For the purpose of setting up the expenditure associated with shares or securities of the same class which are held on 6 April 1982 (1 April 1985 for companies), the expenditure shall consist of the sum of—

- (a) The acquisition cost of all such shares held at that time which were acquired on or after 6 April 1982 (1 April 1982 for companies) together with any subsequent allowable expenditure, and
- (b) the indexation allowance due under the new provisions (i.e. taking account of the abolition of the 12 month rule etc) assuming that all of

the shares were disposed of immediately before 6 April 1985 (1 April 1985 for companies).

Shares acquired prior to 6 April 1982 (1 April 1982 for companies)

A separate pool of expenditure is to be set up for shares and securities of the same class acquired on or before 5 April 1982 (31 March 1982 for companies) which formed part of an existing holding at that date and which are held when the new provisions take effect (the 1982 holding). This will apply therefore to holdings of shares at the onset of the indexation provisions in 1982 which are still retained.

For this pool of expenditure, taxpayers will be able to make a claim for the allowable cost to be based on the 31 March 1982 market value of the shares. Any disposals from this pool will then be treated in the same way as hitherto except that indexation will now run from March 1982 in all cases and losses wil be indexed.

As at present, shares acquired before 6 April 1965 and previously excluded from pooling will continue to be treated as separate assets.

Identification rules

For those securities which are not within the new pooling rules identification rules will remain substantially unchanged. These are in Sections 88 and 89, Finance Act 1982.

For other shares and securities, disposals will be considered in chronological order, with the earliest disposal being taken first. On each disposal, shares will be identified first with shares acquired before 6 April 1965; then with shares in a 1982 pool; and finally with shares in the new pool. These rules will be modified by the provisions which formerly applied to pooled shares e.g. transactions occurring on the same day, and by the rules in the last paragraph.

Short-term transactions

Where there is an acquisition and disposal of shares or securities within a period of 10 days, the Bill provides that if these shares would otherwise have formed part of the new pool, they shall be matched for the purposes of calculating the indexation allowance.

The Bill goes on to provide that where, under the identification rules, a disposal of shares or securities is matched with shares or securities which were acquired within 10 days of the date of disposal, no indexation relief will be given.

(N.B. The foregoing was superseded by a press release of 10 July 1985 (SEE *Finance Act 1985*).)

Indexation of capital gains (p. 104)
The Finance Act 1985 enacts the changes introduced by the Chancellor of the Exchequer in his Budget speech, viz.:

Indexation (SEE *Capital Gains Tax*) is to apply from the date on which an asset is acquired or from March 1982 if later (hitherto indexation began to run only after a 12 month waiting period).

Indexation is to apply to losses (hitherto the indexation allowance did not apply to an asset on which a loss had been made nor could it turn again into a loss as is now possible).

Where an asset is held on 31 March 1982 the taxpayer may claim to have the indexation allowance based on the asset's market value at that date, rather than on expenditure incurred before that date.

The new provisions apply to disposals of assets on or after 6th April 1985, or in the case of companies, on or after 1st April 1985. SEE ALSO *Pooled Assets* (above)

Gilt-edged stocks and corporate bonds
On and after 2 July 1986 these are exempt from Capital Gains Tax even if sold within 12 months of acquisition.

CHEQUE CARD (p. 128) By the end of 1984 there were 19,800,000 cheque cards issued by the English and Scottish clearing banks (including Barclaycards issued to customers of Barclays Bank).

CLEAR DAYS (p. 132) Section 141(2) of the Companies Act 1948, is re-enacted in Section 378(2) of the Companies Act 1985.

COLLECTING BANKER (p. 140) In the case of *Barclays Bank plc.* v *Bank of England* [1985] 1 All ER 385, Bingham, J, acting as arbitrator, held that the collecting banker's duty to its customer was discharged only when a cheque paid in by the customer is physically delivered to the branch of the paying bank for payment. The collecting banker's responsibility to its customer is not discharged when the bank delivers the cheque to the clearing house, nor when the paying bank takes it away from the clearing house. The arbitrator considered that it is the collecting banker's duty to take all reasonable steps to obtain payment, which means that the cheque must be duly presented at the place of payment specified on the cheque, i.e. the branch of the paying bank on which the cheque is drawn.

COMPANIES ACT 1985 (p. 145) This Act, which came into operation on 1st July 1985, repealed and consolidated the Companies Acts of 1948, 1967, 1976, 1980 and 1981. Throughout the Dictionary, references to the 1985 Act have been given wherever practicable but in cases where this would have required substantial reprinting, the references have been included in this Supplement.

SUPPLEMENT

CONSUMER CREDIT ACT 1974 (p. 156) Most of the provisions of the Consumer Credit Act, 1974, came into force on 19th May 1985 (except Statutory Instrument 1983, No. 1571 below which came into effect, in part, on 1 January 1984). Under the Act, the following Statutory Instruments had been made regulating the procedures in relation to consumer credit and hire purchase agreements.

the Consumer Credit (Agreements to Enter Prospective Agreements) (Exemptions) Regulations 1983, SI 1983, No. 1552;
the Consumer Credit (Agreements) Regulations 1983, SI 1983, No. 1553;
the Consumer Credit (Payments Arising on Death) Regulations 1983, SI 1983, No. 1554;
the Consumer Credit (Credit-Token Agreements) Regulations 1983, SI 1983, No. 1555;
the Consumer Credit (Guarantees and Indemnities) Regulations 1983, SI 1983, No. 1556;
the Consumer Credit (Cancellation Notices and Copies of Documents) Regulations 1983, SI 1983, No. 1557;
the Consumer Credit (Notice of Cancellation Rights) (Exemptions) Regulations 1983, SI 1983, No. 1558;
the Consumer Credit (Repayment of Credit on Cancellation) Regulations 1983, SI 1983, No. 1559;
the Consumer Credit (Linked Transactions) (Exemptions) Regulations 1983, SI 1983, No. 1560;
the Consumer Credit (Enforcement, Default and Termination Notices) Regulations 1983, SI 1983, No. 1561;
the Consumer Credit (Rebate on Early Settlement) Regulations 1983, SI 1983, No. 1562;
the Consumer Credit (Settlement Information) Regulations 1983, SI 1983, No. 1564;
the Consumer Credit (Conduct of Business) (Pawn Records) Regulations 1983, SI 1983, No. 1565;
the Consumer Credit (Pawn-Receipts) Regulations 1983, SI 1983, No. 1566;
the Consumer Credit (Loss of Pawn-Receipt) Regulations 1983, SI 1983, No. 1567;
the Consumer Credit (Realisation of Pawn) Regulations 1983, SI 1983, No. 1568;
the Consumer Credit (Prescribed Periods for Giving Information) Regulations 1983, SI 1983, No. 1569;
the Consumer Credit (Running-Account Credit Information) Regulations 1983, SI 1983, No. 1570;
the Consumer Credit (Increase of Monetary Amounts) Order 1983, SI 1983, No. 1571.

The regulations cover virtually every aspect of consumer credit and at the time of going to press they are having a considerable impact on the procedural aspect of lending by banks, hire purchase companies and other consumer credit institutions. In broad terms, the regulations cover such matters as the contents of documents embodying agreements regulated under the Act, the disclosure of prescribed information, cancellable agreements (e.g. if signed away from the lender's premises), the provision of copies of agreements, the form of guarantees for consumer credit, the manner in which agreements may be terminated and the formula for calculation of any rebate due to the customer.

In June 1985, the Government announced that legislation will be introduced to extend the Consumer Credit Act to all second mortgage lending by building societies. The Act already applies to the proposed unsecured lending by building societies. The treatment of first mortgage lending by building societies, banks and licensed deposit takers, will be brought into line but, at the time of writing, a final decision has not been taken on how this is to be achieved.

CURRENT COST ACCOUNTING (p. 184) In May 1985 the Accounting Standards Committe recommended to its component bodies that the mandatory status of SSAP 126 should be suspended.

DATA PROTECTION ACT 1984 This Act received the Royal Assent on 12 July 1984, 'to regulate the use of automatically processed information relating to individuals, and the provision of services in respect of such information'. The Act does not apply to the processing of personal data by manual methods, nor does it apply to information relating to corporate bodies.

The purpose of the legislation is to protect information about private individuals and to enforce standards for the processing of such information.

For the purpose of the Act:

Personal data consists of information about a living individual, including expressions of opinion about him or her, but excluding any indication of the intentions of the *Data-user* (see below) in respect of that individual.

Data-users are organisations or individuals who control the contents and use of a collection of *personal data* processed, or intended to be processed automatically.

A *computer bureau* is an organization or individual who processes *personal data* for *Data-*

users or allows *Data-users* to process *personal data* on his equipment.

A *Data-subject* is an individual to whom personal data relates.

The Act applies to data-users who control the contents of use of data from within the United Kingdom and to computer bureaux providing services in the United Kingdom.

The Act establishes new legal rights for individuals regarding personal data processed by computing equipment and a data subject may seek compensation through the courts for damage and any associated distress caused by the loss, destruction or unauthorized disclosure of data or by inaccurate data, or may apply to the courts for the rectification or erasure of inaccurate data, and may obtain access to data of which he or she is the subject.

The Act imposes obligations on data users and computer bureaux. In particular, a data user must register the personal data held, the purpose for which it is used, the source from which it comes, those to whom it may be disclosed and the countries or territories outside the United Kingdom, to which the date may be transferred. A computer bureau must register its name and address.

Registration must be with the Data Protection Registrar.

Data users must also adhere to certain principles in connection with the personal data which they hold. These principles require broadly that personal data shall be:

Collected and processed fairly and lawfully;
Held only for specified, lawful, registered purposes;
Used only for registered purposes or disclosed to registered recipients;
Be adequate and relevant to the purpose for which it is held;
Be accurate and, where necessary, kept up to date;
Be held no longer than is necessary for the stated purpose; and
Have appropriate security safeguards.

The principles also entitle individuals to have access to data held about themselves.

The rights of a data subject to seek compensation through the courts for damage, etc., caused by the loss, destruction or authorized disclosure of data operates from 12 September 1984. The right to claim in respect of inaccurate data operates from a date six months after the 'appointed day' under the Act, as does the right to rectification or erasure of inaccurate data.

The right of a data subject to obtain access to data of which he or she is the subject operates as from two years after the 'appointed day'.

The appointed day is to be announced by the Home Secretary and, at the time of writing, is expected to be in September 1985. The requirements for registration by data users and computer bureaux commences from the appointed day.

The Act is of particular relevance to banks, finance houses, building societies and others in the financial sector who store personal data on equipment 'operating automatically in response to instructions' which covers, for example, mainframe, mini- and micro-computers, word processors and punched-card processors.

DEPOSIT ACCOUNT (p. 207) At the end of 1984, total sterling deposits of the London Clearing Banks and their subsidiaries amounted to £94,860 million, of which sight deposits were £33,010 million.

DEVELOPMENT LAND TAX (p. 208) In his Budget Statement of 19th March 1985, the Chancellor of the Exchequer announced the abolition forthwith of Development Land Tax.

DOUBLE TAXATION RELIEF (p. 238) In 1985, agreement was reached on a new double taxation agreement with the Republic of Uganda and bilateral agreements were reached between the United Kingdom and Bahrain, Oman, Qatar and the United Arab Emirates in respect of revenues arising from international transport.

EUROBONDS (p. 252) In recent years total issues in the Eurobond market have approximately doubled, viz. from $26.5 billion in 1981 to $45 billion in 1983.

EUROPEAN ECONOMIC COMMUNITY (EEC) (p. 253) In 1985, the Member States agreed to the further enlargement of the Community by the inclusion of Spain and Portugal. This could take place with effect from 1st January, 1986, bringing the number of Member States to 12.

EXPORT CREDIT GUARANTEE DEPARTMENT (p. 258) In May 1985, the ECGD announced a new scheme entered into with a company known as Unicol in the private sector. The scheme called 'Unexis' is to deal with much of the short-term sales business passing through ECGD and is designed to assist in particular those firms which are exporting for the first time. Unexis will provide credit ratings for foreign buyers and will deal with much of the paperwork associated with exporting.

When payment is delayed by foreign buyers, the scheme will provide interim payments of up to 80% of the insured value of shipments. Insurance will be available as hitherto through ECGD.

FINANCIAL TIMES ACTUARIES INDICES (p. 273) With effect from 10th April 1985, the FT Actuaries Shares Indices include an ex-dividend adjustment on the equity stocks in the respective indices, i.e. on the day a stock goes ex-dividend the ex-dividend adjustment is added back in the index, thus avoiding the distortion which hitherto could apply in a sector dominated by a particular stock. The adjustment is on a net basis, i.e. after allowing for basic rate tax of 30%.

FRIENDLY SOCIETY (p. 286) At the time of writing, the 1985 Finance Bill contains provisions to bring the taxation aspects of life business conducted by friendly societies more into line with that of life assurance companies generally. For example, it is provided that societies may write endowment business as well as whole life business and they may issue policies to all adults, i.e. not merely to adults with dependants.

INCOME TAX (p. 322 *et seq.*) With effect from 19th March 1985, new rules applied in relation to tax on partnerships where there is a change of partnership. Hitherto, on any change in the partnership the business was treated as having ceased and a new business was deemed to have come into operation, so that the normal rules of assessment applied as for new businesses (see p. 326).

Under the revised rule, in the income tax year in which the change of partnership takes place and the three following tax years the assessment to tax will be on the actual profits arising in each of those years. The rule applies only where at least one person is a partner in both the old and the new partnerships. The partners still have the option, as under the old rules, to elect to have the partnership treated as a continuing business, in which case the new rule will not apply.

INDUSTRIAL LIFE ASSURANCE (p. 351) The corresponding figures for 1983 are:

In force at end of year	1983
Number of paying policies	46.9 m
Number of free policies	21.9 m
Total number of policies	68.8 m
Yearly premiums (£m)	1,150
Sums insured and bonuses (£m)	20,300

INSIDER DEALING (p. 355) The Company Securities (Insider Dealing) Act, 1985 extends the definition of securities to include 'any right to subscribe for, call for or make delivery of a share or debenture'.

LAND REGISTRATION (p. 384) In December 1984, the Lord Chancellor announced measures to extend compulsory registration of land to the extent that by November 1985 areas containing nearly 80 per cent of the population of England and Wales will be covered. This compares with approximately 73 per cent at the present time.

LIFE OFFICES ASSOCIATION Now part of the Association of British Insurers.

MERCHANT BANKING (p. 440) In May 1985, Lloyds Bank announced the formation of its own merchant banking activities, to be known as Lloyds Merchant Bank.

MORTGAGE INTEREST RELIEF AT SOURCE (MIRAS) (p. 442) From 6 April 1987 qualifying lenders under the MIRAS scheme will be required to include all *new* loans under the scheme, i.e. including those above the current limit of £30,000 for tax relief purposes, and thus basic tax relief up to the permitted maximum will be deducted at source on such loans.

ORDINARY SHARES (p. 480) The value of ordinary shares in private ownership was substantially increased by the British Telecom issue in 1984.

PENSIONS, PENSION SCHEMES (p. 503) The Social Security Bill currently before Parliament proposes the following changes in relation to occupational pension schemes:

(i) Pension benefits to be preserved for early leavers after five years qualifying service (previously only applicable to those over 25 years of age).

(ii) Benefits for early leavers after 1st January 1985 are to be revalued for the number of complete years remaining to normal pension age, the revaluation to be based on the increase in retail prices, up to a maximum of 5 per cent per annum compounded over the period to normal pension age. The revaluation applies to all pensions and retirement benefits, including widows pensions, and these requirements override any provisions in the occupational schemes.

(iii) All schemes must provide transfer options for leaving members who wish to join another approved scheme or take out an annuity policy. The transfer option must provide the cash equivalent of benefits accrued under the scheme.

(iv) The Act provides for disclosure of certain information to members, their wives and representatives and to a new Registry set up for the purpose. The information includes contributions to the scheme, the method of administration, benefits and other financial matters, the rules of the scheme, an annual report, audited accounts and actuarial valuations. The information at the Registry will be available to the public.

In a Green Paper issued in June 1985, the Government outlined major proposals for phasing out the State Earnings-Related Pensions Scheme (SEE ALSO *Social Security*). The main provisions under this heading are:

(*a*) The basic State pension will remain unchanged.

(*b*) The Earnings-Related State Pension will be phased out from April 1987, but men over 50 and women over 45 will continue in the scheme and all existing rights under the Scheme will be honoured.

(*c*) Employers and employees will be required to contribute a minimum of 2% each to an occupational or personal pension scheme, i.e. employers must either arrange their own scheme or contribute to approved schemes of the employees' choice.

(*d*) All pension rights arising under a scheme will be the property of the employee.

(*e*) The new arrangement will apply to all employees earning above the lower earnings limit (q.v.).

Under the new arrangements these 'second tier' pensions will be on a 'money purchase' basis, i.e. the obligation on the employer will be only to provide the minimum pension contribution and the ultimate benefit which the employee receives as pension will depend on the investment performance of the scheme (whether a company scheme or a scheme entered into by the employee privately) and therefore, the total fund available at the time of retirement. The amount of pension which that sum will purchase will depend on available annuity rates at the time.

For younger age groups, i.e. men under 50 and women under 45 (see above), the proposal is that the State Earnings-Related Pension Scheme will be phased out over a 3-year period.

REDUNDANCY PAYMENTS (p. 553) From 1 April 1985, the weekly earnings limit is £152.

REGISTRATION OF BUSINESS NAMES (p. 556) The provisions of the 1981 Companies Act have been substantially re-enacted in the Business Names Act, 1985.

SOCIAL SECURITY (p. 590) A Green Paper published by the Government in June 1985 contains proposals for radical changes in the structure of Social Security benefits. The main proposals are as follows:

(*a*) A new system of Family Credit will provide for low-income working families with children and will replace Family Income Supplement (q.v.).

(*b*) Child Benefit will continue but will not necessarily be indexed in relation to the general index of retail prices.

(*c*) The existing supplementary benefit scheme will be replaced by a more simple structure of Income Support.

(*d*) A new 'Social Fund' will be set up to assist people with special difficulties, such as financial emergencies.

(*e*) Housing Benefit (q.v.) will be simplified. Benefits will be the same for persons in or out of work up to 100% of rent, but everyone will have to pay a minimum, possibly 20%, of rates.

(*f*) Death Grant (q.v.) and Maternity Grant (q.v.) will be replaced by help from the proposed 'Social Fund'.

(*g*) Widows' Allowance (q.v.) will be replaced by a lump sum payment of £1,000.

(*h*) With effect from 1987, Social Security benefits will be uprated in April instead of in November as at present.

The Green Paper is issued in three volumes, viz. *Volume 1: Reform of Social Security*, which sets out the background to the review and the main proposals (Cmnd 9517, HMSO £3). *Volume 2: Reform of Social Security: Programme for Change*, which gives a more detailed account of the main benefits (Cmnd 9518, HMSO £6.60). *Volume 3: Reform of Social Security: Background Papers* (Cmnd 9519, HMSO £10.50).

The Housing Benefit Review is published in a separate paper (Cmnd 9520, HMSO £6.10).

STAMP DUTIES (p. 595) Under the Finance Act, 1985, the following Stamp Duties are abolished:

(*a*) The 1% duty on gifts (effective after 18th March 1985);
(*b*) Stamp duty on instruments transferring property from one partner to a marriage to another, pursuant to a Court Order granting a decree of divorce, nullity or judicial separation, or in pursuance of an agreement between the parties contemplating such divorce, annulment or judicial separation (effective after 25th March 1985);
(*c*) Ad valorem duty on deeds of family arrangement after 25th March 1985—a fixed duty of 50p will be payable.
(*d*) Stamp duty on the following:
 (i) Deed of Appointment of new trustee;
 (ii) Deed of Covenant;
 (iii) Power of Attorney;
 (iv) Hire purchase agreements;
 (v) Stockbrokers contract notes.

A total of 13 fixed duties were abolished, including those listed under (*d*) above.

The Commission of the EEC has proposed to the Council of the EEC that there should be a Directive to all Member States replacing the common rate of capital duties, i.e. duty on the raising of capital, of 1 per cent, by a rate which may be fixed by Member States between 0 per cent and 1 per cent, thus paving the way for the abolition of capital duty.

STOCK EXCHANGE (p. 599) At the time of writing, it is understood that 31 British and overseas securities houses have applied to the Bank of England to become 'market makers', i.e. primary dealers, as provided for in the re-structuring of the market for gilt-edged securities.

On 5th June 1985, the members of the Stock Exchange voted by a large majority to remove the limit of 29.9 per cent on the ownership of Stock Exchange firms by 'outsiders', thus permitting non-Stock Exchange houses, such as banks and other financial institutions, to acquire 100 per cent ownership of Stock Exchange firms. On the same occasion another resolution concerning the internal structure of the Stock Exchange failed to acquire the necessary 75 per cent majority. This resolution would have transferred the ownership and control of the Stock Exchange from individual members to their firms and given the corporate owners voting power in relation to their size.

As at March 1985, there were 4,495 elected members of the Stock Exchange. These represent 199 stockbroking firms, with 2,144 partners and 1,720 associates, and 17 firms of jobbers with 209 partners and 255 associates.

SUPPLEMENTARY BENEFIT (p. 604) A Government Green Paper published in June 1985 (SEE *Social Security* above) provides for the abolition of Supplementary Benefit in its present form and substitution of a system of Income Support. The main proposals under this heading are:

(*a*) There will no longer be two rates of Supplementary Benefit. A new 'Family Premium' will be paid to households with children.
(*b*) Single parents will receive a premium payment.
(*c*) Pensioners will also receive a premium at age 60.
(*d*) The long-term sick and disabled and pensioners over 80 will receive higher premiums.
(*e*) Single parents, disabled people and couples unemployed for two years will be allowed to earn up to a higher figure (probably £15 a week) instead of the present £4.
(*f*) Less rigid rules will apply in relation to the cutting-off of benefit in relation to capital savings.
(*g*) Talks are to be held with building societies and banks to find a formula by which less burden falls on the social security system in respect of mortgage interest payments.
(*h*) People on low incomes will receive help with maternity and funeral costs.

Generally, the aim will be to simplify the present system which, according to the Green Paper, is apparently contained in no less than 16,000 paragraphs of rules and regulations.

TABLE A (p. 608) Table A and the other Tables contained in Schedule 1 of the Companies Act, 1948, were not reproduced in the consolidating Companies Act, 1985, but are now published in Statutory Instruments under Sections 3 and 8 of that Act.

TRUSTEE SAVINGS BANKS (p. 637) At the present time the Trustee Savings Banks Bill is before Parliament. Under an amendment to the Bill it is proposed to preserve the existing four banking subsidiaries, viz. England and Wales, Scotland, Northern Ireland and the Channel Islands and incorporate them in their own countries with their head offices and registered offices also in their respective countries. It is expected that the public flotation of the shares will take place later this year.

UNLISTED SECURITIES MARKET (p. 651) As at March 1985, the Unlisted Securities Market consisted of 282 companies with a total market capitalization of £3,333.6 million.

UPPER EARNINGS LIMIT (p. 651) With effect from 6th October, 1985, the Upper Earnings Limit is removed for the purpose of employers' national insurance contributions. From that date employers' contributions apply to *all* the earnings of employees on a graduated scale.

WILLS (p. 659) In the case of *Re Williams (otherwise Cook) (deceased) Wiles,* v *Madgin* (1984) *Times*, 19 January 1985, it was held that where a home-made will was found to be ambiguous, the condition laid down in Section 21(1)(b) Administration of Justice Act, 1982, was satisfied so that a letter sent by the testatrix to her solicitors giving them instructions regarding her will, was admitted as an aid to the construction of the will.

APPENDIX 1

APPENDIX 1. TAXATION

A. INCOME TAX

The chargeable bands of income and rates of tax for the fiscal year 1985/86 are shown below.

Income Tax Rates:

Band of chargeable income (£)	*Rate* (%)	*Tax payable* 1985–86
1–16,200	30	4,860
16,201–19,200	40	6,060
19,201–24,400	45	8,400
24,401–32,300	50	12,350
32,301–40,200	55	16,695
Over £40,200	60	

Allowances and Reliefs:

	1985–86
Single personal allowance	2,205
Married man's personal allowance	3,455
Wife's earned income allowance	
—maximum	2,205
Age allowance	
Single person	2,690
Married person	4,255
Abatement of relief	
2/3rds excess of income over	8,800
Benefit lost if total income over	
—Single person	9,528
—Married person	10,000
Widow's bereavement allowance	1,250
Additional personal allowance for children	1,250
Housekeeper allowance	100
Dependent relative allowance	
For each dependant	100
Single woman claimant	145
Allowance for son's or daughter's services	55
Blind person's allowance	360

Retirement Annuities Relief:

Year of birth	%	*Year of birth*	%
Since 1933	17½	1912 or 1913	24
1916 to 1933	20	1910 or 1911	26½
1914 or 1915	21	1908 or 1909	29½

APPPENDIX 1

Car Benefits: Scales for 1986–97 (1985–86 figures in brackets)

Cars with original market value up to £19,250 (£17,500) having a cylinder capacity

Cylinder capacity of car in cubic centimetres	*Age of car at end of relevant year of assessment* Under 4 years	4 years or more
Up to 1300cc	450 (410)	300 (275)
1301cc–1800cc	575 (525)	380 (350)
More than 1800cc	900 (825)	600 (550)

Cars with original market value up to £19,250 (£17,500) and not having a cylinder capacity

Original market value of car	*Age of car at end of relevant year of assessment* Under 4 years	4 years or more
Less than £6,000 (£5,500)	450 (410)	300 (275)
£6,000 (£5,500) or more but less than £8,500 (£7,700)	575 (525)	380 (350)
£8,500 (£7,700) or more but less than £19,250 (£17,500)	900 (825)	600 (550)

Cars with original market value more than £19,250 (£17,500)

Original market value of car	*Age of car at end of relevant year of assessment* Under 4 years	4 years or more
More than £19,250 (£17,500) but not more than £29,000 (£26,500)	1320 (1200)	875 (800)
More than £29,000 (£26,500)	2100 (1900)	1400 (1270)

The taxable cash equivalents for the year 1986–87 are shown below. The corresponding figures for the year 1985–86 are shown in brackets.

Cars having a recognised cylinder capacity

Cylinder capacity of car in cubic centimetres	£ £
1300 cc or less	450 (410)
1301 cc–1800 cc	575 (525)
More than 1800 cc	900 (825)

Cars not having a recognised cylinder capacity

Original market value of car	£ £
Less than £6,000 (5,500)	450 (410)
£6,000 (£5,500) or more, but less than £8,500 (7,700)	575 (525)
£8,500 (£7,700) or more	900 (825)

B. CAPITAL GAINS TAX

Rate of Tax: 30%

Small Gains Relief:

Individual and trusts for the mentally disabled or for persons in receipt of an attendance allowance	£5,900
Other trusts	£2,950
Personal representatives in year of death and two following years	£5,900

Retirement Relief for Business Assets:

Retirement at age 60 or over or earlier retirement for reason of ill-health	Gains up to £100,000
Exemption for chattels	£3,000

C. CAPITAL TRANSFER TAX

Rates of Tax:

Transfers on death (£)	*Rate* (%)	*Total tax payable* (£)
0– 67,000	—	—
67,000– 89,000	30	6,600
89,000–122,000	35	18,150
122,000–155,000	40	31,350
155,000–194,000	45	48,900
195,000–243,000	50	73,400
243,000–299,000	55	104,200
Over £299,000	60	

In the case of life transfers, the rate of capital transfer tax is exactly one-half of the percentage rates shown above.

If the general index of retail prices for December each year exceeds that for the previous December, the bands of tax are increased by the percentage increase in the Retail Prices Index. The adjusted rates apply to chargeable transfers made on or after 6th April in the following year.

Exemptions and Reliefs 1985/86

Gifts to spouse domiciled in the UK	Exempt
Annual exemption	£3,000
Small gifts	£250 (to each donee)
Gifts on marriage	£5,000 by a parent £2,000 by a party to the marriage or a grandparent or other antecedent £1,000 by others
Gifts to charities	Exempt
Gifts out of normal expenditure	See text
Agricultural and business property	See text

APPENDIX 2

APPENDIX 2. SOCIAL BENEFIT RATES

	From 26 November 1984 (£)		Proposed rates from 25 November 1985 (where announced) (£)
Illness and Invalidity Benefits			
Sickness benefit			
Man under 65 or woman under 60	27.25		29.15
Wife/adult dependant	16.80		18.00
Each child	0.15		
Man over 65 or woman over 60	34.25		36.65
Wife/adult dependant	20.55		22.00
Each child	7.65		8.05
Invalidity benefit			
Invalidity pension (basic)	34.25		38.30
Wife/adult dependant	20.55		23.00
Each child	7.65		8.05
Severe disablement allowance	21.50		23.00
Wife/adult dependant	12.85		13.75
Each child	7.65		8.05
Invalidity allowance for incapacity beginning:			
Under the age of 40	7.50		8.05
40–49	4.80		5.10
50–59 (men) or 50–54 (women)	2.40		2.55
Maternity benefit			
Maternity grant (single payment)	25.00		
Maternity allowance	27.25		29.15
Adult dependant	16.80		
Each child	0.15		
Mobility allowance	20.00		21.40
War pensioner's private car allowance (per year)	350.00		
Attendance allowance			
Higher rate	28.60		30.60
Lower rate	19.10		20.45
Invalid care allowance	21.50		23.00
Wife/adult dependant	12.85		13.75
Each child	7.65		8.05
Industrial Injuries			
Industrial disablement benefit			
Pension disablement	*Person over 18*	*Person under 18*	
100%	58.40	35.80	62.50
90%	52.56	32.22	
80%	46.72	28.64	
70%	40.88	25.06	
60%	35.04	21.48	
50%	29.20	17.90	
40%	23.36	14.32	
30%	17.52	10.74	

20%	11.68	7.16	
10% or less (payable only for pneumoconiosis assessments)	5.84	—	
Gratuity (lump sum payment)			
19%	3,880.00		
18%	3,686.00		
17%	3,492.00		
16%	3,298.00		
15%	3,104.00		
14%	2,910.00		
13%	2,716.00		
12%	2,522.00		
11%	2,328.00		
10%	2,134.00		
9%	1,940.00		
8%	1,746.00		
7%	1,552.00		
6%	1,358.00		
5%	1,164.00		
4%	970.00		
3%	776.00		
2%	582.00		
1%	388.00		
Special hardship allowance			
Maximum allowance	23.36		25.00
Overall maximum with disablement benefit	58.40		62.50
Constant attendance allowance			
Part time	11.70		12.50
Normal maximum	23.40		25.00
Intermediate rate	35.10		37.50
Maximum in exceptionally severe cases	46.80		50.00
Exceptionally severe disablement allowance	23.40		25.00
Hospital treatment allowance—allowance will bring disablement benefit up to	58.40		
Unemployability supplement	34.25		38.30
Wife/adult dependant	20.55		22.00
Allowance not payable if annual earnings exceed	1,222.00		
Prescribed industrial diseases			
Allowance for the totally disabled	58.40		62.50
Allowance for the partially disabled	21.50		
Industrial death benefit			
Widow's pension—first 26 weeks	50.10		53.60
Widow's pension—			
higher permanent rate	36.35		38.85
lower permanent rate	10.74		11.49
Allowances for children paid with widow's			
pension—each child	7.65		8.05
paid otherwise—each child	0.15		
Family Income Supplement			
Prescribed amount	90.00		97.50
Increase in prescribed amount for each child after first	10.00		11.50
Maximum payment: for family with one child	23.00		25.00
Increase for each additional child	2.00		2.00
Child Benefit			
Each child	6.85		7.00

	From 26 November 1984 (£)	Proposed rates from 25 November 1985 (where announced) (£)
Child benefit increase—first or only child of certain lone parents	4.25	4.55
Child's Special Allowance		
Each child	7.65	8.05
Guardian's Allowance		
Each child	7.65	8.05
Unemployment Benefit		
Man under 65 or woman under 60	28.45	30.45
Wife/adult dependant	17.55	18.80
Each child	0.15	
Man over 65 or woman over 60	35.80	38.30
Wife/adult dependant	21.50	23.00
Each child	7.65	
Retirement Pensions		
Man, woman (own contributions) or widow (late husband's contributions)		
Basic	35.80	38.30
Married woman (husband's contributions)	21.50	23.00
Wife/adult dependant	21.50	
Each child	7.65	8.10
Non-contributory retirement pension for people over 80		
Man, single woman or widow	21.50	
Married woman	12.85	
Age addition for 80 or over	0.25	
Graduated pension		
Amount paid for every unit of £7.50 (man) or £9.00 (woman) graduated contributions paid before 6 April 1975	0.0467	
Widow's Benefits		
Widow's allowance	50.10	
Widowed mother's allowance—basic	35.80	38.30
Widow's pension—basic	35.80	38.30
Age-related widow's pension—basic		
Age at time of husband's death or when widowed mother's allowance stops		
40	10.74	
41	13.25	
42	15.75	
43	18.26	
44	20.76	
45	23.27	
46	25.78	
47	28.28	
48	30.79	
49	33.29	
Each child	7.65	

APPENDIX 2

Earnings Rules

Retirement pension		
For claimants		
The basic pension (including any increase for dependants) will be reduced if a man under 70/woman under 65 earns more than — per week	70.00	75.00
Earnings between	70.00 and 74.00	
5p deducted for each 10p earned over	70.00	
Earnings over	74.00	
5p deducted for each 5p earned over	74.00	
Invalid care allowance		
Allowance is not payable if weekly earnings exceed	12.00	
For spouse or woman caring for claimant's child		
Additional benefit is not payable if weekly earnings of spouse or other adult dependant are more than—		
sickness benefit	16.80	
unemployment benefit	17.55	
claimant—man over 65 or woman over 60		
sickness benefit	20.55	
unemployment benefit	21.50	
Invalidity, retirement, non-contributory invalidity pensions and unemployability supplement		
Increase for dependant wife (or woman having care of child) residing with pensioner is reduced if weekly earnings are more than	45.00	
Earnings between	45.00 and 49.00	
5p deducted for each 10p earned over	45.00	
Earnings over	49.00	
5p deducted for each 5p earned over	49.00	
Increase for a separated wife or other adult dependant is not payable if weekly earnings are more than		
Retirement pension	21.50	
Invalidity pension	20.55	
Severe disablement allowance	21.50	

Death Grant

Single payment depending on age of deceased	
Age under 3	9.00
Age 3–5	15.00
Age 6–17	22.50
Man 18 or over (born after 4 July 1893)	30.00
Woman 18 or over (born after 4 July 1898)	30.00
Man born 5 July 1883–4 July 1893	15.00
Woman born 5 July 1888–4 July 1898	15.00

War Pensions and Allowances

100% disablement pension	58.40	62.50
Unemployability allowance	38.00	40.65
Widow's pension	46.55	49.80

Workmen's Compensation (Supplementation) Scheme

Basic rate inclusive of workmen's compensation	2.00
Major incapacity allowance	58.40
Lesser incapacity allowance (maximum rate)	21.50

	From 26 November 1984 (£)		Proposed rates from 25 November 1985 (where announced) (£)	
	Ordinary (£)	*Long term* (£)	*Ordinary* (£)	*Long term* (£)
Supplementary Benefit				
Couple	45.55	57.10	47.85	60.00
Person living alone	28.05	35.70	29.50	37.50
Non-householder—age 18 and over	22.45	28.55	23.60	30.00
aged 16–17	17.30	21.90	18.20	23.00
Any other person aged:				
11–15 years	14.35		15.10	
Under 11 years	9.60		10.10	
Boarder's personal expenses				
Ordinary—couple	18.50			
Ordinary—single	9.25			
Long term—couple	20.60			
Long term—single	10.30			
Heating additions to supplementary benefit				
Lower rate	2.10		2.20	
Higher rate	5.20		5.45	
Central heating additions				
Lower rate	2.10		2.20	
Higher rate	4.20		4.40	
Estate rate heating additions				
Lower rate	4.20		4.40	
Higher rate	8.40		8.80	
Supplementary benefit				
capital cut-off level	3,000.00*			
capital limit for single payments	500.00			
Housing Benefit Needs Allowances				
Single person	45.10		47.70	
Couple/single parent	66.50		70.20	
Single handicapped person	50.30		53.20	
Couple, one handicapped/single handicapped parent	71.70		75.70	
Couple, both handicapped	74.15		78.25	
Dependant child addition	12.85		14.50	

* The first £1,500 surrender value of life assurance policies will also be disregarded.

N.B. The principal social security benefits are adjusted in November each year in relation to any increase in the Index of Retail Prices for the year to the previous May.